THE LAW
OF CONTRACT
IN CANADA

by G.H.L. FRIDMAN, Q.C., F.R.S.C.,

MA., B.C.L., LL.M.,

of the Ontario Bar, and
of the Middle Temple,
Barrister-at-Law,
Professor of Law, University of Western Ontario

Third Edition

CARSWELL
Thomson Professional Publishing

Canadian Cataloguing in Publication Data

Fridman, G. H. L. (Gerald Henry Louis), 1928-
    The law of contract in Canada

3rd ed.
Includes bibliographical references and index.
ISBN 0-459-55793-9 (bound) ISBN 0-459-55795-5 (pbk.)

1. Contracts - Canada.   I. Title.

KE850.F75   1994   346.71′02   C94-930660-6
KF801.F75   1994

The paper used in this publication meets the minimum requirements of the American National Standard for Information Sciences - Permanence of Paper for Printed Library Materials, ANSI X39.48-1984.

Typesetting: Video Text Inc., Barrie, Ontario, Canada

CARSWELL
Thomson Professional Publishing

One Corporate Plaza, 2075 Kennedy Road, Scarborough, Ontario M1T 3V4
Customer Service:
Toronto 1-416-609-3800
Elsewhere in Canada/U.S. 1-800-387-5164
Fax 1-416-298-5094

Dedicated, with Permission
To
LORD DENNING OF WHITCHURCH

Preface to Third Edition

Several years have gone by since the last edition of this book. In that time there has been much activity in the courts with respect to the law of contract. This edition endeavours to incorporate and discuss some of the major developments. They include some English decisions that are significant for Canada as well as England, and the judgments of the Supreme Court of Canada in the *London Drugs* and *Hunter Engineering* cases, *Air Canada v. British Columbia, Geffen v. Goodman Estate, National Trust v. Mead, Central Trust v. Rafuse, Canadian Pacific Hotels v. Bank of Montreal, BG Checo International v. British Columbia Hydro & Power Authority, Vorvis v. Insurance Corporation of British Columbia.*

Other, perhaps less vital, but nevertheless useful and material decisions from various provincial courts have also been explained or considered. The aim has been to make this edition as up-to-date as possible. Hence new material has been added, for example: discussion of the idea of good faith in contracting, an idea that appears to have become very much *à la mode* at the present time; estoppel by convention; and the recommendations made by the Ontario Law Reform Commission in its *Report on Amendment of the Law of Contract.* References to statutes have been altered to take into account revisions to provincial statute books over the past few years.

I am gratified by the fact that passages in the previous edition of this book have been quoted or referred to in almost one hundred cases across Canada. This means that the work has achieved what was stated to be its purpose in the preface to the second edition, namely, to provide an intelligible account of the present-day norms of the law of contract as they are applied in Canada. As before, that account is intended to be for the benefit not only of courts, and those who appear before them, but also for students in courses on the law of contract in faculties of law in common law Canada. Case-books have their uses. However, a continuous, orderly and logical text, in the end, provides a clearer guide not only to the current state of the law but also to trends indicating where the law may be going in the future.

In preparing this edition I received assistance from Mr. Michael Davies, Ph.D., LL.B., who worked for me one summer preparing a list of cases and articles that had appeared since the last edition. This was most helpful as it provided me with the skeleton of new developments. The flesh I obtained for myself by reading the cases and most of the other material to which I was referred by him, as well as cases and other relevant matters that came to my attention more recently. The activity of Mr. Davies saved me a considerable amount of time, and I am grateful to him and to the Ontario Law Foundation which provided the necessary funding.

I have tried to state the law as of August 1, 1993. But the law of contract is not static. Nor is theorising about the law of contract likely to come to a sudden, sharp end. Text writers and others will continue to examine, analyse, criticise and theorise. The courts will carry on with their everyday business of applying and adapting the law as they have been over the past few years. There is plenty of indication that the Supreme Court of Canada is prepared to make significant changes to the law as it has come down to us from the past in order to make it more relevant, in their view, to current conditions of commerce. What that means, among other things, is that new editions will probably be required in future years. Who can say what will emerge?

London, Ontario
Summer, 1993   G.H.L. Fridman

Contents

Table of Cases

Table of Statutes

1

Introduction

1. Contractual theory

Recent years have seen increasing interest in the underlying theory of the law of contract. Many writers have endeavoured to provide explanations of the principles of law that govern contractual relations, or to consider the true function of the law as it relates to contracts. Despite the quantity, as well as the quality, of the literature in question, the nature and purposes of the law of contract remain a matter of debate. There is no *consensus* among those who have attempted to comment on these issues.[1]

It has been argued, for example, that English courts adopt a positivist approach to the law, basing their decisions and their reasoning upon the formalism of the law of precedent rather than upon any broad, consequential or policy-oriented ideas.[2] The contrary has also been propounded.[3] An approach based more on natural law ideas has also been suggested as more appropriate for a modern law of contract.[4] As might be expected, there have been efforts to base the law of contract upon economic ideas such as "efficiency".[5] By way of contrast others have argued that the essential feature of the law of contract is the idea that morality requires and dictates that promises, or promises of a certain nature, ought to be kept, and therefore the law should enforce them.[6] Modern commentators seem anxious to avoid or

---

1 For a critical discussion of different approaches to contract, see Feinman, "The Significance of Contract Theory" (1989), 58 U. Cinn. L.R. 1283.
2 Phang, "Positivism in the English Law of Contract" (1992), 55 M.L.R. 102.
3 Adams & Brownsword, "The Ideologies of Contract" (1987), 7 J. Leg. St. 205.
4 Herron & Pattison, "Natural Law and Contract: A Time for Redefinition" (1989), 34 Am. J. Jur. 199.
5 See, for example, Wonnall, "The Abstract Character of Contract Law" (1990), 22 Conn. L.R. 437, arguing that the law of contract serves an essential economic function. One example of the application of economic ideas in contract is the idea of so-called "efficient breach": below, pp. 764-765. For criticism of this see Friedmann, "The Efficient Breach Fallacy" (1989), 18 J. Leg. St. 1.
6 See the authorities cited below, notes 13 and 19.

reject the older notion that contracts are based upon agreement or consensus between the parties, who thereby express their respective wills.[7]

Other, metalegal ideas have also been suggested. For example, the view has been expressed that contract performs a regulatory function.[8] It has also been argued that the law of contract is intended to achieve what Aristotle described as "distributive justice," and that an important function or purpose of the law of contract is to perform the kind of function that is otherwise fulfilled by taxation.[9]

A further development in recent times is the emergence of the idea that the older, classicial idea of contracts as, in a sense, static, could be replaced by the idea of "relational contracts," i.e., of contract as being part of an on-going relationship between two or more parties.[10] This would have a significant effect as regards the principles of law governing such relationships, and would require considerable rethinking of the content and application of those principles. It is not surprising, therefore, to find one commentator writing about "the crisis in modern contract theory,"[11] in the course of which discussion he deals with some recent attacks upon the whole concept of contract.[12]

For the purposes of this book it is unnecessary to investigate these various ideas further. The present author is concerned with the principles governing the creation, interpretation, performance and enforcement of contracts and the remedies available to parties in the event of non-performance or breach. In this respect judicial decisions play a vital role in the creation, development and understanding of those principles. Canadian courts, in modern times, may be less positivist in their approach, as compared with courts in England. Nonetheless, by and large, they too are chiefly concerned with the elucidation and application of principles and doctrines that have evolved in the past two centuries, the period of classical contract law in England, from which the courts in common law Canada received the law. By way of introduction to those principles and doctrines it is pertinent to consider certain fundamental characteristics of the modern law of contract, namely promises, agreement, and bargain. It is also relevant to consider the distinctions, as well as the connections, between the nature and scope of the law of contract on the one hand and of the law of restitution and the law of torts on the other.

---

7 Compare below, pp. 15-17. See Hamburger, "The Development of the Nineteenth-Century Consensus Theory of Contract" (1989), 7 Law and Hist. R. 344. For modern criticism see Olsen, "Interpretations of Contract Law" (1992), 77 Cornell L.R. 1043.

8 Braucher, "Contract versus Contractarianism: The Regulatory Role of Contract Law" (1990), 40 Wash. & Lee L.R. 697.

9 Kronman, "Contract Law and Distributive Justice" (1979-80), 89 Yale L.J. 472: on which see Lucy, "Contract as a Mechanism of Distributive Justice" (1989), 9 Ox. J. Leg. St. 132; Richardson, "Contract Law and Distributive Justice Revisited" (1990), 10 Leg. St. 258.

10 See the authorities by Macneil cited below, note 13: note the criticism of Barnett, "Conflicting Visions: A Critique of Ian Macneil's Relational Theory of Contract" (1992), 78 Virginia L.R. 1175.

11 Hillman, "The Crisis in Modern Contract Theory" (1988), 67 Texas L.R. 103.

12 For a very particular attack upon the present-day law of contract and what, it does, see Tidwell & Langer, "The Flesh-Colored Band Aid — Contracts, Feminism, Dialogue and Theory" (1991), 28 Houston L.R. 791; Dow, "Law School Feminist Chic and Respect for Persons: Comments on Contract Theory and Feminism in the Flesh-Colored Band Aid", ibid. at p. 819 (which supports the relational contracts approach).

2. Contract as promise

Promises are fundamental to the idea of contract.[13] A promise is an undertaking as to the future conduct of the party promising, the promisor, with respect to the party to whom the promise is given, the promisee. The former agrees to act, or refrain from acting, in a certain way, to the advantage or for the benefit of the latter. He undertakes to limit his future freedom of action, and to that extent may be said to have accepted or undergone a detriment. A contract consists of a promise, or a set of promises, given by one person in exchange for the promise, or set of promises, made by another person. In some situations the promise is immediately fulfilled, by one or both parties, as when goods are simultaneously exchanged for cash. Nothing remains to be done, in the physical, material sense. Yet, by reason of undertakings which may be expressly given, or, more frequently, implicit in the transaction,[14] there remain as yet unfulfilled or unsatisfied aspects of the transaction, in the form of express or implied promises. To the extent that one party's undertaking is fulfilled or satisfied, his promise, and his side of the contract, are *executed*. To the extent that such party's undertaking remains to be completed, his promise, and his side of the contract are *unexecuted*.

It is the idea of promise which distinguishes contract from representation.[15] A representation is not an undertaking, although, sometimes, it may resemble a promise in its form, for example, where a seller of goods states that the goods in question are "top quality". Representations are statements as to an existing or past fact, not promises as to future events or states of affairs. Although representations can have legal consequences, if made falsely, or negligently, or, on occasion, without either fraud or negligence on the part of the representor, such

---

13 Fried, *Contract as Promise* (1981), Chap. 2. For criticism of Fried's theory see Wellman, "Conceptions of the Common Law: Reflections on a Theory of Contract" (1987), 41 U. Miami L.R. 925. See further Stoljar, "Promise, Expectation and Agreement", [1988] C.L.J. 193; Stoljar, "Keeping Promises: The Moral and Legal Obligation" (1988), 8 J. Leg. St. 258; Barnett, "Some Problems with Contract as Promise" (1992), 77 Cornell L.R. 1022. For an attack on the idea of contract as promise, and the idea that the essence of contractual obligation lies in (i) recompense for benefit and (ii) the protection of reasonable reliance, see Atiyah, *The Rise and Fall of Freedom of Contract* (1979), especially Chap. 22, and, for a more philosophical approach, Atiyah, *Promises, Morals and Law* (1981) (criticized by Raz, "Book Review" (1982), 95 H.L.R. 916). For other expressions of the views of Atiyah see "Contracts, Promises and the Law of Obligations" (1978), 94 L.Q.R. 193; "Book Review" (of Fried, *op. cit.*) (1981), 95 H.L.R. 509; *Essays on Contract*, 1986, especially essays 1, 2 and 5. For another philosophical attack on the idea of contract as promise, see Ardal, "Ought We to Keep Contracts Because they are Promises?" (1983), 17 Valparaiso L.R. 655. A very different view of contract is provided by Macneil, *The New Social Contract* (1980); Macneil, "The Many Futures of Contract" (1974), 47 S. Cal. L.R. 691; Macneil, "Contracts: Adjustment of Long-Term Economic Relations" (1978), 72 N.W.U.L.R. 854. See also Lightsey, "A Critique of the Promise Model of Contract" (1985), 26 Wm. & Mary L.R. 45, attacking the promise model and preferring to describe contract as "the relationship that exists and develops among parties who have made a commitment to a future exchange." See Schwartz, "Relational Contracts in the Courts" (1992), 21 J. Leg. St. 271. And compare Feinman, "The Last Promissory Estoppel Article" (1992), 61 Fordham L.R. 303 at pp. 311-315.

14 Under terms implied by the Sale of Goods Act: below, pp. 485-486.

15 On representations, see below, pp. 450-451.

consequences are non-contractual in their nature. They stem from the misleading nature of a statement, not from any promissory character.

Although promises take the form of undertakings to do, or refrain from doing a specific act or acts, it has been argued that a contract does no more than amount to a promise *either* to do, or refrain from doing the agreed act *or* to pay damages in lieu thereof, the choice being that of the promisor.[16] According to this theory, the function of a contract, at most, is to provide a promisee with the expectation that he will receive a sum of money to represent, so far as the law can do so, what the promisee hoped to obtain from the contract. This approach to contract is very dubious.[17] Its invalidity is highlighted by the doctrine of anticipatory breach or repudiation, and by the doctrine of frustration, as well as by the development of the remedy of specific performance.[18] As an approach it is also extremely antipathetic to the true, essential nature of contract. The common law's purpose was to secure the satisfaction and fulfilment of promises. Damages were, and remain, only a balm, a salve for hurt expectations, as well as other consequences arising from the failure of a party to observe and fulfil his word. The law's intention is to ensure that a person making a promise should keep it in accordance with its letter and spirit. The law of contract is about promises that must be kept.[19]

---

16 Holmes, *The Common Law*, pp. 300-301: and see *Holmes-Pollock Letters*, Vol. I, pp. 21, 79, 119; Vol. II, pp. 55, 200, 233.

17 Buckland, "The Nature of Contractual Obligations" (1942), 8 C.L.J. 247; Fridman, "The Basis of Contractual Obligation" (1974), 7 Loyola of Los Angeles L.R. 1.

18 Below, pp. 600, 623.

19 The idea of promise as "the moral basis of contract law" is promoted by Fried, *op. cit.*, above, note 1. He concludes (*ibid.* at p. 132) as follows: "The law of contracts just because it is rooted in promise and so in right and wrong is a ramifying system of moral judgments working out the entailments of a few primitive principles — primitive principles that determine the terms on which free men and women may stand apart from or combine with each other. These are indeed the laws of freedom." Compare Fridman, "On the Nature of Contract" (1983), 17 Valparaiso L.R. 527. Support for a contract-as-promise interpretation is found in Goddard, "The Myth of Subjectivity" (1987), 7 Leg. St. 263.

Raz (95 H.L.R. 916) criticizes both Fried's view based on the promise principle, and Atiyah's view (*op. cit.*, above, note 13) that contract law is a hybrid of principles of liability based on tort and restitution (as to which see below p. 11). He argues that contract law does not enforce promises; it protects the practice of undertaking voluntary obligations and the individuals who rely on that practice. "One enforces a promise" (*loc. cit.* at p. 933) "by making the promisor perform it, or failing that, by putting the promisee in a position as similar as possible to that he would have occupied had the promisor respected the promise. One protects the practice of undertaking voluntary obligations by preventing its erosion — by making good any harm caused by its use or abuse."

For the philosophical debate about promises and statements (*quaere* representations?) see Ardal, *op. cit.*, above, note 13 at p. 657.

Macneil's thesis (*op. cit.*, above, note 13) is that contract is an exchange relation dealing with the future. Contractual behaviour covers not only promise but also command, status, social role, kinship, bureaucratic patterns, religious obligations and habits. Indeed promise may not be necessary for the emerging exchange relation, the new paradigm of projecting exchange into the future: see Mullock, "The New Paradigm of Contract: A Hermeneutical Approach" (1983), 17 Valparaiso L.R. 677. The theory of contract propounded by Macneil clearly transcends the normal contractual situation with which Canadian lawyers may be faced, and goes far beyond what it is necessary

3. Contract as agreement

The idea of contract is promissory in nature, but, from the standpoint of the law, the essence of contract is agreement, or, as it was put in the classical period of the English common law, from which the law in Canada, outside Quebec, is derived, *consensus ad idem*[20] Contract is a jural relation that is founded upon agreement, that is, upon the manifestation of a mutural concordance between the parties as to the existence, nature and scope of their rights and duties.[21] A contract is a legally recognized agreement between two or more persons, giving rise to obligations that may be enforced in the courts.[22] By such an agreement the parties not only restrict their present or future freedom to act, by the limitations imposed upon themselves by the agreement, they are creating a legal rule, or set of legal rules, a legal regimen, binding as regards themselves and only themselves. It might be suggested that, through the device of contract, parties legislate for themselves, that is to say they create a miniature legal system by and under which they are governed. In truth, however, they are not creating law. Contract, as it has been said,[23] is a form of legal institution. By entering into a contract, parties bring themselves within the ambit of such institution. The parties are taking advantage of the law, and a recognized legal institution, in order to create certain legal consequences.

---

to comprehend in order to understand and appreciate the nature, role and functions of contract law as expressed herein.

For a reconceptualization of contract, by virtue of which "the principles of contract law should be based on conditions of fairness, as determined principally by conventional morality, and of policy, as determined principally by efficiency and administrability," see Eisenberg, "Donative Promises" (1979), 47 U. Chi. L.R. 1; "The Bargain Principle and its Limits" (1982), 95 H.L.R. 741; "The Principles of Consideration" (1982), 67 Cornell L.R. 640; "The Responsive Model of Contract Law" (1984), 36 Stanford L.R. 1107.

20 For the connection between promises and consent, see Atiyah, *Promises, Morals and Law* (1981), pp. 178-180: on which the see Raz, 95 H.L.R. 916 at pp. 921-923: and see Raz, "Authority and Consent" (1981), 67 Virginia L.R. 103 at pp. 118-125.

21 The idea that contractual obligations are based on agreements is qualified in three ways, according to Treitel, *Law of Contract*, 8th ed. (1991), pp. 1-4, namely: (a) the importance of objective appearance rather than the actual fact of agreement (on which see Howarth, "The Meaning of Objectivity in Contract" (1984), 100 L.Q.R. 268; Vorster, "A Comment on the Meaning of Objectivity in Contract" (1987), 103 L.Q.R. 274); (b) the requirement that parties must observe certain standards of behaviour, *e.g.*, implied terms; (c) limitations in modern times on the principle of freedom of contract. In this respect perhaps it should also be noted that some writers have suggested that there is, or ought to be, a doctrine of *good faith* in contracting that would certainly affect the issue of agreement, in that the validity of an apparent agreement might be affected by the presence of "bad faith" in the course of the negotiations, or at some later stage; Reiter, "Good Faith in Contracts" (1983), 17 Valparaiso L.R. 705; compare Powell, "Good Faith in Contracts" (1956), 9 Current Legal Problems 16; Burton, "Breach of Contract and the Common Law Duty to Perform in Good Faith" (1980), 94 H.L.R. 369; Holmes, "A Contextual Study of Commercial Good Faith" (1978), 39 U. Pittsburgh L.R. 381. See also the Ontario Law Reform Commission, *Report on Sale of Goods* (1979), Vol. I, pp. 163-169. See also, below p. 78.

22 This sentence was quoted by Grotsky J. in *Interprov. Concrete Ltd. v. Great West Const. Ltd.* (1987), 23 C.L.R. 123 at 130 (Sask. Q.B.).

23 MacCormick, "Law as Institutional Fact" (1974), 90 L.Q.R. 102.

The fact that contract involves or requires agreement makes it clear that contracts are voluntary. They stem from an exercise of the will of the parties. This differentiates contractual situations, involving contractual rights and duties, from other, seemingly contractual or similar legal relationships in which the obligations and rights come not from any voluntary acts or assumptions but from rules of law imposed without the consent, adherence or volition of the parties.[24] This does not exclude the possibility that some contractual rights or obligations may be created or imposed by the law against the will of one or both parties, for example, by statute.[25] When this occurs, it is not the relationship of contract that is being forced upon the parties, but one or more of the *incidents* of such a relationship. The original contract, which gives rise to the situation in which the imposition of rights and duties occurs, must have come about voluntarily.

One problem that has arisen in relation to the idea of agreement is whether, in discovering such agreement, the courts should be concerned with the knowledge and intent of each individual party, or should determine the existence or non-existence of agreement by reference to some external factors. The difference is between a *subjective* and an *objective* view. What emerges from the cases, and the judicial statements therein, is the attitude that agreement or lack of agreement is to be adjudged, at common law at any rate, by the standards of the reasonable observer, the person on the outside, as it were, of the transaction. Whether parties are in agreement does not depend upon what they themselves knew or understood, rather upon whether in the eyes of the onlooker they appeared to have reached agreement. In this sense, therefore, to the law there may be agreement when, in fact, there is none. The subjective view, however, expresses the attitude that there can only be agreement when the parties actually are in agreement, that is, when each individual party is in accord with the other. Thus a party who labours under a mistake, which is the reason why he contracted, will not be in agreement under the subjective view. The objective view may result in there being a contract as a matter of law, when there is none in fact. This suggests that, in such circumstances, a contract may come about against the volition of one party or both. Equity seems to have taken a more subjective approach to mistake and agreement, as will be examined in due course. It may also be the case that, in modern times, the common law is becoming less attached to the objective view. If this is correct, then the modern law of contract is paying more attention to the actualities of the phenomenon of agreement than to its technicalities.[26]

---

24 *E.g.*, in cases of restitution or unjust enrichment (which formerly was termed "quasi-contract"): below, pp. 11-13.

25 Such as the Sale of Goods Act, below, pp. 485-486.

26 Reference to this passage was made by LaForest J.A. in *Hallmark Pool Corp. v. Storey* (1983), 144 D.L.R. (3d) 56 at 65 (N.B.C.A.), in support of the idea that the duty of the court is to determine contractual rights and obligations *objectively*. On the view that the court recognizes and enforces the "reasonable expectations" of the parties (*i.e.*, an objective approach), see *Cathcart Inspection Services Ltd. v. Purolator Courier Ltd.* (1982), 139 D.L.R. (3d) 371 at 375 (Ont. C.A.), quoting Brooke J.A. in *Leading Invts. v. New Forest Invts.* (1981), 126 D.L.R. (3d) 75 at 85 (Ont. C.A.). See also Reiter & Swan, "Contracts and the Protection of Reasonable Expectations" in Reiter & Swan, *Studies in Contract Law* (1980), pp. 1-22.

This comes into focus in another context. Where it is not the fact of a contract that is in question, but its interpretation or construction, the same problem may arise. Does the contract mean what it appears, on the surface, to mean, or what it was understood or intended by a particular party to mean? There are many facets to the issue of construction, for example, when the problem of certainty is at stake. Here, also, courts may have to face the issue of objectivity or subjectivity. The same is true where there is no allegation of a mistake to prevent the existence of a contract, but the issue is one of deciding whether or not the parties have finalized or reached their agreement. By and large the common law took the view, here as elsewhere, that the only correct and acceptable approach to adopt was to look at the circumstances not in the light of what the parties thought but by the reference to what the reasonable man, external to the situation, would conclude from the facts. Notwithstanding the overt principles stated by the Courts, they are, or may be, substituting their views on whether or not a contract exists or should exist, and what is the nature of the agreement of the parties, for what the parties thought or may have thought, desired or may have desired, intended or may have intended. Indeed, in several areas of the modern law of contract, for example, frustration, implied terms, penalties, unconscionable bargains, the same development may be taking place.[27] Agreement may be changing in its character. The original emphasis by the law upon the need for actual agreement between the parties as the foundation for the existence, meaning and scope of a contract, may have been replaced to some extent by the rising importance of the function of the court in determining whether or not there is a contract between the parties, and, if so, what are its terms and the rights and duties it creates.

There may not be contract without agreement (however that agreement is reached or defined); but there can be agreement without contract. A contract is a species of agreement. It is a legal relationship that is a variety of agreement. Legal relationships are normally founded, or modelled on social, moral and other relationships. But they are special kinds or examples of such relationships. If, as has often been said, nature follows art, it is equally true to say that law follows nature. Thus the idea of contract which is enshrined in modern law, is derived from the concept of agreement which emerged in society. It is based upon a meeting of the minds, intentions, and desires of parties. But it is not limited or regulated solely by these, nor by the general concept of agreement that applies in the world at large. Contracts are agreements that are accepted by the law as being capable and worthy of legal recognition. This means that the law has to acknowlege that the particular promise or promises that are involved, in the context in which they are made or given, should be effectuated in law. An important factor in this respect is the necessity for the parties to intend to create legal relations.[28]

When it is said, therefore, that contract is founded upon promises and upon agreement about promises, this must be understood as subject to the qualification that the promises, and the agreement, are designed and intended to have legal

---

27 Fridman, "Freedom of Contract" (1967), 2 Ottawa L.R. 1.
28 Another is the requirement of consideration: below, pp. 81-136.

effect. This is why, as a matter of law, certain kinds of promises or agreements, cannot ever be regarded or treated as constituting contracts, for example: vows of a religious kind; offers of assistance to charity, whether in the form of work or money; certain kinds of family agreements; undertakings of help or co-operation with friends in a social context. There are instances of promises of a "social" kind which may or may not take on the status and form of contracts. In addition, there are some situations in which what looks as though it might conceivably amount to, or involve a contractual promise or agreement, in fact is not.[29]

4. Contract as bargain

The history of the common law of contract is bound up with the development of remedies in what would now be regarded as a contractual context or situation. There was a "long-drawn-out struggle to supersede the action of debt *sur contract* by assumpsit which culminated in *Slade's Case*[30] in 1602."[31] This "did not involve any extension of liability on informal agreements," that is, agreements not under seal. However, since the concept of a contractual remedy became extended to cases where no debt was involved, in other words, where the liability was founded not upon the fact that one person owed a sum of money to another, but upon a promise made by one to the other, "the rise of assumpsit did involve the recognition by the common law courts of a new liability." This is the basis for the doctrine of consideration.[32]

> The extension of promissory liability into areas previously outside the scope of the common law generated a need for a new set of boundary markers. It was natural that in a doctrinal system of law there should be a place for a new body of doctrine, whose function was to define which promises should be actionable, and which should not give rise to legal liability. Such a corpus of doctrine was evolved in the sixteenth century, and one part of it is the doctrine of consideration, which delimits the actionability of informal promises by *reference to the circumstances in which the promise in question is made.*[33]

Other "limiting doctrines" could have been adopted, and to some extent were adopted, by the common law, for example, the need for writing, or the use of formal words.[34] What the common law did, however, was to concentrate on this one theory under which,

> the actionability of informal promises is made to turn upon an analysis of the motivating reasons which induced the promisor to make the promise — the consideration or considerations for the promise.[35]

---

29 Below, pp. 28-30.
30 (1602), 4 Co. Rep. 91a.
31 Simpson, *A History of the Common Law of Contract* (1975), at p. 316.
32 Below, pp. 81-136.
33 Simpson, above, note 31 at p. 316 (author's italics).
34 *E.g.*, with regards to deeds: below, pp. 117-119.
35 Simpson, above, note 31, at p. 326.

The discussion of the history of the development of this doctrine, and its connection with (a) the doctrine of uses and (b) the canon law[36] reveals that the doctrine of consideration

> is indeed intensely moralistic, and we may disagree with some of its judgments; what is mistaken is to fail to see that a good law of contract has as its function in relation to the commercial world the imposition of decent moral standards.[37]

It is this last remark that is perhaps the most important. It brings home an important feature of the common law of contract, namely the connection between commercial policy or convenience and commercial, and other morality. What the law of contract has been striving for, and what is an essential ingredient of a valid, enforceable, legally acceptable contract, is an agreement that can be called "serious," that is, made with the kind of serious, binding intent that demarcates the casual promise, underserving of legal recognition, from a promise which should be effective in law, and should be obligatory on the future action, as well as the conscience of the promisor.

The idea that contractual promises are founded upon consideration is one that has been subjected to attack in modern times.[38] Such attacks have failed to undermine the essential notion.[39] However, the concept of consideration may be undergoing subtle change, sufficient to make it less serious an obstacle to establishing the existence of a contract; some statutory changes in Canada have removed its need in one area which has given much trouble, that is, in the context of "accord and satisfaction."[40] Moreover, the growth in the United States, and to a more limited extent in England and Canada, of the idea of estoppel, whether it be called equitable estoppel or promissory estoppel, has given greater credence to a different theory of the basis of contract, namely that of "injurious reliance."[41]

According to this theory, so far from there having to be a good reason, in the form of some benefit or detriment, for the giving of a promise which has contractual intent and consequence, all that is necessary is that there should be reliance upon a promise, and resultant injury to the party so relying should the promise not be fulfilled. This theory brings the law of contract much closer, once again, to the law of tort, from which it originally was spawned, procedurally if not, indeed, substantively.[42] This theory would lead to a closer approximation of the common law of tort and contract, such that contract and tort would once again

---

36 *Ibid.*, Part II, Chapters V, VI, VII.

37 *Ibid.*, at p. 488.

38 See the interesting discussion by Gilmore, *The Death of Contract* (1974), pp. 18-34, 55-85.

39 Compare Megaw L.J. in *Harrocks v. Forray*, [1976] 1 All E.R. 737 at 742 (C.A.), on the current relevance of consideration as well as the intention to effect a legal relationship.

40 Below, pp. 551-553.

41 Fridman, "The Basis of Contractual Obligation" (1974), 7 Loyola of Los Angeles L.R. 1. See below, pp. 121-136.

42 Simpson, above, note 31, Part II, Chapters I, II; Milsom, *Historical Foundations of the Common Law* (1969), Chap. 12; Baker, *An Introduction to English Legal History* (1971), pp. 182-198; McLaren, "The Convergence of Tort and Contract: A Return to More Venerable Wisdom?" (1989), 68 Can. Bar Rev. 30.

be different ways whereby obligations could be created and could arise, rather than be different categories of jural relations.[43]

At the present time, however, there is still a clear distinction between the notion of contract and that of tort, and it rests, among other things, upon the concept of consideration. While other features are of great relevance, consideration is the hallmark of contract. It is consideration which functions as a major test of contract; not the sole test, since the necessary intent must also be present.[44] In other words, a promise to pay, give, etc., is nothing more than a bare undertaking, *nudum pactum*, which may bind a party's conscience, and affect him morally, religiously, or otherwise, but never legally. Only if that promise is made for, or supported by consideration, that is, something which is regarded by the law as consideration, will it amount to a contractual promise, and the agreement that results therefrom will be a contract. Only a promise made for, or supported by, consideration is a "serious" promise, of which the law will take official cognizance.[45]

Whether consideration rests upon the idea of *quid pro quo*, that is, giving something in exchange for something else, or upon the idea that there must be a bargain, it is clear that, for an agreement to be a contract, the promise must somehow have been "bought" by the promisee.[46] But this does not necessarily invite the conclusion that only truly commercial agreements are contracts. The law is only drawing a distinction between moral, social or religious agreements or "bargains" and those which have a different force and intent. The idea that moral justification could be the basis of a contract, for example, where a promise was made because of the familial relation of the parties, or out of "natural love and affection," has long since been rejected by the common law.[47] So too, has been the idea that because a person ought to pay or give, his promise to do so should be legally binding. But what is given in return for a promise need not be particularly valuable, monetarily or commercially speaking.[48] In effect, while the courts deny the moral basis of consideration, it may be that underlying some modern cases on consideration is the thought that, since the party in question *ought* to be bound, consideration will somehow be discovered so as to make him bound in law. In subtle ways the law may be making the concept of consideration perform new functions, or, perhaps, revert to an older form. However, the technicalities of the law of consideration will not always permit this; in consequence, it must still be stated that the classical theory of consideration and contractual promises maintains its pre-eminence and its command of the field.

---

43 This is also the thesis of Gilmore, *The Death of Contract* (1974); see *ibid.* at pp. 87-94. Compare Reiter, "Contracts, Torts, Relations and Reliance" in Reiter & Swan, *Studies in Contract Law*, p. 235. See, however, Burrows, "Contract, Tort and Restitution — A Satisfactory Division or Not?" (1983), 99 L.Q.R. 217.

44 Contrast Hepple, "Intention to Create Legal Relations" (1970), 28 C.L.J. 122.

45 This sentence was cited by McLellan J. in *Case's Insulation & Siding Ltd. v. Gordon* (1991), 45 C.L.R. 252 at 255 (N.B.Q.B.).

46 Cited by McLellan J. *loc. cit.* above, note 45.

47 *Eastwood v. Kenyon* (1840), 11 Ad. & E. 438, 113 E.R. 482.

48 Below, pp. 83, 90.

5. Contract and restitution

Earlier it was stated that contract stems from agreement, involving some voluntary act by each of the parties.[49] This vital feature distinguishes the idea of contract from restitution, or, as it is sometimes termed, unust enrichment. The law of restitution is derived from, but now extends beyond, the older law of quasi-contract.[50] Although there are situations in which a restitutionary remedy may arise in a contractual situation, as an alternative possibility to an action for breach of contract,[51] it is important to differentiate the jural relation of contract from the relationship that emerges from the application of the doctrine of restitution. Restitutionary recovery is not based upon contractual notions of damages,[52] but upon the idea that one party must disgorge any benefit by virtue of which he was enriched at the expense of the other party, in circumstances in which it would be unjust for him to retain such benefit. The underlying principle of restitution is not that of promise or agreement: it is the idea of unjust enrichment at another's expense (whether the origin of the particular instance of recovery be common law, for example, where money is paid under a mistake of fact, or equity, as in situations of constructive trust).[53] The necessity for distinguishing contract from quasi-contract, or restitution, arises because of the historical antecedents of the modern law of restitution.

Historians of the common law have shown how, after the emergence of a general contractual remedy, which helped to create the broader concept of contract, there also developed ancillary or additional instances of recovery, where there was no truly contractual relationship between the parties, founded upon an implied contract.[54] The contractual remedy of *assumpsit*, by the inclusion of the so-called "common counts" of *money had and received to the plaintiff's use*, gave rise to a category of quasi-contract, as it became known to theorists of the law, if not by the courts. Though these instances of liability were, superficially at any rate, likened and assimilated to contract, they were not in actuality contractual situations, even where the facts revealed that there was, or had been some contractual relationship between the parties. From the seventeenth to the twentieth centuries, in England, there emerged various groups of cases which applied these principles and exemplified this remedy. Thus recovery was allowed in cases of: mistaken payment of money; money paid upon compulsion; money paid for a consideration that had wholly failed, or for an illegal purpose that was subsequently abandoned in time; money paid in discharge of another party's liability; and many other instances. Recovery was also granted, on equitable principles, for example, trust and account, in other instances. All these various situations, which were formerly thought of as being instances of liability founded upon an "implied promise," or

---

49 Above, p. 5.
50 Fridman, *Restitution*, 2nd ed. (1992), Chap. 1; Goff & Jones, *Law of Restitution*, 3rd ed. (1986), pp. 1-12; Klippert, *Unjust Enrichment*, Chaps. 1, 2.
51 Fridman, *op. cit.* pp. 153-155; Goff & Jones, *op. cit.* pp. 449-483; Klippert, *op. cit.*, Chap. 10.
52 Below, pp. 694, 745.
53 Fridman, *op. cit.* Chaps. 3, 12; Goff & Jones, *op. cit.* Chaps. 3, 34.
54 Simpson, above, note 31, pp. 489-505; Jackson, *History of Quasi-Contract.*

an "implied contract," as the House of Lords stated in *Sinclair v. Brougham*[55] in 1914, are now no longer viewed in the same way.[56]

By virtue of modern developments, in England, the United States and Canada, the better view is that all these instances where recovery is permitted, whether such recovery is based upon the common law or equity, shold be considered as cases of unjust enrichment or restitution. There is no promise, and *a fortiori* no contract. What there is, it should be stated, is an obligation to pay or repay that is imposed by the law, irrespective of agreement, and even by way of contradiction of agreement. The law of unjust enrichment or restitution, terms which appear to be interchangeable, has taken over the field that was once called quasi-contract. It is distinct from the law of contract, even though it stems historically from the law of contract, just as contract is distinct from tort despite their common origin. Restitution, unjust enrichment, or quasi-contract, covers the kinds of situations already mentioned, as well as cases of recovery for services rendered, either in an emergency or otherwise, on the basis of *quantum meruit*, that is, payment calculated on the basis of the worth of the services in question, and incidental expenses, not based upon either agreement or the rules relating to remoteness and measurement of damages where a breach of contract has occurred. The function of the court is not to apply the law of damages in breach of contract cases, but to award what is just and reasonable having regard to the circumstances.

A complication or confusion arises from the fact that there is a contractual *quantum meruit*,[57] as well as quasi-contractual, or restitutionary *quantum meruit*. In some circumstances, for example, where there is a contract between the parties but they have not agreed upon a price for goods or services to be delivered or rendered by one party to the other, the court must award money to the unpaid party on the basis of a reasonable amount for the goods or services. This is a liability that arises from a truly contractual relationship, and the situation between the parties is founded upon the concept of contract as it has been expounded earlier. Where no contract exists between the parties, or such contract as there is cannot be recognized or enforced, for example, because it does not comply with the provisions of the Statute of Frauds,[58] the courts have allowed a deserving party to recover something on a *quantum meruit* basis, which is not the same as what might have been recovered if there had been a valid, enforceable contract upon which the successful party could have sued.[59] The distinction between these cases, as between contract and quasi-contract, lies in the idea that there has to be an

---

55 [1914] A.C. 398 (H.L.).

56 Fridman, *op. cit.* above, note 50; Goff & Jones, *op. cit.* above, note 50; Klippert, *op. cit.*, above, note 50.

57 Below, p. 701.

58 Below, pp. 209-236.

59 See, *e.g., Deglman v. Guar. Trust Co.*, [1954] S.C.R. 725 (S.C.C.); Angus, "Restitution in Canada Since the Deglman Case" (1964), 42 Can. Bar Rev. 529; Fridman, *op. cit.* above, note 50, pp. 285-350.

agreement, between the parties, and such agreement must be in the form of an enforceable contract, to which the law will give effect.[60]

Once the notions of contract on the one hand, and quasi-contract, unjust enrichment or restitution on the other are disentangled, not only does the nature of contract become clearer, but, at the same time, the underlying principles of restitutionary recovery, at common law or in equity, can be revealed, and the body of law which makes up unjust enrichment or restitution can be developed separately, in accordance with its own properly applicable doctrines and rules. Acceptance and understanding of this will remove the confusion of the two streams of the law and will clarify the reasons why the law of quasi-contract is not a part of the law of contract.

6. Contract and tort

Agreement is also a relevant factor in marking the distinction between contractual and tort liability. Rights and liabilities arise from the commission of a tort as they do from the creation of a contract. The difference is that in the case of tort they are created or imposed by the law, whereas in the case of contract those rights and duties stem from the agreement made by the parties, as interpreted and rendered enforceable by the law. In other words, parties can assume or impose obligations on themselves by agreement which would not ordinarily arise in the absence of such agreement. Furthermore, by agreement, and *a fortiori* by contract, parties may sometimes be allowed to affect obligations, rights or duties that arise from the law of torts.[61] Such is the case, for example, where by contract a visitor excludes the duty that would otherwise be owed to him by the occupier of the premises which he is visiting.[62]

Historically the modern law of contract grew out of and developed from the early law of torts.[63] From the fourteenth century, if not before, recognition was given, via the medium of the appropriate writs, to the independence of contractual remedies from those more pertinent to conduct that was tortious. Modern commentators have remarked on the apparent convergence of tort and contract in more recent times, signifying, so it would seem, a reversion to the more ancient intimate connection between these two distinct branches of the law of obligations.[64] Indeed it has been argued by some that, at their present day, it is no longer relevant, nor is it necessary or functional, to differentiate contract from either tort or restitution. This assertion has been as vigorously denied as it has been propounded.[65]

---

60 This passage, beginning with the words "A complication or confusion arises . . ." was cited by Halvorson J. in *Lilly v. Corynthian Restaurant Ltd.; Corynthian Restaurant v. Lilly* (1980), 7 Sask. R. 110 at 115-116 (Sask. Q.B.).

61 Fridman, *Law of Torts*, Vol. 1 (1989), pp. 352-369.

62 *Ibid.*, Vol. 2 (1990), pp. 66-67.

63 Compare McLaren, "The Convergence of Tort and Contract: A Return to More Venerable Wisdom?" (1989), 68 Can. Bar Rev. 30.

64 *Ibid.*; Swanton, "The Convergence of Tort and Contract" (1989), 12 Sydney L.R. 40.

65 Burrows, "Contract, Tort and Restitution — A Satisfactory Distinction or Not?" (1983), 99 L.Q.R. 217.

What is undoubtedly true, however, is that in some circumstances a remedy may be available to a party under both the law of contract and the law of tort.[66] This has led to the problem of determining whether the party in question may be permitted to elect which remedy to pursue, or is obliged to seek relief under the law of contract rather than the law of tort. In such instances the law of contract and the law of tort overlap.[67] Elsewhere they interact,[68] for example, in the case of the tort of inducing, or procuring a breach of contract,[69] which has been extended to other forms of interference with existing, or possibly even contemplated contracts.[70]

Since this book is concerned with the law pertaining to contracts, it is unnecessary to pursue these matters further. What needs to be said, however, is that there are significant differences, just as there are similarities between the scope of the law of contract and that of the law of tort, much as there are important resemblances and differences between contract and restitution.

---

66 See below, pp. 694-701.

67 Bridge, "The Overlap of Tort and Contract" (1982), 27 McGill L.J. 872: Jaffey, "Contract in Tort's Clothing" (1985), 5 J. Leg. St. 77; Markesinis, "An Expanding Tort Law — The Price of a Rigid Contract Law" (1987), 103 L.Q.R. 354.

68 Fridman, "The Interaction of Tort and Contract" (1977), 93 L.Q.R. 422.

69 Fridman, *Law of Torts*, Vol. 2 (1990), pp. 291-306.

70 *Ibid.*, pp. 306-312; Fridman, "Interference with Trade or Business" (1993), 1 Tort Law Review 19-41, 99-122.

2

Agreement

1. Consensus ad idem

(a) The essence of a contract

Agreement is at the basis of any legally enforceable contract. The absence of assent prevents the creation of a binding contract.[1] There must be a substratum of agreement, or *consensus ad idem*. [2] Such agreement must be clearly manifested.

---

1 *Poirier v. Goguen* (1989), 99 N.B.R. (2d) 91 (N.B.Q.B.). The parties' minds must meet on all essential points: compare Osborn J. in *Heron Seismic Services Ltd. v. Muscowpetung Indian Band* (1990), 74 D.L.R. (4th) 308 at 310 (Sask. Q.B.); affirmed (1991), 86 D.L.R. (4th) 767 (Sask C.A.) (no contract); *Island Marine Products Ltd. v. Maxwell* (1991), 101 N.S.R. (2d) 294 (N.S. Co. Ct.) (parties not *ad idem*: no meeting of minds). Contrast *Mark Fishing Co. v. Northern Princess Seafood Ltd.* (1990), 38 F.T.R. 299 (Fed. T.D.); reversed in part (1991), 137 N.R. 151 (Fed. C.A.); *Socanav Inc. v. Greater Sarnia Invt. Corp.* (1988), 21 F.T.R. 162 (Fed. T.D.).

2 See, *e.g., Casey v. Chrysler Can. Ltd.* (1978), 33 N.S.R. (2d) 607 (N.S.T.D.) (no contract concluded about dealership in the defendants' vehicles; no *consensus ad idem*); *Sandy Frank Film Syndication Inc. v. CFQC Broadcasting Ltd.* (1982), 14 Sask. R. 286 (Sask. Q.B.) (no signature on document; no agreement); contrast *Trans Can. Credit Corp. Ltd. v. Tirmer* (1978), 33 N.S.R. (2d) 102 (N.S.T.D.)

"In order to bring a contract into existence there must be a communication of the parties' intention by means of outward expression."[3] It is necessary not only to show an intention in the party to be charged to agree, but also to show an expression of that intention.[4] An inward intent will not suffice. But how does the law determine the existence and nature of a party's intent? In the words of Sirois J. of Saskatchewan in *Gutheil v. Caledonia No. 99 R.M.*: "The law judges of the intention of a person by his outward expression only and it judges of an agreement between two persons exclusively from those expressions of their intentions, which are communicated between them".[5] Hence the requisite agreement may be established by the conduct of the parties subsequent to the alleged contract.[6]

Constantly reiterated in the judgments is the idea that the test of agreement for legal purposes is whether parties have indicated to the outside world, in the form of the objective reasonable bystander, their intention to contract and the terms of such contract. It is not what an individual party believed or understood was the meaning of what the other party said or did that is the criterion of agreement; it is whether a reasonable man in the situation of that party would have believed and understood that the other party was consenting to the identical terms.[7] The

---

(defendant bound by signature, although she claimed no recollection of having signed; a valid agreement). See also *Kawneer Co. v. Bank of Can.* (1982), 40 O.R. (2d) 275 (Ont. C.A.) (no concluded oral collateral contract); *Fraser v. Van Nus* (1983), 45 B.C.L.R. 44 (B.C.S.C.) (no completed agreement, further clarification was necessary).

3 *Thierry v. Thierry* (1956), 2 D.L.R. (2d) 419 at 425 (Sask. C.A.) *per* Martin C.J.S., cited with approval by Tucker J. in *Highland Const. Co. v. Borger Const. Ltd.* (1967), 59 W.W.R. 627 at 633 (Sask. Q.B.).

4 *Per* Stuart J. in *Blackstock v. Williams* (1907), 6 W.L.R. 79 at 82 (N.W.T.C.A.), in which the learned judge relied on the decision of the Privy Council in *Harvey v. Facey*, [1893] A.C. 552 (P.C.) with which compare *Nat. Harbours Bd. v. Northern Sales Ltd.* (1984), 29 Man. R. (2d) 248 (Man. C.A.); leave to appeal to S.C.C. refused (1985), 32 Man. R. (2d) 160n (S.C.C.). But see what is said at pp. 52-55 below, on the subject of acceptance by silence.

5 (1964), 48 D.L.R. (2d) 628 at 635 (Sask. Q.B.). Hence, in *Phillips v. Holmes*, [1988] R.P.C. 613, a sale occurred rendering the defendant guilty of a crime, even though the other party to the contract only argeed to buy the copyrighted goods in order to trap the defendant; and acted under orders from the police.
    This paragraph and part of the next were quoted by Hutchinson J. in *Bate Industrial Services Ltd. v. Enerflex Systems Ltd.* (1992), 132 A.R. 253 at 258-259 (Alta. Q.B.).

6 *Fletton Ltd. v. Peat Marwick Ltd.* (1986), 32 B.L.R. 162 (B.C.S.C.); affirmed on other grounds (1988), 50 D.L.R. (4th) 729 (B.C.C.A.); leave to appeal to S.C.C. refused (1988), 50 D.L.R. (4th) vii (note) (S.C.C.); *Di Giacomo v. Di Giacomo Can. Inc.* (1989), 28 C.P.R. (3d) 77 (Ont. H.C.); additional reasons at (1990), 28 C.P.R. (3d) 447 (Ont. H.C.).

7 *I.T.T. Industries of Can. Ltd. v. Toronto Dominion Bank* (1988), 63 Alta. L.R. (2d) 87 (Alta. Q.B.). Compare *Bate Industrial Services Ltd. v. Enerflex Systems Ltd.*, above, note 5, at 260. The classic formulation is that of Blackburn J. in *Smith v. Hughes* (1871), L.R. 6 Q.B. 597 at 607: "If whatever a man's real intention may be, he so conducts himself that a reasonable man would believe that he was assenting to the terms proposed by the other party and that other party upon that belief enters into a contract with him, the man thus conducting himself would be equally bound as if he had intended to agree to the other party's terms." This has been referred to with approval and quoted in many Canadian cases: see, *e.g.*, the judgment of Ritchie J. in *St. John Tug Boat Co. v. Irving Refining Ltd.*, [1964] S.C.R. 614 at 622 (S.C.C.). Compare La Forest J.A. in *Hallmark Pool Corp. v. Storey* (1983), 144 D.L.R. (3d) 56 at 65 (N.B.C.A.). See however, the discussion of recent English cases involving consent to the *abandonment* of an arbitration agreed upon in a contract,

common law embraced this attitude of objectivity in the determination of contractual relations. However, equitable ideas have infiltrated the law of contract to the extent of permitting a more subjective assessment of the circumstances. In some situations, therefore, the existence of a contract and the nature and content of its terms may be determined by reference to the actual belief and understanding of an individual party rather than by reference to the belief and understanding of a reasonable man hypothetically in the position of such party.[8]

Sometimes it is a simple matter to decide what the parties have manifested to each other, and consequently, whether they have agreed, and if so, upon what. This is especially true where a document containing their agreement has been prepared and signed by the parties. If the plain wording of the document reveals a clear and unambiguous intent, it is not necessary to go further.[9] Indeed, once that has been done, it may not be possible to have recourse outside such document, either to other written material or to parol evidence from the parties or anyone else, in order to explain, or otherwise clarify what is contained in the document.

If there is no single document to which reference can be made in order to decide if a contract exists between the parties, but a series of negotiations, then everything that occurs between the parties relevant to the alleged contract must be considered by the court which is faced with the problem of deciding the issue.[10] From what they have said, done, or written, in combination if necessary, there must be established a bargain or an agreement. Hence in *Pickett v. Love*,[11] where the former lover of the defendant sued for payment in respect of work which he had performed on the defendant's home while they lived together, there was no contract; the relationship between the parties and their general conduct at the time the work was carried out indicated that there was never any agreement to pay for the work, that is, no contract. A different kind of relationship was involved in *Oromocto v. Oromocto Development Corporation*.[12] Here the issue was whether the relationship of debtor and creditor had arisen by agreement between the town of Oromocto and the development corporation for Oromocto. Both were controlled by the federal government. It was held that the transaction under which the town gave a promissory note to the corporation was not a contract; it was a bookkeeping arrangement.

---

by De Moor, "Intention in the Law of Contract: Elusive or Illusory?" (1990), 106 L.Q.R. 632. The leading cases are: *Paul Wilson & Co. A/S. v. Partenreederei Hannah Blumenthal*, [1983] 1 A.C. 854 (H.L.); *Allied Marine Transport Ltd. v. Vale do Rio Doce Navegacao S.A.*, [1985] 1 W.L.R. 925 (C.A.); *Food Corp. of India v. Antclizo Shipping Corp.*, [1988] 1 W.L.R. 603 (H.L.); *Tankrederei Ahrenkeil GmbH v. Frahuil S.A.; The "Multitank Holsatia"*, [1988] 2 Lloyd's Rep. 486 (Q.B.); *Thai-Europe Tapioca Service Ltd. v. Seine Navigation Co., The Maritime Winner*, [1989] 2 Lloyd's Rep. 506.

8 This paragraph was cited by Hoyt J.A. in *Savoie v. Campbellton (City)* (1990), 105 N.B.R. (2d) 333 at 338 (N.B.C.A.).

9 *Central Service Station Ltd. v. Nfld. Light & Power Co.* (1991), 90 Nfld. & P.E.I.R. 118 (Nfld. T.D.).

10 *Baynes v. Vancouver Bd. of School Trustees*, [1927] 2 D.L.R. 698 at 700 (B.C.S.C.) *per* Murphy J. See the cases cited in note 6.

11 (1982), 20 Sask. R. 115 (Sask. Q.B.).

12 (1979), 28 N.B.R. (2d) 78 (N.B.Q.B.). Compare *Skivest Devs. v. Alta.* (1984), 57 A.R. 252 (Alta. Q.B.).

In each instance the courts seek proof of an agreement between the parties involving the necessary exchange of acts and promises, promises and promises, or acts and acts.

A representation of intention, which has not been made into a promise, will not give rise to a contract merely because the one to whom it has been made has acted upon it.[13] Yet it has been suggested that a contract can be formed out of such conduct, giving rise to an estoppel against the one whose expression of intention has led to the subsequent act. There is a hint of this in the judgment of Proudfoot J. in the British Columbia case of *Lawson v. Utan Enterprises Ltd.*[14] This case involved a projected sale of land and buildings. Later there was a purported addition of cattle and an inventory of machinery and equipment to the items to be sold. No final agreement appears to have been reached about these matters. However, the defendant had taken possession of the cattle and sold them, and he had gone onto the farm which was the subject of the sale and had assisted in its operation. It was held that this conduct evidenced the relevant agreement, but it also seems that the court determined the liability of the defendant for breach of contract on the basis of an estoppel founded upon his conduct. As between the necessity for agreement and the application of the doctrine of estoppel, the better view is that there was a concluded agreement in this case evidenced by the conduct of the parties. In other instances courts have been able to find a concluded agreement, without recourse to estoppel, from the conduct of the parties.[15] Despite arguments to the contrary,[16] mere reliance upon the conduct of the other party to an alleged contract will not suffice to establish a contract *de novo*, *i.e.*, where none existed before,[17] in the absence of prior agreement.

---

13 *A.G. Ont. v. Great Lakes Paper Co.* (1921), 64 D.L.R. 159 at 179 (Ont. H.C.) *per* Rose J. Compare *Campbell v. Inverness (County)* (1990), 98 N.S.R. (2d) 330 (N.S.T.D.), a promise to close a dump could not give rise to a binding contractual obligation by the device of promissory estoppel.

   The version of this paragraph in the previous edition was quoted by Hutchinson J. in *Bate Industrial Services Ltd. v. Enerflex Systems Ltd.* (1992), 132 A.R. 253 at 259 (Alta. Q.B.).

14 (1979), 10 B.C.L.R. 163 at 173-176 (B.C.S.C.); damages reduced on appeal (1982), 39 B.C.L.R. 1 (B.C.C.A.). Compare also *Rocca Group Ltd. v. Consumers Distributing Co.* (1977), 21 N.S.R. (2d) 371 (N.S.C.A.).

15 *Adam v. Gen. Paper Co.* (1978), 19 O.R. (2d) 574 (Ont. H.C.). *Byrne v. Napier* (1975), 10 O.R. (2d) 193 (Ont. H.C.). *Bank of Montreal v. Glendale (Atlantic) Ltd.* (1977), 20 N.S.R. (2d) 216 (N.S.C.A.); *Cassidy v. Can. Publishing Corp.* (1989), 41 B.L.R. 223 (B.C.S.C.). Contrast *Zeismann v. W.P.W. Devs. Ltd.* (1976), 78 D.L.R. (3d) 619 (B.C.S.C.); *Stairs v. New Brunswick* (1977), 20 N.B.R. (2d) 553 (N.B.Q.B.).

16 Atiyah, "Contracts, Promises and the Law of Obligations" (1978), 96 L.Q.R. 193; compare Reiter and Swan, "Contracts and the Protection of Reasonable Expectations" in Reiter and Swan, *Studies in Contract Law* at p. 1; Reiter, "Contracts, Torts, Relations and Reliance," *ibid.*. at p. 235.

17 Compare *Fobasco Ltd. v. Cogan* (1990), 72 O.R. (2d) 256 at 260 (Ont. H.C.) *per* Rutherford J. Contrast the situation where modification of an existing contract is involved: below, pp. 121-136. In Australia, however, it would seem that a contractual relationship can be created by the invocation of estoppel (though whether this is common law estoppel, estoppel *in pais* or equitable estoppel is unclear). Moreover it is uncertain whether the remedy is damages for breach of contract or the prevention of detriment to the party relying on the representation, by compensating that party for reliance losses: see *Waltons Stores (Interstate) Ltd. v. Maher* (1988), 164 C.L.R. 387; *Foran v. Wight* (1989), 168 C.L.R. 385; *Commonwealth v. Verwayen* (1990), 170 C.L.R. 394.

(b) Certainty

The court cannot make for the parties a bargain which they themselves did not make in proper time.[18] This means in the first instance, that if a contract is not clearly created by the parties' language or conduct the court cannot construct one.[19] It is for the parties to use such language or employ such conduct as will make plain that they intended to contract.[20] Once they have done so, they will be bound thereby, even if the result is unreasonable. This was stated emphatically by the Supreme Court of Canada in *Steel Co. of Canada v. Willand Management Ltd.*[21] There a building contractor gave what was, in effect, an absolute written guarantee that the building to be constructed would be weather tight, with first class materials being used throughout. Despite the onerousness and gravity of such an undertaking, since the language and intent were clear, the court found that the contractor was bound.

It is different, however, where the language is not unambiguous but vague and uncertain. In the absence of the requisite certainty and clarity the courts will not declare that a contract exists.[22] Another possibility is that the courts will not recognize a particular obligation asserted to be part of a contract. In such instances courts have stated that terms which are uncertain, and therefore not enforceable, may be excised from the contract, if the rest of the agreement is capable of being

---

18 *Murphy v. McSorley*, [1929] 4 D.L.R. 247 at 250 (S.C.C.) *per* Mignault J.; compare *Kelly v. Watson* (1921), 61 S.C.R. 482 at 483 (S.C.C.) *per* Davies C.J.C.; *Gilchrist Vending Ltd. v. Sedley Hotel Ltd.* (1967), 66 D.L.R. (2d) 24 at 28 (Sask. Q.B.) *per* Tucker J.

19 *E.g., Main Line Oil Seeds & Products Ltd. v. Chandler* (1981), 15 Sask. R. 344 (Sask. C.A.); *Kawneer Co. v. Bank of Can.* (1982), 40 O.R. (2d) 275 (Ont. C.A.); *Fraser v. Van Nus* (1983), 45 B.C.L.R. 44 (B.C.S.C.). If such a contract has been partly performed, the court may *strain* to supply the want of certainty: *Sudbrook Trading Estate Ltd. v. Eggleton*, [1982] 3 All E.R. 1 (H.L.); compare Southin J.A. in *304498 B.C. Ltd. v. Garibaldi Whistler Dev. Co.* (1989), 39 B.C.L.R. (2d) 328 at 333-334 (B.C.C.A.), indicating the difference between a claim for damages where performance has occurred and a claim for a decree of specific performance, in which case greater certainty is required.

20 See *Korbin v. Assoc. Homeowners Mtge. Ltd.* (1979), 10 B.C.L.R. 6 (B.C.C.A.); *Bell (C.W.) Hldgs. Ltd. v. Accenter Ltd.* (1978), 31 N.S.R. (2d) 313 (N.S.T.D.) (where reference was made to a draft agreement in earlier negotiations); *Valois v. Dahl* (1981), 15 Sask. R. 357 (Sask. Q.B.) (where reliance was placed on the *subsequent* conduct of the parties); *Scrimes v. Nickle* (1982), 130 D.L.R. (3d) 698 (Alta. C.A.); leave to appeal to S.C.C. refused (1982), 35 A.R. 180 (S.C.C.) (reliance on *prior* conduct of parties).

21 [1966] S.C.R. 746 (S.C.C.). See *R. v. CAE Industries Ltd.* (1985), 20 D.L.R. (4th) 347 (Fed. C.A.); leave to appeal to S.C.C. refused (1985), 20 D.L.R. (4th) 347n (S.C.C.).

22 Contrast *Eng v. Evans* (1991), 83 Alta. L.R. (2d) 107 (Alta. Q.B.) (no intent to create contract out of arrangement to share tickets for hockey games) with *Buchanan v. Hooley* (1991), 95 Nfld. & P.E.I.R. 349 (P.E.I.T.D.) (agreement with realtor involving payment of commission on sale of building, but no commission for making arrangements). See also *Fobasco v. Cogan* (1990), 72 O.R. (2d) 254 (Ont. H.C.). Compare *Leitch (Angus) & Assoc. Ltd. v. Legrand Industs. Ltd.* (1984), 31 Alta. L.R. (2d) 158 (Alta C.A.); leave to appeal to S.C.C. refused (1984), 52 N.R. 396 (S.C.C.) with *Bow Bend Trailer Park Ltd. v. Marasco* (1984), 31 Alta. L.R. (2d) 167 (Alta. C.A.). The same results may follow if a condition precedent is "illusory," *i.e.*, when it involves "fancy or taste": *Wiebe v. Bobsien* (1985), 14 D.L.R. (4th) 754 at 759 (B.C.S.C.).

enforced.[23] Uncertainty about some specific obligation may suffice to make impossible the conclusion that there is a contract in effect between the parties. The test would seem to be whether the term or terms in question relate to *essential* aspects of the alleged contract.[24] Examples of this are the failure of parties to settle the purchase price for goods,[25] the lack of agreement as to the date of commencement and term of a lease.[26]

However, the courts will try to find a clear meaning if at all possible, as clarified by Bull J.A. of the Supreme Court of British Columbia in *Marquest Indust. Ltd. v. Willows Poultry Farms Ltd.*:[27]

---

23 *Br. Amer. Timber Co. v. Elk River Timber Co.*, [1934] 2 W.W.R. 658 (B.C. C.A.). Compare *Nicolene v. Simmonds*, [1953] 1 Q.B. 543 (C.A.); *Re Vince*, [1892] 2 Q.B. 478 (C.A.); *Continental Ins. Co. v. Law Soc. of Alta.* (1984), 34 Alta. L.R. (2d) 214 (Alta. C.A.); leave to appeal to S.C.C. refused (1984), 58 N.R. 78 (S.C.C.). Because there is no agreement on some matters it should not follow that parties had not made a binding agreement: *Boult Enterprises Ltd. v. Bissett*, [1986] 1 W.W.R. 385 (B.C.C.A.); leave to appeal to S.C.C. refused (1986), 65 N.R. 79 (note) (S.C.C.). Parties can intend to be bound though other terms are yet to be agreed upon: *Pagnon S/A v. Feed Products Ltd.*, [1987] 2 Lloyd's Rep. 601 at 611 *per* Bingham L.J.; *ibid.*, at 619 *per* Lloyd L.J. The courts are reluctant to hold a contract void for uncertainty, and, therefore, distinguish between lack of meaning and ambiguity of language: *Greater London Council v. Connolly*, [1970] 2 Q.B. 100 (C.A.); *Brown v. Gould*, [1972] Ch. 53; but see *259596 Alta. Ltd. v. Richards; Richards v. 259596 Alta. Ltd.*, [1983] 2 W.W.R. 592 (Alta. Q.B.). Compare MacDonald J. in *304498 B.C. Ltd. v. Garibaldi Whistler Dev. Co.* (1988), 25 B.C.L.R. (2d) 79 at 84 (B.C.S.C.); affirmed (1989), 39 B.C.L.R. (2d) 328 (B.C.C.A.): " . . . if the real intention of the parties can be collected from the instrument, the court must give effect to it".

24 *Bawitko Invts. Ltd. v. Kernels Popcorn Ltd.* (1991), 79 D.L.R. (4th) 97 (Ont. C.A.); *O'Kennedy v. S. King Holdings Ltd.* (1989), 34 C.L.R. 104 (B.C.S.C.).

25 *Bowden v. Shaw* (1979), 34 N.S.R. (2d) 518 (N.S.T.D.); *Cormier v. Fed. Business Dev. Bank* (1980), 29 N.B.R. (2d) 392 (N.B.Q.B.); reversed on other grounds (1980), 32 N.B.R. (2d) 114 (N.B.C.A.); leave to appeal to S.C.C. dismissed (1980), 35 N.R. 596n (S.C.C.); *Alteen's Jewellers Ltd. v. Cann* (1980), 40 N.S.R. (2d) 504 (N.S. Co. Ct.); compare *Zinman v. Hechter* (1981), 130 D.L.R. (3d) 183 (Man. C.A.); leave to appeal to S.C.C. refused (1982), 14 Man. R. (2d) 360 (S.C.C.); *Jillood v. Quantel Consultants Ltd.* (1984), 59 A.R. 134 (Alta. Q.B.); or upon other financial aspects of the alleged contract: *Pietrobon v. McIntyre* (1987), 15 B.C.L.R. (2d) 350 (B.C.S.C.) (financing) (contrast *Gennis v. Madore* (1988), 72 Nfld. & P.E.I.R. 104 (P.E.I.T.D.)); *304498 B.C. Ltd. v. Garibaldi Whistler Dev. Co.* (1988), 25 B.C.L.R. (2d) 79 (B.C.S.C.); affirmed (1989). 30 B.C.L.R. (2d) 328 (B.C.C.A.) (construction mortgage to be arranged); *L.C.D.H. Audio Visual Ltd. v. I.S.T.S. Verbatim Ltd.* (1988), 40 B.L.R. 128 (Ont. H.C.); affirmed (September 11, 1991), Doc. CA 425/88 (Ont. C.A.) (commission payable); *Morton v. Asper* (1989), 62 Man. R. (2d) 1 (Man. Q.B.).

26 *Can. Square Corp. v. Versafood Services Ltd.* (1979), 8 B.L.R. 21 (Ont. H.C.); affirmed (1981), 34 O.R. (2d) 250 (*sub nom. Can. Square Corp. v. V.S. Services Ltd.*) (Ont. C.A.); compare *Sunshine Vacation Villas Ltd. v. Gov. & Co. of Adventurers of England Trading into Hudson's Bay* (1984), 58 B.C.L.R. 33 (B.C.C.A.); *BCE Dev. Corp. v. Cascade Invts. Ltd.* (1987), 55 Alta. L.R. (2d) 22 (Alta. Q.B.); affirmed (1987), 57 Alta. L.R. (2d) 349 (Alta. C.A.); leave to appeal to S.C.C. refused (1988), 58 Alta. L.R. (2d) xlix (note) (S.C.C.); *Boult Enterprises Ltd. v. Bissett*, [1986] 1 W.W.R. 385 (B.C.C.A.); leave to appeal to S.C.C. refused (1986), 65 N.R. 79 (note) (S.C.C.).

27 (1968), 1 D.L.R. (3d) 513 at 517-518 (B.C.C.A.); followed in *Lanson Homes Ltd. v. Block Bros. Contractors Ltd.* (1972), 28 D.L.R. (3d) 608 (B.C.S.C.); *Boult Enterprises Ltd. v. Bissett*, [1986] 1 W.W.R. 385 (B.C.C.A.); leave to appeal to S.C.C. refused (1986), 65 N.R. 79 (note) (S.C.C.). In this, Canadian courts follow the doctrine enunciated by Lord Wright in *Hillas & Co. v. Arcos Ltd.* (1932), 147 L.T. 503 at 514 (H.L.); "*verba ita sunt intelligenda ut res magis valeat quam pereat*". See also *Ginter v. Sawley Agency Ltd.*, [1967] S.C.R. 451 (S.C.C.).

[i]f the real intention of the parties can be collected from the language within the four corners of the instrument the Court must give effect to such intention by supplying anything necessarily to be inferred and rejecting whatever is repugnant to such real intention so ascertained.

Furthermore,

every effort should be made by a court to find a meaning, looking at substance and not mere form . . .difficulties in interpretation do not make a clause bad as not being capable of interpretation, so long as a definite meaning can properly be extracted.

Thus, if the general intention of the parties can be collected from the language within the four corners of the instrument or document which they have executed, it may be possible for the court to supply what is missing by inference.[28] For example, in *First City Investments Ltd. v. Fraser Arms Hotel Ltd.; Cumberland Management Corporation v. Fraser Arms Hotel Ltd.*,[29] the court could complete the contract by supplying the missing terms relating to the form of the projected mortgage and accumulation clause, liability for taxes, and other items. Such cases appear to be exceptional. For the most part, where terms are missing[30] or have not been finalized,[31] or there is some ambiguity about the precise meaning of what the parties

---

28 As in *Kay Corp. v. Dekeyser* (1977), 76 D.L.R. (3d) 588 (Ont. C.A.), where the necessary term as to when payment of the price of goods was to be made could be implied under the Sale of Goods Act, by which payment of price and delivery of goods are concurrent conditions unless otherwise agreed by the parties. Since there was no such other agreement, the statutory term could be implied. See also *MacIver v. Amer. Motors (Can.) Ltd.* (1976), 70 D.L.R. (3d) 473 (Man. C.A.); *Anderson v. Chaba* (1978), 81 D.L.R. (3d) 449 (Alta. C.A.); *Rocca Group Ltd. v. Consumers Distributing Co.* (1977), 21 N.S.R. (2d) 371 (N.S.C.A.); *R. v. CAE Industries Ltd.*, above, note 21. Compare *Money v. Ven-Lu-Ree Ltd.*, [1988] 1 N.Z.L.R. 685, [1988] 2 N.Z.L.R. 414, [1989] 3 N.Z.L.R. 129 (P.C.); with which contrast *Aotearoa Int. Ltd. v. Scancarriers A/S*, [1985] 1 N.Z.L.R. 510; *Australia & New Zealand Banking Group Ltd. v. Frost Pty. Holdings Ltd.*, [1989] V.R. 695 (no implication of term).

   Note that sometimes a term in the alleged contract that appears to be uncertain, thereby rendering the transaction void for uncertainty, may be capable of ascertainment by some simple process which the courts will invoke; see, *e.g., North West Co. v. Merland Oil Co.*, [1936] 4 D.L.R. 248 (Alta. S.C.); *McVeety v. Draper*, [1944] 2 D.L.R. 741 (Ont. C.A.); *Permo Gas & Oil Ltd. v. Pac. Petroleums* (1963), 40 D.L.R. (2d) 109 (Alta. C.A.); *Coady Store Fixtures & Equipment Co. v. Tosh* (1964), 46 D.L.R. (2d) 368 (Ont. H.C.); affirmed without written reasons (1965), 52 D.L.R. (2d) 506n (Ont. C.A.); *Freeman (Harry) & Sons Ltd. v. Neu* (1984), 66 N.S.R. (2d) 255 (N.S. Co. Ct.). Compare *Sawatzky v. Sawatzky* (1986), 48 Sask. R. 161 (Sask. Q.B.), instalment payments for land related to portion of annual crop price.

29 [1979] 6 W.W.R. 125 (B.C.C.A.); compare *Korbin v. Assoc. Homeowners Mtge. Ltd.* (1978), 10 B.C.L.R. 6 (B.C.C.A.); *Adam v. General Paper Co.* (1978), 85 D.L.R. (3d) 736 (Ont. H.C.); *Byrne v. Napier* (1975), 62 D.L.R. (3d) 589 (Ont. H.C.).

30 *Harrison v. Whitelaw*, [1923] 3 D.L.R. 1183 (Alta. C.A.); *Cummins v. Cummins*, [1934] 2 D.L.R. 228 (Man. C.A.); *Jackson v. Macaulay, Nicolls, Maitland & Co.*, [1942] 2 D.L.R. 609 (B.C.C.A.); contrast *Thomson Groceries Ltd. v. Scott*, [1943] 3 D.L.R. 25 (Ont. C.A.); *Deslippe v. Maguire Const. Ltd.* (1976), 66 D.L.R. (3d) 130 (Sask. Q.B.).

31 *Kelly v. Watson* (1921), 61 S.C.R. 482 (S.C.C.); *Murphy v. McSorley*, [1929] S.C.R. 542 (S.C.C.); *Barker v. Shakespeare; Gill Fuels Ltd. v. Shakespeare* (1956), 2 D.L.R. (2d) 768 (B.C. Co. Ct.); *Causeway Shopping Centre Ltd. v. Thompson & Sutherland Ltd.* (1965), 50 D.L.R. (2d) 362 (N.S.S.C.); affirmed (1965), 54 D.L.R. (2d) 649 (N.S.C.A.); *Causeway Shopping Centre Ltd. v. Muise* (1967), 63 D.L.R.

appear to have agreed to,[32] the general tenor of the decisions is against any possibility of completing the parties' work for them and creating a valid contract out of the vague contractual intent that may be evidenced by their language or conduct.

In other situations the parties may have only agreed to agree. This will be the case where they have left important aspects of the intended contract to be determined by the parties at a later date. Hence it is impossible to conclude that they have arrived at a final, definite contractual relationship.[33] There cannot be a contract to enter into a contract.[34] Nor can there be a contract to negotiate, *i.e.*, an agreement to agree.[35] The underlying principle is that all of the terms of the agreement between the parties must be settled. There must be nothing left for negotiation.[36]

(2d) 26 (N.S.S.C.); affirmed [1969] S.C.R. 274 (S.C.C.); *Re Pigeon & Titley,* [1973] 30 D.L.R. (3d) 132 (Ont. H.C.); *Nemetz (Arnold) Enrg. Ltd. v. Tobien,* [1971] 4 W.W.R. 373 (B.C.C.A.); *Cherewick v. Moore,* [1955] 2 D.L.R. 492 (B.C.S.C.); *Block Bros. Realty Ltd. v. Occidental Hotel Ltd.; Rochelle v. Occidental Hotel Ltd.* (1971), 19 D.L.R. (3d) 194 (B.C.C.A.); *Spur Oil Ltd. v. R.* (1981), 42 N.R. 131 (Fed. C.A.); leave to appeal to S.C.C. refused (1981), 39 N.R. 354 (S.C.C.); *Westward Farms v. Cadieux; Barnabe v. Cadieux* (1982), 138 D.L.R. (3d) 137 (Man. C.A.); leave to appeal to S.C.C. refused (1982), 18 Man. R. (2d) 269 (S.C.C.); *304498 B.C. Ltd. v. Garibaldi Whistler Dev. Co.* (1988), 25 B.C.L.R. (2d) 79 (B.C.S.C.); affirmed (1989), 39 B.C.L.R. (2d) 328 (B.C.C.A.); *Morton v. Asper* (1989), 62 Man. R. (2d) 1 (Man. Q.B.). Contrast *De Laval Co. v. Bloomfield,* [1938] 3 D.L.R. 405 (Ont. C.A.), on which see Gordon (1939), 17 Can. Bar Rev. 204; Wright (1939), 17 Can. Bar Rev. 208; compare *Montana Mustard Seed Co. v. Gates* (1963), 42 W.W.R. 303 (Sask. Q.B.).

32 *Bank of N.S. v. McDougall & Secord Ltd.* (1913), 11 D.L.R. 546 (Alta. C.A.); *Kerr v. Cunard* (1914), 42 N.B.R. 454 (N.B.S.C.); *Fletcher v. Holden* (1914), 19 B.C.R. 567 (B.C.S.C.); *Lethbridge Brewing & Malting Co. v. Webster,* [1919] 49 D.L.R. 250 (Sask. C.A.); *Credit Protectors Ltd. v. MacKay,* [1940] 3 W.W.R. 129 (Sask. Dist. Ct.); *Phibbs v. Choo,* [1977] 69 D.L.R. (3d) 756 (Alta. C.A.); *259596 Alta. Ltd. v. Richards; Richards v. 259596 Alta. Ltd.,* [1983] 2 W.W.R. 592 (Alta. Q.B.); *Rychjohn Invt. v. Hunter* (1979), 100 D.L.R. (3d) 652 (Sask. Q.B.); *Westward Farms Ltd. v. Cadieux; Barnabe v. Cadieux* (1982), 138 D.L.R. (3d) 137 (Man. C.A.); leave to appeal to S.C.C. refused (1982), 18 Man. R. (2d) 269 (S.C.C.); *Spur Oil Ltd. v. R.* (1981), 42 N.R. 131 (Fed. C.A.); leave to appeal to S.C.C. refused (1981), 39 N.R. 354 (S.C.C.). But see *Alta-West Group Invts. Ltd. v. Femco Financial Corp.* (1984), 34 Alta. L.R. (2d) 5 (Alta. Q.B.); *F.M.I. Consultants Ltd. v. Jeanpierre Hldgs. Ltd.* (1985), 57 A.R. 304 (Alta. Q.B.).

33 *Bawitko Invts. Ltd. v. Kernels Popcorn Ltd.* (1991), 79 D.L.R. (4th) 97 at 104 (Ont. C.A.).

34 *Courtney & Fairbairn Ltd. v. Tolaini Brothers (Hotels) Ltd.,* [1975] 1 All E.R. 716 (C.A.); *L.C.D.H. Audio Visual Ltd. v. I.S.T.S. Verbatim Ltd.* (1988), 40 B.L.R. 128 (Ont. H.C.); affirmed (September 11, 1991), Doc. CA 425/88 (Ont. C.A.). But subsequent conduct may lead to a different conclusion: *Cassidy v. Can. Publishing Corp.* (1989), 41 B.L.R. 223 (B.C.S.C.).

35 *Delta Hotels Ltd. v. Okabe Can. Invts. Co.* (1992), 3 Alta. L.R. (3d) 85 (Alta. C.A.); *Walford v. Miles,* [1992] 2 A.C. 128 (H.L.). Nor was it possible to fill in any gaps as to the duration of negotiations by postulating a duty to negotiate in good faith: contrast the obligation to use "best endeavours": *ibid.* at 181 *per* Lord Ackner. See also below, pp. 60-64, dealing with agreements "subject to contract".

36 *Imperial Oil Ltd. v. C. & G. Holdings Ltd.* (1986), 58 Nfld. & P.E.I.R. 326 at 344 (Nfld. T.D.) *per* Goodridge J.; affirmed (1989), 78 Nfld. & P.E.I.R. 1 (Nfld. C.A.). But things can be left to be determined, *e.g.*, price to be decided: *ibid.* Compare *Newfoundland (A.G.) v. Churchill Falls (Labrador) Corp.* (1983), 49 Nfld. & P.E.I.R. 181 at 262-274 (Nfld. T.D.); affirmed (1985), 56 Nfld. & P.E.I.R. 91 (Nfld. C.A.); which was affirmed [1988] 1 S.C.R. 1085 (S.C.C.).

(c) The formalism of agreement

The common law did not, and still does not, require the strict formalities of the old Roman *stipulatio*.[37] In other words, exact linguistic concordance between the parties is not required. However, the common law does require a clear manifestation of agreement.[38] The mechanism of such agreement is contained in the notions of offer and acceptance. Offer and acceptance are the analysis for practical purposes of the normal machinery by which parties manifest their mutual intention. As Lamont J. said in *Acme Grain Co. v. Wenaus*,[39]

> [t]o constitute a contract there must be an offer by one person to another and an acceptance of that offer by the person to whom it is made. A mere statement of a person's intention, or a declaration of his willingness to enter into negotiations is not an offer and cannot be accepted so as to form a binding contract.

Anglin C.J.C. went even further (perhaps too far in the light of what will emerge later with respect to communication of acceptance) when he said in the leading case of *Charlebois v. Baril*,[40]

> [t]o make a contract the law requires communication of offer and acceptance alike either to the person for whom each is respectively intended, or to his authorized agent.

Without an offer and its acceptance, there is no contract.[41] If either or both is missing, there is no proof that the parties were ever *ad idem*, that is, had reached a stage in their negotiations in respect of which it could be said that they had shown not only an intent to be bound together, but the nature, extent, and manner of their being bound so as to give rise to a legally recognizable and enforceable contract. The parties will not be bound *unless* they intend to be bound, nor will they be bound *until* they intend to be bound.[42] Their intentions in these respects are indicated by the features of offer and acceptance. Lord Denning attempted to subvert this notion in *Gibson v. Manchester City Council*.[43] In dealing with a case in which the issue was whether a contract for the sale and purchase of land

---

37 Which required strict correspondence between the language used by the promisor and that of the promisee; see Inst. III, XV, I; Buckland, *Text Book of Roman Law*, 2nd ed. (1950), pp. 434-442.

38 Hence, possibly the reason why sending goods in response to a telegram that X "must have" such goods, was held not to give rise to a contract; *Phillips v. Hatt* (1914), 20 D.L.R. 186 (N.S.S.C.). See also *Eastern Can. Cleaners Ltd. v. S.J. Kernaghan Adjusters Ltd.* (1984), 63 N.S.R. (2d) 299 (N.S.T.D.); additional reasons (1984), 64 N.S.R. (2d) 330 (N.S.T.D.); additional reasons (1985), 68 N.S.R. (2d) 186 (N.S.T.D.).

39 (1917), 36 D.L.R. 347 at 348 (Sask. C.A.).

40 [1928] S.C.R. 88 at 89 (S.C.C.).

41 This paragraph was quoted by Hutchinson J. in *Bate Industrial Services Ltd. v. Enerflex Systems Ltd.* (1992), 132 A.R. 253 at 259-260 (Alta. Q.B.).

42 *Niznick v. Cochlan*, [1948] 2 W.W.R. 856 (Man. K.B.); *Highland Const. Co. v. Borger Const. Ltd.* (1967), 59 W.W.R. 627 (Sask. Q.B.); Galt J. in *St. Denis v. Western Prods. Ltd.*, [1923] 3 W.W.R. 858 at 863 (Man. K.B.); affirmed [1924] 1 W.W.R. 174 (Man. C.A.). But the court will not stop at a point at which the parties appear to have reached agreement and ignore subsequent acts or language which might upset such conclusion; Galt J. in *St. Denis v. Western Prods. Ltd.*, [1923] 3 W.W.R. 858 at 863 (Man. K.B.); affirmed [1924] 1 W.W.R. 174 (Man. C.A.).

43 [1978] 2 All E.R. 583 (C.A.); reversed [1979] 1 All E.R. 972 (H.L.).

could be spelled out of the correspondence between the parties, he said (holding that it was unnecessary for there to be a specific offer and acceptance),[44]

> [t]o my mind it is a mistake to think that all contracts can be analysed into the form of offer and acceptance . . .as I understand the law, there is no need to look for a strict offer and acceptance. You should look at the correspondence as a whole and at the conduct of the parties and see therefrom whether the parties have come to an agreement on everything that was material. If by their correspondence and their conduct you can see an agreement on all material terms, which was intended thenceforward to be binding, then there is a binding contract in law even though all the formalities have not been gone through.

From this attitude the House of Lords recoiled and held, along with the dissentient in the Court of Appeal, Lane L.J., that no firm offer to sell had been made by the Council, therefore, nothing done or said by the purported purchaser could amount to acceptance.[45] The language of the House of Lords indicates that offer and acceptance in the strict classical sense cannot be dispensed with in modern times.[46] This would seem to negate the suggestion made by Rand J. of the Supreme Court of Canada, in *Dawson v. Helicopter Exploration Co.*,[47] that in place of searching for an offer and acceptance, courts should look for acts "instinct with an obligation imperfectly expressed," an expression culled from Cardozo J.[48] This attitude has been welcomed as signifying a willingness to escape from the rigid formalism and strict adherence to the English common law which thus far has been the pattern of judgments in Canada in cases of contract.[49] Apart from the restatement of the traditional view by the House of Lords, in language which will probably be acceptable to Canadian courts, the trouble with this approach is that it would tend to give too paternalistic a role to the courts. As it is, there is much scope for judicial creativity and interference in interpreting the language and conduct of the parties in order to determine whether they have reached a satisfactory and clear agreement that may be termed a contract. Given that the courts will not make a contract for the parties when they have not done so with sufficient clarity for themselves, nor complete an uncompleted transaction to the same end and with the same effect, it seems unlikely that Canadian courts, any more than those in England, will be willing to dispense with the formal requirements of offer and acceptance as guides to the determination of whether a contract has been brought into existence.

---

44 [1978] 2 All E.R. 583 at 586 (C.A.).

45 [1979] 1 All E.R. 972 (H.L.); compare *V.K. Mason Const. Ltd. v. Bank of N.S.*, [1985] 1 S.C.R. 271 (S.C.C.).

46 *Ibid.*, at 974 *per* Lord Diplock; but he does exclude certain "exceptional" types of contracts. Presumably this is a reference to "unilateral" contracts below, pp. 69-76. But there are instances of acceptance by conduct which differ from the kind of case typified by *Gibson v. Manchester City Council*, below, pp. 50-55.

47 [1955] S.C.R. 868 at 874-875 (S.C.C.).

48 *Wood v. Lady Duff-Gordon* (1917), 222 N.Y. 88 at 90; see *Degoesbriand v. Radford* (1985), 41 Sask. R. 43 (Sask. Q.B.).

49 Slayton (1971), 17 McGill L.J. 476 at 480-484.

Despite the seemingly vital necessity for offer and acceptance in the creation of a contract, it must be admitted that sometimes it is difficult to discover these ingredients without some straining of the facts.[50] For the most part, an examination of the facts may indicate or be undertaken so as to indicate where the requisite offer and acceptance may be found. Sometimes achieving that is more difficult. Such is the case where there is a multipartite agreement which is joined by various parties either at the same time or at different times. If there is a prior relationship between some of the parties to which an adjoining party adheres, *who* is offering and *who* is accepting the terms of the contract, and at what times? This problem is illustrated by the English case of *Clarke v. Dunraven*.[51] This concerned an action for damage done to a yacht in a race. The parties were participants in the race. It was argued that the situation was governed by the rules of the race, which were part of the contract entered into by each participant when he agreed to take part. That contract was said to have been made between each and every contestant when he sent a letter signifying his intention to be in the race. But who was the offeror, and who was the offeree? When was the offer made and accepted? A similar situation was involved in a Canadian case, *McCannel v. Mabee McLaren Motors Ltd.*[52] Canadian Studebaker Corporation had made agreements of general application with a number of dealers regulating sales of cars. The parties in this action had associated themselves individually with those agreements in much the same way as the participants in the yacht race had associated themselves with the rules of the race. Hence, it was held that by doing this the participating dealers had contracted among themselves and were bound to each other by contract. Once again it is hard to find in their actions the normally necessary offer to contract, and acceptance of such offer made by one party to the other. One way of solving the problem may be by suggesting that the pre-existing agreement is a standing offer, implied if not express, that is accepted by adherence to such agreement. In this way such situations resemble the case of the passenger who boards a bus, intending to be conveyed, and to pay the appropriate fare for such conveyance, or the customer who puts money in the automatic machine to obtain goods which are shown therein. Whatever the true solution, it can be said that the courts will always try to find offer and acceptance in order to find a contract.

---

50 Compare *New Zealand Shipping Co. v. A.M. Satterthwaite & Co.*, [1975] A.C. 154 at 167 (P.C.) *per* Lord Wilberforce.

51 [1897] A.C. 59 (H.L.); so too, where a party joins an unincorporated association such as a trade union, *Orchard v. Tunney*, [1957] S.C.R. 436 (S.C.C.); or an association of nurses, *Foran v. Kottmeier* (1973), 39 D.L.R. (3d) 40 (Ont. C.A.).

   Where a customer pays for goods or services by a credit card it has been held that this is not a tripartite contract between the customer, the supplier and the credit card company. There are *three* separate, independent contracts, *i.e.*, between customer and supplier, customer and credit card company, supplier and credit card company: *In re Charge Card Services Ltd.*, [1987] Ch. 150 at 158 *per* Millett J.; affirmed [1989] Ch. 497 (C.A.). See also *Customs & Excise Commrs. v. Diners Club Ltd.*, [1989] 1 W.L.R. 1196 (C.A.).

52 [1926] 1 D.L.R. 282 (B.C.C.A.).

2. Offer

(a) Definition

An "offer" means the signification by one person to another of his willingness to enter into a contract with him on certain terms. The language or conduct involved must be capable of being interpreted as revealing an intention to be bound. The courts have distinguished between statements or conduct which manifest such an intention, and statements or conduct which are not intended to have contractual effect at any time, or are intended to have such effect as a result of further clarifying negotiations. In some situations the intended transaction or arrangement is not contractual in nature. In others there is no doubt that the parties had in mind, as the end product of their exchanges, the possibility of a contract; the questions are whether this has crystallized into a definite offer capable of being accepted, and whether such offer has been so accepted as to bring about a contract.

(b) Intention to contract

A contract can only arise if there is the *animus contrahendi* between the parties.[53] Without the expressed or implicit intention that a contract should emerge as a result of the language or conduct of the alleged parties, no contractual obligations can be said to exist and be capable of enforcement.[54] Hence the offer that is made must be an offer to *contract* involving the creation of legal relations. As it was put by Sheppard J.A. in *Arding v. Buckton*,[55]

> a contract may be implied only when the conduct of the parties indicates that they are proceeding on the basis of some legal relation so that the function of the Court is merely to find as a fact that relation with its attendant obligations and rights which the parties have so indicated by implication but have failed to express.

While this is essentially an issue of fact, there are indications that certain parties may be less prone to entering into legal contractual relations than others. A prime illustration is afforded by governments and governmental bodies. Where a government or governmental body has set out its intention of doing something, for example,

---

53 *Vandepitte v. Preferred Accident Ins. Corp.* [1933] A.C. 70 (P.C.). Compare *McKay v. Minard* (1952), 5 W.W.R. 175 (Man. Q.B.), where there was a cost-sharing arrangement to use an automobile, but no contract giving rise to the application of the maxim *volenti non fit injuria* or to legal obligations. On this latter point there have been a number of English decisions of some importance: see *Buckpitt v. Oates*, [1968] 1 All. E.R. 1145; *Albert v. Motor Insurers' Bureau*, [1972] A.C. 301 (H.L.); *Motor Insurers' Bureau v. Meanen*, [1971] 2 All E.R. 1372n (H.L.).

   A *letter of intent* may not suffice, where there is insufficient certainty in the letter to constitute an agreement: *Leitch (Angus) & Assoc. Ltd. v. Legrand Industs. Ltd.* (1984), 31 Alta. L.R. (2d) 158 (Alta. C.A.); leave to appeal to S.C.C. refused (1984), 52 N.R. 396 (S.C.C.). Note, however, the possibility that such a letter of intent may give rise to a valid "unilateral contract": *B.S.C. v. Cleveland Bridge Co.*, [1984] 1 All E.R. 504 at 509-510.

54 Cited by Halvorson J. in *Engel v. Clarkson* (1983), 19 Sask. R. 305 at 311-312 (Sask. Q.B.).

55 (1956), 6 D.L.R. (2d) 586 at 588 (B.C.C.A.); compare *Pickett v. Love* (1982), 20 Sask. R. 115 at 118 (Sask. Q.B.) *per* Sirois J. See also *Re Lincoln R.C. Sep. S. Bd. and Waters*, [1972] 3 O.R. 570 (Ont. Co. Ct.); *Osorio v. Cardona* (1984), 59 B.C.L.R. 29 (B.C.S.C.).

paying subsidies, or allowing remission of taxes *vis-à-vis* members of a certain group, for example, mining companies, or to a specific person or organization, it has been held that such statements of policy, whether contained in a statute or Order in Council, or mere directive, are not offers capable of becoming binding by acceptance by words or conduct or on the part of the specific addressee of the statement or any member of the group affected thereby. This was the case with respect to a section of an Act of British Columbia in *Esquimalt & Nanaimo Railway v. Attorney-General of British Columbia.*[56] In that case a railway company claimed that it was exempted from certain taxation as a result of a contract made between the government of British Columbia and the railway company at some formative stage in the company's development. Although there was a provision of a provincial Act which appeared to create an obligation to allow such exemption, it was held by the Privy Council that the contents of this section did not constitute an offer which was accepted by conduct on the part of the company. Neither the legislature nor the executive of the province, by obtaining the passage of such legislation, intended that a binding legal obligation was going to be created which would affect later provincial governments and provide for the future exemption of the company from the relevant taxation. Similarly in *Lethbridge Collieries Ltd. v. R.*,[57] on a claim by petition of right against the Crown in respect of certain subsidies which the petitioning company alleged the Crown was obliged to pay as a result of an offer made by the Emergency Coal Products Board, it was held that the letter from the Board setting out the terms under which such subsidies would be paid was not an offer. Instead, as Cartwright J. made clear,[58] the letter simply indicated that the Board proposed to follow a certain policy as to payment of subsidies, but reserved to itself throughout the right to say what amount, if any, it would pay from time to time to any operator within the scheme. The same was held, with respect to a comparable policy directive from another Board, in *Joy Oil Co. v. R.*,[59] On the other hand, in a more recent case, *Grant v. New Brunswick*,[60] the Court of Appeal of New Brunswick held that a Government announcement of a scheme for the purchase from farmers of excess potatoes, setting out certain terms and conditions for qualification, was an offer that could be accepted so as to produce a binding contract with a farmer who fulfilled the terms and conditions. The test was said to be objective, that is, not what the party making the statement thoght it meant or intended it to mean, but what a reasonable man in the position of the parties would have thought it meant.[61]

The issue has also arisen where the relationship between the parties to whatever is involved does not seem to indicate anything more than a private arrangement,

---

56 [1948] S.C.R. 403 (S.C.C.); reversed on other grounds, [1950] A.C. 87 (P.C.). See also *Arctic Rentals Inc. v. Canada* (1988), 19 F.T.R. 133 (Fed. T.D.), no contract for use of plaintiff's equipment in building road over reserve and for training Indian band members in the use of such equipment.

57 [1951] S.C.R. 138 (S.C.C.).

58 *Ibid.*, at 151; compare *Skivest Devs. Ltd. v. Alberta* (1984), 57 A.R. 252 (Alta. Q.B.).

59 [1949] Ex. C.R. 136 (Ex. Ct.); affirmed on this point [1951] S.C.R. 624 (S.C.C.).

60 (1973), 6 N.B.R. (2d) 95 (N.B.C.A.).

61 *Ibid.*, at 101 *per* Hughes C.J.N.B. This case was applied in *Ataway v. Stephen Avenue Mall Bd.* (1989), 96 A.R. 138 (Alta. C.A.).

unsupported except by what might be termed "social" or "moral" sanctions. Perhaps the most important illustration of this is to be found in cases concerned with domestic arrangements, that is, between husband and wife,[62] father and son,[63] mother and daughter,[64] or men and women cohabiting.[65] But it is not confined to such instances. In *Fobasco Ltd. v. Cogan*,[66] the agreement among several businessmen with respect to season tickets to Toronto Blue Jays baseball team's home games was a social arrangement, not a legally enforceable contract. In *Charleston v. MacGregor*,[67] there was a direction from the lodge of a trades union to the chairman of a regional grievance committee. On the failure of such chairman to obey the direction, an action was brought by an aggrieved party. It was held that this direction fell short of a legal obligation and gave rise only to an obligation of "honour", or one of "self-interest" or, possibly, both. What was involved here was "a family dispute" between trade unionists, not the breach of a legally binding contract. In cases like this there is said to be a presumption against the arrangement being of a commercial, contractual nature, although, as exemplified by *Dugas v. Dugas*,[68] this presumption can be rebutted or excluded by the circumstances. There a son, who was separated from his wife, went to live with his parents. He paid $25 weekly for his room and board. The father lent money to his son in addition to providing the accommodation. In two years the son only paid the father $100 in respect of everything he had received. He was then killed in a car accident. It was held by Hughes C.J.N.B. that the son's estate was liable to the father for the sums lent and for the unpaid amounts owing in respect of the room and board.

Although cases such as this indicate that there may be situations in which domestic, family, and private agreements can be treated as contractual and involve legal relations that are enforceable in the courts, for the most part, where parties

---

62 *Balfour v. Balfour*, [1919] 2 K.B. 571 (C.A.); *Re MacCulloch; MacCulloch v. MacCulloch* (1980), 44 N.S.R. (2d) 679 (N.S.S.C.); affirmed (1981), 46 N.S.R. (2d) 220 (N.S.C.A.); *Barnett v. Wise*, [1961] O.R. 97 (Ont. C.A.); *Steinberg v. Steinberg* (1963), 45 D.L.R. (2d) 162 (Sask. Q.B.); *Buchmaier v. Buchmaier* (1971), 6 R.F.L. 382 (B.C.C.A.). Contrast the situation where husband and wife were not cohabiting in *Merritt v. Merritt*, [1970] 1 W.L.R. 1211 (C.A.), with *Gould v. Gould*, [1970] 1 Q.B. 275 (C.A.). For a discussion of the leading English decisions, and the view that where family members are involved there is less likelihood of the implication of a contract, see the judgment of Huband J.A. in *Decorby v. Decorby Estate* (1989), 57 Man. R. (2d) 241 at 249-251 (Man. C.A.).

63 *Sanders v. Sanders*, [1965] 1 O.R. 275 (Ont. H.C.); compare *Ross v. Ross* (1973), 33 D.L.R. (3d) 351 (Sask. Q.B.); compare *Posner's Ltd. v. Posner*, [1971] 4 W.W.R. 509 (Man. Q.B.).

64 *Jones v. Padavatton*, [1969] 2 All E.R. 616 (C.A.); *Berryere v. Berryere* (1972), 7 R.F.L. 82 (B.C.S.C.); compare *Rogalsky v. Rogalsky*, [1985] 2 W.W.R. 699 (Man. Q.B.); affirmed [1986] 4 W.W.R. 336 (Man. C.A.).

65 *Arding v. Buckton* (1956), 6 D.L.R. (2d) 586 (B.C.C.A.); *Lazarenko v. Borowsky*, [1966] S.C.R. 556 (S.C.C.); *Swan v. Public Trustee*, [1972] 3 W.W.R. 696 (Alta. S.C.); *Holli (Kost) v. Kost* (1972), 7 R.F.L. 77 (B.C.S.C.); compare *Boutilier v. Everett* (1979), 40 N.S.R. (2d) 527 (N.S.S.C.) (man living with widow); *Pickett v. Love* (1982), 20 Sask. R. 115 (Sask. Q.B.) (ex-boyfriend claiming for work done while living with the defendant).

66 (1990), 72 O.R. (2d) 254 at 259-260 (Ont. H.C.) *per* Rutherford J. Compare *Eng v. Evans* (1991), 83 Alta. L.R. (2d) 107 (Alta. Q.B.), friendly arrangement regarding tickets for hockey games: no intent to create legal relations.

67 (1957), 11 D.L.R. (2d) 78 (Alta. S.C.).

68 (1978), 23 N.B.R. (2d) 199 (N.B.C.A.).

of this kind are involved, the courts have tended to regard their relationship as non-contractual. However, as many modern decisions illustrate,[69] there may be other grounds upon which a claim for recovery of money for services tendered, or goods supplied, can be brought by one such party against the other (or the other's estate). In such "family" cases, whether as between spouses, cohabiting men and women, children and parents, or others, Canadian courts have been prepared to permit recovery on a *quantum meruit* basis by application of restitutionary remedies based on unjust enrichment or constructive trust.[70] The legal obligation to reimburse in such circumstances, or to share the proceeds of work or accumulations of wealth, should not be confused with obligations arising out of contract. Only where it is possible to construe the relationship between the parties as necessarily giving rise to a contract can the latter occur.

The foregoing situations may be looked upon as out of the usual run of commercial transactions. Where the circumstances indicate what would appear, to the ordinary reasonable man looking at the parties' conduct, to be a normal commercial relationship which usually involves a contract with its attendant rights and duties, a binding contract may be the result even where the subject-matter of the alleged contract is speculative. For example, in *Hawrysh v. St. John's Sportsmen's Club*,[71] the plaintiff argued that he had been deprived of the opportunity of winning a contest. It was held that his entry into the competition, under the promulgated rules, amounted to a binding contract to permit him to compete; prevention of such competition was a breach for which the club was liable in damages. Thus in a commercial agreement it will be presumed that the parties intended to create legal relations.[72] This is a presumption that may be rebutted. Such rebuttal occurred in the English case of *Rose & Frank Co. v. J.R. Crompton & Bros. Ltd.*,[73] where the contract in question was expressly stated to be "binding

---

69 *Deglman v. Guar. Trust Co.*, [1954] 3 D.L.R. 785 (S.C.C.); *Ross v. Ross* (1973), 33 D.L.R. (3d) 351 (Sask. Q.B.); *Re Spears* (1973), 40 D.L.R. (3d) 284 (N.S. Co. Ct.); varied (1974), 52 D.L.R. (3d) 146 (*sub nom. Re Spears and Levy*) (N.S.C.A.); *Sikora v. Sikora*, [1977] 6 W.W.R. 580 (Alta. S.C.); *Rathwell v. Rathwell* (1978), 83 D.L.R. (3d) 289 (S.C.C.); *Pettkus v. Becker* (1980), 117 D.L.R. (3d) 257 (S.C.C.); *Murray v. Roty* (1983), 41 O.R. (2d) 705 (Ont. C.A.); *Palachik v. Kiss* (1983), 146 D.L.R. (3d) 385 (S.C.C.). See Fridman, *Restitution*, 2nd ed. (1992), pp. 329-333, 434-440.

70 This paragraph as far as this was quoted in *Decorby v. Decorby Estate* (1989), 57 Man. R. (2d) 241 at 254 (Man. C.A.) *per* Huband J.A.

71 (1964), 46 D.L.R. (2d) 45 (Man. Q.B.); compare *Cipriani v. Burnett*, [1933] A.C. 83 (P.C.). Contrast *Chabinyc v. Western Grocers Ltd.* (1958), 13 D.L.R. (2d) 342 (Man. Q.B.), where the entry into the contest did not create a contract between the parties. Note the reliance on the English case of *Chaplin v. Hicks*, [1911] 2 K.B. 786 (C.A.) with respect to speculative damages; below, pp. 751-753.

72 *Great Georgian Realty Group v. Genesis Marketing Organization Ltd.* (1977), 76 D.L.R. (3d) 592 at 597 (Ont. H.C.) *per* Reid J.

73 [1925] A.C. 445 (H.L.). Compare *Orion Ins. Co. plc. v. Shere Drake Ins. Ltd.*, [1990] 1 Lloyd's Rep. 465, insurance pool arrangement did not involve legal, contractual relations. See also *Kleinwort Benson Ltd. v. Malaysia Mining Corp. Bld.*, [1989] 1 All ER. 785 (C.A.); reversing [1988] 1 All E.R. 714, "letter of intent" did not create contact: a statement of present fact, not a contractual promise. On the subject of the exclusion of contract in such instances, see Holmes, "The Freedom not to Contract" (1985-6), 60 Tulane L.R. 751.

in honour only". It was rebutted in *Stairs v. New Brunswick*,[74] where there was no evidence that the New Brunswick government had ever made any promise to the plaintiff that he would be given a permit to run a refreshment-motel-service station. His acting in certain ways, spending money to his detriment, did not give rise to any contractual liability on the part of the government.

The difficulties involved in this exercise may be illustrated by the decision of the House of Lords in *Esso Petroleum Co. v. Commissioners of Customs & Excise.*[75] The issue was whether coins given away with purchases of petrol were "provided for sale" within the meaning of a statute. In the event it was held that, if a contract were involved in the transfer of such coins, it was not a contract of sale. However, some members of the House thought that the offer to give the coins was an offer to contract, that is, to enter into legal relations. Others thought that the offer involved was not an offer to contract. The reason for the opinion of the second group was the small intrinsic value of the coins to any individual customer of the garage. Hence it was unreasonable to invoke commercial notions into the context. The group who thought there was a contract relied on the presumption referred to earlier, and considered that, since the purpose of the promise to give away the coins was to encourage the purchase of petrol at the garage in question, there was a clear intention to make a legally binding promise to give away the coins with each purchase of a stipulated quantity of petrol.

What appears to be involved is whether the promise in issue was intended to be made for benevolent non-commercial reasons, or may be treated as a serious promise or offer that was expected to be taken seriously and was intended to create a legal relationship between the parties concerned. Two curiously conflicting Canadian cases may be cited in this respect. In *Porter v. Toronto General Trusts Corporation*,[76] employees alleged that their employer had made a promise, that is, an offer to leave them his business in his will, if they continued to work for him until his death. Upon the death of the employer the employees sued to enforce this alleged contract. It was held that the deceased had merely expressed a benevolent intention towards his employees. It was not a definite contractual offer which could be, or had been, accepted by staying in his service for the appropriate period. In this case, Wilson J. of the Supreme Court of British Columbia paid much attention to the fact that the employees were being paid in any event for the work they were doing for the deceased. But the same judge, in the later case of *Sloan v. Union Oil Co.*,[77] came to a different conclusion where the employer company had issued a pamphlet stating that, with respect to certain employees working under certain contracts, such employees would be entitled to a termination

---

74 (1977), 20 N.B.R. (2d) 553 (N.B.Q.B.).

75 [1976] 1 All E.R. 117 (H.L.).

76 [1946] 2 W.W.R. 513 (B.C.S.C.); compare *Blair v. Western Mut. Benefit Assn.*, [1972] 4 W.W.R. 284 (B.C.C.A.); *Moir v. J.P. Porter Co.* (1979), 33 N.S.R. (2d) 674 (N.S.C.A.). Contrast *Maier v. E. & B. Exploration Ltd.*, [1986] 4 W.W.R. 275 (Alta. C.A.) where there was a "unilateral contract" (below, pp. 69-76) arising from the offer of a share option scheme, which was accepted by the employees' continuation in their employment when they could have left.

77 (1955), 16 W.W.R. 225 (B.C.S.C.).

allowance if they remained in the company's employment. One such employee stayed in accordance with the proposal in the pamphlet and then claimed the termination allowance when she left her employment in accordance with the requirements laid down in the pamphlet. It was held that the statement in the pamphlet was an offer, a promise intending to be binding; since it was acted upon by the employee, the company was bound. Yet in this case, also, the employee was paid for her services in the normal way while she was in the company's employment. Why was this not sufficient? Why did her continuation in the company's employ entitle her to the extra benefit whereas similar conduct by the plaintiffs in the *Porter* case did not? It is hard to hold that the deceased was simply benevolent in the *Porter* case, but had a more contractual intent in the *Sloan* case. In both, the desire of the deceased was to ensure that his employees would not prematurely leave their employment, which would have harmful effects upon his business. Yet the results were different.

This requirement of an intention to enter or create legal relations has been the subject of criticism.[78] It has been argued that the idea of *animus contrahendi* adds nothing to the other elements of contract, that indeed it simply duplicates such essential features as offer and consideration.[79] However, even this critic admits that the doctrine may be useful for courts to invoke or employ "because it enables courts to cloak policy decisions in the mantle of private contractual autonomy."[80] To this might be added the comment that, unlike the situation in England, where restitutionary recovery has not been as broadly developed and understood, in Canada some of the more rigorous effects of the doctrine of intention to create legal, that is, contractual, relations have been mollified by the evolution of the extra-contractual remedy first approved by the Supreme Court of Canada in *Deglman v. Guaranty Trust Co.*,[81] and greatly utilised and developed since then.[82]

(c) Invitation to treat

What is sometimes conceived of as an offer, by the alleged offeror or others, may be nothing more than a statement indicating a general commercial intent,

---

78 Tuck (1943), 21 Can. Bar Rev. 123; Shatwell (1954), 1 Sydney L.R. 289; Unger (1956), 19 M.L.R. 96.

79 Hepple, "Intention to Create Legal Relations" (1970), 28 C.L.J. 122.

80 *Ibid.*, at p. 134. An alternative way of regulating transactions may be through the judicial device of "uncertainty". In the law of contract uncertainty encompasses two types of situations: (i) where there is real doubt whether the parties have passed from negotiations to binding consensus (*i.e.*, certainty as to *whether* the parties have finally agreed); and (ii) where vagueness in the language used or omission of essential terms results in uncertainty as to whether the parties have agreed: *Cormier v. Fed. Business Dev. Bank* (1980), 29 N.B.R. (2d) 392 at 414 (N.B.Q.B.) *per* Allen J.; reversed on other grounds (1980), 32 N.B.R. (2d) 114 (N.B.C.A.); leave to appeal to the S.C.C. dismissed (1980), 35 N.R. 596n (S.C.C.). The first situation involves discussion of transactions that are expressed to be "subject to contract", or are still in the stage of negotiation; below, pp. 60-64. The second situation relates to the question of whether the intention to contract has been expressed in sufficiently clear language, above, pp. 19-22.

81 [1954] S.C.R. 725 (S.C.C.).

82 See the cases cited above, note 69: compare Fridman, *Restitution*, 2nd ed. (1992), pp. 288 *et seq.*

a desire to make a contract with the party to whom the statement is addressed if a suitable arrangement can be reached. Such an "offer" is considered to be nothing more than an invitation to treat, which is designed to elicit an offer from the party to whom it is addressed.[83] Such may be the situation where a party submits a design or plan on the basis of which he hopes or expects that a contract to bind the subject-matter of the design, or to undertake the scheme involved in the plan, will emerge.[84] Submissions of this kind have been construed as indicating to the other party the general nature of the former's willingness to contract and the basis upon which he would be willing to contract. They will not amount to offers capable of acceptance so as to create a binding contractual obligation unless they are expressed to be such clearly and unequivocally. A good illustration is provided by *Vail v. Keddy's Motor Inns Ltd.*[85] The defendant paid $1 a year for a right of way across the plaintiff's land and wanted to buy the land. The plaintiff wrote to the defendant, in the course of the negotiations, indicating that a rent of $400 per month would be charged for the use of the right of way. The defendant did not respond but continued to use the right of way. When the plaintiff sued the defendant for trespass, the latter argued that he used the right of way under a contract, namely, to pay $400 per month. It was held that the letter from the plaintiff to this effect was not an offer (and that in any event, the defendant had never accepted it); hence the defendant was liable in trespass.

Clearly this is a matter of construction. Whether a proposal is an offer or not is a question of language and the surrounding circumstances. Hence subsequent conduct by the alleged offeror may clarify his original statement and show that it was an offer. "In each case of this type," as Middleton J. said in *Canadian Dyers Association Ltd. v. Burton*,[86] "it is a question to be determined upon the language used, in the light of the circumstances in which it is used, whether what is said by the vendor is a mere quotation of price or in truth an offer to sell." In that case, and in *Harty v. Gooderham*,[87] there was an offer. In *Johnston v. Rogers*,[88] and the leading case of *Harvey v. Facey*[89] (often cited and relied upon by Canadian courts), there was simply an invitation to make an offer based upon a price quoted by the alleged offeror. Thus, whether a statement made by someone is an offer

---

83 *Reid v. Sinclair* (1910), 14 W.L.R. 478 (B.C.T.D.); *Askwith v. R.* (1918), 18 Ex. C.R. 206 (Ex. Ct.); *Acme Grain Co. v. Wenaus*, [1917] 3 W.W.R. 157 (Sask. C.A.) (telegram instructing an agent to buy grain at a certain price, transmitted to a third party, was held not to be an offer capable of acceptance by such third party).

84 *Mortimer Co. v. Frontenac Breweries Ltd.*, [1930] 1 D.L.R. 182 (S.C.C.).

85 (1981), 38 N.B.R. (2d) 361 (N.B.Q.B.).

86 (1920), 47 O.L.R. 259 at 260 (Ont. H.C.).

87 (1871), 31 U.C.Q.B. 18 (C.A.); and see *McGrath v. Black* (1909), 43 N.S.R. 554 (N.S.C.A.); *Davidson v. Global Gen. Ins. Co.*, [1965] 1 O.R. 505 (Ont. H.C.), where, in fact, the offer to insure was never accepted.

88 (1899), 30 O.R. 150 (Ont. C.A.).

89 [1893] A.C. 552 (P.C.).

may involve a lengthy and complex analysis of the language used by the party in question, and his preceding or later conduct.[90]

An instructive case, which illustrates how courts differentiate clear offers that state with certainty the terms on which the alleged offeror is prepared to contract from statements which invite offers, is *Saltzberg v. Hollis Securities Ltd.*[91] An estate was for sale. There were three equal offers from three different parties. The executors of the estate invited all three to submit new offers, independently, as long as they were over $35,000. It was stated that the estate would go to the highest bidder. In consequence of this, an action was subsequently begun to enforce what was claimed to be a binding contract between the executors of the estate and the bidder who claimed to have made the highest bid. The court held that the letter from the executors to the three participants was not a binding promise to accept the highest offer. Nor was it itself an offer to be accepted by whichever of the three, in the event, made the highest bid. It was only an invitation to the three participants to bid, that is, to offer themselves, as a result of which the executors would or would not accept, and would communicate their acceptance, if any, to the successful bidder.

One situation which has been characterized by the courts as necessarily involving an invitation to treat rather than an offer is the exposure of goods for sale in a shop or other commercial premise, or in a catalogue.[92] In *R. v. Bermuda Holdings Ltd.*,[93] a statute made it illegal to sell or offer to sell cars unless they were equipped as required under statute. The defendants displayed a used car on their premises. An employee of the defendants stated that the car displayed was "for sale". It was held that this was only an invitation to treat, not an offer to sell. Hence the offence had not been committed. This view, that exposing goods to the general public is not an offer to sell such goods but an invitation to members of the public to offer to buy them, is one that is long established by English cases

---

90 As in *Carlill v. Carbolic Smoke Ball Co.*, [1893] 1 Q.B. 256 (C.A.), below, p. 71. See, *e.g., Cummings Grain Co. v. Butcher,* [1922] 1 W.W.R. 243 (Alta. C.A.). The "seller" undertook to let the "buyer" have two cars of grain, stating that he might be able to give him three. It was held that the "buyer" could not bind the "seller" to deliver three cars; if he tried and the "seller" did not agree, there was no contract for *two.*

91 (1964), 48 D.L.R. (2d) 344 (N.S. S.C.). Contrast *Harvela Invts. v. Royal Trust Co. of Can.,* [1985] 1 All E.R. 261 (C.A.); reversed, [1985] 2 All E.R. 966 (H.L.), discussed in Fridman, "Tendering Problems" (1987), 66 Can. Bar Rev. 585 at 593-595. Is the decision in the *Saltzberg* case consistent with *dicta* in some nineteenth century English cases, *viz. Spencer v. Harding* (1870), L.R. 5 C.P. 561; *Johnston v. Boyes,* [1899] 2 Ch. 73; *South Hetton Coal Co. v. Haswell, Shotton & Easington Coal & Coke Co.,* [1898] 1 Ch. 465 (C.A.)? Contrast the decision in *Warlow v. Harrison* (1859), 1 E. & E. 309 as to an auction advertised as "without reserve".

92 *Que. Pharmaceutical Assn. v. T. Eaton Co.* (1931), 56 C.C.C. 172 (Que. C.A.), in which differing opinions were delivered; compare *Spencer v. Harding* (1870), L.R. 5 C.P. 561; *Grainger v. Gough,* [1896] A.C. 325 (H.L.). Contrast the situation in respect of an automatic vending machine. So too, with an automatic parking machine: *Thornton v. Shoe Lane Parking,* [1971] 2 Q.B. 163 (C.A.); and compare a case in which advertising a schedule of trains was an offer: *Denton v. Great Northern Ry. Co.* (1856), 5 E. & B. 860. Contrast the decision in *Harris v. Nickerson* (1873), L.R. 8 Q.B. 286, that advertising an auction was not a promise, *i.e.* offer, to hold the auction.

93 (1970), 9 D.L.R. (3d) 595 (B.C.S.C.); compare *Fisher v. Bell,* [1961] 1 Q.B. 394.

most of which,[94] as the *Bermuda Holdings* case and other more recent Canadian decisions, were concerned with possible criminal, not contractual, liability arisng from such circumstances. It might be thought that the technicalities of the law of contract should not play a significant role in the determination of potential criminal liability. Indeed, in *R. v. Dawood*,[95] Clement J.A., dissenting from the other members of the court, thought that putting goods on display was an offer to sell them (at the advertised price), although the contract was not made until the offer was accepted by taking goods to the sales counter and proffering the money to the cashier. A similar view with respect to goods being sold at a self-service supermarket was expressed *obiter* by Arnup J.A. in *R. v. Steinberg's Ltd.*[96] These opinions contradict the decision of an English court on *Pharmaceutical Society of Great Britain v. Boots Cash Chemists (Southern) Ltd.*[97] Yet they seem more consistent with the practical realities of everyday shopping in such stores. Moreover, in the context of criminal liability for larceny, false pretences, or false advertising, if the question is whether there was an offer, and hence a contract at the material time for criminal purposes, the approach favoured by Clement J.A. and Arnup J.A. would appear more reasonable and sensible. However, even if their approach is ultimately accepted, it remains questionable whether it should apply with equal logic and force to the situation where goods are put in a shop window or a catalogue and are not on view in a self-service store where the customer has to take the goods to a counter to complete the purchase. The traditional English view might be intelligible where the prospective purchaser has to enquire for the goods in a shop or send for them in response to their being advertised in a catalogue. It may not be as relevant where the goods may be physically handled by the prospective customer in the way which is required and involved in self-service transactions. In the former situation the seller may need some protection (for example, from mistakes, or a possible shortfall in the quantities of the advertised goods—even though he might protect himself by a suitably phrased condition as to availability). In the latter situation he may not need such protection. At the moment, however, the prevailing view would seem to be that both situations are to be treated in the same way so far as the distinction between an offer and an invitation to treat is concerned.

Where a property owner advertises for, or otherwise invites tenders from interested parties with the object of producing a contract to do work, buy property, or provide services, the traditional view was that "the advertisement to tender cannot be regarded as anything more than an offer to treat and the tender itself must

---

94 But not all, see *Timothy v. Simpson* (1834), 6 C. & P. 499; *Payne v. Cave* (1789), 3 T.R. 148; *Harris v. Nickerson* (1873), L.R. 8 Q.B. 286; *Warlow v. Harrison* (1859), 1 E. & E. 309.

95 [1976] 1 W.W.R. 262 (Alta. C.A.).

96 (1977), 80 D.L.R. (3d) 741 (Ont. Prov. Ct.).

97 [1953] 1 Q.B. 401 (C.A.).

be regarded as the offer." That was the position as stated in 1960 by Stewart J. of the High Court of Ontario.[98] More recently the Ontario Court of Appeal said,[99]

> [i]t is trite law that an invitation to tender is merely an offer to negotiate. The submission of a tender constitutes an offer which, if accepted by the owner, becomes a binding contract. . . .In legal terms the tenderer is the offeror; the owner is the offeree.

What is interesting about this latter statement is that it was made, thereby reiterating the well-established theory of tenders, after the decision of the Supreme Court of Canada in *R. v. Ron Engineering & Construction (Eastern) Ltd.*[100]

The traditional view of tenders may be illustrated by cases decided not long before the Supreme Court's judgment. These cases rest upon the notion that, since the invitation to tender is not an offer, the tender which results from such invitation, although an offer to contract on the terms contained in the invitation to tender, may be revoked at any time prior to acceptance, that is, before the property owner chooses the tenderer's offer rather than any other bid for the work in issue.[101] In *Metropolitan Toronto v. Poole Construction Ltd.*,[102] for example, the defendants discovered a mistake in their tender and informed the plaintiffs of that mistake within an hour of the opening of the various tenders that had been submitted in response to the plaintiffs' call for tenders. At that time the defendants' tender had not been accepted. Tenders had to be referred to an executive committee for acceptance. The defendants' tender was so referred with the information about the mistake. The plaintiffs' committee approved of the defendants' tender and purported to award the building contract to the defendants on the basis of the tender. The defendants declined, whereupon the plaintiffs awarded the contract to the next lowest bidder and sued the defendants for the amount of the bid bond that was connected with the submission of tenders. The plaintiffs' action was

---

98 In *Hamilton Bd. of Educ. v. U.S. Fidelity & Guar. Co.*, [1960] O.R. 594 at 599 (Ont. H.C.). Nor is there any legal duty owed by the party inviting tenders to provide prospective tenderers with information to assist them to determine whether or not to tender: *Sankey v. Canada (Minister of Transport)*, [1979] 1 F.C. 134 (Fed. T.D.), but see *Mun. Enterprises Ltd. v. Defence Const. (1951) Ltd.* (1985), 28 B.L.R. 263 (N.S.T.D.); affirmed (1985), 23 D.L.R. (4th) 653 (N.S.C.A.).

99 *Kawneer Co. v. Bank of Can.* (1982), 40 O.R. (2d) 275 at 283 (Ont. C.A.). Compare *Re Gibbons* (1977), 22 Nfld. & P.E.I.R. 529 at 537 (Nfld. T.D.). Hence, even if the invitation says that the lowest tender will be accepted, the tender is still an offer and may be rejected, albeit that it is the lowest; *Comeau & Savoie Const. Ltd. v. New Brunswick* (1976), 20 N.B.R. (2d) 258 (N.B.Q.B.); *Lisi (Leo) Ltd. v. New Brunswick* (1975), 11 N.B.R. (2d) 701 (N.B.C.A.). For the application of this to subcontractors dealing with contractors, see *Piggott Structures Ltd. v. Keillor Const. Co.* (1965), 50 D.L.R. (2d) 97 (Ont. C.A.); *M.J. Peddlesden Ltd. v. Liddell Const. Ltd.* (1981), 128 D.L.R. (3d) 360 (B.C.S.C.). On the whole subject see Fridman, "Tendering Problems" (1987), 66 Can. Bar Rev. 582; Henley, "Significant Developments in the Canadian Law of Tenders" (1991), 18 Can. Bus. L.J. 382.

100 (1981), 119 D.L.R. (3d) 267 (S.C.C.); on which see Swan (1981), 15 U.B.C.L.R. 447, Blom (1982), 6 Can. Bus. L.J. 80, Nozick (1982), 60 Can. Bar Rev. 345. See also *Northeast Marine Services Ltd. v. Atlantic Pilotage Authority* (1992), 57 F.T.R. 81 at 97-102 (Fed. T.D.).

101 Compare below, pp. 43-44. In a Quebec case involving a tender and revocation of an offer, *Beaurivage & Méthot Inc. v. Hôpital de St-Sacrement* (1986), 21 C.L.R. 263 at 266-267 (Que. C.A.), Tyndale J.A. said that the ordinary law of offer and acceptance did not apply.

102 (1979), 10 M.P.L.R. 157 (Ont. H.C.).

dismissed. It was held that the defendants could revoke their offer, as contained in their tender, even though the documents relating to the submission of tenders stipulated that tenders were irrevocable until the formal contract was executed. In this instance, however, the fact that the defendants had made a mistake in their tender was relevant because, in consequence, it was held that the plaintiffs could not accept the tender once they knew that it was made in error.[103] However, in *296349 Ontario Ltd. v. Halton Board of Education*,[104] where again there was an error in the tender, the basis of the decision was not that acceptance was not possible but the fact that the tenderer had withdrawn the tender prior to its acceptance by the owner. In this case the mistake was as to the nature of the property in respect of which tenders were invited. This was an invitation to tender to purchase certain land belonging to the Board. The plaintiffs believed that the lands were subdivided when they were not. They tendered accordingly. When they discovered the truth, they withdrew the tender before the defendants had notified the plaintiffs of acceptance by posting such acceptance by registered mail. If they had done so before the plaintiffs withdrew, there would have been a binding contract as stipulated by the tender documents. In this instance, also, neither the tender to purchase nor the offer to purchase said anything as to the offer to purchase being irrevocable until a certain date or event. In these circumstances, the plaintiffs were held to be entitled to recover their deposit sent with their offer to purchase. Their offer was revocable. As O'Leary J. said, "to take away the ordinary right to revoke an offer prior to acceptance of it, requires clear and unequivocal language."[105] Failing such language , the tender submitted by the plaintiffs was a revocable offer until acceptance. As the Court of Appeal made clear on appeal, the Board could have protected itself "in the usual way", by expressly stating that the tenders would be irrevocable for a specified period of time. Since they did not do so, the usual rule applied and the offer to purchase could be withdrawn.

From this it is clear that where an invitation to tender is made, the property owner may lay down the terms on which he will be prepared to consider, and possibly accept, offers made in response. He must do so clearly and unequivocally, but if he does so, then he has effectively dictated to those tendering, that is, offering to contract, that if they do so, their tender will not be subject to the usual rules of offer and acceptance but to the special rules set out in the invitation to tender. Thus, whether a tender is irrevocable or not depends in the first instance upon the language of the invitation to tender.[106] However, such language will not upset the traditional idea that invitations to tender are not offers and that it is the tender itself which is the offer.

That theory, however, appears to have been affected by the decision of the

---

103 Below, pp. 249-250, 261-262.

104 (1980), 126 D.L.R. (3d) 439 (Ont. H.C.); affirmed (1981), 130 D.L.R. (3d) 192 (Ont. C.A.).

105 (1980), 126 D.L.R. (3d) 439 at 444 (Ont. H.C.).

106 But this may not suffice; it may be necessary for the party inviting tenders to provide *consideration* for an irrevocable offer, such that the irrevocable offer is merely an *option* (unless the offer is made in a deed): below, p. 43, compare *Dickinson v. Dodds* (1876), 2 Ch.D. 463 (C.A.); *Goldsbrough, Mort & Co. v. Quinn* (1910), 10 C.L.R. 674 (Aus.).

Supreme Court of Canada in the *Ron Engineering* case. According to the language of Estey J., giving judgment on behalf of the whole court,[107] an invitation to tender, if made in appropriate terms, as it was in that case, can be an offer to contract which becomes a binding contract upon the submission of a tender in conformity with, and in response to, the invitation to tender. This contract, which is distinct from the contract ultimately intended to result from the submission of tenders, belongs to the category of so-called "unilateral contracts".[108]

In the *Ron Engineering* case it was possible for the Supreme Court of Canada to find such a unilateral contract because the tender documents, which contained the invitation to tender, provided that the deposit to be sent with any tender could be forfeited if the tender was withdrawn within 90 days following the close of tenders or if the tenderer failed to execute a construction contract proffered by the owner within the same period. This explanation was accepted by the Ontario Court of Appeal in *Kawneer Co. v. Bank of Canada*[109] where the court found that the facts of the latter case did not involve the application of the principle stated by the Supreme Court. This was because the requirements of the tender documents, as to the specifications to be satisfied before a tender would be accepted, had been followed by the owner—the bank.[110] In the earlier case the terms of the tender documents bound the tenderer and, even though the tenderer had made a mistake in the contents of the tender (which might have precluded the valid creation of a construction contract arising from the tender),[111] the tenderer was bound by the antecedent "unilateral" contract and so forfeited the amount of the deposit sent along with tender. In the *Kawneer* case, the argument by the plaintiff, who was seeking damages for breach of contract, was as follows: the invitation to tender was an offer that had been accepted by the submission of a tender (an instance of a "unilateral contract" as set out in *Ron Engineering*); the terms of this contract required the property owner to award the contract only to tenderers who reached certain stipulated performance specifications; the contract had been awarded to a tenderer who did not achieve those specifications; in consequence, the bank was in breach of this independent unilateral contract. Since the Court of Appeal found that the bank had not downgraded the specifications initially required to be met, it held that, even if such a unilateral contract had existed, its terms had not been

---

107 (1981), 119 D.L.R. (3d) 267 at 272-275 (S.C.C.). Compare the similar approach of the English Court of Appeal in *Harvela Invts. v. Royal Trust Co. of Can.*, [1985] 1 All E.R. 261 (C.A.); reversed [1985] 2 All E.R. 966 (H.L.).

108 Below, pp. 69-76. In a more recent English case, *Blackpool & Fylde Aero Club Ltd. v. Blackpool Borough Council*, [1990] 3 All E.R. 25, the Court of Appeal held that the council was bound by the terms of the invitation to tender to consider a tender that conformed to the conditions of tender. The reasoning of the court, however, was not the same as that of Estey J., even though the English court held that the circumstances gave rise to a contractual obligation distinct from the ultimately intended contract that was to emerge from the tenders. Here the necessary contract was *implied*, not express. The case was recognized by Stocker L.J. above, at 32, as a rare exception to the general rule in such cases as *Spencer v. Harding*, above, note 91, and *Harris v. Nickerson*, above, note 92.

109 (1982), 40 O.R. (2d) 275 at 283-284 (Ont. C.A.).

110 *Ibid.*, at 286.

111 Below, pp. 249-250, 261-262.

broken. Hence the validity and correctness of the approach adopted in the *Ron Engineering* case did not fall to be determined. Although the court seems to cite the reasoning of the Supreme Court with approval, that approbation does not tally with the restatement of the traditional theory of tenders that has been mentioned earlier.

However, the *Ron Engineering* case has been considered and followed in other decisions.[112] It would seem that the analysis adopted by Estey J. has been accepted as the operative and correct one for courts to invoke in such instances. For example, in *R. v. Canamerican Auto Lease & Rental Ltd.*[113] tender specifications for a car rental concession at Canadian airports stated that the concessions would be awarded to parties offering "the highest financial return". They also stated that the Ministry of Transport was not bound to accept the highest or any tender. The plaintiff submitted a tender, but the concessions were not awarded to the highest bidders, with the consequence that a competitor of the plaintiff, who would have been eliminated if the award had been to the highest bidder, was given a concession. The plaintiff sued the Crown for the loss of the increase of business it would have gained if the competitor had been eliminated, or, in the alternative, for the extra amount it bid for the express purpose of outbidding the competitor. The trial judge, applying the *Ron Engineering* case, held that a contract was formed when the tender was submitted by the plaintiff. Therefore the defendant was bound to award concessions to the highest bidders. Hence the defendant was liable, *inter alia*, for breach of this contract. The Federal Court of Appeal affirmed this decision. Heald J. stated that there was a contract in this case of the nature of contract A in the *Ron Engineering* case, *i.e.*, the contract formed by the submission of a tender in response to the invitation to tender.

Although *Ron Engineering* is firmly ensconced, it it also clear that not every invitation to submit tenders will be capable of producing a contract when a tender is submitted.[114] The effect of such a submission will depend on the precise language and intention of the invitation to tender. It has been suggested that the creation of a separate contract out of an invitation to tender followed by a tender may turn upon whether the invitation to tender was couched in terms of the "irrevocability" of the bid.[115] Apart from the language and analysis in the *Ron Engineering* case, it has long been accepted that the terms of an invitation to tender may result

---

112 *Calgary (City) v. Northern Const. Ltd.*, [1986] 2 W.W.R. 426 (Alta. C.A.); affirmed [1988] 2 W.W.R. 193 (S.C.C.); *Northern Const. Ltd. v. Gloge Heating & Plumbing Ltd.* (1986), 27 D.L.R. (4th) 264 (Alta. C.A.); affirming (1984), 6 D.L.R. (4th) 450 (Alta. Q.B.); *Forest Contract Management Ltd. v. C. & M. Elevator Ltd.* (1988), 33 C.L.R. 118 (Alta. Q.B.).

113 (1987), 37 D.L.R. (4th) 591 (Fed. C.A.).

114 Thus in *M.S.K. Financial Services Ltd. v. Alberta* (1987), 23 C.L.R. 172 (Alta. Master), an invitation to tender stated that the lowest tender would not necessarily be accepted. The Minister retained the right to reject any tender or not accept any. The plaintiffs submitted the lowest bid, which was not accepted. The defendant was not liable for breach of contract or otherwise.

115 Above, note 113, at 598-599 in the judgment of Reid J. quoted by Heald J.; compare Henley, *loc. cit.* above, note 99, at pp. 394-395.

in a tender, *i.e.*, a bid or offer, being irrevocable on the part of the tenderer.[116] However, unless such a tender is under seal,[117] problems involving consideration may arise.[118] In the *Ron Engineering* case, Estey J. does not appear to have dealt satisfactorily with the issue of consideration for the obligation undertaken by the tenderer when the tender was submitted. The justification for the treatment accorded that tender in this case, and elsewhere, seems to have been "the integrity of the bidding system",[119] or as expressed elsewhere,[120] customs or practices of the industry.

(d) Communication of offer

Since contract stems from the acceptance of an offer, it would appear to be rational to conclude that there must be knowledge of the offer which is being accepted.[121] Even if the language or conduct of the offeree corresponds to the contents of the offer, there is no necessary connection between the two if the offeree either is ignorant of the offer or is acting despite his knowledge of the offer. In such circumstances, while there is some sort of relation between the offer and the acceptance, no *consensus ad idem* is revealed. There is no Canadian case which makes this clear. However, there is English authority for the proposition that knowledge of the offer is required.

In *Williams v. Carwardine*,[122] a person giving information which led to the conviction of a murderer knew of the reward that was offered for such information. She gave the information thinking that she was soon to die, and to ease her conscience and in hope of forgiveness. This sufficed to entitle her to the reward. She gave the information with intent to fulfil the terms of the offer. Her motives were immaterial. However, in *R. v. Clarke*,[123] an Australian case, the party providing the information which was the subject of the offer of a reward did so to clear

---

116 *Hamilton Bd. of Education v. U.S. Fidelity & Guarantee Co.*, [1960] O.R. 594 (Ont. H.C.). But see *Metropolitan Toronto (Municipality) v. Poole Const. Ltd.* (1980), 10 M.P.L.R. 157 (Ont. H.C.).

117 *Sanitary Refuse Collectors Inc. v. Ottawa (City)* (1971), 23 D.L.R. (3d) 27 (Ont. H.C.); Fridman, *loc. cit.* above, note 99, at p. 598.

118 Below, pp. 81-136.

119 (1981), 119 D.L.R. (3d) 267 at 273 (S.C.C.).

120 *Northern Const. Ltd. v. Gloge Heating & Plumbing Ltd.*, above, note 112.

121 Presumably such communication can be made by fax machine; compare *Rolling v. Willann Invts. Ltd.* (1989), 70 O.R. (2d) 578 (Ont. C.A.). Note, also, the need to communicate all essential terms of the offer: see *Tilden Rent-a-Car Co. v. Clendenning* (1978), 83 D.L.R. (3d) 400 (Ont. C.A.); *Hoffman v. Sportsman Yachts Inc.* (1992), 89 D.L.R. (4th) 600 (Ont. C.A.). This is discussed below, pp. 573-575, in connection with exemption clauses.

122 (1833), 5 C. & P. 566.

123 (1927), 40 C.L.R. 227 (Aus.), with which contrast the American case of *Simmonds v. U.S.* (1962), 308 F. 2d 160. In *Salmond & Spraggon (Aus.) Pty. Ltd. v. Joint Cargo Services Pty. Ltd.*, [1977] 1 Lloyds Rep. 445 (N.S.W.C.A.); eventually reversed by the Privy Council [1980] 3 All E.R. 257 (*sub nom. Port Jackson Stevedoring Pty. Ltd. v. Salmond & Spraggon (Aus.) Pty. Ltd.*) (P.C.), Glass J. relied on *R. v. Clarke* (1924), 40 C.L.R. 227 (Aus.) and said; "It is the rule that where conduct is relied on as the acceptance of . . . an offer, the acceptor must be shown to have acted on the offer."

himself of the alleged crime, he being under suspicion. Here it was held that the reward could not be claimed because the claimant acted not with intent to fulfil the offer, of which he was well aware, but to prove himself innocent. The acceptance was not connected with the offer. Some doubt was cast upon the need for knowledge of the offer, and the subsequent intent to act upon it, by the English case of *Gibbons v. Proctor*[124] in which a policeman claimed a reward for providing information which led to the conviction of a criminal. The offer of the reward was set out in handbills which had not been printed, let alone distributed, at the time the information was given. However, by the material time the plaintiff knew of the offer. The other policemen, through whom the information was conveyed, were considered to be the plaintiff's agents. It was held that the plaintiff was entitled to the reward. At one time it was thought that this case supported the proposition that communication of an offer was unimportant, and a person who acted upon an offer of which he was ignorant could be held to have contracted so as to bind the offeror. It is arguable, however, that this case turned on the fact that the plaintiff acted through agents who provided the information to the appropriate authority *after* the offer was published, hence this case may not be inconsistent with the other decisions referred to above in which knowledge of the offer and the intent to act in accordance with its terms were stressed. On principle, it may be thought, such knowledge should be established if the consent of the offeree is to be proved. Moreover, an act which is performed in isolation, unconnected with the offer to which it is later alleged to relate, ought not to be considered an acceptance since the idea of acceptance necessarily connotes that what is said or done is intended to amount to agreement with the offer that has been made.

In this respect, the alleged offer must also be perceived as being an offer which was intended to be accepted, and to be accepted by the person to whom it was addressed. The strange English case of *Upton-on-Severn R.D.C. v. Powell*[125] illustrates this point. A farmer whose farm caught fire telephoned the police for the fire brigade. If the correct fire brigade had come there would have been no charge to be paid for their services by the farmer. The brigade that came belonged to a different district and would have been able to charge for their services if called by someone outside their district. They sought to recover for their services. Their success depended upon whether the request made for their services could be said to be an offer to such brigade to hire and pay for their services. The fire brigade came in response to the call because they believed they were obliged to come, that is, that the farm was inside their district. Thus, they did not think that they were being offered money to come to put out the fire. Nonetheless it was held that they had the intent to charge if the farm were outside their district and so not susceptible to obligatory services on their part. Since the farm was outside their district, they could recover. In other words, the call by the farmer was held

---

124 (1891), 64 L.T. 594; there is a fuller report in 55 J.P. 616; see Hudson, "Gibbons v. Proctor Revisited" (1968), 84 L.Q.R. 503. Contrast the American case of *Fitch v. Snedaker* (1868), 38 N.Y. 248.
125 [1942] 1 All E.R. 220 (C.A.), on which see Tuck, "Intent to Contract and Mutuality of Assent" (1943), 21 Can. Bar Rev. 123 at 128-130. See also *Daventry Corp. v. Newbury & Wright*, [1926] 1 K.B. 383; *Janes & Egham Fire Brigade v. Staines U.D.C.* (1900), 83 L.T. 426.

by the court to be an offer to pay for services rendered (presumably if payment turned out to be, as it became, obligatory). The test applied was objective, not subjective. Would the reasonable bystander have understood that the farmer intended to pay, that is, was making an offer, and that the brigade was intending to be paid, that is, was accepting the offer.

This decision and the reasoning underlying it seem to invoke a very tortuous approach to, and understanding of, the notion of *consensus ad idem*. It was referred to, and distinguished by a county court judge in Ontario in *Durham v. Carlisle*,[126] where the point at issue was somewhat different. The argument was made that between a negligent driver, who had started a fire, and the town which had paid for the fire services to put out the fire, there was an implied contract that the former would compensate the latter. In the event no such contract could be discovered. The town provided its services under a contract with another township where the incident occurred. It was from the latter, not from the defendant, that the town should have sought recovery. Although not considered from the stand-point of offer and acceptance, it might have been said that when the defendant drove negligently so as to cause the fire, he was not (impliedly) offering to pay for the cost of putting out such fire so as to render the provision of the fire services an acceptance of such offer. The earlier English case simply stresses once again the necessity for finding in a party's language or conduct the requisite offer, whether it be express or implied, from which a contract could arise, and of which the offeree has been made sufficiently aware so as to establish that his own language or conduct was intended to amount to an acceptance of such offer.

It may not suffice that the language or conduct of a party clearly indicates that he is making an offer which the other party can accept or reject. In some circumstances it may be necessary for the offeror to communicate to the offeree notice of a particular term or terms of the offer or provide the offeree with a reasonable opportunity to discover the nature of such term or terms.[127] In general, once the offeree has been made aware that an offer has been made, his acceptance of such offer, especially where the offer is contained in a document and acceptance is evidenced by the offeree's signature on the document, will be conclusive and binding.[128]

---

126 (1975), 63 D.L.R. (3d) 88 (Ont. Co. Ct.).
127 *Tilden Rent-a-Car Co. v. Clendenning* (1978), 83 D.L.R. (3d) 400 (Ont. C.A.), below, pp. 574-575; compare *City Motors (Nfld.) Ltd. v. Alton* (1987), 64 Nfld. & P.E.I.R. 52 (Nfld. T.D.); affirmed on other grounds (1988), 69 Nfld. & P.E.I.R. 161 (Nfld. C.A.) (liability for loss of car); *Hoffman v. Sportsman Yachts Ltd.* (1992), 89 D.L.R. (4th) 600 (Ont. C.A.) (term entitling increase of price of boats purchased by plaintiff: not binding because defendant's agent dissuaded plaintiff from reading contract).
128 *L'Estrange v. Graucob (F.), Ltd.*, [1934] 2 K.B. 394; on which see Samek, "The Objective Theory of Contract and the Rule in L'Estrange v. Graucob" (1974), 52 Can. Bar Rev. 351; see also Spenser, [1973] C.L.J. 104. Note, however, the situation with respect to exemption and similar clauses: below, pp. 573-578.

(e) Duration of offer

Since contract is a personal relationship, it would seem that the death of either offeror or offeree, prior to the completion of a contract, will make the offer lapse, so that it can no longer be accepted and give rise to a binding contract.

If a time for acceptance is specified,[129] and the offeree has not accepted by the expiration of such time, the offer lapses.[130] The time for acceptance may be extended impliedly by the conduct of the parties.[131] If no time is specified, then the offer will only endure and be capable of acceptance for a reasonable time,[132] though it will lapse if in the interim it has been revoked.[133] In *Barrick v. Clark*,[134] A offered to buy B's land in Saskatchewan. B made a counter offer and said that if the price was satisfactory the deal could be closed immediately. A was away from home when B's letter arrived. His wife wrote to tell B to keep the deal open for about 10 days. B did not reply. He offered the land to C who accepted. When A returned home, he purported to accept B's offer, about a month after the offer was originally made. It was held that B's offer was one which had to be accepted, if at all, promptly. More than a reasonable time had elapsed. Therefore acceptance was ineffective. Estey J., in the Supreme Court of Canada,[135] considering what was a reasonable time, made it clear that there was a difference between a case

---

129 In which event the offeror must make it possible for the offer to be accepted: *Carmichael v. Bank of Montreal*, [1972] 3 W.W.R. 175 (Man. Q.B.).

130 *Real Estate Center Ltd. v. Ouellette* (1974), 47 D.L.R. (3d) 568 (N.B.C.A.); *Brookfield Sales & Services Ltd. v. Myers* (1978) 30 N.S.R. (2d) 418 (N.S.C.A.). Such acceptance out of time may be considered a new offer by the other party: (1974), 47 D.L.R. (3d) 568 at 576 (N.B.C.A.) *per* Limerick J.A.

  This sentence was quoted by Virtue J. in *D.M. Vipond Co. v. Rustum Petroleums Ltd.*, [1987] 2 W.W.R. 570 at 574 (Alta. Q.B.).

131 *Imperial Oil Ltd. v. C. & G. Holdings Ltd.* (1986), 58 Nfld. & P.E.I.R. 326 (Nfld. T.D.); affirmed on other grounds (1989), 62 D.L.R. (4th) 261 (Nfld. C.A.).

132 Even if given under seal: *McAlester Can. Oil Co. v. Petroleum Enrg. Co.* (1958), 25 W.W.R. 26 (Sask. C.A.); *Davidson v. Norstrant*, [1921] 1 W.W.R. 993 (S.C.C.) *per* Idington J. Compare *Harkness v. Pleasance* (1913), 12 D.L.R. 842 (B.C.S.C.), where the offeree was to obtain consent of a third party. It was held that this meant that the offer was open for acceptance until a reasonable time had elapsed for the offeree to obtain such consent. See also *D.M. Vipond Co. v. Rustum Petroleums Ltd.*, [1987] 2 W.W.R. 570 (Alta. Q.B.).

133 Which was permitted even where the offeror stated that the offer was to be accepted within 10 days. There could be no obligation to keep the offer open for the whole of such period in the absence of an offer made under seal, or for valuable consideration: *Fraser v. Morrison* (1958), 25 W.W.R. 326 (Man. C.A.). Such offers are *options*, which give the offeree the exclusive right to accept or reject the offer to contract, *e.g.*, to purchase a house. *Options* are distinct contracts, and require an agrement under seal or valuable consideration: *Savereux v. Tourangeau* (1908), 16 O.L.R. 600 (Ont. C.A.); *Gibson v. McVeigh*, [1922] 1 W.W.R. 151 (Alta. S.C.); *Williams v. Keyes*, [1971] 5 W.W.R. 561 (B.C.S.C.). For the duration of an option which is not binding, *i.e.*, is not in a separate contract, see *Beer v. Lea* (1913), 14 D.L.R. 236 (Ont. C.A.).

  This sentence was quoted by Virtue J. in *D.M. Vipond Co. v. Rustum Petroleums Ltd.*, [1987] 2 W.W.R. 570 at 574 (Alta. Q.B.).

134 [1950] 4 D.L.R. 529 (S.C.C.).

135 *Ibid.*, at 537. Hence when an insurance contract was involved the offer of settlement would have been accepted within a reasonable time more than a year after the offer, had it not been for the statutory one-year limitation period: *Mitchell v. Bennett, Cole Adjusters Ltd.* (1986), 33 D.L.R. (4th) 398 (B.C.S.C.).

which concerned shares or stock, or perishable goods, when time might be of great importance in view of the possible fluctuations of price or the character of the goods, and a case involving land, where price might be more stable and certainly the subject-matter of the contract would be.

An interesting question is the effect of an offer rejected by the offeree's counter-offer, which the original offeror refuses to accept. If the original offeree now purports to accept the original offer, will this be valid? It was held in *Livingstone v. Evans*,[136] following the English decision in *Hyde v. Wrench*,[137] that such later acceptance might be good, that is, that the original offer may still be open, depending upon whether the intermediate dealings between the parties, namely, the counter-offer and its rejection, have put an end to the original offer. In that case the refusal on the part of the original offeror of the offeree's counter-offer was contained in a telegram which stated that the original offeror could not reduce his price. In those circumstances, it was held that he was reaffirming his original offer; hence, the offeree could still accept. But the facts were interpreted differently in *Re Cowan and Boyd*,[138] with the result that the original offer had been destroyed by the intervening acts of the parties and thereafter could not be accepted.

(f) Revocation of offer

At any time prior to acceptance, the offeror may withdraw his offer.[139] Once an offer is revoked it can no longer be accepted so as to bind the offeror.[140] There are restrictions upon the freedom of the offeror to revoke his offer without incurring any liability. If the offer was made to an agent who acted without authority in accepting, and the acceptance is subsequently ratified, an intervening revocation of the offer will be ineffective.[141] This will be different where the acceptance is made subject to ratification.[142] An offer under seal, whether in the form of an

---

136 [1925] 3 W.W.R. 453 (Alta. S.C.).

137 (1840), 3 Beav. 334, 49 E.R. 132.

138 (1921), 49 O.L.R. 335 (Ont. C.A.).

139 *Creelman v. R.* (1920), 20 Ex C.R. 198 (Ex. Ct.); compare *1116-9216 Que. Inc. v. R.* (1988), 22 F.T.R. 141 (Fed. T.D.) (offer of government assistance withdrawn prior to advancement of funds because the conditions of the offer were breached by the offeree). But this depends upon whether there has actually been acceptance; hence if an acceptance is qualified, the offeror may still revoke his offer: *Manson v. Pollock* (1914), 6 W.W.R. 205 (Man. C.A.). There appears to be no requirement as to the formality of a revocation, as long as it is made clear to the offeree that the offer is revoked; compare what is said below, p. 46 with respect to the case of *Dickinson v. Dodds* (1876), 2 Ch. D. 463 (C.A.). But an offer to settle made under Rules of Court has to be revoked in writing, as specified in those Rules: *Smith v. Acadia Hotels Ltd.* (1983), 149 D.L.R. (3d) 15 (B.C.C.A.).

140 But this is subject to what will be said to the effect of the offeree's *knowledge* of the revocation, below, p. 46. Note that the position is the same with respect to a *counter-offer*: *O. & M. Invts. Ltd. v. Montreal Trust* (1991), 122 A.R. 345 (Alta. Master).

141 *Bolton Partners v. Lambert* (1889), 41 Ch. D. 295 (C.A.), but the authority of this decision has been qualified; Fridman, *Law of Agency*, 6th ed. (1990), pp. 88-91.

142 *Goodison Thresher Co. v. Doyle* (1925), 57 O.L.R. 300 (Ont. C.A.).

option or not, is irrevocable.[143] So, too, is an option given for valuable consideration. But an option not under seal nor for consideration is always freely revocable before acceptance.[144] Even an offer which appears to be open for a number of days, though there is nothing to bind the offeror to keep it open so long, may be revoked without liability on the part of the offeror, who may recover a deposit which he has given with his offer to purchase.[145]

3. Acceptance

(a) Definition

Acceptance means the signification by the offeree of his willingness to enter into a contract with the offeror on the terms offered to him by the latter. Without an acceptance there can be no contract. In the words of Wilson J. in *Porter v. Toronto General Trusts Corp.*,[146] "a contract consists of an offer and an acceptance." Hence in *Webb & Knapp (Can.) Ltd. v. Edmonton*,[147] the claim of the plaintiffs based on contract failed. The plaintiffs prepared a plan for the city which was never accepted. Later the city used certain parts of the plan of the plaintiffs incorporated into their own plan for the development in question. The Supreme Court of Canada held that whatever claim was available to the plaintiffs was based on breach of copyright, not on contract nor unjust enrichment. Nor was there an acceptance in *Equitable Life Assurance Society of the United States v. British Pacific Building Ltd.*[148] The plaintiffs alleged that there was a binding agreement with the defendants for a loan of money or for long-term financing by mortgage. The defendants' application for a loan was regarded as an offer to borrow, but this was never accepted. Hence there was no contract which could be held to have been broken when the defendants said they would not take up the mortgage in question. So, too, in *Campbell v. Inverness (County)*, [149] the council never contracted to close a certain dump, despite the passage of a resolution indicating the intention of the council to do so. No offer and acceptance could be found to establish any

---

143 *Savereux v. Tourangeau* (1908), 16 O.L.R. 600 (Ont. C.A.). Note the comparison drawn between options and invitations to tender that result in a distinct separate contract upon submission of a tender: above, pp. 34-39.

144 *Gibson v. McVeigh*, [1922] 1 W.W.R. 151 (Alta. S.C.); *Davis v. Shaw* (1910), 21 O.L.R. 474 (Ont. C.A.). This sentence, and the preceding two, were cited by Virtue J. in *D.M. Vipond Co. v. Rustum Petroleums Ltd.*, [1987] 2 W.W.R. 570 at 574 (Alta. Q.B.).

145 *Fraser v. Morrison* (1958), 25 W.W.R. 326 (Man. C.A.).

146 [1946] 4 D.L.R. 345 at 347 (B.C.S.C.).

147 [1970] S.C.R. 488 (S.C.C.). Compare *Iriving (J.D.) Ltd. v. Moncton Flying Club* (1982), 40 N.B.R. (2d) 521 (N.B.Q.B.), where the plaintiffs alleged a contract to rescue the defendants' plane which had made an emergency landing in a bog. By the time the plaintiffs came to the rescue, the defendants' plane had been recovered by a military helicopter. In this case, however, no alternative claims were made on the basis of unjust enrichment. Contrast *Quirk v. Sydney Mines* (1923), 56 N.S.R. 281 (N.S.C.A.); leave to appeal to S.C.C. refused (1923), 56 N.S.R. 571 (S.C.C.).

148 (1980), 33 B.C.L.R. 68 (B.C.S.C.). See also *City Parking Services v. Murray* (1992), 99 Nfld. & P.E.I.R. 11 (Nfld. T.D.).

149 (1990), 98 N.S.R. (2d) 330 (N.S.T.D.).

such contract. By way of contrast, where there are an offer and acceptance the contract is concluded and it will be too late to argue that the contract was subject to some later condition, such as the inspection of property bought in an auction, before the sale could be regarded as agreed.[150]

The response of the offeree must be a clear indication that the offer has been accepted. It must be unconditional, clear and absolute.[151] To reply that the offeree finds the offeror's offer "agreeable" is not acceptance.[152] However, to signify that an offer is "acceptable" was acceptance in *Gateway Industries Ltd. v. MacMillan Bathurst Inc.*[153] Although acceptance may be by way of an oral or written statement, there can be acceptance by conduct. Not all conduct will amount to an acceptance. It must be clear that what the offeree has done is meant by way of acceptance of an offer that has been made. In *Vail v. Keddy's Motor Inns Ltd.*,[154] the defendants did not respond to the plaintiff's letter indicating that the defendants could continue to use a right of way over the plaintiffs' land at a rent of $400 monthly. Apart from the fact that this was not an offer (since the parties were negotiating for the purchase of the land by the defendants) it was also held that the defendants' conduct in continuing to use the right of way was not an acceptance. Whether or not there has been an acceptance depends upon whether the offeree has so conducted himself that a reasonable man would believe that he has accepted, or is accepting, the offer in question, at least as long as the offeror has acted on such belief.[155] The generally adopted theory of offer and acceptance is that the parties' behaviour must be viewed objectively, in terms of how the reasonable man, if he were a bystander, would describe the effect of what he had seen or heard.

(b) The possibility of acceptance

There are several reasons why a purported acceptance may be invalid and not have its normal effect of producing a binding contract between the parties. In the first place, if the offer alleged to have been accepted has been revoked, it is too late for the offeree to accept. Some offers may not be revoked, for instance an offer which is in the form of an option given for valuable consideration. In such circumstances,

---

150 *Squires v. Central Trust Co.* (1986), 58 Nfld. & P.E.I.R. 118 (Nfld. T.D.).

151 *Noel v. Paulin* (1987), 82 N.B.R. (2d) 307 (N.B.Q.B.); *Megill-Stephenson Co. v. Woo* (1988), 55 Man. R. (2d) 81 (Man. Q.B.); affirmed (1989), 59 D.L.R. (4th) 146 (Man. C.A.) (telephone conversation which indicated that a seller's solicitor was to approve did not constitute acceptance). Contrast *Elizabeth Drugs Ltd. v. Bidgood's Wholesale Ltd.* (1991), 91 Nfld. & P.E.I.R. 91 (Nfld. T.D.), where the tenant accepted the landlord's alterations to the lease.

152 *Pelley v. Morguard Trust Co.* (1989), 78 Nfld. & P.E.I.R. 238 (Nfld. T.D.).

153 (1990), 66 Man. R. (2d) 210 (Man. Q.B.); reversed in part (1991), 76 Man. R. (2d) 304 (Man. C.A.); leave to appeal to S.C.C. refused (1992), 78 Man. R. (2d) 237 (note) (S.C.C.); compare *T.D. Bank v. Szilagyi Farms Ltd.* (November 2, 1989), Doc. No. CA 683/87 (Ont. C.A.) ("acknowledged" means "agreed to": therefore acceptance, since it was the reasonable expectation of the parties that the agreement should be binding).

154 (1981), 38 N.B.R. (2d) 361 (N.B.Q.B.).

155 *Greenberg v. Man. Hudson-Essex Ltd.*, [1934] 1 W.W.R. 790 (Man. C.A.); and see the judgment of Disbery J. in *Con-Force Prods. Ltd. v. Rosen* (1967), 61 W.W.R. 129 at 141-145 (Sask. Q.B.).

as Grant J.A. pointed out in *Forrest v. Sollaway*,[156] the offer cannot be revoked "and is open for acceptance by the optionee at any time within the period for which the option is given." A revocable offer which has been revoked, with formal notice to the offeree of such revocation, can no longer be accepted.[157] What if no such notice has been given by the offeror? It was held in the English case of *Dickinson v. Dodds*[158] that as long as the offeree knew of the revocation, even though such knowledge did not come to him directly from the offeror, it was too late for him to be able to accept and bind the offeror. This decision has been followed in England,[159] though it has also been said to be somewhat wide.[160] There appears to be no Canadian case exactly in point, but the view has been expressed by at least one judge, Saunders J. in *Provincial Sanatorium v. McArthur*,[161] that formal notification by the offeror was not necessary. In the words of the learned judge,[162]

> an offer may be revoked before it is accepted and without any formal notice to the person to whom the offer is made. It is sufficient if that person has actual knowledge that the person who made the offer has done some act inconsistent with the continuance of the offer.

Unfortunately the question did not directly and immediately arise in that case. The offer of a subscription to a charitable foundation did not have to be accepted formally as long as the offeree, namely, the council in this case, acted on the strength of the offer of the subscription and continued with its building plans. The decision in *Dickinson v. Dodds* leaves much open to debate. In that case the source of the information as to the revocation of the offer may have been reliable, if not impeccable. What if the source is questionable? Can the offeree ignore the information, accept, and then hold the original offeror bound? It would seem inconsistent with the nature and logic of the idea of *consensus ad idem* to permit an offeree to accept an offer which he knows is no longer extant and operative. To do so would be to create a *consensus* when one party has already intimated his withdrawal of consent. However, in keeping with what has been suggested with respect to the communication of an offer,[163] it would be more reasonable to suggest that, if an offeror wishes to revoke his offer, he should communicate such revocation clearly to the offeree, and in good time, before any acceptance has occurred.

Not only will the offeree find himself precluded from a valid acceptance if

---

156 [1928] 3 D.L.R. 374 at 380 (Ont. C.A.) (sale of a seat on the Toronto Stock Exchange, in respect of which the contract was binding before payment of the purchase price).

157 *Byrne v. Van Tienhoven* (1880), 5 C.P.D. 344. Compare a Quebec case, *Beaurivage & Méthot v. Hôpital de St-Sacrement* (1986), 21 C.L.R. 263 (Que. C.A.). But what is notice to the offeree? Does he have to read it, or only receive it? This must depend upon the contract, *e.g.*, if it is a business communication in the normal way, the offeror may presume that it will have been read by the offeree or his agent.

158 (1876), 2 Ch. D. 463 (C.A.).

159 *Cartwright v. Hoogstoel* (1911), 105 L.T. 628.

160 *Manchester Ship Canal Co. v. Manchester Racecourse Co.*, [1901] 2 Ch. 37 (C.A.).

161 (1934), 7 M.P.R. 225 (P.E.I.S.C.); affirmed (1935), 10 M.P.R. 199 (P.E.I.C.A.); leave to appeal to S.C.C. refused, [1935] 4 D.L.R. 458 (S.C.C.).

162 (1934), 10 M.P.R. 199 at 215 (P.E.I.C.A.).

163 Above, pp. 39-41.

he knows it is too late, he may equally be prevented from binding the offeror, if he, the offeree, knows that the offeror has made a mistake in his offer. A mistake of this kind may relate to the terms of the contract, to the identity of the contracting party, or to the existence of a contract. Some mistakes may render a purported contract a nullity, in consequence of there never having been a valid *consensus ad idem*. Others may render a contract voidable, either at common law, or in equity. The latter will be the case where the offeree knows of the offeror's mistake, the mistake is vital to the contract, and it would be unfair and inequitable to allow the offeree to take advantage of the error made by the offeror when to allow him to do so would bind the offeror to a contract which the offeror would not have made had he been aware of the mistake. Not all mistakes that affect the validity of a contract involve the question whether there has been a valid offer and a valid acceptance. To the extent to which the offeror's error (or, it may be added, the error of the offeree) renders the subsequent acceptance not binding and operative, it may be said that no contract ever comes into existence, or the contract that does is potentially voidable, by reason of mistake.[164] The situation may be illustrated by recent decisions dealing with tenders. In one, *Metropolitan Toronto v. Poole Construction Ltd.*,[165] it was held that the plaintiffs' committe could not validly accept a tender which they knew was mistaken because the defendants had informed the plaintiffs very shortly after all tenders had been opened. However, in *R. v. Ron Engineering & Construction (Eastern) Ltd.*,[166] the tenderers were bound by their tender, despite the mistake made in the tender of which they notified the owner, because of the peculiar decision of the Supreme Court of Canada to the effect that there was a distinct, "unilateral" contract which bound the tenderers the moment they submitted their tender. At that moment of time there was no mistake that operated on an offeree, because the tenderer was the offeree, and not the owner inviting tenders. A similar approach has been adopted where the mistake was on the part of a subcontractor submitting a tender to a contractor who was tendering for the main contract.[167] In such cases it has been held that the general contractor will be taken to have accepted the subcontractor's tender, *i.e.*, offer, when the general contractor's tender, *i.e.*, offer, has been accepted by the owner who initially invited the general contractor to submit a tender.[168]

---

164 See further, below, pp. 247-251, 260-262.

165 (1979), 10 M.P.L.R. 157 (Ont. H.C.).

166 (1981), 119 D.L.R. (3d) 267 (S.C.C.); above, p. 37. Contrast the earlier case of *Belle River Community Arena Inc. v. W.J.C. Kaufmann Co.* (1978), 87 D.L.R. (3d) 761 (Ont. C.A.), with which compare *Imperial Glass Ltd. v. Consolidated Supplies Ltd.* (1960), 22 D.L.R. (2d) 759 (B.C.C.A.). The Nova Scotia Court of Appeal held that the *Ron Engineering* case had not overruled the *Belle River* case (in which the mistake in the tender prevented the creation of a contract): *Mun. Enterprises Ltd. v. Defence Const. (1951) Ltd.* (1985), 28 B.L.R. 263 (N.S.T.D.); affirmed (1985), 23 D.L.R. (4th) 653 (N.S.C.A.).

167 *Northern Const. Co. v. Gloge Heating & Plumbing Ltd.* (1984), 6 D.L.R. (4th) 450 (Alta. Q.B.); affirmed [1986] 2 W.W.R. 649 (Alta. C.A.).

168 *Dave's Plumbing & Heating (1962) Ltd. v. Voth Bros. Const. (1974) Ltd.* (1986), 21 C.L.R. 276 (B.C.S.C.); *Interprov. Concrete Ltd. v. Great West Const. Ltd.* (1987), 23 C.L.R. 123 (Sask. Q.B.); *Custom Iron & Machinery Ltd. v. Calorific Const. Ltd.* (1990), 39 C.L.R. 276 (Ont. Dist. Ct.).

A further ground upon which acceptance may be impossible is that the offeree has neglected to accept within a stipulated time and has delayed too long in accepting.[169] There may be situations in which enough time has elapsed since the offer was communicated to the offeree to render it now unreasonable for the latter to accept,[170] even though no formal revocation of the offer has taken place, and the offeree has no knowledge of any change of circumstances that would indicate that the offer is no longer open. Such would be the case where goods offered for sale were perishable.[171] It was said in *Creelman v. R.*[172] that what would have to be shown was an "oppressive" delay on the part of the offeree before such late acceptance would be inoperative. In that case the Crown was not guilty of any such delay in accepting a tender made by the plaintiffs since the distance between the parties and the fact that the Crown, in the form of a government department, is a slow body to move and make decisions, made the length of time between tender and acceptance not unreasonable. The basis for refusing recognition to a delayed acceptance is the possibility of unfairness against the original offeror. Indeed, it may be argued that an offeree who purports to accept after an unreasonably inordinate delay from receipt of the offer is very much in the position of an offeree who knows that the offer was incorrectly, or inadvertently made to him, or was made in inaccurate terms; the late acceptance, after it may be assumed that an offer can no longer be valid as initially made, because circumstances have, or may have altered, is really an attempt to impose an obligation upon someone who no longer wishes to be bound, just as acceptance of a mistaken offer is an attempt to bind someone in a manner which he never intended.

An acceptance that is unauthorized, where the acceptor is the agent of the true offeree, will not bind either party unless the acceptor was held out as having authority to accept, or the true offeree ratified the unauthorized acceptance.[173]

(c) What is acceptance?

To constitute acceptance, the offeree must signify the assent to the offer in the mode required by the terms of the offer, if any, or else in any manner deemed reasonable. Where no particular mode of acceptance is expressly required, an offer may be accepted in the manner to be implied from the nature of the offer and

---

169 *Real Estate Center Ltd. v. Ouellette* (1974), 8 N.B.R. (2d) 474 (N.B.C.A.); *Mitchell v. Bennett, Cole Adjusters Ltd.* (1986), 33 D.L.R. (4th) 398 (B.C.S.C.); *Case's Insulation & Siding Ltd. v. Gordon* (1991), 45 C.L.R. 252 (N.B.Q.B.); unless the time for acceptance has been extended, expressly or by implication: *Imperial Oil Ltd. v. C. & G. Holdings Ltd.* (1986), 58 Nfld. & P.E.I.R. 326 (Nfld. T.D.); affirmed (1989), 78 Nfld. & P.E.I.R. 1 (Nfld. C.A.).

170 *D.M. Vipond Co. v. Rustum Petroleums Ltd.*, [1987] 2 W.W.R. 570 (Alta. Q.B.).

171 *Shatford v. B.C. Wine Growers Ltd.*, [1927] 2 D.L.R. 759 (B.C.S.C.).

172 (1920), 20 Ex. C.R. 198 (Ex. Ct.).

173 *McIsaac v. Fraser Mach. & Motor Co.* (1910), 44 N.S.R. 290 (N.S.C.A.). Hence, if the principal dies before the agent sends the acceptance, there is no contract: *Re Irvine*, [1928] 3 D.L.R. 268 (Ont. C.A.); or the principal is dead at the time of acceptance: *MacKenzie v. Carroll* (1974), 6 O.R. (2d) 706 (Ont. H.C.).

the surrounding circumstances.[174] This has been held to permit the acceptance of an offer by telegraph rather than by letter[175] or by a telephone message (accompanied by a telegram).[176] Even if the offer is in writing, a written acceptance may not be necessary where the offeror has not stipulated for this method. Commercial expediency may dictate that an offer can be accepted orally, without a formal letter, by the use of telex machines, telegraphs, telegrams, or the telephone.[177] In *Jen-Den Investments Ltd. v. Northwest Farms Ltd.*[178] it was held that an offer to buy land, that had been made in writing, had to be accepted in writing. Hence, the purchaser's oral acceptance of the vendor's written counter-offer did not bind the vendor, who was permitted to revoke his counter-offer before receiving a written acceptance. It would appear, however, that an offer, in this instance a counter-offer, can be accepted orally despite the requirement of a written acceptance, where the requirement of a formal agreement was waived.[179] Where the offeror has not dictated the method of acceptance, the law may consider the conduct of the offeree unreasonable having regard to the circumstances. But the method adopted by the offeree, where he is free to select, must show a clear acceptance of the offer.[180] Hence in *Saperstein v. Drury*,[181] an offer to lease premises was made to one of several co-owners at a certain price for a definite period. The co-owner in question wrote "O.K." on the document and signed it. This was held not to be an acceptance, but only an intimation that the terms were satisfactory to him as long as they were equally satisfactory to the other co-owners. But a notice of intention to accept an offer to sell a seat on the Toronto Stock Exchange, even without tender of the purchase price, was a valid acceptance, since the parties knew that there was usually a delay in paying such purchase prices.[182] An offer may be accepted on the basis or condition that the offeror fulfil certain requirements. If the offeror fails to do so, the acceptance may be inoperative. In *Techni-Metric Inc. v. Canada (Minister of Supply & Services)*,[183] a contractor who tendered a bid

174 *MacIntyre v. Commerce Capital Mtge. Corp.* (1981), 34 O.R. (2d) 104 at 114-115 (Ont. H.C.) *per* Saunders J. This sentence and the one preceding it were cited by Virtue J. in *D.M. Vipond Co., loc. cit.* above, note 170, at 575.

175 *MacIntyre v. Commerce Capital Mtge. Corp.*, above, note 174. Compare *Nfld. v. Symons Gen. Ins. Co.* (1985), 53 Nfld. & P.E.I.R. 232 (Nfld. T.D.).

176 *Island Properties Ltd. v. Entertainment Enterprises Ltd.* (1983), 146 D.L.R. (3d) 505 (Nfld. T.D.); appeal allowed in part on other grounds (1986), 26 D.L.R. (4th) 347 (Nfld. C.A.).

177 Or, presumably, by a fax machine: compare *Rolling v. Willann Invts. Ltd.* (1989), 70 O.R. (2d) 578 (Ont. C.A.). On the use of modern communication methods, compare *Humble Invts. Ltd. v. N.M. Skalbania Ltd.* (1983), 22 Sask. R. 81 at 90 (Sask. C.A.) *per* Tallis J.A.

178 (1979), 81 D.L.R. (3d) 355 (Man. C.A.). Contrast *Whitehall Estates Ltd.v. McCallum* (1975), 63 D.L.R. (3d) 320 (B.C.C.A.); *Williston Basin State Bank v. Shearer* (1983), 53 A.R. 121 (Alta. Q.B.).

179 *Meyer v. Davies* (1989), 45 B.L.R. 92 (B.C.S.C.). Compare *Douglas v. Small* (December 13, 1989), Doc. No. CA009369 (B.C.C.A.), vendor's conduct relieved purchaser from strict compliance with mode of acceptance stipulated in the offer.

180 *Gibbons v. Newfoundland (A.G.)* (1977), 83 D.L.R. (3d) 76 (Nfld. T.D.); *Welton Tool Rental Ltd. v. Douglas Aircraft Co.* (1978), 28 N.S.R. (2d) 636 (N.S.T.D.).

181 [1943] 3 W.W.R. 193 (B.C.C.A.); affirmed [1944] S.C.R. 148 (S.C.C.).

182 *Forrest v. Sollaway*, [1928] 3 D.L.R. 374 (Ont. C.A.); contrast *Bishop v. Gray*, [1944] O.W.N. 435 (Ont. H.C.); affirmed [1944] O.W.N. 700 (Ont. C.A.).

183 (1989), 29 F.T.R. 249 (Fed. T.D.). Compare note 185.

for a contract failed to comply with the scheduling conditions contained in his bid. This justified withdrawal or cancellation of the earlier acceptance of the bid.

If the offeror lays down some special mode of acceptance, just as where he indicates the time within which his offer can be accepted,[184] the position of the offeree is governed by the offeror's conditions. The offeror is in control of the situation; it is he who may regulate, if he so chooses, the details of the creation of the contract.[185] In effect it is a significant part of the role of the offeror, as initiator of an eventual contract, to organize not only what is in the contract but also how the contract is to come about. An offeree who objects to the offeror's requirements may reject the offer, or make a counter-offer of his own. If he does neither, however, he must conform to the prescribed mode of acceptance.

It is clear that, as Wilson J. stated in *Sloan v. Union Oil Co.*,[186] "an offer may be accepted by conduct as well as words." As is the case where acceptance is intended to be, or is appropriately indicated by some statement by the offeree, whether oral or in writing, the nature of acceptance by conduct depends upon the requirements, if any, stipulated by the offeror. In the absence of any special act or conduct prescribed by the offeror, acceptance may be inferred from the offeror's conduct.[187] Yet such conduct must indicate: (a) that the act in question was performed with a view to acceptance of the offer, and not from some other motive or for some other reason;[188] and (b) that it was intended to be acceptance of the offer in question. In such cases the question is whether a reasonable man would interpret the offeree's conduct as an acceptance of the offer.[189] Hence in

---

184 *Brookfield Sales & Services Ltd. v. Myers* (1978), 30 N.S.R. (2d) 418 (N.S.C.A.).

185 *McCool v. Grant* (1921), 48 O.L.R. 630 (Ont. C.A.), bank had to be satisfied that goods would be paid for before acceptance would be valid; *Carr v. Can. Nor. Ry.* (1907), 6 W.L.R. 720 at 722 (Man. K.B.) (offeree had to take possession of offeror's land to indicate acceptance of offer to sell at a certain price). Contrast *Haney v. Winnipeg & Nor. Ry.* (1912), 1 W.W.R. 1046 (Man. K.B.) where the entry of the offeree was attributable to other rights and there did not show acceptance. Note also that the *offeror* may have to fulfil *his own* conditions: *Techni-Metric Inc. v. Canada (Minister of Supply & Services)*, above, note 183.

186 [1955] 4 D.L.R. 664 at 674 (B.C.S.C.); compare the same judge in *Porter v. Toronto Gen. Trusts Corp. (Administrator of Houghton Estate)*, [1946] 4 D.L.R. 345 at 347-348 (B.C.S.C.).

187 *Per* Mulock C.J. Ex. in *Hamilton Gear & Mach. Co. v. Lewis Bros. Ltd.*, [1924] 3 D.L.R. 367 at 369-370 (Ont. C.A.). See, *e.g.*, *Commonwealth Drilling Co. v. Community Petroleums Ltd.*, [1951] 4 D.L.R. 328 (Sask. C.A.), where signing the written version of an orally agreed upon contract was acceptance even though the signer added some alterations to the document. Compare *Fraser v. U-Need-A-Cab Ltd.* (1985), 7 O.A.C. 375 (Ont. C.A.) (passenger entering taxi). See also *Mitchell Energy Corp. v. Canterra Energy Ltd.* (1987), 49 Alta. L.R. (3d) 171 (Alta. Q.B.); *Forest Contract Management Ltd. v. C. & M. Elevators Ltd.* (1988), 33 C.L.R. 118 (Alta. Q.B.); *Di Giacomo v. Di Giacomo Can. Inc.* (1989), 28 C.P.R. (3d) 77 (Ont. H.C.); additional reasons at (1990), 28 C.P.R. (3d) 447 (Ont. H.C.).

188 *Williams v. Carwardine* (1833), 110 E.R. 590; compare *R. v. Clarke* (1927), 40 C.L.R. 227 (Aus.), above, p. 39.

189 *Welton Tool Rental Ltd. v. Douglas Aircraft Co.* (1978), 28 N.S.R. (2d) 636 (N.S.T.D.); see *Dawson v. Helicopter Exploration Co.*, [1955] S.C.R. 868 (S.C.C.); compare *Gibbons v. Newfoundland (A.G.)* (1977), 83 D.L.R. (3d) 76 (Nfld. T.D.); compare *J.K. Campbell & Associates Ltd. v. Lahr Const. Ltd.* (1987), 27 C.L.R. 220 (B.C.S.C.), where the conduct of the general contractor indicated acceptance of new conditions inserted by the subcontractor; he could not argue that they did not form part of the contract with the subcontractor.

Halifax Graving Dock Co. v. R.,[190] the fact that some work was done by the company on repairing docks destroyed in the great Halifax explosion was not acceptance of the government's offer, since the company had also sent a letter of purported acceptance which introduced new terms and conditions. The parties were never *ad idem*.[191] Acknowledging the receipt of an order for goods and despatching them to the buyer was an acceptance.[192] So was paying the entry fee for a competition, which was advertised as open to certain people, as long as the person paying the fee was qualified under the terms of the advertisement, namely, able to play in the bowling competition.[193] Similarly, in *Dunham v. St. Croix Soap Manufacturing Co.*,[194] a person who guessed the weight of a large bar of soap accepted the offer to give the piano to the one who made the nearest guess. So, too, in *D.J. Lowe (1980) Ltd. v. Upper Clements Family Theme Park*,[195] delivery of a crane was acceptance of the counter-offer from the intended lessee of the crane. The lease contract was confirmed by the lessee's use of the crane. In *British Traders Insurance Co. v. Queen Insurance Co. of America*[196] there was an oral agreement by the plaintiff's agent with the insured party. Prior to this the defendant had undertaken to reinsure. As soon as the plaintiff became committed to the insured, the defendant was bound by a contract of reinsurance. As Anglin C.J.C. explained,[197] performance of the condition completed the contract. In much the same way, in *Bank of Montreal v. Glendale (Atlantic) Ltd.*,[198] it was held that there was no need for any formal acceptance of the terms and conditions contained in the invoices sent by the vendor of mobile homes because the purchaser had taken delivery of the homes. As Maloney J. said in *Canadian Market Place Ltd. v. Fallowfield*,[199] "the vital inference of an agreement between the parties may be gleaned from the conduct of the parties, including the communication between them by word or document." In that case the conduct of the parties after the signing of the contract by the offeree indicated the acceptance even though the offeree's agent had failed in his statutory duty to deliver a signed copy of the accepted offer to the offeror, the defendant in this case.

In these cases some positive conduct on the part of the person to whom the offer was made was called for and occurred. What was done by the offeree did not have to be formulated specifically as an acceptance of the offer in the sense of stating precisely, "I accept". It had to take the form of an act or acts referable

190 (1921), 62 S.C.R. 338 (S.C.C.).
191 *Ibid.*, at 382, *per* Sedgwick J.; compare *Eastern Can. Cleaners Ltd. v. S.J. Kernaghan Adjusters Ltd.* (1984), 63 N.S.R. (2d) 299 (N.S.T.D.); additional reasons (1984), 64 N.S.R. (2d) 330 (N.S.T.D.); additional reasons (1985), 68 N.S.R. (2d) 186 (N.S.T.D.).
192 *Re Hudson Fashion Shoppe Ltd.; Ex parte Royal Dress Co.*, [1926] 1 D.L.R. 199 (Ont. C.A.); leave to appeal to S.C.C. refused [1926] S.C.R. 26 (S.C.C.).
193 *Hawrysh v. St. John's Sportsmen's Club* (1964), 49 W.W.R. 243 (Man. Q.B.).
194 (1897), 34 N.B.R. 243 (N.B.C.A.).
195 (1990), 95 N.S.R. (2d) 397 (N.S.T.D.).
196 [1928] S.C.R. 9 (S.C.C.).
197 *Ibid.*, at 13.
198 (1977), 20 N.S.R. (2d) 216 (N.S.C.A.).
199 (1976), 71 D.L.R. (3d) 341 at 345 (Ont. H.C.).

to the offeree's wishing to be bound and wishing to bind the offeror on the terms stipulated by the offeror. The idea that such conduct, without any exact response indicating verbally that the offeree has accepted the offer, suffices to constitute acceptance stems from the decision of the House of Lords in *Brogden v. Metropolitan Railway Co.*[200] There the offeree who signed the written contract failed to return it to the offeror, but continued to act on the basis of the later disputed contract being in existence and being binding upon the parties (as in the *Fallowfield* case referred to above). Hence, a contract was found to exist. Lord Denning relied on this case to find a contract in *Howard Marine v. Ogden & Sons.*[201] There the delivery of barges by the owners and the acceptance of the barges by the charterers was enough to amount to acceptance of a contract of hire; there was no need for a signed charter-party to establish contractual relations between the parties.[202] Lord Denning's reliance on the *Brogden* case in *Gibson v. Manchester City Council*[203] was less fortunate or apt. In the circumstances of that case, which concerned an exchange of correspondence between the parties, relating to the purchase by a tenant of the house which he was renting, some more formal offer and acceptance was required as the House of Lords made plain.[204]

Despite the recognition by the *Brogden* case of the possibility of acceptance of an offer without formal acknowledgement, it has been held that not all conduct will suffice for this purpose. In *Gibbons v. Attorney-General of Newfoundland*,[205] reliance was placed on the *Brogden* case, but the decision was inapplicable. A tender was submitted by Gibbons. The Newfoundland government sent him in reply a form of agreement with some additional information and memoranda not originally supplied in the invitation to tender. This was held not to be an acceptance of the tender proffered by Gibbons. It was a counter-offer. However, the continuation of negotiations on the part of Gibbons did not constitute acceptance of this counter-offer. Hence, there was no contract between Gibbons and the government on which Gibbons could sue. Similarly, in *Welton Tool Rental Ltd. v. Douglas Aircraft Co.*,[206] the performance of work by the plaintiff following upon negotiations about the work to be done by that party did not amount to an acceptance of any offer by the defendant (although, in part, this may have been because it was not clear what the offer was since there was a lack of clarity as to the basis of payment and as to the nature of the expected performance by the plaintiff).

This line of cases reinforces the authority of the English decision in *Felthouse v. Bindley*[207] that the silence of the offeree, his failure to reject an offer, cannot amount to acceptance without more. In that case the offeror specifically stated that if he failed to hear from the offeree to the contrary, he would take the latter's

---

200 (1877), 2 App. Cas. 666 (H.L.); compare *Trinder & Partners v. Haggis* (1951), 95 S.J. 546 (C.A.).
201 [1978] 2 All E.R. 1134 (C.A.).
202 Compare *D.J. Lowe (1980) Ltd. v. Upper Clements Family Theme Park*, above, note 195.
203 [1978] 2 All E.R. 583 (C.A.).
204 [1979] 1 All E.R. 972 (H.L.), above, pp. 23-24.
205 (1977), 83 D.L.R. (3d) 76 (Nfld. T.D.); followed in *J.K. Campbell & Associates Ltd. v. Lahr Const. Ltd.* (1987), 27 C.L.R. 220 (B.C.S.C.).
206 (1978), 28 N.S.R. (2d) 636 (N.S.T.D.).
207 (1863), 11 W.R. 429.

silence as acceptance. No contract resulted from the failure of the offeree to decline the offer. Although the offeror can dictate the time, place, and manner of acceptance, as the Supreme Court of Canada inferentially confirmed in *Schiller v. Fisher*,[208] it seems clear that this will not cover the situation where the offeror says that silence will be enough, even though there are cases in which the nature of the offer reveals that the offeror has dispensed with any formal acceptance or with the need to communicate such acceptance to the offeror prior to performance of the contract on the part of the offeree.[209] The decision in *Felthouse v. Bindley* has been criticized and questioned.[210] Nevertheless, the Supreme Court of Canada has said that something more than a failure to reject an offer is required to constitute a binding contract.

In a number of cases the point has been taken that mere receipt of services from another, without protest, is insufficient to create a contractual liability to pay for such services, or compensate in any way. For this there must be a promise to pay for such services given in advance of the receipt thereof.[211] Hence the importance, in cases such as *Porter v. Toronto General Trusts Corporation*[212] and *Sloan v. Union Oil Co.*,[213] of the question whether the conduct of the employer was actually an offer, which became or could become a binding contract by the employees in question remaining in the service of the employer. If there is no such offer, or the purported offer is simply an expression of benevolent intention, then there is no contract to be spelled out of the fact that services were rendered. The performance of the services is not acceptance. As Ritchie J. said in *St. John Tug Boat v. Irving Refining Ltd.*,[214]

> mere failure to disown responsibility to pay compensation for services rendered is not of itself always enough to bind the person who has had the benefit of those servcies. The circumstances must be such as to give rise to an inference that the alleged acceptor has consented to the work being done on the terms upon which it was offered before a binding contract will be implied.

Even where an offer has obviously been made with intent to create a binding

---

208 (1981), 124 D.L.R. (3d) 577 (S.C.C.).

209 *I.e.*, in the case of so-called "unilateral contracts": below, pp. 69-76. Under the Consumer Protection Act, R.S.O. 1990, c. C.31, s. 36, one who receives goods without any request for them, *i.e.*, unsolicited goods, is not liable to pay for them even if the goods are used, misused, lost, damaged or stolen. This statutory provision alters the old common law relating to the potential liability of involuntary bailees for such goods in certain circumstances. Similar provisions are to be found in British Columbia, Nova Scotia, Prince Edward Island, Newfoundland and Saskatchewan.

210 Miller, "Felthouse v. Bindley Revisited" (1972), 35 M.L.R. 489. But it was accepted and applied by Kerr J. in *Fairline Shipping Corp. v. Adamson*, [1975] Q.B. 180.

211 *I.e.*, an enforceable contract: *Deglman v. Guaranty Trust Co.*, [1954] S.C.R. 725 (S.C.C.): below, p. 231. However, there may be non-contractual, *i.e.*, restitutionary liability to compensate the provider of such services: Maddaugh & McCamus, *Law of Restitution* (1990), Chapters 13, 14, 16, 17; Fridman, *Restitution*, 2nd ed. (1992), Chapter 10.

212 [1946] 2 W.W.R. 513 (B.C.S.C.).

213 [1955] 4 D.L.R. 664 (B.C.S.C.); compare above, p. 50.

214 [1964] S.C.R. 614 at 622 (S.C.C.). See *e.g., Manco Ltd. v. Atl. Forest Prods. Ltd.* (1971), 4 N.B.R. (2d) 100 (N.B.C.A.).

contract, the failure of the offeree to respond may not constitute acceptance. Much depends upon the nature of the offer. In some instances the conduct of the offeree sufficed to amount to acceptance. The failure to make a formal response did not negate a contract. That was not the situation in *Trueman v. Maritime Auto & Trailer Sales Ltd.*[215] The plaintiff purchased a mobile home from a dealer. When he did so he received a warranty card from the manufacturers on which was contained an offer of a warranty in respect of the mobile home. Under the terms of the offer, the card had to be returned to the manufacturers if the warranty was to be effective. The plaintiff failed to return the card. It was held that his failure to do so meant that he had never accepted the manufacturers' offer. Here something more was necessary; a positive act by the plaintiff was called for but was never forthcoming. In other instances, however, what occurred was not mere silence by the offeree, but some positive, unequivocal act in the nature of a response to the other party's offer. For example, in *St. John Tug Boat Co. v. Irving Refining Ltd.*,[216] the plaintiffs offered the use of their tugs to the defendant in a letter to the defendant's agents. No written acceptance of this offer was ever forthcoming. However, the defendant company made use of the plaintiff company's tugs. The general nature of the defendant company's conduct was sufficient to show an acceptance of the offer. Therefore the defendant company was liable to pay for the services rendered by the tugs.

Here there was not just silence, as in *Felthouse v. Bindley*. The whole tenor of the defendant company's behaviour with respect to the use of the tugs evidenced an intention to be bound by the contract offered by the plaintiff company. In coming to this conclusion, the Supreme Court revealed its reliance on the "objective" theory of contract. This was applied in *Irving Oil Ltd. v. Incan Ships Ltd.*[217] The plaintiffs delivered oil to the defendants even though the plaintiffs were told that no subsidy was payable on such shipments. The plaintiffs stipulated that the full price of the oil would be due from the defendants if the subsidy were not allowed. The defendants never expressly accepted and agreed to this, however, they took delivery of the oil. It was held that there was a contract between the parties for the payment of the full price of the oil by the defendants. Relying on the *St. John Tug Boat Co.* case, Barry J. said,[218]

> if a person so conducts himself that a reasonable man would believe that he was assenting to the terms proposed by the other party, and that other party upon that

---

215 (1977), 19 N.B.R. (2d) 8 (N.B.C.A.). See also *Colchester Dev. Ltd. v. Dalfen's Ltd.* (1979), 31 N.S.R. (2d) 684 (N.S. Co. Ct.).

216 [1964] S.C.R. 614 (S.C.C.), followed in *J.K. Campbell & Associates Ltd. v. Lahr Const. Ltd.* (1987), 27 C.L.R. 220 (B.C.S.C.); *Mitchell Energy Corp. v. Canterra Energy Ltd.* (1987), 49 Alta. L.R. (2d) 171 (Alta. Q.B.). Compare also *D.J. Lowe (1980) Ltd. v. Upper Clements Family Theme Park Ltd.* (1990), 95 N.S.R. (2d) 397 (N.S.T.D.).

217 (1979), 26 N.B.R. (2d) 512 (N.B.S.C.); affirmed in part (1980), 30 N.B.R. (2d) 319 (N.B.C.A.).

218 *Ibid.*, at 518; citing also *Clarke v. Kimball* (1883), 23 N.B.R. 412 (N.B.C.A.); *McIntyre v. Hood* (1884), 9 S.C.R. 556 (S.C.C.); *Clarke v. Peabody Overall Co.*, [1931] 2 D.L.R. 832 (Alta. S.C.); *Godson v. McLeod* (1913), 10 D.L.R. 519 (Ont. S.C.).

belief enters into a contract with him, the man thus conducting himself would be equally bound as if he intended to agree to the other party's terms, notwithstanding his real intention.

However, positive conduct has not always been sufficient to indicate this objectively obtained consent. In *J.D. Irving Ltd. v. Fraser-Brace Engineering Co.*,[219] retention of equipment, after the party lending such equipment for rental had demanded higher rates, was not enough to constitute acceptance of the offer to continue to rent the equipment at such higher rental. In *Controlled Parking Systems Ltd. v. Sedgewick*[220] a driver who parked his car in the plaintiff's parking lot had not accepted the contract to park which involved payment of a fee. Hence, he was a trespasser on the parking lot. It was not enough to enter the lot and park the car. The system employed by the plaintiff involved entrance into the lot *and* payment of money in a certain way. The nature of the offer, therefore, indicated that more was required than coming onto the plaintiff's property. Contradictory decisions such as these indicate the difficulties involved in deciding whether silence plus conduct can amount to acceptance of an offer capable of producing contractual liability.

(d) Correspondence with offer

More than once has it been said that an acceptance must correspond precisely to the terms of the offer. In *Harvey v. Perry*,[221] for example, Estey J. in the Supreme Court of Canada referred to " . . .that absolute and unequivocal acceptance of terms required by the authorities to conclude a contract." There must be an acceptance *simpliciter* of the offer.[222] If the acts or language of the offeree do not amount to an absolute and unqualified assent to the material terms and conditions of the offer, there is no acceptance, hence no binding contract.[223]

An example of an equivocal acceptance is provided by *Lefebvre v. Moreau.*[224] There was an exchange of correspondence between the parties. One said he would sell for $1,000. Eventually a response came to this effect: Do you still want to sell? I have $1,000. To this the original offeror replied: I will sell, offer accepted. It was held that there was no contract. The statement, Do you still want to sell? I have $1,000, was not unequivocal acceptance of the original offer. Nor indeed

---

219 (1980), 29 N.B.R. (2d) 147 (N.B.Q.B.); reversed on other grounds (1982), 39 N.B.R. (2d) 181 (N.B.C.A.).

220 [1980] 4 W.W.R. 425 (Sask. Dist. Ct.).

221 [1953] 1 S.C.R. 233 at 237 (S.C.C.); relying on *McIntyre v. Hood* (1884), 9 S.C.R. 556 (S.C.C.); *North Vancouver v. Tracey* (1903), 34 S.C.R. 132 (S.C.C.).

222 *Coulter v. Timlick*, [1919] 2 W.W.R. 736 at 739 (Man. K.B.) *per* Curran J.; compare *Merchants Gas Co. v. Hall*, [1955] O.W.N. 750 at 753 (Ont. H.C.) *per* Smiley J.; affirmed [1955] O.W.N. 888 (Ont. C.A.).

223 *Bishop v. Gray*, [1944] 3 D.L.R. 541 at 544 (Ont. H.C.) *per* Hope J.; affirmed [1944] 4 D.L.R. 743 (Ont. C.A.). Compare *Cole v. Sumner* (1900), 30 S.C.R. 379 (S.C.C.); *Oppenheimer v. Brackman & Ker Milling Co.* (1902), 32 S.C.R. 699 (S.C.C.).

224 [1928] 1 D.L.R. 1019 (Alta. S.C.); compare *Harvey v. Facey*, [1893] A.C. 552 (P.C.).

could it be said to amount to an offer in its own right that could be accepted by the original offeror.

There may be some dilution of this requirement as long as the result would not prejudice the offeror. In *Nieckar v. Sliwa*,[225] an option was exercised otherwise than precisely in compliance with its terms. The variation in the form of exercising the option did not injuriously affect the legal position of the grantor of the option. The theory behind this would appear to be that the grantor of the option was expecting the option to be exercised—indeed, that was his purpose in granting the option. As long as what happened was substantially what he expected and intended to occur, the conduct of the grantee of the option in acting on the option, could suffice to amount to a valid exercise of the option. This conclusion was reached by analogy to the situation with respect to "a simple offer and acceptance".[226] If this is correct, then an offer may be accepted without necessarily exact compliance with the *method* of accepting (as opposed to the *contents* of the acceptance) on the part of the offeree.

The need to show correspondence between offer and acceptance means that even if the statements of the parties in fact tally, there will be no binding contract if the statement by the offeree is made independently of, and not in response to, the offer from the offeror. Thus if the parties write to each other at the same time, in the same terms, but without reference to each other's statement, since each was ignorant of the other's action, there will not be a binding contract. The fact that each party desired and intended to contract on the same terms will not suffice. What has happened in such a case is that each party is offering the other a proposed contract. The cross-offers cannot be conjoined to make a completed contract. Such is the suggestion contained in the English case of *Tinn v. Hoffman*,[227] which has not been commented upon in Canada. However, some criticism of the decision and dicta in that case has been made.[228] It could be argued that, because both parties have evidenced the intention to contract for the same reasons and on the same terms, the situation is not the same as arises where an act is performed in ignorance of an offer, although the act would have amounted to acceptance of the offer if it had been done with knowledge of the offer and with the intention of accepting it.[229] However, as long as the idea of *consensus ad idem* is fundamental to the law of contract, it would seem logical to view a case of cross-offers as not giving rise to a contract. In practical terms what might happen is that one offeror would then write accepting the other offeror's offer, or might act in such a way as amounts to an acceptance of the other's offer in accordance with what has been said earlier.

Such will not be the case, however, where the response to an offer or a cross-offer, made simultaneously with another's offer, is not in sufficiently similar terms to qualify as an acceptance. A statement that purports to be an acceptance of

---

225 (1976), 67 D.L.R. (3d) 378 (Sask. Q.B.).
226 *Ibid.*, at 379 *per* MacLeod J.
227 (1873), 29 L.T. 271.
228 Cheshire, Fifoot & Furmston's *Law of Contract*, 12th ed. (1991), at p. 56.
229 See in reference to *R. v. Clarke* (1927), 40 C.L.R. 227 (Aus.), above, p. 39.

an offer but does not exactly correspond to such offer may itself be treated as an offer susceptible to acceptance by the original offeror. Such "acceptances" are in effect "counter-offers".[230] The roles of the parties are thus reversed, though this makes no difference to the ultimate question of liability, as long as the acceptance of the counter-offer fulfils the requirements of acceptance which have been stated earlier.[231] For example, if the "acceptance" in fact varies the amount of payments to be made under the original offer, and increases the amount of payments to be made under the original offer, and increases the amount of deposit required, or alters the place for payment to occur, it will be a counter-offer, not an acceptance.[232] So, too, where the offer was to buy land which a municipality had bought in a tax sale, the price to include the amount of arrears of tax and costs. The municipality replied accepting the offer to pay "the arrears of taxes, costs *and interest*". This was a counter-offer, not an acceptance.[233] Again in *Parkette Apartments Ltd. v. Masternak*,[234] an offer to purchase, signed by the prospective purchaser, was sent to the vendor, who altered it. This was a counter-offer. Similarly, in *Canada Permanent Mortgage Corporation v. Barnard*,[235] the offeree replied to the offer by requiring a formal agreement to be drawn up in a certain form, such form containing an unusual and onerous clause not previously known to the offeror. This was held to be a counter-offer, not an acceptance. In *Marathon Realty Co. v. Toulon Construction Corporation*[236] the offeree sent a supplementary letter along with his acceptance of a "letter of intent" to sell land. This was a counter-offer. As Goodridge J. said in *Gibbons v. Attorney-General of Newfoundland*,[237] a conditional acceptance is not an acceptance but a counter-offer. In short, therefore, acceptance must tally in all respects with the offer, else there is no evidence of a *consensus ad idem*, and therefore no contract.[238]

(e) The battle of the forms

This issue of correspondence between offer and acceptance has arisen most

---

230 See, *e.g.*, *Humble Invts. Ltd. v. N.M. Skalbania Ltd.* (1983), 22 Sask. R. 81 (Sask. C.A.); *Hume & Rumble v. I.B. of E.W.*, [1954] 3 D.L.R. 805 (B.C.S.C.); *Stewart v. Oscar Fech Const. Ltd.*, [1972] 2 W.W.R. 280 (Alta. S.C.).

231 See, *e.g.*, *Meyer v. Davies* (1989), 45 B.L.R. 92 (B.C.S.C.); above, note 179.

232 *Pearson v. O'Brien* (1912), 4 W.W.R. 342 (P.C.). Compare *Duff v. Rudolph; Adams v. Lunenburg Gas Co.*, [1930] 2 D.L.R. 801 (N.S.C.A.).

233 *North Vancouver v. Tracey* (1903), 34 S.C.R. 132 (S.C.C.). Compare *Island Properties Ltd. v. Entertainment Enterprises Ltd.* (1983), 146 D.L.R. (3d) 505 (Nfld. T.D.) (vendor's response to purchaser including insurance in the purchase price was a counter-offer), appeal allowed in part on other grounds (1986), 26 D.L.R. (4th) 347 (Nfld. C.A.); compare *Goodfellow v. Drschiwiski* (1979), 18 A.R. 561 (Alta. C.A.).

234 [1965] 2 O.R. 350 (Ont. H.C.).

235 [1926] 1 D.L.R. 153 (Sask. K.B.).

236 (1987), 80 N.S.R. (2d) 390 (N.S.T.D.). On letters of intent see below, p. 61.

237 (1977), 22 Nfld. & P.E.I.R. 529 at 534 (Nfld. T.D.); citing *Cole v. Sumner* (1900), 30 S.C.R. 379 (S.C.C.).

238 *Meivre v. Steine* (1912), 20 W.L.R. 687 (Sask. C.A.). Compare *Highland Const. Co. v. Borger Const. Ltd.* (1967), 59 W.W.R. 627 (Sask. Q.B.).

pertinently in what has been called the problem of "the battle of the forms". In the words of one commentator;[239]

> [i]n its simplest form, the buyer sends out his purchase order form to the seller. That form includes a series of terms and conditions which the buyer wants in his sales contract. Usually these terms and conditions are set out on a printed form. Upon receipt of the buyer's form, the seller than sends back his acknowledgement. Typically, it . . . indicates a willingness to accept the buyer's order, but then adds a series of printed terms and conditions . . . which are favourable to the seller. Rather obviously, the terms and conditions set out on the buyer's form will not be exactly the same as those set out on the seller's form. More specifically, there are variances because some of the seller's terms and conditions are in direct conflict with those of the buyer. Others of the seller's terms and conditions add new matters which were not even dealt with on the buyer's form.

The question then arises whether or not there is a contract between the parties, and, if so, what are the terms—those of the seller, or those of the buyer. The problem arose in an English case, *Butler Machine Tool Co. v. Ex-cell-O Corporation (England).*[240] In response to an inquiry by the buyers, the sellers offered to sell goods subject to certain terms and conditions which were to prevail over any terms and conditions in the buyer's order. One of the sellers' conditions was a price variation clause providing that the price of the goods would be the price prevailing on the date of delivery. The buyers placed an order for the goods on which order it was stated that the order was subject to terms and conditions different from those put forward by the sellers. On the buyers' order there was no provision for price variation. At the foot of the buyers' order was a tear-off acknowledgement of receipt of the order. On this it was stated "We accept your order on the Terms and Conditions stated thereon." The sellers completed, signed, and returned the acknowledgement and sent with it a letter saying that the buyers' order was being entered in accordance with the sellers' original quotation. The sellers delivered the goods and claimed an increase in the original price. The buyers refused to pay such increase and the sellers sued. It was held by the Court of Appeal, reversing the trial judge, that the buyers were not bound to pay any extra. The buyers' order was a counter-offer which destroyed the original offer made by the sellers. The sellers' act of completing, signing, and returning the acknowledgement slip was an acceptance of the counter-offer on the buyers' terms. Hence, the contract between the parties was concluded on the terms proposed by the buyers, not those proposed by the sellers. The subsequent letter of the sellers did not reimpose the sellers' original terms; it simply identified the goods and the original price.

---

239 Shanker, "'Battle of the Forms': A Comparison and Critique of Canadian, American and Historical Common Law Perspectives" (1979), 4 Can. Bus. L.J. 263 at 264; see also Vaver, "'Battle of the Forms': A Comment on Professor Shanker's Views," *ibid.*, at 277. For a fuller comparative analysis see Von Mehren, "The Battle of the Forms: A Comparative View" (1990), 38 Am. J. Comp. L. 265.

240 [1979] 1 All E.R. 965 (C.A.). For a discussion of this case in relation to restitutionary recovery, see McKendrick, "The Battle of the Forms and the Law of Restitution" (1988), 8 Ox. J. Leg. St. 197.

The judgments of Lawton and Bridge L.JJ. were expressed in what might be called traditional terms. That of Lord Denning, however, attempted another analysis of the problem. He distinguished three possibilities.[241] In some cases the battle is won by the man who fires the last shot, that is, the man who puts forward the latest terms and conditions. If they are not objected to by the other party, he is taken to have agreed to them. In others, the man who gets the blow in first wins. This would be the case where, although there is a material difference, for example, as to price, the buyer accepting the seller's offer on the buyer's different terms and conditions "ought not to be allowed to take advantage of the difference unless he draws it specifically to the attention of the seller". Thirdly, there is the situation in which shots are fired on both sides. There is a concluded contract but the forms vary. Where this happens the parties' terms and conditions must be construed together. If reconcilable to give a harmonious result, there is a valid contract on such terms. If not, and the terms are mutually contradictory, the conflicting terms must be scrapped and replaced by a reasonable implication.[242]

This analysis, it has been suggested, is inconsistent with traditional views on offer and acceptance. There seems to be no place for forcing the buyer to accept the seller's terms where he did not agree to them without a qualification, nor for creating a contract for the parties when they have not agreed upon one for themselves. This is certainly so where the contract is still completely executory, neither party having done anything such as delivering goods. If one party has performed and the other party has accepted such performance, then it may be unreasonable to hold that there is no contract and to imply a contract on the terms intended by the party performing. In the *Butler* case there was no room for such implication. The proper way of interpreting what had happened is to say that the sellers' act decisively acknowledged that the contract was on the terms stipulated by the buyers. On the other hand, in the Canadian case of *Tywood Industries Ltd. v. St. Anne-Nackawic Pulp & Paper Co.*[243] the court could not find an agreement in such a way.

The *Tywood* case concerned the question of whether a contract between the parties contained a clause referring disputes to arbitration prior to action. The plaintiff's offer to sell goods contained no reference to arbitration, nor did the buyer's original invitation to tender contain such reference, yet the purchase order issued by the buyer, accepting the seller's offer, was in a standard form which required disputes arising from the agreement to be settled by arbitration. The seller sued for the price of the goods sold. The buyer applied for a stay of proceedings

---

241 *Ibid.*, at 968-969. Compare his criticism of traditional offer and acceptance theory in *Gibson v. Manchester City Council*, [1978] 2 All E.R. 583 at 586 (C.A.); reversed [1979] 1 All E.R. 972 (H.L.) above, p. 23.

242 Compare the American U.C.C. 2-207 (I); a definite and seasonable expression of acceptance. . . . operates as an acceptance even though it states terms additional to or different from those offered . . . ; on which see Shanker, *loc. cit.*, above, note 239, at 272-273.

  The Ontario Law Reform Commission (*Report on Sale of Goods* (1979), Vol. I, pp. 83-84) did not favour the adoption of the American approach; on which see Vaver, *loc. cit.*, above, note 239.

243 (1979), 100 D.L.R. (3d) 374 (Ont. H.C.).

pending arbitration. It was held that the application should be dismissed. The parties had not indicted that they had contemplated anything other than the terms relating to the specification of the goods and the price. There was doubt as to whether the arbitration clause could be included in the contract of sale. In this case, unlike the *Butler* case, neither party had indicated the superiority of its terms over those of the other party (a point which was stressed in the English case), nor was attention drawn to the arbitration clause. Also, the buyer did not complain when the seller failed to return the seller's copy of the purchase order with an acknowledgement of the terms sought to be imposed. There was lacking, in this instance, the necessary evidence to permit a court to draw a conclusion as to the inclusion of the disputed term.

However, it may be added that if parties have reached an agreement but left out an important term, there may be occasion for importing such a term by implication. This can certainly be done when the law, that is, a statute, governing the transaction, permits or requires the inclusion by implication of such term in the absence of any express agreement. Thus in *Kay Corporation v. Dekeyser*,[244] a contract of sale of goods failed to include a term as to time of payment for the goods. Under the Sale of Goods Act,[245] where there is no express term to this effect, it is implied that the time for payment is the time of delivery of the goods. Hence it could not be said that the parties had failed to agree on a material term, or had attempted to provide materially different terms on this matter. The Sale of Goods Act term governed the situation. It would seem, therefore, that only where it is possible to construe a purported contract by reference to some rule of law, or the circumstances reveal that the parties have inferentially, if not expressly agreed to the governance of the transaction by one party's terms rather than the other's, a court will be able to create a contract out of what the parties have done, even though there appears to be a conflict between offer and acceptance that would otherwise, and traditionally, spell out a lack of agreement that is necessary to produce the formation of a valid, binding contract. In this latter respect, of course, it may be necessary to refer to the idea that whether there is an agreement, and its precise nature and scope, must be determined having regard to the way a reasonable man would understand and interpret the language and conduct of a given party. If the offeror, or the offeree, would reasonably conclude that the offer was being accepted, or that the counter-offer was to be the basis for the contract and was accepted by the original offeror, then it may be possible for a court to conclude that the parties were *ad idem*.[246]

(f) Agreement "subject to contract"

An acceptance (or an offer) may contemplate something more by way of

---

244 (1977), 76 D.L.R. (3d) 588 (Ont. C.A.).

245 R.S.O. 1990, c. S.1, s. 27.

246 Note also the argument that these problems should be dealt with by the application of "unconscionability"; Vaver, *loc. cit.*, note 239, above, at 286-289. On unconscionability see below, pp. 325-336.

formalization before a binding contract is to come into existence. This may be a formal contract, or it may be something written but not necessarily formal. For example, a document that is expressed to be a "letter of intent" may be accepted by the party to whom it is addressed. If it states or suggests that some further negotiations and discussions are contemplated before any agreement is reached, the "acceptance" of such document will not have the effect of creating a contract.[247] There is no "offer" that can be accepted. However, even if an offer is a true offer in the sense previously considered, the offeree's acceptance may not bind the parties if the expression "subject to contract" or its equivalent has been used either in the offer itself or in the acceptance. In cases of this kind the question is posed whether the result of the offer and acceptance is a contract to enter into a contract, an agreement clarifying the preliminaries to an eventual legally binding agreement, or a binding contract.[248]

An agreement to make an agreement is not enforceable.[249] If parties have purported to contract that they will make a contract in the future, even if they have identified the terms upon which such later contract will be made, there will be nothing as yet that is legally enforceable. The only possible exception to this is where the first agreement amounts to an option given by one party to the other whereby the latter has the opportunity to make a contract with the former if he chooses (whether under certain conditions or not). Such options are genuine contracts, which contemplate the possibility of a further contract emerging, for example, for the purchase of a piece of property. Such options, however, are separate and distinct contracts which must be established by offer and acceptance and either be supported by consideration or be given under seal.[250]

Instances of an agreement to agree must be differentiated from others where there is a possibility that the parties may have reached a final agreement, even

---

247 *Fairport Const. Ltd. v. Fraser Valley Credit Union* (1979), 8 B.L.R. 16 (B.C. Co. Ct.), which relied on *Diamond Dev. Ltd. v. Crown Assets Disposal Corp.*, [1972] 4 W.W.R. 731 (B.C.S.C.), which was rejected by the B.C.C.A. in *First City Invts. Ltd. v. Fraser Arms Hotel Ltd.; Cumberland Mtge. Corp. v. Fraser Arms Hotel Ltd.*, [1979] 6 W.W.R. 125 (B.C.C.A.); compare above, p. 21. For a comparison between the effects of a letter of intent and an agreement subject to contract, *i.e.*, no creation of a legal relationship, see *Marathon Realty Co. v. Toulon Const. Corp.* (1987), 80 N.S.R. (2d) 390 at 403-404 (N.S.T.D.) *per* Davidson J.

248 See Parker J. in *Von Hatzfeldt-Wildenburg v. Alexander*, [1912] 1 Ch. 284 at 288-289, quoted by Judson J. in *Calvan Consol. Oil & Gas Co. v. Manning*, [1959] S.C.R. 253 at 261 (S.C.C.).

See, *e.g., Italian Village Restaurant Ltd. v. Van Ostrand* (1970), 9 D.L.R. (3d) 512 (Alta. S.C.); compare *Lake Ont. Cement Co. v. Golden Eagle Oil Co.* (1974), 3 O.R. (2d) 739 (Ont. H.C.); *M. & M. Drilling Co. v. W.A. Stephenson Const. (Western) Ltd.* (1987), 27 C.L.R. 271 (Alta. C.A.). Compare *Bill Robbins Drilling Ltd. v. Sinclair Can. Oil Co.*, [1973] 2 W.W.R. 515 (Alta. S.C.). See also *Damon Cia Naviera S.A. v. Hepag-Lloyd Int. S.A.*, [1985] 1 All E.R. 475 (C.A.).

249 *Hillas & Co. v. Arcos Ltd.* (1932), 147 L.T. 503 (H.L.); *May & Butcher Ltd. v. R.*, [1934] 2 K.B. 17 (H.L.) (followed in *Spur Oil Ltd. v. R.* (1981), 42 N.R. 131 (Fed. C.A.)); *Diamond Dev. Ltd. v. Crown Assets Disposal Corp.*, [1972] 4 W.W.R. 731 (B.C.S.C.); *Dwinell v. Custom Motors Ltd.* (1975), 12 N.S.R. (2d) 524 (N.S.C.A.); *Skivest Devs. Ltd. v. Alberta* (1984), 57 A.R. 252 (Alta. Q.B.); *Delta Hotels Ltd. v. Okabe Can. Invts. Co.* (1992), 3 Alta. L.R. (3d) 85 (Alta. C.A.); *Walford v. Miles*, [1992] 2 A.C. 128 (H.L.); compare above, p. 22.

250 *Savereux v. Tourangeau* (1908), 16 O.L.R. 600 (Ont. C.A.); *Gibson v. McVeigh*, [1922] 1 W.W.R. 151 (Alta. S.C.); *Williams v. Keyes*, [1971] 5 W.W.R. 561 (B.C.S.C.).

though some additional formality is envisaged. As it was put by Parker J. in an English case, *Von Hatzfeldt-Wildenburg v. Alexander*[251] (which has been cited with approval in Canada),[252]

> if the documents or letters relied on as constituting a contract contemplate the execution of a further contract between the parties, it is a question of construction whether the execution of the further contract is a condition or term of the bargain or whether it is a mere expression of the desire of the parties as to the manner in which the transaction already agreed to will in fact go through. In the former case there is no enforcable contract either because the condition is unfulfilled or because the law does not recognise a contract to enter into a contract. In the latter case there is a binding contract and the reference to the more formal document may be ignored.

In *Bawitko Investments Ltd. v. Kernels Popcorn Ltd.*,[253] where no contract was held to have been concluded on the facts of the case, Robins J.A., speaking for the Ontario Court of Appeal, drew the distinction between situations where parties, after discussing and negotiating the proposed terms of an agreement, bound themselves to execute at a future date a formal written agreement containing specific terms and conditions. They contracted to make a contract. Yet this is not the same as making an agreement to agree.

> When they agree on all of the essential provisions to be incorporated in a formal document with the intention that their agreement shall thereupon become binding, they will have fulfilled all the requisites for the formation of a contract. The fact that a formal written document to the same effect is to be thereafter prepared and signed does not alter the binding validity of the original contract.[254]

Very different is the situation where there is uncertainty as to the terms of the contract, or, though there is no uncertainty as to the terms of the parties' agreement, their understanding and intention "is that their legal obligations are to be deferred until a formal contract has been approved and executed . . .". The original or preliminary agreement cannot constitute an enforceable contract. Such a "contract to make a contract" is not a contract at all.

> The execution of the contemplated formal document is not intended only as a solemn record or memorial of an already complete and binding contract but is essential to the formation of the contract itself.[255]

Where this is the position there is no contract, despite the correspondence between the language of the parties, and the conformity between offer and acceptance, because of the requirement of the added formality.

---

251 [1912] 1 Ch. 284 at 288-289.

252 *Calvan Consol. Oil & Gas Co. v. Manning*, [1959] S.C.R. 253 (S.C.C.); *Lake Ont. Cement Co. v. Golden Eagle Oil Co.* (1974), 3 O.R. (2d) 739 (Ont. H.C.); *Bawitko Invts. Ltd. v. Kernels Popcorn Ltd.* (1991), 79 D.L.R. (4th) 97 (Ont. C.A.).

253 Above, note 252.

254 *Ibid.*, at 104.

255 *Ibid.* See also the distinction between uncertainty of terms and an agreement to be reduced to another document but manifesting a certain agreement, discussed in *Block Bros. Realty Ltd. v. Occidental Hotel Ltd.*; *Rochelle v. Occidental Hotel Ltd.*, [1971] 3 W.W.R. 51 (B.C.C.A.).

This occurred in *Green v. Ainsmore Consolidated Mines Ltd.*,[256] where the agreement to purchase the defendant's mines was included in a letter setting out the terms of the sale, but specifying that this was a draft form of the agreement and the whole thing was subject to a formal agreement. Similarly in *Fry v. Barnes*,[257] an interim agreement was subject to a formal agreement *in futuro* to effectuate the intention of the parties. To the same effect is *Marathon Realty Co. v. Toulon Construction Corporation*,[258] where the formal agreement contemplated did not only embody terms already agreed, but others still to be negotiated. In *Bahamaconsult Ltd. v. Kellogg Salada Canada Ltd.*,[259] the contract contemplated between the parties was for the sale of land. The parties left for later determination in a formal contract the terms concerned with the provision of security for the payment of a deposit as part of the purchase price. It was held by the Ontario Court of Appeal, reversing the trial judge,[260] that matters of substance involving essential terms of the contract had not been agreed upon by the parties, hence, there was no contract. So too, in *Nordex International Development Ltd. v. Texas Industries Ltd.*,[261] the parties intended the execution of a formal contract. Their interim agreement, although an agreement of some sort, was not a binding contract. It did not contain such essential terms as an accurate description of the property to be sold, the rate of interest, the dates for payment of interest, and upon which party the responsibility for registration was to lie.

By way of contrast, a valid contract was held to have come into existence, although the parties agreed that "documents for signature" were to follow, in *Sydney Steel Corporation v. Mannesmann Pipe & Steel Corporation*.[262] Similarly, in *Mark Fishing Co. v. Northern Princess Seafood Ltd.*,[263] the written agreement, which was not executed by the defendant, contained all the necessary and essential terms to which the parties had orally agreed: therefore a valid contract existed. The leading example, in Canada, of an agreement that was binding although the parties contemplated some subsequent formalities, is the decision of the Supreme Court of Canada in *Calvan Consolidated Oil & Gas Co. v. Manning*.[264] Here the correspondence relating to an exchange of interests in different oil and gas permits respectively owned by the parties stated expressly that there was to be a formal agreement to be executed in the future, and that, if the parties could not agree

---

256 [1951] 3 D.L.R. 632 (B.C.S.C.); compare the leading English case of *Chillingworth v. Esche*, [1924] 1 Ch. 97 (C.A.).
257 [1953] 2 D.L.R. 817 (B.C.S.C.); contrast with *Lake Ont. Cement Co. v. Golden Eagle Oil Co.* (1974), 3 O.R. (2d) 739 (Ont. H.C.).
258 (1987), 80 N.S.R. (2d) 390 (N.S.T.D.).
259 (1976), 75 D.L.R. (3d) 522 (Ont. C.A.); leave to appeal to S.C.C. dismissed (1976), 15 O.R. (2d) 276n (S.C.C.).
260 (1975), 61 D.L.R. (3d) 398 (Ont. H.C.).
261 (1981), 12 Sask. R. 353 (Sask. Q.B.). See also *Welton Tool Rental Ltd. v. Douglas Aircraft Co.* (1978), 28 N.S.R. (2d) 636 (N.S.T.D.).
262 (1986), 75 N.S.R. (2d) 211 (N.S.T.D.).
263 (1990), 38 F.T.R. 299 (Fed. T.D.); reversed in part (1991), 137 N.R. 151 (Fed. C.A.).
264 [1959] S.C.R. 253 (S.C.C.); compare *Br. Amer. Timber Co. v. Elk River Timber Co.*, [1933] 4 D.L.R. 286 (B.C.C.A.); *Byrne v. Napier* (1975), 62 D.L.R. (3d) 589 (Ont. H.C.).

on the terms of such agreement, they were to be settled by an aribitrator. It was argued that there was no binding contract *inter alia* because the reference to a later formal contract meant that the interim agreement was not meant to be binding. About this Judson J. said:[265]

> [t]his is not a case of acceptance qualified by such expressed condition as "subject to the preparation and approval of a formal contract", "subject to contract" or "subject to the preparation of a formal contract, its execution by the parties and approval by their solicitors". Here we have an unqualified acceptance with a formal contract to follow.

It was a question of construction, and the court had no doubts with respect to the proper construction to place upon the language of the parties.

The Supreme Court also held that the parties' expressed intention to submit the settlement of the terms of their contract to arbitration did not preclude the conclusion that they had reached a final binding contract. Similarly, in *296440 Ontario Ltd. v. Silverwood Industries Ltd.*[266] the parties had reached an agreement but also provided that it was to be effective only upon approval by a third party. Before such approval was forthcoming, the plaintiff repudiated the agreement and sued for the return of the franchise fee which he had paid to the defendant, as well as for damages. It was held that there was a valid contract between the parties without the third party's approval. The latter's intervention was a condition of performance of the contract, not of its coming into existence.

(g) Communication of acceptance[267]

Whether the offeree must inform or notify the offeror that the former has accepted the latter's offer depends on the nature of the offer. Logically speaking, communication of acceptance ought to be essential.[268] How else is the offeror to know whether he is bound to the original offeree or can safely make his offer to a third party? Statements that communication of acceptance is generally required can be found in many cases.[269] As Cory J.A. explained in *Lanca Contracting Ltd.*

---

265 [1959] S.C.R. 253 at 260 (S.C.C.).

266 (1983), 41 O.R. (2d) 624 (Ont. Co. Ct.); note also the decision in that case that the non-fulfilment of the condition, *i.e.*, the condition precedent, rendered the contract inoperative, not void, applying the decision of the S.C.C. in *Dynamic Tpt. Ltd. v. O.K. Detailing Ltd.*, [1978] 2 S.C.R. 1072 (S.C.C.). See also *Wiebe v. Bobsein*, [1985] 1 W.W.R. 644 (B.C.S.C.).

267 Parts of this section were referred to by Hallett J. in *Eddy MacKay Bldg. Co. v. Nova Scotia (A.G.)* (1982), 52 N.S.R. (2d) 495 (N.S.S.C.).

268 It was in order to satisfy the provisions of the Family Law Reform Act, R.S.O. 1980, c. 152, s. 42(1)(*a*)[see now Family Law Act, R.S.O. 1990, c. F.3, s. 21(1)(a)], see *Bergmann v. Burns* (1982), 134 D.L.R. (3d) 89 (Ont. H.C.).

269 *Sask. Co-op. Wheat Producers Ltd. v. Zurowski*, [1926] 1 D.L.R. 770 at 781 (Sask. K.B.); reversed on other grounds, [1926] 3 D.L.R. 810 (Sask. C.A.). See also *Baston v. Toronto Fruit Vinegar Co.* (1902), 4 O.L.R. 20 (Ont. C.A.); *Fisher v. Schiller* (1979), 100 D.L.R. (3d) 186 at 187 (Ont. C.A.) *per* Morden J.A.; reversed on other grounds (1981), 124 D.L.R. (3d) 577 (S.C.C.); *MacIntyre v. Commerce Capital Mtge. Corp.* (1981), 34 O.R. (2d) 104 at 114 (Ont. H.C.) *per* Saunders J. Unless its necessity is waived: *Shelson Invts. Ltd. v. Durkovich* (1984), 34 Alta. L.R. (2d) 319 (Alta. Q.B.).

v. Brant County Board of Education,[270] notice of acceptance was to protect the offeror. It was unfair to bind an offeror to the terms of his offer until he was aware that his offer had been accepted. Communication will certainly be essential if something in the offer has referred to its necessity. Thus communication was required where an option was expressed as being capable of being exercised by payment of the purchase price to the one giving the option at the office of his solicitor,[271] and where the offeree's alterations to the original offer required acceptance thereof within a specified period.[272] Similarly, in *Thierry v. Thierry*,[273] an agreement between a husband and wife that the husband would transfer property to the wife if the wife had "just cause" in the future was not binding because it had not been accepted within a reasonable period by notification of the husband.

The necessity for communication of acceptance has also been emphasized in cases in which a court has been obliged to determine where a contract was made for the purposes of giving jurisdiction to the court to try the action, or to allow service of a writ out of such jurisdiction. If communication of an acceptance is not required by some written or oral statement or some positive act of which the offeror is aware, then the contract will have been concluded at the place where the offeree is situated, since he accepted there. If the offeror must be made aware of the offeree's acceptance, then the contract will be made where the offeror receives such notification. In *Re Viscount Supply Co.*,[274] the offeror was in Ontario, the offeree in Quebec. The offeree telephoned from Montreal to Toronto. It was held that the contract had been concluded and made in Ontario, not Quebec, because communication of acceptance was necessary and this had occurred in Ontario where the offeror received the call, not in Quebec where the offeree originated the call. A similar result followed in *McDonald & Sons Ltd. v. Export Packers Co.*,[275] where the offer was transmitted from British Columbia, by telephone, and the acceptance came, by telephone, from Ontario. Since the acceptance was received in British Columbia, it was held that the contract was concluded in that province so as to permit service of a writ out of the jurisdiction. The approach taken in cases of this kind is that, where communication between the parties is by some instantaneous, or virtually instantaneous method such as the telephone or telex, it is absolutely essential that the offeror receive a response from the offeree. Without such notification there can be no valid contract.[276] Hence the place where the offeror

---

270 (1986), 26 D.L.R. (4th) 708 at 714-715 (Ont. C.A.).

271 *Knauft v. Bottoms* (1960), 33 W.W.R. 427 (Alta. S.C.).

272 *Parkette Apts. Ltd. v. Masternak*, [1965] 2 O.R. 350 (Ont. H.C.); compare *Schiller v. Fisher* (1981), 124 D.L.R. (3d) 577 (S.C.C.), where the S.C.C. held that as long as the counter-offer was initialled by the stated date, the signed copy did not have to be returned before, or by, that date for a valid acceptance.

273 (1956), 18 W.W.R. 127 (Sask. C.A.).

274 [1963] 1 O.R. 640 (Ont. S.C.); also, see *Williston Basin State Bank v. Shearer* (1983), 53 A.R. 121 (Alta. Q.B.); *Davidson v. Anchorage Inc.* (1980), 23 B.C.L.R. 352 (B.C.S.C.).

275 [1979] 2 W.W.R. 764 (B.C.S.C.).

276 *Entores Ltd. v. Miles Far East Corp.*, [1955] 2 Q.B. 327 (C.A.); for the use of the teletype see *MacIntyre v. Commerce Capital Mtge. Corp.* (1981)), 34 O.R. (2d) 104 (Ont. H.C.); for the use of a fax machine, see *Rolling v. Willann Invts. Ltd.* (1989), 70 O.R. (2d) 578 (Ont. C.A.).

receives such notice must be the place where the contract is finally reached. As it was put by Lord Wilberforce in *Brinkibon v. Stahag Stahl,*[277]

> [t]he general rule . . .is that a contract is formed *when* acceptance of an offer is communicated by the offeree to the offeror. And if it is necessary to determine *where* a contract is formed...it appears logical that this should be at the place where acceptance is communicated to the offeror. In the common case of contracts, whether oral or in writing inter praesentes, there is no difficulty; and again logic demands that even where there is not mutual presence at the same place and at the same time, if communication is instantaneous, for example by telephone or radio communication, the same result should follow.

It might be said that by using such methods of communication the offeror has inferentially, if not expressly, indicated to the offeree that he is willing to receive an acceptance by the same method; indeed that he desires that such method be used for the sake of speed and certainty. Undoubtedly the parties may agree upon any mode of communication they wish. Such agreement may be express or may be implied from the circumstances. The offeror alone may make his intentions or agreement known to the offeree, either by some express statement accompanying the offer as to the way in which, and the time within which the offeree must accept the offer, or in consequence of some reasonable implication that may be drawn from the language or acts of the offeror.

Where such an implication may be made, the result is that the offeror has taken upon himself the risk that he may never actually receive any communication from the offeree. The likelihood of this occurring where communication is instantaneous is small; an offeror who has not received the offeree's answer can quickly inform the offeree. In that way the possibility of the offeror not knowing of the purported acceptance, and the offeree not knowing of the failure of the offeror to receive such acceptance, is lessened. Where the method of communication is not instantaneous, each party may be unaware of what has happened. The offeror may believe that his offer has not been accepted. The offeree may think that his acceptance has been received. Can it be said that there is a contract between the parties in such circumstances? If actual notification to the offeror of the fact of acceptance is a requisite, the answer should be that there is no contract. Such an answer may be unfair to the offeree. To absolve the offeree of any obligation to notify the offeror in fact, rather than transmit an acceptance which may never reach the offeror, might result in unfairness to the offeror. Whichever solution is adopted will not be completely satisfactory to both parties. The common law's answer is to say that the result will depend upon the offeror's conduct. It is his choice of mode of communication that dictates the result. As seen above, where he transacts the negotiations by an instantaneous method of intercommunication, he manifests his desire to have immediate and sure response.[278] Where he adopts

---

277 [1982] 1 All E.R. 293 at 295 (H.L.), italics in the original.
278 Commercial expediency may require such methods of communication and instantaneous replies to offers; *Humble Invts. Ltd. v. N.M. Skalbania Ltd.* (1983), 22 Sask. R. 81 at 90 (Sask. C.A.) *per* Tallis J.A., citing the *Brinkibon* case.

a different mode, he may have indicated to the offeree that such immediacy is not vital. By virtue of the "postal acceptance" rule,[279] where the offeror makes it plain that he is treating the post office, or some similar organization, as his agent for the transmission and receipt of any acceptance, the offeror has then empowered the offeree to utilise such organization as the appropriate agent (and not some other agency). Hence, as long as the offeree uses the nominated agency, the risk of any failure of the acceptance to arrive will be on the offeror, not on the offeree. Should the use of the post, for example, not be contemplated by the parties, the posting of a letter of acceptance will not constitute acceptance. If such a letter is not received, there will be no contract.[280] Where a method of acceptance is stipulated, the risk will be on the offeree if he acts otherwise than in accordance with the stated or impliedly approved method of communication. For example, if the offeror makes an offer in writing for the purchase of shares, he does not by implication state that the telegraph company is his agent for the receipt of an acceptance. Hence an offeree who sends his acceptance by telegram cannot claim that the offeror is bound when the telegram does not arrive at the offeror's premises and in consequence the offeror is ignorant of the acceptance.[281]

By way of contrast in *Magann v. Auger*,[282] where an offer was sent by post, it was held that the offeror had impliedly assented to the offeree's using the post to send the acceptance. Hence putting the acceptance in the hands of the post office was enough to bind the parties, even though the offeror never received the letter of acceptance. The contract was made at the moment when and at the place where the acceptance had actually been sent off to the offeror. In this respect it was held that the law of Quebec was like the law of England, that is, the common law. In the later case of *Charlebois v. Baril*,[283] the Supreme Court qualified this by holding that the above stated principle did not apply where the offer was transmitted by other means, namely, by being actually handed over to the offeree's agent for delivery to the offeree in person. In such a case, posting of the acceptance by the offeree will not suffice, because the offeror has not made the post office his agent.

The situation was summed up by Russell J. in a Nova Scotia case, *Cochrane v. McKay*,[284] in which it was held that posting an acceptance in Nova Scotia of

279 *Adams v. Lindsell* (1818), 1 B. & Ald. 681, 106 E.R. 250; *Household Fire Ins. Co. v. Grant* (1879), 4 Ex. D. 216 (C.A.); *Henthorn v. Fraser*, [1892] 2 Ch. 27 (C.A.); *Holwell Securities v. Hughes*, [1974] 1 All E.R. 161 (C.A.). On this see Gardner, "Trashing with Trollope: A Deconstruction of the Postal Rules of Contract" (1992), 12 Ox. J. Leg. St. 170.

280 *Balfour Grain Ltd. v. Goertz* (1989), 78 Sask. R. 283 (Sask. Q.B.). But if the offeror has stipulated a method of accepting, *e.g.*, initialling changes to an offer made by the purchaser as a counter-offer, posting will not be necessary: *Schiller v. Fisher* (1981), 124 D.L.R. (3d) 577 (S.C.C.).

281 *Smith & Osberg Ltd. v. Hollenbeck*, [1938] 3 W.W.R. 704 (B.C.S.C.).

282 (1901), 31 S.C.R. 186 (S.C.C.). Compare *Ellard v. Waterloo Mfg. Co.*, [1926] 2 W.W.R. 294 (Sask. C.A.). The same result will follow if the use of the post office has been made *express*, as in *Lister v. Bannerman* (1911), 19 W.L.R. 182 (Man. S.C.). For the use of cables, compare *St. Helen's Smelting Co. v. Dom. Antimony Co.* (1908), 42 N.S.R. 385 (N.S.C.A.).

283 [1928] S.C.R. 88 (S.C.C.).

284 (1921), 61 D.L.R. 338 (N.S.C.A.).

an offer sent from Ontario meant that the contract was made in Nova Scotia, since acceptance dated from the time of posting. What the learned judge said is worthy of citation at length:[285]

> Where an offer is made by post the acceptance of that offer is held to be complete when the acceptance is posted, but that rule is fully recognised to be mere "rule of thumb", based on convenience, and an exception to the general rule which I take to be that a communication is not complete until it is brought home to the knowledge of the person to whom it is made. The exception has been extended by Lord Herschell in the case of *Henthorn v. Fraser* . . . to any case "where the circumstances . . . are such that it must have been within the contemplation of the parties that according to the ordinary usages of mankind the post might be used as a means of communicating the acceptance of it, the acceptance is complete as soon as it is posted." Where the communication is not the acceptance of an offer, but the revocation of a letter containing an offer, it has been clearly decided that the communication is not completed by the posting of the letter. It is only completed when the letter containing the revocation is received.

This passage makes certain points very clear. Posting suffices to create a contract, even if the acceptance is never received by the offeror, where the parties by implication have made it so.[286] That will occur when the use of the post (or telegrams in appropriate circumstances)[287] is the normal, accepted, or clearly contemplated means of communication.[288] That rule only applies to acceptances, not to revocations. For obvious reasons, an offeree is free to accept until he actually knows of the revocation, whether or not his knowledge comes directly from the offeror or from other sources.[289]

The law, as thus stated, has been applied in contexts other than that of acceptance of an offer by post, for example, acceptance by or through the medium of some agent,[290] proof of loss of property entitling an assured to claim under a policy of assurance,[291] or serving a specified notice on the corporation.[292] That it is a rule of convenience, at least as regards acceptance of offers, is undeniable. Business could probably not continue in an orderly, straightforward fashion if

---

285 (1921), 61 D.L.R. 338 at 339-340 (N.S.C.A.).

286 See, *e.g., Eddy MacKay Bldg. Co. v. Nova Scotia (A.G.)* (1982), 52 N.S.R. (2d) 495 (N.S.S.C.); compare *Bordo v. 403512 Ont. Inc.* (1983), 41 O.R. (2d) 68 at 73-74 (Ont. H.C.).

287 *E.g., Island Properties Ltd. v. Entertainment Enterprises Ltd.* (1983), 146 D.L.R. (3d) 505 (Nfld. T.D.); appeal allowed in part on other grounds (1986), 26 D.L.R. (4th) 347 (Nfld. C.A.).

288 See, *e.g., Pearce v. Tpt. Fire & Casualty Co.* (1977), 83 D.L.R. (3d) 259 (Ont. Dist. Ct.); *Sibtac Corp. v. Soo* (1978), 83 D.L.R. (3d) 116 (Ont. H.C.); contrast *Brookfield Sales & Services Ltd. v. Myers* (1978), 85 D.L.R. (3d) 525 (N.S.S.C.); affirmed (1978), 30 N.S.R. (2d) 418 (N.S.C.A.) (posting acceptance of insurance premium not enough; premium had to be received by a certain date; therefore premium had to be *received*).

    The previous two sentences in the version of the first edition were cited by the court in *Eddy MacKay Bldg. Co. v. Nova Scotia (A.G.)* (1982), 52 N.S.R. (2d) 495 at 501 (N.S.S.C.).

289 Above, p. 46.

290 *Cowie v. Richards* (1960), 50 M.P.R. 107 (N.B.C.A.), in which Bridges J.A. and McVane C.J.N.B. rely on the postal cases. *Quaere:* was this such a case?

291 *Milinkovich v. Can. Mercantile Ins. Co.,* [1960] S.C.R. 830 (S.C.C.).

292 *Loft v. Physicians' Services Inc.,* [1966] 2 O.R. 253 (Ont. C.A.).

absolute proof of communication of acceptance were always required. But the validity of the extension of this rule of thumb to other, seemingly similar situations, is open to question.[293]

If no particular method of acceptance is prescribed by the offeror, either expressly or by implication, the form that notification must take will depend on the nature of the offer and the circumstances in which it is made. Hence even if written notification would appear to be required by the contract documents, communication by some other method, no less advantageous to the offeror, can be sufficient.[294] That view was adopted by the majority of the Ontario Court of Appeal, following English authority,[295] in preference to an older, stricter view put forward in Ontario. In the earlier Ontario case, *Donovan v. City of Belleville*,[296] it was said that notification of acceptance of a tender had to be given to the successful tenderer by someone who had authority to communicate that acceptance. This view was followed by the dissentient, Zuber J.A., in *Lanca Contracting Ltd. v. Brant Board of Education*.[297] A tender was submitted by the plaintiff company to the defendant board. At a meeting of the board, when the plaintiff company's president was present, the board resolved to accept the plaintiff company's tender. The members of the board knew that the company president was present. After the meeting the chairman of the board, the board's architect and other crucial persons spoke to the plaintiff company's president in terms that implied that the company would be fulfilling the contract for which the plaintiff company tendered. Later the board rescinded its original motion accepting the plaintiff company's tender, and awarded the contract to another tenderer. The plaintiff company sued for breach of contract. The action failed at trial. By a majority the Court of Appeal held that the plaintiff company's tender had been accepted. Therefore the board was contractually bound to the plaintiff company and was liable for breach of the contract. Zuber J.A., dissenting, held that communication was a necessary part of acceptance and involved more than the offeror learning that the offeree had decided to take up the offer. The offeree had to communicate to the offeror his assent to the terms of the offer. Although there were a number of communications from which acceptance could be inferred or would occur in the future, none of them amounted to an expression of acceptance. They did not unequivocally relate to the existence of a contract.

(h) Unilateral contracts

The "postal acceptance" cases do not really state that communication of acceptance is unnecessary where the parties have expressly or impliedly made use

---

293 The previous three sentences were cited by the court in *Eddy MacKay Bldg. Co. v. Nova Scotia (A.G.)*, above, note 288, at 501.

294 *Lanca Contracting Ltd. v. Brant County Bd. of Education* (1986), 26 D.L.R. (4th) 708 (Ont. C.A.).

295 *Manchester Diocesan Council for Education v. Commercial & General Invts., Ltd.*, [1970] 1 W.L.R. 241 (Ch. D.).

296 [1931] O.R. 731 (Ont. C.A.).

297 Above, note 294, at 718.

of the post office or other agency for the transmission of their offer and acceptance. What those cases indicate is that the party who employs such an agency, and permits the other party to do so, undertakes the risk that there will be some malfunction, such that he never receives the offeree's acceptance. He has not dispensed with the necessity for acceptance; he has only undertaken a certain potential risk. In contrast, there are cases which identify situations in which an offeror has either expressly or by implication (more usually the latter) excluded or dispensed with any requirement of communication of acceptance.

The reason why, exceptionally, as Sheppard J.A. indicated in *Wilson v. Clarke Simpkins Ltd.*,[298] the communication of acceptance is not required, is because the intention of the parties is to exclude any such requirement. The intention of the parties as to the manner of contracting, as the learned judge said,[299] is a matter of construction. In that case a contract for the sale of a car, which was signed by the purchaser and a salesman, provided that the contract would not be valid unless it was signed and accepted by the vendor. A space for the vendor's acceptance was left on the document. In these circumstances it was held that once the vendor signed, the contract was binding. There was no need for communication of the acceptance to the purchaser. In *Dominion Building Corporation v. R.*[300] an offer to buy Crown land provided that the offer, if accepted by an order-in-council, would become a binding contract. It was held that the contract was binding when the order-in-council was made, whether or not there was any communication of such order to the purchaser (offeree). As Lord Tomlin indicated,[301] the offer itself removed the need for any communication of acceptance. The same was held true in *Principal Investments Ltd. v. Trevett*,[302] in which an offer stated that the offer, when accepted, would constitute a binding contract of purchase and sale. Once the vendor signed his acceptance it was held that the contract was complete and there was no need for communication of such acceptance to the purchaser.

In such instances the offer or the particular relationship[303] is such as to make it clear that it is the performance of some act by the offeree which concludes the contract and amounts to acceptance, making the contract binding without any requirement of communication of acceptance in advance of the performance of the act. Such contracts have long been designated as "unilateral" contracts. The expression suggests that there is only one party, however, they are not different from normal "bilateral" contracts, except in respect of their lack of any formal

---

298 (1961), 30 D.L.R. (2d) 745 at 746 (B.C.C.A.).

299 *Ibid.*, at 747.

300 [1933] A.C. 533 (P.C.).

301 *Ibid.*, at 545.

302 [1956] O.W.N. 353 (Ont. H.C.). But there must be an acceptance, *e.g.*, payment of a parking fee, the failure to do which meant there was no unilateral contract in *City Parking Services v. Murray* (1992), 99 Nfld. & P.E.I.R. 11 (Nfld. T.D.). Nor was there a bilateral contract.

303 *Turner v. Laurentide Financial Realty Corp. (Western)* (1979), 10 B.C.L.R. 215 at 222 (B.C.S.C.) *per* McEachern C.J. For the possibility of such a contract emerging from a "letter of intent", see *B.S.C. v. Cleveland Bridge Co.*, [1984] 1 All E.R. 504 at 509-510 *per* Goff J. See also *Marathon Realty Co. v. Toulon Const. Corp.* (1987), 80 N.S.R. (2d) 390 at 403-404 (N.S.T.D.) *per* Davidson J. on the nature and function of a "letter of intent".

acceptance prior to the actual performance of the contract by the offeree who has accepted. Because only one party, the offeror, makes a promise, the expression "unilateral" may be justified.[304]

The classic illustration of such contracts is *Carlill v. Carbolic Smoke Ball Co.*[305] The defendant company offered to pay a sum of money to anyone using their product who nonetheless caught influenza. The fact that the company deposited a sum of money at a bank indicated that this was a genuine offer to make a contract and not an advertising trick to induce people to buy the product. This offer was made to the world at large, that is, to anyone who was willing to take up the challenge and use the product for the stipulated time. It did not envisage any acceptance by any particular individual intending to use the product before the product was used. The *nature* of the offer and the surrounding circumstances made it unreasonable to infer that prospective winners of the money should notify the offeror in advance that they agreed to the terms of the contract and intended to perform. This case has been followed by several Canadian courts, in the literal sense where the facts of a Canadian case resembled it,[306] and in the sense of the legal doctrine stated therein.[307] What would seem to be involved are: (i) an indication from the nature of the offer that communication is either impossible or undesirable; and (ii) conduct by the offeree that is consistent only with his having accepted the offer, such that he may be said to have accepted it by what he has done.[308] Hence in *Glaces Rachelli Inc. v. Canada (Minister of Regional Industrial Expansion)*,[309] the government of Canada was bound to confer a grant, on the basis of a unilateral contract, at the most, only if the claimant of the grant fully complied with certain conditions of eligibility for such a grant. Since the claimant did not, no obligation arose.

---

304 For criticism of unilateral contracts and unilateral contract terminology, see Carter, "The Breach of Unilateral Contracts" (1982), 11 Anglo-American L.R. 169 at 170-72.

305 [1893] 1 Q.B. 256 (C.A.) (applied in *Harvela Invts. v. Royal Trust Co. of Can.*, [1985] 1 All E.R. 261 (C.A.); reversed [1985] 2 All E.R. 966 (H.L.)); compare *Great Nor. Ry. Co. v. Witham* (1873), L.R. 9 C.P. 16. Earlier instances are the cases in which a reward has been offered, *e.g.*, for information leading to a conviction.

306 *Dunham v. St. Croix Soap Mfg. Co.* (1897), 34 N.B.R. 243 (N.B.C.A.); see also *Goldthorpe v. Logan*, [1943] 2 D.L.R. 519 (Ont. C.A.) (advertisement offering the clearing of facial hair by electrolysis; offeror held bound when a member of the public undertook treatment and it was not successful). It was probably unnecessary to resort to the idea of "unilateral" contract in this case because there was a "bilateral" contract to perform the treatment, the breach of which, by negligence, supported an action.

307 *Br. Traders Ins. Co. v. Queen Ins. Co.*, [1928] S.C.R. 9 (S.C.C.); *Principal Invts. Ltd. v. Trevett*, [1956] O.W.N. 353 (Ont. H.C.); *Wilson v. Clarke Simpkins Ltd.* (1961), 30 D.L.R. (2d) 745 (B.C.C.A.); *Frankel Structural Steel Ltd. v. Goden Holdings Ltd.* (1969), 5 D.L.R. (3d) 15 (Ont. C.A.); varied on other grounds (1971), 16 D.L.R. (3d) 736 (S.C.C.); *Rusonik v. Can. Trust Co.* (1986), 39 R.P.R. 263 at 278-283 (Ont. H.C.) *per* Henry J.; additional reasons at (December 16, 1986), Doc. No. 40730/79 (Ont. H.C.); affirmed (January 22, 1988), Doc. No. CA 348/86 (Ont. C.A.); *Press Box Inc. v. Berlin* (1988), 85 N.B.R. (2d) 288 (N.B.Q.B.); *Maier v. E & B Exploration Ltd.*, [1986] 4 W.W.R. 275 (Alta. C.A.); compare *McCannel v. Mabee McLaren Motors Ltd.*, [1926] 1 W.W.R. 353 (B.C.C.A.).

308 *Commonwealth Drilling Co. v. Community Petroleums Ltd.*, [1951] 4 D.L.R. 328 (Sask. C.A.).

309 (1989), 29 F.T.R. 169 (Fed. T.D.), a case from Quebec.

Although offers which give rise to such unilateral contracts are accepted by conduct, not by some statement that the offer is being accepted, the importance and uniqueness of such offers lies in the fact that the offeror may become bound without knowing that he is bound. In some cases, where the offer is made to a specific individual, no great inroads are made upon the principle of *consensus ad idem*. The offeror will probably know within a short period of time that his offer has been accepted by the specific offeree's performance of the stipulated act. In *Daulia Ltd. v. Four Millbank Nominees Ltd.*,[310] vendors of property said that they would enter into a contract of sale in respect of the property if the particular prospective purchasers provided a banker's draft for the deposit on sale, came to the vendors' office at a specified time, and tendered to the vendors the purchasers' part of the contract engrossed and signed together with the banker's draft. The Court of Appeal held that this was an offer which could be accepted by the purchasers performing the stipulated acts—a unilateral contract. This was a distinct contract preceding the contract of sale; it was not a contract to enter into a contract.[311]

In *Calgary Hardwood & Veneer Ltd. v. Canadian National Railway*,[312] a vendor agreed to sell land to a purchaser if the latter could obtain municipal approval for the proposed use of the land. It was held that this was not an offer to be accepted before any action by the purchaser, giving rise to a contract subject to a condition precedent (which might have rendered the transaction void if the condition were not satisfied).[313] It was an offer which was accepted without prior notification by the purchaser's obtaining the requisite approval. Thus there was no contract unless, and until, the municipal approval was obtained. In *M.J. Peddlesden Ltd. v. Liddell Construction Ltd.*,[314] the plaintiff, a subcontractor involved in a construction project, submitted a tender through a bid depository system. Under this, sub-contractors deposited sealed tenders valid for 30 days for inspection by the general contractor who then made his own bid for the work to the party wishing the work done. The defendant was the general contractor who successfully bid for the general contract, having told the owner that the plaintiff would be one of the sub-contractors. The defendant informed the plaintiff of his success in the bid for tenders after the expiration of the 30 days within which the plaintiff's sealed tender was valid. Later the defendant repudiated the plaintiff's contract to do the subcontracted work. The issue was whether there was a valid contract between the plaintiff and defendant. If the plaintiff's tender was an offer, the argument was put forward that it was only accepted after the time within which it was operative, that is, when the defendant told the plaintiff of the defendant's success in the bid for the

---

310 [1978] 2 All E.R. 557 (C.A.).

311 Hence it was governed by the Statute of Frauds; below, pp. 213, 220.

312 (1977), 74 D.L.R. (3d) 284 (Alta. S.C.); affirmed [1979] 4 W.W.R. 198 (Alta. C.A.).

313 Below, pp. 437-441.

314 (1981), 128 D.L.R. (3d) 360 (B.C.S.C.), discussed and followed, without distinction, even though it dealt with the "bid depository" system of tendering, rather than the usage in the construction industry, in *Nor. Const. Co. v. Gloge Heating & Plumbing Ltd.* (1984), 6 D.L.R. (4th) 450 (Alta. Q.B.); affirmed [1986] 2 W.W.R. 649 (Alta. C.A.).

general contract. It was held, however, that there was a valid contract. The plaintiff's offer, in his tender to the defendant was, in effect, an offer to contract which would be accepted by the defendant's obtaining a contract with the owner of the property on which the construction was to occur. The plaintiff was dispensing with notification of acceptance. The resulting contract was a unilateral contract. As soon as the owner accepted the defendant's bid for the general contract the plaintiff's offer to do the subcontracted work was also accepted by the defendant without anything further being necessary.

In these cases, however, it was clearly contemplated by the offeror of the unilateral contract that there would be an acceptance if something were done by the offeree. Until such time no obligation existed between the parties. In *A.J. Diamond Associates v. City of Halifax*,[315] no such unilateral contract was held to have arisen when an architect prepared a proposal in response to a call by the city for proposals with respect to an urban renewal project. The city's call for proposals was not an offer to be accepted by preparation or submission of a proposal that could be turned into a unilateral contract by the undertaking of the task. Hence, the city was not obligated to the architect in respect of the proposal. In other words, it is essential that the "offer", if it is to become a unilateral contract by the performance of some act, must be an offer made with intent to enter into legal relations as a consequence of the performance of the stipulated act.[316]

This, clearly, is a limiting factor to be taken into account in determining whether the alleged offeror's statement can mature into a binding contractual obligation whenever someone does whatever is set out in the statement. In the *Carlill* case the nature of the advertisement and the deposit of the money indicated that the smoke ball company was serious in what it said. In other more recent cases involving the liability of manufacturers to consumers, the court, by close analysis of the facts, was able to find that a similar intent lay behind the manufacturers' advertisement of the quality of the goods which were ultimately bought by consumers from dealers in the manufacturers' products. Hence, it was possible to find that there was a valid unilateral contract in the form of a "collateral" contract[317] between the manufacturers in question and the consumers, independent of any contract of sale between the dealers and the consumers. In one case,[318] the advertisement concerned the quality of performance of farm machinery. In another,[319] it dealt with the rustproof nature of the manufacturers' car. The utility of the unilateral contract idea in such cases is obvious. But it has also been invoked in order to escape from the consequences of the privity doctrine[320] so as to permit a stranger to a contract to be entitled to invoke an exemption clause contained in such contract by way of defence to an action brought against him by one of the contracting

315 (1978), 31 N.S.R. (2d) 510 (N.S.T.D.).
316 Compare above, pp. 26-31.
317 Below, pp. 460, 505.
318 *Murray v. Sperry Rand Corp.* (1979), 23 O.R. (2d) 456 (Ont. H.C.).
319 *Naken v. G.M. of Can. Ltd.* (1979), 21 O.R. (2d) 780 (Ont. C.A.); reversed on other grounds not relevant here (1983), 144 D.L.R. (3d) 385 (S.C.C.).
320 Below, pp. 184-191.

parties.[321] The Privy Council, in *New Zealand Shipping Co. v. A.M. Satterthwaite & Co.*,[322] was able to find a separate contract between the holder of a bill of lading relating to goods being shipped and the stevedores who actually unloaded the goods based upon the terms of the bill of lading, including an exemption clause. Although the stevedores were not parties to the bill of lading, it was held that the document clearly contemplated that some stevedores would be involved in the handling of the goods during their passage from consignor to consignee. The terms of the bill of lading, especially the exemption clause, were held to be an offer to exempt anyone who handled the goods from liability for negligence beyond a certain amount. That offer was accepted and became a contract between the holder of the bill of lading and the party handling the goods as soon as the goods were handled in this way, regardless of any prior notification. It turned into a unilateral contract.

These latter examples illustrate the situation where the offer is made to no specific individual. The offeror does not know who will be the offeree, nor does he know within what period of time the offer will be "accepted", yet he takes the risk that someone will accept and that he will be bound thereupon, as long as his "offer" was meant to be taken seriously as such. In the *Satterthwaite* case, the seriousness of the offer was perhaps more obvious than in the advertisement cases. All that was really involved in the latter instances, however, was a little deeper analysis of the facts and circumstances in order to arrive at the conclusion that the manufacturers' statements were not idle expressions designed to promote their goods but were to be taken as binding promises about quality.

In *R. v. Ron Engineering & Construction (Eastern) Ltd.*,[323] such analysis was hardly necessary since the call for tenders required anyone responding to submit the tender in a certain form, deposit a significant sum of money by way of deposit to be forfeited in certain instances, and conform to the detailed terms of the advertisement for tenders. The Supreme Court of Canada held that this was not the usual invitation to treat or chaffer that is involved in such advertisements. It was an offer of a unilateral contract, accepted by submission of the tender by a party even though the latter did not independently inform the owner seeking tenders of the tenderer's intention to submit a tender.[324] In other words, there was no need for the tenderer's intention to submit a tender. In consequence, once the tender was submitted there was a contract between the parties which could not be revoked nor upset by any allegation of mistake in the tender (since any such mistake was irrelevant to the contract involved in the invitation to tender and the subsequent tender, whatever effect it might have had upon any consequent contract to do the construction work).

It may be that the original conception of "unilateral contracts" has been stretched by the courts to provide remedies or create obligations where, by the more usual meaning and application of the ideas of offer and acceptance, there

---

321 Below, pp. 581-588.
322 [1975] A.C. 154 (P.C.).
323 (1981), 119 D.L.R. 267 (S.C.C.), above, pp. 37-39.
324 For criticism of this see Nozick (1982), 60 Can. Bar Rev. 345 at pp. 350-352.

would be no contractual relationship to which effect could be given. Undoubtedly, the "unilateral contract" is a handy tool. However, it is also an uncertain tool. Its applicability in a given situation depends upon: the nature of the alleged "offer" in response to which the self-styled offeree has acted; the feasibility of some notification of acceptance prior to performance; the intention of the "offeror", whether express or implied; and the extent to which the latter has consented to be bound in his ignorance. Perhaps this is more easily concluded in favour of the offeree/acceptor in cases where the offer has been made to the whole world, or the public at large, as in the *Carlill* case and its analogues, than in cases where the offer is made to a specific individual. An offeror in the situation of the manufacturers in that and similar cases would be swamped with large quantities of probably useless communications were it necessary for potential users of the product to inform the manufacturer in advance that they intended to use, buy, consume, or otherwise deal with the product so as to bring themselves within the scope of the offer. What the courts have done through the invention of the "unilateral contract" is to impute to such parties, as reasonable men, the intention to be bound from the fact that the offer has been made, and the willingness to expose themselves to liability because the likelihood of benefit to the offeror far outweighs the possibilities of loss, detriment, or injury. Practical considerations have ousted logical analysis.

However, logical analysis cannot be forgotten entirely. It causes a problem when the question of revocation is considered. An offer can be revoked at any time before acceptance.[325] In the case of offers that are accepted by notification, rather than performance of some act, the offeror will know when acceptance has occurred (except where the "postal acceptance" rule is involved, when for reasons previously discussed,[326] the offeror may be bound even though he is ignorant of the acceptance at the time when he purports to revoke or to act in a manner inconsistent with the existence of a binding contract between himself and the initial offeree). In the case of an offer that is the foundation of a "unilateral contract",[327] when, and how, can the offeror revoke the offer should he decide to do so? If the offer contemplates one single act, for example providing information on the return of a stolen or lost article, presumably the offeror can revoke at any time before he receives the information or article. Presumably he could not do so if he sees the offeree about to provide him with the desired object in order to evade liability to give the latter the reward or other consideration that was offered. As long as the offeror is ignorant of the existence and intentions of the offeree, however, he should have the ability to revoke. The method of revocation would logically seem to be by the equivalent means to those whereby the original offer was made known, for example, advertisement in a newspaper or circulation of handbills. What if the offer requires not just one simple act, for example signing a document, but a series of acts or a prolonged performance, such as the use of the smoke ball

---

325 Above, p. 43.

326 Above, p. 67.

327 Unless such offer is given under seal, when it could be immediately binding and irrevocable; compare above, p. 43-44.

for two weeks? At what moment of time does the offeree who wishes to accept actually accept by commencing performance without previously communicating to the offeror his intention of accepting? To allow the offeror to revoke the offer at any time before the offeree has finished performing the required act or series of acts may leave the offeree in a prejudiced position (unless a court were willing to apply the doctrine of estoppel to create a contract, not to revoke).[328] To say that the offeror may not revoke such an offer once made would run counter to recognized principles of offer and acceptance.

In *Daulia Ltd. v. Four Millbank Nominees Ltd.*[329] Goff L.J., *obiter*, said that once the offeree had commenced performance of the stipulated act, or acts, it was not possible for the offeror to revoke. This was said in the context of a specified offeree and a set of acts which were likely to be performed within a short period of time following upon the making of the offer. Does this dictum also apply to a general offer to the world at large, as in the *Carlill* case? Or would that be too unreasonable *vis-à-vis* the offeror? Would it be possible for the offeror to revoke if he gave appropriate notice of such revocation? If so, what would constitute such notice? How far would the offeree have had to have gone in peformance before it was too late for the offeror to give such notice? Would any slight action on the part of the offeree suffice, or must the offeree have substantially performed the requisite act or acts? These questions remain to be answered by the courts. In order to provide an answer when the appropriate circumstances arise, it may be necessary for the courts to abandon some of the more settled principles of offer and acceptance and achieve a solution that accords with common sense and practical necessity rather than the logical structure of the idea of *consensus ad idem*.

(i) Effect of acceptance

Once an offer has been validly accepted in accordance with the principles considered above, the contract is binding and effective as between the parties. Consequently, the offeror cannot afterwards revoke his offer, nor can the offeree revoke his acceptance. Since under the "postal acceptance" rule, once an acceptance has been posted a binding contract may come into existence before the offeror is aware of such acceptance, it follows that an attempt by the offeror to revoke his offer made between the date of the original offer and the time of receipt of the acceptance will be ineffective if such revocation postdates the moment the letter was posted. In *Ellard v. Waterloo Manufacturing Co.*,[330] a contract under the Saskatchewan Farm Implements Act was held to be binding from the moment

---

328 See the discussion by Wilson J. in *Sloan v. Union Oil Co.*, [1955] 4 D.L.R. 664 (B.C.S.C.). Note, however, the problem of *consideration* for the offeror's promise; below, pp. 86-87. Note also the reluctance of courts to create *new* contractual relations out of estoppel; above, p. 18; below, pp. 121-136; compare *Smokey River Coal Ltd. v. U.S.W.A., Loc. 7621* (1985), 53 A.R. 150 (Alta. C.A.) on the denial of estoppel to regulate relations between employers and a union.

329 [1978] 2 All E.R. 557 at 561 (C.A.).

330 [1926] 3 D.L.R. 207 (Sask. C.A.).

the vendor's acceptance was deposited at the post office. Hence, purported cancellation thereafter by the purchaser did not operate, even though the purchaser's attempt to revoke occurred before the purchaser, who was the offeror, received notification of the acceptance. Notice of revocation must therefore reach the offeree before the latter has posted the letter of acceptance in such cases. By the same process of reasoning, if an offeree has accepted by letter and purports to revoke that acceptance by a telegram (or telephone call, perhaps) which arrives (or is communicated) prior to the arrival of the letter of acceptance, that revocation should be too late to alter the legal situation once the letter is posted. In a New Zealand case,[331] where something of this nature occurred, a contract between offeror and offeree was found to exist and the remarks of the judge suggest support for the proposition set out above. However, there is a Scottish case to the contrary,[332] and differing opinions have been expressed as to the correct attitude for the law to adopt in such circumstances.[333] It may well be that, in this instance, as with the revocation of a "unilateral contract", logical analysis should give way to practical considerations and common sense.

Although parties may subsequently agree to revoke their contract, either in order to replace it with another contract or simply to dissolve their obligations, once a contract has been completed by offer and acceptance neither party can alter or vary the terms of their agreement (except to the extent permitted by the contract itself). In *Ballam v. Hatfield*,[334] the defendant offered to sell 300 tons of hay at $22 per ton. The plaintiff accepted. The defendant then tried to insist upon later shipment of the goods and a deposit by the plaintiff. It was held that it was too late for such variation. The contract was made and the defendant was bound by the original terms. Of course, subsequent variation or alteration may be made by a new contract requiring offer, acceptance, consideration, and, if relevant, conformity with the writing requirements of the Statute of Frauds or some other enactment.[335] Furthermore, under the doctrine of promissory estoppel,[336] there may be variation of a contract without the need for any new, formal contractual agreement between the parties. Such changes involve either a new transaction or some conduct that can permit the invocation of the notion of estoppel. Their admission by the law as modes of altering concluded contracts does not result in the undermining of the basic idea that an acceptance of an offer gives rise to a valid, effective, binding contract that regulates the relationship between the parties.

Two qualifications of this idea must be noted. In the first place, it is possible that, while the contract is binding, a particular term may not be. This can occur if the term in question is an onerous one, favourable to the offeror and unfavourable to the offeree, and reasonable notice of the term was not given to the offeree at the time he accepted. The most usual situation in which this occurs is in respect

---

331 *Wenkheim v. Arndt* (1873), 1 J.R. 73.

332 *Dunmore (Countess) v. Alexander* (1830), 9 Sh. (Ct. of Sess.) 190 (Scot.).

333 Turnbull (1930), 8 Can. Bar Rev. 616; Gordon (1931), 9 Can. Bar Rev. 55.

334 (1922), 55 N.S.R. 508 (N.S.C.A.).

335 Below, pp. 209, 239, 244.

336 Below, pp. 121-136.

of clauses that exempt an offeror from liability in certain circumstances, exclude his liability in whole or in part, or limit the scope and extent of his liability for breach of the contract. Such terms raise special problems which will be noted and discussed in due course.[337]

Secondly, in some contracts the parties may have expressly agreed that the contract should not be binding until a certain event has occurred, or should only be binding until a stipulated event occurs. Contracts that are subject to such conditions precedent or conditions subsequent also raise special problems.[338] In such instances, however, although the parties have reached agreement through the process of offer and acceptance, their resultant contract may not be as completely binding, or possibly even not binding at all, if the nature of their agreement is to produce a conditional contract.

4. Negotiation in good faith

It has been noted earlier that the law does not recognize an agreement to agree or a contract to make a contract.[339] As part of this refusal to accept any obligation to arrive at a concluded agreement on the part of someone who is in the process of negotiation, it is also clear that a party involved in such negotiations is under no obligation with respect to the ultimate conclusion of the negotiations. Despite the suggestions of at least one writer,[340] there is no duty to bargain in good faith giving rise to a contractual remedy when the contract is not completed by reason of the default of one party or the other.[341]

Good faith is relevant where the performance of an already concluded contract is concerned.[342] Where no such contract has emerged, the situation is different. Admittedly it is not open to a party to employ dishonest methods, such as fraud, duress, or some other type of unconscionable behaviour, in order to obtain the consent of another party. Use of such methods may lead to the avoidance of any concluded contract.[343] In the absence of such misconduct it is not possible for a party to maintain an action based upon an allegation that the other negotiating party in the end, refused, for no, or no good, reason, to enter into a projected contract. Contract is a matter of agreement, and such agreement must be achieved before contractual liability can arise. If a party has incurred expenditure during

---

337 Below, pp. 573-578. So, too, in cases of illegality: below, pp. 420-424.

338 Below, pp. 435-446.

339 Above, pp. 22, 61.

340 Belobaba, "Good Faith in Canadian Contract Law," *Special Lectures of the Law Society of Upper Canada*, 1985, pp. 73-92. Contrast Waddams, "Pre-Contractual Duties of Disclosure" in Cane & Stapleton, eds., *Essays for Patrick Atiyah* (1991), Chapter 10, especially at pp. 253-254.

341 *Cineplex Corp. v. Viking Rideau Corp.* (1985), 28 B.L.R. 212 at 216 (Ont. H.C.) *per* Griffiths J., relying on *Courtney & Fairbairn Ltd. v. Tolaini Bros. (Hotels) Ltd.*, [1975] 1 All E.R. 716 (C.A.) (approved by the House of Lords in *Walford v. Miles*, [1992] 2 A.C. 128). See also *MacDougall v. St. Peters Bay (Community)* (1992), 100 Nfld. & P.E.I.R. 45 at 52-59 (P.E.I.T.D.).

342 *Gateway Realty Ltd. v. Arton Holdings Ltd.* (1991), 106 N.S.R. (2d) 180 (N.S.T.D.); affirmed (1992), 112 N.S.R. (2d) 180 (N.S.C.A.). See further below, pp. 522-523.

343 Below, Chapters 8 and 9.

the course of negotiations, in the expectation that a contract will emerge, or money has passed between the negotiating parties, restitutionary remedies may be available to the one who has incurred the expense or parted with the money, on the basis of unjust enrichment.[344] Such a remedy is non-contractual. A restitutionary claim is based, in such circumstances, on the absence of any contractual obligation, whether express or implied, not upon its existence.

The negation of any obligation to negotiate in good faith, which was reiterated by the House of Lords in *Walford v. Miles*,[345] may be exemplified in the decision in *MacDougall v. St. Peters Bay (Community)*.[346] The plaintiff wished to buy village property adjacent to the plaintiff's land. He had informal discussions with village staff who advised him to make a formal request to the council at the annual village meeting, some months away. He did so. At that meeting a motion to sell the lands to the plaintiff was passed, but there was no discussion of price or property survey, nor of any formal purchase and sale agreement. Months later the plaintiff made an offer to buy the land for $5,000. He was asked to re-submit the proposal at the next annual meeting. The plaintiff sued, claiming that the village had breached its duty to negotiate with him in good faith. The village then convened a special meeting at which the council determined to rescind the earlier motion to sell the land to the plaintiff, on two grounds: (i) the motion was ambiguous; and (ii) because of difficulties in the negotiations. The latter allegation was denied by the plaintiff. The plaintiff's new request to buy the land was also denied by the council. On a motion by the village to non-suit the plaintiff, Matheson J. held that the motion should be granted. The plaintiff's action was dismissed. It was not open to the court to review the bona fides or reasonableness of the council's refusal to execute a formal contract with the plaintiff. The council did not have to give any reason for such refusal where no concluded agreement had been reached. In any event no bad faith had been established. Nor could the plaintiff succeed on a restitutionary claim as he had not incurred any pre-contractual expenditures, and the village had not been unjustly enriched at the expense of the plaintiff.

It should be noted that in its *Report on Amendment of the Law of Contract*[347] the Ontario Law Reform Commission considered the issue of good faith in the negotiation or formation of contracts and concluded that, although there was need for legislation on good faith in the performance of concluded contracts, any such legislation, like that in the American Second Restatement of Contracts[348] and in civil law codes,[349] should exclude its application from pre-contractual situations.

---

344 Maddaugh & McCamus, *Law of Restitution* (1990), pp. 463-474; Fridman, *Restitution*, 2nd ed. (1992), pp. 158-161, 300-303.

345 Above, note 341.

346 *Ibid.*

347 Ministry of the Attorney General (1987), at pp. 167, 174-175.

348 Sec. 205; compare U.C.C. s. 1-203; Ontario Law Reform Commission, *Report*, above, note 347, at pp. 170-172.

349 Ontario Law Reform Commission, *Report*, above, note 347, at pp. 169-170.

There can be little doubt that this is a sound conclusion.[350] Unless some misconduct in the nature of fraud, duress, unconscionability or misrepresentation can be alleged, there should not be any restrictions on the freedom of parties to conclude or not conclude a contract on any terms and in such manner as the parties think fit. To impose some kind of obligation of "good faith", the nature of which would appear to be difficult to ascertain in advance, would be to introduce unwelcome hindrance to the freedom of contract.[351]

---

350 For a very different point of view see Brown, "The Contract to Negotiate: A Thing Writ in Water," [1992] J.B.L. 353. And for the more favourable acceptance of the good faith doctrine in Australia, see Finn, "Commerce, the Common Law and Morality" (1989), 17 U. Melb. L.R. 87; Finn, "Australian Developments in Common and Commercial Law," [1990] J.B.L. 265.

351 For the view that the decision in *LAC Minerals Ltd. v. Int. Corona Resources Ltd.* (1989), 61 D.L.R. (4th) 14 (S.C.C.), makes it impossible to say that the doctrine of good faith bargaining forms no part of Canadian law, see Hawkins, "LAC and the Emerging Obligation to Bargain in Good Faith" (1990), 15 Queen's L.J. 65. But the *LAC* case involved the possibility of a fiduciary relationship, or the existence of a fiduciary duty between the negotiating parties, and consequent breach of confidence: see Fridman, *Restitution*, 2nd ed. (1992), at pp. 369-372, 386-389. This may not affect the position stated and discussed in the text.

3

Consideration

1. Importance

The common law distinguishes between gratuitous promises[1] and those which can be the basis of a contractual obligation.[2] What gives the latter their legal character is what is called "consideration". The essence of a valid, binding contract is the idea of a "bargain" between the parties. A contract consists of an exchange of promises, acts, or acts and promises, as a result of which each side receives something from the other. The attempt was made by Lord Mansfield in the

---

1 *I.e.*, promises to confer a benefit by gift, sometimes referred to as "donative promises"; see Eisenberg, "Donative Promises" (1979), 47 U. Ch. L. R. 1; or as "benevolent promises"; see Stoljar, "Enforcing Benevolent Promises" (1989), 12 Sydney L.R. 17; see also Stoljar, "Bargain and Non-bargain Promises" (1988), 18 U. West. Aus. L.R. 119.

2 For an economic analysis of the difference between these, see Posner, "Gratuitous Promises in Economics and Law" (1977), 6 J. Leg. Stud. 411. For an attempt at "reconceptualization", see Eisenberg, "The Principles of Consideration" (1982), 67 Cornell L.R. 640; "The Bargain Principle and Its Limits" (1982), 95 H.L.R. 741; "The Responsive Model of Contract Law" (1984), 36 Stanford L.R. 1107, pp. 1112-1117. See also Cumberbatch, "On Bargains, Gifts and Extortion: An Essay on the Function of Consideration in the Law of Contract" (1990), 19 Anglo-American L.R. 239.

eighteenth century to allow valid contracts to be based upon moral obligation, or to be entirely gratuitous.[3] But in the nineteenth century it was held that there had to be some material advantage passing to or promised by one party before a promise given in exchange could be regarded as a contract.[4] There is no doubt that this doctrine is now firmly established in Canadian law[5] as well as English.[6] If there is no consideration there is no contract; and if there is no contract there is nothing upon or from which to found or create liability.[7] In *Steinberg v. Steinberg*[8] there was a gift of shares between husband and wife. Later the wife signed a promissory note for the value of the shares, this transaction being by way of a device to avoid certain tax liabilities. After the husband and wife separated some time later, the husband brought an action on the note. It was held that he could not sue as there was no consideration for the wife's promise to pay the sum in question. Although some qualifications of the need for consideration have been admitted, by the common law and by statute,[9] the doctrine of consideration remains one of the pillars of the law of contract.[10] However, the nature and content of consideration have undergone change over the years.

2. Meaning

In *Currie v. Misa*[11] in 1875 an English court provided a modern definition

---

3 *Pillans v. Van Mierop* (1765), 3 Burr. 1663. See also Fifoot, *Lord Mansfield* (1936), pp. 126-141. For the earlier history, see Simpson, *A History of the Common Law of Contract* (1975), Chapters 4-7; compare Dawson, *Gifts and Promises* (1980), pp. 199-207.

4 *Rann v. Hughes* (1778), 7 Term. Rep. 350n (H.L.); *Eastwood v. Kenyon* (1840), 11 Ad. & El. 438. See also Atiyah, *The Rise and Fall of Freedom of Contract* (1979), pp. 138-167, 448-454.

5 For recent illustrations see *Blomidon Mercury Sales Ltd. v. John Piercey's Auto Body Shop Ltd.* (1981), 129 D.L.R. (3d) 630 (Nfld. T.D.); *Agrios v. Mediavision Inc.* (1981), 18 Alta. L.R. (2d) 77 (Alta. M.C.); affirmed (1982), 19 Alta. L.R. (2d) 74 (Alta. Q.B.); *Baker v. Neary* ((1984), 51 Nfld. & P.E.I.R. 25 (Nfld. T.D.).

6 *Horrocks v. Forray*, [1976] 1 All E.R. 737 at 742 (C.A.) *per* Megaw L.J.

7 *McPherson v. L'Hirondelle*, [1927] S.C.R. 429 (S.C.C.); *Galpin v. Auld* (1967), 59 W.W.R. 257 (B.C.C.A.); *MacMillan v. MacMillan* (1977), 76 D.L.R. (3d) 760 (Sask. C.A.); *Abraham v. Wingate Properties Ltd.*, [1986] 1 W.W.R. 568 (Man. C.A.); varied on reconsideration [1986] 2 W.W.R. 568 (Man. C.A.). Unless the contract is contained in a deed, *i.e.*, a document under seal: *Hickey v. Hickey* (1986), 86 N.B.R. (2d) 428 (N.B.Q.B.); affirmed (1988), 86 N.B.R. (2d) 421 (N.B.C.A.). On deeds, see below, pp. 117-119.

8 (1963), 45 D.L.R. (2d) 162 (Sask. Q.B.), following the definition of consideration given in *Fleming v. Bank of New Zealand*, [1900] A.C. 577 at 586 (P.C.).

9 Below, pp. 117-136.

10 Whether what is involved is the creation of a contractual relationship between the parties, or the variation of an existing contract (see *Blomidon Mercury Sales Ltd. v. John Piercey's Auto Body Shop Ltd.* (1981), 129 D.L.R. (3d) 630 (Nfld. T.D.)), or the waiver of existing contractual rights (see *Weeks v. Rosocha* (1983), 41 O.R. (2d) 787 (Ont. C.A.)). But *waiver* may be effected differently, without the need for consideration: *Petridis v. Shabinsky* (1982), 132 D.L.R. (3d) 430 (Ont. H.C.); see also below, p. 129.

11 (1875), L.R. 10 Exch. 153; affirmed (1876), 1 App. Cas. 554 (H.L.). For a critical examination of this definition and its consequences in the courts, see Sutton, *Consideration Reconsidered* (1974), pp. 13-33. The learned author concludes that this definition is inaccurate and that consideration should be left undefined.

of consideration which has frequently been cited with approval by courts in Canada.[12] Consideration was there said to consist in,

> some right, interest, profit or benefit accruing to the one party or some forebearance, detriment, loss, or responsibility, given, suffered, or undertaken by the other.[13]

This was expressed by one Canadian judge in the following way:

> The principal requisite and that which is the essence of every consideration, is that it should create some benefit to the party promising or some trouble, prejudice or inconvenience to the party to whom the promise is made.[14]

Such statements reveal the essential ingredients of consideration as it has developed since the early days of truly contractual liability in the common law. The act or promise of one party is, as it were, "bought" or "bargained for" by the act or promise of the other; each party exchanges something of value. To create an enforceable contract there must be, as Lennox J. said in *Loranger v. Haines*,[15] "reciprocal undertakings". So if one party is neither giving anything, nor is promising to do or give anything, there is no consideration for the other party's act or promise.[16] What is meant here by the expression "value" must not be taken in a literal, entirely materialistic sense. In most instances, of course, it will be money or money's worth that is involved. But it is not so exclusive. Consideration means something which is of some value in the eyes of the law.[17] This could include some act, or promise of an act, which is incapable of being given a monetary

---

12 See *Re Desbiens*, [1953] 4 D.L.R. 787 (Man. Q.B.); *Spruce Grove v. Yellowhead Reg. Library* (1982), 143 D.L.R. (3d) 188 at 191 (Alta. C.A.); compare *Bojtar v. Parker* (1979), 99 D.L.R. (3d) 147 (Ont. H.C.); affirmed (1979), 103 D.L.R. (3d) 577 (Ont. C.A.); *Rusonik v. Can. Trust Co.* (1986), 39 R.P.R. 263 at 278-281 (Ont. H.C.), where Henry J. sets out and discusses several definitions of consideration and then applies the doctrine to an instance of a "unilateral" contract, on which see above, pp. 69-76.

13 (1875), L.R. 10 Exch. 153 at 162.

14 Barry C.J. in *Robertson v. Robertson* (1933), 6 M.P.R. 370 at 389 (N.B.C.A.). Hence, in *Can. West Tree Fruits Ltd. v. T.G. Bright & Co.*, [1990] 6 W.W.R. 89 (B.C.C.A.); leave to appeal to S.C.C. refused [1991] 2 W.W.R. lxviii (note) (S.C.C.), there was no valid variation of a contract pertaining to the provision of apple juice. The variation was for the benefit of only one party and the other party derived no benefit at all. Whereas in *Maier v. E & B Exploration Ltd.*, [1986] 4 W.W.R. 275 (Alta. C.A.), the employees obtained the benefit of the variation of their contracts of employment by the inclusion of a share option scheme in return for which the employees continued in their employment when they could have left at any time, since they were originally employed for an indefinite period.

15 (1921), 64 D.L.R. 364 at 372 (Ont. C.A.).

16 See *Spur Oil Ltd. v. R.* (1981), 42 N.R. 131 (Fed. C.A.); leave to appeal to S.C.C. refused (1981), 39 N.R. 354 (S.C.C.); *Blomidon Mercury Sales Ltd. v. John Piercey's Auto Body Shop Ltd.* (1981), 129 D.L.R. (3d) 630 (Nfld. T.D.); *Fobasco Ltd. v. Cogan* (1990), 72 O.R. (2d) 254 (Ont. H.C.) (nothing of value passed from plaintiff to defendant: therefore no contract); contrast *Zinman v. Hechter* (1981), 130 D.L.R. (3d) 183 (Man. C.A.); leave to appeal to S.C.C. refused (1982), 41 N.R. 488 (S.C.C.).

17 *Thomas v. Thomas* (1842), 2 Q.B. 851 at 859; compare *Fobasco Ltd. v. Cogan*, above, note 16, at 259. Sutton, above, note 11, art. 33, prefers to state that whether or not there is a consideration is "a decision in terms of a choice of social policies." This, with respect, seems to go a little too far.

value, though it has value, in the sense of advantage for the party who is the present or future recipient or beneficiary of the act.[18]

A complication arises from the fact that the "value" which is involved may not be going from one party directly to the other.[19] In most instances this is what will happen. A will be giving something to B, or will be doing something for B. But what A gives or does need not come to B, as long as A is undergoing the detriment of giving away what is involved, or performing the act in question in return for an act or promise by B. That detriment to A, without any corresponding benefit to B, is sufficient consideration to support B's promise to perform something for A is well known.

In *Loranger v. Haines*,[20] the plaintiff sued for specific performance of a contract to convey land. The plaintiff and the defendant were friends. The plaintff wished to move and live next door to the defendant. In consequence of this, the plaintiff left Detroit and came to Ontario, where the land was situated; he did things to improve the lot on which he intended to build a house; he paid certain expenses in connection with his move to the land; and he undertook that if he ever wanted to leave the land in question he would give an option to the defendant to buy it from him. Under these circumstances, after the defendant had refused to honour the agreement, it was held that there was a valid contract supported by consideration, namely the acts of the plaintiff referred to above, and the action succeeded. Another more recent example is provided by *Spruce Grove v. Yellowhead Regional Library Board*.[21] The plaintiff municipality transferred land to a library board for one dollar plus other good and valuable consideration on the undertaking of the board that it would build a library on the land. Whether such transfer was *ultra vires* the municipality depended upon whether the transaction was a gift or a sale; in other words, whether it constituted a valid contract. This raised the issue of consideration. The Alberta Court of Appeal held that a sale had taken place, therefore the transaction was not *ultra vires*. There was consideration because there was a promise given for a promise by both parties. The town agreed to provide the land, and the library board agreed to construct a building to be used as regional library headquarters. The promise made by each party met the classic test of "valuable consideration" stated in *Currie v. Misa*.[22] Here, it might be said, the library board's promise involved a detriment to the board, although there might have been a benefit

---

18 See, *e.g., Bank of N.S. v. MacLellan* (1977), 78 D.L.R. (3d) 1 (N.S.S.C.); below, p. 90; *Bank of N.S. v. Hallgarth* (1986), 32 D.L.R. (4th) 158 (B.C.C.A.); *Miller v. Miller* (1991), 103 N.S.R. (2d) 50 (N.S.T.D.).

19 *Trueman v. Maritime Auto & Trailer Sales Ltd.* (1977), 19 N.B.R. (2d) 8 (N.B.C.A.); below, p. 91; *Bank of N.S. v. Drouillard-Potter* (1987), 79 A.R. 2 (Alta. M.C.).

20 Above, note 15. Compare *Brooks Ltd. v. Claude Neon Gen. Advertising Ltd.*, [1932] O.R. 205 (Ont. C.A.); *Westman v. Macdonald*, [1941] 3 W.W.R. 321 (B.C.S.C.); *Press Box Inc. v. Berlin* (1988), 85 N.B.R. (2d) 288 (N.B.Q.B.), consideration for an option to purchase land was found in the optionee's entering into an agreement to lease the land, the lease, and the payment of rent under the lease.

21 (1982), 143 D.L.R. (3d) 188 (Alta. C.A.).

22 Above, note 13.

to the municipality. Similarly, in *Bank of Nova Scotia v. Hallgarth*,[23] a husband who was co-signer of a promissory note for a loan made by the bank to his wife, derived benefit from being relieved of financial pressure, while the bank suffered a detriment in that it gave up its right under previous arrangements with the wife.

Such cases also illuminate the distinction to be drawn between *motive* and consideration. Consideration in a colloquial sense may refer to the reasons why somebody does something — his motives for so acting. In the technical sense it has a more restricted connotation. Prior to the final formulation in modern times of the scope of the doctrine and concept of consideration, it was suggested that a motive for doing or promising something might suffice. For example, the "natural love and affection" which a parent might feel for a child, was sometimes held to be consideration for a promise to give something to the child. While this might be "good" consideration (and therefore could have some effect in situations involving equity), it was eventually held not to be *valuable* consideration, the only kind of consideration to which the common law gave effect. Such other consideration, which was not consideration at all in the eyes of the common law, merely constituted a motive for acting or promising to act. It was a reason why the party acting or promising would want to act or promise as he had done; it could not amount to the price or bargain for the other party's promise or act.[24] So, in *Loranger v. Haines*, for example, it was vital for the court to differentiate true consideration for the defendant's promise to convey the land from any motive on his or the plaintiff's part which might have induced the making of such promise. The mere desire of the parties to live adjoining one another was not consideration; there had to be something of benefit to the defendant or detriment to the plaintiff in return for the promise to convey. This was brought out most strongly in the judgment of Riddell J.[25]

The same is indicated in the judgment of McGillivray J.A. in *Johnson v. Forbes*.[26] In that case, the defendant promised to pay the plaintiff for his past voluntary services as agent for the defendant. But the promise was not expressed in precise terms. What was stated was that the plaintiff "would be taken care of". In an action brought by the plaintiff for some recompense for what he had done, it was held that there was no contract upon which an action could be founded. There was no consideration for the plaintiff's performance of services; the promise made by the defendant expressed a "moral obligation of gratitude",[27] a motive for

---

23 Above, note 18; compare *Miller v. Miller*, above, note 18.
24 For discussion of this historical development, see Stoljar, "No Obituary for Wennall v. Adney" (1990), 11 J. Leg. Hist. 250.
25 Above, note 15, at 371. Compare Ruttan J. in *Harding v. Harding* (1972), 28 D.L.R. (3d) 358 at 364 (B.C.S.C.) (a case of husband and wife).
26 [1931] 3 W.W.R. 757 (Alta. C.A.). *Rogalsky v. Rogalsky*, [1985] 2 W.W.R. 699 (Man. Q.B.); affirmed [1986] 4 W.W.R. 336 (Man. C.A.).
27 *Johnson v. Forbes*, above, note 26, at 762.

promising, not consideration.[28] In *Fobasco Ltd. v. Cogan*,[29] the fact that the parties did business together was the reason or motive behind the defendant's offer to permit the plaintiffs to use some of the season's tickets for baseball games purchased by the defendant. This was distinct from consideration.

Some uncertainty may be said to have been thrown upon this whole view of what is meant by consideration by Wilson J. in *Sloan v. Union Oil Co.*[30] Consideration consisted of, or in, a promise intended to be binding, intended to be acted upon, and in fact acted upon. Insofar as this merely refers to an act which is given in return for a promise or another act from the other party, it does not appear to be revolutionary; as long as it is recalled that the act in question can be detrimental to one party without having to be beneficial to the other. If, on the other hand, this analysis or definition is meant to include or refer to a bare, valueless promise it may go too far. On the facts of the case in question, there was no need to look beyond the doing of an act by the promisee in return for the promise by the defendant company to pay the financial benefits in issue. Hence, it was not strictly necessary for the learned judge to employ any novel concepts of consideration.[31]

3. Mutuality

The language of Wilson J. seems to undermine the idea that to establish a valid contract each party must give or promise something in return for the other's act or promise. A bare, voluntary, gratuitous act or promise, unsupported by any reciprocal undertaking will not be enough. There must be mutuality; a contract must show that both parties are bound in some way.[32] The act or promise of one party must be performed or given in exchange for something actually done or promised by the other. Hence an offer to sell goods is not binding if there is no corresponding undertaking to buy.[33] However, the undertaking may not be very onerous, for example, as in an English case,[34] an undertaking by a mother to see that the promisor's child was well and happy. Moreover, the undertaking may be implied from the circumstances in which event the transaction has been said to

---

28 Compare *Agrios v. Mediavision Inc.* (1981), 18 Alta. L.R. (2d) 77 (Alta. M.C.); affirmed (1982), 19 Alta. L.R. (2d) 74 (Alta. Q.B.) (benefits attainable under the Income Tax Act did not constitute consideration from the defendant to the maker of a promissory note).

29 Above, note 16, at 259.

30 [1955] 4 D.L.R. 664 at 678-679 (B.C.S.C.); see above, p. 30, for the facts of this case.

31 Compare *Zinman v. Hechter* (1981), 130 D.L.R. (3d) 183 (Man. C.A.); leave to appeal to S.C.C. refused (1982), 41 N.R. 488 (S.C.C.); with which contrast *Ben Plastering Ltd. v. Global Dixie Ltd. (No. 2)* (1979), 33 C.B.R. (N.S.) 253n (Ont. H.C.); see also below, p. 124.

32 *Young v. Can. Nor. Ry.*, [1930] 1 W.W.R. 446 (Man. C.A.); affirmed on other grounds, [1931] 1 W.W.R. 49 (P.C.).

33 *Greenberg v. Lake Simcoe Ice Supply Co.* (1917), 39 O.L.R. 32 (Ont. H.C.); *Brantford, Waterloo & Lake Erie Ry v. Huffman* (1891), 19 S.C.R. 336 (S.C.C.); compare *Tobias v. Dick & T. Eaton Co.*, [1937] 4 D.L.R. 546 (Man. K.B.). Contrast the situation where the offeror promises to buy what he wants exclusively from the offeree; there is an implied promise that he will buy from no one else: *Brandon Gas Co. v. Brandon Creamery* (1912), 8 D.L.R. 191 (Man. C.A.).

34 *Ward v. Byham*, [1956] 1 W.L.R. 496 (C.A.).

be "instinct with an obligation".[35] It is clear that whatever the intent, however great the motive or desire to be bound, there will be no legal obligation unless the strict, technical requirement of consideration is met. Hence, in *Citibank Canada v. Cameron*,[36] the operative reason for denying the plaintiff a summary remedy against the defendant in respect of the loan made to the defendant's wife by the plaintiff bank was because the wife never requested the loan, *i.e.*, the detriment suffered by the plaintiff. When she signed a promissory note and other documents without reading them, she was not aware that she was asking the plaintiff bank to do anything, since she did not understand what the documents meant.

In this regard two particular problems may be mentioned. One relates to what are sometimes called "firm offers".[37] A promise to keep an offer open for acceptance for a prescribed or reasonable period is not binding (where it is not made under seal) unless it is supported by consideration. The possibility that this might lead to injustice, as where a merchant acts to his detriment in reliance on such a promise only to find that the offeror is not bound, has led to a change in the law, at least as it affects merchants, in the Uniform Commercial Code in the United States;[38] a change that was also recommended by the Ontario Law Reform Commission in relation to sale of goods.[39] But the dangers of opening up the law in this way have also been stressed and the view has been expressed that it would be more suitable to prevent any injustice by permitting the enforcement of such a promise or offer to a limited extent "if justice so requires in view of the subsequent reliance of the promisee."[40] The adoption of such an approach, while understandable, is itself open to criticism. There may be grounds for eradicating the doctrine of consideration from the law. To treat so-called "firm offers" as justifying something akin to a contract, however, while leaving the law of consideration, in general, undisturbed, would be to permit an exception to the doctrine in a context in which, it might be thought, the parties are or should be well aware of the demands of the law, and may well have transacted with the deliberate purpose of not intending to create binding, legal obligations. A more appropriate remedy would be one in tort, where fraud, or possibly negligence, had induced the alleged loss.

A very special problem in this respect has arisen with regard to a promise by someone to donate money to a charitable organization or institution. Is such a promise a mere offer of a gift not capable of constituting a contractual obligation

---

35 *Dawson v. Helicopter Exploration Co.*, [1955] S.C.R. 868 (S.C.C.); *Great Eastern Oil & Import Co. v. Chafe* (1956), 4 D.L.R. (2d) 310 (Nfld. S.C.); followed in *Hickman (A.E.) Co. v. Roses Aluminum Ltd.* (1981), 36 Nfld. & P.E.I.R. 206 (Nfld. Dist. Ct.); distinguished in *Case's Insulation & Siding Ltd. v. Gordon* (1991), 45 C.L.R. 252 (N.B.Q.B.).

36 (1991), 4 O.R. (3d) 526 (Ont. Master); affirmed (1991), 7 O.R. (3d) 777 (Ont. Gen. Div.).

37 See Ontario Law Reform Commission, *Report on Sale of Goods* (1979), Vol. I, pp. 91-96; Ontario Law Reform Commission, *Report on Amendment of the Law of Contract* (1987), pp. 20-25; see also Swan, "Consideration and the Reasons for Enforcing Contracts" (1976), 15 U.W.O.L. Rev. 83 in Reiter and Swan, *Studies in Contract Law* (1980), 23 at pp. 41-52.

38 U.C.C. §2-205.

39 Draft Bill, s. 4.3; *loc. cit.* above, note 37, Vol. III, p. 18, compare *Report on Amendment of the Law of Contract*, pp. 23-25, 33-34.

40 Waddams, *Law of Contracts*, 2nd ed. (1986), p. 97.

that may be enforced if it is not honoured? Or can there be circumstances under which any such promise or offer, if accepted by the offeree, attains the status of a contract? For this there must be consideration for the promise (unless it is contained in a deed).[41] The difficulty is to identify what possible consideration there can be for such a promise, having regard to the definition of consideration in terms of benefit or detriment.

The English cases in which this problem was raised[42] made it clear that, in the absence of a deed, the mere desire to give to a charity would not suffice. This was simply sentiment, or, to put it another way, a promise to give from the motive of achieving a laudable purpose. The desire to promote charity is not sufficient to create a binding legal obligation (unless the formality of a deed is also employed). The Canadian authorities appear to have found ways of circumventing this barrier to the enforceability of such promises by discovering something more than a charitable motive or intent as the wellspring of the donor's promise.

In *Sargent v. Nicholson*,[43] in reliance upon a document promising a subscription to the Y.M.C.A., that organization undertook certain liabilities in respect of a new building. It was held that this made the promise a binding contract which could not be revoked and was enforceable against the promisor. So, too, in *Y.M.C.A. v. Rankin*,[44] where the only difference was that the building that was going to be constructed from the various subscriptions was not actually completed, although commitments had been entered into on the faith of the promise. Once the promise was acted upon to the extent of the making of such commitments, it was too late for the promise to give to be revoked. In *Re Ross; Hutchison v. Royal Institution for the Advancement of Learning*[45] a promise to pay a sum of money to McGill University towards the buildng of a gymnasium, if the University would provide an additional sum for the same purpose, was held to constitute an actionable contract. It was an offer made for consideration, as long as the University proceeded with the stipulated work. Hence, a subsequent agreement under which the promisor withdrew his earlier promise on condition that he made a fresh promise for a different sum of money, though this was to be given for an unrestricted purpose, was held to be a binding contract; each party had provided valuable consideration for the promises contained in the second agreement. In *Re Loblaw*,[46] there was a promise by a testator to give money to Victoria University within two years, the money to be used for a specific purpose. This was held to be a good contract. But in this case there was never any actual undertaking of the work involved in achieving the purpose. The learned judge in *Re Loblaw* took the view that there was an *implied* promise to undertake the purpose envisaged by the testator and

---

41 Or statutory change has occurred; below, note 49.

42 *Re Hudson* (1885), 33 W.R. 819; *Re Corey* (1912), 29 T.L.R. 18.

43 (1915), 9 W.W.R. 883 (Man. C.A.). See also *Berkeley Street Church Trustees v. Stevens* (1875), 37 U.C.Q.B. 9 (C.A.).

44 (1916), 10 W.W.R. 482 (B.C.C.A.).

45 [1932] S.C.R. 57 (S.C.C.) (an appeal from Quebec, but the Supreme Court of Canada said it involved the common law).

46 [1933] O.R. 764 (Ont. S.C.).

such implied promise was consideration for the promise to give the money. While this might have been valid where a specific purpose had originally been mentioned by the parties, it would seem that if there were simply a general intent to benefit the charity, without the promise of money being tied to any particular end to be achieved, there would be no contract. All that would emerge from the testator's or donor's expression of willingness to give would be a gratuitous promise to give, unsupported by consideration, and therefore not actionable. This is what the Supreme Court decided in *Governors of Dalhousie College v. Boutilier*,[47] where nothing was tied in with the offer of a gift of money. Crockett J. said: "There is no doubt . . . that an express agreement by the promisee to do certain acts in return for a subscription is a sufficient consideration for the promise of the subscriber."[48] But there would seem to be no basis for implying any such promise merely from the offer of a gift of money and that would mean that there was no consideration for such a promise. Hence, in that case, the general promise to give money was not enforceable.

The last case in which this problem was considered, and in which it was dealt with at some length, was *Provincial Sanatorium v. McArthur*.[49] There the defendant signed a subscription list set up under a campaign to build a sanatorium for tuberculosis patients and promised to pay the treasurer of the commission, set up under a provincial statute to run the institution, the sum of $200 payable in three instalments. Under the statute the commission was empowered to solicit subscriptions from the public. When called upon to honour his pledge, the defendant refused on the ground that he was offended by a political article published in a local newspaper. He said he would give the money when the conditions under which he had promised to give, namely, the building and equipping of the sanitorium, were complied with and not before. When sued for the money, he pleaded *inter alia* that his promise was given without consideration and was therefore not binding. Judgment was given for the plaintiff. In other words, there was a binding contract. While the subscriptions of others was not consideration for the promise made by one subscriber,[50] if a subscriber made a promise and it was acted on by the promisee, the promisor could not revoke his promise but he could be sued if the work had been completed.[51] In this instance, the trial judge found that the defendant's offer of money had been accepted and was used for the purpose for which the money was subscribed, namely, to set up a fund to build a sanatorium. It was too late

---

47 [1934] S.C.R. 642 (S.C.C.) (on which see a note by C.A.W. (1935), 13 Can. Bar Rev. 108). Despite the American authorities to the contrary which were discussed in that case, Crockett J. points out that to hold otherwise would be to make a bare promise that was acted upon actionable. Compare also below p. 121, as to what is now said on the subject of *promissory estoppel*.

48 [1934] S.C.R. 642 at 648 (S.C.C.).

49 [1935] 4 D.L.R. 255 (P.E.I.C.A.); leave to appeal to S.C.C. refused, [1935] 4 D.L.R. 458 (S.C.C.). To some extent, this case was based on legislation. Consideration is not necessary in such situations: Statute of Frauds, R.S.P.E.I. 1988, c. S-6, s. 4, which goes back to an Act of 1872 (35 & 36 Vict., c. 28). The same is true in N.S.: Public Subscriptions Act, R.S.N.S. 1989, c. 378, which goes back to R.S.N.S. 1881, c. 60.

50 [1935] 4 D.L.R. 255 at 264 (P.E.I.C.A.), relying on the *Boutilier* case, above, note 47.

51 *Ibid.*, at 265, relying on the *Stevens, Sargent* and *Rankin* cases, above.

to revoke the promise after it had been accepted. While there was criticism of the judicial statements that an implied promise to use money subscribed for a particular purpose could be spelled out of a general intention to use the money charitably, nonetheless, if there was a specific purpose in mind at the time of the promise to subscribe, there could be an implied promise that the money would be used for such purpose.

It would see, therefore, that a promise to give money to a charity may become an enforceable promise: (1) if the promisee completes the purpose the subscriber had in mind; (2) if the promisee begins to undertake the fulfilment of such purpose; (3) if nothing has yet been done, but there is a clear, if implied undertaking that money provided as a result of such promise will be used for the specific purpose the subscriber had in mind when he made his offer. In such circumstances, consideration for the promise to give exists.

4. Sufficiency

(a) Adequacy and sufficiency contrasted

The adequacy of the consideration is normally irrelevant.[52] As was said in the English case of *Bolton v. Madden*,[53]

> . . .the adequacy of the consideration is for the parties to consider at the time of making the agreement, not for the Court when it is sought to be enforced.

This was cited with approval and adopted in *Fleming v. Mair*.[54] In the later case of *Robertson v. Robertson*[55] it was emphasized that it was not necessary that the consideration and promise should be equivalent in actual value. So in *Scivoletto v. DeDona*[56] the plaintiff paid for a girl to come from Italy to Canada to marry his son. Instead, the defendant married her. Both plaintiff and defendant believed that when the girl did not marry the plaintiff's son the plaintiff was entitled to return her to Italy. They therefore agreed that the defendant would reimburse the plaintiff in respect of the passage money. It was held that this was an enforceable contract—the adequacy of the consideration for the promise, namely, that the plaintiff would not send the girl back to Italy, was irrelevant.

An even stronger illustration is provided by *Bank of Nova Scotia v. MacLellan*.[57] There a wife agreed to co-operate with her ex-husband's creditors in order for them to obtain the balance of a debt owed by her husband. In return for her offer

---

52 *I.e.*, as long as there exists consideration; the contrast is noted in *Can. West Tree Fruits Ltd. v. T.G. Bright & Co.*, [1990] 6 W.W.R. 89 at 96 (B.C.C.A.); leave to appeal to S.C.C. refused [1991] 2 W.W.R. lxvii (note) (S.C.C.).

53 (1873), L.R. 9 Q.B. 55 at 56.

54 [1921] 2 W.W.R. 421 (Sask. C.A.). Compare *Weston (George) Ltd. v. Baird* (1916), 31 D.L.R. 730 at 735 (Ont. C.A.) *per* Lennox J.

55 (1933), 6 M.P.R. 370 at 389 (N.B.C.A.).

56 (1961), 35 W.W.R. 44 (Alta. Dist. Ct.).

57 (1977), 78 D.L.R. (3d) 1 (N.S.S.C.); contrast *MacMillan v. MacMillan* (1977), 76 D.L.R. (3d) 760 (Sask. C.A.). But compare *Miller v. Miller* (1991), 103 N.S.R. (2d) 50 (N.S.T.D.).

to assist the creditors in finding her former husband, the creditors agreed to accept part of the debt which the wife also owed as joint debtor with her husband, in settlement of the wife's liabilities. This was held to be a binding contract resulting in the release of the wife from her liabilities to the creditors, although, at first sight, it would seem to be an instance of acceptance of a smaller sum instead of the larger amount owed (which, at common law, would not have amounted to a binding contract).[58] Hence, the wife could not be sued for the balance of the debt left unpaid when the former husband could not be traced. The promise by the wife to help find her ex-husband was held to be consideration for the release of the wife, even though that promise was slight and of little real value. It was sufficient to meet the legal standards of consideration. The wife had undertaken something to her detriment. In much the same way courts have been prepared to accept that consideration for a manufacturer's guarantee of the quality of goods could take the form of a customer's purchase of those goods from a dealer who sold them.[59] The underlying theory in such instances is that the manufacturer will ultimately obtain a benefit in that he will be able to sell more goods to the dealer in question, once the latter had disposed of his current stock to customers.[60]

Thus the courts do not inquire as to the adequacy or inadequacy of the consideration; they leave the parties to form their own judgment as to this and to make their own bargain. This is one, and a very important aspect of the common law doctrine of freedom of contract. However, this lack of interference only occurs, as was pointed out in *Loranger v. Haines*,[61] "where the parties are equally capable of looking after their own interests and in the absence of evidence of fraud." Inadequacy of consideration may be so gross as to be evidence of fraud. This is what occurred in *McCarthy v. Kenny*,[62] where worthless shares were exchanged for valuable ones. But in *MacLauchlan v. Soper*,[63] a conveyance expressed to be for the consideration of one dollar was not upset for inadequacy. There may be a general equitable jurisdiction to upset a contract for inadequate consideration, but such inadequacy will not vitiate a contract unless it is such that it indicates a strongly unconscientious transaction or one involving fraud.[64] While there is nothing in the common law similar to the provision of the American Uniform Commercial Code[65] which entitles a court to strike down a contract which is

---

58 Below, pp. 104-106. But see *Robichaud v. Caisse populaire de Pokemouche Ltée* (1990), 105 N.B.R. (2d) 227 (N.B.C.A.).

59 *Murray v. Sperry Rand Corp.* (1979), 23 O.R. (2d) 456 (Ont. H.C.); *Trueman v. Maritime Auto & Trailer Sales Ltd.* (1977), 19 N.B.R. (2d) 8 (N.B.C.A.) where there was no contract because the customer never returned the warranty card to the manufacturer, *i.e.*, never accepted the offer of a guarantee; but in any event, the purchase of the vehicle took place *before* the customer obtained the card and the warranty. Compare *Roenisch v. Bangs* (1993), 8 Alta. L.R. (3d) 148 (Alta. Q.B.).

60 This is of great importance in relation to "collateral contracts": below, pp. 509-510.

61 (1921), 64 D.L.R. 364 at 372 (Ont. C.A.).

62 [1939] 3 D.L.R. 556 at 566 (Ont. H.C.) *per* Hogg J.

63 (1965), 50 M.P.R. 339 (P.E.I.S.C.).

64 *Fleming v. Mair* (1921), 58 D.L.R. 318 at 325 (Sask. C.A.) *per* Turgeon J.A.; and see, generally, *MacLacuhlan v. Soper*, note 63, above; compare *Paris v. Machnick* (1972), 32 D.L.R. (3d) 723 (N.S.S.C.).

65 Art. 2, 2-302.

unconscientious, this, presumably equitable doctrine, limited though it may be, goes some way towards achieving this result.[66]

Adequacy of consideration may not be the test of a valid contract but reality or sufficiency of consideration is. There must be something which is being given in exchange for the act or promise that is alleged for there to be contractual obligation.[67] Hence, in one case,[68] where an option was given to a certain company to buy shares in another, the alleged consideration for the option was the agreement of the optionee to make a similar proposition, namely, grant a similar option to a third party. It was held that this was not valuable consideration capable of supporting the grant of the first option. All the original optionee was doing was passing on his rights or option to a third party. So, too, in *Tobias v. Dick & T. Eaton & Co.*[69] under an agreement, X was given the exclusive right to sell (and to buy for this purpose) machines manufactured by Y in a certain area and for a stated time period. It was held that since the agreement contained no promise to *sell* the machines on the part of X, there was no contract and therefore no agency between Y and X. In other words, in these cases there was really nothing that was being given as the price of the promise by the other party. However, in *Federal Business Development Bank v. F.B. Holdings Ltd.*,[70] a different attitude appears to have been taken. This involved a contract of loan by which the defendant agreed to borrow and the plaintiffs agreed to lend money. The defendant also agreed that if he cancelled the agreement and did not borrow, he would pay various fees to the plaintiffs. The defendant cancelled and the plaintiffs sued for the fees. It was argued, *inter alia*, that there was no contract because the alleged contract did not oblige the defendant to borrow nor the plaintiffs to lend. However, it was held that there was a contract, with mutuality of obligation. By the term as to cancellation, the parties had not negated any contractual obligations; they had provided a way to determine, or extricate themselves from the contract. Similarly, in *Maier v. E & B Exploration Ltd.*,[71] the consideration for the promise to vary the amount paid to employees by the inclusion of a share option scheme was the continuation by those employees in their employment. As they were not employed for a definite period, they could have left their employment.

However, what is involved may be slight in value or in detrimental quality (whichever is appropriate to the circumstances). In the famous English case of

---

66 See what is said, pp. 325-326, with respect to the doctrine of "unconscionability", and compare the legislation on unconscionable transactions: pp. 337-342.

67 *Abraham v. Wingate Properties Ltd.*, [1986] 1 W.W.R. 568 (Man. C.A.); *Can. West Tree Fruits Ltd. v. T.G. Bright & Co.*, [1990] 6 W.W.R. 89 (B.C.C.A.); leave to appeal to S.C.C. refused [1991] 2 W.W.R. lxvii (note) (S.C.C.); *Case's Insulation & Siding Ltd. v. Gordon* (1991), 45 C.L.R. 252 (N.B.Q.B.) (in none of which consideration was established). See also *Waldock v. Bissett* (1992), 67 B.C.L.R. (2d) 389 (B.C.C.A.), rescission of old agreement in consideration of new one: sufficient consideration.

68 *Gibson v. McVeigh*, [1922] 1 W.W.R. 151 (Alta. S.C.).

69 [1937] 4 D.L.R. 546 (Man. K.B.).

70 [1979] 2 W.W.R. 445 (Sask. Dist. Ct.).

71 [1986] 4 W.W.R. 275 (Alta. C.A.).

Bainbridge v. Firmstone,[72] A lent two boilers to B to be weighed. B promised that they would be returned in good condition. It was held that the parting with possession was a sufficient detriment to A to provide consideration for B's promise as to the return of the boilers. So, too, the retention of a right to cancel a contract, if such cancellation might involve loss, was sufficient consideration for a counter-promise;[73] not buying another plot of land in a cemetery was sufficient consideration for an agreement to give the defendant a plot and its appurtenant rights;[74] undertaking to employ someone, even though the employee could be dismissed at any time without notice, was sufficient consideration for the employee's counter-promise;[75] preparing a *pro forma* balance sheet at the request of the promisor was sufficient consideration for a promise to forgive certain debts;[76] undertaking to provide a home and support for grandparents was sufficient consideration for the transfer of a house to the grandchildren.[77] In all these situations, as well as many other, what was given or promised was truly, upon analysis, of little or no worth, but it was sufficient to amount to consideration.[78]

The distinction between sufficient (even though inadequate) consideration and insufficient consideration has given rise to problems and has stimulated some very fine, not to say subtle, distinctions. Many of these are illustrated in English cases which have not been paralleled by Canadian decisions.[79] Although it is sometimes difficult to justify the conclusion that consideration was present so as to permit the recognition of a contractual relationship, as in the bailment cases previously cited,[80] it seems clear that the feature which marks the difference between contractual obligations and those arising otherwise, for example, under the law of tort or the law of bailment, is the presence or absence of consideration as previously defined and explained. That this distinction is sometimes artificial is undeniable. That it may cause difficulty is equally undeniable. Hence, the suggestions that have been made that the difference between gratuitous obligations and those undertaken for some reward, however trifling, should no longer be vital.[81] At the present time, however, such an attitude, which stresses the importance of

---

72 (1838), 8 Ad. & El. 743; compare *Coggs v. Bernard* (1703), 2 Ld. Raym. 909.

73 *Colwood Cemetery Co. v. Pub. Utilities Comm.* (1961), 36 W.W.R. 283 (B.C.C.A.).

74 *Hubbs v. Black* (1918), 44 O.L.R. 545 (Ont. C.A.).

75 *Weston (George) Ltd. v. Baird* (1916), 37 O.L.R. 514 (Ont. C.A.); *Skeans v. Hampton* (1914), 31 O.L.R. 424 (Ont. C.A.).

76 *Regehr v. Ketzakey Silver Mines Ltd.* (1970), 10 D.L.R. (3d) 171 (Alta. C.A.).

77 *Hickey v. Hickey* (1986), 86 N.B.R. (2d) 428 (N.B.Q.B.); affirmed (1988), 86 N.B.R. (2d) 421 (N.B.C.A.).

78 Hence, in the English case of *Chappell & Co. v. Nestle Co.*, [1960] A.C. 87 (H.L.) the wrappers of chocolate bars could be part of the consideration for the purchase of records at a low money price; and in *Indevco Properties Ltd. v. J.B. Franks Management Co.* (1989), 63 D.L.R. (4th) 398 (B.C.C.A.), the purchaser's promise to use due diligence to obtain rezoning of the land that was the subject of the contract could be part of the consideration for the contract.

79 *E.g.*, the distinction between a contract and a conditional gift: see Cheshire, Fifoot and Furmston, *Law of Contract*, 12th ed. (1991), p. 87.

80 Above, note 72.

81 Reiter, "Contracts, Torts, Relations and Reliance," in Reiter & Swan, *Studies in Contract Law* (1980), Study 8.

the "reasonable expectations" of the parties and reduces the materiality of some kind of bargain between them, is not one that has appealed to the courts to the extent of inducing them to abandon the notion of consideration. There are situations in which factors other than consideration may be relevant in determining the nature and extent of the legal rights and obligations of the parties. Such is the case where a party is said to be estopped by virtue of his conduct and its effect upon the other party.[82] The courts have not yet replaced the doctrine of consideration by the notion that whether or not a bargain of some kind has been reached between them, the parties' relationship is to be regulated by their "reasonable expectations". To discover whether an obligation may be said to have arisen by reason of a contract between the parties, it is still necessary to determine whether sufficient consideration has been given or promised for the obligation in question. Such determination involves courts in decisions as to whether the party seeking to benefit from the obligation has provided some benefit, however minimal or artificial, or undergone some detriment, however trifling, in return for the undertaking of the obligation.

(b) Forbearance to sue

A series of cases in England in the latter part of the nineteenth century established that a compromise of a serious claim, if honestly made, could be valuable consideration at common law, whether or not the claim would have been successful if it had ever been tried in court. Such compromise can take one of two forms. The prospective litigant can refrain from taking an action in return for the promise of the intended defendant; or an action once commenced can be settled by such an agreement. Either way, in appropriate circumstances, the resulting agreement will be valid and enforceable. As was said in *Miles v. New Zealand Alford Estate Co.*,[83]

> [i]f an intended litigant *bona fide* forbears a right to litigate a question of law or fact which is not vexatious or frivolous to litigate, he does give up something of value.

The effect of these English decisions has been accepted in Canada. For example, in *Francis v. Allan*[84] the Supreme Court upheld the argument that an agreement not to press a claim against an estate was consideration for an undertaking to settle the claim. Some years later, in *Attorney General of British Columbia v. Deeks Sand & Gravel Co.*,[85] Kellock J., citing and following the decisions referred to above, held that a claim which was subsequently determined to be unfounded in law could validly form the basis of an agreement of compromise under which the claimant surrendered any potential rights he might have had under such claim. As the learned judge explained, the common law had once been different; only the surrender of

---

82 Below pp. 121-136: compare the remarks of Rice J.A. in *Robichaud v. Caisse populaire de Pokemouche Ltée* (1990), 105 N.B.R. (2d) 227 at 246-248 (N.B.C.A.).

83 (1886), 32 Ch. D. 266 at 291 (C.A.) *per* Bowen L.J.; see also *Callisher v. Bischoffsheim* (1870), L.R. 5 Q.B. 449; and *Jayawickreme v. Amarasuriya*, [1918] A.C. 869 (P.C.).

84 (1918), 57 S.C.R. 373 at 376 (S.C.C.) *per* Idington J.

85 [1956] S.C.R. 336 at 343 (S.C.C.).

good claims could be consideration. It had changed as a consequence of the English decisions previously cited. So there are several instances of compromises being upheld as good contracts, notwithstanding the possible, or even actual invalidity of the claim which was being compromised.[86]

However, the claim must be made *bona fide*, not with the knowledge that it was unfounded and as an attempt to obtain something fraudulently.[87] Nor will a compromise agreement be upheld if the contract on which the compromise was based was an illegal contract.[88] To permit a party to gain from the compromise of a threatened action upon an illegal contract would indirectly recognize and enforce the original illegal contract. It must also be shown that the forbearance to sue was undertaken at the express or implied request of the party who pays or does something for the compromising party.[89] However, the circumstances may establish that the forbearance was in consideration of what the other party did or promised.[90] It has also been held that, despite the so-called "parol evidence rule", which normally precludes extrinsic oral evidence where there is a written contract,[91] such evidence is admissible to prove that a forbearance to sue was undertaken in consideration of a promise from the other party, in this instance, a guarantee.[92] If a compromise agreement is entered into as a result of duress, including economic duress,[93] that agreement will not be upheld and enforced, unless the victim of the duress subsequently does something that amounts to affirmation of the agreement, as long as that party was aware of the duress at the time of the conduct that constitutes affirmation.[94]

A more important qualification of the validity of such compromises may also exist. In *Magee v. Pennine Insurance Co.*[95] the parties entered into a compromise

---

86 *Beer v. McLeod* (1890), 22 N.S.R. 535 (N.S.C.A.); *Drewry v. Percival* (1909), 19 O.L.R. 463 (Ont. C.A.); *Adams v. Craig* (1911), 24 O.L.R. 490 (Ont. C.A.); *Leslie v. Stevenson* (1915), 34 O.L.R. 473 (Ont. C.A.); *Famous Foods Ltd. v. Liddle*, [1941] 3 W.W.R. 708 (B.C.C.A.); *Walters v. Walters*, [1946] 3 W.W.R. 497 (Sask. C.A.); *Bilodeau v. McLean*, [1924] 2 W.W.R. 631 (Man. C.A.) (mutual abandonment of claims by each party against the other was consideration for settlement of new clauses); *Sovereign Gen. Ins. Co. v. Fizzard* (1977), 14 Nfld. & P.E.I.R. 175 (Nfld. Dist. Ct.). Compare *T.D. Bank v. Nova Entertainment Inc.* (1992), 7 Alta. L.R. (3d) 132 (Alta. Q.B.) (for the purpose of "value" in the PPSA). But the position is different if there is mutual mistake: *Husky Oil Operations Ltd. v. Forest Oil Corp.* (1991), 79 Alta. L.R. (2d) 134 (Alta. C.A.); leave to appeal to S.C.C. refused (1991), 81 Alta. L.R. (2d) lxvii (note) (S.C.C.); compare below. It has been said that a request for forebearance to sue will suffice: and there is no need for an actual agreement not to sue; *Commodity Broking v. Meehan*, [1985] I.R. 12 at 21 *per* Barron J.

87 *Lister (R.E.) Ltd. v. Dunlop Can. Ltd.* (1982), 135 D.L.R. (3d) 1 (S.C.C.).

88 *Metlege v. Ryan* (1980), 113 D.L.R. (3d) 248 (N.S.C.A.); on illegality, see pp. 344-388 below.

89 *Niagara Structural Steel Ltd. v. Bellows* (1965), 46 D.L.R. (2d) 705 (Ont. H.C.).

90 *Logini Const. Inc. v. Harris; Circosta (N.J.) & Assoc. Realty Ltd. v. Harris; Centreby Enterprises Inc. v. Harris* (1982), 35 O.R. (2d) 633 (Ont. Co. Ct.); compare *Cities Service Oil Co. v. Rubel*, [1931] 2 D.L.R. 183 (Ont. C.A.).

91 Below, pp. 455-462.

92 *Hickman (A.E.) Co. v. Roses Aluminum Ltd.* (1981), 36 Nfld. & P.E.I.R. 206 (Nfld. Dist. Ct.).

93 Below, pp. 314-320.

94 *Stott v. Merit Invt. Corp.* (1988), 48 D.L.R. (4th) 288 (Ont. C.A.); leave to appeal to S.C.C. refused (1988), 49 D.L.R. (4th) viii (note) (S.C.C.).

95 [1969] 2 Q.B. 507 (C.A.).

agreement in settlement of an insurance claim which both parties, under common fundamental mistake, believed was enforceable. Looking at the "equities" of the situation, the majority of the English Court of Appeal held that the settlement contract could not be upheld once the discovery was made by the parties of the falsity of the application for insurance on which the alleged settlement arose (though there was no allegation of fraud against the assured, nor any proof that he had acted fraudulently). In that case, which raises difficult questions relating to the operation of mistake upon what appear to be validly made contracts,[96] the majority of the court refused to uphold a settlement that had been entered into *bona fide*, if erroneously, by the claimant and the party on whom the claim was made. This was followed by Andrews J. of the Supreme Court of British Columbia in *Toronto-Dominion Bank v. Fortin (No. 2)*.[97] A compromise agreement was reached between the receiver-manager of a company and a party who had previously agreed to buy the companies of which the receiver-manager was in control as a result of liquidation proceedings. That settlement was founded upon the buyer's desire to repudiate the contract. He paid a large sum of money to be released from potential liability. Later it was discovered that the contract in question was *ultra vires* the receiver-manager. Consequently the contract was void. The buyer claimed the return of the money he had paid, claiming that the compromise agreement was also invalid, and that the money had been paid under a mistake. It was held that the receiver-manager was liable to return the money on the ground that, being an officer of the court, he owed a higher duty than other contractors might have owed the buyer and could not rely on the apparent agreement between the parties to retain the money. However, it was also held that the compromise agreement could not be upheld, despite the *bona fides* of the parties, because it was invalidated by mistake. The judge distinguished this case from other instances of compromise agreements on two grounds; first, that the receiver-manager lacked capacity to enter into the original contract, hence, *any* contract relating to the companies, including the compromise agreement, was invalid; second, that, unlike the *Deeks* case,[98] legal advice had not been taken before the compromise was reached. Reliance was placed upon the decision in *Magee* for the purpose of establishing that a compromise agreement entered into under a mistake could be upset even though it was otherwise agreed upon in good faith. The approach of Lord Denning M.R., in that case was founded upon the idea that it would be unfair to hold a mistaken party to such an agreement (although this seems to counter the earlier compromise decisions). It was this approach that appealed to the Supreme Court of Canada in *R.E. Lister Ltd. v. Dunlop Canada Ltd.*[99] On that basis the compromise agreement involved in that case was upheld following the earlier English cases on such agreements with respect to sufficiency of consideration. Here the equities were in favour of the validation of the agreement. The agreement had been fully

---

96 See p. 252-254.
97 (1977), 88 D.L.R. (3d) 232 (B.C.S.C.); below, pp. 256-257. See also *Husky Oil Operations Ltd. v. Forest Oil Corp.*, above, note 86.
98 Above, note 85.
99 Above, note 87.

executed on both sides. It had been entered into after both parties had obtained legal advice, including independent legal advice for one of the parties. All the facts were fully known. There was no reason in equity for allowing such an agreement to be set aside. What emerges from the judgment of the court[100] is that, to set aside such a contract when it has been reached in a written contract drawn by the parties' solicitors, for parties experienced in business, is very difficult. Nevertheless, it may be possible, in a suitable case, for such compromise agreements to be invalidated on general equitable grounds.

(c) Existing obligation

(i) General

Can the promise to do what a party is already bound to do ever amount to consideration for a promise by the other party? The promisor could already be obliged to the same promisee to do what he *now* promises. Such obligation might arise from a prior contract between the parties or from some public duty under which the promisor is already bound, or the promisor may be purporting to promise the new promisee that he will perform an obligation which is already owed to a *third* party. Since at first sight what the promisor is giving, or is purporting to give, is not anything new by way of undertaking a fresh burden or detriment but merely a repetition of an already binding duty, is the "new" promise really consideration?

Lord Denning clearly thought that it could be. In *Ward v. Byham*[101] he said that "a promise to perform an existing duty, or the performance of it, should be regarded as good consideration, because it is a benefit to the person to whom it is given." In that case the father of an illegitimate child offered to let the mother have the child and pay a weekly sum for its maintenance, provided that the mother could prove that the child would be well looked after and happy and allowed to decide for herself whether she wished to live with the mother. This was held to be a good contract, so that the mother could sue for unpaid maintenance. Although the mother was under a statutory duty to maintain the child, the majority of the English Court of Appeal held that the mother had promised more than the performance of her statutory duty; she had undertaken to look after the child, satisfy the father that the child was happy, and let the child decide where she wanted to live. In a subsequent case, *Williams v. Williams*,[102] Lord Denning qualified his previous statement. There, a wife was claiming under an alleged agreement to pay her maintenance. She was actually in desertion, so the husband was under no duty to maintain her; she was under a duty to maintain herself. Nevertheless, Lord Denning was prepared to hold that there was consideration for the promise

---

100 *Ibid.*, at 15-16.
101 [1956] 2 All E.R. 318 and 319 (C.A.); compare *Horrocks v. Forray*, [1976] 1 All E.R. 737 (C.A.). See the comments by Mocatta J. in *North Ocean Shipping Co. v. Hyundai Const. Co.*, [1978] 3 All E.R. 1170 at 1177, and those of the Court of Appeal in *Williams v. Roffey & Nicholls (Contractors)*, [1990] 1 All E.R. 512 at 519-520, 525.
102 [1957] 1 All E.R. 305 at 306-307 (C.A.).

to pay maintenance. The benefit to the husband was that, while she was paid, she would not pledge his credit or otherwise trouble him or put him to expense. The other members of the court found consideration in her promise not to return or offer to return to him as long as he paid the agreed sum. In giving judgment, Lord Denning again said that a promise to perform an existing duty was good consideration for a new promise but added, "as long as there is nothing in the transaction which is contrary to public interest."

The views of Lord Denning were critically examined and discussed in *Williams v. Roffey & Nicholls (Contractors) Ltd.*[103] From what is said by the English Court of Appeal in that case, it is clear that consideration remains a fundamental requirement before a contract not under seal can be enforced. However, there has been development, and the rigid approach to consideration found in the early nineteenth century is no longer necessary or desirable.[104] Courts are more ready to find consideration so as to reflect the intentions of the parties, unless there is an element of fraud, duress, or inequality of bargaining power present.[105] Nevertheless, the broad statements of Lord Denning appear to have been regarded as going too far. The most one member of the court, Purchas L.J., would appear to accept was "that where there were benefits derived by each party to a contract of variation even though one party did not suffer a detriment this would not be fatal to the establishing of sufficient consideration to support the agreement".[106]

Although it may not be valid to state the law in the general terms of Lord Denning, it is certainly true that in recent years there has been development by virtue of which it can be said that there are circumstances in which a promise to perform an obligation already binding on a party who makes that promise in return for a new promise from the other party can be sufficient consideration for that new, additional, or varying contract between the parties.

(ii) *Promise to perform existing duty to the same promisee*

The origins of the present law are to be found in two English cases, *Harris v. Watson*[107] and *Stilk v. Myrick*.[108] In *Harris v. Watson* the captain of a ship, acting on behalf of the owners during a voyage for which the plaintiff had already contracted to serve as a seaman, promised the seaman five guineas over and above his common wages if he would perform some extra work. The plaintiff's claim

---

103 [1990] 1 All E.R. 512; below, p. 99.

104 *Ibid.*, at 524 *per* Russell L.J.

105 On these, see below, pp. 245, 313, 328.

106 Above, note 103, at 527.

107 (1791), Peake 72.

108 (1809), 2 Camp. 317. For criticism of the way this case has been interpreted, see Gilmore, *The Death of Contract* (1974), pp. 22-28, and see Swan, "Consideration and the Reasons for Enforcing Contract" in Reiter & Swan, *Studies in Contract Law* (1980), 23 at pp. 27-29. That the case is still good law seems clear from *Arrale v. Costain*, [1976] 1 Lloyd's Rep. 98 at 106 (C.A.) *per* Lane L.J., *North Ocean Shipping Co. v. Hyundai Const. Co.*, [1978] 3 All E.R. 1170 at 1177 *per* Mocatta J; and *Williams v. Roffey*, above, note 103, at 518, 522 *per* Glidewell L.J., at 525 *per* Purchas L.J.

for the five guineas was non-suited. The language of Lord Kenyon suggests that the grounds for such dismissal of the action were akin to duress and derived from ideas of public policy. In the later similar case of *Stilk v. Myrick*, the plaintiff again was non-suited. But the reason for this has been variously reported. One report indicates that the claim failed for want of consideration. Another suggests that the earlier case was founded on just and proper policy. The Privy Council, in *Pao On v. Lau Yiu Long*,[109] said that these cases were explicable on the basis of an absence of fresh consideration for the captain's promise but were an unsure foundation for a rule of public policy in invalidating contracts where, save for the rule, there would be valid consideration. It is all the more surprising how *Stilk v. Myrick* has become the accepted honoured doctrine when, in the twentieth century, in *Raggow v. Scougall*,[110] another court refused to deny validity to a promise by a seaman to take *less*, not more, money for doing the work he was already contracted to do. When the seaman sued for the larger amount, presumably relying on the *Stilk* case, he was told that he was doing "a very dishonest thing", and was denied a remedy. More recently, in *North Ocean Shipping Co. v. Hyundai Construction Co.*,[111] fresh consideration for a promise to pay more than the originally contracted price was found in an undertaking to increase the amount of a letter of credit issued by the party seeking more money.

Still more recently the decision in *Stilk v. Myrick* was again approved and confirmed by the English Court of Appeal in *Williams v. Roffey & Nicholls Ltd.*[112] Nevertheless, it was possible for the court to find that a valid, enforceable contract existed when, in return for a promise of extra payment for work already contracted to be performed, the sub-contractor who had agreed to do certain work on a block of flats being refurbished by the defendants, the main, general contractors, undertook to finish the work on time. In this case the plaintiff ran into financial difficulties prior to completing the work, and the defendants would have been liable to pay a penalty for non-completion on time under the main contract. Hence, the parties agreed that the defendants would pay an extra sum if the plaintiff completed his work on time. The defendants failed to pay the extra sum, as well as one of the originally agreed instalments. Consequently, the plaintiff refused to finish the work and sued for the outstanding amounts. He was successful at trial, subject to a minor qualification, and the defendants' appeal was dismissed.

Glidewell L.J. expressed the governing principle as follows:[113]

> (i) if A has entered into a contract with B to do work for, or to supply goods or services to, B in return for payment by B and (ii) at some stage before A has completely performed his obligations under the contract B has reason to doubt whether A will, or will be able to, complete his side of the bargain and (iii) B thereupon promises A an additional payment in return for A's promise to perform his contractual obligations on time and (iv) as a result of giving his promise B obtains in practice a benefit, or obviates a

---

109 [1979] 3 All E.R. 65 at 76-77 (P.C.).
110 (1915), 31 T.L.R. 564.
111 [1978] 3 All E.R. 1170.
112 [1990] 1 All E.R. 512 (C.A.).
113 *Ibid.*, at 521-522.

disbenefit, and (v) B's promise is not given as a result of economic duress or fraud on the part of A, then (vi) the benefit to B is capable of being consideration for B's promise, so that the promise will be legally binding.

Russell L.J. put this more succinctly. Where a party undertakes to make a payment because by so doing it will gain an advantage arising out of the continuing relationship with the promisee, the new bargain will not fail for want of consideration.[114] Purchas L.J., while stating that *Stilk v. Myrick* was still the governing principle,[115] was prepared to accept, as the other members of the court, that in modern times a different attitude to consideration was more appropriate. To him, as long as both parties acquired benefits under a new agreement varying an earlier one, it was not necessary that each should also suffer a detriment.[116] In consequence of this case, where a contractual duty already exists it may be possible, in the absence of some vitiating factor such as duress or fraud,[117] to vary the original agreement without necessarily establishing a whole new contract with fresh consideration on both sides. As pointed out in this case[118], most modern situations before the courts involved an element of duress, the presence of which would result in the strict application of the doctrine of *Stilk v. Myrick*.

The foregoing cases all involved an existing contractual duty. In another instance, the court had to contend with a promise to do something which the promisor was already bound to do under a public, not contractual, duty. The case in question is a decision of the House of Lords, *Glasbrook Brothers v. Glamorgan County Council.*[119] A private coal company offered to pay the police to give it certain protection during a strike. The police were already bound, by virtue of their statutory duties, to provide some such service for the company. But the police authority's promise to provide a stationary guard, not just a mobile force, was consideration for the company's promise to pay. The police were providing special, unusual, different services, which they were not under any public duty to give or provide. Hence, something new was introduced so that there was fresh consideration.

The ideas either inherent or expressed in these cases may be seen in operation in Canadian decisions. Two cases from the early part of the century, both from Nova Scotia, illustrate the attitude of the courts in Canada. In *Dempster v. Bauld*[120] it was said that a promise to perform an existing duty would not be consideration for a new promise.[121] However, if there were a *bona fide* dispute between the parties as to the meaning of a term in the original contract, that is, as to the duty owed

---

114 *Ibid.*, at 526.

115 *Ibid.*, at 525-526.

116 *Ibid.*, at 527.

117 Below, pp. 295, 313.

118 *E.g.*, above, note 112, at 520 *per* Glidewell L.J., at 526 *per* Purchas L.J. On this case, see Hooley, "Consideration and the Existing Duty", [1991] J. Bus. L. 19.

119 [1925] A.C. 270 (H.L.). Discussed in *Harris v. Sheffield United Football Club*, [1988] Q.B. 77 (C.A.), where the issue was determined under the provisions of the Police Act, 1964, c. 48.

120 (1905), 37 N.S.R. 330 (N.S.C.A.).

121 *E.g.*, to build the house the promisor was already contractually obliged to build: *Smith v. Dawson* (1923), 53 O.L.R. 615 (Ont. C.A.) (the owner's promise to pay over insurance money collected from the burning down of the *first* building put up by the builder was not enforceable).

by the promisor, then a renewed promise, which clarified that duty, might possibly be consideration for a further promise from the original promisee. In *DeWolfe v. Richards*[122] a new promise which involved a change in the promisor's duty or liability under the original agreement was capable of being consideration. The change in question took the form of giving up some wagons in return for the promisee's agreement to release the promisor from an existing liability. It might not have been of benefit to the promisee, nonetheless, it sufficed as fresh cosideration. Similarly, in a more modern case, *Snell Lumber Ltd. v. Teed*,[123] a party was under a duty to supply goods to another. X wished to guarantee payment of the purchase price, but he did not do so by a contract under seal. In order for such guarantee to be an enforceable contract there had to be consideration from the one under the duty to supply the goods. It was not sufficient for the supplier merely to supply the original goods envisaged in the contract between the parties; he had to supply *fresh* goods.

In cases involving employees agreeing to continue to work for more pay or extra advantages not contained in the original contract of employment, it has been held that the promise to pay or provide more would not be enforceable unless the employee also gave something additional in return, such as the performance of additional duties. Such would be the situation where the employee would have, or could have, terminated his employment if the employer had not entered into the new agreement.[124] In *Maguire v. Northland Drug Co.*,[125] for example, an employee entered into a covenant in restraint of trade during the period of his employment, not prior to his being employed. Dysart J. said,[126]

> . . . the employee was given to understand, and did understand, that his refusal to execute the covenant would lead to an early termination of his employment, and . . . the employer tacitly promised that if the bond were signed, the employment would not soon be terminated. . . . This continuance of employment constitutes legal consideration, the adequacy of which will not be inquired into by the courts.

A more recent illustration, involving facts akin to those in the *Snell Lumber* case arose in *Gilbert Steel Ltd. v. University Construction Ltd.*[127] The parties agreed that one would supply the other with steel at a stipulated price. Later the supplier asked for a higher price for delivery of the same quantity of the same steel, alleging changes in the price structure that made such additions desirable. The buyer of

---

122 (1908), 43 N.S.R. 34 (N.S.C.A.).

123 (1959), 43 M.P.R. 304 (N.B.C.A.). See also *Burton v. Brook* (1956), 6 D.L.R. (2d) 464 (B.C.S.C.).

124 *Peerless Laundry & Cleaners Ltd. v. Neal*, [1953] 2 D.L.R. 494 (Man. C.A.); *Sloan v. Union Oil Co.*, [1955] 4 D.L.R. 664 (B.C.S.C.). *Maier v. E & B Exploration Ltd.*, [1986] 4 W.W.R. 275 (Alta. C.A.), above, p. 92.

125 [1935] S.C.R. 412 (S.C.C.).

126 *Ibid.*, at 415.

127 (1973), 36 D.L.R. (3d) 496 (Ont. H.C.); affirmed (1976), 67 D.L.R. (3d) 606 (Ont. C.A.). See the discussion of this case, and the question of modification of contracts in Ontario Law Reform Commission, *Report on Amendment of the Law of Contract* (1987), pp. 13-18, 33 recommending change that would permit modification without consideration, with some qualifications. The *Gilbert Steel* case was followed in *Lewitski v. Ogilvie* (1992), 56 O.A.C. 69 (Ont. Div. Ct.).

the steel agreed, so as to obtain the steel. The action by the supplier for the new price was dismissed at trial and this dismissal was upheld on appeal. In the Ontario Court of Appeal it was argued first that there was a new contract, that is, that the original contract for the purchase of the steel had been replaced by a new one involving the higher price. This was not accepted as an explanation of what had occurred. Had it been, there would have been no difficulty since it is always open to parties to discharge their original agreement and make a new one.[128] The second argument was that there was consideration for the promise by the buyer to pay the increased price. It was alleged that the promise to pay that price was supported by a promise by the supplier to give increased credit to the buyer — the construction company. Both arguments were rejected. With respect to the second argument it is instructive to compare this decision with that of an English court in *North Ocean Shipping Co. v. Hyundai Construction Ltd.*[129] There the contract was for the building of a ship at an agreed price. The builder of the ship agreed to open a letter of credit corresponding to the contract price. Later, in view of the devaluation of the American dollar, the builder sought an increase in the price. To this the ultimate owner agreed, in order to obtain the ship which was needed to fulfil charters made by the ultimate owner with third parties. When the builder sued for the increase in price it was held that there was a good contract because, as part of the agreement as to the new price, the builder also agreed to extend the scope of the letter of credit. However, the contract might have been voidable for duress (had it not been that the subsequent conduct of the ultimate owner amounted to affirmation of the transaction).[130]

Attempts have been made to argue that the *Gilbert Steel* case might well have been decided, as the English case might have been, on the basis of "duress", that is, the attempt to force the buyer to agree to accept the steel at a new price, founded on the supplier's knowledge of the difficulties that would be created for the buyer if the steel were not supplied as originally agreed.[131] This approach was not raised or dealt with in the decision. Instead, the court based their disposition of the case firmly on the basis of the doctrine in *Stilk v. Myrick.* The same approach was adopted in later cases in which the problem of finding new consideration for a promise to do something the promisor was already bound to do was raised.[132] In view of

---

128 Below, pp. 549-557.

129 [1978] 3 All E.R. 1170.

130 As to *duress*, see pp. 313-320. Compare the remarks as to the effect of duress in some situations in *Williams v. Roffey & Nicholls (Contractors) Ltd.*, above, note 112.

131 Swan, "Consideration and the Reasons for Enforcing Contracts," in Reiter & Swan, *Studies in Contract Law* (1980), p. 23; Reiter, "Courts, Consideration and Common Sense" (1977), 27 U.T.L.J. 439.

132 *R.C.H. Enterprises Ltd. v. Batisse D'Acier Hercule Ltée* (1977), 16 N.B.R. (2d) 338 (N.B.C.A.); *Ben Plastering Ltd.v. Global Dixie Ltd. (No. 2)* (1979), 33 C.B.R. (N.S.) 253n (Ont. H.C.); *Blomidon Mercury Sales Ltd. v. John Piercey's Auto Body Shop Ltd.* (1981), 129 D.L.R. (3d) 630 (Nfld. T.D.); *Zinman v. Hechter* (1981), 130 D.L.R. (3d) 183 (Man. C.A.); leave to appeal to S.C.C. refused (1982), 41 N.R. 488 (S.C.C.); compare the dissenting judgment of Nemetz C.J.B.C. in *Delaney v. Cascade River Holidays Ltd.* (1983), 44 B.C.L.R. 24 at 33-35 (B.C.C.A.).

the decision *Williams v. Roffey & Nicholls (Contractors) Ltd.*,[133] the doctrine in *Stilk v. Myrick* is still valid and operative; but the effect of duress may have become more relevant and important.

However, the doctrine has been criticized as standing in the way of a realistic, sensible, modern method of dealing with what have been called "going transaction adjustments" or "contract modification". Although there is some purpose to the rule, namely, to prevent the possibility that one party will take undue advantage of the comparatively weak, exposed position of the other party, there may be situations where modification is legitimate and excusable, for example, if the work to be done turns out to be more expensive and costly than the party providing the work originally conceived, as was the case in *Williams v. Roffey & Nicholls (Contractors) Ltd.*, where, as previously noted, the Court of Appeal was prepared to modify the strictness of a doctrine applicable in Napoleonic times to then operative conditions on the high seas. As indicated there, improperly forced modifications can be dealt with by doctrines of duress, fraud or unconscionability. Valid or justifiable modifications would not fall within such grounds for disapprobation or disavowal. Since the decision in *Williams v. Roffey & Nicholls (Contractors) Ltd.* it would seem then the law will give effect to such modifications, at least in some circumstances. This, in fact, has long been recognized by the American *Restatement of Contract*, Second Edition.[134] Such modifications will be recognized if they are fair and equitable in view of circumstances not anticipated by the parties when the contract was made, or to the extent provided by statute, or to the extent that justice requires enforcement in view of material changes of position in reliance on the promise to pay more, or perform something extra over and above what the party in question was obliged to give or do under the contract. The first situation, it may be suggested, may have grave consequences with respect to the law of frustration.[135] The second needs no comment. The third seems to rely heavily on doctrines of estoppel, particularly promissory estoppel.[136] This, too, was raised as a possible answer to *Stilk v. Myrick* situations by the plaintiff in *Williams v. Roffey & Nicholls (Contractors) Ltd.*[137] However, the court found it unnecessary and undesirable to pursue this, especially in view of the way that doctrine has so far been accepted and adopted.[138]

---

133 Above, note 112.

134 (1981), Section 89. Hillman, "Policing Contract Modifications under the U.C.C." (1979), 64 Iowa L.R. 849; Brody, "Performance of a Pre-Existing Contractual Duty as Consideration" (1975), 52 Denver L.J. 433; Muris, "Opportunistic Behaviour and the Law of Contracts" (1981), 65 Minn. L.R. 521; Posner, "Gratuitous Promises in Economics and Law" (1977), 6 J. Leg. Stud. 411; Posner & Rosenfeld, "Impossibility and Related Doctrines in Contract Law: An Economic Analysis" (1977), 6 J. Leg. Stud. 83.

135 Below pp. 623 *et seq.*.

136 Below pp. 121-136.

137 [1990] 1 All E.R. 512 at 520, 523, 526-527 (C.A.).

138 Below p. 125. See the discussion in the *Report on Amendment of the Law of Contract*, above, note 127.

(iii) *Promise to pay an existing debt*

A special instance of the situation discussed above arises where the obligation which the promisor already owes to the promisee is to pay an agreed sum of money and the new promise is to pay a portion of that sum. Is such a promise valid and binding since the debtor is simply promising to pay what he already is bound to pay the creditor?

Very early in the history of the law of contract, in *Pinnel's Case*,[139] it was held that such a promise was not enforceable. If A owed B money, a promise by A to B to pay him the money, or any smaller sum, in return for a new promise by B to A, was not a good contract. This was of special importance, as the facts of that case showed, where A promised to pay B a smaller sum, in return for B's releasing A from liability to pay him the larger sum. An attempt was made to argue that this was a valid "accord and satisfaction," thereby discharging A from his former liability, since where A is liable to B, it is possible for A and B, by contract, to discharge that liability. The agreement between the two is an "accord", and what is given for the release of the debtor is the "satisfaction".[140] However, *Pinnel's Case* laid down that, in the absence of a deed, a promise of such smaller sum could not be "satisfaction", that is, consideration, for the release. This was a doctrine that was repeated and given its modern form by the House of Lords in *Foakes v. Beer*.[141] Even in *Pinnel's Case* it was recognized that if some *new* obligation or thing were introduced, however trivial or insignificant its value or worth, as the price of the promise to release the debtor from all or part of his original debt, a valid contract would have been created, that is, there would be accord and satisfaction.[142] Hence, in a recent case, *Robichaud v. Caisse populaire de Pokemouche Ltée*,[143] an agreement to pay $1,000 in settlement of a judgment for $3,000 was held binding. The agreement was made between the judgment creditor and a finance company which had undertaken to resolve the debtor's financial problems. By agreeing to this settlement the creditor was saved time, effort and inconvenience. This was sufficient consideration to allow the agreement to be a valid accord and satisfaction. Such a result flows from the artificial nature of consideration previously discussed.[144] Hence, it is not surprising that the common law refused to accept as a good contract an agreement whereby a creditor undertook to release his debtor from the original debt in return for payment of at least some of which was owed, which had the merit of assuring the creditor that the debt was not altogether lost, but treated as valid an agreement under which the creditor discharged his debtor from liability in return for something of no real value, for

---

139 (1602), 5 Co. Rep. 117a.

140 *Udy v. Doan*, [1940] 2 W.W.R. 440 (Sask. K.B.). See, further, below, pp. 551-553.

141 (1884), 9 App. Cas. 605 (H.L.). In Ontario, the effect of this decision was overcome by the Administration of Justice Act, 1885 (48 Vict., c. 13), s. 6: see further, below, pp. 119-121.

142 See, *e.g., Kaulbach v. Eichel*, [1930] 1 D.L.R. 983 (N.S.C.A.). See also, and compare, *Bank of N.S. v. MacLellan* (1977), 78 D.L.R. (3d) 1 (N.S.S.C.), and *MacMillan v. MacMillan* (1977), 76 D.L.R. (3d) 760 (Sask. C.A.); above, p. 90.

143 (1990), 105 N.B.R. (2d) 227 (N.B.C.A.).

144 Above, pp. 82-86.

example, a peppercorn.[145] The one exception of this appears to have been with respect to arrangements between a debtor and his various creditors, that is, composition. The courts in the nineteenth century gradually concluded that such agreements were enforceable, despite the doctrine of *Pinnel's Case*, possibly on the basis that each *creditor* provided consideration, or possibly, on the ground of commercial convenience or possibly fraud, which outweighed strict logic.[146]

Certainly the courts also accepted, but as a genuine qualification of the doctrine of *Pinnel's Case*, that payment of the original debt in some new form, for example, by way of negotiable instrument instead of cash, or payment at some accelerated time, even if of a smaller amount than the original debt, might be sufficient advantage to the creditor, or detriment to the debtor, to constitute consideration for the promise by the former to release the latter from the full debt. So it was held in *Sibree v. Tripp*[147] in 1846 that payment in such new form or at such new date could substitute an accord and satisfaction that was binding. This approach was adopted and accepted by the Supreme Court of Canada in *Foot v. Rawlings*,[148] in which the debtor gave the creditor a series of post-dated cheques in settlement of his original debt that was contained in several promissory notes. As long as the cheques were being given and paid on presentation by the debtor's bank, the creditor could not enforce his originally owed debt. However, in *D. & C. Builders v. Rees*[149] in 1965, the Court of Appeal in England held that payment by *cheque* was not sufficiently different to amount to a *new* consideration under the doctrine of *Pinnel's Case*. Hence an agreement to accept payment of part of a debt by cheque did not subsequently prevent the creditor from successfully suing for the remainder of what was owed, even though the payment was said to be in discharge of the original debt. It remains to be seen what view will be adopted by Canadian courts, if it ever becomes necessary to decide the issue.[150]

It may never be. As will be seen, certain inroads have been made upon this view of the law of consideration by the doctrine of promissory estoppel.[151] Furthermore, perhaps more importantly, in several provinces of Canada there is

---

145   On peppercorns see Lord Somervell in *Chappell & Co. v. Nestle Co.*, [1960] A.C. 87 at 114 (H.L.).

146   *Hirachand Punamchand v. Temple*, [1911] 2 K.B. 330 (C.A.).

147   (1846), 15 M. & W. 23, overruling *Cumber v. Wane* (1721), 1 Stra. 426. *Cumber v. Wane* was specifically "abrogated" in British Columbia: Law and Equity Act, R.S.B.C. 1979, c. 224, s. 40.

148   [1963] S.C.R. 197 (S.C.C.).

149   [1966] 2 Q.B. 617 (C.A.) in which Lord Denning announced a doctrine repeated by him in *Arrale v. Costain*, [1976] Lloyd's Rep. 98 at 102 (C.A.) to the effect that there might be equitable reasons for not allowing the creditor to claim the whole sum; see also below, p. 135. In particular, in *D. & C. Bldrs. v. Rees*, there was an element of intimidation, or duress, by the debtor towards the creditor, which might have invalidated the agreement by the creditor to accept the lesser sum in settlement of the entire debt. This alone might have determined the case; compare pp. 313-320.

150   If the debtor obtains an extension of time for the payment of his debt in return for giving security for the existing debt, this *new* arrangement will be an enforceable contract: *O'Brien v. Stebbins*, [1927] W.W.R. 176 (Sask. C.A.); *McCoy v. Hop*, [1923] 2 W.W.R. 801 (Sask. C.A.).

151   Below, pp. 121-136. See also the remarks of Rice J.A. on the use of promissory estoppel in this kind of situation in *Robichaud v. Caisse populaire de Pokemouche Ltée* (1990), 105 N.B.R. (2d) 227 at 246-248 (N.B.C.A.).

legislation which has recognized the incongruity and illogicality of the rule in *Pinnel's Case*, and its subsequent history, and has attempted to reverse that doctrine. Wherever such a statutory provision exists in Canada, it is possible for a debtor to obtain a satisfactory and binding release from his original debt, whether that debt involves payment of money or some other kind of performance, and the fact that the new agreement, whether totally executory or partially executed, is founded upon the promise by the debtor to give money which he is already bound to pay the creditor, or do something he is already bound to do for the other party, will not invalidate the agreement on the ground of there being no consideration.[152] Some Canadian legislatures, therefore, in anticipation of changes in the law in England which were suggested in 1937[153] but so far have not been made, may have eradicated at least one unfortunate result of the strictness of the doctrine of consideration.

(iv) *Promise to perform duty owed to a third party*

A different attitude was taken by the courts on the question whether a promise made to X to perform a duty which the promisor already owes to Y can amount to consideration for a promise by X to the party previously bound to Y. In this respect, the distinction must be noted between that situation and the situation where the promise made to X is an undertaking to enter into a contract with Y. Such a promise, the fulfilment of which would involve the promisor in undertaking a new obligation to a third party, can certainly be consideration for X's promise even though there may be no tangible, measurable benefit to X in the making of the contract with Y.[154] The situation now under discussion arises where there is already a contract with Y. For example, as in the famous English case of *Shadwell v. Shadwell*,[155] the promisor was bound to marry Y and then promised X that, in return for something from X, the promisor would carry out his obligation to marry Y. It was held that, in those circumstances, the second promise was enforceable.[156] In other words, the undertaking to fulfil the earlier obligation to the third party was consideration for the new promise. This was followed in Canada in the Supreme Court in *Heichman v. National Trust Co.*[157] In that case a father promised land and chattels to H when H had offered to marry his daughter. The marriage took place as arranged before the promise with respect to the property. But the father never made good his promise. When H died, his estate was held

---

152 Below, pp. 119-121.

153 Law Revision Committee, Sixth Interim Report, 1937, Cmd. 5449, pp. 20-21.

154 *Lysnar v. Nat. Bank of New Zealand*, [1935] 1 W.W.R. 625 (N.Z.). Note also the question of "collateral" contracts, below, pp. 505-515. Note also the doctrine of implied warranty of authority in agency which seems exceptional; Fridman, *Law of Agency*, 6th ed. (1990), pp. 218-221.

155 (1860), 9 C.B.N.S. 159.

156 Compare *Scotson v. Pegg* (1861), 6 H. & N. 295; *Chichester v. Cobb* (1866), 14 L.T. 433. See also *Ward v. Byham*, [1956] 1 W.L.R. 496 (C.A.).

157 (1920), 60 S.C.R. 428 (S.C.C.).

able to enforce the promise against the wife's father. Mignault J.[158] specifically cited, relied upon, and followed the decision in *Shadwell v. Shadwell*.

There is a degree of illogicality about this approach. Indeed, it has been referred to as "a secret paradox of the common law".[159] There appears to be something wrong in principle about treating such promises as consideration.[160] If the repetition of X's promise to Y is not consideration for a second promise of something new by Y to X, then the repetition of X's promise to Z should not be consideration for a promise of something by Y to X. If X were to undertake some new obligation to Z, and not just reiterate the existing obligation, there would be justification for calling such a promise or undertaking consideration for Y's promise to X. Notwithstanding such doubts, the Privy Council upheld this approach to situations of this kind in *New Zealand Shipping Co. v. A.M. Satterthwaite & Co.*,[161] a decision concerned with the scope of exemption clauses as a result of which an important qualification of the doctrine of privity of contract was introduced in relation to such provisions in a contract. There it was said,[162]

> [a]n agreement to do an act which the promisor is under an existing obligation to a third party to do, may quite well amount to valid consideration . . . the promisee obtains the benefit of a direct obligation. . . . This proposition is illustrated and supported by *Scotson v. Pegg*,[163] which their Lordships consider to be good law.

Despite the possibility that the so-called benefit to the promisee, called Y above, is merely illusory or fictitious, the endorsement of the earlier case-law by the Privy Council in the *Satterthwaite* case was reiterated by the Privy Council in *Pao On v. Lau Yiu Long*.[164] The only qualification that could be made of the principle so endorsed was where some ground of public policy could be invoked or relied upon to invalidate the transaction. One such ground that was clearly accepted as applicable in that case was duress, whether of the physical or economic kind.[165] It was argued that this should be extended to include "extortion by the abuse of a dominant bargaining position to threaten the repudiation of a contractual obligation." The argument was supported by reference to American cases and text-writers. The Privy Council refused to agree that the law could be developed along such lines.[166] To invoke such a rule of public policy would be unhelpful and would create an unacceptable anomaly. It was also unnecessary, because if the party exercising pressure were guilty of duress or coercion, the contract would be vitiated. If there were no coercion there would be no reason for avoiding a contract supported

---

158 *Ibid.*, at 440.
159 Bronaugh, "A Secret Paradox of the Common Law" (1983), 2 Law and Philosophy 193.
160 Compare Cheshire, Fifoot and Furmston, *Law of Contract*, 12th ed. (1991), pp. 107-108, and the authorities there cited.
161 [1975] A.C. 154 (P.C.); below, pp. 583-584.
162 *Ibid.*, at 168.
163 Above, note 156.
164 [1979] 3 All E.R. 65 at 76-77 (P.C.).
165 As to which see pp. 313-320. See also the discussion of the relevance of duress in *Williams v. Roffey & Nicholls (Contractors) Ltd.*, [1990] 1 All E.R. 512 at 520-521 (C.A.) *per* Glidewell L.J.
166 Above, note 164, at 77-78.

by real, and otherwise legal, consideration. The suggested doctrine was unhelpful because it would render the law uncertain. It would create an anomaly because, whereas duress would make a contract voidable at the option of the affected party, the kind of behaviour that was argued would make the doctrine of *Scotson v. Pegg* and *Shadwell v. Shadwell* inapplicable and would make the contract void for want of consideration. Hence, it would be possible for conduct less heinous or reprehensible than duress to have a greater effect in law than actual duress.

The result of these decisions is that, unless the transaction is affected by some vitiating element such as mistake, duress, or fraud, a promise to perform an existing duty owed to a third party can be consideration for a new contract between the party already bound to the third party and a party contracting with the one previously so bound. Logical or not, paradoxical or not, intelligible or not, that would seem to be the common law.

5. Past consideration

Consideration is said to be *executory* when it consists of a promise to do, pay, or give something in the future as, for example, if A agrees that he will pay B in return for something from B. Consideration is said to be *executed* when it consists of the performance of some act by a party, for example, when there is a promise which is given in consideration of A's services to B. From these, valid kinds of consideration must be distinguished *past* consideration which will not suffice to support a promise and create an enforceable contract. Hence, executed consideration must be differentiated from past consideration (although the two appear to resemble each other). The test would seem to be whether the act, which is the consideration, and the promise dependent upon such act are part and parcel of the same transaction. Thus if A promises to pay B if and when B produces A's lost dog, the consideration, namely, the production of the dog by B, is executed; but if B first produces the dog and then A promises to pay B in consideration of B's having already produced the dog, the consideration is past.

The point at issue here is that, if there is to be a valid, enforceable contract, the promises, or the promise and the act, must have been exchanged in return for each other. If something is done first and then there is a promise relating to such act or performance, the two are not tied together by the notion of agreement. One thing has not necessarily been done in consideration of the other. In consequence, anything promised as a result of the past performance of the act in question is simply promised gratuitously not in a binding contractual way. There is no mutuality between the act of performance and the subsequent promise from the recipient of the benefit of the act of performance. The detriment suffered by the performer of the act was not suffered in return for anything, or the promise of anything, from the other party. There may have been a hope of something; even, possibly, the expectation of something. But there was no promise of anything.

The importance of the distinction between past and executed consideration lies in the fact that past consideration is not regarded as sufficient to support a

promise and create a valid contract.[167] It is vital to show that the promise sought
to be enforced was made in exchange for some present or future act to be performed
by the other party. Whether the contract in issue was entered into for present,
not past, consideration divided the British Columbia Court of Appeal in *Delaney
v. Cascade River Holidays Ltd*.[168] The plaintiff was injured while a passenger on
a raft which was travelling on "white water" during the course of an adventure
organized by the defendants. Before he was permitted to board the raft, he was
asked to sign a release which discharged the defendants from liability. If he had
not signed the release, he would not have been allowed to go on the raft and
participate in the trip. He signed, boarded the raft, and was injured by reason of,
he alleged, the defendants' breach of duty. When sued, the defendants pleaded
that they had been exempted from liability by the release. The plaintiff argued
that the release had not been agreed to by him for consideration. The consideration
for going on the raft was payment of the purchase price, which had occurred in
the past, before the signing of the release. The plaintiff was contractually entitled
to board the raft because he had paid the appropriate sum. In agreeing to let the
plaintiff on the raft, the defendants were only agreeing to what they were already
bound contractually to do.[169] This argument was accepted by Nemetz C.J.B.C.,
who dissented from the majority of the court. The latter, MacFarlane and Taggart
JJ.A., held that at the time he paid the purchase price the plaintiff had actual or
imputed knowledge that a liability waiver would be required of him before
embarkation. Therefore, the granting of such a waiver or release by him was part
of the consideration which the plaintiff was providing for the right to go on the
voyage. The factual analysis of the case according to these judges indicated that
the payment of the price for the trip occurred at or about the time the release
was signed. The immediate consideration which the plaintiff received, therefore,
was that he was permitted to enter the van and carry on with the venture, that
is, embark on the raft. It is possible, therefore, that the difference of opinion in
this case stemmed from a slightly different emphasis on certain facts or evidence
rather than upon any divergent views about the law or its application.

The distinction between truly past consideration and consideration which only
appears to be past but was provided at the request of the promisor, so as to rank
as executed consideration, may be illustrated by cases involving employment.
Promises by an employer to pay an employee in consideration of his employment
by the promisor or by an employee, to do or refrain from doing something when
the employee was already engaged in such employment, were gratuitous, not

---

167 *Eastwood v. Kenyon* (1840), 11 Ad. & El. 438 (Q.B.). Or a variation of a contract: *Ataway v.
    Stephen Avenue Mall Bd.* (1989), 96 A.R. 138 (Alta. Q.B.). There are some exceptions, *viz.*, (i)
    a subsequent promise by a discharged bankrupt to pay debts although the discharge may be enforced:
    (b) a promise to pay a statute-barred debt: (c) a promise by a minor who has reached majority
    affirming an unenforceable promise made for consideration during minority: Ontario Law Reform
    Commission, *Report on Amendment of the Law of Contract* (1987), at p. 19: compare below, pp.
    149-150. The Report recommends that promises made in recognition of a past benefit should
    be binding to the extent necessary to prevent unjust enrichment: *ibid.*, at p. 25.
168 (1983), 44 B.C.L.R. 24 (B.C.C.A.).
169 Compare above, pp. 98-103.

supported by consideration, unless some new factor was introduced, such as that the employee agreed to continue working, or that the employer would continue to employ the person in question.[170] In these cases, if the new promise was made in consideration of what had been done by the employer or employee in the past, such new promise was not supported by consideration capable of making it enforceable. Similarly, if a new promise were made to pay a past debt, that is, where the debtor promised the creditor something in consideration of the fact that the creditor, in the past, had advanced money to the debtor, such fresh promise by the debtor was given in consideration of a *past* act of the creditor. If some new factor were introduced, for example, an extension of time, or the giving of security, there would be sufficient difference or novelty to entitle a court to hold that there was fresh consideration for a new promise, not past consideration.[171]

The situation is different where the originally past consideration was rendered at the request of the present promisor *and* under such circumstances that even in the absence of an express promise the law will imply a promise in return for the act. In such circumstances, that is, where a promise would and could be implied, a subsequent express promise in respect of such past act may be treated,

> either as an admission which evidences, or as a positive bargain which fixes the amount of that reasonable remuneration on the faith of which the service was originally rendered.[172]

This statement was made in a nineteenth century English case, *Stewart v. Casey*, in which the court recognized the validity of a principle going back as far as the decision in 1615 in *Lampleigh v. Brathwait*.[173] There, services were rendered in an effort to prevent the execution of someone. Later a promise was made to pay the one giving the services in respect of what he had done. It was held that at the time he gave the services he did so at the request of the subsequent promisor, and it was implicit that there would be payment. Hence the later promise was actionable. But in *Roscorla v. Thomas*,[174] where a warranty as to the fitness of a horse was given *after* the conclusion of the contract of sale of the animal, it was decided that the only consideration for such warranty was the sale, and this was past. Therefore, the warranty was not binding, since it was not part of the original contract of sale and was given for no consideration capable of making it into a separate, distinct, and enforceable contract.

For an act done before the giving of a promise to make a payment or to confer some other benefit to be consideration for that promise, three factors or

---

170 *Maguire v. Northland Drug Co.*, [1935] S.C.R. 412 (S.C.C.); *Peerless Laundry & Cleaners Ltd. v. Neal*, [1953] 2 D.L.R. 494 (Man. C.A.). Compare *Maier v. E & B Exploration Ltd.*, [1986] 4 W.W.R. 275 (Alta. C.A.), above, p. 92.

171 *O'Brien v. Stebbins*, [1927] 2 W.W.R. 176 (Sask. C.A.); *McCoy v. Hop*, [1923] 3 D.L.R. 873 (Sask. C.A.).

172 *Stewart v. Casey*, [1892] 1 Ch. 104 at 116 (C.A.) *per* Bowen L.J. This was cited with approval by the P.C. in *Pao On v. Lau Yiu Long*, [1979] 3 All E.R. 65 at 74 (P.C.).

173 (1615), Hob. 105.

174 (1842), 3 Q.B. 234; compare *Delaney v. Cascade River Holidays Ltd.*, above, note 168.

conditions must be satisfied, as the Privy Council pointed out in *Pao On v. Lau Yiu Long*,[175]

> [t]he act must have been done at the promisor's request, the parties must have understood that the act was to be remunerated either by payment or the conferment of some other benefit, and payment, or the conferment of a benefit, must have been legally enforceable had it been promised in advance.

These three conditions were satisfied in that case. The complex facts concerned a guarantee given to a contract relating to the sale of shares by the defendants to the plaintiffs and the undertaking by the defendants to buy back some of the shares. The plaintiffs subsequently demanded that the defendants give them a guarantee as to the price at which the shares would be repurchased. This was because of the plaintiffs' fears about the market price of the shares in the future. One of the arguments raised by the defendants by way of defence to an action brought on the guarantee[176] was that it was given for past consideration and was therefore invalid. This defence was rejected by the Privy Council on the grounds that the promise given under the main agreement not to sell the shares for a year was at the request of the defendants; the parties understood at the time of the main agreement that the restriction on selling must be compensated for by the benefit of a guarantee against a drop in price and such a guarantee would be legally enforceable.

Some Canadian cases illustrate this doctrine. In *Grant v. Van Alvensleben*,[177] a promise was given to pay for past services which were originally rendered out of friendship, and without any request for their being proffered. It was held that this promise was made without consideration and was unenforceable. In *Johnson v. Forbes*,[178] a promise that P "would be taken care of" in respect of his past services to the defendant was not enforceable, as it was made without consideration. There was only a moral obligation, stemming from gratitude for what P had done, not a legal one arising from any undertaking to pay. A final excellent example is *Re Grosch*.[179] There was an agreement made between the two daughters of a testator, who were the beneficiaries under his will, and their uncle, who was the executor and trustee of the will, to pay him for services which he had rendered to them under the will while they were still infants. It was held that the consideration for this agreement was past, hence the agreement was unenforceable. The services were *not* rendered at the request of the daughters, therefore no promise to pay could be implied. In effect, the facts of this case are the complete opposite of those in the old English case of *Lampleigh v. Brathwait*. It is hardly surprising, therefore, that the court concluded that it did not come within any possible exception to the past consideration rule.

---

175 [1979] 3 All E.R. 65 at 74 (P.C.).
176 Others involved duress, see p. 318-319, and insufficiency of consideration, above p. 90.
177 (1913), 4 W.W.R. 1303 (B.C.C.A.).
178 [1931] 3 W.W.R. 757 (Alta. C.A.); compare *Rogalsky v. Rogalsky*, [1985] 2 W.W.R. 699 (Man. Q.B.); affirmed [1988] 4 W.W.R. 336 (Man. C.A.).
179 [1945] 2 W.W.R. 252 (Alta. C.A.).

6. Legality

The consideration proffered for the making of a contract must not be illegal, immoral, or contrary to public policy.[180]

What is illegal scarcely needs elaboration. The performance of an act, or the offer to perform an act which is contrary to law is illegal consideration, incapable of supporting a valid enforceable contract.[181] So too, if the proffered consideration, though not illegal, contravenes accepted morality, for example, an offer of illicit intercourse in return for the payment of money. A good illustration is provided by *Frere v. Shields*.[182] In that case the defendant promised the plaintiff an interest in his estate to induce her to return to him. The parties were married, but the marriage was bigamous. In effect, therefore, the offer was made for the purpose of obtaining the continuance or resumption of illicit cohabitation. It was held that the consideration for the promise to give the plaintiff the share of the estate was immoral, and therefore invalid. Hence an action based on an alleged contract was not available to the plaintiff.

If the consideration, though neither strictly illegal or immoral, nonetheless in some way offends public policy, it will not be regarded as capable of supporting a contract. The doctrine of public policy is not an easy one to explain or expound. However, the notion of something being contrary to public policy is well-accepted and understood in the law. For example, a compellable witness promised to give evidence in a divorce action in return for a promise by the party for whom the witness was to testify to leave the witness something in his will. Though this amounted to a larger sum of money than the cost of a subpoena under which the witness could have been forced to testify, the alleged contract was held bad and unenforceable.[183] First of all, it was a promise by the potential recipient of testamentary benefits to do something which he was already obligated to do by law, namely, give evidence, and so could be regarded, as already seen, as a gratuitous promise.[184] Secondly, since what was involved was an agreement which could have affected the course of justice, it was contrary to public policy. On the other hand in *Main v. Main*,[185] a wife agreed with her husband to assume responsibility for the child of the marriage after the marriage broke up. The husband agreed, in return, to pay a monthly amount by way of maintenance for the wife and child. It was held that this was a valid, enforceable contract. The promise to be responsible for the child was valuable consideration for the promise to pay maintenance. It was argued that this agreement was contrary to public policy as it purported to exclude the jurisdiction of the court to award maintenance to a wife. Nonetheless, the contract was valid. The parties attempted to fix the amount of maintenance

---

180 See Chapter 10.
181 *Metlege v. Ryan* (1980), 113 D.L.R. (3d) 248 (N.S.C.A.) (compromise of claim based on illegal contract was invalid since made for illegal consideration); compare above, p. 95.
182 [1939] 2 W.W.R. 396 (Sask. C.A.). *Quaere*: would this kind of case be decided the same way today? See below, pp. 387-388.
183 *Hendry v. Zimmerman*, [1948] 1 W.W.R. 385 (Man. C.A.).
184 *Ibid.*, at 293-294 *per* Coyne J.A.; compare above, p. 100.
185 [1955] 2 D.L.R. 588 (B.C.S.C.); affirmed (1956), 2 D.L.R. (2d) 341 (B.C.C.A.).

by agreement. If appropriate, the court could still have intervened at the suit of a party.

So too, in *Scivoletto v. DeDona*,[186] the contract to reimburse the plaintiff for the expenses of bringing the girl who was intended for the plaintiff's son from Italy to Canada, although she ultimately married the defendant, was not contrary to public policy. It was not a contract relating to the marriage, which might have been illegal if it purported to regulate which party the girl should marry, rather it was a contract relating to certain travelling expenses. In *Burton v. Brook*[187] the original creditor who had assigned his claim to the plaintiff—his counsel—had murdered the original debtor. Was the claim barred by the doctrine of public policy? The murder and the fact that the claimant was the murderer's counsel undoubtedly muddied the issue of whether there was consideration for the promise to pay the sum of money involved. In view of the decision with regard to consideration generally, it was not necessary to determine the question of legality.

7. Source

In the nineteenth century, decisions in England indicated that a contract could not be enforced by someone who had not provided consideration. It was necessary to show that consideration had moved from the promisee who later sought to uphold the promise.[188] A stranger to the consideration could not take advantage of a contract, even if it was intended to operate for his benefit.[189] The House of Lords endorsed this proposition in *Dunlop Pneumatic Tyre Co. v. Selfridge*.[190] At the same time, both in the earlier cases and in the *Selfridge* case, another, perhaps even older proposition of law, was stated. A contract is a personal matter between the parties who are privy to its making; only such a party can acquire rights or be subjected to liabilities under it. As Lord Haldane said in 1915: "Our law knows nothing of a *jus quaesitum tertio* arising by way of contract."[191] The nature of the doctrine of privity, its consequences, and its qualification or modifications in recent years, are matters dealt with elsewhere.[192] The relevance of that doctrine in the present context lies in the argument that the doctrine of privity and the doctrine that "consideration must move from the promisee" are merely two way of expressing the same idea, namely, that someone has to be a party to a contract, providing consideration, before he may sue or be sued on such contract. This view has been put forward, contrary to the opinion expressed by the House of Lords in the *Selfridge*

---

186 (1961), 35 W.W.R. 44 (Alta. Dist. Ct.); above, p. 90.

187 (1956), 6 D.L.R. (2d) 464 (B.C.S.C.).

188 *Price v. Easton* (1833), 4 B. & Ad. 433. Compare *Bank of N.S. v. Drouillard-Potter* (1987), 79 A.R. 2 (Alta. M.C.). But it does not matter who receives the benefit of that consideration: *ibid.* Compare *Bank of N.S. v. Hallgarth* (1986), 32 D.L.R. (4th) 158 (B.C.C.A.).

189 *Tweddle v. Atkinson* (1861), 1 B. & S. 393.

190 [1915] A.C. 847 (H.L.).

191 *Ibid.*, at 853.

192 Chapter 5.

case, and adopted by the English Law Revision Committee in 1937,[193] that privity is distinct from the requirements of the doctrine of consideration.[194]

The traditional view requires that a person claiming the benefit of a promise in a contract: (a) must be named as a party to the contract; and (b) must have provided consideration. The more modern view would require only that the claimant be a party, as long as some other party to the contract had provided consideration. Another way of expressing these views might be to say that only promisors are parties to contracts, others named in a contract as participants or beneficiaries not being parties in a true legal sense. Alternatively, not every party, in the sense of participant or beneficiary, needs to be a promisor.[195] The traditional view is clearly supported by English authority and has been reaffirmed and rationalized[196] despite some textual and judicial support for the contradictory opinion.[197] Support for the modern view, which would negate the idea that consideration must move from the promisee, can be found in dicta in England and Australia. Those dicta may be said to have attracted at least one Canadian judge.

The English decision in which there are indications supporting the modern view is *McEvoy v. Belfast Banking Co.*[198] The father of the plaintiff transferred his money on deposit with the defendant bank to an account in the name of himself and the son (at that time an infant). The father then died. The father's executors were permitted by the bank to withdraw the money and put it in their own names, losing the money in the attempt to maintain the family business. The son sued the bank. One of the problems raised by this action was whether the bank was contractually bound to the son, which, in turn, raised the issue of consideration. In the judgment of Lord Atkin,[199] the view is propounded that if the contract is made by one party with two others (A and B), jointly and severally, then A purports to make the contract on behalf of B as well as himself "and the consideration supports such a contract." The Australian case of *Coulls v. Bagot's Executor & Trustee Co.*[200] also contains statements that promote a similar attitude although the actual decision did not require the High Court of Australia to adopt such an approach to resolve the issue. However, the language of the different judges (those in the majority as well as those dissenting) indicates that the wife did not have to supply consideration since the husband had done so. The difference of opinion

---

193 Cmd. 5449, pp. 22, 25-30.

194 Compare Flannigan, "Privity — The End of an Era (Error)" (1987), 103 L.Q. Rev. 564 at 568-569. It has been recommended that lack of consideration (and want of privity) should not render unenforceable a contract for the benefit of a third party: Ontario Law Reform Commission, *Report on Amendment of the Law of Contract* (1987), pp. 49-71.

195 Coote, "Consideration and the Joint Promisee," [1978] C.L.J. 301 at pp. 309-310.

196 *Ibid.*

197 See the references in Coote, *loc. cit.* above, note 195, at 302, notes 11-20. Compare Flannigan, *loc. cit.* above, note 194, at 564-568, 569-572.

198 [1935] A.C. 24 (H.L.), discussed by Cullity, "Joint Bank Accounts With Volunteers" (1969), 85 L.Q.R. 530 at 531-533.

199 [1935] A.C. 24 at 43 (H.L.); see also Lord Thankerton, *ibid.*, at 52; *New Zealand Shipping Co. v. A.M. Satterthwaite & Co.*, [1975] A.C. 154 at 180 (P.C.) *per* Lord Simon of Glaisdale.

200 [1967] A.L.R. 385 (Aus. H.C.).

was over the question of whether the wife was a party. The contract in this case was between the husband and a company whereby the husband gave the company the right to quarry on his land in return for a payment of royalty. The husband authorized the company to pay the money to himself and his wife jointly. The wife, as well as the husband, signed the contract (thus she was a party in one sense, if not in what has been termed the true legal sense). The issue arose, after the husband's death, of whether the company should pay the money to the wife or only to the husband's executors. In the event, for reasons not apposite here, the court held that the money was not payable to the wife. However, there are suggestions in the judgments of some members of the court that since the husband had provided consideration, the wife did not have to do so; she could be a party and could acquire rights to the money. This decision, as well as the subsequent case of *Beswick v. Beswick*[201] in the House of Lords, were utilized by Bouck J. of the Supreme Court of British Columbia in *Waugh v. Slavick*,[202] to enable plaintiffs who were signatories of a contract, but had not provided consideration, to maintain an action for specific performance of the contract. The learned judge left open the question of whether an action by those parties could have succeeded had the claim been for damages at common law for breach of contract. The reason for this distinction was that in the *Beswick* case the plaintiff was held able to sue for specific performance in her capacity as personal representative of the deceased contracting party and thus enforce the contract which was intended to confer a benefit on her in her personal, rather than representative, capacity. In the words of Bouck J.,[203]

> *Beswick v. Beswick* decided that specific performance of a contract can be ordered where the persons between whom consideration passed or their personal representatives are parties to the action. This is so despite the fact that strangers to the contract who have not given consideration may benefit from the decree. The minority came to the same conclusion in *Coulls*. The reasoning from these two authorities is attractive and I can see no reason why it should be applied in Canada. It will do justice between the parties in this action by holding them to their bargain.

The contract in this case was between various members of the family of a man who had been killed, with his infant son, in a plane accident. The purpose of the contract was to deal with the deceased man's estate, bearing in mind that this passed to the infant son and the deceased man's parents. The agreement was later repudiated by the ex-wife of the deceased man. The other parties to the agreement brought the action for specific performance which was awarded by Bouck J. The various arguments of the ex-wife, including the issue of consideration, were rejected by the judge.

These indications, taken into conjunction with the various ways in which the strictness of the privity doctrine has been modified in recent years, suggest that perhaps, the older traditional view that consideration must move from the promisee

---

201 [1968] A.C. 58 (H.L.); below, pp. 181-182.
202 (1976), 62 D.L.R. (3d) 577 at 585-587 (B.C.S.C.).
203 *Ibid.*, at 587.

is declining in importance. However, it may be premature to regard it as having completely lost all force.[204]

8. Proof

(a) Express

Normally the consideration will be expressly stated in the written document containing the contract, or in the oral exchanges that contain its terms. In some instances, however, it may be necessary to explain what the parties had in mind. Parol evidence may sometimes be admitted to explain the meaning of a written document. Parol evidence will always be admissible to prove the contents of a contract that is wholly parol and not contained in any writing.[205] Thus in *Crippen v. Hitchner*,[206] parol evidence was introduced to show the real consideration, as opposed to what appeared to be the consideration on the face of the agreement. So too, in *Kuball v. Prudential Trust Co.*,[207] the written agreement stated that the consideration for a contract was one dollar. Evidence was admissible to prove that the parties intended something larger as the true consideration for the contract. Even where no consideration is shown on the face of the document, parol evidence may establish what the consideration is, as long as the contract was not intended to be gratuitous.[208]

(b) Implied

Without specific language or parol evidence, consideration may be implicit in the agreement or bargain struck by the parties. An agreement that does not expressly reveal any consideration for a promise which one of the parties is seeking to enforce can be shown to have been made for an implied consideration. An old case which supports this is *Brownell v. Raworth*.[209] By an agreement in writing the defendant agreed to convey certain land, subject to two mortgages, to the plaintiff. No request was ever made by the defendant to the plaintiff to take the conveyances, only that the plaintiff should accept a deed from the defendant and allow the latter to remain in possession of the land for a certain time. It was held that there was sufficient consideration for the defendant's promise to convey. A request from him to the plaintiff to take the conveyances could be implied into the arrangement and the detriment involved in his doing this was sufficient to constitute consideration. The court followed the old English case of *Bainbridge*

---

204 See, *e.g.*, *Bank of N.S. v. Drouillard-Potter*, above, note 188.
205 Below, pp. 455 *et seq.*
206 (1911), 18 W.L.R. 259 (B.C. Co. Ct.).
207 (1957), 21 W.W.R. 273 (Sask. Q.B.).
208 *Niagara Structural Steel Ltd. v. Bellows*, [1965] 1 O.R. 89 (Ont. H.C.). Compare *Great Eastern Oil & Import Co. v. Chafe* (1956), 4 D.L.R. (2d) 310 at 316 (Nfld. S.C.) *per* Walsh C.J.; *Hickman (A.E.) Co. v. Roses Aluminum Ltd.* (1981), 36 Nfld. & P.E.I.R. 206 (Nfld. Dist. Ct.).
209 (1881), 21 N.B.R. 11 (N.B.C.A.).

v. Firmstone.[210] The mere acceptance of the conveyance subject to the mortgages was enough detriment to amount to consideration moving from the promisee.

Similarly, a contract under which the plaintiff company agreed to ship the defendant company's goods at certain rates and with the benefit of certain deductions was a good contract which bound the defendant company.[211] It was implied from the agreement that the plaintiff company would always ship the defendant company's goods for the duration of the contract. The fact that the plaintiff company had never expressly undertaken to do this, whereas the defendant company had expressly agreed to ship all their products through the plaintiff company's ships, did not matter. The contrary undertaking by the plaintiff company was implied. In the same way, in *Great Eastern Oil & Import Co. v. Chafe*[212] a contract involving the sale of petrol was "instinct with obligation". Hence, although the contract only expressly referred to one party's undertaking to *purchase* the petrol, it was implied that the other party would *sell* the petrol to the one who had agreed to purchase. Therefore there was mutuality and consideration.

9. Exceptions

(a) Contracts under seal[213]

If a contract is contained in a deed, that is, a document under seal, there is no need for there to be consideration moving from either party towards the other.[214] It is only in the absence of such a deed that consideration is required.[215] The converse of this, as was pointed out by Hunt J. in *Yellowega v. Yellowega,*[216]

---

210 (1838), 3 Ad. & El. 743; above, p. 93.

211 *Can. Pac. Navigation Co. v. Victoria Packing Co.* (1889), 3 B.C.R. 490 (B.C.C.A.).

212 Above, note 208, applied in *Case's Insulation & Siding Ltd. v. Gordon* (1991), 45 C.L.R. 252 (N.B.Q.B.). Compare *Caisse Populaire Notre Dame Ltée v. Moyen* (1967), 59 W.W.R. 129 (Sask. Q.B.) which raised, *inter alia*, the effect of a loan without an express promise to pay; *held*, such a promise could be implied, though whether on the basis of consideration, *i.e.*, contract, or restitution, *i.e.*, quasi-contract, is uncertain.

213 For the recommendation that the seal should be denied legal effect, *i.e.*, its replacement by a witnessed signed document, see *Report on Amendment of the Law of Contract*, above, note 194, Chapter 3. Compare the discussion and conclusions by Herschorn, "Documents Under Seal: Consequences and Complications" (1989), 10 Advocates' Q. 129.

214 *Bay v. Three Hebemick Enterprises Ltd.* (1983), 21 Man. R. (2d) 51 (Man. Q.B.) (even if the consideration is not paid as stated in the deed); *Hickey v. Hickey* (1988), 86 N.B.R. (2d) 421 (N.B.C.A.); affirming (1988), 86 N.B.R. (2d) 428 (N.B.Q.B.). As to what is sufficient for a document under seal, see *Bank of N.S. v. Forest F. Ross & Son Ltd.* (1982), 40 N.B.R. (2d) 563 (N.B.Q.B.) (no need for a proper wafer); *C.I.B.C. v. Dene Mat Const. Ltd.*, [1988] 4 W.W.R. 344 (N.W.T.S.C.) (no need for formation of sealing and delivery; anything on the document can be a seal). On deeds, see Youdan, "The Formal Requirements of a Deed" (1979), 5 B.L.R. 71. Note that the seal itself may not be necessary if the intention was clear: *N.B. v. Olson* (1984), 57 N.B.R. (2d) 321 (N.B.Q.B.); *e.g.*, if the document states it was given under seal: *C.I.B.C. v. Dene Mat Const. Ltd.*, above. Contrast *Royal Bank of Can. v. Kiska* (1967), 63 D.L.R. (2d) 582 (Ont. C.A.) with *Linton v. Royal Bank of Can.* (1966), 60 D.L.R. (2d) 398 (Ont. H.C.).

215 *Re/Max Garden City Realty Inc. v. 828294 Ont. Ltd.* (1992), 8 O.R. (3d) 787 at 790 (Ont. Gen. Div.).

216 (1968), 66 W.W.R. 241 at 242 (Man. Q.B.).

is that a seal is not necessary when valuable consideration is given by one party to the other.

Why contracts under seal are regarded in this special light by the common law is not altogether clear. It may be that such instruments record the seriousness of the parties' intentions, thus replacing the necessity for consideration as evidence of an intent to enter into legal relations. But it has long been recognized that the purpose served by consideration is not to establish such an intent; despite the presence of consideration, the intent to enter into legal relations must also be shown.[217] Hence, the presence of a seal affixed to a document should not remove the need to show that intent. It has also been suggested that a seal "imports" consideration.[218] That, too, is questionable. There are cases which indicate that even if a contract is under seal, it may be possible, indeed even necessary, to go behind the seal and investigate whether or not there was consideration for the making of the contract. Thus in *Maguire v. Northland Drug Co.*,[219] Dysart J., in the Supreme Court of Canada said,

> [t]here was ample consideration for the bond. Although the necessity of proving consideration for the covenant is not dispensed with by the presence of a seal *in a case of this kind.* . . .[220]

He then went on to explain that the circumstances indicated that there was consideration, based on the promise not to dismiss the employee.

A more revealing decision is that of Egbert J. of the Supreme Court of Alberta in *Chilliback v. Pawliuk*.[221] The plaintiff signed a release, purporting to be under seal, in respect of his potential claim for damages against the defendant. When he sued for such damages, the defendant raised the plea that the claim was precluded by reason of this agreement. On its face the document expressly stated that there was no consideration for the agreement. The defendant argued that as the document was under seal the lack of consideration did not matter. The learned judge held that the release was not an instrument under seal; hence, because there was no consideration, it was not enforceable against the plaintiff. However, he went on to hold that even if it had been a document under seal, it would not have been enforceable for want of consideration. He said,[222]

> the document itself, as well as the surrounding evidence, negatives consideration, so that the mere presence of a seal cannot "import" consideration, or raise an irrebuttable presumption of a consideration which did not, in fact, exist. The Court, in the exercise of its equitable jurisdiction may look at the true bargain between the parties, and refuse to enforce an otherwise unenforceable agreement, merely because it is under seal.

This is a strange doctrine. It appears to run contrary to every fundamental principle

---

217 Above, pp. 26-31.

218 *Alberta (Dir. of Employment Standards) v. Sanche* (1992), 2 Alta. L.R. (3d) 14 (Alta. Master); affirmed (1992), 5 Alta. L.R. (3d) 243 (Alta. Q.B.).

219 [1935] S.C.R. 412 (S.C.C.); above, p. 101.

220 [1935] S.C.R. 412 at 415 (S.C.C.); emphasis added.

221 (1956), 17 W.W.R. 534 (Alta. S.C.).

222 *Ibid.*, at 540.

of the common law. While there may be a general equitable jurisdiction to relieve a party from an onerous or unconscionable transaction,[223] to state that a document under seal is not conclusive of the bargain or agreement between the parties, and that consideration may still be required, is perhaps going rather far. In cases of contracts not under seal, there have been instances of courts treating the stipulated consideration as not being the true consideration, especially if it can be regarded as nugatory, though not illusory, and this despite the doctrine that adequacy of consideration is not usually a matter for a court to determine. Such instances may be said to involve some fraud, or equally unconscionable conduct on the part of one side to the bargain.[224] Nor did they concern contracts under seal.

It is not surprising that the dicta and reasoning of Egbert J. in this case were subjected to critical examination.[225] That comment expressed the view that the decision of Egbert J. confused the status and effect of a seal and rendered an important historical institution no longer valid or useful. A subsequent comment[226] considered the role of the seal in modern times to be a fiction and a deception; if a gratuitous promise was to be enforced, other means should be devised to do so, not the retention of the archaic concept of the document under seal. Therefore, the decision and language of Egbert J. were justified and desirable as being more in conformity with reality and everyday practice.

The judgment of Egbert J., it is suggested, is based upon historical and doctrinal misconceptions, in that it confuses a well-accepted distinction between a parol contract and one under seal. If there is to be relief from transactions, whether under seal or not, it should not be on the basis of adequacy of consideration but on some more general equitable notion of unconscionability that recognizes common-law principles but provides relief from their strict application in appropriate circumstances.

(b) Statutory changes

In Canada the harshness of the rule in *Pinnel's Case*[227] has been alleviated by statutory alteration of the law relating to consideration.[228] In Ontario, Manitoba, Saskatchewan, Alberta, and British Columbia as well as the Northwest Territories and the Yukon, provision has been made by statute[229] to permit an accord and

---

223 Below, pp. 325-336.

224 Above, p. 91.

225 Weston (1956), 34 Can. Bar Rev. 453.

226 Helman (1956), 34 Can. Bar Rev. 873.

227 (1602), 5 Co. Rep. 117a.

228 For the fate of *Pinnel's Case* in Canada, at common law and under the statutes, see Brenner, "Part Payment of a Debt by Accord and Satisfaction: The Canadian Experience" (1980), 18 U.W.O.L.R. 369.

229 Alberta: Judicature Act, R.S.A. 1980, c. J-1, s. 13(1); B.C.: Law and Equity Act, R.S.B.C. 1979, c. 224, s. 40; Manitoba: Mercantile Law Amendment Act, R.S.M. 1987, c. M120, s. 6; Ontario: Mercantile Law Amendment Act, R.S.O. 1990, c. M.10, s. 16; Saskatchewan: Queen's Bench Act, R.S.S. 1978, c. Q-1, s. 45(7). Compare also Judicature Act, R.S.Y.T. 1986, c. 96, s. 25; Judicature Act, R.S.N.W.T. 1988, c. J-1, s. 40.

satisfaction to occur when a smaller sum is given or promised in the place of the originally larger amount owed by the debtor.[230] The language of one such statute (there are minor differences in some provinces)[231] reads as follows:

> Part performance of an obligation either before or after a breach thereof when expressly accepted by the creditor in satisfaction or rendered in pursuance of an agreement for that purpose, though without any new consideration, shall be held to extinguish the obligation.[232]

It will be seen that the wording refers to "an obligation", suggesting that it covers more than the payment of money. However, it would seem that the cases decided under these statutes have been concerned with the problem raised in *Pinnel's Case* and *Foakes v. Beer*,[233] rather than with any other sort of obligation.[234]

The part performance must be in satisfaction of the whole obligation, and not for any other reason,[235] and it must be in pursuance of the new agreement.[236] It will be ineffective unless what is agreed is performed.[237] What was the intention of the parties in making this new arrangement is a question of fact.[238] The question was raised, however, though not answered by the court in *Rommerill v. Gardener*,[239]

---

230 The effect of these statutes is to change the principle of *accord and satisfaction* in these instances: *Udy v. Doan*, [1940] 2 W.W.R. 440 at 443 (Sask. K.B.) *per* Anderson J.; *Mason v. Johnston* (1893), 20 O.A.R. 412 at 417 (Ont. C.A.) *per* Osler J.A. Compare *Bell v. Quagliotti*, [1918] 2 W.W.R. 915 (B.C.S.C.). There must be an *agreement*, however, see *Brock and Can. Bank of Commerce v. Faider*, [1948] 2 W.W.R. 581 (Alta. C.A.). The statutory defence is different from the plea of accord and satisfaction: *Esquire Heating & Air Conditioning Ltd. v. Hoffman*, [1984] 6 W.W.R. 730 (Alta. M.C.). On accord and satisfaction, see below, pp. 551-553.

231 *E.g.*, in Manitoba the acceptance must be in writing: see *MacKiw v. Rutherford*, [1921] 2 W.W.R. 329 (Man. K.B.).

232 Mercantile Law Amendment Act, R.S.O. 1990, c. M.10, s. 16, on which see Ontario Law Reform Commission, *Report on Amendment of the Law of Contract* (1987), pp. 9-13. See also Manitoba Law Reform Commission, Report No. 62, *Report on Small Projects, Part I* (1985), O.L.R.C. *Report*, p. 12, note 33.

233 (1884), 9 App. Cas. 605 (H.L.).

234 *Rommerill v. Gardener* (1962), 40 W.W.R. 265 (B.C.C.A.); but see *Bell v. Quagliotti*, above, note 230.

235 *Hermiston v. Bulych* (1954), 14 W.W.R. 47 (Sask. C.A.); compare *Somers v. Liberty School Dist.*, [1928] 1 W.W.R. 884 (Alta. Dist. Ct.); *Kelly, Douglas & Co. v. Simister* (1954), 13 W.W.R. 107 (B.C.S.C.); affirmed (1954), 13 W.W.R. 494 (B.C.C.A.).

236 *Williams (A.R.) Mach. Co. v. Winnipeg Storage Ltd.*, [1926] 3 W.W.R. 451 (Man. K.B.); reversed without affecting this point, [1927] 3 W.W.R. 665 (Man. C.A.). Even, possibly, when this was not known; see *Blair v. Mut. Supplies Ltd.*, [1935] 3 W.W.R. 578 (Alta.S.C.).

237 *Udy v. Doan*, [1940] 2 W.W.R. 440 at 446 (Sask. K.B.); criticized by Brenner, *loc cit.* above, note 228, at 406-411. The O.L.R.C. *Report*, above, note 232, recommends (pp. 10-12, 32) that the statute should apply to *executory* as well as executed agreements. It also recommends (pp. 12-13, 33) that such an agreement should be revocable by the obligee for a breach that is not merely trivial or technical. It is also recommended that no consideration should be necessary for an agreement to waive performance of an obligation (pp. 10-12, 32).

238 *Cohen & Sweigman, Re; Ex parte Gelman*, [1925] 4 D.L.R. 359 (Ont. S.C.); compare *Phillip v. Massey-Ferguson Finance Co.*, [1973] 1 W.W.R. 443 (Sask. Dist. Ct.) where the debtor gave more than he owed at the material time and the conduct of the creditor was held to amount to acceptance as accord and satisfaction of the entire debt.

239 (1962), 40 W.W.R. 265 (B.C.C.A.), on which see Brenner, *loc. cit.* above, note 228, at 420-422.

whether the creditor could demand the payment of the greater sum and so determine the agreement for payment of the lesser amount in settlement despite such agreement, as long as the agreement remained unperformed. In the earlier case of *Hoolahan v. Hivon*[240] it was held that part performance of an obligation extinguishes it: (1) when the part performance is accepted by the creditor in lieu of full performance;[241] or (2) where a pre-existing agreement to substitute part performance for full performance without there being any new consideration for such agreement, is undertaken by the debtor. As long as the debtor is carrying out such agreement, which might presumably involve some period of time, for example, where payment is on a monthly basis, it was said that the creditor could not revoke the agreement for lack of consideration. This still leaves undecided what would happen if the creditor, having agreed to accept the lesser sum, perhaps on certain conditions, changes his mind and revokes his agreement before the debtor has started, or has had the opportunity to start to fulfil the part performance agreed upon in the second "contract".[242]

There are problems raised by this statutory alteration of the law which have not been resolved by the courts.[243] The outer limits of the sections have yet to be defined.[244]

(c) Promissory estoppel[245]

If the first exception to the necessity for proving that there was consideration for a contract existed at common law, and the second has been the product of statutory intervention, the third is, in a way, the offspring of equity, although in more recent times it may have become firmly enshrined as a part of the common

---

240 [1944] 3 W.W.R. 120 (Alta. S.C.); Brenner, *loc. cit.* above, note 228, at 415-417.

241 Compare *Woodlot Services Ltd. v. Flemming* (1977), 83 D.L.R. (3d) 201 (N.B.C.A.) a New Brunswick case where there was no reference to any statute, but the issue was whether the creditor accepted part payment as discharging the full debt; in the event he did not, so he could cash the cheque in part payment and sue for the balance of the debt.

242 See, on revocation the recommendations of the Ontario Law Reform Commission, above, note 232.

243 Brenner, *loc. cit.* above, note 228, at pp. 423-426.

244 *Ibid.*, at 426. Hence, the recommendations by the Ontario and Manitoba Law Reform Commissions, above, note 232.

245 Fridman, "Promissory Estoppel" (1957), 35 Can. Bar Rev. 279; Fridman, "The Basis of Contractual Obligation" (1974), 7 Loyola of Los Angeles L.R. 1. Reference may also be made to Jackson, "Estoppel as a Sword" (1968), 81 L.Q.R. 84, 223; Atiyah, *Consideration in Contracts: A Fundamental Restatement* (1971); Sutton, *Consideration Reconsidered* (1974), especially pp. 37-142; Thompson, "From Representation to Expectation: Estoppel as a Cause of Action," [1983] C.L.J. 257; Manwaring, "Promissory Estoppel in the Supreme Court of Canada" (1987), 10 Dalhousie L.J. No. 3, 43. See also Feinman, "Promissory Estoppel a Judicial Method" (1984), 97 H.L.R. 678; Feinman, "The Meaning of Reliance: A Historical Perspective" [1984] Wisconsin L.R. 1373.

For the attempt to use the doctrine of promissory estoppel in the context of labour law, in cases involving the application of a collective agreement, see, *e.g.*, *Smoky River Coal Ltd. v. U.S.W.A., Local 7621* (1985), 53 A.R. 150 (Alta. C.A.).

law.[246] It is hardly strange, therefore, that the doctrine to be discussed in this section of this chapter, has been variously called "quasi-estoppel", "equitable estoppel"[247] and "promissory estoppel".[248]

Although the idea of estoppel is an old one, long-established in the common law, and although there are cases going back to the seventeenth century in which courts of equity have given a slightly different interpretation and application to that common law idea,[249] the modern concept of promissory estoppel as it affects the creation and continuance of contractual rights and duties really stems from the decision of the House of Lords in *Hughes v. Metro. Railway Co.*[250] At common law, "estoppel" simply refers to the notion that once a man has told a lie he cannot afterwards tell the truth if, in the meantime, the innocent victim of the lie has acted on it in a significant manner. Put in more precise legal terms, as was indicated in the House of Lords in *Jorden v. Money,*[251] if one party makes a representation as to present or past fact upon which the other party relies to his detriment, the representor cannot afterwards repudiate the representation and allege the true facts. What *Jorden v. Money* clarified, however, was that any such representation had to be as to the past or present if, without being put in a strictly contractual form, it was going to be binding upon the representator. If a representation were as to the *future* state of things it would have to be made contractually if it was to be binding and have legal effect. In other words it would have to be supported or "bought" by consideration.[252] Promises as to the future are contracts or they are nothing. Indeed it has been stressed that even to vary an existing contract or to produce a valid waiver of contractual rights which would result in a kind of variation

---

246 There is now no real distinction between common law and equity: *United Scientific Hldgs. v. Burnley Borough Council,* [1978] A.C. 904 (H.L.).

247 In *Baxter (M.L.) Equip. Ltd. v. GEAC Can. Ltd.* (1982), 36 O.R. (2d) 150 at 157-159 (Ont. H.C.) *per* Rutherford J., the doctrine is described as "equitable estoppel"; compare *Owen Sound Pub. Library Bd. v. Mial Dev. Ltd.* (1979), 102 D.L.R. (3d) 685 at 690 (Ont. C.A.); compare Goff J. in *Société Italo-Belge pour le Commerce et l'Industrie S.A. v. Palm & Vegetable Oils (Malaysia) Sdn Bhd,* [1982] 1 All E.R. 19 at 25. But equitable estoppel may also include "proprietary estoppel" (below): *Vandervell's Trusts (No. 2), Re,* [1974] Ch. 269 at 300-301 (C.A.). It should be differentiated from "estoppel by convention", which is a rare type of estoppel described as estoppel arising from contract: *Colchester Borough Council v. Smith,* [1991] 2 All E.R. 29 at 63 *per* Ferris J.; affirmed [1992] 2 All E.R. 561 (C.A.). See further below p. 129, note 285.

248 *Woodhouse A.C. Israel Cocoa S.A. v. Nigerian Produce Marketing Co.,* [1972] A.C. 741 at 758 (H.L.) *per* Lord Hailsham L.C.; *Ajayi v. Briscoe (R.T.) (Nigerian),* [1964] 3 All E.R. 556 at 559 (P.C.) *per* Lord Hodson.

249 Fridman, 35 Can. Bar Rev. 279 at 291-292.

250 (1877), 2 A.C. 439 (H.L.).

251 (1854), 5 H.L. Cas. 185 (H.L.).

252 Sometimes this has been achieved by treating the situation as involving a "unilateral" contract (above, pp. 69-76), in which the performance of the requested act is the consideration: *Frankel Structural Steel Ltd. v. Goden Holdings Ltd.* (1969), 5 D.L.R. (3d) 15 (Ont. C.A.); varied (1971), 16 D.L.R. (3d) 736 (S.C.C.): followed in *Rusonik v. Can. Trust Co.* (1986), 39 R.P.R. 263 (Ont. H.C.); additional reasons (December 16, 1986), Doc. No. 40730/79 (Ont. H.C.); affirmed (January 22, 1988), Doc. No. CA348/86 (Ont. C.A.).

of the original contract between the parties, the common law requires that there be consideration for such new arrangement to be valid and binding.[253]

This common-law position has been affected by the equitable doctrine enunciated by Lord Cairns in the *Hughes* case.[254] This was stated in these words:

> ... but it is the first principle upon which all Courts of Equity proceed, that if parties who have entered into definite and distinct terms involving certain legal results — certain penalties or legal forfeiture — afterwards by their own act or with their own consent enter upon a course of negotiation which has the effect of leading one of the parties to suppose that the strict rights arising under the contract will not be enforced, or will be kept in suspense, or held in abeyance, the person who might otherwise have enforced those rights will not be allowed to enforce them where it would be inequitable having regard to the dealings which have taken place between the parties.

The effect and function of the doctrine in the *Hughes* case was to allow courts some flexibility when dealing with strict legal rights arising out of contract where the conduct of the parties could be interpreted so as to make such flexibility legitimate.[255] The courts gave effect to the language and intentions of the parties, not to some equitable doctrine that could permit a court to distort contractual rights and obligations if it were reasonable to do so. The language of Lord Cairns in the *Hughes* case does not suggest that the courts of equity have the power to override the strict common-law requirement of consideration in order to create contractual rights and obligations where none might have existed. Such equitable estoppel, in the words of a Canadian judge,[256] might be "a means of circumventing the common-law requirement of consideration to make a promise binding." However, historically, "the concern has been to avoid going so far as to grant relief in situations where a plaintiff not in a legal relationship with the defendant acts to his detriment upon a promise made by the defendant and then sues the defendant because of the promise."[257]

The turning point in the modern law of equitable estoppel[258] was the decision

---

253 *Blomidon Mercury Sales Ltd. v. John Piercey's Auto Body Shop Ltd.* (1981), 129 D.L.R. (3d) 630 (Nfld. T.D.); *Weeks v. Rosocha* (1983), 41 O.R. (2d) 787 (Ont. C.A.). But there may be waiver without consideration if the waiver is treated in the same way as representations are under the doctrine of equitable or promissory estoppel: *Petridis v. Shabinsky* (1982), 35 O.R. (2d) 215 (Ont. H.C.); compare *Rickards (Charles) Ltd. v. Oppenhaim*, [1950] 1 K.B. 616 at 623 (C.A.) *per* Denning L.J.; *Tudale Explorations Ltd. & Bruce, Re* (1979), 20 O.R. (2d) 593 at 598-599 (Ont. Div. Ct.). See also below, pp. 543-549, on the relations between estoppel, performance of a contract, waiver of rights thereunder, and variation.

254 Above, note 250, at 448. For the suggestion that the sort of conduct justifying estoppel approximates to fraud, see *Voyager Petroleums Ltd. v. Vanguard Petroleums Ltd.*, [1982] 2 W.W.R. 36 (Alta. Q.B.), and the cases cited there.

255 *Birmingham & Dist. Land Co. v. L. & N.W. Ry.* (1888), 40 Ch. D. 268 at 286 (C.A.) *per* Bowen L.J.

256 Rutherford J. in *Baxter (M.L.) Equip. Ltd. v. GEAC Can. Ltd.* (1982), 36 O.R. (2d) 150 at 157 (Ont. H.C.).

257 *Ibid.*

258 Lloyd J. in *Syros Shipping Co. S.A. v. Elaghill Trading Co.; Proodos C., The*, [1981] 3 All E.R. 189 at 190.

of Denning J. in *Central London Property Trust Ltd. v. High Trees House Ltd.*[259] In that case and later,[260] Lord Denning gave wider effect to the *Hughes* principle. "There has been a series of decisions," he said in the *High Trees* case,[261]

> ... in which a promise was made which was intended to create legal relations and which, to the knowledge of the person making the promise, was going to be acted on by the person to whom it was made, and which was in fact so acted on. In such cases the courts have said that the promise must be honoured ... they are not cases of estoppel in the strict sense. They are really promises—promises intended to be binding, intended to be acted on, and in fact are acted on. ... The courts have not gone so far as to give a cause of action in damages for the breach of such a promise, but they have refused to allow the party making it to act inconsistently with it. It is in that sense, and that sense only, that such a promise gives rise to an estoppel.

This language led Wilson J. of the Supreme Court of British Columbia in *Sloan v. Union Oil Co.*[262] to interpret the language of an employer as creating a contractual liability to make good his "promise" or "representation" with respect to the future payment of fringe benefits to his employees, even though there was no consideration in the strict sense for such promise. Cases subsequent to the *High Trees* decision, both in England and in Canada, have corrected the impression that the words of Denning J. might have conveyed and have shown that the only true function of this doctrine is to affect existing contractual rights, not to manufacture contracts out of such "promises" or "representations". Numerous statements in English and Canadian cases can be cited to support the proposition that this use of estoppel can be made only to affect accrued or inchoate rights, not to produce contractual relations where the essential ingredients of a contract, such as consideration or a clear and ascertained agreement as to terms, are lacking.[263]

There may be the possibility of creating proprietary rights out of estoppel where the party alleging the estoppel was not invested with any such rights at common law or in equity. English decisions illustrate how the doctrine of "proprietary estoppel" has also developed from the language of Lord Cairns in the *Hughes* case.[264] The effect of this development has been to permit a party

---

259 [1947] K.B. 130.

260 *Rickards (Charles) Ltd. v. Oppenhaim*, [1950] 1 K.B. 616 (C.A.); *Combe v. Combe*, [1951] 2 K.B. 215 (C.A.); *D. & C. Bldrs. v. Rees*, [1966] 2 Q.B. 617 (C.A.); *Crabb v. Arun Dist. Council*, [1976] Ch. 179 (C.A.); *Arrale v. Costain*, [1976] 1 Lloyd's Rep. 98 at 102 (C.A.).

261 Above, note 259, at 134.

262 [1955] 4 D.L.R. 664 at 674-79 (B.C.S.C.); compare above, p. 86.

263 *Syros Shipping Co. S.A. v. Elaghill Trading Co.*, above, note 258; *Brikom Invts. v. Carr*, [1979] 2 All E.R. 753 (C.A.); *United Overseas Bank v. Jiwani*, [1977] 1 All E.R. 733; *Petridis v. Shabinsky*, above, note 253; *Gilbert Steel Ltd. v. University Const. Ltd.* (1976), 67 D.L.R. (3d) 606 (Ont. C.A.); *Zeisman v. W.P.W. Devs. Ltd.* (1976), 78 D.L.R. (3d) 619 (B.C.S.C.); *Byrne v. Napier* (1975), 62 D.L.R. (3d) 589 (Ont. H.C.); *Stairs v. N.B.* (1977), 20 N.B.R. (2d) 553 (N.B.Q.B.); *Fobasco Ltd. v. Cogan* (1990), 72 O.R. (2d) 254 at 260 (Ont. H.C.); *Campbell v. Inverness (County)* (1990), 50 M.P.L.R. 296 at 317-326 (N.S.T.D.).

264 *Inwards v. Baker*, [1965] 2 Q.B. 29 (C.A.); *Ives (E.R.) Invts. v. High*, [1967] 2 Q.B. 379 (C.A.); *Siew Soon Wah v. Yong Tong Hong*, [1973] A.C. 836 (P.C.); *Crabb v. Arun Dist. Council*, above, note 260; *Pascoe v. Turner*, [1979] 2 All E.R. 945 (C.A.); *Greasley v. Cooke*, [1980] 3 All E.R.

to maintain some kind of proprietary interest in land against the assertion of the owner's strict legal rights, where the owner's conduct has misled the party alleging estoppel. There has been reliance by such party to his detriment, and it would be inequitable to allow the owner to resile from his representation or promise and assert his rights as an owner against the other party.[265] The possibility that some sort of proprietary right may emerge from estoppel should not lead to the conclusion that from such estoppels may emerge a contract. In the context of contract, such estoppels operate "as a shield and not a sword". They may be raised by way of defence to an action brought on the original contract. They may not be utilized to create a contractual right upon which an action for breach of such contract can be founded.[266]

This has been denied by some commentators.[267] Their view has been given credence and seemingly, acceptance, by the Ontario Division Court in *Re Tudale Explorations Ltd. and Bruce*.[268] Tudale Explorations was the owner of certain mining claims. They gave a company called Teck the right and option to explore and develop the claims for three years. The agreement between the parties provided that the shares were held by an escrow agent and Teck and at its option could require the claims be transferred into the name of a company to be incorporated in a certain manner, the shares of which would be issued in certain proportions to the parties. This option had to be exercised within three years. On failure by

---

710 (C.A.). See also Thompson, "From Representation to Exception: Estoppel as a Cause of Action," [1983] C.L.J. 257 at 266-275. In *Crabb v. Arun Dist. Council*, above, note 260, at 193, Scarman L.J. questioned the validity of the distinction between proprietary and promissory estoppel; see also Thompson, *loc. cit.*, above, at pp. 275-278; compare *Attorney-General of Hong Kong v. Humphrey's Estate (Queen's) Gardens Ltd.*, [1987] A.C. 114 (P.C.); *Gillies v. Keogh*, [1989] 2 N.Z.L.R. 327 at 331 *per* Cooke P., at 344-346 *per* Richardson J.

265 In this respect, note *Hastings Minor Hockey Assn. v. Pac. Nat. Exhibition* (1981), 129 D.L.R. (3d) 721 (B.C.C.A.), where the plaintiff failed to establish the estoppel.

266 To quote Denning L.J. in *Combe v. Combe*, above, note 260, at 220: "The doctrine of consideration is too firmly fixed to be overthrown by a sidewind . . .it still remains a cardinal necessity of the formation of a contract, though not of its modification or discharge." In *Secretary of State for Employment v. Globe Elastic Thread Co.*, [1979] 2 All E.R. 1077 at 1082 (H.L.) Lord Wilberforce said: "Even if an estoppel may give rise to a contractual obligation, it does not follow . . . that a contract gives rise to an estoppel." The meaning of this is not clear. However, Lord Wilberforce relied on the remarks of Lord Hailsham L.C. In *Woodhouse A.C. Israel Coca S.A. v. Nigerian Produce Markeint Co.*, [1972] A.C. 741 at 758 (H.L.) where the cases on promissory estoppel were said to be in need of review and reduction to a coherent body of doctrine. They were not to be regarded with suspicion, but they raised problems of coherent exposition. Is this implied criticism of the doctrine, or only of its scope and effect?

267 Waddams, *Law of Contracts*, 3rd ed. (1993), paras. 197-200; Reiter, "Courts, Consideration and Common Sense" (1977), 27 U.T.L.J. 439 at 480. See also Estey J. in *Fort Francis v. Boise Cascade Can. Ltd.; Boise Cascade Can. Ltd. v. Ont.; Ont. v. Boise Cascade Can. Ltd.* (1983), 46 N.R. 108 at 136 (S.C.C.) on the "uncertainty" of the doctrine.

268 (1978), 20 O.R. (2d) 593 (Ont. Div. Ct.). See also the comments by Rice J.A. in *Robichaud v. Caisse populaire de Pokemouche Ltée* (1990), 105 N.B.R. (2d) 227 at 246-248 (N.B.C.A.), where the idea of estoppel as a sword as well as a shield is supported. See also the comments of Lord Denning in *Evenden v. Guildford City Assn. Football Club*, [1975] 3 All E.R. 269 at 273 (C.A.), on which see *Co-op. Trust Co. of Can. and Atl. Steel Bldgs. Ltd., Re* (1982), 134 D.L.R. (3d) 316 at 322 (N.S.C.A.).

Teck to exercise the option, the shares would revert to Tudale. The agreement also provided that it could only be modified by instrument in writing signed by the parties. The original time for the exercise of the option was later extended by a few months. Before the expiration of the extended time for exercise of the option, there were conversations between officers of the two companies, the ultimate result of which was that the president of Tudale rejected the request for a further 60-day extension of that option period, but said in a letter that Tudale would allow Teck "sufficient time to submit your proposal for a joint venture." That letter arrived after the time for exercise of the option had expired. A few days later Teck purported to exercise the option, although Tudale had previously stated that the agreement was terminated. Tudale applied for a vesting order, claiming that Tudale was entitled to the mining claims. The Mining and Lands Commissioner found in favour of Tudale and issued the order. Teck appealed to the Divisional Court. The appeal was allowed. The ground of this decision was that Tudale had agreed to extend the time for exercising the option and then had repudiated the agreement on the basis of expiration of the time for its exercise. Teck had acted on the representation to its detriment. On the application of the case law that was extensively examined by the court, Tudale could not deny the extension or refuse to give Teck a reasonable time to regain its position. That the promise was oral, lacked consideration, and related to a future event, was not material. The doctrine of estoppel applied to assist Teck. Nor, according to the court, did it matter that the estoppel was being used as a sword and not a shield. This suggests, as the court earlier stated, that the distinction was of no importance.[269] However, it was also said by the court that the position of Teck in this case was such that it was not the plaintiff seeking to wield the sword, but the defendant claiming the benefit of a shield. Teck's claim was based upon the contract. "The promise of extension is set up only as a defence of Tudale's assertion that the rights under that contract had expired."[270] Hence, it is suggested, the decision in this case did not require the conclusion that the conduct of the parties created a contract by estoppel; the facts involved a variation or waiver of strict contractual rights in consequence of conduct which could involve an estoppel. The case, in fact, is yet another illustration of the application of the doctrine as a "shield" in the way in which other decisions have stated and used the doctrine. Secondly, the *dicta* in that case, which seem to support the use of estoppel as a "sword" as well as a "shield", contradict decisions and *dicta* in other Canadian cases, including decisions of courts higher in rank than the Divisional Court.[271] Whatever was said in the *Tudale* case to suggest that contracts can arise

---

269 *Re Tudale Explorations & Bruce* (1978), 20 O.R. (2d) 593 at 597 (Ont. Div. Ct.); compare *Conwest Exploration Co. v. Letain*, [1964] S.C.R. 20 (S.C.C.).

270 (1978), 20 O.R. (2d) 593 at 597 (Ont. Div. Ct.).

271 *E.g., Gilbert Steel Ltd. v. University Const. Ltd.*, above, note 263; *MacLeod v. Dom. (Town) School Commrs.* (1958), 16 D.L.R. (2d) 587 (N.S.S.C.); *Causeway Shopping Centre Ltd. v. Thompson & Sutherland Ltd.* (1965), 54 D.L.R. (2d) 649 (N.S.C.A.); *Watson v. Can. Permanent Trust Co.* (1972), 27 D.L.R. (3d) 735 (B.C.S.C.); affirmed (1974), 66 D.L.R. (3d) 85 (B.C.C.A.); *Bank of Montreal v. Glendale (Atlantic) Ltd.* (1977), 76 D.L.R. (3d) 303 (N.S.C.A.); *Can. Superior Oil Ltd. v. Paddon-Hughes Dev. Co.*, [1970] S.C.R. 932 (S.C.C.). Contrast, however, the contrary view expressed in

out of estoppel cannot stand with the manifold indications in Canadian cases, echoing what has been said in English decisions, that the doctrine of "promissory estoppel" or "equitable estoppel" operates only to modify or qualify previously created contractual rights and obligations and can provide only a defence to an action brought on duly and validly created contracts.[272]

The situation is somewhat different in the United States.[273] The *Second Restatement of Contract*[274] reformulated the original way in which the promissory estoppel doctrine was put in the *First Restatement*,[275] to the extent of modifying the enforceability of such "promises" by limiting the remedy of the promisee to whatever justice required, which does not necessarily involve an action for enforcement. However, there are authorities which suggest, though this is neither clear nor unanimous, that under the *Second Restatement*, as under the *First Restatement*, there is greater scope for the enforcement of such "gratuitous" promises unsupported by consideration, than in England or Canada.[276] The Americans appear

---

Baxter (M.L.) Equip. Ltd. v. GEAC Can. Ltd. (1982), 36 O.R. (2d) 150 at 158 (Ont. H.C.); *Edwards v. Harris-Intertype (Can.) Ltd.* (1983), 40 O.R. (2d) 558 at 570 (Ont. H.C.); affirmed (1984), 46 O.R. (2d) 286 (Ont. C.A.); compare *Petridis v. Shabinsky* (1982), 35 O.R. (2d) 215 at 221 (Ont. H.C.) ("even if the doctrine can be used as a sword to establish a claim rather than as a shield in defence of a claim"); *Robichaud v. Caisse Populaire de Pokemouche Ltée*, above, note 268.

272 Compare some other illustrations of the use of promissory estoppel: *C.N.R. and Beatty, Re* (1981), 128 D.L.R. (3d) 236 (Ont. H.C.) (labour relations and arbitration); *Gillis v. Bourgard* (1983), 145 D.L.R. (3d) 570 (Ont. C.A.) (insurance); but see *Smokey River Coal Ltd. v. U.S.W.A. Loc. 7621* (1985), 53 A.R. 150 (Alta. C.A.).

273 Compare Rutherford J. in *Baxter (M.L.) Equip. Ltd. v. GEAC Can. Ltd.* (1982), 36 O.R. (2d) 150 at 157 (Ont. H.C.): "In the United States, relief in this situation would be granted pursuant to their doctrine of injurious reliance. Equitable estoppel does not go nearly so far."

274 Paragraph 90, which reads,
> a promise which the promisor should reasonably expect to induce action or forbearance on the part of the promisee or a third person and which does induce such action or forbearance is binding if injustice can be avoided only by enforcement of a promise. The remedy granted for breach may be limited as justice requires.

For discussion of the position in the U.S., see: Knapp, "Reliance in the Revised Restatement: The Proliferation of Promissory Estoppel" (1981), 8 Col. L.R. 52; Metzger & Phillips, "The Emergence of Promissory Estoppel as an Independent Theory of Recovery" (1983), 35 Rutgers L.R. 472; and for an argument against continuance of the doctrine, Feinman, "The Last Promissory Estoppel Article" (1992), 61 Fordham L.R. 303. See also, Herman, "Detrimental Reliance in Louisiana Law" (1984), 58 Tulane L.R. 707 (for a discussion of the issue in a civil law jurisdiction). See also Ontario Law Reform Commission, *Report on Amendment of the Law of Contract* (1987), pp. 29-30.

275 Which was in the following terms,
> any promise which the promisor should reasonably expect to induce action or forbearance of a definite and substantial character on the part of the promisee and which does induce such action or forbearance is binding if injustice can be avoided only by enforcement of the promise.

See Fridman, "Promissory Estoppel" (1957), 35 Can. Bar Rev. 279 at 282-290 for the original *Restatement* proposition, its background, and its application. See also Sutton, *Consideration Reconsidered*, pp. 145-187.

276 Fridman, "The Basis of Contractual Obligation" (1974), 7 Loyola of Los Angeles L.R. 1 at 16-17. It is to be noted that in the U.S. strong support for the positive enforcement of such promises is to be found in cases concerned with charitable subscriptions, on which see above, pp. 87-90.

to have developed a notion of "injurious reliance" that has attracted considerable attention on the part of some writers who have attempted to propound the view that contracts can emerge from reliance on the conduct of another party where such reliance would cause injury if the "promise" were not recognized and enforced in some way by the court, even though there was no contract in the strict technical sense between the parties, and where such reliance and possible injury, in consequences, were within the reasonable expectations of the party whose promise was relied on by the other party.[277] Notwithstanding the strong arguments put forward in support of such proposition and the occasional suggestion by courts that "reasonable expectations" are a criterion for determining the effect of parties' conduct,[278] the better view is that the law in Canada, as well as England, has not yet accepted that there can be contracts, or relationships akin to contracts, between parties merely in consequence of some statement or other conduct by one party which induces another party to act, or refrain from acting, in reliance on such statement or conduct.[279] Situations like that might give rise to some liability in tort (if there were fraud or negligence), or to possible restitutionary recovery where one party has been unjustly enriched or benefited by the other; or possibly, one party has been unjustly impoverished; or to the modification or qualification or suspension of contractual rights and obligations as between the parties in question, where there was such a contract already between them. Beyond these possibilities, the law has not proceeded.

Such is the current status of the doctrine. The essential features of promissory estoppel must now be examined.[280]

---

277 Reiter, "Contracts, Torts, Relations and Reliance" in Reiter & Swan, *Studies in Contract Law* (1980), p. 235; compare Reiter & Swan, "Contracts and the Protection of Reasonable Expectations", *ibid.*, p. 1. See also the discussion of promissory estoppel and reliance in *Mentuck v. Canada*, [1986] 3 F.C. 249 at 261-269 (Fed. T.D.).

278 See, *e.g., Leading Invts. Ltd. v. New Forest Invts., Ltd.; Liebig (H.W.) & Co. v. Leading Invts. Ltd.* (1981), 126 D.L.R. (3d) 75 at 85 (Ont. C.A.); *Cathcart Inspection Services Ltd. v. Purolator Courier Ltd.*. (1982), 139 D.L.R. (3d) 371 at 375-376 (Ont. C.A.).

279 Change, to this effect, similar to the provisions of s. 90(1) of the *Second Restatement*, has been recommended by the O.L.R.C., *Report on Amendment of the Law of Contract* (1987), pp. 30-32, 34.

A different view appears to have been adopted in Australia by the High Court in *Waltons Stores (Interstate) Ltd. v. Maher* (1988), 62 A.L.J.R. 110: compare *Je Maintiendrai Pty. Ltd. v. Quaglia* (1980), 26 S.A.S.R. 101; *Legione v. Hateley* (1983), 152 C.L.R. 406. See Bagot, "Equitable Estoppel and Contractual Obligations in the Light of Waltons v. Maher" (1988), 62 Aust. L.J. 926; Lindgren, "Estoppel in Contract" (1989), 12 U.N.S.W.L.J. 153. See also *Silovi Pty Ltd. v. Barbaro* (1988), 13 N.S.W.L.R. 466; *Austrotel Pty Ltd. v. Franklins Selfserve Pty. Ltd.* (1989), 16 N.S.W.L.R. 582. On estoppel generally, see *Commonwealth of Australia v. Verwayen* (1980), 170 C.L.R. 394; *Foran v. Wight* (1989), 168 C.L.R. 385. The uncertainty of the law in Australia was discussed by Kirby J. in *Lorimer v. State Bank of New South Wales* (1991), CA 40092/89: CD 284123/87 (N.S.W.C.A.).

280 Compare *Voyager Petroleums Ltd. v. Vanguard Petroleums Ltd.*, [1982] 2 W.W.R. 36 (Alta. Q.B.), applying *Willmott v. Barber* (1880), 15 Ch. D. 96 at 105-106 *per* Fry J; *Holder v. Holder*, [1968] Ch. 353 at 394 (C.A..) *per* Harman L.J.; *Can. & Dom. Sugar Co. v. C.N. (West Indies) S.S.*, [1947] A.C. 46 (P.C.); *Celona v. Kamloops Centennial (Pac. No. 269) Branch of Royal Can. Legion* (1972), 31 D.L.R. (3d) 305 (B.C.S.C.).

(1) There must have been an existing legal relationship between the parties at ✓ the time the statement on which the estoppel is founded was made.

This is clearly set out in several recent Canadian decisions[281] following that of the Supreme Court of Canada in *Canadian Superior Oil Ltd. v. Paddon-Hughes Development Co.*[282] A petroleum and natural gas lease had been extended beyond its original term until drilling was completed. The lease provided that the term would only be extended further if the property was in production. Since this had not occurred, the lease terminated. The appellant sought a declaration that the lease was valid and subsisting, arguing that the respondent was estopped from asserting that it had terminated. This was based on a representation made by the respondent after the termination date to the effect that the lease was still in existence. The court held that the lease could only be revived after its termination date by an agreement supported by consideration. The appellant could not base its action on promissory estoppel. There had to be a subsisting legal relationship between the parties when the representations, relied upon as creating an estoppel, were made. As it was put by Grange J. in *Petridis v. Shabinsky,*[283] the doctrine of promissory estoppel as it is generally understood involves an assurance by one party that it will not enforce its legal rights with the intention that the assurance be acted upon by the other party.

(2) There must be a clear promise or representation[284] made by the party against whom the estoppel is raised, establishing his intent to be bound by what he has said.[285]

---

281 *Owen Sound Pub. Library Bd. v. Mial Dev. Ltd.* (1979), 102 D.L.R. (3d) 685 (Ont. C.A.); *Petridis v. Shabinsky* (1982), 35 O.R. (2d) 215 (Ont. H.C.); *Baxter (M.L.) Equip. Ltd. v. GEAC Can. Ltd.* (1982), 36 O.R. (2d) 150 (Ont. H.C.); *Edwards v. Harris-Intertype (Can.) Ltd.* (1983), 40 O.R. (2d) 588 (Ont. H.C.); affirmed (1984), 46 O.R. (2d) 286 (Ont. C.A.). See also *Re Co-op. Trust Co. of Can. and Atl. Steel Bldgs. Ltd.* (1982), 134 D.L.R. (3d) 316 (N.S.C.A.); *Maracle v. Travellers Indemnity Co. of Can.* (1991), 80 D.L.R. (4th) 652 at 656 (S.C.C.).

282 [1970] S.C.R. 932 (S.C.C.). See also *Conwest Exploration Co. v. Letain,* [1964] S.C.R. 20 (S.C.C.); *John Burrows Ltd. v. Subsurface Surveys Ltd.,* [1968] S.C.R. 607 (S.C.C.).

283 (1982), 35 O.R. (2d) 215 at 221 (Ont. H.C.).

284 A "conditional" promise or representation will not suffice: *Colchester Dev. Ltd. v. Dalfen's Ltd.* (1979), 31 N.S.R. (2d) 684 (N.S. Co. Ct.) (promise to accept notice to vacate premises was conditional upon lessee's paying certain dues, therefore no estoppel to prevent landlord from suing for lessee's abandonment of premises).

285 This requirement of a representation or promise marks the distinction between promissory estoppel now under discussion and what has been termed "estoppel by convention". This operates where there has been an agreed statement of facts, the truth of which has been assumed by the convention of the parties as the basis of transaction into which they are about to enter: *Amalgamated Invt. & Property Co. v. Texas Commerce Int. Bank Ltd.,* [1982] Q.B. 84 (C.A.); *Norwegian American Cruises A/S v. Paul Mundy; The "Vistafjord",* [1988] 2 Lloyds Rep. 343 at 349 *per* Bingham L.J.; *Furness Withy (Australia) v. Metal Distributors (U.K.); The "Amazonia",* [1990] 1 Lloyds Rep. 235 at 246 (C.A.) *per* Staughton L.J., at 251 *per* Dillon L.J.; *Orion Ins. Co. plc. v. Sphere Drake Ins.,* [1990] 1 Lloyds Rep. 465 at 505 (C.A.) *per* Hirst J.; *The "Captain Gregos" (No. 2),* [1990] 2 Lloyds Rep. 399 at 405 (C.A.) *per* Bingham L.J. See also *Colchester Borough Council v. Smith,* [1991] 2 All E.R. 29 at 61-63 *per* Ferris J.; Treitel, *Law of Contract,* 8th ed. (1991), pp. 111-115. Estoppel by convention is a version of estoppel *in pais, i.e.,* common law estoppel: *Thompson v. Palmer* (1933), 49 C.L.R. 507 at 567 (Aust. H.C.) *per* Dixon J.; *Grundt v. Great Boulder Property*

The function of promissory estoppel is to alter or affect the legal relations between the parties. Therefore it is essential that the statement or conduct that grounds the estoppel be intended to have such consequence.[286] As Judson J. said in *Conwest Exploration Co. v. Letain*,[287] there must be "an unambiguous representation of intention . . . which was intended to be acted upon and was acted upon. . . .". This was put by Lord Denning, in an earlier English case,[288] cited by the Supreme Court of Canada in *Engineered Homes Ltd. v. Mason*,[289] as follows:

> . . . this type of equitable defence cannot be invoked unless there is some evidence that one of the parties entered into a course of negotiation which had the effect of leading the other to suppose that the strict rights under the contract would not be enforced, and I think this implies that there must be evidence from which it can be inferred that the first party intended that the legal relations created by the contract would be altered as a result of the negotiations.

In *Engineered Homes Ltd. v. Mason* three building contractors, the trustee in bankruptcy of a land development company, and a mortgagee agreed that each of the building contractors was to purchase certain lots from land originally owned by the mortgagor — the land development company. The purchase price was to be paid to the trustee in trust for the mortgagee. The trustee pressed a claim for fees. One of the contractors agreed to pay the price for lots to be purchased by him earlier than required under the agreement. The money was duly paid but not sent by the trustee to the mortgagee as stipulated in the agreement. Later the contractor claimed return of the money from the trustee. The trustee's defence was that, although the agreement by the contractor to pay the money in advance was not supported by consideration, the money had been advanced on the understanding that it would be applied to the trustee's claim for fees. Therefore the contractor was estopped from asserting his strict rights under the agreement which would have entitled the contractor to the return of the money. The Supreme Court of Canada, reversing the decision of the British Columbia Court of Appeal, held that the trustee had failed to prove a clear and unambiguous promise on the part of the contractor, whether by words or conduct, that the trustee would be released from his obligations under the agreement to transmit the money to the mortgagee. Consequently there was no estoppel and the contractor was entitled to the money.

Gold Mines Ltd. (1937), 59 C.L.R. 641 (Aust. H.C.). It has been invoked only by English courts: see, however, *Litwin Const. (1973) Ltd. v. Kiss* (1988), 52 D.L.R. (4th) 459 at 464-469 (B.C.C.A.). In any event, it is not a doctrine that affects the law relating to consideration, *i.e.*, the legal effects of a promise that has been proved to have been made. It operates to prevent a party from denying that a promise has been made, without specifying the legal effects of the assumed promise: *Amalgamated Invt. & Property Co. v. Texas Commerce Int. Bank Ltd.*, above.

286 The intent may be inferred from the evidence, even though no direct statement to such effect was made. Knowledge by the promisor that the promisee is likely to regard the promise as affecting their legal relations constitutes an appropriate basis from which to draw an inference of the necessary intent: *Owen Sound Pub. Library Bd. v. Mial Dev. Ltd.* (1979), 102 D.L.R. (3d) 685 at 693 (Ont. C.A.).

287 [1964] S.C.R. 20 at 28 (S.C.C.); compare *Pentagon Const. (1969) Co. v. U.S. Fidelity & Guar. Co.* (1977), 77 D.L.R. (3d) 189 at 205 (B.C.C.A.).

288 *Combe v. Combe*, [1951] 1 All E.R. 767 at 770 (C.A.).

289 (1983), 146 D.L.R. (3d) 577 at 581 (S.C.C.).

Similarly in *Bank of Montreal v. Loomis Armoured Car Service Ltd.*,[290] the plaintiff's action for breach of contract was not defeated by the defendants' claim of estoppel. The defendants contracted to guarantee delivery of sealed bags from the plaintiff to the consignees. The bags contained marked bills for delivery to the Bank of Canada. The bags were never in fact delivered, nor were they ever found. The defendants' employee was suspected. The plaintiff conducted investigations, including submitting the employee to polygraph tests. The plaintiff's security manager verbally informed the defendants' branch manager of the results of the investigations and that the plaintiff was closing the file on the case. The defendants later conducted their own investigations in consequence of which the employee was subsequently convicted of theft. The plaintiff then sued for breach of contract, alleging that the defendants were liable for the misconduct of their employee. The defendants pleaded that the plaintiff was estopped from suing by reason of its prior conduct and the representation that it was closing the file on the case. It was held that no promissory estoppel arose from the statement made by the plaintiff's security manager. There was no intention that the defendants should believe that the plaintiff would not enforce its rights under the contract. There was no promise that the plaintiff was abandoning its rights. It was an informal statement with no legal significance, nor did the security manager have any authority, as an agent, to grant a release from liability. As is made clear by the Supreme Court of Canada in *John Burrows Ltd. v. Subsurface Surveys Ltd.*,[291] equitable or promissory estoppel does not arise because one party has taken advantage of an indulgence granted by the other. The party in question must have believed that strict rights under the contract would not be enforced and the contractual relationship between the parties would be altered. Hence, in that case, the defence could not be raised when late payments of interest under promissory notes given for the purchase price of a corporation were accepted. This did not mean that the payees were estopped from relying on the strict terms of the contract and demanding payment of the full amount, not just the interest, upon the default of the maker of the promissory note whose tardiness in paying interest had brought about the situation.

(3) There must have been reliance, by the party raising the estoppel, upon the statement or conduct of the party against whom the estoppel is raised.[292]

The representation which forms the basis for a claim of estoppel must not only be intended to be acted upon in a manner that would alter the legal relations between the parties; it must have been acted upon by the promisee — the one to whom the representation is made. In *Edwards v. Harris-Intertype (Canada) Ltd.*,[293] the plaintiff agreed to buy four machines from the defendants. Although the machines had been delivered, the plaintiff had not yet paid for them. Payment

---

290 (1980), 21 B.C.L.R. 247 (B.C.S.C.).

291 [1968] S.C.R. 607 (S.C.C.).

292 *Fort Francis v. Boise Cascade Can. Ltd.; Boise Cascase Can. Ltd. v. Ont.; Ont. v. Boise Cascade Can. Ltd.* (1983), 46 N.R. 108 at 137 (S.C.C.) *per* Estey J.

293 (1983), 40 O.R. (2d) 558 (Ont. H.C.); affirmed (1984), 46 O.R. (2d) 286 (Ont. C.A.).

was due on May 31st, but the defendants agreed to an extension of time for payment until June 8th. The plaintiff sued for breach of alleged contract to extend the time for payment. Osborne J. held that there was no contract because the promise to extend the time had been given without consideration. The plaintiff argued in the alternative that, under the doctrine of promissory estoppel, the defendants were liable. Osborne J. seems to have been willing to accept that promissory estoppel could be used as a sword, not only as a shield.[294] However, regardless of this, the plaintiff's claim on the basis of estoppel failed. The plaintiff was an insolvent company at the time payment was originally due, as well as at the later date. Hence, the plaintiff had not acted in any way in reliance upon the alleged promise not to demand payment before the June date. Therefore the doctrine of promissory estoppel did not apply.

In an English case of 1979,[295] Lord Denning, returning to the principle of the *High Trees* case, seems to have attempted to extend its scope. Having said that the principle extended to all cases where one party makes a promise or representation intending that it should be binding, intending that the other should rely on it and on which the other does in fact rely, by acting on it, by altering his position on the faith of it, by going ahead with a transaction then under discussion, or by any other way of reliance,[296] Lord Denning then went on,[297]

> [i]t is no answer for the maker to say: 'You would have gone on with the transaction anyway.' That must be mere speculation. No one can be sure what he would, or would not, have done in a hypothetical state of affairs which never took place. . . . Once it is shown that a representation was calculated to influence the judgment of a reasonable man, the presumption is that he was so influenced.

This case concerned a claim by landlords against tenants for repairs to the roof of a building in which the tenants had flats. The tenants' plea of estoppel succeeded, according to Lord Denning, because of the irrelevance of the fact that one of the tenants would have taken the lease whether or not the landlord had made oral representations that the landlord would repair the roof. The plea of the other tenants succeeded because the estoppel was not personal to the original representee but was an equity intended for the benefit of those from time to time holding the leases, so that the benefit of the estoppel passed to the assignees of the original tenants just as its burden passed to any assignee of the original landlord.[298] However the other members of the Court of Appeal reached the same decision in favour of the tenants by other means involving waiver, not promissory estoppel. The statement of Lord Denning, therefore, must be considered only as a *dictum*. Moreover, Roskill L.J. was dubious whether the doctrine of promissory estoppel could be extended

---

294 *Ibid.*, at 570 (Ont. H.C.), relying on *dicta* in *Re Tudale Explorations Ltd. and Bruce* (1978), 20 O.R. (2d) 593 (Ont. Div. Ct.); *Petridis v. Shabinsky*, above, note 283; *Baxter (M.L.) Equip. Ltd. v. GEAC Can. Ltd.*, above, note 281.

295 *Brikom Invts. v. Carr*, [1979] 2 All E.R. 753 (C.A.).

296 *Ibid.*, at 758-59.

297 *Ibid.*, at 759.

298 *Ibid.*, at 760.

in the ways suggested by Lord Denning. " [I]t would be wrong," he said,[299] "to extend the doctrine of promissory estoppel, whatever its precise limits at the present day, to the extent of abolishing in this back-handed way the doctrine of consideration." In this regard he also adopted the remarks of Lord Hailsham in *Woodhouse A.C. Israel Cocoa Ltd. S.A. v. Nigerian Produce Marketing Co.*,[300] to the effect that the sequence of cases based on promissory estoppel needed to be reviewed and reduced to a coherent body of doctrine by the courts. Given this approach, it is hardly likely that English courts will be prepared to extend the scope of promissory estoppel as widely as Lord Denning indicated it might reach. Whether Canadian courts will go further than those of England is a matter for debate. If they do ultimately acknowledge that the sword/shield dichotomy is neither justifiable nor reasonable, they might go further and adopt the notion that a representation calculated to induce some act or forbearance by the party to whom it is made may be presumed to have this effect. They might also be prepared to adopt the idea that the benefit and burden of such an estopel can pass to assignees or successors in title in the way Lord Denning argued.[301]

(4) The party to whom the representation was made must have acted upon it to his detriment.

This is still a matter of dispute. *Dicta* can be cited from cases in England and Canada to the effect that the promisee must have acted in reliance on the representation or promise to his detriment.[302] Some statements merely speak in terms of the promisee's altering his position which has been assumed to mean that he altered it detrimentally.[303] Certainly where estoppel is invoked in other contexts, not that of promissory estoppel, the element of detriment has been emphasized. However, there are also judicial statements which deny that detriment is a necessary element in a successful plea of promissory or equitable estoppel.[304]

---

299 *Ibid.*, at 761.

300 [1972] A.C. 741 at 758 (H.L.).

301 The change recommended by the Ontario Law Reform Commission, above, note 279, would not have these consequences.

302 *E.g., Hughes v. Metro. Ry. Co.* (1877), 2 A.C. 439 (H.L.); *Birmingham & Dist. Land Co. v. L. & N.W. Ry.* (1888), 40 Ch. D. 268 (C.A.); *Salisbury v. Gilmore*, [1942] 2 K.B. 38 (C.A.); *Tool Metal Mfg. Co. v. Tungsten Elec. Co.*, [1955] 2 All E.R. 657 (H.L.); *Can. Superior Oil Ltd. v. Paddon-Hughes Dev. Co.*, [1970] S.C.R. 932 at 939 (S.C.C.) *per* Martland J. (quoting from *Greenwood v. Martins Bank Ltd.*, [1933] A.C. 51 at 57 (H.L.)); *Edwards v. Harris-Intertype (Can.) Ltd.* (1983), 40 O.R. (2d) 558 at 566 (Ont. H.C.); affirmed (1984), 46 O.R. (2d) 286 (Ont. C.A.); *Pentagon Const. (1969) Co. v. U.S. Fidelity & Guar. Co.* (1977), 77 D.L.R. (3d) 189 at 206 (B.C.C.A.). Compare a New Zealand case, *Budget Rent A Car v. Goodman*, [1991] 2 N.Z.L.R. 715 at 724, citing an earlier decision, *Gillies v. Keogh*, [1989] 2 N.Z.L.R. 327 for the proposition that underlying the three essential elements of encouragement of a belief or expectation, reliance on that and detriment, is a general test of unconscionability. Compare what is said below, pp. 135-136, on the issue of equitable behaviour of the promisee.

303 *Ajayi v. Briscoe (R.T.) (Nigeria)*, [1964] 3 All E.R. 566 (P.C.).

304 Criticized by Atiyah, *The Rise and Fall of Freedom of Contract* (1979), at p. 777, note 71, on the ground that this would permit a promisee to improve his rights by acting on a promise in a manner beneficial to himself.

Lord Denning, for example, in *W.J. Alan & Co. v. El Nasr Export & Import Co.*[305] suggested that detriment was not required, as long as the promisee had altered his position in reliance on the representation or promise. The same judge, in *Brikom Investments v. Carr,*[306] in a passage to which reference has been made, again stated that the recipient of the representation need only act on the representation "by altering his position on the faith of it, by going ahead with a transaction then under discussion, or by any other way of reliance." In that case, as previously noted, the other members of the court did not accede to Lord Denning's viewpoint and decided the case on other grounds, nor did they go along with his ideas in the earlier decision, again coming to the same resolution of the issue before the court on different grounds from those of Lord Denning. Such contradictory *dicta* leave the present state of the law in some doubt.

In *Société Italo-Belge pour le Commerce et l'Industrie S.A. v. Palm & Vegetable Oils (Malaysia) Sdn Bhd,*[307] Goff J. seems to have adopted a view more consistent with that of Lord Denning than with that of other judges. Under a contract of sale of goods, the sellers were obliged to declare to the buyers, in writing, the ship on which the goods were being carried as soon as possible after the vessel's sailing. The sellers gave such a declaration more than one month after the ship had sailed. On receipt of the declaration the buyers did not protest about the lateness of the declaration, nor did they state that they were accepting the declaration under reserve of their contractual rights. The buyers also requested the sellers to hand over to their sub-buyers documents covering the consignment. The sub-buyers rejected the documents. The buyers immediately rejected them also, and the sellers were forced to resell the goods elsewhere for less than the contract price. The sellers claimed the difference in an action for breach of contract against the buyers. One of the points in issue was whether the buyers had waived their right to reject the sellers' tender of the documents. This was based upon the buyers' conduct in not protesting the late declaration and not protesting, but requesting, the delivery of the documents. Because of the short period of time between the date of the representation by the buyers, that is, that they would not object to the late declaration, and the date of the rejection of the documents, the sellers had not suffered any detriment even though they had relied on that represenation. Therefore it was argued that there was no basis for a plea of promissory estoppel under the *High Trees* principle. However, Goff J. held that detriment was not necessary for a valid promissory estoppel. The fact that the sellers had not suffered any such detriment would not have been a barrier to the success of the sellers' argument that the buyers were estopped from denying the validity of the declaration and, therefore, the conclusion that the buyers were in breach of contract. Goff J. took a different point. Citing the language of Lord Cairns in the *Hughes* case, he said that a representor will not be allowed to enforce his rights where it would be inequitable

---

305 [1972] 2 Q.B. 189 at 213 (C.A.).
306 [1979] 2 All E.R. 753 at 758-759 (C.A.).
307 [1982] 1 All E.R. 19.

having regard to the dealings which have taken place between the parties.[308] "To establish such inequity," said Goff J.,[309]

> it is not necessary to show detriment; indeed the representee may have benefited from the representation, and yet it may be inequitable, at least without reasonable notice, for the representor to enforce his legal rights.

But it did not follow that in every case in which the representee acted, or failed to act, in reliance on the representation, it would be inequitable for the representor to enforce his rights; for the nature of the action, or inaction, might be insufficient to give rise to the equity. On the facts of this case, there was nothing inequitable in allowing the buyers to enforce their legal right to reject the documents, even though they had made a representation which indicated that they were not going to enforce those rights. The sellers had not been prejudicied by the buyers' conduct nor by the sellers' reliance on the representation. Therefore, the buyers could still insist on their right to reject and the sellers could not maintain an action for breach of contract.

If Goff J. is correct in his analysis of the *Hughes* doctrine and its relationship with the later *High Trees* principle, the only issue on which a court must be satisfied, once the other elements of promissory estoppel have been established, is whether or not allowing the estoppel to succeed would produce an inequitable result as between the parties.

(5) The promisee must have acted equitably.

This is another issue which remains unresolved. As just noted, it has been suggested that a representee who had incurred no detriment might be able to plead estoppel if it would be inequitable to allow the representor/promisor to refute the representation or promise. There might be situations in which the equities were all on the other side, in that the representee/promisee would obtain an unfair advantage over the representor/promisor if the former were permitted to raise and rely on the plea of promissory estoppel. This was hinted at as a possibility by Lord Denning in *D. & C. Builders v. Rees*,[310] which was decided on other grounds. There, a creditor was told by the debtor that the debtor would pay a lesser sum than the amount owing or nothing at all. The debtor knew that the creditor was in a difficult financial situation, such that the creditor would be glad to get anything. The creditor agreed to take, and received, the lesser sum but later sued for the full amount. The action was successful, having regard to the English position under *Pinnel's Case*[311] and *Foakes v. Beer*.[312] However, the point was taken that even though there might sometimes be a valid agreement to accept a lesser sum in place of a greater sum, this would not be so where the agreement was obtained improperly, that is, by duress or intimidation or, as later said by Lord Denning,[313] by some

---

308 Compare *P. v. P.*, [1957] N.Z.L.R. 854 (N.Z.).
309 Above, note 307, at 27.
310 [1966] 2 Q.B. 617 at 625 (C.A.).
311 (1602), 5 Co. Rep. 117a.
312 (1884), 9 App. Cas. 605 (H.L.); above, p. 104.
313 *Arrale v. Costain*, [1976] 1 Lloyd's Rep. 98 (C.A.); see also p. 105, note 149.

unconscionable conduct. In the *Rees* case the debtor who might have pleaded promissory estoppel to preclude the action for the outstanding amount of the debt, was tainted by his "misuse of the delicate financial position of the creditor". Hence the suggestion that any such "agreement", arising by way of estoppel, might be nugatory. In Canada, in view of the statutory provisions previously discussed,[314] there might be no need to invoke the doctrine of promissory estoppel, but the otherwise operative agreement might be vitiated by duress or similar conduct, just as any contract might be affected.

One final matter requires mention. There is some dispute as to whether the effect of the doctrine, where it is applicable and may be invoked, is to suspend or to abrogate the rights of the representor/promisor. In a New Zealand case, *P. v. P.*,[315] it was suggested that the latter was the correct way of interpreting the doctrine. Once the party making the representation has caused the other party to act thereon to his detriment (or in circumstances which made it inequitable for the former party to deny his promise), then the original rights no longer exist in their pristine state; they must be taken as having been modified or qualified forever by the representation or promise. Such, also, appears to have been the view of Lord Denning in the *High Trees* case.[316] with respect to the rent which was originally agreed to be paid by the tenant. The landlord lost the right to the proper amount as soon as each underpayment of rent was made. However, other decisions and *dicta* in England[317] suggest that the effect of the doctrine is only to suspend the strict legal rights of the promisor until such time as he gives reasonable notice to the other party terminating the effect of the representation.[318] That he may do so is subject to the qualification that the promisee can resume his original position; if he cannot, then the representation or promise becomes final and irrevocable. This accords with the general, equitable nature of the doctrine. If the promisee cannot resume his original situation without some hardship then it would be inequitable to permit the promisor to reaffirm his original strict rights, albeit with notice of his intention to do so, and so put the promisee into just as difficult a situation as he was in before the making of the representation on which he relied. Indeed the promisee might well be worse off than before. As yet, however, there is no clear authority one way or the other. It may be suggested that, given the nature and purposes of the doctrine, it would be more consistent to hold that the effects of the estoppel could be reversed as long as such reversal were effected reasonably and without giving rise to some inequity.

---

314 Above, pp. 119-121.

315 [1957] N.Z.L.R. 854 (N.Z.).

316 [1947] K.B. 130.

317 *Tool Metal Mfg. Co. v. Tungsten Elec. Co.*, [1955] 2 All. E.R. 657 (H.L.); *Ajayi v. Briscoe (R.T.) (Nigeria)*, [1964] 3 All E.R. 556 at 559 (P.C.) *per* Lord Hodson.

318 Support for this proposition is also to be found in the argument in *Edwards v. Harris-Intertype (Can.) Ltd.* (1983), 40 O.R. (2d) 558 at 570-571 (Ont. H.C.); affirmed (1984), 46 O.R. (2d) 286 (Ont. C.A.) that the vendors should have given reasonable notice of their intention to repossess the machinery that was the subject of the sale, once they had agreed to extend the time for payment. This was *obiter* because the estoppel did not cause reliance by the purchasers to their detriment.

4

Capacity

1. Contractual capacity

Since a contract is an agreement between two or more persons, and involves the idea of *consent*, only those who have the power to give consent can contract. This excludes those considered as lacking such power through being under the age of majority or through having a disordered mind.[1] At various times, however, even adults of sound mind have been placed under disability. For example, married women were treated very differently from their unmarried sisters until recent times.[2] Even today, aliens, at least in time of war, may be deprived of the contractual capacity which they enjoy in time of peace while they are considered friendly.[3] Foreign sovereigns, their ambassadors and other, similar diplomatic persons, under the rules of international law, may be able to make contracts, but may be exempt from liability to suit thereunder.[4] Reasons of State make it desirable and necessary to ignore the usual rules of the law and make exceptions. However, it should be pointed out that in such cases it is probably correct to state that there is a contract between the foreign sovereign, ambassador, etc., on the one hand and the other, undifferentiated party on the other. However, the contract may be unenforceable in the courts against the foreign sovereign or other specially treated party. The contract may have some effect in law as long as there is no attempt at its enforcement in the courts against that particular party. The limitation that arises from the status of the party in question is not so much a matter of the substantive law of contract as of the law of procedure, as affected by, for example, international law.

The law has widened the scope of personality to include artificial persons among those who have contractual capacity. Such juristic persons as corporations never suffer from the defects of minority or mental incompetence (albeit that their managers may). However, there are other circumstances in which a juristic person is denied full contractual capacity—which may be likened to the effects of minority or incompetency upon a natural person. The extent of such limitations on contractual capacity depends on the kind of corporation that is involved.

Consideration must also be given to groups which do not enjoy corporate status of personality in law. Nonetheless, the may have to be treated differently from the individuals who make up such groups, where contractual capacity is concerned.

---

1 For the position of *convicts, i.e.*, those under lawful restraint in prison, see *Young v. Carter* (1912), 26 O.L.R. 576 (Ont. H.C.).

2 The law now gives married women full contractual capacity: see, *e.g.*, in Alberta the Married Women's Act, R.S.A. 1980, c. M-7 [am. 1990, c. 22]; in British Columbia, the Married Women's Property Act, R.S.B.C. 1979, c. 252, s. 25, added by the Law and Equity Act, R.S.B.C. 1979, c. 224 [en. 1985, c. 68]; in Ontario, the Family Law Act, R.S.O. 1990, c. F.3; in Saskatchewan, the Equality of Status of Married Persons Act, S.S. 1984-85-86, c. E-10.3.

3 *Janson v. Driefontein Consol. Mines Ltd.*, [1902] A.C. 484 (H.L.); *Porter v. Freudenberg*, [1915] 1 K.B. 857 (C.A.); *Lampel v. Berger* (1917), 40 O.L.R. 165 (Ont. H.C.); *Re Cimonian* (1915), 34 O.L.R. 129 (Ont. H.C.); *Bauer Chemical Co. v. Sanatogen Co. of Can.* (1920), 20 Ex. C.R. 123 (Ex. Ct.). For the situation of enemy corporations see *Daimler Co. v. Continental Tyre Co.*, [1916] 2 A.C. 307 (H.L.).

4 See, *e.g.*, *Mighell v. Sultan of Johore*, [1894] 1 Q.B. 149 (C.A.).

2. Contracts with a common party[5]

At common law it was not possible for a person to contract with himself. This meant that A could not contract with A and B jointly; nor could A and B contract with A, B and C. Hence, also A and B could not contract with B and C. Any attempt to make such a contract resulted in a legal nullity, a transaction that was void. For these propositions of law, criticized though they have been as disfiguring the law of a great commercial nation,[6] there is ample English authority[7] which has been followed by courts in Canada.[8] Only if the contracts concerned involved covenants that were several and not joint, could there be any effect given to such agreements.[9] It might appear that to forbid a person to contract with himself is neither unreasonable, in logical terms, nor unfortunate in a practical sense. However, there have been, and are still, situations in which the denial of this capacity to an otherwise capable party is both an inconvenience and a commercial hindrance. This is especially true where the contracting party, though the same person, is really contracting in two different capacities, for example, as a principal on one side and a trustee on the other,[10] as a partner on one side and as the owner of premises on the other.[11] There may be good reason why this sort of arrangement is required, but the common law prevented this from being done.

A change in the law was made in England in 1925, by section 82 of the Law of Property Act.[12] The effect of that section is not entirely clear. While it makes a contract to which there is a common party, for example, A and B with A, valid, the problem is raised whether the common party drops out of the transaction. A further question is whether that statute validates a contract of this kind: A and B contracting with B and C. The second issue was settled in favour of the application of the statute in the New South Wales case of *Stewart v. Hawkins*,[13] in relation to a similar provision of a local Act. The first question was answered by the decision that the common party remained a party.

In the United States the problem has been more clearly and fully dealt with by the Model Interparty Agreement Act, prepared by the Uniform Law Commissioners and passed in a handful of states.[14] In Canada, while there has been legislation dealing with conveyances between parties one of whom is common

---

5 See the *11th Report of the Institute of Law Research and Reform*, University of Alberta (1972).

6 Glanville Williams, *Joint Obligations*, at p. 47.

7 *Ellis v. Kerr*, [1910] 1 Ch. 529, *Napier v. Williams*, [1911] 1 Ch. 361; *Rye v. Rye*, [1962] A.C. 496 (H.L.).

8 *Burdick v. Mills*, [1923] 1 W.W.R. 283 (Sask. K.B.). Compare *Re Sherrett & Grey*, [1933] O.R. 690 (Ont. H.C.); *Re Sutherland and Volos*, [1967] 1 O.R. 611 (Ont. C.A.).

9 *Ellis v. Kerr*, [1910] 1 Ch. 529 at 538-539.

10 *Ellis v. Kerr*, above.

11 *Rye v. Rye*, above, note 7.

12 15 & 16 Geo. 5, c. 20.

13 (1960), 60 S.R. (N.S.W.) 104.

14 Uniform Laws Annotated, vol. 9B 303.

to both sides,[15] in terms which are similar to those contained in English legislation,[16] there has been nothing dealing with contracts only, until the passage in Alberta of the Common Parties Contracts and Conveyances Act.[17] By this statute

> A contract is valid and enforceable in accordance with its terms notwithstanding that in or by the contract
>> (a) one of the parties enters into a convenant, promise or agreement with himself and some other person, or
>> (b) one of the parties and some other person enter into a covenant, promise or agreement with that same party and a different person, or,
>> (c) one of the parties and some other person enter into a covenant, promise or agreement with that same party.

This statute is retroactive[18] and it applies to contracts conveying interests in real or personal property.[19] Thus in Alberta, if not in other provinces, there is no longer any such limitation upon contractual capacity as existed at common law. A person may contract with himself.

3. Incapacities of natural persons

(a) Minors

The common law from earliest times drew a distinction between minors and those of mature age and limited the extent to which a minor could make a contract by which he would be bound. While the age of majority may have been altered in many common-law jurisdictions, including the provinces of Canada, and lowered from 21 to 18 (or possibly 19),[20] the distinction between those under and those over such age, so far as the law of contract is concerned, still exists. Some change in the law has been presaged in England[21] (though not yet enacted); it has occurred

---

15 Ontario: Conveyancing and Law of Property Act, R.S.O. 1990, c. C.34, ss. 41, 42, 43; Manitoba: Real Property Act, R.S.M. 1988, c. R30, s. 88; New Brunswick: Property Act, R.S.N.B. 1973, c. P-19, s. 23; Prince Edward Island: Real Property Act, R.S.P.E.I. 1988, c. R-3, s. 13.

16 Law of Property Act, 1925 (15 & 16 Geo. 5, c. 20), s. 72.

17 Law of Property Act, R.S.A. 1980, c. L-8, s. 10(1), incorporated from the Common Parties Contracts and Conveyances Act, S.A. 1974, c. 20.

18 *Ibid.* s. 13(1).

19 *Ibid.* s. 10(3).

20 See, *e.g.*, Age of Majority and Accountability Act, R.S.O. 1990, c. A.7.

21 Report of Lord Chancellor's Committee on the Age of Majority (Latey Committee) (1967) Cmnd. 3342; Law Commission *Working Paper on Minors' Contracts*, No. 81, 1982. And Scotland, Scottish Law Commission, Consultative Memorandum No. 65, *Legal Capacity and Responsibility of Minors and Pupils*, 1985; Ontario Law Reform Commission, *Report*, below, note 22, at pp. 198-202. The English Law Commission suggested the radical approach of giving full capacity to minors 16 or over, and making contracts by those over 16 unenforceable. In the alternative it suggested "qualified unenforceability".

in Australia,[22] New Zealand,[23] and British Columbia.[24] At the present time, however, save in British Columbia, the common law, as it was in England prior to the passing of the Infants' Relief Act, 1874, applies in Canada.[25] In British Columbia, the capacity of minors is now regulated by the provisions enacted in 1985,[26] following the recommendations of the Law Reform Commission of British Columbia.[27] A distinction must therefore be made between the situation in other provinces and that which obtains in British Columbia.

(1) Provinces other than British Columbia

(i) *Effect of the law*

The attitude and effect of the law were explained thus by Laidlaw J.A. in the leading case of *McBride v. Appleton*:[28]

> The contract of an infant is considered in law as different from the contracts of other persons. The law exercises as it were a guardianship of the infant, using its power in some cases to nullify completely contractual transactions with an infant, and in other cases giving the privilege to the infant of saying during his infancy and for a reasonable time thereafter that he could not be bound by a contract to which he was a party.

What this quotation suggests is that at common law there are two categories of minors' contracts: those which are void and those in respect of which the law grants the minor a privilege, namely, to avoid the contract if he so desires.[29] The first class of contracts does not involve the minor in making any decision; indeed he is precluded from choosing. The second class does invite him to exercise a freedom of choice, but the privilege is his. He may avoid the contract and recover

---

22 Minors (Property and Contracts) Act, N.S.W. 1970, No. 60. See Ontario Law Reform Commission, *Report on Amendment of the Law of Contract*, 1987, pp. 189-192.

23 Minors' Contracts Act, 1969, No. 41; O.L.R.C., *Report*, above, note 22, at pp. 187-189.

24 Law Reform Amendment Act, 1985, S.B.C. 1985, c. 10, ss. 1, 2, and S.B.C. 1987, c. 42, s. 47; c. 59, s. 10, amending the Infants Act, R.S.B.C. 1979, c. 196. For other proposals for reform elsewhere in Canada see O.L.R.C., *Report*, above, note 22, at pp. 202-213; 14th Report of the Institute of Law Research and Reform, 1975.

25 In *Brand v. Griffin* (1908), 9 W.L.R. 427 (Alta. S.C.), it was held that the Infants' Relief Act, 1874, did not apply in Alberta or the North-West Territories, which received English law as it was in July 1870. Other provinces, which antedate the passing of that statute, would clearly not have received it into their law without the enactment of comparable legislation.

   British Columbia originally enacted the English statute. Those provisions were repealed in 1985 by S.B.C. 1985, c. 10, s. 2.

26 Above, note 24.

27 *Report on Minors' Contracts*, 1976.

28 [1946] 2 D.L.R. 16 at 24 (Ont. C.A.). Compare *R. v. Rash* (1923), 53 O.L.R. 245 at 255 (Ont. C.A.) *per* Masten J.; *Ivan v. Hartley*, [1945] 4 D.L.R. 142 at 143 (Ont. H.C.) *per* Hogg J.

29 But sometimes the distinction is between valid and void contracts: *Butterfield v. Sibbitt & Nipissing Elec. Supply Co.*, [1950] 4 D.L.R. 302 at 307 (Ont. H.C.) *per* Ferguson J.

anything he has paid under it,[30] or he may raise his minority by way of defence to an action brought on by such a contract. But he may sue to enforce the contract, in which event the other, adult party may not plead that the contract was made with a minor. It is the minor's privilege, not the adult's.

However, this account of the law is not entirely accurate. In the first place, there are undoubtedly some contracts which at common law were binding on a minor and could not be treated as voidable at the option of the minor either during minority or within a reasonable time after the minor attained majority. Secondly, some voidable contracts could be ratified by a minor after majority so as to make them valid, enforceable contracts binding on the minor. Thirdly, there has been considerable debate as to whether there was, and still is at common law a category of contracts which were absolutely void.[31]

(ii) *Enforceable contracts*

(A) *Necessaries* A contract for necessaries is binding upon a minor, to the extent that he may be made liable to pay for any necessaries which he purchases. It is less clear whether a minor may be made liable on an executory contract for the purchase or supply of necessaries, that is, before the goods, etc., have actually been delivered or provided to or for him. Under the various provincial Sale of Goods Acts,[32] a minor is only liable for necessaries in the form of goods which have been sold *and delivered* to the minor. With respect to other types of necessaries, there is not even such slender statutory authority for one view or the other. Since there may be liability on other executory contracts which are binding on a minor, there is some ground upon which to base the argument that an executory contract for necessaries is binding and enforceable.[33] However, it must be acknowledged that there is respectable judicial and textual authority for the proposition that the minor's liability is not contractual but quasi-contractual, or *real*, in the Roman law sense, that is, based upon actual enjoyment of the goods or services which

---

30 See further, below, but note that he will be prevented from doing so if he, the infant, has been guilty of fraudulent conduct; *Gregson v. Law* (1913), 5 W.W.R. 1017 (B.C.S.C.); *Robinson v. Moffatt* (1915), 35 O.L.R. 9 (Ont. C.A.).

31 See *Toronto Marlboro Major Junior "A" Hockey Club v. Tonelli* (1977), 18 O.R. (2d) 21 at 36 (Ont. H.C.) *per* Lerner J.; affirmed on appeal (1979), 23 O.R. (2d) 193 (Ont. C.A.). Compare *R. v. Rash*, above, note 28, at 256-257 *per* Rose J.; *Miller v. Smith & Co.* [1925] 2 W.W.R. 360 at 377 (Sask. C.A.) *per* Martin J.A.

32 Fridman, *Sale of Goods in Canada*, 3rd ed. (1986), pp. 33-35. Note the liability of parents for necessaries supplied to minors; parents are obliged to support minors under the Ontario Family Law Act, R.S.O. 1990, c. F.3, s. 31.

33 Those in favour of such liability include Hamilton L.J. in *Roberts v. Gray*, [1913] 1 K.B. 520 at 530 (C.A.); Buckley L.J. in *Nash v. Inman*, [1908] 2 K.B. 1 at 12 (C.A.); Goff & Jones, *Law of Restitution*, 3rd ed. (1986), p. 427; Percy, "The Present Law of Infants' Contracts" (1975), 53 Can. Bar Rev. 1 at 7-8.

constitute the necessaries.[34] The problem remains an unsolved one at common law.[35]

Meanwhile, it becomes important to determine what are necessaries. In the Sale of Goods Act of the various provinces they are defined as "goods suitable to the condition of life of . . .(the) infant . . .and to his actual requirements at the time of sale and delivery." Everything depends upon the social and economic position of the minor as well as upon what would be regarded as essential for life. Curiously enough, a car has been held not a necessary, even in these days,[36] even, as in *Pyett v. Lampman*[37] where the car was used by the minor in the business of selling fish by which he earned a living.[38]

It would seem that a trading contract will not bind a minor.[39] Any such contract is not for necessaries. This seems a strange attitude for the law to adopt, since it might preclude a minor from engaging in a legitimate business on his own behalf.[40] However, a possible explanation is that minors do not commence business in their own names, and with the lowering of the age of majority, the problem may have been outflanked.

That the goods should fall into the category of necessaries is not sufficient. It must also be shown that the minor was not already adequately supplied with such goods at the material time. The time of sale and time of delivery are both material. If at either moment the minor does not require the goods, despite the fact that ordinarily they would be considered as necessaries, the contract falls outside this common-law exception.

---

34 Miles, "The Infant's Liability For Necessaries" (1927), 43 L.Q.R. 389; Wright, (1935), 13 Can. Bar Rev. 319 at 320-322; Edwards, *Infants' Liability in Contract.* Isaac Pitblado Lectures (1970), 1 at p. 8; Rose J. in *R. v. Rash* (1923), 53 O.L.R. 245 at 256 (Ont. C.A.); McCamus, "Restitution of Benefits Conferred Under Minors' Contracts" (1979), 28 U.N.B. L.J. at pp. 96-98.

35 Winfield, "Necessaries Under the Sale of Goods Act" (1942), 58 L.Q.R. 82; *Toronto Marlboro Major Junior "A" Hockey Club v. Tonelli* (1979), 23 O.R. (2d) 193 at 200 (Ont. C.A.) *per* Zuber J.A.

36 *Coull v. Kolbuc* (1969), 68 W.W.R. 76 (Alta. Dist. Ct.); *Fannon v. Dobranski* (1970), 73 W.W.R. 371 (Alta. Dist. Ct.); *Noble's Ltd. v. Bellefleur* (1963), 37 D.L.R. (2d) 519 (N.B.C.A.); *First Charter Financial Corp. v. Musclow* (1974), 49 D.L.R. (3d) 138 (B.C.S.C.).

37 (1923), 53 O.L.R. 149 (Ont. C.A.). Compare *Mercantile Union Guar. Corp. v Ball*, [1937] 2 K.B. 498 (C.A.). Contrast the odd case of *McGee v. Cusack*, [1936] 1 D.L.R. 157 (P.E.I. Co. Ct.).

38 There are decisions which held, *e.g.*, that a house qualifies as necessaries: *Soon v. Watson* (1962), 33 D.L.R. (2d) 428 (B.C. S.C.) a decision which may not be of general application since it turned on the B.C. Infant's Relief Act (since repealed: above, note 25). Another decision held that a contract for education was a contract for necessaries (although also not a contract for goods): *Wong v. Kim Lee* (1961), 34 W.W.R. 506 (Sask. Dist. Ct.). But a policy of insurance was not a contract for necessaries: *Wong v. Kim Lee*, above; nor was a contract to provide a correspondence course in accounting: *Int. Accountants' Soc. v. Montgomery*, [1935] O.W.N. 364 (Ont. C.A.).

39 See the English case of *Cowern v. Nield*, [1912] 2 K.B. 419, followed in *Pyett v. Lampman*, above (unless, perhaps, the contract is beneficial to the minor, below, p. 146; *McGee v. Cusack*, above). But see below, note 40. For the difficulties involved in deciding what is a trading contract see *Chaplin v. Frewin*, [1966] Ch. 71 (C.A.), in which the minor wrote his life story and contracted for its publication. It was held that this was a valid contract of service made by the minor, not a trading contract, and therefore could not be avoided by the minor.

40 Contrast the case of *Re Smith and Link* (1911), 17 W.L.R. 550 (Alta. Dist. Ct.) (which may be distinguished in that it dealt with liability under a Workmen's Compensation Act, not under contract).

The category of "necessaries" includes more than goods. Martin J.A., in *Miller v. Smith & Co.*,[41] said that an "infant may bind himself to pay for his necessary meat, drink, clothing, medicines and likewise for his teaching or instruction." A contract to provide medical or dental services or treatment to the minor will be binding upon him[42] (unless, perhaps, it contains penal or disadvantageous terms, such as a waiver by the minor of the doctor's or dentist's liability in tort for negligence[43]). How far this goes is uncertain.[44] From cases referred to earlier,[45] it may be inferred that a contract to work as an employee for a minor will not come within the scope of "necessaries", even though a contract by a minor under which he works for someone else could be binding, because trading contracts made by minors are not caught by the concept of necessaries. The test of what are necessaries appears to be whether the services provided by the adult are vital to the health or other welfare of the minor. Minors may require to be kept healthy, or, sometimes, to be educated, just as they require food and drink (or shelter[46]). They do not require to maintain businesses and so employ workers.

It may be that contracts for necessary services, in contrast with contracts for goods, are binding contractually on the minor, who can be liable on the executory contract if in breach.[47]

(B) *Contracts of service* One separate group of contracts, which could be considered as contracts for necessaries, are those under which a minor is employed. A minor can validly contract in such a way, provided that the contract, as a whole, is for the minor's benefit and is in no way derogatory to his position.[48] In *Johnston v. Keenan*,[49] an old case from the Northwest Territories, the minor agreed that he would be liable, as a shepherd, for any sheep lost during the period of the herding. It was held that this was utterly unconscionable and therefore unenforceable against the minor. Similarly, in *Miller v. Smith & Co.*,[50] a contract under which a minor was employed limited the employer's liability in respect of any negligence on the part of the employer which resulted in injury to the minor. It was held that this was not for the minor's benefit and was therefore not binding on him so as to prevent his bringing an action for his injuries.

---

41 [1925] 2 W.W.R. 360 at 377 (Sask. C.A.); above, note 38 (education), with which contrast *Int. Accountants' Soc. v. Montgomery*, above, note 38.

42 *Re Oberth*, [1936] 3 W.W.R. 474 (Man. K.B.).

43 *Miller v. Smith & Co.*, above, note 41.

44 It does not include a contract of insurance: *Wong v. Kim Lee*, above, note 38.

45 Above, note 39.

46 *Soon v. Watson*, above, note 38. In *Sherdley v. Sherdley*, [1987] 2 All E.R. 54 at 63 (H.L.), Lord Brandon adverted to the "artificiality of contracts entered into by young children with the schools which they attend." But an order of the court which contemplates the making of such contracts was not a sham in the legal sense of that term.

47 *Roberts v. Gray*, [1913] 1 K.B. 520 (C.A.); O'Connor, "Liability of an Infant Upon His Contract of Service" (1926), 4 Can. Bar Rev. 365.

48 *Miller v. Smith & Co.*, [1925] 3 D.L.R. 251 at 267 (Sask. C.A.) *per* Morton J.A. For statutory provisions dealing with apprenticeship see, *e.g.*, Trades Qualification Act, R.S.O. 1990, c. T.17, s. 14.

49 (1894), 3 Terr. L.R. 239 (N.W.T.S.C.).

50 Above, note 41.

In coming to such conclusion, Canadian courts followed English authorities,[51] which indicated that a beneficial contract of service, in the pecuniary sense of "beneficial",[52] would be binding on a minor, as well as on the other party.

A more recent discussion of this problem is found in *Toronto Marlboro Major Junior "A" Hockey Club v. Tonelli*.[53] A player who was under 18 at the time signed a contract with an amateur hockey club. He agreed to play for the club for three, or at his option, four years for minimal remuneration. He also agreed to pay the club 20 per cent of his earnings during his first three years as a professional hockey player. Other terms favourable to the player were inserted into the contract, which was signed by his father as well as by himself. When he reached 18, the player repudiated the contract and entered into an agreement with a professional club. The amateur club sought first to obtain an injunction to restrain the former minor from playing for the second club. Morden J. refused to grant such injunction. He held that the contract was not beneficial to the minor because its terms were not "reasonable". The argument of the amateur club that the contract was beneficial because the minor was receiving valuable training by virtue of which he was enabled to earn large sums of money was rejected by the judge. So, too, was the argument that it would be unfair to the club not to enforce the contract since they had undertaken the training of the minor from whom they would receive little or no benefit until later, at a time when, under the contract he would have been able to terminate the contract and take his services elsewhere. The subsequent action for damages against the former minor, his father, and the professional club (for inducing a breach of contract) was also dismissed, by Lerner J. at first instance and by the majority of the Ontario Court of Appeal. Again the conclusion was that the contract was not beneficial to the minor.

Lerner J. took the view that "benefit" meant "pecuniary benefit". On the facts of this case such benefit was obtained by the amateur club; the minor derived few pecuniary benefits or little compensation for his natural skills, application to his task and desire to excel.[54] In the Court of Appeal,[55] Blair J.A., speaking for the majority, disagreed with this limited, one-dimensional view of "benefit", which had been embraced by Morden J. as well as Lerner J., in reliance upon the views expressed by the English Court of Appeal in *Chaplin v. Frewin*.[56] In coming to this conclusion, thought Blair J., the two other judges had been misguided. Their decisions were correct, however, because they had taken other, valid considerations into account. These were that the contract was not to the minor's advantage, indeed

---

51 *Clements v. London & North Western Ry.*, [1894] 2 Q.B. 482 (C.A.); *De Francesco v. Barnum* (1890), 45 Ch. D. 430; *Doyle v. White City Stadium*, [1935] 1 K.B. 110; *Roberts v. Gray*, above, note 47.

52 Contrast Lord Denning M.R. in the *Chaplin* case, above, note 39 at 88, where *beneficial* was interpreted in a *moral* or *social* sense.

53 (1977), 18 O.R. (2d) 21 (Ont. H.C.); affirmed (1979), 23 O.R. (2d) 193 (Ont. C.A.).

54 (1977), 18 O.R. (2d) 21 at 34 (Ont. H.C.). Note that Lerner J. also considered alternate claims in equity and *quantum meruit*, which were not discussed in the Court of Appeal, and are very questionable.

55 (1979), 23 O.R. (2d) 193 at 207-208 (Ont. C.A.).

56 Above, note 39.

may have hindered him in the advancement of his aims and desires,[57] and it was made between parties who were on unequal terms.[58] This was an onerous and one-sided contract made all the more questionable because one party was a minor. Hence, it was not binding on the minor if he chose to repudiate it.

The dissent of Zuber J.A. was not founded upon any different view as to the basic law, but on a different approach to the meaning of "benefit". To Zuber J.A. the task of a court in determining whether or not a contract was for a minor's benefit was to put itself in the position of a "prudent and informed parent" of a minor, having regard to the nature and purpose of the contract, and to decide whether such parent would have approved of the contract in question.[59] This test was based on the language of Fry L.J. in *De Francesco v. Barnum*.[60] It is obvious that the difference between the two points of view in this case was not one of principle but related to the question of how to apply the principle to the facts.

(C) *Beneficial contracts* It is questionable whether other contracts, which are neither for necessaries, strictly speaking, nor for the employment of a minor (which may also be regarded as a kind of contract for necessaries), can be binding and enforceable without more, even if to be regarded as for the benefit of the minor. In *Johannson v. Gudmunson*,[61] which is a leading case on the power of a minor to appoint an agent to act on his behalf,[62] it was held that since the contract concluded by the father, the alleged agent for minor principals, was one for the purchase of land which was for the benefit of the minors, it was a valid enforceable contract. However, in *Butterfield v. Sibbitt & Nipissing Electric Supply Co.*[63] it was said that contracts with a minor were either void as being contrary to the minor's interests (as was the contract in that case, by which the minor purported to settle and compromise a tort claim), or were for the minor's benefit. If for his benefit they were still voidable unless for necessaries.[64] It may be that the better view is that all such contracts as are neither void *ab initio*, of which more will be said later, nor valid as being for necessaries, including contracts of service, are capable of being valid and enforceable in one of two instances. First, there are those contracts

---

57 (1979), 23 O.R. (2d) 193 at 210-211 (Ont. C.A.).

58 *Ibid.* at 211-212, relying on *A Schroeder Music Publishing Co. v. Macaulay*, [1974] 3 All E.R. 616 (H.L.), on which see p. 329.

59 (1979), 23 O.R. (2d) 193 at 203 (Ont. C.A.).

60 (1890), 45 Ch. D. 430 at 442.

61 (1909), 19 Man. R. 83 (Man. C.A.); compare *Short v. Field* (1915), 32 O.L.R. 395 (Ont. C.A.), minor had taken possession of real property and had controlled it to detriment of the vendor: therefore repudiation of the contract by the minor and recovery of the deposit money were not allowed.

62 Compare Fridman, *Law of Agency*, 6th ed. (1990), at pp. 50-51. See the recommendations on powers of attorney given by a minor by the Ontario Law Reform Commission, *Report*, above, note 22, at pp. 207-208.

63 [1950] O.R. 504 (Ont. H.C.).

64 Contrast *Henderson v. Nor. Trusts Co.*, [1953] 1 D.L.R. 108 at 121-122 (Sask. Q.B.), but the case could have been decided on the basis of failure to repudiate within a reasonable time after the attainment of majority. This was a case of a separation agreement between a husband and his wife, who soon after making the agreement reached her majority. It was held that the agreement was reasonable and for her benefit. Therefore it was valid.

which will bind a minor unless *repudiated* during minority or within a reasonable time of attaining majority. Second, there are those contracts which will not be binding unless they are ratified after the attainment of majority. Both categories, however, are better regarded as *voidable* contracts, than as enforceable ones. They are capable of becoming or of being treated as valid, but the minor has the option of avoiding them, either by repudiation or by failing to ratify.[65]

(iii) *Voidable contracts*

(A) *Those valid unless repudiated* There appears to be a class of contracts, under which a minor acquires an interest in permanent property to which a continuing obligation is attached, in respect of which a rule emerged at common law that repudiation was required for any such contract to be invalidated. Four different types of contracts are involved, namely, contracts concerning land,[66] share contracts, partnership agreements, and marriage settlements.[67]

(1) *Land.* At common law, where a minor contracted to purchase land, as long as the minor had not taken possession and rendered it impossible to reinstate the vendor, or had otherwise acted to the latter's detriment,[68] repudiation was possible during infancy or within a reasonable time thereafter.[69] Statute has made

---

65 It would seem that there is some dispute as to whether the English distinction applies in Canada. See, *e.g.*, Edwards, above, note 34 at p. 5; Payne, "The Contractual Liability of Infants" (1966), 5 West. Ont. L.R. 136 at 143; *R. v. Rash* (1923), 53 O.L.R. 245 at 263 (Ont. C.A.) *per* Rose J. Contrast *Blackwell v. Farrow*, [1948] O.W.N. 7 (Ont. H.C.); *Fannon v. Dobranski*, above, note 36; *Coull v. Kolbuc, ibid.; Noble's Ltd. v. Bellefleur, ibid.; Lafayette v. W.W. Distributors Ltd.* (1965), 51 W.W.R. 685 (Sask. Dist. Ct.). Note also that in Ontario a minor with capacity to marry has capacity to enter into a marriage contract or separation agreement with the court's approval; Family Law Act, R.S.O. 1990, c. F.3, s. 55(2).

The Ontario Law Reform Commission, *Report*, above, note 22, at pp. 202, 204-206 recommends: (i) as a general rule minors' contracts should not be enforceable against them, but should be enforceable by them; (ii) that a contract should be enforced against a minor if the court is satisfied that the contract was in the best interests of the minor; (iii) this should apply to executory *and* executed contracts; (iv) contracts should be enforceable against a minor if approved by the court as being for the benefit of the minor; and (v) a court should be able to grant a minor capacity to enter into contracts generally, or any description of contract, on terms the court thinks fit.

66 Which include mortgages; *Foley v. Can. Permanent Loan & Savings Soc.* (1983), 4 O.R. 38 (Ont. C.A.); conveyances: *Whalls v. Learn* (1888), 15 O.R. 481 (Ont. C.A.); quit-claims: *Lauzan v. Menard* (1923), 25 O.W.N. 387 (Ont. H.C.); purchase: *Hagerman v. Siddall & Johnson Ltd.*, [1924] 2 D.L.R. 755 (Sask. K.B.).

67 In view of its general recommendation about the unenforceability of minors' contracts, above, note 65, the Ontario Law Reform Commission also recommended that a person contracting with a minor should be able to require the minor to affirm or repudiate the contract by a notice in writing, to be answered within 30 days: *Report*, at pp. 203-204. No distinction would then exist between different kinds of voidable contracts, as at present.

68 As in *Short v. Field* (1915), 32 O.L.R. 395 (Ont. C.A.).

69 *Foley v. Can. Permanent Loan & Savings Co.* (1883), 4 O.R. 38 (Ont. C.A.); *Whalls v. Learn* (1888), 15 O.R. 481 (Ont. C.A.); *Lauzon v. Menard* (1923), 25 O.W.N. 387 (Ont. H.C.); *Hagerman v. Siddall & Johnson*, [1924] 2 D.L.R. 755 (Sask. K.B.). But if the contract was not for the minor's benefit, repudiation was not necessary; the contract was already unenforceable: *Nicklin v. Longhurst*, [1917] 1 W.W.R. 439 (Man. C.A.).

it possible for minors to make fully binding dispositions of land, immediately effective, subject to the involvement of the court in the making of such disposition.[70]

(2) *Shares.* Many cases establish that an agreement by a minor to purchase shares in a company may be repudiated, even after majority, as long as this is done within a reasonable time.[71] However, if the minor has affirmed the contract, it is too late for him to repudiate liability under such contract. Acceptance of a dividend after attainment of majority, for example, is definite affirmation of such a contract.[72]

(3) *Partnership agreements.* Since capacity to become a partner is governed by the common law, there are no statutory provisions to govern the situation. In an English case on point, (there appears to be no Canadian case that might be relevant[73]) *Lovell & Christmas v. Beauchamp,*[74] it was held that a minor could be bound by a partnership contract until he repudiated it, though, since a minor cannot enter into a valid trading contract, he could not be liable as a debtor in respect of goods ordered for the firm.

(4) *Marriage settlements.* The voidability of such a settlement within a reasonable time after attainment of majority was settled by the House of Lords in *Edwards v. Carter,*[75] in which it was held that four and one half years after reaching 21 was too late, being an unreasonable delay. Legislation in, for example, Alberta,[76] has empowered minors to make bindng marriage settlements subject to intervention and approval by the court. However, the effect of the Age of Majority Act in Alberta[77] has meant that the earlier legislation will only affect such settlements if made by a female minor of between 17 and 18.[78]

Repudiation means repudiation of all the contract, not just those parts which are intended to be for the benefit of the adult party, while keeping alive those parts which are, or appear to be for the minor's benefit.[79] The act of repudiation must involve something that clearly indicates the minor's intention not to be bound

---

For the application of this to personalty that was non-necessary, see *Lafayette v. W.W. Distributors & Co.,* above, note 65.

70 See, *e.g.,* Children's Law Reform Act, R.S.O. 1990, c. C.12, s. 59; Minors' Property Act, R.S.A. 1980, c. M-16; Infants Act, R.S.S. 1978, c. I-9, s. 9; R.S.B.C. 1979, c. 196, s. 20. Note problems relating to land titles and registration: see, *e.g.,* Land Titles Act, R.S.O. 1990, c. L.5, s. 28; Registry Act, R.S.O. 1990, c. R.20, s. 47.

71 *Re Sovereign Bank; Clark's Case* (1916), 35 O.L.R. 448 (Ont. C.A.); *Re Central Bank and Hogg* (1890), 19 O.R. 7 (Ont. Ch.); *Re Prudential Life Ins. Co.; Re Paterson,* [1918] 1 W.W.R. 105 (Man. K.B.).

72 *Re Prudential Life Co.; Re Paterson,* [1918] 1 W.W.R. 105 (Man. K.B.). Are these, then, truly cases of "repudiation" or of "ratification"?

73 But see *Woods v. Woods* (1885), 3 Man. L.R. 33 (Man. Q.B.).

74 [1894] A.C. 607 (H.L.).

75 [1893] A.C. 360 (H.L.).

76 Minors' Property Act, R.S.A. 1980, c. M-16, ss. 12, 13 [am. 1985, c. 15, s. 25].

77 R.S.A. 1980, c. A-4.

78 For the situation with respect to *separation agreements* made by a minor see *Henderson v. Nor. Trust Co.,* above, note 64. In Ontario, see the Family Law Act, R.S.O. 1990, c. F.3, s. 55(2).

79 *Henderson v. Minneapolis Steel & Machinery Co.,* [1931] 1 D.L.R. 570 (Alta. S.C.).

by the contract.[80] Hence the problem which arose in cases concerning shares of deciding whether the acceptance or use of dividends was an affirmation of the contract, negating any subsequent attempt at repudiation.[81] Furthermore, any repudiation must occur "promptly", that is within a reasonably short time after the minor has attained majority.[82] Eight years has been held to be too long,[83] as has two years.[84] Two and a half months has been considered to be prompt,[85] as has a few weeks.[86]

(B) *Those invalid unless ratified* It would seem that all other contracts made by a minor, that is, for non-necessaries, are capable of being ratified once the minor attains majority, and consequently, of becoming valid and enforceable, unless the contract is so prejudicial to the minor as to be utterly void *ab initio*.[87] Hence, at common law, a minor's settlement of a tort acton, for example, for personal injuries, might be ratifiable,[88] or it might be completely void, as was held in *Butterfield v. Sibbitt & Nipissing Electric Supply Co.*[89] For this reason legislation, for example, the Minors' Property Act in Alberta,[90] has made such settlements binding if made under the auspices of the court, at least where personal injuries actions are concerned. But a judgment of a court which approves a settlement of an action, of any kind, may well be binding, since it is not simply an agreement between the parties but a judgment of the court itself.[91]

The problem of what amounts to ratification is complicated by the provisions of an English statute, namely, Lord Tenterden's Act, under which

---

80 *Phillips v. Sutherland* (1910), 15 W.L.R. 594 (Man. K.B.) (failure to return what the minor had received precluded a valid repudiation). Suing for negligence after signing a contract of release in respect of claims have been made is repudiation: *Butterfield v. Sibbitt and Nipissing Elec. Supply Co.*, [1950] 4 D.L.R. 302 (Ont. H.C.).

    The Ontario Law Reform Commission, *Report*, above, note 22, at p. 204, recommended that legislation should provide that repudiation include: (i) refusal to perform all or a material term of a contract; (ii) claiming relief under a contract unenforceable by a minor; and (iii) giving an oral or written notice of repudiation to the other party.

81 See the cases cited above, note 71.

82 The expression is that of Barlow J. in *Hilliard v. Dillon*, [1955] O.W.N. 621 at 623 (Ont. H.C.).

83 *Lauzon v. Menard* (1923), 25 O.W.N. 387 (Ont. H.C.).

84 *Foley v. Can. Permanent Loan & Savings Soc.* (1883), 4 O.R. 38 (Ont. C.A.); *Phillips v. Greater Ottawa Dev. Co.* (1916), 33 D.L.R. 259 (Ont. C.A.).

85 *Whalls v. Learn* (1888), 15 O.R. 481 (Ont. C.A.).

86 *Murray v. Dean* (1926), 30 O.W.N. 271 (Ont. H.C.).

87 Compare *Soon v. Watson* (1962), 33 D.L.R. (2d) 428 at 432 (B.C.S.C.) *per* Munroe J.A. See below, on the existence and nature of such a category of void contracts. There are dicta, however, to the effect that such contracts, *i.e.*, those requiring ratification, are binding unless and until repudiated: *Blackwell v. Farrow*, [1948] O.W.N. 7 (Ont. H.C.); *Noble's Ltd. v. Bellefleur* (1963), 37 D.L.R. (2d) 519 (N.B.C.A.); *Lafayette v. W.W. Distributors & Co.* (1965), 51 W.W.R. 685 (Sask. Dist. Ct.); *Coull v. Kolbuc* (1969), 68 W.W.R. 76 (Alta. Dist. Ct.); *Fannon v. Dobranski* (1970), 73 W.W.R. 371 (Alta. Dist. Ct.) This must be incorrect. But it does point out the curiously extended meaning given in ths context to the expression "voidable contracts".

88 *Carey v. Freeman*, [1938] O.R. 713 (Ont. C.A.).

89 [1950] O.R. 504 (Ont. H.C.).

90 R.S.A. 1980, c. M-16, s. 15.

91 *Poulin v. Nadon*, [1950] O.R. 219 (Ont. C.A.).

no action shall be brought whereby to charge any person upon any promise made after full age to pay any debt contracted during infancy or upon any ratification after full age of any promise or simple contract made during infancy, unless such promise or ratification shall be made by some writing signed by the party to be charged therewith.[92]

While this statute no longer applies in England, it probably still does in those parts of Canada which (a) received English law after 1829 or (b) have enacted it in their own Statute of Frauds.[93] Thus Alberta, for example,[94] and Saskatchewan[95] are probably governed by Lord Tenterden's Act. Since the effect of the statute is to render an informal ratification "unenforceable", any such ratification may still be effective despite the statutory requirements.[96] In any event the provisions of this statute appear very archaic and ought to be repealed. Whether formal or informal, however, a ratification, to be effective, must be "an admission of existing liability" rather than a mere recognition of a debt or contract made during minority.[97] Helping the lender of money used to buy a car and motorcycle, the loan being secured by a chattel mortgage, to recover possession and then sell the goods, was not ratification. It would have been anomalous to hold the owner worse off for co-operating with the lender than if he had not done so.[98]

(iv) Void contracts[99]

Whether there is a category of void minors' contracts has been the subject of some controversy among textbook writers.[100] In Canada, where the Infants' Relief Act has not been enacted to settle the issue, there are cases which establish that

---

92 Statute of Frauds Amendment Act, 1828 (9 Geo. 4), c. 14, s. 5.

93 *E.g.*, Nova Scotia, R.S.N.S. 1989, c. 442, s. 9, Ontario, R.S.O. 1990, c. S.19, s. 7 (which the Ontario Law Reform Commission, *Report on Amendment of the Law of Contract*, 1987, p. 203, recommended should be repealed).

94 *Brand v. Griffin* (1908), 9 W.L.R. 427 (Alta. S.C.).

95 *Molyneux v. Traill* (1915), 9 W.W.R. 137 (Sask. Dist. Ct.).

96 *Re Hutton; Re Flynn; Swift Can. Co. v. Bull*, [1926] 6 D.L.R. 108 (Alta. S.C.): with which contrast *Molyneux v. Traill*, above, note 95. But see *Blackwell v. Farrow*, below.

97 *Blackwell v. Farrow*, [1948] O.W.N. 7 (Ont. H.C.); *Loudon Mfg. Co. v. Milmine* (1907), 14 O.L.R. 532 (Ont. H.C.); affirmed (1908), 15 O.L.R. 53 (Ont. C.A.) (with which contrast *Lynch Bros. Dolan Co. v. Ellis* (1909), 7 E.L.R. 14 (P.E.I.S.C.). In *Great West Implement Co. v. Grams* (1907), 1 Alta. L.R. 11 (Alta. S.C.) it was held that if a minor purchased goods, which were not necessaries, and retained them after attaining majority without disaffirming the contract within a reasonable time, this was ratification; but on appeal this was reversed on the facts: (1908), 8 W.L.R. 160 (Alta. C.A.). Surely this would not be enough under Lord Tenterden's Act?

98 *Bayview Credit Union Ltd. v. Daigle* (1983), 3 D.L.R. (4th) 95 (N.B.Q.B.).

99 In Ontario it would seem that prior to Part III Children's Law Reform Act, R.S.O. 1990, c. C.12 (originally enacted in 1982: S.O. 1982, c. 20, s. 1), a disposition of land by a minor, unless in accordance with the Infants Act, was void, but see *Re Leblanc* (1977), 75 D.L.R. (3d) 518 (Ont. H.C.); affirmed on other grounds (1978), 83 D.L.R. (3d) 151 (Ont. C.A.) (which dealt with property devised to a minor).

100 Pollock, *Principles of Contract* (13th ed. 1950), pp. 47-48; Wright (1935), 13 Can. Bar Rev. 319 at 323; *Williston on Contracts* (3rd ed. 1959), ss. 223, 226. See the differing views of the judges in *McBride v. Appleton*, [1946] O.R. 17 (Ont. C.A.).

some contracts by minors can be void *ab initio*. Such contracts do not need avoidance, nor can they be made valid by post-majority ratification. A prime source for this view is the Ontario case of *Beam v. Beatty*,[101] in which a bond given by a minor to secure the purchaser of shares from a minor against any loss the former might suffer was held to be invalid.

However two views have since appeared as to when a minor's contract will be void. According to one, this will occur only when the contract is prejudicial to the minor.[102] According to the other, wider view, this will occur whenever the contract is not for the minor's benefit.[103] This latter opinion seems too wide for the purposes of any such rule. Moreover it seems to conflict with cases which clearly indicate that a non-beneficial contract may still be capable of being ratified, or even of being valid unless and until repudiated. Hence, it is suggested, the category of void contracts (if required at all, which is debatable[104]) ought to be restricted to those which are clearly prejudicial to the best interests of the minor, and not simply lacking in any benefit to him.[105]

(v) *Consequences of invalid contracts*

(A) *General* A contract with a minor, if enforceable in accordance with what has earlier been stated, is valid for all purposes (though in the case of a contract of sale of goods the only price for necessaries sold and delivered to the infant that may be recovered from the infant is "a reasonable price", not the agreed price under the contract).[106]

(B) *Voidable contracts* As already indicated these may be valid as far as the minor's liability is concerned,[107] until repudiated or invalid unless ratified. If there

---

101 (1902), 3 O.L.R. 345 (Ont. H.C.); reversed on other grounds (1902), 4 O.L.R. 554 (Ont. C.A.). See also *Phillips v. Greater Ottawa Dev. Co.* (1916), 38 O.L.R. 315 (Ont. C.A.); *McKay v. McKinley*, [1933] O.W.N. 392 (Ont. H.C.); *Re Staruch*, [1955] 5 D.L.R. 807 (Ont. C.A.); *Ivan v. Hartley*, [1945] O.W.N. 627 (Ont. H.C.). Compare *R. v. Leduc*, [1972] 1 O.R. 458 (Ont. Dist. Ct.). See also *Toronto Marlboro Major Junior "A" Hockey Club v. Tonelli* (1978), 18 O.R. (2d) 21 at 34 (Ont. H.C.) *per* Lerner J.

102 *R. v. Rash* (1923), 53 O.L.R. 245 at 255 (Ont. C.A.) *per* Martin J.A.; *Hagerman v. Siddall & Johnson*, [1924] 2 D.L.R. 755 (Sask. K.B.); *McKay v. McKinley*, [1933] O.W.N. 392 (Ont. H.C.); *McBride v. Appleton*, [1946] 2 D.L.R. 16 at 30 (Ont. C.A.) *per* Roach J.A., and at 26-27 *per* Laidlaw J.A. (even if the contract is for the minor's benefit: *ibid.*); *Re Staruch*, [1955] 5 D.L.R. 807 (Ont. C.A.).

103 This can be deduced from the breadth of interpretation of what is prejudicial: see *Re Staruch*, above; *Altobelli v. Wilson*, [1957] O.W.N. 207 (Ont. C.A.); *Upper v. Lightning Fastener Employees' Credit Union (St. Catharines)* (1966), 9 C.B.R. (N.S.) 211 (Ont. Co. Ct.). See also Ferguson J. in *Butterfield v. Sibbett & Nipissing Elec. Supply Co.*, [1950] 4 D.L.R. 302 at 307 (Ont. H.C.); compare *R. v. Leduc*, [1972] 1 O.R. 458 at 459 (Ont. Dist. Ct.).

104 Hartwig, "Infants' Contracts in English Law: With Commonwealth & European Comparisons" (1966), 15 I.C.L.Q. 780 at 793.

105 Under the recommendations of the Ontario Law Reform Commission, *Report*, above, note 93, no such category would exist.

106 Under the Sale of Goods Act, see Fridman, *Sale of Goods in Canada*, 3rd ed. (1986), pp. 33-34.

107 The minor may enforce the contract against the other party, which may amount to ratification or negate repudiation, but he cannot obtain specific performance: *Melville v. Stratherne* (1878), 26 Gr. 52 (Ont. Ch.).

is no repudiation, the contract will have its normal, full effect. If the minor repudiates, he will be relieved from all future liabilities not yet due at the time of the repudiation. In respect of accrued liabilities, not yet discharged, *Re Central Bank and Hogg*[108] is authority for the proposition that repudiation brings them to an end. In that case, a minor purchased shares in the company, which was in the process of being wound up. Prior to her attaining 21, the then age of majority, there was an order for calls against contributories, including the minor. Before the date of her majority, she repudiated the share contract by seeking to have her name removed from the list of contributories. It was held that this discharged her obligations both future and existing. Money already paid over by the minor, however, prior to repudiation, may not always be recoverable. Much depends upon whether or not the adult party has performed his part of the bargain, that is, whether or not there has been what the common law called a total failure of consideration.[109] In cases involving the purchase of realty, the fact that the minor has exercised possession and control, with the permission of the adult vendor, has meant loss of any right of recovery of a deposit paid on such realty.[110] However, the recovery of property other than money, whether it be goods or land, after repudiation of the contract under which the minor transferred the property to the adult, may depend upon the possibility that, applying equitable, not common-law principles, complete *restitutio in integrum* can be made.[111] The validity of such distinction, and its operation may both be questioned.[112]

Turning to contracts which require ratification for their validity, it would seem that even before any such act on the part of the minor it may be possible for the minor to enforce the contract against the adult (other than by specific performance by reason of lack of mutuality in this respect[113]). Moreover, a third party cannot rely on the invalidity of the contract. Thus in *McBride v. Appleton*,[114] the sale of motorcycle under a conditional sales agreement, which provided that title remained in the original seller, may have been void (or voidable) so far as the minor was concerned, but that did not assist a third party to whom, eventually, the motorcycle had been sold, when repossession was claimed by the original seller, following default in payment on the part of the minor. If the minor never ratifies, then he can not be sued in respect of accrued or future liabilities.[115] Recovery

---

108 (1890), 19 O.R. 7 (Ont. Ch.).
109 Compare *Steinberg v. Scala (Leeds) Ltd.*, [1923] 2 Ch. 452 (C.A.). This is the view of Payne, "The Contractual Liability of Infants" (1966), 5 Western L.R. 136 at 144.
110 *Short v. Field* (1915), 32 O.L.R. 395 (Ont. C.A.); *Robinson v. Moffatt* (1915), 35 O.L.R. 9 (Ont. C.A.).
111 See, *e.g.*, *Whalls v. Learn* (1888), 15 O.R. 481 (Ont. C.A.). This is the view of Percy, "The Present Law of Infants' Contracts" (1975), 53 Can. Bar Rev. 1 at 21. It is also favoured by McCamus, "Restitution of Benefits Conferred Under Minors' Contracts" (1979), 28 U.N.B.L.J. 89, at pp. 99-103.
112 *Pearce v. Brain*, [1929] 2 K.B. 310 at 314, *per* Swift J.
113 *Lumley v. Ravenscroft*, [1895] 1 Q.B. 683; compare below, p. 796.
114 [1946] O.R. 17 (Ont. C.A.). Hence the original seller still retained his title as agreed in the conditional sales contract, and could recover the goods from the innocent third party.
115 *Pyett v. Lampman*, [1923] 1 D.L.R. 249 (Ont. C.A.).

of money paid or property transferred by the minor under such a contract has been said to depend upon *either* total failure of consideration *or* the possibility of *restitutio in integrum*.[116] Cases may be cited in support of both propositions.[117] Perhaps both may be involved, as was suggested in *Sturgeon v. Starr* in 1911:

> If an infant pay money without valuable consideration he can get it back; and if he pay money for valuable consideration he may also recover it; but subject to the condition that he can restore the other party to his former position.[118]

In support of the *restitutio* principle as the basis for recovery is the majority decision in the English case of *Chaplin v. Frewin*,[119] which was concerned with recovery of copyright which had been assigned by the minor to the publishers. It was held that by reason of contracts made with other publishers on the faith of the assignment, *restitutio* was not possible. In consequence, nor was recovery by the minor.

There appears to be some uncertainty in the law where the minor has partly paid for goods which he has received, and then refused to ratify the contract (or wishes to repudiate or rescind it). What if *restitutio* is not completely possible? Can it be said that there is total failure of consideration? It may be that in these situations the minor, while capable of rescinding, or not being bound by the contract, must return the property to the adult party, and may not be able to recover his deposit or part payment.[120]

(C) *Void contracts* Since any such contract is not binding upon a minor, he is not bound by it to the adult party, and may recover back money paid or property transferred, apparently regardless of any benefits he may have received or his ability to make *restitutio*.[121] This may support those who argue that a category of void contracts by minors is undesirable, or even non-existent, since to permit the minor to despoil the adult party may wreak injustice and so be contradictory to the spirit of law relating to minors' contracts, which is to protect the minor not penalize the adult.

This may have especial consequences where a minor has purchased goods under such a "prejudicial" contract and then sells them to a third party who is an innocent purchaser for value. If the original contract is void the latter should obtain no title; only if the original title is voidable might he conceivably acquire a good title if the transaction took place before the minor avoided *his* contract

---

116 McCamus, *loc. cit.*, perfers the *restitution* approach.
117 Failure of consideration: *McDonald v. Baxter* (1911), 46 N.S.R. 149 (N.S.C.A.); *Phillips v. Greater Ottawa Dev. Co.* (1916), 33 D.L.R. 259 at 263 (Ont. C.A.) *per* Masten J.; *Noble's Ltd. v. Bellefleur* (1963), 37 D.L.R. (2d) 519 (N.B.C.A.); *Nicklin v. Longhurst*, [1917] 1 W.W.R. 439 (Man. C.A.); *Coull v. Kolbuc* (1969), 68 W.W.R. 76 (Alta. Dist. Ct.); *Fannon v. Dobranski* (1970), 73 W.W.R. 371 (Alta. Dist. Ct.). *Restitutio: Bo-Lassen v. Josiassen*, [1973] 4 W.W.R. 317 (Alta. Dist. Ct.). See Percy, *loc. cit.*, at pp. 25-30.
118 (1911), 17 W.L.R. 402 at 404 (Man. K.B.) *per* Prendergast J.
119 [1966] Ch. 71 (C.A.).
120 Percy, *loc. cit.*, at pp. 27-30.
121 *Re Staruch*, [1955] 5 D.L.R. 807 (Ont. C.A.). But see *Phillips v. Greater Ottawa Dev. Co.*, above, note 117. See Percy, *loc. cit.*, at p. 35.

with the first seller.[122] In *McBride v. Appleton*,[123] Roach J.A. dissenting, having held that the purchase by the minor amounted to a void contract, got around this problem by applying the doctrine of estoppel to prevent the original owner, that is, the seller to the minor, from relying upon the voidness of that contract as against an innocent third party purchasing from the minor. But the extent to which such doctrine is applicable is questionable and third parties have not always been easily protected.[124]

(vi) *Alternate liability in tort*

Minors may be sued in tort, except where liability depends upon some state of mind or type of conduct, such as negligence, which is not attributable to a minor of the particular age group involved. However, an adult cannot evade the immunity of a minor under a contract by suing in tort in respect of the wrongful act which allegedly constituted the breach of contract. This is so even if the act in question could be characterized as tortious as well as in breach of contract. A distinction is drawn between acts arising out of the performance of the contract and acts independent of the contract. Thus driving a car negligently, when there was an express or implied term in a contract of hire that it would not be damaged, is not actionable in negligence thereby avoiding the minor's contractual immunity.[125] But deliberately destroying the car might well be an actionable tort, namely, trespass, despite the unavailability of any contractual remedy to the adult party.[126] This distinction was also drawn in two cases in British Columbia. In *Victoria U Drive Yourself Auto Livery v. Wood*,[127] the minor hirer of a car was liable for the damage caused to it by *another* minor to whom he had given the car to drive in contravention of the contract, that is, it was outside the purview of the contract. In *Dickson Bros. U-Drive Ltd. v. Woo Wai Jing*,[128] the hirer himself, a minor, was guilty of negligently causing damage to the car. There was no liability in tort. The *Wood* case is a very dubious decision; the point about tort liability was never argued or dealt with by the court. Nonetheless, the distinction apprears to be well accepted. It has been pointed out[129] that these different and illogical results may depend upon the drafting of the contract under which the minor obtains possession of the chattel. In any

---

122 Fridman, *Sale of Goods in Canada*, 3rd ed. (1986), pp. 132-135.
123 [1946] O.R. 17 (Ont. C.A.).
124 The minor may be compensated if he has acted under a void contract and conferred a benefit on the other party: *Altobelli v. Wilson*, [1957] O.W.N. 207 (Ont. C.A.).
125 *Jennings v. Rundall* (1799), 101 E.R. 1419; *Fawcett v. Smethurst* (1914), 84 L.J.K.B. 473; *Noble's Ltd. v. Bellefleur*, above, note 117.
126 *Burnard v. Haggis* (1863), 14 C.B.N.S. 45; *Ballett v. Mingay*, [1943] K.B. 281 (C.A.); *McCallum v. Urchak*, [1926] 1 W.W.R. 137 (Alta. C.A.).
127 [1930] 1 W.W.R. 522 (B.C.C.A.); compare *McCallum v. Urchak*, above.
128 (1957), 23 W.W.R. 485 (B.C.C.A.).
129 Percy, *loc. cit.*, at p. 40.

event the capricious effects of this legal doctrine lead to the conclusion that there is something very amiss with the law.[130]

A further consequence of the principle that contractual immunity cannot be outflanked by invoking the law of tort is that an action cannot be brought against a minor in deceit alleging fraudulent misrepresentation of his age.[131] Nor will such misrepresentation prevent the minor, in a contract action brought against him, from pleading his minority.[132] However, the fraud of a minor may have consequences in equity.[133] A fraudulent minor may not be able to bind the adult to the contract,[134] he may have to restore goods purchased under a contract induced by his fraudulent misrepresentation as to his age,[135] he may also have to disgorge the proceeds of goods obtained in this way.[136] So far as this last point is concerned, it was held in the English case of *Leslie (R.) Ltd. v. Sheill*[137] that this did not mean that a minor could be compelled to restore money which he had already disposed of prior to the discovery of his fraud. In the famous words of Lord Sumner, "restitution stopped where repayment began."[138]

(vii) *Liability of adult guarantor or surety*

The position adopted by the law with respect to the immunity of minors led to the introduction of methods by which tradesmen could be protected. This was

---

130 Hence the recommendations of the Ontario Law Reform Commission, *Report on Amendment of the Law of Contract* (1987), pp. 208-210, agreeing with the change of the law in New South Wales and the position of the Alberta Institute of Law Research & Reform, that a minor should be liable for independent torts and torts connected with contracts, subject to two limitations: (i) a minor should be liable for a false representation as to his age only where the person to whom the representation was made had reasonable grounds for believing the representation to be true; and (ii) a minor should not be liable for such a representation only because he signed or adopted a document prepared and tendered by the person to whom the representation was made or with whom the minor contracted, and the document was preprinted and used in all such transactions. These limitations were necessary to protect minors from exploitation and were consistent with the general policy, affirmed by the Commission, of protecting minors from contractual liability.

131 *Stocks v. Wilson*, [1913] 2 K.B. 235; *Re Darnley and C.P.R.* (1908), 9 W.L.R. 20 (B.C.S.C.) (with which contrast *Continental Guar. Corp. of Can. v. Mark*, [1926] 4 D.L.R. 707 (B.C.C.A.)). Compare the recommendations above, note 130.

132 *Jewell v. Broad* (1909), 19 O.L.R. 1 (Ont. H.C.); affirmed (1909), 20 O.L.R. 176 (Ont. C.A.).

133 Compare Lerner J. in *Toronto Marlboro Major Junior "A" Hockey Club v. Tonelli* (1978), 18 O.R. (2d) 21 at 35 (Ont. H.C.).

134 Compare *Robinson v. Moffatt* (1915), 35 O.L.R. 9 (Ont. C.A.); *Gregson v. Law* (1913), 5 W.W.R. 1017 (B.C.S.C.).

135 *Noble's Ltd. v. Bellefleur*, above, note 125.

136 *Stocks v. Wilson*, above, note 131.

137 [1914] 3 K.B. 607 (C.A.).

138 *Ibid.*, at 618. The possibility of a quasi-contractual remedy, *i.e.*, for money had and received, is still uncertain. Much depends upon whether this is thought of as "contractual" in nature or independent. If the latter, then there may be no reason why such recovery should not be permitted despite the infant's contractual incapacity; compare Percy, *loc. cit.*, at pp. 45-46. See further for full discussion, McCamus, *loc. cit.*, pp. 110-115; Payne, *loc. cit.*, pp. 150-152; Atiyah, "The Liability of Infants in Fraud and Restitution" (1959), 22 M.L.R. 273 at 282-290; Goff and Jones, *Law of Restitution*, 3rd ed. (1986), pp. 428-439.

sought to be achieved by the involvement of an adult third party. Two ways of doing this developed. First, someone dealing with a minor took an indemnity from an adult. Secondly, the tradesmen or businessman made the adult a principal contracting party.

If the adult is involved under some independent arrangement, much may depend upon whether this is a guarantee or an indemnity. There is authority for the proposition that a guarantor will not be liable if the debt guaranteed is void or voidable;[139] therefore a minor's contract which falls within either of these two categories is one in respect of which an adult's guarantee will be invalid to protect the adult contracting with the minor.[140] The essence of a guarantee is that there is an enforceable obligation of a principal debtor. Therefore, failing such enforceable obligation on the part of a minor, there is nothing that can be guaranteed.[141] If the same result is sought to be achieved by an indemnity, however, then the adult underwriting the non-performance of the minor, that is, his non-payment, will be liable.[142] The problem here is that the distinction between guarantee and indemnity is extremely technical and artificial.[143] The protection of an adult contracting with a minor may depend upon factors and language which are beyond the control or comprehension of the adult contracting party. A perfectly legitimate conclusion may be precluded and frustrated by the application of some complex law. It might be better simply to permit adult guarantors of minors to be liable whenever the minor defaults, not just where the contract is one which is enforceable against the minor. On the other hand, the policy of the law as it now is, namely, to prevent the contractual adventures of minors beyond a limited sphere of activity, might itself be foiled if the easy method of guarantee were available. Minors might cajole, coerce, or persuade adults to undertake such guarantees on their behalf in circumstances in which it would be better if the minor were not encouraged to indulge his or her tastes. This might result in greater harm to more people, as

---

139 *Ins. Office of Australia Ltd. v. T.M. Burke Pty. Ltd.* (1935), 35 S.R. (N.S.W.) 438; *McDonald v. Dennys Lascelles Ltd.* (1933), 48 C.L.R. 457; *MacDonald-Crawford Ltd. v. Burns*, [1924] 2 W.W.R. 413 (Sask. C.A.). Contrast *Edmonton Airport Hotel Co. v. Crédit Foncier Franco-Canadien*, [1965] S.C.R. 441 (S.C.C.); *Hagan Tpt. Ltd. v. Can. Accept. Corp.*, [1974] S.C.R. 491 (S.C.C.).

140 *Coutts & Co. v. Browne-Lecky*, [1947] K.B. 104. See the discussion of this and other cases by Steyne (1974), 90 L.Q.R. 246 at 251-254. But there appears to be no *Canadian* authority to this effect. Indeed in *R. v. Novak*, [1920] 1 W.W.R. 136 (Man. C.A.), the surety of a debt owed by a minor to the Crown was liable on the minor's default. But as this was a debt incurred by way of loan to enable the minor to study to become a teacher, perhaps the contract was not an unenforceable one, on the part of the minor. Moreover, (i) the debt was incurred with the Crown under statute, (ii) the adult may have been an independent or principal party, see below, rather than a guarantor.

141 But why extend the minor's personal immunity to an adult? Compare *McBride v. Appleton*, [1946] 2 D.L.R. 16 (Ont. C.A.). Hence the recommendation of the Ontario Law Reform Commission, *Report*, above, note 130, p. 208, that a guarantor should be bound by the guarantee as if the minor were an adult, and may be indemnified by the minor if the obligation was enforceable against the minor, or be granted relief as the court thinks just, if the obligation is not enforceable against the minor. "Guarantee" here should include indemnity or any other undertaking of responsibility.

142 *Yeoman Credit v. Latter*, [1961] 2 All E.R. 294 (C.A.).

143 See the recommendation of the Ontario Law Reform Commission, above, note 141.

well as the possible encouragement of methods of tradesmen to obtain such guarantees.

All these problems are avoided if the adult contracting with a minor finds an adult who will undertake primary, not secondary liability on behalf of the minor, for example, by becoming a party to the contract between the adult and the minor.[144] In *Feldman v. Horn & Rae*[145] the plaintiff sold a car to a minor under a conditional sale contract. A promissory note was given for the debt. Both documents were signed jointly by the minor and an adult, the second defendant. When the minor defaulted in payment, it was held that the adult was liable for the balance owing. By signing the note she had become a principal party, jointly and severally liable with the minor. Therefore this was not an instance of guarantee, such that the unenforceability of the contract as against the minor relieved the adult from alternative liability. This was a case of personal, primary liability on the part of the adult. The only possible way for an adult to escape such liability in those circumstances is if the adult can establish that he was really a surety, a secondary party, even though described in the contract as a principal.[146] This would seem unlikely, however, as it might lead to fraud, and since the defence is equitable, such a result would seem to be unconscionable.[147]

(2) British Columbia

The earlier law was changed as a consequence of the Report of the provincial Law Reform Commission[148] by the Law Reform Amendment Act, 1985,[149] which amended the Infants Act[150] in two ways. It repealed certain sections[151] and added new sections 16.1-16.11. The situation may be summarized as follows.

A contract by a minor, *i.e.*, someone who was an infant at the time the contract was made, is unenforceable against him unless: (a) the contract is enforceable against him by some statute; (b) the minor affirms the contract on attaining majority;[152] (c) it is wholly or partially performed by the minor after majority; or (d) it is not repudiated by the minor within a year after majority.[153] However,

---

144 *MacDonald-Crawford Ltd. v. Burns*, [1924] 2 D.L.R. 977 at 985-988 (Sask. C.A.) *per* Lamont J.A.

145 (1960), 33 W.W.R. 568 (Alta. Dist. Ct.); compare *Pearson v. Calder* (1916), 35 O.L.R. 524 (Ont. C.A.).

146 See, *e.g.*, *Eldridge & Morris v. Taylor*, [1931] 2 K.B. 416 (C.A.).

147 *Wauthier v. Wilson* (1912), 28 T.L.R. 239 (C.A.).

148 Report on Minors' Contracts, 1976.

149 S.B.C. 1985, c. 10, s. 1.

150 R.S.B.C. 1979, c. 196. Note how some of these changes have been reflected in the *Report* of the Ontario Law Reform Commission, above, notes 65, 67, 80, 130, 141.

151 *Viz.*, ss. 17-19.

152 Within one year of the minor's attaining majority the adult party may give a notice in writing requesting the minor to affirm or repudiate the contract. If nothing is done within 60 days the minor is deemed to have repudiated the contract.

153 A minor is deemed to have repudiated a contract after attaining majority if the minor refuses to perform the contract or a material term; makes a claim for relief under the statute; or gives or makes reasonable efforts to give oral or written notice of repudiation to another party.

the minor can enforce the contract against the adult party as if the minor had been an adult at the time of contracting. In the case of an unenforceable contract the minor or another party (if the minor has repudiated the contract or is in breach) can apply to a court for relief against a party to the contract or someone who has acquired a right or interest in property transferred under the contract (except a stranger to the contract who, or whose predecessor in title, acquired the property *bona fide* and for value). The court has wide powers in respect of the relief that may be given, including ordering compensation, restitution of property, and discharge of parties from contractual obligations. Various factors must be taken into consideration by the court, including the circumstances surrounding the making of the contract, whether the minor induced the contract by a misrepresentation of age, the subject matter and nature of the contract, the nature and value of property if the contract concerns property, the age and means of the minor, or a change of position that might make any grant of relief inequitable as far as any party to the application is concerned. A minor does not induce the making of a contract by making a representation as to age for this purpose where the one to whom the representation was made did not have reasonable grounds for believing the representation was true; or the minor signed or adopted a document relating to the contract and the document contained a statement that the minor was 19 or otherwise had contractual capacity, the document was prepared and tendered by the other party, and was prepared and used in other similar transactions. If property is transferred under a contract unenforceable against a minor, title will pass unless and until an order about the transfer is made under these provisions.

A court can give a minor full capacity to enter any contract, or capacity to enter a specific contract or class of contracts. So can the Public Trustee.

A guarantor or one who indemnifies or otherwise undertakes responsibility for the failure of a minor to perform a contractual obligation will be liable as if the minor were an adult when the contract was made.

However, (i) the minor is not deprived of any defence that would be available to an adult of full capacity; and (ii) a minor may not be sued in tort where the tort is connected with, arises out of, was contemplated by, or is an indirect means of enforcing an unenforceable contract.[154]

(b) Insane persons[155]

(i) *Effect of insanity*

A contracting party may have been declared or found insane by some judicial determination prior to the making of the contract which is in question. In such event, there is authority to the effect that such a person cannot enter into any

---

154 Note that the Ontario Law Reform Commission's recommendations differ, above, note 130.

155 Fridman, "Mental Incompetency" (1963), 79 L.Q.R. 502 at 509-516; compare Browne, "Can the Insane Contract?" (1933), 11 Can. Bar Rev. 600. See also the judgment of Nicholson J. in *Bank of N.S. v. Kelly* (1973), 41 D.L.R. (3d) 273 (P.E.I.S.C.). Note the situation in respect of marriage contracts, separation agreements and cohabitation agreements in Ontario under the Family Law Act, R.S.O. 1990, c. F.3, s. 55(3).

contract. Hence such a contract will be void.[156] Once a person has been found by a court to be wanting in intellect, then it would seem to follow that such person lacks contractual capacity. He or she is not able to consent.

A person may be lacking in mental competence,[157] that is, incapable of appreciating what he was doing or the nature and effects of what he was doing, without there ever having been any judicial determination of this question.[158] If such a person enters into a contract, what is its effect? Following English authorities,[159] it would seem that Canadian courts agree that the contracts of such a person are not void *ab initio*. They are voidable at the option of the insane person.[160] Hence that party may enforce the contract against the other whose sanity was never in issue. For this reason, in one case[161] a lease to a municipal corporation made by the plaintiff's attorney, at the time the plaintiff was insane, was valid and enforceable against the corporation.

(ii) *Relevant factors*

(A) *Knowledge of other party* The insanity must have been known to the other party at the time of contracting. In *Hardman v. Falk*,[162] the fact that the grantor of an option to purchase some land was insane at the time of such grant under a contract was not enough to invalidate the contract. It was a fair contract, made in good faith by the optionee, without any knowledge on his part of the insanity of the grantor. For this reason, Sheppard J.A. dissented in the case of *Re Rogers*.[163]

---

156 *Monticello State Bank v. Baillee*, [1922] W.W.R. 894 (Alta. C.A.); *Rourke v. Halford* (1916), 37 O.L.R. 92 (Ont. C.A.). Unless, possibly, if the contract is made during a "lucid interval": see *Moore v. Confederation Life Assn.*, [1918] 2 W.W.R. 895 (B.C.S.C.). For the situation under the Patients Property Act in British Columbia, see *Taylor v. Jenkins* (1986), 1 B.C.L.R. (2d) 207 (B.C.S.C.).

157 This will be a question of fact: *Peters v. Rocher* (1982), 15 Man. R. (2d) 168 (Man. Q.B.). On the issue of evidence see *Sawatzky v. Sawatzky* (1986), 48 Sask. R. 161 (Sask. Q.B.); *Thom v. Saltner*, [1989] 1 W.W.R. 456 (Man. Q.B.) (woman suffering from Alzheimer's disease transferring assets). See also the detailed discussion of the evidence in *C.I.B.C. v. Dzeryk (Public Trustee)* (1993), 8 Alta. L.R. (3d) 86 (Alta. Q.B.).

158 *Wilson v. R.*, [1938] S.C.R. 317 (S.C.C.).

159 *Imperial Loan Co. v. Stone*, [1892] 1 Q.B. 599 (C.A.); *York Glass Co. v. Jubb* (1925), 134 L.T. 36 (C.A.). But see *Daily Telegraph Newspaper Co. v. McLaughlin*, [1904] A.C. 776 (P.C.); *Gibbons v. Wright* (1954), 91 C.L.R. 423.

160 *Fyckes v. Chisholm* (1911), 3 O.W.N. 21 (Ont. H.C.); *Hardman v. Falk*, [1955] 3 D.L.R. 129 (B.C.C.A.); *Re Rogers* (1963), 42 W.W.R. 200 (B.C.C.A.); *Sawatzky v. Sawatzky*, above, note 157. But some English authorities suggest that there may be situations in which an insane person is so unsound of mind as to be utterly incapable of contracting, *i.e.*, where a purported contract is void; Fridman, above, note 155 at pp. 513-515. This seems to be an outmoded view: it is questionable in view of the approach to contracts made by drunkards, where the test *now* seems to be unconscionability rather than appreciation of the legal quality of the act: below, p. 162.

161 *Kerr v. Petrolia* (1921), 51 O.L.R. 74 (Ont. H.C.). Compare *Cameron v. Dorcic* (1987), 80 N.S.R. (2d) 152 (N.S.T.D.); affirmed (1988), 83 N.S.R. (2d) 85 (N.S.C.A.).

162 [1955] 3 D.L.R. 129 at 133 (B.C.C.A.). Compare *Hill Estate v. Chevron Standard Ltd.* (1991), 74 Man. R. (2d) 162 (Man. Q.B.); reversed [1993] 2 W.W.R. 545 (Man. C.A.); leave to appeal to S.C.C. refused [1993] 4 W.W.R. lxvii (note) (S.C.C.).

163 (1963), 39 D.L.R. (2d) 141 (B.C.C.A.) (followed in *Schultz v. Ruzas* (1982), 40 A.R. 60 (Alta. Q.B.)).

The question was whether a change in the beneficiary clause in an insurance policy had been validly made. Since the party making the change was insane at the time the court had to decide whether the appropriate test was the test applicable in contract cases or in those concerned with testamentary capacity. The latter simply involved capacity: knowledge of third parties was immaterial. The contractual test, following the decision in *Imperial Loan Co. v. Stone*,[164] also required evidence of knowledge on the part of the other party to the transaction. The majority of the court held that the testamentary test applied. Therefore the change was invalid. Sheppard J.A.[165] held that the contractual test was involved; hence the change was operative. So, too, in *Ridgley v. M. & M. Holdings Ltd.; Ridgley v. McGrath*,[166] a party who was mentally incompetent because of alcohol addiction entered into a fair lease with some long-term business associates who were ignorant of his incapacity. He also conveyed land to some friends who knew he might be incompetent. It was held that the lease was valid. It was fair and the lessors did not know of the incapacity. But the conveyance was invalid since it was unfair to the incompetent party as the grantees knew of his want of capacity.

Actual knowledge of the other party's insanity is not necessary. It is enough if there is wilful disregard of the facts.[167] This was illustrated by the decision of the Appellate Division of the Supreme Court of Alberta in *Hunt v. Texaco Exploration Co.; Hunt v. Thom*[168] in which it was held that actual or constructive notice sufficed. There was constructive notice where the circumstances gave rise to suspicion but the party contracting with the ultimately proved insane party deliberately refrained from inquiring or satisfying himself about the other party's capacity.

(B) *Fairness* In addition to the requirement that the sane party have knowledge of the other party's insanity, it has been suggested that there must be evidence that the contract was unfair.[169] If this is so, then adequacy of consideration, not usually a factor of which the courts will take notice, may be extremely relevant.[170]

---

164 Above, note 159.

165 Above, note 163, at 145.

166 (1982), 39 Nfld. & P.E.I.R. 232 (Nfld. T.D.).

167 *Grant v. Imperial Trust Co.*, [1934] O.W.N. 370 (Ont. C.A.); affirmed [1953] 3 D.L.R. 660 (S.C.C.); *i.e.*, constructive notice: *Bank of N.S. v. Kelly* (1973), 41 D.L.R. (3d) 273 (P.E.I.S.C.); compare *Lingard v. Thomas* (1984), 46 Nfld. & P.E.I.R. 245 (Nfld. T.D.); *Sawatzky v. Sawatzky*, above, note 157.

168 [1955] 3 D.L.R. 555 (Alta. S.C.); followed in *Schultz v. Ruzas*, above, note 163. But is such notice only effective where the consideration was inadequate? See *Lingard v. Thomas* (1984), 46 Nfld. & P.E.I.R. 245 (Nfld. T.D.). Compare, *Fyckes v. Chisholm* (1911), 19 O.W.R. 977 at 980 (Ont. H.C.) *per* Mulock C.J. Ex. Ct.

169 See the cases cited above, notes 162, 166; see *Walker v. Cusack* (1982), 16 Man. R. (2d) 114 at 121 (Man. Q.B.); *Schultz v. Ruzas* (1982), 40 A.R. 60 at 66 (Alta. Q.B.); *Wilson v. R.*, [1938] S.C.R. 317 (S.C.C.). This was left unsettled in *Moore v. Confederation Life Assn.*, [1918] 2 W.W.R. 895 (B.C. S.C.). But the question of taking advantage was not held important by Nicholson J. in *Bank of N.S. v. Kelly* above, note 167, only knowledge of the incompetency. Fairness was only relevant when there is a lesser degree of incompetency not amounting to incapacity to contract: *ibid.* at 6.

170 *Hardman v. Falk*, [1955] 3 D.L.R. 129 (B.C.C.A.).

It has also been said that, besides knowledge of the insanity, and the fairness or otherwise of the contract considered objectively, regard should also be paid to whether the contract was unconscionable, that is to say, whether the sane party took advantage of the insane one.[171] The relevance of these additional elements is open to question, especially in light of the decision of the Privy Council in *Hart v. O'Connor.*[172] There the Privy Council, hearing an appeal from New Zealand, overruled the earlier New Zealand decision by McMullin J. in *Archer v. Cutler.*[173] In the earlier case it was held that a contract for the sale of land could be invalidated by a party claiming that he was insane at the material time *either* if the other party knew of the unsoundness of mind *or* if the contract was unfair to the insane party, even though the other party did not know of the insanity. The Privy Council refused to accept that this was the law in England or New Zealand. After considering at length and in detail the English, Canadian and Australian decisions, Lord Brightman, delivering the opinion of the Board,[174] said that to accept the proposition enunciated in *Archer v. Cutler* that a contract with a person ostensibly sane, but actually of unsound mind can be set aside because it is "unfair" to the person of unsound mind in the sense of contractual imbalance was unsupported by authority, was illogical and would distinguish the law in New Zealand from the law of Australia[175] for no good reason as well as from the law of England from which the law of Australia and New Zealand and other "common-law" countries (which would include common-law Canada) has stemmed.

In sum, the validity of a contract entered into by a lunatic ostensibly sane is to be judged by the same standards as a contract by a person of sound mind. It is not voidable by the lunatic or his representatives by reason of "unfairness" unless such unfairness amounts to equitable fraud which would have enabled the complaining party to avoid the contract even if he had been sane.[176] Similarly, unconscionable conduct on the part of the sane party was not a necessary ingredient that had to be established before an insane party could avoid a transaction. In *Hart v. O'Connor,* therefore, the transaction, an agreement to buy farmland which was the subject matter of a testamentary settlement, was a valid contract, not to be avoided by the representatives of the sole trustee of the estate (who had entered into the contract with the appellant) on the ground of the trustee's insanity, a fact unknown to the appellant at the material time. There was no evidence of unconscionable conduct nor of equitable fraud, therefore there were no grounds for upsetting the transaction. This case has been followed in Canada.[177] If the insanity of the other party is not known the transaction will not be voidable on the ground of insanity. The fairness of the transaction with an insane party is not

---

171 *Wilson v. R.,* above; *Marshall v. Can. Permanent Trust Co.* (1968), 69 D.L.R. (3d) 260 (Alta. S.C.).

172 [1985] 2 All E.R. 880 (P.C.).

173 [1980] 1 N.Z.L.R. 386 (N.Z.).

174 [1985] 2 All E.R. 880 at 894 (P.C.).

175 *McLaughlin v. Daily Telegraph Newspaper Co.* (1904), 1 C.L.R. 143 (Aus. H.C.); *Tremills v. Benton* (1892), 18 V.L.R. 607.

176 [1985] 2 All E.R. 880 at 894 (P.C.).

177 *Cameron v. Dorcic* (1987), 80 N.S.R. (2d) 152 (N.S.T.D.); affirmed (1988), 83 N.S.R. (2d) 85 (N.S.C.A.); *Halifax West Aquinas Credit Union Ltd. v. Owens* (1989), 91 N.S.R. (2d) 256 (N.S.T.D.).

material to its validity, unless the transaction would be voidable on other grounds, such as equitable fraud, victimization, taking advantage or unconscionability, in the same way as a contract between two sane parties.[178]

(iii) *Liability for necessaries*

Notwithstanding what has been said above, that is, even when there was knowledge of the insanity, where necessaries have been sold and delivered to an insane person, there is liability at common law and under various provincial Sale of Goods Acts to pay a reasonable price.[179] Hence the estate of the insane person will be liable.[180]

(c) Drunkards

(i) *Voidability of contracts*

During the course of the nineteenth century, the English courts eventually decided that a contract entered into by someone who was drunk was not void, but was capable of being avoided at the suit of the drunkard, when he regained his sobriety, if his intoxication led him into not knowing what he was doing, and the other contracting party was aware of such state.[181] This is clearly also the law in Canada.[182] The basis of such voidability appears to be not lack of capacity to contract but the possibility of fraud by the other, sober party.[183] Hence the contract might be voidable even if the other party were ignorant of the drunkenness, if the contract was not fair or made *bona fide*.[184] In *Black v. Wilcox*,[185] the Ontario Court of Appeal placed emphasis upon the unconscionability of the contract, or the lack of equality of bargaining power between the parties.[186]

---

178 *Halifax West Aquinas Credit Union Ltd. v. Owens*, above, note 177, which concerned a contract with a chronic schizophrenic — which was upheld: on grounds for avoiding a contract between sane parties, below, pp. 325-336. See also *Hill Estate v. Chevron Standard Ltd.* (1991), 74 Man. R. (2d) 162 (Man. Q.B.); reversed [1993] 2 W.W.R. 545 (Man. C.A.); leave to appeal to S.C.C. refused [1993] 4 W.W.R. lxvii (note) (S.C.C.).

179 Fridman, *Sale of Goods in Canada*, 3rd ed. (1986), p. 33, note 2.

180 *Morrow v. Morrow* (1920), 47 O.L.R. 222 (Ont. C.A.). Compare *Re Rhodes* (1890), 44 Ch. D. 94 (C.A.). The incompetent will be liable to reimburse the lender of money which has been spent by the incompetent on necessities or in the conduct of the incompetent's estate: *Bank of N.S. v. Kelly*, above, note 169. See, further, Fridman, *Restitution*, 2nd ed. (1992), pp. 273-275; Maddaugh & McCamus, *Law of Restitution* (1990), pp. 693-696.

181 *Gore v. Gibson* (1845), 13 M. & W. 623; *Matthews v. Baxter* (1873) L.R. 8 Ex. 132.

182 *Bawlf Grain Co. v. Ross* (1917), 55 S.C.R. 232 (S.C.C.). This and the preceding sentence were cited by McQuaid J. in *Murray v. Smith* (1980), 32 Nfld. & P.E.I.R. 191 (P.E.I.S.C.); affirmed (1981), 35 Nfld. & P.E.I.R. 382 (P.E.I.C.A.).

183 *Bawlf Grain Co. v. Ross*, above, note 182, at 262 *per* Anglin J.

184 *Watmough v. Cap's Const. Ltd.*, [1977] 1 W.W.R. 398 (Alta. Dist. Ct.).

185 (1977), 70 D.L.R. (3d) 192 (Ont. C.A.).

186 Compare *Blomley v. Ryan* (1956), 99 C.L.R. 362; *Peeters v. Schimonoski*, [1975] 2 N.Z.L.R. 328 (N.Z.); *Fleury v. Homocrest Dairy Co-op.* (1958), 15 D.L.R. (2d) 161 (Ont. H.C.) (drugs).

The proof of lack of knowledge appears to be on the party attempting to enforce the contract. Hence, in an old Northwest Territories case, *Alloway v. Hutchison (No. 2)*,[187] one who took from the payee a bill of exchange and who could not prove that the payee lacked knowledge of the drunkenness of the maker of the bill, was not a holder in due course, and was therefore unable to claim on the bill.

But before any such contract can be avoided, there must be evidence that the party was so drunk as not to know what he was doing. In *McLaren v. McMillan*,[188] another old case from the West, the purchaser who signed a promissory note for the price of a share in a horse was held not to be so intoxicated as not to know what he was doing at the time. He was excited by his excessive drinking, and made more pliable in consequence, but he knew what was going on.[189]

Furthermore, the party who contracted while drunk must avoid the transaction promptly, after becoming sober; if he fails to do so, he will not be allowed to avoid.[190]

(ii) *Ratification*

Such contracts are not void but voidable. The majority of the Supreme Court of Canada held in *Bawlf Grain Co. v. Ross*,[191] that any such contract could be ratified by the drunkard when he became sober. Furthermore, a failure to repudiate within a reasonable time after becoming sober, when the circumstances were such that promptness of repudiation would be expected, amounted to ratification.[192] In that case, there was a sale of wheat by a man who was drunk. By the time he repudiated the price of wheat had changed, that is, had risen. It was held that the seller was bound by his contract. Since the price of wheat fluctuated, it was only reasonable that, if he intended and desired not to be bound by the contract made while he was intoxicated, the seller should have done something fairly quickly. His delay made it too late for him to repudiate, as it indicated that he was waiting to see how the price went, not that he was repudiating because he had realized immediately when he was sober that he had made an improvident deal while drunk. The majority judges in the Supreme Court equated this sort of contract with contracts by persons of unsound mind, or contracts that were for any reason voidable.[193]

---

187 (1898), 6 Terr. L.R. 425 (N.W.T.S.C.).

188 (1907), 5 W.L.R. 336 (Man. K.B.).

189 *Ibid.* at 337 *per* Macdonald J. Contrast *Watmough v. Cap's Const. Ltd.*, above, note 184, where long and excessive drinking was held to render a man incapable of entering into a contract.

190 *Landry v. Takiff* (1979), 24 N.B.R. (2d) 553 (N.B.Q.B.).

191 Above, note 182.

192 Compare *Imperial Life Assur. Co. v. Audette* (1912), 1 W.W.R. 819 (Alta. S.C.), on the validity of an insurance policy, entered into while drunk. It was held that failure to repudiate when the policy was delivered amounted to ratification of the contract. See also *Landry v. Takiff*, above, note 190.

193 See, *e.g., Bawlf Grain Co. v. Ross* (1917), 55 S.C.R. 232 at 238-239 (S.C.C.) *per* Idington J.

(d) The aged and the handicapped

There appear to be no special common-law principles governing the contractual capacity of those affected in any way by age or physical disability. The age of a party might be relevant to the issue of sanity or mental competence (when the rules previously discussed would be applicable). Or a party's age might have a bearing on the question whether a contract was voidable on the grounds of unconscionability or "inequality of bargaining power".[194] Instances may be found in which the age of a party was a factor to be taken into account in determining whether advantage had been taken of such person by the other contracting party.

So, too, where a party was suffering from a physical, as contrasted with a mental disability.[195] Some disabilities will not affect the physical or mental capacity of a party to make a contract, unless in consequence such party were subjected to treatment, by way of analgesic or sedation, that had the effect of rendering the party in question incapable of appreciating the nature and consequences of what he was doing. This occurred in *Fleury v. Homocrest Dairy Co-Operative.*[196] The release of a claim for negligence was set aside because the victim of the negligence had agreed to the release when she was heavily affected by the drugs she was taking for medical reasons. Other physical disabilities may affect a party's contractual capacity, for example, according to some old Scottish cases, being in labour.[197] Deafness might render a person incapable of hearing or understanding correctly an offer that was being made, so that the handicapped person's acceptance could be called into question. Blindness, too, might have the same effect. Indeed the plea of *non est factum*, now of wider import and relevance, was first introduced into the law to cope with just such situations.[198] In cases of this kind, it might be more appropriate to invalidate the contract in question on the grounds of lack of consent, or mistake, or possibly, in more modern parlance, unconscionability, than by treating the handicapped person as lacking in contractual capacity, or having only a qualified capacity.

4. Artificial persons

(a) Introduction

The law recognizes other kinds of "persons" besides human beings. The legal concept of incorporation has the effect of making certain individuals, or groups of individuals, into distinct legal persons, enjoying capacities apart from those which

---

194 See below, pp. 328-330. But not always: compare *370866 Ont. Ltd. v. Chizy* (1987), 57 O.R. (2d) 587 (Ont. H.C.).

195 *E.g.*, where the relevant party was the victim of a stroke: the situation was treated as one involving a party suffering mental incapacity: *Sawatzky v. Sawatzky* (1986), 48 Sask. R. 161 (Sask. Q.B.).

196 (1958), 15 D.L.R. (2d) 161 (Ont. H.C.).

197 *Belford v. Scot* (1683), Mor. 6297; *A. v. B.* (1686), Mor. 6298; *Mason v. Mason* (1686), 2 B.S. 89.

198 Below, pp. 282-283.

the individuals concerned may enjoy as human beings.[199] Since it is a person in law, artifical though such personality may be, a corporation may enter into contracts of all kinds, save those which, by their very nature, are inapplicable to a corporation, such as a contract to marry. However, there are restrictions upon the capacity of a corporation to contract. Those restrictions depend upon the type of corporation which is involved.

In the first place, there is the distinction between corporations sole and corporations aggregate. A corporation sole arises at common law where an individual natural person is endowed by the law with corporate status distinct from that individual's natural personality. The chief remaining illustration of this, at least so far as Canada is concerned, is the Crown. The monarch himself or herself is one legal person; the Crown, as a distinct legal person, embodies the formal, legal capacities of the monarch. Thus, the personality of the Crown transcends and continues after the termination of the personality of the individual monarch who temporarily occupies the throne.

Corporations aggregate (which are by far the more important in modern life and law) either arise at common law by being created by the Crown in the exercise of its Royal Prerogative, or are created by, and under, the terms of some statute. Chartered companies, such as the Hudson's Bay Company, are examples of the former. Limited liability companies under federal or provincial legislation, such as the Canada Business Corporations Act,[200] or the Ontario Business Corporations Act,[201] are examples of the latter. Such corporations, which are intended to carry on business activities of various kinds, have been characterized in modern terms as "business corporations".

(b) The Crown

(i) *Formalities*[202]

The Crown being a corporation at common law has capacity to enter into a contract. In Canada the situation is complicated by the fact that there is a Dominion or federal Crown and there are several provincial Crowns. Each has sovereignty in respect of those matters placed under its supervision and control by what was formerly the British North America Act, 1867.[203]

Hence it is necessary to determine in every instance whether the contract in

---

199 *Salomon v. Salomon & Co.*, [1897] A.C. 22 (H.L.). But where enemy status is involved, in the case of business corporations, the court can go behind the corporate "veil" and look at the real nature of the corporation's personality, in terms of those who continue to make up the corporation: *Daimler Co. v. Continental Tyre Co.*, [1916] 2 A.C. 307 (H.L.); Fridman, "Enemy Status" (1955), 4 I.C.L.Q. 613.

200 R.S.C. 1985, c. C-44.

201 R.S.O. 1990, c. B.16.

202 See Jackett C.J. in *R. v. Transworld Shipping Ltd.* (1976), 61 D.L.R. (3d) 304 (Fed. C.A.); Arrowsmith, "The Contractual Liability of the Crown and its Agents" (1990), 28 Osgoode Hall L.J. 571.

203 Now the Constitution Act, 1867; see the Schedule to the Constitution Act, 1982, as enacted by the Canada Act, 1982.

question is one over which a particular "Crown" has the constitutional power, and therefore the capacity to make.

There is another way in which such distinction becomes important. The legislature that is appropriate in the circumstances, for example, the Parliament of Canada, the Legislative Assembly of Alberta, the Ontario Provincial Parliament, may have the constitutional power and right to pass legislation controlling or regulating the powers and capacities of the Crown in respect of contracts in general, or contracts in particular. It becomes vital to decide whether such legislation is *intra vires* the legislative body concerned, as was discussed by the Exchequer Court of Canada in *Dimensional Investments Ltd. v. R.*[204] Once the body in question has such power, then whatever formalities it prescribes must be followed.[205] Thus if the contract is one which is made by a "provincial" Crown, the law governing the contract, including the formalities to be adopted, will be the appropriate provincial law. If it is a federal contract, made by the Crown in Right of Canada, then general Canadian law will be applicable, that is, legislation of the Parliament of Canada.[206]

(ii) *Enforcement*

At common law, in England and Canada, there was no right to sue the Crown in contract. In the event that the Crown was alleged to be in breach of contract the subject could only petition for some redress, by a procedure known as petition of right.[207] It was a matter of grace on the part of the Crown whether permission was granted to allow the proceedings to continue, although it would appear that this was probably more normal than unusual. However, the subject had no clear right of action but was dependent upon the clemency of the Crown. Even then, the only possible remedy was damages. Under no circumstances could specific performance of a contract be obtained as it might against a private citizen or corporation.[208]

Statute has now changed this situation. In most, if not all provinces (as well as under the law of Canada itself), there is a right to sue the Crown for breach

---

204 [1966] Ex. C.R. 761 (Ex. Ct.); affirmed (1967), 64 D.L.R. (2d) 632 (S.C.C.).

205 *Mackay v. A.G. B.C.*, [1922] 1 A.C. 457 (P.C.); *Dom. Bldg. Corp. v. R.*, [1933] 2 W.W.R. 417 (P.C.).

206 *Bank of N.S. v. R.* (1961), 27 D.L.R. (2d) 120 (Ex. Ct.); *Bartlet v. Osterhout*, [1931] O.R. 358 (Ont. H.C.). See *R. v. CAE Industries Ltd.* (1985), 20 D.L.R. (4th) 347 (Fed. C.A.); leave to appeal to S.C.C. refused (1985), 20 D.L.R. (4th) 347n (S.C.C); *J.E. Verreault & Fils Ltée v. A.G. Que.*, [1977] 1 S.C.R. 41 (S.C.C.).

To determine whether a contract exists the general law of contract, including the doctrine of promissory estoppel (above, pp. 121-136) is also applicable, *e.g.*, where a contract was alleged to arise between a treaty Indian and the Crown: *Mentuck v. Canada*, [1986] 3 F.C. 249 (Fed. T.D.).

207 *Thomas v. R.* (1874), L.R. 10 Q.B. 44; *Windsor & Annapolis Ry. v. R.* (1886), 11 App. Cas. 607 (P.C.).

208 *Dom. Bldg. Corp. v. R.*, above, note 205, at 548.

of contract.[209] The exact nature of the right, and the procedure relating to its exercise are contained in the specific provisions of the Act. The effect of this legislation, however, subject to the exclusion of specific performance and injunctions as possible remedies,[210] is to place the Crown in as close as possible the same position as any other corporation or individual when it comes to the making and enforcement of contracts.

(c) Business corporations

(i) *Powers*

At common law there was an important distinction between chartered companies, or corporations, and companies or business corporations owing their existence, legality and personality to some statute under the terms of which they were incorporated.

Common-law, that is, chartered corporations had and continue to have the capacity of a natural person to contract save for such contracts as are impossible for an artificial person. In other words, such a corporation has the same powers to contract business as an individual. This was settled in the seventeenth century in *Sutton's Hospital Case.*[211] If the charter of such a corporation prohibits the doing of a certain act, the effect of a breach of the charter is to entitle the Crown to forfeit the charter. But any contract made in breach of the charter will be binding. This is made clear in the opinion of the Judicial Committee given by Lord Haldane in *Bonanza Creek Gold Mining Co. v. R.,*[212] in which it was held that the Lieutenant-Governor of Ontario, acting in pursuance of the Royal prerogative, could create a company with powers which extended beyond the province of Ontario. This was a chartered, not a statutory company.[213]

By contrast, statutory corporations are only legal persons insofar as they are empowered by the statute which creates them. Anything done beyond such powers was *ultra vires* at common law. It was *void*, not on the ground of being illegal (though the same act may also be illegal for other reasons), but simply for want of legal capacity. This doctrine of *ultra vires*, which did not and still does not apply to common-law and chartered corporations, provided an importnt restriction upon the contractual capacity of such bodies.

---

209 Petition of Right Act, R.S.C. 1970, c. P-12 [repealed R.S.C. 1970 (2nd Supp.), c. 10, s. 64(1)]; Federal Court Act, R.S.C. 1985, c. F-7, s. 17(2) [re-en. 1990, c. 8, s. 3]. Compare Proceedings Against the Crown Act, R.S.O. 1990, c. P.27; this statute was based upon an Act drafted by the Canadian Commissioners on Uniformity. Other provinces with similar legislation are Alberta, British Columbia, Manitoba, New Brunswick, Nova Scotia, and Saskatchewan.

210 See, *e.g.*, R.S.O. 1990, c. P.27, s. 18.

211 (1612), 10 Co. Rep. 1, 30b, 77 E.R. 960.

212 [1916] 1 A.C. 566 especially at 584 (P.C.).

213 As to whether a company incorporated by letters patent under the Dominion Companies Act was a common law company, see *Nat. Land & Loan Co. v. Rat Portage Lbr. Co.*, [1917] 3 W.W.R. 269 (Man. K.B.). On common law corporations and the doctrine of *ultra vires* see *Communities Economic Dev. Fund v. Can. Pickles Corp.* (1991), 85 D.L.R. (4th) 88 at 96-97 (S.C.C).

It was settled by the House of Lords in *Ashbury Carriage Co.v. Riche*[214] that a company created under the English Companies Act could not validly contract in respect of something which it was not within its legal objects and purposes to do. In that case, a company formed to make and supply materials for railway construction could not contract to construct a railway. Hence the other contracting party could not recover damages for breach of such contract. It did not make any difference that the company had purported to ratify the contract made by the directors. The important issue was whether the company itself, not the directors, had the power. Hence, if a contract was *intra vires* a company, but *ultra vires* the directors, the contract might be made and ratified by an appropriate shareholders' meeting. This was, and is an agency question, not one relating to general contractual capacity.[215]

The doctrine of *Riche's* case was early adopted by the Supreme Court of Canada in *Cie de Villas du Cap Gibraltar v. Hughes*[216] in which it was held that a contract for the purchase of tiles to be used for erection of buildings was not *ultra vires* the company, since it was within the purpose of the company.[217] The distinction drawn was between something implicit and necessary for the proper carrying out of the objects for which the company was incorporated, and something totally unconnected with such objects.[218] Hence the necessity for drafting the constitutional documents of a company, that is, the Memorandum and Articles of Association, with great care in order to protect the company, its officers, agents and servants, and to give the company as wide a sphere of operations as possible.

In some jurisdictions, however, the common-law doctrine has been abolished by legislation dealing with business corporation. Such is the situation in Ontario,[219]

---

214 (1875), L.R. 7 H.L. 653 (H.L.); see also *Wenlock v. River Dee Co.* (1885), 10 App. Cas. 354 (H.L.).

215 See Fridman, *Law of Agency*, 6th ed. (1990), pp. 76-77, 323-324, on the changes now contained in the Companies Act, 1985. Note also the problem of ratification by a company of a contract made prior to the legal existence of the company: *ibid.*, pp. 75-76. See also *Repetti Ltd. v. Oliver Lee Ltd.*, [1923] 3 D.L.R. 1100 (Ont. C.A.); *Hudson-Mattagami Exploration Mining Co. v. Wettlaufer Bros. Ltd.*, [1928] 3 D.L.R. 661 (Ont. C.A.). See, generally, Getz, "Pre-Incorporation Contracts: Some Proposals" (1967), U.B.C. Law R. 381: Gosse, "Liability on Pre-Incorporation Contracts" (1972), 18 McGill L.J. 512. For statutory changes in the law see the Ontario Business Corporations Act, R.S.O. 1990, c. B.16, s. 21. Compare Canada Business Corporations Act, R.S.C. 1985, c. C-44, s. 14(2).

216 (1884), 11 S.C.R. 537 (S.C.C.).

217 *Ibid.*, at 551 *per* Ritchie C.J.

218 Compare *Nat. Land & Loan Co. v. Rat Portage Lbr. Co.*, above, note 213; *Carter Dewar Crowe Co. v. Columbia Bitulithic Co.* (1914), 6 W.W.R. 1215 (B.C.C.A.); *Pac. Coast Coal Mines Ltd. v. Arbuthnot*, [1917] A.C. 607 (P.C.). See also *Canadian Pacific Railway Co. v. Winnipeg (City)*, [1952] 1 S.C.R. 424 (S.C.C.); *Communities Economic Dev. Fund v. Can. Pickles Corp.*, above, note 213, at 99-100. Compare *Hazell v. Hammersmith & Fulham London Borough Council*, [1991] 1 All E.R. 545 (H.L.).

219 Business Corporations Act, R.S.O. 1990, c. B.16, s. 15. Compare Business Corporations Act, S.A. 1981, c. B-15, s. 15; Company Act, R.S.B.C. 1979, c. 59, s. 21; Corporations Act, R.S.M. 1987, c. C225, s. 15; Business Corporations Act, S.N.B. 1981, c. B-9.1, s. 13; Corporations Act, R.S.N. 1990, c. C-36, s. 27; Business Corporations Act, R.S.S. 1978, c. B-10, s. 15; Business Corporations Act, R.S.Y. 1986, c. 15, s. 18.

and in respect of corporations incorporated under federal Canadian legislation.[220] Not all the provinces have thus far copied this example. Hence in some provinces the *ultra vires* doctrine may still be in operation, and will affect the capacity of a business corporation to enter into a valid, binding contract.[221]

Where the doctrine still applies, a contract that is *ultra vires* a company may not be altogether ineffective. If goods are supplied to a company under such a contract, then, despite the voidness of the contract, there will be an obligation to make restitution in compensation for the value received by the company.[222] This is very similar to the situation with respect to contracts made by minors.[223] The doctrine of restitution in this regard may be said to stem from the decision of the House of Lords in *Sinclair v. Brougham*[224] in which the House had to consider the effect in equity, if not common law, of *ultra vires* contracts made by a building society which was ultimately wound up and liquidated. From that decision, and others, it is clear that *ultra vires* transactions are not entirely without legal effect, although this may involve the law of restitution rather than the law of contract.

(ii) *Formalities*

There may be further control upon the power of a statutory business corporation to make a contract. At common law a corporation could only contract under its corporate seal. Some exception was made to this in the case of certain everyday, commonplace transactions on the part of trading companies. These could be entered into by writing or parol (if no other requirement of the law made writing necessary).[225] By statute, for example, the Alberta Companies Act,[226] companies created under such legislation may now contract under seal, in writing, or orally, in the same way as natural persons. In other words, where a seal would be required by an individual it must be used by the corporation, and similarly with writing. Where no formalities would be needed for a natural person, they are not required for a company. This is a great simplification and improvement of the law.[227]

---

220 R.S.C. 1985, c. C-44, s. 15.
221 Nova Scotia, Northwest Territories and Prince Edward Island (which is a "letters patent jurisdiction", *i.e.*, governed by the law relating to common law, not statutory corporations: above, p. 167); see *Communities Economic Dev. Fund v. Can. Pickles Corp.*, above, note 213, at 100.
222 *Trades Hall Co. v. Erie Tobacco Co.* (1916), 10 W.W.R. 846 (Man. C.A.). See Fridman, *Restitution*, 2nd ed. (1992), pp. 176-179; Maddaugh & McCamus *Law of Restitution* (1990), pp. 325-333. Note also the possibility of recovery of money paid or given under such a contract: *Caledonia Community Credit Union Ltd. v. Haldimand Feed Mill Ltd.* (1974), 45 D.L.R. (3d) 676 (Ont. H.C.).
223 Above, p. 153.
224 [1914] A.C. 398 (H.L.). See Goff & Jones, *Law of Restitution*, 3rd ed. (1986), Chapter 1.
225 *South of Ireland Colliery Co. v. Waddle* (1869), L.R. 4 C.P. 617. See the discussion in *Bernardin v. N. Dufferin* (1891), 19 S.C.R. 581 (S.C.C.).
226 R.S.A. 1980, c. C-20, s. 165(1); compare R.S.O. 1990, c. B.16, s. 15. See, on earlier legislative provisions, *Can. Market Place Ltd. v. Fallowfield* (1976), 71 D.L.R. (3d) 341 (Ont. H.C.).
227 On whether an individual has contracted with a corporation or its representative, see *MacMullin v. A. & B. Miller Contracting Ltd.* (1987), 78 N.S.R. (2d) 48 (N.S.T.D.).

(d) Municipal corporations

Special mention must be made of the constitutional authorities which regulate local government. Municipal corporations provide another instance of corporations which are creatures of statute. Their function is to carry out the government of some urban or rural district within the jurisdiction of a province. It was made clear by the Privy Council in *John Mackay Co. v. Toronto*[228] that such bodies are subject to the doctrine of *ultra vires* that applies to other statutory corporations, such as trading companies, *and* to the particular provisions of the statute under which such a municipal corporation is instituted, so far as concerns contractual capacity. As Martin J.A. said in *Hiller v. Shamrock*,

> [a] rural municipality being a creation of statute can only enter into binding and valid contracts by complying with the statutory provisions.[229]

This has two effects or applications. On the one hand, such a corporation can only contract within the scope of its statutory powers and in accordance with the *ultra vires* doctrine. Thus, in *Campbell v. Inverness (County)*,[230] a municipal corporation had the power to enter into a contract pertaining to a garbage dump, though, on the facts, no such contract had been made. The original resolution in favour of such a contract had been revoked by a later resolution. Secondly, it can only contract, even in respect of matters within its powers and scope, in a manner permitted by the governing statute.[231]

As the cases seem to indicate, these are, in some respects, only different aspects of the same problem, namely, the construction and interpretation of the statutory powers of a municipal corporation. Whether a by-law is required,[232] or ratification by the council,[233] what is the effect of the lack of such requirement?[234] All these raise at one and the same time the issue of *ultra vires* and the question whether proper formalities have been observed. Perhaps, however, it might be said that cases of this kind are really concerned with substantive, not procedural questions, since they involve what the corporation may do, in terms of the way it must conduct its business if its efforts are to be effective in law.

More vitally concerned with formalities, such as the necessity for a given contract with such a corporation to be made under the seal of the corporation,

---

228 [1919] 3 W.W.R. 253 (P.C.). For a more modern, English, discussion of the position of municipal corporations, see *Hazell v. Hammersmith & Fulham London Borough Council*, [1991] 1 All E.R. 545 (H.L.).

229 [1930] 4 D.L.R. 276 at 285 (Sask. C.A.). See also *Waterous Engine Works Co. v. Palmerston* (1892), 21 S.C.R. 556 (S.C.C.).

230 (1990), 50 M.P.L.R. 296 at 310-312 (N.S.T.D.).

231 But in *Campbell v. Inverness (County)*, above, note 230, at 313, it was held that no special method of contracting was required, such as a seal. Promissory estoppel might have been involved if the circumstances had so warranted, which they did not: *ibid.*, 317-324.

232 *Donovan v. Belleville*, [1930] 3 D.L.R. 434 (Ont. H.C.); affirmed [1931] 4 D.L.R. 268 (Ont. C.A.).

233 *Hiller v. Shamrock*, above, note 229.

234 *Burnaby v. B.C. Elec. Ry. Co.* (1913), 3 W.W.R. 628 (B.C.S.C.). Note also the possibility of tracing in equity even if the contract is *ultra vires* and void: *Lamb v. Estevan*, [1922] 3 W.W.R. 1187 (Sask. C.A.).

are such cases as *Manning v. Winnipeg*.[235] The question there was whether the city could be liable for the plaintiff's services in court on its behalf when the contract under which the plaintiff was employed was not given under the seal of the city. It was held that there was no liability. Two conflicting principles of law, which derived from English cases, were considered: on the one hand, that a corporation, which had accepted the benefit of a contract which ought to have been made under the corporation's seal, would be liable on a *quantum meruit* for the value of the benefit received;[236] and on the other hand, that where a statute requires the corporation to contract under seal, work done under a verbal contract (even if accepted by the corporation) does not lead to liability on the part of the corporation.[237] The former notion was adopted and utilized by the Supreme Court of Canada in *Bernardin v. North Dufferin*.[238] In the *Winnipeg* case the latter view appears to have been accepted and applied. However, in *Campbell v. Inverness (County)*,[239] no seal was required for a contract pertaining to the disposition of a garbage dump. Such a contract could have been made by a resolution of the council. If this is correct, it would seem that, consistent with the modern disfavour of the seal and revision of its nature,[240] the absence of a seal will not affect the validity of a contract otherwise effectively made by a municipal council.

5. Unincorporated associations

(a) Generally

There are many organizations which, although not incorporated under any statute or by common law, carry on what is, morally, if not legally speaking a corporate kind of existence. Chief among these are private clubs and religious societies. Legislation in many provinces, such as the Alberta Societies Act,[241] enables some of these, namely, those concerned with educational, charitable, religious, and similar activities, to acquire a sort of corporate status which enables them to contract very much like a true corporation, and sue and be sued upon such contracts. However, at common law, and this would still apply to such unincorporated associations as do not or cannot come under the shelter of a Societies Act, such bodies have no separate existence in law and cannot therefore contract except as a group.[242] An unincorporated body is incapable of contracting and is not recognized by the law. Hence where the officers of an unincorporated lodge signed notes for

---

235 (1911), 21 Man. R. 203 (Man. C.A.).

236 *Clarke v. Cuckfield Union Guardians* (1852), 21 L.J.Q.B. 349; *Lawford v. Billericay, R.C.*, [1903] 1 K.B. 722 (C.A.).

237 *Hunt v. Wimbledon Local Bd.* (1878), 4 C.P.D. 48 (C.A.); *Young & Co. v. Royal Leamington Spa Corp.* (1883), 8 App. Cas. 517 (H.L.).

238 (1891), 19 S.C.R. 581 (S.C.C.); see also *Witherspoon v. East Williams* (1918), 44 O.L.R. 584 (Ont. C.A.).

239 Above, note 230.

240 Above, p. 169.

241 R.S.A. 1980, c. S-18.

242 Hence a "sale" of liquor by the bartender of a club to a member was not a sale; it was a *release* of the joint interest of all other members: *Graff v. Evans* (1882), 8 Q.B.D. 373.

the repayment of money lent to the lodge, they were personally liable. They could not plead that they had signed as agents on behalf of any principal, thereby excluding their liability on the contracts.[243] In *Canada Morning News Co. v. Thompson*,[244] the question was whether an unincorporated society could enter into a lease. Anglin C.J.C., giving the judgment of the Supreme Court of Canada, said,

> [that] an unincorporated society . . . cannot become a lessee is established by several judgments, of which it is only necessary to refer to two — *Jarrott v. Ackerley*[245] and *Henderson v. Toronto General Trusts Corporation*.[246] These decisions rest upon the incapacity of an unincorporated and unregistered society to assert any position which is maintainable in law only by a legal entity. In principle, therefore, they are equally applicable whether the position asserted be that of landlord or tenant.[247]

Such organizations, in consequence, can only contract through agents, and all the members of such an organization will be liable to jointly and severally.[248] It may be that under procedural rules in any given province, a representative action may be brought by or against any such association.[249] Whether or not this be so, all the membership are involved, not simply those who happen to represent the association as plaintiffs or defendants. There is no separate corporate status. Consequently, no doctrine of *ultra vires* can apply to such bodies.

(b) Trade unions

(i) *At common law*

Trade unions are one kind of voluntary association, like private clubs, which at common law have no separate distinct legal identity. Such bodies, like those associations which have been referred to in the previous section, are not legal entities, even though they may appear to be and behave like corporate bodies.[250] Hence such a body cannot make contracts in its own name, nor can it sue and be sued in its own name as distinct from that of its members.[251] As McDonald C.J.B.C. said in *Stephen v. Stewart*,

> [it] is clear that any indication that a union is a legal entity must be found in some

---

243 *Finlay v. Black*, [1921] 2 W.W.R. 907 (Y.T.S.C.).

244 [1930] S.C.R. 338 (S.C.C.).

245 (1915), 85 L.J. Ch. 135.

246 (1928), 62 O.L.R. 303 (Ont. C.A.).

247 *Can. Morning News v. Thompson*, [1930] S.C.R. 338 at 342 (S.C.C.).

248 See *e.g.*, *Bradley Egg Farm Ltd. v. Clifford*, [1943] 2 All E.R. 378 (C.A.); compare Fridman, *Law of Agency*, 6th ed. (1990), p. 212.

249 See *e.g.*, *Demarchi v. Spartari* (1914), 5 W.W.R. 1336 (B.C. Co. Ct.).

250 *Clay Prods. Wkrs. Union v. Dom. Fire Brick & Clay Prods. Ltd.*, [1946] 3 W.W.R. 798 (Sask. C.A.); *Amalgam. Bldrs. Council v. Herman*, [1930] 2 D.L.R. 513 (Ont. C.A.); *Orchard v. Tunney*, [1957] S.C.R. 436 (S.C.C.).

251 *Int. Ladies Garment Wkrs. Union v. Rothman*, [1941] S.C.R. 388 at 391 (S.C.C.) *per* Rinfret J. Compare *Orchard v. Tunney*, above, with which contrast the decision of the House of Lords in *Bonsor v. Musicians' Union*, [1956] A.C. 104 (H.L.).

statute, though this has always been a matter of inference, as from provisions allowing the union to hold property, act by agents, etc.[252]

Thus, in many of the cases the task of the court has been to determine whether there are any statutory provisions that might have the effect of making a trade union into a legal, juridical person, a quasi-corporation, capable of separate existence in law.

However, there are decisions in which it has been held that, for the purposes of protecting union property, and to enable criminal and other proceedings to be brought against defaulters (such as officers of the union who had made off with union funds) a union could bring appropriate action.[253] In *Polakoff v. Winters Garment Co.*,[254] Reaney J., following the decision of the House of Lords in *Russell v. Amalgamated Society of Carpenters & Joiners*,[255] held that a trade union was illegal at common law, and therefore could not bring an action in the courts of Ontario. Other cases, in other jurisdictions, make it plain that actions can be brought by a union for such a purpose, even apart from any statute.[256] Of course such decisions do not fundamentally affect the common-law position with respect to the capacity of a trade union, as such, to enter into a contract in its own name; their purpose and extent are limited. For changes in the common-law attitude it is necessary to look to statute.

(ii) *Under statute*

Both federal and provincial legislation has been passed in order to create a structure for collective bargaining between unions and employers. In consequence of this, it would seem, some kind of corporate, quasi-corporate or similar status has been bestowed on unions in the various jurisdictions, so as to cloak them with sufficient legal personality to enable them to enter into valid, binding collective agreements, capable of being enforced by and against such unions. The nature of the status or personality, that is, its scope and consequences, will depend upon the exact language used by the legislation in question, as interpreted by the courts.

A distinction may be drawn between a union that is certified in accordance with the provisions of such a statute, and one which is not. It is clear that an uncertified union will have no personality of any kind, whether for the purposes of the statute, that is, for collective bargaining, or for others, for example, the making

---

252 [1944] 1 D.L.R. 305 at 308 (B.C.C.A.).

253 *Starr v. Chase*, [1924] S.C.R. 495 (S.C.C.); *Amalgam. Soc. of Carpenters & Joiners v. Sinclair*, [1925] 2 D.L.R. 774 (Ont. C.A.) (following *Yorkshire Miners' Assn. v. Howden*, [1905] A.C. 256 (H.L.)); *Senkiw v. Utility Glove (1961) Ltd.* (1966), 58 D.L.R. (2d) 754 (Man. Q.B.); affirmed (1967), 62 D.L.R. (2d) 48 (Man. C.A.); *Contr. Equip. & Supply (1965) Ltd. v. Bldg. Material Drivers, Warehousemen & Helpers, Loc 914* (1965), 53 W.W.R. 702 (Man. C.A.).

254 [1928] 2 D.L.R. 277 (Ont. H.C.).

255 [1912] A.C. 421 (H.L.).

256 Cases cited above, note 253.

of any other kind of contract.[257] Even certification might not confer general personality upon a trade union, to enable it to sue and be sued in its own name, that is, to permit it to enter into contracts.[258] The cases suggest that, in the words of Riley J. of the Supreme Court of Alberta,

> for limited purposes of Labour Acts and proceedings thereunder a Union is a legal statutory entity separate and distinct from the membership that comprises it.[259]

The cases which support such a proposition are not of general application. In other words, they do not substantiate any suggestion that a trade union which is certified under a federal or provincial Labour Act is a distinct legal personality for all normal purposes, for example, the making of contracts other than collective agreements. If this is indeed so, then it follows that trade unions, save for matters governed by the appropriate legislation, are in no better position than any other unincorporated association. Indeed, they might be worse off, insofar as a trade union might be illegal at common law and therefore totally incapable of entering into a legal contract, which it might enforce, other than a transaction which requires judicial protection so as to prevent any fraudulent or other criminal activity of which the union, that is, its members, might be the innocent victim.

---

257 *Local 1562 United Mine Wkrs. v. Williams* (1919), 59 S.C.R. 240 (S.C.C.); *Soc. Brand Clothing Ltd. v. A.C.W.A.*, [1931] S.C.R. 321 (S.C.C.); *Perrault v. Poirer*, [1959] S.C.R. 843 (S.C.C.).

258 *Amalgam. Bldrs. Council v. Herman*, [1930] 2 D.L.R. 513 (Ont. C.A.) where, however, the provincial statute was held to be *ultra vires*, therefore, the purported certification was invalid.

259 *Charleston v. MacGregor* (1957), 11 D.L.R. (2d) 78 at 88 (Alta. S.C.). See *Re Patterson & Nanaimo Dry Cleaning & Laundry Wkrs. Union Loc. No. 1*, [1947] 2 W.W.R. 510 (B.C.C.A.). *Vancouver Mach. Depot Ltd. v. United Steel Wkrs. of Amer.*, [1948] 2 W.W.R. 325 (B.C.C.A.); *Re Int. Nickel Co.; Shedden v. Kopinak*, [1950] 1 D.L.R. 381 (Ont. H.C.). Compare *Walker v. Billingsley* (1952), 5 W.W.R. 363 (B.C.S.C); *Peerless Laundry & Cleaners Ltd. v. L.W.I.U.* (1952), 6 W.W.R. (N.S.) 443 (Man. Q.B.).

5

Privity

1. The concept of privity

(a) What is privity?

As the word would suggest, "privity" involves the idea of being *privy* to a contract, that is, being a party to, or participant in a contractual arrangement. The common law drew, and still draws a distinction between (1) those who are involved in a contract, as being signatories (if the contract is in writing, whether with or without a seal), or, if it is oral, as being among those assenting to the contractual undertakings, and (2) those who claim rights under a contract, or upon whom it is sought to impose liabilities under a contract, when they were not involved in the original making of the contract and were not expressly engaged to or in it by their participation. An agreement between A and B involves only A and B as parties: there is privity of contract between them. A contract between A and B which requires that A do something for C or that C do something for A creates no privity of contract between A and C or B and C.[1] The contract may mention C and may purport to confer a benefit upon C or impose an obligation upon C,

---

[1] *Datile Financial Corp. v. Royal Trust Corp. of Can.* (1991), 5 O.R. (3d) 358 (Ont. Gen. Div.); reversed in part on other grounds (1992), 11 O.R. (3d) 224 (Ont. C.A.); *MacDonald v. Matheson* (1986), 57 Nfld. & P.E.I.R. 268 (P.E.I.C.A.), contract for supply of dentures between patient and dentist: payment to be made by the Department of Veteran Affairs: only the patient and the dentist were parties to the contract. Compare *Watson v. C.F. Hart Ltd.* (1986), 59 Nfld. & P.E.I.R. 308 (Nfld. Dist. Ct.); *Iampen v. Royal Bank* (1987), 79 A.R. 305 (Alta. Master). Contrast *Moss v. Richardson Greenshields of Can. Ltd.*, [1988] 4 W.W.R. 15 (Man. Q.B.); affirmed [1989] 3 W.W.R. 50 (Man. C.A.), where the broker was held to be privy to an options trading agreement entered into by the plaintiff, an investor.

but it cannot result in C's being a party to the contract in the ordinary, usual sense. As will be seen, there may be situations in respect of which the involvement of C in this kind of way can produce consequences of a legal kind *vis-à-vis* C. For the moment, however, the question is not what are the consequences of a person not being a party to a contract, but rather, when is a person a party.[2]

In most instances this is clear. Some situations have given rise to difficulty. One concerns contracts between A and B under which B promises A to pay A's widow after the death of A. When A dies, his widow becomes A's personal representative, either as administratrix or executrix. If B fails to fulfil his promise to pay A's widow, and the widow sues, it has been held that she may do so in her capacity as personal representative, but not in her personal capacity.[3] The law draws a distinction between the widow as standing in the shoes of the deceased (and therefore as privy to the contract) and the widow wishing to bring an action herself. The widow is thus privy to the contract and not privy to it at one and the same time. Another curious situation arises where tenants of separate premises in a shopping centre contract with the landlord individually to restrict their activities to a particular business. It has been held that a community of interest arises among the various tenants sufficient to create privity of contract between *them* (as well as between each of them and the landlord). Thus each tenant has a direct interest in the performance of the terms of each one's lease by all the other tenants. Consequently, one tenant may sue another tenant for an injunction to restrain that other tenant from competing with the plaintiff tenant contrary to the terms of the defendant tenant's lease.[4] This notion of an indirect privity seems somewhat strange, albeit that there is a practical reason for allowing the action in such instances. Equally strange was the version of privity that appears to have been adopted in *Centennial Realties Ltd. v. Westburn Industrial Enterprises Ltd.*[5] The plaintiff wished to buy a boiler for his apartment building. He could not buy directly as a retail purchaser from the defendant wholesaler. As a consequence the sales transaction was actually arranged between the defendant and a contractor engaged by the plaintiff. The invoice was made out to the contractor, but the purchase price was paid by the plaintiff. When the boiler turned out to be unsatisfactory, the plaintiff wished to sue for breach of the implied term as to fitness of the boiler incorporated

---

2 If a party to a contract dies, the contract may be terminated under the doctrine of frustration: below, p. 646. However, rights and duties under the contract may continue to bind a party's heirs, executors or administrators: (a) if the contract specifically provides; and (b) even if it does not: *Rettie Estate v. Tsawwassen Gardens Ltd.* (1989), 42 B.L.R. 78 (B.C.S.C.). On the effect of death see further, below, p. 690.

3 *Beswick v. Beswick*, [1968] A.C. 58 (H.L.); *Waugh v. Slavik* (1976), 62 D.L.R. (3d) 577 (B.C.S.C.); *Gasparini v. Gasparini* (1978), 87 D.L.R. (3d) 282 (Ont. C.A.); see, further, below, pp. 180-182, 188. See also *Scrimes v. Nickle* (1982), 130 D.L.R. (3d) 698 (Alta. C.A.); leave to appeal to S.C.C. refused (1982), 41 N.R. 572 (S.C.C.).

4 *Re Spike and Rocca Group Ltd.* (1979), 107 D.L.R. (3d) 62 (P.E.I.S.C.).

5 (1978), 31 N.S.R. (2d) 64 (N.S.T.D.). See also, for a very different situation, *Holland v. St. John Toyota Ltd.* (1981), 130 D.L.R. (3d) 156 (N.B.Q.B.) (dealer giving rustproof guarantee in the name of X, for whom dealer acts as a franchised dealer, guarantee part of contract of sale between dealer and customer, *i.e.*, "agent" is really party to the contract).

in the contract under the Nova Scotia Sale of Goods Act. He was successful. Since the defendant knew that the boiler was supplied to the plaintiff to be installed in the plaintiff's apartment building, the transaction was such that a warranty of fitness could be considered to have been given by implication by the defendant to the plaintiff. It is hard to find any true privity here, unless the contractor whose name appeared on the invoice is treated as the agent of the plaintiff. This was not made explicit by the judge, although it may be implicit in his language. In contrast, in *International Airport Industrial Park Ltd. v. Tanenbaum*[6] the defendant was in partnership with F, who later agreed with the plaintiffs to share the benefits of the partnership with them. This was held not to give rise to any contract between the plaintiffs and the defendant. Consequently, the plaintiffs could not sue the defendant. There was no partnership between them. There was no original privity, nor any subsequent privity by way of novation or assignment.[7]

What such cases indicate is that courts can sometimes stretch the notion of privity in order to effect justice, but will not always do so.[8] However, as exemplified by *Trans Canada Credit Corporation Ltd. v. Royal Insurance Co. of Canada*,[9] the rigours of the doctrine of privity will sometimes be ineffective to preclude a remedy. Here the plaintiff was the chattel mortgagee of an automobile, shown on the policy of insurance effected on the automobile as a lienholder, to whom loss was payable in the event of damage. The automobile was damaged. The insurance company made a cheque payable to the mortgagor and the repairer of the vehicle jointly. The repairs were not carried out and the mortgagor became bankrupt. As a result the plaintiff sued the insurance company on the policy. It was held that the insurance company was liable for the cost of the repairs. Although there was no privity of contract between the plaintiff and the insurance company, and despite the impossibility of applying any of the recognized exceptions or qualifications of the privity doctrine to the facts of this case,[10] Nathanson J. of the Nova Scotia Supreme Court held that the plaintiff mortgagee could sue under the "loss-payee" clause in the policy. There was a recognized commercial practice for over 100 years in Canada and the United States to give legal effect to such clauses. "It would be

---

6 (1976), 69 D.L.R. (3d) 1 (S.C.C.). Compare, as to the absence of a valid assignment that could create the necessary privity of contract, *Watson v. C.F. Hart Ltd.* (1986), 59 Nfld. & P.E.I.R. 308 (Nfld. Dist. Ct.).

7 On novation see below, pp. 539-542; on assignment below, Chapter 17.

8 For example, in *Roman Corp. v. Peat Marwick Thorne* (1992), 11 O.R. (3d) 248 (Ont. Gen. Div.), Farley J. refused to hold that shareholders in a company were privy to the contract between the company and its auditors so as to permit the shareholders an action for breach of contract when the alleged negligence of the auditors resulted in the loss of the shareholders' investment. The learned judge ruled on *dicta* in *Caparo Industries plc. v. Dickman*, [1990] 1 All E.R. 568 (H.L.), a case on negligent misrepresentation, *i.e.*, *tort*, by auditors.

9 (1983), 143 D.L.R. (3d) 296 (N.S.T.D.); affirmed (1983), 149 D.L.R. (3d) 280 (N.S.C.A.). A more liberalizing attitude to privity was adopted by the High Court of Australia in *Trident General Ins. Co. v. McNiece Bros Pty. Ltd.* (1988), 165 C.L.R. 107: on which see Kincaid, "Privity and the Essence of Contract" (1989), 12 U.N.S.W.L.J. 59; and Kincaid, 48 C.L.J. 243.

10 On which see below, pp. 194-200.

disruptive of those commercial practices," said the judge,[11] "as they exist today if, suddenly, the validity of policies of insurance containing mortgage clauses or loss-payee clauses was called into question." Although it might have been better had the legislature amended the Insurance Act to effect a statutory solution to the problem, in the absence of such legislation, "the courts have a duty to ensure that all parties to substantial obligations live up to the covenants which they have made and which they know or should know will be relied upon by others." With respect, however, the learned judge was deciding the issue on grounds that contradict the basic idea of privity. The solution may well have been reasonable and warranted, but it was inconsistent with the common law. Other instances may be cited where a statute has altered the privity doctrine in relation to specific contracts.[12] This might have been achieved in this instance. The fact that it had not been should have controlled the situation. What the learned judge was doing was utilizing a commercial practice, which contradicted the common law, and giving it legal effect. It is questionable whether the doctrine of privity should be ousted in this way. If the case is rightly decided, it suggests that there may be qualifications of the strict application of the doctrine of privity stemming from the realties of the commercial world, and that the technicalities of the doctrine should not be allowed to stand in the way of achieving substantial justice. Unfortunately, however, as will be seen, this has not always been the view adopted by the courts.

(b) Consideration

For there to be a valid, enforceable contract an essential ingredient, though not the only one, is that consideration should have been given for the promise or the act involved in the allged contract.[13] Without consideration the agreement involves merely a gratuitous promise that is incapable of being enforced in the courts. One requirement of the doctrine of consideration was stated in the past to be that "consideration must move from the promisee."[14] On this basis, it would seem, if there are several parties on one side of the contract, for example, several creditors, then, if the debtor is to be bound to *all* of them, all the creditors must provide or have provided consideration for the debtor's undertaking to be bound. In most, if not all cases, this will probably be the situation. In practical terms, however, it need not be the case. For example, it might be that A, B, and C all agree that between them they will lend a sum of money to D. D is then bound to reimburse them all. They have all furnished consideration for D's promise to repay. Suppose that A and B are the only ones who actually advance the money,

---

11 Above, note 9, at 307, relying on *Coleman v. Northern Assur. Co.*, [1950] 3 D.L.R. 556 (Ont. H.C.); *Kuprowski v. Indust. Accept. Corp.* (1964), 48 D.L.R. (2d) 73 (Sask. C.A.); *London & Midland Gen. Ins. Co. v. Bonser*, [1973] S.C.R. 10 (S.C.C.).

12 Below, p. 194.

13 See Chapter 3.

14 See, *e.g.*, *Dunlop Pneumatic Tyre Co. v. Selfridge & Co.*, [1915] A.C. 847 at 853 (H.L.) *per* Viscount Haldane; compare *Fleming v. Bank of New Zealand*, [1900] A.C. 577 at 586-587 (P.C.) *per* Lord Lindley.

but the contract stipulates that A, B and C are the lenders and D is bound to repay all three, does the requirement about consideration mean that C, although named as a party to the contract, is not entitled to anything from the repayment by D?[15]

The difficulties have stemmed from the confusion that has occurred in the cases, and the books, between two distinct legal doctrines which to some extent overlap or coalesce to produce the same result, namely, the exclusion of strangers to a contract. In the first place there is the doctrine of consideration, that is, the need for consideration to create a valid, binding legal contractual obligation. Secondly, there is the doctrine of privity of contract under which only parties to a contract acquire rights or are subjected to liabilities thereunder.[16] In many instances a person is, or has been held unable to enforce a contract which purports to be for his benefit, and this refusal could have been on *either* ground. Indeed in one nineteenth century English case, *Price v. Easton*,[17] judgment was given against the plaintiff, in one such case, by different judges for each of these reasons. It was in the later case of *Tweddle v. Atkinson*[18] that the doctrine of privity appears to have been relied upon as the chief reason for denying an action to a person who was not a party to a contract, but claimed a benefit under it, and not the fact that such person had not provided consideration.

For reasons which will emerge later, the notion of privity has loomed larger in such situations than the doctrine of consideration. Hence, possibly, arose the failure to realize the true scope of the doctrine of consideration in multipartite situations, because there was no need to analyze the consideration aspect of such problems in any depth since they could be disposed of more easily and simply in accordance with the requirements of the doctrine of privity. The consequence may well have been to confuse the requirement of privity with that of consideration, and, therefore, to produce the idea that only someone who has given consideration (even if he were expressed to be, and was a party to a contract) could take the benefit of any promise in a contract, that is, could claim to be a creditor. In fact, as more modern thought on the subject is beginning to appreciate, there is a clear difference between the requirements of the doctrine of consideration and those of the doctrine of privity, and they should be kept separate and not confused.[19]

---

15 This would appear to be the conclusion drawn in the Sixth Interim Report of the Law Revision Committee in England, (1937) Cmd. 5449.

16 For discussion of the connection between these two doctrines, see Flannigan, "Privity — The End of an Era (Error)" (1987), 103 L.Q.R. 564, especially at pp. 568-572. The Ontario Law Reform Commission, *Report on Amendment of the Law of Contract* (1987), at pp. 68-71 recommended that legislation should provide that in contracts for the benefit of third parties, below, pp. 185-191, lack of consideration and want of privity should not make the contract unenforceable, *viz.*, by the third party.

17 (1833), 4 B. & Ad. 433; below, p. 185.

18 (1861), 1 B. & S. 393; compare below, p. 186.

19 Compare above, p. 114. In *Birkdale Realty v. McLean* (1984), 64 N.S.R. (2d) 409 (N.S. Co. Ct.) it was said that privity is a matter of substance, not form, and is closely connected with consideration. Contrast the views expressed by Adams & Brownsword, "Privity and the Concept of a Network Contract" (1990), 10 Leg. St. 12 at pp. 21-25.

In the present context, the issue is whether *every party*, that is, every one who is *privy*, in the strict sense, to a contract, must provide consideration, or whether it is sufficient if one of the parties on one side, that is, one creditor, has provided consideration for the promisor's (that is the debtor's) promise or undertaking to all the creditors. The better view would seem to be that the latter is correct, and that as long as someone from among various promisees has provided consideration for the promise made to them, the contract will be valid and enforceable. There is authority for this proposition in the decision of the House of Lords in *McEvoy v. Belfast Banking Co.*[20] In that case a father made a deposit with the bank in the names of himself and his infant son. When the son sued the bank for the money it was argued that the son was not a party to the transaction because he had given no consideration. This was not accepted by the House. The contract by the bank was held to be made with father and son, jointly and severally; hence the consideration moving from the father supported the contract with the son as well as himself. More recently, in the High Court of Australia, at least two members of that court, Barwick C.J. and Windeyer J., were able to decide the issue before them along the same lines. In *Coulls v. Bagot's Executor & Trustee Co.*,[21] the deceased granted a right to quarry his land to a company in return for a certain royalty payment for a stipulated period. It was provided in the contract that the company was authorized to pay the money to the deceased and his wife jointly. The contract was in writing and was signed by the deceased, his wife, and the company. When the deceased died the question arose whether the company was bound to pay the royalty to the wife. The majority of the Court held that the wife had no claim because the husband had given the company a revocable *mandate* to pay the wife and this was terminated by his death. But one member of the court, dissenting, held that if the wife was to be regarded as a party to the agreement, the fact that she had given no consideration for the promise to pay the royalty (such consideration having been given exclusively by the deceased, who was the owner of the land on which the quarrying was to take place) was not a barrier to her claim on the contract to pay the royalty. In the words of Windeyer J.:[22]

> [t]he promise is made to them collectively. It must, of course, be supported by consideration, but that does not mean by considerations furnished by them separately. It means a consideration given on behalf of them all and, therefore, moving from them all. In such a case the promise of the promisor is not gratuitous; and, as between him and the joint promisees, it matters not how they were able to provide the price of his promise to them.

Until recently this issue does not seem to have been discussed in Canadian courts. The decision of Brouck J. in *Waugh v. Slavik*[23] suggests that there is nothing

---

20 [1935] A.C. 24 (H.L.).

21 (1967), 40 A.L.J.R. 471 (Aust. H.C.) (on which see, Winterton, (1969), 47 Can. Bar Rev. 493).

22 (1967), 40 A.L.J.R. 471 at 483.

23 [1976] 1 W.W.R. 273 (B.C.S.C.).

in this analysis that cannot be accepted by those courts,[24] and that, so far as concerns cases involving a plurality of creditors or debtors, as long as one of the group has provided the necessary consideration, there will be a good and enforceable contract between all the creditors on the one hand and all the debtors on the other. There what happened was as follows. X and his infant son were killed in a plane crash. Under X's will his estate was to go to the son after some cash payment to X's parents. X had prepared a different will, but that had not yet been executed. Under that projected will, other beneficiaries were included, namely, in addition to the parents, X's sister, a friend of X, and the woman with whom X was living at the time of his death. In the aftermath of the accident, an agreement was reached between these "beneficiaries" on the one hand and the ex-wife of X, who would have succeeded to all X's property through the infant son, who would have acquired that property first under the valid will. This agreement involved a sharing of X's property. Later the ex-wife repudiated the agreement, and the suit was brought by the "beneficiaries" to obtain specific performance of this agreement. The argument was raised that, although the mistress of X had given consideration, namely, surrendering whatever rights to claim under the will of X that she might have possessed as X's "common-law wife," the other parties had not. Hence they could not enforce the agreement. The learned judge, applying what had been said by Windeyer J. and Barwick C.J., as well as dicta of the other judges, in the *Coulls* case, and the speeches in the *Beswick* case,[25] held that, as long as one of the "beneficiaries" had given consideration, it did not matter that the others had not. He enforced the agreement.

The reliance placed by Bouck J. on *Beswick v. Beswick* makes it relevant to consider the facts and decision in that case. Peter Beswick sold his business as a coal merchant to his nephew in consideration that the nephew would pay Peter a weekly sum as long as Peter lived, and thereafter, if Peter's wife survived him, an annuity to Peter's widow. The nephew paid Peter the weekly sum until Peter died, paid the widow one week's money, and then refused to pay any more. She sued the nephew for arrears of the annuity and specific performance of the contract between Peter and the nephew. The action was brought by her in two capacities, as administratrix of Peter's estate and on her own behalf. Ultimately the House of Lords held that she could obtain specific performance of the contract under which she could force the nephew to perform the provision of the contract which produced a benefit for herself in her personal capacity. Her success depended on her suing as administratrix, that is, as standing in the shoes of Peter, who could have brought an action for specific performance himself, had he been alive. Unlike certain members of the Court of Appeal, the House of Lords held that she had no personal action, at common law, on equitable grounds, or by virtue of statute.[26] In a situation somewhat similar to that in the Australian case of *Coulls v. Bagot's*

---

24 Compare the dicta of Lord Simon of Glaisdale (dissenting) in *New Zealand Shipping Co. v. A.M. Satterthwaite & Co.*, [1974] 1 All E.R. 1015 at 1030-1031 (P.C.).

25 Above, note 3.

26 Below, p. 200.

Executor & Trustee Co.,[27] a different result was achieved by a different approach. Had the widow not been the administratrix of the deceased's estate, she might not have had a remedy in England, though she would have had according to the minority in the Australian case.

The approach of the House of Lords in *Beswick* was unusual. Normally courts will not grant decrees of specific performance of obligations to pay money; the appropriate remedy is an action for damages.[28] In *Beswick*, had damages been awarded, the administratrix, suing as such, could have claimed only nominal damages, because the estate of Peter Beswick had lost nothing by the nephew's failure to pay the widow. Such a result, although technically correct, would have resulted in injustice. Consequently, the House of Lords allowed the equitable form of relief which ensured that the nephew would be obliged to pay the widow what was due under the contract. In view of the point that an award of damages would have been technically valid and correct, although lacking in utility, it is interesting to note that Bouck J. in *Waugh v. Slavik* might have taken a different approach had the action in that case been for damages for breach of contract rather than for specific performance. It is difficult to see the juridical basis for that distinction. The learned judge also thought that there was a "body of case law," to use his language, attempting to protect third party beneficiaries. This, it is suggested, is far from correct, as the *Beswick* case indicates. That decision, and the others relied on by Bouck J., do not undermine the traditional common-law principles. They restate and reinforce them. Furthermore, Bouck J. misunderstood what the House of Lords did in *Beswick*, and treated the "beneficiaries" in the case before him, incorrectly it is suggested, as being in the same legal situation as the administratrix in *Beswick*. While his initiative is to be respected, it is unfortunate that the reasoning of Bouck J., by the use of which he arrived at a satisfactory solution, is open to question.

(c) Joint and several parties

Where there are several creditors or debtors, they may engage as parties to the contract jointly or severally.[29] If they are joint parties, then their obligation (or benefit, as the case may be) is one and indivisible.[30] Thus if one joint debtor dies, the obligation totally falls on the survivor, and the deceased debtor's executors

---

27 Above, note 21.

28 Below, p. 790.

29 Or jointly *and* severally: *Thompson & Purcell Surveying Ltd. v. Burke* (1977), 39 N.S.R. (2d) 181 (N.S. Co. Ct.) in which situation a personal judgment against one debtor is *not* necessarily a bar to judgment against the others. Contrast the situation where the liability is joint alone: *Mann v. Kotch* (1981), 10 Man. R. (2d) 373 (Man. Co. Ct.); compare *Murray v. Delta Copper Co.*, [1926] S.C.R. 144 (S.C.C.).

30 Hence, if the intention is to create a joint obligation and some of the intended parties do not join, there will be no contract at all: see *United Nickel Copper Co. v. Dom. Nickel Copper Co.* (1913), 24 O.W.R. 462 (Ont. H.C.); affirmed (1913), 25 O.W.R. 948 (Ont. C.A.). As to the effect of judgment against one debtor, see *Mann v. Kotch* (1981), 10 Man. R. (2d) 373 (Man. Co. Ct.).

are not liable.[31] If they are several parties, then the obligation or benefit is capable of severance or separation as between them.[32] It is question of construction of the contract whether their participation in the contract is joint or several.[33] In some circumstances, for example, where the contract referred to "A and B and each of them,"[34] it may be held that they are joint and several contractors. The importance of the distinction lies in the consequences which flow with respect to (1) the right of each individual contractor to sue on the contract individually, or his obligation to be sued individually and (2) the effect which settlement *with* one creditor or settlement *by* one debtor may have upon rights or liabilities respectively of the other creditors or debtors.

If the parties are jointly creditors or debtors, then one single creditor may not sue on his own behalf, unless he can establish that he has suffered some specific, separate damage by the debtor's wrongdoing, not a damage common to all the creditors.[35] Similarly, if each debtor is jointly liable then the proper action is against all jointly.[36] On the other hand if there are separate liabilities each must be sued separately, and there can be no joint action against the joint debtors, or by and on behalf of the various creditors.[37] Where there are separate liabilities, the damages payable to the different creditors may be different amounts.[38]

It is also important to bear in mind the difference that results from a settlement made by or with one of several creditors or debtors, depending upon whether the obligation (on either side) is joint or several. Take the case where one of several creditors releases the debtor; what is the effect on the other creditors' rights? It would seem, from what was said in *Larose v. Ocean Accident & Guarantee Corporation*,[39] that a release given by two of three joint judgment creditors will not necessarily mean that the debtor is also released from further liability at the hands of the third such creditor. It seems to be a matter of construction. This is certainly true of the situation in reverse, that is, where there are a number of debtors

---

31 *Robert Porter & Sons Ltd. v. Armstrong*, [1926] S.C.R. 328 (S.C.C.) (following *White v. Tyndall* (1888), 13 App. Cas. 263 (H.L.)).

32 The effect of this is still a matter of consideration: see *Russian Mercantile Co. v. Achtemijczuk*, [1925] 3 W.W.R. 701 (Alta. S.C.). See also *Baldwin v. Chalker* (1984), 48 Nfld. & P.E.I.R. 86 (Nfld. C.A.) where distinct contracts were involved.

33 *No. 1 Yamaha Ltd. v. Russon Sports Centre Ltd.* (1981), 8 Sask. R. 22 (Sask. Q.B.); *Plow & Watters Printing Can. Ltd. v. Merrill Lynch Royal Securities Ltd.* (1983), 22 B.L.R. 108 (Ont. H.C.). In *Helm v. Simcoe & Erie Gen. Ins. Co.* (1979), 19 A.R. 326 (Alta. C.A.) a surety was held bound even though the bond had not been signed by principal debtor.

34 *E.A. Towns Ltd. v. Harvey*, [1945] 2 D.L.R. 782 (B.C.S.C.); affirmed [1946] 2 D.L.R. 72 (B.C.C.A.); affirmed [1946] 4 D.L.R. 160 (S.C.C.). Compare *Thompson & Purcell Surveying Ltd. v. Burke*, above, note 29.

35 *Elliott v. Parks* (1884), 23 N.B.R. 611 (N.B.C.A.).

36 Hence, if a creditor obtains something from one joint debtor he must bring this into account before suing the other joint debtor: *Advance Rumely Thresher Co. v. Bain*, [1920] 3 W.W.R. 840 (Sask. C.A.).

37 *True and Stairs v. Atherton* (1875), 16 N.B.R. 90 (N.B.C.A.).

38 *Campbell Flour Mills Ltd. v. Bowes; Campbell Flour Mills Ltd. v. Ellis* (1914), 32 O.L.R. 270 (Ont. C.A.).

39 [1918] 1 W.W.R. 616 (Alta. C.A.); affirmed (1918), 59 S.C.R. 663 (S.C.C.).

and one, for example, is released by the creditor or creditors. As long as the debtors are several, and not joint, it will be possible, provided that it is expressly or impliedly agreed to such effect, to release one such debtor while reserving rights of action against the other or others.[40] If the liability is joint, however, a release of one debtor will also affect the liabilities of the others. So, too, if the debtors are jointly and severally liable, an unsatisfied judgment obtained against one such debtor will not operate as a bar to prevent the creditor whose debt remains unpaid from suing the other, hitherto unsued debtor.[41]

Thus, while the law recognizes that there may be a plurality of parties on one side or other of a contract (in the same way that there may be a plurality of injured parties, or tortfeasors, in consequence of the commission of some tort)[42] it has had to provide special rules relating to the nature, scope, extent, and duration of the liabilities and rights of the different parties. However, all such parties, whether creditors or debtors, as they have been termed in this context, are privies to the contract. Their existence and involvement in the contract do not raise any problems as to the acquisition of rights or the imposition of liabilities. It is otherwise in respect of "creditors" or "debtors," as they may be called for this purpose, who are referred to and provided for in the contract, but are not parties, either jointly or severally.

2. The doctrine of privity

(a) Contracts under seal

The common law has always taken a particularly narrow view with respect to contracts under seal. In relation to such contracts, the doctrine of privity has been carried to what might be considered extreme lengths, in consequence of which some of the exceptions to the general principle of privity,[43] do not apply where the parties have put their agreement in a deed.

No person can sue or be sued, by action at common law, upon a contract under seal unless he is a party to the contract in the sense that he is a *signatory* of the contract.[44] This means, as pointed out, for example, by the Supreme Court

---

40 *Lonergan v. Saskatoon & Sutherland, Contr. Co.* (1915), 8 Sask. L.R. 201 (Sask. K.B.); *Bueckert v. Friesen (No. 2)*, [1927] 1 W.W.R. 825 (Man. C.A.).

41 *Hough Lithographing Co. v. Morley* (1910), 20 O.L.R. 484 (Ont. C.A.); compare *Thompson & Purcell Surveying Ltd. v. Burke*, above, note 29; contrast *Mann v. Kotch*, above, note 29. For the effect of *payment* of a judgment, see *Prince Albert v. Underwood, McLellan & Assoc. Ltd.*, [1969] S.C.R. 305 (S.C.C.); *Imperial Bank of Can. v. Begley*, [1935] S.C.R. 89 (S.C.C.); affirmed [1936] 2 W.W.R. 243 (P.C.). But a judgment against one *joint* debtor will bar an action against the other: *Birkdale Realty v. McLean* (1984), 64 N.S.R. (2d) 409 (N.S. Co. Ct.).

42 In respect of which the common-law rules as to *liabilities* have had to be altered by statutes; see *e.g.*, Negligence Act, R.S.O. 1990, c. N.1.

43 Below, pp. 191-200.

44 See *Winnett v. Heard* (1928), 62 O.L.R. 61 (Ont. H.C.). But in respect of a separation agreement under seal between a husband and wife, in which the infant children were named as parties, even though they did not sign the deed, it was held that a daughter did acquire a right of action to sue for the husband's (*i.e.*, her father's) breach, by not fulfilling his obligation to provide her with

of Canada in *Margolius v. Diesbourg*,[45] where the problem was raised in precise terms, that a person who claims to be the *principal* of a signatory to the contract, cannot sue or be sued on such contract. The law of agency, therefore, which does permit of the acquistion of rights or imposition of liabilities with respect to those not parties to a contract,[46] does not have quite the same effect where a contract is under seal. Only the *agent* can sue or be sued by the third party since only they have signed the contract.[47] Nor does it matter whether the contract was required by law to be under seal. If in fact the parties have chosen to contract in that form, then the rule stated above will apply. Further, it was held in *Hart v. Great West Securities & Trust Co.*,[48] that even a party to a deed will not be able to sue on it, and will not be exposed to liability under it, where he has not *executed* the deed at the material time. However, if such a party has performed or observed all the stipulations contained in the deed which he undertook therein, such a party may enforce the contract against the other party, irrespective of execution of the deed. The rationale of this apparent exception to the strict common-law doctrine appears to be that a party who has accepted a benefit under a contract cannot take advantage of the technical objection that the other party, who conferred the benefit, omitted to execute the deed.

(b) Other contracts

The general principle at common law, as it developed early in the nineteenth century in England, was that none but parties to a contract can sue on the contract or any of its terms, and consequently none but a party may be subjected to liability.[49]

In *Price v. Easton*[50] B promised X that if X worked for him, that is, B, he, B, would pay A a sum of money. It was held that A could not sue on this contract, he being a stranger alike to the contract and the consideration. In the seventeenth century case of *Dutton v. Poole*,[51] at a time when "natural love and affection", that is, some moral obligation, was thought sufficient to establish valuable consideration, a similar promise, namely, to give money to a third person, was held enforceable by such third person. The denial of the basis or *ratio* for such

---

a college education: *Selby v. Selby* (1956), 3 D.L.R. (2d) 275 (N.B.C.A.). Admittedly the fact that the contract was under seal removed the need for *consideration* from the daughter (compare, above, p. 117); but she had not signed the contract. Can this be explained on the basis of the infancy of the child, and by treating the mother as having signed not just as an *agent* of the child, but in the *capacity* of the child? Or is the case wrongly decided?

45 [1937] S.C.R. 183 (S.C.C.). Note, however, the statement by Davis J., *ibid.*, at 189, that the position is different *in equity*: as to which see below, pp. 196-200.

46 *Smith v. Yorkshire Guarantee Co.* (1915), 10 W.W.R. 475 (B.C.C.A.).

47 *Porter v. Pelton* (1903), 33 S.C.R. 449 (S.C.C.).

48 [1918] 2 W.W.R. 1061 (Sask. C.A.).

49 *Bilson v. Kokotow* (1975), 8 O.R. (2d) 263 (Ont. H.C.); affirmed (1978), 23 O.R. (2d) 720 (Ont. C.A.); leave to appeal to S.C.C. refused (1978), 23 O.R. (2d) 720n (S.C.C.). Apparently this was not the rule in the seventeenth century, until *Bourne v. Mason* (1669), 1 Vent. 6; Flannigan, "Privity — The End of an Era (Error)" (1987), 103 L.Q.R. 564 at pp. 564-566.

50 (1833), 4 B. & Ad. 433, above, p. 179.

51 (1678), 2 Lev. 210.

decision, in the early nineteenth century, led to the refusal by the court in *Tweddle v. Atkinson*[52] to follow the earlier precedent. Instead the attitude adopted in *Price v. Easton* was confirmed, though no longer on the twin bases of no consideration and the plaintiff not being a party to the contract, but on the simpler ground that the plaintiff was a stranger to the contract. In *Tweddle v. Atkinson* X was A's father. He agreed with Y, who was A's father-in-law, that Y should pay A £200 and that A should have suit on this contract at law or in equity. When Y died, not having paid A the money, A sued Y's executor in assumpsit, that is, at common law. The executor demurred to the suit, alleging by this that the action was not maintainable by A. It was held that assumpsit would not lie.

In England the doctrine received its final approval and most elaborate exposition in the case of *Dunlop Pneumatic Tyre Co. v. Selfridge & Co.*,[53] in which the House of Lords stated categorically that, "our law knows nothing of a '*jus quaesitum tertio*' arising by way of contract."[54] In that case B promised Dew & Co. to sell tyres at list prices, and to pay £5 for each breach of that agreement to A. When A sued B for breach of this agreement, the House of Lords held that there was no privity between A and B. It was also held that, even if there had been privity of contract between them (on the basis that A were undisclosed principals of Dew & Co.[55]) no consideration moved from A, through Dew & Co. to B. On agency principles, or on the basis of the statements in the *Coulls* case,[56] consideration may not be a relevant reason for denying an action in a case of this kind.[57]

While there may be dispute as to the effect of this decision in relation to the idea that "consideration must move from the promisee,"[58] there can be no doubt that the House of Lords clearly and decisively affirmed the proposition that there must be privity of contract between parties if one is to be able to make the other liable on a contract or otherwise enforce benefits alleged to accrue to him under such contract.

That doctrine has unquestionably been received and adopted by Canadian courts.[59] As long ago as 1872, in *Mulholland v. Merriam*,[60] a Canadian court accepted the decision in *Tweddle v. Atkinson* in preference to earlier English cases. There are several more modern decisions in which a third party who attempted to enforce

---

52 (1861), 1 B. & S. 393, above, p. 179: see the discussion in Flannigan, above, note 49, at pp. 569-571.

53 [1915] A.C. 847 (H.L.).

54 *Ibid.*, at 853 *per* Lord Haldane L.C. For an argument that this is not an absolute rule see Andrews, "Does a Third Party Beneficiary Have a Right in English Law?" (1988), 8 J. Leg. St. 14.

55 Compare below, pp. 195-196, on agency.

56 Above, pp. 114, 180.

57 See, also, below, pp. 201-205, in respect of the regulation of the terms and conditions under which chattels are sold, so as to restrict subsequent resales of such chattels.

58 Above, pp. 113-116; compare Flannigan, above, note 49, at pp. 571-572.

59 *London Drugs Ltd. v. Kuehne & Nagel Int. Ltd.* (1992), 97 D.L.R. (4th) 261 at 343-344 (S.C.C.) *per* Iacobucci J.

60 (1872), 19 Gr. 288 (Ont. Chan.); affirmed (1873), 20 Gr. 152 (Ont. C.A.). Contrast *Faulkner v. Faulkner* (1893), 23 O.R. 252 (Ont. C.A.). See also *Kendrick v. Barkey* (1907), 9 O.W.R. 356 (Ont. H.C.); *Edmison v. Couch* (1899), 26 O.A.R. 537 (Ont. C.A.).

a contract or a contractual term expressed to be for his benefit was denied any remedy.[61] For example, in *Smith v. Rae*,[62] a doctor agreed with a husband to deliver his wife when she was in childbirth. The doctor was held not liable for negligent breach of contract at the suit of the wife. Generally speaking it may be said that the *ratio decidendi* of these cases, even where consideration is raised in issue, is that the plaintiff was never a party to the contract, or, if a party through the agency of one of the original parties, ceased to be so when the agency was revoked by some event such as the death of the party in question.[63] In many cases, the problem of consideration has never been raised, the decision being based entirely upon the fact that the plaintiff was not considered to be a party. In one such case, *Great Northern Railway Co. v. Cole Agencies Ltd.*,[64] a successor in title to one of the original parties to a contract was being sued by the other original party. The pleadings were struck out on the ground of lack of privity, thereby rendering the defendant not liable for alleged breach of contract. Disbery J. appears to have based his decision solely on the issue of privity, not discussing the relevance of consideration:

> Under the general doctrine of privity of contract no one who is not an original party to a contract is entitled to seek to enforce the terms of the contract or is bound by any of its provisions. Such third parties are strangers to the contract.[65]

In *Sears v. Tanenbaum*,[66] after somewhat different approaches had been taken by the trial judge and the Ontario Court of Appeal, basing their opinions on the reasoning and effect of *Beswick v. Beswick*,[67] the majority of the Supreme Court

---

61 *Van Hemelryck v. New Westminister Const. & Enrg. Co.*, [1920] 3 W.W.R. 709 (B.C.C.A.); *Bryson v. Glenlawn School Dist.*, [1944] 3 W.W.R. 156 (Man. C.A.); *Young v. Can. Nor. Ry.*, [1931] 1 W.W.R. 49 (P.C.) (as to the effect of a collective agreement upon individual contracts, where the agreement had not been incorporated into such individual agreements); *Northwestern Securities v. White* (1962), 35 D.L.R. (2d) 666 (B.C.C.A.) (in which it was held that lack of privity did not need to be pleaded; it was a question of law which arose anyway); *General Securities Ltd. v. Brett's Ltd.* (1956), 19 W.W.R. 385 (B.C.S.C.) with which compare *Bill Boivin Plumbing & Heating Ltd. v. Flatt*, [1965] 2 O.R. 649 (Ont. C.A.). *Watson v. C.F. Hart Ltd.* (1986), 59 Nfld. & P.E.I.R. 308 (Nfld. Dist. Ct.); *Iampen v. Royal Bank* (1987), 79 A.R. 305 (Alta. Master); *Misener Financial Corp. v. McDonald Chevrolet Oldsmobile Ltd.* (1988), 83 N.S.R. (2d) 249 (N.S. T.D.). Contrast the curious case of *Vipond v. Ramsay*, [1934] 4 D.L.R. 84 (S.C.C.) from Quebec. Contrast also *Moss v. Richardson Greenshields of Can. Ltd.*, [1988] 4 W.W.R. 15 (Man. Q.B.); affirmed [1989] 3 W.W.R. 50 (Man. C.A.), where the broker was held to be a party to the agreement that was in issue.

62 (1919), 46 O.L.R. 518 (Ont. C.A.).

63 *E.g.*, *McIntyre v. Royal Trust Co.*, [1945] 2 W.W.R. 364 (Man. K.B.); affirmed [1946] 1 W.W.R. 210 (Man. C.A.); compare the decision with respect to the status of the plaintiff as an *undisclosed principal* in the *Van Hemelryck* case, above; below, p. 195.

64 (1964), 49 W.W.R. 153 (Sask. Q.B.). Contrast *Rettie Estate v. Tsawwassen Gardens Ltd.* (1989), 42 B.L.R. 78 (B.C.S.C.), where the right to sue passed to the heirs, executors or administrators of a deceased party, even though the contract did not mention them.

65 (1964), 49 W.W.R. 153 at 159 (Sask. Q.B.). Compare Egbert J. in *Merrill Petroleums Ltd. v. Seaboard Oil Co.* (1957), 22 W.W.R. 529 at 555-556 (Alta. S.C.); affirmed (1958), 25 W.W.R. 236 (Alta. C.A.).

66 (1968), 70 D.L.R. (2d) 126 (Ont. H.C.); varied (1970), 9 D.L.R. (3d) 425 (Ont. C.A.); reversed (1971), 18 D.L.R. (3d) 709 (S.C.C.).

67 [1968] A.C. 58 (H.L.); above, p. 181.

of Canada finally held that the plaintiff had no right of action, for reasons which had nothing to do with the doctrine of privity. The *Tanenbaum* case involved an agreement between four people part of which called for the payment of commission on certain dealings by a company of which one of the four was a director to a company of which another of the four was director. When the commissions were not paid, the plaintiff, whose company was the payee, sued the defendant, whose company was supposed to make the payments. At the trial it was held that specific performance of the contract between the four participants could not be granted, because it was unenforceable.[68] However, following the *Beswick* case, damages could be awarded to the plaintiff, which he would hold in trust for his company. The Court of Appeal, also following the *Beswick* case, held that specific performance could be granted to force the defendant's company to pay the money in question directly to the plaintiff's company. In the Supreme Court of Canada, although Spence J., and others in the minority, thought that the appropriate remedy was to force the defendant to get his company to pay the plaintiff's company the money alleged to be owing, the majority decided the litigation by an interpretation of the original four-party agreement, to which neither company was privy. The issues dealt with in *Beswick* did not arise. At the very least, however, the *Tanenbaum* case inferentially supports the doctrine of privity that has been stated above.

However, as far as the High Court and the Court of Appeal decisions are concerned, the case also recognizes that there may be some apparent exceptions to the doctrine, apart from what might be considered true exceptions to the doctrine. Thus, as previously mentioned, in the *Beswick* case and others,[69] the courts have accepted that a party to a contract may sue on it for the purpose of enforcing obligations due to a third party, who is, in fact, the same person as the plaintiff, although occupying a different capacity.[70] The widow in the *Beswick* case was her deceased husband's personal representative; she was also herself. She could sue in her first capacity to benefit herself in her second capacity. The contracting party in the *Tanenbaum* case could sue in his personal capacity in order to benefit himself as director of his company, that is, in his second capacity. The concept of privity may have been stretched, or the doctrine of privity qualified, by the technical differentiation of the two capacities of the plaintiff, in this and similar cases, as well as in others where what might be thought of as practical necessities or community of interest made up for what was a technical lack of privity.[71] A similar attitude was expressed in the *Trans Canada Credit Corporation* case[72] where

---

68 For reasons involving company law not the law of contract.

69 Above, p. 176, note 3.

70 And, therefore, by obtaining specific performance of the contract enforce the payment of money to the third party stranger, the beneficiary under the contract. In *Beswick* the House of Lords regarded the situation as justifying a decree of specific performance where normally the plaintiff's remedy would be damages. This was because the actual damage suffered by the plaintiff in her representative capacity was nominal.

71 *Centennial Realties Ltd. v. Westburn Industrial Enterprises Ltd.* (1978), 31 N.S.R. (2d) 64 (N.S.T.D.); *Re Spike and Rocca Group Ltd.* (1979), 107 D.L.R. (3d) 62 (P.E.I.S.C.) above, p. 176.

72 (1983), 143 D.L.R. (3d) 296 (N.S.T.D.); affirmed (1983), 149 D.L.R. (3d) 280 (N.S.C.A.), above, p. 177.

the realities of insurance practices seem to have outflanked the strictness of the doctrine of privity.[73] In the English case of *Snelling v. John G. Snelling Ltd.*,[74] the doctrine of privity was technically applicable, because the agreement between the brothers could confer no benefits on the company which they incorporated, that company not being a party to the brothers' contract. However, as the judge pointed out, to have given judgment in favour of the plaintiff, and allowed the counterclaim of his brothers (without any possibility of their being reimbursed by the company) would have produced absurdity. Under the contract what was owed to the plaintiff on his resignation from the company should have gone to the company, and he was not entitled to be paid what he had earned. But this could not provide the company with a defence to his action for the money. Yet he failed in his action, and his brothers were able to have the action dismissed, rather than simply apply for a stay of proceedings. This was because all the relevant parties were before the court. Notwithstanding the technicalities of the doctrine of privity, which appear to have been set aside or waived by the judge, the plaintiff was not permitted to recover money which had been paid over to a third party, the company, which had acquired no rights to that money under a contract to which it was not privy. A decision which was plainly contradictory of the doctrine of privity could be justified once again on grounds of practicality and elementary justice. There was no point in making the parties go through a complex procedure when the issue between them could be resolved satisfactorily notwithstanding the seeming strictness of the law.

A further instance of practical necessity overriding the doctrine of privity is provided by the English case of *Jackson v. Horizon Holidays Ltd.*[75] An action was brought by a man who had booked a holiday for breach of contract by his travel agency. The claim was successful for reasons not relevant here. Damages were recovered not only for the injuries or loss incurred by the plaintiff personally, but also on behalf of his wife and children. The reasoning of Lord Denning, which appears to apply some broad statements in a nineteenth century English case, *Lloyd's v. Harper*,[76] has been rejected by the House of Lords,[77] who said that Lord Denning had misapplied the earlier decision.[78] However the actual decision in the *Jackson* case was not overruled, its correctness being based either as a broad decision on

---

73 Compare *J. Clark & Son Ltd. v. Finnamore* (1973), 32 D.L.R. (3d) 236 (N.B.C.A.). But this case seems to conflict with the later Supreme Court decision in *Greenwood Shopping Plaza Ltd. v. Beattie* (1980), 111 D.L.R. (3d) 257 (S.C.C.) below, pp. 585-586; as well as with the earlier decisions in *General Securities Ltd. v. Brett's Ltd.* (1956), 5 D.L.R. (2d) 46 (B.C.S.C.), and *Bill Boivin Plumbing & Heating Ltd. v. Flatt* (1965), 51 D.L.R. (2d) 574 (Ont. C.A.). Another "insurance" case, which may involve the "trust" exception to the doctrine of privity (below, pp. 196-200) rather than a contractual qualification, is *Re Scott and Mfrs. Life Ins. Co.* (1973), 41 D.L.R. (3d) 296 (Man. Q.B.).

74 [1973] 1 Q.B. 87; *quaere* whether this case would be applied in Canada.

75 [1975] 3 All E.R. 92 (C.A.); see further below, p. 738.

76 (1880), 16 Ch. D. 290, especially at 321 (C.A.) *per* Lush L.J.

77 *Woodar Invt. Dev. Ltd. v. Wimpey Const. (U.K.) Ltd.*, [1980] 1 All E.R. 571 (H.L.).

78 By treating remarks which applied where the agency or trust qualifications of the doctrine (below, pp. 194-200) were apposite as justifying a broader qualification of the doctrine: see [1980] 1 All E.R. 571 at 576 *per* Lord Wilberforce, 585 *per* Lord Russell, and 588 *per* Lord Keith.

measure of damages or as an example of a type of contract calling for special treatment, such as persons contracting for family holidays, ordering meals in restaurants for a party, hiring a taxi for a group. It might be reasonable to describe such instances as involving an implicit agency relationship between the contracting party and those who later seek a remedy in damages.[79] Whatever be the proper explanation of the *Jackson* case, the later House of Lords comments were intended to uphold the present doctrine of privity (and its acknowledged qualifications), even though criticism of the doctrine was expressed by Lord Scarman.[80]

By way of final comment, reference should be made to the way in which the privity doctrine has interacted with the law relating to exception, exclusion and limitation clauses. The problem here has been whether someone not a party to a contract containing such a clause could take advantage of the clause when later sued by a contracting party. This may be called the problem of "vicarious immunity," the contrary or opposite of vicarious liability. A fuller examination of this issue is undertaken in a later chapter, where such clauses are analyzed and discussed.[81] In the present context, however, it should be said that recent developments may have made inroads in the strict doctrine of privity that was applied to such situations by the House of Lords in *Scruttons Ltd. v. Midland Silicones Ltd.*,[82] and by subsequent Canadian cases.[83] The later Privy Council decision in *New Zealand Shipping Co. v. A.M. Satterthwaite & Co.*,[84] applying *dicta* in the *Scruttons* case, held that it was possible to permit the extension of the benefit of an exemption or similar clause to a third party by the invocation of the law of agency in appropriate circumstances. This has sometimes been done, and sometimes has been refused.[85] However, at least one recent Canadian decision, perhaps going beyond the strict doctrines of agency (or trusts), has been prepared to allow a third party stranger to a contract to cloak himself in the protection of such a clause on the ground that it was commercially expedient and part of the intentions of the parties, and the general commercial background against which the contract was made, that such protection should be extended in this way.[86] Insofar as such

---

79 Thereby bringing the agency qualification (below, pp. 194-196) into operation.

80 Above, note 77, at 591; compare *Swain v. Law Society*, [1983] 1 A.C. 598 at 611 (H.L.) *per* Lord Diplock.

81 Below, pp. 581-588.

82 [1962] A.C. 446 (H.L.).

83 *Can. Gen. Elec. Co. v. Pickford & Black Ltd.*, [1971] S.C.R. 41 (S.C.C.); *Bill Boivin Plumbing & Heating Ltd. v. Flatt*, above, note 73; *ITO-Int. Terminal Operators Ltd. v. Miida Electronics Inc.* (1986), 28 D.L.R. (4th) 641 (S.C.C.); *Christian Vision Book Store Supplies (1983) Ltd. v. Avatex Management Ltd.* (1986), 50 Alta. L.R. (2d) 359 (Alta. Q.B.); *London Drugs Ltd. v. Kuehne & Nagel Int. Ltd.* (1992), 97 D.L.R. (4th) 261 at 358-370 (S.C.C.).

84 [1975] A.C. 154 (P.C.). See *e.g.*, *L. & B. Const. Ltd. v. Nor. Can. Power Comm.; Nor. Can. Power Comm. v. L. & B. Const. Ltd.*, [1984] 6 W.W.R. 598 (N.W.T.S.C.).

85 Below, pp. 582-586.

86 *Marubeni Amer. Corp. v. Mitsui O.S.K. Lines Ltd.* (1979), 96 D.L.R. (3d) 518 (Fed. T.D.); appeal allowed in part (1981), 124 D.L.R. (3d) 33 (*sub nom. Miida Electronics v. Mitsui O.S.K. Lines Ltd.*) (Fed. C.A.); appeal allowed in part (1986), 28 D.L.R. (4th) 641 (*sub nom. ITO-Int. Terminal Operators Ltd. v. Miida Electronics Inc.*) (S.C.C.). On this case in relation to privity of contract see a comment by Reif (1988), 26 Alta. L. Rev. 372. See now, especially, *London Drugs Ltd. v. Kuehne & Nagel*

decisions abandon the solid ground of agency or trust law (on which certain well-accepted qualifications of the privity doctrine are based), and purport to oust the strict application of the doctrine of privity for practical reasons, they may be said to enshrine exceptions to, qualifications of, or limitations upon the doctrine of privity that are more apparent than real, in a doctrinal sense.[87]

3. Modifications of the doctrine

(a) In general

The restrictive character of this common-law doctrine needs no emphasis. It clearly manifests a very narrow, rigid approach to contractual obligations.[88] Other systems of law have discovered that to adopt the idea that contracts are personal to the contracting parties is to frustrate the object of contract, and to cause very practical difficulties, which the demands of logic, as it were, do not justify, having regard to legitimate commercial and other needs. Hence their acceptance of the notion of stipulations for third parties.[89]

Even the common law recognized the defects of this lately developed doctrine.[90] To prevent a third person not a party to an original contract, though named in it and governed by it, from being able to enforce that contract, and to

---

Int. Ltd. (1992), 97 D.L.R. (4th) 261 (S.C.C.) below, pp. 586-588. See also the refusal of an English court to be bound by the strict doctrine of privity in *Norwich City Council v. Harvey*, [1989] 1 All E.R. 1180 (C.A.).

87 But the strictness of the doctrine and its exceptions were insisted upon by the Federal Court of Appeal in *St. John Shipbuilding & Dry Dock Co. v. Kingland Maritime* (1981), 43 N.R. 1 (Fed. C.A.); leave to appeal to S.C.C. refused (1981), 126 D.L.R. (3d) 332n (S.C.C.).

88 Compare the discussion of criticism of the doctrine, and the way it has been dealt with in some jurisdictions, by Iacobucci J. in *London Drugs Ltd. v. Kuehne & Nagel Int. Ltd.*, above, note 86, at 345-352. See, *e.g.*, the recommendation that the law be changed by the Law Revision Committee, 6th Interim Report, 1937. Cmd. 5449, para. 50(9), which would have given the third party certain direct rights of action under contracts. In the *Woodar Invt.* case, above, note 77, at 591, Lord Scarman referred to this Report and the fact that nothing had been done in consequence, which was a matter for regret.

   Similar change was recommended by the Ontario Law Reform Commission, *Report on Amendment of the Law of Contract*, 1987, after discussing legislative change in New Zealand, Western Australia, Queensland and Quebec: *ibid.*, at pp. 58-65, and American developments, *ibid.*, at pp. 55-58, which have eroded, or in some instances abandoned, privity of contract. For a discussion of the situation in the United States, see Eisenberg, "Third Party Beneficiaries" (1992), 92 Col. L.R. 1358: compare earlier comments in Williston, "Contracts for the Benefit of a Third Person" (1902), 15 H.L.R. 767; Corbin, "Contracts for Benefit of Third Persons" (1918), 27 Yale L.J. 1008. See also *Restatement of Contracts* (2d), para. 133.

89 Buckland and McNair, *Roman Law and Common Law*, 2nd ed. pp. 214-217; Amos and Walton, *Introduction to French Law*, pp. 170-174. For Quebec see c.c. art. 1029: on which see Irving (1963) 9 McG. L.J. 337. Note the alteration recommended by the Civil Code Revision Office, *Committee on Law of Obligations*, pp. 133-139; Report on the Quebec Civil Code, 1977, Vol. I pp. 366-369, Vol. II, pp. 616-618; Ontario Law Reform Commission, *Report*, above, note 88, at pp. 64-65.

90 Hence, perhaps, the development of various ways to circumvent the strictness of the doctrine, *e.g.*, the dual capacity of the plaintiff in *Beswick v. Beswick*, [1968] A.C. 58 (H.L.); the measurement of damages in *Jackson v. Horizon Holidays Ltd.*, [1975] 3 All E.R. 92 (C.A.); the procedural devices employed in *Snelling v. John G. Snelling Ltd.*, [1973] Q.B. 87, above, pp. 176, 188, 189.

make such a person immune from any liability upon it, has long been accepted by the common law as impractical in certain contexts, such as the law of real property. Side by side with the doctrine of privity of contract, the common law created the notion of "privity of estate," by which a third party could be affected by agreements between the landlord and the original tenant of the property.[91]

Another development, that is partly common law and partly stems from the law merchant, is the idea of agency. The growth of the law of agency enabled third parties to become involved in contracts by the expedient of using an "agent" to contract on their behalf, with the consequence, as the law emerged, that the "principal," the one who employed the "agent," could sue and be sued on the contract thus made. There were, and still are, other limitations on the utility of the agency doctrione to avoid the strict effects of the doctrine of privity of contract.[92] But, there can be no doubt that agency at least helped to alleviate some of the more stringent consequences of privity at common law, and gave some greater flexibility to the law of contract.[93]

Other developments in the law merchant helped to cure the defects from which the common law of contract suffered as a result of the idea of privity. The needs of the business community made it essential to create some means whereby the strict notion of privity could be overcome. One vital development was the emergence and recognition of negotiable instruments, namely bills of exchange, cheques, promissory notes.[94] These are documents which both are, and evidence contractual transactions. They have many of the same characteristics and qualities as currency, that is, money. The rise of the idea of negotiability, under which title to such documents, and the money which they represent, may be passed by the transfer of such documents, that is, "negotiation," was an important stage in the transformation of the law of contract and the development of commercial law. It made the conduct of business and the growth of commercial life possible. Once the strict limitations of the common law of contract were broken by this new notion, the

---

91 This is paralleled by the *equitable* doctrine of *restrictive covenants* in relation to the use of land; below, p. 201.

92 Below, p. 194, note also the situation with respect to contracts under seal: above, p. 184.

93 As did the development of the idea of assignment: below, Chapter 17.

94 On promissory notes see now a decision under the Interest Act, R.S.C. 1985, c. I-15, s. 4, which regulates the amount of interest that may be charged: see *Elcano Acceptance Ltd. v. Richmond, Richmond, Stambler & Mills* (1989), 68 O.R. (2d) 165 (Ont. H.C.); additional reasons at (1989), 68 O.R. (2d) 641 (Ont. H.C.); affirmed (1991), 3 O.R. (3d) 123 (Ont. C.A.). For earlier cases, see *Barton v. Paradis*, [1930] C.S. 31; *Douville v. Guyon*, [1967] S.C. 378 (Que. S.C.); *Can. Permanent Trust Co. v. Kowal* (1981), 32 O.R. (2d) 37 at 65-66 (Ont. H.C.) *per* Boland J.; compare *Massey Manufacturing Co. v. Perrin* (1892), 8 Man. R. 457 (Man. Q.B.); see also the dissenting judgment of Mahony J. in *Kobi's Cabinets Ltd. v. Can. Permanent Trust Co.* (1980), 27 O.R. (2d) 717 (Ont. H.C.); upheld on appeal (1980), 115 D.L.R. (3d) 256 (Ont. C.A.).

They are also contracts under the Bills of Exchange Act, R.S.C. 1985, c. B-4 in relation to conflict of laws provisions. However, whether or not a promissory note was a contract it was not affected by a British Columbia statute; since promissory notes fall within the legislative jurisdiction of the federal government; *John Deere Plow Co. v. Agnew* (1913), 48 S.C.R. 208 (S.C.C.), discussed by O'Leary J. in *Elcano Acceptance Ltd. v. Richmond, Richmond, Stambler & Mills*, above, at 68 O.R. (2d) 165 at 169.

way was made easy and clear for the gradual elaboration of commercial relationships and the advance of commercial transactions.[95]

In more recent times a new development may be in the process of occurring. This is the rise of bankers' commercial credits, which, for the purposes of international transactions, such as sales, may have taken the place formerly occupied by such negotiable instruments as bills of exchange. Under these arrangements, when there is a sale of goods, especially between countries, the seller arranges to be paid by a bank, with which the buyer has an agreement, under the terms of which, on the happening of a certain event, for example, the shipment of goods by the seller to the buyer, an *irrevocable* credit is opened at the bank in favour of the seller, who can draw on it to the extent of the buyer's indebtedness to the seller for the price of the goods. The contractual situation is very complex, since it involves "transgresssion" of the doctrines of consideration and privity. In strict law, it would seem, there may be no rights of action to recover the money from the bank (although there would be actions by seller against buyer, buyer against seller, and buyer against bank, in the event of a breach of one of the constituent contracts). But the system appears to work in practice and may have been recognized by the courts to the extent of there being customary rules now governing these various transactions, such as to bind the parties.[96] However, it may be too soon to accept that the law has recognized another true exception to the privity doctrine.

Insurance affords another example of the way in which the strict common law of contract has been unable to provide a satisfactory legal background for the exigencies of everyday life. In the first place, a person not a party to an insurance contract may be the beneficiary thereunder.[97] Secondly, because of the privity doctrine it was necessary for the law to invent another idea, that of "subrogation" to enable an insurer to have a right of action against a third party, by reason of whose conduct, for example, a tort, the insurer may have been obliged to pay the assured under the terms of the contract between insurer and assured. Either as a consequence of the terms of the contract between insurer and the assured or as a result of the law itself, the insurer has been "subrogated" to whatever rights the assured would have had against the third party, for example, to sue for negligence.[98] In this manner equity, if not common law has managed to outflank the strict common-law doctrine of privity in certain situations.[99]

The common law of negligence which was once hampered by the doctrine

---

95 On "negotiability" and its difference from assignment, see below, p. 672.

96 See, *e.g.*, *Malas v. British Imex Indust. Ltd.*, [1958] 1 All E.R. 262 (C.A.); *United Dominions Trust Ltd. v. Kirkwood*, [1966] 1 All E.R. 968 (C.A.). See also *United City Merchants (Invts.) Ltd. v. Royal Bank of Can.*, [1982] 2 All E.R. 720 (H.L.). Compare the situation with respect to "performance bonds": *Edward Owen Engr. Ltd. v. Barclays Bank Int. Ltd.*, [1978] Q.B. 159 (C.A.).

97 *P. Samuel & Co. v. Dumas*, [1924] A.C. 431 (H.L.); compare *Trans Can. Credit Corp. Ltd. v. Royal Ins. Co. of Can.* (1983), 143 D.L.R. (3d) 296 (N.S.T.D.); affirmed (1983), 149 D.L.R. (3d) 280 (N.S.C.A.) above, p. 177.

98 See *J. Clark & Son Ltd. v. Finnamore* (1973), 5 N.B.R. (2d) 467 (N.B.C.A.). For the doctrine of subrogation, see Goff & Jones, *Law of Restitution*, 3rd ed. (1986), pp. 523-549; Fridman, *Restitution*, 2nd ed. (1992), pp. 398-402; Maddaugh & McCamus, *Law of Restitution* (1990), pp. 159-181.

99 Goff & Jones, above, note 98, pp. 551-567; Fridman, above, note 98, pp. 412-414.

of privity of contract, at least throughout the nineteenth and early twentieth centuries, cast off the shackles of that doctrine in *Donoghue v. Stevenson*,[100] a decision which marked the start of the idea that a person not a party to a contract might have rights of action *in tort* arising from the negligent breach of a contract *between two other parties*. The law of negligence has grown a long way from that quintessential idea at this time, but it should not be forgotten that it was the breach of the citadel of privity which marked the commencement of the modern tort of negligence, the development of which has still not ended.[101]

In some situations statute law has been enacted to avoid the consequences of the common-law doctrine of privity, for example, in relation to insurance with respect to injuries caused by driving a motor vehicle. Legislatures have acknowledged the impracticability of the common law in relation to the realities of modern life. However, where a statute does give a third party a right under a contract between other parties, then the right of action has been held to be statutory not contractual (which suggests that the exception or modification of the common-law doctrine is more apparent than real).[102]

Finally, mention must be made of an equitable development which has done much to undermine or limit the strength of the common-law doctrine. By the employment of the *trust* concept, equity has enabled third parties sometimes to acquire enforceable rights under contracts to which they were not signatories or parties.[103]

(b) Some specific qualifications

(i) *Agency*[104]

Under the law of agency, a principal may contract with another party through an agent. In such circumstances, even though the contract is negotiated between the agent and the third party (and may even be signed by the agent, not the principal), the contract which comes about is held to be between the principal and the third party, not the agent and the third party.[105] There are, of course, qualifications to this general principle. Thus, as seen earlier, if the contract is by deed, the agent

---

100 [1932] A.C. 562 (H.L.).

101 Fridman, *Law of Torts in Canada*, Vol. 1 (1989), pp. 231-232.

102 *Metro. Loan Co. v. Can. Security Assur. Co.*, [1934] 2 W.W.R. 422 (Man. C.A.); compare *Davis & Sons v. Taff Vale Ry. Co.*, [1895] A.C. 542 at 560 (H.L.) *per* Lord Macnaghten.

103 Below, pp. 196-200; compare also the equitable doctrine of *restrictive covenants*: below, p. 201.

104 See, generally, Fridman, *Law of Agency*, 6th ed. (1990). Nothing decided in *London Drugs Ltd. v. Kuehne & Nagel Int. Ltd.* (1992), 97 D.L.R. (4th) 261 (S.C.C.) affects this qualification of the privity doctrine.

105 Fridman, *op. cit.*, at pp. 193-200. Of course, it must be shown that the relationship of principal and agent existed, which can cause problems in some circumstances: *ibid.*, pp. 47-52. In this respect can it be said that the requisite relationship existed in *Centennial Realties Ltd. v. Westburn Indust. Enterprises Ltd.* (1978), 31 N.S.R. (2d) 64 (N.S.T.D.), above p. 176. Note also that if an agent employs a sub-agent this may not produce privity between the sub-agent and the principal: Fridman, *op. cit.*, pp. 150-154; *S/S Steamship Co. v. "Alchatby" (The)* (1986), 5 F.T.R. 253 (Fed. T.D.); affirmed (1989), 101 N.R. 384 (Fed. C.A.).

alone will acquire rights and be subjected to liabilities thereunder.[106] The principal has no direct rights or liabilities with respect to the third party. Secondly, there are situations in which the agent does not drop out, as it were, but remains a party to the transaction, capable of suing, and being sued by the third party.[107] However, the more normal position is that the principal, on whose behalf the agent contracts, is the one entitled to take the benefit of the contract so negotiated, as well as being the one liable in the event of default.

This will only be the result when the agent, in contracting, has acted within the scope of his authority.[108] An agent who contracts without authority does not achieve the result of making his principal a party to the contract[109] (and may be liable himself to the third party, on the basis of contract, that is, as the only other contracting party, or for breach of the implied warranty of authority, by representing that he had authority to contract).[110] What is meant by authority? This concept breaks down into various categories, namely, express, implied, usual, customary, and apparent or ostensible authority.[111] As long as the agent has acted in accordance with one of these various types of authority when he contracted, then the contract will bind the principal (though it must be noted that if the agent acted with apparent or ostensible authority this may result in the principal's being liable, without any corresponding right to sue the third party). Mention should also be made of the doctrine of ratification.[112] By virtue of this, an originally unauthorized act or transaction on the part of the agent may become valid by subsequent authorization or ratification, which will have the effect (in almost all cases) of rendering the transaction as good as if the agent had been authorized in advance. This is not always true, for example, where an offer has been accepted subject to ratification and the offer has been withdrawn between the original unauthorized acceptance by the agent and the later ratification by the principal.[113] Nor will an undisclosed principal be able to ratify an unauthorized contract made by his agent.[114]

An important distinction is drawn between a disclosed and an undisclosed principal. An undisclosed principal is one whose existence is not made known by the agent to the third party; the latter therefore is contracting with the agent under the belief that the agent is the other party, that is, a principal in his own right. While, exceptionally, the common law permits an undisclosed principal to acquire rights and be subjected to liabilities as a consequence of a contract made by his

---

106 Above, p. 184; compare *Margolius v. Diesbourg*, [1937] S.C.R. 183 (S.C.C.).

107 Fridman, above, note 104, at pp. 207-228; compare *Holland v. St. John Toyota Ltd.* (1981), 130 D.L.R. (3d) 156 (N.B.Q.B.), above p. 176, note 5.

108 Hence if the agent's authority is *revoked* before he contracts, the principal will not be bound: *McIntyre v. Royal Trust Co.*, [1946] 1 W.W.R. 210 (Man. C.A.).

109 Fridman, above, note 104, at pp. 195-196.

110 *Ibid.*, pp. 207, 218.

111 *Ibid.*, pp. 52-69, 107-118.

112 *Ibid.*, pp. 74-97.

113 *Ibid.*, pp. 87-92.

114 *Ibid.*, pp. 78-80. See, *e.g.*, *Eckroyd v. Rodgers* (1913), 4 W.W.R. 601 (Man. K.B.); *Van Hemelryck v. New Westminister Const. & Enrg. Co.*, [1920] 3 W.W.R. 709 (B.C.C.A.).

agent on his behalf, in some circumstances this will not be so.[115] If the identity of the contracting party is important to the third party transacting with the agent, if the agent was unauthorized in what he did, if the existence of some other principal is expressly or impliedly excluded by the contract between agent and third party, the undisclosed principal is precluded from being a party to the contract. The anomalous position of the undisclosed principal (which compounds the anomaly of agency) has not been extended to cover all possible situations.

Subject to such limitations, however, namely, authority, disclosure of the existence of a principal, the intention of the parties, the concept of agency, and the rules which have been developed with respect to its use in the law, have made important inroads upon the doctrine of privity of contract. By using someone to transact on one's behalf, even to the extent of concealing that interrelationship, it is possible for one person to be a party to a contract which he has not made. In a sense, however, the exception is more imaginary than real. The true party is the principal; the agent is only a sort of amaneuensis or instrument. The consideration is furnished by the principal; it is only transmitted on his behalf by the agent. What the law of agency achieves, it may be suggested, is a mechanical, rather than a truly substantive qualification of the privity doctrine. Nonetheless, it is important to bear agency in mind; commercially speaking, it may be stated categorically that without the development of the notion of agency, business would have been seriously hampered, the law might have been kept in an immature, undeveloped condition, and it would have been impossible for commerce, trade, and everyday life generally, to have emerged as we know it in modern times.[116]

(ii) *Trust*[117]

In 1893 Street C.J. said in an Ontario case, *Faulkner v. Faulkner*,[118]

> In all the cases since *Tweddle v. Atkinson* . . . in which a person not a party to a contract has brought an action to recover some benefit stipulated for him in it, he has been driven, in order to avoid being shipwrecked upon the common-law rule which confines such an action to parties and privies, to seek refuge under the shelter of an alleged trust in his favour.

This charming comment, as it was called by Disbery J. in *Tobin Tractor (1957) Ltd. v. Western Surety Ltd.*[119] expresses very succinctly the effect of the English

---

115 Fridman, above, note 104, at pp. 228-236.

116 For the application of the agency principle to attempts to invoke the protection of an exemption or similar clause by someone not a party to the original contract, see below, pp. 581-588. Compare *Christian Vision Book Store Supplies (1983) Ltd. v. Avatex Management Ltd.* (1986), 50 Alta. L.R. (2d) 359 (Alta. Q.B.) with *Moss v. Richardson Greenshields of Can. Ltd.*, [1988] 4 W.W.R. 15 (Man. Q.B.); affirmed [1989] 3 W.W.R. 50 (Man. C.A.).

117 Nothing decided in *London Drugs Ltd. v. Kuehne & Nagel Int. Ltd.* (1992), 97 D.L.R. (4th) 261 (S.C.C.) affects this qualification of the privity doctrine.

118 (1893), 23 O.R. 252 at 258 (Ont. C.A.).

119 (1963), 40 D.L.R. (2d) 231 at 235 (Sask. Q.B.).

cases from 1880[120] to the 1933 Privy Council decision in the Canadian case of *Vandepitte v. Preferred Accident Insurance Corporation.*[121] In those cases it was held that "where a contract is made for the benefit and on behalf of a third person, there is an equity in that third person to sue on the contract, and the person who has entered into the contract may be treated as a trustee for the person for whose benefit it has been entered into."[122] Prior to the more recent English cases, Canadian courts were prepared to apply the notion of trust, even where the expresssion "trust" was not to be found in the contract. Indeed the use of that term was unimportant. So it was said in an early Canadian case, *Mulholland v. Merriam.*[123] There a man gave all his property to his son-in-law with directions to pay the donor's heirs in a specified manner after the donor was dead. When the donor died, it was held that the intended beneficiaries could sue the son-in-law even though they were not parties to the contract under which the deceased donor gave his property to the defendant, the son-in-law. It is arguable that this case involved a gift of the property rather than a contract between the donor and his son-in-law. However, if the existence of a contract is inferred from the facts, the basis of the son-in-law's liability to the beneficiaries was the notion of trust. The son-in-law had accepted the property with the intention of carrying out the instructions and wishes of the donor. Nor was it always necessary to have an ascertained fund or property out of which the payment was to be made.[124] But not all cases were viewed the same way. It was not always a simple matter to establish such a "trust".[125] In *Faulkner v. Faulkner,*[126] for example, such a trust could not be created to enable the brother to sue on the contract made by the father and mother with respect to the education of the brother in question. The action had to be brought by the executors of the mother.

However, enshrined in these decisions, and those in England of the same period,[127] there can be found clearly enunciated a doctrine that if a party to a contract can properly be treated as having contracted as a "trustee" for a third person, who is the real and true beneficiary of the promise made to the "trustee," then that beneficiary may enforce the contract, albeit that this will involve making

---

120 *Lloyd's v. Harper* (1880), 16 Ch. D. 290 (C.A.); *Re Empress Engineering Co.* (1880), 16 Ch.D. 125 (C.A.); and see *Gandy v. Gandy* (1885), 30 Ch. D. 57 (C.A.) which was misinterpreted and misapplied by Lord Denning in *Jackson v. Horizon Holidays Ltd.*, [1975] 3 All E.R. 92 (C.A.), above, p. 189. For earlier equity cases see *Tomlinson v. Gill* (1756), Amb. 330; *Gregory v. Parker* (1808), 1 Comp. 394.

121 [1933] A.C. 70 (P.C.).

122 *Lloyd's v. Harper* (1880), 16 Ch. D. 290 at 309 (C.A.) *per* Fry L.J.

123 (1872), 19 Gr. 288 at 293 (Ont. Chan.); on appeal (1873), 20 Gr. 152 (Ont. C.A.).

124 *Dawson v. Dawson* (1911), 23 O.L.R. 1 at 12 (Ont. C.A.) *per* Meredith C.J.

125 Contrast *Dawson v. Dawson*, above, note 124, and *Mitchell v. London Assur. Co.* (1888), 15 O.A.R. 262 (Ont. C.A.) (where a trust was admitted), with *Osborne v. Henderson* (1889), 18 S.C.R. 698 (S.C.C.) (no trust). See also *Kendrick v. Barkey* (1907), 9 O.W.R. 356 (Ont. H.C.); *Edmison v. Couch* (1899), 26 O.A.R. 537 (Ont. C.A.).

126 (1893), 23 O.R. 252 (Ont. C.A.).

127 And later: see *Royal Exchange Assur. v. Hope*, [1928] 1 Ch. 179 (C.A.); *Harmer v. Armstrong*, [1934] 1 Ch. 65 (C.A.). Contrast, however, *Morley v. Moore*, [1936] 2 All E.R. 79 (C.A.).

the trustee a nominal party to the action, either as plaintiff or as defendant.[128] The idea that this test of "trusteeship" could be viewed as a pure formality, which the courts would gladly and easily invoke in order to achieve the possibility of a third party deriving a benefit from the contract, was shown to be unjustified by the Privy Council decision in the *Vandepitte* case.[129] Although the actual decision may have been reversed, on very practical grounds, by statute in many jurisdictions, it still stands as a valid statement of the law in this matter. In that case the issue was whether an insurance policy taken out by X, the owner of a motor car, could be held to cover the liability of X's daughter who was driving the car at the time of the accident out of which the claim arose. The liability of the insurance company depended upon whether the policy covered the daughter, that is, the driver, as well as the actual insured. For this purpose it was argued that the contract of insurance notionally made or could be treated as making the insured party a trustee for *anyone* who drove the vehicle with his consent. The Judicial Committee, through Lord Wright, denied that there could be any such trust. In other words, what the court was deciding was that the courts will not create a trust out of nothing, as it were: there must be some clear indication that the intention of the parties to the contract was that one party should be regarded as having contracted on behalf of another, specified person, as a trustee. In Lord Wright's words, "the intention to constitute the trust must be affirmatively proved: the intention cannot necessarily be inferred from the mere general words of the policy."[130]

The issue in a number of Canadian cases, as in England,[131] has been whether it was possible to construe the contents of the contract before the court as creating such a trust. By and large it would appear that attempts to achieve such a result, at least in more modern Canadian cases, have been unsuccessful.[132] The difficulty of establishing such a trust was pointed out by Disbery J. in *Tobin Tractor (1957)*

---

128 But this procedure was not required by the House of Lords in *Les Affréteurs Réunis S.A. v. Leopold Walford (London) Ltd.*, [1919] A.C. 801 (H.L.) (shipowners liable to charter-party brokers for the latter's commission promised by the shipowners to the charterers).

129 [1933] A.C. 70 (P.C.). Compare *Crown Bakery v. Preferred Accident Ins. Co.*, [1933] 2 W.W.R. 33 (Sask. C.A.); *Comer v. Bussell*, [1940] S.C.R. 506 (S.C.C.).

130 [1933] A.C. 70 at 79-80 (P.C.). Was the reluctance of courts to infer a trust based on the unwillingness of judges to assume that the parties intended to deprive themselves of their ability to alter their arrangements?

131 See *Re Schebsman*, [1943] 2 All E.R. 768 (C.A.): *Re Miller's Agreement*, [1947] 2 All E.R. 78; *Green v. Russell*, [1959] 2 All E.R. 525 (C.A.).

132 See *Royal Bank v. Eastern Trust Co.*, [1951] 3 D.L.R. 828 (P.E.I.S.C.); *Thorne v. Livingston*, [1952] O.W.N. 773 (Ont. C.A.); *Merrill Petroleums Ltd. v. Seaboard Oil Co.* (1957), 22 W.W.R. 529 above; affirmed (1958), 25 W.W.R. 236 (Alta. C.A.) in which Egbert J. at first instance (22 W.W.R. 529 at 561) had followed *Re Schebsman*, above. In none of these cases was the argument in favour of a constructive trust successful. See also *Christian Vision Book Store Supplies (1983) Ltd. v. Avatex Management Ltd.* (1986), 50 Alta. L.R. (2d) 359 (Alta. Q.B.), where no trust could be created out of the relationship and connection between the owner of property, the lessor, and the management company that looked after the property in question: the latter could not claim the protection of a clause in the lease in respect of negligence causing damage through burst pipes. Contrast *J.A. Johnston Co. v. E.R. Taylor Const. Ltd.* (1965), 52 D.L.R. (2d) 20 (Ont. H.C.) where the contract between a construction company and the lessee of a building created a trust in favour of the building owner which could sue for damage caused by the construction company.

Ltd. v. Western Survey Ltd.,[133] in which the unpaid suppliers of a construction company wished to sue the person who had gone surety for a performance bond entered into by the company with the municipality for which the company was working. It was held that the surety could not be sued, as the supplier of the goods was not a party to the contract under which the surety was bound, and the concept of trust could not provide a basis for any claim against him by the suppliers of the goods. The learned judge made it clear that evidence and documents were not to be manipulated in order to discover a trust where none was ever intended to be created, simply to avoid the common-law doctrine of privity of contract. Sympathy for the third party beneficiary should not encourage unjustified extensions of the idea.[134] The same point was made by Henry J. in *Fournier Van & Storage Co. v. Fournier.*[135] In that case there was an agreement between X and the defendant that the defendant would discharge the plaintiff company's obligation under a bond. When the defendant did not do so, the plaintiff company sued to obtain performance of this promise. It was held that the company, not being a party to the agreement, could not sue. No trust relationship could be inferred from the circumstances. In the language of the learned judge,[136]

> the courts are reluctant to find that a trust has been created so as to allow the stranger to a contract to bring an action in his own name. It must clearly have been within the contemplation of the parties that one of them be a trustee of the chose in action for the benefit of the third party.

However, a different view was taken more recently in Ontario, where the contract in question expressly provided for a stranger to the contract, which was a bond, to sue "as a beneficiary of the trust herein provided for." In *Johns-Manville Canada Inc. v. John Carlo Ltd.,*[137] the defendants entered into a contract to do work for the Ministry of the Environment. In conjunction with this contract the defendants entered into a "labour and material payment bond" with a surety under which a claimant, as defined in the bond, could sue. A claimant for this purpose was someone having a direct contract with the defendants for labour, material or both, used or reasonably required for use in the defendants' performance of their contract with the Ministry. The plaintiffs were claimants within the meaning of this contract. When they sued for the money owing to them under contracts with the defendants, the surety pleaded that the plaintiffs were not parties to the contract of surety between the defendants and the surety. Despite the privity doctrine, R.E. Holland J. held that the surety contract had created a trust, under which the plaintiffs were entitled to sue. The distinction between this case and others referred to by the

---

133 (1963), 40 D.L.R. (2d) 231 (Sask. Q.B.).

134 *Ibid.,* at 238.

135 [1973] 3 O.R. 741 (Ont. H.C.); compare *Datile Financial Corp. v. Royal Trust Corp. of Can.* (1991), 5 O.R. (3d) 358 at 369 (Ont. Gen. Div.) *per* Hollingworth J.; reversed in part on other grounds (1992), 11 O.R. (3d) 224 (Ont. C.A.).

136 *Fournier Van & Storage Co. v. Fournier,* above, note 135, at 746.

137 (1980), 113 D.L.R. (3d) 686 (Ont. H.C.); affirmed (1981), 123 D.L.R. (3d) 763 (Ont. C.A.).

learned judge[138] was that in them no trust could be established, whereas in this instance the language of the bond clearly created a trust which permitted the application of this exception to, or modification of the principle in *Dunlop Pneumatic Tyre Co. v. Selfridge & Co.*[139]

(iii) *Statute*

In England this has taken the form of an attempt to utilize certain statutory provisions as the source of a more general exception. There is no doubt that, in appropriate circumstances, a statute may enable a third person to sue or be sued on a contract to which he is not a party. This will happen, in the words of Disbery J.,[140] "in those spheres where statutory provisions have been enacted to relieve against the application of the doctrine." Insurance, especially motor vehicle insurance provides one illustration of such statutory activity.[141] So, too, in relation to the rights of members of unincorporated associations to sue, and in respect of representative actions, where these are allowed in a particular jurisdiction.[142]

However, in England, Lord Denning, in a series of cases, culminating in *Beswick v. Beswick*,[143] when it was in the Court of Appeal, attempted to create a more sweeping doctrine based upon the provisions of section 56 of the 1925 English Law of Property Act.[144] The House of Lords rejected his suggestion,[145] although it was not necessary for their decision to come to any conclusion on this matter. In effect, the House of Lords reaffirmed the basic common-law doctrine and despite the efforts of Lord Denning refused to recognize or accept any new qualification founded upon the interpretation or construction of a statutory provision.

By and large this dispute is not relevant in Canada. With one exception, there are no provincial statues which are in the same form as the language of the English section referred to above. Hence, in general, there is no possibility of arguing that, as distinct from specific statutory exceptions to the doctrine, there is any broad qualification achieved by statute. The exception is Prince Edward Island. There a statutory provision emulates the language of the English Real Property Act of 1845,[146] which is re-enacted in the 1925 Act. In *Keoughan v. Holland*[147] an attempt was made to utilize this provision in much the same way that, subsequently in

---

138 *Can. Oil Companies Ltd. v. Scottish Can. Assur. Corp.* (1960) (unreported); *Re Bodner Rd. Const. Co.; R. v. Can. Indemnity Co.* (1963) 41 D.L.R. (2d) 617 (Man. Q.B.); *Tobin Tractor (1957) Ltd. v. Western Survey Ltd.*, above, note 133.

139 [1915] A.C. 847 (H.L.), above, p. 186.

140 In *Great Nor. Ry. Co. v. Cole Agencies Ltd.* (1964), 49 W.W.R. 153 at 159 (Sask. Q.B.).

141 See, *e.g.*, Insurance Act, R.S.O. 1990, c. I.8, ss. 190, 193.

142 Compare also the situation in Canada with respect to collective agreements: *Bryson v. Glenlawn School District*, [1941] 3 W.W.R. 156 (Man. C.A.).

143 [1966] Ch. 538 (C.A.); see also *Smith & Snipes Hall Farm Ltd. v. River Douglas Catchment Bd.*, [1949] 2 K.B. 500 (C.A.); *Drive Yourself Hire Co. (London) Ltd. v. Strutt*, [1954] 1 Q.B. 250 (C.A.); *Stromdale & Ball Ltd. v. Burden*, [1952] Ch. 223.

144 15 & 16 Geo. 5, c. 20.

145 [1968] A.C. 58 (H.L.) for the facts and decisions in that case, see above, p. 181.

146 8 & 9 Vict., c. 106.

147 [1948] 1 D.L.R. 605 (P.E.I.S.C.).

England, Lord Denning tried. In that case there was a conveyance under which the grantor agreed with the grantee that he would provide maintenance to X, someone who was not a party to the deed. It was held that X was not able to enforce this agreement. Not being a party to the contract, X was precluded by the common-law doctrine of privity. Nor could any trust be created out of the situation, in accordance with the doctrine previously examined. Under the provincial statute, in the language of the English Act, it was provided that,

> a person may take an immediate or other interest in land or other property, or the benefit of any condition, right of entry, covenant or agreement over a respecting land or other property, although he may not be named as a party to the conveyance or other instrument.

This was prayed in aid as a source of X's right to sue. But the Canadian court, rejecting the argument then, as English courts did later, held that a statute dealing with conveyancing could not, by a side-wind as it were, completely alter a fundamental doctrine of the common law, namely the doctrine of privity.

(iv) *Restrictions upon chattels*

Attempts have been made in some courts to permit an exception or qualification of the privity doctrine where what is involved is a contract that affects property, as opposed to a contract that involves the performance of some act such as the payment of money to a third party.[148]

Courts of equity developed the doctrine that a contract which involved a restriction upon the use of *land* was enforceable not only against the original contracting party but also, in some situations, against anyone who succeeded the original contracting party, contractually or otherwise, in title to the land that was affected by the contract. The decision in *Tulk v. Moxhay*[149] in 1848, marked the modern beginning of the doctrine of covenants running with the land under which a restriction upon the use of land could be enforced, in equity, against successors in title, even if there were no privity of contract between the beneficiary of the covenant and the party in possession of the land. The issue that has been raised is whether the same doctrine, now firmly enshrined as part of the law of real property, can be extended to other kinds of property. To do so would involve somewhat more extensive qualification of the common-law doctrine of privity of contract.

As long ago as 1858, in *De Mattos v. Gibson*[150] this was attempted. In that case a charter-party was entered into between two parties. During the life of the charter-party, the owner of the ship mortgaged it to a third party, who knew of the existence of the charter-party. The plaintiff, the charterer, alleged that the

---

148 Tettenborn, "Covenants, Privity of Contract and the Purchaser of Personal Property" (1982), 41 C.L.J. 58; Ogilvie, "Privity of Contract and the Third Party Purchaser" (1987-88), 13 Can. Bus. L.J. 402, and see the authorities cited *ibid.*, p. 405, note 19.

149 (1848), 2 Ph. 774.

150 (1958), 4 De G. & J. 276, critically examined and analyzed by Ogilvie, *loc. cit.* above, note 148, at pp. 412-417.

mortgagee was threatening to sell the ship in disregard of the charterer's contractual rights. He attempted to obtain an injunction to restrain this activity. Eventually, after several stages of litigation, the plaintiff failed, on the ground that there was no evidence of interference with performance of the charter-party. But it seems that, had there been, such an injunction might well have been issued. The subsequent history of this part of the law seems to be founded upon a dictum of Knight-Bruce L.J. at one stage in the proceedings:[151]

> Reason and justice seem to prescribe that, at least as a general rule, where a man, by gift or purchase, acquires property from another, with knowledge of a previous contract, lawfully and for valuable consideration made by him with a third person, to use and employ the property for a particular purpose in a specified manner, the acquirer shall not, to the material damage of the third person, in opposition to the contract and inconsistently with it, use and employ the property in a manner not allowable to the giver or seller.

After some dispute and uncertainty, this appears to have been given support by a decision of the Privy Council upholding the courts of Nova Scotia in *Lord Strathcona Steamship Co. v. Dominion Coal Co.*,[152] which does seem to enunciate something approaching a *Tulk v. Moxhay* doctrine for chattels, or at least chattels of peculiar and particular value,[153] or possibly, as was later said to be the case by Lord Wright "to the very special case of a ship under a charter-party."[154] In the *Lord Strathcona* case, A chartered a ship to B. Under the charter-party A, the owner, was prevented from using the ship in a manner inconsistent with the charter-party. A sold the ship to C, who bought it with notice of the charter-party and its terms. It was held that B could be granted an injunction against C, to prevent C from using the ship in any inconsistent manner.

Unfortunately, while one may have great sympathy with this approach, it does not seem to have any proper or logical basis. A charter-party creates no proprietary interest in the ship being chartered: the charterer's rights are contractual. Hence, the *Tulk v. Moxhay* doctrine hardly seems appropriate in the context of a contract concerning the use or the restrictive use of a *chattel*. The law has not assimilated real property and chattels for many purposes. To permit the kind of control allowed in the *Lord Strathcona* case, indeed, seems to conflict with both the decision and the *ratio decidendi* in *Dunlop v. Selfridge*.[155] Such was, in effect the later decision

---

151 *Ibid.*, at 282. See the decision in *Messageries Imperiales Co. v. Baines* (1863), 7 L.T. 763.

152 [1926] A.C. 108 (P.C.), critically examined and analyzed by Ogilvie, *loc. cit.* above, note 148, at pp. 418-421. Contrast the view that *De Mattos v. Gibson* was wrong, expressed in *Lord Strathcona S.S. v. Dom Coal Co.*, at 143.

153 *Per* Lord Chelmsford in *De Mattos v. Gibson*, above, note 150 at 299; *e.g.*, copyrights: *MacDonald v. Eyles*, [1921] 1 Ch. 631; shares: *Ont. Jockey Club v. McBride*, [1927] S.C.R. 86 (S.C.C.); affirmed on other grounds, [1927] A.C. 916 (P.C.); goodwill of a business: *Can. Brotherhood of Railway Transport & Gen. Workers v. B.C. Air Lines Ltd.*, [1971] 1 W.W.R. 39 (B.C. Chambers); reversed [1971] 2 W.W.R. 466 (B.C.C.A.).

154 *Clore v. Theatrical Properties Ltd.*, [1936] 3 All E.R. 483 at 491 (C.A.). To the contrary, Tettenborn, *loc. cit.* above, note 148 at p. 74.

155 Above, p. 186.

of Diplock J., in *Port Line Ltd. v. Ben Line Steamers Ltd.*[156] Various reasons were given in that case for denying the proposition that a qualification of the use of a ship between A and B could affect C. One, perhaps an important one in the context, was that such proposition could not allow a claim in damages, or for compensation, to be predicated upon such an arrangement; the most that the earlier decision allowed was that C could be restrained with respect to the use to which he put the chattel. But the learned judge also disallowed the claim for money paid by the Government when the ship chartered to the plaintiffs was requisitioned (after X had sold the ship to the defendants, who had chartered it back to X) on the ground of lack of proprietary interest and lack of knowledge on the part of the defendants of the plaintiffs' rights, despite awareness of the charter between X and the plaintiffs. In the view of Diplock J. the principle in *De Mattos v. Gibson* was severely limited in scope, if, indeed, it could be said to have any valid existence.[157] Insofar as the *Lord Strathcona* case purported to be based on *De Mattos v. Gibson*, it was wrongly decided.

However, a different view was taken by Brown-Wilkinson J. in *Swiss Bank Corporation v. Lloyd Bank Ltd.*[158] This case involved a very complicated fact situation concerning the acquisition of securities in an Israeli company by means of money borrowed from a Swiss Bank with Bank of England approval and permission., Ultimately the borrower sold the securities and the issue involved the freedom of the defendant bank, which had granted credit to another company, of which the borrowing bank was a subsidiary, to dispose of the proceeds of the sale of the securities notwithstanding the Swiss bank's rights over the money in question. The trial judge held, *inter alia*, that the plaintiffs could succeed in obtaining an injunction to restrain the disposition of the money by the defendant bank, because the defendant bank's charge on the money was invalid. However, if the charge had been valid, no injunction would have been granted, since the defendant bank did not have actual notice of the Swiss bank's right in relation to the securities being sold, at the date when the defendant bank took out its charge on the securities. Therefore, under the principle in *De Mattos v. Gibson*, the defendant bank would not have been bound or affected by the previously existing rights of the plaintiffs over the securities. In the course of the judgment, the learned judge considered the *De Mattos* principle at some length and concluded as follows:[159] the *De Mattos* principle was good law (Diplock J. notwithstanding); it represented the equitable counterpart of the tort of knowing interference with contractual rights; a person proposing to deal with property so as to cause a breach of contract will be restrained by injunction from doing so if he had knowledge of the contract when he acquired

---

156 [1958] 1 All E.R. 787, critically examined and analyzed by Ogilvie, *loc. cit.* above, note 148, at pp. 421-426.

157 Tettenborn, *loc. cit.* above, note 148, attempts to put the doctrine on a firm and well-organized basis.

158 [1979] 2 All E.R. 853, critically examined and analyzed by Ogilvie, *loc. cit.* above, note 148, at pp. 406-412.

159 [1979] 2 All E.R. 853 at 876. See also Hoffman J. in *Law Debenture Trust Corp. plc v. Ural Caspian Oil Corp. Ltd.*, [1993] 2 All E.R. 355 at 361-362 (Ch. Div.).

the property; a plaintiff does not have to have a proprietary interest in the property to obtain such an injunction; it is enough that he has an interest in the performance of the contract; constructive notice of the contract affecting the property is insufficient; there must be actual notice. When the case reached the Court of Appeal, it was held that there was no substance in the *De Mattos v. Gibson* point, so it was disregarded.[160] Nor did the House of Lords have to consider this aspect of the case.[161] The present situation, therefore, is that there are two conflicting judgments at first instance, leaving the present day status of the *De Mattos* principle, as approved and applied in the *Lord Strathcona* case, open to doubt. From the point of view of privity of contract, leaving aside questions of property, equitable relief, or actions for interference with contractual rights (which raise different issues), it would seem to be contrary to settled common-law principles to accept the qualification that appears to have been introduced by Knight-Bruce L.J.[162]

It is interesting to note, therefore, that in some early twentieth century cases in England, the attempt was made, unsuccessfully in the event, to stretch the *Tulk v. Moxhay* principle of restrictive convenants, even before the *Lord Strathcona* decision, and make it apply to allow some kind of price regulation on the sale of goods.[163] Thus where A and B agreed on the sale of goods by A to B, one term being that B could only resell those goods at not less than an agreed price, this agreement could not bind a subsequent purchaser from B. Such a person was free to resell those goods at whatever price he desired. There could be no control over chattels except by contract and such contract could only bind the immediate parties (or their principals if they were agents). A Canadian case which makes the same point, though not with respect to price, is *General Securities Ltd. v. Brett's Ltd.*[164] The seller of a car stipulated in the contract, which was a conditional sale, that the buyer would not permit any liens to be created over and in respect of the car. The buyer had the vehicle repaired and when the repairer sought to claim his common-law lien over the car in respect of the cost of the repairs, it was argued that this could not happen by virtue of the agreement between seller and buyer. It was held that such agreement could not affect a third party who was not privy to the agreement. Consequently the repairer could exercise his lien. In coming to this conclusion the court expressly followed the earlier English authority on

---

160 [1980] 2 All E.R. 419 (C.A.). But Ogilvie argues, *loc. cit.* above, note 148, at p. 412 that the Court of Appeal *appears* to have agreed with the trial judge that the *De Mattos* principle was good law.

161 [1981] 2 All E.R. 449 (H.L.).

162 In *Law Debenture Trust Corp. plc v. Ural Caspian Oil Corp. Ltd.*, above, note 159, Hoffmann J. held that under this principle a court could not impose upon the third party a positive duty to perform covenants entered into by his predecessor; it could only grant a negative injunction to restrain such third party from doing acts inconsistent with the performance of the contract by his predecessor.

163 *Taddy & Co. v. Sterious & Co.*, [1904] 1 Ch. 354; *McGruther v. Pitcher*, [1904] 2 Ch. 306 (C.A.). See Tettenborn, *loc. cit.* above, note 148, at pp. 66-68, pointing out that statute has overtaken the common law in this regard. See also Ogilvie, *loc. cit.* above, note 148, at pp. 427-428. She also considers cases involving copyright, options to purchase chattels, and restrictions on share transfers: *ibid.*, pp. 428-433.

164 (1956), 19 W.W.R. 385 (B.C.S.C.).

price control. But it might be argued that the court was also impliedly stating that the *Lord Strathcona* doctrine was of limited value, if operative at all. Admittedly, there appears to have been no actual notice of the term as to liens in this case on the part of the repairer.[165] Hence, it might be said that, even on the *Lord Strathcona* principle the repairer should have succeeded. The better view is that, regardless of the issue of notice, the law is reluctant to extend the *Tulk v. Moxhay* principle, in any degree, to chattels. Despite the arguments of Browne-Wilkinson J., it is doubtful whether that principle can apply to ships which have been chartered, let alone other chattels. The doctrine of privity of contract seems to be more powerful, by and large, than any other.[166]

---

165 In this regard note the argument by Browne-Wilkinson J., above note 159, that constructive notice would be insufficient, and compare *Joseph v. Lyons* (1884), 15 Q.B.D. 280 (C.A.); *Manchester Trust v. Furness*, [1895] 2 Q.B. 539 (C.A.).

166 But it is ripe for reform, even overripe: compare Lord Scarman in *Woodar Invt. Dev. Ltd. v. Wimpey Const. (U.K.) Ltd.*, [1980] 1 All E.R. 571 at 591 (H.L.); Ontario Law Reform Commission, *Report on Amendment of the Law of Contract* (1987).

6

Writing

1. The Statute of Frauds

(a) Its origins and authority

Deeds, that is, documents that were signed and sealed by one or both parties, were the only kind of contract originally recognized and enforced by the common law. The common law accepted that there could be other forms of contractual obligation, created either in writing or orally, only at the beginning of the seventeenth century.[1] At that time there was no requirement that a contract should be in writing,

---

1 *Slades's Case* (1602), 4 Co. Rep. 91a. The history of the development of contract is summarized in Cheshire, Fifoot & Furmstom's *Law of Contract*, 12th ed. (1991), pp. 1-9. See also Simpson, *A History of the Common Law of Contract: The Rise of Assumpsit*; Stoljar, *A History of Contract at Common Law*; Milsom, *Historical Foundations of the Common Law*, Chapters 10-12; Baker, *An Introduction to English Legal History*, Chapters 9, 10, & 16.

nor even that it be evidenced by writing. The introduction of any such formality came about by statute. Significant, and still vitally important among such enactments, is the Statute of Frauds[2] passed in the reign of Charles II, some sections of which yet govern most of the common-law provinces of Canada, in their original form[3] or through the medium of local statutes.[4]

Suggestions have been made that the Statute of Frauds was passed to create new law in order specifically to control juries and to deal with the problems of perjury and instability which succeeded the troubled time of the Civil War in England and the return to the Stuarts in 1660.[5] It has also been surmised that the relevant sections to be examined in this chapter merely codified the law or practice which existed prior to the Statute.[6] Despite much critical commentary and many suggestions for reform,[7] an important area of the law of contract in much of Canada is still regulated in many provinces by the original archaic language of a seventeenth century statute that has given rise to much convoluted judicial interpretation.

Two sections of the Act are relevant to the general law of contract. One will be dealt with at a later stage, namely, section 17,[8] since it has been re-enacted in the Sale of Goods Acts of the various common-law provinces.[9] The other, section 4, refers to a variety of contracts. One category, namely, contracts relating to land, has been dealt with in England now by section 2 of the Law of Property (Miscellaneous Provisions) Act, 1989.[10] In Canada, comparable legislation may be found in specific property legislation in different provinces. For present purposes, however, the appropriate provision will be discussed in the context of, and by reference to, the Statute of Frauds. In a given jurisdiction, however, it may be

---

2 1677, (29 Cha. 2) c. 3.

3 *E.g.*, in Alberta.

4 In Ontario, R.S.O. 1990, c. S.19; Prince Edward Island, R.S.P.E.I. 1988, c. S-6 (which has removed many of the original requirements of the old English statute); New Brunswick, R.S.N.B. 1973, c. S-14; Nova Scotia, R.S.N.S. 1989, c. 442. British Columbia and Manitoba have both repealed the Statute: S.B.C. 1985, c. 10, s. 8 and S.M. 1982-83-84, c. 34, s. 1 respectively. In British Columbia, the Law and Equity Act, R.S.B.C. 1979, c. 224, ss. 57, 58, enacted by S.B.C. 1987, c. 42, s. 51, provides for contracts concerning land or dispositions of land to be proved by some form of writing or else by acts of acquiescence by the defendant, or reliance by one party on the other.

5 Holdsworth, *History of English Law*, Vol. vi, at p. 388. See also Willis, "The Statute of Frauds — A Legal Anachronism" (1928), 3 Indiana L.J. 427; Stevens, "Ethics and the Statute of Frauds" (1952), 37 Cornell L.Q. 355. For an analysis of the functions performed in modern times by writing in relation to contracts, see Fuller, "Consideration and Form" (1941), 41 Col. L.R. 799, discussed and criticized in Fridman, "The Necessity for Writing in Contracts Within the Statute of Frauds" (1985), 35 U.T.L.J. 43 at pp. 48-53.

6 Rabel, "The Statute of Frauds and Comparative Legal History" (1947), 63 L.Q.R. 174 at 177. And was founded upon earlier legislation on the continent of Europe, which still exists; see French *Code Civile*, Art. 1341; B.G.B. (Germany), para. 313.

7 Below, pp. 236-238.

8 Though this should be s. 16 of the Statute of Frauds, since later editions of the Statutes of the Realm of England combined ss. 13 and 14 of the original Statute.

9 Below, p. 239.

10 1989, c. 34.

necessary to refer to some other statutory enactment which contains the original wording, or has the same effect as the seventeenth century statute.

(b) The provisions of the Statute

The relevant section, that is, section 4,[11] is worded as follows:

No action shall be brought whereby to charge any executor or administrator upon any special promise to answer damages out of his own estate; or whereby to charge the defendant upon any special promise to answer for the debt, default or miscarriage of another person; or to charge any person upon any agreement made upon consideration of marriage;[12] or upon any contract or sale of lands, tenements or hereditaments, or any interest in or concerning them;[13] or upon any agreement that is not to be performed within the space of one year from the making thereof; unless the agreement upon which such action shall be brought, or some memorandum or note thereof, shall be in writing and signed by the party to be charged therewith or some other person thereunto by him lawfully authorized.

(c) Contracts within the Statute[14]

(i) *Contracts of guarantee*

The Statute refers to an action "whereby to charge the defendant upon any special promise to answer for the debt, default or miscarriage of another person." There must be an original obligation in existence, which remains in existence throughout.[15] As was stated in an old case, *Forth v. Stanton,* "The Statute applies

---

11 Note, however, in Ontario, s. 5 (added by S.O. 1929, c. 23, s. 6) which states:

A promise, contract or agreement to pay a sum of money by way of liquidated damages or to do or suffer any other act, matter or thing based upon, arising out of, or relating to a promise, contract or agreement dealt with in section 4 is not of any greater validity than the last-mentioned promise, contract or agreement.

For the meaning and relevance of this curious provision see Ontario Law Reform Commission, *Report on Amendment of the Law of Contract,* (1987), at p. 83.

Two other sections may be mentioned: (i) section 7, on ratification of contracts by minors: above p. 149; (ii) section 8 dealing with representations as to the character, conduct, credit, ability, trade or dealings of another to enable that other to obtain credit: O.L.R.C., *Report,* pp. 84-85. This deals only with fraud, not negligence: *ibid.* Repeal of this is recommended.

12 The words "any agreement made upon consideration of marriage" do not apply in Ontario, having been deleted from the Ontario Statute by S.O. 1978, c. 2, s. 88; see further below, p. 217.

13 The word "or" has been read traditionally as "for": O.L.R.C., *Report,* above, note 11, at pp. 79-80.

14 In *Rimer v. Rimer* (1981), 119 D.L.R. (3d) 579 (Alta. Q.B.) it was held that an oral settlement of a wife's claim against her husband, in a divorce action, merged in the judgment; it was no longer a contract within the scope of the Statute. Nor does the Statute apply to a promissory note given in relation to an agreement for the sale of land: *Wong v. Sawyer* (1990), 110 A.R. 378 (Alta. Master), although a promissory note is a contract, above, p. 192, note 94.

15 But the provisions of the Statute of Frauds relating to guarantees do not apply to guarantees which comply with the Ontario Personal Property Security Act, R.S.O. 1990, c. P.10; *Re M.C. United Masonry Ltd.; Peat Marwick Ltd. v. Goldfarb* (1983), 142 D.L.R. (3d) 470 (Ont. C.A.).

only to promises made to the person to whom another is answerable."[16] In other words, the Statute refers only to contracts of guarantee and not to contracts of indemnity — a distinction and terminology suggested in the English case of *Mountstephen v. Lakeman*[17] and followed in Canadian cases.[18] The person to whom the promise within the Statute is made must already be, or be about to become, a creditor, not the original debtor or anyone else.[19] It is a *collateral* liability, that is, one conditional on the non-performance of some other person, that is created by the promise within the Statute, not an *original* liability. In *Beattie v. Dinnick*[20] the plaintiff was the holder of a promissory note given by an insurance company. The defendant was the president of the company. The plaintiff was pressing for payment. The defendant orally promised to see him paid if he were not otherwise successful in obtaining his money. The court held that this was a guarantee, not an indemnity. Hence it was within the Statute and unenforceable, being oral. In contrast, in *Active Customs Brokers Ltd. v. Sack*,[21] the president of a company gave an oral guarantee of the company's debt. This was held not within the Statute. The defendant had a substantial benefit or self-interest in the matter to indicate that he was really undertaking his own debt, not the debt of another. The distinction between these cases seems difficult to explain. In both instances the defendant was seeking to protect the situation of "his" company. The later Ontario decision is supported by the case of *Sarbit v. Hanson & Booth Fisheries (Canada) Co.*,[22] where the defendant promised to pay a supplier for goods supplied to fishermen if they did not pay. He had an interest in their business. At first instance this was held to be a contract of guarantee not indemnity. The Manitoba Court of Appeal took a different view. The Statute does not apply to a contract creating a liability in a promisor which is not dependent on the liability of some other person.[23] In such instances, the obligation is "direct" (a phrase preferred by the court in *Sarbit v. Hanson & Booth Fisheries (Canada) Co.*,[24] to the term "indemnity"). It is not the requisite collateral obligation or liability that has been expounded as being the essence of guarantee in many leading English cases, relied upon and followed in Canada.

Nothing turns upon the use, or otherwise, by the parties of the term "guarantee".

---

16 (1669), 1 Wms. Saund. 210, 85 E.R. 217 at 224.

17 (1871), L.R. 7 Q.B. 196; affirmed (1874), L.R. 7 H.L. 17 (H.L.). See the annotation, "Guarantees and The Statute of Frauds" by Falconbridge in (1920), 55 D.L.R. 1.

18 See, *e.g. Ideal Plumbing & Heating Ltd. v. Pearce* (1957), 24 W.W.R. 320 (Sask. C.A.). In *Kamitomo v. Pasula* (1983), 50 A.R. 280 (Alta. Q.B.) an indemnity agreement was held not to fall within the Statute.

19 Compare *Beattie v. Dinnick* (1896), 27 O.R. 285 at 292 (Ont. C.A.) *per* Street J.; *Wagner v. Heidt*, [1931] 2 D.L.R. 680 at 684 (Sask. C.A.) *per* Martin J.A. See also *Gillies v. Brown* (1916), 53 S.C.R. 557 especially at 560 (S.C.C.) *per* Davies J.

20 (1896), 27 O.R. 285 (Ont. C.A.).

21 (1987), 25 O.A.C. 305 (Ont. Div. Ct.).

22 [1950] 2 W.W.R. 545 (Man. K.B.); reversed on other grounds (1951), 1 W.W.R. (N.S.) 115 (Man. C.A.).

23 *Ideal Plumbing & Heating Ltd. v. Pearce*, above, note 18, following the old English case of *Birkmyr v. Darnell* (1704), 1 Salk. 27, 91 E.R. 27.

24 Above, note 22, at 117 *per* Coyne J.A.

Even if the word is not used, the promise may be a guarantee.[25] So too, if the contract is called an "indemnity agreement". It may still be a guarantee.[26] In *Sarbit v. Hanson & Booth Fisheries (Canada) Co.*,[27] Coyne J.A., following language used by the English Court of Appeal in *Harburg India Rubber Comb Co. v. Martin*,[28] stated that the application of the Statute involved the

> . . . determination of what language was used by the parties and its interpretation. If there is any doubt of the proper interpretation of that language, the acts of the parties and the surrounding circumstances may be looked at in aid. It is the substance and intent of the admission, not its particular form, that is material.

Thus, for example, in one case,[29] where one party, for independent consideration, undertook to pay an existing debt owed by X to the plaintiff, it was held that this was not a guarantee, nor, indeed, was it an indemnity. It was a *novation* of the original debt, that is, the extinction of the first obligation and the creation of a new one, between different parties. Hence the Statute of Frauds did not apply.

Moreover, if the guarantee is merely an ancillary term in some contract, the main purpose of which is outside the Statute, the courts will apply the Statute to the term as to the guarantee. If the object of the contract is, for example, the purchase of property, the introduction of business into a stockbroker's office, etc., as Vaughan Williams L.J. said in the *Harburg* case, "the mere fact that as an incident to it . . . the debt of another to a third person will be paid does not bring the case within the section."[30] This has meant that in certain situations a contract which might otherwise be one of guarantee is interpreted and regarded differently. One such situation is that of "*del credere*" agency,[31] where the agent undertakes to secure the performance of the contract himself if the principal does not.[32] Another is where the "guarantor" has certain proprietary rights which he is trying to protect by the "guarantee".[33] A recent Canadian illustration of this is provided by *Travel Machine Ltd. v. Madore*.[34] This involved an oral guarantee given by an employee of the plaintiff travel agency in respect of a customer's debt. Sutherland J. held, following the leading English cases,[35] that the guarantee was given as incident

---

25 *Fleetwood Corp. v. Imp. Invt. Corp.* (1965), 51 D.L.R. (2d) 654 (B.C.C.A.).

26 *Bank of B.C. v. Hayes* (1980), 116 D.L.R. (3d) 726 (Alta. Q.B.) dealing with the Alberta Guarantees Acknowledgement Act, but applying the concepts of the Statute of Frauds.

27 Above, note 22, at 125; compare *Guild & Co. v. Conrad*, [1894] 2 Q.B. 885 (C.A.).

28 [1902] 1 K.B. 778 (C.A.).

29 *Wagner v. Heidt*, above, note 19; compare *Guthrie v. Mod-Vic Co.* (1972), 6 N.B.R. (2d) 434 (N.B.S.C.).

30 Above, note 28, at 786.

31 A *del credere* agent is one who for an extra commission undertakes responsibility for the due performance of the contract by persons whom he introduces to his principal: see Fridman, *Law of Agency*, 6th ed. (1990), pp. 38-40.

32 *Sutton & Co. v. Grey*, [1894] 1 Q.B. 285 (C.A.).

33 *Fitzgerald v. Dressler* (1859), 141 E.R. 861 — indemnity, not guarantee. But contrast the *Harburg* case, above, note 28.

34 (1983), 143 D.L.R. (3d) 94 (Ont. H.C.). Note the reasons given why the doctrine of part performance (below, pp. 227-236) does not apply to oral contracts of guarantee within the Statute of Frauds: *ibid.*, at 100.

35 *Sutton & Co. v. Grey*, above, note 32; the *Harburg* case, above, note 28.

to a wider and ongoing relationship, very similar to that involved in a *del credere* agency. The object of the giving of the guarantee, as a result of which the travel agency exended credit to the customer contrary to its normal practice, was to effect the sale of travel services and the oral guarantee arose in a pre-existing commercial relationship. The employee had an interest in the subject-matter, since it was related to her regular work and the regular business of her employer, from whom she earned her remuneration.

Since the Statute refers to "miscarriage" of another as well as "debt or default", it has been held[36] that a promise to satisfy the liability of another person for a tort committed by him to the promisee is within the Statute. Thus, while it may be conjectured that the Statute originally intended to deal with contractual obligations that were supported by a second undertaking made to the creditor, interpretation has broadened the scope of the Statute's operation.

(ii) *Contracts for sale of land or any interest in land*[37]

It is necessary to differentiate land from *goods*.[38] Even though some sales of goods may require writing to be enforceable,[39] there are sufficient distinctions between the statutory requirements to merit drawing a line between one category of property and the other. What is involved here is the old common-law distinction between *fructus industriales*, that is, "cultivated produce", and *fructus naturales*, that is, "spontaneous produce of the soil". This was, and remains an artificial, and probably unjustifiable differentiation, which caused untold problems in the courts. The provisions of the Sale of Goods Act under which *goods* are defined for the purposes of that Act clarify the previous confusion and lay down a settled and more workable rule which sweeps within the definition of "goods" not only "industrial crops", but also severable natural produce.

There are other problems. What is encompassed in the notion of land, or any interest in or concerning land? An agreement to give possession of new premises is within the Statute.[40] But not an agreement to support X for life in consideration of a conveyance of land to the promisor.[41] Such a contract was not one dealing

---

36 *Kirkham v. Marter* (1819), 2 B. & Ald. 613, 106 E.R. 490.

37 This does not include a lease of land for not more than three years at a rent of two-thirds the value of the property. But see *Hoj Industries Ltd. v. Dundas Shepard Square Ltd.* (1978), 23 O.R. (2d) 295 (Ont. Co. Ct.), where such a lease was held to fall within the Statute, *i.e.*, it concerned the disposition of an interest in land.

On this part of the Statute, see Bridge, "The Statute of Frauds and Sale of Land Contracts" (1986), 64 Can. Bar Rev. 58. Note that in England the law has been altered by the Law of Property (Miscellaneous Provisions) Act, 1989, c. 34, s. 2.

38 See Fridman, *Sale of Goods in Canada*, 3rd ed. (1986), pp. 17-19; see also Ontario Law Reform Commission, *Report on Sale of Goods* (1979), Vol. I, pp. 57-65; *Report on Amendment of the Law of Contract* (1987), pp. 80-82.

39 Below, pp. 239-244.

40 *Jones v. Caple* (1959), 29 W.W.R. 310 (B.C.S.C.).

41 *Spencer v. Spencer* (1913), 4 W.W.R. 7875 (Man. K.B.). Nor a contract to form a partnership or to receive shares in a company, each of which involves land: *Gray v. Smith* (1889), 43 Ch. D. 208 (C.A.); *Archibald v. McNerhanie* (1899), 29 S.C.R. 564 (S.C.C.).

with land or any interest in or concerning land. It was a collateral agreement,[42] (though reading the judgment in that case the impression is gained that the real purpose of the classification of the contract was to prevent the Statute being used to cover or cause a fraud). An agreement to sell a half-interest in land purchased from a vendor to another purchaser was within the Statute, but not a transaction where the seller in the second contract originally bought on behalf of himself and the buyer in the second contract, for then a trust would have existed prior to that contract and the agreement between the two purchasers, namely, the trustee and his beneficiary, would not be one concerning land but the subject-matter of the trust.[43] In much the same way, while the contract for the sale of land must be made in accordance with the Statute a contract of agency, under which the vendor appointed an agent to sell the land, does not itself require to conform to the Statute.[44]

An agreement involving the right to the proceeds of a sale of land may or may not be within the ambit of the Statute.[45] But an agreement to settle an action for a declaration that certain land was held on a resulting trust was not within the provisions of the Statute relating to contracts (although it was within those dealing with trusts).[46] The Statute did not apply to a repurchasing option in favour of the original grantor of the land, since this was contained in a registered deed of conveyance.[47] Nor did the Statute apply to an agreement postponing an existing mortgage in favour of a new mortgagee;[48] or to an agreement to extend the time for completion of a purchase of land.[49] However, a contract to make a contract for the sale of land was itself a contract concerning land, and so within the Statute. This, said the English Court of Appeal,[50] was because the contract in question would be specifically enforceable as a contract relating to the sale of land, or because, if this "introductory" contract had been performed, it would have created a proper written contract which could have been specifically performed. Any other decision might have opened the way for fraudulent evasion of the Statute.

In *Van Berkel v. De Foort*[51] there was an oral contract to permit the defendant to cut and remove one year's crop of hay from the plaintiff's land. The question arose in the course of litigation whether this was enforceable as there was no memorandum as required by the Statute. It was held that this was not a sale of goods but a contract concerning an interest in land; therefore, the Statute applied.

---

42 See also *Brymer v. Thompson* (1915), 34 O.L.R. 194 (Ont. H.C.); affirmed (1915), 34 O.L.R. 543 (Ont. C.A.).

43 *Morris v. Whiting* (1913), 5 W.W.R. 936 (Man. K.B.).

44 *Standard Realty Co. v. Nicholson* (1911), 24 O.L.R. 46 (Ont. H.C.); *McIlvride v. Mills* (1906), 16 Man. R. 276 (Man. C.A.). Compare Fridman, above, note 31, at p. 48.

45 *Stuart v. Mott* (1894), 23 S.C.R. 384 (S.C.C.); *Harris v. Lindeborg*, [1931] S.C.R. 235 (S.C.C.); *Cooper v. Critchley*, [1955] 1 All E.R. 520 at 524 (C.A.) *per* Jenkins L.J.

46 *McKenzie v. McKenzie* (1976), 69 D.L.R. (3d) 765 (B.C.C.A.).

47 *Indust.-Devs. Mall Ltd. v. Barbieri* (1978), 88 D.L.R. (3d) 156 (Ont. H.C.).

48 *Fed. Savings Credit Union Ltd. v. Hessian* (1979), 8 R.P.R. 32 (N.S.T.D.). But it does to the *variation* of a mortgage: *T.D. Bank v. Lenec* (1984), 60 B.C.L.R. 36 (B.C.C.A.).

49 *Jenkins v. Strickland* (1990), 83 Nfld. & P.E.I.R. 30 (Nfld. T.D.).

50 *Daulia v. Four Millbank Nominees*, [1978] 2 All E.R. 557 (C.A.).

51 [1933] 1 W.W.R. 125 (Man. C.A.) following two cases in Manitoba: *Sharpe v. Dundas* (1911), 18 W.L.R. 86 (Man. C.A.); *Decock v. Barrager* (1909), 10 W.L.R. 709 (Man. C.A.).

But in *Smith v. Curry*,[52] following the English decision of *McManus v. Cooke*,[53] it was suggested, though without any firm decision, that the Statute did not apply to a contract dealing with an easement. There was a decision of the Supreme Court of Canada[54] which said that the Statute does not apply to a contract referring to a right of way. However, it seems strange to think that contracts which dispose of the power to use land in a certain way, namely, to use it in pursuance or enjoyment of what is clearly at common law an interest in land, which is what an easement is, do not fall within the language of the Statute. A distinction can be seen between such instances, on the one hand, and those exemplified both by the pre-Sale of Goods Act cases on *fructus industriales* and *fructus naturales* and the provisions of that Act, and by the decision in *Emerald Resources Ltd. v. Sterling Oil Properties Management Ltd.*[55] The statutory provisions and the pre-statute cases, as well as the *Emerald* case, concern "things", that is, tangible matter which is in, on, or attached to the land, as opposed to the intangible concept of "user", or enjoyment of the benefit of land. In the *Emerald* case, for example, it was not incomprehensible that the court should hold that a claim to royalty on petroleum, natural gas and related hydrocarbons which emanated from certain land was not a claim to an interest in land, thereby escaping the clutches of the Statute of Frauds. But that an easement, such as a right of way, should not escape these clutches is mystifying, especially as in the *Van Berkel* case what was a profit *à prendre* appears to have attracted the Statute. Clearly here is another example of the confusion and possibilities for illogicality and injustice that can result from the language and interpretation of the Statute, much as the alleged difference between a guarantee and an indemnity or novation is easier to state in simple terms than to identify in actual fact and apply in individual instances.

(iii) *Contracts not to be performed within a year*

This is a strange category. It might be thought that contracts which bound one person to guarantee another's debt and contracts relating to land were clear instances of the need to establish liability by some form of writing. To extend the Statute to all contracts, whatever their subject-matter, if they involve a longer period than a year for their completion, seems an unnecessary extravagance. Perhaps the situation at common law, long since changed, by which the parties to a contract (although potentially the best witnesses) were excluded from giving testimony, may explain this inclusion within the Statute of Frauds.[56] Furthermore, the chances of false or perjured evidence, or merely mistaken evidence, when the contract had

---

52 [1918] 2 W.W.R. 848 (Man. C.A.).

53 (1887), 35 Ch. D. 681.

54 *Acton Tanning Co. v. Toronto Suburban Ry.* (1918), 56 S.C.R. 196 (S.C.C.).

55 (1969), 3 D.L.R. (3d) 630 (Alta. C.A.); affirmed (1970), 15 D.L.R. (3d) 256 (S.C.C.).

56 The original justification was "not to trust the memory of witnesses for a longer time than one year": *Smith v. Westhall* (1697), 1 Ld. Raym. 316, 91 E.R. 1106. For criticism see the English Law Revision Committee's report, *The Statute of Frauds and the Doctrine of Consideration*, 1937 (Cmd. 5499) at pp. 9-11.

been made some years before the litigation to which it gave rise, were high (although if the contract were within the Statute it did not matter that the action arose the day after the contract was made, and, if such a thing were possible, the case was heard the very next day, that is, while recollection was still fresh and clear). It suffices to say that, perhaps because of the strangeness of the statutory provision, and the dislike of the courts of the technical defence of the statute succeeding where it lacked merit, the decisions reveal a peculiar interpretation of the phrase "not to be performed within a year."

To begin with there are clear instances where a contract is for more, or, as the case may be, less than a year. Thus the contract, from its terms may be incapable of being performed by either party within the year from its making. This is exemplified by the old English case of *Boydell v. Drummond*,[57] which concerned a subscription to a forthcoming edition of Shakespeare that would have taken longer than 12 months to appear. Or the contract cannot be performed by one of the parties within the year and it does not manifest any intention that the other party should fully perform his side of the bargain within the year. Thus a contract for a two-year period under which one party agrees to take orders for, and sell to customers the maximum volume possible of the other party's product was within the Statute.[58] So was a contract under which the plaintiff was to pursue training as a nurse in the defendant's hospital for two years.[59] So, too, was a contract of employment under which the employee's salary was to rise from $700 per annum to $1,000 per annum by annual increases.[60] Another example is provided by a contract for a perpetual term under which one party was to pay the other $10,000 per year for ten years.[61]

On the other hand the contract may be intended to be performed and may actually be performed by one party within the year. Thus in *Spencer v. Spencer*,[62] in which there was a promise to convey land in return for a promise to support for life, it was held that the contract was one to be performed within the year, as the conveyance would clearly occur within the requisite period; so, too, where the contract is one of service for one year commencing the day after that on which the contract is made.[63]

In contradistinction, however, are cases where it is not clear whether the contract is to be performed within or beyond the statutory period. If the contract is for an indefinite period which (according to circumstances that may or may not occur) may or may not be coterminous with the statutory year, then the contract

---

57 (1809), 11 East. 192, 103 E.R. 958.
58 *Sherman v. Monarch Chrome Furniture Co.* (1958), 15 D.L.R. (2d) 6 (Ont. C.A.). Compare *Reeve v. Jennings*, [1910] 2 K.B. 522 (covenant in restraint of trade for 36 months after employee left service of employer).
59 *McKay v. St. Joseph's Hosp. Bd.* (1921), 54 N.S.R. 140 (N.S.C.A.).
60 *Fairgrieve v. O'Mullin* (1896), 40 N.S.R. 215 (N.S.S.C.).
61 *Color Your World Inc. v. Robert F. Avery Holdings Ltd.* (1988), 88 A.R. 163 (Alta. Q.B.).
62 Above, note 41.
63 *Beller v. Klotz*, [1917] 1 W.W.R. 585 (Sask. C.A.).

is not within the Statute of Frauds.[64] On the other hand, if the contract is so worded as to show distinctly that the parties contemplated the duration of the contract for a definite period of more than one year, although it contains an express or implied term by which it *may* be terminated within the year, then the contract is within the Statute. As Lord Alverstone said in the leading case of *Hanau v. Ehrlich*, which has been approved and followed in Canada,

> . . . if there is no mention of time, and the time is uncertain, the agreement is not within the Statute . . . if the time mentioned is more than one year, but there is power to determine, the agreement is within the Statute.[65]

In the words of Kerwin J. of the Supreme Court of Canada,[66] the Statute does not apply if it is possible that the provisions can be performed or are not incapable of being performed within a year.

Thus, where there was a contract of employment to last for the life of the employee, though the employee could terminate it at any time if not satisfied with the salary or bonuses, it was held that the contract was not within the Statute because it might be wholly performed within a year, since the employee might terminate it, or might die[67] (a lugubrious thought which was instrumental in another case[68] involving a contract for the support of a child — who, it was said, might not live for more than one year). As Mackay J.A. said,[69]

> . . . [t]he statute has no reference to cases in which the whole contract may be performed within one year, but there is no definite provision as to its duration, even though it may appear as a fact that the performance has extended beyond that time; . . . where the contract is such that the whole may possibly be performed within a year and there is no express stipulation to the contrary, the statute does not apply. . . .

So, too, an agreement to pay a stated price for milk from a herd of Guernsey cows, in consideration of the owner of the herd taking stock in a dairy company, was not within the Statute, despite the vagueness of the period, since the owner might sell the herd within the year, have no milk to deliver, or could die before the year was out.[70] Where one contracting party obliged himself not to do a certain thing, no time limit being mentioned,[71] and where one party made a promise to

---

64 *Quance v. Brown*, [1926] 2 D.L.R. 824 (Ont. C.A.) which was concerned with when a dividend was payable. Since it *could* have been paid within one year, and not five, the Statute did not apply. Compare *Van Snellenberg v. Cemco Elec. Mfg. Co.*, [1945] 3 W.W.R. 369 at 385 (B.C. C.A.) *per* Robertson J.A., at 395-396 *per* Sidney Smith J.A.; affirmed [1947] S.C.R. 121 (S.C.C.). As to the effect of an implied annual hiring after the original period of one year see *Jaremy v. Vita Co-op. Ltd.*, [1942] 3 W.W.R. 513 (Man. K.B.); affirmed [1943] 1 W.W.R. 1 (Man. C.A.).

65 [1912] A.C. 39 at 42 (H.L.).

66 *Mott v. Trott*, [1943] S.C.R. 256 at 260 (S.C.C.); compare *Richmond Wineries Western Ltd. v. Simpson*, [1940] S.C.R. 1 (S.C.C.).

67 *Campbell v. Bus. Fleets Ltd.*, [1954] O.R. 87 (Ont. C.A.); *Van Snellenberg v. Cemco Elec. Mfg. Co.*, above, note 64.

68 *Kijko v. Bacyzki* (1921), 51 O.L.R. 225 (Ont. C.A.).

69 *Campbell v. Bus. Fleets Ltd.*, above, note 67, at 94.

70 *Shaver v. Hamilton Corp. Creameries Ltd.*, [1936] O.W.N. 645 (Ont. C.A.).

71 *MacIntosh v. Hotham*, [1933] 2 W.W.R. 383 (Sask. C.A.).

marry, without mentioning when the marriage was to take place,[72] the Canadian court accepted the principles laid down in *Hanau v. Ehrlich*,[73] which involved an employment contract for two years that could have been terminated at any time. Similarly, in *Boutilier v. Everett*,[74] a contract of loan was an agreement capable of being performed within a year from its making because the borrower was at liberty to pay off the loan at any time; therefore, he could have paid it within a year. The Statute did not apply.

It would seem, therefore, that, in the absence of some definite stipulation as to time, which undoubtedly decides the issue, and leaves no room for judicial manoeuvres, there is considerable scope for interpretation of contractual terms as to duration or the time of performance, in such a way as to provide maximum flexibility and allow the courts to prevent the abuse of the Statute.

(iv) *Other contracts*[75]

The remaining categories need no elaborate discussion. The very first clause of the section, which deals with promises by executors and administrators, relates to the personal liability of such representatives for the debts or liabilities of the testator or intestate only to the extent of the assets which have come into their hands. The Statute applies only to a special promise by such a representative, to be personally liable out of *his own* estate. There is little practical utility for such a provision in modern times.[76]

Contracts made "upon consideration of marriage" do not include contracts of marriage themselves.[77] The contracts with which the Statute is concerned are those which involve, for example, the settlement of property by one person upon another in consideration of marriage, which does not appear to be a very customary or frequent occurrence in Canada. Indeed in Ontario, this category has been deleted;[78] in its place certain contracts, namely, marriage contracts, separation agreements, and cohabitation agreements,[79] must be in writing and signed by the person to be bound, as well as being witnessed.[80] If not, they will be unenforceable.[81]

By way of contrast there are contracts to which the Statute does not, and

---

72 *Sheehan v. Mercantile Trust Co.* (1919), 45 O.L.R. 422 (Ont. H.C.); reversed on other grounds (1920), 46 O.L.R. 581 (Ont. C.A.).

73 Above, note 65.

74 (1979), 40 N.S.R. (2d) 527 (N.S.T.D.).

75 Note also the situation with regard to ratification of an infant's contract, which also requires to be in writing under Lord Tenterden's Act, 1829 (10 Geo. 4) which has been incorporated in some provincial Statutes of Frauds: above, p. 149; and representations of creditworthiness, above, p. 209, note 11.

76 It has been deleted in England (by the Law Reform (Enforcement of Contracts) Act, 1954 (2 & 3 Eliz. 2) c. 34; New Zealand (by the Contracts Enforcement Act, 1956); and Western Australia (by the Law Reform (Statute of Frauds) Act, 1962).

77 See the *Sheehan* case, above, note 72.

78 S.O. 1978, c. 2, s. 88.

79 Defined in the Family Law Act, R.S.O. 1990, c. F.3, s. 51.

80 *Ibid.*, s. 55(1).

81 *Ibid.* This applies also to agreements to amend or rescind a domestic contract.

can never apply. For example, if the contract is not one which is being enforced by an action, then, even if it falls within one of the stated categories, it is outside the confines of the statutory requirements.[82] Nor will the Statute apply to an agreement the purpose of which is to terminate an action between the parties, that is, a settlement of litigation.[83]

(d) Requirements of the Statute

(i) *General*

The Statute requires that the agreement, or some memorandum or note thereof, must be in writing, signed by the defendant or his lawfully appointed agent. Without this, "no action shall be brought to charge" the defendant. In effect, therefore, to enforce any contract within the categories previously discussed, the plaintiff must produce either a signed written contract or a "memorandum or note" which will satisfy the language of the Statute.[84]

(ii) *The contents of the note or memorandum*

The Statute of Frauds does not contemplate that the agreement itself must be completely in writing. If it is, then there are no problems; the Statute will be satisfied. But the decisions reveal that a good deal less than a written contract will suffice, provided that all the essential terms of the contract are contained in the appropriate note or memorandum.[85] For example, the essential terms of a contract of sale of land are the parties, the property to be sold, and the purchase price.[86] The arrangements for completion (as long as they do not significantly vary

---

82 *Johnston v. Block*, [1945] 3 W.W.R. 244 (Sask. K.B.).

83 *R.C. Archiepiscopal Corp. of Winnipeg v. Rosteski* (1958), 26 W.W.R. 82 (Man. C.A.); *Rimer v. Rimer* (1981), 119 D.L.R. (3d) 579 (Alta. Q.B.). Nor to a promissory note, above, p. 209, note 14.

84 *Freeland v. Freeland* (1982), 19 Alta. L.R. (2d) 180 (Alta. Q.B.). An oral contract that does not satisfy these requirements may be raised as a defence: *Barber v. Glen* (1987), 59 Sask. R. 49 (Sask. C.A.).

85 *Eaton v. Crook* (1910), 12 W.L.R. 658 (Alta. C.A.); *Rogers v. Hewer* (1912), 3 W.W.R. 477 (Alta. C.A.); *Smith v. Spencer* (1918), 42 D.L.R. 269 (Sask C.A.); *Saperstein v. Drury*, [1943] 3 W.W.R. 193 (B.C.C.A.); affirmed on other grounds [1944] S.C.R. 148 (S.C.C.). Compare *Chapman v. Kopitoski*, [1972] 6 W.W.R. 525 (Sask. Q.B.). Terms implied by law need not be in the memorandum: *Peterson v. Bitzer*, [1922] 1 W.W.R. 141 (S.C.C.). If a term is omitted by the plaintiff, the memorandum will not satisfy the Statute, but, if the plaintiff agrees to an oral term submitted by the defendant, then the contract may be enforced: *Huttges v. Verner* (1975), 12 N.B.R. (2d) 473 (N.B.C.A.).

   If a contract has not in fact been concluded, *e.g.*, because of lack of certainty of terms, or a mistake which negates consensus, the Statute becomes irrelevant: *Lensen v. Lensen*, [1987] 2 S.C.R. 672 (S.C.C.); *Costin v. Blois* (1988), 84 N.S.R. (2d) 126 (N.S.T.D.).

86 *MacLean v. Ritchie* (1977), 21 N.S.R. (2d) 446 (N.S.T.D.) where the written agreement also included the closing date, and certain of the conditions of the contract; compare *Babcock v. Carr* (1981), 127 D.L.R. (3d) 77 (Ont. H.C.) (where parol evidence was admitted to identify the property that was the subject-matter of the contract); and, in another connection, *Can. Square Corp. v. Versafood Sevices Ltd.* (1981), 130 D.L.R. (3d) 205 (Ont. C.A.).

what has been agreed) are not so essential that they must be contained in the note.[87] Even a receipt can suffice as a note or memorandum if it is evident that it is not merely a receipt for a part payment or deposit, but a document which sets out all the essential terms of the agreement in respect of which the payment so acknowledged was made.[88]

What, then, are essential terms? The identity of the parties, that is, their names or a sufficient description whereby they can be, or are, identified must be classified as essential. In *Litras v. Mattern*,[89] for example, the memorandum stated that the offeror was a client of the brokers who signed the offer. It was held that this was a sufficient description of the identity of the offeror to make the memorandum acceptable under the Statute. In this case it was held that parol evidence was admissible to establish the existence of a principal and his identity, once the agent had signed the memorandum. In *Dynamic Transportation Ltd. v. O.K. Detailing Ltd.*,[90] parol evidence was admitted to identify the lot intended to be the subject of the sale. There are limits to the extent to which such evidence will be permitted for the purpose of filling gaps left by the note or memorandum. As Orde J.A. said in *Imperial Bank of Commerce v. Nixon*,[91]

> . . . where you have a memorandum or note in writing which completely satisfies the requirements of the statute, you may by oral evidence identify the parties or the subject-matter. The evidence must be such as of necessity will fit the contract and exclude any alteration.

This has become an important point with respect to the consideration for the contract. It must be stated in the note or memorandum, and parol evidence will not be admitted to prove it.[92] But there are cases which suggest that the precise amount of consideration may not be necessary to state in the written document, such as the amount of an employee's salary, as long as it is stated that he is to be paid a salary.[93] Nor need the exact price for goods be stated if the price has been paid. Under an alteration to the Statute of Frauds introduced in England in

---

87 *McKenzie v. Walsh* (1921), 61 S.C.R. 312 (S.C.C); leave to appeal refused, March 16, 1921; compare *Rowe v. Fidelity-Phenix Fire Ins. Co. of N.Y.*, [1944] 3 D.L.R. 441 at 447 (Ont. H.C.); which was reversed without reasons [1944] 4 D.L.R. 265 (Ont. C.A.); *Gutheil v. Caledonia No. 99 (R.M.)* (1964), 50 W.W.R. 278 (Sask. Q.B.).

88 Contrast *Knight v. Cushing* (1912), 1 W.W.R. 563 (Alta. S.C.); reversed on grounds which made it unnecessary to consider the Statute of Frauds (1912), 2 W.W.R. 704 (S.C.C.), with *Kirkland v. Smith* (1911), 16 W.L.R. 530 (B.C.S.C.); *Babcock v. Carr*, above, note 86. See also *Costin v. Blois*, above, note 85, where the receipt referred only to "land" and did not identify what was being sold: hence the statutory requirements were not satisfied.

89 [1938] 1 W.W.R. 381 (B.C.S.C.). Compare *Bennett v. Stodgell* (1916), 36 O.L.R. 45 (Ont. C.A.). Contrast *Imp. Bank of Commerce v. Nixon*, [1926] 4 D.L.R. 1052 (Ont. C.A.) where the guarantee omitted the name of the principal debtor, it was insufficient under the Statute of Frauds.

90 (1978), 85 D.L.R. (3d) 19 (S.C.C.). Contrast *Costin v. Blois*, above, note 85.

91 Above, note 89, at 1054. Compare *Eaton v. Crook*, above, note 85; *Smith v. Spencer*, above, note 85.

92 *Quance v. Brown*, [1926] 2 D.L.R. 824 at 827 (Ont. C.A.) *per* Riddell J.A. See also *Hutchison v. Paxton*, [1928] 2 D.L.R. 485 (Ont. H.C.); affirmed [1928] 4 D.L.R. 704 (Ont. C.A.). Similarly, if payment is to be made in instalments: *Tweddell v. Henderson*, [1975] 1 W.L.R. 1496.

93 *Jaremy v. Vita Co-op. Ltd.*, [1942] 3 W.W.R. 513 (Man. K.B.); affirmed [1943] 1 W.W.R. 1 (Man. C.A.).

1856 by the Mercantile Law Amendment Act,[94] the consideration need not be stated in a document offered in support of an agreement "to answer for the debt, default or miscarriage of another person," that is, a guarantee. But this is a special statutory exception introduced to prevent fraud, that is, the opportunity to evade responsibility by a technicality.

Questions of time in relation to the performance of the contract have been dealt with in different ways. Thus the time of completion of a contract for the sale of land was held not essential in *McKenzie v. Walsh*,[95] but in that instance it was held by the Supreme Court of Canada that the date was only a matter of convenience and arrangement, not an important and vital term of the contract between the parties. On the other hand, in *Mitchell v. Mortgage Co. of Canada*,[96] a memorandum was held to be insufficient when it omitted to identify when a term of years would commence. So, too, in *Ackerman v. Thomson & McKinnon, Auchincloss Kohlmeyer Inc.*,[97] the contract in question was for the employment of the plaintiff as a commission salesman by the defendant stockbrokers. The contract was within the Statute of Frauds. But the written document that was tendered as evidence of the contract made no mention of the duration of the appointment of the plaintiff to the institutional sales department. The Ontario Court of Appeal held that this was a defective memorandum as it omitted a reference to a material term of the contract. By way of contrast, where the contract was for an *indefinite* hiring, such memorandum as was required would not have to include any reference to the duration of the employment.[98] Hence, it is clearly a matter of fact whether, given the nature and circumstances of the particular contract, time is sufficiently important to warrant being included in the written terms.[99]

---

94 19 & 20 Vict., c. 60, s. 3: in Ontario this is in the Statute of Frauds, R.S.O. 1990, c. S.19, s. 6.

95 (1921), 61 S.C.R. 312 (S.C.C.). See also *Ford v. Keller* (1979), 9 Alta. L.R. (2d) 346 (Alta. T.D.).

96 [1919] 3 W.W.R. 324 (S.C.C.). But there is no need for a written extension of time: *Holmes v. Alexson* (1974), 7 O.R. (2d) 11 (Ont. H.C.); affirmed (1976), 12 O.R. (2d) 431 (Ont. C.A.); compare *Jenkins v. Strickland* (1990), 83 Nfld. & P.E.I.R. 30 (Nfld. T.D.).

97 (1974), 4 O.R. (2d) 240 (Ont. C.A.).

98 *Connell v. Bay of Quinte Country Club* (1923), 24 O.W.N. 264 (Ont. H.C.).

99 The requirements of the Statute of Frauds, where an agreement was expressed to be "subject to contract" (on which see pp. 60-64), were considered by the English Court of Appeal in two cases: *Law v. Jones*, [1974] Ch. 112, and *Tiverton Estates Ltd. v. Wearwell Ltd.*, [1975] Ch. 146 (C.A.) in which the court came to opposite conclusions. In the first case it was decided that as long as the document said to be "subject to contact" contained the terms of the contract that might ultimately become binding between the parties, there was sufficient note or memorandum to satisfy the Statute; hence, the document could result in a binding contract notwithstanding the qualifying words.

This was repudiated in the subsequent case in which decisions founded upon the similar provisions of the Sale of Goods Act (namely, *Buxton v. Rust* (1872), L.R. 7 Exch. 279; *Thirkell v. Cambi*, [1919] 2 K.B. 590 (C.A.); *Societe Capa v. Acatos & Co.*, [1953] 2 Lloyd's Rep. 185) were followed.

Reconciliation of these cases was attempted by Buckley L.J. in *Daulia v. Four Millbank Nominees*, [1978] 2 All E.R. 557 at 570 (C.A.). The document "subject to contract" could only become part of the written memorandum of a later oral contract. The later note or memorandum of the second oral contract had to record the essential terms of the earlier document that was "subject to contract". As to the second point, however, see *Adam v. Gen. Paper Co.* (1978), 85 D.L.R. (3d) 736 (Ont. H.C.), below, note 102.

(iii) *Its form*

Any form of memorandum is admissible if it is in writing and signed by the party making it, and it contains all that the Statute of Frauds requires.[100] So said Strong C.J. of Canada in a case[101] in which just such a document established a contract within the Statute even though the document purported to *repudiate* the sale referred to therein.[102] As long as the essential terms are contained in the document, it does not matter what sort of form it takes.[103] Even a receipt may suffice.[104] So may a testamentary writing, for example, a codicil.[105] Indeed in one English case, *Farr, Smith & Co. v. Messers Ltd.*,[106] a statement of defence signed by the party's agent, namely, his counsel, operated as the note or memorandum under the Statute. Nor does the note or memorandum have to be delivered by one party to the other. It is enough if it is in existence before the commencement of the action to enforce the contract.[107]

By way of alleviation of the strict doctrine the courts have sometimes permitted the note or memorandum to be contained in more than one document. Originally, this could not be done since the courts refused to permit oral evidence to prove the connection between two such documents from which the requisite note or memorandum could be formed. Thus, in *Boydell v. Drummond*[108] the defendant agreed to buy a number of Shakespearean engravings over a number of years. The terms of the agreement were in a prospectus which had been seen by the defendant in the plaintiff's shop. The defendant had only signed a book entitled "Shakespeare Subscribers, their Signatures". This contained no terms and did not refer to the prospectus. The court refused to allow the plaintiff to prove the

---

100 *Harvie v. Gibbons* (1980), 12 Alta. L.R. (2d) 72 (Alta. C.A.).

101 *Martin v. Haubner* (1896), 26 S.C.R. 142 at 148 (S.C.C.).

102 Hence, a signed letter which repudiated an agreement alleged to have been reached by the parties, referred to a draft prepared by the other party's solicitor which contained the terms of an oral agreement satisfied the Statute: *Adam v. Gen. Paper Co.* (1978), 85 D.L.R. (3d) 736 (Ont. H.C.). Contrast *Daulia v. Four Millbank Nominees*, above, note 99; compare *Basbey v. Sweating* (1861), 9 C.B.N.S. 843. There appears to be a difference of opinion between Canadian and English courts on this point.

103 Quoted by Hamilton J. in *A.G. Man. v. Love* (1982), 20 Man. R. (2d) 220 at 222 (Man. Q.B.) (description of land in preamble to contract, not in body of contract, enough to fulfil the Statute). So, too, a notice of approval of a mortgage may be sufficient: *Jenkins v. Strickland* (1990), 83 Nfld. & P.E.I.R. 30 (Nfld. T.D.).

104 Above, note 88.

105 *Re Hoyle*, [1893] 1 Ch. 84 (C.A.). Even if the will is later revoked: *Johnson v. N.S. Trust Co.* (1973), 6 N.S.R. (2d) 88 (N.S.C.A.). But not if the will has been destroyed: *Devereux v. Devereux* (1978), 2 E.T.R. 164 (Ont. H.C.). Moreover, in *Pople v. Cowan Estate* (1986), 39 Man. R. (2d) 136 (Man. Q.B.), a will which left property to the plaintiff and a later will which revoked and replaced the earlier one, and did not leave the property to the plaintiff, did not constitute a sufficient memorandum.

106 [1928] 1 K.B. 397.

107 *Pooler v. Patricia*, [1934] 3 W.W.R. 754 at 757 (Alta. S.C.) *per* Ewing J.

108 (1809), 11 East. 142, 103 E.R. 958. Compare *Peirce v. Corf* (1874), L.R. 9 Q.B. 210; *Rishton v. Whatmore* (1878), 8 Ch. D. 467.

connection between the two different writings, by oral evidence, and so satisfy the Statute.

A later series of cases, commencing with *Long v. Millar*[109] in 1879, and culminating in the decision of Russell J. in *Stokes v. Whicher*[110] in 1920 made inroads upon the strictness of ths doctrine. The attitude was summarized by Russell J. thus:

> If you can spell out of the document a reference to some other transaction, you are at liberty to give evidence as to what that other transaction is, and if that other transaction contains all the terms in writing, you then get a sufficient memorandum with the Statute by reading the two together.[111]

This doctrine was accepted by the Supreme Court of Canada in *Doran v. McKinnon*,[112] in which parol evidence was admitted to show that the terms of a contract within the Statute had been accepted by the defendant over his signature and that these were the terms referred to in litigation between the defendant and the defendant's partners. In the words of Davies J.:

> Parol evidence may be given to connect two documents together which do not expressly refer to each other, but which connection and reference is a matter of fair and reasonable inference.[113]

The purpose of such evidence, admitted where there is an express cross-reference or where such reference may be "spelled out", that is, inferred from the nature of the document, is not to show what were the terms of the contract, but to show what was the writing which is referred to and constitutes the note or memorandum within the Statute.[114]

In one instance, this took the form of connecting a document and a letter,[115] in another, two documents which between them provided a vital term, namely, the date for possession of premises,[116] in another, a payment of a deposit by the defendant, by cheque, and an interim agreement unsigned by the defendant.[117] But

---

109 (1879), 4 C.P.D. 450 (C.A.). See also *Sheers v. Thimbleby* (1897), 76 L.T. 709 (C.A.); *Pearce v. Gardner*, [1897] 1 Q.B. 688 (C.A.); *Oliver v. Hunting* (1890), 44 Ch. D. 205.

110 [1920] 1 Ch. 411; see also *Fowler v. Bratt*, [1950] 1 All E.R. 662 (C.A.); *Burgess v. Cox*, [1950] 2 All E.R. 1212.

111 [1920] 1 Ch. 411 at 418.

112 (1916), 53 S.C.R. 609 (S.C.C.). See also *Rattenbury (N.) Ltd. v. Winchester* (1953), 31 M.P.R. 69 (P.E.I.C.A.); *White v. Carson* (1975), 13 N.B.R. (2d) 357 (N.B.Q.B.); *C.I.B.C. v. Titus* (1980), 28 O.R. (2d) 52 (Ont. H.C.); *Abernethy Credit Union Ltd. v. Flavel* (1983), 25 Sask. R. 310 (Sask. Q.B.).

113 (1916), 53 S.C.R. 609 at 611 (S.C.C.). But there have to be two *existing* documents: *Devereux v. Devereux* (1978), 2 E.T.R. 164 (Ont. H.C.).

114 *Ibid.* See, *e.g.*, *Can. Law Book Co. v. Butterworth & Co.* (1913), 3 W.W.R. 1014 (Man. K.B.), for the later appellate decisions which did not raise this question, see (1913), 4 W.W.R. 237 (Man. C.A.); affirmed (1914), 5 W.W.R. 1217 (P.C.).

115 *Steine v. Mathieu*, [1923] 3 W.W.R. 493 (Sask. C.A.).

116 *Peterson v. Bitzer*, [1922] 1 W.W.R. 141 (S.C.C.); see also *Moojelsky v. Rexnord Can. Ltd.* (1989), 96 A.R. 91 (Alta. Q.B.); compare *Jenkins v. Strickland* (1990), 83 Nfld. 7 P.E.I.R. 30 (Nfld. T.D.).

117 *E. & B. Mtges. Ltd. v. Skrivanos* (1980), 118 D.L.R. (3d) 139 (B.C.S.C.); compare *Harvie v. Gibbons* (1980), 12 Alta. L.R. (2d) 72 (Alta. C.A.); and *Re Quieting of Titles Act (Nfld.); Maguire v. Patey* (1987), 66 Nfld. & P.E.I.R. 15 (Nfld. T.D.); affirmed (1989), 81 Nfld. & P.E.I.R. 312 (Nfld. C.A.).

in *Fennell v. Fisher*[118] (in somewhat similar circumstances to those of the later English case of *Timmins v. Moreland Street Property Co.*[119]) it was not possible to connect a cheque for $5,000 given by the purchaser and endorsed by the vendor "in full for house and contents" with a transfer of land, not mentioning contents, where the consideration was stated to be $5,500 so as to establish a contract for the contents of the buildings which were sold and enable the plaintiff to recover the value of such contents.[120]

(iv) *The signature*

Only the person who is being sued on the contract need have signed.

> A plaintiff may sue upon a contract required to be in writing by the Statute of Frauds even though he has not signed it providing that the defendant has signed the memorandum or contract upon which he is sought to be charged.[121]

Nor need the party himself have signed the contract, note or memorandum. It is enough if it is signed by "some other person thereunto lawfully authorized." Hence the signature of an agent with authority to do so will satisfy the Statute.[122] If he lacked authority in the first instance,[123] or his authority was revoked prior to his signing the document,[124] then the signature will be to no avail. But it does not matter whether the agent himself was appointed by a document which satisfied the Statute of Frauds;[125]nor indeed does it matter how the agent obtained the

---

118 [1947] 2 W.W.R. 1007 (Sask. C.A.).

119 [1957] 3 All E.R. 265 (C.A.) discussed in Fridman, "Joinder of Documents to Form a Memorandum" (1958), 22 Conveyancer 275.

120 In effect, the court was adopting the *narrow* view of clear reference, rather than the more liberal "side-by-side" principle which has sometimes been stated: see Fridman, note 119, above, at pp. 277-279. Contrast the more "liberal" approach in the cases referred to above in note 117. However, there must be an express or implied reference that is real, not imaginary: see *Columbia Caterers Ltd. v. Famous Restaurants Ltd.* (1956), 18 W.W.R. 577 (B.C.C.A.); *Walker v. Copp Clark Publishing Co.*, [1962] O.R. 622 (Ont. H.C.); and by implication *Moojelsky v. Rexnord Can. Ltd.*, above, note 116.

121 *McGarry v. Richards, Akroyd & Gall Ltd.*, [1954] 2 D.L.R. 367 at 377 (B.C.S.C.) *per* Davey J. As long as the document satisfies the requirements of the Statute: *Ford v. Keller* (1979), 9 Alta. L.R. (2d) 346 (Alta. T.D.). Hence, a signature on a *cheque* will do, as long as the cheque can be connected with another document that contains the essential terms: *Harvie v. Gibbons* (1980), 12 Alta. L.R. (2d) 72 (Alta. C.A.); compare above, p. 221. If there is no signature the memorandum will be insufficient, as in *Harvey v. McCarthy* (1988), 86 N.B.R. (2d) 438 (N.B.Q.B.), where a rough document was prepared by the parties but unsigned.

122 *Litras v. Mattern*, [1938] 1 W.W.R. 381 (B.C. S.C.). Compare *Wilson & Sons v. Pike*, [1948] 2 All E.R. 267 (C.A.). The agent may also be liable: *Basma v. Weekes*, [1950] 2 W.W.R. 784 (P.C.); see Fridman, *Law of Agency*, 6th ed. (1990), pp. 207-218.

123 *Lloydminster v. Acme Dept. Stores (1958) Ltd.* (1964), 49 W.W.R. 18 (Sask. Q.B.). Compare *Harris v. Mohawk Oil Co.* (1979), 103 D.L.R. (3d) 171 (B.C.S.C.).

124 *Moyer & Co. v. Smith & Goldberg Ltd.*, [1929] S.C.R. 625 (S.C.C.).

125 *McIlvride v. Mills* (1906), 16 Man. R. 276 (Man. C.A.).

necessary authorization. Hence a signature by counsel to a pleading will be enough.[126]

It is immaterial whether the name is written or printed. Thus the defendant's name printed at the head of an invoice,[127] or on a catalogue (the leaves of which were used by an auctioneer as bills or receipts),[128] was sufficient. But the name must be the proper name of the defendant, not some false name which he is using for the purpose of this particular contract.[129]

Nor is it material where the name appears on the document as long as it refers to and governs the whole document. Therefore in the English case of *Caton v. Caton*,[130] although the names of the parties appeared at various points in the document, which was an agreement in consideration of marriage, there was no signature that governed the entire document. However, as long as the signature has this effect it can be at the beginning, instead of at the foot of the document,[131] or, indeed, anywhere else.[132]

(e) The effect of non-compliance

(i) *At common law*

There is no question but that a contract within the Statute, even if not formally evidenced as set out in the Statute, is a valid contract, not one that is illegal, void or voidable.[133] It was held, in the nineteenth century, in *Leroux v. Brown*,[134] that failure to perform the requirements of the Statute led to procedural problems, not substantive ones. As Lord Blackburn said in the later case of *Maddison v. Alderson*,[135] the section "applies not to the solemnities of the contract but to the procedure." In the words of Riddell J.A. in an Ontario case,

> it must never be forgotten that the Statute of Frauds does not deal with the validity of the transaction, but only with the evidence to prove an agreement.[136]

---

126 *Farr, Smith & Co. v. Messers Ltd.*, [1928] 1 K.B. 397.
127 *Schneider v. Norris* (1814), 105 E.R. 388. Or at the top of a memorandum connected to an unenforced sub-contract: *Moojelsky v. Rexnord Can. Ltd.*, above, note 116.
128 *Cohen v. Roche*, [1927] 1 K.B. 169. Or on a cheque: above, note 121.
129 *McMeekin v. Furry* (1907), 5 W.L.R. 487 (B.C.S.C.); affirmed on other grounds (1907), 39 S.C.R. 378 (S.C.C.).
130 (1867), L.R. 2 H.L. 127 (H.L.).
131 *McIlvride v. Mills*, above, note 125; compare *Moojelsky v. Rexnord Can. Ltd.*, above, note 116.
132 *Swim v. Amos* (1895), 33 N.B.R. 49 (N.B.C.A.); *Standard Realty Co. v. Nicholson* (1911), 24 O.L.R. 46 (Ont. H.C.).
133 *Maloughney v. Crowe* (1912), 6 D.L.R. 471 at 473 (Ont. H.C.) *per* Middleton J. This is referred to by Godin J. in *Maritime Orthopedic Co. v. Moncton Prosthetics & Orthotics Clinic Ltd.* (1992), 127 N.B.R. (2d) 44 at 81 (N.B.Q.B.).
134 (1852), 12 C.B. 801, 138 E.R. 1119.
135 (1883), 8 App. Cas. 467 at 488 (H.L.).
136 *Standard Realty Co. v. Nicholson* (1911), 24 O.L.R. 46 at 53 (Ont. H.C.).

The contract will be unenforceable if it does not comply with the terms of the Statute as discussed earlier in this chapter; it will not be void.[137]

What that means is that no action can be brought to enforce the contract against the other party, unless that other party has signed the requisite note or memorandum.[138] But if the contract is not being enforced, although it is otherwise a part of the case the plaintiff is making against the defendant, it may be proved without writing and used by the plaintiff.[139] For example, it may be treated as good consideration for *another* contract which is either not within the Statute or conforms to the Statute's requirements.[140] So, too, a contract which is not duly and properly evidenced is not rendered useless by the Statute and may be pleaded as a defence[141] or by way of set-off to an action brought against the defendant.[142] Nor can the Statute be raised if the action is one for dissolution of a partnership and an accounting, rather than the enforcement of a contract.[143] Nor is the Statute a bar to an action for rectification of a contract based upon fraud or mistake.[144] Nor will the Statute bar an action in quasi-contract (or restitution).[145] Nor will it operate to bar an action that is based on waiver.[146]

However, it is to be noted that even at common law there may be other qualifications upon the effects of the Statute. Thus the defence of the Statute is not just technical, but it must be pleaded.[147] Yet even if pleaded it might not be

---

137 *Wauchope v. Maida* (1972), 22 D.L.R. (3d) 142 (Ont. C.A.); *Re Yale and MacMaster* (1974), 46 D.L.R. (3d) 167 (Ont. H.C.); *Re M.C. United Masonry Ltd.; Peat Marwick Ltd. v. Goldfarb* (1983), 142 D.L.R. (3d) 470 (Ont. C.A.).

138 *McGarry v. Richards, Akroyd & Gall Ltd.*, [1954] 2 D.L.R. 367 (B.C.S.C.).

139 *Johnston v. Block*, [1945] 3 W.W.R. 244 (Sask. K.B.). Money paid under such a contract is irrecoverable, even though the contract could not have been enforced if the money had not been paid: *Switzer's Invts. Ltd. v. Burn* (1964), 49 W.W.R. 627 (Alta. S.C.).

140 *Kinzie v. Harper* (1908), 15 O.L.R. 582 (Ont. C.A.).

141 *Re Whissel Enterprises Ltd. and Eastcal Dev. Ltd.* (1980), 116 D.L.R. (3d) 174 (Alta. C.A.); *Barber v. Glen* (1987), 59 Sask. R. 49 (Sask. C.A.).

142 *Frith v. Alliance Invt. Co.* (1914), 6 W.W.R. 981 (S.C.C.). Compare *Coady v. J. Lewis & Sons*, [1951] 3 D.L.R. 845 (N.S.S.C.) in which the defendant could not raise an unenforceable contract against the plaintiff to defeat the plaintiff's claim by a set-off under which the defendant sought to recover money paid the plaintiff under such unenforceable contract.

143 *Wong v. Hou*, [1928] 1 W.W.R. 480 (B.C.S.C.).

144 *Fordham v. Hall* (1914), 6 W.W.R. 769 (B.C.C.A.); *U.S.A. v. Motor Trucks Ltd.*, [1924] A.C. 196 (P.C.); compare *Alvi v. Lal* (1990), 13 R.P.R. (2d) 302 at 307-312 (Ont. H.C.).

145 *Palachik v. Kiss* (1983), 146 D.L.R. (3d) 385 (S.C.C.); compare *Deglman v. Guar. Trust Co.*, [1954] S.C.R. 725 (S.C.C.).

146 *Petridis v. Shabinsky* (1982), 132 D.L.R. (3d) 430 (Ont. H.C.); compare *Crosby v. Temple*, [1940] 2 D.L.R. 554 (N.S. C.A.); *Iwanczuk v. Center Square Dev. Ltd.* (1967), 61 D.L.R. (2d) 193 (Ont. H.C.). For waiver see pp. 544-545.

147 *Beemer v. Brownridge*, [1934] 1 W.W.R. 545 at 549 (Sask. C.A.) *per* Turgeon J.A.; *Ethier v. Ethier*, [1987] 4 W.W.R. 641 (Sask. Q.B.). This, and the succeeding sentence were quoted by Chrumka J. in *Conmac Western Industries v. Robinson* (1993), 9 Alta. L.R. (3d) 232 at 308 (Alta. Q.B.), and by Godin J. in *Maritime Orthopedic Co. v. Moncton Prosthetics & Orthotics Clinc Ltd.* (1992), 127 N.B.R. (2d) 44 at 81 (N.B.Q.B.). Even if the party relying on the Statute previously admitted the contract: see Stevens, "Ethics and the Statute of Frauds" (1952), 37 Cornell L.Q. 355 at 361-371.

allowed to bar an action, if to do so would be to perpetrate a fraud upon, or an injustice against, the other party.[148]

There is another important qualification upon the apparent ineffectiveness of a contract not properly evidenced under the Statute. This relates to the way in which such a contract can operate upon a prior contract which itself did not offend the Statute and could have been enforced.[149] The effects of such second contract will depend upon whether the parties' intention was: (i) to vary, but not destroy the first contract; (ii) to discharge, that is, end the first contract without anything further; or (iii) to discharge the first contract and replace it by a new, second contract.

If the second, and unenforceable contract was intended merely to vary the terms of the original and enforceable one, then the cases reveal that the second contract is ineffective. The parol variation must be ignored.[150] However, if one party wishes to enforce the first contract, it may be that a court will refuse specific performance of such contract unless the party seeking such specific performances also undertakes to accept the variations in the second contract, if the other party so desires, and the variations are for the party's benefit.[151]

If the second contract was intended expressly or by implication to discharge the first contract, that is, to rescind it, then it will be effective for that purpose, even though it is otherwise unenforceable by reason of the provisions of the Statute. This was clearly established by the House of Lords in *Morris v. Baron & Co.*[152] in 1918, a case which has been accepted and followed in Canada.[153]

Thirdly, if the second contract was intended to be a substitute for the first contract, that is, to rescind the first contract and create a new contractual arrangement between the parties, it will be effective to discharge the first contract

---

148 *Per* Coyne J.A. in *Int. Associated Hairdressers v. Glasgow* (1957), 9 D.L:.R. (2d) 615 at 628 (Man. C.A.); therefore a third party could rely on an oral agreement between two *other* parties for a lease of goods with power to resell, as a defence to an action for repossession brought against him. Compare also *Wong v. Hou*, above, note 143; *Devine v. Somerville*, [1931] 3 W.W.R. 264 (B.C.S.C.). This has been much developed in the U.S.: see *e.g.*, Summers, "The Doctrine of Estoppel Applied to the Statute of Frauds" (1931), 79 U. Penn. L.R. 440; Note, "Promissory Estoppel as a Means of Defeating the Statute of Frauds," 44 Fordham L.R. 114; Edwards, "The Statute of Frauds of the Uniform Commercial Code and the Doctrine of Estoppel" (1978), 62 Marquette L.R. 205.

149 Distinguish the situation where the *original* contract is orally altered but the contract is signed; the distinction is drawn between rectification of an inaccurate formulation and variation: *New Hart Bldrs. v. Brindley*, [1975] Ch. 342 on which see Emery in (1975), 39 Conveyancer 336.

150 *Brooks v. Stainer*, [1963] 2 O.R. 481 (Ont. H.C.) following the English case of *Goss v. Nugent* (1833), 110 E.R. 713. Compare *King v. Freeman*, [1942] O.R. 561 (Ont. H.C.); *Shook v. Munro & Davidson*, [1948] S.C.R. 539 at 543 (S.C.C.) *per* Kellock J. But an agreement to extend the time for completion of a contract was not a variation of the original contract; hence it did not have to satisfy the Statute: *Jenkins v. Strickland* (1990), 83 Nfld. & P.E.I.R. 30 (Nfld. T.D.).

151 *Maloughney v. Crowe* (1912), 26 O.L.R. 579 (Ont. H.C.).

152 [1918] A.C. 1 (H.L.) and see *British & Benington's Ltd. v. North Western Cachar Tea Co.*, [1923] A.C. 48 (H.L.). See Fridman, *Sale of Goods in Canada*, 3rd ed. (1986), pp. 25, 272.

153 See, *e.g.*, *Johnson Invts. Ltd. v. Pagratide*, [1923] 2 W.W.R. 736 (Alta. C.A.); *Mason v. Scott*, [1934] 3 D.L.R. 769 (N.S.S.C.); reversed on other grounds [1935] 2 D.L.R. 641 (S.C.C.).

but, without satisfying the Statute of Frauds, it will be ineffective to create an enforceable obligation between the parties.[154]

Obviously, much depends upon the intention of the parties as manifested by their conduct.[155] Sometimes, even if the second contract is ineffectual, the conduct of one of the parties in consequence of such contract can give rise to some form of estoppel which might be effective against the party seeking to enforce his strict contractual rights under the first contract.[156] What is, or may, be involved in such instances is *waiver*, not variation — a different, if allied, concept.[157]

(ii) *In equity*

Whatever the effect of the Statute of Frauds at common law, and however strictly the statute was construed and applied by common-law courts, it was decided quite early after the passage of the Statute,[158] by courts of equity, that defendants would not be allowed to plead and rely upon the Statute if to permit them to do so would be to allow the Statute "to be used as an engine of fraud."[159] Since a contract which did not conform to the Statute was merely unenforceable, equity invented a doctrine under which, in appropriate circumstances, a defendant was not allowed to rely upon the technical defence of the Statute. In the language of Lord Simon of Glaisdale in *Steadman v. Steadman*,

> [w]here . . . a party to a contract unenforceable under the Statute of Frauds stood by while the other party acted to his detriment in performance of his own contractual obligations, the first party would be precluded by the Court of Chancery from claiming exoneration, on the ground that the contract was unenforceable, from performance of his reciprocal obligations; and the court would, if required, decree specific performance of the contract . . . This became known as the doctrine of part performance — the 'part' performance being that of the party who had, to the knowledge of the other party, acted to his detriment in carrying out irremediably his own obligations (or some significant part of them) under the otherwise unenforceable contract.

As Lord Reid said in the same case,[160] "There is nothing about part performance in the Statute of Frauds. It is an invention of the Court of Chancery. . . ." Hence,

---

154 See the cases cited in the last two notes.
155 Contrast, *e.g.*, *Morris v. Baron*, above, note 152, with *United Dom. Corp. (Jamaica) v. Shoucair*, [1969] 1 A.C. 340 (P.C.) a case arising not out of the Statute of Frauds but the Moneylenders Act, 1927 (17 & 18 Geo. 5), c. 21, though the same principles were involved.
156 See *Brooks v. Stainer*, note 150, above, where there was no such estoppel arising from the oral variation of a mortgage by way of extension of time in consideration of an increase in the rate of interest. Compare *Imp. Grain & Milling Co. v. Slobinsky Bros. & Sons*, [1922] 3 W.W.R. 221 (Man. K.B.); *Sierichs v. Hughes* (1918), 42 O.L.R. 608 (Ont. C.A.); *Patterson v. Scott*, [1922] 2 W.W.R. 700 (Man. K.B.). But see *Jenkins v. Strickland*, above, note 150.
157 Below, pp. 543-546. See, *e.g.*, *Petridis v. Shabinsky* (1982), 132 D.L.R. (3d) 430 (Ont. H.C.).
158 *Butcher v. Stapley* (1685), 1 Vern. 363, 23 E.R. 524. Compare *Maddison v. Alderson* (1883), 8 App. Cas. 467 at 477 (H.L.).
159 *Steadman v. Steadman*, [1974] 2 All E.R. 977 at 996 (H.L.) *per* Lord Simon. (This sentence was cited by MacIntosh J. in *Wilson v. Harrison* (1979), 35 N.S.R. (2d) 499 at 509 (N.S.T.D.).
160 [1974] 2 All E.R. 977 at 981 (H.L.).

in deciding any case not clearly covered by authority, the equitable nature of the remedy was to be kept in mind.

The whole nature of this doctrine is to prevent one party from fraudulently taking advantage of the other, as the examples put by Lord Salmon in the *Steadman* case[161] indicate and prove. Coyne J.A., in one Canadian case,[162] referred to the equitable principles

> which hold that the Statute of Frauds does not apply where there has been performance or part performance of the oral contract by, *or where otherwise the result would be fraud against, or injustice to,* the other party. . . .

The italicized phrases might be construed as a somewhat wide statement of principle, but there is no doubt whatsoever as to the doctrine of part performance. The problems which have arisen, however, relate not to the existence of the doctrine, but to the situations to which it applies and the requirements of the doctrine. Dispute has also raged as to the true juridical nature of the doctrine.

In the first place, it would seem that, while most of the decisions relate to contracts concerning land or interests in land, the doctrine may not be limited in its scope to such transactions.[163] Thus, it has been applied: (i) in a case concerning goods[164] (though probably, the provisions of the Sale of Goods Act[165] provide a sufficiently similar exception or qualification not to necessitate reliance on this equitable doctrine); and, (ii) in some English cases,[166] to contracts involving personal services, though, possibly, the decisions therein can be justified or substantiated on other principles.[167] However, since the basis of the doctrine is that the contract to which the acts of part performance refer must be such as in their own nature

---

161   *Ibid.*, at 1006-1007. These involve payment of the total purchase price of a house when there was no written contract or memorandum. Compare *Bunka v. Ruttle Estate* (1987), 62 Sask. R. 129 (Sask. Q.B.); *Re Quieting of Titles Act (Nfld.)*; *Maguire v. Patey* (1987), 66 Nfld. & P.E.I.R. 15 (Nfld. T.D.); affirmed (*sub nom. Paton v. Patey*) (1989), 81 Nfld. & P.E.I.R. 312 (Nfld. C.A.); *Nicol v. Weigel* (1991), 17 R.P.R. (2d) 213 (B.C.C.A.), in all of which the act of paying money together with *other* acts amounted to part performance. Contrast *Alvi v. Lal* (1990), 13 R.P.R. (2d) 302 (Ont. H.C.), where it was not.

162   *Int. Assoc. Hairdressers v. Glasgow* (1957), 9 D.L.R. (2d) 615 at 628 (Man. C.A.) (italics supplied).

163   Contrast the views of Lord Selborne against such extension in *Maddison v. Alderson* (1883), 8 App. Cas. 467 at 480 (H.L.) (repeating what was said in *Britain v. Rossiter* (1879), 11 Q.B.D. 123 (C.A.)) with those in favour of extension expressed by Kay L.J. in *McManus v. Cooke* (1887), 35 Ch. D. 681 at 697 (a case which was followed in Canada in *Smith v. Curry*, [1918] 2 W.W.R. 848 (Man. C.A.)). See also the judgment of LeBel J. in *Foster v. Royal Trust Co.*, [1951] 1 D.L.R. 147 at 152 (Ont. H.C.). *Britain v. Rossiter*, above, was followed in *Color Your World Inc. v. Robert F. Avery Holdings Ltd.* (1988), 88 A.R. 163 (Alta. Q.B.).

164   *Can. Law Book Co. v. Butterworth & Co.* (1913), 3 W.W.R. 1014 (Man. K.B.); reversed on other grounds (1913), 4 W.W.R. 237 (Man. C.A.); affirmed (1914), 5 W.W.R. 1217 (P.C.).

165   Below, pp. 239-244.

166   Contrast *Britain v. Rossiter*, above, note 163; *Scott v. Pattison*, [1923] 2 K.B. 723; *James v. Kent (Thomas) & Co.*, [1951] 1 K.B. 551 (C.A.).

167   *E.g., quantum meruit: quasi-contract*; compare *Deglman v. Guar. Trust Co.*, [1954] S.C.R. 725 (S.C.C.); below, pp. 701-702.

are enforceable by the court, namely, a court of equity,[168] it seems most likely that the proper scope of the doctrine is or, perhaps, should be, restricted to contracts dealing with interests in land.[169] What happens in these cases is that the contract is sufficiently established by the act of part performance to let in proper parol evidence of the contract such that a court can charge the defendant upon the "equities" arising out of the conduct in question, and decree specific performance of the alleged, and in effect proven, contract.[170] Hence, the contract ought to be of the kind which could be made the subject of a decree of specific performance,[171] and that would seem to preclude the extension of the doctrine to contracts concerning personal services or contracts for more than a year, an exclusion that has been queried as explicable historically but undesirable functionally.[172]

Second, what are the requirements of the doctrine? In other words, what sort of conduct suffices to amount to part performance of an alleged contract that is not evidenced by a note or memorandum within the Statute?[173] In answer to this question it must be pointed out, as it was by McDonald J. of the Supreme Court of Alberta in *Toombs v. Mueller*,[174] that there have been two different views —

---

168   *Fry on Specific Performance*, 6th ed. (1921), at pp. 276-277; cited with approval in several cases, *e.g., per* Viscount Dilhorne in *Steadman v. Steadman*, above, note 159, at 991. This would also exclude contracts lacking in "mutuality" (below, p. 796): *Robinson v. MacAdam*, below, note 171; *Carter v. Irving Oil Co.*, below, note 171.

169   Compare Sutherland J. in *Travel Machine Ltd. v. Madore* (1983), 143 D.L.R. (3d) 94 at 100 (Ont. H.C.) denying that the doctrine can apply to contracts of guarantee, both for historical reasons and because otherwise it would be easy to take a case out of the Statute, amounting to a judicial repeal of the provisions of the Statute dealing with guarantees. But it has been applied to other contracts: see *Maritime Orthopedic Co. v. Moncton Prosthetics & Orthotics Clinic Ltd.* (1992), 127 N.B.R. (2d) 44 (N.B.Q.B.); *Hoeppner v. Horstman Contracting Ltd.* (1992), 79 Man. R. (2d) 257 (Man. Q.B.).

170   Compare Lord Selborne in *Maddison v. Alderson* (1883), 8 App. Cas. 467 at 475 (H.L.). This sentence was cited by Proudfoot J. in *Harris v. Mohawk Oil Co.* (1979), 103 D.L.R. (3d) 171 at 179 (B.C.S.C.). On the way to prove or establish the oral contract see *Steadman v. Steadman*, above, note 159, at 990-991 *per* Viscount Dilhorne, and 997-999 *per* Lord Simon of Glaisdale; compare *Carvery v. Fletcher* (1987), 34 D.L.R. (4th) 739 at 742-743 (N.S.T.D.) *per* Hallett J.

171   Compare *Robinson v. MacAdam*, [1948] 2 W.W.R. 425 (B.C.S.C.); *Carter v. Irving Oil Co.*, [1952] 4 D.L.R. 128 (N.S.S.C.). Therefore, it is inapplicable where damages are being sought under the "unenforceable" contract (except possibly, under the provisions of Lord Cairns' Act, 1858 (21 & 22 Vict.), s. 2, if and where this is applicable in Canada. Compare *Lavery v. Pursell* (1888), 39 Ch. D. 508). But in *Nicol v. Weigel* (1991), 17 R.P.R. (2d) 213 (B.C.C.A.), damages were awarded: and *Lavery v. Pursell* was said not to apply. On the difference of opinion as to whether the contract should be one where a decree of specific performance could actually have been made or a contract in respect of which a court of equity would have assumed jurisdiction, whether or not a decree would have been made, see Ontario Law Reform Commission, *Report on Amendment of the Law of Contract* (1987), at pp. 92-93.

172   O.L.R.C. *Report*, above, note 171, at p. 92.

173   The discussion of acts of part performance in the succeeding pages is referred to by Huband J.A. in *Decorby v. Decorby* (1989), 57 Man. R. (2d) 241 at 253 (Man. C.A.). He considers the apparent division of opinion between English and Canadian cases (which is denied by O'Sullivan J.A., *ibid.*, at 243), but does not decide the issue since, on either view, there were no acts of part performance in the case before the court: *ibid.*, at 253.

174   [1974] 6 W.W.R. 577 (Alta. S.C.); reversed without written reasons [1975] 3 W.W.R. 96 (Alta. C.A.). But see the additional editor's note in [1975] 5 W.W.R. 520.

a narrow one, and a broader, more generous one. Each stems from the speeches in the House of Lords in *Maddison v. Alderson*.[175] The narrow view regards the evidence strictly and cautiously; the broader view accepts much looser evidence as establishing sufficient acts of part performance.

In *Maddison v. Alderson*, Lord Selborne L.C. said[176]

> [a]ll the authorities show that the acts relied upon as part performance must be unequivocally, and in their own nature, referable to some such agreement as that alleged.

Elsewhere in his speech he said[177]

> [a]ll the acts done must be referred to the actual contract, which is the measure and test of their legal and equitable character and consequences. . . .

Comparison of these passages led Lord Simon in the *Steadman* case[178] to pose several questions. One of these concerned Lord Selborne's reference to "*res gestae*" subsequent to and arising out of the contract. What did that mean?[179] Was it necessary for the *reg gestae*, whatever they were, to refer to some such agreement as alleged or the actual agreement? The specific term or some contract? What was, or is meant by "unequivocally"? "Of their own nature"? The other speeches in the *Maddison* case, such as that of Lord O'Hagan[180] and that of Lord Blackburn[181] also use the kind of language which has posed for English and Canadian judges alike the problem of determining just how specific the act or acts of part performance must be.

In Canada the Supreme Court adopted the narrow view in *McNeil v. Corbett*[182] in 1907, where Duff J. interpreted Lord Selborne's language as meaning "an agreement respecting the lands themselves."[183] This view was followed in later cases.[184] As McRuer C.J.H.C. said in *McMillen v. Chapman*, "The part performance must be referable to the oral agreement that is relied on."[185] Hence, payment of rent and remaining in possession were not sufficient acts of part performance of

175 (1883), 8 App. Cas. 467 (H.L.).
176 *Ibid.*, at 478-479 (relied on by Estey J. in *Willits v. Dixon* (1981), 128 D.L.R. (3d) 436 at 444 (Sask. Q.B.) where the acts alleged, including the cohabitation of the woman with the man, did not constitute sufficient acts of part performance).
177 *Ibid.*, at 475-476.
178 [1974] 2 All E.R. 977 at 996-997 (H.L.).
179 *Ibid.*, at 998, for a full discussion of this *evidentiary* expression as used in the context of the doctrine of part performance.
180 (1883), 8 App. Cas. 467 at 485 (H.L.).
181 *Ibid.*, at 489-490.
182 (1907), 39 S.C.R. 608 (S.C.C.).
183 *Ibid.*, at 611.
184 See, *e.g.*, *McGillivray v. Shaw* (1963), 39 D.L.R. (2d) 660 (Alta. C.A.); *Erb v. Wilson* (1969), 69 W.W.R. 126 (Sask. Q.B.); *Hurd v. Roy* (1970), 74 W.W.R. 363 (B.C.S.C.). Compare, more recently, after the decision in *Steadman v. Steadman*, [1974] 2 All E.R. 977 (H.L.), *Alvi v. Lal* (1990), 13 R.P.R. (2d) 302 at 312-313 (Ont. H.C.).
185 [1953] 2 D.L.R. 671 at 679 (Ont. C.A.). Compare more recently, *Hansen v. Price* (1981), 14 Sask. R. 430 (Sask. Q.B.); *Syhlonyk v. Syhlonyk* (1982), 20 Sask. R. 354 (Sask. Q.B.); *Willits v. Dixon* (1981), 128 D.L.R. (3d) 436 (Sask. Q.B.). But see *Lensen v. Lensen* (1984), 14 D.L.R. (4th) 611 (Sask. C.A.).

an oral agreement which neither party had in contemplation in that case during the alleged part performance. Nor was allowing haystacks to remain on the land in *Van Berkel v. De Foort*[186] evidence of an oral contract to permit the defendant to cut and remove the crop of hay from the plaintiff's land. There was not the necessary act or change of position by the party relying on the contract.[187] In several cases the issue was whether acts of service performed by one party for another over a period of years, sometimes a very long period, were referable to an alleged oral contract to leave land to the party providing the services after the death of the beneficiary of the services. In *Deglman v. Guaranty Trust Co. of Canada*,[188] such acts were held not to amount to part performance. That decision unquestionably rejected some earlier Canadian cases[189] in which a broader view had been taken. But later decisions in the Supreme Court of Canada[190] appear to have made inroads upon *Deglman*, and are either distinguishable very narrowly on the facts or, which is more probable, represent the undermining of the narrower view.[191]

Prior to the *Steadman* case there were indications in England of a broader view of the decision and *dicta* in *Maddison v. Alderson*. In *Kingswood Estate Co.*

---

186 [1933] 1 W.W.R. 125 (Man. C.A.). For other cases where insufficient acts of part performance occurred, see, *e.g., Erb v. Wilson,* above, note 184; *Roberts v. Colwell* (1932), 5 M.P.R. 451 (N.B. S.C.); *Baker v. Neary* (1984), 51 Nfld. & P.E.I.R. 25 (Nfld. T.D.) (acts of surveying not sufficient). For cases where what had been done satisfied the requirements of the doctrine, see *Briese v. Dugard,* [1936] 1 D.L.R. 723 (Man. C.A.); *McLaughlin v. Mayhew* (1903), 6 O.L.R. 174 (Ont. C.A.); *Hudon v. Cyr* (1973), 40 D.L.R. (3d) 366 (N.B.C.A.); *McGillivray v. Shaw* (1963), 39 D.L.R. (2d) 660 (Alta. C.A.); *Hurd v. Roy* (1970), 74 W.W.R. 363 (B.C.S.C.); *Kramaruk v. Kushnir* (1956), 2 D.L.R. (2d) 452 (Ont. C.A.); *Freeland v. Freeland* (1982), 19 Alta. L.R. (2d) 180 (Alta. Q.B.); *Harris v. Mohawk Oil Co.* (1979), 103 D.L.R. (3d) 171 (B.C.S.C.); *Lee v. Shore* (1984), 29 Man. R. (2d) 191 (Man. Q.B.); *Lensen v. Lensen,* above, note 185.

187 Compare *Hawkesworth v. Turner* (1930), 46 T.L.R. 389.

188 [1954] S.C.R. 725 (S.C.C.); compare *Baker v. Guar. Trust Co.,* [1956] O.W.N. 120 (Ont. H.C.).
      Yet in *Taylor v. Rawana* (1990), 74 O.R. (2d) 357 (Ont. H.C.); affirmed (1992), 10 O.R. (3d) 736 (Ont. C.A.), Clarke J., while professing to follow the *Deglman* case, concluded that the acts of the plaintiff amounted to part performance. He had moved into the defendant's property, cleaned it up and repaired it. The defendant claimed the plaintiff was only a tenant. The judge held that the alleged contract to sell the property to the plaintiff was proved and could be enforced despite the fact that it was oral and did not comply with the Statute. Compare *Re Quieting of Titles Act: Maguire v. Patey* (1987), 66 Nfld. & P.E.I.R. 15 (Nfld. T.D.); affirmed (*sub nom. Paton v. Patey*) (1989), 81 Nfld. & P.E.I.R. 312 (Nfld. C.A.). Contrast with *Taylor v. Rowana* the decision that there were no sufficient acts of part performance in *Mid Park Const. Ltd. v. Cleland* (1992), 27 R.P.R. (2d) 68 (Ont. Gen. Div.) (which seems to have followed the narrower, stricter doctrine of the *Deglman* case).

189 Namely, *Wilson v. Cameron* (1913), 30 O.L.R. 486 (Ont. C.A.); *Coyle v. McPherson,* [1944] 1 W.W.R. 552 (B.C.S.C.); *Foster v. Royal Trust Co.,* [1950] O.R. 673 (Ont. H.C.).

190 *Brownscombe v. Pub. Trustee (Admin. of Vercamert Estate),* [1969] S.C.R. 658 (S.C.C.); *Thompson v. Guar. Trust Co.,* [1973] 6 W.W.R. 746 (S.C.C.) (followed in *Orange v. Swierz Estate* (1986), 54 Sask. R. 195 (Sask. Q.B.). With which contrast *Erb v. Wilson,* above, note 184; *Swan v. Pub. Trustee,* [1972] 3 W.W.R. 696 (Alta. S.C.).

191 See also *Hink v. Lhenen* (1975), 52 D.L.R. (3d) 301 (Alta. C.A.); *Devereux v. Devereux* (1978), 2 E.T.R. 164 (Ont. H.C.); *Hansen v. Price* (1981), 14 Sask. R. 430 (Sask. Q.B.); *Orange v. Swierz Estate,* above, note 190, with which contrast *Ross v. Ross* (1973), 33 D.L.R. (3d) 351 (Sask. Q.B.); *Syhlonyk v. Syhlonyk* (1982), 20 Sask. R. 354 (Sask. Q.B.); *Willits v. Dixon* (1981), 128 D.L.R. (3d) 436 (Sask. Q.B.).

v. Anderson,[192] Upjohn L.J. said that the contention that the acts of part performance had to be referable to no other title than the alleged was "a long exploded idea." The true rule was that the acts in question should "be such as must be referred to some contract, and may be referred to the alleged one; that they prove the existence of some contract, and are consistent with the contract alleged."[193] This was applied in *Wakeham v. MacKenzie*.[194] The plaintiff agreed orally with X, after the death of X's wife, that she would move into X's house and look after him and the house, paying her own share of the food and coal, if X would leave her the house in his will. She did so, giving up her own flat in order to do so. After two or three years X died but did not leave her anything in his will. She now sought specific performance of the oral contract. This was granted. Unlike the acts of the "housekeeper" in *Maddison v. Alderson*, those of the plaintiff in this case established the contract alleged. She had given up her home, had looked after the home of the deceased, and had contributed to the common fund out of which she and X had lived. Her acts were explicable by reference only to some contract and were consistent with the contract alleged. Unquestionably, this was a departure from earlier authority.

The issue came before the House of Lords in *Steadman v. Steadman*.[195] The case arose out of a dispute between a husband and wife who were joint owners of a house. The wife started proceedings under the Married Women's Property Act, 1882,[196] for the house to be sold and the proceeds divided between the spouses. The husband was in arrears in paying the wife's maintenance. They agreed tentatively to the transfer of the wife's interest in the house to the husband for £1,500. When the parties came before the magistrates in respect of the maintenance order they came to an oral agreement, subject to the approval of the justices, that: (1) the wife would surrender her interest in the house for £1,500; (2) she would consent to the discharge of the maintenance order in her favour; (3) both would consent to the continuance of the order in favour of the child; (4) the husband would pay part of the arrears and the wife would remit the balance. This was approved by the justices, insofar as they had jurisdiction to do so. They varied the maintenance order and adjourned the proceedings with regard to the arrears. The court officially wrote to the husband to such end. He paid the amount he had agreed to pay the wife from the arrears, and his solicitors sent a form of transfer of her interest in the house to the wife's solicitors for her signature. She returned the transfer saying that she did not find the terms acceptable. When she subsequently

---

192 [1963] 2 Q.B. 169 at 189 (C.A.). Contrast the views of Warrington L.J. in *Chaproniere v. Lambert*, [1917] 2 Ch. 356 at 361 (C.A.).

193 Fry, *Specific Performance*, 5th ed. (1911), p. 278, section 582.

194 [1968] 2 All E.R. 783. Compare the facts in the *Kingswood Estate* case, above, note 192.

195 [1974] 2 All E.R. 977 (H.L.). Contrast the decision in *Rimer v. Rimer* (1981), 119 D.L.R. (3d) 579 (Alta. Q.B.) that an agreement merged in the judgment or order of the court. Compare with the *Steadman* case, *Ethier v. Ethier*, [1987] 4 W.W.R. 641 (Sask. Q.B.), wife sending transfer of her interest in the matrimonial home; *Re Quieting of Titles Act; Maguire v. Patey* (1987), 66 Nfld. & P.E.I.R. 15 (Nfld. T.D.); affirmed (*sub nom. Paton v. Patey*) (1989), 81 Nfld. & P.E.I.R. 312 (Nfld. C.A.), payment of purchase price, taking possession, spending money on improvements.

196 45 & 46 Vict., c. 75.

had the proceedings under the 1882 Act restored for hearing, she contended that the agreement relating to the transfer of her share, being an agreement for the disposition of an interest in land was unenforceable under the provisions of section 40 of the Law of Property Act, 1925[197] which had replaced the relevant passage in section 4 of the Statute of Frauds. She claimed that there was no note or memorandum, nor any act of part performance. By a majority, Lord Morris of Borth-y-Gest dissenting, the House of Lords held that there were sufficient acts of part performance to render the agreement enforceable.

Although the payment of the money by the husband was insufficient in itself, such payment taken into conjunction with the announcement of the oral agreement to the magistrates, the abandonment by the husband of his claim to full remission of the arrears of maintenance, and the preparation and delivery to the wife of a form of transfer for her signature, would indicate that the husband had acted to his detriment in reliance upon a contract of the nature alleged.[198] It was enough for the acts of part performance alleged to point, on the balance of probabilities, to their having performed in reliance on a contract which was consistent with the contract alleged. They did not have to point to the exact contract, or even to a contract of the general nature alleged. What was important was whether, in the circumstances, it was inequitable to allow the defendant, in this instance the wife, to rely on the statutory defence under the 1925 Act (or the Statute of Frauds). Hence payment of a sum of money might, in itself, amount to part performance under the doctrine, even though, in this instance, payment by itself was not enough, and was accompanied by other material and evidentiary acts.[199]

To arrive at this determination, the House had to accept the broader doctrine or version of what had been held in *Maddison v. Alderson*. This is made clear most explicitly in the speech of Lord Simon of Glaisdale.[200] What emerges from that speech in particular is the equitable nature of the doctrine, and the need to interpret and apply it broadly, without requiring too specific a reference from the act or acts of part performance, if jusice is to be done and a defendant prevented from relying unfairly upon the technical defence of the Statute.

The problem is to determine whether, currently in Canada, the more relaxed view of the doctrine is the law, or the older, narrower, stricter version. Not long after the decision in the *Steadman* case authority in favour of its approach was

---

197 15 & 16 Geo. 5, c. 20.

198 Compare the idea that the party performing the act of part performance would be prejudiced if the alleged contract was not recognized and enforced: *Fed. Savings Credit Union Ltd. v. Hessian* (1979), 8 R.P.R. 32 (N.S.T.D.).

199 Contrast the later decisions in *Daulia v. Four Millbank Nominees*, [1978] 2 All E.R. 557 (C.A.); *Re Gonin*, [1977] 2 All E.R. 720 (with which compare *Starlite Variety Stores Ltd. v. Cloverlawn Invt. Ltd.* (1978), 92 D.L.R. (3d) 270 (Ont. H.C.); affirmed (1979), 103 D.L.R. (3d) 192 (Ont. C.A.) in respect of the payment of money as an act of part performance). Compare *Ethier v. Ethier*, above, note 195; *Re Quieting of Titles Act*, above, note 195. In contrast, payment of money, *e.g.*, a share of the deposit on the purchase price of property, was not enough in *Alvi v. Lal*, above, note 184.

200 [1974] 2 All E.R. 977 at 998-1000 (H.L.).

forthcoming in Alberta.[201] In an Ontario case, *Starlite Variety Stores Ltd. v. Cloverlawn Investments Ltd.*,[202] it was held that the payment of money, plus the performance of certain other acts, amounted to sufficient part performance to bring the doctrine into play.[203] More recent decisions also approve and follow the *Steadman* case and adopt a more liberal or relaxed attitude to what are acts of part performance for the purposes of the doctrine.[204] While these decisions point towards the view that reference to some contractual relationship may suffice, there are other cases in which it has been suggested that the acts alleged to be acts of part performance must unequivocally refer to the alleged or asserted contract.[205] Hence in one case,[206] the conduct of the plaintiff, in running his sick brother's farm, was consistent either with an alleged contract of sale of the farm to the brother or with the relationship of landlord and tenant between the brothers. Consequently, the doctrine of part performance was not applied. So, too, building a house on land bought from the defendant was not referable to an alleged contract that the defendant would not build a marina.[207] Nor was making improvements to property referable to a contract of sale as opposed to a tenancy.[208] Moreover, in *Alvi v. Lal*[209] an Ontario judge specifically rejected the *Steadman* case to hold that payment of money cannot constitute part performance of a contract with respect to a contract involving land.

In view of these varied decisions it is suggested that in Canada the question remains unresolved. No clear, undisputed authority has settled whether the proper attitude for courts to adopt is that the acts relied upon must point to the specific contract alleged, or some contract of that type, or need only establish some sort of contract between the parties, thereby permitting the admission of parol evidence to supply the missing information as to the contract and its terms.

---

201 *Colberg v. Braunberger* (1978), 12 A.R. 183 (Alta. C.A.) (where the discussion was *obiter* because there never was any agreement, oral or otherwise; the court did not discuss the Canadian cases); *Re Shillabeer* (1979), 18 A.R. 173 (Alta. S.C.). Contrast the decision of McDonald J. in *Toombs v. Mueller*, [1974] 6 W.W.R. 577 (Alta. S.C.) in favour of the stricter approach; apparently agreed to by the Appellate Division, [1975] 5 W.W.R. 520 (although the trial judge's decision was reversed on other grounds [1975] 3 W.W.R. 96 (Alta. C.A.)). But see *Lensen v. Lensen*, above, note 185. See also *Decorby v. Decorby* (1989), 57 Man. R. (2d) 241 (Man. C.A.).

202 (1978), 92 D.L.R. (3d) 270 (Ont. H.C.); affirmed (1979), 103 D.L.R. (3d) 192 (Ont. C.A.): compare *Severin v. Vroom* (1977), 76 D.L.R. (3d) 427 (Ont. C.A.); *Bunka v. Ruttle Estate* (1987), 62 Sask. R. 129 (Sask. Q.B.).

203 Compare a British Columbia case, *Currie v. Thomas* (1985), 19 D.L.R. (4th) 594 (B.C.C.A.), and one in Saskatchewan, *Bell v. Guaranty Trust Co. of Can.* (1984), 13 D.L.R. (4th) 476 (Sask. C.A.); leave to appeal to S.C.C. refused (1984), 36 Sask. R. 80 (note) (S.C.C.).

204 *Von Richter v. Flett Estate* (1987), 77 N.B.R. (2d) 401 (N.B.C.A.); *Ethier v. Ethier*, above, note 195; *Re Quieting of Titles Act*, above, note 195; *Jenkins v. Strickland* (1990), 83 Nfld. & P.E.I.R. 30 (Nfld. T.D.). See also *Basha v. Basha Estate* (1990), 88 Nfld. & P.E.I.R. 194 (Nfld. T.D.).

205 *Koskolos v. Richard Fry Devs. Ltd.* (1988), 30 C.L.R. 11 (N.S.T.D.); *Carvery v. Fletcher* (1987), 34 D.L.R. (4th) 739 (N.S.T.D.). Contrast the view that both tests must be satisfied; *Harris v. Mohawk Oil Co.* (1979), 103 D.L.R. (3d) 171 (B.C.S.C.).

206 *Syhlonyk v. Syhlonyk* (1982), 20 Sask. R. 354 (Sask. Q.B.).

207 *Koskolos v. Richard Fry Devs. Ltd.*, above, note 205.

208 *Carvery v. Fletcher*, above, note 205.

209 (1990), 13 R.P.R. (2d) 302 at 313 (Ont. H.C.).

Two other points should be mentioned. First, paralleling the issue just debated, there is uncertainty as to whether the alleged acts of part performance must "necessarily imply" the existence of the contract in question (or "a" contract, depending upon whether the narrow or broad view is valid) or support the reasonable inference of a contract on the balance of probability.[210] Second, there is doubt as to whether, once the doctrine is successfully invoked, the court can award damages rather than a decree of specific performance. Canadian cases have gone in both directions.[211] The issue arises from the application of legislation permitting courts of equity to award damages in certain circumstances, and the proper interpretation of the power so conferred on courts.[212] Should the Statute remain in effect in jurisdictions where it has not been repealed, it would seem that the more accepted view is that damages may be awarded for breach of contract where the contract can be established under the doctrine of part performance, regardless of the technicalities of equity and the legislation which extended the remedies available in courts of equity.

Apart from the scope and requirements of the doctrine, there is debate about its juridical nature. One view is that the Statute of Frauds itself is an evidentiary statute only. Therefore, if a contract within its scope is not evidenced by the appropriate writing it may be evidenced otherwise, namely, by acts of part performance. Thus the doctrine is nothing more than a doctrine of evidence, having no substantive effect.[213] A second view is that acts of part performance raise "equities" which render it unjust not to enforce the contract.[214] The purpose of the doctrine is to preclude a defendant from behaving unconscionably, and so causing hardship or prejudice to a plaintiff who has acted on the faith of there being a valid contract between the parties.[215] This view may have been given implicit, if not express, approval by the House of Lords in *Steadman v. Steadman.* Another explanation of the doctrine is that it is a form or variety of "equitable

---

210 Compare *Maddison v. Alderson* (1883), 8 App. Cas. 467 at 483 (H.L.) *per* Lord O'Hagan with *ibid.*, at 476 *per* Lord Selborne. The latter would seem to be the appropriate test in England after the *Steadman* case.

211 In favour of awarding damages: *McIntyre v. Stockdale* (1912), 27 O.L.R. 460 (Ont. H.C.); *Pfeifer v. Pfeifer*, [1950] 2 W.W.R. 1227 (Sask. C.A.); *Brownscombe v. Pub. Trustee (Admin. of Vercamert Estate)*, [1969] S.C.R. 658 (S.C.C.); *Starlite Variety Stores Ltd. v. Cloverlawn Invt. Ltd.*, above, note 199; *Nicol v. Weigel* (1991), 17 R.P.R. (2d) 213 (B.C.C.A.): compare above, note 171. Against *Bennett v. Stodgell* (1916), 36 O.L.R. 45 (Ont. C.A.); *Robinson v. MacAdam*, [1948] 2 W.W.R. 425 (B.C.S.C.); *Carter v. Irving Oil Co.*, [1952] 4 D.L.R. 128 (N.S.S.C.); *Pearson v. Skinner School Bus Lines (St. Thomas) Ltd.*, [1968] 2 O.R. 329 (Ont. H.C.).

212 Below, pp. 706-709; compare above, note 171.

213 See the reference to this statement, and its attribution to the "narrow" view of the doctrine of part performance, above, p. 230, in *Alvi v. Lal* (1990), 13 R.P.R. (2d) 302 at 312 (Ont. H.C.). Compare the remarks of O'Sullivan J.A. in *Decorby v. Decorby* (1989), 57 Man. R. (2d) 241 at 241 (Man. C.A.), that part performance does not prove a contract; it only supplies the want of paper required by the Statute.

214 *Maddison v. Alderson* (1883), 8 App. Cas. 467 (H.L.); *Lensen v. Lensen* (1984), 14 D.L.R. (4th) 611 (Sask. C.A.).

215 Compare *Fed. Savings Credit Union Ltd.v. Hessian* (1979), 8 R.P.R. 32 (NS.T.D.) following and applying *Lohnes v. Daw* (1968), 68 D.L.R. (2d) 730 (N.S.S.C.).

estoppel". The defendant is estopped, even though it is not he, but the plaintiff who has acted, provided that he knew what the plaintiff was doing, acquiesced in such acts, or gave his consent. Even if the defendant did not directly benefit from the plaintiff's acts, the doctrine may be applicable. This seems to be a strange kind of estoppel, which has support in the United States,[216] but not in England, nor in Canada. That the doctrine is equitable in nature is incontrovertible. Hence, it rests upon part performance; full performance by one party of his obligations will not *per se* entitle that party to enforce the contract if the Statute of Frauds requirements have not been satisfied.[217] Since the doctrine is equitable, there may be validity in any one of the notions set out above. Unconscionable behaviour, the creation of "equities", the idea of "estoppel", all relate to, and stem from, the essential basic concept of equity. Which view is the more correct, however, and provides the best explanation of the rationale of the doctrine, is more questionable.

(f) Reform of the law

The Statute of Frauds has been changed in England,[218] its original home, and elsewhere in the common law world, for example, New Zealand[219] and Western Australia.[220] Change has been suggested in other parts of Australia[221] and in the United States.[222] Within Canada, the Statute has been repealed in British Columbia[223] and Manitoba.[224] Reform has also been recommended in Newfoundland[225] and in Ontario.[226]

These developments raise the question whether what is desirable is some reform of the Statute or its total repeal, leaving writing as not a requisite for contracts, unless some other statute, for special reasons, makes such a requirement mandatory. In this respect it is worthy of note that, despite the criticism expressed by the English Law Revision Committee in 1937, total abolition of the requirement of writing did not occur. England has abolished that requirement save in respect of contracts concerning land and contracts that guarantee another's debt. Retention of the

---

216 Above, note 148.

217 *Cocking v. Ward* (1845), 1 C.B. 858 at 868 *per* Tindal C.J.; *Sanderson v. Graves* (1875), L.R. 10 Exch. 234. For a contrary view see *Kinsey v. Nat. Trust Co.* (1904), 15 Man. R. 32 (Man. K.B.); *Spencer v. Spencer* (1913), 4 W.W.R. 785 (Man. K.B.).

218 Law Reform (Enforcement of Contracts) Act, 1954 (2 & 3 Eliz. 2) c. 34; Law of Property (Miscellaneous Provisions) Act, 1989 (U.K.), c. 34.

219 Contracts Enforcement Act, 1956, No. 23, s. 2.

220 Law Reform (Statute of Frauds) Act, 1962, No. 66, s. 2.

221 Law Reform Commission of Queensland, A *Review of the Statute of Frauds* (1970); Law Reform Committee of South Australia, 34th Report, *Statute of Frauds and Cognate Enactments* (1975).

222 Uniform Land Transactions Act: Iowa Code Ann. §622.34, 35 (1950); Alaska Statutes Ann. §09.25.020 (1962).

223 S.B.C. 1985, c. 10, s. 8. Compare above, note 4.

224 S.M. 1982-83-84, c. 34, s. 1.

225 Newfoundland Law Reform Commission, *Discussion Paper on the Statute of Frauds, 1677* (1991).

226 Ontario Law Reform Commission, *Report on Amendment of the Law of Contract* (1987), Chapter 5. See also Bridge, "The Statute of Frauds and Sale of Land Contracts" (1986), 64 Can. Bar Rev. 58.

requirement of writing in relation to land was said to be justified by the need to secure ample time for investigation and reflection. However, the doctrine of part performance may be considered to have outflanked the legislative requirement of writing, and is not based on the ideas of investigation and reflection, but rather on the need to prevent fraud or other unconscionable conduct.

How the statutory provision relating to writing as a requirement of certain contracts has been dealt with in various jurisdictions was described and discussed in the *Report on Amendment of the Law of Contract* produced by the Ontario Law Reform Commission in 1987, which is the latest in a series of such reports that have come out of various jurisdictions. Unlike Manitoba and British Columbia, the Ontario body did not recommend the complete repeal of the Statute. Instead a number of amendments were suggested, with a view to eradicating some of the illogicalities, inconsistencies and difficulties produced by the current law, as contained in the legislation and the case law decided thereunder.[227] These may be summarized as follows.

First it is recommended that the provisions dealing with promises by executors and administrators should be repealed. This is something that is universally recommended even where total repeal is not. In Ontario the provisions of section 5, referred to earlier,[228] are also recommended for repeal. So, too, are the provisions dealing with representation concerning another's creditworthiness and those dealing with contracts not to be performed within a year. As regards the latter, repeal of which has also been recommended in Newfoundland[229] (they have been already in England and New Zealand), repeal is a better solution than that suggested by the New York Law Revision Committee.[230] They proposed retention of this category within the Statute subject to the exemption of contracts fully performed on one side where there was some memorandum, even if an inaccurate one, or the defendant admitted the agreement was a contract of employment for not more than one year from commencement of the work.

With respect to contracts of guarantee, retained within the Statute in England, subject to some modification, the Ontario Commission recommend that contracts of indemnity should be included, that a writing requirement should only be imposed where a guarantee or indemnity is given by someone otherwise than in the course of business to a person acting in the course of business, that such a guarantee or indemnity should be evidenced by some writing signed by the person to be charged or an agent, and that the writing should identify the parties and reasonably indicate that a guarantee has been or is being given. In this regard "given in the course of a business" would include a guarantee or indemnity given by a shareholder, officer or director of a company who guarantees or indemnifies a debt or other obligation of the company. In Alberta the Guarantees Acknowledgement Act[231] makes a guarantee void, not just unenforceable, if certain formalities are not fulfilled,

---

227 *Report*, above, note 226, at pp. 116-117.
228 Above, p. 209, note 11.
229 Above, note 225, at p. 87.
230 *Report*, Leg. Doc. 1957, No. 65A.
231 R.S.A. 1980, c. G-12: compare below, p. 245.

including the notarized signature of the guarantor. The purpose of this legislation is to safeguard people from the indiscreet and foolish undertaking of obligations as guarantors. In Newfoundland it has been suggested that the requirement of writing should be extended to contracts of indemnity and that consideration be given to enacting consumer protection legislation which also goes beyond the limited protection of the writing requirement of the present Statute and the proposed amendment by the Ontario Law Reform Commission. Other suggestions have been that a defendant who admitted the contract in his pleading or testimony could not rely on the Statute, which might lead to perjury or concealment of evidence, evils against which the original Statute was meant to guard. It has also been suggested that a higher standard of proof should be introduced, which would suffice for evidentiary purposes but not others. Alternatively it was suggested that a standard form for guarantees should be created, as in Alberta. The Ontario proposal is somewhat like that contained in the minority report in the English Law Revision Committee's document of 1937, by which contracts of guarantee would be void unless their terms were embodied in a written document. In this respect it is to be noted that the Ontario *Report* also recommends that part performance should not be admitted as a substitute for writing whether such part performance was by the party seeking to enforce the guarantee or indemnity or by the guarantor or indemnitor.

As regards the provisions of the Statute dealing with contracts relating to land, repeal is recommended by the Ontario *Report* subject to a requirement that a contract concerning land should not be enforceable on the evidence of the party alleging the contract unless that evidence is corroborated by some other material evidence. No definition of "land" should be included in any legislation effecting such repeal. This suggestion also appears to receive support and approbation in Newfoundland.[232] The purpose behind the Ontario proposals seems to be to retain the need for some basic substantial proof of the existence of a contract concerning land without necessitating writing, and without utilizing the doctrine of part performance, although acts of part performance might come within the scope of the other corroborating material evidence referred to in the Ontario Law Reform Commission's recommendations.

It is obvious that there are many conflicting views about what should be done with the present law in Ontario, and other provinces where the Statute has not been repealed in its entirety. Although much doubt has been expressed on the issue of abolishing a writing requirement for guarantees and contracts concerning land, the consequences of the repeal of the Statute in Manitoba and British Columbia do not seem to have been harmful to either the legal system or the economy. Perhaps after all the best solution is the simplest.[233]

---

232 Above, note 225, at p. 87.

233 See also Fridman, "The Necessity for Writing in Contracts within the Statute of Frauds" (1986), 35 U.T.L.J. 43.

2. The Sale of Goods Act

(a) The current provisions

Originally the Statute of Frauds also applied to certain contracts for the sale of goods. By section 17,[234]

> No contract for the sale of goods, ware or merchandizes for the price of £10 sterling or upwards shall be allowed to be good except the buyer shall accept part of the goods so sold and actually receive the same, or give something in earnest to bind the bargain or in part payment, or that some note or memorandum in writing of the said bargain be made and signed by the parties to be charged by such contract or their agents thereunto lawfully authorized.

This provision differed from that of section 4. It applied only to sales over a certain sum (which in 1677 was probably quite a large sum). It did not require that the contract be evidenced in writing; there were several alternative grounds upon which the contract could be established. Contracts within this section were also not void or illegal, but simply unenforceable unless the provisions of the Statute were fulfilled.[235]

The English Sale of Goods Act, 1893,[236] replaced this provision with an equivalent one. Canadian statutes which follow the 1893 Act, other than Manitoba and British Columbia,[237] adopted the Statute of Frauds requirement, though some provinces have elaborated upon what is meant by "acceptance".[238] In 1954, England repealed this provision of the 1893 Act[239] so that contracts of sale of goods in England no longer require to be evidenced by writing or otherwise under the Sale of Goods Act. However, no Canadian province other than Manitoba and British Columbia as yet has done the same,[240] with the result that in Canada, except for Manitoba and British Columbia, contracts for the sale of goods for $50 and upwards, which in these days is not a large sum, unlike the original £10 sterling of 1677, must comply with statutory provisions if they are to be enforceable.

This will not prevent property in goods from passing under a contract of sale even if the provisions in question have not been fulfilled. It simply means that neither party will be able to enforce the contract against the other, except where one of the requirements of the appropriate section in the provincial Sale of Goods Act has been met.[241]

---

234 Which ultimately became s. 16 and was amended in England by the Statute of Frauds Amendment Act, 1828 (9 Geo. 4) c. 14, s. 7.

235 *Martin v. Haubner* (1896), 26 S.C.R. 142 (S.C.C.).

236 56 & 57 Vict., c. 71(a).

237 Which exclude any such provision in their statutes, see S.M. 1982-83-84, c. 34; S.B.C. 1958, c. 52, s. 17.

238 See, *e.g.*, R.S.O. 1990, c. S.1, s. 5(3).

239 Law Reform (Enforcement of Contracts) Act, 1954 (2 & 3 Eliz. 2) c. 34.

240 But repeal is recommended by the Ontario Law Reform Commission in its *Report on Sale of Goods* (1979), Vol. I, pp. 107-110; and in Newfoundland (*Discussion Paper* (1991), at p. 79) and Alberta (Alberta Institute of Law Research and Reform, Report No. 44, at p. 28).

241 *Taylor v. Reid* (1906), 13 O.L.R. 205 (Ont. Div. Ct.).

(b) Scope of statute

The Statute of Frauds in its original provision, and the Sale of Goods Act today, refer to "goods". Contracts respecting other types of property may fall within the other section of the Statute of Frauds, but not this one. Hence, the importance of the distinction between "goods" and "land" or "interest in land". This is especially vital because of: (i) the doctrine of part performance in equity,[242] and (ii) the application of alternative modes of proof of a contract of sale of goods.

The Sale of Goods Act defines goods as including "emblements, industrial growing crops and things attached to or forming part of the land which are agreed to be severed before sale or under the contract of sale."[243] Emblements, that is, what is produced annually as a result of agricultural labour, with "industrial growing crops", make up *fructus industriales*, the other crops being products which are not annual or permanent. *Fructus naturales* cover all such natural products as grow on land, even if originally sown by man, according to the leading pre-1893 case of *Marshall v. Green*[244] which has been followed in Canada.[245] Sales of such things will not be sales of goods unless the things in question are to be severed from the land by virtue of the contract under which they are sold (no matter at what time the severance is to take place). This suggests that *all* such contracts will be sales of goods, since there is no point in selling such things unless the intention is that they should be severed from the land and ultimately delivered to, or taken by the buyer. So much follows from a number of Canadian cases, in which English authority before and after the 1893 Act was followed.[246] However, there is at least one decision, *Sharpe v. Dundas*,[247] in which a sale of *fructus naturales* was a sale of an interest in land, not a sale of goods. There the contract was for the sale of hay grown one year on a stipulated piece of land. At the time of the contract no grass or hay was growing on the land. Hence, the contract was held not to be one for the sale of goods.

Contracts under which the "seller" is to manufacture and then deliver some chattel to the buyer also raise the problem of whether "goods" are involved. It has been argued in certain instances that the contract is one for work and labour, that is, for services, not one for the sale of goods, even though incidentally something

---

242 Which probably only applies to land, above, pp. 228-229.

243 Fridman, *Sale of Goods in Canada*, 3rd ed. (1986), pp. 16-17.

244 (1875), 1 C.P.D. 35; distinguished in *Lavery v. Pursell* (1888), 39 Ch. D. 508.

245 *Gardner v. Staples* (1915), 8 W.W.R. 397 (Sask. C.A.).

246 The intention may be implied, see *Fredkin v. Glines* (1908), 9 W.L.R. 393 (Man. C.A.). Compare *Messervey v. Central Can. Canning Co.*, [1923] 3 W.W.R. 365 (Man. K.B.). In *Hingley v. Lynds* (1918), 44 D.L.R. 743 (N.S.C.A.) this was the decision on an equal division of the Nova Scotia court. Compare further *Jones & Sons v. Tankerville*, [1909] 2 Ch. 440 with *Morgan v. Russell*, [1909] 1 K.B. 357 (followed in *Saskatoon Sand & Gravel Ltd. v. Steve* (1973), 40 D.L.R. (3d) 248 (Sask. Q.B.); affirmed (1979), 97 D.L.R. (3d) 685 (Sask. C.A.) in which an agreement to dig and remove gravel was held to be the grant of a *profit à prendre*).

247 (1911), 18 W.L.R. 86 (Man. C.A.).

tangible changes hands at the end of the "seller's" work.[248] Thus, if S paints B's portrait, there is work which also involves the transfer of property in the canvas and paints used. But such a contract may or may not be one of sale of goods.[249] Only if the "essential character" of the agreement is for the sale of goods will it fall within the Act. In saying this Culliton J.A. of the Saskatchewan Court of Appeal, in a case upheld by the Supreme Court of Canada on other grounds, *Preload Co. of Canada v. Regina (City),*[250] was following English authority, in particular the decision in *Clay v. Yates*[251] which was followed more recently in *Robinson v. Graves.*[252] Despite some differing English and Canadian expression of opinion, this appears to be the better and the more acceptable test of the distinction between a contract of sale of goods and a contract for services.[253]

(c) Requirements of the statute

(i) *General*

For a contract to be enforceable under the Sale of Goods Act, one of three alternatives must be satisfied. The buyer must accept part of the goods sold and actually receive them, or the buyer must give something by way of earnest or in part payment, or there must be some note or memorandum signed by the party to be charged or his agent.

(ii) *Acceptance*

What is meant by "acceptance" under this provision of the Sale of Goods Act is not the same as acceptance for the purposes of the sections of the Act which relate to the buyer's performance of his duties and the extinction of his remedies against the seller in the event of acceptance by the buyer of faulty goods.[254] What

---

248 See, *e.g., Scott Maritimes Pulp Ltd. v. B.F. Goodrich Can. Ltd.* (1977), 72 D.L.R. (3d) 680 (N.S.C.A.); *Markland Assoc. Ltd. v. Lohnes* (1973), 33 D.L.R. (3d) 493 (N.S.S.C.); *Brunswick Glass Ltd. v. United Contractors Ltd.* (1975), 12 N.B.R. (2d) 631 (N.B. Co. Ct.); *Hodgkinson v. Hitch House Ltd.* (1987), 60 O.R. (2d) 793 (Ont. Div. Ct.). Compare *Gee v. White Spot Ltd.* (1986), 32 D.L.R. (4th) 238 (B.C.S.C.), where it was argued, successfully, that where a customer was served food in a restaurant this was a contract of sale, not a contract for services.
249 *Isaacs v. Hardy* (1884), Cab. & E. 287.
250 (1958), 13 D.L.R. (2d) 305 at 314 (Sask. C.A.); affirmed (1959), 20 D.L.R. (2d) 586 (S.C.C.).
251 (1856), 1 H. & N. 73. But contrast the view in *Lee v. Griffin* (1861), 30 L.J.Q.B. 252, approved by Chisholm C.J. in *Ross v. Sadofsky,* [1943] 1 D.L.R. 334 (N.S.C.A.).
252 [1935] 1 K.B. 579 (C.A.). Compare *Marcel (Furriers) v. Tapper,* [1953] 1 W.L.R. 49.
253 *Kellion West Ltd. v. Sportspage Enterprises Ltd.* (1982), 23 Alta. L.R. (2d) 99 (Alta. Q.B.); *Unident Ltd. v. Delong, Joyce & Ash Temple Ltd.* (1981), 50 N.S.R. (2d) 1 (N.S.T.D.).
    Note that the contract must be a contract of sale and not, *e.g.,* an executory agreement for a future sale: *Royal Bank v. Gerald C. Sarchfield & Sons Ltd.* (1986), 72 N.B.R. (2d) 124 (N.B.Q.B.); but the seller need not be the owner, as long as he is acting as the owner's agent, *e.g.,* in the case of a sale on consignment for the owner: *Yellowknife Auto Body (1983) Ltd. v. Poluk,* [1987] N.W.T.R. 143 (N.W.T. Terr. Ct.).
254 Fridman, above, note 243, at pp. 45, 247-254; *Abbott & Co. v. Wolsey,* [1895] 2 Q.B. 97 (C.A.); *Ross v. Sadofsky,* above, note 251.

is involved here is some act done in relation to a completed chattel. Hence, a statement made by the buyer to the seller as to the proper size of a refrigerator box that was being manufactured by the seller for the buyer, such statement being made while the box was in the process of manufacture, was not an act of acceptance so as to evidence the oral contract and make it thereby enforceable.[255] But payment for part of an order of goods which had been delivered was acceptance not only of the part delivered but of all the goods.[256] It has also been held that *rejection* of goods can be acceptance of them for this purpose.[257] And this may be especially true where the defendant later sets out this rejection in his pleadings.[258] Such acts constitute evidence of the existence of the contract that is being alleged and that appears to be the function of the alternative requirements of the Act.[259]

What is meant by "actual receipt"? The cases indicate that it imports delivery,[260] that is, that the buyer must acquire some sort of possession at some time, even if he later rejects. This may include some act which evidences control or purported control over the goods on the part of the buyer. Thus in *McLean v. McGhee*[261] the buyer attempted to sell the goods to a third party and allowed such third party to take and try the goods. This was acceptance and receipt for the purposes of the Statute of Frauds and the Sale of Goods Act. Here the buyer's conduct evidenced a pre-existing contract of sale. He was dealing with the goods as if they were in his actual possession. Hence in *Woods v. James*[262] there was no acceptance and receipt of goods in the possession of X which had been sold by the seller to the buyer where the buyer did not take possession of them from X and X had not acknowledged that he held them on the buyer's behalf, having previously held them on behalf of the seller.

(iii) *Earnest or part payment*

Earnest is something given by the buyer, at the time of the contract, and

---

255 *Ross v. Sadofsky*, above, note 251. See also *Unident Ltd. v. Delong, Joyce & Ash Temple Ltd.*, above, note 253.

256 *Slobodian v. Knight*, [1921] 3 W.W.R. 399 (Alta. C.A.).

257 *Thames Canning Co. v. Eckardt* (1915), 34 O.L.R. 72 (Ont. H.C.). But this would seem to involve examination of the goods *first*. If all that occurs is that the buyer is provided with an opportunity to examine, but does not do so, this is insufficient for the Statute: compare *Sears Ltd. v. Hacker*, [1946] O.W.N. 201 (Ont. H.C.); affirmed [1946] O.W.N. 352 (Ont. C.A.).

258 *Materne (J.) Design & Const. Ltd. v. Gendel*, [1971] 2 O.R. 176 (Ont. C.A.); *Brunswick Glass Ltd. v. United Contractors Ltd.*, above, note 248.

259 Hence, if the consideration for the sale is wholly executed on one side, written proof of the contract is not required; this is either part performance or something similar: *Covlin v. Covlin*, [1920] 3 W.W.R. 812 (Sask. C.A.). Compare *Lavery v. Turley* (1860), 6 H. & N. 239. Contrast *Sears Ltd. v. Hacker*, above. note 257, on what is part performance under the Sale of Goods Act. Compare also *Freedman v. French* (1921), 50 O.L.R. 432 (Ont. C.A.), citing *Plevins v. Downing* (1876), 1 C.P.D. 220; *Sierichs v. Hughes* (1918), 42 O.L.R. 608 (Ont. C.A.).

260 *Woods v. James*, [1946] O.W.N. 101 (Ont. C.A.).

261 [1920] 2 W.W.R. 394 (Man. C.A.), following *Chaplin v. Rogers* (1800), 1 East. 192; *Abbott & Co. v. Wolsey*, [1895] 2 Q.B. 97 (C.A.); *Taylor v. Great Eastern Ry. Co.*, [1901] 1 K.B. 774.

262 Above, note 260.

accepted by the seller as indicating the completion of the contract. To be earnest it must be given outright by the buyer to the seller with no hope or intention of being returned. A part payment, on the other hand, is made *after* the contract and is not made as part of the process of contracting. It is a question of fact whether anything which may have gone from buyer to seller is given as either earnest or part payment.

(iv) *A note or memorandum*

The note or memorandum must contain the essential terms of the contract. These include the identity of the parties, the subject matter of the sale, the consideration, that is, the price, if it was agreed upon,[263] and possibly the place of delivery of the goods[264] where that differs from the statutory place of delivery, which is the seller's place of business if he has one.[265] What is involved are all the terms which are agreed upon between the parties at the time the memorandum was made and signed.[266] This will suffice even if the contract does not specify precisely the consideration. Thus, in one case[267] the memorandum spoke of a consideration of "one dollar and other valuable consideration (the receipt whereof is hereby acknowledged)." It was held that this was enough to fulfil the requirements of the Statute.

The document may in fact consist of more than one piece of writing (just as in cases under the Statute of Frauds).[268] But one piece of writing must refer to the other so as to enable or permit them to be joined together to form the requisite memorandum.[269] This may be done by parol evidence, as long as such evidence does not vary the terms of a document which clearly manifests the original agreement between the parties.[270] This is true even if the variation refers only to a part of the contract that need not itself be evidenced in writing.[271] Even if the document repudiates the contract, it will be a sufficient note or memorandum, as long as in the course of repudiating the contract the document sets out the terms which are being repudiated.[272]

---

263 *Berry v. Robinson* (1921), 49 N.B.R. 166 (N.B.C.A.).

264 *Calgary Grain Co. v. Nordness*, [1917] 2 W.W.R. 713 (Alta. C.A.); *Calgary Grain Co. v. Liddle*, [1917] 2 W.W.R. 717 (Alta. C.A.).

265 Fridman, above, note 243, p. 228.

266 *Berry v. Robinson*, above, note 263. Note that what suffices under this provision might not be enough under s. 4 of the Statute of Frauds: *Sarl v. Bourdillon* (1856), 1 C.B.N.S. 188 at 196 *per* Cresswell J. As to reference to *part* of the goods, see *Slobodian v. Knight*, above, note 256.

267 *Can. Williston Minerals Ltd. v. Forseth* (1962), 33 D.L.R. (2d) 72 (Sask. C.A.). Contrast *Fennell v. Fisher*, [1947] 2 W.W.R. 1007 (Sask. C.A.).

268 Above, pp. 221-223.

269 *Smith v. Spencer* (1918), 42 D.L.R. 269 (Sask. C.A.); *Steine v. Mathieu*, [1923] 3 W.W.R. 493 (Sask. C.A.). Contrast *Fennell v. Fisher*, above, note 267.

270 *Smith v. Spencer*, above, note 269.

271 *Nugent v. Davies*, [1923] 1 D.L.R. 1040 (Ont. C.A.). Compare *Freedman v. French*, above, note 259.

272 *Martin v. Haubner* (1896), 26 S.C.R. 142 (S.C.C.); *Sears Ltd. v. Hacker*, above, note 257, following *Thirkell v. Cambi*, [1919] 2 K.B. 590 (C.A.).

The signature does not have to be a signature in the strict sense, as long as it applies to the whole document and indicates who is to be charged, that is, who is the defendant. It may be that of an agent of the defendant,[273] as long as he has authority to sign at the time he appends his signature. Hence, in *Moyer & Co. v. Smith & Goldberg Ltd.*,[274] since the agent's authority had been removed prior to his signing the contract, the Statute had not been fulfilled.

(d) **Reform of the law**

It has been suggested that the provisions of the Act, like those of the Statute of Frauds, are useful and serve an important function. Hence, the Statute should not be tampered with, or its provisions cavalierly interpreted and applied, in order to do justice in a particular case, even at the expense of the strict law.[275] It is not surprising, however, that this provision of the Statute of Frauds (now the Sale of Goods Act) has come under criticism in the same way as those of section 4 of the original Statute.

In the United States, the Uniform Commercial Code[276] attempted to clarify and reorganize the law in the light of social and commercial needs and practice, without going to the extreme of removing the requirement of writing altogether from the law of sale of goods. England, on the other hand, abolished these provisions of the Sale of Goods Act.[277] So too have Manitoba, British Columbia, and New Zealand. It may be suggested that in modern society no very important purpose is achieved, and no interest is protected, by retention of this provision. The value of the goods which it excludes is almost derisory in a modern inflationary economy; important contracts will probably be in writing in any event and many transactions involving goods now come within the purview of other statutes which in some way or other require writing, and other formalities, which make the requirements of the Sale of Goods Act somewhat outmoded and archaic. It is suggested that the time has come for the removal of these provisions from the law relating to sale of goods.[278]

3. Other statutes

In many jurisdictions in Canada there are statutes of more modern origin, apart from those which have amended or repealed in part the Statute of Frauds, under the provisions of which some kind of writing (and possibly something even more formal, such as a deed which requires registration with a public functionary or on a public register), must be made by one or both parties to a transaction

---

273 Or of both parties: *May v. Conn* (1911), 23 O.L.R. 102 (Ont. Dist. Ct.).

274 [1929] S.C.R. 625 (S.C.C.).

275 *Thirkell v. Cambi*, above, note 272, at 596-597 *per* Scrutton L.J.

276 U.C.C. §2-201.

277 Law Reform (Enforcement of Contracts) Act, 1954 (2 & 3 Eliz. 2) c. 34.

278 Compare Ontario Law Reform Commission, *Report on Sale of Goods* (1979), Vol. I, pp. 107-110, recommending repeal of these provisions in Ontario.

if the transaction in question is to have any, or some certain legal effect. Since there are statutes which are commonly found across Canada and there are also some which are unique to one province or only found in a few provinces, it consequently is unnecessary to do more than to alert the reader to the possibility that, within his particular jurisdiction, there may be certain other contracts, over and above those within the Statute of Frauds or the Sale of Goods Act, in respect of which some documentary evidence is required.[279]

One statute which stands out as unique and as a gloss upon the Statute of Frauds is the Guarantees Acknowledgement Act of Alberta.[280] Under this Act contracts of guarantee have to be in specified form, with a statement sworn before a notary public to the effect that the guarantor understood what he was doing, or else the guarantee will be void. A contract will be within this Act even if it is described as an "indemnity".[281] Certain guarantees are exempt from the Act's requirements.[282] Where the Act applies, however, its requirements relate to the evidence of a satisfactory guarantee.[283]

Other statutes have a wider import and relate to such diverse types of contracts as insurance,[284] door-to-door sales, assignment, hiring of teachers, carriage of goods or passengers by rail, bills of sale, and deductions from employees' wages. In all these instances (and there may be more depending upon the province) it is important to have regard to the specific statutory provisions in order to understand exactly what is required of the parties to make a valid, enforceable contract.

---

279 See, for example, Consumer Credit Transactions Act, S.A. 1985, c. C-22.5, s. 21; Consumer Protection Act, R.S.B.C. 1979, c. 65, s. 12 [am. 1986, c. 5, s. 2]; Consumer Protection Act, R.S.M. 1987, c. C200 [am. 1989-90, c. 53, s. 7]; Direct Sellers Act, R.S.S. 1978, c. D-28, s. 22 [am. 1986, c. 29, s. 6]; Prepaid Funeral Services Act, S.S. 1986, c. P-22.3, ss. 13-15; Prepaid Services Act, R.S.O. 1990, c. P.22, ss. 3-6.

280 R.S.A. 1980, c. G-12.

281 *Crown Lbr. Co. v. Engel* (1961), 36 W.W.R. 128 (Alta. C.A.); *Bank of B.C. v. Hayes* (1980), 116 D.L.R. (3d) 726 (Alta. Q.B.).

282 *Goodyear Tire & Rubber Co. v. Knight* (1960), 33 W.W.R. 287 (Alta. C.A.).

283 *Gen. Tire & Rubber Co. v. Finkelstein* (1967), 62 W.W.R. 380 (Alta. S.C.); *Indust. Accept. Corp. v. Hepworth Motors Ltd.* (1965), 52 W.W.R. 555 (Alta. S.C.). See generally, *Edmonton Airport Hotel Co. v. Crédit Foncier Franco-Canadien*, [1965] S.C.R. 441 (S.C.C.).

284 *Green Forest Lbr. Ltd. v. Gen. Security Ins. Co.* (1980), 34 N.R. 303 (S.C.C.), dealing with the Ontario Marine Insurance Act.

7

Mistake

1. General principles

(a) Mistake and agreement

Contract depends upon agreement.[1] There must be *consensus ad idem.*[2] Sometimes what appears to be a valid contract is the product of a mistake by one or both parties. Such a mistake may pertain to the terms of the contract, or it may relate to the existence or nature of the subject-matter of the contract. The former has been described[3] as a mistake in contractual terms, the latter as a mistake in assumptions. Whichever kind of mistake it may be, the problem arises whether a contract negotiated under such circumstances can be considered a valid, binding agreement, enforceable in law.[4] In this regard recent developments, arising from

---

1 This and the next five sentences were quoted by Hunter J. in *Building Design 2 Ltd. v. Wascana Rehabilitation Centre*, [1992] 6 W.W.R. 343 at 358 (Sask. Q.B.).

2 Above, pp. 15-18. If there is no mistake, then it is unnecessary to consider these issues: *Husky Oil Operations Ltd. v. Forest Oil Corp.* (1991), 79 Alta. L.R. (2d) 134 (Alta. C.A.); leave to appeal to S.C.C. refused (1991), 81 Alta. L.R. (2d) lxvii (note) (S.C.C.).

3 Palmer, *Mistake and Unjust Enrichment* (1962): see Waddams, *Law of Contracts*, 3rd ed. (1993), pp. 207-271. This differentiation is also adopted in the Ontario Law Reform Commission, *Report on Amendment of the Law of Contract* (1987), pp. 253-270, and the reforms recommended are based thereon: *ibid.*, pp. 264-266, 270. See also *Vandekerhove v. Litchfield* (1993), 103 D.L.R. (4th) 739 at 750 (B.C.S.C.) *per* Skipp J.

4 It has given rise to a voluminous literature: see, *e.g.*, Weir, "Mistake in the Law of Contracts" (1941), 19 Can. Bar Rev. 391; Shatwell, "The Supposed Doctrine of Mistake in Contract: A Comedy of Errors" (1955), 33 Can. Bar Rev. 166; Cartwright, "Solle v. Butcher and the Doctrine of Mistake in Contract" (1987), 103 L.Q.R. 594. Compare also Treitel (1988), 104 L.Q.R. 501. For the notion

the equitable jurisdiction of the courts, have modified earlier, stricter doctrines of the common law.

Two opposing principles may be seen operating in cases in which mistake has been pleaded in order to relieve a party from liability, or potential liability, under a contract. On the one hand, there is the attitude that agreements must be kept, that there is a sanctity about contract which makes it important, indeed imperative not to permit a party to resile from an agreement once it has been made.[5] On the other hand, even prior to equitable developments, the common law was prepared to accept that there might be circumstances in which it would be unjust to hold a party to a bargain which he had made, in consequence of a mistake. The operation of any doctrine or doctrines of mistake had to be kept within narrow limits, however, because of the dangerous confusion that would arise if a man were able to disown a contract which he had once made by accepting an offer.[6]

One interpretation of the common-law doctrine of mistake is to regard it as an aspect of offer and acceptance. An offer that is made in error, for example, as where the offeror intended to say $200 a ton but wrote $20 by mistake, may be an offer that cannot be validly accepted by the other party.[7] An acceptance that is in error, for example, where the offeror intended to offer rolled gold and the offeree intended to accept pure gold, may not be a valid acceptance.[8] Such

of "risk" in relation to mistake, see Swan, "The Allocation of Risk in the Analysis of Mistake and Frustration," Reiter and Swan, *Studies in Contract Law*, p. 182. For economic analysis of the mistake problem, see Kronman, "Mistake, Disclosure, Information and the Law of Contracts" (1978), 7 J. Legal Stud. 1; Smith and Smith, "Contract Law, Mutual Mistake and Incentives to Produce and Disclose Information" (1990), 19 J. Leg. Stud. 467.

5 Compare Steyn J. in *Associated Japanese Bank (Int.) v. Crédit du Nord S.A.*, [1988] 3 All E.R. 902 at 912 (Q.B.D.): "The first imperative must be that the law ought to uphold rather then destroy apparent contracts."

6 Compare Munroe J. in *Royal Bank v. Hale* (1961), 30 D.L.R. (2d) 138 at 150 (B.C.S.C.). Hence, possibly, the idea that any discussion of the effect of the mistake may be unnecessary because the contract itself, by express or implied condition precedent, may provide who bears the risk of a mistake: *Associated Japanese Bank* case, above, note 5, at 912: compare *Can. Medical Laboratories Ltd. v. Stabile* (1992), 25 R.P.R. (2d) 106 at 132-134 (Ont. Gen. Div.) *per* Mandel J. In that case the doctrine of common law mutual mistake was not available to the plaintiff, because the risk was on the plaintiff. On the issue of risk, see the Ontario Law Reform Commission *Report*, above, note 3, at p. 256. For an instance of a decision based on the implication of a condition precedent see *Centurion Invts. Ltd. v. N.M. Skalbania Ltd.* (1983), 22 Sask. R. 241 (Sask. C.A.).

7 This sentence was quoted by Estey J. in *R. v. Ron Engineering & Const. (Eastern) Ltd.* (1981), 119 D.L.R. (3d) 267 at 277 (S.C.C.).

8 E.g., *Dalewood Invts. Ltd. v. Maida* (1982), 40 O.R. (2d) 472 (Ont. C.A.); affirmed (1985), 50 O.R. (2d) 223 (S.C.C.) (error about subdivision plans); *Sinnott v. Amaria* (1981), 29 Nfld. & P.E.I.R. 428 (Nfld. Dist. Ct.). See, however, *Walton v. Landstock Invts. Ltd.* (1976), 72 D.L.R. (3d) 195 (Ont. C.A.) in which a counter-offer made changes in the original offer, not noted by the original offeror; he accepted, under a mistaken belief of the contents of the offer. It was held that the contract was valid, but subject to avoidance on the part of the original offeror, i.e., the acceptor of the counter-offer, on the ground of innocent misrepresentation. It was also said, at 199 by Houlden J.A., that the party adding a term by innocent misrepresentation could not rely on such term. Is this a suggestion of invalidity by reason of mistake? See also a case which did turn on mistake, entitling the mistaken party to *equitable* relief: *Stepps Invt. Ltd. v. Security Capital Corp.* (1976), 73 D.L.R. (3d) 351 (Ont. H.C.).

situations are illustrated by the "tender" cases, those in which a party tendering for a contract has submitted an incorrect tender in consequence of a mistake in calculating the price at which the work is to be done.[9] The party calling for tenders accepts the tender and is then informed by the tenderer of the mistake. Is the purported acceptance of the tender valid so as to produce a binding contract between the parties? Prior to the decision of the Supreme Court of Canada in *R. v. Ron Engineering & Construction (Eastern) Ltd.*,[10] the case law indicated that in such situations "an offeree cannot accept an offer which he knows has been made by mistake and which affects a fundamental term of the contract."[11] In the *Ron Engineering* case, however, the facts of which have been analyzed elsewhere,[12] the court construed the situation as giving rise to two distinct contracts. The first came into existence when the tender was submitted. Although this tender may have contained a mistake, that mistake did not affect the validity of the contract under which the tenderer could not withdraw the tender for 60 days after the date of the opening of tenders. The reason assigned by the court for this was because the tenderer intended to submit the very tender submitted, including the price (that is, the erroneous price) therein stipulated.[13] Although the "acceptance" of the offer contained in the property owner's advertisement for tenders was therefore based

---

9 *Hamilton Bd. of Education v. U.S. Fidelity & Guar. Co.*, [1960] O.R. 594 (Ont. H.C.); *Metro. Toronto v. Poole Const. Ltd.* (1979), 10 M.P.L.R. 157 (Ont. H.C.); *296349 Ont. Ltd. v. Halton Bd. of Education* (1980), 126 D.L.R. (3d) 439 (Ont. H.C.); affirmed (1981), 130 D.L.R. (3d) 192 (Ont. C.A.); *Kawneer Co. Can. v. Bank of Can.* (1982), 40 O.R. (2d) 275 (Ont. C.A.); *Belle River Community Arena Inc. v. W.J.C. Kaufmann Co.* (1978), 87 D.L.R. (3d) 761 (Ont. C.A.); *Defence Const. (1951) Ltd. v. Municipal Enterprises Ltd.* (1985), 23 D.L.R. (4th) 653 (N.S.C.A.). Contrast *Custom Iron & Machinery Ltd. v. Calorific Const. Ltd.* (1990), 39 C.L.R. 276 (Ont. Dist. Ct.), where the party tendering for the sub-contract was bound by his error in the tender: compare *Northern Const. Co. v. Gloge Heating & Plumbing Ltd.* (1984), 6 D.L.R. (4th) 450 (Alta. Q.B.); affirmed (1986), 27 D.L.R. (4th) 264 (Alta. C.A.); *Calgary (City) v. Northern Const. Co.*, [1986] 2 W.W.R. 426 (Alta. C.A.); affirmed [1987] 2 S.C.R. 757 (S.C.C.). See Fridman, "Tendering Problems" (1987), 66 Can. Bar Rev. 582 at pp. 607-613; Blom (1987-88), 13 Can. Bus. L.J. 203; (1988-89), 14 Can. Bus. L.J. 494.

Another illustration may be the English case of *Upton-on-Severn Rural District Council v. Powell*, [1942] 1 All E.R. 220 (C.A.). There the farmer whose farm caught fire telephoned the police for the fire brigade. If the correct fire brigade had come there would have been no charge to be paid for their services by the farmer. The brigade that came sought to recover a charge for their services. This depended upon whether the request made by the farmer could be said to be an offer to such brigade to hire their services. The fire brigade came because they believed they were obliged to come, because of the erroneous understanding that the farm was inside their district. Thus, the brigade in question was not really accepting an offer to pay for their services. Nonetheless recovery was permitted. It was held that the brigade that came had the intention of charging if the farm were outside their district (as it turned out to be), and so not entitled to free, obligatory services. The test applied was an objective one, namely, would the reasonable bystander have understood that the farmer intended to pay and the brigade intended to be paid (a strange concept to apply in the emergency situation that had arisen). A better approach would have been to say that the farmer, the alleged offeror, had no intention of offering to pay for fire brigade services, or that the brigade had no intention of accepting an offer to pay.

10 (1981), 119 D.L.R. (3d) 267 (S.C.C.).

11 (1980), 98 D.L.R. (3d) 548 at 550 (Ont. C.A.) *per* Arnup J.A.; reversed [1981] 1 S.C.R. 111 (S.C.C.).

12 Above, pp. 36-39, 74.

13 Above, note 10, at 275.

on a mistake, it was not a mistaken acceptance. Hence, that contract was not to be impugned on the ground of mistake. The second, or construction contract came into existence at the time when the property owner accepted the tender. This was not invalidated for mistake for two reasons.[14] First, the tenderer intended to submit the tender in form and substance as it was. Second, there was no principle of law which rendered the tender incapable of acceptance by the property owner. The latter had not been informed about the mistake at the time the tender was submitted, nor at the time of the tender's acceptance. The situation was not governed by the law of mistake in contracting; it was regulated by the forfeiture provisions contained in the tender documents.[15]

Not all instances of operative mistake concern errors in relation to offer or acceptance. Offer and acceptance may correspond, and may therefore appear to reveal all the features of a valid contract. However, offer and acceptance alike may be founded upon some mistake. This can occur, for example, where offeror and offeree purport to contract about an object which both believed to be in existence, when in fact it had been destroyed by fire.[16] Such instances do not support the theory or view that mistake relates to offer and acceptance. What, perhaps more correctly, is happening in such an instance is that there is a factor present which *nullifies* consent, rather than *negatives* it, as in the other cases. Such a distinction has been drawn.[17] In *McMaster University v. Wilchar Construction Ltd.*,[18] Thompson J. of the Ontario High Court suggested that only mistake nullifying consent was truly mistake in law. Mistake which negatived consent did not share this status,

> . . . as it prevents the formation of contract due to the lack of consensus and the parties are never *ad idem*. It is rather an illustration of the fundamental principle that there can be no contract without consensus of all parties to the terms intended. This is but another way of saying that the offer and the acceptance must be coincident or must exactly correspond before a valid contract results.

Between nullifying and negativing consent there is a fine, even nebulous distinction. Despite the authority of Lord Atkin's statement in *Bell v. Lever Brothers Ltd.*,[19] it is a questionable mode of differentiating mistakes which affect the validity of a contract and mistakes which do not. A mistake with respect to an offer or an acceptance does affect the extent to which parties have fulfilled their contractual intentions. So, too, does a mistake that does not relate to either offer or acceptance but destroys the basis on which the parties have contracted, for instance where they are contracting about something that does not exist, or ceased to exist at the time of contracting, or where they are contracting about different things, though

---

14 *Ibid.*

15 *Ibid.*, at 276.

16 Compare *Centurion Invts. Ltd. v. N.M. Skalbania Ltd.* (1981), 12 Sask. R. 79 (Sask. Q.B.); affirmed (1983), 22 Sask. R. 241 (Sask. C.A.).

17 *Bell v. Lever Brothers Ltd.*, [1932] A.C. 161 at 217 (H.L.) *per* Lord Atkin.

18 (1971), 22 D.L.R. (3d) 9 at 18 (Ont. H.C.); affirmed (1973), 69 D.L.R. (3d) 400n (Ont. C.A.).

19 Above, note 17.

their errors do not precisely correspond. Analytically speaking, there are more appropriate distinctions that will be drawn later.

The common law has insisted upon there being an error which is fundamental in character, something essential, going to the root of the contract.[20] Only such a mistake will destroy the intent of the party in question, so as to invalidate his offer or acceptance. Only such a mistake will destroy the apparent agreement of the parties, that is, will undermine the appearance of *consensus* which is manifested to the outside world by their language or conduct. There must be what was called by Wills J.A., in *R. v. Ontario Flue-cured Tobacco Growers' Marketing Board; Ex parte Grigg*,[21] "a false and fundamental assumption", under which the parties contracted.[22] In *Bell v. Lever Brothers Ltd.*,[23] a decision of the House of Lords which has been frequently cited and followed with approval in Canadian courts, Lord Atkin analyzed the nature of fundamental error at common law and went to great pains to point out the distinction between a mistake which went to the root of a contract so as to make it void *ab initio*, and a mistake which had no such effect. In essence, it would seem, the common law was attempting to draw a distinction between a mistake which affected the *intention to contract* and a mistake which operated on the mistaken party's *motive for contracting*.[24] Only the former relieves him from his apparent obligation; the latter is not something of which the common law will take cognizance (in the absence of fraud, that is, a misrepresentation, which may entitle the mistaken party to avoid the transaction).[25]

It is now clear that the approach adopted by the common law has been affected by equitable doctrines. "Today, it is clear that mistake in equity is not circumscribed by common law definitions."[26] Hence, it is necessary to consider the common law and equitable approaches to mistake separately, although the two disctinct views will be applicable in appropriate situations. Fundamental mistake is still relevant. But other factors may play apart.

---

20 *Morrison v. Burton* (1955), 15 W.W.R. 667 at 671 (Alta. S.C.) *per* Egbert J. Hence, the death of one of the principals to a projected contract was a material fact, the concealment of which meant that no contract was concluded: *MacKenzie v. Carroll* (1974), 6 O.R. (2d) 706 (Ont. H.C.).

21 (1965), 51 D.L.R. (2d) 7 at 14 (Ont. C.A.). This case was referred to and followed in *Can. Medical Laboratories Ltd. v. Stabile*, above, note 6, at 128-130.

22 This sentence was cited by Glube J. in *Clintar Spray & Environmental Ent. Inc. v. Municipal Spraying & Contracting Ltd.* (1978), 27 N.S.R. (2d) 682 at 693 (N.S.T.D.); affirmed on other grounds (1978), 30 N.S.R. (2d) 451 (N.S.C.A.).

23 [1932] A.C. 161 at 217-218, 224-226 (H.L.).

24 Compare Coady J.A. in *Imperial Glass Co. v. Consol. Supplies Ltd.* (1960), 22 D.L.R. (2d) 759 at 763, 765 (B.C.C.A.); see also *Clintar Spray & Environmental Ent. Inc. v. Municipal Spraying & Contracting Ltd.* (1978), 27 N.S.R. (2d) 682 (N.S.T.D.); affirmed on other grounds (1978), 30 N.S.R. (2d) 451 (N.S.C.A).

25 This and the previous sentence were cited by Glube J. in the *Clintar Spray* case, above, note 24, at 696.

26 *Associated Japanese Bank (Int.) Ltd. v. Crédit du Nord S.A.*, [1988] 3 All E.R. 902 at 911 (Q.B.D.) *per* Steyn J. This case was cited and referred to by Mandel J. in *Can. Medical Laboratories Ltd. v. Stabile*, above, note 6.

(b) Fundamental mistake in England

The doctrine of fundamental or substantial error going to the root of the contract, as explained in *Bell v. Lever Brothers Ltd.*,[27] stems from earlier English cases connecting mistake and total failure of consideration.[28] The real issue was whether a contracting party had obtained what he had intended to obtain by the bargain into which he entered. If the answer to this question was in the negative, and the reason for this discrepancy was that such party was mistaken, the contract might be void at common law, or voidable (if the mistake had been induced by some misrepresentation, either fraudulent or innocent). If the party alleging mistake had obtained what he had contracted to obtain, but it later turned out to be different in some way, not as valuable, not as good, not as useful, then, even though there had been a mistake, it would not affect the binding nature of the transaction (unless fraud could be established, or there was another kind of misrepresentation that justified equitable rescission). The meaning of the language of the House of Lords in *Bell v. Lever Brothers Ltd.*[29] was subsequently subjected to exegesis, with a view to salvaging contracts from a finding of fundamental mistake that would render them void, and to empower courts to qualify or control contracts.

The starting point of what might be termed the "revaluation" or "reinterpretation" of *Bell v. Lever Brothers Ltd.* is the judgment of Lord Denning in *Solle v. Butcher.*[30] The correct interpretation of *Bell v. Lever Brothers Ltd.*, according to Lord Denning,[31] was that "once a contract has been made, that is to say, once the parties, whatever their inmost states of mind, have to all outward appearances agreed with sufficient certainty in the same terms on the same subject-matter, then the contract is good unless and until it is set aside for failure of some condition on which the existence of the contract depends, or for fraud, or on some equitable ground." Moreover neither party could rely on his own mistake to say it was a nullity from the beginning, no matter that it was a mistake that was fundamental in his mind, or that the other party knew he was under a mistake. The situation was even stronger if the other party did not know of the mistake but shared it. The trend of Lord Denning's judgment was towards the idea that, by and large, mistake rendered a contract voidable in equity rather than void at common law, save in some exceptional instances, namely those which Lord Denning referred to in the passage cited.

The watering down of the idea of "fundamental mistake" was further advanced by the judgment of Goff J. in *Grist v. Bailey.*[32] There, the parties' mistake as to

---

27 Above, note 23, at 224-227 *per* Lord Atkin.
28 *Gompertz v. Bartlett* (1853), 2 E. & B. 869; *Gurney v. Womersley* (1854), 4 E. & B. 133; *Downes v. Ship* (1868), L.R. 3 H.L. 343 (H.L.); *Kennedy v. Panama Royal Mail Co.* (1867), L.R. 2 Q.B. 580. Compare Canadian cases to the same effect: *Alta. North West Lumber Co. v. Lewis* (1917), 38 D.L.R. 228 (B.C.C.A.); *Caldwell v. Cockshutt Plow Co.* (1913), 18 D.L.R. 722 (Ont. C.A.); *Northey Mfg. Co. v. Sanders* (1899), 31 O.R. 475 (Ont. Div. Ct.).
29 Above, note 23.
30 [1950] 1 K.B. 671 (C.A.).
31 *Ibid.*, at 691.
32 [1967] Ch. 532.

the nature of the tenancy to which the property being sold was subject was held not to be a fundamental mistake at common law, in the sense used in *Bell v. Lever Brothers Ltd.* The parties in this case believed that the sitting tenant was protected under special legislation, when in fact he was an ordinary contractual tenant who could have been dispossessed. This would have affected the value of the property. When the vendor discovered the truth he wished to rescind the contract, so as to be able to obtain a higher price. This was held not possible at common law, since the mistake did not render the contract void. But it was possible in equity, because: (a) there was a common mistake; and (b) the mistake was fundamental. It follows, therefore, that a mistake not fundamental at common law may be fundamental in equity. The same approach is evident in a later English decision, *Magee v. Pennine Insurance Co.*[33] The mistake involved in this case closely resembled that which occurred in *Bell v. Lever Brothers Ltd.*[34] The issue was whether an agreement to settle what was thought to be a valid claim by one party against the other, in this instance in respect of a claim under a motor vehicle insurance policy (in *Bell v. Lever Brothers Ltd.* in respect of the early termination of a contract of employment), was binding on the parties when it was later discovered that the first contract, namely, the insurance policy in the *Magee* case (like the employment contract in *Bell v. Lever Brothers Ltd.*), was itself voidable at the option of the party agreeing to make a payment under the settlement. In *Bell v. Lever Brothers Ltd.* the House of Lords held that the settlement was binding; the mistake in question did not affect its validity as an operative contract. In the *Magee* case the majority of the English Court of Appeal held that the mistake did have the effect of entitling the insurance company to avoid the settlement, and so escape liability to pay the agreed amount. However, Lord Denning took the view that the settlement was not void at law but voidable in equity. Lord Denning, relying on his earlier comments in *Solle v. Butcher*, said:[35] "A common mistake, even on a most fundamental matter, does not make a contract void at law: but it makes it voidable in equity." The common mistake in this instance did not make the agreement to pay money to the assured a nullity, but made it liable to be set aside in equity. Winn L.J. dissented, on the ground that the speeches and decision in *Bell v. Lever Brothers Ltd.* were applicable to the facts of the *Magee* case. The two situations were virtually indistinguishable. The doctrine of fundamental mistake as enunciated in *Bell v. Lever Brothers Ltd.* was the governing principle, which meant that the settlement in the *Magee* case was not void at law. In Winn L.J.'s words: "there was a misapprehension as to rights, but no misapprehension whatsover as to the subject-matter of the contract, namely the settlement of the rights of the assured with regard to the accident that happened."[36]

A conflict, therefore, emerged in England between two views. On one side,

---

33 [1969] 2 Q.B. 507 (C.A.).

34 For the facts of which see below, p. 275.

35 [1969] 2 Q.B. 507 at 514 (C.A.). Compare *Laurence v. Lexcourt Holdings Ltd.*, [1978] 2 All E.R. 810 (Ch. D.), discussing equitable relief such as rectification (below, pp. 821-832) or modification by the exercise of the equitable jurisdiction of the court.

36 Above, note 35, at 516.

Bell v. Lever Brothers Ltd. drew a sharp distinction between mistakes in contracting and mistakes in motives for contracting. On the other side, the reinterpretation of *Bell v. Lever Brothers Ltd.* obliterated this distinction, treating mistakes in motives for contracting, when sufficiently vital and effective, as being sufficient to entitle a party to invoke equitable relief, such as rescission, to escape from the binding effects of a contract, or certain parts or terms of a contract. In *Amalgamated Investment & Property Co. v. John Walker & Sons Ltd.*[37] the English Court of Appeal adverted to this conflict, but did not resolve it. There was no need for the court to do this, since, on the facts, there was no mistake at the time of contracting. The change in the character of the building that was the subject of the sales contract occurred after the contract was made. Hence, there could be no basis for any allegation that the transaction was entered into as the result of any mistake by either party or both.

The Court of Appeal has not considered this further. However, the conflict between the cases, and between different views of what was said in *Bell v. Lever Bros. Ltd.*, was discussed at length by Steyn J. in *Associated Japanese Bank International Ltd. v. Crédit du Nord S.A.*[38] He made it clear that the interpretation placed by Lord Denning on the speeches of the majority in *Bell v. Lever Bros. Ltd.* was incorrect. The principles enunciated in that case still govern mistake at common law. What has happened is that equitable developments have affected the position at common law. If mistake was relevant, *i.e.*, if no express or implied condition precedent governed the situation, common law mistake had first to be examined, where it had been pleaded. If the contract was void at common law no question of mistake in equity arose. But if the contract was held to be valid, a plea of mistake in equity might still be considered.

As far as common law mistake was concerned, Steyn J. set out several propositions of law, over and above the notion that contracts should be upheld rather than destroyed.[39] Thus the common law rules, like those of frustration, were designed to deal with the impact of unexpected and wholly exceptional consequences on apparent contracts. A mistake to have legal consequences must be shared substantially by both parties and must relate to facts as they existed at the time the contract was made. The mistake must render the subject-matter of the contract essentially and radically different from the subject-matter the parties believed to exist, which was the point established in *Bell v. Lever Bros. Ltd.* But a party cannot be allowed to rely on a common mistake where the mistake consists of a belief he entertains without reasonable grounds. Policy and good sense dictate the qualification of the positive rules regarding common mistake.[40]

---

37 [1976] 3 All E.R. 509 (C.A.).

38 *Associated Japanese Bank (Int.) Ltd. v. Crédit du Nord S.A.*, [1988] 3 All E.R. 902 at 911 (Q.B.D.): see also, on equitable mistake, *ibid.*, at 914.

39 *Ibid.*, at 912-913.

40 *Ibid.* at 913. Note his comparison with the approach in equity where fault on the part of the mistakenly affected party will preclude relief: *Solle v. Butcher*, [1950] 1 K.B. 671 (C.A.). On this case see Cartwright, "Solle v. Butcher and the Doctrine of Mistake in Contract" (1987), 103 L.Q.R. 594. It has been suggested that this requirement makes the common law test of operative mistake no

(c) Fundamental mistake in Canada

The original common-law approach to fundamental mistake has recently been reaffirmed.[41] However, there is also one Canadian case in which the approach found in *Solle v. Butcher*,[42] *Grist v. Bailey*[43] and the *Magee* case[44] was adopted and applied. Furthermore, the doctrine of *error in substantialibus*,[45] which appears to be distinct from the equitable principles on which a contract may be rectified, modified or set aside,[46] makes inroads on the differentiation between fundamental mistake and other inoperative mistakes at common law, as explained in *Bell v. Lever Bros. Ltd.*

The more traditional view of mistake is exemplified by three cases. In *McCarthy v. Godin Mining & Exploration Ltd.*,[47] the plaintiff took a lease of land in order to mine silica deposits. The parties thought that silica was a reserved mineral under a provincial statute, with the result that the owner of the land could not prevent mining of silica on his land. In fact silica was not reserved; therefore, the owner of the land owned the silica and was not obliged to let the rights to mining to the plaintiff. In an action to enforce the contract, it was held that this mistake went to the root of the contract and rendered it void *ab initio*. The parties were contracting about something both thought the owner was obliged to allow another person to do, when he did not have to, and would not have done so had he known the truth, that is, the legal status of silica. In *Clintar Spray & Environmental Enterprise Inc. v. Municipal Spraying & Contracting Ltd.*,[48] a contractor made an error in calculating the price for work done. It was argued that the contract had been entered into by mistake, therefore it ought not to be binding. The court held that the mistake as to price affected the motive of the other party in making the contract. He did so because he thought he was getting a bargain price. It did not affect the intention to contract. Hence, the contract could not be invalidated for mistake. The distinction between intention and motive was accepted and applied. Similarly, in *A.L. Gullison*

---

different from the test in equity: *Can. Medical Laboratories Ltd. v. Stabile* (1992), 25 R.P.R. (2d) 106 at 132 (Ont. Gen. Div.) *per* Mandel J.: see Guest, ed., *Chitty on Contracts*, 26th ed. (1989), Vol. 1 at p. 401.

41 *Can. Medical Laboratories Ltd. v. Stabile*, above, note 40, at 126, 128, citing both *Bell v. Lever Bros. Ltd.* and *R. v. Ontario Flue-Cured Tobacco Growers' Marketing Bd.* (1965), 51 D.L.R. (2d) 7 (Ont. C.A.).

42 [1950] 1 K.B. 671 (C.A.).

43 [1967] Ch. 532.

44 [1969] 2 Q.B. 507 (C.A.).

45 Below, pp. 257, 306-308.

46 Below, pp. 808-832.

47 (1978), 20 N.B.R. (2d) 676 (N.B.Q.B.). Compare *First City Capital Ltd. v. B.C. Building Corp.* (1989), 43 B.L.R. 29 (B.C.S.C.): purchaser of building not entitled to buy it, therefore contract of purchase not valid. Contrast *Can. Medical Laboratories Ltd. v. Stabile*, above, note 40, where mistake was not relevant because the plaintiff, who tried to rely on mistake to avoid the contract, inserted the relevant clause into the contract, and, therefore, accepted the risk that the provision would not be satisfied. *Caveat emptor* applied.

48 (1978), 27 N.S.R. (2d) 682 (N.S.T.D.); affirmed on other grounds (1979), 30 N.S.R. (2d) 451 (N.S.C.A.).

& *Sons Ltd. v. Cory*,[49] the owner of a house under construction and the builder he employed both mistakenly believed that the plans used in the construction would produce a house of a certain size. When they did not, the question arose whether the contract was binding on the ground of this mistake. It was held that the mistake did not affect the parties' intention to contract it. It went only to questions of quality not to the essential nature of the contract. Hence, the mistake did not affect the contract as it stood.

Such instances illustrate the hold the traditional views of fundamental mistake have upon Canadian courts. However, there are other Canadian decisions which cast doubt upon the common-law approach based on the distinction between intention and motive, or that between quality and substance.

First, in *Toronto-Dominion Bank v. Fortin (No. 2)*[50] F agreed to buy a group of companies from a receiver-manager when they were in the process of liquidation. Later he repudiated the agreement. He paid $10,000 to the receiver-manager in settlement of a threatened action for breach of contract. This was in the nature of a compromise. Subsequently, in litigation between other parties, the Supreme Court of British Columbia held that the receiver-manager had no legal power to offer the companies for sale, or to agree to sell them. Consequently the original contract between F and the receiver-manager had been void. F sued for the return of the $10,000, pleading that the money had been paid under a mistake of fact in that, the original contract being void, a purported compromise of a suit for breach of such contract was itself void. Andrews J. held that there was a fundamental mistake as to the validity of the claim by the receiver-manager. This was grounds for setting aside the compromise and permitting recovery of the money. It should be noted that the receiver-manager, being an officer of the court, was said to be under a higher duty than an ordinary contracting party not to take unfair advantage of a mistake as to his legal position. If this is the true ground for the decision, it is acceptable. If the basis of the decision is mistake, then the decision is more questionable. It does not seem to be consistent with the decision, as well as the principles involved in *Bell v. Lever Brothers Ltd.* Andrews J. followed the *Magee* case. But the idea that the mistake in this case, as to the validity of the earlier contract and therefore of the compromise contract, was fundamental when the mistake as to the validity of the employment contract, in respect of which the compromise of settlement was reached in *Bell v. Lever Brothers Ltd.* was not so fundamental as to permit treating the settlement as void (so as to allow recovery of sums paid under the settlement), raises the issue of the applicability of *Bell v. Lever Brothers Ltd.* in modern times in Canada. In particular the decision seems to equate a mistake as to motive, namely, agreeing to compromise in order to escape liability on the contract to buy the companies, with mistake as to intention,

---

49 (1979), 24 N.B.R. (2d) 638 (N.B.Q.B.); reversed in part (1980), 29 N.B.R. (2d) 86 (N.B.C.A.). Contrast *Seppanen v. Seppanen* (1991), 59 B.C.L.R. (2d) 26 (B.C.S.C.), where the parties never intended that the settlement made between the husband and wife should have the effect of releasing the husband from the unpaid portion of a judgment debt owed by the husband to the wife.

50 (1978), 88 D.L.R. (3d) 232 (B.C.S.C.); compare *Vandekerhove v. Litchfield* (1993), 103 D.L.R. (4th) 739 (B.C.S.C.).

namely, the intent of F to enter into a compromise of a threatened suit for breach of contract.

Secondly, there are cases which confuse a mistake as to the identity or substance of the subject-matter of a contract with a mistake as to some quality or characteristic which it possesses. In *Bell v. Lever Brothers Ltd.* this differentiation was stressed, notably in the speech of Lord Atkin. The post-*Bell* cases already discussed seem to indicate that a mistake as to quality or characteristic can justify some form of equitable relief, such as rescission, even though it will not make the purported transaction a legal nullity. There is a series of Canadian cases in which courts have allowed rescission of a contract, or modification of its terms in favour of the mistaken party, where the mistake was as to some feature of the subject-matter, for example, its size, the age of a vehicle, the presence of some defect in a building, even though there was no mistake as to the existence or identity of the subject-matter.[51] Moreover, in such cases, Canadian courts have been prepared to allow relief to the mistaken party even though it could not be said that there was a total failure of consideration, in the sense that the mistaken party was obtaining something totally different from that for which he bargained. Not all cases have gone along with this point of view.[52] But there is certainly support for the idea that a mistake need not be fundamental, in the *Bell v. Lever Brothers Ltd.* sense, for it to have some effect upon the validity of a contract. There may be good reason for the development of this doctrine of *error in substantialibus*, since it may enable a party to evade one of the consequences of a contract concerning land being executed prior to the discovery of the mistake that induced its being made (where fraud cannot be alleged or proved and the gravamen of the affected party's claim is innocent misrepresentation).[53] If this is the extent of the operation of this doctrine, then it will not completely overthrow or weaken the common law idea of fundamental mistake. However, it does modify the strictness of that common law doctrine, as do other equitable principles.

To appreciate the effects of these it is necessary to draw a distinction between two types of mistake that can occur, depending on whether both parties are in error, or only one is mistaken.[54]

---

51 *Redican v. Nesbitt*, [1924] S.C.R. 135 (S.C.C.); *Alessio v. Jovica* (1974), 42 D.L.R. (3d) 242 (Alta. C.A.); *Hyrsky v. Smith* (1969), 5 D.L.R. (3d) 385 (Ont. H.C.); *Gronau v. Schlamp Invts. Ltd.* (1975), 52 D.L.R. (3d) 631 (Man. Q.B.); *O'Flaherty v. McKinlay*, [1953] 2 D.L.R. 514 (Nfld. C.A.); *Nor. & Central Gas Corp. v. Hillcrest Collieries Ltd.; Byron Creek Collieries Ltd. v. Coleman Collieries Ltd.* (1976), 59 D.L.R. (3d) 533 (Alta. S.C.); *Conkin v. Konschuh* (1984), 54 A.R. 326 (Alta. Q.B.). See, generally, Fridman, "Error in Substantialibus: A Canadian Comedy of Errors" (1978), 56 Can. Bar Rev. 603, referred to by Glube J. in *Aberg v. Refuse* (1979), 8 R.P.R. 216 at 228 (N.S.T.D.), where rescission of an executed contract was refused.

52 See *Aberg v. Refuse* (1979), 8 R.P.R. 216 (N.S.T.D.); compare *Hudson v. Watson Motor Co.*, [1931] 3 W.W.R. 621 (Man. C.A.); *R. v. Ont. Flue-cured Tobacco Growers' Marketing Bd.; Ex parte Grigg* (1965), 51 D.L.R. (2d) 7 (Ont. C.A.).

53 Below, pp. 306-308.

54 For an excellent succinct discussion of the distinction see the judgment of Maclean J. in *Sykes v. R.*, [1939] Ex. C.R. 77 at 85-86 (Ex. Ct.); affirmed [1945] 4 D.L.R. 807 (S.C.C.), followed in *Commercial Credit Corp. v. Newall Agencies Ltd.* (1981), 126 D.L.R. (3d) 728 (B.C.S.C.).

(d) Bilateral and unilateral mistake

(i) *Bilateral mistake*

Bilateral mistakes fall into two categories. First, both parties are in error, but their mistakes are different.[55] For example, A believes that B wishes to buy a second-hand car, which is what he is selling, while B wishes to buy a new car and believes that the car A is selling is a new car. Second, the error in the minds of both parties is the same, as, for example, where A and B believe that the car is a new car when in fact it is second-hand. The former has been termed "mutual" mistake, the latter "common" mistake. A theoretical distinction might be made between these two kinds of bilateral mistake. In mutual mistake the issue would seem to be: what would a reasonable person infer from the words and conduct of the parties? If, despite their different mistakes, it would appear to the outside world that the parties were in agreement as to a contract and its terms, then a contract would exist at common law.[56] As it was put in one Canadian case, "mutual assent is not required for the formation of a valid contract, only a manifestation of mutual assent. . . . Whether or not there is a manifestation of mutual assent is to be determined from the overt acts of the parties."[57] The source of this approach to cases of this kind is the language of Blackburn J. in the English case of *Smith v. Hughes*,[58] which has frequently been cited and followed in Canadian courts:

> If whatever a man's real intention may be, he so conducts himself that a reasonable man would believe that he was assenting to the terms proposed by the other party, and that other party upon that belief enters into the contract with him, the man thus conducting himself would be equally bound as if he had intended to agree to the other party's terms.

Such instances of mistake may be regarded in two ways. In the first place, it could be said that as long as there was an apparent correspondence of offer and

---

55 *Indust. Tanning Co. v. Reliable Leather Sportswear Ltd.*, [1953] 4 D.L.R. 522 (Ont. C.A.); affirmed [1955] 2 D.L.R. 284 (S.C.C.). Compare O'Leary J. in *Re Gabriel and Hamilton Tiger-Cat Football Club Ltd.* (1975), 57 D.L.R. (3d) 669 at 677 (Ont. H.C.): "In mutual mistake the parties misunderstand each other and are at cross-purposes." See also *Patterson v. Anderson* (1987), 80 N.S.R. (2d) 80 (N.S.T.D.), father intended and believed he was agreeing to transfer of control over management of property to daughter: daughter thought the land was being conveyed to her. Compare *Can. Medical Laboratories Ltd. v. Stabile*, above, note 40, alleged mutual mistake regarding the meaning of a use clause in a lease. Contrast *Associated Japanese Bank (Int.) Ltd. v. Crédit du Nord S.A.*, above, note 38, where the parties believed that the precision engineering machines that were the subject of a sale and leaseback existed — when they did not: this was an instance of common mistake.

56 *Staiman Steel Ltd. v. Commercial & Home Bldrs. Ltd.* (1976), 71 D.L.R. (3d) 17 at 22 (Ont. H.C.) *per* Southey J. See and compare *Raffles v. Wichelhaus* (1864), 2 H. & C. 906; *Scriven Bros. v. Hindley*, [1913] 3 K.B. 564; *Lindsay v. Heron & Co.* (1921), 64 D.L.R. 92 (Ont. C.A.); *Twin City Equipment Sales & Rental Ltd. v. Mid West Pipeline Contractors Ltd.* (1980), 2 Sask. R. 421 (Sask. Q.B.); *Dalewood Invts. Ltd. v. Maida* (1982), 40 O.R. (2d) 472 (Ont. C.A.); affirmed (1985), 59 N.R. 81 (S.C.C.). But equity might intervene to set aside the contract: as in *Patterson v. Anderson*, above, note 55. See also below, pp. 263-265.

57 *Walton v. Landstock Invts. Ltd.* (1976), 72 D.L.R. (3d) 195 at 198 (Ont. C.A.) *per* Houlden J.A.

58 (1871) L.R. 6 Q.B. 597 at 607; compare *Tamplin v. James* (1880), 15 Ch. D. 215 at 217-218 (C.A.) *per* Baggallay L.J.

acceptance, the inward, secret beliefs of one or both parties were irrelevant. Objectively speaking, the parties have arrived at a *consensus ad idem*, which is the foundation of contract at common law. Hence, even if parties have been mistaken, a court may be able to find that they have in effect validly contracted, either by the appearance of agreement, or by some kind of estoppel, arising from the belief that was induced in one party by the language or acts of the other party.[59] However, if no such *consensus* can be discovered, for example, where there is an obvious ambiguity about the terms of the purported contract, no objectively ascertained agreement can be inferred or concluded. Second, it could be said that, as long as the parties intended to contract in the manner and on the terms indicated by their acts or language, the fact that both had different motives for contracting, based on their mistaken beliefs, albeit that their mistakes were different ones, would have no effect upon the validity of the apparent contract. The first approach emphasizes the connection between mistake and correspondence of offer and acceptance. The second approach underlines what has been said earlier as to the distinction between intention and motive. With regard to both, the impact of equitable developments has been to give greater flexibility to the courts to uphold, modify or set aside contracts where there has been a mutual mistake.

In common mistake cases, the issue would seem to be whether the existence of such shared mistake destroyed the basis of the contract. In these instances there is no question of a lack of *consensus ad idem*. The parties have clearly agreed on the contract and its terms. However, there may be no contract, or the contract may be affected by some equitable remedy such as rectification, because the real, underlying intentions of the parties have been foiled.[60] It is to this situation that Thompson J. was referring when he said, in *McMaster University v. Wilchar Construction Ltd.*[61]

> [i]n mutual or common mistake the error or mistake in order to avoid the contract at law must have been based either upon a fundamental mistaken assumption as to the subject-matter of the contract or upon a mistake relating to a fundamental term of the contract.

In some Canadian cases there appears to be confusion between common and mutual mistake. Courts have referred to the mistake in issue as being mutual when

---

59 *Sinnott v. Amaria* (1981), 29 Nfld. & P.E.I.R. 428 (Nfld. Dist. Ct.).

60 Compare *A.L. Gullison & Sons Ltd. v. Cory* (1979), 24 N.B.R. (2d) 638 (N.B.Q.B.); reversed in part (1980), 29 N.B.R. (2d) 86 (N.B.C.A.); *Brooklin Heights Homes Ltd. v. Major Hldgs. & Devs. Ltd.* (1977), 80 D.L.R. (3d) 563 (Ont. H.C.), with *McCarthy v. Godin Mining & Exploration Ltd.* (1978), 20 N.B.R. (2d) 676 (N.B.Q.B.).

    This and the previous two sentences, were cited by Hunter J. in *Building Design 2 Ltd. v. Wascana Rehabilitation Centre*, [1992] 6 W.W.R. 343 at 358 (Sask. Q.B.), and by Lane J. in *Law-Woman Management Corp. v. Peel (Regional Municipality)* (1991), 17 R.P.R. (2d) 62 at 92 (Ont. Gen. Div.).

61 (1971), 22 D.L.R. (3d) 9 at 17 (Ont. H.C.); affirmed (1973), 12 O.R. (2d) 512n (Ont. C.A.). See, generally, McTurnan, "An Approach to Common Mistake in English Law" (1963), 41 Can. Bar Rev. 1.

essentially it was more appropriately described as common.[62] Other courts, consistently with the distinguishing features of such mistakes, have treated the mistake before them as mutual rather than common, and have determined whether the contract in issue was valid or not by reference to the question whether objectively speaking the parties had reached an agreement.[63] In effect, what the courts in these cases did was to apply the distinction between quality and substance (or identity) to which reference has been made. By doing so, the courts were able to decide whether the parties had objectively agreed upon the substance and identity of the subject-matter of a contract, even though they were under different misapprehensions as to some characteristic or quality of that subject-matter.

Whether the kind of mistake that is involved is described as "mutual" or as "common", it is suggested that, in the final analysis, the rationale for invalidating the alleged contract at common law is the same: was there any error as to the intention to contract, or, putting this slightly differently, did the contracting party seeking to avoid the contract for mistake obtain the consideration for which he had bargained? The answers to these questions involve examination of the nature of "fundamental" mistake, and its application to the facts in issue.

(ii) Unilateral mistake

Little, if any, theoretical or practical effect may flow from the differentiation of common and mutual mistake. However, it is important to distinguish these various kinds of bilateral mistake from unilateral mistake, where only one party is in error. Here it may be vital to the final result whether the party not in error is aware or unaware of the other party's mistake.[64] If the party not in error knows or ought to know of the other's mistake, any purported agreement between them may not be enforceable in equity (whatever its effects may be at common law), on the ground that equity will not permit a party to take advantage of the error in offering or accepting by the other party.[65] The rationale of such cases is that equity penalizes unconsionable conduct, whether it actually constitutes fraud or involves something amounting to fraud in the view of equity.[66]

---

62 *E.g.*, *A.L. Gullison & Sons Ltd. v. Cory*, above, note 60; *Centurion Invsts. Ltd. v. N.M. Skalbania Ltd.* (1981), 12 Sask. R. 79 (Sask. Q.B.); affirmed (1983), 22 Sask. R. 241 (Sask. C.A.); *McCarthy v. Godin Mining & Exploration Ltd.*, above, note 60.

63 *Sinnott v. Amaria*, above, note 59; *Dalewood Invts. v. Maida*, above, note 56.

64 Hence, there was no unilateral mistake as to the number of games in the schedule for 1974 in *Re Gabriel*, above, note 55, since the manager of the club did not know that the player was mistaken as alleged; compare *Sign-O-Lite Signs Ltd. v. Windsor Plywood (Kelowna) Ltd.* (1988), 61 Alta. L.R. (2d) 21 (Alta. Q.B.). This passage was referred to in *Commercial Credit Corp. v. Newall Agencies Ltd.* (1981), 126 D.L.R. (3d) 728 at 733 (B.C.S.C.) *per* Hyde L.J.S.C.

65 Equity will set aside the contract: *First City Capital Ltd. v. B.C. Building Corp.* (1989), 43 B.L.R. 29 (B.C.S.C.), following *Taylor v. Johnson* (1983), 57 A.L.J.R. 197 (Aust. H.C.). Or will dismiss a claim for specific performance of an alleged contract to sell land where the vendor was mistaken as the purchaser knew: *Santini v. Catenacci* (1991), 21 R.P.R. (2d) 111 (Ont. Gen. Div.); compare *Glasner v. Royal LePage Real Estate Services Ltd.* (1992), 28 R.P.R. (2d) 72 (B.C.S.C.).

66 *Ibid.*; *BCE Dev. Corp. v. Cascade Invts. Ltd.* (1987), 55 Alta. L.R. (2d) 22 (Alta. Q.B.); affirmed (1987), 56 Alta. L.R. (2d) 349 (Alta. C.A.); leave to appeal to S.C.C. refused (1988), 58 Alta. L.R. (2d) xlix (note).

It is not necessary for the party seeking to avoid the contract on the ground of mistake to prove that the other party caused or induced the mistake (although if such causation is established it might lead to rescission for fraud, or for innocent misrepresentation[67]). As long as the unmistaken party knows of the mistake, without having caused it, that party cannot resist a suit for rectification on the grounds of mistake.[68] The converse of the proposition as to knowledge of the other party's mistake is that if the unmistaken party is ignorant of the other's mistake the contract will be valid and neither rescission nor rectification will be possible. Such was the case in *Commercial Credit Corporation v. Newall Agencies Ltd.*[69] The lessor of an automobile, at the lessee's request, indicated the price at which the lessee could purchase the vehicle. The price was erroneously understated. That fact was unknown to the lessee, who paid the stipulated amount and took a transfer of title to the vehicle. It was held that the lessor who sold the vehicle was not entitled to rely on the doctrine of mistake and claim the difference between the sale price and the correct price.

The same result can be found to have been reached in what have been called the "tender" cases.[70] If the party calling for tenders knew of the tenderer's mistake at the time the tender was accepted, the purported acceptance did not produce a valid binding contract. The only situation of this kind where this result was not

---

67 In *Walton v. Landstock Invts. Ltd.* (1976), 72 D.L.R. (3d) 195 at 199 (Ont. C.A.) Houlden J.A. suggested that even though there was a valid contract, if a term was added to a contract by an innocent misrepresentation, the party responsible for the misrepresentation was not entitled to rely upon *that* term.

68 *Nfld. Liquor Corp. v. N.P.A.E.* (1980), 22 Nfld. & P.E.I.R. 62 (Nfld. T.D.), where a party to a collective agreement failed to point out to the other party a clause granting benefits to employees to which the employer had not agreed in the negotiations; the employer was entitled to rectification. Compare *Beverley Motel (1972) Ltd. v. Klyne Properties* (1981), 126 D.L.R. (3d) 757 (B.C.S.C.), reconveyance ordered of property sold by vendor who made a mistake as to scope of offer, known to purchaser. Compare *Hayes v. Butler* (1982), 40 Nfld. & P.E.I.R. 43 (Nfld. Dist. Ct.), signature to contract void because of mistake by party signing, therefore the other party to contract obtained no title to land which was the subject of the contract and was a trespasser. But see *Avco Financial Services Realty Ltd. v. Tracey* (1979), 59 N.S.R. (2d) 333 (N.S.T.D.). Sometimes the court will apply the doctrine of estoppel to prevent the unmistaken party from taking advantage of the mistake: *Becker Milk Co. v. Goldy* (1977), 82 D.L.R. (3d) 598 (Ont. H.C.); affirmed (1978), 87 D.L.R. (3d) 608n (Ont. C.A.). The first two sentences of this paragraph were quoted in *Montreal Trust Co. v. Maley* (1992), 99 D.L.R. (4th) 257 at 262 (Sask. C.A.); leave to appeal to S.C.C. refused (1992), 102 D.L.R. (4th) vii (note) (S.C.C.), in which rectification was granted of a contract to buy land from the plaintiff when, by mistake, as known to the defendant, oil leases were not reserved from this sale, although it was the plaintiff's general policy to do so.

69 (1981), 126 D.L.R. (3d) 728 (B.C.S.C.).

70 Above, pp. 249-250: see *Belle River Community Arena Inc. v. W.J.C. Kaufmann Co.* (1978), 87 D.L.R. (3d) 761 (Ont. C.A.) following *McMaster Univ. v. Wilchar Const. Ltd.*, above, note 61, not following *Imperial Glass Co. v. Consol. Supplies Ltd.* (1960), 22 D.L.R. (2d) 759 (B.C.C.A.); below, p. 276. See also *Metro. Toronto v. Poole Const. Ltd.* (1979), 10 M.P.L.R. 157 (Ont. H.C.). Contrast *Nor. Const. Co. v. Gloge Heating & Plumbing Ltd.* (1984), 6 D.L.R. (4th) 450 (Alta. Q.B.) where the offeree had insufficient notice of the mistake, the contract was valid; compare *Calgary v. Northern Const. Co.*, [1986] 2 W.W.R. 426 (Alta. C.A.); affirmed [1987] 2 S.C.R. 757 (S.C.C.); *Custom Iron & Machinery Ltd. v. Calorific Const. Ltd.* (1990), 39 C.L.R. 276 (Ont. Dist. Ct.).

reached was the *Ron Engineering* case,[71] where the property owner did not know of the tenderer's mistake at the time of acceptance, and where, moreover, the Supreme Court held that the tender was a valid acceptance, albeit founded on mistake, of the property owner's offer contained in the tender advertisement.

Ignorance of the other party's mistake will not protect the mistaken party from the possibility of equitable interference, if that party ought to have been aware of the mistaken party's belief, *i.e.*, where the non-mistaken party has constructive notice of the other party's error.[72]

There has been some dispute as to the nature of the relief or remedy available to the mistaken party in cases of this kind. A Canadian case, *Devald v. Zigeuner*,[73] held that the mistaken party had the option to seek rectification or rescission. This was denied by a subsequent English decision, *Riverlate Properties Ltd. v. Paul*,[74] on the ground that, where unilateral mistake was shown, only rectification should be possible. However, in a later Canadian case, *Stepps Investments Ltd. v. Security Capital Corporation*,[75] Grange J. held that there was a distinction between cases where the unmistaken party knew of the other party's mistake and cases where he ought to have known of it, because a reasonable man in the unmistaken party's position would have realized that the mistake was made.[76] In the latter situation, the learned judge held, the mistaken party did have the right to choose his remedy. In that case changes were made in a contractual document whereby a contract to buy certain shares was no longer conditional upon the closing of an agreement between the prospective purchaser of the shares and a third party, X. These changes were not brought to the attention of the prospective purchaser (the defendant in the action) or his solicitor.[77] The purchaser always intended that the contract to purchase the shares would be conditional upon such extrinsic acts with X. Grange J. held that there was no fraud, but there was a mistake on the part of the defendant. This mistake was known to the plaintiff, the prospective vendor of the shares, or ought to have been known by him. Consequently, the defendant was entitled to equitable relief; he could obtain rectification of the contract, or its rescission, at his option. He could not be bound by the contract as it stood. If the vendor wanted to hold the defendant to the contract, he would have to submit to the contract's being altered so as to become conditional upon the event with X, as the purchaser always intended.[78]

Where there is a bilateral mistake or a unilateral mistake that is unknown

---

71 (1981), 119 D.L.R. (3d) 267 (S.C.C.); above, pp. 36, 74, 249.

72 *BCE Dev. Corp. v. Cascade Invts. Ltd.*, above, note 66; *First City Capital Ltd. v. B.C. Building Corp.*, above, note 65.

73 (1958), 16 D.L.R. (2d) 285 (Ont. H.C.).

74 [1975] Ch. 133 (C.A.), on which see Waddams, (1975), 53 Can. Bar Rev. 339.

75 (1976), 73 D.L.R. (3d) 351 (Ont. H.C.).

76 *Ibid.*, at 364.

77 Compare *Walton v. Landstock Invts. Ltd.* (1976), 72 D.L.R. (3d) 195 (Ont. C.A.) where the basis for *rescission* was the innocent misrepresentation of the unmistaken party.

78 Release from liability was the form of relief obtained in *First City Capital Ltd. v. B.C. Building Corp.*, above, note 65; whereas rectification was obtained in *BCE Dev. Corp. v. Cascade Invts. Ltd.*, above, note 66.

to the unmistaken party, the approach of the common law is objective. The courts do not try to find the real, underlying intention of each party, but have "applied the dispassionate and objective test of the reasonable man." The courts examine all the circumstances and decide what sense, if any, must be ascribed to the parties.[79] Where the mistake of one party is known to the other party, the courts will apply a subjective test and will permit evidence of the real intention of the mistaken party to be introduced. The difference in these approaches is explained by the difference between the common-law attitude to mistake and the attitude of equity to which reference has earlier been made.

(e) Common law and equity

To the common law a contract either existed or it did not; if there was fundamental mistake there was no contract and any purported agreement was void, a nullity.[80] In equity, however, it would seem that, even where a mistake would not invalidate a contract *ab initio*, under common-law rules, if it would be inequitable or unconscientious for a party to be permitted to take advantage of another's mistake, even if not induced by him, then equity would come to the rescue of the mistaken party, at least to the extent of providing an equitable remedy,[81] for example, rescission or rectification, or allowing an equitable defence to an equitable remedy, such as specific performance, which the non-erring party was attempting to invoke.[82] A series of English equity decisions[83] shows that where one party knows that another understands his offer in a sense different from that in which it is manifested, the contract will not be allowed to stand (at least in the form that was misunderstood).[84] These cases have been followed and applied in Canada.[85]

---

79 *Indust. Tanning Co. v. Reliable Leather Sportswear,* [1953] 4 D.L.R. 522 at 525 (Ont. C.A.) *per* Hope J.A.; affirmed [1955] 2 D.L.R. 284 (S.C.C.), followed in *Santini v. Catenacci* (1991), 21 R.P.R. (2d) 111 (Ont. Gen. Div.).

80 This and the next sentence were quoted in *Montreal Trust Co. v. Maley* (1992), 99 D.L.R. (4th) 257 at 262 (Sask. C.A.); leave to appeal to S.C.C. refused (1993), 102 D.L.R. (4th) vii (note) (S.C.C.).

81 This passage beginning with "To the common law" was cited by Huband J.A. in *Granville Savings & Mortgage Corp. v. Slevin* (1992), 12 C.C.L.T. (2d) 275 at 297 (Man. C.A.); reversed (November 2, 1993), Doc. 23210, La Forest, Sopinka, Gonthier, Cory, McLachlin, Iacobucci & Major JJ. (S.C.C.).

82 See, *e.g., Ivanochko v. Sych* (1967), 58 W.W.R. 633 (Sask. C.A.), where equitable relief was granted. Contrast *Schonekess v. Bach* (1968), 62 W.W.R. 673 (B.C.S.C.), where the mistake was not substantial enough to justify rescission. See, further, below, pp. 792-793, 808-814.

83 *E.g., Webster v. Cecil* (1861), 54 E.R. 812; *Garrard v. Frankel* (1862), 54 E.R. 961; *Craddock Bros. v. Hunt,* [1923] 2 Ch. 136 (C.A.). The foregoing sentences were cited by Glube J. in *Clintar Spray & Environmental Ents. Inc. v. Mun. Spraying & Contracting Ltd.* (1978), 27 N.S.R. (2d) 682 at 698 (N.S.T.D.); affirmed on other grounds (1978), 30 N.S.R. (2d) 451 (N.S.C.A.).

84 This passage from the beginning of the paragraph, as it appeared in the first edition of this book, was cited in *Patterson v. Anderson* (1987), 80 N.S.R. (2d) 80 at 84 (N.S.T.D.).

85 *Bennett v. Adams River Lbr. Co.* (1910), 15 W.L.R. 383 at 387 (B.C. Co. Ct.); *Morgan v. Hudson Bay Mining & Smelting Co.,* [1930] 2 D.L.R. 587 (Man. K.B.); *Walton v. Landstock Invts. Ltd.* (1976), 72 D.L.R. (3d) 195 (Ont. C.A.); *Stepps Invts. Ltd. v. Security Capital Corp.* (1976), 73 D.L.R. (3d) 351 (Ont. H.C.); *Patterson v. Anderson,* above, note 84. Contrast *Imperial Glass Co. v. Consol. Supplies Ltd.* (1960), 22 D.L.R. (2d) 759 (B.C.C.A.) (below, p. 276), which has been severely criticized; see (1961), 39 Can. Bar Rev. 625.

In one such case it was suggested that only where there was such *mala fides* would there be relief for a unilateral mistake.[86] But this may be too restrictive. There appears to be much more scope for the operation of error in equity, even where such error does not exactly fall within the ambit of the stricter, common-law doctrine, that is, a fundamental mistake affecting intention. Possibly equity adopted and followed the broader concepts enunciated, so far as the civil law was concerned, by the French jurist Pothier in the eighteenth century.[87] This would seem to be particularly true in respect of mistakes as to *personality*, as opposed to the identity, of a contracting party.[88] The difference, and the more lenient attitude of equity, are perhaps justified by the fact that the broader concept of equitable mistake is only applicable, either by way of remedy or defence to an action, where a party is invoking equitable remedies (on the ground that "he who seeks equity must do equity"), or an equitable defence can be raised to a common-law action in which the plaintiff is seeking to enforce his strict legal rights. Equitable mistake, in short, relates to, and affects remedies much more directly than mistake at common law. Hence the affirmation of the contract by a mistaken party will jeopardize his right to rescind for mistake.[89] The common law is more stringent, and prevents the contract from coming into existence where the common-law doctrine of mistake operates.

This point of view was expressed by Thompson J. in *McMaster University v. Wilchar Construction Ltd.*:[90]

> As a general rule, equity follows the law in its attitude towards contracts which are void by reason of mistake. If the contract is void at common law, equity will also treat it as a nullity. Equity, however, will intervene in certain cases to relieve against the rigours of the common law, even though the mistake would not be operative at law. If, for lack of consensus, no contract comes into existence, there, of course, is nothing to which an equity can attach. It is only in cases where the contract is not

---

86 *Sykes v. R.*, [1939] Ex. C.R. 77 at 85-86 (Ex. Ct.); affirmed [1945] 4 D.L.R. 807 (S.C.C.).

87 *Traité des Obligations*, (1806) ed., s. 19. The passage is as follows:

> Whenever the consideration of the person with whom I am willing to contract enters as an element into the contract which I am willing to make, error in regard to the person destroys my consent, and consequently avoids the contract. . . . On the contrary, when the consideration of the person with whom I thought I was contracting does not enter at all into the contract, and I should have been equally willing to make the contract with any person whatsoever, as with him whom I thought I was contracting, the contract ought to stand.

This has been cited in English cases, *e.g., per* Viscount Haldane, in *Lake v. Simmons*, [1927] A.C. 487 at 501 (H.L.). See also the judgment of Tucker J. in *Sowler v. Potter*, [1940] 1 K.B. 271, in which the learned judge probably came to the *wrong* conclusion, namely that the lease was void for mistake in that there was error as to the person contracting, as a consequence of such reliance. There really was no mistake as to *identity* there, only as to the attributes of the tenant. Compare *Page & Jacques v. Clark* (1914), 19 D.L.R. 530 at 538-539 (Ont. C.A.) *per* Meredith C.J.O.

88 In respect of which note "the statement by Pothier has given rise to such refinements that it is time it was dead and buried altogether": *Lewis v. Averay*, [1971] 3 All E.R. 907 at 910 *per* Lord Denning M.R. On mistake as to identity see below, pp. 267-271.

89 Compare *Can. Medical Laboratories Ltd. v. Stabile* (1992), 25 R.P.R. (2d) 106 at 134-136 (Ont. Gen. Div.) at 134-136.

90 (1971), 22 D.L.R. (3d) 9 at 18-19 (Ont. H.C.); affirmed (1973), 69 D.L.R. (3d) 400n (Ont. C.A.).

void at law that equity . . . may afford relief by declaring the contract voidable. It gives relief for certain types of mistakes which the common law disregards and its remedies are more flexible. Thus, equity does not require the certainty which has led to the narrow common law doctrine of fundamental mistake. It seeks rather the more broad and more elastic approach by attempting to do justice and to relieve against hardship. In equity, to admit of correction, mistake need not relate to the essential substance of the contract, and provided that there is mistake as to the promise or as to some material terms of the contract, if the Court finds that there has been honest, even though, inadvertent, mistake, it will afford relief in any case where it considers that it would be unfair, unjust or unconscionable not to correct it.

Developments in England,[91] however, indicate that the common-law doctrine of mistake and its effects may be modified by a more "equitable" approach even where the issue relates to the existence of a valid contract rather than to the possibility of some equitable relief from an otherwise binding transaction. The weakening of the stricter common-law doctrine may have the effect of enabling a party to escape from liability on a contract where the error is not one of substance, but amounts only to an error as to some quality or characteristic which previously, at common law, would not have permitted the invalidation of the contract. Whether this more generous view of the effects of mistake will ultimately prevail remains to be seen. Those who favour a less formalistic approach to the law readily welcome such a more relaxed attitude.[92] Those who still stress the element of consent in contract view such developments as potentially dangerous, in that they could result in the undermining of traditional common-law approaches to the essential idea of contract as an objectively established agreement evidencing consent.

(f) Mistake of fact and mistake of law

The common law recognized a distinction between mistakes of fact and mistakes of law. The former might render a contract void or voidable, as previously seen. The latter would not have the same effect.[93] The reason usually given for this distinction was that everyone was presumed to know the law: ignorance of the law was neither excuse nor defence. This rationale, which supported the attitude of the criminal law to the plea of mistake, was inappropriate in the realm of contract. Nonetheless it was accepted as justifying the difference between two types of mistake. Just as a mistake of law would not allow the mistaken party to rely on the doctrine of mistake at common law to nullify a contract, so it would not permit someone who had paid money to another under such a mistake to recover that

---

91 *Associated Japanese Bank (Int.) Ltd. v. Crédit du Nord S.A.*, [1988] 3 All E.R. 902 (Q.B.D.); *Solle v. Butcher*, [1950] 1 K.B. 671 (C.A.); *Grist v. Bailey*, [1967] Ch. 532; *Magee v. Pennine Ins. Co.*, [1969] 2 Q.B. 507 (C.A.); above, pp. 252-254.

92 In this respect see the recommendations of the Ontario Law Reform Commission, *Report on Amendment of the Law of Contract* (1987), at pp. 251-270, that the distinction between common law and equitable remedies be abolished and courts have more power to order relief for mistakes in assumption or mistakes in understanding (on the difference between which see *ibid.*, pp. 253, 266).

93 *Bilbie v. Lumley* (1802), 2 East 469.

money under the law of what was quasi-contract and is now restitution.[94] However, there were two major exceptions to this preclusion of recovery. One was where the non-mistaken party exercised some form of compulsion over the mistaken one. The other was where the parties were not *in pari delicto*.[95] Furthermore, it was held in *Re Diplock*[96] that a mistake of law would not preclude recovery of money paid thereunder under equitable, as contrasted with common-law doctrines.

Drawing a distinction between what was a mistake of law and what was a mistake of fact was often very difficult. An illustration is provided by *Solle v. Butcher*.[97] The English Court of Appeal was divided over the question whether the mistake in that case was one of fact or law. The mistake concerned the status of premises under the Rent Restriction Acts. The majority of the court held the mistake to be one of fact, based upon the structural change to the premises. Jenkins L.J. dissented, holding the mistake to be one of law.

The doctrine that a mistake of law would not operate to permit recovery of money was subjected to much criticism.[98] It resulted in statutory change in some jurisdictions.[99] In Canada the Supreme Court held in *Hydro Electric Commission of Nepean v. Ontario Hydro*[100] that the doctrine applied, and none of the exceptions or qualifications of the doctrine applied to the facts of that case. Dickson J. dissented, and considered that the archaic distinction should be abolished. His suggestion was taken up by the court in the later decision in *Air Canada v. British Columbia*.[101] In relation to the recovery of money paid under a mistake the court held that it did not matter whether the mistake were of fact or law (although there were reasons for denying recovery in that instance — reasons that are not relevant to the law of contract). It is a matter of debate whether this decision also applies to questions relating to the validity of a contract, as opposed to the recovery of money.[102] If it should be so applied, then the ancient difference will disappear. At the moment there is no decision that has this effect. On principle, however, on the same grounds as have been suggested for abolishing the distinction as regards restitutionary remedies, it appears both reasonable and sensible to eradicate this distinction from the law of contract. The Ontario Law Reform Commission's *Report*[103] recommends that there be no such distinction with respect to what is there referred to as a

---

94 Goff & Jones, *Law of Restitution*, 3rd ed. (1986), pp. 117-127; Maddaugh & McCamus, *Law of Restitution* (1990), pp. 256-262; Fridman, *Restitution*, 2nd ed. (1992), pp. 94-96.

95 *Kiriri Cotton Co. v. Dewani*, [1960] A.C. 192 (P.C.); *George (Porky) Jacobs Enterprises Ltd. v. City of Regina* (1964), 44 D.L.R. (2d) 179 (S.C.C.); *Eadie v. Brantford (Twp.)*, [1967] S.C.R. 573 (S.C.C.); Goff & Jones *op cit.*, above, note 94, pp. 128-135; Maddaugh & McCamus, *op. cit.*, pp. 262-267, 273-276; Fridman, *op cit.*, pp. 96-98.

96 [1948] Ch. 465 (C.A.); affirmed [1951] A.C. 251 (H.L.).

97 [1950] 1 K.B. 671 (C.A.).

98 Law Reform Commission of British Columbia, *Report on Benefits Conferred under a Mistake of Law* (1981).

99 *E.g.*, Western Australia, Law Reform (Property, Perpetuities & Succession) Act, 1962, s. 23.

100 (1982), 132 D.L.R. (3d) 193 (S.C.C.); Fridman, above, note 94, pp. 100-105.

101 (1989), 59 D.L.R. (4th) 161 (S.C.C.); Fridman, above, note 94, pp. 105-109.

102 See the suggestion to the contrary by Taylor J.A. in *Mayer v. Mayer Estate* (1993), 106 D.L.R. (4th) 353 at 367 (B.C.C.A.).

103 Above, note 92, at pp. 264-265.

mistake in assumption. Such a mistake relates to the creation or formation of a contract, and is the logical situation in which the mistake might be either of fact or law. Hence the relevance of the recommendation. It remains to be seen whether this recommendation will ever become law. The decision in the *Air Canada* case, if applied more generally, may render this particular recommendation otiose.

2. Particular kinds of mistake

(a) Identity of a party[104]

In *Lewis v. Averary*,[105] Lord Denning M.R. refused to accept the theory that a mistake as to identity renders a contract void. It is suggested that such a statement, which was probably not necessary for the decision in the case, tends to make nonsense of more than a hundred years of development by the courts in England and Canada.[106] On the contrary, there would appear to be abundant authority for the view that there are indeed circumstances in which a mistake as to the identity of the other contracting party will render a purported contract a nullity. The distinction is drawn between a mistake as to identity of personality and a mistake as to attributes.[107] This distinction was attacked by Lord Denning in the case just cited as being

> a distinction without a difference. A man's very name is one of his attributes. It is also a key to his identity. If then he gives a false name, is it a mistake as to his identity? or a mistake as to his attributes? These fine distinctions do no good to the law.

It is possible to sympathize with the sentiment expressed in that last remark, particularly in the case of *Lewis v. Averay*. This concerned the rights of an innocent third party who purchased goods from a rogue who obtained them from the innocent seller on the basis of a false representation as to who he was. Nonetheless, it is correct to state that, fine and subtle as the distinction may be, it is part of the law. In Canada, it was applied in 1967 by Disbery J. in *Con-Force Products Ltd. v. Rosen*.[108] The learned judge held that a contract was made with X personally, not as the agent of a corporation. There may have been a mistake as to an attribute of X, namely, was he an agent or not, but there was no mistake as to his identity

---

104 See Williams, "Mistake as to Party in the Law of Contracts" (1945), 23 Can. Bar Rev. 271, 380; Samek, "Some Reflections on the Logical Basis of Mistake of Identity of Party" (1960), 38 Can. Bar Rev. 479; Coote, "Mistake as to Identity Again" (1973), 11 Alta. L. Rev. 161; McLauchlan, "Mistake of Identity after the Contractual Mistakes Act" (1983), 10 N.Z.U.L.R. 199 at 206-216 for a discussion of the earlier English cases. For a philosophical view, see Bronaugh, "The Place of Identity in Contract Formation" (1978), 18 U.W.O.L.R. 185.

105 [1971] 3 All E.R. 907 at 911 (C.A.).

106 Compare McLauchlan, *loc. cit.*, above, note 104, at pp. 213-214.

107 This has been said to be illogical and unsatisfactory, Williams, *loc. cit.*, above, note 104, at p. 280, cited by Hickling, Book Review (1977), 12 U.B.C.L.R. 140 at 143. Even Hickling admits that there are judicial opinions which support it. See also Bronaugh, *loc. cit.*, above, note 104, at pp. 187-189.

108 (1967), 64 D.L.R. (2d) 63 at 74 (Sask. Q.B.); applied in *Twin City Equipment Sales & Rental Ltd. v. Mid West Pipeline Contractors Ltd.* (1980), 2 Sask. R. 421 (Sask. Q.B.).

so as to induce the contract.[109] Similarly, in *Vancouver Motors U-Drive Ltd. v. Terry*[110] the question involved determination of whether there had been consent to the possession of a vehicle given by a car-drive company to a negligent driver, who lacked a licence to drive. The driver had obtained such possession by falsely pretending that he was another, to whom the company had hired the vehicle. It was held that possession passed with consent. The company's servant intended to deal with the person in front of him, even though he did so only because he possessed certain attributes. Hence liability under the Motor-Vehicle Act resulted. Taschereau J. dissented in this case from the majority of the Supreme Court, following English decisions, such as *Lake v. Simmons*,[111] in which a similar question had arisen with respect to passing of possession of certain jewellery to a man's mistress under the belief that: (a) she was his wife; and (b) they were being sold on approval, when the mistress was stealing them.

The English cases of the nineteenth and early twentieth centuries[112] clearly established a difference between intending to contract with the person with whom one was face to face, or with whom one was corresponding, possibly under the mistaken belief, which might have been induced fraudulently by that other person, that he possessed certain characteristics, such as wealth, a business, or a title, and intending to contract with such person, but only because of the belief that he was somebody else. The question in each case was whether the exact identity of the party was material. The non-materiality of the other contracting party was established in such cases as *King's Norton Metal Co. v. Eldridge, Merrett & Co.*,[113] where the rogue in the case invented a company in which he claimed partnership, so that the innocent seller must have intended the person who sent him the order for goods, whoever he was, even though it was only because he thought there was a wealthy partnership behind the order. So, too, in *Phillips v. Brooks Ltd.*,[114] it was *after* the sale of the jewellery to the customer was concluded that the customer claimed to be Sir George Bullough, with the result that the jeweller surrendered possession of the ring on credit. In other words, the jeweller intended to contract with the rogue before him, though only because he believed him to possess the attributes, especially in terms of cash, of Sir George Bullough. On the other hand,

---

109 Compare the language of Perdue J.A., as to the need to show conduct which induced a contract that otherwise would not have been made or to obtain better terms, in *Kelly v. Enderton* (1912), 2 W.W.R. 453 at 459 (Man. C.A.); affirmed [1913] A.C. 191 (P.C.).

110 [1942] S.C.R. 391 (S.C.C.).

111 [1927] A.C. 487 (H.L.), which was also applied in *Atl. Shopping Centres Ltd. v. Hutton* (1980), 25 Nfld. & P.E.I.R. 320 (Nfld. T.D.). See the explanation of this case by Waller J. in *Citibank NA v. Brown Shipley & Co.*, [1991] 2 All E.R. 690 at 700 (Q.B.D.).

112 *Cundy v. Lindsay* (1878), 3 App. Cas. 459 (H.L.); *Phillips v. Brooks Ltd.*, [1919] 2 K.B. 243; *Ingram v. Little*, [1961] 1 Q.B. 31 (C.A.), on which see McLauchlan *loc. cit.*, above, note 104. The facts and decisions in these and other cases are notoriously difficult to reconcile. For change in the law in New Zealand, by the Contractual Mistakes Act, 1977, see McLauchlan, *loc. cit.*, above, note 104, at pp. 216-220. The Act is criticized *ibid.*, pp. 220-231.

113 (1897), 14 T.L.R. 98 (C.A.), distinguished in *Hector v. Lyons* (1988), 58 P. & C.R. 156 (C.A.).

114 [1919] 2 K.B. 243; compare *Dennant v. Skinner*, [1948] 2 All E.R. 29.

in the famous case of *Cundy v. Lindsay*[115] Blenkarn fraudulently induced B to sell him linen in the mistaken belief that he, B, was selling to Blenkiron & Co., a highly respectable firm in the same street. The House of Lords held that there was no sale as B intended Blenkiron (with whom he did not deal) and never thought of Blenkarn (with whom he did deal). Again in *Boulton v. Jones*,[116] B ordered goods from Brocklehurst (who had sold his business to A on the previous day). A supplied the goods, which B consumed in the belief that they came from Brocklehurst. It was held that B was not liable to A for their price, as he proved that his order was meant for Brocklehurst personally and not for the casual owner of the business. It would seem that Bramwell B. relied on a set-off between B and Brocklehurst to establish this personal relationship. This has been utilized in several cases involving undisclosed principals, where the courts have had to decide whether or not to permit the principal to bring an action on a contract made by the agent on his behalf, without disclosing the fact of agency to the other party.[117] The test which has been invoked and applied is whether there was some personal factor or feature about the actual contracting party (or about the principal) which made the actual contracting party attractive and desirable as a contracting party (or which, if known, would have made the principal an unattractive and undesirable contracting party).[118] In *Ingram v. Little*,[119] the identity of the person with whom the old ladies dealt was held to be important to them, hence his fraud, which induced their mistake, rendered the contract invalid so as not to give the rogue any property which he could pass to an innocent third party.

Two more recent English cases underline the point that a mistake about the identity of a contracting party will only render the purported contract void and of no effect if the identity of the party in question was fundamental. Other mistakes of identity may render the transaction voidable, but will not be incapable of passing title to property that has been transferred under the contract that is in issue. In *Hector v. Lyons*[120] the contract was for the purchase of property. The vendor believed that A was buying the property. A told his solicitors that A's son (under age) was the buyer. The contract was drawn up accordingly, and A signed the purchaser's copy of the contract, not in the presence of his solicitors, and with his usual signature. When the vendor refused to complete the transaction, A sued for specific performance. This was denied on two grounds (one of which was concerned with

---

115 (1878), 3 App. Cas. 459 (H.L.), approved by Perdue J.A. in *Boyd v. South Winnipeg Ltd.*, [1917] 2 W.W.R. 489 at 501 (Man. C.A.). On *Cundy v. Lindsay* see *Citibank NA v. Brown Shipley & Co.*, above, note 111, at 699.

116 (1857), 2 H. & N. 564, 157 E.R. 232; *Hardman v. Booth* (1863), 1 H. & C. 803, 158 E.R. 1107, on which see McLauchlan, *loc. cit.*, above, note 103, at pp. 206-207.

117 See *Smith v. Wheatcroft* (1878), 9 Ch. D. 223 (applied in *Atl. Shopping Centres Ltd. v. Hutton* (1980), 25 Nfld. & P.E.I.R. 320 (Nfld. T.D.)); *Archer v. Stone* (1898), 78 L.T. 34; *Gordon v. Street*, [1899] 2 Q.B. 641 (C.A.); *Nash v. Dix* (1898), 78 L.T. 445; *Dyster v. Randall*, [1926] Ch. 932; *Said v. Butt*, [1920] 3 K.B. 497. Compare Fridman, *Law of Agency*, 6th ed. (1990), pp. 233-235.

118 Compare *Alexander v. Enderton* (1914), 5 W.W.R. 1022 (Man. K.B.); affirmed (1914), 25 Man. R. 82 (Man. C.A.); *Page & Jacques v. Clark* (1914), 31 O.L.R. 94 (Ont. C.A.).

119 [1961] 1 Q.B. 31 (C.A.).

120 (1988), 58 P. & C.R. 156 (C.A.).

the law relating to undisclosed principals). As far as mistake is concerned, the Court of Appeal made the point that where an oral contract was involved, *i.e.*, one made between persons contracting face to face, a mistake as to identity was of no effect unless the mistake induced the making of the contract. That principle did not apply to a written contract, where the writing, as in the instant case, identified the parties who were vendor and purchaser. What is important in the judgment in this case is the recognition of the point that identity only makes a contract void where it is fundamental to the making of the contract.

This is also the message of the other decision, *Citibank NA v. Brown Shipley & Co.*[121] The facts involved a fraud which resulted in the issuance of a banker's draft to a rogue who cashed it with a receiving bank. The issuing bank (in fact there were several since more than one transaction was involved) sued the receiving bank to recover the value of the draft. It was alleged that title to the draft never passed to the receiving bank because the latter could only obtain title through the fraudulent party who never received title. The issuing bank claimed that by virtue of the law of mistake, the purported contract with the rogue was a nullity. For this to be the case it was necessary to establish that the identity of the party with whom the issuing bank transacted was of fundamental importance. This was not the case. At the most the mistake was about the attributes of the person to whom the drafts were delivered. The issuing bank believed that person had the authority of a customer of the bank, which he did not. But they intended to give that person the draft. Hence the mistake was not operative to invalidate the transaction and prevent the passage of title to an innocent third party, namely the receiving bank.

Waller J. explained that *Ingram v. Little, Lewis v. Averay* and *Phillips v. Brooks Ltd.* emphasized, *inter alia*, that to establish that there is no contract under which title can pass, as contrasted with a voidable contract, it must be shown that it is fundamental to the contract that one party to the contract should be who he says that he is. That is easier to establish where contracts are made entirely by documents and is less easy to establish in an *inter praesentes* position.[122]

The mistaken identity cases consequently illustrate the common-law doctrine of mistake previously discussed. Where a mistake about the other party's identity has persuaded a court to hold the transaction void, the effect of the mistake has been to negate the apparent contract, rather than nullify it. This is because the offeror intended his offer for one particular person, and it was accepted by someone else (that is, an impersonator of the intended offeree), or the offeror pretended to be someone else, knowing that the offeree was only accepting because he believed that the offeror was that other person. Offer and acceptance did not correspond, as they must for *consensus ad idem* to be established. Another way of analyzing these situations is in terms of unilateral mistake. The offeree cannot accept an offer which he knows is intended for someone else; an acceptance based upon a misconception of the identity of the offeror, where that is a vital term of the

---

121 [1991] 2 All E.R. 690 (Q.B.D.).
122 *Ibid.*, at 700.

contract, is an invalid acceptance because the offeror knows that the offeree is affected by the mistake at the time of acceptance. In all these situations, it must be stressed, the mistake was "fundamental", in that the identity of the other contracting party was vital to the formulation of the intent to contract by the mistaken party.[123] Furthermore, the mistake affected the mistaken party's *intention* to contract with the other party, not the mistaken party's *motive* for contracting.

(b) Identity of subject-matter

Here we are concerned with mistake about the terms of the contract, namely, what is it about? what obligations does it involve? what is its subject? "Subject-matter" must be given a very broad connotation, ranging from the identity of the goods or land with which the transaction is concerned, to such questions as the price to be paid, or any of the other obligations of the transferee or beneficiary. But it must be stressed again that only *fundamental* terms count for this purpose. A mistake about an ancillary term might have some legal effect, but at common law, whatever its effect in equity, it will not render the purported contract a nullity. And a mistake about something which is wholly extrinsic to the contract, even though it goes to a fact which induced the making of the contract, will have no legal effect at all (in the absence of fraud or some other vitiating conduct).

Once again the search is for *consensus ad idem*. Have the parties agreed upon what is fundamental to their contract? If so, then irrespective of the *reasons* or *motives* for such agreement, which may differ from party to party and may, indeed, be founded upon error, and as long as this is not the product or consequence of fraud, the contract will be good and will bind. If they are contracting about different things, or upon different terms, then there is no contract.

The problem, which corresponds to the issue where the personality of a contracting party is involved, is whether the mistake in question relates to something substantial or something merely qualitative. Identity is once again contrasted with attribute, except that in the present context we are considering the "thing", that is, the contract itself or the subject-matter of the contract, instead of the other party to the contract. A mistake as to the "quality" of the contract or its subject-matter might have effect if it involves a term of the contract. In such circumstances, there might be liability on the part of one party for breach of such term (without proof of fraud or negligence). This does not effect the validity, that is, the existence, of the contract. An operative mistake as to the identity of the subject-matter of the contract, or some term or terms, would render the contract non-existent. There would be no breach, nor any form of liability (in the absence of fraud). There simply would not be any contractual obligation between the parties.

Thus in *Scriven Brothers v. Hindley*,[124] in an auction to B of a "lot" consisting of Russian tow, B's bid was intended for Russian *hemp*. Evidence showed that this

---

123 If identity is immaterial, the mistake will be inoperative: *Indust. & Educational Publishing Co. v. Gold Medal People Ltd.* (1927), 32 O.W.N. 228 (Ont. C.A.).

124 [1913] 3 K.B. 564 (distinguished in *Staiman Steel Ltd. v. Commercial & Home Bldrs. Ltd.* (1976), 71 D.L.R. (3d) 17 (Ont. H.C.), below, note 142).

mistake was genuine and reasonable, having regard to the contents of a misleading catalogue and various markings on the goods. It was held that there was no contract. So, too, in *Van Praagh v. Everidge*,[125] where the mistake was of a similar kind. This was followed in a Canadian case, *Cancilla v. Orr*,[126] where P intended to bid for lot 4 (which he was induced by the mistake of V to believe that he was buying). In fact V did not own lot 4, but owned lot 2. P took a receipt for a deposit on lot 2 and signed an agreement for the sale to himself of lot 2. It was held that there was no valid contract. Rescission and the return of the money paid, with interest, were granted to P. To the same effect was the decision in *Murray v. Jenkins*,[127] where the Supreme Court of Canada avoided a purported contract which dealt with the purchase of some land. The parties were mistaken as to the exact identity of the land to be sold. Again in *Barron v. Morgan*,[128] there was a common or mutual mistake between the parties as to the existence or continuance of Crown grants relating to land which was being sold. In the circumstances the court ordered rectification of the contract, rather than its avoidance. But the principles applicable were the same. In *Industrial Tanning Co. v. Reliable Leather Sportswear*,[129] S said the contract was for S's stock, that is quantity X. B said it was a contract for the sale of 8X. Held: there was a mutual mistake because both parties were in error as to the nature of each other's intentions, and neither realized that what he intended was misunderstood by the other. In all these cases, as in *R. v. Ontario Flue-cured Tobacco Growers' Marketing Board; Ex parte Grigg*,[130] there was a "mistake as to an essential subject-matter, in fact the essence of the thing they contracted for."

Several other Canadian cases illustrate the same situation. *Hayes v. Butler*[131] involved an action for trespass. The liability of the defendant depended upon whether the defendant's claim that the land in question belonged to him could be substantiated. This, in turn, depended upon the validity of a contract of sale. The defendant argued that the disputed piece of land, which was adjacent to land which he had bought from the plaintff, had been conveyed with the sale of the other land. An affidavit was signed by the previous owner of this piece of land agreeing that there was no dispute over the terms of the contract between the parties. In fact the affidavit conveyed an interest in the disputed land to the defendant, but it had been signed by the previous owner under the influence of a mistake. He did not appreciate that he was conveying the land in question. Hence, the conveyance and the affidavit were void. In consequence, the defendant was guilty of trespass. So, too, in *McCarthy v. Godin Mining & Exploration Ltd.*,[132] a lease of land for mining was assigned. Both parties and the owner of the land

---

125 At least at first instance: [1902] 2 Ch. 266. It was different on appeal: [1903] 1 Ch. 434 (C.A.).
126 (1914), 5 W.W.R. 1294 (Man. K.B.); affirmed (1914), 24 Man. R. 355 at 360 (Man. C.A.).
127 (1898), 28 S.C.R. 565 (S.C.C.).
128 [1930] 3 W.W.R. 65 (B.C.S.C.).
129 [1953] O.W.N. 921 (Ont. C.A.); affirmed [1955] 2 D.L.R. 284 (S.C.C.).
130 (1965), 51 D.L.R. (2d) 7 at 15 (Ont. C.A.) *per* Wills J.A.
131 (1982), 40 Nfld. & P.E.I.R. 43 (Nfld. Dist. Ct.).
132 (1978), 20 N.B.R. (2d) 676 (N.B.Q.B.).

believed that silica was a reserved mineral under statute, with the result that the owner of the land could not prevent the mining of the silica, which was the object of the lease. Silica was not a reserved mineral; therefore, the owner of the land owned the silica. Therefore, the assignment was void for mistake. It was founded upon a mistake that went to the root of the contract; it affected the very nature of the subject-matter of the contract. Similarly in *Dalewood Investments Ltd. v. Maida*[133] the parties had in mind different plans of subdivisions of the land being sold by the contract. Consequently there was no valid contract between the parties.

In contrast, there are cases in which quality, not identity, was involved, a distinction which was pointed out by Rinfret J. of the Supreme Court of Canada in *Clay v. Powell & Co.*,[134] in which the learned judge relied upon *Smith v. Hughes*, in the days before the judgment of Lord Atkin in *Bell v. Lever Brothers Ltd.* That this is not an easy difference to apply can be seen, first of all, in a comparison of an English and a Canadian case in which the mistake in question could easily be interpreted, so it is suggested, as either one relating to identity or as one relating to quality. In *Raffles v. Wichelhaus*,[135] the parties contracted for the sale of some cotton cargo "ex Peerless Bombay". One party meant one ship by that name leaving Bombay: the other intended a different ship, of the same name, also leaving Bombay. But the dates were different. The English court held that there was no contract as the parties were not *ad idem*. In *Lindsay v. Heron & Co.*[136] the contract was for the purchase of shares in a named company. There were in fact two companies with the same, or a similar name. One party intended one of these companies; the other understood and intended the contract to refer to the other. Notwithstanding such error, the Canadian court held that there was *consensus ad idem*, and there was a valid contract.[137] It would seem, in the light of some English decisions, that as long as on the face of the circumstances, there appears to be consensus, that is, mutual reference to the same object, the fact that each party intends his language to refer to another object will be to no effect. This was held in one case involving a mistake as to the brand of "Kapok" to be purchased,[138] and in another relating to two different kinds of "horsebeans".[139]

Similarly, in some other Canadian cases, although there may have been a subjective mistake on the part of one party as to the precise scope or contents of the intended contract, the fact that a reasonable man could properly interpret the agreement between the parties as referring to certain matters entitled the court to conclude that there was an objectively reached agreement with respect to those

---

133 (1982), 40 O.R. (2d) 472 (Ont. C.A.); affirmed (1985), 50 O.R. (2d) 223 (S.C.C.).

134 [1932] S.C.R. 210 at 217 (S.C.C.).

135 (1864), 2 H. & C. 906 (distinguished in *Staiman Steel Ltd. v. Commercial & Home Bldrs. Ltd.*, below, note 141). For a critical account of this case and the theories to which it has given rise, see Gilmore, *The Death of Contract* (1974), pp. 35-40.

136 (1921), 50 O.L.R. 1 (Ont. C.A.) (followed in *Staiman Steel Ltd. v. Commercial & Home Bldrs. Ltd.*, below, note 142).

137 Compare *Twin City Equipment Sales & Rentals Ltd. v. Mid West Pipeline Contarctors Ltd.* (1980), 2 Sask. R. 421 (Sask. Q.B.).

138 *Harrison & Jones v. Bunten*, [1953] 1 Q.B. 646.

139 *Frederick E. Rose (London) Ltd. v. William H. Pim Jr. & Co.*, [1953] 2 Q.B. 450 (C.A.).

matters.[140] Hence, in *Brooklin Heights Homes Ltd. v. Major Holdings & Developments Ltd.*,[141] there was a valid contract of sale between the parties and this included the vendor's obligation to pay "lot levies" in respect of the issuance of building permits. The purchaser's understanding that the vendor's undertaking to pay the municipality to obtain the release of a residential subdivision agreement was a reasonable one, given that such release could not be obtained from the municipality without the payment of the "lot levies". In *Staiman Steel Ltd. v. Commercial & Home Builders Ltd.*,[142] goods were sold by auction. The seller argued that certain goods were not included in the lot sold to the buyer. The latter said that they were. It was held that a reasonable man observing what had been said and done by the parties at the time of the auction could reasonably infer that the disputed goods were not included in the sale. Hence, the buyer had not bought them. But he had bought the lot in question without the disputed goods. Whatever the subjective intent of the buyer as to the inclusion of the disputed goods, he had manifested to the outside world his intention to buy the offered lot minus the disputed goods. Hence objectively speaking the parties were *ad idem* as to the undisputed part of the lot. *A.L. Gullison & Sons Ltd. v. Cory*[143] is another example. The parties agreed on the plans for a house to be built for one of the contracting parties by the other. Both mistakenly believed that these plans would produce a house of a certain size, as desired by the ultimate owner of the house. In fact they did not. Nonetheless, the owner was bound by the contract. In effect, in all these cases the buyer obtained what he had bargained for, and there was no failure of consideration.[144]

The explanation of these cases may be that, applying an objective test, the parties really were *ad idem*, or would appear to have been so to the reasonable bystander. Another way of explaining them might be to say that the mistake involved related to the quality of the goods to be bought rather than their identity. Would one not think, however, that the question as to which company's shares were being bought, would relate to identity and not quality? Yet, in *Leaf v. International Galleries*,[145] an even stronger case of mistaken identity appears to have been treated as one of mistake as to quality. In that case A bought a picture from B, both believing it to be a Constable. In fact it later turned out to be a copy. In such circumstances it was held that the purchaser could not avoid the contract on the ground of mistake, and, as it happened, was unable to obtain damages for innocent misrepresentation. What might seem to be underlying such decisions is the notion that the courts

---

140 Compare *Clintar Spray & Environmental Ents. Inc. v. Mun. Spraying & Contracting Ltd.* (1978), 27 N.S.R. (2d) 682 (N.S.T.D.); affirmed on other grounds (1979), 30 N.S.R. (2d) 451 (N.S.C.A.); *Walton v. Landstock Invts. Ltd.* (1976), 72 D.L.R. (3d) 195 (Ont. C.A.); *Sinnot v. Amaria* (1980), 29 Nfld. & P.E.I.R. 428 (Nfld. Dist. Ct.).

141 (1977), 80 D.L.R. (3d) 563 (Ont. H.C.).

142 (1978), 71 D.L.R. (3d) 17 (Ont. H.C.).

143 (1979), 24 N.B.R. (2d) 638 (N.B.Q.B.); reversed in part (1980), 29 N.B.R. (2d) 86 (N.B.C.A.).

144 Compare *Selesse v. Central Garages Sales & Services Ltd.* (1977), 18 N.B.R. (2d) 64 (N.B.Q.B.); see also below, p. 305.

145 [1950] 2 K.B. 86 (C.A.) (on certain aspects of which, not relevant here, see *Shapiro v. Banque Canadienne Nationale* (1981), 123 D.L.R. (3d) 630 (Man. Q.B.)).

will not intervene (in the absence of fraud) to relieve a party of a bargain which was not as good as he originally thought it was going to be. His mistake is as to "value" of the subject-matter of the contract, that is, the quality of the contract, rather than as to the nature of what he was going to obtain, that is, the identity of the subject-matter. Hence in *Kennedy v. Royal Mail Co. of Panama*,[146] there was no mistake as to the *identity* of the shares bought by the purchaser, even though they were not as valuable as they were thought to be by reason of the failure of a lucrative government contract to materialize. A similar attitude has been adopted in relation to claims for the recovery of money paid on the basis of a failure of consideration. The party in question got what he bargained for, even though he was in error as to what it was truly worth. The real question was, as Blackburn J. said,[147]

> whether the misapprehension as to the contract goes to the root and substance of the matter so as to make the shares which the applicant has obtained in a company with this questionable contract substantially different things from shares in a company with a valid contract. . . .

The leading case, which has been followed and accepted in Canada, is *Bell v. Lever Brothers Ltd.*[148] B sought to recover £30,000 paid to A under a compensation agreement releasing B from service contracts under which A managed B's African interests. It was alleged that the money had been paid under a mistake of fact. The fact in issue was the validity of the agreement. The service contracts had become voidable in consequence of A's failure to account to B for sums of money made in a cocoa pool. Consequently, so B alleged, they had paid out money when there was no need for them to have done so. The majority of the House of Lords held that the compensation agreement was valid, as to its subject-matter, that is, that the service contracts had not lost their validity, and had therefore been discharged in the manner B intended. The mistake of B was merely as to the quality of the compensation agreement and B's notice of the acts outside the compensation agreement was immaterial. Thus there was no duty on A to bring to B's attention any facts that would or mioght have been relevant to the making of the agreement. A had not deliberately induced the mistake. Even if they had known about it, they

---

146 (1867), L.R. 2 Q.B. 580.

147 *Ibid.*, at 589.

148 [1932] A.C. 161 (H.L.). This statement of the facts in this case, and the following passage down to the phrase "not in the intention of B to make the agreement in question," were cited by Glube J. in *Clintar Spray & Environmental Ents. Ltd. v. Mun. Spraying & Contracting Ltd.*, above, note 139, at 694-695 (N.S.T.D.).

In *Courtright v. C.P. Ltd.* (1983), 5 D.L.R. (4th) 488 (Ont. H.C.); affirmed (1985), 18 D.L.R. (4th) 639 (Ont. C.A.), it was held that a solicitor owed a high fiduciary duty to a potential employer, therefore non-disclosure of possible criminal acts by the solicitor affected the validity of the contract. Contrast *Queen v. Cognos Inc.* (1990), 74 O.R. (2d) 176 at 187-188 (Ont. C.A.); reversed [1993] 1 S.C.R. 87 (S.C.C.).

did not have to enlighten B. They could, in effect, take advantage of the mistake. What this case decides, it has been said,[149] is that

> once a contract has been made, that is to say, once the parties whatever their state of mind, have to all outward appearances agreed with sufficient certainty in the same terms on the same subject-matter, then the contract is good unless and until it is set aside for failure of some condition on which the existence of the contract depends on for some fraud or on some equitable ground. Neither party can rely on his own mistake to say it was a nullity from the beginning, no matter that it was a mistake which to his mind was fundamental, and no matter that the other party knew that he was under a mistake. A fortiori if the other party did not know of the mistake but shared it.

In *Bell v. Lever Brothers Ltd.* the error was in the motive or reason for making the compensation agreement, not in the intention of B to make the agreement in question.[150]

This was adopted and followed in *Imperial Glass Co. v. Consolidated Supplies Ltd.*[151] In that case, as Thompson J. explained in the *McMaster University* case,[152]

> the offeror, through error or mistake, misquoted the price of glass to the offeree, who upon the basis of such quotation, tendered upon a subcontract. Its tender having been accepted, the offeree then requested and received written confirmation of the quotation. This was held to be an offer to contract. The offeree then placed an order for the glass with the offeror which was held to amount to an acceptance of the offer. The mistake was known to the offeree before acceptance but the offeror was unaware of or did not realize its mistake before the placing of the order. Upon becoming aware of the mistake the offeror refused to deliver and the offeree then commenced the action to recover damages for non-delivery.

It was held that the contract was valid and there could be liability for its non-

---

149 *Per* Lord Denning in *Solle v. Butcher*, [1950] 1 K.B. 671 at 691 (C.A.). See the same judge in *Magee v. Pennine Ins. Co.*, [1969] 2 Q.B. 507 (C.A.) and Goff J. in *Grist v. Bailey*, [1967] Ch. 532. See also the discussion of this case by Steyn J. in *Associated Japanese Bank (Int.) Ltd. v. Crédit du Nord S.A.*, [1988] 3 All E.R. 902 (Q.B.D.).

150 Contrast, however, *T.D. Bank v. Fortin (No. 2)* (1977), 88 D.L.R. (3d) 232 (B.C.S.C.); above, p. 256. And see the discussion of the conflict between the *Bell* case and later English cases, above, pp. 252-254.

151 (1960), 22 D.L.R. (2d) 759 (B.C.C.A.); criticized in (1961), 39 Can. Bar Rev. 625. Compare *R. v. Kimbley*, [1945] 3 W.W.R. 232 (Sask. C.A.) (not followed in *Belle River Community Arena Inc. v. W.J.C. Kaufmann* (1978), 87 D.L.R. (3d) 761 (Ont. C.A.)). Contrast *Devald v. Zigeuner*, [1958] O.W.N. 381 (Ont. H.C.), where the purchaser knew that the vendor wanted to keep a piece of land that was erroneously included in the offer. The purchaser was allowed to choose between submitting to rectification of the contract, or accepting rescission at the consent of the vendor. If this was based on *common* mistake, it was good, according to Russell L.J. in *Riverlate Properties Ltd. v. Paul*, [1974] 2 All E.R. 656 at 664-665 (C.A.), otherwise if it was based on *unilateral* mistake.

152 (1971), 22 D.L.R. (3d) 9 at 24 (Ont. H.C.); affirmed (1973), 12 O.R. (2d) 512n (Ont. C.A.).

performance. The mistake was held to be in the motive or reason for making the offer and not in the offer itself.[153]

But in the *McMaster University* case,[154] the mistake, in this instance, the omission of a vital term of the offer which the offeror intended to make, was an error in the making of or in the words of the offer. And the mistake in the offer was known to the offeror before acceptance and the fact of the mistake was communicated to the offeree before acceptance. Hence, the situation was different. The offeree was aware of the lapse on the part of the offeror, and a reasonable person in the position of the offeree would have realized that the offeror, who was tendering for a construction contract, would not have omitted an escalation clause to cover foreseeably higher costs of labour for the duration of the intended contract. Such an offer could not be accepted in such a way as to bind the offeror, whether such result was achieved by applying common-law principles or on the basis of the equitable approach to mistake.[155]

This is an important point. In *Bell v. Lever Brothers Ltd.*, the plaintiffs were relying on the common law to nullify the contract. This required the House of Lords to declare and apply the strict common-law doctrine of mistake in formation of a contract. And the nature of that doctrine, if not absolutely clear beforehand, was made abundantly plain by the House of Lords, in terms of fundamental mistake, not motive or reason. But the doctrine enunciated in that case does not oust the equitable notion of relief where there has been an unconscionable attempt to bind a party to an offer or bargain which has been made in error, *to the knowledge* of the other party. Indeed even at common law, as indicated by the language of the court in *Smith v. Hughes*,[156] many years before *Bell v. Lever Brothers Ltd.*, there was scope for refusing to give effect to a contract based upon an acceptance of an offer which was mistaken. In that case the question (which was sent back for a new trial) was whether the offeree accepted on the basis of an offer which was mistaken, to the offeree's knowledge, or not. This was the foundation of holding that there was no contract in *Hartog v. Colin & Shields*.[157] The offeror offered Argentine hair skins at a certain price per pound, instead of per piece. This was, in effect, offering the goods at a third their normal value. The offeree, from his knowledge of the trade, must have realized that there was a mistake. Hence, his acceptance was not valid (anymore than there could be acceptance of an offer known by the offeree to have been revoked at the time of acceptance). In the

---

153 See the *Imperial Glass* case, above, note 151, at 763 *per* Coady J.A. The comparison with *Bell v. Lever Bros.* is made, *ibid.*, at 765. On the distinction between motive and intention to contract, compare the *Clintar Spray* case above, note 140.

154 Followed in *Belle River Community Arena Inc. v. W.J.C. Kaufmann*, above, note 151; compare *Becker Milk Co. v. Goldy* (1977), 82 D.L.R. (3d) 598 (Ont. H.C.); affirmed (1978), 87 D.L.R. (3d) 608n (Ont. C.A.); *Metro. Toronto v. Poole Const. Ltd* (1978), 10 M.P.L.R. 157 (Ont. H.C.).

155 In the *McMaster University* case probably it was on the basis of the common law; for an example of the same result being achieved by the application of equitable doctrines and remedies see *Devald v. Zigeuner*, above, note 151. On the subject of such "unilateral mistake", see above, pp. 260-262.

156 (1871), L.R. 6 Q.B. 597.

157 [1939] 3 All E.R. 566.

same way, as noted in connection with cases of mistaken identity of a party,[158] an offer made to B cannot be accepted by B if he knows it was really intended for A. The test is objective, as elaborated in the famous case of *Upton-on-Severn Rural District Council v. Powell.*[159]

As Thompson J. said in the *McMaster University* case:[160] "If by any means he [that is, the promisee] knows there was no real agreement between him and the promisee [*sic*: but promisor must be meant], he is not entitled to insist that the promise be fulfilled in a sense to which the mind of the promisor did not assent." The chief difference between common law and equity in this respect, it would seem, is in the greater flexibility of equity. An error may not have to be quite so fundamental to be operative in equity. In other words, there may be scope in equity for giving effect to motive or reason for contracting, even if there is no fraud in the strict common-law sense, when there is no such scope, after the decision in *Bell v. Lever Brothers Ltd.* for any such leniency at common law.[161] Furthermore, there is room for the introduction of a more *subjective* approach where equity is involved, so that when, on even the objective test of *Smith v. Hughes*, there is a valid contract, a subjective, unilateral mistake can be relied upon to upset the contract, if it would be unfair to deny relief to a mistaken party.[162]

(c) Existence of subject-matter

The cases examined in the previous pages fall into two classes. On the one hand, there are those in which the parties have been contracting about two different objects, that is, there is no concordance between the offer and acceptance. On the other, there are those in which there is no mistake about or lack of correspondence in respect of the subject-matter of the contract, but the parties have different beliefs about such subject-matter, and, consequently, different reasons or motives for entering into the contract. There is a third possibility; the parties may intend to contract about the same subject-matter, but they are both mistaken as to its existence.[163] In this instance, too, distinct situations may occur.

---

158 Above, pp. 267-271.

159 [1942] 1 All E.R. 220 (C.A.); above, p. 249, note 9.

160 Above, note 152, at 18, relying on *Colonial Invt. Co. v. Borland* (1911), 1 W.W.R. 171 (Alta. S.C.); affirmed (1912), 2 W.W.R. 960 (Alta. C.A.); *Smith v. Hughes*, above, note 156.

161 Compare the discussion of "fundamental mistake", above, pp. 252-257.

162 See *Bennett v. Adams River Lbr. Co.* (1910), 15 W.L.R. 383 (B.C. Co. Ct.), relying on *Webster v. Cecil* (1861), 54 E.R. 812; *Tamplin v. James* (1880), 15 Ch. D. 215 (C.A.); compare the exercise of equitable jurisdiction to release from a contract entered into by mistake where one party knew or ought to have known of the other's fundamental error in *First City Capital Ltd. v. B.C. Building Corp.* (1989), 43 B.L.R. 29 (B.C.S.C.).

163 Into this category *might* fall such cases as *T.D. Bank v. Fortin (No. 2)* (1977), 88 D.L.R. (3d) 232 (B.C.S.C.) (above, pp. 256-257); and *McCarthy v. Godin Mining & Exploration Ltd.* (1978), 20 N.B.R. (2d) 676 (N.B.Q.B.) (above, pp. 237, 272), but neither case was actually decided on such basis. So, too, in *First City Capital Ltd. v. B.C. Building Corp.*, above, note 162, the case might have been decided as it was on the ground that the parties believed they could contract about the property in issue when, in fact, the purchaser was not entitled to buy the property.

The "thing" about which they are contracting may not now, if it ever did, exist. Second, they may both believe that they can contract about it, but it is not something legally capable of being the subject of a contract. Third, they may contemplate the possibility of non-existence of the "thing", and agree either that if it does not exist there is to be no contract or that if it does exist the parties are to be bound by their respective agreements or undertakings. Fourth, they may not be *ad idem* as to what is to happen if the "thing" does not exist, that is, one party may believe and intend that in such event there will be no contract, while the other may believe and intend that there will be a binding contract.

These different problems are susceptible to different legal solutions. Some of these involve the application of the law of mistake; others involve distinct legal doctrines.

The clearest case, possibly, is where the parties contracted about something which both believed existed whereas it had never done so, or has perished or been destroyed prior to the making of the contract. A classic instance is *Couturier v. Hastie*.[164] There was a sale of a cargo of corn believed to be en route to London. Unknown to the parties it had become overheated on the voyage and to prevent total loss had been sold by the ship's captain. The House of Lords held that there was no sale; therefore, there could be no liability for the price of the goods. This decision was followed in Canada in *Judgment Recovery (Nova Scotia) Ltd. v. Dominion Insurance Corporation*,[165] where an insurance agent issued endorsements to a policy that had already been cancelled by the insurer. Since the policy to be amended no longer existed, the amendments were held to have no effect, and provided no cover for the insured party. The court took the view that there was no subject-matter for the contract; therefore, what was purported to have been done was void, a legal nullity.[166] This interpretation of *Courturier v. Hastie*, however, has been disputed.[167]

Some writers consider that the true *ratio decidendi* is that the contract was subject to a condition precedent, namely, the existence of the goods. In other words, whether or not there is a contract in such circumstances will depend upon how the contract is construed by the courts, and not upon any notions of mistake. This appears to be the view adopted by the High Court of Australia in *McRae v. Commonwealth Disposals Commission*.[168] In that case a contract was entered into for the sale of a sunken tanker on a particular reef. It emerged that there was no such wreck on the reef in question. Was there a contract? This was said to depend upon what the parties could be said to have intended by their agreement. In the event it was held that there was a contract, in the form of an implied promise as to the existence of the sunken ship.

---

164 (1856), 5 H.L. Cas. 673 (H.L.); compare *Scott v. Coulson*, [1903] 2 Ch. 249 (C.A.).

165 (1978), 79 D.L.R. (3d) 648 (N.S.T.D.).

166 *Ibid.*, at 651-653.

167 See Atiyah, "Couturier v. Hastie and the Sale of Non-Existent Goods" (1957), 73 L.Q.R. 34.

168 (1951), 84 C.L.R. 377 (Aust. H.C.). Compare also *Associated Japanese Bank (Int.) Ltd. v. Crédit du Nord S.A.*, [1988] 3 All E.R. 902 at 912 (Q.B.D.) *per* Steyn J.; compare above, p. 254.

The Sale of Goods Act[169] stipulates that a sale of goods which have perished at the time of the sale, unknown to the parties, is void. This may not be as absolute a statutory provision as it seems at first sight. For it could nonetheless be agreed between the parties that one is to take the risk of the thing being "sold" not actually being in existence. This would be a question of construction; it would mean construing the contract as an *emptio spei,* that is, a sale on the terms that the buyer took a chance that the subject-matter of the sale existed, and would bear the loss if it did not (as contrasted with an *emptio rei speratae* — when the existence and scope of the contract would depend upon what, if anything, existed or emerged).[170] Furthermore, the contract might be made dependent upon there actually being something to contract about, in which event the existence of the "thing" would be a condition precedent.

Some of the language used by Fitzpatrick C.J. and Davies J. of the Supreme Court of Canada in *Roche v. Johnson*[171] supports this. In that case, there was an agreement to sell coal mines to a company in return for cash and stock in the company. No such company existed at the time, as both parties knew. Therefore, they were aware that the stock which was part of the consideration for the price was not in existence. In such circumstances it was held by a majority of the court in an action for breach of the contract to deliver the stock, that there was no enforceable contract. In the words of Fitzpatrick C.J.[172]

> [i]f a party to a contract is relieved of his obligation to deliver when the goods though existing at the time of the contract have been subsequently destroyed as where though non-existent at the time of the contract they have subsequently come into existence and been destroyed, much more would it seem is he entitled to relief if the goods never were in existence at all. It seems indeed almost necessary in such case to imply a condition in the contract that the goods will come into existence, for no man could be supposed to bind himself to such an impossibility as the delivery of a non-existent thing.

More recently, in *Centurion Investments Ltd. v. N.M. Skalbania Ltd.,*[173] the Saskatchewan Court of Appeal employed the notion of condition precedent, rather than the doctrine of mistake, to deal with a situation where parties had contracted for the sale and purchase of land under the belief that a prior contract between the vendor and X was invalid. Later it was held that the first contract was good. In an action brought by the second purchaser against the vendor it was held that their contract was void. There was what the trial called a "mutual mistake" (which should perhaps more properly have been termed a "common mistake")[174] that was fundamental to the contract. On appeal, however, although the decision that the alleged contract was void was upheld, the basis for such determination was that the contract was subject to a condition precedent as to its possibility or legality.

---

169 Fridman, *Sale of Goods in Canada,* 3rd ed. (1986), pp. 59-63.
170 *Ibid.,* at p. 55.
171 (1916), 53 S.C.R. 18 (S.C.C.).
172 *Ibid.,* at 24-25; compare Davies J., *ibid.,* at 26, 27.
173 (1981), 12 Sask. R. 79 (Sask. Q.B.); affirmed (1983), 22 Sask. R. 241 (Sask. C.A.).
174 Above, pp. 258-260.

The approach of the Court of Appeal in that case, the language of Fitzpatrick C.J. cited above, and similar language and decisions in other cases,[175] reveals the strong connection between mistake insofar as it relates to the existence of the subject-matter of a contract, construction of contract, and the doctrine of frustration or impossibility of performance.[176] Indeed some of the cases could be equally as well decided on one ground as upon another. This possibility makes it all the more difficult to acknowledge and apply any doctrine of mistake to such instances. As Lord Denning said in *Solle v. Butcher*,[177]

> [t]he cases where goods have perished at the time of sale . . . are really contracts which are not void for mistake but are void by reason of an implied condition precedent, because the contract proceeded on the basic assumption that it was possible of performance.

Those remarks referred also to cases where the goods at the time of the sale "belong to the buyer". This could be extended to include cases not only where the sale is of such a *res sua*, but also where, for some other reason, it was not possible, in law for the buyer to buy the goods from the seller. In one sense, it could be said, they are only other illustrations of the sale of a non-existent thing. In another sense, however, it could be argued that the mistake is one of *law*, not fact. For example, in *Cooper v. Phibbs*,[178] the contract concerned a lease of salmon fishing rights for three years. Unknown to both parties the lease was already owned by the intended lessee. It was held that the contract could be set aside, on the ground of mistake. Though it was argued that the mistake was one of law, not fact, in that it concerned ownership, it was held that a mistake about *private rights* was a mistake of fact. But supposing that the mistake were as to the legality of a sale to the purported buyer, or as to the legality of any sale of the thing in question, for example, where both parties were ignorant that the law forbade such sales? What kind of mistakes are these? They might be excluded from the operation of the law of mistake on the ground that they concerned law, not fact.[179] They might come within the scope of the law relating to sales of non-existent things, on the basis that a thing which legally cannot be sold, either to a specific individual or to anyone generally, is not a thing which exists for the purposes of the law of contract (something corresponding to the Roman notion of *res extra commercium*).

---

175 See *McKenna v. F.B. McNamee & Co.* (1888), 15 S.C.R. 311 (S.C.C.); *Carr v. Berg*, [1917] 3 W.W.R. 1037 (B.C.C.A.); affirmed [1918] 2 W.W.R. 368 (S.C.C.); *Kerrigan v. Harrison* (1921), 62 S.C.R. 374 (S.C.C.).

176 As to which see below, p. 623 *et seq.*

177 [1950] 1 K.B. 671 at 691 (C.A.).

178 (1867), L.R. 2 H.L. 149 (H.L.). In *McCarthy v. Godin Mining & Exploration Ltd.* (1978), 20 N.B.R. (2d) 676 (N.B.Q.B) (above, pp. 237, 272), Barry J. suggested that the case could be determined along the lines of *Cooper v. Phibbs, i.e.*, as a case involving the purchase of a *res sua*, therefore the contract would be invalid because there was nothing that could be purchased by one party from the other, since it was not in existence as a piece of property capable of becoming the property of the purchaser.

179 Above, pp. 265, 266. But note the question of the relevance of the distinction today: above, p. 267.

What if the thing exists, but there is something about it which could be made use of to render the sale a nullity, if only it were known about by one of the contracting parties? The facts of *Bell v. Lever Brothers Ltd.*[180] spring to mind in this context. The service agreements about which the parties contracted undoubtedly existed, but they were capable of being avoided if only Lever Brothers had known of the conduct of the employees whose contracts were being terminated by the compensation agreement. Notwithstanding the questions of law that were involved in the validity and enforceability of the service contracts, the mistake in question was one of fact, not law. Hence, it had to be dealt with on the basis of the law of mistake. Does this mean that the question whether or not a legal obligation exists, so as to be susceptible to being rescinded by subsequent agreement, or else requiring a payment thereunder, is always one of fact, not law? Many of the cases in which the repayment of money is being claimed on the ground that it was originally paid under a mistake are cases of this sort, and have been held to involve a mistake of fact.[181] But in others it has been said that the mistake was one of law, thereby excluding recovery[182] (unless on some alternative ground, such as compulsion). It is now clear that, in Canada, recovery of money paid under mistake will be possible whether the mistake was one of fact or law.[183] The common law has arrived at the same conclusion as equity, as set out in the *Diplock* case.[184] It is now a matter of doubt whether this attitude will also be adopted to determine whether or not a contract is in existence between the parties in the light of the error under which it was negotiated.

(d) Identity of transaction

Another possibly operative kind of mistake occurs when a party has mistaken the kind of contract, that is, transaction, that is involved. For example, a party believes that he is giving a guarantee for another's debt, when he is in fact selling his property. Originally, where a contract was by deed, that is, *under seal*, a party could plead such error in certain limited circumstances, by alleging, *non est factum*, that is, that the deed, though appearing to be his, was in fact not his, as he had assented and affixed his seal to something other than what he had intended. Such a plea was a denial of consent. In more modern times, the plea has been allowed to be raised in the case of *any* written contract, not necessarily one under seal.

The doctrine of *non est factum*, as stated in a recent Canadian case,[185] has had a long and elastic history:

There have been times when the interpretation given by the courts has been so narrow

---

180 [1932] A.C. 161 (H.L.) (above, p. 275) contrast *Magee v. Pennine Ins. Co.*, [1969] 2 Q.B. 507 (C.A.); *T.D. Bank v. Fortin (No. 2)* (1978), 88 D.L.R. (3d) 232 (B.C.S.C.).
181 Goff & Jones, *Law of Restitution*, 3rd ed. (1986), pp. 119-120.
182 *Ibid.*, pp. 120-127.
183 Above, p. 266.
184 *Re Diplock*, [1948] Ch. 465 (C.A.); affirmed [1951] A.C. 251 (H.L.).
185 *C.I.B.C. v. Shotbolt*, [1981] 5 W.W.R. 738 at 747 (Man. Q.B.) *per* Kroft J. See also *Cameron v. Dorcic* (1987), 80 N.S.R. (2d) 152 at 157 (N.S.T.D.); affirmed (1988), 83 N.S.R. (2d) 85 (N.S.C.A.).

as to apply to only those persons demonstrating a disability akin to blindness or mental infirmity. At other times the doctrine has been used with a more curative philosophy. Both approaches are understandable. On the one hand, it is of importance particularly in the world of commerce that documents apparently signed and executed in the ordinary course should be relied upon. On the other, there is a reluctance to impose a burden on someone who probably would never have affixed his signature to a document had he understood its true nature and intent. This is particularly so when the gain or benefit attached to the signing is small in relation to the burden imposed.

This plea was originally available only to the blind and the illiterate, as stated in the old English decision in *Thoroughgood's Case; Thoroughgood v. Cole*.[186] Since then it has undergone considerable development, culminating in the decision of the House of Lords in *Saunders v. Anglia Building Society*.[187] The law in Canada has been based upon the English developments. Therefore, it is of some importance to see what was decided in the latter part of the nineteenth century and early part of the twentieth by courts in England, and the effect of the more recent case, before looking at the approach of the Canadian decisions.

What started, in the medieval period, as a plea putting in issue the validity of a particular party's signature, became in the nineteenth century, when the consensual contract, as opposed to the contract under seal, was the chief form of manifestation of agreement, a doctrine which could be made applicable to all written contracts.[188] In doing this, the courts made adaptations which, as Lord Wilberforce pointed out in the *Saunders* case,[189] were not always logical. Parallelling other similar distinctions which were operative in relation to mistake, the courts drew a difference between mistakes as to the character of a document and mistakes as to its contents. If a party had been misled into thinking that a document was quite different in legal character from what it actually was, then, even in the absence of fraud, he would be able to resist liability under such a document. By way of a novel development since the early days of the plea (which only operated *inter partes*), he could also claim back property from some third party into whose hands it had come as a result of transactions by the one who orginally had induced the making of the contract in respect of which the plea could be raised. This was because any such contract would be void *ab initio*. If all that had happened was that a party was misled as to some contents of the document, then, at the most, the contract was voidable. The problem of making this differentiation was first stated in its modern form in *Foster v. MacKinnon*[190] and later restated, with some terminological changes that may have rendered the whole thing confusing and illogical, in *Howatson v. Webb*.[191] It was discussed at some length by Lords

---

186 (1582), 2 Co. Rep. 9a, 76 E.R. 408.
187 [1971] A.C. 1039 (H.L.); applied in *United Dominions Trust Ltd. v. Western*, [1975] 3 All E.R. 1017 (C.A.).
188 The chief source of this was the decision in *Foster v. Mackinnon* (1869), L.R. 4 C.P. 704. Later important decisions were *Hunter v. Walters* (1871), 7 Ch. App. 75; *Nat. Prov. Bank of England v. Jackson* (1886), 33 Ch. D. 1 (C.A.).
189 Above, note 187, at 970.
190 Above, note 188.
191 [1907] 1 Ch. 537; affirmed [1908] 1 Ch. 1 (C.A.).

Wilberforce and Pearson in the *Saunders* case,[192] where the most modern view of this doctrine was clarified.

In *Saunders v. Anglia Building Society* the plaintiff, a 78-year-old woman, executed an assignment of her leasehold interest in a certain house to Lee, the first defendant. She stated that she intended to give the house to her nephew Walter on condition that Walter permit her to live in the house for the rest of her life: and that she handed the title deeds to Walter believing that this action was all that was necessary to make him owner of the house. In signing the assignment, which she did voluntarily, she believed that all she was doing was signing a deed of gift giving effect to the intended granting of the house to Walter. In consequence of all this, Lee was able to raise money on the security of the house from a building society. But other arrangements which had been made between Lee and Walter, to achieve which they had induced the plaintiff to sign the document, fell through. Instead of Walter obtaining the intended benefit of the whole transaction, the money obtained by Lee paid off the latter's creditors. In consequence, while Walter would have indirectly got some financial advantage from the assignment to Lee (and it must be remembered that the plaintiff wanted ultimately to benefit Walter), he got nothing. Subsequently the plaintiff brought an action to have the assignment to Lee declared void, as well as return of the title deeds and damages for fraudulent misrepresentation, as well as damages from the building society for detention of the title deeds. The action was brought against Lee and the building society. The basis of the claim was *non est factum*. The plaintiff's action succeeded at trial. On appeal the building society was successful in having the original judgment upset. The House of Lords upheld the Court of Appeal on the ground that the evidence did not establish the necessary mistake. Thus the plaintiff was unable to invoke the plea.

The House of Lords agreed that the operation of the doctrine should be limited in scope. It would be dangerous to extend it too far. Hence it was not to be applied where the person signing the document could easily have ascertained its true nature by reading it and has taken on himself the risk of not reading it.[193] There had to be a difference either in the whole document or as to a particular which went to the substance of the whole consideration or to the root of the matter; points of detail in the contents of the document would not be enough.[194] In the words of Lord Pearson[195]

> the plea of *non est factum* ought to be available in a proper case for the relief of a person who for permanent or temporary reasons (not limited to blindness or illiteracy) is not capable of both reading and sufficiently understanding the deed or other document to be signed. By 'sufficiently understanding' I mean understanding at least to the point of detecting a fundamental difference between the actual document and the document as the signer had believed it to be.

---

192 Above, note 186, at 970-971, 977-980.
193 *Ibid.*, at 978-979 *per* Lord Pearson.
194 *Ibid.*, at 965 *per* Lord Hodson.
195 *Ibid.*, at 979.

What would be a proper case for relief? In view of the language of Lord Pearson this would seem to indicate a case where the document was fundamentally or radically different from what the signer believed and intended it to be, and where the signature was not brought about by negligence of the signer failing to take precautions he ought to have taken.[196] How does one ascertain the signer's intention? Again, from what Lord Pearson said, it would seem that this is to be done by applying the subjective, not the objective test, that is, the intention which he has in his own mind, rather than the intention which he manifests to others.[197]

The problem of negligence requires some separate and special discussion. In the course of the modern development of this doctrine, the notions of duty of care, negligence and estoppel became mixed together and were introduced into the elaboration of the circumstances in and under which the doctrine might be applicable or inapplicable. The speeches in the *Saunders* case elucidated much that was confused, and have shown the extent to which, and the way in which, the negligence of the signer of the document may be relevant in deciding whether or not the plea should be allowed. Prior to the *Saunders* case, the cases, and in particular the decision in *Carlisle & Cumberland Banking Co. v. Bragg,*[198] appeared to have distinguished between documents which were bills of exchange and those which were not. In the case of the former, the cases suggested that the maker, that is, signer of the document owed a duty of care to persons who might subsequently take the bill of exchange for value and so possibly lose if the bill were declared to be void on the basis of *non est factum.* Other documents, however, involved no such duty. Hence, with bills of exchange negligence could destroy the plea, but not with other documents. The same point was sometimes expressed in the language of estoppel, thereby creating confusion.[199] On the one hand there was the idea that "negligence" in its full technical meaning, involving duty of care and so forth, was necessary to defeat the plea; on the other hand there was the notion that conduct which might not amount to negligence could still found an estoppel. Not only did this produce problems of substantive law; it also meant that the burden of proof was on the innocent party who wished to uphold the validity of the original contract. The House of Lords made it plain that what may be involved is not negligence in the technical sense, but negligence in the sense of "carelessness". Furthermore, this can defeat any plea of *non est factum,* whatever the nature of the document in question, and the onus of proof is on the party raising the plea of *non est factum* so as to have the document held to be a nullity.[200] The *Bragg* case is no longer good law. Indeed, in view of the fact that the House of Lords approved a passage in the judgment of Lord Denning M.R. in the Court

---

196 *Ibid.*; compare Lord Wilberforce, at 972.

197 *Ibid.*, at 980. This and the previous three sentences were cited in *Duck Lake Feed Processors Ltd. v. Folliet* (1982), 16 Sask. R. 355 at 370 (Sask. Q.B.).

198 [1911] 1 K.B. 489 (C.A.). See also *Lewis v. Clay* (1897), 67 L.J.O.B. 224.

199 See, *e.g., Howatson v. Webb,* above, note 191; *Blay v. Pollard,* [1930] 1 K.B. 628 (C.A.); *Muskham Finance Ltd. v. Howard,* [1963] 1 Q.B. 904 (C.A.).

200 See the detailed discussion by Stone, "The Limits of Non Est Factum After Gallie v. Lee" (1972), 88 L.Q.R. 190.

of Appeal, it would seem that the *prima facie* rule is that a document will be good unless and until the party alleging its invalidity proves that there are reasons, including the absence of any carelessness on his part, which justify the application of the plea. What Lord Denning said was[201]

> Whenever a man of full age and understanding, who can read and write, signs a legal document which is put before him for signature — by which I mean a document which, it is apparent on the fact of it, is intended to have legal consequences — then, if he does not take the trouble to read it, but signs it as it is, relying on the word of another as to its character or contents or effect, he cannot be heard to say that it is not his document.

Such has been the English development of this doctrine. What has now to be considered is the way the law developed in Canada and the effect of the decision in the *Saunders* case upon the Canadian situation.[202]

In some of the earlier cases, in which *Foster v. Mackinnon, Howatson v. Webb* and the *Bragg* case, were cited with approval and followed,[203] there are many references to blindness and illiteracy, and especially inability to read and write English, as being the basis for this plea.[204] While it was unnecessary for a party pleading *non est factum* to prove fraud or misrepresentation on the part of the other party in order to succeed,[205] "mere lack of explanation and understanding of a document does not entitle a party making it to relief from its obligations," as was said by Smith J.A. in the leading case of *Bradley v. Imperial Bank*.[206] But refusal to read over a document, when the signer cannot read or write, or misreading the document, or misrepresenting its contents, would all be grounds for holding that a document which had been executed in fact was not executed in law.[207] Ignorance of English, however, was held not in itself capable of supporting a presumption that the signer was defrauded.[208] Moreover, except where there was a positive request for the document to be read or explained there would seem to have been no duty to make the contents of the document clear to the signer, such that failure to do so permitted the application of the plea.[209]

---

201 *Gallie v. Lee*, [1969] 2 Ch. 17 at 36-37 (C.A.).

202 The discussion of the Canadian development in the first edition of this book was referred to by Stratton J. in *Zed v. Zed* (1980), 28 N.B.R. (2d) 580 at 586 (N.B.Q.B.).

203 The leading case is *Martin v. Nat. Union Fire Ins. Co.*, [1923] 3 W.W.R. 897 (Alta. C.A.); affirmed [1924] S.C.R. 348 (*sub nom. Nat. Union Fire Ins. Co. of Pittsburg v. Martin*) (S.C.C.).

204 *J.R. Watkins Co. v. Jansen*, [1928] 1 W.W.R. 199 (Sask. C.A.); affirmed [1928] S.C.R. 414 (*sub nom. J.R. Watkins Co. v. Minke*) (S.C.C.).

205 *Imperial Bank v. McLellan*, [1934] 1 W.W.R. 65 (Alta. S.C.). But fraud could be: *Can. Bank of Commerce v. McGillivray*, [1922] 3 W.W.R. 527 (Sask. K.B.).

206 [1926] 3 D.L.R. 38 at 65-66 (Ont. C.A.) (followed in *Bank of N.S. v. Forest F. Ross & Son Ltd.* (1982), 40 N.B.R. (2d) 563 (N.B.Q.B.), where the facts entitled the court to apply both the *Saunders* case and the earlier Canadian decisions); compare *Int. Loan Co. v. Kostniuk*, [1936] 3 D.L.R. 227 (Man. K.B.); reversed on other grounds [1936] 4 D.L.R. 764 (Man. C.A.).

207 *Letourneau v. Carbonneau* (1904), 35 S.C.R. 110 at 111 (S.C.C.) *per* Nesbitt J.

208 *Lasby v. Johnson*, [1928] 3 W.W.R. 447 (Sask. C.A.).

209 *Can. Bank of Commerce v. Dembeck*, [1929] 4 D.L.R. 220 at 228 (Sask. C.A.) *per* Mackenzie J.A.

Such ideas were reiterated in cases occurring in the 1940's and early 1950's. There had to be a mistake for the plea to be successful; hence, even if fraud were lacking, there must have been some misrepresentation.[210] Consensus was the test; therefore a signer who was not Canadian in origin, or whose knowledge of English was totally or partially defective, might well raise the plea by way of defence.[211] In such instances, as was stated in *Michels v. Miner*,[212] speaking of the signer, "his mind did not go with the pen". But the mistake had to be about the nature of the document, not its contents. And, as Macdonald J. said in *Hankinson v. Royal Bank of Canada*,[213] there must be no negligence on the part of the signer if he is to be allowed to escape being bound by his signature. In that case the signer was misled not as to the nature of the document he was signing, which was a promissory note, but as to its contents. In such case, he could not plead *non est factum*.[214] So, too, in *Bank of Nova Scotia v. Canadian Road Equipment Ltd.*,[215] the signer of the document knew he was signing a guarantee of the company's indebtedness to the plaintiff bank. He was ignorant as to the extent of his undertaking; indeed he was negligent. Hence, the plea could not be raised. Furthermore, it would seem, the plea could not be raised, irrespective of the question of the kind of mistake or the signer's negligence, if the documents were a negotiable instrument. So much Coady J.A. said in *Ostrikoff v. Vancouver Finance Co.*[216]

Ultimately, by reason of problems arising from the discovery of oil in the prairie provinces, a number of cases reached the Supreme Court of Canada, and led to a further statement of the basic and English-derived principles. The first leading decision was *Prudential Trust Co. v. Cugnet.*[217] H (acting as agent for the A Co.) persuaded C to sign an agreement and transfer of his share in certain mineral rights. He represented that the document was a mere grant of an option on the rights. A Co. assigned the transfer to the plaintiff company. In an action based on the transfer it was held that the defendants (who were C and his son) could

---

210 *Rayfuse v. Mugleston*, [1954] 3 D.L.R. 360 (B.C.C.A.); *Maloney v. Eldorado Mining & Refining Ltd.* (1954), 11 W.W.R. 49 (Alta. S.C.). Compare *Sumner v. Bonser*, [1949] 1 W.W.R. 676 (Sask. C.A.).

211 *De Koning v. Boychuk*, [1951] 3 D.L.R. 624 (Alta. S.C.); *Serbu v. Feinstein* (1951), 3 W.W.R. (N.S.) 545 (Sask. C.A.). For a more modern approach, namely, along the lines that the transaction was unconscionable, see *Cymbaluk v. Lewicki*, [1973] 3 W.W.R. 169 (B.C.S.C.).

212 [1949] 2 W.W.R. 269 (Alta. S.C.); compare *Prudential Trust Co. v. Hjertaas* (1953), 9 W.W.R. (N.S.) 8 (Sask. Q.B.).

213 [1954] 2 D.L.R. 345 at 352-353 (N.S.C.A.).

214 Contrast *Marks v. Imp. Life Assur. Co.*, [1949] O.R. 49 (Ont. H.C.); affirmed [1949] O.R. 564 (Ont. C.A.), where the wife did not realize that she was signing a document which affected *her* insurance policies, therefore she could plead *non est factum*.

215 [1951] O.R. 288 (Ont. H.C.).

216 (1955), 17 W.W.R. 248 (B.C.C.A.).

217 [1956] S.C.R. 915 (S.C.C.); compare *Hase v. Prudential Trust Co.; Fichter v. Prudential Trust Co.* (1956), 20 W.W.R. 337 (Sask. Q.B.); *Perry v. Prudential Trust Co.; Thomas v. Crown Trust Co.* (1957), 21 W.W.R. 685 (Man. Q.B.); affirmed (1958), 25 W.W.R. 193 (Man. C.A.). Contrast *Rogers v. Nfld. Light and Power Co.* (1957), 9 D.L.R. (2d) 56 (Nfld. S.C.), where the plaintiff knew he was granting rights in and over his land, namely, to put up electrical works, etc., and was not misled into misunderstanding the document, except possibly the extent of its contents: *ibid.* at 63-64. *per* Walsh C.J. Held, *non est factum* could not be pleaded.

plead *non est factum* as a good defence. Here there was a mistake as to the nature and character of the document itself, not merely as to its contents.[218] Even if C had been negligent, which does not appear to have been the case in the circumstances, such negligence would not estop him from raising the plea, as there was no general duty of care in these situations.[219] On the other hand, in *Prudential Trust Co. v. Forseth*,[220] a wife signed a document under the Saskatchewan Homestead Act, under which she assented to the disposition of her rights in property in respect of which she had certain statutory rights. As a result she lost those rights which were assigned to the trust company. She argued *non est factum*, and her plea was disallowed. In this case she may have had difficulty in comprehending what the document meant, but she was under no misconception as to the nature of the document, that is, what it was intended to achieve. Hence the plea could not stand.

Subsequent cases seem to have polarized around these two decisions. Either the party raising the plea was sufficiently ignorant and overreached to justify granting the defence, or, as in *Forseth*, a party who read a document or had it read through (in the absence of deception) and was literate enough to entitle the court to infer understanding of the general nature of the document, was bound. Thus in *Dorsch v. Freeholders Oil Co.*,[221] where the plaintiff refused or neglected to have the contract read to him or to read it himself, but simply obtained some explanation of some of the conditions, it was held that he knew he was disposing of his royalty under a lease and was granting a further lease to the defendants, hence he could not rely on *non est factum*. In contrast in *Stearns v. Ratel*,[222] which concerned a contract under which the plaintiff purported to release the defendant from liability to the plaintiff in respect of an accident, it was held that while this could cover repairs to the plaintiff's car, it did not affect the plaintiff's rights in respect of personal injuries. The plaintiff had been misled by the garage operator acting as agent for the defendant's insurers. The majority of the British Columbia Court of Appeal followed the *Cugnet* case, to hold that the plaintiff knew it was a release of some sort, but not what kind of release was involved. Davey J.A. dissented, and was prepared to follow the reasoning and decision in the *Forseth* case.

The Canadian situation, prior to the *Saunders* case, would appear to have been that there was considerable sympathy for the position of some illiterate, ill-educated, or otherwise disadvantaged parties, who signed a document, perhaps not fully realizing what was involved. But for *non est factum* to be pleaded successfully, the party raising the plea would have to show some kind of misconception, not necessarily fraudulently induced, as to the intended legal effect

---

218 [1956] S.C.R. 915 at 925 (S.C.C.) *per* Nolan J.

219 *Ibid.*, at 929 *per* Locke J.

220 [1960] S.C.R. 210 (S.C.C.); compare *Prudential Trust Co. v. Olson*, [1960] S.C.R. 227 (S.C.C.); *Homeplan Realty Ltd. v. Rochon* (1972), 30 D.L.R. (3d) 748 (Sask. Q.B.).

221 [1965] S.C.R. 670 (S.C.C.); compare *Pepper v. Prudential Trust Co. Ltd.*, [1965] S.C.R. 417 (S.C.C.). Note the effect of *adoption* of the contract on the plea of *non est factum* unless there has been fraud: *ibid.*, affirming (1964), 45 W.W.R. 275 (Sask. C.A.).

222 (1961), 29 D.L.R. (2d) 718 (B.C.C.A.).

of the document. Negligence does not seem to have played a very large part in the thinking of Canadian judges in this context, although they were concerned with the sort of *intent* shown by the signer of the document.[223]

Between 1971 and 1983 Canadian courts were faced many times with the problem of deciding whether to follow the English approach in the *Saunders* case or that of the Supreme Court of Canada in *Cugnet*. In several decisions from various provinces courts accepted and followed the House of Lords,[224] notwithstanding the binding nature of the *Cugnet* case as compared with the decision in *Saunders*. In other instances[225] a provincial court followed *Cugnet*, or else was able to distinguish the Supreme Court case, and, indirectly follow the lead of the House of Lords.[226] Sometimes a court faced with the issue of *non est factum* was able to determine the problem without reference to either the House of Lords or the Supreme Court of Canada.[227] The plea of *non est factum* was not always successful.[228] The crucial issues in any case in which the plea was raised were

---

223 This paragraph was cited by Estey J. in *Marvco Color Research Ltd. v. Harris* (1982), 141 D.L.R. (3d) 577 at 586 (S.C.C.).

224 *Hall v. Watton* (1973), 4 Nfld. & P.E.I.R. 587 (Nfld. S.C.); affirmed (1975), 8 Nfld. & P.E.I.R. 1 (Nfld. C.A.); *Custom Motors Ltd. v. Dwinell* (1975), 61 D.L.R. (3d) 342 (N.S.C.A.); *Prov. Bank of Can. v. Whiteoak Const. Ltd.* (1976), 15 N.B.R. (2d) 408 (N.B.Q.B.); *Bank of Montreal v. Crosby Group Ltd.* (1977), 26 N.S.R. (2d) 331 (N.S.T.D.); *Van de Sande v. Kirk* (1976), 22 N.S.R. (2d) 339 (N.S.T.D.); *C.I.B.C. v. Kanadian Kiddee Photo Ltd.*, [1979] 3 W.W.R. 256 (B.C.S.C.); *C.I.B.C. v. Dura Wood Preservers Ltd.* (1979), 14 B.C.L.R. 338 (B.C.S.C.); *Zed v. Zed* (1980), 28 N.B.R. (2d) 580 (N.B.Q.B.); *Royal Bank v. Smith* (1980), 27 Nfld. & P.E.I.R. 40 (Nfld. T.D.) (following *Bank of N.S. v. Battiste* (1979), 22 Nfld. & P.E.I.R. 192 (Nfld. T.D.), which followed the *Saunders* case); *Royal Bank v. Churchill* (1980), 27 Nfld. & P.E.I.R. 31 (Nfld. T.D.); *Firestone of Can. Ltd. v. Smith* (1978), 24 N.S.R. (2d) 578 (N.S.T.D.); *Royal Bank v. Gannon* (1980), 42 N.S.R. (2d) 526 (N.S.T.D.); *Island Glass Ltd. v. O'Connor* (1980), 28 Nfld. & P.E.I.R. 377 (P.E.I. S.C.); *C.I.B.C. v. Shotbolt*, [1981] 5 W.W.R. 738 (Man. Q.B.); *Royal Bank v. Mahoney* (1982), 38 Nfld. & P.E.I.R. 179 (Nfld. C.A.); *Bank of Montreal v. Dodds* (1982), 55 N.S.R. (2d) 392 (N.S.T.D.).

225 *Reichelt v. West-Gro Hldgs. Ltd.*, [1978] 4 W.W.R. 484 (B.C.S.C.); *MacEachern v. Bancroft* (1977), 27 N.S.R. (2d) 407 (N.S.T.D.); *Marchand v. Marchand* (1979), 36 N.S.R. (2d) 264 (N.S.T.D.); *Horvath v. Young* (1980), 15 R.P.R. 266 (Ont. H.C.); *Bank of Montreal v. Taurus Tpt. Ltd.* (1980), 22 B.C.L.R. 154 (B.C.S.C.); *Duck Lake Feed Processors Ltd. v. Folliet* (1982), 16 Sask. R. 355 (Sask. Q.B.); *Bank of N.S. v. Omni Const. Ltd.*, [1981] 3 W.W.R. 301 (Sask. Q.B.; affirmed [1983] 4 W.W.R. 577 (Sask. C.A.).

226 *Bank of N.S. v. Forest F. Ross & Son Ltd.* (1982), 40 N.B.R. (2d) 563 (N.B.Q.B.); compare *C.I.B.C. v. Shotbolt*, [1981] 5 W.W.R. 738 at 748-749 (Man. Q.B.).

227 *Lomas v. DiCecca* (1978), 88 D.L.R. (3d) 434 (Ont. H.C.); *Household Finance Corp. v. Adams* (1976), 16 N.B.R. (2d) 149 (N.B.Q.B.); *Butt v. Humber* (1976), 17 Nfld. & P.E.I.R. 92 (Nfld. T.D.); *Taylor v. Armstrong* (1979), 24 O.R. (2d) 614 (Ont. H.C.); *Ghadban v. Bank of N.S.* (1982), 132 D.L.R. (3d) 475 (Ont. H.C.).

228 Cases where it succeeded: *C.I.B.C. v. Kanadian Kiddee Photo Co.*, above, note 224; *Marchand v. Marchand*, above, note 225; *Royal Bank v. Gannon*, above, note 224; *Horvath v. Young*, above, note 225; *Island Glass Ltd. v. O'Connor*, above, note 224; *C.I.B.C. v. Shotbolt*, above, note 226; *Duck Lake Feed Processors Ltd. v. Folliet*, above, note 225; *Ghadban v. Bank of N.S.*, above, note 227; *Beaulieu v. Nat. Bank of Can.* (1983), 47 N.B.R. (2d) 220 (N.B.Q.B.); reversed (1984), 55 N.B.R. (2d) 154 (N.B.C.A.). Cases where it failed: *Butt v. Humber*, above, note 227; *C.I.B.C. v. Dura Wood Preservers Ltd.*, above, note 224; *Royal Bank v. Smith*, above, note 224; *Royal Bank v. Churchill*, above, note 224; *Bank of Montreal v. Taurus Tpt. Ltd.*, above, note 225; *Bank of N.S. v. Omni Const. Ltd.*, above, note 225; *Royal Bank v. MacPhee* (1981), 33 N.B.R. (2d) 370

these: was there a significant difference between the document actually signed by the party raising the defence and the document he or she believed was being signed and had the intent to sign: was the party signing guilty of the carelessness in appending his or her signature? In 1981 Kroft J., in Manitoba, after looking at the *Saunders, Cugnet* and *Forseth* decisions, concluded that the current state of the law could be summarized as follows:[229]

> 1. Where the defendant failed to understand the precise meaning and content of a document, but did have a good idea as to its nature and purpose, the defence will not succeed.
>
> 2. Where there is an absence of intention by virtue of the fact that the instrument signed is fundamentally different from that which the party believed he was signing, and where the defendant demonstrates an absence of carelessness, the defence will succeed.

Proof that the defendant thought the document he or she was signing was fundamentally different from the document he or she was in fact signing depended upon evidence as to the state of mind and knowledge of the party whose signature was in issue.[230] Was such party experienced in business? Was it a novel situation for such party? What, if any, representations were made by the other party to the document, that party's solicitor, or someone else? Whether the party signing was careless depended upon such matters as his or her age, literacy, standard of education, experience in business, normal standards of behaviour for a person in such situation, reasonableness of his or her reliance upon the other party's statements or representations, or those of a solicitor, bank manager or similar person, ability of such person to understand the nature and effect of what he or she was signing, and whether or not it was reasonable for such party to sign without reading the document or asking to have its nature and effect explained.[231]

The issue did not reach the Supreme Court of Canada until the case of *Marvco*

(N.B.Q.B.); *Gillis v. McDonald* (1980), 44 N.S.R. (2d) 60 (N.S.T.D.); *Alcan Can. Prod. Ltd. v. Burin Peninsula Aluminum Prods. Ltd.* (1980), 31 Nfld. & P.E.I.R. 181 (Nfld. T.D.); *Bank of N.S. v. Forest F. Ross & Son Ltd.*, above, note 226; *Royal Bank v. Mahoney*, above, note 224; *Bank of Montreal v. Dodds*, above, note 224.

229 *C.I.B.C. v. Shotbolt*, [1981] 5 W.W.R. 738 at 748 (Man. Q.B.).

230 Compare *C.I.B.C. v. Kanadian Kiddee Phot Co.*, above, note 224; *C.I.B.C. v. Dura Wood Preservers Ltd.*, above, note 224; *Zed v. Zed*, above, note 224; *Royal Bank v. Gannon*, above, note 224; *Horvath v. Young*, above, note 225; *Royal Bank v. MacPhee*, above, note 228; *Wardley Can. Ltd. v. Gelzinger* (1981), 28 A.R. 595 (Alta. Q.B.); *Island Glass Ltd. v. O'Connor*, above, note 224; *C.I.B.C. v. Shotbolt*, above, note 226; *Duck Lake Feed Processors Ltd. v. Folliet*, above, note 225; *Royal Bank v. Mahoney*, above, note 224; *Bank of Montreal v. Dodds*, above, note 224. See also *Royal Bank v. Savage* (1983), 48 N.B.R. (2d) 117 (N.B.Q.B.).

231 Compare *Bank of N.S. v. Forest F. Ross & Son Ltd.*, above, note 226; *Bank of Montreal v. Dodds*, above, note 224; *Royal Bank v. Churchill*, above, note 224; *Beaulieu v. National Bank of Can.*, above, note 228, with *C.I.B.C. v. Kanadian Kiddee Photo Co.*, above, note 224; *Bank of N.S. v. Omni Const. Ltd.*, above, note 225; *C.I.B.C. v. Shotbolt*, above, note 226; *Duck Lake Feed Processors Ltd. v. Folliet*, above, note 225; *Royal Bank v. Mahoney*, above, note 224; *Ghadban v. Bank of N.S.*, above, note 227.

Color Research Ltd. v. Harris[232] in 1983. As a result of that case at least one of the issues dealt with by the House of Lords in *Saunders* may be said to have been resolved in Canada. In effect the Supreme Court refused to uphold the *Cugnet* case in the light of *Saunders*, accepted the overruling of the decision in the *Bragg* case, and held that careless behaviour by the party who had signed a document and now wished to plead *non est factum* might defeat the defence regardless of whether the document was a negotiable instrument or something else. This principle of law, as Estey J. pointed out,[233] is based not only upon the principle of placing the loss on the person guilty of carelessness, but also upon a recognition of the need for certainty and security in commerce. That has been recognized since the earliest days of the plea. In the *Marvco* case the parties signing the document, which was a collateral security granted by them in favour of the appellants securing the performance by certain convenantors under another transaction, did not read the document. They relied upon representations as to its nature made to them by one of the convenantors whose performance was being guaranteed by the document in question. In reliance upon this document the appellants released one of the covenantors from liability under a chattel mortgage he had given them. The appellants adjusted their affairs on the basis that the security was valid.[234] On those facts the Supreme Court held the parties who had signed the security liable.

Subsequent cases have accepted and applied the *Saunders* and *Marvco* cases. In the latter Estey J. used language that indicated the Supreme Court viewed with favour the approach in *Saunders* to the nature of a mistake that will allow a party to plead *non est factum*.[235] It is a difficult matter to invoke the plea successfully. The onus of proof is heavy upon a party raising the plea.[236] Most of the cases in which it has been raised resulted in lack of success for the party seeking to rely on the plea. Various reasons were given for this. In some instances there was

---

232 (1982), 141 D.L.R. (3d) 577 (S.C.C.), applied in *Slattery Mgmt. & Realty (1978) Ltd. v. Archie Colpitts Ltd.* (1983), 48 N.B.R. (2d) 244 (N.B.Q.B.); *Beaulieu v. Nat. Bank of Can.* (1983), 47 N.B.R. (2d) 220 (N.B.Q.B.); reversed (1984), 55 N.B.R. (2d) 154 (N.B.C.A.); *Harvest Hldgs. Ltd. v. Bohun* (1984), 34 Sask. R. 127 (Sask. Q.B.); *Sullivan v. Crnogorac* (1983), 60 N.S.R. (2d) 201 (N.S.T.D.). See also the comments of Prowse J. in *C.I.B.C. v. Chang*, [1986] 1 W.W.R. 326 (Alta. Q.B.).
233 (1982), 141 D.L.R. (3d) 577 at 586 (S.C.C.).
234 *Ibid.*, at 589.
235 *Ibid.*, at 585-585. In *Avco Financial Services Realty Ltd. v. Tracey* (1979), 59 N.S.R. (2d) 333 (N.S.T.D.), a mother who knew she was signing a deed dealing with land, but believed it related to other land owned by her son, not the land which the deed conveyed, was not able to plead *non est factum*; she knew what she was signing and was mistaken only about the contents. This looks like an application of the older rule, but it could be rationalized under the recent English rule. See also *Caisse-Populaire de Ste-Anne du Madawaska Ltée v. Cormier* (1983), 53 N.B.R. (2d) 1 (N.B.Q.B.).
236 *Prentice v. Barrie Community Credit Union Ltd.* (1988), 26 C.P.C. (2d) 178 (Ont. Dist. Ct.); *Castle Building Centres Group Ltd. v. Da Ros* (1990), 95 N.S.R. (2d) 24 (N.S.T.D.); affirmed (1990), 97 N.S.R. (2d) 270 (N.S.C.A.). See, *e.g.*, *Russell v. S.W. Mifflin Ltd.* (1991), 89 Nfld. & P.E.I.R. 168 (Nfld. T.D.); *Coleman v. Bishop* (1991), 103 N.S.R. (2d) 265 (N.S.T.D.).

no mistake.[237] In others the mistake that was made did not go to the nature of the document that was signed, but either to its contents[238] or to its legal consequences,[239] neither of which would suffice to satisfy the test in *Saunders*. In other instances the plea failed because of the carelessness of the party raising the plea.[240] Where the plea has been successful, it has been because the party signing the document was ignorant of the English language and did not know what was going on;[241] or was of limited education and reading ability and was mistaken as to what the document was;[242] or relied on what she was told by her husband to whom she was subservient in business matters, so she did not know what she was signing.[243]

The Canadian experience since *Saunders* and *Marvco* seems to suggest that the alteration to the doctrine made by the House of Lords may have resulted in its now being much more difficult to raise the plea of *non est factum* successfully.

---

237 *Columbia Trust Co. v. Solihull Enterprises Ltd.* (1986), 3 B.C.L.R. (2d) 123 (B.C.S.C.); *General Motors Acceptance Corp. of Can. v. Lawson* (1986), 74 N.B.R. (2d) 191 (N.B.Q.B.); affirmed on other grounds (1988), 52 D.L.R. (4th) 385 (N.B.C.A.); leave to appeal to S.C.C. refused (1989), 90 N.B.R. (2d) 360 (note) (S.C.C.); *Clowater v. Banque nationale du Can.* (1987), 82 N.B.R. (2d) 243 (N.B.Q.B.); reversed in part on other grounds (1988), 88 N.B.R. (2d) 279 (N.B.C.A.); *Sewid v. Ocean Fisheries Ltd.* (1987), 20 B.C.L.R. (2d) 201 (B.C.S.C.); *Hickey v. Hickey* (1988), 86 N.B.R. (2d) 421 (N.B.C.A.); *Bank of N.S. v. Toytman* (1989), 74 Nfld. & P.E.I.R. 53 (Nfld. T.D.); *Granville Savings & Mortgage Corp. v. Slevin* (1992), 12 C.C.L.T. (2d) 275 (Man. C.A.); reversed (November 2, 1993), Doc. 23210, La Forest, Sopinka, Gonthier, Cory, McLachlin, Iacobucci & Major JJ. (S.C.C.); *Farm Credit Corp. v. Miller* (1992), 126 A.R. 335 (Alta. Q.B.).

238 *Eagle Const. Ltd. v. Chaytor* (1986), 58 Nfld. & P.E.I.R. 23 (Nfld. T.D.); *Bank of N.S. v. Drouillard-Potter* (1987), 79 A.R. 2 (Alta. Master); *Cameron v. Dorcic* (1987), 80 N.S.R. (2d) 152 (N.S.T.D.); affirmed (1988), 83 N.S.R. (2d) 85 (N.S.C.A.); *Royal Bank v. Gill*, [1988] 3 W.W.R. 441 (B.C.C.A.); *N.S. Savings & Loan Co. v. Gorman* (1988), 86 N.S.R. (2d) 132 (N.S.T.D.); *MacDonald v. Creelman* (1989), 88 N.S.R. (2d) 403 (N.S.C.A.); affirming (1988), 83 N.S.R. (2d) 415 (N.S.T.D.); *Castle Building Centres Group Ltd. v. Da Ros* (1990), 95 N.S.R. (2d) 24 (N.S.T.D.); affirmed (1990), 97 N.S.R. (2d) 270 (N.S.C.A.); *Gorman v. Gorman* (1991), 90 Nfld. & P.E.I.R. 263 (Nfld. T.D.).

239 *Jenkins v. Strickland* (1990), 83 Nfld. & P.E.I.R. 30 (Nfld. T.D.), especially at 34 *per* Barry J.

240 *C.I.B.C. v. Chang*, [1986] 1 W.W.R. 326 (Alta. Q.B.); *Associate Capital Services Corp. v. Multi-Geophysical Services Inc.* (1987), 54 Alta. L.R. (2d) 85 (Alta. Q.B.); *Bank of N.S. v. Drouillard-Potter*, above, note 238; *Prince Albert Credit Union v. Diehl*, [1987] 4 W.W.R. 419 (Sask. Q.B.); *Vukomanovic v. Cook Bros. Transport Ltd.* (1987), 65 Nfld. & P.E.I.R. 181 (Nfld. T.D.); *Royal Bank v. Gill* (1987), 31 D.L.R. (4th) 61 (B.C.S.C.); affirmed (1987), 47 D.L.R. (4th) 466 (B.C.C.A.); *Citibank Can. v. Cameron* (1991), 4 O.R. (3d) 526 (Ont. Master); affirmed (1991), 7 O.R. (3d) 777 (Ont. Gen. Div.) (with which contrast *Wellington Trust Co. v. Scavuzzo* (1992), 26 R.P.R. (2d) 206 (Ont. Master)); *TSC Shannon Corp. v. Dial-A-Video Ltd.* (1992), 99 Nfld. & P.E.I.R. 326 (Nfld. T.D.). Contrast a New Zealand case in which there was no negligence: *Chiswick Invts. v. Pevats*, [1990] 1 N.Z.L.R. 169. Negligence in this context has been defined as the failure to take reasonable precautions to ascertain the character of a document before signing it: *Patelin v. Cullen* (1975), 132 C.L.R. 355.

241 *Garcia v. Garcia* (1986), 72 A.R. 180 (Alta. Q.B.). Contrast *Farm Credit Corp. v. Miller* (1992), 126 A.R. 335 (Alta. Q.B.), where the document was signed in a lawyer's office and the defendants knew what they were signing: *non est factum* could not be pleaded successfully: compare *Araki v. Wlodyka*, [1993] 5 W.W.R. 360 (B.C.S.C.).

242 *Meunier v. Meunier* (1988), 84 N.S.R. (2d) 86 (N.S.T.D.).

243 *Northside Economic Dev. Assistance Corp. v. Strickland* (1990), 96 N.S.R. (2d) 4 (N.S.T.D.).

8

Misrepresentation

1. Nature and types of misrepresentation[1]

A misrepresentation is a misstatement of some fact which is material to the making or inducement of a contract.[2] Complexity results from the very close relationship between misrepresentations, statements which are terms of a contract, and other statements which can form the basis for an estoppel against the party making them.[3] In each instance, one party has led the other into entering into a contract with the former, to some extent on the basis of the statement made by the former. The status of such statement is very important when it comes to considering: (a) whether or not a valid contract has been made; (b) what are its terms; and (c) the nature of the remedy open and available to the aggrieved party. If a statement can be regarded as a *term of the contract*,[4] then the position of a party who has suffered loss by reason of the breach of such term, that is, the failure of the other party to live up to his promise, is clearer to expound and easier

---

1 Reference was made to this section, and reliance placed upon it by Stratton J.A. in *Thomas Equip. Ltd. v. Sperry Rand Can. Ltd.* (1982), 40 N.B.R. (2d) 271 at 287 (N.B.C.A.).
2 Compare Miffin C.J. in *Paragon Entertainment Prods. Inc. v. McDonald's Wholesale & Retail Ltd.* (1978), 19 Nfld. & P.E.I.R. 181 at 181 (Nfld. T.D.). See, for example, *Eisenschiml v. Western Drilling Co.*, [1943] 1 W.W.R. 605 (Alta. C.A.); *Shortt v. MacLennan*, [1959] S.C.R. 3 (S.C.C.); *Comeller v. Billinkoff* (1952), 11 W.W.R. 279 (Man. Q.B.); contrast *Leggett v. Taylor* (1965), 50 D.L.R. (2d) 516 (B.C.S.C.).
   Note the extension of the scope and effect of misrepresentation, in relation to certain types of contracts, by the Business Practices Acts of Alberta, British Columbia, Newfoundland, Ontario and Prince Edward Island: below, pp. 340-342.
3 See Atiyah, "Misrepresentation, Warranty and Estoppel" (1971), 9 Alta. L. Rev. 347.
4 Below, pp. 449-453. See *Gill v. Kittler* (1983), 21 B.L.R. 108 (Alta. Q.B.).

to rectify. Misrepresentations do not necessarily qualify as terms of a contract.[5] Notwithstanding this, some misrepresentations can have an important effect upon the validity of the contract which results from their being made.[6]

A distinction must be made between misrepresentations which are fraudulent and those which are not. A fraudulent misrepresentation is one which is made with knowledge that it is untrue and with the intent to deceive. It may even constitute a term of the contract. Whether it does or not is immaterial, since fraud gives rise to effects in the law of contract and the law of tort. A contract resulting from a fraudulent misrepresentation may be avoided by the victim of the fraud. In such instances the apparent consent by the innocent party to the contract and its terms, is not a real consent.[7] Whether or not the effect of such fraud is to induce a mistake (which might render the contract *void*[8]), the consent of the innocent party may be revoked at his option.

Non-fraudulent misrepresentations have a different effect. At common law only fraud entitles an innocent party to upset his apparent consent and avoid a contract which originally was validly created. At common law an innocent misrepresentation, that is, where the party making it was unaware that what he was stating was untrue, could not render the resulting contract either void or voidable, unless the effect of such misrepresentation was to produce an operative mistake. Equity took a different view of such misrepresentations, whether or not their result was to induce a mistake. This distinction has had an important effect upon the remedies available for innocent misrepresentation.

A further complication has been introduced in more recent times. Until 1963, it might have been said that it did not matter whether an innocent misrepresentation was or was not made negligently. Indeed, so far as the law of contract is concerned, there is still no difference. The important distinguishing factor is fraud. Since the decision of the House of Lords in *Hedley Byrne & Co. v. Heller & Partners*[9] (which has been followed many times in Canada), a *negligent*, but non-fraudulent misrepresentation may give rise to a remedy in *tort*, whether or not a contract

---

5 The distinction between terms and misrepresentations, especially innocent misrepresentations, is the subject of discussion in the Ontario Law Reform Commission's *Report on Amendment of the Law of Contract* (1987), chapter 12. The Commission's recommendations for reform, which enlarge the scope of the remedy of rescission (below, pp. 808-821) are found on pp. 242-243 of the *Report*.

6 Note that an exemption or exclusion clause (below, pp. 571-600) cannot preclude an action for fraudulent misrepresentation, though a suitably worded clause may affect claims for innocent misrepresentation, just as it might oust liability for breach of contract: *Ballard v. Gaskill*, [1955] 2 D.L.R. 219 (B.C.C.A.); *Campbell v. Hamill*, [1925] 4 D.L.R. 958 (Sask. C.A.).

7 This and the previous sentence were cited in *TWT Enterprises Ltd. v. Westgreen Devs. (North) Ltd.* (1991), 78 Alta. L.R. (2d) 62 at 78 (Alta. Q.B.) *per* Picard J; affirmed (1992), 3 Alta. L.R. (3d) 124 (Alta. C.A.).

8 Above, pp. 247-251. For some illustrations of the overlap of misrepresentation and mistake, see *Zed v. Zed* (1980), 28 N.B.R. (2d) 580 (N.B.Q.B.); *Island Glass Ltd. v. O'Connor* (1980), 28 Nfld. & P.E.I.R. 377 (P.E.I. S.C.); *Kozina v. Trans-Alta. Mortgage & Financing Services Ltd.* (1979), 24 A.R. 405 (Alta. Q.B.); *Ghadban v. Bank of N.S.* (1982), 132 D.L.R. (3d) 475 (Ont. H.C.); *MacEachern v. Bancroft* (1978), 27 N.S.R. (2d) 407 (N.S.T.D.).

9 [1964] A.C. 465 (H.L.). On negligent misrepresentation, see Fridman, *Law of Torts in Canada*, Vol. 1 (1989), at pp. 263-276.

has resulted from such misrepresentation.[10] A whole new field of judicial action has been opened by this decision, the effects and consequences of which are still not entirely settled.[11]

2. Fraudulent misrepresentation[12]

(a) General

A fraudulent misrepresentation consists of a representation of fact made without any belief in its truth, with intent that the person to whom it is made shall act upon it and actually causing that person to act upon it.[13] In *United Shoe Machinery Co. v. Brunet*,[14] the defendants wanted to raise the defence of fraudulent misrepresentation to an action for an injunction and damages based upon a contract under which the plaintiffs leased to the defendants machines for performing a certain process in the making of shoes. In the event, the Privy Council held that the defendants could not raise and rely on the defence because they had adopted and affirmed the contract despite the fraudulent misrepresentations. In holding that the defence had been made out, and would have operated had it not been for the subsequent conduct of the defendants, Lord Atkinson made it clear that to establish a case of false or fraudulent misrepresentation the following had to be established: (1) that the representations complained of were made by the wrongdoer to the victim; (2) that these representations were false in fact; (3) that the wrongdoer, when he made them, either knew that they were false or made them recklessly without knowing whether they were false or true; (4) that the victim was thereby induced to enter into the contract in question.[15]

---

10 For example, see *Walter Cabott Const. Ltd. v. R.* (1974), 44 D.L.R. (3d) 82 (Fed. T.D.); reversed in part (1975), 69 D.L.R. (3d) 542 (Fed. C.A.). See also *A.L. Gullison & Sons Ltd. v. Corey* (1980), 29 N.B.R. (2d) 86 (N.B.C.A.); *Carman Const. Ltd. v. C.P.R.* (1982), 136 D.L.R. (3d) 193 (S.C.C.). *Rainbow Industrial Caterers Ltd. v. Can. National Railway Co.* (1988), 54 D.L.R. (4th) 43 (B.C.C.A.); *Rainbow Industrial Caterers Ltd. v. Can. National Railway Co.* (1990), 67 D.L.R. (4th) 348 (B.C.C.A.); affirmed (1991), 84 D.L.R. (4th) 291 (S.C.C.). See also, below, p. 700.

11 Two issues are of great importance: (1) the relations between actions in tort and actions in contract, where the parties have contracted on the basis of the misrepresentation (below, pp. 694-701); (2) the effect of an exclusion clause where there has been a negligent misrepresentation (below, pp. 512-516, 571); see also *Carman Const. Ltd. v. C.P.R.*, above, note 10; *Peters v. Parkway Mercury Sales Ltd.* (1976), 58 D.L.R. (3d) 128 (N.B.C.A.).

12 Reference to the opening paragraph of this section was made in *Pare v. Soon* (1982), 16 Sask. R. 154 at 160 (Sask. Q.B.).

13 This sentence was quoted in *Roussel v. Saunders* (1990), 85 Nfld. & P.E.I.R. 228 at 238 (Nfld. T.D.) *per* Adams J.

14 [1909] A.C. 330 (P.C.); followed in *Paragon Entertainment Prods. Inc. v. McDonald's Wholesale & Retail Ltd.* (1979), 19 Nfld. & P.E.I.R. 181 (Nfld. T.D.).

15 [1909] A.C. 330 at 338 (P.C.). This sentence was quoted in *Linfield v. Walker* (1986), 71 N.B.R. (2d) 413 at 420 (N.B.C.A.) *per* Ayles J.A. Note also the point that on discovery of the fraud, or within a reasonable time thereafter, the victim must avoid the contract: compare below, p. 302. As to the standard of proof of fraud, see *Scott v. Cresswell*, [1975] 3 W.W.R. 193 (Alta. C.A.); *Northern & Central Gas Corp. v. Hillcrest Collieries Ltd.; Byron Creek Collieries Ltd. v. Coleman Collieries Ltd.*, [1976] 1 W.W.R. 481 at 528-529 (Alta. S.C.). Fraud must be strictly pleaded and strictly proven: *Rainbow Industrial Caterers Ltd. v. Can. National Railway Co.*, above, note 10, at 69 *per* Esson J.A.; compare *ibid.*, at 81 *per* Wallace J.A.

(b) Fact

There must be a positive misstatement of *fact*. "Representation to give grounds for the avoidance of a contract must be matters of fact and this means either an existing fact or a past event." Thus spoke Martin J.A. in *Enfield v. London Guarantee & Accident Co.*[16] However, an intention as to the future may in some instances be treated as a fact. For example, in *International Casualty Co. v. Thomson*[17] the plaintiff contracted to buy shares in an insurance company on condition that within a fixed time the company would be in business in Vancouver and the plaintiff would be made the medical examiner of the company for that city. When the stipulated event did not happen it was held that the contract could be rescinded for fraudulent misrepresentation. The "intention" of the company to do business in the future, was a misstatement as to fact, that is, its *present* state of mind.

Facts must also be differentiated from opinion.[18] In several cases courts have made quite clear that a party who expresses views as to the value of property, whether currently or in the future, is not guilty of any misrepresentation.[19] The courts have been anxious lest a party who found he had not obtained as good a bargain as he expected be permitted to avoid the contract, on the basis of misrepresentation, merely by alleging that he was misled.[20] Fraud is something to be proved very strictly, not lightly alleged and accepted.[21] Indeed on occasion

---

16 [1926] 4 D.L.R. 37 at 42 (Sask. C.A.); compare *Ry. Passengers Assur. Co. v. Standard Life Assur. Co.* (1921), 65 D.L.R. 470 at 477-478 (S.C.C.) *per* Duff J.; *Arnprior v. U.S. Fidelity & Guar. Co.* (1915), 21 D.L.R. 343 at 349-350 (S.C.C.) *per* Duff J. Note that an express representation, *e.g.*, as to the rents payable on a certain property, may include an implied representation *viz.*, that such rents were properly and legally changed, which was not true: *Congiusti v. Guriel* (1989), 34 O.A.C. 306 (Ont. C.A.). Contrast *Jetaway Invts. Ltd. v. Salah* (1986), 73 N.S.R. (2d) 12 (N.S.T.D.), no misrepresentation by vendor who advised agent to tell prospective purchaser that rents charged were not the registered rents.

17 (1913), 48 S.C.R. 167 (S.C.C.); compare *Prather v. King Resources Co.*, [1973] 1 W.W.R. 700 (Alta. C.A.).

18 *Allen v. Allen* (1976), 15 Nfld. & P.E.I.R. 362 (Nfld. Dist. Ct.); compare *Cancarp Const. Ltd. v. P.D.I. Structures (1982) Inc.* (1987), 62 O.R. (2d) 161 at 168 (Ont. H.C.), opinions distinguished from promises; *Mayer v. Mayer Estate* (1993), 106 D.L.R. (4th) 353 (B.C.C.A.). In *Roussel v. Saunders* (1990), 85 Nfld. & P.E.I.R. 228 (Nfld. T.D.), the statement that there was no formaldehyde was a misrepresentation of fact, not an opinion.

19 *Stewart v. Cunningham* (1915), 8 W.W.R. 579 (B.C.C.A.); *Can. West Loan Co. v. Virtue*, [1921] 1 W.W.R. 730 (B.C.S.C.); *Jackson and Lacey v. People's Trust Co.* (1912), 22 W.L.R. 325 (B.C. Co. Ct.); *Berge v. Grew*, [1927] 3 W.W.R. 811 (Alta. C.A.). But if one party knows the facts best, his opinion may be fact: *Smith v. Land & House Property Corp.* (1885), 28 Ch. D. 7 at 15 (C.A.) *per* Brett L.J.: *Bissett v. Wilkinson*, [1927] A.C. 177 (P.C.); *Northern & Central Gas Corp. v. Hillcrest Collieries*, above, note 15, at 530.

20 *Knox v. Bunch* (1913), 24 W.L.R. 265 (Alta. S.C.).

21 *Jackson v. People's Trust Co.*, above, note 19 following *Schultz v. Wood* (1881), 6 S.C.R. 585 (S.C.C.); *Beatty v. Neelon* (1886), 13 S.C.R. 1 (S.C.C.); *Lasby v. Johnson*, [1928] 4 D.L.R. 956 (Sask. C.A.). See also *Prudential Trust Co. v. Olson*, [1960] S.C.R. 227 (S.C.C.). The onus is on the plaintiff: *Popowich v. Dromarsky*, [1946] 1 W.W.R. 570 (Alta. C.A.); *Alexander v. Enderton* (1914), 15 D.L.R. 588 at 591 (Man. K.B.); affirmed (1914), 19 D.L.R. 897 (Man. C.A.). But this does not mean that the *criminal* standard of proof is involved: see the cases cited in note 15 above.

For cases when fraud was established, see *Reichelt v. West-Gro. Hldgs. Ltd.*; *West-Gro Indust. Ltd. v. Reichelt*; *Reichelt v. Mount Lehman Equitable Mtge. Co.*, [1978] 4 W.W.R. 484 (B.C.S.C.);

courts have been prepared to accept that what a party said amounted only to "puffing", *simplex commendatio*, the mere aggrandizement of his own wares or property, out of a desire to do business, not a fraudulent deception.[22]

Clearly, while the courts will protect an innocent party from gross fraud, they will not attempt to protect a contracting party from all types of conduct. In accordance with the general principles of the law of contract, a party is expected to look out for himself, and make his own bargains. If he has done foolishly, this is his own fault and he is left to his own devices. Only from totally improper conduct, in this instance fraud, will he be granted protection and a remedy by the courts. To such an extent is this so, that even if the victim of the misrepresentation could have found out that it was fraudulent, but did not do so, and thus could have avoided the consequences of the deception, he will not be deprived of a remedy. Following the leading English decision in *Redgrave v. Hurd*[23] the Supreme Court of Canada held in *Sager v. Manitoba Windmill Co.*[24] that the plaintiff's own negligence in this respect will not be a defence to an allegation that the defendant was fraudulent. Even a term in the contract that each party will rely on his own judgment will not excuse a fraudulent party.[25] Thus, where fraud is established, the fault lies squarely on the guilty party.

A distinction must be made between misrepresentations of fact and those

---

Smith v. Porter (1978), 21 N.B.R. (2d) 170 (N.B.S.C.); reversed (1979), 27 N.B.R. (2d) 439 (N.B.C.A.); *MacEachern v. Bancroft* (1978), 27 N.S.R. (2d) 407 (N.S.T.D.); *Kisil v. John F. Stevens Ltd.* (1981), 42 N.S.R. (2d) 148 (N.S.T.D.). For cases when fraud was not proved, see *R.E. Lister Ltd. v. Dunlop Can. Ltd.* (1978), 85 D.L.R. (3d) 321 (Ont. H.C.); reversed (1979), 105 D.L.R. (3d) 684 (Ont. C.A.); reversed [1982] 1 S.C.R. 726 (S.C.C.); *Van Der Kuilen v. Todd*, [1979] 3 W.W.R. 165 (Sask. Q.B.); *Paragon Entertainment Prods. Inc. v. McDonald's Wholesale & Retail Ltd.*, above, note 14; *Consumer Glass Co. v. D'Aragon* (1979), 6 B.L.R. 114 (Ont. H.C.); *Lakex Mines Ltd. v. Marathon Realty Co.* (1980), 24 B.C.L.R. 332 (B.C.S.C.). *Aucoin v. Young* (1987), 79 N.B.R. (2d) 374 (N.B.Q.B.); reversed (1988), 87 N.B.R. (2d) 170 (N.B.C.A.); leave to appeal to S.C.C. refused (1988), 89 N.B.R. (2d) 116n (S.C.C.).

22 *Rasch v. Horne*, [1930] 1 W.W.R. 816 (Man. C.A.). Also on the ground that this kind of statement is something that can be tested by the plaintiff; compare the decision of the Privy Council in the New Zealand case of *Bisset v. Wilkinson*, [1927] A.C. 177 (P.C.). Contrast the situation with respect to the experience of a party in the coal business in the relevant locale: *Northern & Central Gas Corp. v. Hillcrest Collieries; Byron Creek Collieries Ltd. v. Coleman Collieries Ltd.*, above, note 15, at 530.

23 (1882), 20 Ch. D. 1 (C.A.). Compare *Directors of Central Rly. Co. of Venezuela v. Kisch* (1867), L.R. 2 H.L. 99.

24 (1913), 4 W.W.R. 1078 (Sask. S.C.); affirmed (1914), 6 W.W.R. 265 (Sask. C.A.); affirmed (1914), 7 W.W.R. 1213 (S.C.C.); compare *United Services Funds (Trustees of) v. Richardson Greenshields of Can. Ltd.* (1988), 48 D.L.R. (4th) 98 at 109-111 (B.C.S.C.) *per* Southin J.; compare *Banque National du Can. v. Wood Trucking Ltd.* (1990), 112 N.B.R. (2d) 142 at 148 (N.B.Q.B.). But knowledge that a representation is false may result in the conclusion that the plaintiff with such knowledge did not rely on the representation, *i.e.*, the representation did not induce the plaintiff to act: *RMI Properties Ltd. v. Can. Mortgage & Housing Corp.* (1989), 103 A.R. 179 (Alta. Q.B.).

25 *Campbell v. Hamill*, [1925] 3 W.W.R. 628 (Sask. C.A.). So, too, a clause which purported to exclude liability for fraud was not operative; the fraud of a party vitiated the whole contract, including the exclusion clause: *Ballard v. Gaskill*, [1955] 2 D.L.R. 219 (B.C.C.A.); compare *TWT Enterprises Ltd. v. Westgreen Devs. (North) Ltd.* (1991), 78 Alta. L.R. (2d) 62 (Alta. Q.B.); affirmed (1992), 3 Alta. L.R. (3d) 124 (Alta. C.A.).

relating to law.[26] Since everyone is supposed to know the law, there can be no misrepresentations as to the state of the law. This is really a very questionable proposition. However, a distinction has been drawn between a misstatement as to the law and a misstatement as to legal consequences. In *Rule v. Pals*,[27] a party was misled as to the legal qualifications for call to the Bar of Saskatchewan. This led to a contract to provide a correspondence course for the Bar. His action for fraudulent misrepresentation failed. In *Graham v. Legault*,[28] however, there was a failure to disclose that a basement was illegally rented. Here there was a misrepresentation not as to law, that is, as to when a permit was required, but as to fact, namely, the legal consequences of the lack of a permit. Hence, a remedy was given.

(c) No belief in truth

The misstatement must be made dishonestly or recklessly, with lack of belief in its truth. This was the effect of the leading English case of *Derry v. Peek*[29] in 1889. By a private Act of Parliament, A obtained the power to run a tramway at Plymouth. With the consent of the Board of Trade A would have been empowered to use steam instead of animal propulsion. A issued a prospectus stating it to be a great advantage that A *had* the power to use steam. This statement involved the assumption that the consent of the Board of Trade had been obtained. In fact it was refused (because of the narrow, steep streets). The company was wound up. B, who had bought shares on the faith of the prospectus, sued for deceit. The House of Lords held that the finding that A *honestly* believed that he and the others who had issued the prospectus had the power in question was conclusive. In other words, an honest, if mistaken belief as to the truth of an assertion did not amount to fraud. Though the actual point in issue, as to the liability of company directors for untrue statements in a prospectus, has been changed by legislation, in Canada as well as England, the substantive point of law has not been altered. For there to be fraud there must be dishonesty, or such recklessness as to the truth as is tantamount to dishonesty. This decision as to what is "false" was followed without reservation by the Supreme Court of Canada in *Nesbitt, Thomson & Co. v. Pigott*.[30] It is clear that for a party to be liable for fraudulent misrepresentation there must be evidence of knowledge that the representation was untrue, and an intent to defraud, or the absence of an honest belief in the truth of the representation.[31]

---

26 The recommendations of the Ontario Law Reform Commission would abolish the distinction between misrepresentation of fact and misrepresentation of law: *Report*, above, note 5, at p. 243.

27 [1928] 2 W.W.R. 123 (Sask. C.A.).

28 [1951] 3 D.L.R. 423 (B.C.S.C.).

29 (1889), 14 App. Cas. 337 (H.L.).

30 [1941] S.C.R. 520 (S.C.C.); compare *Lakex Mines Ltd. v. Marathon Realty Co.* (1980), 24 B.C.L.R. 332 (B.C.S.C.).

31 *Dufour v. Sunbay Foods Inc.* (1986), 48 Sask. R. 33 (Sask. Q.B.); *Webster v. Steeves* (1987), 80 N.S.R. (2d) 419 (N.S. Co. Ct.); *Brenton Grays Boatyard Ltd. v. Ocean Bounty Seafoods Ltd.* (1990), 98 N.S.R. (2d) 1 (N.S.T.D.); *Marble Mountain Enterprises Ltd. v. Gillies* (1990), 105 A.R. 321 (Alta. Q.B.); *TWT Enterprises Ltd. v. Westgreen Devs. (North) Ltd.* (1991), 78 Alta. L.R. (2d) 62 (Alta.

However, in some instances conduct that does not amount to fraud can be considered as negligence,[32] which may give rise, now,[33] to an action for damages, and, insofar as such a misrepresentation is an innocent misrepresentation, can permit rescission.[34]

(d) Intent that plaintiff should act

The misrepresentation must be material. In other words, it must be as to something which was intended to induce the other party to enter into a contract.[35] For example, if there is a misrepresentation as to the identity of a contracting party, it will not be effective, in the legal sense, even if false, unless it was known to the person making the misrepresentation that the identity of the party with whom he was contracting was important to the victim of the misrepresentation, and it was intended to influence what he did.[36] In this respect, as the English case of *Andrews v. Mockford*[37] shows, a misrepresentation may be made to the world at large, not merely one party, so that any injured party may have a remedy. In that case, false statements were made in a prospectus and repeatedly published to rig the market. Hence, anyone who purchased the shares had a remedy. In contrast, in *Peek v. Gurney*[38] only original allottees of shares were able to sue on false statements in the prospectus, not someone who purchased shares from an original allottee.

But the false representation must be made before the contract is formed. If it occurs afterwards it cannot be considered an inducement to act, *i.e.*, by entering the contract.[39] Moreover, there must be a communication between the fraudulent representor and the party who sues in respect of the misrepresentation. Hence, in *White v. Pellerine*,[40] the action would not lie. Here the defendant sold property

---

Q.B.); affirmed (1992), 3 Alta. L.R. (3d) 124 (Alta. C.A.). Hence, a statement not made recklessly did not lend to liability: *Bresson v. Ward* (1987), 79 N.S.R. (2d) 156 (N.S. Co. Ct.).

32 See, *e.g.*, *Congiusti v. Guriel* (1989), 34 O.A.C. 306 (Ont. C.A.); *Dixon v. Deacon Morgan McEwan Easson* (1990), 70 D.L.R. (4th) 609 (B.C.S.C.); reversed (1993), 102 D.L.R. (4th) 1 (B.C.C.A.); *TWT Enterprises Ltd. v. Westgreen Devs. (North) Ltd.*, above, note 31; *Lafferty v. Gurylo* (1991), 17 R.P.R. (2d) 250 (Ont. Gen. Div.). But there may be fraud and negligence in the same case: *Roussel v. Saunders* (1990), 85 Nfld. & P.E.I.R. 228 (Nfld. T.D.).

33 Since *Hedley, Byrne & Co. v. Heller & Partners*, [1964] A.C. 465 (H.L.); see Linden, *Canadian Tort Law*, 5th ed. (1993), Chapter 12, especially pp. 423-427; Fridman, *Law of Torts in Canada*, Vol. 1 (1989), pp. 263-276.

34 Below, pp. 305-308: compare *Grossman v. Woolf* (1990), 40 O.A.C. 154 (Ont. Div. Ct.).

35 *Alexander v. Enderton* (1914), 15 D.L.R. 588 at 591 (Man. K.B.) *per* Matthews C.J., upheld by (1914), 25 Man. R. 82 (Man. C.A.). See *Consumer Glass Co. v. D'Aragon* (1979), 6 B.L.R. 114 (Ont. H.C.); *Dixon v. Deacon Morgan McEwan Easson* (1990), 70 D.L.R. (4th) 609 at 614-615 (B.C.S.C.) *per* Spencer J.; reversed (1993), 102 D.L.R. (4th) 1 (B.C.C.A.); compare *Grossman v. Woolf*, above, note 34.

36 *Love v. Lynch*, [1920] 2 W.W.R. 538 (Sask. C.A.).

37 [1896] 1 Q.B. 372 (C.A.).

38 (1873), L.R. 6 H.L. 377 (H.L.).

39 *Currie v. MacFarlane* (1989), 92 N.S.R. (2d) 343 (N.S.T.D.); additional reasons at (1989), 94 N.S.R. (2d) 177 (N.S.T.D.).

40 (1988), 84 N.S.R. (2d) 330 (N.S. Co. Ct.); affirmed (1989), 90 N.S.R. (2d) 212 (N.S.C.A.).

to X who sold it to the plaintiff. The defendant never made any representation to the plaintiff, only to X.

(e) Plaintiff must act on representation

The obverse of the intent of the maker of the representation that it should influence the other party is that it should have such effect. Only in that way can the representation truly be material. Even if no loss was suffered by the innocent party, as long as it can be shown that it was a false misrepresentation that induced the making of the contract, for example, the sale of a car as in *Pomehichuk v. Gale*,[41] the contract may be avoided for fraud. Where there was no such effect as a consequence of a false statement, as in *Nelson v. Gagnon*,[42] there will be no remedy. Reliance by the plaintiff is crucial.[43] Without such reliance there can be no legal effect of a fraudulent misrepresentation;[44] it establishes the causal connection between the defendant's fraud and the harm resulting, such as the granting of a loan by a bank.[45]

The onus is on the party alleging fraudulent misrepresentation to prove that the misrepresentation was relied upon by him in entering into the contract.[46] Hence, in *Timmins v. Kuzyk*[47] a claim based upon fraudulent misrepresentation with respect to the sale of a motel to the plaintiffs was unsuccessful. There was no proof that the alleged fraud had induced the sale in the first place or caused any damage. The price paid for the motel was a proper price, not in any way inflated or untoward. Indeed the plaintiffs had not repudiated the contract as soon as the alleged fraud had been discovered. They had continued to operate the motel and collect rents.

The issue of reliance is a question of fact to be inferred from all the circumstances of the case and evidence at the trial. It is not a question of law. Hence, an appellate court should not reverse the trial judge without good reason.[48]

(f) Effect of fraud and remedies

Fraud has effects both at common law and in equity, and gives rise to remedies under the law of tort and the law of contract. A fraudulent misrepresentation amounts to the tort of deceit, for which the injured party will receive damages

---

41 [1950] 2 W.W.R. 66 (Man. K.B.).

42 (1915), 22 D.L.R. 179 (B.C.C.A.).

43 See *Ghadban v. Bank of N.S.* (1982), 132 D.L.R. (3d) 475 (Ont. H.C.) as to the duty on a bank not to misrepresent the nature of a guarantee signed by the father-in-law of the bank's customer.

44 Compare *Holt Renfrew & Co. v. Henry Singer Ltd.* (1982), 135 D.L.R. (3d) 391 (Alta. C.A.); leave to appeal to S.C.C. refused (1982), 22 Alta. L.R. (2d) xxxvi (S.C.C.); *Roussel v. Saunders* (1990), 85 Nfld. & P.E.I.R. 228 (Nfld. T.D.); *Currie v. MacFarlane*, above, note 39.

45 *Banque Nationale du Can. v. Wood Trucking Ltd.* (1990), 112 N.B.R. (2d) 142 (N.B.Q.B.).

46 *Mankovsky v. Jacob*, [1922] 2 W.W.R. 684 (Man. K.B.); *L.K. Oil & Gas Ltd. v. Canalands Energy Corp.* (1989), 60 D.L.R. (4th) 490 at 496 (Alta. C.A.) *per* Harradence J.A.; leave to appeal to S.C.C. refused [1990] 1 W.W.R. lxxin (S.C.C.). This sentence and the prior paragraph were cited by Campbell J. in *Hyndman v. Jenkins* (1981), 29 Nfld. & P.E.I.R. 331 at 339-340 (P.E.I. S.C.).

47 (1962), 32 D.L.R. (2d) 207 (B.C. S.C.).

48 *L.K. Oil & Gas Ltd. v. Canalands Energy Corp.*, above, note 46, at 497-501. No inference can be drawn from the fact that the other party acted as the representor intended.

from the misrepresentor.[49] A contract induced by fraud is voidable at the election of the defrauded party.[50] It is not void *ab initio*; it is liable to be upset.[51] Rescission may be granted.[52] But the equitable remedy of rescission is discretionary.[53]

Damages may be awarded as well as rescission.[54] Such damages will be calculated on the basis of the loss suffered through the deceit, so as to put the injured party into the position he would have been in had the fraud not occurred.[55] In *Smith v. Porter*,[56] for example, the vendor of an insurance agent falsely stated that the business was "current", that is, that all premiums payable to insurance companies had been paid up to 60 days of the take-over date. This statement was made to a banker approved by the parties to finance the transaction. The plaintiff, who was purchasing the agency, relied on the statement in agreeing to purchase the business. In fact substantial sums were in arrears. It was held that the contract was rescindable for fraudulent misrepresentation and the defendant was entitled to damages in the amount of the arrears which he had been obliged to pay.

Rescission will not be granted unless the parties can be put back into their previous situations. *Restitutio in integrum* must be possible.[57] Hence if a third party

---

49 On the measure of damage for deceit, see *RMI Properties Ltd. v. Can. Mortgage & Housing Corp.* (1989), 103 A.R. 179 (Alta. Q.B.). Contributory negligence is inapplicable: *Linfield v. Walker* (1986), 71 N.B.R. (2d) 413 (N.B.C.A.); reversing (1986), 71 N.B.R. (2d) 428 (N.B.T.D.). A defendant who concedes that the contract may be rescinded for deceit does not deprive the plaintiff of the right to damages for deceit, including aggravated damages (but not in the circumstances punitive or exemplary damages): *Archer v. Brown*, [1984] 2 All E.R. 267; compare *Smith v. Lasko*, [1987] 5 W.W.R. 412 (Man. C.A.).

50 This sentence and the next three were quoted by Picard J. in *TWT Enterprises Ltd. v. Westgreen Devs. (North) Ltd.* (1991), 78 Alta. L.R. (2d) 62 at 78 (Alta. Q.B.).

51 *Wallbridge v. W.H. Moore & Co.; W.H. Moore & Co. v. Bradley* (1964), 48 W.W.R. 321 (B.C.S.C.), citing *Clough v. London & North Western Ry.* (1871), L.R. 7 Ex. 26; *United Shoe Mach. Co. v. Brunet*, [1909] A.C. 330 (P.C.); *Morin v. Anger*, [1931] 1 D.L.R. 827 (Ont. C.A.); *Bawlf Grain Co. v. Ross* (1917), 55 S.C.R. 232 (S.C.C.); *McCarthy v. Kenny*, [1939] 3 D.L.R. 556 (Ont. H.C.); *Perry v. Thompson* (1957), 7 D.L.R. (2d) 556 (B.C.S.C.).

52 *Burns v. Ambler* (1963), 42 W.W.R. 254 (B.C.S.C.); or a defence to an action for specific performance or damages: *Cload v. Ferguson* (1953), 10 W.W.R. 426 (Alta. Dist. Ct.).

53 *Jarvis v. Maguire* (1961), 35 W.W.R. 289 (B.C.C.A.); *Alex v. Tiede*, [1986] 5 W.W.R. 599 (Man. Q.B.). Hence, it may be denied on various grounds: *ibid.*, at 608 *per* Monnin J. See below, pp. 301-303; and compare pp. 817-819. Nor will rescission be granted where the defect that was not disclosed was patent, *i.e.*, was discoverable by the party seeking rescission: *Stotts v. McArthur* (1990), 63 Man. R. (2d) 46 (Man. Q.B.); additional reasons at (1990), 64 Man. R. (2d) 171 (Man. Q.B.); reversed (1991), 75 Man. R. (2d) 212 (Man. C.A.).

54 *Muise v. Whalen* (1990), 96 N.S.R. (2d) 298 (N.S.T.D.).

55 *Newbigging v. Adam* (1886), 34 Ch. D. 582 (C.A.); affirmed (1888), 13 App. Cas. 308 (H.L.); *Redgrave v. Hurd* (1882), 20 Ch. D. 1 (C.A.). For example, the difference between the actual value of property and what was paid as well as consequential loss: *Frawley v. Buckley* (1988), 93 N.B.R. (2d) 139 (N.B.Q.B.). Any benefit received by the plaintiff must be taken into account: *Jarvis v. Maguire*, above, note 53.

56 (1980), 27 N.B.R. (2d) 439 (N.B.C.A.); compare *Kisil v. John F. Stevens Ltd.* (1980), 42 N.S.R. (2d) 148 (N.S.T.D.); *Desautels v. Zeemel Enterprises Ltd.* (1981), 8 Man. R. (2d) 91 (Man. Q.B.).

57 *Morin v. Anger*, above, note 51; *Trans. Can. Trading Co. v. M. Loeb Ltd.*, [1947] O.W.N. 432 (Ont. H.C.); *Paragon Entertainment Prods. Inc. v. McDonald's Wholesale & Retail Ltd.* (1978), 19 Nfld. & P.E.I.R. 181 at 191 (Nfld. T.D.) *per* Miffin C.J. Unless the third party would be better served by rescission, as was the case in *Stewart v. Complex 329 Ltd.* (1990), 109 N.B.R. (2d) 115 (N.B.Q.B.).

has acquired rights, in consequence of the contract entered into originally as a result of a fraudulent misrepresentation, as against the party induced to enter into the original contract, no rescission of such original contract will be possible. In such circumstances, the only remedy available will be damages.[58] So, too, if the victim of the fraudulent misrepresentation has delayed unduly in pursuing a remedy. However, there is a suggestion, by implication, in the decision in *Kingstone v. Dominion Alloy Steel Corporation*,[59] that even twelve years' delay might not prevent rescission of a contract obtained through a fraudulent misrepresentation, as contrasted with a misrepresentation that was innocent. In that case the contract was for the purchase of shares in a company. Presumably, despite the passage of such a length of time, it might have been possible to put the parties back where they were. In other instances, probably, too long a delay might have irreparable consequences, thereby making rescission an inappropriate and undesirable remedy. Delay will not prevent rescission, however, where the defendant's conduct was the reason for the delay. In *Stewart v. Complex 329 Ltd.*,[60] the plaintiff attempted to rescind the contract when he discovered the misrepresentation. The defendant did not respond for three months. The plaintiff sold the property to a receiver in bankruptcy. In these circumstances rescission was allowed.

Finally, rescission will be denied where the injured party has affirmed or adopted the contract by words or conduct.[61] The extent to which passage of time might amount to such affirmation or adoption has just been considered. In such cases the denial of rescission, that is, upholding the contract, even though damages may still be awarded on the basis of either misrepresentation or breach of contract.[62] could be founded on the equitable doctrine of *laches*, that is, unreasonable delay, or upon the notion that the originally injured party has affirmed the contract, or, at the very least, by his long endurance of the fraud, may have made it impossible to achieve substantial *restitutio in integrum*. Delay is not the only basis for alleging affirmation or adoption. More positive conduct may be shown, thereby making it easier for a court to conclude that the necessary affirmation had taken place. It would seem, however, that the courts will not lightly or easily make such a determination or arrive at such a conclusion where the defendant has been fraudulent. Thus, painting a house which had been purchased after a misrepresentation was not enough to prevent subsequent rescission (and in that case the misrepresentation was probably only innocent, not fraudulent).[63] Nor was granting a lease of a farm which had been bought as a consequence of misrepresentation.[64] The Court of Appeal of British Columbia, in *Kupchak v. Dayson Holdings Ltd.*; *Dayson Holdings Ltd. v. Palms Motel Ltd.*,[65] suggested that equivocal acts could

---

58 This and the previous three sentences were cited by MacIntosh J. in *Wilson v. Harrison* (1979), 35 N.S.R. (2d) 499 at 507-508 (N.S.T.D.).

59 [1939] O.R. 286 (Ont. C.A.).

60 Above, note 57.

61 *Dodds v. Millman* (1964), 47 W.W.R. 690 (B.C.S.C.).

62 *Barron v. Kelly* (1918), 56 S.C.R. 455, especially at 478-479 (S.C.C.), *per* Anglin J.

63 *Guest v. Beecroft* (1957), 22 W.W.R. 481 (B.C.S.C.).

64 *Boulter v. Stocks* (1913), 47 S.C.R. 440 (S.C.C.).

65 (1965), 53 W.W.R. 65 (B.C.C.A.), followed in *Stewart v. Complex 329 Ltd.*, above, note 57.

not amount to affirmation, and that whether rescission should be granted depended upon its practicability having regard to the circumstances. In that case, where the injured party dealt with the property after the transaction had been completed, it was held that rescission would not be denied; there was nothing inequitable about rescinding the contract despite what the plaintiff had done. Therefore, damages were not an adequate remedy.

3. Innocent misrepresentation

(a) At common law and in equity

Statements which mislead another contracting party may not be made with the kind of intent, previously described, that results in a finding of fraud. Such "innocent" misrepresentations may be made negligently or in circumstances which do not substantiate an allegation of negligence. So far as the law of contract is concerned, there is no reason for distinguishing between negligent and non-negligent misrepresentations, where fraud is absent. However, a negligently made misrepresentation may result in tort liability for damages.[66] For present purposes, therefore, a distinction should be made between a negligent misrepresentation and what will be termed a "pure", i.e., non-negligent, innocent misrepresentation. Two important features of non-negligent, innocent misrepresentation must be acknowledged. First of all, there is a clear distinction between statements which are intended to be, and are regarded as being terms of the contract, and statements which are not terms but merely inducements to the making of the contract.[67] Second, there is a difference between the approach at common law and the attitude of equity towards innocent misrepresentation.

At common law an innocent, non-negligent misrepresentation would not, and still does not entitle the victim to any relief unless the statement concerned can be regarded as constituting a term of the contract. If the statement can be regarded as more than an assertion but as a definite part of the bargain, that is, as one of the promises made by one party to get the consent of the other, then it will be a term.[68] Its exact status is another matter, and one upon which the nature of the victim's remedy will depend. In such instances the contract is perfectly valid, though there may have been a breach which justified some sort of remedial action. The injured party may be able to repudiate the contract and claim damages for breach, or he may be restricted to a claim for damages, or to the return of his

---

66 In the law of tort, negligent misrepresentation is of great importance as a form of liability: see Fleming, *Law of Torts*, 8th ed. (1992), pp. 640-651; *Salmond & Heuston on the Law of Torts*, 20th ed. (1992), pp. 214-219; Linden, *Canadian Tort Law*, 5th ed. (1993), Chapter 12. See also, below, note 77.

67 This distinction is referred to by the Ontario Law Reform Commission, *Report on Amendment of the Law of Contract* (1987), pp. 236-237, as is the possibility of treating such misrepresentations as contractual terms: *ibid.*, pp. 236-237, a solution that is rejected: *ibid.*, p. 241.

68 *Heilbut, Symons & Co. v. Buckleton*, [1913] A.C. 30 (H.L.): Fridman, *Sale of Goods in Canada*, 3rd ed. (1986), pp. 156-161. See *Behn v. Burness* (1863), 122 E.R. 281: *Bannerman v. White* (1861), 142 E.R. 685.

money on the basis of failure of consideration. He cannot allege that the contract is bad and liable to be avoided on the ground of misrepresentation. At common law, it was and remains of crucial importance to determine the precise juridical nature of a statement, assertion, or representation made by one party to another. This is a matter of construction.[69] Nor is it an easy matter.[70] In one curious case, *Hurt v. Keroack*[71] a statement that there were no bed bugs in a rooming house that was being sold was held to be an innocent misrepresentation, not a term in the contract, even though it might have been thought that this was an essential part of the condition of the premises rather than a mere inducement to make the contract. The task of distinguishing one sort of statement from another is made imperative by the state of the law under which, as was pointed out in *Paproski v. Neuman*,[72] it is only where the innocent misrepresentation does not constitute a term of the contract that the representee is limited to an action to avoid the contract.

Here is the vital point. Where what has been made is a "pure" innocent misrepresentation, that is, a non-negligent misrepresentation, then, in equity, the victim is entitled to rescind the contract, in other words to repudiate his original and apparent consent.[73] He may also be allowed something by way of an indemnity to restore him to the position in which he was prior to the making of the contract,[74] including the restitution of benefits obtained through the contract.[75] But he will not be allowed to claim damages in respect of any loss he may allege has resulted from the deception.[76] For damages to be awarded, the representation must be fraudulent, or it must constitute a term, or there must be negligence constituting a breach of duty, and resulting in tort liability.[77]

---

69 Below, pp. 451-453.

70 See, *e.g.*, the different ways in which the various courts interpreted the same set of facts in *Franz v. Hansen*, [1917] 3 W.W.R. 77 (Alta. C.A.); reversed [1918] 2 W.W.R. 40 (S.C.C.); leave to appeal to Privy Council refused (1918), 57 S.C.R. vii (S.C.C.).

71 [1943] 1 W.W.R. 715 (Man. C.A.).

72 (1956), 20 W.W.R. 294 at 299 (Sask. C.A.). See *e.g.*, *Walton v. Landstock Invts. Ltd.* (1976), 72 D.L.R. (3d) 195 (Ont. C.A.).

73 On the correct use of "rescission", see *Andronyk v. Williams* (1986), 21 D.L.R. (4th) 557 at 564-565 (Man. C.A.) *per* O'Sullivan J.A.; leave to appeal to S.C.C. refused (1986), 42 Man. R. (2d) 242n (S.C.C.). Note the effect of affirmation. Partial rescission cannot be ordered: *Kingu v. Walmar Ventures Ltd.* (1986), 38 C.C.L.T. 51 at 57-58 (B.C.C.A.), where the requirements for rescission for innocent misrepresentation are set out.

74 *Fleischhaker v. Fort Garry Agencies Ltd.* (1957), 23 W.W.R. 390 (Man. C.A.).

75 *Walters v. Capron* (1964), 50 W.W.R. 444 (B.C.S.C.).

76 See *Kooiman v. Nichols* (1991), 75 Man. R. (2d) 298 (Man. C.A.); compare *Irvine v. Thornhill* (1987), 49 M.V.R. 270 (Ont. Prov. Ct.). But see the suggestion to the contrary in *Gill v. Kittler* (1983), 21 B.L.R. 108 (Alta. Q.B.).

77 Above, p. 294; see *e.g.*, *Walter Cabott Const. Ltd. v. R.* (1974), 44 D.L.R. (3d) 82 (Fed. T.D.); reversed in part (1975), 69 D.L.R. (3d) 542 (Fed. C.A.). And see *Congiusti v. Guriel* (1989), 34 O.A.C. 306 (Ont. C.A.); *TWT Enterprises Ltd. v. Westgreen Devs. (North) Ltd.* (1991), 78 Alta. L.R. (2d) 62 (Alta. Q.B.); affirmed (1992), 3 Alta. L.R. (3d) 124 (Alta. C.A.); *Lafferty v. Gurylo* (1991), 17 R.P.R. (2d) 250 (Ont. Gen. Div.); *Roussel v. Saunders* (1990), 85 Nfld. & P.E.I.R. 228 (Nfld. T.D.); *Pizzo v. Crory* (1986), 71 N.S.R. (2d) 419 (N.S.T.D.); *Kingu v. Walmar Ventures Ltd.*, above, note 73.

Another possibility is that the statement can be treated as a "collateral warranty", on which see, below, pp. 459-462. For examples, see *Cancarp Const. Ltd. v. P.D.I. Structures (1982) Inc.*

(b) Operative innocent misrepresentation and its effects

For an innocent misrepresentation to be operative in this way, as was explained in *Alberta North West Lumber Co. v. Lewis*,[78] following the leading English case of *Kennedy v. Royal Mail Co. of Panama*,[79] there must be, generally speaking, a substantial difference between what the victim bargained for and what he obtained, such as to constitute a failure of consideration.[80] Hence in *Komarniski v. Marien*[81] rescission was not obtained. The land purchased was represented as covering 4.8 acres. In fact it was only 2.6 acres. The misrepresentation was innocent, not fraudulent. The purchaser had not obtained something different from what he had bargained for in the contract. The difference related to the *size* of the land, not the land itself.[82] The party alleging innocent misrepresentation, producing a mistake, must have been seriously inconvenienced by the mistake in question.[83] Another way of expressing this is to speak in terms of material inducement that makes a mistake or misapprehension affecting the expectation of the party.[84] In such instances the injured party is entitled, in equity, to be restored to the position he would have been in had he not been affected by the innocent misrepresentation.[85]

(1987), 62 O.R. (2d) 161 (Ont. H.C.); *Bresson v. Ward* (1987), 79 N.S.R. (2d) 156 (N.S. Co. Ct.); *Jetaway Investments Ltd. v. Salah* (1986), 73 N.S.R. (2d) 12 (N.S.T.D.); *Dellelce Const. & Equipment v. Portec Inc.* (1990), 73 O.R. (2d) 396 (Ont. H.C.); additional reasons at (1990), 73 O.R. (2d) 396 at 440 (Ont. H.C.). Note also the possibility of an action in equity based upon breach of a fiduciary duty: see *Canson Enterprises Ltd. v. Boughton & Co.* (1992), 85 D.L.R. (4th) 129 (S.C.C.), discussing the appropriate measure of damages in such a case.

78 [1917] 3 W.W.R. 1007 (B.C.C.A.).

79 (1867), L.R. 2 Q.B. 580; compare above, p. 275.

80 Compare *Caldwell v. Cockshutt Plow Co.* (1913), 18 D.L.R. 722 at 734 (Ont. C.A.); *Northey Mfg. Co. v. Sanders* (1899), 31 O.R. 475 at 478 (Ont. Div. Ct.). See also the judgment of Sinclair J.A. in *Alessio v. Jovica* (1974), 42 D.L.R. (3d) 242 at 256-257 (Alta. C.A.), which refers to the doctrine of *error in substantialibus*; the judgment of Lieberman J. in *Northern & Central Gas Corp. v. Hillcrest Collieries; Byron Creek Collieries Ltd. v. Coleman Collieries Ltd.*, [1976] 1 W.W.R. 481 at 553-554 (Alta. S.C.); *Gronau v. Schlamp Invts. Ltd.*, [1975] W.W.D. 47 (Man. Q.B.). Note that in the *Alessio* case there was a difference of opinion between the majority and Allen J.A. (dissenting) as to whether the lack of sewage facilities made the land sufficiently different to warrant rescission, even though the land was zoned as it had been stated to be by the vendor and his agent. But see below, as to the doctrine of *error in substantialibus*.

81 [1979] 4 W.W.R. 267 (Sask. Q.B.); compare *John Bosworth Ltd. v. Pro. Syndicated Devs. Ltd.* (1979), 24 O.R. (2d) 97 (Ont. H.C.).

82 But how does this equate with the doctrine of *error in substantialibus*? See, *e.g., Hyrsky v. Smith* (1969), 5 D.L.R. (3d) 385 (Ont. H.C.); compare, above, pp. 256-257.

83 *Field v. Zien*, [1963] S.C.R. 632 (S.C.C.).

84 *449576 Ont. Ltd. v. Bogojevski* (1984), 9 D.L.R. (4th) 109 (Ont. H.C.); see, *e.g., C.I.B.C. v. Kennedy* (1988), 50 R.P.R. (2d) 298 (B.C.S.C.).

85 *Newbigging v. Adam* (1886), 34 Ch. D. 582 at 592-593 (C.A.) *per* Bowen L.J.; affirmed (1888), 13 App. Cas. 308 (H.L.); *Corbeil v. Appell*, [1950] 1 D.L.R. 159 (B.C.S.C.). Or to refuse to perform: *W.W. Distributors & Co. v. Thorsteinsson* (1960), 33 W.W.R. 669 (Man. C.A.). But rescission will be refused if there has been undue delay: *Terri-Grant Enterprises Inc. v. 82506 Can. Ltd.* (1986), 47 Sask. R. 63 (Sask. Q.B.).

Restitutio in integrum must be possible.[86] However, it was said by Dysart J. in *Hines v. McCallum*[87] in 1925, that the tendency of modern cases was to relax the strictness of the notion of *restitutio in integrum*, such that as long as substantial restitution is possible it should be granted even if strict *restitutio* cannot be made.[88] What must be done, so far as possible, is to indemnify the injured party against obligations or liabilities resulting from the contract which has been rescinded and set aside as a consequence of the innocent misrepresentation. Damages for resultant loss may *not* be awarded.[89] While this may still involve the injured party in some loss, for example, of expected profit, which might be recoverable if he were bringing an action for breach of contract or for fraud, or, possibly, in modern times, for negligence, the maker of a misrepresentation who is guiltless of fraud or the breach of a term of the contract is not to be compelled to make good all loss and so be held responsible in the same way as one who would be liable at common law. The equitable relief is based on freeing the victim from the unfortunate consequences of another's innocent error, not in punishing that innocent party. Hence, the limitations on the kind of relief available.[90]

Developments in the English courts,[91] which have been followed in Canada, have placed limitations upon the extent to which the victim of an innocent misrepresentation can avoid the contract. It was held by the Supreme Court of Canada,[92] in *Redican v. Nesbitt*,[93] that once a contract was executed, the fact that it was induced by an innocent misrepresentation would not entitle the victim to rescind, if the contract was concerned with real property. Cases in England and Canada indicate that this much criticized doctrine applies only to conveyances of real property[94] and does not apply where the contract concerns a chattel or

---

86 There was no problem about a guarantor's rescission of a guarantee resulting from such a misrepresentation: *C.I.B.C. v. Larsen*, [1983] 5 W.W.R. 179 (B.C.C.A.). But rescission was not available where the plaintiff could not return benefits he had received: *Terri-Grant Enterprises Inc. v. 82506 Can. Ltd.*, above, note 85. See also *Samardziya v. Judd* (1986), 40 Man. R. (2d) 253 (Man. Q.B.).

87 [1925] 1 W.W.R. 838 (Man. K.B.). Is this still true today?

88 The question is what is substantial? See *Thurston v. Streilen*, [1951] 4 D.L.R. 724 (Man. K.B.).

89 *Comeller v. Billinkoff* (1953), 11 W.W.R. 279 (Man. Q.B.); compare the English case of *Whittington v. Seale-Hayne* (1900), 82 L.T. 49.

90 But the remedy is not limited by any neglect on the part of the victim. As with fraud, his failure to take care of himself will not deprive him of an otherwise available remedy: *Comeller v. Billinkoff*, above; *Bevan v. Anderson & Peace River Gravel Co.* (1957), 23 W.W.R. 508 (Alta. S.C.); *Gill v. Kittler* (1983), 21 B.L.R. 108 (Alta. Q.B.). However, the right to rescind for innocent misrepresentation may be lost by affirmation of the contract by the victim: *Panzer v. Zeifman* (1978), 88 D.L.R. (3d) 131 (Ont. C.A.). Or by undue delay: above, note 85.

91 Altered, however, in England, by the Misrepresentation Act, 1967 (U.K.), c. 7.

92 Following the English decisions of *Seddon v. North Eastern Salt Co.*, [1905] 1 Ch. 326; *Angel v. Jay*, [1911] 1 K.B. 666; see now the Misrepresentation Act, 1967 (U.K.), c. 7, s. 1(*b*).

93 [1924] S.C.R. 135 (S.C.C.), reaffirmed by Judson J. in *Shortt v. MacLennan*, [1959] S.C.R. 3 (S.C.C.). Compare *Panzer v. Zeifman*, above, note 90. See also *Abraham v. Wingate Properties Ltd.* (1984), 30 Man. R. (2d) 309 (Man. Q.B.); varied [1986] 1 W.W.R. 568 (Man. C.A.); varied on reconsideration [1986] 2 W.W.R. 568 (Man. C.A.).

94 And may be explained by the doctrine of "merger": on which see below, p. 553.

other personal property.[95] In such instances, at least as long as the claim for rescission is brought within a reasonable time, even if there has been "acceptance" of goods within the meaning of the Sale of Goods Act, there may still be rescission, though, naturally, no claim for damages.[96] Furthermore, there are cases in Canada, going back to the Supreme Court's decision in 1898 in *Cole v. Pope*,[97] which hold that even where the contract is a conveyance and has been executed, if the victim gets nothing of what he bargained for in the contract, and there has been a total failure of consideration, he may still rescind. The rationale for not applying the doctrine adopted by the Supreme Court of Canada in *Redican v. Nesbitt* is the idea of *error in substantialibus*.[98] As it was put more recently in *Adams v. Canadian Co-Operative Implements Ltd.*,[99] " . . . rescission is a remedy available for innocent misrepresentation even in the case of an executed contract, where the resulting error is an error *in substantialibus*, that is, an error as to substantial matters." In that case the plaintiff, a farmer, bought a new haystacker from the defendants, who represented that it would work with the 54 r.p.m. power take-off on the plaintiff's own tractor. In fact the haystacker would only operate on a 1000 r.p.m. power take-off. Hence, it was useless for the plaintiff. It was held that the contract could be rescinded for innocent misrepresentation and the purchase price could be recovered. However, the problem in all such cases is whether the error in question is sufficiently material to render what the plaintiff obtained under the contract substantially different in nature from what he believed he was going to obtain. In *Komarniski v. Marien*,[100] for instance, the difference in area of the purchased land did not amount to such a substantial difference as to permit the invocation of the notion of *error in substantialibus*. To the contrary was the earlier decision of Lieff J. in *Hyrsky v. Smith*.[101]

The notion of *error in substantialibus*, as developed by Canadian courts, seems in conflict with classical ideas of fundamental mistake in two ways.[102] First of all, it appears that sometimes even where there is only a partial failure of consideration, rescission may be permitted on this basis (or some modification of the original contract), where, under common-law ideas of mistake this should not be possible in the absence of fraud. Second, the kind of mistake induced by the relevant innocent misrepresentation may relate only to the quality of the subject-

---

95 For a detailed discussion see Bridge, "Misrepresentation and Merger: Sale of Land Principles and Sale of Goods Contracts", (1986), 20 U.B.C. L. Rev. 53.

96 See, *e.g., Ennis v. Klassen*, (1990), 70 D.L.R. (4th) 321 (Man. C.A.); Fridman, *Sale of Goods in Canada*, 3rd ed. (1986), p. 421-424.

97 (1898), 29 S.C.R. 291 (S.C.C.); see also *Ruscheinsky v. A. Spencer Co.*, [1948] 2 W.W.R. 392 (B.C.S.C.). Compare *O'Flaherty v. McKinlay*, [1953] 2 D.L.R. 514 (Nfld. C.A.); *O'Connor v. Sturgeon Lake Lbr. Co.* (1914), 17 D.L.R. 316 (Sask. S.C.); affirmed (1914), 7 W.W.R. 64 (Sask. C.A.).

98 On which see Fridman "Error in Substantialibus: A Canadian Comedy of Errors" (1978), 65 Can. Bar Rev. 603; compare the comments of Huband J.A. and Twaddle J.A., dissenting, on the doctrine in *Ennis v. Klassen*, above, note 96, at 331-332, 339.

99 (1980), 20 A.R. 533 at 537 (Alta. Q.B.) *per* McFadyen J.

100 Above, note 81.

101 (1969), 5 D.L.R. (3d) 385 (Ont. H.C.); criticized in Fridman, *loc. cit.*, above, note 98, pp. 616-620.

102 Compare above, pp. 255-257.

matter of the contract, not its identity or existence. Again to permit such errors to support rescission is contrary to the common-law doctrine of fundamental mistake, at least as it developed prior to recent English decisions which have been discussed in an earlier chapter.[103] *Error in substantialibus* as a ground for upsetting a completed transaction may be acceptable, however, despite its incursion upon basic conceptions of mistake, because it does provide a means of escaping from the unfortunate consequences of the English doctrine about executed contracts (which has itself been abrogated by statute in England) and because it does not *per se* determine the contract, but only allows a court to exercise its equitable discretion to rescind (or modify the terms of the contract) in appropriate circumstances.

The recognition and development of the doctrine of *error in substantialibus*, however, does emphasize the questionable nature of the original limitation of the operation of the equitable notion of rescission for innocent misrepresentation in cases of executed contracts relating to real property.

There is no greater reason for protecting a completed transaction concerning realty than one dealing with personalty. Moreover, once exceptions are permitted the rule is subject to such restriction that it loses much of its force. Indeed, Riley J. of the Supreme Court of Alberta refused to accept and follow the doctrine in *Bevan v. Anderson & Peace River Sand & Gravel Co.*[104] There an innocent misrepresentation was made as to the condition of certain equipment and the prospects of the enterprise about which the parties were contracting. The defendant was entitled to repudiate, that is, to claim rescission, notwithstanding that the contract was executed. This approach, it is suggested, is by far the more logical and acceptable one bearing in mind that rescission, as an equitable remedy, is discretionary, depending upon the possibility of *restitutio*, whether complete or substantial, and the protection of innocent third parties who may have acquired rights in the meanwhile, and may be refused if it is impracticable or inequitable in the circumstances. Hence, there is, or should be, no danger that injustice will result to either party or to a stranger from the granting of rescission. To agree with this, however, is not also to agree with the application of the doctrine of *error in substantialibus* to achieve this result. As indicated in an Ontario decision,[105] *error in substantialibus* may not, and perhaps should not be employed over-generously. It would appear to be far better and less harmful a principle to allow what is now permitted by statute in England, namely, the rescission of an executed contract, whatever the nature of the subject-matter, in suitable instances of contracts entered into in consequence of an innocent misrepresentation. That would mean the possibility of rescission unless: (a) *restitutio* was impossible; (b) third parties had acquired legitimate rights; or (c) damages would be a sufficient remedy for the injured party.

---

103 Above, pp. 252-254.
104 (1957), 23 W.W.R. 508 (Alta. S.C.).
105 *John Bosworth Ltd. v. Pro. Syndicated Devs. Ltd.* (1979), 24 O.R. (2d) 97 (Ont. H.C.).

4. Non-disclosure

The situations so far discussed have been those in which a positive misstatement has been made. The question has also arisen whether a failure to disclose, without any accompanying misstatement, can ever suffice to found a case of fraudulent or innocent misrepresentation.

A distinction must be made between a failure to disclose which in effect renders what has been stated a misrepresentation, and a failure to disclose which leaves anything said or written as true, but results in some misconceptions since the whole truth has not been told. The former kind of non-disclosure if fraudulent is fraudulent misrepresentation. For this to occur there must be what Lord Cairns in *Peek v. Gurney*[106] described as "some active misstatement of fact or, at all events, such a partial and fragmentary statement of fact as that the withholding of that which is not stated makes that which is stated absolutely false."[107] So, too, if the statement was true when made, but subsequently became untrue through a change which was known to the maker of the statement but not revealed by him to the representee, a dishonest failure to report the change may amount to fraud.[108] This is what occurred in the English case of *With v. O'Flanagan*[109] in which the value of a medical practice which was being sold dwindled through the vendor's illness between the statement of its estimated value at the date of the contract and the subsequent date for completion. In such circumstances there were grounds for rescission. Another illustration of failure to disclose the whole truth is provided by *Graham v. Legault*,[110] in which on the sale of some premises, the basement suite of which was rented, the vendor did not disclose that the renting in question was illegal, as no permit had been obtained as required in the circumstances. This was held to be a fraudulent misrepresentation of fact (not of law), and grounds for rescission.[111]

As constrasted with such instances of telling a half-truth or failing to correct a statement which has become untrue are cases in which there is complete silence

---

106 (1873), L.R. 6 H.L. 377 at 403 (H.L.).

107 See, *e.g.*, *Desautels v. Zeemal Enterprises Ltd.* (1981), 8 Man. R. (2d) 91 (Man. Q.B.); *Renaissance Resources v. Metalore Resources* (1984), 53 A.R. 289 (Alta. Q.B.); *Frawley v. Buckley* (1988), 93 N.B.R. (2d) 139 (N.B.Q.B.). Contrast cases in which no misrepresentation occurred: *Ens v. deVries* (1986), 75 A.R. 227 (Alta. Q.B.); *Daeyoo Enterprises Co. v. Long* (1986), 75 A.R. 47 (Alta. Q.B.). Compare *Olson v. New Home Certification Program of Alta.* (1986), 44 Alta. L.R. (2d) 207 (Alta. Q.B.); *Reidy v. Bramalea Ltd.* (1988), 73 Sask. R. 22 (Sask. Q.B.).

    Not all non-disclosure will be fraud, though non-disclosure may involve a breach of duty: *Williamson Bros. Const. Ltd. v. British Columbia* (1990), 41 C.L.R. 192 (B.C.S.C.).

108 *Brownlie v. Campbell* (1880), 5 App. Cas. 925 at 950 (H.L.) *per* Lord Blackburn; see *K.R.M. Const. Ltd. v. B.C. Railway* (1982), 40 B.C.L.R. 1 (B.C.C.A.); *Rainbow Industrial Caterers Ltd. v. Can. National Railway Co.* (1988), 54 D.L.R. (4th) 43 at 64, 78 (B.C.C.A.).

109 [1936] Ch. 575 (C.A.).

110 [1951] 3 D.L.R. 423 (B.C.S.C.); compare *Atomic Interprov. Transport (Eastern) Ltd. v. Paul Geiger Trucking Ltd.* (1987), 47 Man. R. (2d) 42 (Man. Q.B.): misrepresentation by omission, which rendered a surcharge clause in an insurance contract inoperative. On appeal, the decision was affirmed on other grounds: (1988), 45 D.L.R. (4th) 312.

111 This passage, commencing with "So, too, if the statement was true when made", was quoted in *Mun. Enterprises Ltd. v. Defence Const. (1951) Ltd.* (1985), 71 N.S.R. (2d) 59 at 67 (N.S.C.A.).

not affecting in any comparable way something which previously or concurrently has been said. Such silence will not amount to misrepresentation (whether fraudulent or innocent) unless it relates to some material fact which there is a duty on the silent party to disclose to the other.[112]

The issue of duty has been raised frequently in the context of the sale of real property. One question is whether the vendor is obliged to reveal to the purchaser latent defects rendering the premises unfit for habitation? Where the premises are not new, but have been lived in by the vendor for some time prior to the sale, there is authority for the propositions that the vendor must disclose such defects if they are known to him, and that the vendor will be liable if he was guilty of concealment or reckless disregard of the truth or falsity of any representation made by him respecting the premises.[113] There would also appear to be a duty on the vendor to disclose a defect that renders the premises dangerous in themselves, or that the circumstances are such as to disclose the likelihood of such danger.[114] This duty, and the liability which flows therefrom, are not based upon negligence, but on fraud.[115] For example, in *Rowley v. Isley*,[116] after completion, it was discovered that the house being sold was infested by cockroaches, rendering it uninhabitable. Non-disclosure of that defect was held to amount to fraudulent misrepresentation. However, Weatherston J.A., in *McGrath v. MacLean*,[117] was not prepared to hold that there could be rescission of a completed transaction concerning realty where the non-disclosure did not amount to fraud. There had to be active concealment, that is, fraudulent behaviour, not simply a failure to disclose. In *Hansen v. Twin City Construction Co.*,[118] Feehan J. of the Alberta Queen's Bench, appears to have accepted that the failure to disclose the known existence of a latent defect could be fraud, and suggested that showing a purchaser what appeared to be a

---

112 *Bank of N.S. v. Boehm*, [1973] 3 W.W.R. 757 (B.C.S.C.). Hence, if there is no duty to disclose there can be no misrepresentation by silence: *Robb v. Yukon Territory* (1987), 2 Y.R. 224 (Y.T.C.A.); additional reasons at (1987), 3 Y.R. 43 (Y.T.C.A.). Such a duty arose between the negotiating parties in *B.G. Preeco I (Pacific Coast) Ltd. v. Bon Street Holdings Ltd.* (1989), 60 D.L.R. (4th) 30 (B.C.C.A.). Here it did not matter whether the defendant's agents made an explicit misrepresentation or simply omitted to tell the plaintiff what the circumstances called for, namely the true identity of the offering company: *ibid.*, at 34 *per* Seaton J.A., quoting the trial judge, Paris J. On the issue of identity, see also *Curtis v. Dupuis* (1991), 112 N.B.R. (2d) 361 (N.B.Q.B.), where the manager's silence about his status was not a misrepresentation. There must be reliance on the silence if the misrepresentation is to have any legal effect: *Hoy v. Lozanovski* (1987), 43 R.P.R. 296 (Ont. Dist. Ct.).

113 *McGrath v. MacLean* (1979), 95 D.L.R. (3d) 144 (Ont. C.A.); *Sevidal v. Chopra* (1988), 64 O.R. (2d) 169 (Ont. H.C.); *Jung v. Ip* (1988), 47 R.P.R. 113 (Ont. Dist. Ct.); additional reasons at (1988), 50 R.P.R. 180 (Ont. Dist. Ct.).

114 *E.g.*, radioactivity: *McGrath v. MacLean*, above, note 113, at 152 *per* Dubin J.A.; compare *Heighington v. Ontario* (1987), 60 O.R. (2d) 641 (Ont. H.C.); additional reasons at (1987), 60 O.R. (2d) 641 at 655 (Ont. H.C.); affirmed (1989), 61 D.L.R. (4th) 190 (Ont. C.A.); *Sevidal v. Chopra*, above, note 113.

115 Compare *Sevidal v. Chopra*, above, note 113, at 183-189 *per* Oyen J.

116 [1957] 3 D.L.R. 766 (B.C.S.C.). See also *Danforth Heights Ltd. v. McDermid Bros.* (1922), 52 O.L.R. 412 (Ont. C.A.).

117 Above, note 113, at 155-157.

118 (1982), 136 D.L.R. (3d) 111 at 113-114 (Alta. Q.B.).

genuine fireplace, complete with ashes, without disclosing that it was an artificial fireplace, could possibly be a fraudulent misrepresentation. The claim in that case arose from the fact that, because the fireplace was not genuine, a fire started in the house, causing considerable damage; however, the learned judge did not determine the case on this ground, to some extent, because fraud had not been pleaded, and the plaintiff had not claimed rescission.

The duty to disclose, and not remain silent, arises in contracts *uberrimae fidei*, that is, where the parties must show the utmost good faith towards each other.[119] Dealings involving family arrangements and compromises are one category of contracts that attract this duty. Transactions between persons in a fiduciary relationship with one another are another category.[120] Such a relationship refers to a relation of confidence or authority of such a nature that the law recognizes a duty on the part of him in whom the confidence is reposed or the authority is vested to use his position for the benefit of the other party and not to abuse it for his own.[121] Confidence means any form of trust or reliance; authority means any form of power, control, dominion or personal influence. Good examples of this are: trustee and beneficiary, principal and agent, companies and directors, solicitors and their clients, partners, doctors and their patients. A third category involving *uberrima fides* comprises all contracts of insurance in which everything must be disclosed which would affect the judgment of the insurer in deciding whether or not to accept the risk proposed by the intended assured.[122] The foregoing list may not be exclusive. It is always open to the courts to declare that some new relationship or new situation should give rise to this high obligation.[123]

---

119 Contrast *Can. Farm Implement Co. v. Alta. Foundry etc. Co.*, [1927] 1 W.W.R. 1025 (Alta. S.C.), and *Young v. Cross & Co.*, [1927] 2 D.L.R. 373 at 379 (B.C.C.A.) *per* Macdonald J.A.; compare *Reidy v. Bramalea Ltd.*, above, note 107.

120 *Revell v. O'Brien Financial Corp.* (1988), 30 B.C.L.R. (2d) 330 (B.C.C.A.); affirmed (1991), 62 B.C.L.R. (2d) 314 (B.C.C.A.). On the issue of damages in such a case, see *Canson Enterprises Ltd. v. Boughton & Co.* (1992), 85 D.L.R. (4th) 129 (S.C.C.), which discusses how damages in equity should be calculated *viz.*, by analogy with contract or tort, or distinctly.

121 Hence, the attempt to bring a contract for personal services as a football player within this category failed in *Re Gabriel & Hamilton Tiger-Cat Football Club Ltd.* (1975), 8 O.R. (2d) 285 (Ont. H.C.). But in *Can. Kawasaki Motors Ltd. v. McKenzie* (1981), 126 D.L.R. (3d) 253 (Ont. Co. Ct.) a County Court Judge in Ontario suggested that such a relationship might exist between a manufacturer arranging to grant a franchise and the guarantors of the prospective franchise.

122 See, *e.g., Case Existological Laboratories Ltd. v. Foremost Ins. Co. of Can.* (1982), 133 D.L.R. (3d) 727 (B.C.C.A.), where non-disclosure was not established.

123 See *Can. Kawasaki Motors Ltd. v. McKenzie*, above, note 121.

9

Duress, Undue Influence, Unconscionability

1. Introduction

There are other grounds which, either at common law or in equity, may justify the repudiation of consent once given so as to vitiate an otherwise valid contract. Whether what is involved is duress in the strict sense, undue influence as that notion was developed in equity, or the more modern, perhaps vaguer and more generalized idea of unconscionability, the essence of granting rescission of, or similar relief from an otherwise binding contract is that the victim's consent was not obtained or given when he or she was physically, emotionally, or intellectually free and competent to give it, but was the product of some minatory, overweening or improperly persuasive conduct on the part of the guilty party.[1]

2. Duress

(a) Duress to the person

At common law a contract induced by actual or threatened physical violence

---

1 This paragraph was cited by Kelly J. in *Royal Bank v. Savage* (1983), 48 N.B.R. (2d) 117 at 120 (N.B.Q.B.) and by Gerein J. in *Superior Dev. Ltd. v. Brown; Brown v. Superior Dev. Ltd.* (1984), 34 Sask. R. 74 at 77 (Sask. Q.B.).

or unlawful imprisonment of the other party, his wife, children, or near relative, could be avoided on the ground of duress.[2] The threats need not have been made against the other contracting party directly, as long as the threat of harm to another is acted upon by the party against whom the agreement is sought to be enforced.[3] Hence, threats made against a child or children, if they affect the parents, will permit a plea of duress.[4] Since the effect of duress was to render the apparent consent of the threatened party not a true consent to the transaction, it might be thought that, on proof of duress the alleged contract would be void, a legal nullity. Such was the view of a Canadian judge in 1976,[5] where a distinction was drawn between duress, making a purported contract void, and undue influence,[6] making a purported contract voidable at the option of the party subjected to such influence. However, the Privy Council, in *Barton v. Armstrong*,[7] adopted the view that duress only made the subsequent contract voidable. The parallel was drawn between duress and fraud.[8] Just as proof of deception destroyed the foundations of a contract, so, too, once there were threats of violence (in that case of death) and those threats were a reason for the victim to execute the contract in question (albeit not the only reason), the contract could be avoided by the victim. By a majority in that case, the Privy Council held that the contract which was entered into after threats had been made to kill the plaintiff could be avoided by the plaintiff, even though there was evidence that the plaintiff might well have entered into the contract had the defendant not uttered the threats in question so as to induce the plaintiff to contract. That a contract effected by duress is voidable, not void, was accepted by the British Columbia Court of Appeal in *Byle v. Byle*,[9] pointing out the error of the judge in *Saxon v. Saxon*,[10] based upon some language of the Privy Council in *Barton v. Armstrong*,[11] which does not concur with other, later interpretations.[12]

Most instances of duress involving threats of physical violence, which is a rare occurrence in these days, concern threats made by one contracting party against the other. There are situations in which the alleged threat was made by a third party, not the party now seeking to enforce a contract alleged to have been entered into as a result of the threats. Where this is the case, it has been said that the party suing, who was not the party guilty of making the threats, must know about

---

2 See, *e.g.*, *Colp v. Hunker* (1911), 1 W.W.R. 314 (Sask. S.C.) (threat to shoot). Compare *J.H. Samuels & Co. v. Crown Trust Co.* (1959), 27 W.W.R. 160 (Alta. S.C.). See also *Brooks v. Alker* (1975), 9 O.R. (2d) 409 (Ont. H.C.). For a recent reference to this passage, see *Campbell v. Campbell* (1990), 83 Nfld. & P.E.I.R. 340 at 348 (Nfld. U.F.C.) *per* Barry J.

3 *Byle v. Byle* (1990), 65 D.L.R. (4th) 641 at 649 (B.C.C.A.).

4 Below, note 5; *Byle v. Byle*, above, note 3.

5 *Saxon v. Saxon*, [1976] 4 W.W.R. 300 (B.C.S.C.); affirmed [1978] 4 W.W.R. 327 (B.C.C.A.).

6 Below, pp. 320-325.

7 [1975] 2 All E.R. 465 (P.C.).

8 *Ibid.*, at 474-475.

9 Above, note 3, at 650.

10 Above, note 5.

11 Above, note 7.

12 *North Ocean Shipping Co. v. Hyundai Const. Co.*, [1978] 3 All E.R. 1170; see below, p. 000; *Dir. of Public Prosecutions for Northern Ireland v. Lynch*, [1975] A.C. 653 at 695 (H.L.) *per* Lord Simon of Glaisdale.

the threats if the defence of duress is to succeed against such party.[13] As was said by Meldrum J. in *Canadian Imperial Bank of Commerce v. Boudreau,*[14] "To establish duress against a third party there must be duress and it must be known to the third party at the time the contract was entered into." In that case the plaintiff sued the co-signer of a conditional sales contract for the balance due under the contract. She was the mother of the male defendant who was the principal debtor under the contract. She pleaded duress, and argued that she feared that her son would get back at her if she did not co-sign the contract. It was held that this was not sufficient to show duress, as there was no evidence of what the son would do if she did not sign.[15] Moreover, the bank did not know about any such threats or fears at the time the contract was signed by the mother and her son. Hence, the plea of duress failed. Similarly, in *Bank of Nova Scotia v. Drouillard-Potter,*[16] the bank was unaware of any pressure exerted on the wife by the husband to co-sign a bank loan. The husband was not the agent of the bank. Therefore, a plea of duress could not succeed.

Since duress renders the contract voidable, not void, the subsequent conduct of the party alleging duress may affect the right to avoid the transaction. If that party's conduct can be regarded as affirming, condoning, or ratifying the contract, the plea of duress will fail. In *Byle v. Byle,*[17] the conduct of the parents was not affirmation, even though they allowed the party, whose duress was alleged, to work on the land that was the subject-matter of the contract, and to receive rents in respect of it, for two years after the contract. They did not know they had any alternative course of action.

(b) Extension of duress at common law

The scope of duress at common law was very limited.[18] Hence, the development by courts of equity at a comparatively early date of the idea that relief might be granted where a disposition were procured by the exercise of pressure which the Chancellor considered illegitimate, although it might not have amounted to common-law duress.[19] However, the common law has not stood still. From being concerned originally with duress of the person, that is, threats of physical violence,

---

13 *Wilgross Invts. Ltd. v. Goldshlager* (1974), 5 O.R. (2d) 687 (Ont. Div. Ct.); *Bank of Montreal v. Lynn* (1976), 23 O.R. (2d) 667 (Ont. H.C.); *Bank of N.S. v. MacLellan* (1980), 30 N.B.R. (2d) 596 (N.B.C.A.); *Royal Bank v. Mahoney* (1982), 38 Nfld. & P.E.I.R. 179 (Nfld. C.A.); *Bank of Nova Scotia v. Drouillard-Potter* (1987), 79 A.R. 2 (M.C.).

14 (1982), 41 N.B.R. (2d) 365 at 368 (N.B.Q.B.).

15 Contrast *E. & R. Distributors v. Atlas Drywall* (1980), 118 D.L.R. (3d) 339 (B.C.C.A.), invoking a special rule as between a husband and wife.

16 (1987), 79 A.R. 2 (M.C.)

17 Above, note 3, especially at 653-654; contrast *North Ocean Shipping Co. v. Hyundai,* above, note 12; *Victorov v. Davison* (1988), 20 C.P.R. (3d) 481 (Ont. H.C.); *Stott v. Merit Invt. Corp.* (1988), 48 D.L.R. (4th) 288 (Ont. C.A.); leave to appeal to S.C.C. refused (1988), 49 D.L.R. (4th) viii (note) (S.C.C.).

18 *Barton v. Armstrong,* above, note 7.

19 Below, pp. 320-325.

it has extended its scope to take into account, first of all, threats to another's property, and, in more modern times, what has been termed "economic duress". Indeed, there are indications that the ultimate scope of the concept of duress is still undetermined.[20]

One previously disputed point seems now to have been settled. At one time it was thought that mere duress of goods would not invalidate a contract induced by such pressure, though it would permit the recovery of money paid to the other, threatening party, by the threatened party, in what was originally an action for money had and received.[21] Such quasi-contractual recovery is now recognized as one head of restitutionary recovery, independent of any contractual remedies or relief that might be available to the party subjected to the threats.[22] But it has also been conceded that there is something illogical about upholding a contract entered into as a result of duress of goods while permitting the recovery of money paid in consequence of such duress.[23] Hence, it may now be stated that any kind of recognized duress will have the same effect as the original common-law duress to the person.

The essential idea behind the plea of duress is that improper, wrongful pressure has been brought to bear by one person upon another so as to make the latter unwillingly do something against his interest.[24] Two particular situations have caused problems. One concerns the compromise of a threatened civil action. A legitimate compromise, based upon a *bona fide* belief by both parties that a suit is maintainable, has been held valid, whether it has been executed, by the payment of money, or remains executory.[25] Even though the compromise is founded upon a threat to sue, it has been determined that the party paying or agreeing to pay for the withdrawal of the suit cannot subsequently plead duress to recover the payment or avoid the agreement.[26] A distinction must be drawn between such legitimate compromises and payments or agreements exacted by demands made in bad faith, that is, with the knowledge that the claim was unfounded, or made

---

20 Rafferty, "The Element of Wrongful Pressure in a Finding of Duress" (1980), 18 Alta. L. Rev. 431.

21 *Skeate v. Beale* (1840), 11 Ad. & El. 983; Beatson, "Duress as a Vitiating Factor in Contract" (1974), 33 C.L.J. 97.

22 Fridman, *Restitution*, 2nd ed. (1992), Chapter 5; Goff & Jones, *Law of Restitution*, 3rd ed. (1986), Chapter 9; Maddaugh & McCamus, *Law of Restitution* (1990), Chapter 24.

23 *Siboen v. Skibs*, [1976] 1 Lloyd's Rep. 293 at 334-336 *per* Kerr J; *R.E. Lister Ltd. v. Dunlop Can. Ltd.* (1978), 85 D.L.R. (2d) 321 at 348 (Ont. H.C.) *per* Rutherford J.; reversed (1979), 105 D.L.R. (3d) 684 at 694-696 (Ont. C.A.) *per* Weatherston J.A.; reversed on other grounds (1982), 135 D.L.R. (3d) 1 (S.C.C.).

24 Whether it is correct to speak of a party's will being coerced so as to vitiate his consent is a matter of debate: see *Dimskal Shipping Co. S.A. v. Int. Transport Workers' Federation*, [1991] 3 W.L.R. 875 at 883 (H.L.) *per* Lord Goff. But see *Pao On v. Lau Liu Long*, [1979] 3 All E.R. 65 at 78 (P.C.); *Stott v. Merit Invt. Corp.*, above, note 17, at 305 *per* Finlayson J.A.; *Gordon v. Roebuck* (1989), 64 D.L.R. (4th) 568 at 572 (Ont. H.C.) *per* Fitzpatrick J.; reversed in part (1992), 92 D.L.R. (4th) 670 (Ont. C.A.).

25 Above, pp. 94-97.

26 But he might be able to plead mistake: *T.D. Bank v. Fortin (No. 2)* (1978), 88 D.L.R. (3d) 232 (B.C.S.C.); above, p. 96.

with the addition of some improper threat, such as a threat to prosecute.[27] Secondly, a threat not to fulfil a contractual obligation, so as to compel the promisee to pay or agree to pay something additional to secure performance, or to make some other modification of the contract, will not be valid on the ground that there was no new consideration for such payment or agreement.[28] However, there is another reason why such modificatory agreements may be invalid and unenforceable against the party promising the additional payment or other new undertaking. It has been held that promises exacted in such circumstances have been made under duress, even though no threats of physical violence to the promisor or the promisor's goods or property may be involved. This development has involved the creation or recognition of "economic duress".

(c) Economic duress[29]

The idea that threats other than of physical violence to a person or his property, or the abuse or misuse of public office or the legal process, could be the basis of a plea of duress, and in particular that the threat to break a contract, without any lawful justification, could serve such purpose, was first mooted by Kerr J. in the English case of *Siboen v. Skibs*.[30] In that case the threat in question was the refusal by charterers to pay the charges under a charterparty unless the owners of the ship performed certain acts. On the facts of the case it was held that duress was not an available plea, because what had occurred amounted only to commercial pressure, not the sort of coercion that could support a plea of duress. However, the idea was implanted that, in appropriate instances, threats of this kind might permit the invocation of the defence of duress to render an agreement so produced voidable. In *North Ocean Shipping Co. v. Hyundai Construction Ltd.*,[31] another English judge was faced with a similar problem, and held that duress could certainly be pleaded to avoid a contract reached after threats to break an existing agreement had been made by a party already obliged. There was a contract to build a ship

---

27 Rafferty, *loc. cit.*, above, note 20 at pp. 441-446, 448-449.

28 Above, pp. 101-103.

29 Fridman, *Restitution*, 2nd ed. (1992), pp. 137-140; Goff & Jones, *Law of Restitution*, 3rd ed. (1990), pp. 222-240; Maddaugh & McCamus, *Law of Restitution* (1990), pp. 557-562; Ogilvie, "Economic Duress, Inequality of Bargaining Power and Threatened Breaches of Contract" (1982), 26 McGill L.J. 289. Macdonald, "Duress by Threatened Breach of Contract", [1989] J. Bus. L. 460; Halson, "Opportunism, Economic Duress and Contractual Modifications" (1991), 107 L.Q.R. 649. See also Muris, "Opportunistic Behaviour and the Law of Contracts" (1981), 65 Minn. L. Rev. 521. For an American view based on economic analysis, see Dalzell, "Duress by Economic Pressure" (1942), 20 N. Car. L. Rev. 237, reprinted in Kronman & Posner, *The Economics of Contract Law*, 1979, pp. 67-72. This section of the chapter was referred to by Barry J. in *Campbell v. Campbell* (1990), 83 Nfld. & P.E.I.R. 340 at 348 (Nfld. U.F.C.).

30 [1976] 1 Lloyd's Rep. 293; compare *Sundell (T.A.) & Sons Pty. Ltd. v. Emm Yannoulatos (Overseas) Pty. Ltd.* (1956), S.R. (N.S.W.) 323 (N.S.W. Sup. Ct.). See the discussion by Lord Goff in *Dimskal Shipping Co. S.A. v. Int. Transport Workers' Federation*, [1991] 3 W.L.R. 875 at 883 (H.L.).

31 [1978] 3 All E.R. 1170. See *Nfld. & Labrador Drilling Ltd. v. Miller* (1992), 97 Nfld. & P.E.I.R. 140 (Nfld. T.D.), where economic duress was successfully pleaded to preclude payment of an additional sum which was agreed in the original contract.

for a specified price. Before the contract was completed, the U.S. dollar underwent devaluation, with the result that the price, in U.S. dollars, was worth less. The shipbuilders then told the owners that they would not complete the contract unless an additional percentage was added to the original price to take the devaluation into account. The builders knew that the owners needed the ship to fulfil certain contracts they had with third parties. The owners agreed to pay the extra money (reserving their rights, whatever they were, in the meantime). In subsequent litigation, which raised the issue whether the extra money could be obtained by the builders, it was held that there was consideration for the promise to pay more (in that the builders agreed to extend the original letter of credit).[32] However, it was also held that the conduct of the builders amounted to economic duress which could operate to entitle the owners to avoid the agreement to pay more money. What was involved in this instance was more than simple commercial pressure. The builders were using their knowledge of the economic circumstances of the owners to compel or coerce them into agreeing to something they would otherwise not have assented to in the absence of the threats.[33] However, it was also held that the conduct of the owners after the making of the agreement amounted to affirmation of the transaction. Hence, since duress only rendered a contract voidable, not void *ab initio*, such affirmation could destroy the owners' privilege of electing to avoid the agreement to pay extra money.

The suggestion in these cases that sometimes commercial pressure might amount to duress entitling the victim to avoid a contract was approved and adopted in Canada in *R.E. Lister Ltd. v. Dunlop Canada Ltd.*,[34] even though, ultimately, the Supreme Court of Canada resolved the litigation on other grounds.[35] In any event, as the lower courts held in that case, the principle of economic duress through business or commercial pressure was not applicable on the facts since the debtors who had agreed to certain compromise agreements had obtained independent advice and were able to make decisions freely. The test for economic duress, as accepted in that case, was the test laid down by the Privy Council in *Pao On v. Lau Yiu Long.*[36] Once again the issue related to a threat to break a contract, this time in order to compel or force the other party to sign a guarantee that the price of certain shares, which were the subject-matter of the main transaction, would not be less than a stipulated price on a particular material date (requiring the defendants to indemnify the plaintiffs should the shares fall below such price).

---

32 Compare *Gilbert Steel Ltd. v. University Const. Ltd.* (1976), 67 D.L.R. (3d) 606 (Ont. C.A.); above, pp. 101-102.

33 Compare *Atlas Express Ltd. v. Kafco Ltd.*, [1989] 1 All E.R. 641 (Q.B.).

34 (1978), 85 D.L.R. (3d) 321 (Ont. H.C.); reversed (1979), 105 D.L.R. (3d) 684 (Ont. C.A.); reversed on other grounds (1982), 135 D.L.R. (3d) 1 (S.C.C.). See, *e.g., Modular Windows of Can. v. Command Const.* (1984), 11 C.L.R. 131 (Ont. H.C.) (defendant, having no alternative but to sign agreement to pay more money, able to rely on defence of economic duress). *R.E. Lister Ltd. v. Dunlop Can. Ltd.* was applied in *De Wolfe v. Mansour* (1986), 73 N.S.R. (2d) 110 (N.S.T.D.).

35 (1982), 135 D.L.R. (3d) 1 (S.C.C.).

36 [1979] 3 All E.R. 65 (P.C.), on which see England and Rafferty, "Contractual Variations: Consideration and Duress" (1980), 18 O.H.L.J. 627.

The Privy Council held that the defence of duress had not been established.[37] However, while doing so, the Board also: (i) recognized the existence of a plea of economic duress; (ii) set out the nature of the pressure that constituted such duress; and (iii) identified the underlying notion of duress in such instances.

> Duress, whatever form it takes, is a coercion of the will so as to vitiate consent . . .in a contractual situation commercial pressure is not enough. There must be present some factor which could in law be regarded as a coercion of his will so as to vitiate his consent. . . .In determining whether there was a coercion of will such that there was no true consent, it is material to enquire whether the person alleged to have been coerced did or did not protest; whether, at the time he was allegedly coerced into making the contract, he did or did not have an alternative course open to him such as an adequate legal remedy; whether he was independently advised; and whether after entering the contract he took steps to avoid it.[38]

These various factors have long been recognized, in England and in Canada, as the essential ingredients of a valid claim for recovery of money paid under duress, or compulsion, in a restitutionary action. They have now been accepted as the true bases for a valid plea of duress involving threats of an economic or commercial kind, without any suggestion of physical harm to a person or his property. As the Privy Council said: " . . .there is nothing contrary to principle in recognizing economic duress as a factor which may render a contract voidable, provided always that the basis of such recognition is that it must amount to a coercion of will, which vitiates consent. It must be shown that the payment made or the contract entered into was not a voluntary act."[39]

In a subsequent decision of the House of Lords, *Universe Tankships Inc. of Monrovia v. International Transport Workers' Federation*,[40] Lord Scarman, who had delivered the opinion of the Privy Council in *Pao On v. Lau Yiu Long*, returned to the question of economic duress. He identified two elements, culled from earlier authorities on which the decisions in *Barton v. Armstrong* and *Pao On v. Lau Yiu Long* were based. The first was pressure amounting to compulsion of the will of the victim. This involved the absence of any practical choice other than of submission to the threat of the other party, proved by protest, by the absence of independent advice, or the absence of a declaration of intention to go to law to recover money paid or property transferred. However, the second element was perhaps more essential. This was the illegitimacy of the pressure exerted. Lord Diplock, in this case,[41] was not prepared to hold that any commercial pressure, even where the parties were not in an equal bargaining position,[42] might amount to illegitimate pressure constituting duress. In life, including life in commerce and finance, many acts are done under pressure, sometimes overwhelming pressure.

---

37 See also above, pp. 107, 111, for other defences which failed.
38 *Pao On v. Lau Yiu*, above, note 36, at 78 *per* Lord Scarman, referring to *Siboen v. Skibs*, above, note 30, and *Barton v. Armstrong*, [1975] 2 All E.R. 465 (P.C.).
39 Above, note 36, at 79.
40 [1982] 2 All E.R. 67 at 88 (H.L.).
41 *Ibid.*, at 76.
42 See below, pp. 328-330.

They are not necessarily done under duress.[43] That depended, according to Lord Scarman,[44] on whether the circumstances were such that the law regarded the pressure as legitimate. This involved first of all, the nature of the pressure, which might be decisive in many instances, and second, the nature of the demand which the pressure was applied to support.

> The origin of the doctrine of duress in threats of life or limb, or to property, suggests strongly that the law regards the threat of unlawful action as illegitimate, whatever the demand. Duress can, of course, exist even if the threat is one of lawful action; whether it does so depends on the nature of the demand. Blackmail is often a demand supported by a threat to do what is lawful, e.g., to report criminal conduct to the police. In many cases, therefore, what one has to justify is not the threat, but the demand . . .[45]

These two ideas, (a) that there must be the required amount of coercion, and (b) that the pressure exerted must be regarded by the law as not legitimate, were stressed in two Canadian cases, *Stott v. Merit Investment Corporation*[46] and *Gordon v. Roebuck*.[47] In the first, economic duress was established as a result of the statement that all would not go well with the plaintiff if he did not sign an agreement acknowledging his liability for a client's losses. But the subsequent conduct of the plaintiff amounted to affirmation. In the second case, no exercise of economic duress was proved.[48] Nevertheless, the doctrine is firmly established in Canada, as it is in England. Societal pressures can be every bit as effective if improperly used, as those flowing from threats of physical abuse.[49]

3. Undue influence

Equity went further than the common law of duress and developed the doctrine that contracts entered into as a result of moral coercion could also be avoided where it would be inequitable and unconscionable to hold the victim bound by his agreement. The doctrine of undue influence reached beyond the boundaries of physical duress on person or property. Equity was concerned with the more subtle effects of non-physical pressure upon the mind and ultimate consent of the party being influenced. The use by one contracting party of any form of oppression, coercion, compulsion or abuse of power or authority for the purpose of obtaining the consent of the other party may result in avoidance of the resulting contract

---

43 [1982] 2 All E.R. 67 at 89 (H.L.) *per* Lord Scarman, citing Lords Wilberforce and Simon in *Barton v. Armstrong*, [1975] 2 All E.R. 465 at 476-477 (P.C.).

44 [1982] 2 All E.R. 67 at 89 (H.L.).

45 *Ibid.*, citing *Thorne v. Motor Trade Assn.*, [1937] A.C. 797 at 828 (H.L.) *per* Lord Atkin.

46 (1988), 48 D.L.R. (4th) 288 at 308 (Ont. C.A.) *per* Finlayson J.A.; leave to appeal to S.C.C. refused (1988), 49 D.L.R. (4th) viii note (S.C.C.).

47 (1989), 64 D.L.R. (4th) 568 at 572 (Ont. H.C.), *per* Fitzpatrick J.; reversed in part (1992), 92 D.L.R. (4th) 670 (Ont. C.A.).

48 Compare *Victorov v. Davison* (1988), 20 C.P.R. (3d) 481 (Ont. H.C.); *Adanac Realty Ltd. v. Homes Dev. Ltd.* (1986), 43 R.P.R. 88 (Ont. H.C.); *N.A.B.E.T., Loc. 913 v. Cramm* (1986), 63 Nfld. & P.E.I.R. 347 (Nfld. T.D.), in none of which was economic duress established.

49 *Stott v. Merit Invt. Corp.*, above, note 46, at 305 (Ont. C.A.).

on the ground of undue influence.[50] As the House of Lords explained in *National Westminster Bank v. Morgan*,[51] the principle justifying the court in setting aside a transaction for undue influence is the need to save persons from being victimized by others, not some vague "public policy".

The equitable doctrine of undue influence is older than the decision in *Allcard v. Skinner*.[52] However, it was in that case that the doctrine was established in its modern form, according to which there are two classes of cases in which the doctrine applies: (1) those where the court has been satisfied that the transaction (which may be either a gift, as in *Allcard v. Skinner* itself, or a commercial contract) was the result of influence expressly used by the donee (or promisee) for the purpose; (2) those where the relations between the donor (or promisor) and donee (or promisee) have at, or shortly before, the execution of the transaction been such as to raise a presumption that the donee (or promisee) had influence over the donor (or promisor). The first class consists of cases of "actual undue influence". The second consists of cases of "presumed undue influence". The difference between these cases lies in the burden of proof. In the first class, the onus is on the party claiming undue influence entitling him to avoid the transaction to prove that such influence was actually exerted by the other party. In the second class, once the relationship giving rise to the presumption is proved to exist, the onus is on the party alleged to be guilty of undue influence to rebut the presumption by suitable and appropriate evidence, such as that the other party obtained independent legal or financial advice.[53]

There are well-established categories of relationships that give rise to the presumption of undue influence. These include family relationships,[54] such as parent and child,[55] brothers and sisters.[56] Others include trustee and beneficiary; solicitor

50 *Burris v. Rhind* (1899), 29 S.C.R. 498 (S.C.C.); *McKay v. Clow*, [1941] S.C.R. 643 (S.C.C.). A plea of undue influence attacks the sufficiency of consent: *Morrison v. Coast Furnace Ltd.* (1965), 55 D.L.R. (2d) 710 (B.C.C.A.) *per* Davey J.A. The plea is not available against a third party ignorant of the undue influence: *Domenco v. Domenco* (1963), 41 D.L.R. (2d) 267 (Man. Q.B.); compare *Bank of Credit & Commerce Int. S.A. v. Aboody*, [1992] 4 All E.R. 955 at 980-981 (C.A.) (overruled by the House of Lords in *C.I.B.C. Mortgages plc v. Pitt*, [1993] 4 All E.R. 433 (H.L.)).

51 [1985] 1 All E.R. 821 at 827-828 (H.L.) *per* Lord Scarman, citing *Allcard v. Skinner* (1887), 36 Ch. D. 145 at 183 *per* Lindley L.J.

52 (1887), 36 Ch. D. 145.

53 *Bank of Credit & Commerce Int. S.A. v. Aboody*, [1992] 4 All E.R. 955 at 964 (C.A.) *per* Slade L.J. (on which see above, note 50).

54 *McKay v. Clow*, [1941] S.C.R. 643 (S.C.C.); *Lato v. Lato* (1982), 19 Sask. R. 271 (Sask. Q.B.). See, for different applications of the doctrine of presumed undue influence: *Wheeler v. Wheeler* (1978), 20 N.B.R. (2d) 399 (N.B.Q.B.); affirmed (1978), 25 N.B.R. (2d) 374 (N.B.C.A.); *Provender v. Lavoie* (1980), 5 Sask. R. 119 (Sask. Q.B.); *McArthur v. McArthur* (1982), 45 N.B.R. (2d) 10 (N.B.Q.B.); *Randall v. Nicklin* (1984), 58 N.B.R. (2d) 414 (N.B.C.A.); *Matheson v. Johnston* (1984), 66 N.S.R. (2d) 19 (N.S.T.D.); *Gammon v. Steeves* (1986), 72 N.B.R. (2d) 239 (N.B.Q.B.); reversed in part (1987), 83 N.B.R. (2d) 397 (N.B.C.A.); *Tulick Estate v. Ostapowich* (1988), 62 Alta. L.R. (2d) 384 (Alta. Q.B.); *Kielly Estate v. Knox* (1989), 76 Nfld. & P.E.I.R. 96 (P.E.I.T.D.).

55 *Laderoute v. Laderoute* (1978), 81 D.L.R. (3d) 433 (Ont. H.C.); *Sawatzky v. Sawatzky* (1986), 48 Sask. R. 161 (Sask. Q.B.); *Goguen v. Goguen* (1988), 92 N.B.R. (2d) 158 (N.B.Q.B.); *Green v. Perley* (1989), 103 N.B.R. (2d) 181 (N.B.Q.B.). Contrast *Anderson v. Carter* (1986), 68 A.R. 100 (Alta. Q.B.); *Johnson v. Johnson Estate* (1986), 69 N.B.R. (2d) 408 (N.B.Q.B.); *Shoop v. Tanner* (1986),

and client; doctor and patient; guardian and ward; future husband and fiancee.[57] In more recent times, since 1961, according to Wilson J. in *Geffen v. Goodman Estate*,[58] the relationships in which undue influence will be presumed are not confined to fixed categories, but may be extended where the facts make such a conclusion appropriate. Some "special" relationship must be shown, though what constitutes such a "special" relationship is not clear. One suggested test is whether the parties were in a fiduciary relationship. Another is that influence flows from a confidential relationship. Another is that the relationship should be advisory. Another is that the test of "dominating influence" should be applied to create the necessary relationship giving rise to a presumption of undue influence.[59] Although it was decided in *Bank of Montreal v. Stuart*[60] that no presumption of undue influence arose as between husband and wife, it was recently held by the English Court of Appeal, and the House of Lords, in *Barclays Bank plc. v. O'Brien*,[61] that a married woman who provides surety for her husband's debts, as well as others in analogous positions, such as elderly parents on whom pressure might be brought by adult children, were to be treated as a specially protected class of sureties. Hence, where the relationship between the debtor and the surety was one in which influence by the debtor over the surety and reliance by the surety on the debtor were natural and probable features of the relationship, the security given by the surety might be unenforceable, even if the creditor suing the surety had no knowledge of the vitiating circumstances, and was not responsible for those circumstances, as for instance, if the husband were the agent of the creditor such as a bank. Although this is not exactly a case of presumed undue influence, it comes very close to it.

An issue that has arisen recently and was considered at some length by the

---

53 Sask. R. 293 (Sask. Q.B.); affirmed (1988), 69 Sask. R. 307 (Sask. C.A.); *MacDonald v. Creelman* (1988), 83 N.S.R. (2d) 415 (N.S.T.D.); affirmed (1989), 88 N.S.R. (2d) 403 (N.S.C.A.).

56 *Thom v. Saltner*, [1989] 1 W.W.R. 456 (Man. Q.B.). Contrast *Geffen v. Goodman Estate* (1991), 81 D.L.R. (4th) 211 (S.C.C.); reversing (1989), 61 D.L.R. (4th) 431 (*sub nom. Goodman Estate v. Geffen*) (Alta. C.A.); which reversed [1987] 4 W.W.R. 730 (*sub nom. Goodman v. Geffen*) (Alta. Q.B.).

57 *Geffen v. Goodman Estate*, above, note 56, at 221 (S.C.C.); see also *Treadwell v. Martin* (1976), 67 D.L.R. (3d) 493 (N.B.C.A.); *G. Mida Const. Ltd. v. Imperial Devs. (Int.) Ltd.*, [1978] 5 W.W.R. 577 (Man. C.A.) (with which contrast *Green v. Charterhouse Group Can. Ltd.* (1976), 68 D.L.R. (3d) 592 (Ont. C.A.); *Allen v. Allen* (1976), 15 Nfld. & P.E.I.R. 362 (Nfld. Dist. Ct.); *Tannock v. Bromley* (1979), 10 B.C.L.R. 62 (B.C.S.C.); *Malicki v. Yankovich* (1981), 33 O.R. (2d) 537 (Ont. H.C.); additional reasons at (1982), 42 O.R. (2d) 522 (Ont. H.C.); affirmed (1983), 41 O.R. (2d) 160 (Ont. C.A.); *Rochdale Credit Union Ltd. v. Barney* (1984), 48 O.R. (2d) 676 (Ont. C.A.); leave to appeal to S.C.C. refused (1985), 8 O.A.C. 320 (S.C.C.). Contrast *Land v. McPherson* (1989), 42 B.L.R. 23 (B.C.S.C.); affirmed (May 10, 1990), Doc. No. V00960 (B.C.C.A.).

58 Above, note 56, at 221.

59 Above, note 56, at 222.

60 [1911] A.C. 120 (P.C.); *Harding v. Harding* (1972), 28 D.L.R. (3d) 358 (B.C.S.C.).

61 [1992] 4 All E.R. 983 (C.A.); affirmed [1993] 4 All E.R. 417 (H.L.); compare an earlier Canadian case, *E. & R. Distributors v. Atlas Drywall* (1980), 118 D.L.R. (3d) 339 (B.C.C.A.). See also *Bertolo v. Bank of Montreal* (1986), 33 D.L.R. (4th) 610 especially at 618-620 (Ont. C.A.).

Supreme Court of Canada in *Geffen v. Goodman Estate*,[62] is whether, in order to establish a presumption of undue influence, it is necessary to prove that the transaction was to the manifest disadvantage of the plaintiff seeking to have it upset.

This requirement was made pertinent by the House of Lords in *National Westminister Bank plc. v. Morgan*.[63] It was also applied to an instance of "actual", not "presumed", undue influence by the English Court of Appeal in *Bank of Credit & Commerce International S.A. v. Aboody*,[64] which was overruled by the House of Lords in *C.I.B.C. Mortgages plc v. Pitt*,[65] in which proof that the transaction was manifestly disadvantageous was held not to be required where there was *actual* undue influence. Earlier, in *Geffen v. Goodman Estate*, Wilson J. pointed out that the requirement that a plaintiff demonstrate manifest disadvantage had come under heavy criticism.[66] However, although the circumstances in the *Geffen* case did not seem to necessitate examination of the *Morgan* decision *in toto*, bearing in mind that the Supreme Court of Canada was not bound by that decision, Wilson J. deemed it relevant to investigate the purpose to be served by the doctrine of undue influence. After considering some expressed views, she concluded that neither a result focused approach nor a process focused approach fully captured the true purport of the equitable rule because the doctrine applied to a wide variety of transactions from pure gifts to classic contracts.[67] To her, the nature of the relationship that had to exist before a presumption of undue influence could be made was not to be found in the ideas of "confidence" or "reliance", but was to be discovered by interpreting "influence" to mean "the ability of one person to dominate the will of another, whether through manipulation, coercion, or outright, but subtle abuse of power."[68] Disadvantage was not particularly appropriate a concept for general application to the situations in which the doctrine of undue influence could apply. It was appropriate in a commercial setting, but not necessarily elsewhere. The potential for domination inherent in a given relationship was the first crucial issue.[69] Once this was established it was necessary to examine the nature of the transaction. In commercial transactions the party seeking to upset the contract had to show that the contract worked unfairness in the sense that the plaintiff was unduly disadvantaged by it or in the sense that the defendant was unduly benefited by

---

62 Above, note 56: applied in *Roenisch v. Bangs* (1993), 8 Alta. L.R. (3d) 148 (Alta. Q.B.); *Lynch Estate v. Lynch Estate* (1993), 8 Alta. L.R. (3d) 291 (Alta. Q.B.).

63 [1985] A.C. 686 (H.L.); the limits of which was indicated by Lord Browne-Wilkinson in *C.I.B.C. Mortgages plc v. Pitt*, above, note 50, at 439.

64 Above, note 53.

65 Above, note 50.

66 Above, note 56, at 224, citing Dixon, "The Limits of Undue Influence Explained", [1989] C.L.J. 359; Dale, "Undue Influence and Manifest Disadvantage" (1988), 52 Conveyancer & Property Lawyer 441; Tiplady, "The Limit of Undue Influence" (1988), 48 M.L.R. 579; Ogilvie, "Undue Influence in the House of Lords" (1986), 11 Can. Bus. L.J. 503; Andrews, "Undue Influence and Contracts of Loan", [1985] C.L.J. 192. The judgment of Wilson J. was concurred in by Cory J.

67 Above, note 56, at 226.

68 *Ibid.*, at 227.

69 *Ibid.*

it. This was acceptable in commercial transactions, where a court of equity had to accord some degree of deference to the principle of freedom of contract and the inviolability of bargains while, at the same time, tempering the harshness of the common law. The same was not true where gifts were concerned. Here the concern of the court was that acts of beneficence not be tainted. Hence, it was enough to establish the presence of a dominant relationship.[70]

LaForest J., with whom McLachlin J. agreed, did not think that the issue of manifest disadvantage arose for decision on the facts of this case, which was not a commercial transaction, involving as it did a gift of property by a woman to her brothers.[71] He expressed the opposing points of view, which stemmed from differences as to what the doctrine is designed to protect. He did not come down on either side with certainty, yet he seems to be in favour of playing down the role of disadvantage, in that he did not agree with the proposition that the law will not interfere with a contract that does not necessarily lead to material disadvantage, even where it was clear that the process by which it was made was tainted.[72] In other words, it is abuse of power, trust or confidence that is the test of voidability for undue influence, not the unreasonableness of the bargain.

The judgment of Sopinka J. does nothing to resolve this dispute, since he concluded that no presumption arose in this case once the trial judge found that there was no undue influence.[73] The judgment deals solely with the question of burden of proof: it does not attempt to deal with the issues that occupied the attention of the other members of the court.

In view of the disagreement outlined above, and the way the case was ultimately decided, it would seem that the true nature of the doctrine of undue influence, and the requirements for invocation of the presumption remain unresolved as far as Canada is concerned.[74] What can be stated with certainty is that the distinction between the two categories of undue influence cases originating in the nineteenth century is still relevant, and that the burden of proof will depend on whether undue influence can or cannot be presumed from the relationship of the parties rather than established by positive evidence.

Where the presumption applies, the transaction will be set aside unless the beneficiary under the contract establishes the independence of the other party or that he had independent legal advice, as long as this was based on knowledge of all the relevant circumstances and was honest and competent advice.[75] But lack of independent advice may not support a plea of undue influence, where the parties

---

70 *Ibid.*, at 227-228.

71 *Ibid.*, at 240.

72 *Ibid.*

73 *Ibid.*, at 241.

74 The decision in *C.I.B.C. Mortgages plc v. Pitt*, above, note 50, may exercise considerable influence in the future.

75 *Inche Noriah v. Shaik Allie Bin Omar*, [1929] A.C. 127 (P.C.); see *Treadwell v. Martin*, above, note 57; *Provender v. Lavoie*, above, note 54. *Sawatzky v. Sawatzky*, above, note 55. Contrast *Clements v. Mair* (1980), 2 Sask. R. 1 (Sask. Q.B.); *Gammon v. Steeves*, above, note 54; *Green v. Perley*, above, note 55.

knew what they were doing.[76] In other situations, some facts may invite a conclusion of undue influence and require the beneficiary to show the fairness of the transaction, for example, where the other party lacked intelligence, was ignorant of the language in which the transaction was conducted,[77] or was illiterate.[78] But even with such extensions, the courts will not relieve a party from his contractual obligations merely because the party in question has been foolish. Some unconscionable conduct by the other party must be shown.[79]

4. Unconscionability[80]

(a) The traditional view

The equitable doctrine of undue influence has been stretched, or reinterpreted. Although the relationship between the parties is not one which can raise a presumption of improper conduct, calling into question the desirability of upholding and enforcing a contract, there may be present features which encourage and entitle a court applying equitable principles to intervene and grant rescission. Those features are the ingredients of what might be termed "equitable fraud". It is not fraud in the classical, common-law sense, involving misrepresentations of the truth. Nor is there any improper application of pressure amounting to duress or its equitable analogue of undue influence. Nonetheless, the conduct of one party in obtaining the assent of the other to a particular contract was of such a character that a court might well consider that to uphold the ensuing contract would be to perpetrate an injustice and produce an unfair result. A contract may be rescinded if the behaviour of one contracting party was unconscionable.[81]

Wide though this jurisdiction may be, and broad though its application can

---

76 *Murray v. Smith* (1980), 32 Nfld. & P.E.I.R. 191 (P.E.I.S.C.); affirmed (1981), 35 Nfld. & P.E.I.R. 382 (P.E.I.C.A.); *Malicki v. Yankovich*, above, note 57.

77 Compare *Iwanchuk v. Iwanchuk* (1919), 48 D.L.R. 381 (Alta. C.A.).

78 *Gladu v. Edmonton Land Co.* (1914), 7 W.W.R. 279 (Alta. S.C.); contrast *Cripps v. Woessner*, [1917] 2 W.W.R. 1072 (Man. C.A.). Even where no independent legal advice was obtained, a wife was not acting under the undue influence when she mortgaged her own separate property without actually going security for her husband: *Wilgross Invts. Ltd. v. Goldshlager* (1974), 5 O.R. (2d) 687 (Ont. Div. Ct.); contrast *E. & R. Distributors v. Atlas Drywall*, above, note 61.

79 That the contract was advantageous to the defendant did not suffice in *Sutherland v. Sutherland*, [1946] 4 D.L.R. 605 (B.C.S.C.); *Brock & Petty v. Gronbach*, [1953] 1 S.C.R. 207 (S.C.C.). Contrast *Hnatuk v. Chretian* (1960), 31 W.W.R. 130 (B.C.S.C.); *Mulholland v. Bartsch*, [1939] 1 D.L.R. 795 (Alta. S.C.); compare the views of the Wilson J. in *Geffen v. Goodman Estate*, above, note 56.

80 Note the wider use of the idea as developed in Waddams, "Unconscionability in Contracts" (1976), 39 M.L. Rev. 369. See also Tiplady, "The Judicial Control of Contractual Unfairness" (1983), 46 M.L. Rev. 601; Enman, "Doctrines of Unconscionability in Canadian, English and Commonwealth Contract Law" (1987), 16 Anglo-Am. L.R. 191. For economic analysis see Trebilcock, "The Doctrine of Inequality of Bargaining Power" (1976), 26 U.T.L.J. 359; *idem*, "An Economic Approach to the Doctrine of Unconscionability" in Reiter and Swan *Studies in Contract Law*, 1980, Study 11.

81 The paragraph was referred to and part of it quoted by Matthews J.A. in *Atlas Supply Co. of Can. v. Yarmouth Equipment Ltd.* (1991), 103 N.S.R. (2d) 1 at 16 (N.S.C.A.); leave to appeal to S.C.C. granted (1991), 108 N.S.R. (2d) 270n (S.C.C.); appeal to S.C.C. discontinued April 1, 1992.

sometimes appear, even a court applying equitable powers is not able, nor is it willing, to interfere with a concluded contract, otherwise not exceptionable, merely on the ground that one party now finds that the original bargain he made is not to his taste, or will not be as profitable or as valuable as he had hoped and intended. As Wilson C.J. of the Supreme Court of British Columbia said,[82]

> [t]he court exists for many purposes and one of those purposes is the protection of unsophisticated and defenceless persons against the exactions of conscienceless persons who seek to take advantage of them. . . . But the courts are not empowered to relieve a man of the burden of a contract he has made under no pressure and with his eyes open merely because his contract is an act of folly.

The equitable power is to give relief in cases involving unconscionable transactions, not all those which, originally or subsequently, may prove to be foolhardy, burdensome, or otherwise undesirable and improvident.[83]

Cases involving parties who were under the influence of drink (or drugs) at the time of contracting, or were feeble-minded (although perhaps not technically insane or mentally incompetent), or illiterate, ignorant, uneducated, or otherwise mentally or intellectually disadvantaged, clearly qualify as instances of situations where the other party might be characterized as behaving unconscionably if he knows of such impairment, and deliberately uses his knowledge to achieve a bargain for himself.[84] Quite apart from any possibility of avoidance on the grounds of drunkenness or mental incompetence,[85] such transactions are liable to defeasance on the broader basis of "unconscionability". However, the avoidance of a contract for drunkenness or mental incompetence, and the avoidance of a contract for undue influence or duress, must be differentiated from avoidance for unconscionable behaviour. This was pointed out in a leading Canadian case, *Morrison v. Coast Finance Ltd.*[86] Rescission of a contract on the ground that it is the product of undue influence (or, it may be added, the other grounds mentioned above) is founded upon the validity of the consent which one party has manifested. The fact that such consent was obtained by such means, or resulted from the state of mind of the affected party, vitiates the apparent agreement between the parties. Where a bargain is held to be unconscionable, it is not the consent of the victim that is impugned, but the reasonableness of the bargain, the conscientiousness of the other

---

82 *Miller v. Lavoie* (1966), 63 W.W.R. 359 at 365 (B.C.S.C.).

83 *Stepper v. Laurel Credit Plan Ltd.* (1968), 63 W.W.R. 168 at 171 (Sask. Dist. Ct.).

84 See, *e.g., Black v. Wilcox* (1977), 70 D.L.R. (3d) 192 (Ont. C.A.); *Hall v. Grassie* (1982), 16 Man. R. (2d) 399 (Man. Q.B.); *Stubbs v. Erickson* (1981), 34 B.C.L.R. 45 (B.C.S.C.); *Tweedie Estate v. Geib* (1982), 19 Sask. R. 48 (Sask. Q.B.); *Dom. Home Improvements Ltd. v. Knuude* (1986), 20 C.L.R. 192 (Ont. Dist. Ct.); *Bertolo v. Bank of Montreal* (1986), 33 D.L.R. (4th) 610 (Ont. C.A.); *Thom v. Saltner*, [1989] 1 W.W.R. 456 (Man. Q.B.); *Turner Estate v. Bonli Estate* (1990), 77 Sask. R. 49 (Sask. Q.B.); affirmed (1990), 86 Sask. R. 235 (Sask. C.A.).

85 Above, pp. 158-163.

86 (1965), 54 W.W.R. 257 at 259 (B.C.C.A.) *per* Davey J.A. (cited and relied on by Hinkson J.A. in *Cougle v. Maricevic*, [1992] 3 W.W.R. 475 — a case involving the conduct of an insurance adjuster, who proved the agreement was fair, just and reasonable).

party, the equitable character of the transaction.[87] In making such decisions, a court may be concerned with the internal state of mind of the party seeking rescission. But it is also concerned with external matters, the state of affairs surrounding the making of the contract, to the extent that such externalities operated on the mind of the party seeking rescission.[88] Moreover a finding that there had not been undue influence does not preclude a decision in favour of a party who also alleges unconscionable conduct. In contrast with an attack upon consent, which is what is involved in a plea of undue influence, a plea that a bargain is unconscionable, or has been obtained by unconscionable means or methods, permits a court to invoke relief against an unfair advantage gained by an unconscientious use of power by a stronger party against a weaker. Where such misuse of power is shown, it creates a presumption of fraud, in the equitable not common-law sense.[89] That presumption the stronger party must repel by proving that the bargain was fair, just and reasonable. The two doctrines are closely related. Indeed the latter is obviously an offshoot of the former. But they are distinct, even though their parentage is the same.[90]

Prior to the decision of Lord Denning in *Lloyd's Bank v. Bundy*,[91] there were many instances in Canada where relief was given from a contract on this basis.[92] Not every claim for rescission on the ground of unconscionability succeeded. Sometimes trading on the victim's need for money resulted in rescission.[93] Sometimes, where the contract was not bad in itself, the fact that the party claiming rescission negotiated from the need for money did not lead a court to upset the transaction.[94] High-pressure salesmanship led to rescission of a contract for the

---

87 This sentence, beginning with the words "but the reasonableness", was quoted by Barry J. in *Campbell v. Campbell* (1990), 83 Nfld. & P.E.I.R. 340 at 349 (Nfld. U.F.C.).

88 This and the previous two sentences were quoted by Matthew J.A. in *Atlas Supply Co. of Can. v. Yarmouth Equipment Ltd.*, above, note 81, at 16 (N.S.C.A.).

89 *Ahone v. Holloway* (1988), 30 B.C.L.R. (2d) 368 at 375 (B.C.C.A.).

90 The passage commencing, "Moreover a finding", down to the end of the paragraph, was quoted by Matthews J.A. in *Altas Supply Co. of Can. v. Yarmouth Equipment Ltd.*, above, note 81, at 16.

    Note that the distinction between substantive and procedural unconscionability is considered to be inappropriate for use in the new formulation of the doctrine recommended by the Ontario Law Reform Commission, *Report on Amendment of the Law of Contract* (1987), at p. 128. For the distinction in question, compare Kerans J.A. in *Calgary (City) v. Northern Const. Co.*, [1986] 2 W.W.R. 426 at 442-443 (Alta. C.A.); affirmed [1988] 2 W.W.R. 193 (S.C.C.). See also, on the connection between undue influence, unconscionable behaviour, and the gaining of an advantage by one party or the suffering of a disadvantage by the other party, *Cameron v. Dorcic* (1987), 80 N.S.R. (2d) 152 (N.S.T.D.); affirmed (1988), 83 N.S.R. (2d) 85 (N.S.C.A.); *Principal Invts. Ltd. v. Thiele Estate* (1987), 12 B.C.L.R. (2d) 258 (B.C.C.A.).

91 [1974] 3 All E.R. 757 (C.A.).

92 *Waters v. Donnelly* (1884), 9 O.R. 391 (Ont. Ch.); *Knupp v. Bell* (1968), 67 D.L.R. (2d) 256 (Sask. C.A.); *Mundinger v. Mundinger* (1969), 3 D.L.R. (3d) 388 (Ont. C.A.); affirmed (1970), 14 D.L.R. (3d) 256n (S.C.C.); *Marshall v. Can. Permanent Trust Co.* (1968), 69 D.L.R. (2d) 260 (Alta. S.C.); *Morrison v. Coast Finance Ltd.*, above, note 86; *Paris v. Machnick* (1972), 32 D.L.R. (3d) 723 (N.S. T.D.); *Adams v. Fahrngruber* (1975), 62 D.L.R. (3d) 256 (Ont. H.C.).

93 *Mulholland v. Bartsch*, [1939] 2 D.L.R. 747 (Alta. C.A.); compare *Pridmore v. Calvert* (1975), 54 D.L.R. (3d) 133 (B.C.S.C.).

94 *Sloan v. Maude-Roxby*, [1940] 1 W.W.R. 206 (B.C.S.C.).

sale of cooking utensils to a bride and her mother in *W.W. Distributors & Co. v. Thorsteinsson.*[95] Similar salesmanship did not compel a court to rescind a contract for dancing lessons in *Griesshammer v. Ungerer*[96] (although, where additional elements tantamount to establishing fraud could be shown, in *Gaertner v. Fiesta Dance Studios,*[97] rescission was granted). Although the possibility of rescission for unconscionable behaviour of a party is derived from authority that goes back many years, the judgment of Lord Denning in the *Bundy* case gave a new meaning and direction to an older doctrine. It may also have led to the enlargement of the categories of misconduct which can defeat an otherwise valid apparent consent to a contract. Hence, the questionable nature of that judgment and its effects. First of all, it may have broadened the concept of what is unconscionable beyond what is reasonable and necessary for the purpose of achieving justice and preventing unfairness. Second, by doing so, it may have rendered the law of contract more uncertain, and provided too clumsy or unpredictable an instrument for the courts to employ for the purpose of controlling what may be considered unsuitable, unreasonable, unfair, or unjust contracts. Some Canadian cases, since the *Bundy* decision, have proceeded on the basis of the older, more traditional notion of what is unconscionable, without recourse to, or reliance upon the development contained in Lord Denning's judgment. Others have adopted the latter approach, and, indeed, have expanded and elaborated upon it.

(b) Inequality in bargaining power

In *Lloyd's Bank v. Bundy,*[98] the English Court of Appeal set aside a charge given by the plaintiff, an elderly man, over his house, which had been a family possession for some time, to his bank, in order to secure a loan to the plaintiff's son made by the bank. The son had been in financial difficulty, and his father earnestly desired to help his son, and was highly emotional about the transaction. The majority of the court allowed rescission of the contract on the ground that there had been undue influence, in the traditional equitable sense, and a failure by the bank to afford the plaintiff the chance to seek independent advice. The conduct of the bank involved a breach of the fiduciary duty which the bank owed the plaintiff, its customer. Lord Denning, however, found in favour of rescission on the basis of a wider conception of undue influence. This broader approach, which he based upon several disparate doctrines under which courts could upset

---

95 (1960), 26 D.L.R. (3d) 365 (Man. C.A.).

96 (1958), 14 D.L.R. (2d) 599 (Man. C.A.).

97 (1972), 32 D.L.R. (3d) 639 (B.C.S.C.).

98 Above, note 91. On the majority judgments, and the *correct* way to approach cases of undue influence, see *Nat. Westminister Bank v. Morgan,* [1985] 1 All E.R. 821 especially at 830-831 (H.L.). See Slayton, "The Unconscionable Bargain Doctrine" (1976), 22 McGill L.J. 96; Sealy, "Undue Influence and Inequality of Bargaining Power" (1975), 34 C.L.J. 22; Clarke, "Unequal Bargaining Power in the Law of Contract" (1975), 44 Aust. L.J. 221; Carr, "Inequality of Bargaining Power" (1975), 38 M.L. Rev. 463; Tiplady, *loc. cit.,* above, note 80; Beatson, "Unconscionability: placebo or pill?" (1981), 1 Oxford J. of Leg. Studies 426; Hasson, Reiter and Leff, "Unconscionability: Symposium on Unconscionability in Contract Law" (1980), 4 Can. Bus. L.J. 383, 403, 424.

concluded transactions, he expressed under the general rubric or formula of "inequality of bargaining power".

> . . .the English law gives relief to one who, without independent advice, enters into a contract on terms which are very unfair or transfers property for a consideration which is grossly inadequate, when his bargaining power is grievously impaired by reason of his own needs or desires, or by his own ignorance or infirmity, coupled with undue influences or pressures brought to bear upon him by or for the benefit of the other.[99]

This principle, which, in a sense seems to resemble the traditional English doctrine of undue influence and the traditional Canadian doctrine of unconscionability, has been invoked in some subsequent English cases, notably by Lord Denning himself.[100] However, in *A. Schroeder Music Publishing Co. v. Macaulay*,[101] the language of Lord Diplock suggests that there may be some wider support for this principle in England. It is in Canada, however, where the principle enunciated by Lord Denning has enjoyed greater esteem and employment. In this respect it must be noted that one source of Lord Denning's principle was the Canadian doctrine of unconscionability. However, it should also be noted that subsequent Canadian decisions have not always applied the principle of "inequality of bargaining power", even though some have adopted and utilized it in place of older ideas of what is and what is not unconscionable.

As noted earlier, the traditional view of unconscionability is that it involves conduct that is tantamount to fraud in a moral, if not strictly legal sense.[102] The principle of inequality of barganing power involves something different. It requires that the bargain that was made was somehow unfair, that advantage was being taken, knowingly, of a gullible, ignorant, or particularly vulnerable or susceptible party, that there was some dire need on the part of the victim which rendered him incapable of making a sound decision, that his emotional state was such that he could not appreciate and weigh the advantages and disadvantages of the contract, and that he was not allowed or encouraged to seek independent advice.[103] Despite criticism which has been raised against the doctrine,[104] suggesting, for example, that it was nothing more than "a slogan for unstructured distributive justice", or "an emotionally satisfying incantation", it may be suggested that between traditional conceptions of what is unconscionable and the reformulation of what is unjust

---

99 [1974] 3 All E.R. 757 at 765 (C.A.). For the rejection of this approach by the House of Lords, see *Nat. Westminster Bank v. Morgan*, [1985] 1 All E.R. 821 at 830 (H.L.). There it was said that no such principle was needed, as the doctrine of undue influence had been sufficiently developed.

100 *Clifford Davis Management Ltd. v. W.E.A. Records*, [1975] 1 All E.R. 237 (C.A.); *Re Brocklehurst*, [1978] 1 All E.R. 767 (C.A.); *Arrale v. Costain Civil Engineering Ltd.*, [1976] 1 Lloyd's Rep. 98 (C.A.).

101 [1974] 3 All E.R. 616 (H.L.).

102 This sentence was quoted by Matthews J.A. in *Atlas Supply Co. of Can. v. Yarmouth Equipment Ltd.* (1991), 103 N.S.R. (2d) 1 at 16 (N.S.C.A.); leave to appeal to S.C.C. granted (1991), 108 N.S.R. (2d) 270n (S.C.C.); appeal to S.C.C. discontinued April 1, 1992.

103 This sentence was quoted by Jewers J. in *Boisonault v. Block Bros. Realty Ltd.* (1987), 47 Man. R. (2d) 148 at 153 (Man. Q.B.).

104 Tiplady, *loc. cit.*, above, note 80, at pp. 611, 612.

in terms of inequality of bargaining power there is not a wide gap. To judge by recent Canadian authority, the two notions appear to be almost interchangeable.[105]

(c) The two approaches

The cases in which unconscionability has been found to exist exhibit a variety of situations. In one a transaction was upset because of the behaviour of a forceful and overbearing solicitor, representing the other party.[106] In another a Hungarian who could not understand English sold his land at a price far below its true market value. The illiteracy of the plaintiff, as well as his age and physical condition, rendered the conduct of the defendant unconscionable.[107] Sometimes the unconscionability stems from the mental condition of the weaker party,[108] sometimes from the fact that there was a family relationship between the parties of which advantage was taken, by relying on the family factor to obtain the assent of the other, perhaps emotionally weaker, party.[109] There have been cases, however, where there was no such mental or emotional weakness. The argument as to the unconscionable behaviour was based upon some other relationship between the parties, involving a kind of dependence. For example, in *Davidson v. Three Spruces Realty Ltd.; Farr v. Three Spruces Realty Ltd.; Edlson v. Three Spruces Realty Ltd.*,[110] one ground upon which an exemption clause in a contract was successfully attacked was that the clause was unconscionable. The contract was one under which a bailee took care of some valuable deposited by the bailor. When the goods were stolen, and the bailor sued for breach of contract, the bailee pleaded the exemption clause under which he would not have been liable for such loss. In denying the plea, Anderson J.[111] held, *inter alia*, that the clause was unconsionable. It was contained in a standard form contract, which was not truly negotiated by the parties. It negated the very essence of the contract, which was to provide for the safety of the valuables.

---

105 This sentence, and the previous one, beginning with "it may be suggested", were quoted by Matthews J.A., above, note 102.

106 *Junkin v. Junkin* (1978), 86 D.L.R. (3d) 751 (Ont. H.C.).

107 *Fusty v. McLean Const. Ltd.* (1978), 6 Alta. L.R. (2d) 216 (Alta. Dist. Ct.); compare *Taylor v. Armstrong* (1979), 24 O.R. (2d) 614 (Ont. H.C.); *Turner Estate v. Bonli Estate*, above, note 84; contrast *Eagle Const. Ltd. v. Chaytor* (1986), 58 Nfld. & P.E.I.R. 23; *Kielly Estate v. Knox* (1989), 76 Nfld. & P.E.I.R. 96 (P.E.I.T.D.).

108 *Hall v. Grassie* (1982), 16 Man. R. (2d) 399 (Man. Q.B.); *Tweedie v. Gerb* (1982), 19 Sask. R. 48 (Sask. Q.B.); compare *Stubbs v. Erickson* (1981), 34 B.C.L.R. 45 (B.C.S.C.) (alcoholic). But the nervousness of the elderly woman did not have this effect in *370866 Ont. Ltd. v. Chizy* (1987), 57 O.R. (2d) 587 (Ont. H.C.).

109 *Bomeck v. Bomeck* (1983), 146 D.L.R. (3d) 139 (Man. C.A.) (though Hubbard J.A. dissented). Contrast *Re McCormack Estates* (1986), 59 Nfld. & P.E.I.R. 215 (P.E.I.S.C.), where it was usual for the family farm to go to the son who stayed and worked it. The relationship may exist between one of the contracting parties and someone not the other contractor, but causing the contracting party to feel compelled to contract: see, *e.g.*, *Buchanan v. C.I.B.C.* (1980), 125 D.L.R. (3d) 394 (B.C.C.A.).

110 (1977), 79 D.L.R. (3d) 481 (B.C.S.C.).

111 *Ibid.*, at 492-493.

It was unusual in character and the bailor's attention was not drawn to it.[112] Representations were made which would lead the bailor to believe that the clause would not apply. The enforcement of the clause would be a tacit approval by the courts of unacceptable commercial practices. Hence, the clause was void for unconscionability.

In the same way courts have held contracts unconscionable where one party was not able to have independent legal or other advice which placed that party in a position of inequality, for example, where a woman gave a promissory note to a bank as security for a loan to her son;[113] or conjoined parties released a negligent defendant under the terms of a settlement that was inadequate.[114]

Another instructive group of cases involves the relationship of employer and employee. In one instance the issue was whether the terms of a contract of employment were unconscionable.[115] The contract provided for four weeks notice of termination, or salary in lieu. It was argued that this was unconscionable. The majority of the Ontario Court of Appeal disagreed with this contention; the terms were clear and intelligible, and no influence had been brought to bear on the employee to accede to the contract. Houlden J.A. dissented on the ground that the full effect of the contract had not been explained to the employee. The facts of this case involve a situation which appears to be far removed from what might be called the usual case of unconscionable behaviour, if it may be suggested that there is such a thing as a "usual" case of unconscionability. More appropriate for the invocation of this idea are other cases in which the problem has involved contracts concerning land, arising out of the employment of one person by a large, powerful company. There have been several decisions in which courts have been asked to declare unconscionable, and therefore not binding upon an employee, a contract under which an employee, as part of his employment, has been obliged to buy a house from his employer, on terms which involve the right of the employer to repurchase the house when the employee/purchaser ceased to be employed by the employer/vendor. In each instance the details of the term relating to the repurchase differed, and that difference was enough in one situation to permit the court to declare the term oppressive and unconscionable,[116] whereas in other cases

---

112 Compare *Tilden Rent-a-Car v. Clendenning* (1978), 83 D.L.R. (3d) 400 (Ont. C.A.); below, pp. 574-575.

113 *Bertolo v. Bank of Montreal* (1986), 33 D.L.R. (4th) 610 (Ont. C.A.). Contrast *DeWolfe v. Mansour* (1986), 73 N.S.R. (2d) 110 (N.S.T.D.).

114 *Doan v. Ins. Corp. of B.C.* (1987), 18 B.C.L.R. (2d) 286 (B.C.S.C.). Contrast *Sebastian v. Bonitatibus* (1988), 31 C.C.L.I. 80 (Ont. Dist. Ct.); *Century 21 Campbell Munro Ltd. v. S. & G. Estates Ltd.* (1992), 89 D.L.R. (4th) 413 (Ont. Gen. Div.), settlement of a commercial dispute was not unconscionable.

115 *Wallace v. T.D. Bank* (1983), 41 O.R. (2d) 161 (Ont. C.A.); compare *Lott v. Angelucci* (1982), 36 B.C.L.R. 273 (B.C.C.A.) (sale of home to vendor's employee was not unconscionable, there was no proof of any unconscientious use of power by the stronger party against the weaker, and therefore no fraud); compare also *Boisonault v. Block Bros. Realty Ltd.*, above, note 103 (no advantage taken of real estate salesman where contract required that he forfeit commissions when he left his employment).

116 *Laurin v. Iron Ore Co. of Can.* (1977), 82 D.L.R. (3d) 634 (Nfld. T.D.).

the term did not offend.[117] The distinction appears to turn on the price at which the repurchase was to take place, and whether the purpose of the transaction was to protect the employee and give him some security of tenure or to protect the employer from possible diminution in the value of the property by reason of the employee's occupation of the house during the period of his employment. The mere fact that the parties were employer and employee, and the obvious inequality of their respective situations, did not of itself raise any presumption of unconscionability (especially if that is equated with some kind of fraud). There had to be something which indicated that unfair advantage was being taken of the employee's situation, in particular, his need to be employed, and his inability to bargain with respect to the transaction[118] concerning the house and its original and repurchase prices.

Perhaps the most elaborate discussion of the doctrine of unconscionable behaviour is to be found in the British Columbia case of *Harry v. Kreutziger*.[119] The plaintiff, an Indian, sold a boat together with a fishing licence, to the defendant. The real interest of the defendant was in the licence, not the boat, for without the licence the defendant could not engage upon the fishing enterprise that he had in mind. The price given by the defendant was not inadequate or unreasonable for the boat, but it was far below the true market value of the licence. The plaintiff changed his mind and wanted to rescind the contract. He argued that the transaction was, *inter alia*, unconscionable. He was in financial difficulties, arising from his situation with respect to government assistance. The defendant knew of this. The plaintiff was an illiterate Indian, and advantage was taken of him by the defendant. At trial the plaintiff was unsuccessful. The British Columbia Court of Appeal held that the transaction could be rescinded as it involved an unconscionable bargain. In coming to this conclusion, McIntyre J.A. said[120]

> [w]here a claim is made that a bargain is unconscionable, it must be shown for success that there was inequality in the position of the parties due to the ignorance, need, or distress of the weaker, which would leave him in the power of the stronger, coupled with proof of substantial unfairness in the bargain. When this has been shown a presumption of fraud is raised and the stronger must show, in order to preserve his bargain, that it was fair and reasonable.

This statement of the principle suggests that there is a close connection between unconscionable behaviour in the traditional sense and inequality of bargaining power as expounded by Lord Denning. It also indicates that the essential idea of unconscionability is that of fraud. Lambert J.A. declared that whether or not a contract was unconscionable was to be tested by the community standards of commercial morality.[121] For this purpose Canadian cases were to be examined

---

117 *Athabasca Realty Co. v. Lee* (1976), 67 D.L.R. (3d) 272 (Alta. T.D.); *Athabasca Realty Co. v. Graves* (1979), 11 Alta. L.R. (2d) 135 (Alta. Q.B.).

118 This sentence, as far as "to the transaction" was quoted by Hallett J. in *Stephenson v. Hilti (Can.) Ltd.* (1989), 93 N.S.R. (2d) 366 at 370 (N.S.T.D.).

119 (1977), 3 B.C.L.R. 348 (B.C.S.C.); reversed (1978), 9 B.C.L.R. 166 (B.C.C.A.).

120 *Ibid.*, at 173.

121 *Ibid.*, at 177.

rather than cases in other jurisdictions, modern instances rather than older ones, and legislation which related to similar issues as providing guidance to what the community considered was acceptable commercial practice and behaviour.[122] The judgment of Lambert J.A. suggests that what is unconscionable, or what amounts to inequality, depends upon the current views of any given community rather than upon classical ideas of what is equitable or inequitable. The doctrine is a peculiarly modern one, though it may be derived in principle from traditional notions. Hence, it must be interpreted and applied in a modern fashion, not by reference to possibly outmoded ideas of "right" and "wrong".

In this respect, perhaps the doctrine of inequality of bargaining power can be regarded as an updated version of the traditional notion of what is unconscionable. Indeed in *Athabasca Realty Ltd. v. Lee*[123] it was said that to invoke the doctrine successfully there must be proof of unconscionability *arising* from inequality of bargaining power. Lord Denning's formulation was quickly approved and adopted by some Canadian courts. Sometimes, as in *McKenzie v. Bank of Montreal*,[124] it was applied where a party agreed to a transaction while under emotional pressure, in that particular instance arising from the plaintiff's involvement with a man known to the bank to have committed several fraudulent transactions. Sometimes it was applied to a situation where the consideration for a contract was grossly inadequate, for example, the payment of $500 in settlement of an accident claim worth $50,000.[125] In another instance, the doctrine was applied as between a bank and its customer, the latter being the widow of a debtor to the bank.[126] However, while accepting the validity of Lord Denning's approach, some courts did not apply the doctrine so as to invalidate a transaction.[127] The test appears to have been whether the stronger party took unfair advantage of the weaker one.[128] In one instance, where rescission of the satisfaction of a first mortgage was granted, Campbell J. said

[f]actors which the courts have deemed to constitute inequality of bargaining power

---

122 *Ibid.*, at 177-178.

123 Above, note 117.

124 (1975), 55 D.L.R. (2d) 641 (Ont. H.C.); affirmed (1977), 70 D.L.R. (3d) 113 (Ont. C.A.); compare, the emotional involvement of the father and mother of an inexperienced young man eager to obtain a franchise from the defendant in *Can. Kawasaki Motors Ltd. v. McKenzie* (1981), 126 D.L.R. (3d) 253 (Ont. Co. Ct.). This led them to provide personal guarantees that were not upheld and enforced. Compare *Bertolo v. Bank of Montreal*, above, note 113.

125 *Beach v. Eames* (1976), 82 D.L.R. (3d) 736 (Ont. Co. Ct.); leave to appeal to Ont. C.A. dismissed (1976), 82 D.L.R. (3d) 736n (Ont. C.A.). Compare *Doan v. Ins. Corp. of B.C.*, above, note 114, and contrast *Sebastian v. Bonitatibus*, above, note 114.

126 *Royal Bank v. Hinds* (1978), 88 D.L.R. (3d) 428 (Ont. H.C.); compare *Bank of Montreal v. Hancock* (1982), 137 D.L.R. (3d) 648 (Ont. H.C.).

127 *R.E. Lister Ltd. v. Dunlop Can. Ltd.* (1978), 85 D.L.R. (3d) 321 (Ont. H.C.); reversed (1979), 105 D.L.R. (3d) 684 (Ont. C.A.); reversed on other grounds (1982), 135 D.L.R. (3d) 1 (S.C.C.). *Thermo-Flo Corp. v. Kuryluk* (1978), 84 D.L.R. (3d) 529 (N.S.T.D.), with which contrast *A. & K. Lick-A-Chick Franchise Ltd. v. Cordiv Enterprises Ltd.*, below, note 130; *Athabasca Realty Ltd. v. Lee*, above, note 117; *Lott v. Angelucci*, above, note 115.

128 *Natuk v. Kawula* (1979), 1 Man. R. (2d) 25 (Man. C.A.); compare *Hall v. Grassie* (1982), 16 Man. R. (2d) 399 (Man. Q.B.); compare *De Wolfe v. Mansour*, above, note 113.

include lack of independent advice; lack of business experience; limited education; distress or need; ignorance of the true effect of the transaction.[129]

Reading these cases, and those which have turned on the traditional idea of unconscionability, the impression is obtained that, whichever test is being utilized and applied, the basic question for the court is the same: has there been an unconscientious use or abuse of power or position by one party against the other.[130] In the final analysis, there does not seem to be too vast a difference, if any at all, between rescission for unconscionable behaviour and rescission for taking advantage of an inequality of bargaining power. Whichever test is used, however, one issue does arise. How far is it valid and desirable for courts to exercise some discretionary power over contracts that have been negotiated without fraud, duress or undue influence in the classical sense, and without there having been some kind of misrepresentation, albeit innocent, giving rise to a mistake that induced the making of the contract?[131]

(d) The utility and disutility of unconscionability

A doctrine of unconscionability has been part of the law for several centuries. The strictness and harshness of the common law of contract was alleviated by equitable ideas long before Lord Denning's principle of inequality of bargaining power was injected into the modern law. It would appear necessary and legitimate to have some doctrine that can be invoked whenever adherence to the basic principle of consent giving rise to the contract could result in injustice or unfairness.[132] The problem has been to determine the nature and boundaries of such doctrine. The legal history of the past two hundred years indicates that courts in England, whether courts of equity before the fusion of the two systems or modern courts administering equity and common law as one system, and courts in Canada whether before or since Lord Denning rephrased the idea of unconscionability, have experienced great difficulty over steering a straight and secure course between the Scylla of strict enforcement of agreements reached without fraud, duress, mistake or misrepresentation, and the Charybdis of rescission or avoidance of contracts that are considered to be unconscientious or unfair. There is general agreement amongst lawyers in England, Canada and the United States that some method must be found to permit the regulation of contracts that favour one party unduly at the expense

---

129 *Moore v. Fed. Business Dev. Bank* (1981), 30 Nfld. & P.E.I.R. 91 at 98 (P.E.I.S.C.).

130 Compare *A. & K. Lick-A-Chick Franchises Ltd. v. Cordiv Enterprises Ltd.* (1981), 119 D.L.R. (3d) 440 at 449 (N.S.T.D.), suggesting that Lord Denning's principle and Lambert J.A.'s idea of divergence from community standards of commercial morality as constituting unconscionable behaviour (see *Harry v. Kreutziger*, above, note 119) are only slightly different approaches to the same principle; presumably both would be rejected by the House of Lords on the basis of what is said in *Nat. Westminster Bank v. Morgan*, [1985] 1 All E.R. 821 (H.L.).

131 The passage beginning, "Reading these cases", was quoted by Hallett J. in *Stephenson v. Hilti (Can.) Ltd.*, above, note 118, at 370.

132 For discussion of the use of the doctrine of unconscionability in relation to exclusion clauses, see the different views of Dickson C.J. and Wilson J. in *Hunter Engineering Co. v. Syncrude Can. Ltd.* (1989), 57 D.L.R. (4th) 321 at 341-342 and 378-381 (S.C.C.); below, pp. 597-600.

of the other, as long as there are some other factors present indicating that this unbalanced state has not been arrived at in a totally free and legitimate manner. But there is no such general agreement as to the validity of the way in which English, Canadian, or American law has solved the problem.

The attempt to provide some method of what has been termed[133] "the judicial control of contractual unfairness" has met with comment by academic writers,[134] even though it seems to enjoy widespread approval by the courts. Sometimes this adverse comment takes the form of objection to the methods employed by the courts to justify what they are doing, rather than to the very notion of some sort of control. Thus, it has been said[135] that judges have formulated the test of unconscionability in semi-procedural terms ("taking advantage"), avoiding any distinction between procedural and substantive unconscionability. The former involving fraud, duress or misrepresentation, indirectly promotes efficiency by protecting the integrity of the bargaining process. The latter is solely concerned with the result, that is, the price in the broadest sense. Consequently, the failure to separate substance from procedure leads to the elusiveness of unconscionability. It is precisely that quality of elusiveness that provides that basis for criticisms of judicial efforts to regulate unfairness in modern times. A very different criticism[136] is founded upon the attitude that unconscionability, inequality of bargaining power, and similar related equitable doctrines are necessary because traditional methods of adjudication, when applied to issues of fairness, are essentially dishonest. The attitude depends upon the postulate that traditional methods of adjudication emanate from obsolescent philosophical notions, namely, freedom of contract, *laisser faire*, the sanctity of contract; this causes judges to dissemble the true reason for a decision. Hence, only a full break from traditional methods can restore judicial integrity and re-establish sound doctrine, even at the price of a period of uncertainty. The critic who attacks this attitude asserts that justice or fairness are not instruments of contract law, nor do they constitute doctrine; they are descriptions of the way in which lawyers handle the instruments of the law. To elevate justice or fairness to ends in themselves, brings in its train the danger that judges will begin to make choices they are ill-equipped to make.

There are consequently two major alleged defects of the modern idea of unconscionability, whether expressed in traditional terms or in the more modern vestments of inequality of bargaining power. The first is the insubstantial, elusive character of the ideas which the courts are invoking and applying to resolve

---

133 Tiplady (1983), 46 M.L. Rev. 601.
134 See, *e.g.*, Hasson, Reiter and Leff (1980), 4 Can. Bus. L.J. 383, 403, 424; Thal, "The Inequality of Bargaining Power Doctrine: The problem of Definining Contractual Unfairness" (1988), 8 Ox. J. Legal St. 17.
135 Beatson (1981), 1 Oxford J. of Leg. Studies 426 at 431. See the Report of the Ontario Law Reform Commission (1987) above, note 90, that the distinction should be ignored in the legislation that is proposed.
136 Tiplady, *loc. cit.*, above, note 133 at p. 618. Tiplady argues that justice and certainty are not opposed but are close approximations or harmonious objectives, and that traditional methods of adjudication already incorporate to a sufficient degree the end of justice, so that the rejection of these methods is misguided and itself a source of potential injustice: *ibid.*, at p. 602.

individual cases. The second is the danger inherent in this process of the courts arrogating to themselves a power that will be impossible for them to deploy or to control, with the result that no one, whether lawyer or litigant, will eventually be able to know in advance which contracts will be upheld and enforced and which will be subject to rescission or modification.

Both these defects ultimately can be reduced to one characteristic: uncertainty. The argument is between supporters of certainty in commercial transactions and supporters of the desire to achieve justice or fairness. It has been alleged that certainty in contract law is a myth.[137] Hence, to found any contractual doctrine, or to dismiss any new doctrine, on the basis of the criterion of certainty is invalid and inaccurate. However, certainty has also been described as "a protean concept".[138] What may be acceptable in the name of certainty in one context may not be in others. Indeed the quest for certainty and the antinomies of certainty and flexibility in the name of "justice" or "fairness" are crucial features of modern contract law generally, not only in the context of contract formation or existence. The only way in which the two ideas can be reconciled in relation to unconscionability may be by some requirement of the content of unconscionability itself. The decisions which have been examined indicate that there are several factors, not uncertain in themselves, and capable of being identified as present or absent by an examination of the facts of an individual case, the invocation and application of which can provide meaning and content to what is otherwise an elusive, questionable, uncertain, and potentially meaningless concept, the use of which might cause problems for the law. It is now too late to object to the introduction of such ideas into the mainstream of contract law. Indeed, as will be seen, legislation has also been founded upon the idea of penalizing unconscionable behaviour in negotiating contracts, and has invoked the concept of unconscionability to allow a court to upset what would be otherwise valid and acceptable transactions. Unconscionability must now be accepted as one of the cornerstones of the law of contract. However, there is room for debate on the question of what constitutes unconscionable behaviour. In the settlement of that question lies the task of the courts for the future.[139]

---

137 This is the view of the American Realists: see Tiplady, *loc cit.*, above, note 133, at pp. 602-603.

138 *Ibid.*, at p. 603, citing Megaw L.J. in *Maredelanto Co. Naviera S.A. v. Bergbau-Handel G.m.b. H. (The "Mihalis Angelos")*, [1971] 1 Q.B. 164 (C.A.); *Bunge Corp. v. Tradax Export S.A.*, [1981] 2 All E.R. 513 at 536 (H.L.).

139 Unless legislation along the lines proposed by the Ontario Law Reform Commission in 1987, *Report on Amendment of the Law of Contract*, pp. 136-138, is enacted. Its purpose is to create more definitive decisional criteria for determining questions of unconscionability; to permit a court to raise the issue itself; to apply the doctrine to all types of contracts; and to give courts a variety of remedies that may be ordered. On these proposals, see Vaver, "Unconscionability: Panacea, Analgesic or Loose Can(n)on?" (1989), 14 Can. Bus. L.J. 40.

(e) Legislation on unconscionability

(i) *Introduction*

In modern times, legislatures have been compelled to intervene and create remedies (and sometimes rules of law) which enable courts to ameliorate the situation of certain parties who have contracted unwisely, though not in any way that would invite the application of common-law or equitable principles of relief. In earlier periods of Canadian history there were statutes which intervened on behalf of debtors, either generally or in respect of certain groups of society, such as farmers. Perhaps the most important class of statutes belonging to this category are the Acts which deal with what have been termed "unconscionable transactions". Such statutes were designed to cope with the position of those forced by circumstance to borrow money, at a time when they lacked the necessary bargaining power or economic position to make terms which were reasonable, satisfactory and acceptable to society at large. The aim of the legislation, which followed English statutes dealing with money-lenders,[140] was to provide a measure of protection for the borrower who might be disadvantaged in his dealings with the lender. More recently, both with respect to the substantive law and the law relating to remedies, the emphasis has been upon protecting the consumer, rather than the debtor. Legislatures in Canada, following the example of legislatures in other parts of the common-law world, have enacted statutes which imply or impose terms in particular types of contracts. Statutes pertaining to sale of goods, conditional sales, or contracts creating or granting credit, make full disclosure of certain facts (for example, the cost of borrowing) an essential ingredient of the legality and validity of the contract and, quite apart from any suggestion of fraud, require advertisements and information about products to be accurate and not misleading. Recent legislation in British Columbia, Alberta, Newfoundland, Ontario and Prince Edward Island has a wider impact. First of all, it appeals to a wide range of contractual situations. Second, it affects the remedies available to a party alleging that he has been damnified by some breach of the statute.

(ii) *Unconscionable transactions*

Every province has legislation which applies to money-lending transactions, and permits intervention by the court where such a contract is harsh and unconscionable and the cost of the loan is excessive.[141] In an Ontario case,[142] Grant

---

140 Hence the relevance of English decisions: see, *e.g., Miller v. Lavoie* (1966), 63 W.W.R. 359 (B.C.S.C.); *Morehouse v. Income Invts. Ltd.*, [1966] 1 O.R. 229 (Ont. Co. Ct.).

141 Unconscionable Transactions Act, R.S.A. 1980, c. U-2; R.S.N. 1990, c. U-1; Consumer Protection Act, R.S.B.C. 1979, c. 65; Unconscionable Transactions Relief Act, R.S.M. 1987, c. U20; R.S.N.S. 1989, c. 481; R.S.N.B. 1973, c. U-1; R.S.P.E.I. 1988, c. U-2; R.S.S. 1978, c. U-1; R.S.O. 1990, c. U.2.

142 *Adams v. Fahrngruber* (1975), 10 O.R. (2d) 96 at 102 (Ont. H.C.). See also *McHugh v. Forbes* (1991), 83 D.L.R. (4th) 184 (Ont. C.A.), where the defence under the Act was held not to be available. A party may rely on the provisions of the Act without the Act being pleaded: *Almas v. Spenceley* (1972), 25 D.L.R. (3d) 653 (Ont. C.A.); *Marinis v. Third Generation Realty Ltd.* (1991), 38 C.C.E.L. 197 (Ont. Gen. Div.); *Milani v. Banks* (1992), 98 D.L.R. (4th) 104 (Ont. Gen. Div.).

J. said that the right to grant relief under this legislation " . . .is confined to cases where the terms of the bargain are grossly unfair and were procured by the one party as a result of the other's weakness or necessity being taken advantage of."

Such legislation was attacked in the courts as being *ultra vires* of provincial legislatures. It was argued that statutes of this kind were really dealing with the rate of interest that could be charged on a loan, and as such could not operate where the federal Interest Act[143] operated in sole command of the legislative field. In *Attorney General of Ontario v. Barfried Enterprises Ltd.*,[144] the Supreme Court of Canada, by a majority, held that the Ontario statute was *intra vires* and constitutional. This would seem to mean that all the provincial statutes in the same terms are valid. It was said by the majority that the legislation did not deal with interest but with the annulment or reformation of a contract of loan on the two grounds set out in the Act, namely, harshness and excessive cost. The vice was in the *bonus* which the lender collected by the high charge he imposed for lending the money in question, not in the interest. A bonus was not interest.[145]

The validity of these statutes not now being questionable,[146] it remains to be seen what these statutes do by way of providing a party who claims their benefit with a remedy. Where a transaction comes within the statute, the court can: (1) reopen any account already taken and relieve the debtor from payment of any sum in excess of the sum adjudged by the court to be fairly due in respect of the principal and the cost of the loan;[147] (2) order the creditor to repay such excess; (3) set aside, wholly or in part, revise, or alter any security given or agreement made in respect of the money lent, or, order the creditor to indemnify the debtor if the security has gone.[148] Thus the court has wide powers, exceeding what would be available at common law or in equity, to deal with any injustice created by a transaction that falls foul of the statute.

What sort of transactions do this? As pointed out by Grant J. in the case previously cited,[149]

> [i]t is a condition precedent to the jurisdiction of the Court to grant relief . . .that it find two conditions existed, namely, that the cost of the loan was excessive and that the transaction was harsh and unconscionable.

It has been held that whether the cost of a loan is excessive, that is, whether the rate of interest is too high, depends upon whether it could have been obtained

---

143 R.S.C. 1985, c. I-15.

144 [1963] S.C.R. 570 (S.C.C.).

145 *Ibid.*, at 575 *per* Judson J.

146 They have been held to apply to a transaction closed prior to the coming into force of the statute: *Stepper v. Laurel Credit Plan Ltd.* (1968), 63 W.W.R. 168 (Sask. Dist. Ct.).

147 Even if the loan has been repaid in full and the mortgage given to secure it has been discharged: *Churchill v. Le Barron Mtges Ltd.* (1978), 86 D.L.R. (3d) 538 (Nfld. Dist. Ct.).

148 See, *e.g., Milani v. Banks*, above, note 142, where the court set aside a charge on the defendant's property as security for a loan, and revised a promissory note to make the borrower liable only for the principal sum.

149 Above, note 142, at 101.

for a lesser rate.[150] In *Adams v. Fahrngruber*,[151] however, it was held that this test was not applicable where the lender would not make the loan if he was aware, as he was not in that case, or might have suspected that the proceeds of the loan were to be used for some improper purpose. However, the rate of interest may not be excessive in light of the risk to the lender that he might not be repaid and the nature of the security offered to, and taken by him, in conjunction with the loan.[152]

The rate of interest may in itself prove that the transaction was harsh and unconscionable. In cases which have been decided on that basis,[153] the rate of interest was exacted from the borrower who was in dire need of the money and there was an element of unfairness about the loan. In none of these transactions was the borrower in a position to make his own bargain on terms of equality with the money-lender.[154] But even where the loan, which takes the form of mortgages, has interest rates varying between 60 per cent and 74 per cent, these rates would not necessarily put the transaction within the statute as being harsh and unconscionable. This possibility was admitted by Cozens-Hardy L.J. in a case concerned with the English Money-Lenders Act, *Poncione v. Higgins*.[155] In *Adams v. Fahrngruber* the defendant did not receive large bonuses for the loans he made to the plaintiff, but the transaction was not categorized as being harsh and unconscionable on a number of grounds. Among these were the following factors: the plaintiff had no urgent need for the money for an obligation that was pressing (which is often the case); he hoped to make a substantial profit if the money were lent to him (which he had done on previous occasions); and there was no inequality between the parties (both being shrewd men of business[156]). It is not surprising that for these, and other reasons, the learned judge did not give the plaintiff the statutory relief, which was designed to relieve a debtor from an obligation to which in all the circumstances he could not be said to have given a free and valid consent. In coming to a conclusion in any case under the statute it is necessary for the court to balance a number of factors, including whether full disclosure has been made between the parties, the fiduciary character of the relationship between them, the expense of borrowing, and the urgency of the borrower's need, along with the risk involved to the lender, etc. As was said in one case,[157] a lender is entitled

---

150 *Re Scott & Manor Invts. Ltd.*, [1961] O.W.N. 210 (Ont. Co. Ct.).

151 Above, note 142.

152 *Miller v. Lavoie*, above, note 140, applying *Poncione v. Higgins* (1904), 21 T.L.R. 11 (C.A.); *Samuel v. Newbould*, [1906] A.C. 461 (H.L.).

153 *Re Scott & Manor Invts. Ltd.*, above, note 150; *Collins v. Forest Hill Invt. Corp.*, [1967] 2 O.R. 351 (Ont. Co. Ct.); *Morehouse v. Income Invts. Ltd.*, above, note 140; compare *Samuel v. Newbould*, above, note 152, at 470; *Krocker v. Midtown Mortgage & Loans Ltd.*, [1975] W.W.D. 63 (Alta. T.D.). See also *Central & Eastern Trust Co. v. Stonehouse Motel & Restaurant Ltd.* (1980), 47 N.S.R. (2d) 493 (N.S.T.D.); *Slattery Management & Realty (1978) Ltd. v. Archie Colpitts Ltd.* (1983), 48 N.B.R. (2d) 244 (N.B.Q.B.). Contrast *Trans. Can. Credit Corp. v. Ramsay* (1980), 27 Nfld. & P.E.I.R. 144 (P.E.I.S.C.) when 25.72 per cent interest was not excessive, harsh or unconscionable.

154 *Adams v. Fahrngruber*, above, note 142, at 103.

155 Above, note 152, at 12. And see *Trans. Can. Credit Corp. v. Ramsay*, above, note 153.

156 Compare *Trans. Can. Credit Corp. v. Ramsay*, above, note 153.

157 *Morehouse v. Income Invts. Ltd.*, above, note 140, at 119.

to adequate protection by the terms of the contract of loan, but protection is one thing and harshness is another.

(iii) *Unfair business practices*

The British Columbia Trade Practice Act, the Alberta Unfair Trade Practices Acts, the Ontario Business Practices Act, the Newfoundland Trade Practices Act, and the Prince Edward Island Business Practices Act,[158] make great changes in the substantive, procedural and remedial law relating to a specific class of contracts, for example, those called "consumer transactions" in the British Columbia Act, and those involving "consumer representations" under the Ontario Act.[159] These changes affect: (1) the nature, scope and extent of the law relating to misrepresentation, by creating liability, for the purposes of the statutes, in respect of statements that might not have been operative misrepresentations, as well as those which undoubtedly would have been, at common law, or in equity; (2) the law of evidence by permitting the admission of oral or parol evidence to prove that some wrongdoing has taken place within the meaning of the statute, in an action brought under the statute,[160] where the common law would not have allowed such evidence to be adduced under the parol evidence rule;[161] (3) the remedies available to an injured party by (a) creating wide powers of rescission, as well as damages, restitution of money, etc., (b) making certain contracts that might have been valid at common law or equity into unenforceable contracts, (c) permitting recovery where rescission would not have been available because restitution was not possible, or third party rights might be prejudiced, (d) allowing punitive or exemplary damages, though these would not be awarded at common law, (e) permitting persons not necessarily parties to the contract that is being attacked to undertake the appropriate action under the statute (that is, possibly, a class action). The statutes make it impossible to exclude or limit the operation of the statute by agreement, waiver, or otherwise. A party protected under the statute can never forego his protection.

Under the British Columbia Act a consumer transaction means

(A) a sale, lease, rental, assignment, award by chance, or other disposition or supply of any kind of personal property whether tangible or intangible, including chattels that are, or are intended to be, affixed to land upon or after delivery, or services, or any right, title, or interest therein . . .; or

(B) the granting, or provision of credit, other than credit extended solely on the security of real property, to an individual for purposes that are primarily personal, family, or household, or relate to a business opportunity requiring both expenditure of money or property and personal services by that individual and in which he has not been previously engaged.

---

158 R.S.B.C. 1979, c. 406; R.S.A. 1980, c. U-3; R.S.O. 1990, c. B.18; R.S.N. 1990, c. T-7; R.S.P.E.I. 1988, c. B-7. In the Northwest Territories, the Insurance Act, R.S.N.W.T. 1988, c. I-4, ss. 239-243 make provision for such practices in relation to insurance contracts.

159 S. 1 (B.C.); s. 1(1)(c) (Alta.); s. 1(c) (Ont.).

160 But not in Alberta.

161 Below, pp. 455-462.

It also means "a solicitation or promotion by a supplier with respect to a transaction" that is within the above definition. It may be seen that what the Act is striking at are transactions between business people, who are engaged in business for profit, and the ordinary, average man in the street, the everyday consumer, who lacks the knowledge and expertise to understand and appreciate the niceties of the transaction. It is not intended to deal with business people dealing at arms' length, on an equal financial or economic basis.[162]

The Ontario statute refers to consumers, that is, natural persons, except those, whether partners or otherwise, acting in the course of carrying on business, and a consumer representation is

a representation, statement, offer, or request or proposal

(i) made respecting or with a view to the supplying of goods or services, or both, to a consumer, or

(ii) made for the purpose of or with a view to receiving consideration for goods or services, or both, supplied or purporting to have been supplied to a consumer.

That statute attacks "false, misleading or deceptive consumer representations," which are called or deemed "unfair practices",[163] and so can be the subject of action or prosecution.[164] It and the British Columbia Act also deal with an "unconscionable consumer representation".[165] These expressions are illustrated in the statute, though the illustrations are not intended to be exhaustive of the respective categories.[166]

Where a transaction falls within such statutes, and offends their provisions by involving the proscribed misconduct, the consumer, that is, the member of the public dealing with the person under the statutory liability, will be able to escape from the consequences of the transaction, and possibly even obtain damages or compensation for loss.[167] What is more, and this is an interesting development, the statutes create an administrative process, in the form of a Director, whose function is to supervise the compliance of the business community with the statute. The Director has wide statutory powers of investigation, action, prosecution, and so on.[168] It is clearly intended that over and above what might be called the "ordinary" contractual remedies of a party to such a transaction, which are only

---

162 For cases on the B.C. statutes, see *Findlay v. Couldwell* (1976), 69 D.L.R. (3d) 320 (B.C.S.C.); *Dir. of Trade Practices v. Household Finance Corp.*, [1977] 3 W.W.R. 390 (B.C.C.A.); *Stubbe v. P.F. Collier & Son Ltd.* (1977), 74 D.L.R. (3d) 605 (B.C.S.C.); *Pac. Finance Accept. Co. v. Turgeon* (1978), 93 D.L.R. (3d) 301 (B.C.S.C.); *Rushak v. Henneken* (1992), 84 D.L.R. (4th) 87 (B.C.C.A.).

163 R.S.O. 1990, c. B.18, s. 2. Compare the Alberta Act, s. 4(1)(a), (b), (c). See *Motor Vehicle Manufacturers' Assn. v. Ontario (Min. of Consumer & Commercial Relations)* (1988), 49 D.L.R. (4th) 592 (Ont. H.C.), sales incentive program did not fall foul of the Ontario Act.

164 *Ibid.*, ss. 3, 4, 17(2); compare the B.C. statute ss. 16, 20, 21, 24, 25.

165 *Ibid.*, ss. 2(b), 3(1) respectively.

166 *Ibid.*, ss. 2(b) (i)-(viii), 3(2) (a)-(b) respectively.

167 See, *e.g.*, B.C. Act, ss. 20, 21. For these and other remedies see also the Ontario Act, s. 4; the P.E.I. statute s. 5.

168 The Alberta statute does not go as far as the legislation in British Columbia and Ontario.

an extension of the older common-law and equitable remedies, there will be extraordinary, non-contractual remedies, for example, declarations, injunctions, restraints, etc., to compel suppliers within the statute to observe its requirements and maintain fair and proper standards of business. In a sense, therefore, the statutes are designed to prevent improprieties as much as, or maybe even more than to cure harms already suffered. Such an approach is undoubtedly novel in respect to contractual relationships. Perhaps it is an augury for the future.[169]

---

169 Similar legislation has been enacted in Australia *viz.*, Trade Practices Act, 1974 (Cth), on which see Duggan (1991), 13 Sydney L.R. 138, Goldring (1988), 13 Sydney L.R. 514. In England, the most important statute is the Unfair Contract Terms Act, 1977, c. 50, dealing with exclusion clauses (below, pp. 592-593). On this statute, see Brown, [1988] J.B.L. 386; Adams & Brownsord (1988), 106 L.Q.R. 94; Macdonald, "Exclusion Clauses: The Ambit of s. 13(1) of the Unfair Contract Terms Act 1977" (1992), 12 Legal Studies 277.

10

Illegality

1. Invalidity through illegality

(a) The requirement of validity

To be acceptable, a contract must be capable of recognition by the law, not prohibited by the law. Stretching back to the eighteenth century, to look no further, are dicta which establish categorically that the courts will not recognize and effectuate an improper purpose.[1] What this means is that certain agreements, though otherwise and in all other respects acceptable, will not qualify as valid contracts, if they contravene the law.[2] This may not have the result that for all purposes any such agreement will be treated as if it had never occurred. On the contrary, in some circumstances, and for some limited purposes a contract which is invalid can still have certain legal consequences. Indeed, sometimes, in accordance with settled principles, the invalid parts of a contract can be severed from the rest, so that the valid part can be recognized and given effect by the courts, while leaving the invalid part to one side. Such consequences, however, are exceptional, and for given reasons.[3] The basis for the doctrine is that illegal agreements are invalid.

(b) Illegality and other kinds of invalidity

A contract may be, or become, invalid for various reasons. Sometimes the parties' attempt to enter into a valid, operative contract can be unsuccessful by reason of their inability to achieve the requisite degree of certainty.[4] Sometimes a purported consent may be inoperative because one, or both, of the parties was giving consent while affected by the kind of mistake that renders a contract a nullity.[5] Such invalidity makes the purported contract void *ab initio*. It is without legal effect so far as concerns the law of contract, although the conduct of the parties may have other consequences of a legal nature, for example, under the law of restitution where money has been transferred by the mistaken party to the

---

1 *Collins v. Blantern* (1767), 2 Wils. 341, 95 E.R. 847; *Lowe v. Peers* (1768), 4 Burr. 2225, 98 E.R. 160; *Holman v. Johnson* (1775), 1 Cowp. 341, 98 E.R. 1120.
2 This and the previous two sentences were quoted by Stratton C.J. in *Tucker Estate v. Gillis* (1989), 53 D.L.R. (4th) 688 at 691 (N.B.C.A.).
3 Below, pp. 420-424.
4 Above, pp. 19-22.
5 Above, Chapter 7.

other.[6] On other occasions a contract may be *prima facie* valid, but one party is accorded the privilege of avoiding the contract by reason of his lack of capacity,[7] or because the other party was guilty of fraud, duress, undue influence or some other form of unconscionable conduct.[8] Where this is the case the contract is voidable, but not void *ab initio*. If the party permitted to avoid the contract does not do so (or is not allowed to do so by reason of his delay, his own inequitable conduct, or the impossibility of making full restitution), the contract remains valid and fully effective. Even if avoidance takes place, there may be some legal consequences of the transaction that can not be reversed, for instance, property transferred under the contract may already have been transferred to an innocent third party without notice of what went before, in which circumstances the third party transferee will be considered to have obtained a valid, indefeasible title.

A contract for an illegal purpose, *i.e.*, a purpose regarded by the law as improper, though it conforms to all other requirements of a valid transaction, will be void. Invalidity through illegality refers to the infringement by a contract of some statute or doctrine of the common law relating to the purpose or object to be achieved by such contract. The term "illegality", in this sense, does not mean "criminal". An illegal contract, though invalid and therefore void, does not necessarily involve the contracting parties in liability for criminal conduct. However, the term "illegality" has been used to cover contracts which may have consequences in the criminal law, under the Criminal Code in Canada (or under statute or the common law in England), as well as the consequence of contractual invalidity.

(c) Illegality and voidness

In the history of contracts which are invalid at common law the courts have frequently used the expression "illegal" to mean not only a contract which is undoubtedly illegal under statute or under one of the heads of public policy to be examined later, but also a contract which at common law is not completely and truly illegal. As clarified by Denning L.J. in the English case of *Bennett v. Bennett*,[9] some of these "illegal" contracts at common law were not, and are not now, illegal in the fullest sense. They are really void to the extent of their illegality, but may be enforced as to the rest, if the illegal part can be severed from the legal. Thus, a contract in restraint of trade is void, but not illegal; insofar as it is possible to excise the illegal restraint from the rest of the contract, this will be done.[10] In the more sophisticated language and ideas of the twentieth century, contracts may be invalid, in whole or in part, without being illegal, and such invalidity may arise under statute or by virtue of the common law. Canadian cases,

---

6 Goff & Jones, *Law of Restitution*, 3rd ed. (1986), pp. 87-116; Fridman, *Restitution*, 2nd ed. (1992), pp. 43-92; Maddaugh & McCamus, *Law of Restitution* (1990), pp. 207-251.
7 Above, pp. 140-164.
8 Above, Chapters 8 and 9.
9 [1952] 1 K.B. 249 at 160 (C.A.). See also *Goodinson v. Goodinson*, [1954] 2 Q.B. 118 at 120-121 (C.A.) *per* Somervell L.J.
10 Below, pp. 420-424.

however, do not appear to make the same subtle distinctions. They seem to use the phrases "illegal" and "void" interchangeably, and to make no real differentiation between different classifications of invalidity,[11] even though they apply the English doctrine of severability[12] upon the basis of which the distinction between voidness and illegality may be said to rest.

It may be questioned, however, how far the distinction between voidness and illegality is useful and important in modern law. It has been argued that, by reason of the difference in the legal consequences, the distinction has relevance.[13] A void, but not illegal contract is not necessarily as ineffective for all purposes as one which is totally illegal. Is there a real difference? Or is what occurs merely a difference in the scope of the public policy that is being invoked? Since such contracts are void because of the doctrine of public policy, it must be conceded that the definition of the public policy involved in such instances may be slightly different from that which is involved in others. The common law could, and did, develop different doctrines to suit different situations. There is no reason why it cannot be said that in respect of all "illegal" contracts the public policy that is being served, and the consequences which should follow, are necessarily uniform or rigid. What is really in issue is the degree of seriousness with which the law views a particular kind of "illegality", and the extent, therefore, to which it should nullify or negate any contractual intent. Perhaps what is needed for analytical purposes is simply to categorize the different classes of contracts "illegal" at common law, with their respective consequences, rather than to distinguish illegal contracts at common law from void, but not illegal contracts. Alternatively, maybe a more subtle analysis should be developed, not so much from the standpoint of illegality or voidness but from the point of view of the ultimate policy that is being served, with special regard to the consequences of striking down a contract and declaring it invalid, for whatever reason and on whichever basis.[14]

One distinction that does merit recognition, is that between invalidity under statute and invalidity at common law. There are sufficient differences between the nature of the invalidity in question and the operation of the relevant doctrines to justify classification of the types of invalidity in accordance to whether the source is some statute or some rule of the common law.

---

11 But see the judgment of Lamont J. in *George White & Sons v. Jashansky*, [1917] 2 W.W.R. 173 (Sask. S.C.) distinguishing illegal from invalid (but not illegal) contracts. Both are void, but in respect of an invalid, but not illegal contract there is an equitable right to the return of property. See also *Ciz v. Hauka* (1953), 11 W.W.R. 433 (Man. Q.B.), where money paid under a contract was illegal under the statute dealing with dower (compare *Demchenko v. Fricke*, [1926] 2 W.W.R. 221 (Sask. C.A.)) was recoverable. This, with respect, is a questionable decision: see further below, pp. 432-434.

12 Below, pp. 420-424.

13 Cheshire, Fifoot and Furmston, *Law of Contract*, 12th ed. (1991), pp. 356-362.

14 See, *e.g.*, Furmston, "The Analysis of Illegal Contracts" (1967), 16 U.T.L.J. 267, in which many of the leading English cases are analyzed and criticized.

2. Statutory illegality

(a) Prohibition by statute[15]

The concern here is not with the Criminal Code,[16] but with statutes of a regulatory nature, the infringement of which may involve illegality.[17] The prohibition of a contract by such a statute renders the contract void and of no effect. So said Lord Russell of Killowen, speaking for the Judicial Committee of the Privy Council, in *Montreal Trust Co. v. Canadian National Railway.*[18] In that case the Canadian National Railway took a lease of a house to be occupied by the chairman of the company as his official residence from a nominee of a director of the Canadian National Railway. This kind of transaction was prohibited under the provisions of the Canadian Railways Act then in force. It was held that the lease was void for illegality. In stating this principle and applying it, the Privy Council was simply putting into effect a long-standing doctrine, under which statutory illegality is very potent in its effects (and cannot even be cured by, for example, the agreement

---

15 Reference to this and the succeeding section was made by Bouck J. in *Cyprus Anvil Mining Corp. v. White Pass & Yukon Corp.* (1980), 21 B.C.L.R. 93 at 102 (B.C.S.C.); affirmed (1980), 21 B.C.L.R. 282 (B.C.C.A.).

16 Contracts in breach of which are illegal and invalid: below, pp. 373-374. Compare *Exhibition Advertising Enterprises v. Victoria Exhibition* (1962), 132 C.C.C. 303 (B.C.S.C.), holding invalid an agreement which involved participation in a lottery illegal under the Criminal Code applying *Dream Home Contests Ltd. v. R.; Hodges v. R.,* [1960] S.C.R. 414 (S.C.C.). See also *Mira Design Co. v. Seascape Hldgs. Ltd.,* [1982] 1 W.W.R. 744 (B.C. Chambers), (contract illegal under s. 305.1 of the Criminal Code, R.S.C. 1970, c. C-34 [see now R.S.C. 1985, c. C-46, s. 347] as charging an excessive rate of interest). On appeal this was reversed, *inter alia* by the *severance* of the invalid provision: [1982] 4 W.W.R. 97 (B.C.S.C.); see also *William E. Thomson Associates Inc. v. Carpenter* (1989), 61 D.L.R. (4th) 1 (Ont. C.A.); leave to appeal to S.C.C. refused (1990), 105 N.R. 397 (note) (S.C.C.); *BCORP Financial Inc. v. Baseline Resort Devs. Inc.,* [1990] 5 W.W.R. 275 (B.C.S.C.); and *Milani v. Banks* (1992), 98 D.L.R. (4th) 104 (Ont. Gen. Div.); *Vandekerhove v. Litchfield* (1993), 103 D.L.R. (4th) 739 (B.C.S.C.).

17 *E.g.,* the Ontario Human Rights Code, R.S.O. 1990, c. H.19, from the requirements of which the parties could not contract out by a collective agreement which provided for compulsory retirement of firefighters at age 60, despite the Code's prohibition of discrimination on the grounds of age: *Ont. Human Rights Comm. v. Etobicoke* (1982), 40 N.R. 159 (S.C.C.); compare *Kuun v. Univ. of N.B.* (1984), 56 N.B.R. (2d) 430 (N.B.C.A.); compare *Potash v. Royal Trust Co.* (1983), 28 Man. R. (2d) 1 (Man. Q.B.); reversed, [1984] 4 W.W.R. 210 (Man. C.A.) (no contracting out of the Mortgage Act, R.S.M. 1987, c. M200 and the Interest Act, R.S.C. 1985, c. I-15); see also *Morton v. Asper* (1989), 62 Man. R. (2d) 1 (Man. Q.B.); additional reasons at (1991), 72 Man. R. (2d) 184 (Man. Q.B.) (contract that was contrary to the Manitoba Companies Act); *Mack v. Harman* (1990), 87 Sask. R. 136 (Sask. Q.B.) (contract that infringed Income Tax Act and Wheat Board Act); *Maksymetz v. Kostyk,* [1992] 2 W.W.R. 354 (Man. Q.B.) (contract contrary to Manitoba Liquor Control Act). But note the possibility of waiving statutory rights if not against public policy: *MacDonald v. Royal Trust; Young v. Royal Trust* (1984), 54 A.R. 116 (Alta. Q.B.). See also *Re Nfld. Telephone Co. and Memorial Univ.* (1984), 46 Nfld. & P.E.I.R. 76 (Nfld. T.D.). But waiver will be allowed where a collective agreement provides greater benefits than a statute, *e.g.,* an Employment Standards Act: *Can. Co-op. Implements Ltd. v. U.S.W.A., Loc. 3960* (1984), 29 Man. R. (2d) 198 (Man. Q.B.).

18 [1939] A.C. 613 at 627 (P.C.) with which contrast *Foster v. Oxford Ry. Co.* (1853), 13 C.B. 200, 138 E.R. 1174. Compare however, *Oliver v. Wottonville,* [1943] S.C.R. 118 (S.C.C.). "Statute" here includes orders, rules or regulations made in pursuance of statutory or prerogative powers and having the force of law.

or assent of some body which has quasi-legislative powers, such as a municipal corporation).[19] As Anglin C.J.C. said in *Advance Rumely Thresher Co. v. Yorga*,[20] relying upon the nineteenth century English case of *Cope v. Rowlands*,[21] in which the fundamental principle was stated in its modern form, " . . .we have here a contract to the enforcement of which by the vendor no court of justice should lend its hand." The contract in question was one which infringed the provisions of the Saskatchewan Farm Implements Act, by virtue of which if the agreement was not read over to a buyer in a manner in which he could understand it, the contract was illegal. This resulted in the inability of the seller to hold the buyer in this instance bound by the contract.[22]

It might be thought, from these and other statements and examples, that the doctrine was clear and uncomplicated, that whenever a statute prohibited a certain course of conduct, or required a particular course of conduct, the failure to observe which resulted in a penalty of some kind, a contract which infringed the statutory prohibition or requirement would be illegal and therefore void. The situation is not as straightforward as that. In some instances a statute will make a contract void, but not necessarily illegal in the sense of rendering the parties liable to criminal prosecution. Furthermore, in some instances a statute while involving illegality, in the sense of prescribing penalties for certain conduct, will not have the effect of rendering void a contract entered into in breach of the statute.[23] The former distinction may not have much effect, in terms of the validity of the contract, but the latter distinction is of great importance.

---

19 *John Mackay Co. v. Toronto*, [1920] A.C. 208 (P.C.); compare the *Seydelman* case below, note 45; or the agreement of the parties, above, note 17; compare *Hashim v. Costain Ltd.* (1986), 54 O.R. (2d) 790 (Ont. H.C.) on the effect of the Condominium Act, R.S.O. 1980, c. 84, s. 61 (not contained in R.S.O. 1990, c. C.26).

20 [1926] S.C.R. 397 at 401 (S.C.C.); see also *Brown v. Moore* (1902), 32 S.C.R. 93 (S.C.C.); *Wirth v. Kutarna*, [1955] 5 D.L.R. 785 (Sask. C.A.). Compare *Consumers Cordage Co. v. Connolly* (1901), 31 S.C.R. 244 (S.C.C.); new trial ordered on other grounds (1901), 89 L.T. 347 (P.C.).

21 (1836), 2 M. & W. 149 150 E.R. 707; see also *Langton v. Hughes* (1813), 1 M. & S. 591 at 596 *per* Lord Ellenborough C.J.

22 Note the statement by Newcomb J., [1926] S.C.R. 397 at 407 (S.C.C.) that the statute in question did not make the contract illegal, as did statutes such as the Gaming Act. But, with respect, the Gaming Acts do exactly the same: below, pp. 358-366. Hence, it is suggested, the distinction between voidness and illegality is unsound and unproductive.

23 *E.g.*, where the statute has its own enforcement provisions, such as the Manitoba statute considered in *Westward Farms Ltd. v. Cadieux; Barnabe v. Cadieux*, [1981] 3 W.W.R. 673 at 692 (Man. Q.B.) *per* Wright J.; appeal allowed on other grounds (1983), 138 D.L.R. (3d) 137 (Man. C.A.); leave to appeal to S.C.C. refused (1982), 18 Man. R. (2d) 269 (S.C.C.); see also *Friesen v. Bomok* (1979), 95 D.L.R. (3d) 446 at 455-457 (Sask. Q.B.). Nor will a statute render a contract void if for other reasons the *court* will enforce the agreement, *e.g.*, a promise by a liquidator, an officer of the court, to pay commission to a real estate broker that contravened the relevant statute: *Springer v. Higgins Co.* (1979), 5 B.L.R. 302 (Ont. Div. Ct.).

(b) Express and implied prohibitions

(i) *In general*

Illegality avoids a contract *ab initio* if the making of the contract is expressly or impliedly prohibited by statute.[24] A distinction must therefore be drawn between a statute which expressly avoids a transaction, by declaring it illegal, and one which only makes conduct illegal, if at all, by implication. If a contract is expressly prohibited it is void in law: it can only be saved if the legislation expressly provides to the contrary.[25] Thus, if a statute provides that only licensed persons may do certain acts, such as deal in potatoes,[26] buy and sell linseed oil,[27] make a charter-party,[28] perform electrical work,[29] work on drains,[30] act as a mortgage broker,[31] drill a well,[32] such statute expressly forbids contracts which are made in contravention of its provisions, that is, by people without the requisite licence or official approval.[33] The same is the case if a statute requires certain affidavits to be truly

---

24 *Archbolds (Freightage) Ltd. v. S. Spanglett Ltd.*, [1961] 1 Q.B. 374 at 381 (C.A.) *per* Pearce L.J. 388 *per* Devlin L.J. Contrast *Bedford Ins. Co. v. Instituto de Resseguros de Brasil*, [1984] 3 All E.R. 766 with *Stewart v. Oriental Fire & Marine Ins. Co.*, [1984] 3 All E.R. 777, dealing with the *same* provision of the Insurance Companies Act, 1974, c. 49 (U.K.). See also *Ernst v. Dumlich* (1984), 55 B.C.L.R. 285 (B.C.S.C.); reversed (1985), 19 B.C.L.R. (2d) 155 (B.C.C.A.); leave to appeal to S.C.C. refused (1985), 19 B.C.L.R. (2d) 155n (S.C.C.).

But there must be a breach of an express statutory provision if the contract is to be declared illegal on the ground that it violates a statute; or else there must be something illegal implied in the performance of the contractual obligations: *B.C. Packers Ltd. v. Sparrow* (1988), 22 B.C.L.R. (2d) 302 (B.C.S.C.); affirmed (1989), 35 B.C.L.R. (2d) 334 (B.C.C.A.); leave to appeal to S.C.C. refused (1989), 38 B.C.L.R. (2d) xxxii (note) (S.C.C.); compare *Fauman v. Cooks* (1986), 41 M.V.R. 60 (Ont. Dist. Ct.); affirmed (January 15, 1988), Doc. No. 13739/82 (Ont. Div. Ct.). See *Lantz v. Hansen* (1987), 82 N.S.R. (2d) 392, 207 A.P.R. 392 (N.S. Co. Ct.), where the fulfilment of the contract required the parties to commit an illegal act, *viz.*, occupying premises without a valid occupancy permit as required by a municipal ordinance.

25 *Shopsky v. Danyliuk* (1959), 23 D.L.R. (2d) 501 at 503 (Alta. S.C.) *per* Milvain J; compare *Pinsky v. Wass*, [1953] 1 S.C.R. 399 (S.C.C.); *Meduk v. Soja*, [1958] S.C.R. 167 (S.C.C.). Compare also *North-Sask. Seeds Ltd. v. Couch* (1960), 32 W.W.R. 253 (Sask. Dist. Ct.); *Vita Food Products Inc. v. Unus Shipping Co.*, [1938] 2 D.L.R. 372 (N.S.S.C.); affirmed, [1939] A.C. 277 (P.C.) or is to be enforced in other ways: *Westward Farms Ltd. v. Cadieux*, above, note 23.

26 *MacNaught v. Rayner*, [1954] 1 D.L.R. 844 (P.E.I.C.A.).

27 *Re Mahmoud and Ispahani*, [1921] 2 K.B. 716 (C.A.).

28 *Picbell Ltd. v. Pickford & Black Ltd.*, [1951] S.C.R. 757 (S.C.C.).

29 *Horlock v. Pinerich Dev. Ltd.* (1978), 84 D.L.R. (3d) 413 (Ont. Div. Ct.); *Laliberte v. Blanchard* (1979), 28 N.B.R. (2d) 394 (N.B.Q.B.); affirmed (1980), 31 N.B.R. (2d) 275 (N.B.C.A.).

30 *Monticchio v. Torcema Const. Ltd.* (1979), 8 B.L.R. 225 (Ont. H.C.).

31 *Leaper v. Grenadier Dev. Ltd.* (1981), 22 B.C.L.R. 354 (B.C.S.C.); varied on other grounds (1982), 38 B.C.L.R. 125 (B.C.C.A.).

32 *Sprague's Well Drilling Ltd. v. Mills* (1990), 38 C.L.R. 150 (N.S.T.D.).

33 Compare *Johnstone Fabricators Ltd. v. Can. Credit Men's Trust Assn.* (1964), 47 W.W.R. 513 (B.C.S.C.), no inspector of bankruptcy appointed at the material time under the Bankruptcy Act: contrast *Pimvicska v. Pimvicska* (1974), 50 D.L.R. (3d) 569 (Alta. S.C.) (lack of written permission under the Alberta Bee Act, S.A. 1972, c. 15). See also *Diversified Crops Ltd. v. Patton Farms Ltd.; Diversified Crops Ltd. v. Rosgen* (1975), 61 D.L.R. (3d) 749 (Alta. S.C.); affirmed (1976), 67 D.L.R. (3d) 190 (Alta. C.A.): contract under Canada Grain Act, S.C. 1970-71-72, c. 7 [see now R.S.C. 1985, c. G-10] made by licence but not in authorized form was held to be illegal and unenforceable. A

sworn on the transfer of property,[34] or requires that land must be subdivided and registered before it can be sold.[35]

However, sometimes it is not clear whether a statute is actually prohibiting a contract, or merely exacting a penalty from someone who contracts in a manner contrary to the statute, for example, without having the requisite licence. Then the problem arises whether by implication a contract so made is illegal and void. The proper way to resolve this question may have been changing in recent years.

(ii) *Construction*

The following, oft-cited test was laid down by Lord Esher in *Melliss v. Shirley and Freemantle Local Board of Health*:[36]

> . . . although a statute contains no express words making void a contract which it prohibits, yet, when it inflicts a penalty for the breach of the prohibition, you must consider the whole Act as well as the particular enactment in question, and come to the decision, either from the context or the subject matter, whether the penalty is imposed with intent merely to deter persons from entering into the contract, or for the purposes of revenue, or whether it is intended that the contract shall not be entered into so as to be valid at law.

Applying this test, the factors that must be taken into consideration in determining whether a statute impliedly makes a contract illegal and void are therefore: (1) whether it is designed for the protection of the public generally rather than a particular group; (2) whether the penalty imposed by the statute necessarily implies a prohibition or is simply for the purpose of inflicting some punishment upon infringers of the law,[37] (3) whether the purpose of the statute is simply to obtain revenue by the creation of some licence which must be purchased from the state in order to carry on a particular kind of activity which involves the making of contracts. It is a matter of construction. There must be a clear implication or necessary inference from the statute that contracts which infringe it should be void.[38]

A leading Canadian case, which has been followed, distinguished, and

---

compromise based on a contract which infringes such licensing registration will also be illegal: *Metlege v. Ryan* (1980), 113 D.L.R. (3d) 248 (N.S.C.A.).

34 Hence, such a contract may not be specifically enforced: *Stuart v. Kingman* (1978), 91 D.L.R. (3d) 142 (Ont. H.C.).

35 Hence, the party obliged to register a plan could not rely on the sale as a defence to an action: *Hands v. Sutherland* (1976), 66 D.L.R. (3d) 40 (Alta. S.C.).

36 (1885), 16 Q.B.D. 446 at 451-452 (C.A.), cited with approval in *Pimvicska v. Pimvicska*, above, note 33, at 572.

37 This passage, beginning with the words "whether it is designed . . .", was cited in *Mira Design Co. v. Seascape Hldgs. Ltd.*, [1982] 4 W.W.R. 97 (B.C.S.C.).

38 *Lasenby v. Lamp Hldgs. & Devs. Ltd.* (1980), 117 D.L.R. (2d) 181 (Ont. Div. Ct.), citing Devlin J. in *St. John Shipping Corp. v. Joseph Rank*, [1956] 3 All E.R. 683 at 690-691. This paragraph was cited in *Perry Engineering Ltd. v. Farrage* (1989), 28 C.P.R. (3d) 221 at 225 (B.C.S.C.). There it was held that the illegality of a contract did not affect a claim by someone who was not a party to the impugned contract.

discussed in subsequent decisions, is *Kocotis v. D'Angelo*.[39] An electrician did not have a licence as required under statute. Nonetheless he performed work for the defendant. When the electrician sued for the payment involved he was met with the defence of illegality. It was held that the defence should succeed. The statute in question not only prohibited unlicensed people from working, under payment of a penalty if they did so, it also meant that such people should not be allowed to sue for work so done. It was a statute passed to protect the public from improper workmen, that is, unqualified, since unlicensed; it was not just intended to provide revenue for the Province of Ontario. Here a penalty implied a prohibition.[40] The decision in this case follows the judgment of the Supreme Court of Canada in *Commercial Life Assurance Co. v. Drever.*[41] There a real estate agent, who had no licence, was held unable to claim his commission on a transaction which he effected professionally. A different conclusion was reached by the Supreme Court in the later case of *Meyers v. Freeholders Oil Co.*,[42] which involved a section of the Saskatchewan Securities Act. There it was held that the statute only involved a penalty for breach of the law; it did not render invalid a contract made in breach. Martland J., after referring to the situation where a statute clearly forbids the making of a certain kind of contract.[43] went on to consider the position where there was no express prohibition:

> ...some statutes have been construed as only imposing a penalty, where the Act provides for one, although that is not necessarily the result of a penalty provision being incorporated in the Act.[44]

In *Maschinenfabrik Seydelman K-G v. Presswood Brothers Ltd.*[45] a statute required certain contracts to have the approval of the Hydro-Electric Power Commission of Ontario. The contract in issue was not made with such approval. Consequently it was held to be void by the court at first instance, and no property passed under it to the defendants. The fact that the Commission subsequently approved the

---

39 [1958] O.R. 104 (Ont. C.A.); followed and applied with respect to a by-law of Toronto requiring renovators to have licences, in *Calax Const. Inc. v. Lepofsky* (1974), 5 O.R. (2d) 259 (Ont. H.C.); compare *C. Battiston & Sons Inc. v. Mauti* (1986), 34 D.L.R. (4th) 700 (Ont. Div. Ct.); compare *Horlock v. Pinerich Dev. Ltd.* (1978), 84 D.L.R. (3d) 413 (Ont. Div. Ct.). Note the distinction of this case in *Day & Night Heating Ltd. v. Brevick* (1961), 35 D.L.R. (2d) 436 (B.C. Co. Ct.). See also *Turner v. Rose-Alta. Const. Ltd.* (1984), 31 Sask. R. 145 (Sask. Q.B.); *Sprague's Well Drilling Ltd. v. Mills*, above, note 32.
40 Applying a principle going back to *Bartlett v. Vinor* (1692), Carth. 252, 90 E.R. 750, *per* Lord Holt C.J.
41 [1948] S.C.R. 306 (S.C.C.); compare *Brown v. Moore* (1902), 32 S.C.R. 93 (S.C.C.); *Wasel Bros. v. Laskin*, [1934] 3 D.L.R. 798 (Sask.C.A.); *Montreal Trust Co. v. C.N.R.*, [1939] A.C. 613 (P.C.); *MacNaught v. Rayner*, [1954] 1 D.L.R. 844 (P.E.I.C.A.); *Prince Albert Properties & Land Sales Ltd. v. Kushneryk*, [1955] 5 D.L.R. 458 (Sask. C.A.). See also *Leaper v. Grenadier Devs. Ltd.* (1980), 114 D.L.R. (3d) 171 (B.C.S.C.); varied on other grounds (1982), 38 B.C.L.R. 125 (B.C.C.A.). Contrast *Lasenby v. Lamp Holdings & Devs. Ltd.*, above, note 38.
42 [1960] S.C.R. 761 (S.C.C.).
43 *Ibid.*, at 774, citing *McAskill v. Northwestern Trust Co.*, [1926] S.C.R. 412 (S.C.C.).
44 [1960] S.C.R. 761 at 775 (S.C.C.), relying on the judgment of Lord Esher M.R. cited above, note 36.
45 [1965] 1 O.R. 177 (Ont. H.C.).

contract did not save it from illegality. A new agreement would have to be shown. Once again what was stressed was the distinction between the mere imposition of a penalty, without more, and the desire to protect the public from the improper activity by the licensing or approving of certain conduct of professional or similar behaviour. The decision was reversed on appeal on the basis of the parties' lack of intention to act illegally.[46] Similarly, in *Color Your World Inc. v. Robert F. Avery Holdings Ltd.*,[47] failure to comply with the requirements of a Franchise Act, and provide certain statements, did not render the franchise agreement unlawful and void. At first instance, in *Ames v. Investo Plans Ltd.*,[48] the court held that a contract not made in accordance with the requirements of the British Columbia Securities Act was void *ab initio*, that is, illegal. That Act was passed to protect the public against schemes to sell shares of doubtful value. It was not passed merely to necessitate certain formalities, nor to obtain revenue. But, on appeal, this decision was reversed. The statute was construed differently, so as to make the contract neither void nor, save in certain circumstances, voidable.[49]

(iii) *Policy*

The test which was used and applied in these cases may be characterized as one that inclines towards a strictly "constructionist" approach to the problem. A different way of looking at such statutes, or at least a way which emphasizes a different, less technical method, was expressed by the Ontario Court of Appeal, whose judgment was approved by the Supreme Court of Canada, in *Sidmay Ltd. v. Wehttam Investments Ltd.*[50] That case concerned the validity of a mortgage and several collateral mortgages given to a privately controlled Ontario corporation that had not been registered under an Ontario statute which prohibited a corporation, other than a registered corporation, from undertaking or transacting in Ontario the business of a loan corporation, or of a loaning corporation, or of a trust company. The borrower sought to have the mortgages declared illegal and void by reason of the contravention of the statutory provision. He succeeded at trial. But the mortgagee's appeal was successful before the Court of Appeal, and that reversal of the trial judge was upheld in the Supreme Court. Thus the mortgages were not illegal and invalid despite the failure to comply with the statute. In arriving at this conclusion, and the interpretation of the statute which justified such

---

46 [1966] 1 O.R. 316 (C.A.).

47 (1988), 88 A.R. 163 (Alta. Q.B.).

48 [1972] 3 W.W.R. 443 (B.C.S.C.); reversed, [1973] 5 W.W.R. 451 (B.C.C.A.), following *McAskill v. Northwestern Trust Co.*, [1926] S.C.R. 412 (S.C.C.); *Meyers v. Freeholders Oil Co.*, [1965] S.C.R. 761 (S.C.C.); distinguishing the statute in *Dorsch v. Freeholders Oil Co.*, [1965] S.C.R. 670 (S.C.C.); *Direct Lbr. Co. v. Western Plywood Co.*, [1962] S.C.R. 646 (S.C.C.) (with which compare *Wilkinson v. Harwood*, [1931] S.C.R. 141 (S.C.C.)); *Philco Prods. Ltd. v. Thermionics Ltd.*, [1940] S.C.R. 501 (S.C.C.).

49 [1973] 5 W.W.R. 451 (B.C.C.A.); compare *Rogers v. Leonard* (1973), 1 O.R. (2d) 57 (Ont. Div. Ct.).

50 (1967), 61 D.L.R. (2d) 358 (Ont. C.A.); affirmed, [1968] S.C.R. 828 (S.C.C.). Compare *C. Battiston & Sons Inc. v. Mauti*, above, note 39.

conclusion, the Court of Appeal looked at the underlying purpose of the statute. This was "to afford greater security to the depositors, creditors and security holders of the corporation."[51] That purpose would be defeated if the corporation's assets became depleted by the inability to recover from the borrower the money lent on the security of real estate. To permit a borrower to retain the amount of the loan made to it from the funds entrusted to the corporation for investment would produce exactly the opposite of the result sought to be obtained by the Act. Laskin J.A.[52] cited the relevant statement of principle in the American *Restatement of the Law of Contracts*,[53] as applying to the facts of this case: "If refusal to enforce or to rescind an illegal bargain would produce a harmful effect on the parties for whose protection the law making the bargain illegal exists, enforcement or rescission, whichever is appropriate, is allowed."

This approach to illegal contracts was considered by Krever J., in the later case of *Royal Bank v. Grobman*,[54] to be "the modern judicial view." He summarized it in these words: "The serious consequences of invalidating the contract, the social utility of those consequences, and a determination of the class of persons for whom the prohibition was enacted, are all factors which the Court will weigh." Hence, in that case, a mortgage which infringed provisions of the Bank Act was not invalid on the grounds of illegality. The purpose of the loan-to-value ratio established by the Act, which ratio was not maintained by the mortgage in issue, was to protect banks, depositors and shareholders. It was inconsistent with, indeed inimical to that purpose if the collateral security taken by the bank by way of protection of its loan were held to be unenforceable because the extension of credit exceeded 75 per cent of the value of the borrower's equity in the real property secured.

The issue in cases of illegality, therefore, according to cases which adopt and follow this approach, is whether the contract which is at stake falls within or outside the scope of the purpose or policy which is being advanced or promoted by the statute that is alleged to make the contract illegal and therefore invalid. The policy of the statute is the chief factor that must concern a court where an indirect, or implied prohibition is said to arise with respect to a particular contract, and not such matters as the relative significance of the penalty, or whether the statute is a revenue-raising enactment, or even whether the statute is designed to protect the public generally or a class or group in particular. These matters may not be completely irrelevant, but their importance is less than the overall ambit of the statute having regard to its purposes and the consequences that would follow from a refusal to accept a contract that seems to be impliedly illegal under the statute as a valid, enforceable agreement. Some subsequent decisions illustrate the operation of this approach.

---

51 (1967), 61 D.L.R. (2d) 358 at 375 (Ont. C.A.) *per* Kelly J.A.

52 *Ibid.*, at 387-388.

53 § 601.

54 (1977), 83 D.L.R. (3d) 415 at 432 (Ont. H.C.); see also *Re Lambton Farmers Ltd.* (1978), 91 D.L.R. (3d) 290 (Ont. H.C.). Contrast the view taken by the majority of the British Columbia Court of Appeal of the policy and effect of the B.C. Real Estate Act in *Chambers v. Pennyfarthing Dev. Corp.* (1985), 20 D.L.R. (4th) 488 (B.C.S.C.).

Thus, in *Albert E. Daniels Ltd. v. Sangster*[55] a corporation failed to register its business name as required by an Ontario statute. This failure did not invalidate a contract made by the corporation. The statute was designed to gather information, not to protect the public from unqualified persons or to protect registered corporations from commercial competition. Consequently it was no defence to an action brought by the corporation on the contract that its business name, in which the contract was made, was unregistered. In *Re H.A. Walker & Associates Ltd. and Trustee for Waltson Properties Ltd.*[56] a breach of the Ontario Real Estate and Business Brokers Act occurred. There was no signed statement giving the details of the price of a transaction made by the broker to procure a loan facilitating the real estate transaction involved. This did not invalidate the loan. The broker, who was the lender of the money, could recover for his services as a real estate broker. The illegality under the contract was merely collateral to the contract. So, in *Edmonds v. Perth County Board of Education*[57] a collective agreement between teachers and the board of education transgressed the provisions of the Anti-Inflation Act; to such extent it was illegal, and the payment or receipt of payments over the permissible limits were prohibited and illegal. This did not affect the collective agreement as a whole. The provisions of that agreement relating to life insurance benefits were valid and enforceable against the Board. In *Re Ontario Securities Commission and British Canadian Commodity Options Ltd.*[58] a contract to trade in securities was made with a trader not registered under the Ontario Securities Act. It was illegal under that statute for an unregistered trader to make such contracts. However, the purchaser of the securities was entitled to rescind the contract and recover what he had paid. The purpose of the Act was to protect purchasers of securities. A distinction was to be drawn between the prohibited party and the party protected by the prohibition. In much the same way, the court was entitled to enforce an agreement by a liquidator of a company (considered to be an officer of the court) with an unlicensed real estate broker, despite the prohibition in the relevant statute,[59] although the same result would not have

---

55 (1976), 12 O.R. (2d) 512 (Ont. Co. Ct.); compare *Lasenby v. Lamp Hldgs. & Devs. Ltd.* (1980), 117 D.L.R. (3d) 181 (Ont. Div. Ct.); compare the right of the unlicensed contractor to recover for goods supplied in the performance of an illegal contract in *Horlock v. Pinerich Devs. Ltd.* (1978), 84 D.L.R. (3d) 413 (Ont. Div. Ct.); and *Monticchio v. Torcema Const. Ltd.* (1979), 8 B.L.R. 225 (Ont. H.C.).

56 (1978), 90 D.L.R. (3d) 294 (Ont. S.C.); affirmed (1979), 30 C.B.R. (N.S.) 112 (*sub nom. Re Waltson Properties (No. 2); Walker (H.A.) & Assoc. Ltd.v. Trustee*) (Ont. C.A.). Compare the situation where there was a breach of the Motor Vehicle Dealers Act, R.S.O. 1980, c. 299 in *Fauman v. Cooks* (1986), 41 M.V.R. 60 (Ont. Dist. Ct.); affirmed (January 15, 1988), Doc. No. 13739/82 (Ont. Div. Ct.); the dealer's commission was recoverable.

57 (1978), 91 D.L.R. (3d) 108 (Ont. H.C.); compare *Re Libby, McNeil & Libby of Can. Ltd. v. U.A.W.* (1978), 91 D.L.R. (3d) 259 (Ont. Div. Ct.); reversed (1978), 21 O.R. (2d) 362 (Ont. C.A.).

58 (1979), 93 D.L.R. (3d) 208 (Ont. H.C.).

59 *Springer v. Higgins Co.* (1979), 5 B.L.R. 302 (Ont. Div. Ct.); applying *Ex parte James* (1874), 9 Ch. App. 609.

followed had the action been brought by the broker against the liquidator.[60] The
purpose of the Act was to protect those who purchased real estate.[61] The liquidator
was not to be equated with an ordinary purchaser; it was not contrary to the policy
of the Act to allow the liquidator to remunerate someone who had performed a
service for him. Similarly, in *Canada Permanent Trust Co. v. MacLeod*,[62] an executor
who failed to obtain consent to a transfer as required under the Nova Scotia
Succession Duty Act before mortgaging property belonging to the deceased did
not thereby invalidate the mortgage. The object of the statute was to enable the
Crown to collect tax on the succession of property after the death of the property-
holder; it was outside the ambit of the statute to strike down a transfer that did
not conform to its requirements. The purpose of the statute, the Franchises Act,
in *Nike Infomatic Systems Ltd. v. Avac Systems Ltd.*,[63] was to regulate and control
the selling of franchises: it was not to prevent the enforcement of liabilities against
persons required to comply with the Act. Hence, a contract for the sale of a franchise
which did not comply with the Alberta Franchises Act was not void under that
statute. It was extremely relevant in this respect that the statute did not declare
such contracts as failed to comply with its requirements to be void, or provide
for special remedies of its own.[64] However, in *Ontario Human Rights Commission
v. Etobicoke*,[65] the fact that the Ontario Human Rights Code provided for
administrative methods for its enforcement did not result in a decision that a
collective agreement that purported to oust provisions of the Code relating to
discrimination on the grounds of age was valid. On the contrary the agreement
that stipulated for mandatory retirement of firefighters at age 60 was held to be
illegal and therefore void. It as against public policy as set out in the provisions
of the Code. Here the policy of the relevant statute clearly indicated that the contract
in issue must be understood as being invalid, and not just as entitling a person
aggrieved by the contract's provisions to proceed before the Human Rights
Commission as set out in the Code.[66]

What these decisions illustrate is that, recently, courts in Canada have been

60 *Commercial Life Assur. Co. v. Drever*, [1948] S.C.R. 306 (S.C.C.); *Prince Albert Properties & Land
Sales Ltd. v. Kushneryk*, [1955] 5 D.L.R. 458 (Sask. C.A.); compare the services of an unlicensed
mortgage broker in *Leaper v. Grenadier Devs. Ltd.* (1980), 114 D.L.R. (3d) 171 (B.C.S.C.); varied
on other grounds (1982), 38 B.C.L.R. 125 (B.C.C.A.).
61 *Simpson v. Toronto Factory Properties Ltd.* (1974), 48 D.L.R. (3d) 48 (Ont. H.C.).
62 (1980), 39 N.S.R. (2d) 629 (N.S.C.A.); compare *Color Your World Inc. v. Robert F. Avery Holdings
Ltd.* (1988), 88 A.R. 163 (Alta. Q.B.); contrast *Halifax Relief Comm. v. Halifax* (1965), 50 D.L.R.
(2d) 69 (N.S.C.A.); *Reid v. Reid* (1976), 22 N.S.R. (2d) 361 (N.S.T.D.).
63 (1980), 16 B.C.L.R. 139 (B.C.S.C.).
64 Compare *Westward Farms Ltd. v. Cadieux*, [1981] 3 W.W.R. 673 (Man. Q.B.); appeal allowed on
other grounds (1982), 138 D.L.R. (3d) 37 (Man. C.A.); leave to appeal to S.C.C. refused (1982),
18 Man. R. (2d) 269 (S.C.C.); *Friesen v. Bomok* (1979), 95 D.L.R. (3d) 446 (Sask. Q.B.).
65 (1982), 40 N.R. 159 (S.C.C.); compare *Kuun v. Univ. of N.B.* (1984), 56 N.B.R. (2d) 430 (N.B.C.A.).
66 Contrast the decision that a breach of the Code did not create a right of action for damages in
tort, the basis for which being that the statute provided for relief and remedies, thereby negating
the possibility that a separate civil action could be maintained: *Bd. of Govs. of Seneca College v.
Bhadaura*, [1981] 2 S.C.R. 181 (S.C.C.); Fridman, "Civil Liability for Criminal Conduct" (1984),
16 Ottawa L.R. 34 at pp. 39-40, 44-46.

placing more emphasis upon the underlying policy and aims of a statute than upon other factors which previously were invoked to determine the legality of a contract that infringed the statute. The courts appear to be playing a more interpretive role in these instances, and are being less technical in their approach to the problem of construction of the statutes. The language of McIntyre J. of the Supreme Court of Canada in the *Ontario Human Rights Commission* case[67] suggests that the true basis for declaring a contract invalid for infringement of a statute is the common-law doctrine of "public policy".[68] If public policy, rather than the construction of the statute in terms of an "implied prohibition" of a contract (as suggested by Devlin J.[69]), is the correct rationale for statutory illegality in such instances, then it becomes clear that the proper function of a court is to determine the policy behind the statute in question, to discover whether it is in accordance with that policy, or outside that policy's ambit or scope, to hold the allegedly offending contract to be illegal and therefore invalid.

(c) Illegal performance

A further distinction had been drawn, at least in the English cases.[70] This is the difference between illegality at the outset and illegality in consequence of the mode of performance of a contract. A contract may be illegal from the moment of its inception, on the ground that, either expressly or impliedly, a statute makes the making of such a contract illegal. Hence, no rights or liabilities emerge from such contract, even if the parties are ignorant of the illegality and have no intention of breaking the law.[71] The situation may be different where a contract is not in itself illegal, but is performed in an illegal manner or to effect an illegal purpose. A party who knowingly performs the contract illegally, as did the sellers in *Anderson Ltd. v. Daniel*,[72] when they failed to provide the buyer of manure with an invoice stating the percentage of certain chemical substances in the goods sold, will be unable to enforce the contract, although the innocent party may.[73] But participation in the illegal purpose or performance (even if the illegality is unknown, since the parties believed at the time that what they were doing was lawful), will render the contract void as regards both parties.[74] Hence, in *Lantz v. Hansen*,[75] the lease

---

67 Above, note 65 at 170.

68 Below, pp. 370-372.

69 In the *St. John Shipping* case, above, note 38.

70 But see *Rogers v. Leonard* (1973), 39 D.L.R. (3d) 349 (Ont. Div. Ct.).

71 Below, pp. 416-420. Hence, it may taint *collateral* transactions: *Spector v. Ageda*, [1973] Ch. 30; contrast *Strongman (1945) Ltd. v. Sincock*, [1955] 2 Q.B. 525 (C.A.); *Leaper v. Grenadier Devs. Ltd.* (1980), 22 B.C.L.R. 354 (B.C.S.C.); varied on other grounds (1982), 38 B.C.L.R. 125 (B.C.C.A.).

72 [1924] 1 K.B. 138 (C.A.).

73 Compare *Mason v. Clarke*, [1955] A.C. 778 (H.L.); *Marles v. Phillip Trant & Sons*, [1954] 1 Q.B. 29 (C.A.).

74 *J.M. Allan (Merchandising) Ltd. v. Cloke*, [1963] 2 Q.B. 340 (C.A.), where the parties to the hire of the roulette wheel did not know at the time (but discovered subsequently) that the use of the wheel was still in contravention of the Betting and Gaming Act. Compare *Laliberte v. Blanchard* (1979), 28 N.B.R. (2d) 394 (N.B.Q.B.); affirmed (1980), 31 N.B.R. (2d) 275 (N.B.C.A.). See also *Ouston v. Zurowski* (1985), 18 D.L.R. (4th) 563 (B.C.C.A.), where the plaintiff's ignorance that

was illegal because its performance involved the parties in committing an illegal act, namely, occupying the legal leased premises in the absence of a valid occupancy permit required by a local law, whereas, in *British Columbia Packers Ltd. v. Sparrow*,[76] the sale of the use of a roe herring licence did not involve any illegality in the performance of the contractual obligations arising from the sale. So, too, in *BCORP Financial Inc. v. Baseline Resort Developments Inc.*,[77] the loan that was made was not made for an illegal purpose. Therefore the principal sum could be recovered, although the illegal interest could not.

However, it would seem that here, too, the distinction must be drawn between a statute which makes any infringement, however collateral, in the course of performance of the contract capable of rendering the contract illegal and void, and a statutory provision which may penalize infringements but will not destroy the validity of a contract performed illegally. Once again it is a question of interpretation, this time, perhaps, requiring the court to test the relative importance of the infringement, the nature of the infringement on the particular case, and the hardship that would be inflicted if the contract as a whole were rendered illegal and void on the ground that, during its performance, this infringement of the law occurred. This emerges clearly in two English cases, *St. John Shipping Corporation v. Joseph Rank*[78] and *Shaw v. Groom.*[79] In the former a ship was loaded beyond the limits permitted by statute. The ship, which was under charter, only exceeded these limits during the course of the voyage, that is, originally the charter was lawful. It was held that the illegal loading was only incidental to the performance of the contract, the charter, and could not make the performance so illegal as to deprive the shipowners of the right to sue the cargo owners for freight. In the latter case a landlord sued for arrears of rent. He had not issued his tenant with a proper rent book as required by statute. Again it was held that this illegality, which, as in the previous case could lead to criminal prosecution, did not make the contract illegal as to its mode of performance. One reason for permitting the landlord to recover the unpaid rent was that, in contrast to *Anderson Ltd. v. Daniel*,[80] the legislation in this instance was not intended to prevent the enforcement of all contracts which were performed in a manner illegal under the statute.

---

the "pyramid" scheme was illegal did not save the contract; but the plaintiff recovered his money under the "repentance" doctrine: below pp. 429-430.

75 (1988), 82 N.S.R. 392 (N.S. Co. Ct.).

76 (1988), 22 B.C.L.R. (2d) 302 (B.C.S.C.); affirmed (1989), 35 B.C.L.R. (2d) 334 (B.C.C.A.); leave to appeal to S.C.C. refused (1989), 38 B.C.L.R. (2d) xxxii (note) (S.C.C.).

77 [1990] 5 W.W.R. 275 (B.C.S.C.); compare the judgment of Macfarlane J.A. in *Dodge v. Eisenman* (1985), 23 D.L.R. (4th) 711 (B.C.C.A.) where the defendant did not have a licence under the Canadian Mining Regulations: the agreement was not illegal. See also *Vandekerhove v. Litchfield* (1993), 103 D.L.R. (4th) 739 (B.C.S.C.).

78 [1957] 1 Q.B. 267.

79 [1970] 1 All E.R. 702 (C.A.).

80 Above, note 72.

(d) Gaming and wagering contracts[81]

(i) *What is a wagering contract?*

A wagering contract consists in mutual promises under which either party may gain or lose according to the ascertainment of an event uncertain to their knowledge, the promise of each providing his sole interest in the transaction.[82] "It is essential," Lord Denning M.R. said in a modern case,[83] "that each party may either win or lose. If one party can neither win or lose then it is not 'gaming' or 'wagering'." In that case the defendant bet on the totalizator in England through the plaintiff, a licensed bookmaker. He lost and did not pay. When the plaintiff sued, the defendant pleaded that it was a gaming or wagering contract within the legislation that will be examined below. If it had been, the defendant's contention would have been correct. The Court of Appeal held that the contract was between the defendant and the Totalizator Board (not the plaintiff). Under the provisions which set up that Board it could neither win nor lose in any transaction. Therefore, the contract was not a wagering contract and the defendant was liable to reimburse the plaintiff who had paid the Board.[84] So, too, in the Alberta Case of *Lyman v. Kuzik*[85] the plaintiff could sue on a contract under which the finalists in a competition agreed to divide the proceeds between them, whichever one actually

---

81 See Ross, "Anomalies in the Law of Wagering Contracts" (1930), 8 Can. Bar Rev. 718; Falconbridge, "More Anomalies in the Law of Wagering Contracts" (1931), 9 Can. Bar Rev. 331; Osborne & Campbell, "Recent Amendments to Canadian Lottery and Gaming Laws: The Transfer of Power Between Federal and Provincial Governments" (1988), 26 Osgoode Hall L.J. 19.

　　For a discussion of the public policy and morality aspects of the law relating to such contracts, see *Boardwalk Regency Corp. v. Maalouf* (1992), 88 D.L.R. (4th) 612 (Ont. C.A.), where the Ontario Court of Appeal was divided on the enforceability of a cheque given in respect of gambling in New Jersey, where gambling is legal. For a different view of public policy, by which a loan for gambling in Nevada, where gambling is legal, was unenforceable in Ontario, see *M. & R. Investment Co. v. Marsden* (1987), 63 O.R. (2d) 509 (Ont. Dist. Ct.).

82 *Carlill v. Carbolic Smoke Ball Co.*, [1893] 1 Q.B. 256 (C.A.). Note that the event does not have to be future or uncertain despite the statement to that effect by Hawkins J. in that case. In *Osorio v. Cardona* (1984), 59 B.C.L.R. 29 (B.C.S.C.), the agreement to pool winnings on horse races was *not* a wager, but a valid pooling arrangement.

83 *Tote Investors Ltd. v. Smoker*, [1968] 1 Q.B. 509 at 516 (C.A.). See further *Ellesmere v. Wallace*, [1929] 2 Ch. 1 (C.A.).

84 This is presumably why betting on horse races in Canada, within and under the provisions of the Criminal Code, is valid and, if need be, enforceable. Only totalizator betting is permitted. Hence, all transactions are cash transactions, which may preclude any legal problems. But if a bettor were not paid he might be able to sue on the contract in question, provided the rules of the appropriate board did not result in his being deprived of any remedy.

　　Note also the remarks of Stevenson J. in *Velensky v. Hache* (1981), 121 D.L.R. (3d) 747 at 752 (N.B.Q.B.): "Except as provided in ss. 185 to 192 [see now R.S.C. 1985, c. C-46, ss. 201 to 209] of the Criminal Code gambling is not an illegal activity in Canada." Note also legislation relating to lotteries, both federal and provincial.

85 (1965), 57 W.W.R. 110 (Alta. C.A.); compare *Osorio v. Cardona*, above, note 82, where the plaintiff was able to claim the total amount of his share in a win on horse races, despite his agreement to accept a smaller amount in settlement, which agreement was unconscionable because it was the result of a threat to pay nothing. Contrast, *Breitmeier v. Batke* (1966), 56 W.W.R. 678 (Alta. Dist. Ct.).

won the competition. By reason of this requirement of the possibility of gain or loss, such cases as *Carlill v. Carbolic Smoke Ball Co.*[86] may be differentiated from wagering situations. The plaintiff there could only win if she acted in the way stipulated by the defendant's advertisement. Either she would contract the illness, and so become entitled to the money, or she would remain healthy, which would not amount to any detriment but a benefit from using the defendant's product. Another reason was that the stake was not the only interest of the parties in the contract. The defendant stood to sell his product by the transaction, the plaintiff to maintain her health or obtain the "reward".

Insurance contracts, as long as the assured has an "interest" in the subject-matter of the contract, are outside the scope of wagering or gaming transactions. Dealing in stocks and shares on *margin* may be wagering transactions. This occurs where a client of a stockbroker instructs his broker to buy and sell shares by a *contract for differences*, under which the parties agree to pay or receive the differences between the price of shares on one day and their price on another.[87] If this is a genuine transaction, made in anticipation of a rise or fall in the stock market, the contract will not be a wager: if it is a colourable sale, under which it is not intended that the buyer will ever obtain the shares, then it will be a wager.[88] Even if the buyer only intends to sell the shares forward, that is, before the settling day, in the hope of making a gain by the fall of the market in the interim, the contract may still not be a wager.[89]

One specific type of stock market transaction has been made illegal by the Criminal Code in Canada: this is the sale involving dealings in shares, etc., on margin, where no delivery of the shares, etc., is contemplated by the parties.[90] In such instances the applicable law is not that which relates to gaming and wagering, but the general law as to illegality by infringement of a criminal statute.[91] Accordingly, it would seem that such a transaction is illegal and void on grounds other than that it involves wagering.[92]

If the contract does not fall into a well-organized category of wagering contract, for example, a bet on a card game, then whether it is a wagering transaction or not must be determined upon the substance of the agreement, rather than its

---

86 Above, note 82; see above, p. 71.
87 *Grizewood v. Blane* (1852), 11 C.B. 538, 138 E.R. 578.
88 *Barnett v. Sanker* (1925), 41 T.L.R. 660; *Ironmonger & Co. v. Dyne* (1928), 44 T.L.R. 597 (C.A.).
89 *Thacker v. Hardy* (1878), 4 Q.B.D. 685 (C.A.).
90 Criminal Code, R.S.C. 1985, c. C-46, s. 383.
91 Below, pp. 373-374.
92 So held in the Manitoba Court of Appeal in *Prudential Exchange Co. v. Edwards*, [1938] 1 W.W.R. 22 (Sask. C.A.); reversed without affecting this point, [1939] S.C.R. 135 (S.C.C.); see further, *Beamish v. Richardson* (1914), 49 S.C.R. 595 (S.C.C.); *Maloof v. Bickell* (1919), 59 S.C.R. 429 (S.C.C.); *Topper Grain Co. v. Mantz*, [1926] 2 W.W.R. 140 (Alta. S.C.); *Medicine Hat Wheat Co. v. Norris Comm. Co.*, [1919] 1 W.W.R. 161 (Alta. C.A.); *Woodward & Co. v. Koefoed*, [1921] 3 W.W.R. 232 (Man. C.A.); *Nelson v. Baird* (1915), 8 W.W.R. 144 (Man. K.B.); *Turner v. Alta. Pac. Grain Co.*, [1936] 3 W.W.R. 260 (Alta. S.C.); reversed, [1938] 1 W.W.R. 97 (Alta. C.A.).

In *Prudential Exchange Co. v. Edwards*, [1939] S.C.R. 135 (S.C.C.) the Supreme Court of Canada did not have to determine the issue, because the contract called for delivery of and payment for the wheat, and so was neither a wagering transaction nor illegal under the Code.

form.[93] Hence, in *Brogden v. Marriott*,[94] a contract under which one party agreed to buy a horse for £200 if the horse could trot at 18 miles per hour, but for a shilling if it could not, was held to be a wager, not a *bona fide* conditional contract for the sale of the horse.

(ii) *The effect of such contracts*

(A) *In general* At common law, it would seem wagering or gaming contracts were perfectly valid and enforceable.[95] But the judges discouraged litigation on such contracts if they were frivolous, vexatious, involved indecent evidence,[96] or perhaps touched upon public policy.[97] Eventually the legislature stepped in and, in England, there is a series of statutes stretching back to the time of Charles II, which affect the validity of such contracts, and, in particular, the validity of securities, etc., given in consequence of wagers or gaming agreements. The problem which arises in Canada, except in Ontario, is whether those statutes apply. Ontario is governed by the Gaming Act,[98] which re-enacts provisions of the various English statutes. Outside Ontario much may depend upon the date when, under the laws of a province, English law was received. In Alberta, for example, it would seem that the Acts of 1710, 1835 and 1845 apply (but not that of 1892, since the law in Alberta states that English law was received as of 1870).[99] In British Columbia, on the other hand, it would seem that the English statutes do not bind the courts.[100] Nor do they apply in New Brunswick.[101] Therefore, in what follows it will be assumed that either: (i) the English Acts apply to a province; or (ii) the province is Ontario, in which event the provincial legislation has the same, indeed a wider effect, since Ontario has legislated in the terms of the English Act of 1892 as well as others.

What these various legislative provisions achieve, in effect, is as follows. (1) They render *gaming* contracts, that is, wagers made on gaming, and in particular "playing at cards, dice, tables, tennis, or bowls," illegal, in the sense that if the consideration for a contract is money or something valuable won by such gaming,

---

93 *Carlill v. Carbolic Smoke Ball Co.*, above, note 82; *Universal Stock Exchange Ltd. v. Strachan*, [1896] A.C. 166 (H.L.).
94 (1836), 3 Bing N.C. 88, 132 E.R. 343.
95 See *e.g.*, *Earl of March v. Pigot* (1771), 5 Burr. 2802, 98 E.R. 471.
96 *Da Costa v. Jones* (1778), 2 Cowp. 729, 98 E.R. 1331; *Ditchburn v. Goldsmith* (1815), 4 Camp. 152, 171 E.R. 49.
97 *Gilbert v. Sykes* (1812), 16 East. 150, 104 E.R. 1045.
98 R.S.O. 1990, c. G.2.
99 *Breitmeier v. Batke* (1966), 56 W.W.R. 678 (Alta. Dist. Ct.); compare *DeJardin v. Roy* (1910), 12 W.L.R. 704 (Sask. Dist. Ct.).
100 *Carr Bros. v. Abbs*, [1939] 1 W.W.R. 249 (B.C. Co. Ct.), in which the action was held not to be one to recover money lent for gambling, so that the statutes would not have been relevant if they had applied.
101 *Velensky v. Hache* (1981), 121 D.L.R. (3d) 747 (N.B.Q.B.), where reference is made to New Brunswick statutes going back to 1786, the first session of the New Brunswick legislature. In Newfoundland it would seem to depend on whether the statutes were passed in England before the institution of a local legislature: *Young v. Blaikie* (1822), 1 Nfld. L.R. 277 at 283 (Nfld. S.C.).

it is deemed to be a contract made for an illegal consideration. The same is true of an agreement to reimburse or repay money knowingly lent or advanced for such gaming or betting (whether before or at the time of the gaming or play). (2) They make contracts by way of wagering or gaming generally void, so that no action can be brought to recover money etc., alleged to have been won by the wager, either from the other party or a stakeholder. (3) They render void any express or implied promise to refund money "paid under or in respect of" a contract that is void as being a wagering or gaming contract, or to pay commission or reward for such a contract, or for services rendered in connection with it (this only applies in Ontario, since it is drawn from the 1892 English statute). It follows, therefore, that the situation with respect to these kinds of contracts must be viewed from different angles: as between the parties, in respect of a transaction between principal and agent, with respect to securities, in relation to loans made for wagering or gaming purposes.

(B) *As between the parties* The statutes made all such contracts void (in the English statute the phrase is "null and void").[102] Hence, no action can be brought by either party to enforce any such contract. In *Breitmeier v. Batke*[103] three people qualified as potential winners of a $2,000 Bingo game. They all agreed that the winner of the play-off would give one-third of the prize money to each of the other two. The defendant won and gave cheques for the appropriate amount to the plaintiff and the third person. Then he stopped payment on the cheques. The plaintiff sued on his cheque and it was held that the action was not maintainable by reason of the English Gaming Act of 1845. In other words a party to such a contract who claims to have won under it or to be entitled to the proceeds of the wager cannot enforce his claim by action (though if he is paid it would seem that the money is irrecoverable by the loser).[104] Therefore, it is suggested that these contracts are void, but not illegal. Their invalidity does not affect collateral transactions. Hence, in *Bridger v. Savage*[105] a principal could recover from his turf commission agent, that is, bookmaker, what he had won, and was in the agent's hands, as money had and received to the principal's use, that is, on the basis of what would now be called unjust enrichment or restitution, and was formerly termed quasi-contract. As to whether wagering and gaming contracts are merely void under statute, and not illegal, this is a semantic, fruitless differentiation,[106] since, even where contracts are truly illegal some collateral transactions may be valid and enforceable, even where the main one is not.[107]

The House of Lords, resolving an argument that persisted for many years since

---

102 Gaming Act, R.S.O. 1990, c. G.2, s. 3; Gaming Act, 1845 (8 & 9 Vict.) c. 109, s. 18. But note that under the Act of 1710 (9 Ann.) c. 19, and the Ontario Gaming Act, s. 3, a player who pays a bet on a game may recover in excess of $40 (in Ontario) within 3 months of payment.

103 (1966), 56 W.W.R. 678 (Alta. Dist. Ct.).

104 But note the situation if the money was paid to the winner by a *stakeholder.* below.

105 (1885), 15 Q.B.D. 363 (C.A.).

106 Above, pp. 345-346.

107 Below, pp. 418-420.

a decision of the English Court of Appeal in 1908,[108] decided that the statute avoids more than the actual, original wager. A contract that appears to be a fresh agreement, made for new consideration, but which is still fundamentally a promise to pay the wager that was first involved, will be void under the Act. In *Hill v. William Hill (Park Lane) Ltd.*[109] the defendant had not paid off his debts to a bookmaker. It was decided by Tattersalls, the club that deals with betting arrangements at racecourses in England, that he must pay, failing which he would be posted as a defaulter and warned off Newmarket racecourse. He agreed to pay the amount owing to the plaintiffs in monthly instalments and gave them a post-dated cheque for one amount in consideration that they would refrain from enforcing the order from Tattersalls about posting him as a defaulter. When the instalments were not paid, the plaintiffs sued. It was held by a majority of the House of Lords that this new agreement was also affected by the statute and was void. The test of validity of any such new agreement is not whether there is fresh consideration, since this may formally be present: it is whether in substance and intention the new agreement is meant to be an alternative method of enforcing a contract which is caught by the statute, as being a wager, and therefore void.[110]

Nor may the winner of the wager recover his money from a stakeholder with whom the loser has deposited the amount wagered prior to the event. But either party may recover his *own* deposited amount from such stakeholder, and if the stakeholder does pay the winner, the stakeholder will be liable to account for such payment to the loser, if the latter gave instructions not to pay which were disregarded by the stakeholder.[111]

The statutes exempt from their provision "a subscription or contribution, or agreement to subscribe or contribute for or towards any plate, prize, or sum of money to be awarded to the winner or winners of any lawful game, sport, pastime or exercise."[112] This would seem to make a prize for such a game irrecoverable; the transaction would still be a wager, at least if two parties were involved.[113] If it were a multi-partite arrangement, and the ultimate prize was the stakes of all the participants, the decision in *Ellesmere v. Wallace*[114] suggests that such an agreement would not be a wager.[115] It is hard to accept that there cannot be a

---

108 *Hyams v. Stuart King*, [1908] 2 K.B. 696 (C.A.). For earlier decisions to like effect, see *Bubb v. Yelverton* (1870), L.R. 9 Eq. 471; *Re Browne*, [1904] 2 K.B. 133. Compare *Poteliakhoff v. Teakle*, [1938] 2 K.B. 816 (C.A.). As to whether this kind of conduct constitutes *blackmail*, see *Burden v. Harris*, [1937] 4 All E.R. 559, with which compare *Norreys v. Zeffert*, [1939] 2 All E.R. 187.

109 [1949] A.C. 530 (H.L.).

110 See, *e.g.*, *Coral v. Kleyman*, [1951] 1 All E.R. 518. Contrast the situation where the contract is one of loan made in connection with gambling or wagering below, p. 365. If new consideration can be found, immunizing the loan contract from gambling or wagering, the loan may be recoverable.

111 *Diggle v. Higgs* (1877), 2 Ex D. 422 (C.A.).

112 (8 & 9 Vict.) c. 109, s. 41, quoted in *Diggle v. Higgs, ibid.*

113 *Ibid.*

114 [1929] 2 Ch. 1 (C.A.); but the case was decided on other grounds and is questionable as regards this point.

115 Though it might involve a *lottery* and therefore be illegal; compare *Exhibition Advertising Enterprises Ltd. v. Victoria Exhibition* (1962), 132 C.C.C. 303 (B.C.S.C.).

wager involving more than two persons; indeed the Alberta Appellate Division seems to have accepted that there could be in *Breitmeier v. Batke*.[116] The true test surely is whether one person can win and other lose. Hence, in the case of a lawful game, the prize money may still be the result of a wager, and the statute simply validates agreements *to provide* such money, not agreements as to what is to happen to it.

(C) *Situations involving principal and agent* If a person is appointed as a stakeholder, to keep the money for both sides while the wager is being determined, either principal can recover his money back from the stakeholder, and the agent who disregards instructions will be liable if he pays over to the winner.[117] If he has paid before receiving instructions to the contrary, however, he will be immune from liability, since, being a stakeholder and therefore an agent to pay over the sums deposited to the winner of the bet or wager, he acted with authority.[118] But no action can be brought against the stakeholder by the winner to recover the loser's deposit, as well as the winner's own deposit; that contravenes the statutes.[119]

If the agent is not a stakeholder, that is, an agent for both parties, but simply agent for one, the situation is different. The agent would be entitled at common law to be indemnified by his principal if he carried out his principal's instructions, for example, paid the bet to the winner, even though the payment of the winner could not have been enforced by him through an action. This decision, in *Read v. Anderson*,[120] could lead to the circumvention of the Gaming Acts. Hence, in England, which Ontario has followed,[121] there is the provision of the 1892 Act, which reverses the decision in the case just cited and renders such an action impossible. The agent cannot now be indemnified in England or Ontario (though presumably he can where the 1892 Act is not in effect). But he cannot be sued if he fails to carry out his instructions, that is, to make the bet in question, since then he would be liable for doing something which is void.[122] On the other hand, the agent will not be able to resist a claim by his principal in respect of money actually won by the principal by the wager and paid over to the agent. The principal's action is not contractual in nature, and is therefore not caught by the legislation making such contracts void.[123]

(D) *Securities* Under the Act of 1710, securities, for example, a cheque, for bets by, or on the players, and for loans for *gaming* (that is, wagers involved in

---

116 Above, note 103.
117 *Burge v. Ashley & Smith Ltd.*, [1900] 1 Q.B. 744 (C.A.), even after the 1892 English Act.
118 *Varney v. Hickman* (1847), 5 C.B. 271, 136 E.R. 881.
119 *Diggle v. Higgs*, above, note 111.
120 (1882), 10 Q.B.D. 100 (C.A.).
121 Gaming Act, R.S.O. 1990, c. G.2, s. 5.
122 *Cohen v. Kittell* (1889), 22 Q.B.D. 680.
123 *Bridger v. Savage*, above, note 105; even after the 1892 Act; *De Mattos v. Benjamin* (1894), 63 L.J. Q.B. 248; contrast *Morgan v. Ashcroft*, [1938] 1 K.B. 49 (C.A.).

games), were made void.[124] The avoidance of gaming securities worked great hardship on innocent holders of such a cheque, who could therefore obtain no satisfaction on the bill because it was given for no consideration, even though the holder in due course was ignorant of the origins of the bill. Hence, section 1 of the Gaming Act 1835, in England, which is contained in section 1 of the Ontario Gaming Act, stated that such securities are "deemed" to have been given for an *illegal* consideration. This means that a holder in due course of a cheque or other bill given in payment of a gaming debt, provided he established that he gave value for the bill and took it in good faith, will be protected and can sue on it.[125] Hence, in *Woolf v. Hamilton*,[126] since the endorsee of a cheque knew that it had been given in payment of a lost bet on a horse, he was prevented from enforcing it against the drawer.

If a cheque is given in payment of a non-gaming wager, it will be caught by the provisions of the 1845 Act, or secton 4 of the Ontario Act (whichever is applicable) by which the contract is void. Hence, it was given for no consideration. This means that a holder in due course will be able to enforce the security unless the drawer of the cheque, in the case of a cheque, or such party as would be liable on the security, can prove that the holder had given no consideration. Thus, in *Fitch v. Jones*,[127] the holder in due course of a promissory note originally given in settlement of a bet on the rise and fall of the hop duty (a non-gaming wager) could recover on the note, consideration being presumed, as this was under the 1845 Act, and the defendant was not able to prove that the holder had not given value. Indeed it may be that proof that the holder knew that the security had been given in respect of a wager will not of itself take away the holder's right to enforce the security.[128]

Of course as between the winner and the loser, if the latter pays the former by a security, for example, a cheque, the winner will not be able to enforce it. Only a transferee may acquire rights under these statutory provisions. However, there is one curiosity which has been altered by statute in England, but appears

---

124 See also the New Brunswick Act Respecting Gambling Transactions, R.S.N.B. 1923, c. 156; *Velensky v. Hache* (1981), 121 D.L.R. (3d) 747 (N.B.Q.B.), though the loan for gambling was recoverable as a *debt*. *Quaere*: Does the statute still exist? It is not contained in the Revised Statutes of New Brunswick.

125 *Bank of N.S. v. Edwards* (1981), 126 D.L.R. (3d) 615 at 622 (Ont. Co. Ct.). In that case it was held that the plaintiff bank's position as holder in due course was not affected by an endorsement of the cheque which said "re Aruba gambling loss," because in ordinary banking practice only the front of a cheque was examined. Moreover the consideration for the cheque was the surrender of the gambler's I.O.U.'s, not the promise to repay money lent for gaming.

126 [1898] 2 Q.B. 337 (C.A.). Compare *Moulis v. Owen*, [1907] 1 K.B. 746 (C.A.). But if the game was abroad and the gaming contract would be upheld abroad, the situation will be different: the *Baumgart* case (1927), 96 L.J.K.B. 789; *Harold Meyers Travel Service Ltd. v. Magid* (1977), 77 D.L.R. (3d) 32 (Ont. C.A.). *Boardwalk Regency Corp. v. Maalouf* (1992), 88 D.L.R. (4th) 612 (Ont. C.A.); additional reasons at (1992), 88 D.L.R. (4th) 612 at 632 (Ont. C.A.). Note, however, the dissenting opinion of Arbour J.A., refusing to uphold the contract on grounds of public policy: compare *M. & R. Investment Co. v. Marsden* (1988), 63 O.R. (2d) 509 (Ont. Dist. Ct.).

127 (1855), 5 E. & B. 238, 119 E.R. 470.

128 *Lilley v. Rankin* (1886), 56 L.J.Q.B. 248.

still to be law in Canada. Under section 2 of the 1835 Act (and section 2 of the Ontario Act), if a loser *pays* the amount of a bill, etc., for example, a cheque, not to the winner himself but to an endorsee, that is, the innocent assignee of the security, that money is recoverable from the winner. This led to some strange decisions in England, where a cheque had been given to the winner, the amount being credited to the payee's account before the clearance with the payor's, that is, the loser's bank. It was held that this resulted in the loser being able to recoup from the winner.[129] This was changed by a statute in 1922 in England.[130] But since no such change has occurred in Canada it may be that these decisions are still law in Canadian jurisdictions (at least where bank practice produces a similar effect).

(E) *Loans* Money that is lent to play on an illegal game is irrecoverable.[131] Even if the game is not *per se* illegal it would seem that the 1835 Act in England, or section 1 of the Ontario Act, will render money lent for such gaming to be irrecoverable[132] if the defendant proves that the plaintiff, the lender, knew that the borrower was going to use it for such purpose and the money was used for such purpose.[133] Hence, in *Norley v. Skillman*[134] the defendant, who could not establish such knowledge, was liable to repay the loan, according to the County Court Judge who tried the issue, because the lender believed that all gambling had stopped.[135] But, in a British Columbia case, *Carr Bros. v. Abbs*,[136] where the money was not lent for illegal gambling, even though it may have been used to play poker (and in the lender's store, to boot!), the lender, who took no share in

---

129 *Dey v. Mayo*, [1920] 2 K.B. 346 (C.A.); *Sutters v. Briggs*, [1922] 1 A.C. 1 (H.L.).

130 Gaming Act, 1922 (12 & 13 Geo. 5) c. 19; repealed by the Statute Law Revision Act, 1953 (2 & 3 Eliz. 2) c. 5, its effect having expired by the effluxion of time.

131 *M'Kinnell v. Robinson* (1838), 3 M. & W. 434, 150 E.R. 1215. But not if the gaming is to be carried on in a jurisdiction where the money is recoverable, see, *e.g.*, *Saxby v. Fulton*, [1909] 2 K.B. 208 (C.A.). Hence, a travel agent who paid gaming debts incurred by a client in the Bahamas where gaming is legal, was able to recover in Ontario from the client on the client's promise to reimburse him: *Harold Meyers Travel Servcie Ltd. v. Magid* (1975), 9 O.R. (2d) 200 (Ont. H.C.); affirmed (1977), 77 D.L.R. (3d) 32 (Ont. C.A.).

   So, too, in *Boardwalk Regency Corp. v. Maalouf*, above, note 126, the majority of the Ontario Court of Appeal held that a cheque given in New Jersey to consolidate earlier cheques written by the defendant to cover his gambling debts, whereupon further credit was extended to the defendant, could be sued upon in Ontario. The proper law of the contract was New Jersey law and the Ontario Gaming Act did not apply, since gambling was permitted to some extent in Canada, public policy did not dictate that the action on the New Jersey judgment should not be enforced. In any event, according to Lacourcière J.A., the action would have been maintainable on the debt.

132 But in New Brunswick it has been held that money lent to enable a player to continue to play poker could be recovered as a *debt*, not by an action on the cheque given to secure the loan: *Velensky v. Hache* (1981), 121 D.L.R. (3d) 747 (N.B.Q.B.).

133 See *e.g.*, *Thomas v. Parley*, [1929] 2 W.W.R. 317 (Sask. C.A.); *Miller v. Wall*, [1933] 2 W.W.R. 574 (Man. C.A.).

134 [1973] 1 O.R. 303 (Ont. Co. Ct.).

135 This was applied in *Bank of N.S. v. Edwards* (1981), 126 D.L.R. (3d) 615 (Ont. Co. Ct.) where the consideration for the cheque given to pay past gambling debts was the surrender of the debtor's I.O.U.s, and the bank did not lend or advance the money for gaming.

136 [1939] 1 W.W.R. 249 (B.C. Co. Ct.).

the gaming or its product, was able to sue for recovery of the money lent in an earlier case. Poker, it was held, was not illegal,[137] nor was the action one to recover money lent for gambling, which meant that the transaction was not within the English statutes of 1710, 1835 or 1845 (which were applicable in British Columbia where the case was being heard). It would seem that this conflicts with the basis for the decision in the *Norley* case (even though the actual decision is reconcilable with the earlier British Columbia one)[138] and with the decision of an English court in *Carlton Hall Club v. Laurence*,[139] which held that, when a cheque given in repayment of a loan to play poker was caught by the English statutes, so that the lender could not sue on it, the lender could not sue on the contract of loan, even though the statutes do not expressly cover loans for gaming purposes.

There are English decision[140] which establish that if money is given not to the loser to pay his debts, but directly to the winner, it may not be recoverable from the loser, that is, the borrower, because of the provisions of the 1892 Gaming Act in England, which is contained in section 5 of the Ontario Act. This renders void "any promise, express or implied, to pay any person a sum of money paid by him under or in respect of a contract or agreement" that is itself void because it involves gaming or wagering. This would certainly be the situation: (a) where the payment was made at the request of the borrower: (b) if the lender knew that the money was going to be used by the borrower to such effect: and (c) where the 1892 Act or its equivalent are in force in a given jurisdiction.[141] Do these decisions, therefore, mean that *Carr Bros. v. Abbs*[142] is wrong? Or can that case be reconciled with other decisions by saying that the lender did not know what use was being made of his money or did not intend it to be used for gaming (both of which conclusions would seem to be excluded by the facts as found and stated in the case)? Or is the real test whether what was going on was known to be a *criminal* activity, namely, maintaining a common gaming house, rather than the mere indulgence by the borrower in gaming or wagering, so that recovery of the loan depended upon proof that the lender was a party to an illegal act?

---

137 But it was illegal in the *Norley* case!

138 Perhaps they are reconcilable on the basis of a different view as to the legality or illegality of the game in progress.

139 [1929] 2 K.B. 153, with which contrast *Cumming v. Mackie*, [1973] S.L.T. 242.

140 *Tatam v. Reeve*, [1893] 1 Q.B. 44; *Woolfe v. Freeman*, [1937] 1 All. E.R. 178; *McDonald v. Green*, [1951] 1 K.B. 594 (C.A.); *C.H.T. Ltd. v. Ward*, [1965] 2 Q.B. 63 (C.A.). But the loan is recoverable if the money is used by the borrower to pay debts already lost and it is no term of the contract of loan that the money shall be used for such bets: *Re O'Shea*, [1911] 2 K.B. 981 (C.A.).

141 But the money is recoverable if the gaming was carried on in a country where gaming was legal, *e.g.*, the Bahamas; s. 5 of the Ontario Act only applies to gaming contracts in Ontario: *Harold Meyers Travel Service Ltd. v. Magid*, above, note 131. See *Boardwalk Regency Corp. v. Maalouf*, above, note 131.

142 Above, note 136.

(e) Contracts made on a Sunday

At common law a contract made on a Sunday was perfectly valid.[143] In Canada, the federal Lord's Day Act[144] affected the legality and validity of contracts made on Sundays. That statute was declared unconstitutional by the Supreme Court of Canda in *R. v. Big M Drug Mart Ltd.*,[145] as a result of the provisions of the Charter of Rights and Freedoms. The attempt by the federal statute to regulate the conduct of business on Sunday, subject to certain exceptions, was held to infringe religious freedom as protected by the Charter. Subsequently, the Act was repealed.[146] The complex law and contradictory decisions that formerly were necessary to understand have now been rendered irrelevant. However, provincial legislation that purports to affect the extent to which business (including the making of contracts) on Sundays and other statutory holidays is lawful, may continue to be material.

Some provincial legislation which used to render unlawful the making of certain contracts on a Sunday has been repealed, as a consequence of the decision with respect to the effect of the Charter on the federal Act.[147] Other provincial legislation has survived attacks upon its constitutionality.[148] In various decisions different provincial courts, as well as the Supreme Court of Canada, have held that the particular provincial statute involved was neither *ultra vires* the provincial legislature nor invalid on the grounds that it entailed interference with religious freedom or resulted in inequality.[149] Where such legislation did contravene the provisions of the Charter, it was sometimes upheld on the basis of the general preservation of legislation under article 1.[150] In one instance, however, one such statute was successfully challenged.[151]

---

143 *Drury v. Defontaine* (1880), 1 Taunt. 131, 127 E.R. 781; see also *Broome v. Swan* (1766), 6 Bro. P.C. 333, 2 E.R. 1115 (H.L.); *R. v. Walden* (1914), 6 W.W.R. 850 (B.C.C.A.); *Cudney v. Gives* (1890), 20 O.R. 500 (Ont. C.P.).

144 R.S.C. 1970, c. L-13, s. 4.

145 (1985), 18 D.L.R. (4th) 321 (S.C.C.); compare *Principal Invts. Ltd. v. Thiele Estate* (1987), 37 D.L.R. (4th) 398 (B.C.C.A.).

146 R.S.C. 1985, Appendix I, Schedule.

147 *Viz.*, Law of Property Act, R.S.A. 1980, c. L-8, s. 58, repealed by the Charter Omnibus Act, S.A. 1985, c. 15, s. 49; Sale of Goods Act, R.S.A. 1980, c. S-2, s. 5, repealed by S.A. 1985, c. 15, s. 41.

148 *E.g.*, Retail Business Holidays Act, R.S.O. 1990, c. R.30; Remembrance Day Act, R.S.M. 1970, c. R80; Days of Rest Act, S.N.B. 1985, c. D-4.2; Holiday Shopping Regulation Act, S.B.C. 1980, c. 17.

149 *R. v. Edwards Books & Art Ltd.* (1987), 35 D.L.R. (4th) 1 (S.C.C.); *R. v. Sobeys Stores Ltd.* (1986), 69 N.B.R. (2d) 246 (N.B.Q.B.); affirmed (1986), 73 N.B.R. (2d) 234 (N.B.C.A.); *London Drugs Ltd. v. Red Deer (City)* (1987), 44 D.L.R. (4th) 264 (Alta. Q.B.); affirmed (1988), 52 D.L.R. (4th) 203 (Alta. C.A.); *R. v. Myrrmidon Inc.*, [1987] 6 W.W.R. 204 (Man. Q.B.); affirmed [1988] 5 W.W.R. 385 (Man. C.A.); *Peel (Regional Municipality) v. Great Atlantic & Pacific Co. of Can.* (1991), 78 D.L.R. (4th) 333 (Ont. C.A.); leave to appeal to S.C.C. granted 85 D.L.R. (4th) viii (note) (S.C.C.).

150 *R. v. Paul Magder Furs Ltd.* (1989), 69 O.R. (2d) 172 (Ont. C.A.); leave to appeal to S.C.C. refused (1989), 37 O.A.C. 159 (note) (S.C.C.); *R. v. Westfair Foods Ltd.* (1989), 65 D.L.R. (4th) 56 (Sask. C.A.).

151 *Can. Safeway Ltd. Store No. 252 v. R.* (1988), 25 B.C.L.R. (2d) 29 (B.C. Co. Ct.); affirmed (1988), 37 B.C.L.R. (2d) 199 (B.C.C.A.).

The cases referred to concern prosecutions for violation of the relevant statutes or by-laws: or the rights of a particular business which a tradesman or company wished to pursue on a prohibited day. There do not appear to be any decisions involving the validity of a contract made in contravention of the legislation. However it would seem logical to conclude that, if the legislation in question is valid, a contract that is made on a Sunday, or other prohibited day for doing business, would be illegal and therefore void. The issue would then arise whether the contract was truly made on the day in question. Hence, it is possible that decisions rendered in connection with the application of the original federal statute might be relevant. These consider if and when a contract has been made on a Sunday so as to come within the scope of the prohibition contained in that Act. In consequence, it is suggested, they could be very pertinent to the same question in the context of a provincial statute or some municipal by-law that was to the same effect as the now-repealed federal statute. Therefore, it is necessary to give an account of such decisions.

There are possibilities that a contract which seems to have been made on a Sunday will be held not to have been. Indeed Canadian courts have often attempted to avoid holding a contract invalid where it is possible to say that the making of the contract was spaced over several days, including some acts occurring on a Sunday.[152] In *Olliviere v. Durand*,[153] for example, it was held that the negotiations took place on a Sunday but the actual contract was made on a weekday. Similarly in *Re Grier and Krivak*[154] a contract made on Sunday, which was subject to a condition that financing be arranged within ten days, was held not to be within the Act. In *Angevaare v. McKay*[155] on the other hand, a contract which was agreed to on a Sunday (a contract for the sale of a car), was dated two days later, and the conditional sale agreement that accompanied the sale was entered into on a weekday. This contract was held made on a Sunday.[156]

---

152 *McDonald v. Fellows* (1979), 17 A.R. 330 (Alta. C.A.); *Bergen v. Billingham* (1972), 28 D.L.R. (3d) 49 (Man. Q.B.); *Holmes v. Alexson* (1974), 54 D.L.R. (3d) 175 (Ont. H.C.); affirmed (1976), 12 O.R. (2d) 431 (Ont. C.A.); *Cari-Van Hotel Ltd. v. Globe Estates Ltd.*, [1974] 6 W.W.R. 707 (B.C.S.C.).

153 (1953), 9 W.W.R. (N.S.) 53 (Man. C.A.); compare *Gamble v. Wright* (1927), 31 O.W.N. 482 (Ont. H.C.); affirmed (1927), 32 O.W.N. 193 (Ont. C.A.); compare *Roman Hotels Ltd. v. Desrochers Hotels Ltd.* (1976), 69 D.L.R. (3d) 126 (Sask. C.A.), where the offer was accepted on a Monday, though the document was signed on a Sunday.

154 (1973), 31 D.L.R. (3d) 381 (Man. Q.B.). Compare *Rai v. Csapo* (1981), 21 R.P.R. 122 (B.C.S.C.), and *Yaschuk v. Hammett* (1981), 11 Sask. R. 282 (Sask. Q.B.); *Ball v. Crawford* (1983), 53 B.C.L.R. 153 (B.C.C.A.).

155 [1961] O.R. 34 (Ont. Co. Ct.).

156 Compare *Worton v. Sauve* (1977), 80 D.L.R. (3d) 382 (Alta. Dist. Ct.), where the contract made on a Sunday was invalid, although the purchaser's cheque in payment of the deposit was post-dated to the Monday; compare *MacLean v. Ritchie* (1977), 21 N.S.R. (2d) 446 (N.S.T.D.). So, too, was a contract of sale of goods invalid when it was made on a Sunday, even though the seller's obligation was conditional on the happening of a future event; this did not postpone the date of the formation of the contract; *Serendipety Pools (West) Ltd. v. Goodman's Indust. Maintenance Ltd.* (1981), 126 D.L.R. (3d) 140 (Man. C.A.).

A leading case is *Aconley v. Willart Holdings Ltd.*[157] The vendor of land brought an action for specific performance of the contract of sale. The agreement was signed on a Sunday. But the vendor was unaware of the fact that the purchaser had completed the execution of the contract on a Sunday. The documents had been left with the purchaser on a weekday and the purchaser's solicitor had stated to the vendor that the purchaser would complete the agreement on a Friday. The agreement had been partly performed, therefore, before the Sunday. The vendor was held entitled to specific performance as the parties had agreed before Sunday, and there had been partial completion before Sunday.

(f) Agreements within the Competition Act[158]

Certain agreements or contracts which had as their purpose the regulation of trade, for example, by creating monopolies or fixing the price at which goods sold, were formerly illegal under the Criminal Code. More recently these have been dealt with by provisions of what is now the Competition Act, which replaced the former Combines Investigation Act. There is no doubt that agreements which come within the purview of this statute are unlawful, and may give rise to criminal liability.[159] However, the question is whether such agreements, if criminal, are affected civilly. A provision of that statute purports to state that the Act does not affect civil rights.[160] This may mean only that an agreement within the statute is not an actionable conspiracy. Does it also mean that such an agreement is illegal and cannot therefore give rise to rights or liabilities?

In *Weidman v. Shragge*[161] in 1912, the Supreme Court had to deal with a contract between two Winnipeg dealers under which prices to be paid for certain articles were fixed, with the object of restraining competition and establishing a monopoly. This was at a time when the relevant statutory provisions were in the Criminal Code. A majority of the court held that such an agreement was not void at common law, because it was not in unreasonable restraint of trade, and therefore could not be void under the statute. In 1912, by virtue of earlier English decisions, combinations between traders, etc., to maintain prices or control the market, were not bad,[162] even though similar combinations by workmen to keep up the price of their labour or otherwise to control the labour market were in unreasonable restraint of trade and therefore void.[163]

---

157 (1964), 49 W.W.R. 46 (Man. Q.B.); distinguished in *Perry v. Anderson* (1990), 12 D.L.R. (3d) 414 (B.C.S.C.); compare *Allistone & Cunningham Ltd. v. Wallace*, [1951] 4 D.L.R. 608 (B.C. Co. Ct.).

158 R.S.C. 1985, c. C-34, ss. 45-51.

159 As to which see *Aetna Ins. Co. v. R.* (1977), 75 D.L.R. (3d) 332 (S.C.C.); *Atl. Sugar Refineries Co. v. Canada (A.G.)* (1980), 115 D.L.R. (3d) 21 (S.C.C.); *Sumner Sports Inc. v. Pavillon Chasse & Pêche (440) Inc.* (1990), 72 D.L.R. (4th) 317 (Que. C.A.) (contract not in breach of s. 32(1) of the original Act).

160 Constitutionally the federal Parliament cannot legislate with reference to "property and civil rights".

161 (1912), 46 S.C.R. 1 (S.C.C.).

162 See, *e.g., Mogul S.S. Co. v. McGregor, Gow & Co.*, [1892] A.C. 25 (H.L.).

163 *Hilton v. Eckersley* (1855), 6 E. & B. 47, 119 E.R. 781; see also *Russell v. Amalgam. Soc. of Carpenters and Joiners*, [1912] A.C. 421 (H.L.). For Canadian cases, see *Chase v. Starr*, [1923] 3 W.W.R.

Subsequently, however, the Supreme Court of Canada held that the relevant provisions of the Criminal Code did not give rise to a defence to a counter-claim for money alleged to be the price of goods sold and delivered on the basis of the illegality of the contract under the statute.[164] Those provisions made illegal conspiracies or combinations to limit production or control prices. It was held in this case that there was no illegality alleged by the vendor that was connected with the transaction in question. Even before the provisions were taken out of the Criminal Code and put into the Combines Investigation Act, therefore, it may have been a doubtful question whether any such agreements could give rise to a defence of illegality, in the event of an action being brought thereon. Now that the matter is no longer dealt with in the criminal statute, even though infringement still can involve an offence and the imposition of penalties, it is still a question whether the effect of those provisions is to enable a party to such an agreement to raise the plea of illegality.

3. Common-law illegality

(a) The doctrine of public policy

Public policy, as distinguished from what might be called "political policy," with which it has often been confused, is that principle of law which holds that

> no subject can lawfully do that which has a tendency to be injurious to the public or against the public good which may be termed, as it sometimes has been, the policy of the law or public policy in relation to the administration of the law.[165]

Such a principle is necessarily incident to every state governed by law.

As English cases since the eighteenth century, and Canadian cases following them, have established, the courts may declare a contract invalid and illegal on the ground that its very nature, or the purpose which it is designed to achieve, whether directly or indirectly, contravenes the ends of society.[166] Such contracts offend the basis of legal order, which is founded upon justice, legality, and morality.

---

500 (Man. C.A.); affirmed, [1924] S.C.R. 495 (*sub nom. Starr v. Chase*) (S.C.C.); *Polakoff v. Winters Garment Co.*, [1928] 2 D.L.R. 277 (Ont. H.C.).

164 *Direct Lbr. Co. v. Western Plywood Co.*, [1962] S.C.R. 646 (S.C.C.). Compare *Wilkinson v. Harwood*, [1931] S.C.R. 141 (S.C.C.); *Philco Prods. Ltd. v. Thermionics Ltd.*, [1940] S.C.R. 501 (S.C.C.).

165 *Egerton v. Brownlow* (1853), 4 H.L. Cas. 1, 10 E.R. 359 at 437 (H.L.) *per* Lord Truro. Hence, a contract that infringed the law of the state of Washington could not be enforced in British Columbia, according to one member of the court, Southin J.A., on the ground that to have done so would have been against the public policy of British Columbia: *Gillespie Management Corp. v. Terrace Properties* (1989), 62 D.L.R. (4th) 221 at 222 (B.C.C.A.).

166 Or does something which contradicts some basic idea of society, such as freedom of government bodies to make decisions on the ground of what is beneficial and desirable to the public: *Finney v. Twp. of McKellar* (1982), 133 D.L.R. (3d) 351 (Ont. C.A.) (contract not specifically enforceable, because it fettered the freedom of a municipality to be influenced by the public hearing regarding road diversion to be held under a provincial statute). So, too, a transaction that is a sham, designed to conceal its real purpose, may be invalid and unenforceable: *Small v. Sonnenberg* (1990), 104 N.B.R. (2d) 395 (N.B.Q.B.); reversed on other grounds (1990), 111 N.B.R. (2d) 117 (N.B.C.A.) (agreement with regard to payment for use of an unlicensed airport).

The doctrine of public policy is concerned with the fundamentals of the legal system. What offends against public policy are acts which support, encourage, permit and foster conduct which is injurious to the very foundations upon which society exists. To recognize and enforce contracts that do this would be to offend the public conscience.[167]

There is some dispute on the question whether the scope of the doctrine at common law is now settled, such that it is incapable of wider expansion. In England, appeals have been made to the courts to strike down transactions or practices on the basis that they offend public policy, even though the situations in question were novel applications of the doctrine. In one instance, for example, it was suggested, and held, that it was discriminatory, and therefore illegal at common law, to refuse a licence as a horse trainer to a woman.[168] In another instance, though the more traditional grounds of restraint of trade might be the basis for the decision, a contract which restricted the freedom of a football player to join other football clubs at the end of his service with one such club was held invalid and unenforceable.[169] In a third instance, an attempt to alter the rules of the Pharmaceutical Society, by making it improper to sell pharmaceutical products in the same place and at the same time as non-pharmaceutical products (which would have hampered the trade of members of the Society and might have led to a decline in the provision of service to the public) was frustrated by the courts which held that the proposed and adopted rule was *ultra vires* of the Society, on the grounds, *inter alia*, of public policy.[170]

Such uses of the doctrine, however, may be questioned.[171] In certain respects, such matters as sexual or racial discrimination, for example, or the regulation of industry, business and commerce, are better dealt with by legislatures, which can consult with different potentially affected interests, than by the judicial, nebulous and "unruly" doctrine of public policy, enunciated, interpreted and applied by judges who need consult with nobody, except themselves and their precedents, cannot make adequate inquiries into the desirability or otherwise of their decision, in social,

---

167 Compare *Howard v. Shirlstar Container Transport Ltd.*, [1990] 1 W.L.R. 1292 (C.A.) where this did not apply because the plaintiff acted illegally to escape imminent danger: below, note 248. However, the idea that the test of illegality is whether the contract would offend the public conscience has been criticized, and seemingly rejected as inconsistent with the settled law, in *Tinsley v. Milligan*, [1993] 3 All E.R. 65 (H.L.), especially at 75-78 *per* Lord Goff, dissenting.

168 *Nagle v. Feilden*, [1966] 2 Q.B. 633 (C.A.). Contrast the decision in respect of discrimination against Chinese and Japanese in *Brooks-Bidlake & Whittal Ltd. v. A.G. B.C.* (1922), 63 S.C.R. 466 (S.C.C.); affirmed [1923] A.C. 450 (P.C.). Would this still be true where a province has legislation against discrimination: compare *Ont. Human Rights Comm. v. Etobicoke* (1982), 40 N.R. 159 (S.C.C.); above, p. 355.

169 *Eastham v. Newcastle United Football Club*, [1963] 3 All E.R. 139.

170 *Pharmaceutical Soc. of G.B. v. Dickson*, [1970] A.C. 403 (H.L.).

171 Unless, possibly, they can be viewed as applications of the doctrine of restraint of trade: see further below, pp. 407-415. For the effect of an illegal, because fraudulent, contract between the parties on one party's action in tort against the other, see *Saunders v. Edwards*, [1987] 2 All E.R. 651 (C.A.), where the English Court of Appeal considers the nature of the doctrine *ex turpi causa non oritur actio*: below p. 425. On this case, see the remarks of Lord Goff in *Tinsley v. Milligan*, above, note 67, at 76.

as contrasted with legal terms, and may be applying outmoded (or in some instances *avant-garde*) notions of what is in the public interest. Judges are not legislators, even though, explicitly in some cases, impliedly in others, they may apply notions of policy in the making of their decisions.[172]

The desirability of limiting the scope of the doctrine of public policy, at least in relation to contracts, was stated by members of the House of Lords in *Fender v. St. John-Mildmay*.[173] Even clear and accepted instances of the doctrine should not be applied unnecessarily, but only if there is evidence of the dangerous or injurious consequences of permitting the validity and enforceability of a contract that would come within the doctrine. The need to approach such matters with caution, and not to expand the doctrine beyond what has been accepted in the past or what is absolutely essential for the future, was stressed by the majority of the Supreme Court of Canada in *Re Millar*.[174] This case concerned not a contract but a disposition in a will. The applicable principles of law were the same. Duff C.J., and Davis, Kerwin and Hudson JJ. stated that public policy was limited to decided cases and instances, and there was no power in the courts to create new kinds of situations which contravened public policy. Moreover, even within the specified instances when the doctrine applied, if application of the doctrine was sought for the purpose of invalidating a transaction, it had to be shown that: (1) the prohibition was imposed in the interests of the safety of the state, or the economic and social well-being of the state and its people as a whole; and (2) it was imposed only in clear cases, in which harm to the public was substantially incontestable and did not depend upon what were termed the idiosyncratic inferences of a few judicial minds. The Supreme Court, therefore, as the House of Lords before it, was cognizant of the dangers inherent in riding the "unruly horse" of public policy, which, once mounted, could lead to unforeseen destinations and terminations. There is grave risk in permitting the judges to strike down contracts at will, whenever in their opinion some jealously guarded tenet which they favour and approve is under attack, whether or not the public generally would agree with their assessment of the potential consequences. Nor do the judges want a very wide power in this respect. Even where no statute governs, the precedents of the past may have presented the judges with enough power and flexibility, in undisputed instances, to enable them to regulate and control attempts to undermine society by acting illegally.[175]

---

172 Compare the remarks of Lord Simon of Glaisdale in *Miliangos v. George Frank (Textiles) Ltd.*, [1975] 3 All E.R. 801 at 821-825 (H.L.).

173 [1938] A.C. 1 (H.L.): see also *Janson v. Driefontein Consol. Mines Ltd.*, [1902] A.C. 484 (H.L.); *Egerton v. Brownlow*, above, note 165; *Rodriguez v. Speyer Bros.*, [1919] A.C. 59 (H.L.); *Geismar v. Sun Alliance & London Ins.*, [1977] 3 All E.R. 570 at 575 *per* Talbot J. Presumably this renders ineffective the contrary view expressed by McCardie J. in *Naylor, Benzon & Co. v. Krainische Industrie Gessellschaft*, [1918] 1 K.B. 331 at 342; affirmed, [1918] 2 K.B. 486 (C.A.), relying on, *e.g., Neville v. Dom. of Can. News Co.*, [1915] 3 K.B. 556 (C.A.).

174 [1938] S.C.R. 1 (S.C.C.).

175 For an interesting example, from Quebec, of a plea of illegality on the grounds of public policy being raised unsuccessfully, see *Angers v. Gauthier*, [1924] S.C.R. 479 (S.C.C.); leave to appeal to Privy Council refused (1924), 26 Que. P.R. 106 (P.C.), where the licensed pilots of Montreal

(b) Contracts to commit illegal acts

An agreement to do anything which is criminal or tortious is illegal and cannot be enforced by the courts.[176] Thus, a contract to undertake broadcasting, when it was illegal to do so by reason of a failure to obtain the necessary licence, was held void in *Agathos v. Community Communications Inc.*,[177] as was a contract with an unlicensed medical practitioner.[178] So, too, were a mortgage which was entered into to avoid, *inter alia*, the payment of income tax,[179] and a contract which purported to avoid federal and provincial sales tax.[180] So, too, was a contract to employ someone to sell stamps to retailers, to be given by the retailers to customers and be redeemable for premiums.[181] Since the use of such stamps was illegal under the Criminal Code,[182] so, too, was the contract of employment. Its ultimate purpose was illegal. Even if there was no intention on the part of the contracting parties to violate the law, the contract will still be invalid, whether or not they knew of the law in question. But if the contract could be performed legally, it must be shown that there was an intent to infringe the law for it to be held void (at least as against a particular party), and, in this respect, knowledge of the law will be important.[183]

---

agreed to combine their earnings and divide the net product equally among themselves. When the association sued a pilot for failure to fulfil the agreement, his plea of illegality failed. See also a curious case in which it was alleged that a clause preventing fraternization between employees in the North and local Indians and Eskimos was not valid under the Canadian Bill of Rights; the claim was not upheld: *Whitfield v. Can. Marconi Co.* (1967), 68 D.L.R. (2d) 251 (Que. Q.B.); affirmed (1968), 68 D.L.R. (2d) 766n (S.C.C.); application for rehearing dismissed, [1968] S.C.R. 960 (S.C.C.). But see the *Ont. Human Rights Comm.* case, above, note 168, on the use of an anti-discrimination statute. Note also the possible effects of: (a) the Charter of Rights; and (b) Federal and provincial human rights, or anti-discrimination legislation.

176 *E.g.*, a contract which infringed a temperance statute *Chechik v. Bronfman*, [1924] 2 W.W.R. 1165 (Sask. C.A.); or one infringing provisions relating to the issue of shares: *Re Bluebird Corp.*, [1926] 2 D.L.R. 484 (Ont. C.A.). Compare an agreement involving the taking or giving of a bribe: *Insco Sarnia Ltd. v. Polysar Ltd.* (1990), 49 B.L.R. 122 (Ont. Gen. Div.).

177 (1974), 3 O.R. (2d) 316 (Ont. H.C.).

178 *Tannock v. Bromley* (1979), 10 B.C.L.R. 62 (B.C.S.C.), where property given to the defendant by the plaintiff was recoverable, but not the fees paid; compare below, p. 426.

179 *Williams v. Fleetwood Hldgs. Ltd.* (1973), 41 D.L.R. (3d) 636 (Sask. C.A.); compare *Squires v. Fong* (1983), 25 Sask. R. 273 (Sask. Q.B.).

180 *Matereux de Const. Castonguay Inc. v. Pelletier* (1982), 38 N.B.R. (2d) 111 (N.B.Q.B.). Compare *Tucker Estate v. Gillis* (1988), 53 D.L.R. (4th) 688 (N.B.C.A.), transaction to avoid provincial sales tax, hence chattel mortgage void and unenforceable. See also below, pp. 416-418.

181 *United Dom. Promotion Sales Inc. v. Shaw* (1957), 119 C.C.C. 380 (N.B. Co. Ct.). Compare *C.M.H.C. v. Co-op. Colleges Residences Ltd.* (1974), 3 O.R. (2d) 142 (Ont. H.C.); affirmed (1975), 13 O.R. (2d) 394 (Ont. C.A.). But the mortgage in *Mira Design Co. v. Seascape Hldgs. Ltd.*, [1982] 4 W.W.R. 97 (B.C.S.C.) (reversing [1982] 1 W.W.R. 744 (B.C. Chambers)) did not infringe s. 305.1 [now s. 347] of the Code.

182 See now R.S.C. 1985, c. C-46, ss. 305, 364.

183 *One Hundred Simcoe St. Ltd. v. Frank Burger Contractors Ltd.*, [1968] 1 O.R. 452 (Ont. C.A.); affirmed, [1969] I.L.R. 1-257 (*sub nom. Dom. Ins. Corp. v. One Hundred Simcoe Street Ltd.*) (S.C.C.). See also the case of *Engleblom v. Blakeman*, [1930] 1 W.W.R. 565 (B.C.C.A.), where the defence of illegality failed because the defendant had ratified the agreement to buy licensed premises

In some instances, the purpose of the contract is at once criminal *and* tortious, for example, where goods are obtained by fraud,[184] or fraud is employed to obtain a large loan from a mortgage company,[185] or a bank,[186] or the arrangement is to "rig" the Stock Market by artificially enhancing the true value of shares by entering into a contract to buy them at a fictitious premium.[187] In other situations, the contract has as its object the commission of what is a tort, for example, when it is to assault[188] or libel[189] a third party. It would seem also that if the purpose of a contract is to get one party to break his contract with a third party, the second agreement will be invalid. In such a situation, the contract is made for the purpose of inducing the breach of an already existing contract, which is a tort.[190]

A problem that may be raised is whether agreements which involve maintenance or champerty are illegal. Maintenance is improperly stirring up litigation by aiding a person to bring a civil suit or defend a claim when the supporter has no just cause or excuse for so doing[191] (for example, he would have a common interest in the result, or he is acting out of charity).[192] Champerty involves the further agreement that the party providing the support, usually financial, should receive a share of whatever is recovered in the action.[193] These were crimes, as well as torts, at common law.[194] In England, they are no longer crimes,[195] but it would seem that the statutory removal of their criminal nature may not have affected the illegality of such contracts on the grounds of public policy[196] (though

---

and taken a transfer of the plaintiff's bar licence, when the defendant *knew* that he was not qualified to accept such licence. *Sed quaere?* Was the contract not invalid?

184 *Berg v. Sadler & Moore*, [1937] 2 K.B. 158 (C.A.).

185 *Zimmerman v. Litkeman*, [1978] 1 S.C.R. 1097 (S.C.C.).

186 *Thompson v. Biensch* (1980), 3 Sask. R. 353 (Sask. C.A.); leave to appeal to S.C.C. refused (1980), 34 N.R. 357n (S.C.C.); compare *Menard v. Genereaux* (1982), 138 D.L.R. (3d) 273 (Ont. H.C.); contrast *Insta-Matic Finance Ltd. v. Domensky* (1982), 20 Man. R. (2d) 306 (Man. Co. Ct.).

187 *Scott v. Brown, Doering, McNab & Co.*, [1892] 2 Q.B. 724. Or to defraud the vendor's estranged wife: *Cerilli v. Klodt* (1984), 48 O.R. (2d) 260 (Ont. H.C.).

188 *Allen v. Rescous* (1676), 2 Lev. 174, 83 E.R. 505.

189 *Apthorp v. Neville & Co.* (1907), 23 T.L.R. 575.

190 *Wanderers' Hockey Club v. Johnson* (1913), 5 W.W.R. 117 (B.C.S.C.) following *Harrington v. Victoria Graving Dock. Co.* (1878), 3 Q.B.D. 549.

191 *Neville v. London Express Newspaper Ltd.*, [1919] A.C. 368 (H.L.). See *Pettey v. Avis Car Inc.* (1993), 13 O.R. (3d) 725 at 741-742 (Ont. Gen. Div.) and cases there cited.

192 *Martell v. Consett Iron Co.*, [1955] Ch. 363 (C.A.); compare *Alabaster v. Harness*, [1895] 1 Q.B. 339 (C.A.).

193 *Re Trepca Mines Ltd. (No. 2)*, [1963] Ch. 199 (C.A.). Compare *Pettey v. Avis Car Inc.*, above, note 191, at 742. On champerty, see Tan, "Champertous Contracts and Assignments" (1990), 106 L.Q.R. 656.

194 This sentence and the next two were quoted in *Pielak v. Crown Forest Industries Ltd.*, [1992] 3 W.W.R. 592 at 604 (B.C.S.C.).

195 Since the Criminal Law Act 1967 (U.K.), c. 58, ss. 13(1), 14(1).

196 *Ibid.*, s. 14(2). Hence, a solicitor could not be indemnified against costs incurred under a champertous agreement, even when he was not a party of that agreement: *Re Trepca Mines Ltd. (No. 2)*, above, note 193. Contrast the validity of the assignment in *Trendtex Trading Corp. v. Credit Suisse*, [1982] A.C. 679 (H.L.).

this may be, now, in England, not because they involve criminality or tortiousness, but because such agreements may interfere with the administration of justice).[197]

The situation in Canada is more complex, and perhaps more uncertain. In the first place, these offences do not exist under the Criminal Code, although champerty is still illegal in Ontario.[198] Secondly, to the extent to which a particular province permits contingent fees to be agreed upon between a lawyer and his client, for example, in Alberta such *prima facie* "champertous" agreements will not be invalid. However, the question may still be asked whether, at least in the provinces other than Ontario where such arrangements are not permitted, a contract to such effect, whether or not involving a lawyer, would be illegal. This question was raised but not answered in *Amacher v. Erickson.*[199] The defendant who had a tax case pending in Oregon, hired the plaintiff, an accountant, to act on his behalf and promised to pay him $5,000 if the defendant regained $25,000 in the proceedings. When the defendant did not pay the plaintiff, who was in British Columbia, the latter sued. It was held that, whatever was the situation in British Columbia with regard to such agreements, and this was never resolved, since the contract was to be performed in Oregon where it was legal, there was no barrier to the enforcement of the contract in British Columbia. While there is no clear authority, it is suggested that, unless such agreements come within the contingency fee rules, they should be outlawed on the ground that they offend against what was, and to even a limited extent, still is the policy of law. Unless there is a valid, legally acceptable reason for permitting a party to undertake the support of another, for financial reward or otherwise, in the conduct of that other's litigation, agreements to such effect should not be recognized and enforced by the law. From more recent discussions, however, it would appear that the illegal nature of agreements that involve maintenance or champerty, *e.g.*, in cases of assignments where no proper interest to be protected can be proved, is still recognized.[200]

The refusal by the law to enforce contracts which involve the commission of a crime or tort has led to some problems. What if the contract itself does not directly require the commission of any such unlawful act, but is said to come into force when an act occurs, and such act takes the form of a crime? Can a party benefit under such contract? Clearly, a party who claims to benefit as a result of his own wrongful act, especially one that is criminal, such as murder or manslaughter, cannot be allowed to succeed. This has been held true where the

---

197 *Rees v. De Bernardy,* [1896] 2 Ch. 437.

198 By the Champerty Act, R.S.O. 1897, c. 32. The illegality of champerty has been continued in every version of the consolidated statutes of Ontario since that date. See *Buday v. Locator of Missing Heirs Inc.* (1993), 16 O.R. (3d) 257 (Ont. C.A.).

199 (1963), 42 W.W.R. 348 (B.C.S.C.). Contrast the situation in *Gillespie Management Corp. v. Terrace Properties* (1989), 62 D.L.R. (4th) 221 (B.C.C.A.), where the law in British Columbia was the same as the law in the State of Washington, where the control was illegal. Hence, according to Southin J.A., the public policy of B.C. would not allow the contract to be enforced in that province.

200 *Fredrickson v. Ins. Corp. of B.C.* (1986), 28 D.L.R. (4th) 414 (B.C.C.A.); affirmed (1988), 49 D.L.R. (4th) 160 (S.C.C.); *Pielak v. Crown Forest Industries Ltd.,* above, note 194.

claim is made under a will.[201] What if the claim is based on a contract? This was discussed in the well-known and much debated case of *Beresford v. Royal Insurance Co.*[202] The defendant company was being sued by the personal representatives of a man who had insured himself with the company and committed suicide minutes before the policy would have expired for want of payment of premiums. Since suicide was a crime (at least in England at that time),[203] it was argued that the personal representatives, who stood in the same position legally speaking as the deceased himself, could not require payment. The contract of insurance stipulated that the company would pay the deceased's representatives even though he should die by his own hand, whether sane or insane. The suit for the insurance money failed. Here the contract itself was not illegal *ab initio*. Hence, it was not totally void, and might have had some validity, for example, if assigned as security for a loan. What the House of Lords seem to have said in this instance is that an agreement not essentially illegal and void can become so, at least for some purposes, if its enforcement would have the effect of permitting a wrongdoer to benefit thereunder by his own wrongful act, if the act in question would bring the contract into operation and affect or cause the liability of the other party to accrue. In *Gray v. Barr*,[204] the plaintiff, found innocent of the murder or manslaughter of X, was seeking indemnity from his insurance company, under a policy of insurance in respect of liability to third parties, when the widow of the man he killed claimed damages for his negligence in causing that death. Notwithstanding the acquittal, the plaintiff was held to have caused the deceased's death in an unlawful way and should not be allowed to benefit under the contract of insurance.[205] Since the plaintiff had been acquitted at the criminal trial, it was curious that a civil court should hold that he was guilty of wrongful conduct, other than the kind of tortious conduct which would give rise to the duty to indemnify under the policy of insurance. The assured in the *Beresford* case was guilty of a crime, but the plaintiff in this one was not; a jury at the criminal trial had so declared.

---

201 *Cleaver v. Mutual Reserve Fund Life Assoc.*, [1892] 1 Q.B. 147 (C.A.); *Re Crippen*, [1911] P. 108; *Re Giles*, [1971] 3 All E.R. 1141 (where the criminal was of diminished responsibility, yet this did not affect the inability to succeed under the will of the husband she had killed); *Lundy v. Lundy* (1895), 24 S.C.R. 650.

202 [1938] A.C. 586 (H.L.).

203 Not now: Suicide Act, 1961 (9 & 10 Eliz. 2) c. 60. Nor is it now a crime in Canada, since 1972.

204 [1970] 2 Q.B. 626; affirmed on other grounds, [1971] 2 Q.B. 554 (C.A.). Note the distinction of this case by the minority of the Supreme Court of Canada in *Co-op. Fire & Casualty Co. v. Saindon*, [1976] 1 S.C.R. 735 (S.C.C.) on the ground that in the *Gray* case the mere perpetration of an act that had foreseeable consequences sufficed, whereas in the *Saindon* case "intent" was specifically in issue, namely, whether the assured brandished the lawn-mower and hit the injured party with the requisite statutory intent.

205 Compare the decision in *Geismar v. Sun Alliance & London Ins. Ltd.*, [1977] 3 All E.R. 570 that an assured could not collect on an insurance policy (not itself illegal and invalid) in respect of goods that had been smuggled into England without payment of customs duties, *i.e.*, illegally. Contrast the decision in *Euro-Diam Ltd. v. Bathurst*, [1987] 2 All E.R. 113, affirmed [1988] 2 All E.R. 23 (C.A.), where the illegality was unconnected with the plaintiffs' claim on the insurance policy on diamonds that were stolen in Germany. Hence, the action did not fail. On this case, see the remarks of Lord Goff in *Tinsley v. Milligan*, [1993] 3 All E.R. 65 at 76-77 (H.L.).

This decision may be supported by cases which have been concerned with the liability of an insurance company to indemnify a policyholder in respect of his liability to third parties injured or killed as a result of the policyholder's conduct.

The English cases appear to distinguish between criminal conduct which is deliberate and that which is criminal because it is the result of negligence, for example, in the case of manslaughter resulting from the gross negligence of the driver of a car (so called "motor manslaughter").[206] Canadian cases may depend upon the language of the policy or the relevant Insurance Act. In *Home Insurance Co. v. Lindal*,[207] the Supreme Court of Canada was faced with the question whether the intoxication of a driver (which resulted in his causing injury to his passenger) affected the driver's claim for indemnity under his policy of insurance in respect of the passenger's claim for damages. The court held that it did on the grounds of public policy, because the driver was committing a criminal act, namely, driving while intoxicated. Similar behaviour did not result in the exclusion of the insurance company's liability in *Mutual of Omaha Insurance Co. v. Stats*,[208] because the assured's drunken driving causing the death in question was treated as an "accident" within the meaning of the policy. In *Langley v. Fidelity Insurance Co.*,[209] a judge at first instance was unwilling to take the doctrine of public policy too far, and interfere unduly with the sanctity of the contract, under which the insurance company was liable to pay on the very event that occurred, for example, negligence. Hence, the rule that it is contrary to public policy to indemnify a person against his own criminal act (which means that he would benefit by his criminality) was not extended to a case where the assured acted inadvertently and did not know that what he was doing was unlawful, and where his conduct was not patently criminal or unlawful. The insurance company was liable when the assured caused injury to himself while he was carrying a loaded gun, which was against an Ontario statute, and it accidently went off. The decision was different in *Co-operative Fire & Casualty Co. v. Saindon*[210] where the assured's wielding of the lawnmower which caused the injured party's damage was held to have been perpetrated with the necessary statutory intent as set out in the New Brunswick Insurance Act. In *Wakeling v. Insurance Corporation of British Columbia*,[211] on the other hand, the plaintiff was not operating his vehicle for an illicit or prohibited trade or transportation,

---

206 *Tinline v. White Cross Ins. Co.*, [1921] 3 K.B. 327; *James v. Br. Gen. Ins. Co.*, [1927] 2 K.B. 311; see also *Hardy v. Motor Insurers' Bureau*, [1964] 2 Q.B. 745 (C.A.). But in *Marcel Beller Ltd. v. Hayden*, [1978] 3 All E.R. 111 the conduct of the assured, namely dangerous driving while under the influence of alcohol, precluded the insurance company's liability under the policy, regardless of the assured's intent, although his conduct was not deliberate.

207 [1934] S.C.R. 33 (S.C.C.). Compare also *Amer. Auto. Ins. Co. v. Dickson*, [1943] S.C.R. 143 (S.C.C.); *La Foncière Cie D'Assur. v. Perras*, [1942] Que. K.B. 231 (Que. K.B.); affirmed [1943] S.C.R. 165 (S.C.C.).

208 (1978), 87 D.L.R. (3d) 169 (S.C.C.). Compare the decision in *Can. Indemnity Co. v. Walkem Mach. & Equip. Ltd.*, [1976] 1 S.C.R. 309 (S.C.C.) where only *criminal* negligence would have precluded liability under the insurance policy.

209 [1935] 4 D.L.R. 89 (Ont. C.A.).

210 [1976] 1 S.C.R. 735 (S.C.C.); contrast the view of "accident" taken in *Marcel Beller Ltd. v. Hayden*, above, note 206.

211 (1988), 44 D.L.R. (4th) 335 (B.C.S.C.).

which would have protected the insurer from liability for the injuries inflicted by the plaintiff on two people, under the terms of regulations made under the provincial Insurance (Motor Vehicle) Act.[212] It is clear that the person alleged to have been acting illegally must have been doing so at the time, and in the course or for the purposes of performing the acts on which liability is based, if the illegality is to affect the relevant insurance coverage.[213]

(c) Contracts that interfere with the administration of justice

Any agreement that has as its purpose the performance of an act which would affect the proper administration of justice by the courts is illegal and void as against public policy.[214] For example, an agreement not to appear at the public examination of a bankrupt and oppose his discharge, was held invalid in *Kearley v. Thomson*.[215] So, too, an agreement to pay a witness an amount of money more than the statutory fee to which he was entitled, when such witness was within the jurisdiction and subject to the judicial process, was held invalid in *Hendry v. Zimmerman*,[216] presumably on the ground that this might influence both the attendance and the evidence of the witness. On this principle, in *Flexi-Coil Ltd. v. Smith Roles Ltd.*,[217] a contract which provided that X would not give any assistance to a party who might be sued for infringement of the plaintiff's patent was contrary to public policy. It might have interfered with the right of a litigant to produce a witness on his behalf, that is, it could have interfered with the administration of justice.

In *Campbell v. Campbell*,[218] an action was brought on a contract to pay alimony. This agreement was part of a broader transaction under which the parties agreed to a collusive divorce with the object that the husband, the defendant in the action, when free from his first marriage, would marry the plaintiff's daughter (the plaintiff being the defendant's current wife). This was held against public policy as affecting the proper administration of justice. Contracts that promote maintenance or champerty, even if not invalid on the ground that they are agreements to commit criminal or tortious acts[219] should certainly be susceptible of attack on the ground that they interfere with the proper administration of justice.

In the same way, a contract which results in the stifling of a prosecution for a criminal offence may also be illegal and invalid, as it prevents the making of correct decisions as to social and legal policy and the fulfilment of a person's duty to society. So, if the purpose of an agreement is to interfere with the proper institution

---

212 R.S.B.C. 1979, c. 204.

213 Compare *Blackstock v. Ins. Corp. of B.C.* (1983), 143 D.L.R. (3d) 743 (B.C.S.C.).

214 *Flexi-Coil Ltd. v. Smith Roles Ltd.* (1981), 50 C.P.R. (2d) 29 (Fed. T.D.); affirmed, [1982] 1 F.C. 533 (Fed. C.A.).

215 (1890), 24 Q.B.D. 742 (C.A.). Compare also a contract which provided for the distribution of an insolvent's property in a manner which ran counter to insolvency legislation: *Br. Eagle Int. Airlines Ltd. v. Air France*, [1975] 2 All E.R. 390 (H.L.).

216 [1947] 2 W.W.R. 358 (Man. K.B.); affirmed [1948] 1 W.W.R. 385 (Man. C.A.).

217 Above, note 214.

218 [1936] 4 D.L.R. 52 (N.S.C.A.).

219 Above, p. 374. But note the possible exception of legal agreements to pay contingency fees.

or completion of proceedings to prosecute someone accused of a criminal offence, even if the one who agrees not to prosecute, or to refrain from continuation with the proceedings, obtains no financial or other gain, such agreement will be void. No action may be brought upon it, nor may it be used by way of a defence in any proceedings. As was said by Walsh J. in *Johnson v. Musselman*[220]

> [i]t is the agreement not to prosecute at which the law baulks, and once the fact of such an agreement having been made is established there is an end to any liability founded upon or arising out of it.

Whether a promise not to prosecute is express or implied in the agreement, such agreement will be made for an illegal consideration. Hence, in *People's Bank v. Johnson*[221] a bond given by a father-in-law was not binding on him, since it was given for an illegal consideration, namely, the undertaking to compound a felony.[222]

The offence which is not going to be prosecuted in consequence of the agreement must be one that is of a public nature.[223] This was the basis of the division of the court in *Johnson v. Musselman*.[224] A promissory note was given in consideration of an agreement to stifle criminal proceedings for wilfully killing a horse which was the property of another. It was held by a majority of the court that this involved a public offence, not merely a private trespass, and the note was unenforceable, except by a transferee in due course who had given value. The contrast was drawn between this kind of case and a compromise of a civil suit, or the settlement of other, non-public offences. The suggestion has been made that the distinction depends upon whether a civil remedy is given in respect of the wrong done, which might lead to valid compromise.[225] But many crimes also amount to torts for which there may be a remedy in damages, yet the public nature of the wrong is unaffected. In *Jones v. Merionethshire Permanent Benefit Building Society*,[226] the offence was obtaining money or credit by false pretenses, the damage resulting from which being certainly remediable by civil action, yet the agreement not to prosecute in return for the money taken was unenforceable. This was followed in *Hawkes v. Waugh*,[227] the facts being somewhat similar. Even where the offence was only of a quasi-criminal nature, namely a breach of the provisions of the Customs Act, and the agreement involved the provision of evidence *for* the prosecution of an accused (the amount to be paid to the plaintiff being dependent

---

220 (1917), 37 D.L.R. 162 at 163 (Alta. C.A.). But if pressure were brought to bear on one party to agree, this could result in securities given under such agreement being recoverable at the suit of the party thus compelled to agree: *Steinberg v. Cohen*, [1930] 2 D.L.R. 916 (Ont. C.A.); compare *Erwin v. Snelgrove*, [1927] 4 D.L.R. 1028 (Ont. C.A.).

221 (1892), 20 S.C.R. 541 (S.C.C.).

222 *Ibid.*, at 543 *per* Ritchie C.J.

223 *Keir v. Leeman* (1846), 9 Q.B. 371, 115 E.R. 1315.

224 Above, note 220.

225 *Keir v. Leeman*, note 223; *Flower v. Sadler* (1882), 10 Q.B.D. 572 (C.A.).

226 [1892] 1 Ch. 173 (C.A.). But this will not follow if there has been undue influence: compare *Williams v. Bayley* (1866), L.R. 1 H.L. 200 (H.L.); *Burris v. Rhind* (1898), 29 S.C.R. 498 (S.C.C.); *Fairweather v. McCullough* (1918), 43 O.L.R. 299 (Ont. C.A.).

227 [1948] 3 D.L.R. 397 (N.B.C.A.).

upon the length of the accused's eventual prison sentence), it was held that the agreement was unenforceable and void as against public policy.[228] If this case is to be followed, it would seem that any agreement not to prosecute might be invalid. It was suggested in *Fuller v. Stoltze*[229] that there is a distinction between a legitimate compromise of a claim and a compromise produced as a result of a threat to prosecute for misfeasance, for example, in the handling of a company's affairs. The plaintiff succeeded in having the agreement overthrown in that case on the ground of compulsion, the parties therefore not being *in pari delicto*.[230] But, in the Supreme Court,[231] Davis J. referred to the principle that a compromise will be valid if there is a just and *bona fide* doubt as to the existence of liability (whether criminal or civil) and there is a civil, as well as possibly criminal liability for the acts in question. This will not operate, however, where it can be shown that, in effect, what was taking place was an agreement to stifle the prosecution.[232] It seems that there may be situations in which, even though some criminal or potentially criminal conduct is involved on the part of the defendant, an agreement to pay the plaintiff money if the plaintiff does not institute or continue with criminal proceedings, may nonetheless be valid and legal.[233]

While it is clear that contracts which purport to oust the jurisdicton of the courts will be invalid as against public policy,[234] it has been suggested that such agreements are not *illegal*, but void, *i.e.*, not recognizable or enforceable by the courts.[235] In other words, if sued, a party cannot raise as a defence that the other party agreed that resort would not be had to the courts. By way of response it may be said that there seems little point, in a practical sense, in distinguishing between a void and an illegal contract for this purpose. In any event, such an agreement is invalid. But a more important distinction can, and has been drawn. This is the distinction between an agreement to oust the jurisdiction of the courts altogether, in respect of the settlement of disputes as to the law, and an agreement to leave the settlement of disputed questions of fact to another body, or to submit a dispute to arbitration. Indeed, it may be lawful to make submission to arbitration a condition precedent to approaching the courts, such that if a party does so before

---

228 *Symington v. Vancouver Breweries*, [1931] 1 W.W.R. 410 (B.C.C.A.).

229 [1938] 1 W.W.R. 241 (Sask. C.A.); affirmed, [1939] S.C.R. 235 (S.C.C.).

230 Below, pp. 431-432: compare *Steinberg v. Cohen*, above, note 220.

231 [1939] S.C.R. 235 at 243 (S.C.C.).

232 *Bow v. Pfeiffer & Gilbert*, [1924] 2 W.W.R. 1149 (Sask. C.A.).

233 *E.g. Fisher & Co. v. Apollinaris Co.* (1875), 10 Ch. App. 297, where the offence in question was under the Trade Marks Act, *i.e.*, presumably, almost a *private* offence.

234 *Lee v. Showmen's Guild of Great Britain*, [1952] 2 Q.B. 329 (C.A.); *Baker v. Jones*, [1954] 2 All E.R. 553, *Re Davstone Estate's Leases*, [1969] 2 Ch. 378. This is the reason why some agreements between separating or divorcing spouses as to payment of maintenance may be invalid, if the contract provides, as part of the consideration for the promise to pay, a promise by the wife not to resort to the courts: see *Hyman v. Hyman*, [1929] A.C. 601 (H.L.); *Bennett v. Bennett*, [1952] 1 K.B. 249 (C.A.) (which has been reversed by statute in England). But not when (a) the court is a foreign court: *Addison v. Brown*, [1954] 2 All E.R. 213; or (b) the invalid term is severable: *Goodinson v. Goodinson*, [1954] 2 Q.B. 118 (C.A.).

235 Cheshire, Fifoot and Furmston, *Law of Contracts*, 12th ed. (1991), pp. 393-395.

the arbitration, such proceedings may be stayed by the court.[236] Further, if there is a procedure for the settlement of disputed questions of fact (and even law, as long as nothing is said as to finality) by a particular domestic tribunal or set of tribunals, the courts have held that recourse to them may not be made unless and until all domestic tribunals have been applied to by the complainant and he still has a grievance, whether it be of law or interpretation of fact.[237]

(d) Contracts injurious to the state

There are other ways in which society may be harmed in its corporate sense or character besides through conduct which upsets the due administration of justice, especially criminal justice.[238] For example, transactions which involve trading in public office are obviously and justifiably illegal and void. This was carried perhaps a stage further by Meredith C.J.C.P. in Ontario (though not by the other members of the court, some of whom dissented from the actual decision) in *Carr-Harris v. Canadian General Electric Co.*[239] The plaintiff was employed on a commission basis. The contract stemmed from the belief of the employers that the plaintiff had connections with and influence upon the government in the United Kingdom, for the purpose of obtaining orders from that government for munitions to be manufactured and supplied by the employer. When the plaintiff sued for commission which had not been paid, he failed. The reasoning of the Chief Justice was that the transaction contravened public policy and was therefore illegal and void. It involved underhand activities, possibly detrimental to the well-being of Canada, as well as to the United Kingdom, a friendly state. Added to which, it might be said that there was an element of corruption, actual or intended, about the employment of the plaintiff, to the knowledge and with the intent of the employer.

The courts have always treated corrupt transactions as illegal and void. A contract which involves bribery is clearly unlawful.[240] Indeed, statute has made such activity criminal.[241] The courts appear to have enlarged the notion of bribery and corruption for the purposes of the law of contract, if not for the purposes of criminal liability. Thus, in *Vancouver v. Registrar of Vancouver Land Registration District*[242] a municipality undertook that its council would pass a particular by-law involving the exercise of discretion in order to do so. The agreement which was made in consideration of this promise or undertaking was held to be illegal as against public policy. Such a promise involved the possibility of an action against the municipality for breach of contract if the by-law were not passed. Hence, there was great inducement to pass such by-law, which tended to restrain the freedom

---

236 *Scott v. Avery* (1856), 10 E.R. 1121 (H.L.); *Czarnikow v. Roth, Schmidt & Co.*, [1922] 2 K.B. 478 (C.A.).

237 *White v. Kuzych*, [1951] A.C. 585 (P.C.).

238 Compare the idea that a contract which fettered the freedom of a municipality was against public policy: *Finney v. Twp. of McKellar* (1982), 133 D.L.R. (3d) 351 (Ont. C.A.).

239 (1921), 49 O.L.R. 351 (Ont. C.A.).

240 Compare *Insco Sarnia Ltd. v. Polysar Ltd.* (1990), 49 B.L.R. 122 (Ont. Gen. Div.).

241 Criminal Code, R.S.C. 1985, c. C-46, ss. 119-125.

242 (1955), 15 W.W.R. (N.S.) 351 (B.C.C.A.), applied in *Finney v. Twp. of McKellar*, above, note 238.

of members of the council to exercise their discretion in such matters honestly and to the best of their ability. They were officials with a public duty, and could not therefore bargain away their obligations. In coming to this conclusion the court followed the lead, with respect to the fettering of a discretion that was to be exercised in the public interest, for example, by Members of Parliament,[243] or advisers of the Crown,[244] given in earlier English authority. The doctrine is plain. Someone who is elected or appointed to act in the public interest generally cannot so bind himself as to prevent the proper exercise of his abilities or discretion in that general public or state interest. The position with respect to contracts thus resembles the general rule that applies in many fiduciary situations against permitting a conflict of duty and interest and making secret or improper profits (whether fraud in the common law sense is involved, or not).[245]

Another important illustration of contracts inimical to the best interests of the state is provided by the situation with respect to contracts made with alien enemies. A contract with a foreign person, whether a private individual or corporation, or a foreign state, is not in itself invalid. Such contracts are perfectly good, even though they might not be governed by the law of a Canadian province, but by some foreign law, either by agreement between the parties or as a consequence of the operation of the conflict of laws doctrine of "the proper law of contract".[246] However, a contract with a foreign state or sovereign might not be enforceable as against the state or sovereign.[247] Second, if the contract involves illegality by the law of the foreign state, that is, its purpose was to infringe that law, or it can only be performed by such infringement, then the contract will be illegal and void under the common law.[248] Thus, a contract to import liquor into the United States during the prohibition period was held invalid by the English Court of Appeal in *Foster v. Driscoll*,[249] a decision which was followed for much the same reasons,

---

243 *Amalgam. Society of Ry. Servants v. Osborne*, [1910] A.C. 87 (H.L.).

244 *Egerton v. Brownlow* (1853), 4 H.L. Cas. 1, 10 E.R. 359 (H.L.), in which the point was that a disposition dependent upon a person's obtaining a certain degree of nobility was invalid since it might lead to improper conduct and anti-social ambitions on his part.

245 See Fridman, *Law of Agency*, 6th ed. (1990), pp. 161-168; Fridman, *Restitution*, 2nd ed (1992), pp. 367-384; Maddaugh & McCamus, *Law of Restitution* (1990), Chap. 25.

246 Dicey-Morris, *Conflict of Laws*, 11th ed. (1987), Vol. 2, pp. 1161-1168; Morris, *The Conflict of Laws*, 3rd ed. (1984), pp. 265-282.

247 Above, p. 138.

248 See *e.g.*, *Regazzoni v. K.C. Sethia (1944) Ltd.*, [1958] A.C. 301 (H.L.). However, in *Howard v. Shirlstar Container Transport Ltd.*, [1990] 1 W.L.R. 1292 (C.A.), although the contract involved illegality under a foreign law, the defence of *ex turpi causa* was not applicable; the plaintiff's criminal act was committed to escape from imminent danger. Hence, it would not affect the public conscience to enforce the defendant's obligations: compare above, p. 371.

Nor will the illegality under the foreign law prevent an action if that illegality was not directly and proximately connected with the plaintiff's claim, *e.g.*, for indemnity under a policy of insurance as in *Euro-Diam v. Bathurst*, [1987] 2 All E.R. 113, affirmed [1988] 2 All E.R. 23 (C.A.), where the plaintiff issued a false invoice for diamonds sent to Germany, the purpose being to enable the customer to avoid payment of German customs duty (which was illegal). But see *Tinsley v. Milligan*, [1993] 3 All E.R. 65 at 76-77 (H.L.) *per* Lord Goff.

249 [1929] 1 K.B. 470 (C.A.).

COMMON-LAW ILLEGALITY   383

and in the same sort of situation by a Canadian court in *Shiesel v. Kirsch*.[250] There it was said that an improper motive did not make a contract illegal; what was important and effective was the true nature of the transaction, that is, was it intended to break the law of a friendly foreign state?[251] Third, if the state of which the other contracting party is a national becomes involved in war with Canada, the contract will be "abrogated".[252] Under this doctrine the contract becomes frustrated so far as anything unperformed is concerned.[253] Accrued rights under such a contract become suspended, so far as their enforcement is concerned, until the end of hostilities.[254] Obviously, the alien enemy, even if present in the country,[255] cannot sue in a court in Canada. If he sues in a neutral country the decision of the courts of that country cannot be enforced in any province in Canada, else assistance to the enemy might be the unfortunate, and illegal result.[256] If the Canadian citizen sues the enemy alien in a court in Canada, which could occur if the alien enemy were present in the country, judgment is possible.[257] For the purposes of all this, an enemy is defined as a person residing or carrying on business in an enemy country (which can therefore include Canadian citizens who happen to be in such territory at the outbreak of a war).[258]

(e) Contracts which involve or encourage immorality

It has long been said that a court will not enforce a contract which is *contra bonos mores*.[259] Hence, even though certain conduct is not illegal, in the sense

---

250 [1931] O.R. 41 (Ont. C.A.).

251 Hence, in *Westgate v. Harris*, [1929] 4 D.L.R. 643 (Ont. C.A.) the lease of a dock was not illegal despite the defendant's allegation that it was for the purposes of a company to import liquor illegally into the U.S.A., because there was no evidence of a violation of the law of the U.S.A. There may have been knowledge of, but there was no participation in the ultimate illegality. Compare *Harwood & Cooper v. Wilkinson*, [1930] 2 D.L.R. 199 (Ont. C.A.); affirmed [1931] S.C.R. 141 (S.C.C.), mortgagee did not know that the money was being used for an illegal purpose, namely, exporting liquor to the U.S.A. during the Prohibition era.

252 *Esposito v. Bowden* (1857), 7 E. & B. 763, 119 E.R. 1430; *Ertel Bieber & Co. v. Rio Tinto Co.*, [1918] A.C. 260 (H.L.); *Schering Ltd. v. Stockholms Enskilda Bank*, [1946] A.C. 219 (H.L.). This will be especially true if the other contracting party is the state itself or the sovereign.

253 For the doctrine of frustration see below, Chapter 16. But note the decision in *Bevan v. Bevan*, [1955] 2 Q.B. 227, as to the duty of a husband to pay sums falling due to his wife under a separation agreement, even if the wife becomes an "alien enemy".

254 *Ottoman Bank v. Jebara*, [1928] A.C. 269 (H.L.); *Arab Bank Ltd. v. Barclays Bank*, [1954] A.C. 495 (H.L.).

255 *Porter v. Freudenberg*, [1915] 1 K.B. 857 (C.A.).

256 *Lampel v. Berger* (1917), 40 O.L.R. 165 (Ont. H.C.).

257 *Porter v. Freudenberg*, above, note 255.

258 *Lampbel v. Berger*, above, note 256; *Sovfracht V/O v. Van Udens Scheepvaart En Agentuur Maatschappij*, [1943] A.C. 203 (H.L.); *Hangkam Kwingtong Woo v. Liu Lan Fong*, [1951] 2 All E.R. 567 at 571-572 (P.C.) *per* Lord Simonds. See, generally, Fridman, "Enemy Status" (1955), 4 I.C.L.Q. 613.

259 See *per* Lord Kenyon C.J. in *Girardy v. Richardson* (1793), 1 Esp. 13, 170 E.R. 265. Hence the refusal of the court in *Kijko v. Bacyzski* (1921), 51 O.L.R. 225 (Ont. C.A.) to enforce a promise made by the father of an illegitimate child to the mother for the support of the child; the child

of being contrary to the criminal law or tortious, if it is inherently immoral then a contract to promote or further such conduct will be illegal and void.

For the most part, contracts of this kind are contracts which relate to sexual misconduct, even where such behaviour is not inherently criminal. If a contract also involves criminality, for example, a contract to undertake the seduction of a girl under the lawful age of consent, it will be invalid as being against the criminal law. Contracts involving sexual immorality have been held to be illegal and invalid without this criminal element. On this basis, the courts in the past refused to enforce contracts relating to future cohabitation between parties who were not married. So in *Prokop v. Kohut*[260] the plaintiff sought to claim a half interest in the estate of the deceased on the basis of an agreement between them that they would live together as man and wife. The terms of the agreement were that the plaintiff would perform services for the deceased, and in return he would leave her such half interest in his will. The claim failed on the ground that, at best, it was an illegal contract. A very different attitude was shown by Kindred J. at first instance in *Chrispen v. Topham*[261] with regard to a similar written agreement between an unmarried man and woman. Present day social acceptance of common law living countered the argument that the agreement was made for an immoral purpose and therefore illegal and unenforceable. Hence, the woman was bound by her agreement and liable for a debt arising from her share of the cost of utilities.

This change in judicial attitudes and by statute may make it unnecessary for a party to rely on older cases in which, despite the previously considered immoral cohabitation between the parties, a successful contractual claim was made, as long as the plaintiff did not have to rely upon the cohabitation and the agreement in respect thereof in order to establish a cause of action.[262]

There are other indications in recent case law that older ideas of morality may be outmoded.[263] The fact that parties were living together without being married will not of itself deprive a woman of any rights to property that may have been acquired by the joint efforts of the parties. If such a right can be derived from an express or implied contract, without the claimant having to plead or rely upon the cohabitation as the basis of such contract, the claimant will succeed on that contract. There is an implicit recognition in the cases that the length of the

---

was born while the mother was still living with her husband. *Quaere*: would this decision be the same today?

260 (1965), 54 D.L.R. (2d) 717 (B.C.S.C.).

261 (1986), 28 D.L.R. (4th) 754 (Sask. Q.B.); affirmed (1987), 39 D.L.R. (4th) 637 (Sask. C.A.), on other grounds. The woman was entitled to a counterclaim for compensation based on an oral collateral agreement; compare below, p. 462. See also the legalization of such agreements under the Ontario Family Law Act, R.S.O. 1990, c. F.3, ss. 53, 54.

262 *E.g., Baker v. Balderston*, [1936] 4 D.L.R. 439 (Man. K.B.); reversed [1937] 1 D.L.R. 736 (*sub nom. B. v. B.*) (Man. C.A.); *Kutsenko v. Wasilenko* (1959), 19 D.L.R. (2d) 665 (Sask. C.A.); *Stanley v. Stanley* (1960), 30 W.W.R. 686 (Alta. S.C.); (1960), 39 W.W.R. 640 (Alta. C.A.); *Spurgeon v. Aasen* (1965), 52 W.W.R. 641 (B.C.S.C.); *Niederberger v. Mamnook* (1981), 130 D.L.R. (3d) 353 (B.C.S.C.). Compare *Greasley v. Cooke*, [1980] 3 All E.R. 710 (C.A.), involving the application of proprietary estoppel despite the fact that the plaintiff had cohabited with the previous owner of the house she was claiming.

263 Compare Dwyer, "Immoral Contracts" (1977), 93 L.Q.R. 386.

relationship is important.[264] It shows that what was involved was not just a temporary sexual liaison, but a long-standing connection akin to a marriage. However, in many instances the claimant's rights may depend on the law of trusts, or, as more recently revealed, the law of unjust enrichment or restitution.[265] There seems to be a greater acceptance today of the concept of sharing as between those cohabiting as if they were spouses, in the same way as statutory change has given enlarged rights in matrimonial property to wives, even though the legal owner of the property in issue may be the husband.

However, a distinction would still appear to be drawn between more permanent relationships between men and women and those which involve merely temporary arrangements. Even though sometimes a more permanent relationship can give rise to a contractual liability, or more usually to rights arising under the law of trusts or restitution, a temporary relationship will not. Thus, any agreement for sexual intercourse outside matrimony is bad at common law, even if the intercourse is not forbidden by the criminal law, for example, on grounds of age. The law appears to go further, however, and to strike down contracts which, while not themselves designed to provide for such intercourse, do enable a party to participate therein. While prostitution may not be illegal *per se*, a contract which enables a woman to ply the trade of prostitute, for example, by providing her with premises or equipment necessary for her trade, may be invalid on the grounds of illegality since it is entered into for an immoral purpose. Much will depend upon the extent to which the contracting party seeking to enforce the contract against the prostitute can be said to be involved in her immoral trade by such contract. In *Miller v. Wall*,[266] which was concerned with the effects of a loan for gaming, not a contract with a prostitute, it appears to have been held that knowledge of the immorality or illegality to be effected by the loan suffered to make the loan invalid. In coming to this conclusion, the Court followed the English case of *Pearce v. Brooks*,[267] which illustrates this point very well. The plaintiffs supplied the defendant with a coach of a new and intriguing design. The defendant was a prostitute and intended to use the coach to attract men for business purposes. One of the two plaintiffs knew that she was a prostitute, but there was no evidence that either knew of her intentions with respect to the coach. The jury found that the plaintiffs were aware of her design. On that basis, judgment was given for the defendant in an action to recover money due under the contract. This was upheld on appeal.

Thus, the moment there is participation, through knowledge and the assistance provided by the contract, in the immoral purpose or intentions of a contracting party, the contract will be invalid and illegal as being against public policy. Perhaps

---

264 *Niederberger v. Memnook*, above, note 259, at 358.

265 *Pettkus v. Becker*, [1980] 2 S.C.R. 834 (S.C.C.); *Murray v. Roty* (1983), 41 O.R. (2d) 705 (Ont. C.A.); *Palachik v. Kiss* (1983), 146 D.L.R. (3d) 385 (S.C.C.); *Sorochan v. Sorochan* (1986), 29 D.L.R. (4th) 1 (S.C.C.); Fridman, *Restitution*, 2nd ed. (1992), at pp. 332-333; Maddaugh & McCamus, *Law of Restitution* (1990), pp. 660-670.

266 [1933] 2 W.W.R. 574 (Man. C.A.).

267 (1866), L.R. 1 Exch. 213; compare *Upfill v. Wright*, [1911] 1 K.B. 506.

the leading Canadian case in this respect is *Clark v. Hagar*.[268] A house was sold and a mortgage given in respect of the sale. In fact, the house was intended for use as a brothel. But the question whether the mortgage was void or valid depended upon the knowledge and intentions of the transferor of the property. In the circumstances of this case, it was held that the mortgage was valid, notwithstanding that the property in fact was being used for the immoral, indeed illegal purpose.

A distinction must therefore be drawn between the intentions of one party (which may be to act immorally in consequence of the contract) and the common or mutual intentions of the parties. Only if the latter correspond and there is knowledge and actual or presumed intention to promote an immoral act or immoral conduct, then the contract will be invalid as against public policy. Hence, the importance of the question whether the acts intended by one or both parties are inherently criminal (as well as being immoral) or merely immoral. Once the acts in question are illegal, in the sense of criminal, knowledge is irrelevant. If immorality alone is the basis for the alleged invalidity of the contract, knowledge and intent must be shown. Put succinctly, the issue is this: does the mere supply of certain goods, property or services, to a person who is immoral or is leading an immoral way of life, necessarily invalidate the contract under which the goods, etc., are supplied? The answer is: no, since, unless there are special circumstances that point to the *only* use of the goods, etc., in question being an immoral use, there is no necessary connecton between the contract of supply and the immoral conduct of the one to whom the goods, etc., are supplied. Thus, a prostitute must eat, therefore a contract to sell food to a prostitute is not of itself against public policy. It would be different, for example, if the supplier of the food knew that the food in question was to be used at an orgy where prostitution was going to take place.

(f) Contracts affecting marriage

The law is deeply concerned with the status of marriage. Hence, contracts which relate to the creation and continuance of that status have long come under the scrutiny of the common law.

Three different classes of agreements may be noted.

First, there are those which relate to marriage in the future between presently unmarried parties. A contract which prevents or prohibits a person, not currently married, from marrying in the future is invalid. A contract in restraint of marriage is contrary to the law.[269] Further, a contract under which a person undertakes, for reward, to arrange a marriage for another party, a marriage brokerage contract,

---

268 (1894), 22 S.C.R. 510 (S.C.C.); compare *Dom. Fire Ins. v. Nakata* (1915), 52 S.C.R. 294 (S.C.C.), where the insurance company knew that the premises were used as a bawdyhouse; it was so stated in the application form! The company could cancel the contract on the grounds of illegality. Note however, the dissent of Duff J. based on the decision in *Pearce v. Brooks* and the doctrine of collateral purposes.

269 *Lowe v. Peers* (1768), 4 Burr. 2225 98 E.R. 160. Note, however, the provision of a statute such as the Ontario Family Law Act, R.S.O. 1990, c. F.3, Part IV, dealing with "marriage contracts" between spouses or intended spouses which relate to rights and obligations under the marriage or on separation, annulment or divorce.

is also invalid, even if the broker gives the prospective spouse a wide selection of possible mates.[270]

Second, there are contracts between currently married spouses relating to their marriage, for example, an agreement to separate or to refrain from seeking certain judicial remedies such as maintenance. While an agreement under which spouses agree immediately to separate, and which contains the terms of such separation, for example, financial arrangements, custody of the children, is valid,[271] an agreement under which spouses agree that they will separate *in the future* is against public policy, as it tends towards the disruption of matrimony.[272] A separation agreement (or an agreement made on or before divorce), under which a wife undertakes not to pursue a remedy in the courts, even if made for good consideration, namely a promise to make regular payments to the wife, is against public policy and unenforceable.

The third class of agreements consisted of promises to marry while the promisor was already married to someone else. It was held in England in two cases in 1908[273] that any such promise would be against public policy and invalid, at least where the proposed future spouse was aware of the married status of the person promising to marry him or her in the future.[274] The reason for this was the possibility that the promisor might thereby be induced to immorality or even crime. This was followed in Canada in *Sheehan v. Mercantile Trust Co.*,[275] in which a testator was said to have promised to marry the plaintiff when his current wife died, the promise being made during the lifetime of the present wife. It was alleged by the plaintiff that the testator had subsequently agreed to pay the plaintiff $10,000 in lieu of marriage, that is, that he had contracted to obtain release from the promise of marriage. This alleged promise was held invalid. The original promise to marry was an illegal contract, therefore release therefrom could not be consideration for the promise to pay the money in issue.[276] However, in *Fender v. St. John-Mildmay*[277] the House of Lords held that, if the promise to marry were made after the promisor had obtained a decree *nisi* of divorce, even before such decree was made absolute, then, even though he was still married to the first wife, the promise was not invalid. It did not violate the ideas of public policy, since it would not necessarily lead

---

270 *Hermann v. Charlesworth*, [1905] 2 K.B. 123 (C.A.).

271 *Wilson v. Wilson* (1848), 1 H.L. Cas. 538 (H.L.).

272 *Brodie v. Brodie*, [1917] P. 271. But see *Harrison v. Harrison*, [1910] 1 K.B. 35 for an apparent exception to this. In *Brooks v. Alker* (1975), 9 O.R. (2d) 409 (Ont. H.C.), it was argued that a contract of sale of a house, jointly owned by a husband and wife, was void and against public policy, because it might have hastened or encouraged the separation of the spouses and the breakdown of their marriage. This argument failed.

273 *Spiers v. Hunt*, [1908] 1 K.B. 720; *Wilson v. Carnley*, [1908] 1 K.B. 729 (C.A.).

274 For the situation where the party was ignorant of the marital status of the promissor, see *Shaw v. Shaw*, [1954] 2 Q.B. 429 (C.A.). For a curious case which raises the possibility of other means of enforcing a promise made by a party already married where the other party was ignorant of the prior marriage, see *Re Spears and Levy* (1974), 52 D.L.R. (3d) 146 (N.S.C.A.).

275 (1920), 52 D.L.R. 538 (C.A.).

276 Compare the illegality of the compromise agreement which was tainted by the illegality of the original, later compromised, contract in *Metlege v. Ryan* (1980), 113 D.L.R. (3d) 248 (N.S.C.A.).

277 [1938] A.C. 1 (H.L.).

to immorality; nor interefere with the matrimonial life of the promisor, such matrimonial life having come to an end for practical purposes, despite the temporary continuation of the marriage legally speaking. Consequently, no harm was done to either the married state or morality in general by giving effect to such promises of marriage. These English or Canadian authorities would seem no longer to be relevant in jurisdictions where an action for breach of promise of marriage will no longer be maintainable. Moreover, even if such an action is still possible, the changed social attitudes referred to earlier would seem to make any such agreements to marry binding, no matter when made, *i.e.*, before, during or after divorce proceedings to terminate a previous marriage.

(g) Contracts in restraint of trade

(i) *The development of the doctrine*

The doctrine of restraint of trade purports to be derived from the notion of public policy, in that it is in the interests of society that men should be free to trade or to employ their skill and labour as they feel fit, and should not be inhibited from doing so by any agreement to the contrary.[278] In modern times, it has undergone considerable change from the doctrine as it emerged in the early part of the eighteenth century in *Mitchel v. Reynolds*.[279] Fundamentally, however, the justification of the courts' interference with contracts, otherwise freely entered into, that have the effect of restricting a party's future use of his time, skill, and expertise, is still that society will suffer. Admittedly, there are situations in which other interests, namely those of the contracting parties, can be permitted to outweigh any possible interests of society. The courts seem to be striking a balance between conflicting interests. On the one hand is the collective need or desire of society as a whole, the public, that men should be free to go and live as they please, not made into slaves of any degree or sort,[280] and that men should be able to benefit the state and the people generally by their talents and labour. On the other hand, is the individual desire for protection or regulation of potential competition, and the desire of some for legitimate immediate advantages that can only be achieved by the surrender of other future ones. These, too, are ends or aims which, in themselves, are not necessarily contrary to law or to public policy. What we see in operation in the law relating to contracts or covenants in restraint of trade is not so much public policy in it fullest sense, in the sense of a doctrine that protects society from transactions which offend against its vital interests and would, if unchecked, possibly lead to the destruction or breakdown of society. The public policy that substantiates and purports to justify the doctrine of restraint of trade, is something different; it is a doctrine that seeks to rationalize and harmonize the conflicting

---

278 See the speeches in *Nordenfelt v. Maxim Nordenfelt Guns & Ammunition Co.*, [1894] A.C. 535 (H.L.); *A.G. of Australia v. Adelaide S.S. Co.*, [1913] A.C. 781 (P.C.); *Mason v. Provident Clothing & Supply Co.*, [1913] A.C. 724 (H.L.); *Herbert Morris Ltd. v. Saxelby*, [1916] 1 A.C. 688 (H.L.).

279 (1711), P. Wms. 181, 24 E.R. 347.

280 Compare *Horwood v. Millar's Timber & Trading Co.*, [1917] 1 K.B. 305 (C.A.), which virtually involved a kind of slavery.

interests of the parties. However, the public interest must also be satisfied before a contract in restraint of trade will be accepted.[281]

A contract, or covenant, in restraint of trade is one by which a party restricts his future freedom to act in relation to his trade, business or profession.[282] He thereby limits what he may do, how he may carry on his business or professional life, where or with whom he may transact such business or profession, or under what conditions. By such an agreement, therefore, he curtails his liberty in a particular way. It is clear that any curtailment which goes beyond what might be called the "remunerative" aspects of a man's life, and affects his whole personal behaviour, may be invalid on the grounds that it is, or is tantamount to a voluntary assumption of slavery, which is contrary to common law.[283] But, in its earliest beginnings the common law of contract went further than attacking personal slavery, and struck down agreements which restricted a man's "business" freedom. Indeed, Lord Hodson in the *Esso Petroleum* case[284] believed that this had its origin in Magna Carta.

The basis for this dislike of such agreements was twofold. On the one hand was the belief in personal freedom and the right of every man to act as he pleased, as long as he acted lawfully. On the other hand, particularly in the time of Elizabeth I, there was the dislike of "monopolies", by which one person could control a trade, business or profession, either generally or in a particular locality. Certain monopolies may have been permitted or accepted on grounds of public policy, for example, the monopoly of the legal or medical professions (since it was in the public interest that standards be maintained and this could best be done by special organizations of these professionals). Others might have been allowed by the Crown, again for the public interest. But, in general, they were not favoured. The first inroads into this were made in 1711 in the case of *Mitchel v. Reynolds*.[285] It became realized and accepted that even in the public interest some restraints were necessary. The two situations in respect of which some alleviation of the strict doctrine was recognized were: (1) where the purchaser of a business sought to protect himself against future competition by the seller of the business in the same locality and; (2) where a master whose apprentice or servant left his service might have utilized secrets or processes discovered while in the course of the prior

---

281 *Esso Petroleum Co. v. Harper's Garage (Stourport) Ltd.*, [1968] A.C. 269 (H.L.); below, pp. 402-407; *Stephens v. Gulf Oil Can. Ltd.* (1974), 3 O.R. (2d) 241 (Ont. H.C.); reversed (1975), 11 O.R. (2d) 129 (Ont. C.A.); leave to appeal to S.C.C. refused (1976), 11 O.R. (2d) 129n (S.C.C.) without affecting the point discussed in the text; *Tank Lining Corp. v. Dunlop Industries Ltd.* (1982), 140 D.L.R. (3d) 659 (Ont. C.A.). Note that in relation to restraint of trade "illegality" does not mean "criminal": *A.G. of Australia v. Adelaide S.S. Co.*, above, note 278.

282 Compare Diplock L.J. in *Petrofina (G.B.) Ltd. v. Martin*, [1966] Ch. 146 at 180 (C.A.) (cited with approval by Lord Hodson in the *Esso Petroleum* case, above, note 281 at 317): "A contract in restraint of trade is one in which a party (the convenantor) agrees with any other party (the covenantee) to restrict his liberty in the future to carry on trade with other parties not parties to the contract . . .as he chooses."

283 *Horwood v. Millar's Timber & Trading Co.*, [1917] 1 K.B. 305 (C.A.); with which contrast *Denny's Trustee v. Denny*, [1919] 1 K.B. 583.

284 Above, note 281, at 317.

285 Above, note 279.

service and so affected his former master's business. Hence, in 1711 Lord Macclesfield accepted that a restraint might be valid and acceptable if it was proper and to prevent injury to a "fair contractor" and as long as it was *partial* and not general, that is, "not to exercise a trade throughout the kingdom." This judgment introduced certain concepts into the law of restraint, namely: the distinction between general and partial restraints; the distinction between covenants that were oppressive or injurious and those made on good consideration; the notion of reasonableness. Once a start had been made in the allowance of such covenants or contracts, it was possible for the law to develop away from the older, stricter attitude and towards a modern realization that not all restrictions on liberty are bad. However, the present law really began to take shape towards the end of the nineteenth century and the earlier years of the present one.

This modern development began with the decision of the House of Lords in *Nordenfelt v. Maxim Nordenfelt Guns & Ammunition Co.*[286] In this case, a manufacturer of guns and other war material sold his business to a company and agreed to restrain his future activities. Later the purchasing company amalgamated with another company and Nordenfelt was employed as managing director. In his contract of employment he undertook that for twenty-five years, except for the company in question, he would not carry on the business of manufacturing arms, etc., or any business competing, or liable to compete in any way with the business being carried on by the company. This really meant that Nordenfelt was agreeing not to compete anywhere in the world for the next twenty-five years. No greater example of a wide, general restraint could be imagined. It would seem that this offended against earlier principles, such as those stated by Tindal C.J. in *Horner v. Graves*,[287] when he said

> [w]hatever restraint is larger than the necessary protection of the party can be of no benefit to either, it can only be oppressive; and if oppressive, it is, in the eye of the law, unreasonable. Whatever is injurious to the interest of the public is void, on the grounds of public policy.

Yet the House of Lords held the *Nordenfelt* restraint valid, to the extent to which Nordenfelt was obliged not to compete in the gun business. The covenant which affected his ability to engage in any other business was severed from the rest of the contract and held void. The importance of the case lies in the fact that Lord Macnaghten (but not the other members of the House of Lords) stated that there was no difference between general and partial restraints; both equally depended upon whether they were reasonable. In his frequently quoted words,[288]

---

286 [1894] A.C. 535 (H.L.); for some earlier decisions which form the basis of this case see *Hinde v. Gray* (1840), 1 Man. & G. 195, 133 E.R. 302; *Whittaker v. Howe* (1841), 3 Beav. 383, 49 E.R. 150; *Ward v. Byrne* (1839), 5 M. & W. 548, 151 E.R. 232; *Leather Cloth Co. v. Lorsont* (1869), L.R. 9 Eq. 345. For an early Canadian case following the *Nordenfelt* decision, see *McCausland v. Hill* (1896), 23 O.A.R. 738 (Ont. C.A.), where the court upheld a covenant not to compete in any part of Canada as being reasonable in the interests of the parties; contrast the decision in *Ergonic Resources Inc. v. Waker* (1982), 19 Sask. R. 128 (Sask. Q.B.).

287 (1831), 7 Bing. 735 at 743.

288 Above, note 286 at 565.

[t]he public have an interest in every person's carrying on his trade freely; so has the individual. All interference with individual liberty of action in trading, and all restraints of trade themselves, if there is nothing more, are contrary to public policy, and therefore void. That is the general rule. But there are exceptions: restraints of trade and interference with individual liberty of action may be justified by the special circumstances of a particular case. It is a sufficient justification, and indeed it is the only justification, if the restriction is reasonable—reasonable, that is, in reference to the interests of the parties concerned and reasonable in reference to the interests of the public, so framed and so guarded as to afford adequate protection to the party in whose favour it is imposed, while at the same time it is in no way injurious to the public.

The statement of the law in the *Nordenfelt* case was repeated and underlined by Lord Parker of Waddington speaking for the Privy Council in *Attorney General of Australia v. Adelaide Steamship Co.*[289] Further development, however, occurred in two subsequent House of Lords decisions.[290] In the first, *Mason v. Provident Clothing & Supply Co.*,[291] it was held that Lord Macnaghten was correct: that there was no distinction between general and partial restraints. Either could be void if it offended against the notions of reasonableness. In the second, *Herbert Morris Ltd. v. Saxelby*,[292] the House, taking up the suggestion in the earlier case, held firmly and decisively what had been undecided before, that there was a distinction between a contract which restrained the competition of a vendor of a business (which will increase the alienability of the good-will of the business, that is, make it more valuable) and a contract which prevents competition by an ex-employee or apprentice. In these cases, therefore, which stemmed from the decision in the *Nordenfelt* case, the framework of the modern law was stated. Modern Canadian cases have indicated that the law applicable in Canada stems from, and is to be found in, these decisions, and others which follow them.[293]

From the various cases the judicial idea of restraint of trade may be derived. The basic principles are conveniently summarized in the speech of Lord Parker of Waddington in *Herbert Morris Ltd. v. Saxelby*.[294] They enshrine the elements of the doctrine of restraint of trade, and they have been restated and applied many times since then, in Canada as well as England:

(1) All restraints of trade themselves are contrary to public policy and therefore void[295] if there is nothing more.[296]

---

289 [1913] A.C. 781 (P.C.).

290 See also *North Western Salt Co. v. Electrolytic Alkali Co.*, [1914] A.C. 461 (H.L.).

291 [1913] A.C. 724 (H.L.).

292 [1916] 1 A.C. 688 (H.L.).

293 *Elsley v. J.G. Collins Ins. Agencies Ltd.* (1978), 83 D.L.R. (3d) 1 (S.C.C.); *Doerner v. Bliss & Laughlin Indust. Inc.* (1980), 117 D.L.R. (3d) 547 (S.C.C.); *Tank Lining Corp. v. Dunlop Indust. Ltd.* (1983), 140 D.L.R. (3d) 659 (Ont. C.A.).

294 [1916] 1 A.C. 688 at 706-707 (H.L.). See the comprehensive discussion of these principles and the elements of liability by Puddester J. in *Reed Stenhouse Ltd. v. Learning* (1990), 87 Nfld. & P.E.I.R. 271 at 300-318 (Nfld. T.D.).

295 For the view that contracts in restraint of trade are not valid or invalid *per se* and *ab initio* but are "unenforceable", see *Shell U.K. Ltd. v. Lostock Garage Ltd.*, [1977] 1 All E.R. 481 (C.A.) *per* Lord Denning M.R. The idea that such contracts could change their character depending on the way the circumstances changed, was regarded by Bridge L.J. as "a complete novelty in law":

(2) The onus of proving special circumstances is on the party alleging them, that is, endeavouring to uphold the restraint.[297]

(3) Such facts, when proved, leave it as a matter of law whether they do or do not justify the restraint.

(4) For a restraint to be valid: (i) it must be reasonable in the interests of the contracting parties; and (ii) it must be reasonable in the interests of the public.

(5) To be reasonable in the interests of the parties the restraint must afford adequate protection to the party in whose favour it is imposed.

(6) To be reasonable in the interests of the public it must in no way be injurious to the public.

(7) The two interests are quite distinct and must be investigated and determined independently.

The doctrine requires a four-stage inquiry. First, is the covenant under review in restraint of trade? Second, is the restraint one that is against public policy and therefore void? Third, can the restraint be justified as reasonable in the interests of the parties? Fourth, can it also be justified as reasonable with reference to the interests of the public?[298] But covenants in restraint of trade must not be examined in a disembodied manner, as if they were some strange scientific specimen under microscopic scrutiny. The validity, or otherwise, of a covenant of this kind can be determined only upon an overall assessment of the covenant, the agreement in which it is found, and all of the surroundings circumstances.[299]

(ii) *The primary instances of restraint of trade*

(A) *Introduction* The two classic situations which raised the problems that are set out above, with which most cases were concerned until recent times, were those of the sale of a business and the attempt in a contract of employment to regulate the after-termination conduct of the employee. As the cases reveal, while the principles applying to these cases were the same, some slight difference of emphasis may be seen in operation between them. In the words of Dysart J. of the Supreme Court of Canada in *Maguire v. Northland Drug Co.*[300]

---

ibid., at p. 493. See further Fridman, "Some Polemical Thoughts on the Subject of Restraint of Trade" (1978), 2 Can. J. of Bus. L. 303. The views of Lord Denning cannot be regarded as consistent with the established principles. Compare *Cradle Pictures (Can.) Ltd. v. Penner (No. 2)* (1977), 34 C.P.R. (2d) 34 at 50 (Ont. H.C.).

296 *E.g.*, if the restraint is coupled with a mortgage or lease of new property: *Stephens v. Gulf Oil Can. Ltd.* (1975), 65 D.L.R. (3d) 193 (Ont. C.A.); leave to appeal to S.C.C. refused (1976), 65 D.L.R. (3d) 193n (S.C.C.); below, pp. 412-414.

297 Compare *Petrofina Can. Ltd. v. Gionet* (1973), 9 N.B.R. (2d) 65 at 70 (N.B.Q.B.) *per* Barry J.

298 *Tank Lining Corp. v. Dunlop Indust. Ltd.* (1982), 140 D.L.R. (3d) 659 at 663-664 (Ont. C.A.) *per* Blair J.A.; *Barsman v. Deloitte Haskins & Sells of Can. Ltd.* (1984), 4 D.L.R. (4th) 558 at 561 (Ont. H.C.).

299 *Elsley v. J.G. Collins Ins. Agencies Ltd.*, [1978] 2 S.C.R. 916 at 923-924 (S.C.C.) *per* Dickson J.

300 [1935] S.C.R. 412 at 416 (S.C.C.); compare *Deacons v. Bridge*, [1984] 2 All E.R. 19 at 22 (P.C.) *per* Lord Fraser.

[p]ublic policy, as interpreted by the courts, requires on the one hand that employers be left free to protect from violation their proprietary rights in business, and on the other hand, that every man be left free to use to his advantage, his skill and knowledge in trade. In the weighing and balancing of these opposing rights, the whole problem in cases of covenants in restraint of trade is to be found. Less latitude is allowed in the enforcement of restrictions as between employer and employee than as between vendor and purchaser of good will.

In these two instances, however, it was accepted that a measure of interference with freedom of trade was not within the field of restraint, as long as the degree of interference did not exceed the accepted standard.[301] The burden of establishing that, while reasonable between the parties, the covenant is against the public interest or injurious to the public, is on the covenantor, the one undertaking the restraint.[302] So far as the situation between the parties is concerned, a restraint will not be reasonable unless it provides no more than what is adequate for the protection of the covenantee. He must show his need for protection and that the protection provided by the covenant is no wider than is necessary.[303]

There are a number of policies or principles that affect the operation of the doctrine, which are as follows: (1) the basic desire of the law to protect individual freedom and avoid restraints; (2) the public interest in freedom of action by owners of businesses, employers, and employees; (3) the notion that contracts freely entered into without fraud, duress, etc., should be upheld and not destroyed by the courts at will; (4) the recognition that proprietary interests can and should be protected by the law, to the extent of permitting a party to achieve this by a covenant that is in restraint; (5) the elucidation of what are proprietary interests capable and worthy of being protected; (6) the dislike of the courts for covenants which are simply designed to prevent competition, that is, which are purely and simply monopolistic in character.

(B) *Reasonableness as between the parties*

(I) Employer-employee cases: In *Elsley v. J.G. Collins Insurance Agencies Ltd.*,[304] Dickson J. formulated several questions that were to be asked when assessing the

---

301 *Deacons v. Bridge*, [1984] 2 All E.R. 19 at 21 (P.C.) *per* Lord Fraser. This case was concerned with *partners*, and the situation did not conform to either of the types of referred to in the text, though it had some resemblance to both; compare *Baker v. Lintott* (1981), 117 D.L.R. (3d) 465 (Alta. Q.B.), reversed, [1982] 4 W.W.R. 766 (Alta. C.A.); *Bassman v. Deloitte, Haskins & Sells of Can.* (1984), 44 O.R. (2d) 329 (Ont. H.C.); *Ernst & Young v. Stuart* (1993), 79 B.C.L.R. (2d) 70 (B.C.S.C.).

302 *Tank Lining* case, above, note 298 at 665. Reasonable depends on the circumstances at the time the contract is made, including the parties' expectations of what might happen in the future: *ibid.*

303 *Lock v. Nelson & Harvey Ltd.; Nelson & Harvey Ltd. v. Lock* (1959), 33 C.P.R. 138 (B.C.S.C.); *Friesen v. McKague* (1993), 96 D.L.R. (4th) 341 at 345 (Man. C.A.); *Rapid-Med Plus Franchise Corp. v. Elliott* (1991), 73 Man. R. (2d) 150 (Man. C.A.). Preventing competition *per se* is not sufficient reason: *Vancouver Malt & Sake Brewing Co. v. Vancouver Breweries Ltd.*, [1934] A.C. 181 (P.C.). Compare *Dyform Enrg. Ltd. v. Ittup Hollowcore Int. Ltd.* (1983), 19 B.L.R. 1 (B.C.S.C.), with *Culzean Inventions Ltd. v. Midwestern Broom Co.* (1984), 31 Sask. R. 180 (Sask. Q.B.), both of which concerned agreements relating to *patents*.

304 (1978), 83 D.L.R. (3d) 1 at 7 (S.C.C.).

reasonableness of a clause which attempted to restrain an ex-employee after he left the employment governed by the covenant in restraint of trade.

(a) Did the employer have a proprietary interest entitled to protection? Such an interest might consist of trade secrets or processes developed by the employer.[305] It could relate to the names of customers who dealt with the employer during the currency of the employment.[306] But it would not go so far as to include potential customers or clientele.[307] Nor could it comprehend methods of work, production, or management that were not capable of being considered in any way private to the employer, or specially developed by him.[308] (b) Were the temporal or spatial features of the covenant in restraint too broad? As will be seen, many decisions have turned on the time within which the restraint was to operate, or the area within which it was to be effective, rather than upon the inherent nature of the restraint having regard to the business the employer was endeavouring to protect.[309] (c) Was the covenant against competition generally, and not limited to proscribing solicitation of clients of the former employer? Although, normally, only existing customers could be shielded from subsequent solicitation by the ex-employee, there might be circumstances where the interests of the employer were such that it would not be unreasonable to extend the protection to which he was legitimately entitled to other, future, potential customers. "Whether a restriction is reasonably required

---

305 *E.g.*, the mail-order business in *Littlewoods Organisation Ltd. v. Harris*, [1978] 1 All E.R. 1026 (C.A.). The interest to be protected must exist at the time the contract is made: *Chicago Blower Corp. v. 141209 Can. Ltd.*, [1989] 6 W.W.R. 210 (Man. Q.B.), applying *Tank Lining Corp. v. Dunlop Industries Ltd.* (1982), 140 D.L.R. (3d) 659 (Ont. C.A.).

306 *W.R. Grace & Co. of Can. v. Sare* (1980), 28 O.R. (2d) 612 (Ont. H.C.); *Western Inventory Service Ltd. v. Sager* (1983), 42 O.R. (2d) 166 (Ont. H.C.); *Western Inventory Service Ltd. v. Flatt* (1979), 9 B.C.L.R. 282 (B.C.S.C.); compare *Deacons v. Bridge*, [1984] 2 All E.R. 19 (P.C.); *Deloitte, Haskins & Sells v. Brooker* (1982), 20 B.L.R. 252 (Sask. Q.B.); *J.L.R. Hldgs. Ltd. v. Wiseberg* (1977), 79 D.L.R. (3d) 305 (Ont. H.C.); affirmed (1978), 92 D.L.R. (3d) 416 (Ont. C.A.); *Reed Stenhouse Ltd. v. Learning*, above, note 294; *Sunsweet Fundraisers Inc. v. Moldenhauer* (1991), 98 Sask. R. 81 (Sask. Q.B.); *Friesen v. McKague*, above, note 303; or the environment in a restaurant resulting from the reputation of a musician who performed there and attracted customers: *Nili Hldgs. Ltd. v. Rose* (1981), 123 D.L.R. (3d) 454 (B.C.S.C.).

307 *Creditel of Can. Ltd. v. Faultless* (1977), 81 D.L.R. (3d) 567 (Ont. H.C.); *Craig Agency of Ont. Ltd. v. Bennett* (1977), 74 D.L.R. (3d) 562 (Ont. H.C.). Nor *former* customers of whom the ex-employee would be ignorant: *Bassman v. Deloitte, Haskins & Sells of Can.* (1984), 44 O.R. (2d) 329 (Ont. H.C.). Compare *Ernst & Young v. Stuart*, above, note 301.

308 *Arvak Mgmt. Inc. v. McKee* (1983), 40 Nfld. & P.E.I.R. 116 (Nfld. T.D.); *Cradle Pictures (Can.) Ltd. v. Penner (No. 2)* (1977), 34 C.P.R. (2d) 34 (Ont. H.C.). Compare *Dyform Enrg. Ltd. v. Ittup Hollowcore Int. Ltd.* (1983), 19 B.L.R. 1 (B.C.S.C.), with which compare *Culzean Inventions Ltd. v. Midwestern Broom Co. Ltd.* (1984), 31 Sask. R. 180 (Sask. Q.B.).

309 Compare *Maxwell v. Gibsons Drugs Ltd.* (1979), 16 B.C.L.R. 97 (B.C.S.C.); *Ergonic Resources Inc. v. Waker* (1982), 19 Sask. R. 128 (Sask. Q.B.) with *Mezaros v. Barnes*, [1977] 2 W.W.R. 376 (Man. Q.B.); *Baker v. Lintott*, [1981] 2 W.W.R. 385 (Alta. Q.B.); reversed, [1982] 4 W.W.R. 766 (Alta. C.A.); *Big Iron Drilling Ltd. v. Standard Hldgs. Ltd.*, [1981] 1 W.W.R. 599 (Sask. Q.B.). See also *Nelson Burns & Co. v. Gratham Industries Ltd.* (1983), 150 D.L.R. (3d) 692 (Ont. H.C.); affirmed (1986), 30 D.L.R. (4th) 158 (Ont. C.A.); leave to appeal to S.C.C. refused (1986), 72 N.R. 364 (S.C.C.); *Can. American Financial Corp. (Can.) v. King* (1989), 60 D.L.R. (4th) 293 (B.C.C.A.); *Rapid-Med. Plus Franchise Corp. v. Elliott*, above, note 303.

for the protection of the covenantee," said Dickson J.[310] "can only be decided by considering the nature of the covenantee's business and the nature and character of the employment." To protect the employer's proprietary interest it may be necessary to prevent the ex-employee from establishing his own business or working for others so as to be likely to appropriate the employer's trade connection through his acquaintance with the employer's customers.[311] Since the parties may be unequal, a covenant in restraint of trade may be oppressive to the employee. It will be acceptable, however, when its purpose is not to prohibit the employee from exploiting the skills he has acquired during the employment, but to protect the former employer against competition where the scope and and nature of the employee's work and and his contact with clients and customers of his former employer is such that he could readily do harm to his employer.[312]

Not surprisingly, in cases involving employers and employees the courts have been most strict in their application of the doctrine, and, in particular, the idea of reasonableness as between the parties. In the early cases of *Mason* and *Morris*, the House of Lords struck down covenants by an ex-canvasser who agreed not to act for similar firms within 25 miles of London for three years after the termination of his service with his employers, and by an ex-draughtsman employed in the manufacturing and sale of lifting machinery when he agreed not to engage in competition.

Canadian courts have not been slow to follow these examples and apply them to fact-situations before them. The actual decision has depended upon whether the restraint in question was too wide in terms of physical or geographical extent, too broad in terms of the kind of competition that was involved, or too long in its intended duration. Thus, in *New Method Cleaners & Launderers Ltd. v. Hartley*[313] the defendant was employed by the plaintiffs who had a business in Winnipeg. The covenant in the contract of employment purported to prevent the defendant, after his employment with the plaintiffs, from trading in a similar business in *Manitoba*. This was held to be too wide. The question was whether the defendant's employment was of such a nature as to warrant such a wide covenant to protect the plaintiffs.[314] The mere fact that the defendant had contact with customers of the plaintiffs was not enough to justify such a wide restraint.[315] Similarly, in *Rapid-*

---

310 Above, note 304.

311 *Berthe v. Greggor*, [1983] 2 W.W.R. 515 (Man. Q.B.); *Acadia Forest Products Ltd. v. Neal Forest Products Ltd.* (1983), 48 N.B.R. (2d) 429 (N.B.Q.B.). Contrast *Investors Syndicate Ltd. v. Versatile Invts. Ltd.* (1982), 126 D.L.R. (3d) 451 (Ont. H.C.); reversed in part on other grounds (1983), 149 D.L.R. (3d) 46 (Ont. C.A.).

312 *Doerner v. Bliss & Laughlin Indust. Ltd.* (1980), 117 D.L.R. (3d) 547 at 552 (S.C.C.).

313 [1939] 1 D.L.R. 711 (Man. C.A.). Compare *Kelly v. McLaughlin* (1911), 1 W.W.R. 309 (Man. C.A.); *Hall v. More*, [1928] 1 W.W.R. 400 (B.C.C.A.) (where *severance* was possible); *Maxwell v. Gibsons Drugs Ltd.* (1979), 16 B.C.L.R. 97 (B.C.S.C.), where the area of the restraint, 25 miles, was too wide and was reduced: *Cradle Pictures (Can.) Ltd. v. Penner (No. 2)* (1977), 34 C.P.R. (2d) 34 (Ont. H.C.).

314 [1939] 1 D.L.R. 711 at 717 (Man. C.A.) *per* Richards J.A.

315 *Ibid.*, at 718.

Med Plus Franchise Corp. v. Elliott,[316] a restraint was supposed to apply, to Manitoba and elsewhere, for three years after the employee left the employment. The restraint was reasonable only in respect of its application to Manitoba. A covenant not to engage in similar work for two years after the termination of the defendant's employment by the plaintiff within Canada or Bermuda was also too excessive and unreasonable in *Canadian American Financial Corp. (Canada) Ltd. v. King*.[317] A restraint that extended to the employee's "territory", after he ceased being an employee, was too wide, as there was no clear definition of the "territory".[318] But a covenant restricted in scope to Ontario, and in time by reference to customers for whom the employee had performed services within the preceding 12 months was not unreasonable and could be enforced.[319] So was a covenant restricting the appellant from practising veterinarian medicine for three years within a 25-mile radius of Steinbach, Manitoba upheld as being reasonable having regard to the direct personal relationships made by the appellant with customers consequent upon the appellant's employment by the respondent.[320]

Sometimes scope and length of duration have combined to make the restraint invalid. In the *Maguire* case,[321] the defendant entered into a bond that he would not compete by setting up in business or working for himself within 25 miles of Flin Flon for 25 years. It was held by the Supreme Court, reversing the Manitoba Court of Appeal, that there was consideration for the bond, in the promise to employ or continue to employ the defendant, but that the consideration, namely the covenant in restraint was unreasonable and unenforceable. Dysart J., relying on earlier English and Canadian authorities, made it plain that an employer by such a covenant could only protect his property,[322] such as trade secrets, or possibly information about customers.[323] Bare competition could never be prevented.[324] Nor could an employer

---

316 Above, note 303.

317 Above, note 309; nor was severance possible: below, pp. 420-424.

318 *W.R. Grace & Co. of Can. Ltd. v. Sare* (1980), 28 O.R. (2d) 612 (Ont. H.C.).

319 *Western Inventory Service Ltd. v. Sager* (1983), 42 O.R. (2d) 166 (Ont. H.C.); compare *Mezaros v. Barnes*, [1977] 2 W.W.R. 376 (Man. Q.B.).

320 *Friesen v. McKague* (1993), 96 D.L.R. (4th) 341 (Man. C.A.); compare *Sunsweet Fundraisers Inc. v. Moldenhauer* (1991), 98 Sask. R. 81 (Sask. Q.B.) (duration of two years for a limited distance).

321 Above, note 300. See also *Can. Fur Auction Sales Co. v. Neely*, [1954] 2 D.L.R. 154 (Man. C.A.). Contrast *K.M.A. Caterers Ltd. v. Howie*, [1969] 1 O.R. 131 (Ont. C.A.), where the restraint would only apply, under the terms of a collective agreement, if the employment was terminated for just cause, but the restraint was only for one year; compare *Reed Stenhouse Ltd. v. Learning* (1990), 87 Nfld. & P.E.I.R. 271 (Nfld. T.D.).

322 Hence the decision in *City Dray Co. v. Scott*, [1950] 2 W.W.R. 913 (Man. K.B.). *Note* in respect of this case: (1) at the time of the agreement the employee was no longer an employee of the plaintiff in whose favour the contract was intended (would this mean there was no consideration?); (2) it concerned the payment of a *pension* as to which compare *Taylor v. McQuilkin* (1968), 2 D.L.R. (3d) 463 (Man. Q.B.); *Bull v. Pitney-Bowes Ltd.*, [1966] 3 All E.R. 384. See below, p. 403.

323 Compare the cases cited above in note 306; contrast *Arvak Mgmt. Inc. v. McKee* (1983), 40 Nfld. & P.E.I.R. 116 (Nfld. T.D.), where the employer established no proprietary interests which required protection from the ex-employee; and *Craig Agency of Ont. Ltd. v. Bennett* (1977), 74 D.L.R. (3d) 562 (Ont. H.C.).

324 Hence, the decision against the covenant in *Sherk v. Horwitz*, [1972] 2 O.R. 451 (Ont. H.C.); affirmed on other grounds, [1973] 1 O.R. 360 (Ont. C.A.); leave to appeal to S.C.C. refused (1972), 9

control or restrict the use and enjoyment of an employee's skill, even if that skill had been obtained while working for the employer. Such skill was the employee's property.[325]

Thus, where there are no trade secrets which come into the possession of the employee during his employment, the employer can hardly argue that it is reasonable to prevent the employee from later setting up in competition or working for another firm. This is particularly true when customers' names are the issue. Sometimes the names of customers are not considered to be trade secrets. Such was the case with respect to such names and the methods of performing janitorial services in *American Building Maintenance Co. v. Shandley*.[326] What appears to be relevant with respect to customers' names is whether the employee made personal contact with such customers during his employment.[327] Thus, where a covenant prohibited an ex-employee from dealing with customers of the employer for whom the employee had performed personal services within twelve months prior to his leaving the employment, the covenant was not unreasonable.[328] But it was unreasonable to prohibit the employee from dealing with customers who had gone to the employer prior to the employee's employment,[329] or from dealing with potential customers.[330] Knowledge about customers with whom the employee has dealt may be considered confidential information, capable of being protected,[331] whereas knowledge of other customers is much more in the "general domain", such that the employer cannot prevent the employee from utilizing it in the future.

Another relevant consideration is whether the employee is being restrained from acting in *any* capacity whatsoever or simply in capacities or businesses which

---

C.P.R. (2d) 119n (S.C.C.). Compare *Investors Syndicate Ltd. v. Versatile Invts. Ltd.* (1981), 126 D.L.R. (3d) 451 (Ont. H.C.); reversed in part on other grounds (1983), 149 D.L.R. (3d) 46 (Ont. C.A.).

325 Compare with respect to an employment or personnel agency, *Drake Int. Ltd. v. Miller* (1975), 9 O.R. (2d) 652 (Ont. H.C.) with *Mgmt. Recruiters of Toronto Ltd. v. Bagg*, [1971] 1 O.R. 502 (Ont. H.C.) and *Computer Centre Personnel Ltd. v. Lagopoulos* (1975), 8 O.R. (2d) 480 (Ont. H.C.).

326 (1966), 57 W.W.R. 133 (B.C.C.A.). Compare *Fisher v. Rosenberg* (1960), 67 Man. R. 336 (Man. Q.B.); see also *Nor. Messenger (Calgary) Ltd. v. Frost* (1966), 56 W.W.R. 412 (Alta. S.C.); *Nor. Messenger & Transfer Ltd. v. Fabbro* (1964), 49 W.W.R. 115 (Man. Q.B.).

327 *Elsley v. J.G. Collins Ins. Agencies Ltd.* (1978), 83 D.L.R. (3d) 1 (S.C.C.); *Cradle Pictures (Can.) Ltd. v. Penner (No. 2)* (1977), 34 C.P.R. (2d) 34 (Ont. H.C.); *Friesen v. McKague*, above, note 320. Compare *Reed Stenhouse Ltd. v. Learning*, above, note 321, where the ex-employee took one of his former customers with him when he left the covenantee's employment. Compare the issuance of an injunction to prevent an ex-employee from contracting with former customers of the employer in *John Michael Design plc. v. Cooke*, [1987] 2 All E.R. 332 (C.A.).

328 *Western Inventory Service Ltd. v. Sager* (1983), 42 O.R. (2d) 166 (Ont. H.C.); compare, as to solicitation of customers of the covenantee, *Sunsweet Fundraisers Inc. v. Moldenhauer*, above, note 320.

329 *Bassman v. Deloitte, Haskins & Sells of Can.* (1984), 44 O.R. (2d) 329 (Ont. H.C.); *Ernst & Young v. Stuart* (1993), 79 B.C.L.R. (2d) 70 (B.C.S.C.).

330 *Creditel of Can. Ltd. v. Faultless* (1977), 81 D.L.R. (3d) 567 (Ont. H.C.); *Cradle Pictures (Can.) Ltd. v. Penner (No. 2)*, above, note 327.

331 *Commercial Plastics Ltd. v. Vincent*, [1965] 1 Q.B. 623 (C.A.). On this basis see *Gestetner (Can.) Ltd. v. Henderson*, [1948] 2 W.W.R. 84 (Alta. C.A.): *Nelsons Laundries Ltd. v. Manning* (1965), 51 W.W.R. 493 (B.C.S.C.).

do, or might legitimately compete with that of the employer. Thus, in *T.S. Taylor Machinery Co. v. Biggar*,[332] a sales manager covenanted: (i) not to work in any capacity for any of his employer's principals or other firms with which the employer *had negotiated* to act as agent (though not employed as such); (ii) not to carry on any similar business to that of the employer for five years after termination of the employment. This was held to be unreasonable and invalid. The question to be asked, in the words of Dickson J.A. (as he then was),[333] was whether the restraint was excessive as regards area, time of operation, and scope. On this basis the restraint was held bad in *Portage Mobilehome Co. v. Challenger Home Builders Ltd.*,[334] where a salesmanager agreed not to sell mobile houses or compete with his employer within 100 miles of Portage La Prairie, where the employers were located, for three years after leaving the employment. This was too wide in area, and covered too much by way of activity to protect the employers within reason. A similar answer was given in respect of a restriction on a franchisee, prohibited from competing in respect of any other area in whch he could have been granted a franchise as well as in the current authorized location of the franchise.[335] But a franchisee in Saskatchewan could be precluded from competition in the same business within Saskatchewan,[336] or within Manitoba.[337] Even if a restraint may not be too wide in terms of time, it may cover too much in terms of the scope of the activity prohibited, as shown by *Gibbons v. Drew Chemical Ltd.*,[338] where the employee was prevented from working for another employer (but only for a year) for the purpose of selling a product sold by the employee while in the first employer's employment. It was held that this could not stop the employee working for a company whose products were not the same as those of the first employer.

Sometimes where the need for protection is established and the methods adopted relate clearly to such protection, a restraint will be reasonable and therefore valid. This will turn upon the scope and content, in area, time, and type of activity of the restraint. In other words the converse situation will emerge: that the employer has a protectable interest, whether it be termed proprietary or otherwise, and that the protection involved in the restraint is reasonable and not too excessive. Thus, in *Lock v. Nelson & Harvey Ltd.; Nelson & Harvey Ltd. v. Lock*,[339] the employee

---

332 (1968), 2 D.L.R. (3d) 281 (Man. C.A.); compare as to too great a scope, *Acorn Products (Can.) Ltd. v. Adler* (1973), 10 C.P.R. (2d) 162 (Ont. H.C.); compare also *Gledhow Autoparts Ltd. v. Delaney*, [1965] 3 All E.R. 288 (C.A.).

333 (1968), 2 D.L.R. (3d) 281 at 289 (Man. C.A.).

334 (1972), 29 D.L.R. (3d) 191 (Man. C.A.). Contrast *Whitehorse Lounge Ltd. v. Bennett* (1984), 51 Nfld. & P.E.I.R. 91 (Nfld. T.D.), agreement not to compete within ten miles for ten years, the sale of the business occurring in a small town, was *not* in restraint of trade.

335 *Ergonic Resources Inc. v. Waker* (1982), 19 Sask. R. 128 (Sask. Q.B.).

336 *Big Iron Drilling Ltd. v. Standard Hldgs. Ltd.*, [1981] 1 W.W.R. 599 (Sask. Q.B.).

337 *Rapid-Med Plus Franchise Corp. v. Elliott* (1991), 73 Man. R. (2d) 150 (Man. C.A.).

338 (1972), 8 C.P.R. (2d) 105 (B.C.S.C.).

339 (1959), 33 C.P.R. 138 (B.C.S.C.); compare *Reliance Cordage Co. v. Hetterly* (1969), 5 D.L.R. (3d) 297 (Sask. Q.B.). Compare *Baker v. Lintott* (1981), 117 D.L.R. (3d) 465 (Alta. Q.B.); reversed [1982] 4 W.W.R. 766 (Alta. C.A.), where the covenant was reasonable as between the parties, but not in the public interest; compare *Deacons v. Bridge*, [1984] 2 All E.R. 19 (P.C.). Both these cases involved partners, not employers and employees, but the principles would seem to be the same.

was the manager of the local office of the employers. He agreed that for two years after the termination of his employment he would not solicit customers of his employers known to him during his employment, and that he would not directly or indirectly engage in a rival business within 30 miles of the local office. In this instance it was held that the restraint was reasonable. Similarly, a restraint which covered employment in all the Atlantic provinces was too wide, but it could be made good by severing Newfoundland from the scope of the covenant, since, in other respects, namely the length of the covenant's duration, two years, it was reasonable as between the parties.[340] The same happened in *Garbutt Business College Ltd. v. Henderson*,[341] in which the restraint was valid in respect of time, namely, five years,[342] and place, namely, Calgary, but had to be severed in relation to the scope of the activity covered by the restraint. In cases such as this, the prime consideration is the need to protect the employer from unreasonable exposure to competition from the ex-employee. As it was put in *Jiffy Foods Ltd. v. Chomski*,[343] is the ex-employee guilty of a flagrant breach of a voluntary covenant which was legitimately designed to protect the employer?

As between employer and employee, a restraint unlimited as to time may be reasonable.[344] As long as the restraint is restricted in other ways, a restraint may be reasonable even if it is very broad as to the area within which the employee may pursue the activity in the future.[345] But an employer may not be able to achieve the same result by a contract which guarantees an ex-employee a pension in return for a covenant against future competition.[346] Nor will an employer evade the doctrine by containing his restraint not in a contract with the employee but with another *employer*. This was attempted in *Kores Manufacturing Co. v. Kolok Manufacturing Co.*,[347] where two employers agreed that neither would employ an ex-employee

---

340 *E.P. Chester Ltd. v. Mastorkis* (1968), 70 D.L.R. (2d) 133 (N.S.C.A.); compare *Can. Linen Co. v. Mole*, [1938] 1 W.W.R. 491 (B.C.C.A.); *Greening Indust. Ltd. v. Penny* (1965), 53 D.L.R. (2d) 643 (N.S.S.C.); *Carruthers Clinic Ltd. v. Herdman*, [1956] O.R. 770 (Ont. H.C.). But the attempt to get a restrictive covenant expressed in terms of Canada and Bermuda to apply only to British Columbia and Alberta failed in *Can. American Financial Corp. (Can.) Ltd. v. King* (1989), 60 D.L.R. (4th) 293 (B.C.C.A.).

341 [1939] 3 W.W.R. 257 (Alta. C.A.).

342 Compare *Nor. Messenger (1965) Ltd. v. Cartney* (1971), 4 C.P.R. (2d) 80 (Alta. T.D.), as to a restraint valid in terms of its duration.

343 [1973] 3 O.R. 955 (Ont. Div. Ct.), applied in *J.L.R. Hldgs. Ltd. v. Wiseberg* (1977), 79 D.L.R. (3d) 305 (Ont. H.C.); affirmed (1978), 92 D.L.R. (3d) 416 (Ont. C.A.), where the employee was held in breach of an implied term in the contract of employment.

344 *Fitch v. Dewes*, [1921] 2 A.C. 158 (H.L.).

345 Compare *Connors Bros. v. Connors*, [1941] 3 W.W.R. 666 (P.C.), a case of sale of a business, but the principle seemed the same.

346 *Bull v. Pitney-Bowes Ltd.*, [1966] 3 All E.R. 384, following, but distinguishing *Wyatt v. Kreglinger & Fernau*, [1933] 1 K.B. 793 (C.A.). Compare *Furlong v. Burns & Co.*, [1964] 2 O.R. 3 (Ont. H.C.); *Taylor v. McQuilkin* (1968), 2 D.L.R. (3d) 463 (Man. Q.B.); *City Dray Co. v. Scott*, [1950] 2 W.W.R. 913 (Man. K.B.).

347 [1959] Ch. 108 (C.A.). Contrast the strange case of *Hivac v. Park Royal Scientific Instruments Ltd.*, [1946] 1 Ch. 169 (C.A.), in which *employees* were restrained from working at night for another employer, even though no trade secrets were being disclosed; cited with approval in *State Vacuum Stores of Can. Ltd. v. Phillips*, [1954] 3 D.L.R. 621 (B.C.C.A.).

of the other when such employee had been employed by the other during the previous five years. It was held by the English Court of Appeal that this was unreasonable as between the parties; it was not necessary to protect either party's trade secrets or confidential information.

(II) Vendor and purchaser cases: The courts are more disposed to uphold covenants in restraint of trade as between a party who is selling a business, including its goodwill,[348] and the purchaser of such business. The courts have long recognized the greater need of the new owner to protect himself against potential future competition from the previous owner, who may be in an excellent position, by virtue of his long experience, his years in the business, his contacts, and his knowledge of methods and people, to render nugatory the intended benefit to be obtained by the purchaser from the sale of the business. As Lord Wilberforce pointed out in the *Esso Petroleum Case*,[349] it was established in 1620 that, on the sale of the goodwill of a business, a promise might validly be given not to carry on the relevant trade, and general recognition was given to this type of covenant in 1711. So the rule has become accepted that, in the interest of trade itself, restrictions may be imposed upon the vendor of goodwill provided that they are fairly and properly ancillary to the sale. If they exceed this limit the "doctrine" may be applied. As long as the restraint is reasonable in the circumstances, for example, by being limited in time and place in a manner which is relevant to the type of business involved, any such covenant will be enforceable.[350] In this regard, as long as the parties are bargaining equally, they may be treated as being the best judges of their interests and of what is reasonable as between them. This was the conclusion of the court in *Dale & Co. v. Land*[351] where on the sale of the business of insurance a covenant against competition in Alberta to last for five years was upheld as being reasonable between the parties.

It has been held that a restraint to endure for the vendor's lifetime is reasonable.[352] In *Connors Brothers Ltd. v. Connors*,[353] a restraint that was to operate over the whole of Canada, even though the vendor was situated in New Brunswick, was valid. In that case the business sold was that of a sardine canning company, and the vendor promised that he would not be directly or indirectly engaged in any other sardine business in the Dominion of Canada. In view of the fact that

---

348 Hence the importance of the purchase of the goodwill of the business stressed by the Supreme Court of Canada in *Doerner v. Bliss & Laughlin Indust. Inc.* (1980), 117 D.L.R. (3d) 547 at 553 (S.C.C.).

349 [1968] A.C. 269 at 335 (H.L.).

350 See, *e.g., Fluorescent Sales & Services Ltd. v. Bastien* (1958), 39 W.W.R. 659 (Alta. C.A.); *Hecke v. Cie de Gestion Maskoutaine Ltd.*, [1972] S.C.R. 22 (S.C.C.); *Bard Tpt. Ltd. v. Bard* (1978), 23 N.B.R. (2d) 304 (N.B.Q.B.); contrast, *Pellow v. Ivey* (1933), 49 T.L.R. 422; *Goldsoll v. Goldman*, [1915] 1 Ch. 292 (C.A.); *Reed Shaw Osler Ltd. v. Wilson* (1981), 17 Alta. L.R. (2d) 81 (Alta. C.A.), where the clause in restraint went even further than that in *Stenhouse Australia Ltd. v. Phillips*, [1974] A.C. 391 (P.C.).

351 (1987), 56 Alta. L.R. (2d) 107 (Alta. C.A.), applying the *Tank Lining Corp.* case, below, note 354.

352 *Cope v. Harasimo* (1964), 50 W.W.R. 639 (B.C.C.A.).

353 [1941] 3 W.W.R. 666 (P.C.).

the operations of the purchasing company were more extensive than the province of New Brunswick, and the possibilities for intervention that could arise if the convenantor were not limited in the way prescribed by the contract, the restraint was reasonable as between the parties. This was hardly a surprising decision in light of the actual resolution of the problem in the *Nordenfelt* case.

Similarly, in *Tank Lining Corporation v. Dunlop Industrial Ltd.*,[354] a clause preventing a party from engaging in the business of lining tank cars in Canada for two years after the termination of the agreement was upheld as reasonable in the interests of the parties (as well as being reasonable in the interests of the public). Under the agreement the plaintiff licensed the defendant the use of its processes, trade secrets and "know-how" with respect to the business of lining or relining railway tank cars to protect them from corrosion from chemical cargoes. The defendant's objection was that the clause was wider than was necessary for the protection of the plaintiff's interests, since it prohibited the defendant from doing business in all of Canada, when, before and after termination of the agreement, the great bulk of the work was done for tank car owners and lessees in Ontario and Quebec. Very little business was done in western or Atlantic provinces and no orders were ever taken from Alberta, Newfoundland or Prince Edward Island. However, the evidence revealed that, when the agreement was made, the parties expected to serve the whole Canadian chemical industry, throughout the country, and this was a reasonable expectation. Hence, this case differed from the usual sale of an existing business confined to all small area, in which instances a purchaser could not enforce a non-competition clause covering a much wider area. The purpose of the restraint clause was to protect the plaintiff against the very event that happened: the exploitation of its trade secrets by the defendant without compensation. By the same agreement, however, the defendant was protected against the exploitation of its efforts in creating a Canadian market if the plaintiff had attempted to carry on the business, contrary to the clause which precluded *both* of them from engaging in the business for two years after the agreement was determined.

On the other hand there are decisions which reveal the limits of this more liberal attitude. Thus, there must be some interest of the purchaser to protect by the restraint. In *Newhook v. Elson*,[355] the facts were as follows. There was a sale of a taxi business. The vendor convenanted not to operate a taxi business in the town in question, Gander, or within 15 miles for a period of 25 years, except for *one* taxi. It was held that this covenant was void and could not bind the former owner of the business who now wished to set up a new undertaking. In the circumstances of this case, bearing in mind the nature of the business that was

---

354 (1982), 140 D.L.R. (2d) 659 (Ont. C.A.). Compare the validity of a world-wide convenant to protect a patentee, limited to operate for eight years, in *Dyform Enrg. Ltd. v. Ittup Hollowcore Int. Ltd.* (1983), 19 B.L.R. 1 (B.C.S.C.). Contrast the invalidity of a Canada-wide prohibition imposed on a franchisee in *Ergonic Resources Inc. v. Waker* (1982), 19 Sask. R. 128 (Sask. Q.B.); see also *Can. American Financial Corp. (Can.) Ltd. v. King*, above, note 340 (invalid prohibition against competition throughout Canada and in Bermuda.
355 (1959), 44 M.P.R. 258 (Nfld. S.C.).

being sold, the locality, and the time period stated in the contract, there was no goodwill that was being sold and that needed protection once it was transferred to the buyer of the business. It was only a means of preventing competition from the ex-owner of the taxi business.

Second, there must be a genuine sale, a proper transaction, not something colourable. In *Vancouver Malt & Sake Brewing Co. v. Vancouver Breweries Ltd.*,[356] a covenant contained in the sale of the goodwill of a brewer's licence under which the sellers were restricted for 15 years from brewing beer was held invalid. The sellers in fact never brewed beer, although their licence was for such manufacture. They made sake, for the Japanese in Vancouver. Consequently, they were not selling their business of beer brewing; they had none. They were not even selling their sake brewing business; since the right to brew sake was excepted from the restraint. What was involved was an agreement not to compete in the manufacture of beer for the contractual period. It was a bare covenant against competition, not a sale of business. Moreover, it was unreasonable as between the parties because it purported to be unrestricted as to area of operation, even though the licence that was being "sold" was a licence for Vancouver City only.

Third, despite the more lenient attitude adopted by courts when dealing with the sale of a business, covenants in restraint of trade given by the vendor will be strictly construed. Thus, in *Chamberlain v. Parsons*,[357] the covenant was against "[setting] up a business" after the vendor had sold to the purchaser. It was held that this was not infringed when the vendor did electrical work, with which the business sold was concerned, out of his own home. He was not setting up in business: he was "[carrying] on business." This was not prohibited by the covenant.[358]

Thus, even though there may be less need to preserve the liberty of action of a vendor of a business, such leniency on the part of the law will not go to the extent of overlooking what is in reality a concealed attempt to stifle competition. Covenants of that sort really offend the basic notion and purpose of the doctrine of restraint of trade. In a sense, it might be said, such covenants are objectionable more because they are unreasonable in relation to the public interest than because they are unreasonable as between the parties. Indeed, they may be perfectly reasonable as between the parties. This leads to the question of what is meant by unreasonable in the public interest, and just how important such unreasonableness is.

(C) *Unreasonableness as respects the public interest* The public interest was stressed in the early leading cases. Yet frequently, in both English and Canadian cases, the determination of the validity of a restraint was made on the basis that it was reasonable or unreasonable as between the parties. The question of public interest was seldom to the fore. Although the difference was drawn between the

---

356 [1934] A.C. 181 (P.C.).

357 (1978), 91 D.L.R. (3d) 590 (N.S.C.A.).

358 Hence, restraints that are "uncertain" or "too vague" will not be regarded as reasonable and enforceable: compare *Reed Shaw Osler Ltd. v. Wilson* (1981), 17 Alta. L.R. (2d) 81 (Alta. C.A.); *Ergonic Resources Inc. v. Waker* (1982), 19 Sask. R. 128 (Sask. Q.B.).

two types of "reasonableness", greater emphasis was placed upon the situation as between the parties; if that were satisfactory the restraint was probably acceptable.[359]

Some cases promoted the notion of "reasonableness in the public interest", and discussed the validity of a restraint in such terms.[360] Occasionally the results of a court's interpretation of the idea of "reasonableness in the public interest" were susceptible to criticism. An example of this is the English case of *Wyatt v. Kreglinger & Fernau*.[361] There a pension scheme was struck down because it involved an undertaking by the pensioner not to enter the trade in question again after retirement, which was considered to be a restraint of trade and against the public interest. This was followed in England,[362] and in Canada.[363] But the view in Canada would seem to be that the restraint in issue was invalid because it was unreasonable as regards the parties. In *Taylor v. McQuilkin*,[364] a clause under which a pension payable to a retired member of the company could be suspended if the retired member in the course of subsequent employment acted to the prejudice of the company, was void as in unreasonable restraint of trade. The reasoning of Matas J. makes it clear that this decision was based upon the lack of any proprietary interest to be protected, and the unlikelihood that the ex-employee would use confidential information. Despite the arguments put forward against the proposition that pension schemes of the "Wyatt" kind are void as against the public interest, any agreement which hinders a man, even if after retirement, from using his time and skill as he wishes, and to achieve something which might benefit the public, generally offends against the accepted principles of the restraint doctrine. However, the invalidity of such restraint is preferably to be determined from the point of view of the individual's interest rather than those of the public generally. Appeals to "public interest" in such cases may be suspect. At the very least, such an approach may mislead or open up avenues of development that could finish in strange conclusions.

Although this attitude may have appealed to judges in the decades following the *Nordenfelt* case, it now seems to be inappropriate. Such is the conclusion to be drawn from the *Esso Petroleum* case.[365] Indeed, it was suggested there that at

---

359 Contrast the view expressed by Blair J.A. in *Tank Lining Corp. v. Dunlop Indust. Ltd.* (1982), 140 D.L.R. (3d) 659 at 668-669 (Ont. C.A.) that Canadian courts took a different view, because of the criminal law prohibition of combines in restraint of trade in 1889.

360 See, *e.g., Great Eastern Oil & Import Co. v. Chafe* (1956), 4 D.L.R. (2d) 310 (Nfld. S.C.) (though this may be because the facts in that case took it into another, newer, category of restraint, as to which see below); *Reliance Cordage Co. v. Hetterly* (1969), 5 D.L.R. (3d) 297 (Sask. Q.B.), in which Bence C.J.Q.B. relied heavily upon statements in earlier cases as to the concept of public policy and the need for a covenant in restraint to be consistent with the interest of the public; *Financial Credit Bureau Services Ltd. v. Credit Bureau of Gloucester Ltd.* (1975), 10 N.B.R. (2d) 249 (N.B.S.C.); affirmed (1975), 11 N.B.R. (2d) 570 (N.B.C.A.).

361 [1933] 1 K.B. 793 (C.A.).

362 *Bull v. Pitney-Bowes Ltd.*, [1966] 3 All E.R. 384.

363 *Furlong v. Burns & Co.*, [1964] 2 O.R. 3 (Ont. H.C.); *Taylor v. McQuilkin* (1968), 2 D.L.R. (3d) 463 (Man. Q.B.).

364 Above, note 363.

365 [1968] A.C. 269 (H.L.).

least one case decided on the basis of unreasonableness between the parties[366] should have been disposed of on the ground of the arrangement being against the public interest. In the judgment of the Ontario Court of Appeal in *Stephens v. Gulf Oil Canada Ltd.*,[367] reference was made to the second limb of the *Nordenfelt* test, that is, the concept of reasonableness in the public interest. The second limb was equally important and could be determinative of a case, and the onus was on the plaintiff, seeking to uphold a restraint, rather than on the defendant, seeking to defeat. With respect to the content of the test, Lord Pearce in the *Esso Petroleum* case[368] had suggested that the two tests of reasonableness were really only one, namely, is it in the interests of the community that this restraint should, as between the parties, be held to be reasonable and enforceable? The Ontario Court of Appeal preferred the approach of Ungoed-Thomas J. in *Texaco Ltd. v. Mulberry Filling Station Ltd.* According to this,[369]

> in applying the second limb of the Nordenfelt test of reasonableness, one has to consider whether the restrictions were reasonable in reference to the interests of the public as expressed in one or more propositions of law, rather than in reference to the interests of the public at large.[370]

The proposition of law which emerged in this case was

> the right of men to trade freely, subject to reasonable restraints which are in keeping with the contemporary organization of trade.

It was recognized, however, that other propositions of law might emerge in the future in the wider aspect of the public interest, either as a result of a public inquiry authorized by statute, or a detailed judicial inquiry.

In the *Stephens* case, it was argued against the validity of the *solus* agreement that it was injurious in relation to the interests of the public, in the light of the evidence, by reason of the impairment of the dynamic operation of the competitive market as a result of the surrender by the individual entrepreneur on an industry-wide basis of his ability to exercise his competitive initiative. To the Court of Appeal, this could not be concluded. Nor could the injurious character of the agreement be inferred or deduced without much more complete evidence as to the economic and social benefits and detriments of *solus* agreements. This case, therefore, seems to state that just because freedom of trade is restrained does not make a contract to such effect against the reasonable interests of the public. The public is not necessarily injuriously affected by such agreements. If, as a matter of public,

---

366 *Kores Mfg. Co. v. Kolok Mfg. Ltd.*, [1958] 2 All E.R. 65 (C.A.); above, p. 399.
367 (1976), 11 O.R. (2d) 129 (Ont. C.A.); leave to appeal to S.C.C. refused (1976), 11 O.R. (2d) 129n (S.C.C.) (reversing the original decision of Henry J. on the ground that the restraint was not unreasonable as between the parties); below, pp. 412-414. See also the judgment of Puddester J. in *Reed Stenhouse Ltd. v. Learning* (1990), 87 Nfld. & P.E.I.R. 271 at 300-318 (Nfld. T.D.).
368 Above, note 365, at 324.
369 [1972] 1 All E.R. 513.
370 Above, note 367, at 149.

statutory resolution,[371] or judicial decision, it can be said in relation to any particular situation that it imports harm to the public at large to contract for a restraint, such a covenant will be bad. Restraint may be both valid and in the public interest. Restraint *per se* is not invalid: only such restraints as are proved to be injurious will be so.

The reasoning of the Ontario Court of Appeal in the *Stephens* case is by no means decisive. Stress was placed upon the element of reasonableness in the public interest, which was once again brought to the fore, after having been reduced in importance by earlier decisions, as a result of the language of the House of Lords in the *Esso Petroleum* case. At the same time, however, the Ontario Court of Appeal appears to have suggested that the element of reasonableness in the public interest can be harmonized successfully with the notion of reasonableness as between the parties, so as to lessen the effect of the public interest aspect. To adopt such a view reduces the thrust of the remarks in the *Esso Petroleum* case and the *Stephens* case with regard to the requirement that a restraint, to be valid and enforceable, must also be reasonable in the public interest.

Recent cases have re-affirmed the importance of this element of public interest. In *Baker v. Lintott*,[372] for example, a covenant between a physician and his partners that he would not compete within 25 miles of Medicine Hat for two years after voluntarily leaving the partnership was originally held to be against the public interest in that it unduly restricted the access of the public to the physician's medical services. This was reversed on appeal; the effect of the covenant was not to impose an unreasonable restriction on the community's choice of doctors. Similarly, in *Elsley v. J.G. Collins Insurance Agencies Ltd.*,[373] where the employee was precluded from competing as an insurance agent against the employer for five years after the termination of the employment in certain specified places in the County of Welland, the Supreme Court of Canada held that this was not unreasonably against the public interest. There was nothing in the evidence to suggest that the people of Niagara Falls would suffer through the loss, for a limited period, of the services of the employee in the general insurance business.[374] Nor was the covenant against competition extracted from the vendor of a business in *Doerner v. Bliss & Laughlin*

---

371 See the Competition Act, R.S.C. 1985, c. C-34, s. 35; but see *Culzean Inventions Ltd. v. Midwestern Broom Co.* (1984), 31 Sask. R. 180 (Sask. Q.B.), where an agreement for the payment of royalty on a patent after the expiration of the patent was not a covenant in restraint of trade, nor was it an attempt to create a monopoly contrary to the Combines Investigation Act [now the Competition Act].

372 (1981), 117 D.L.R. (3d) 465 (Alta. Q.B.); reversed on appeal, [1982] 4 W.W.R. 776 (Alta. C.A.); compare *Maxwell v. Gibsons Drugs Ltd.* (1979), 16 B.C.L.R. 97 (B.C.S.C.); compare also *Dyform Enrg. Ltd. v. Ittup Hollowcore Int. Ltd.* (1982), 19 B.L.R. 1 (B.C.S.C.). Contrast with the *Baker* case the earlier decision in *Sherk v. Horwitz* (1972), 25 D.L.R. (3d) 675 (Ont. H.C.); affirmed on other grounds (1973), 31 D.L.R. (3d) 152 (Ont. C.A.); leave to appeal to S.C.C. refused (1972), 9 C.P.R. (2d) 119n (S.C.C.), where a similar kind of covenant, for five years, was held invalid on the basis of a change in the attitude of public policy from 1952 (when *Mills v. Gill*, [1952] 3 D.L.R. 27 (Ont. H.C.) was decided), in consequence of the creation of the Ontario Health Scheme and other developments in Ontario. See also *Deacons v. Bridge*, [1984] 2 All E.R. 19 at 25 (P.C.).

373 (1978), 83 D.L.R. (3d) 1 (S.C.C.).

374 *Ibid.*, at 9.

Industries Ltd.[375] against the public interest. The covenantor argued that after taking control of the business that was involved the purchasers followed policies which were corrupt, monopolistic, and generally contrary to public policy. These general and some more specific allegations were not made out to the satisfaction of the court at the trial. The Supreme Court would not interfere with those findings of fact.[376] Hence, there were no bases upon which to found a holding that the public interest was affected by the covenant. In any event, it was added,[377] the monopoly, that was said to have resulted from the sale of the business, existed prior to the sale. It had been created by the vendors themselves, and they could not be heard to say subsequently that their creation was evil and contrary to public policy.

The most comprehensive discussion of this matter is to be found in the judgment of the Ontario Court of Appeal in *Tank Lining Corporation v. Dunlop Industrial Ltd.*[378] As noted previously, it was held that the restraint in that case was reasonable as between the parties.[379] It became necessary for the court to consider the second limb or branch of Lord Macnaghten's test in the *Nordenfelt* case.[380] Various matters were made clear. First of all, the broad issues of public policy which determine whether a restraint is *prima facie* void are not to be confused with the more detailed considerations of the public interest which might justify it.[381] Second, the suggestion by Lord Pearce in the *Esso Petroleum* case that the two tests of reasonableness were really one had been rejected not only by the Ontario Court of Appeal in the *Stephens* case, as already seen,[382] but by the Supreme Court of Canada in the *Elsley*[383] and *Doerner* cases.[384] "The considerations relevant to the interests of the parties and of the public are separate and distinct and this has become more apparent in recent years. The dual test in the doctrine recognizes that the assertion of a private right can create a public wrong." Next, even if a covenant did not contravene the Combines Investigation Act (and now the Competition Act[385]) it might still be unreasonable in the public interest. Finally, the court addressed the question raised also in the *Stephens* case, whether the public interest had to be expressed in propositions of law. The court was not able to arrive at any definite conclusion on this, nor was it required to do so, since the covenantor was not able to demonstrate any injury to the public from the mutual exchange of promises in this case not to engage in the business in question for the period stated in the contract.

---

375 (1980), 117 D.L.R. (3d) 547 (S.C.C.).
376 *Ibid.*, at 553-554.
377 *Ibid.*, at 555.
378 (1982), 140 D.L.R. (3d) 659 (Ont. C.A.); followed and applied in *Dale & Co. v. Land* (1987), 56 Alta. L.R. (2d) 107 (Alta. C.A.); *Chicago Blower Corp. v. 141209 Can. Ltd.*, [1989] 6 W.W.R. 210 (Man. Q.B.).
379 Above, p. 401.
380 Above, p. 391.
381 Above, note 378, at 670.
382 Above, p. 404.
383 Above, note 378 at 671.
384 *Ibid.*, at 671-672.
385 R.S.C. 1985, c. C-34.

However, it was pointed out by the court[386] that to restrict the doctrine to a proposition of law such as that set out in the *Texaco* case,[387] namely, to economic and social effects that in some fashion have acquired the status of legal dogmas, might result in the doctrine losing its utility as a valuable instrument for adjusting this branch of the law to changing economic and social conditions. For example, a reciprocal restrictive covenant, of the kind in this case, might produce economic and social effects demonstrably harmful to the public interest. The cessation of business might deprive the nation or a region of an essential industry, an important source of wealth and employment, or vital technology. This would make it hard to ignore those effects as regards the public interest even though they might not be included in "those expressed in propositions of law which tend to be concerned with abhorrence of monopoly or the advancement of freedom to trade and competition".[388] Thus, the view of the Ontario Court of Appeal now appears to be that the doctrine of public interest in relation to restraints of trade should be left as open and flexible as possible, lest it become too curtailed, or too identified with static principles of law, economics, or social policy, and thus be rendered incapable of coping with new variations on some ancient themes. This would seem to be a reasonable attitude for the courts to adopt, even though it may leave the resolution of specific instances of restraint unclear, unless and until they have been litigated.

(iii) *Other instances of restraint of trade*

(A) *Introductory* "It is much too late now," said Lord Reid in the *Esso Petroleum* case,[389] "to say that this rather anomalous doctrine of restraint of trade can be confined to the two classes of case to which it was originally applied." But he went on to add that the cases outside those two classes gave little guidance as to the circumstances in which it should be applied. Lord Wilberforce[390] referred to the fact that the courts are not lacking in tools which

> enable them to select from the whole range of those contracts, which in one way or another limit freedom in trading, segments of current and recognisably normal contracts which are not currently liable to be subjected to the necessity of justification by reasonableness. Such contracts may even be listed, provisionally, in categories . . . but the classification must remain fluid and the categories can never be closed.

These two statements suggest: (1) that there are other instances where the courts have invalidated, and will continue to invalidate contracts or covenants which they regard as being in restraint of trade, even where such contracts do not fall into what may be termed the "traditional" categories; and (2) they have recognized

---

386 Above, note 378, at 674.

387 *Texaco Ltd. v. Mulberry Filling Station Ltd.*, [1972] 1 All E.R. 513; above, p. 404.

388 Above, note 378, at 674.

389 [1968] A.C. 269 at 295 (H.L.).

390 *Ibid.*, at 337; cited with approval in *Tank Lining Corp. v. Dunlop Indust. Ltd.* (1982), 140 D.L.R. (3d) 659 at 664 (Ont. C.A.).

and will continue to recognize contracts which, at first sight, seem to be as equally in restraint of trade as those within the "traditional" categories, yet, for various reasons are exempted or excluded from the normal treatment of covenants or contracts in restraint. It would appear, from the speeches in the *Esso Petroleum* case, to mention no other, that the underlying notion of public interest can be utilized to achieve whatever result be desired. Furthermore, what is or is not in the public interest will depend upon the social and economic climate of the time: the various policies that are to be supported or frustrated: the kind of activity which is worthy of encouragement or deserving of curtailment.

(B) *Restraints affecting personal relations* There are decisions which indicate that the doctrine of restraint of trade can reach out to render invalid a contract which involves a party in binding himself with respect to his entire way of life, not simply his trading or business conduct. In *Horwood v. Millar's Timber & Trading Co.*,[391] a clerk who agreed with a moneylender that he would not change his employment or residence, part with property or incur obligations, legal or moral, without the assent of the moneylender, was able to have that agreement declared invalid and not binding. It had the effect of making him into virtually the slave of the moneylender. Whether this could, properly or not, be described as a covenant in restraint of trade, it was certainly an abuse of freedom of contract, and resulted in unprecedented restrictions on the liberty of the clerk in numerous ways. On the other hand, where such restrictions may be described as necessary and reasonable in the interests of the parties concerned, they would not be invalid. This occurred in *Denny's Trustee v. Denny*,[392] in which a spendthrift son agreed with his father that he would keep away from the temptations of London.

(C) *Restraints involving trade regulation* At common law, combinations amongst producers or traders, designed to control the output of a certain item, or to regulate the level of the price at which it was sold, were not *per se* illegal. Hence, a combination between such parties which had as its object, *inter alia*, the exclusion of another trader, was not a tortious conspiracy.[393] As long as the parties involved were bargaining at arms' length and on equal terms, their arrangements would probably not be attacked, since, as was said in one case,[394] the parties were the best judge of what was reasonable as between themselves; it would seem that the public interest was not so greatly emphasized in such context. Thus, an agreement to restrict the sale of a hop producer's crop to a particular association was upheld;[395] so, too, were agreements on price maintenance;[396] even a "knockout" agreement amongst bidders at an auction was acceptable and enforceable, unless prohibited by statute.[397] But even an agreement of the sort permitted in the "hop" case, could

---

391 [1917] 1 K.B. 305 (C.A.).
392 [1919] 1 K.B. 583.
393 *Mogul S.S. Co. v. McGregor, Gow & Co.*, [1892] A.C. 25 (H.L.).
394 *North Western Salt Co. v. Electrolytic Alkali Co.*, [1914] A.C. 461 at 471 (H.L.) *per* Lord Haldane.
395 *English Hop Growers v. Dering*, [1928] 2 K.B. 174 (C.A.).
396 *Dunlop Pneumatic Tyre Co. v. Selfridge & Co.*, [1915] A.C. 847 (H.L.).
397 *Rawlings v. Gen. Trading Co.*, [1921] 1 K.B. 635 (C.A.).

be invalid as being in restraint, where its terms went beyond what was reasonable to protect the legitimate interests of the association, and went too far in limiting the freedom of the individual trader.[398] In the same way, in a New Brunswick case, a convenant against competition which was against the interests of a trade association, its subscribers, and the customers of such subscribers, was held invalid as an unreasonable restraint. It is one thing to attempt to regulate trade relations. It is quite another to do so at the expense of either an individual covenantor or the public generally.[399]

Such attempts at controlling the way a particular trade, business or profession is regulated may infringe the common law, if they go beyond *either* what is reasonable in the interests of the parties *or* if they offend some other principle of the law, such as the notion that there should not be discrimination on a sexual or racial basis,[400] or the doctrine of *ultra vires* in relation to the powers of corporations.[401] They may also conflict with some statutory provision or policy, designed to promote freedom of trade and the prevention of monopolies or monopolistic control. In such circumstances they would be invalid for statutory reasons, and would only be valid if within the scope of the legislation, to the extent to which it does or might permit some element of combination.[402]

(D) *Restraints by mortgage*[403] In some situations, a restraint is attempted by means of a mortgage on property, a term of which may involve the mortgagor in fettering his freedom of action in respect of trading.[404] To quote Lord Wilberforce,

---

398 *McEllistrim v. Ballymacelligott Co-op. Agriculture & Dairy Society*, [1919] A.C. 548 (H.L.).

399 *Financial Credit Bureau Services Ltd. v. Credit Bureau of Gloucester Ltd.* (1974), 10 N.B.R. (2d) 249 (N.B.S.C.); affirmed (1975), 11 N.B.R. (2d) 570 (N.B.C.A.). Compare the decision with respect to the restraint on the cricketers in *Greig v. Insole*, [1978] 3 All E.R. 449.

400 *Nagle v. Feilden*, [1966] 2 Q.B. 633 (C.A.). Compare the invalidity of a collective agreement that infringed the provisions of the Human Rights Code with respect to discrimination on the grounds of age: *Ont. Human Rights Comm. v. Etobicoke* (1982), 40 N.R. 159 (S.C.C.); above, p. 355.

401 *Dickson v. Pharmaceutical Society of Great Britain*, [1970] A.C. 403 (H.L.). But the doctrine of restraint of trade is inapplicable in relation to membership in a voluntary association where such membership is not a pre-requisite to carrying on a business or profession: *Pimentel v. Winnipeg Real Estate Bd.* (1991), 72 Man. R. (2d) 64 (Man. Q.B.); affirmed (1992), 83 Man. R. (2d) 164 (Man. C.A.). Compare *GKO Associates Ltd. v. Parrish* (1977), 35 C.P.R. (2d) 22 (Ont. H.C.).

402 Hence, in *Trudel v. Clairol Inc.*, [1975] 2 S.C.R. 236 (S.C.C.), an agreement to control the price at which certain goods were to be resold was not invalid, since the agreement did not offend what, formerly, was the Combines Investigation Act, and was not otherwise unreasonable at common law.

403 Compare the same situation in respect of leases: *Spike v. Rocca Group Ltd.* (1980), 109 D.L.R. (3d) 89 (P.E.I. S.C.); see also *Amoco Australia Pty. Ltd.v. Rocca Bros. Motor Engr. Co. Pty.*, [1975] 1 All E.R. 968 (P.C.). But such was not the case where the lease was of a public house, and included the sale therein only the *lessor's* beer (*i.e.*, it was a "tied" house); such leases have long been held valid: *Catt v. Tourle* (1869), 4 Ch. App. 654; *Clegg v. Hands* (1890), 44 Ch. D. 503 (C.A.).

404 *Biggs v. Hoddinott*, [1898] 2 Ch. 307 (C.A.); *Bradley v. Carritt*, [1903] A.C. 253 (H.L.); *Morgan v. Jeffreys*, [1910] 1 Ch. 620: *Knightsbridge Estates Trust Ltd. v. Byrne*, [1940] A.C. 613 (H.L.); *Clark v. Supertest Petroleum Corp.* (1958), 14 D.L.R. (2d) 454 (Ont. H.C.); *Re Moore and Texaco Can. Ltd.*, [1965] 2 O.R. 253 (Ont. H.C.).

. . .as part of a transaction of mortgage, it is permissible, so far as the rules of equity are concerned, both to postpone the date of repayment and, at any rate during the period of the loan, to tie the mortgagor to purchase exclusively the products of the mortgagee . . . But just as provisions contained in a lease . . . which pass beyond what is normally found in and ancillary to this type of transaction and enter upon the field of regulation of the parties' trading activities, may fall to be tested as possible restraints of trade, so . . . may those in a mortgage. The mere designation of a transaction as a mortgage, however true, does not ipso facto protect the entire contents of the arrangements from examination, however fettering of trade these arrangements may be, if their purpose and nature is found not to be ancillary to the lending of money on security, as, for example, to make the lending more profitable or safer, but some quite independent purpose, they may and should be independently scrutinised.[405]

Such scrutiny, indeed, was necessary in the *Esso Petroleum* case itself, where the arrangements between the parties did involve mortgages. The agreement involved the owner of the garage in conforming to the requirements of the Esso Company including buying all its motor fuel from Esso. The fact that, in part at any rate, this was included in or connected with a mortgage did not take the agreement out of the purview of the doctrine of restraint of trade, by virtue of which one, though not the other agreement, was invalid.[406]

(E) *Restraints involved in distribution agreements*[407] A development that has occurred in the years since the *Nordenfelt* case has involved agreements under which a manufacturer or wholesaler supplies a distributor with his product, on condition that the distributor, that is, the trader, accepts the obligation of selling only the manufacturer's or wholesaler's product, or otherwise fetters his, the trader's, future liberty with respect to trading. Such cases are not examples of a vendor and purchaser of business, nor do they involve the relationship of master and servant. The parties are, in one sense, bargaining equally.[408] In some instances it is clear that the trader would not be engaged in the trade in question were it not for the arrangements with the manufacturer or wholesaler. Indeed the latter might be setting up the former in business, providing him with premises, as well as a product to sell, possibly at a competitive, fair, even generous price or on eminently advan-

---

405 *Esso Petroleum Co. v. Harper's Garage (Stourport)*, [1968] A.C. 269 at 342 (H.L.).

406 Compare *Shell U.K. Ltd. v. Lostock Garage Ltd.*, [1977] 1 All E.R. 481 (C.A.), where the agreement was not necessarily bad under the doctrine of restraint of trade, but was nonetheless unenforceable; *Alec Lobb (Garages) Ltd. v. Total Oil G.B. Ltd.*, [1983] 1 All E.R. 944, where the charge on the property was in the form of a lease and a lease-back, by an underlease, which contained a tie covenant that was held to be an unreasonable restraint of trade and therefore void; on appeal [1985] 1 All E.R. 303 (C.A.), the transaction was held not to be in restraint of trade by reason of the special circumstances of the case; see, *e.g., ibid.* at 315 *per* Dunn L.J.

407 These may now be dealt with by the Restrictive Trade Practices Commission under R.S.C. 1985, c. C-34, s. 39.

408 But if they are not, then different considerations may apply, see *e.g., Clifford Davis Mgmt. Ltd. v. W.E.A. Records*, [1975] 1 W.L.R. 61 (C.A.) in which an agreement to give copyrights in music written by the members of a "pop" group for a period of years was for too long a time, having regard to the inequality of bargaining power of the parties, and was therefore unenforceable against a third party accused of "infringing" such copyrights. Compare what is said about the importance of equality of bargaining in *Dale & Co. v. Land* (1987), 56 Alta. L.R. (2d) 107 (Alta. C.A.).

tageous terms. This was the situation in *Great Eastern Oil & Import Co. v. Chafe*,[409] where the defendant was set up in a service station by the plaintiff company, on favourable terms as to equipment, etc., in return for which the defendant agreed to buy only the plaintiff company's gasoline for a period of five years. It was held that this was not an invalid agreement. It was not an unreasonable restraint of trade. It did not interfere with the public interest, since there was no evidence that it produced overly high prices. It was not unreasonable as between the parties since it was to last only for five years, and it did not affect the defendant's activities as a repairman and motor mechanic.

Even without such advantages to the covenantor, an agreement of this kind was held valid in *United Shoe Machinery Co. v. Brunet*,[410] which involved a party's tying himself up to one manufacturer for 20 years under circumstances which, according to the Privy Council, did not reveal any illegal methods used to obtain the agreement. But much may depend upon the nature of the agreement in each case, as Lord Wilberforce explained in the *Esso Petroleum* case.[411] There are cases in which such agreements have been upheld[412] (like agreements under which a principal appoints someone a "sole" agent),[413] and there are instances of such agreements going beyond what was necessary, as stifling competition and being too restrictive.[414] It would seem that the test is reasonableness. But reasonable in the interests of the parties or in the public interest?

One would have thought the former. The decision in the *Esso Petroleum* case[415] suggests possibly the latter as being the true and correct basis for any such decision. In that case the House of Lords had to consider the validity of an agreement between the petroleum company and a company which was operating two garages. The agreement was one under which the company agreed to take its motor fuel exclusively from Esso; it was a "solus" agreement, which involved the "tying covenant", the price-maintenance clause, the continuity covenant and the compulsory trading covenant. There were, in fact, two agreements, relating to two separate garages owned by the garage company. One was secured by a mortgage to last five years: the other was secured by another mortgage to last for 21 years. The net effect of all these arrangements was that, under the agreements, the garage company was bound to maintain the covenants with Esso for the duration of the respective mortgages. It was, in effect, an arrangement under which the garage company was enabled to carry on business. When the cheaper petrol came on the market, the garage company wanted to stop selling Esso's petrol and deal with

---

409 (1956), 40 M.P.R. 21 (Nfld. S.C.). Compare *Hiebert v. Pac. Petroleums Ltd.* (1980), 109 D.L.R. (3d) 137 (Man. Q.B.).

410 [1909] A.C. 330 (P.C.).

411 Above, note 405, at 332-333.

412 *Bouchard Servais v. Prince's Hall Restaurants Ltd.* (1904), 20 T.L.R. 574 (C.A.); *Foley v. Classique Coaches Ltd.*, [1934] 2 K.B. 1 (C.A.).

413 *W.T. Lamb & Sons v. Goring Brick Co.*, [1932] 1 K.B. 710 (C.A.); *Br. Oxygen Co. v. Liquid Air Ltd.*, [1925] Ch. 383.

414 See, *e.g.*, *A.G. of Australia v. Adelaide S.S. Co.*, [1913] A.C. 781 (P.C.).

415 *Esso Petroleum Co. v. Harper's Garage (Stourport) Ltd.*, above, note 405; see also the earlier decision of the English Court of Appeal in *Petrofina (G.B.) Ltd. v. Martin*, [1966] Ch. 146 (C.A.).

the other petrol company. The Esso company sought to restrain this by injunctions, claiming that the garage company was bound by the agreements. In the event the House of Lords, applying the doctrine of restraint of trade, held that the first agreement, for five years, was not unreasonable and was enforceable but the second for the longer period was too long, and hence was void as being in unreasonable restraint of trade. In reaching this conclusion the House of Lords canvassed the entire law of restraint of trade, and the speeches in the House have many illuminating, as well perhaps as confusing, things to say about the nature and scope of the doctrine, its application in particular cases, its foundation and rationale.

One important distinction emerges from the case. This is the difference between an agreement under which a current trader agrees to give up some of his *present* freedom to trade in return for some advantage from the party claiming the benefit of the covenant in restraint, and an agreement under which a person not a trader obtains the ability to trade, for example, the possession of the trading premises, on the terms which include a restraint. The former surrenders his prior freedom; this will only be good if the degree of surrender is reasonable. The latter has lost no freedom; hence, he may be subjected to restraints (at least as long as they are not so onerous as to amount to slavery or perhaps are otherwise detrimental to public policy).[416]

The *Esso Petroleum* case reveals that agreements which tie up a trader's freedom of action in respect of the goods which he sells, even if the restraint is connected with a mortgage, that is, a loan of money to enable the trader to engage in trade, may still be invalid under the doctrine of restraint of trade.[417] The test is what is reasonable, bearing in mind much the same considerations as in other, more traditional instances of restraint of trade, namely, the notion of liberty to trade, freedom of contract, sanctity of contract, protection of legitimate trade interests, etc. While the language employed by some of their Lordships had led at least one commentator to consider some of the suggestions in the case to be novel, sweeping, perhaps even illogical and wrong,[418] the actual decision appears to be founded upon well-organized and accepted ideas as to the balance between restraints and liberty.

Not surprisingly, the decision has been applied in Canada. Both Henry J. and the Ontario Court of Appeal in *Stephens v. Gulf Oil Canada Ltd.*,[419] accepted and followed the decision and the language of the House of Lords. However, whereas

---

416   *Cleveland Petroleum Co. v. Dartstone*, [1969] 1 W.L.R. 116; *Hiebert v. Pac. Petroleums Ltd.* (1980), 109 D.L.R. (3d) 137 at 139-140 (Man. Q.B.), where, in a case of the first kind, surrender of present freedom, the court held that five years was the longest time that the court would consider the restraint to be reasonable.

417   But not always: *Alec Lobb (Garages) Ltd. v. Total Oil G.B. Ltd.*, [1983] 1 All E.R. 944; reversed on this point, [1985] 1 All E.R. 303 (C.A.).

418   Heydon, "The Frontiers of the Restraint of Trade Doctrine" (1969), 85 L.Q.R. 229.

419   (1974), 3 O.R. (2d) 241 (Ont. H.C.); reversed on appeal (1976), 11 O.R. (2d) 129 (Ont. C.A.); leave to appeal to S.C.C. refused (1976), 11 O.R. (2d) 129n (S.C.C.). See also above, p. 404. The provisions of the Competition Act, R.S.C. 1985, c. C-34, s. 39 may make this decision unnecessary and wrong. The *Esso Petroleum* case was also followed and applied in *Hiebert v. Pac. Petroleums Ltd.*, above, note 416.

Henry J. held that the restraint in that case was unreasonable and therefore invalid, the Court of Appeal came to a different conclusion. Interestingly enough, the case is only indirectly concerned with restraint of trade in the usual sense, and only collaterally with restraints involving distribution agreements. However, it would appear that what was said and held in the case can apply not only to an option to purchase, that is, of first refusal, which was the real subject matter of the litigation, but, more generally, to contracts of the kind now under discussion. In *Stephens* there was a contract of loan from the oil company to the owner of a garage, with the usual sort of *solus* agreement, similar to the one found in the *Esso Petroleum* case. The loan was secured by a mortgage for ten years, renewable thereafter at the option of the oil company for a further ten years, if the loan were not repaid at that date. The contract also gave the oil company the right of first purchase should the garage owner want to sell. Some time later the garage owner wanted to sell part of the premises to the plaintiff, to use as a repair shop. A contract was entered into between the garage owner, the plaintiff, and the oil company. The latter agreed to the sale by the garage owner to the plaintiff. The contract provided that, if either subsequently decided to sell the part of the property they owned, they would give each other the right of first refusal. It was also agreed that the purchase by the plaintiff was subject to the terms of the original loan made by the oil company to the garage owner. Further, the consideration for the oil company's agreeing to the sale to the plaintiff, thereby foregoing its right of first refusal, was the undertaking that the purchase would be subject to the terms of the original loan to the garage owner, including the right of first refusal given therein by the garage owner to the oil company.

Subsequently, the garage owner sold his interest in the remainder of the property to the oil company, without first offering it to the plaintiff. The latter brought an action to enforce his contract with the garage owner, that is, the terms of the purchase he made of the part of the premises. This action raised the issue whether the terms of the loan made between the garage owner and the oil company, and the terms incorporated into the three-party agreement, were valid and enforceable or infringed the law of restraint of trade by reason of the fact that they tied up the property for a considerable term of years, namely, at least the original ten years of the mortgage, and even the subsequent ten, a total of twenty years.

Henry J. held that the agreements were void as against public policy, because they were contrary to both limbs of the *Nordenfelt* rule. They were unreasonable as between the parties. They were also contrary to the public interest. The Court of Appeal reversed this judgment on both grounds. As already seen, that court took a different view of what was involved in the test of public interest. They also came to an opposite conclusion on the issue of reasonableness as between the garage owner and the oil company, in light of the fact that, at the time of the three-party agreement, only six years of the original ten years of the mortgage remained to run. Hence, it would seem, the Court of Appeal was of the opinion that what was involved at the time of that three-party agreement, which was material since it was the validity of the terms of the three-party agreement that was in question, was a restraint as to the right to sell the property that was to last for *six* years, not ten or twenty. It was also material to the Court of Appeal that the plaintiff had purchased the property, that is, the part of the premises, with knowledge of the existing tie between the garage owner and the oil company, and with consent to the right of first refusal as an integral part of the restrictions. Furthermore, the provisions of the various agreements did not go too far in their effort to protect the oil company, which was lending the money to the garage owner, and did not amount to an imposition by one party on another, the two being unequal as bargainers. In the event, therefore, the option given to the oil company was valid, and bound all the parties. Hence, the plaintiff could not succeed in his action against the garage owner and the oil company.

The importance of this case lies, *inter alia*, in its acceptance of the reasoning and principles in the *Esso Petroleum* case, and in the way the decision in that case was utilized, including the distinction made by the House of Lords between different periods, that is, the two contracts, and between buying property subject to a restraint and granting a restraint on property already owned by the covenantor.

(iv) *Present scope of the doctrine*

Various statements of principle were made in the House of Lords, by virtue of which, it may be supposed, new situations as well as the previously accepted categories of contracts in restraint of trade may be swept into the orbit of the doctrine, and thus, in individual instances, be compelled to satisfy the tests of reasonableness. Thus: (1) there is the test of fettering existing freedom to differentiate one type of tie from another;[420] (2) there is the test of sterilization of a party's capacity to serve the public; (3) there is the more pragmatic and flexible test of Lord Wilberforce that turns upon whether a class of contracts has passed into "the accepted and normal currency of commercial or contractual or conveyancing relations." If so then, unless there is something exorbitant about an individual contract in such class or there is a change in social or economic circumstances such as to merit a new view of such contracts, a contract in such class will never be required to be justified on grounds of reasonableness.

All these tests have been subjected to criticism.[421] However, in reality, what the House of Lords was doing in the *Esso Petroleum* case was endorsing or justifying the addition of one additional example of a contract in restraint of trade to the hitherto accepted categories, while at the same time suggesting that the categories of invalid restraint, like those of negligence (and for much the same reasons) are never closed. The House of Lords accepted that there were several situations in respect of which it could be said what seems at first sight to be a restriction on freedom of trading does not amount to a covenant in restraint of trade such as to attract the operation of the common-law doctrine.

One excellent example of this is the case of a contract of employment under which the employee agrees to give his services exclusively to one employer for

---

420 *Cleveland Petroleums Co. v. Dartstone*, [1968] 1 All E.R. 201 (C.A.); *Hiebert v. Pac. Petroleums Ltd.* above, note 416; in both of which this test was invoked and applied.

421 Heydon, above, note 418.

a long period of time[422] (to which may be added the instance of a party granting exclusive copyright rights to one party for a period of time[423]). In the words of Lord Pearce,[424]

> [t]he doctrine does not apply to ordinary commercial contracts for the regulation and promotion of trade during the existence of the contract, provided that any prevention of work outside the contract, viewed as a whole is directed towards the absorption of the parties' services and not their sterilisation. Sole agencies are a normal and necessary incident of commerce and those who desire the benefits of a sole agency must deny themselves the opportunities of other agencies. So, too, in the case of a film star who may tie herself to a company in order to obtain from them the benefits of stardom . . .and partners habitually fetter themselves to one another.

The very next paragraph in this speech clarifies the circumstances under which such restraints are not treated as within the ambit of the doctrine but are accepted as valid in themselves even without passing any test as to reasonableness:

> When a contract only ties the parties during the continuance of the contract, and the negative ties are only those which are incidental and normal to the positive commercial arrangements at which the contract aims, even though those ties exclude all dealings with others, there is no restraint of trade within the meaning of the doctrine and no queston of reasonableness arises.

But this will be different if: (1) the contract ties the activities of a party *after* the determination of the contract; or (2) if *during* the contract one party is too unilaterally fettered so that the contract no longer regulates and promotes trade but takes on the predominating character of restriction.[425]

Thus, the exclusive service agreement (like, possibly, the exclusive purchase of product type of agreement) is not invalid *per se*. It may be to encourage trade or business; it may afford the restricted party a unique opportunity to perform his business or profession, without which he would be in limbo. But, if the purpose of any such contract is to stifle enterprise, opportunity, development, if it is to *conceal*, rather than to expose the party under restriction, as for example, where an inventor agrees to have his invention put away for a period, lest its development interfere with the existing trade of the purchaser of the invention or of the inventor's services, then, such an agreement may be within the doctrine.[426] It is a question of degree, about which there may be disagreement.[427]

---

422 *Gaumont-British Picture Corp. v. Alexander*, [1936] 2 All E.R. 1686; *Warner Bros. Pictures Inc. v. Nelson*, [1937] 1 K.B. 209. These cases, and others, raise issues with respect to the enforcement of negative obligations by means of an injunction: as to which see below, pp. 800-801.

423 *Clifford Davis Management Ltd. v. W.E.A. Records*, [1975] 1 All E.R. 237 (C.A.); compare *A. Schroeder Music Publishing Co. v. Macaulay*, [1974] 3 All E.R. 616 (H.L.).

424 [1968] A.C. 269 at 328 (H.L.).

425 As in *Young v. Timmins* (1831), 1 C. & J. 331, 148 E.R. 1446, discussed by Heydon, above, note 418, at pp. 240-241.

426 This and the preceding two sentences were cited with approval by Kelly J. in *Acadia Forest Products Ltd. v. Neal Forest Products Ltd.* (1983), 48 N.B.R. (2d) 429 at 436 (N.B.Q.B.).

427 Witness the discussion by Heydon, above, note 418.

4. The consequences of illegality

(a) **Voidness of transaction**

A contract which is illegal either at common law or under statute is void and unenforceable by either party.[428] While the burden may be upon the defendant to establish that the plaintiff is relying upon an illegal contract to prove his case,[429] it would seem that the court is entitled to take note of an illegality that is obvious on the face of the contract.[430] The House of Lords in *North Western Salt Co. v. Electrolytic Alkali Co.*,[431] held that a defendant could not elicit the illegality of

---

428 See *U.S. Fidelity & Guar. Co. v. Cruickshank*, [1919] 3 W.W.R. 821 (Sask.C.A.) (contract to stifle a prosecution, illegal at common law); *Ernest v. Christian*, [1929] 1 D.L.R. 207 (N.S.C.A.) (contract which violated a provincial temperance statute); *Menard v. Genereux* (1982), 138 D.L.R. (3d) 273 (Ont. H.C) (contract which involved fraud on a bank); *Berne Dev. Ltd. v. Haviland* (1983), 40 O.R. (2d) 238 (Ont. H.C.) (contract which involved deception of mortgagee); *Cerilli v. Klodt* (1984), 48 O.R. (2d) 260 (Ont. H.C.) (contract intended to defraud vendor's estranged wife; *Mazerolle v. Day & Ross Inc.* (1986), 70 N.B.R. (2d) 119 (N.B.Q.B.) (purchase of cigarettes through Indians to avoid payment of provincial taxes; no claim against insured when the cigarettes were stolen); *Tucker Estate v. Gillis* (1989), 53 D.L.R. (4th) 688 (N.B.C.A.) (chattel mortgage unenforceable since made in connection with, and in pursuance of, an illegal scheme to avoid payment of provincial sales tax); *Ace Asphalts & Maintenance (Products) Ltd. v. O'Neill* (1991), 114 N.B.R. (2d) 168 (Alta. Q.B.), plaintiff could not claim unpaid wages because he was accepting unemployment insurance (where the contract was valid but to have allowed an action would have infringed the *ex turpi causa* doctrine: below). Even if the contract is made expressly subject to the proviso that it is to conform to a provincial statute's requirements: see *Trusteel Corp. v. Queensway Const. Corp; Trusteel Corp and Truman, Re* (1960), 22 D.L.R. (2d) 616 (Ont. C.A.); reversed, [1961] S.C.R. 528 (S.C.C.); *Murray Elias Ltd. v. Walsam Invts. Ltd.*, [1964] 2 O.R. 381 (Ont. H.C.); affirmed, [1965] 2 O.R. 672n (Ont. C.A.). But it must be shown to be illegal; hence the different decision at different levels in *Howard Sand & Gravel Co. v. Gen. Security Ins. Co.*, [1953] 3 D.L.R. 633 (Ont. H.C.); reversed, [1954] 1 D.L.R. 99 (Ont. C.A.); which was affirmed, [1954] 4 D.L.R. 682 (S.C.C.). Hence also a contract that is valid within the jurisdiction will be enforceable even if it is invalid elsewhere; compare *Bigelow v. Craigellachie Glenlivet Distillery Co.* (1905), 37 S.C.R. 55 (S.C.C.); *Nat. Surety Co. v. Larsen*, [1929] 3 W.W.R. 299 (B.C.C.A.).

But what may not be achieved though a convenant in restraint of trade may be achieved by the invocation of an agent's fiduciary duty precluding his competing in certain ways after employment: *Investors Syndicate Ltd. v. Versatile Invts. Ltd.* (1983), 149 D.L.R. (3d) 46 (Ont. C.A.).

Note the recommendation of the Ontario Law Reform Commission, *Report on Amendment of the Law of Contract* (1987), at p. 236, that legislation should provide that the court should be empowered to grant relief by way of restitution and compensation for loss as it thinks just, as long as this would be consistent with the policy underlying the unenforceability of the contract.

429 *Wilkinson v. Harwood*, [1931] S.C.R. 141 (S.C.C.).

430 *Rodrigue v. Dostie*, [1927] S.C.R. 563 (S.C.C.); *Scott v. Brown, Doering, McNab & Co.*, [1892] 2 Q.B. 724 (C.A.). Absence of knowledge of the illegality will not affect the issue; the transaction will still be illegal: *Laliberte v. Blanchard* (1979), 28 N.B.R. (2d) 394 (N.B.Q.B.); affirmed (1980), 31 N.B.R. (2d) 275 (N.B.C.A.), quoting Lord Denning M.R. in *J.M. Allan (Merchandising) Ltd. v. Cloke*, [1963] 2 All E.R. 258 at 261 (C.A.); *Central Trust Co. v. Rafuse* (1983), 147 D.L.R. (3d) 260 at 270-271 (N.S.C.A.) *per* Jones J.A. But such lack of knowledge may permit the ignorant party to pursue a remedy despite the illegality: see *First Nat. Bank of Oregon v. Watson Ranching Ltd.* (1984), 34 Alta. L.R. (2d) 110 (Alta. Q.B.).

431 [1914] A.C. 461 (H.L.); applied in *Uruski v. Hnatiw* (1956), 6 D.L.R. (2d) 441 (Sask. C.A.). See also *Zimmerman v. Letkeman*, [1978] 1 S.C.R. 1097 (S.C.C.), unlawful purpose of the parties disclosed by the evidence; therefore, contract of sale of land not specifically enforceable; compare *Cerilli v. Klodt*, below.

a contract in the course of cross-examination unless the illegality was clear on the face of the contract, or pleaded in defence, or appeared from the plaintiff's examination-in-chief. Thus, if illegality is not pleaded, and the plaintiff's case does not obviously appear to rest and be based upon an illegal transaction, the issue of illegality may never come before the court.[432] Everything may depend, therefore, as Gwynne J. pointed out in *Clark v. Hagar*,[433] upon whether or not the plaintiff has to rely upon the illegal transaction to establish his case.[434]

This major consequence of such a contract is often expressed in one of two ways. The first is, *ex turpi causa non oritur actio*. This means that a claim cannot be founded upon a base cause, namely, the breach of a statute or a contract that is against public policy. The second is, *in pari delicto potior est conditio defendentis*. This means that where the parties are equally at fault in their participation in illegality, the position of the defendant is the superior. It may be seen that these are two ways of saying the same thing, that rights or claims may not be founded upon illegality. Hence, in *Jackson v. Jackson*,[435] the defendant was unable to plead by way of defence to an action for the recovery of a loan that the transaction was in reality a gift in a form and manner designed to protect the father, who gave the money, from liability for gift taxes, that is, an illegal transaction. He could not rely upon the illegality to *prevent* his liability any more than in *North-Western Construction Co. v. Young*,[436] the plaintiff, an extra-provincial company which was unregistered under the British Columbia Companies Act, and therefore was not entitled to carry on business in British Columbia, could sue, that is, *establish* liability, on a contract it had made with the defendant company.[437] At the same time, if the parties are *in pari delicto*, no restitution will be possible. Hence, money paid under such a contract will be irrecoverable from the other party.[438] Thus, unless

---

432 But if the illegality is obvious, the party affected by such illegality does not have to be a party to the action; the court can give effect to the illegality and avoid the contract: see *Cerilli v. Klodt* (1984), 48 O.R. (2d) 260 (Ont. H.C.) (contract to defraud estranged wife avoided, even though wife not a party to the purchaser's action for specific performance).

433 (1893), 22 S.C.R. 510 at 523 (S.C.C.). Hence, in *Mack v. Edenwold Fertilizer Services Ltd.*, [1987] 5 W.W.R. 469 (Sask. C.A.); reversing [1986] 3 W.W.R. 741 (Sask. Q.B.), the Saskatchewan Court of Appeal held that an agreement to pay interest on money received by the seller, under a contract of sale that was illegal because it was framed so as to avoid paying income tax, was also illegal and unenforceable. The two contracts were not independant. Contrast *Major v. C.P.R.*, [1922] 3 W.W.R. 512 (S.C.C.), with *Elford v. Elford*, [1922] 3 W.W.R. 339 (S.C.C.). See also *Amar Singh v. Kulubya*, [1964] A.C. 142 (P.C.). Hence, the plaintiff could be successful in *Kirzinger v. Kalthoff* (1964), 46 W.W.R. 547 (Sask. Q.B.); below, p. 425.

434 *Euro-Diam Ltd. v. Bathurst*, [1988] 2 All E.R. 23 at 29 (C.A.) *per* Kerr L.J.

435 (1960), 34 W.W.R. 431 (B.C.S.C.).

436 (1908), 13 B.C.R. 297 (B.C.C.A.).

437 Compare *Wasel Bros. v. Laskin*, [1934] 2 W.W.R. 577 (Sask. C.A.) no action for price of transportation of goods under a contract invalid by statute.

438 *Taylor v. Chester* (1869), L.R. 4 Q.B. 309; *Parkinson v. College of Ambulance Ltd.*, [1925] 2 K.B. 1; compare *Rose v. Donaldson; Rose v. Briscoe; Rose v. Yates*, [1931] 3 W.W.R. 480 (Alta. S.C.). Nor will money owing to the plaintiff representing the value of goods delivered: *Kingshott v. Brunskill*, [1953] O.W.N. 133 (Ont. C.A.). The situation may be different if the defendant would be unjustly enriched as long as the illegality was not too gross and vicious; see the remarks of Saunders J. in *Berne Dev. Ltd. v. Haviland*, above, note 428 at 250-251 (relying on *Menard v. Genereux*,

one of the exceptional circumstances to be considered later can be held to operate, the parties must be left in the situation in which they find themselves after the making of the contract and any partial or entire performance of it by one or both. They cannot come to the courts to enforce any unfulfilled promises, recover any money or property which has been transferred thereunder, or obtain damages.[439]

While recognizing that a transaction which directly infringes the common law or a statute is illegal and void, the common law has been less clear where the transaction is not quite so obviously illegal. Admittedly, if the transaction, as entered into by the parties, is fundamentally illegal or for an illegal purpose, even though it appears to be legitimate in character, it will be tainted with illegality. Thus, contracts which are intended to enable a party to participate in gaming will themselves be void and unenforceable even if they appear to be simple loans.[440] Hence, in the English case of *Fisher v. Bridges*,[441] a contract which purported to be a sale of land was unenforceable, since it was intended that the land should be used for an illegal lottery. So, too, in the Canadian case of *Exhibition Advertising Enterprises v. Victoria Exhibition*[442] there was an agreement to lease land at an agricultural fair, during the period of the fair. The lessee wanted to exhibit on the land a model home, for which he would sell tickets to the public, who would see it, with the object of drawing a winner from among the ticket-holders. It was held that this amounted to a lottery illegal under the Criminal Code. Hence, there could be no action for breach of the option to renew a clause in the agreement. Even if the agreement is between other parties, that is, not those who were originally participants in the illegality, it will be tainted with the same defect, if the parties to the collateral agreement knew that they were assisting to effect an illegal purpose,[443] for example, by lending money to a debtor to pay off a loan which was illegal under statute, namely, by reason of the fact that it included compound interest.[444]

Two qualifications must be introduced. The first is that the transaction must have been intended to effect an illegal purpose, even if, on the face of it, there is no illegality. In such circumstances it will become sufficiently collateral to the illegality to be considered void on the same ground. This is well illustrated by contracts which, in the end, are contracts to assist in the promotion or encour-

---

above, note 428, *Steinberg v. Cohen*, [1930] 2 D.L.R. 916 at 928 (Ont. C.A.) *per* Masten J.; *Sidmay Ltd. v. Wehttam Invts. Ltd.*, [1967] 1 O.R. 508 at 531 (Ont. C.A.) *per* Kelly J.A.; affirmed, [1968] S.C.R. 828 (S.C.C.)).

439 Hence, in *Zimmerman v. Letkeman*, [1978] 1 S.C.R. 1097 (S.C.C.), a contract of sale, which involved recording a false price to enable the purchaser to obtain a larger loan from a mortgage company, was not specifically enforceable at the suit of the purchaser when the vendor subsequently changed his mind and did not want to be a party to fraud.

  The passage from "At the same time" to "or other damages" was quoted by Monnin J. in *Gateway Hotel (1985) Ltd. v. Schur* (1990), 66 Man. R. (2d) 305 at 315 (Man. Q.B.).

440 *Miller v. Wall*, [1933] 2 W.W.R. 574 (Man. C.A.); compare above, pp. 365-366.

441 (1854), 3 E. & B. 642, 118 E.R. 1283.

442 (1962), 132 C.C.C. 303 (B.C.S.C.).

443 *Cannan v. Bryce* (1819), 3 B. & Ald. 179, 106 E.R. 628. Contrast *Leaper v. Grenadier Dev. Ltd.* (1980), 22 B.C.L.R. 354 (B.C.S.C.); varied on other grounds (1982), 38 B.C.L.R. 125 (B.C.C.A.).

444 *Spector v. Ageda*, [1973] Ch. 30.

agement of immorality.[445] If a contract is made with a prostitute, for example, it will not necessarily be illegal and void. Only if both parties intended that the subject-matter of the contract should be utilized for the immoral acts or behaviour of the prostitute will the contract be illegal. If one party had such intention and the other did not, then, so far as the innocent party is concerned, the contract is not illegal, even though it may be collateral to an illegal purpose.[446] So in *Clark v. Hagar*,[447] the Supreme Court held *valid* a mortgage given on a house which was sold for the purpose of being a brothel, a purpose which was known to the mortgagor but not the mortgagee. Surprisingly enough, in a later case, *Dominion Fire Insurance Co. v. Nakata*,[448] the Supreme Court, over the dissent of Duff J., came to the opposite conclusion in a similar situation. An insurance company knew that the house being insured with it was going to be used as a brothel, because, strangely, the application form informed the insurance company to such effect. The policy was illegal and invalid and the insurance company could cancel it. In one sense the company was being allowed to take advantage of its own knowledge that it was participating collaterally in an illegal purpose.

The second qualification is concerned more with illegality in performance than illegality at the inception of a contract. If the contract is potentially illegal, in the sense that it will be so if it is not performed in accordance with statutory requirements, a party who wishes to avoid illegality may expressly contract that the performance should be in such a manner as to keep away from illegality. Where this promise by the other party is made a condition of the other party's entering the contract, it will be enforceable and valid, even though it is collateral to a contract that ends in being illegally performed. But this must be distinguished from a contract which is still illegal, even though one party stipulated that it was subject to compliance with a particular statute. The distinction may lie in the fact that in the former instance, which is founded upon an English decision,[449] one party undertook the duty of obtaining the necessary statutory licence, in the latter, a Canadian case,[450] the obligation was not specifically alloted to, or undertaken by one particular party. It would also appear that only exceptionally will such a collateral undertaking relieve a party from the consequences of being a party to what culminates in being an illegal contract. It really must be shown that he legitimately and innocently believed that he was freed from any statutory obligation to ensure legal performance.

445 Above, pp. 383-386.
446 *Pearce v. Brooks* (1866), L.R. 1. Exch. 213; above, p. 385. See also *First Nat. Bank of Oregon v. Watson Ranching Ltd.* (1984), 34 Alta. L.R. (2d) 110 (Alta. Q.B.), promissory note enforceable by plaintiff, which was not a party to the deception practised by the maker of the note to obtain a guarantee.
447 (1894), 22 S.C.R. 510 (S.C.C.) with which contrast *Rose v. Donaldson; Rose v. Briscoe; Rose v. Yates*, [1931] 3 W.W.R. 480 (Alta. S.C.).
448 (1915), 52 S.C.R. 294 (S.C.C.).
449 *Strongman (1945) Ltd. v. Sincock*, [1955] 2 Q.B. 525 (C.A.).
450 *Murray Elias Ltd. v. Walsom Invts. Ltd.*, [1964] 2 O.R. 381 (Ont. H.C.); affirmed, [1965] 2 O.R. 672n (Ont. C.A.).

An example of this is provided by *Central Trust Co. v. Rafuse*.[451] A firm of solicitors acted for the plaintiff trust company in connection with a mortgage loan to a motel and restaurant company. The trust company and the solicitors knew that the proceeds of the loan were to be used to assist certain individuals to buy shares in the motel and restaurant company. Unknown to the trust company and its solicitors, this infringed provisions of the Nova Scotia Companies Act. Subsequently, it was held that the mortgage arranged by the solicitors was void and unenforceable because, since it contravened the Companies Act, it was against public policy and illegal. The trust company sued the solicitors for losses incurred in consequence of the mortgage being declared void. The trust company lost at trial, and its appeal was dismissed, because the company's claim was statute-barred. However, in the Court of Appeal, Jones J.A. considered the question whether the fact that the solicitors were engaged by the trust company in effecting what ultimately turned out to be an illegal transaction was enough in itself to bar any action by the trust company against the solicitors, whether in contract or tort.[452] In this regard, the fact that neither of the parties was aware that what they were effecting was illegal did not make any difference. However, such illegality did not suffice to make the contract for the solicitors' services to advise on the transaction itself an illegal contract, the effect of which would be to bar any action against the solicitors. It was clear that, if either party had known the loan was illegal, the transaction would not have proceeded. That being so, it could not be said that the engagement of the solicitors was for the purpose of carrying out an illegal transaction. Consequently, applying the reasoning of the English court in the *Strongman* case,[453] the trust company could sue the solicitors for breach of the contract to provide legal services, which breach occurred by reason of the solicitors' negligence in not knowing about the relevant statutory provisions. The ultimate illegality did not prevent or preclude an action for damages for breach of the contract, the performance of which involved the illegality. Although the Supreme Court of Canada allowed the plaintiff's appeal from the dismissal of his claim by the Nova Scotia Court of Appeal, which agreed with the trial judge, they did not disagree with the views of the lower court on the issue of illegality.[454]

(b) The doctrine of severance[455]

A further, and very important qualification of the doctrine of the voidness of illegal contracts is the idea of *severance*. Sometimes a court will recognize the separation of valid from objectionable parts of a contract, and, while refusing to

---

451 (1983), 147 D.L.R. (3d) 260 (N.S.C.A.); reversed on other grounds by the Supreme Court of Canada, (1987), 31 D.L.R. (4th) 481: on which, see below, p. 695.

452 *Ibid.*, 270-273 (N.S.C.A.).

453 Above, note 449.

454 (1987), 31 D.L.R. (4th) 481 at 530 (S.C.C.).

455 This section was referred to by Cooper J.A., dissenting, in *Harrietsfield-Grandlake Community Assn. v. Halifax County* (1978), 26 N.S.R. (2d) 198 at 221 (N.S.C.A.).

enforce the latter, will give effect to the former.[456] In this connection it should be mentioned that the argument that there is a distinction between illegal and void (but not illegal) contracts, whether by statute or common law, may depend upon the application of the idea of severance. If the consideration for a promise or set of promises is illegal, then all the promises which rest on, or are dependent upon such consideration will be invalid. If some of the promises are dependent upon such illegal consideration, whether illegal at common law or under statute, while others have an independent existence, and rest upon consideration which is not itself illegal, then such independent promises may be enforceable against the other party.[457] This distinction lies at the root of the illegal-void dichotomy.[458] To quote from one English case which is said to support this[459]

> ... there are two kinds of illegality of differing effect. The first is where the illegality is criminal, or *contra bonos mores*, and in those cases ... such a provision, if an ingredient in a contract, will invalidate the whole, although there may be other provisions in it. There is a second kind of illegality which has no such taint; the other terms in the contract stand if the illegal portion can be severed, the illegal portion being a provision which the court, on the grounds of public policy, will not enforce.

Whether an agreement is capable of severance and partial enforcement depends on the object and policy of the law that is being infringed; whether that object or policy would be subverted by partial performance of the agreement; whether one or both parties intended to breach the law; whether one party would be unjustly enriched if the contract were not enforced.[460] These features have been particularly important in cases involving the charging of interest that violates the

---

456 This sentence was quoted by Mercier J. in *Huppe v. Huppe* (1990), 66 Man. R. (2d) 241 at 246 (Man. Q.B.). In *Littlewoods Organisation Ltd. v. Harris*, [1978] 1 All E.R. 1026 (C.A.), the English Court of Appeal considered achieving much the same result by the process of "construing" the contract so as to limit the meaning and scope of an excessively wide covenant in restraint of trade. Only one judge, Browne, L.J., thought that this involved rewriting the contract, which could not be done. Compare *Amoco Australia Pty. Ltd. v. Rocco Bros. Motor Engr. Co. Pty.*, [1975] A.C. 561 at 578 (P.C.) *per* Lord Cross. See also *Carney v. Herbert*, [1985] 1 All E.R. 438 at 443-444 (P.C.) *per* Lord Brightman.

457 *Kearney v. Whitehaven Colliery Co.*, [1893] 1 Q.B. 700 at 711 (C.A.) *per* Lord Esher M.R., cited with approval in *St. Gabriel Land & Hydraulic Co. v. Consumers Cordage Co.*, [1944] Qué. K.B. 305 (Qué. K.B.); affirmed, [1945] S.C.R. 158 (S.C.C.). See also *Brooks-Bidlake & Whittal Ltd. v. A.G. B.C.* (1922), 63 S.C.R. 466 (S.C.C.); affirmed, [1923] A.C. 450 (P.C.). Contrast *Wallis v. Day* (1837), 2 M. & W. 273, 150 E.R. 759 with *Vancouver Malt & Sake Brewing Co. v. Vancouver Breweries Ltd.*, [1934] A.C. 181 (P.C.); above, p. 402. See also *Investors Syndicate Ltd. v. Versatile Invts. Ltd.* (1981), 126 D.L.R. (3d) 451 (Ont. H.C.); reversed in part on other grounds (1983), 149 D.L.R. (3d) 46 (Ont. C.A.).

458 There is also an argument based upon the idea of *mutuality*, whereby a *void* promise can become the basis of an action if it is actually performed; an *illegal* promise cannot: see this discussed by Treitel, "Mutuality in Contract" (1961), 77 L.Q.R. 83. Is this not another way of saying the same thing?

459 *Goodinson v. Goodinson*, [1954] 2 Q.B. 118 at 120-121 (C.A.) *per* Somervell L.J.

460 *William E. Thomson Associates Inc. v. Carpenter* (1989), 61 D.L.R. (4th) 1 at 8 (Ont. C.A.) *per* Blair J.A.; leave to appeal to S.C.C. refused (1990), 105 N.R. 397 (note) (S.C.C.). See *Bon Street Devs. Ltd. v. Terracan Capital Corp.* (1992), 76 B.C.L.R. (2d) 90 (B.C.S.C.), where there was no oppression by the lender which ousted the operation of the Criminal Code provisions.

provisions of the Criminal Code. In these the interest provision was severed, enabling the lender of the money to recover the principal sum.[461]

A very important instance of the availability and application of the doctrine is provided by contracts in restraint of trade.[462] Frequently, the attempt is made to have something saved from a contract which contains provisions that infringe the doctrine of restraint of trade by applying the idea of severance, and seeking to have the restraint provision or provisions excised from the contract, leaving the remainder intact and enforceable. In one such case in England, *Putsman v. Taylor*,[463] the scope and application of the doctrine were described in language which summarizes the effect of earlier decisions.[464]

> If a promisee claims the enforcement of a promise, and the promise is a valid promise and supported by consideration, the Court will enforce the promise, notwithstanding the fact that the promisor has made other promises, supported by the same consideration, which are void, and has included the valid and invalid promises in one document. But if the promise sought to be enforced is invalid, as being under restraint of trade or for any other reason, the Court will not invent a valid promise by the deletion, alteration, or addition of words, and thus enforce a promise which the promisor might well have made, but did not make. The promise to be enforceable must be on the face of the document a separate promise, a separate compact, the subject of separate consideration and accord, the performance of which is independent of the performance of any other promises which the promisor may have made. If the promise is a separate promise and valid, the Court will enforce it. Whether it is separate or not depends on the language of the document. Severance . . . is the act of the parties, not of the court.[465]

This last phrase seems very important. The issue is whether the parties have by their language identified separate promises. The promise must appear severable. In other words, if a blue pencil could be put through the allegedly invalid promise without disturbing the rest of the contract, it looks *prima facie* as if the cancelled words, that is, the promise being struck out, constituted a separate promise. This is the so-called "blue pencil" rule, which is a rule of thumb only. However, that test is insufficient by itself.[466] The true test emerges as being whether the subtraction of the void part of a contract affects the *meaning* of the remainder, or merely the *extent*. It is not permitted to change radically the purport and substance of

---

461 *Ibid., BCORP Financial Inc. v. Baseline Resort Devs. Inc.*, [1990] 5 W.W.R. 275 (B.C.S.C.); *Milani v. Banks* (1992), 98 D.L.R. (4th) 104 (Ont. Gen. Div.).

462 Note the recommendations of the Ontario Law Reform Commission, above, note 428, that would give courts wider power to alter contractual provisions so as to give some effect to the contract.

463 [1927] 1 K.B. 637 (D.C.); affirmed [1927] 1 K.B. 741 (C.A.); applied by Cartwright J. in *Pauzé v. Gauvin*, [1954] S.C.R. 15 (S.C.C.).

464 Such as, *Goldsoll v. Goldman*, [1915] 1 Ch. 292 (C.A.); *Attwood v. Lamont*, [1920] 3 K.B. 571 (C.A.).

465 Above, note 463, at 639-640 (D.C.) *per* Salter J., part of which was quoted by Hinkson J.A. in *Can. American Financial Corp. (Can.) v. King* (1989), 60 D.L.R. (4th) 293 at 300 (B.C.C.A.).

466 Compare Lambert J.A. in *Can. American Financial Corp. (Can.) v. King*, above, note 465, at 306.

the original contract.[467] As it was put more recently,[468] the issue is whether the deletion of the invalid obligation "alters entirely the scope and intention of the agreement" so that what is left is no longer "a reasonable arrangement between the parties" or an "intelligible economic transaction."

Thus, in *Putsman v. Taylor* itself, severance was permitted of a covenant not to be employed in any capacity with any tailor in certain named places. This left the employee bound by covenants not for a period of five years from the termination of his employment to set up as a tailor or enter the employment of the neighbouring trade rival in the places in question. Competition with the local branch of a multiple business where the employee had previously been employed in tailoring might be restrained, but not competition with the *other* branches of that business. That was going too far in extent. Similarly in *Goldsoll v. Goldman*,[469] where the covenant in restraint purported to apply to dealing in imitation and real jewellery in England and certain other named countries, the court severed the part which related to "real" jewellery and to the countries other than England, and enforced the rest. Again in the *Nordenfelt* case,[470] the covenant to carry on *any business* that *might compete* anywhere in the world was severed from the rest of the agreement relating to arms manufacture which, in the circumstances, as already seen, was reasonable and enforceable. On the other hand, in *Attwood v. Lamont*,[471] a covenant not to enter into the drapery and cognate trades within ten miles of Kidderminster was held to be too wide a restraint in the circumstances, and the court would not carve out from this broad restraint a reasonable one, namely, a prohibition as to tailoring. That was a case in which the court refused to cut down a restraint too wide as to its scope. In *Empire Meat Co. v. Patrick*,[472] the court refused to cut down a restraint that was too wide as to physical area, even though it would have been reasonable, having regard to the extent of the employer's business, to protect him within one mile of Cambridge, as opposed to the five miles mentioned in the contract.

These principles had been applied in Canada. In *Garbutt Business College Ltd. v. Henderson*,[473] the covenant which purported to apply to the principal of a business college covered and included a prohibition against the principal's having a "financial interest" in such an establishment for the period of the restraint and within the area of restraint. It was held that this could be severed from the rest of the contract, which was then enforceable. In other instances, courts have severed provisions in

---

467 Compare *Mason v. Provident Clothing & Supply Co.*, [1913] A.C. 724 (H.L.).

468 *Amoco Australia Pty. Ltd. v. Rocca Bros. Motor Engr. Co. Pty.*, [1975] A.C. 561 at 578 (P.C.) where deletion of the invalid covenant, *i.e.*, the tie, made the lease and lease-back unintelligible and the transaction as a whole made no commercial sense. Contrast *Alec Lobb (Garages) Ltd. v. Total Oil G.B. Ltd.*, [1983] 1 All E.R. 944; where deletion of the tie left the lease at a premium and the lease-back at a rack rent was a recognizable and commercially intelligible transaction; severance was possible. Note the reversal of this decision, with respect to the invalidity of the contract, by the Court of Appeal, [1985] 1 All E.R. 303 (C.A.).

469 Above, note 464.

470 [1894] A.C. 535 (H.L.); above, p. 390.

471 Above, note 464; compare *Routh v. Jones*, [1947] 1 All E.R. 758 (C.A.).

472 [1939] 2 All E.R. 85 (C.A.).

473 [1939] 3 W.W.R. 257 (Alta. C.A.).

covenants in restraint of trade which have purported to extend the restraint to, for example, Newfoundland as well as the mainland Atlantic provinces, or to "similar" businesses to the one sought to be protected.[474] It may be seen, therefore, that the problems are common to England and Canada, and the solutions are the same.[475]

(c) Recovery despite illegality

(i) *Exceptions to the strict doctrine*

To the ideas of *ex turpi causa* and *in pari delicto*, there are qualifications or exceptions, some of which may be more apparent than real. These are situations in which an illegal contract may not stand in the way of some kind of remedy or recovery, with the result that a party is not necessarily deprived of rights or claims because he has participated in something which is illegal at common law or by statute.[476] Where this is so, then the party in question can recover property or money, and might even be able to sue for damages for breach of the contract.[477] If damages are being sought, then it must be possible for the plaintiff to maintain his action without having to rely upon the illegal contract. Where the return of property or money is involved, then, as Saunders J. stated in *Berne Developments Ltd. v. Haviland*,[478] the courts have developed three exceptions to the general rule that the court will not order the return of property transferred under an illegal contract. These are: (1) where the party claiming is less at fault; (2) where the party claiming repents before the contract is performed; and (3) where the party claiming has an independent right to recover. However, the door may not be closed to further exceptions. There may be other situations beyond the recognized exceptions where a court may lend assistance to a party to recover property

---

474 *E.P. Chester Ltd. v. Mastorkis* (1968), 56 C.P.R. 139 (N.S.C.A.); *Can. Linen Co. v. Mole*, [1938] 1 W.W.R. 491 (B.C.C.A.); *Greening Indust. Ltd. v. Penny* (1965), 53 D.L.R. (2d) 643 (N.S.S.C.); *Carruthers Clinic Ltd. v. Herdman*, [1956] O.R. 770 (Ont. H.C.); *Rapid-Med Plus Franchise Corp. v. Elliott* (1991), 73 Man. R. (2d) 150 (Man. C.A.). Contrast *Can. American Financial Corp. (Can.) v. King*, above, note 465.

475 See, *e.g.*, a case which permitted severance so as to allow a restraint that would cover the legitimate interests of the plaintiff: *Betz Laboratories Ltd. v. Klyn* (1969), 70 W.W.R. 304 (B.C.S.C); varied (1969), 70 W.W.R. 742 (B.C.C.A.), which followed *Taylor (T.S.) Mach. Co. v. Biggar* (1968), 67 W.W.R. 246 (Man. C.A.). In *Investors Syndicate Ltd. v. Versatile Invts. Ltd.* (1982), 126 D.L.R. (3d) 451 (Ont. H.C.) the offending clause was severed, thereby disentitling the plaintiffs (covenantees) from suing for damages for breach of the covenant that was in restraint, without affecting the rest of the contract; on appeal, however, (1983), 149 D.L.R. (3d) 46 (Ont. C.A.) the plaintiffs were able to found their claim to damages on the defendant's breach of his fiduciary duty as an agent, reversing the trial judge's decision that no implied item relating to such duty could exist because it would *also* be contrary to public policy.

476 If he has *not* participated in the illegality a party will not be defeated by a plea of *ex turpi causa*: *First Nat. Bank of Oregon v. Watson Ranching Ltd.* (1984), 34 Alta. L.R. (2d) 110 at 144-145 (Alta. Q.B.).

477 Or include money due under such a contract in an *account stated*: see *Owens v. Denton* (1835), 1 Cr. M. & R. 711, 149 E.R. 1266.

478 (1983), 40 O.R. (2d) 238 at 249 (Ont. H.C.).

transferred under an illegal contract. In recent years there has been a recognition of the desirability of balancing the need to preserve public policy by not enforcing illegal agreements and the need to avoid unjust enrichment.[479] The striking of this balance may depend in each case on the extent of the illegality and the unjust enrichment.[480]

(ii) *Independence of action*

By way of exception to the doctrine of *ex turpi causa*, if the plaintiff does not have to set up the illegal contract as an integral part of his claim against the defendant, he is not affected by the doctrine, because, in such circumstances, he is not relying upon *turpis causa*, an improper cause of action.[481] Thus, in *Kirzinger v. Kalthoff*[482] there was a sale of shares, in breach of the Saskatchewan Securities Act. It was also invalid as being brought about by fraud. The defendant obtained a loan from the plaintiff under a written agreement for repayment either by cash or in shares, that is, the shares sold by the defendant to the plaintiff in the manner described above. When the plaintiff sued on the loan, it was held that the loan agreement was not illegal, but a *bona fide* transaction untainted by the previous illegal sale and the purchase of the shares. The plaintiff did not have to rely on the original share purchase to support his claim against the defendant. It was immaterial that these shares were or might be used to repay the loan. Hence, his action was maintainable. So too, in *Keystone Fisheries Ltd. v. Leftrook*,[483] an action in negligence, that is, in tort, was available where none in contract could have been permitted since the contract of carriage was illegal.

There is also the possibility that a contract was intended to be performed in a legal manner, but became illegal by reason of the way it was performed. Much here depends upon the intentions of the parties. If there was an alternative mode of performance which was legal, and this was intended by one party as the correct method, that party will be able to sue. If both parties so intended, then the contract

---

479 *Ibid.*, at 250 relying on *Zimmerman v. Letkeman*, [1978] 1 S.C.R. 1097 (S.C.C.); *Williams v. Fleetwood Hldgs. Ltd.* (1973), 41 D.L.R. (3d) 636 (Sask. C.A.). Such a broad basis for recovery was denied by Krever J. in *Menard v. Genereux* (1982), 138 D.L.R. (3d) 273 (Ont. H.C.). Contrast, however, *dicta* in *Monticchio v. Torcema Const. Ltd.* (1980), 8 B.L.R. 225 (Ont. H.C.) on the availability of a *quantum meruit* claim. See Maddaugh & McCamus, *Law of Restitution* (1990), at pp. 373-374.

480 Above, note 478, at 250. This paragraph was quoted by Monnin J. in *Gateway Hotel (1985) Ltd. v. Schur* (1990), 66 Man. R. (2d) 305 at 315 (Man. Q.B.).

481 *Elford v. Elford* (1922), 64 S.C.R. 125 (S.C.C.). See also *Tucker Estate v. Gillis* (1988), 53 D.L.R. (4th) 688 at 695 (N.B.C.A.); compare *Spiers v. Hunt*, [1908] 1 K.B. 720 at 723 *per* Phillimore L.J.; namely, an action for damages for breach of the implied warranty that the defendant was unmarried, even though the contract for marriage was void as the defendant was already married, above, p. 387. Compare *Siveyer v. Allison*, [1935] 2 K.B. 403. Compare also *Shaw v. Shaw*, [1954] 2 Q.B. 429 (C.A.); above, p. 387. See also *Clay v. Yates* (1856), 1 H. & N. 73, 156 E.R. 1123, which involved a contract to print a libellous book.

482 (1964), 46 W.W.R. 547 (Sask. Q.B.). Contrast *Zimmerman v. Letkeman*, above, note 479.

483 (1959), 16 D.L.R. (2d) 680 (Man. C.A.).

may still be good. The leading authority is *Waugh v. Morris*.[484] That case concerned a contract to deliver French hay alongside one party's ship in the Thames. Although the importation of such hay in England was prohibited, it was held that the contract was not illegal, since the owner of the ship need not have imported the hay once he was in possession of it; he could have re-exported it to another country, and there was no evidence that either party intended that the illegal purpose was to be the one effected by the contract. So, too, in *Hindley & Co. v. General Fibre Co.*,[485] the buyers nominated a German port as the one to which the goods were to be delivered (they having a choice of four named ports). It was illegal to deliver to such a port. However, alternative performance was possible, since the buyers subsequently nominated Antwerp, a valid port, as the destination of the goods. Hence, the contract was not illegal, and the sellers were liable for non-delivery of the goods. In *J.M. Allan (Merchandising) Ltd. v. Cloke*,[486] however, even though the parties did not appreciate that the roulette wheel that was being hired involved illegality, they intended it to be used in the illegal manner. Their ignorance was no defence or excuse, nor could they assert that there was an alternative mode of performance.

Finally, there is the possibility that, even though the transaction is illegal and void, goods[487] which have been transferred thereunder may become the property of the buyer in such a manner as to give him title enforceable even as against the other party to the illegal transaction (though it will only be enforceable if this may be done without asserting the illegal transaction[488]). In *Singh v. Ali*,[489] Lord Denning, giving the opinion of the Privy Council, stated that despite the illegality in that case (which involved the breach of some regulations made in Malaya concerned with obtaining a haulier's permit), the sale of the lorry which the plaintiff desired to use without the required permit did have the consequence that the plaintiff acquired title to the lorry. Therefore, he could sue for its return from the defendant who had taken possession of it without consent, even though the entire transaction

---

484 (1873), L.R. 8 Q.B. 202.

485 [1940] 2 K.B. 517. Compare *Mason v. Clarke*, [1955] A.C. 778 (H.L.).

486 [1963] 2 Q.B. 340 (C.A.); followed in *Laliberte v. Blanchard* (1979), 28 N.B.R. (2d) 394 (N.B. Q.B.); affirmed (1980), 31 N.B.R. (2d) 275 (N.B.C.A.). Contrast *Marles v. Phillip Trant & Co.*, [1954] 1 Q.B. 29 (C.A.), where the party innocent of the illegal performance could sue for breach of contract.

487 Or a lease, see *Feret v. Hill* (1854), 139 E.R. 400, where a tenant obtained a lease by fraudulently concealing that he was going to use the premises as a brothel; he could recover possession when he was ejected by the landlord. Contrast the probably wrongly decided case of *Sowler v. Potter*, [1940] 1 K.B. 271, where the fraud as to the identity of the tenant entitled the landlord to treat the lease as void. For the transference or acquisition of land, despite involvement in illegality, see *Tinsley v. Milligan*, [1993] 3 All E.R. 65 (H.L.), where the distinction was drawn between situations when the presumption of advancement applied and those where it did not.

488 Hence the failure of the plaintiff to recover half the banknote deposited as security for a night in a brothel in *Taylor v. Chester* (1869), L.R. 4 Q.B. 309. So, too, no claim on insurance could be made in respect of cigarettes that had been purchased in a manner designed to avoid provincial taxes: *Mazerolle v. Day & Ross Inc.* (1986), 70 N.B.R. (2d) 119 (N.B.Q.B.).

489 [1960] A.C. 167 (P.C.).

under which the plaintiff bought the lorry was illegal and could have involved the plaintiff in criminal liability. In the words of Lord Denning,

> [t]here are many cases which show that when two persons agree together in a conspiracy to effect a fraudulent or illegal purpose — and one of them transfers property to the other in pursuance of the conspiracy — then, so soon as the contract is executed and the fraudulent or illegal purpose is achieved, the property . . .which has been transferred by the one to the other remains vested in the transferee, notwithstanding its illegal origin . . . The reason is because the transferor, having fully achieved his unworthy end, cannot be allowed to turn round and repudiate the means by which he did it — he cannot throw over the transfer. And the transferee, having obtained the property, can assert his title to it against all the world, not because he has any merit of his own, but because there is no one who can assert a better title to it.[490]

The court does not confiscate the property because of the illegality (something which could not be done in any event, as well as being totally impracticable). What is said, in the words of Lord Eldon,[491] is, "Let the estate lie where it falls."

Some difficulty is inherent in this decision, and, indeed, in the whole issue. If the defendant's title is founded upon the contract, which is illegal, how can it be said that he acquires title against the plaintiff (or anyone else)? If there is some independent ground for an assertion of title, for example, it is a gift which is perfected by delivery, then the conclusion is both more consistent with principle and more acceptable. However, it would now seem established that, in whatever manner the title was transferred, the intent of the parties will be effectuated, even though illegality was committed in the process.[492] This is suggested by a more recent decision of the English Court of Appeal, in which Lord Denning participated, *Belvoir Finance Co. v. Stapleton.*[493] There was an illegal sale and hire-purchase arrangement of three cars, followed by a fraudulent transfer of the cars by the assistant manager of the company which was taking the cars on hire-purchase from the plaintiffs. When they sued the assistant manager for conversion, the question of title arose. Did the plaintiffs acquire title under the illegal transactions such that they could enforce it against the defendant (the innocent purchaser being otherwise protected)? Following *Singh v. Ali*, even though the cars in the *Belvoir* case had never been delivered to the plaintiffs (unlike the lorry in *Singh v. Ali* which had been possessed by the plaintiff, though later taken by the defendant without the plaintiff's consent), the court held that the plaintiffs in the *Belvoir* case had acquired title to the cars. This acquisition of title could be the basis of an action for conversion against the defendant. This is an even stronger authority than the *Singh* case, since the court had to invoke the provisions of the Sale of Goods Act with respect to passing of property where no physical possession had been given to the buyer, and had to decide the issue by reference to the intention of the parties as to passing of

---

490 *Ibid.*, at 176. Compare *Euro-Diam Ltd. v. Bathurst*, [1988] 2 All E.R. 23 at 29 (C.A.) *per* Kerr L.J.

491 *Muckleston v. Brown* (1801), 6 Ves. 52 at 69.

492 This sentence was quoted by Stratton C.J. in *Tucker Estate v. Gillis*, above, note 481, at 697.

493 [1971] 1 Q.B. 210 (C.A.); see also *Belvoir Finance Co. v. H.G. Cole & Co.*, [1969] 2 All E.R. 904.

property,[494] even though that intention was based upon, and involved an illegal contract of sale. The decision can be supported on the grounds that: (1) the plaintiffs did not have to rely on *turpis causa*, but upon the intention of the seller to transfer property in the cars to the plaintiffs (the *motive*, that is, the illegal transaction being immaterial for this purpose); and (2) the defendant was not *in pari delicto*: as he was only an official of the company which was involved in the illegal transaction, he was not the other party to such transaction.

So far as the first point is concerned, it has already been seen that, as long as the plaintiff does not have to set up the illegal transaction as the basis of his claim, he will be able to succeed.[495] Hence, in *Amar Singh v. Kulubya*,[496] since the plaintiff's claim to return of land was based upon his registered ownership of it, the fact that the plaintiff was also the landlord of the defendant under an illegal tenancy agreement was not material to his claim for repossession. Similarly in *Neider v. Carda of Peace River District Ltd.*,[497] the plaintiff could succeed not on the basis of any illegal contract, but simply because the plaintiff was still the registered owner of the land in question. In *Clelland v. Clelland*,[498] a man believed he was married to the woman to whom he had transferred some property. The property was recoverable, even though their relationship was immoral, such that there was no lawful consideration for the transfer, because the "husband's" claim was not founded upon the illegality, but upon the transfer under what was held to be a mistake of fact, namely, that the parties were lawfully married. A leading, but sometimes criticized case, is *Bowmakers Ltd. v. Barnet Instruments Ltd.*,[499] in which the plaintiffs had acquired title to machine tools under an illegal contract. When they delivered the tools to the defendants under a hire-purchase agreement, the latter, after paying some instalments, sold some of the tools to third parties and refused to re-deliver the others. The plaintiffs could sue the defendants in conversion, notwithstanding that the original sale to the plaintiffs was illegal (although this did not prevent their obtaining title from their vendor) as were the hire-purchase agreements with the defendants. The latter illegality is perhaps more in point. Yet it should not have prevented a claim for conversion by selling the goods, in breach of bailment, to third parties. It might have stopped the claim in respect of the other, that is, the remainder of the goods, still in the defendants' possession. However, it might still be said that the plaintiffs' claim was founded

---

494 Compare Fridman, *Sale of Goods in Canada*, 3rd ed. (1986), pp. 70-95.
495 Hence, the plaintiff could recover his down-payment in *Osmack v. Stan Reynolds Auto Sales Ltd.*, [1974] 1 W.W.R. 408 (Alta. C.A.); affirmed, [1976] 2 W.W.R. 576 (S.C.C.).
496 [1964] A.C. 142 (P.C.), with which contrast *Chettiar v. Chettiar*, [1962] A.C. 294 (P.C.).
497 [1972] S.C.R. 678 (S.C.C.); compare where the transfer involved illegality at common law, not under statute: *Elford v. Elford*, above, note 481.
498 [1944] 3 W.W.R. 234 (B.C.S.C.); affirmed, [1945] 2 W.W.R. 399 (B.C.C.A.). See also *Re Spears and Levy* (1974), 52 D.L.R. (3d) 146 (N.B.C.A.).
499 [1945] K.B. 65 (C.A.); on which see Coote, "Bowmakers Ltd. v. Barnet Instruments Ltd." (1972), 35 M.L.R. 38. Compare a Canadian case in which the plaintiff could ignore the legal contract of carriage and sue in tort for negligence in causing the loss of the goods being transported by the common carrier under such contract: *Keystone Fisheries Ltd. v. Leftrook* (1959), 27 W.W.R. 289 (Man. C.A.).

upon the improper action of the defendants in denying the plaintiffs the return of the latter's goods.

So far as concerns the second point mentioned above in relation to the *Belvoir* case, it raises the issue whether parties are truly *in pari delicto*. In the *Belvoir* case the defendant might not be considered such a party. But, even in cases where the parties to an action are parties to the illegal transaction, such that *prima facie* the doctrine *in pari delicto potior est conditio defendentis* applies so as to defeat the plaintiff's claim, there are exceptional circumstances in which this does not hold true.[500]

(iii) *Repentance*

Where illegality has not yet intervened, that is, the contract is not executed, any property which has been transferred by the plaintiff to the defendant in pursuance of the illegal agreement is recoverable.[501] In such circumstances it is said that there is a *locus poenitentiae*. The repenting party, however, must do so in time, before the illegal purpose has been effectively performed. When this occurs he may come to the court for assistance in recovering his property. So, in *Taylor v. Bowers*,[502] the plaintiff believed that he was insolvent. To avoid payment of his creditors he assigned goods to X who mortgaged them to the defendant, with knowledge that all this was to defraud the plaintiff's creditors. When the plaintiff did not become insolvent so as to involve the consequence of bankruptcy, he was held able to recover his goods from the defendant. But, in *Kearley v. Thomson*,[503] the defendants agreed not to appear at the public examinations of the plaintiff, a bankrupt, and also agreed not to oppose his discharge in due course. In return, the plaintiff agreed to pay a sum of money for their costs, the defendants being the solicitors for the petitioning creditor. The defendants did not appear, but before the plaintiff applied for discharge he sued the defendants for the return of the money paid them by him. It was held that he could not recover. The illegality must be substantially, even if not completely performed, for the money to be irrecoverable. Hence the difference between these two cases. Hence also the refusal to permit the bettor in *Parker v. Mason*[504] to recover the money given to the bookmaker for illegal bets, even though the bets had not been placed by the latter. In one sense, the contract had been executed. But in *Ouston v. Zurowski*[505] the illegal purpose had not been effectuated before the plaintiff repented. The plaintiff had given the defendant money to participate in a pyramidal sale which was illegal. Before anything had been done under this illegal scheme, the plaintiff abandoned

---

500 Below, pp. 431-432.

501 *Lawson v. Farley*, [1924] 1 W.W.R. 243 (Sask. C.A.). Hence the possibility of an action for the return of the deposit in *Stuart v. Kingman* (1979), 91 D.L.R. (3d) 142 (Ont. H.C.), even though the contract of sale was illegal because it violated the Ontario Land Transfer Tax Act.

502 (1876), 1 Q.B.D. 291 (C.A.).

503 (1890), 24 Q.B.D. 742 (C.A.).

504 [1940] 2 K.B. 590.

505 (1985), 63 B.C.L.R. 89 (B.C.C.A.); compare *McDonald v. Fellows* (1979), 105 D.L.R. (3d) 434 (Alta. C.A.).

any involvement and sought to recover the money. This was enough to permit such recovery.

Another point also emerges from these cases: the reason why the contract is not executed must be because of repentance by the plaintiff, not because its execution has been "frustrated" irrespective of the desires of the plaintiff. Frustration is what occurred in *Bigos v. Bousted*,[506] namely the failure by the other contracting party to perform his side of the illegal bargain (like the bookmaker in *Parker v. Mason*). As Pritchard J. said in that case,

> ... there is a distinction between what may ... be called the repentance cases ...and the frustration cases ... If a particular case may be held to fall within the category of repentance cases, I think the law is that the court will help a person who repents, provided his repentance comes before the illegal purpose has been substantially performed.[507]

There may be some problem about determining what is partial, as opposed to substantial performance of an executory contract. But, it is suggested that the difficulty is not so great as to prevent the courts from being able to decide when money transferred under an illegal contract is recoverable.

The requirement that the plaintiff must repent was the reason why the plaintiff could not succeed in his action for specific performance of a contract for the sale of land in *Zimmerman v. Letkeman*.[508] This involved a sale of land, the purchase price for which was falsely stated in the contract as being other than what it was in fact so that the purchaser could obtain a larger loan from a mortgage company. The vendor subsequently repudiated the contract on the ground that he did not wish to be party to a fraud. The vendor's repentance did not aid the purchaser. In effect the purchaser was still attempting to enforce an illegal contract. The Supreme Court of Canada reversed the Saskatchewan Court of Appeal,[509] which had held, by a majority, that the plaintiff could invoke the *locus poenitentiae* doctrine, and eschew the illegal acts in his claim for specific performance. Instead the Supreme Court arrived at the same conclusion as the dissentient, Bayda J.A., who applied the English case of *Alexander v. Rayson*,[510] which was indistinguishable in principle from the *Zimmerman* case. It also involved an unsuccessful attempt to enforce a land contract, in that instance a lease, not, however, by seeking specific performance but by an action for unpaid rent. Because of the fraudulent intent of the landlord, his claim failed. To the Supreme Court of Canada the plaintiff in *Zimmerman* was not founding his claim on any repudiation of his erstwhile fraudulent intent or purpose. He was continuing to rely on a contract that was illegal, in the light of the evidence, even though the documents on which he relied did not disclose his unlawful purpose.

---

506 [1951] 1 All E.R. 92.
507 *Ibid.*, at 100.
508 [1978] 1 S.C.R. 1097 (S.C.C.).
509 [1977] 1 W.W.R. 408 (Sask. C.A.), applying *Elford v. Elford* (1922), 64 S.C.R. 125 (S.C.C.) and reversing, [1975] 4 W.W.R. 216 (Sask. Q.B.).
510 [1936] 1 K.B. 169 (C.A.).

(iv) *Parties not equally in fault*

There may be a reason why the parties should not be treated as equally responsible for the illegal transaction into which they have entered. In such event, the one who is singled out for such special consideration will be able to sue on the contract, at least to the extent of recovering what he has paid the other party.[511] This will occur where one party has been the victim of fraud, duress, or some similar conduct on the part of the other party. An example is provided by *Steinberg v. Cohen*.[512] There was an agreement to stifle a prosecution. The money agreed to be paid was given, as was a security which was part of the bargain. The payee exerted pressure on the party paying the money and giving the security. Hence, it was held that they were not *in pari delicto*. The security was set aside. But the money was not recoverable. This latter part of the decision is strange, in view of earlier[513] as well as later cases[514] in which money obtained by duress has been held recoverable, even where some illegality was involved. It would appear that, in this regard, this decision is now doubtful. A stronger case is *Erwin v. Snelgrove*,[515] in which the consideration for a mortgage given by the plaintiff to the defendant was the stifling of a prosecution against a relative of the plaintiff. Although this was an illegal transaction, the plaintiff was not *in pari delicto* with the defendant, because he could show that he was induced by undue influence and pressure to make the contract. Hence, the mortgage was invalid.

The parties will also not be *in pari delicto* if one party can show that the contract infringed a statute that was passed to protect a class of persons of which the plaintiff was a member. In such instances, he can claim the protection of the statute, despite his own participation in the illegality.[516] This has been held to be the situation in England under legislation dealing with money-lenders,[517] and under

---

511 Hence, the plaintiff could have recovered his cheque, despite the illegality under the Alberta Land Titles Act, since the parties were not *in pari delicto*, in *Hands v. Sutherland* (1976), 66 D.L.R. (3d) 40 (Alta. S.C.). Perhaps, also this was the reason why the plaintiff could recover the price of the advertising in *Lunenburg County Press Ltd. v. Demone* (1978), 26 N.S.R. (2d) 179 (N.S.C.A.), even though the contract contravened a statute. The defendant had induced the contract by misrepresentation. Compare *Tannock v. Bromley* (1979), 10 B.C.L.R. 62 (B.C.S.C.).

512 [1930] 2 D.L.R. 916 (Ont. C.A.); compare *Johnson v. Musselman*, [1917] 2 W.W.R. 444 (Alta. C.A.).

513 *Smith v. Cuff* (1817), 6 M. & S. 160, 105 E.R. 1203; *Atkinson v. Denby* (1862), 7 H. & N. 934, 158 E.R. 749; *British Workman's & Gen. Ins. Co. v. Cunliffe* (1902), 18 T.L.R. 502 (C.A.); *Harse v. Pearl Life Assur. Co.*, [1904] 1 K.B. 558 (C.A.). See also *Jones v. Merionethshire Permanent Bldg. Society*, [1892] 1 Ch. 173 (C.A.).

514 *E.g., Kiriri Cotton Co. v. Dewani*, [1960] A.C. 192 (P.C.).

515 [1927] 4 D.L.R. 1028 (Ont. C.A.); compare *Burris v. Rhind* (1899), 29 S.C.R. 498 (S.C.C.); *Fairweather v. McCullough* (1918), 43 O.L.R. 299 (Ont. C.A.). See also *Fuller v. Stoltze*, [1938] 1 W.W.R. 241 (Sask. C.A.); affirmed, [1939] S.C.R. 235 (S.C.C.).

516 *Browning v. Morris* (1778), 2 Cowp. 790, 98 E.R. 1364; *Barclay v. Pearson*, [1893] 2 Ch. 154.

517 *Lodge v. Nat. Union Invt. Co.*, [1907] 1 Ch. 300; *Kasamu v. Baba-Egbe*, [1956] A.C. 539 (P.C.).

landlord and tenant legislation by which premiums for granting tenancies were illegal.[518] The same approach applies in Canada in such circumstances.[519]

Parties will be *in pari delicto*, equally at fault, where they contract with their eyes open, knowing of the illegality. In *Rosemay v. Nuberg & Dale Construction Ltd.*,[520] the plaintiff employed the defendant as its agent to obtain tenants for its apartments. Both parties knew that the defendant was not registered under the Ontario Real Estate and Business Brokers Act. Consequently, the defendant was acting illegally. The plaintiff paid the defendant the agreed commission on one lease. Later the tenant defaulted and the plaintiff sought to recover the commission. The County Court Judge's decision in favour of the plaintiff was reversed on appeal by the Divisional Court. In this instance there were no grounds for asserting that the plaintiff was not equally involved with the illegality along with the defendant, and as much to blame for the breach of the statute. Hence, recovery was not possible. It would have been unjust to allow the plaintiff to rely on the statute to require the defendant to disgorge the fruits of her performing her part of the bargain even though that bargain was illegal.

(v) *Equitable relief*

It seems that equity may go further than the common law, at least in some instances. In marriage brokerage contracts, for example, which were invalid at common law on grounds of public policy,[521] it has been held that money paid in pursuance of such a contract, for example, in order to obtain the initial services of the broker, was recoverable, although the plaintiff in that case could hardly be described as an innocent party to the transaction. Since the broker did not produce a spouse for the plaintiff it might have been argued that the money was recoverable on the ground of failure of consideration (though this is difficult to sustain since the broker had done something to obtain a spouse, and could therefore legitimately argue that he had provided consideration for the initial payment). In any event, it was held, in *Hermann v. Charlesworth*,[522] that the money was recoverable on equitable grounds.

Another possible equitable basis for providing relief from the consequences

---

518 *Kiriri Cotton Co. v. Dewani*, [1960] A.C. 192 (P.C.).

519 *Sidmay Ltd. v. Wehttam Invts. Ltd.*, [1967] 1 O.R. 508 (Ont. C.A.); affirmed, [1968] S.C.R. 828 (S.C.C.). Contrast *Bon Street Devs. Ltd. v. Terracan Capital Corp.* (1992), 76 B.C.L.R. (2d) 90 (B.C.S.C.) where the parties contracted to pay interest that was illegal under the Criminal Code; the plaintiff was not a weak borrower and the defendant was not an oppressive lender; therefore they were *in pari delicto*: the exception did not apply.

520 (1982), 40 O.R. (2d) 152 (Ont. Div. Ct.). Contrast *First Nat. Bank of Oregon v. Watson Ranching Ltd.* (1984), 34 Alta. L.R. (2d) 110 (Alta. Q.B.) (where the plaintiff was ignorant of the deception which gave rise to the illegality).

521 Goff & Jones, *Law of Restitution*, 3rd ed. (1986), p. 419; but the cases cited there are old, belonging to the seventeenth, eighteenth and early nineteenth centuries. It is questionable whether this long dormant doctrine may be extended very generally. It appears to be based on, or explained in, some remarks of Lord Eldon in *Vauxhall Bridge Co. v. Spencer (Earl)* (1821), Jac. 64 at 67.

522 [1905] 2 K.B. 123 (C.A.).

of an illegal transaction was illustrated in *Springer v. Higgins Co.*[523] This is the doctrine that an officer of the court cannot take advantage of any mistake or other invalidating cause to avoid his otherwise existing liabilities or responsibilities. To permit him to do so would be contrary to the high principles of equity.[524] In that case the liquidator of a company sought directions of the court as to whether he was obliged to pay commission on a contract for the sale of property to an agent who was not licensed under provincial legislation dealing with real estate brokers and agents. Because of this the contract to pay commission was illegal. Notwithstanding this illegality, the court held the liquidator liable to pay the "agent". The liquidator had accepted the benefit of the efforts of the agent, that is, the product of the sale. Therefore, he was obliged to act as a "high-principled" person. It might have been different if the agent had sued the liquidator for the unpaid commission. In such a situation, presumably, the normal effects of an illegal contract would have ensued.

Lamont J. in a Saskatchewan case,[525] said that there was a distinction between illegal and void, but not illegal contracts. The former were bad at common law and equity and could found no relief; the latter, though bad in law could give rise to an equitable right to the return of property parted with under the agreement. It is suggested that this distinction is not entirely well-founded.[526] Even at common law there might be recovery of money or goods transferred under an illegal or a void, but not necessarily illegal contract.[527] In a subsequent Saskatchewan case, *Schuman v. Drab*,[528] it was held that where goods were sold and delivered under a contract which was contrary to a Saskatchewan statute, the goods must be returned or else paid for. This suggests that in some cases of illegality, at any rate, the defendant cannot enjoy the fruits of the contract without payment, even if both parties are cognizant of the illegality. It would seem, therefore, that, to a certain extent, even where a party is not totally innocent, which is the common-law requirement for recovery, in equity such a party might have some limited right to the return of his property or payment in lieu. Possibly, this might depend upon the comparative guilt of the plaintiff as against the defendant, and upon whether, in all the other circumstances, it would not be against the public interest to permit such recovery. However, the possibility of such lenience in equity must be noted.[529]

5. Conclusions

Some final comments may be made upon the whole subject of illegality in relation to the law of contract.

---

523 (1979), 5 B.L.R. 302 (Ont. Div. Ct.).

524 *Ex parte James* (1874), 9 Ch. App. 609; *Re Tyler*, [1907] 1 K.B. 865 (C.A.).

525 *George White & Sons v. Jashansky*, [1917] 2 W.W.R. 173 (Sask. S.C.).

526 Compare *Ciz v. Hauka* (1953), 11 W.W.R. 433 (Man. Q.B.).

527 Above, pp. 426-429.

528 [1919] 3 W.W.R. 588 (Sask. C.A.).

529 A proposed new view of the law and the treatment of payments under illegal contracts based on this broad, equitable principle is considered and expounded in Maddaugh & McCamus, *Law of Restitution* (1990), pp. 366-374.

At the present time there are some areas of the law that remain uncertain. The law of restraint of trade potentially is in a state of flux in view of recent decisions, which appear to broaden its scope, or to open the way to a broadening of scope. It is also far from clear just how far a contract may be illegal either under statute or at common law, or how far a party may be penalized as a result of being "involved" in a transaction which subsequently materializes as being illegal in inception or performance. The courts appear to have developed several rules or doctrines under which, if it be desired, a party can be relieved of the consequences of illegality.[530] While some guidance is provided in the cases, there is room for an authoritative statement not only of the principles of illegality but also of the principles relating to the effects of illegality. Until this has been done, there will continue to be a degree of uncertainty about the entire question, not only theoretically but also in terms of the decision of any given case or the resolution of any individual problem.[531]

---

530 This and the previous sentence were cited by Bouck J. in *Cyprus Anvil Mining Corp. v. White Pass & Yukon Corp.* (1980), 21 B.C.L.R. 93 at 102 (B.C.S.C.); affirmed (1980), 21 B.C.L.R. 282 (B.C.C.A.).

531 The Ontario Law Reform Commission, *Report on Amendment of the Law of Contract* (1987), Chapter 11, did not recommend any alteration of the doctrine with respect to illegal contracts, but did suggest giving broad powers to courts to deal with such contracts generally and contracts in restraint of trade in particular. For discussion of these proposals, see Trakman, "Porridge or Scrambled Eggs" (1988-89), 14 Can. Bus. L.J. 75.

11

Conditional Contracts

1. The older law
2. "True" conditions precedent
3. Waiver
4. Obligations under true conditions precedent
5. The present status of the *Turney* doctrine

1. The older law

Prior to the English Sale of Goods Act, 1893, the expression *condition* was employed by the courts to refer to a term in a contract by virtue of which the contract could be postponed, so far as its taking effect was concerned, unless or until a certain event or occurrence took place, or could be rendered invalid and non-binding *ab initio* if a certain event or occurrence happened.[1] The former types of condition were called "conditions precedent",[2] the latter "conditions subsequent".[3] An alternative form of language was to refer to the former class of conditions as *suspensive* (because they acted to suspend the potential operation of the contract), and the latter *resolutive* (because they acted to dissolve or render ineffective a contract that had already become operative).[4] It was a question of construction, either from the express language of the contract, or by admitting parol evidence of some such agreement between the parties, as in *Pym v. Campbell*,[5] whether the contract as it stood was absolute, that is, immediately binding and incapable of being upset by any circumstances or events, or was conditional.[6]

---

1 See the history related by Diplock L.J. in *Hong Kong Fir Shipping Co. v. Kawasaki Kisen Kaisha*, [1962] 2 Q.B. 26 (C.A.); and Reynolds, "Warranty, Condition and Fundamental Term" (1963), 79 L.Q.R. 534 at 535.

2 What Lord Reid presumably was referring to in *Schuler A.G. v. Wickman Machine Tool Sales Ltd.*, [1973] 2 All E.R. 39 at 44 (H.L.) when he spoke of "a pre-condition: something which must happen or be done before the agreement can take effect." See *e.g., Bettini v. Gye* (1876), 1 Q.B.D. 183, where, in fact, the obligation to arrive in London a stated number of days prior to the performance was *not* a condition precedent; compare also *Behn v. Burness* (1863), 3 B. & S. 751, 122 E.R. 281.

3 *Head v. Tattersall* (1871), L.R. 7 Exch. 7; *i.e.*, what Lord Reid, above, called "some state of affairs which must continue to exist if the agreement is to remain in force."

4 This passage was inferentially referred to by Dube J. in *Imperial General Properties Ltd. v. R.* (1983), 143 D.L.R. (3d) 735 at 740 (Fed. T.D.).

5 (1856), 6 E. & B. 370, 119 E.R. 903; compare below, pp. 455-459.

6 For an older pair of illustrative English cases, see *Poussard v. Spiers* (1876), 1 Q.B.D. 410 and *Bettini v. Gye*, above, note 2.

A new use of the terminology was introduced by the Sale of Goods Act in 1893.[7] Notwithstanding this development, further examples, on both sides of the line,[8] can be found of the pre-1893 use of the expressions condition precedent and condition subsequent. In one Canadian case,[9] decided before the decision of the Supreme Court in *Turney v. Zhilka*[10] a term was held not to be a condition precedent because it was not a material term related to a guarantee, but only provided machinery to facilitate the delivery of certain shares. In *Hong Kong Fir Shipping Co. v. Kawasaki Kisen Kaisha Ltd.*,[11] it was held that in a charter-party there was no condition precedent as to the seaworthiness of the ship to be chartered, such that the charterers could repudiate the charter when it turned out that the ship was not ready on time. Hence, the latter were liable for wrongful repudiation of the contract at the suit of the owners. In another English case,[12] however, a condition that would have been a condition precedent was held to be void for uncertainty. There it was supposed to be a term of a contract of sale of a house that a "satisfactory" mortgage would be arranged. It was held that this was so vague as to be bad. In consequence the contract of sale never came validly into existence, with the result that the party ultimately in possession was not lawfully in possession.

With these may be contrasted clear instances of such conditions precedent.[13] In *The "Mihalis Angelos"*,[14] for example, the expected readiness of a chartered ship to load was a condition precedent of the charter-party, unlike the alleged condition as to seaworthiness in the *Hong Kong Fir* case. Hence, the *owners* were in breach. Similarly, with the obligation to open an irrevocable sight credit before fish could be delivered under a contract.[15] So, too, in a case concerned with the lease of a house, the payment of a deposit was not just earnest of the good intentions of the lessee; it was a condition precedent to the contract taking effect. Hence, when the deposit was not paid by the purported lessee, he had no interest in land capable of being registered under the English Land Charges Act, so as to permit

---

7 Below, pp. 488-489.

8 And some narrow decisions: see, *e.g.*, *Davidson v. Norstrant*, [1921] 1 W.W.R. 993 (S.C.C.). Compare *Battle v. Willox* (1908), 40 S.C.R. 198 (S.C.C.).

9 *Brunt v. Fairley; Birge v. Fairley*, [1955] O.W.N. 248 (Ont. H.C.); affirmed [1955] O.W.N. 677 (Ont. C.A.).

10 [1959] S.C.R. 578 (S.C.C.), discussed below, pp. 437-441.

11 [1962] 2 Q.B. 26 (C.A.).

12 *Lee-Parker v. Izzet (No 2)*, [1972] 2 All E.R. 800; with which contrast the situation where the party had to obtain "an acceptable offer" in the Canadian case of *Lestrange v. Juda*, [1973] 1 O.R. 588 (Ont. H.C.), in which the condition surely ought to have been void for uncertainty. Compare as to a condition *subsequent* that was *ultra vires*, *Alta. Rolling Mills Co. v. Christie*, [1919] 1 W.W.R. 572 (S.C.C.).

13 See, *e.g.*, *Chase v. Campbell*, [1962] S.C.R. 425 (S.C.C.); *McBride v. Johnson*, [1962] S.C.R. 202 (S.C.C.).

14 [1970] 3 All E.R. 125 (C.A.); compare as to condition of thickness of materials in a construction contract; *Laminated Structures & Holdings Ltd. v. Eastern Woodwkrs. Ltd.*, [1962] S.C.R. 160 (S.C.C.).

15 *Nfld. Associated Fish Exporters Ltd. v. A.T. Karelas* (1963), 49 M.P.R. 49 (Nfld. S.C.); *Trans Trust S.P.R.L. v. Danubian Trading Co.*, [1952] 2 Q.B. 297 (C.A.). Compare as to foreign exchange, *Bank of China, Japan & The Straits v. American Trading Co.*, [1894] A.C. 266 (P.C.).

him to enter a caution against the plaintiff's title.[16] Again, in *Bentworth Finance Ltd. v. Lubert*,[17] the failure of the seller of a car to deliver the buyer its log-book (even though this was not a document of title) was a breach of a suspensive condition, that is, a condition precedent. Therefore, a contract of hire-purchase never came into existence, in consequence of which the defendant, the one wishing to buy the vehicle the log-book of which was never delivered, was not liable for arrears under the hire-purchase agreement, nor for damages.

A similar situation can arise with respect to a condition subsequent, as shown by the English case of *Smallman v. Smallman*.[18] There an agreement between a husband and wife, in the process of separating and divorcing, under which the husband was making a settlement with the wife, was said to be "subject to approval" by the court. It was held that there was a binding agreement right away, but it became invalid if the court did not approve. Lord Denning M.R. said that the agreement was suspended in *operation* until the court approved its terms, but in the meantime, neither party could disavow it. He compared this situation with a sale of goods which was agreed to be subject to a party's obtaining an export or import licence, and with a sale of land "subject to title being approved by our solicitor".[19] The latter instance is very different from a contract of sale which is subject to a condition precedent.[20]

2. "True" conditions precedent

A radical change in the approach to conditions precedent was effected by the Supreme Court of Canada in *Turney v. Zhilka*.[21] The court differentiated what was called "a true condition precedent — an external condition upon which the existence of the obligation depends"[22] from an ordinary or *internal* condition, which, in effect, was a condition in the sense in which that term was understood after the Sale of Goods Act.[23] If a condition is a true condition precedent, there is no contract until it is satisfied. If a condition is the other sort of condition, then, in the event of its non-fulfilment, there may still be a binding contract between the parties, depending on the way in which the innocent party, guiltless of any breach, reacts to a breach of the condition.[24] It follows from *Turney v. Zhilka*, therefore,

16 *Myton Ltd. v. Schwab-Morris*, [1974] 1 All E.R. 326. Compare as to the valuation of property to be sold, *Harcourt v. Craddock*, [1954] O.R. 308 (Ont. C.A.).

17 [1968] 1 Q.B. 680 (C.A.).

18 [1971] 3 All E.R. 717 (C.A.).

19 *Ibid.*, at 720.

20 On which see *Aberfoyle Plantations Ltd. v. Cheng*, [1960] A.C. 115 at 124-125 (P.C.) per Lord Jenkins. Until the condition is fulfilled there is no contract of sale to be completed: *ibid.*, at 126. Compare with respect to a deed given in escrow: *Kingston v. Ambrian Invt. Co.*, [1975] 1 All E.R. 120 (C.A.).

21 [1959] S.C.R. 578 (S.C.C.).

22 *Ibid.*, at 583 per Judson J.

23 What is here said about conditions precedent also applies, *mutatis mutandis*, to conditions subsequent: see *Raysun Pty. Ltd. v. Taylor*, [1971] Qd. R. 172 (Aust.); *Gange v. Sullivan* (1966), 116 C.L.R. 418 (Aust.); cited in *Matrix Const. Co. v. Chan*, below, note 28. See also *296440 Ont. Ltd. v. Silverwood Industries Ltd.* (1983), 41 O.R. (2d) 624 (Ont. Co. Ct.).

24 Below, pp. 529-534.

that a distinction now exists between a condition relating to the *existence* of any contractual obligation and a condition that is precedent to *performance* of a contractual obligation by the other party, not the one subject to fulfilment of the condition precedent.[25]

Although the notion of "true" conditions precedent has been subjected to criticism,[26] Dickson J., speaking for the majority of the court in *Barnett v. Harrison*,[27] held that the idea was firmly enshrined in Canadian law. The many cases in which the nature of a condition precedent has been argued make the difference between the two kinds of such conditions clear, even though the actual determination of the correct character of the condition under consideration by a court in any given instance may not always be simple and straightforward.[28]

---

25 This paragraph was quoted in *Ponoka Savings & Credit Union Ltd. v. Urban Core Developers Ltd.*, [1988] 6 W.W.R. 321 at 324 (Sask. Q.B.) *per* Wright J.

For an example of a *performance condition*, in this instance the provision of adequate insurance, see *Fletton Ltd. v. Peat Marwick Ltd.* (1986), 32 B.L.R. 162 (B.C.S.C.); affirmed (1988), 50 D.L.R. (4th) 729 (B.C.C.A.); leave to appeal to S.C.C. refused (1988), 50 D.L.R. (4th) vii (note) (S.C.C.). Compare also, *Maritime Couriers (Int.) Inc. v. Woodstock Int. Export Ltd.* (1986), 33 B.L.R. 309 (B.C.S.C.), commission payable only on performance of sales contract: therefore not payable when that contract not performed because of lack of a compliance bond; *Wolf Mountain Coal Ltd. Partnership v. Netherlands Pacific Mining Co.* (1988), 31 B.C.L.R. (2d) 16 (B.C.S.C.); affirmed (1989), 36 B.C.L.R. (2d) xxxvii (note) (B.C.C.A.), failure of plaintiff to produce feasibility study to obtain bank financing for sale of one-half of defendant's interest in coal-producing property: therefore plaintiff's claim for breach of contract dismissed; *Thornitt v. Watson Projects Inc.* (1989), 27 C.P.R. (3d) 270 (B.C.S.C.), lessors failed to provide property to lessee, therefore defendant, sub-lessor, liable to sub-lessee.

Contrast *McCaig v. Nimmo* (1987), 85 N.B.R. (2d) 132 (N.B.Q.B.): true condition precedent, *viz.*, that purchaser of land could find purchaser for his Nova Scotia property on or before a stipulated date; *Crerar v. Credit Foncier Trust Co.* (1987), 37 B.L.R. 1 (Ont. H.C.), true condition precedent, *viz.*, opening of letter of credit before mortgage could be renewed.

26 Davies, "Conditional Contracts for the Sale of Land" (1977), 55 Can. Bar Rev. 289; see also Reiter and Swan, "Contracts and the Protection of Reasonable Expectations," in Reiter and Swan, *Studies in Contract Law*, at pp. 12-15. Note also the attempt by Laskin C.J.C. in *Barnett v. Harrison* (1976), 57 D.L.R. (3d) 225 at 230-234 (S.C.C.) to distinguish *Turney v. Zhilka* in such a way as to render the approach in that case nugatory.

27 (1976), 57 D.L.R. (3d) 225 at 246-247 (S.C.C.). He gave five reasons: (1) the distinction between two types of "waiver" situations (below, p. 441) was valid; (2) the court should not interfere with agreements made by parties legally advised; (3) to find waiver despite the *Turney* doctrine would allow a party to enforce or upset a contract if it were profitable to do so, despite an express agreement that bound him; (4) the *Turney* doctrine avoided difficult questions of construction of an agreement; (5) the doctrine has been in effect since 1959 and has been followed, therefore it should continue unless compelling reasons to the contrary were shown, and parties could exclude the doctrine by express agreement.

With respect, these reasons are weak and unconvincing. In British Columbia the doctrine has been changed by statute: below, p. 447.

28 *Turney v. Zhilka*, above, note 21; *Barnett v. Harrison*, above, note 26; on which see (1976), 8 Ottawa L. Rev. 82; *F.T. Dev. Ltd. v. Sherman*, [1969] S.C.R. 203 (S.C.C.); *O'Reilly v. Marketers Diversified Inc.*, [1969] S.C.R. 741 (S.C.C.); *Metro. Trust Co. of Can. v. Pressure Concrete Services Ltd.*, [1973] 3 O.R. 629 (Ont. H.C.); affirmed on appeal (1975), 60 D.L.R. (3d) 431 (Ont. C.A.); *Matrix Const. Ltd. v. Chan* (1974), 51 D.L.R. (3d) 284 (B.C.S.C.); reversed on appeal [1976] 2 W.W.R. 764 (B.C.C.A.); *Whitehall Estates Ltd. v. McCallum* (1975), 63 D.L.R. (3d) 320 (B.C.C.A.); *100 Main St. Ltd. v. W.B. Sullivan Const. Ltd.* (1978), 20 O.R. (2d) 401 (Ont. C.A.); leave to appeal to S.C.C.

One way of differentiating the two types of conditions precedent is to distinguish "contingent" from "promissory" conditions.[29] The former are "true" conditions precedent in the sense indicated in *Turney v. Zhilka*: the latter are not and relate to the promises of the parties, that is, to the consideration provided by one party for performance of his obligations by the other party.[30] That the determination of the nature of a condition precedent can be a difficult task may be illustrated by reference to *McCauley v. McVey*.[31] A contract for the sale of land, in respect of which time was of the essence,[32] was stated to be contingent upon the vendor's having title to the land by the date set for closing. The vendor did not acquire title by that date because of his own failure to arrange the surveys necessary to effect the transfer of title to the vendor from a third party. The vendor then claimed that the contract was not binding because it was subject to a "true" condition precedent which had not been fulfilled. The purchaser sued for specific performance. At the trial of the action he failed. The dismissal of the claim for specific performance was upheld by the Ontario Court of Appeal. In the Supreme Court of Canada, however, the purchaser was successful. The majority of the court held that the condition was not a "true" condition precedent, with the consequence that the purchaser could keep the contract in force and demand performance when the vendor obtained the necessary title. McIntyre J. dissented. In his opinion, echoing the views of the Ontario Court of Appeal, this was a true condition precedent of the type characterized in *Turney v. Zhilka* and other decisions of the Supreme Court of Canada. The condition in this instance did not provide that the vendor was to acquire title. It was not promissory in nature. It referred merely to the vendor having title. It was contingent.[33]

Sometimes, it would seem, such "true" conditions precedent may be implied[34] (in the same way that the different category of *internal* conditions precedent may

refused (1978), 20 O.R. (2d) 401n (S.C.C.); *Great Georgian Realty Group v. Genesis Marketing Organization Ltd.* (1977), 76 D.L.R. (3d) 592 (Ont. H.C.); *O'Leary v. G.M. Gaudet Enterprises Ltd.* (1977), 27 N.S.R. (2d) 95 (N.S.T.D.); *Davis v. Prince* (1977), 21 N.S.R. (2d) 140 (N.S.C.A.); *Chaulk v. Fairview Const. Ltd.* (1977), 14 Nfld. & P.E.I.R. 13 (Nfld. C.A.); *Sky Ranches Ltd. v. Nelson* (1977), 4 B.C.L.R. 97 (B.C.S.C.); affirmed (1980), 30 B.C.L.R. 162 (B.C.C.A.); *Ed Sinclair Const. & Supplies Ltd. v. Grunthaler* (1979), 18 A.R. 162 (Alta. C.A.); *Amic Mortgage Invt. Corp. v. Marquette Financial Services Ltd.* (1982), 36 A.R. 501 (Alta. Q.B.); *Westwood Farms v. Cadieux; Barnabe v. Cadieux,* [1982] 5 W.W.R. 1 (Man. C.A.); leave to appeal to S.C.C. refused (1982), 18 Man. R. (2d) 269 (S.C.C.); *Hechter v. Thurston* (1979), 98 D.L.R. (3d) 329 (Man. C.A.); reversed (1981), 34 N.R. 181 (S.C.C.); *Haupt v. Westcott* (1981), 116 D.L.R. (3d) 585 (Alta. Q.B.); reversed (1981), 140 D.L.R. (3d) 573 (Alta. C.A.); leave to appeal to S.C.C. refused (1981), 39 N.R. 540n (S.C.C.); *King v. Holsmer* (1982), 44 N.B.R. (2d) 290 (N.B.Q.B.); *Fed. Business Dev. Bank v. Hoydalo* (1983), 23 Man. R. (2d) 256 (Man. Q.B.). Contrast *Lewis Realty Ltd. v. Skalbania* (1980), 23 B.C.L.R. 336 (B.C.C.A.); *White v. Big River Sports & Equipment Ltd.* (1980), 28 N.B.R. (2d) 308 (N.B.C.A.); *296440 Ont. Ltd. v. Silverwood Industries Ltd.* (1983), 41 O.R. (2d) 624 (Ont. Co. Ct.). Compare the cases cited above, note 25.

29 *Carlson v. Big Bud Tractors of Can. Ltd.* (1981), 7 Sask. R. 337 at 350-352 (Sask. C.A.).
30 *Inkster v. Waite* (1980), 22 B.C.L.R. 213 (B.C.C.A.).
31 (1980), 98 D.L.R. (3d) 577 (S.C.C.).
32 Below, pp. 525-529.
33 Above, note 31, at 582-583.
34 *Oserberg v. Wolfman* (1982), 15 Man. R. (2d) 263 (Man. Q.B.).

be implicit or implied in the contract where it is necessary to do so to make a contract effective).[35] Once again, it is a question of construction to be determined by a court, whether the obligations in a contract are absolute and immediately binding, or are contingent upon some external event.

When a contract is subject to such a "true" condition precedent, the question has been raised whether any contract exists between the parties before the condition is satisfied. Some cases suggest the view that it would be logical and correct to conclude that until the satisfaction of the condition precedent, there is no binding contract between the parties.[36] The alternative view, approved it would appear by the Supreme Court of Canada in *Dynamic Transport Ltd. v. O.K. Detailing Ltd.*,[37] is that if a condition precedent fails the contract may loosely be described as void, but it is not entirely accurate to say that the actual validity of a contract depends upon the condition precedent. Once the parties have complied with the rules of offer and acceptance, the contract is concluded in the sense that neither party is free to withdraw from it pending fulfilment or non-fulfilment of the condition. As a result it is preferable to say that non-fulfilment of the condition makes the contract inoperative as opposed to void.[38] As Dickson J. said in the case just cited,[39]

> [i]t is true that the performance of some of the provisions of that agreement [to obtain planning permission before an agreed sale of land could go through] was not due unless and until the condition was fulfilled, but that in no way negates or dilutes the force of the obligations imposed by those provisions. . . .These obligations were merely in suspense pending the occurrence of the event constituting the condition precedent.

For reasons which will later appear,[40] the Supreme Court may not have been obliged to come to such a conclusion in this case. Hence, the statement by Dickson J. may go further than was necessary. Moreover, it may be suggested that to say that a contract exists, where it is subject to a true condition precedent in the *Turney* sense, obfuscates the distinction that has been made between such true conditions precedent and conditions precedent to the performance of a contract,[41] rather than to its existence or validity. The former, if they are to be distinguished at all, must be so on the basis that their inclusion in an agreement renders that agreement ineffective to bind the parties until the event contemplated by the condition. What

---

35 Below, pp. 475-481.
36 Compare *Garner v. Lee*, [1977] 3 W.W.R. 760 (B.C.S.C.); *Phipps v. Pickering* (1978), 8 B.C.L.R. 101 (B.C.S.C.); *Hechter v. Thurston* (1980), 98 D.L.R. (3d) 329 (Man. C.A.); reversed [1980] 2 S.C.R. 254 (S.C.C.); *Ed Sinclair Const. & Supplies Ltd. v. Grunthaler* (1978), 8 Alta. L.R. (2d) 244 (Alta. S.C.); reversed in part (1979), 10 Alta. L.R. (2d) 326 (Alta. C.A.); compare *Serendipity Pools (West) Ltd. v. Goodman's Industrial Maintenance Ltd.* (1982), 126 D.L.R. (3d) 140 at 147 (Man. C.A.); *Triple Five Corp. v. Crown Zellerbach Stores Ltd.* (1981), 17 Alta. L.R. (2d) 178 (Alta. Q.B.).
37 [1978] 2 S.C.R. 1072 (S.C.C.).
38 *296440 Ont. Ltd. v. Silverwood Industries Ltd.* (1983), 41 O.R. (2d) 624 at 627 (Ont. Co. Ct.) *per* Weiler Co. Ct. J., referring to Atiyah, *An Introduction to the Law of Contract*, 3rd ed. (1981), at pp. 146-147. For the admission of parol evidence to prove that a condition precedent has not been satisfied, see *Samoth Financial Corp. Ltd. v. Todd* (1979), 14 B.C.L.R. 266 (B.C.S.C.).
39 Above, note 37 at 1082.
40 Below, pp. 443-446.
41 Above, p. 436.

other reason would there be for including such a condition? Indeed in cases where contracts for the sale of land are subject to such conditions, the whole point is that the parties have taken steps to protect themselves by the inclusion of such a term, and their arrangements should not be upset by the courts, as Dickson J. himself pointed out in *Barnett v. Harrison*,[42] where one reason for upholding the *Turney* categorization was that it was consistent with the desires of the parties as expressed in their agreement. In contrast with such true conditions precedent, other conditions precedent do not affect the validity or binding quality of a contract, but simply suspend performance of the obligations arising under the contract on the part of one, or other, of the parties, or both, until the stipulated condition is fulfilled.

The effect of the subjection of a contract to a true condition precedent can best be clarified by reference to two important issues which have arisen in connection with such contracts. Indeed the nature of such conditions precedent is vital only in relation to these issues. Moreover, what has developed in the courts in Canada since the *Turney* case in respect of these issues may be said to have had a profound effect upon the validity of the *Turney* distinction between "true" conditions precedent and others. The issues in question are: (1) whether a condition precedent can be waived by one party; and (2) whether any particular duties are imposed upon either party or both where a contract is subject to a condition precedent.

3. Waiver

The chief point about the distinction made by the Supreme Court of Canada in *Turney v. Zhilka* was that "true" conditions precedent could never be waived unilaterally,[43] whereas other conditions precedent could be waived by the party for whose benefit such condition had been introduced into the contract.[44] In *Barnett v. Harrison*,[45] Dickson J. adverted to the correctness of the distinction made in the *Turney* case between the manifest right of A to waive default by B in the performance of a severable condition intended for the benefit of A and the attempt by A to waive his own default or the default of C, upon whom depended the performance which gave rise to the obligation, that is, the true condition precedent.

The *Turney* doctrine also resulted in avoidance of two difficult questions: (a) whether the condition precedent was for the benefit of the purchaser alone or the joint benefit of purchaser and vendor; and (b) whether the condition precedent was severable from the balance of the agreement.[46] In *Turney v. Zhilka*,[47] Judson

---

42 (1976), 57 D.L.R. (3d) 225 at 246 (S.C.C.).

43 *Barnett v. Harrison* (1976), 57 D.L.R. (3d) 225 (S.C.C.); *Lestrange v. Juda* (1973), 31 D.L.R. (3d) 684 (Ont. H.C.).

44 Contrast *Crerar v. Credit Foncier Trust Co.* (1987), 37 B.L.R. 1 (Ont. H.C.), and *McCaig v. Nimmo* (1987), 85 N.B.R. (2d) 132 (N.B.Q.B.) with *Dolan v. Patton* (1986), 75 N.S.R. (2d) 399 (N.S.T.D.). On waiver generally see below, pp. 544-546.

45 Above, note 43 at 246.

46 *Ibid.*, at 247.

47 [1959] S.C.R. 578 at 586 (S.C.C.).

J. had pointed out that waiver was permissible where a condition was severable from the remainder of the contract, that is, where it was not really a true condition precedent but a distinct obligation, or a condition precedent to performance. Many cases have been concerned with the issue whether a condition precedent that was before the court could be a "true" condition precedent, therefore not unilaterally waivable, or a severable or "ordinary" condition precedent, and therefore potentially capable of being waived by one party despite its non-fulfilment or the disagreement of the other party. One way of outflanking the strictness of the *Turney* doctrine has been by distinguishing the facts of a particular case from the situation that arose in *Turney v. Zhilka*. This was the method unsuccessfully employed by Laskin C.J., dissenting in *Barnett v. Harrison*. It has been more successfully employed in other instances.[48]

Where such a distinction cannot be drawn, the court is forced to declare the condition precedent effective and binding. A "true" condition precedent, in the *Turney* sense, goes to the root of the contract, and the only way that its fulfilment can be dispensed with so as to leave the contract intact and valid is if the parties make a new or further agreement, either varying the original contract by omitting or bilaterally waiving the condition precedent, or rescinding the original agreement and replacing it with a new one, from which the condition precedent of the first contract is lacking. If the condition in question is one which is not a condition precedent to the coming into effect of a binding contract, then such condition may be waived by both parties agreeing together, or by conduct which indicates such waiver by all of them;[49] or it may be waived unilaterally, as long as such waiver is by the party in whose favour the condition was inserted into the contract.[50]

In *Anglo-Newfoundland Industrial Resources Ltd. v. Hiscock*,[51] for example, a sale of land was conditional upon the purchaser's obtaining the necessary building permits. The purchaser decided not to apply for the permits and purported to waive the condition, calling upon the vendor to complete. The latter refused to do so. When the purchaser sued for specific performance, the vendor argued that, since the condition as to the permits was a true condition precedent, it could not be waived unilaterally, even if the purchaser alleged that it was included solely for his benefit. The vendor's argument was successful and specific performance was

---

48 *E.g. McCauley v. McVey* (1980), 98 D.L.R. (3d) 577 (S.C.C.). Indeed the inclusion in a contract of an express waiver clause may indicate that the condition precedent is not a true condition precedent in the *Turney* sense: see *Imperial Gen. Properties Ltd. v. R.* (1983), 143 D.L.R. (3d) 735 at 742 (Fed. T.D.) *per* Dube J., citing *Genern Invts. Ltd. v. Back* (1969), 3 D.L.R. (3d) 611 at 616-617 (Ont. H.C.) *per* Hartt J.; *Dennis v. Evans* (1972), 23 D.L.R. (3d) 625 (Ont. H.C.); affirmed (1972), 27 D.L.R. (3d) 680n (Ont. C.A.).

49 *Pizzo v. Crory* (1986), 71 N.S.R. (2d) 419 (N.S.T.D.).

50 See *e.g., Beauchamp v. Beauchamp*, [1973] 2 O.R. 43 (Ont. C.A.); affirmed (1974), 40 D.L.R. (3d) 160 (S.C.C.). For a case where there was no waiver see *Blanco v. Nugent*, [1949] 1 W.W.R. 721 (Man. K.B.). For a case where the vendor was asked to waive a condition as to forfeiture of a deposit if the purchaser did not pay, see *Beitel v. Sorokin*, [1973] 5 W.W.R. 639 (Alta. C.A.); affirmed [1974] 2 W.W.R. 767 (S.C.C.).

51 (1976), 14 Nfld. & P.E.I.R. 235 (Nfld. T.D.); compare *Hobart Invt. Corp. v. Walker* (1977), 76 D.L.R. (3d) 156 (B.C.C.A.); leave to appeal to S.C.C. refused (1977), 76 D.L.R. (3d) 156n (S.C.C.); *Ed Sinclair Const. & Supplies Ltd. v. Grunthaler* (1980), 18 A.R. 162 (Alta. C.A.).

refused. Similarly, government approval of a mortgage agreement by a certain date was also a true condition precedent, which could not be waived by either party, in *Amic Mortgage Investment Corporation v. Marquette Financial Services Ltd.*[52] In *Westward Farms Ltd. v. Cadieux; Barnabe v. Cadieux*,[53] the contract expressly stated that it would be void if the condition in question was not fulfilled; hence, there was no right to waive compliance with the condition even though the condition was included for the benefit of the plaintiff seeking to enforce the contract.

The above instances involved an attempt at unilateral waiver which was not agreeable to the other party. It would appear, however, that, in certain cases, a unilateral waiver of a "true" condition precedent may be "accepted" by the other party, in which event it will be effective to make the contract valid and enforceable, despite non-fulfilment of the condition precedent.[54] Such was the approach adopted by Goodman J. in *Smale v. Van der Weer*,[55] following a decision of the Ontario Court of Appeal in the earlier case of *Giaouris v. Pristouris*.[56] In the *Smale* case, the purchaser's waiver of a condition precedent to the operation of an agreement for the sale of land was accepted by the vendor, each party treating the contract as existing and enforceable. The waiver was effective and the vendor was able to enforce the contract against the purchaser. This may exemplify the idea of mutual agreement mentioned above. Or it may indicate that there has been some softening of the original strictness of the *Turney* doctrine. It might seem that Canadian courts, while accepting the *Turney* doctrine in principle, are endeavouring to escape from its trammels either by distinguishing cases on their facts or by permitting informal bilateral waiver without some formal agreement replacing the earlier one that was subject to the condition precedent.

There is another way in which the courts have succeeded in diminishing the significance of the *Turney* doctrine, and creating some liability despite the failure of a condition precedent to be fulfilled or to be complied with by the party, or the stranger to the contract, who was to perform something before the contract could be effective. This involves consideration of the duties which impliedly, if not expressly, arise when a contract is made subject to a condition precedent.

4. Obligations under true conditions precedent

Once a condition has been correctly characterized as a true condition precedent, the obligations of the respective parties may be clarified. Such a condition may expressly impose duties on one party or on both.[57] For example, it may be that the seller of goods has to have them valued in order to discover the price

---

52 (1982), 36 A.R. 501 (Alta. Q.B.); compare *Fed. Business Dev. Bank v. Hoydalo* (1983), 23 Man. R. (2d) 256 (Man. Q.B.).

53 [1982] 5 W.W.R. 1 (Man. C.A.); leave to appeal to S.C.C. refused (1982), 18 Man. R. (2d) 269 (S.C.C.).

54 Compare *Matrix Const. Ltd. v. Chan*, [1976] 2 W.W.R. 764 at 767 (B.C.C.A.).

55 (1977), 80 D.L.R. (3d) 704 (Ont. H.C.).

56 (1976), 2 R.P.R. 81 (Ont. C.A.); leave to appeal to S.C.C. refused (1977), 2 R.P.R. 81n (S.C.C.).

57 *Dynamic Tpt. Ltd. v. O.K. Detailing Ltd.* (1978), 85 D.L.R. (3d) 19 at 26 (S.C.C.) *per* Dickson J.; see, *e.g., Steiner v. E.H.D. Invts. Ltd.* (1977), 78 D.L.R. (3d) 449 (Alta. C.A.).

at which they are to be sold. Or the parties may have agreed that they will appoint an arbitrator to settle some vital term of their eventual contract. The consequences of such duties will depend on what happens. Thus, the party obliged to perform the condition precedent may neglect to do so, or may so act as to make it impossible for himself to fulfil it. He may be prevented from doing so by some act by the other party which makes it impossible for the first party to fulfil the condition precedent. They may *both* neglect or ignore their mutual obligation, or some intervening event or occurrence may make it impossible to fulfil the condition.

If the party obliged fails to perform,[58] or the party not obliged prevents the *other* party from performing the condition,[59] then he will not be able to enforce the contract as against the other party, on the ground that "a party shall not take advantage of his own wrong, or of an event brought about by his own act or omission."[60] Consequently the other, that is, innocent party, is relieved from the obligations of the contract. The same result will follow if the party obliged under the condition makes it impossible for himself to perform it, that is, if he is guilty of what has been called "self-induced frustration."[61] The converse of this is that the party leaving a condition precedent unfulfilled when it was his obligation to perform it, or preventing its fulfilment, will not be able to defend himself against an action for breach of the main contract.[62] But, in some circumstances, it may be that the condition itself is a separate obligation, the breach of which gives rise

---

58 As in *Jack Wookey Holdings Ltd. v. Tanizul Timber Ltd.* (1988), 27 B.C.L.R. (2d) 221 (B.C.C.A.).

59 *Harcourt v. Craddock*, [1954] O.R. 308 (Ont. C.A.); *McColl-Frontenac Oil Co. v. Angel*, [1948] 1 W.W.R. 169 (Man. Q.B.); affirmed [1948] 2 W.W.R. 127 (Man. C.A.); *Yukon Gold Co. v. Can. Klondike Power Co.*, [1919] 2 W.W.R. 814 (B.C.C.A.); *Boone v. R.*, [1934] S.C.R. 457 (S.C.C.).

60 *Metro Trust Co. of Can. v. Pressure Concrete Services Ltd.*, (1973), 37 D.L.R. (3d) 649 (Ont. H.C.); affirmed (1975), 60 D.L.R. (3d) 431 (Ont. C.A.) *per* Holland J., citing and relying on *New Zealand Shipping Co. v. Société Des Ateliers et Chantiers de France*, [1919] A.C. 1 (H.L.); *Commr. of Agricultural Loans of Ont. v. Irwin*, [1940] O.R. 489 (Ont. C.A.); affirmed [1942] S.C.R. 196 (S.C.C.). See also *Cheall v. Assn. of Professional, Executive, Clerical & Computer Staff*, [1983] 2 A.C. 180 (H.L.); *Alghussein Establishment v. Eton College*, [1988] 1 W.L.R. 587 (H.L.). See the various reasons given by the different members of the court for allowing the plaintiff to recover in *Whitehall Estates Ltd. v. McCallum* (1975), 63 D.L.R. (3d) 320 (B.C.C.A.). But if he has acted in good faith and the condition was for *his* benefit, then he may not be prevented from other advantages under the contract such as the recovery of his deposit, on the ground that the contract did not become effective by reason of the non-fulfilment of the condition precedent: see, *e.g.*, *Astra Trust Ltd. v. Adams*, [1969] 1 Lloyd's Rep. 81. Compare as to the performance of conditions *subsequent*, the remarks of Lord Denning M.R. in *Smallman v. Smallman*, [1971] 3 All E.R. 717 at 720 (C.A.); as to (1) licences, see *Brauer & Co. (G.B.) Ltd. v. James Clark (Brush Materials) Ltd.*, [1952] 2 All E.R. 497 (C.A.); *Pound & Co. v. Hardy Co.*, [1956] A.C. 588 (H.L.); (2) the purchase of property subject to approval of title, *Marten v. Whale*, [1917] 2 K.B. 480 (C.A.); *Branca v. Cobarro*, [1947] K.B. 854 (C.A.).

61 *Halifax v. Vaughan Const. Co.* (1957), 9 D.L.R. (2d) 431 (N.S.S.C.) a case of expropriation of property (reversed on other grounds (1958), 41 M.P.R. 19 (N.S.C.A.)). On frustration, see below, pp. 623 *et seq.* The situation will be different if the condition precedent becomes impossible to fulfil through the fault of *neither* party: *Focal Properties Ltd. v. George Wimpey Ltd.* (1975), 73 D.L.R. (3d) 387 (Ont. C.A.); affirmed on appeal [1978] 1 S.C.R. 2 (S.C.C.).

62 *Morse v. Mac & Mac Cedar Co.*, [1918] 2 W.W.R. 205 (B.C.S.C.); compare *Meeker v. Nicola Valley Lbr. Co.* (1917), 55 S.C.R. 494 (S.C.C.); leave to appeal to the Privy Council refused (1918), 55 S.C.R. vii.

to an action or some other remedy.[63] Indeed, this might be the only operative obligation, if the condition precedent remains unfulfilled, in accordance with what has been said earlier, since the main contract will not become effective failing performance of the condition. However, a party who has benefited from a contract over several years cannot subsequently plead that the other party did not perform or fulfil a condition precedent, in the event of later litigation on the contract.[64] In effect there is a new contract without the condition precedent. If there are obligations on *both* sides, that is, conditions precedent that must be fulfilled by each of the parties, then they must *both* carry out such obligations, or neither will be able to enforce the contract.[65]

Decisions in the past few years have drawn attention to the fact that, where a contract is subject to a true condition precedent, even though failure of the condition to be fulfilled might result in there being no binding contract between the parties, some liability may emerge from the lack of compliance with the condition. Indeed, there are even suggestions that the party who was not obliged to do anything under the contract, might be able to enforce the contract by a decree of specific performance, although the condition precedent to which the contract was subjected has not been fulfilled. The basis of such liability is the doctrine of implied terms, previously considered. By virtue of such an implication a party may come under a duty to act in good faith, to co-operate with the other party to obtain the assent or approval of a third party whose approval is a prerequisite of the contract, or to use his best efforts to achieve compliance with, or fulfilment of the condition precedent.

Recognition of this can be found in the judgment of Dickson J. in *Dynamic Transport Ltd. v. O.K. Detailing Ltd.*[66] "In appropriate circumstances," he said, "the Courts will find an implied promise by one party to take steps to bring about the event constituting the condition precedent." He gave as illustrations a contract where land was sold "subject to planning permission," into which contract courts have frequently implied a promise by the purchaser to use his best endeavours to obtain planning permission (no promise to obtain such permission could be implied since this would be without the control of the parties), and contracts subject to the condition precedent of an approval or licence being obtained, one party, by inference in the circumstances, being held to have undertaken to apply for the approval or licence. This type of case was a specific instance of the general principle that the court will readily imply a promise on the part of each party to do all that is necessary to secure performance of the contract.[67] As explained in a later

---

63 *Harcourt v. Craddock*, above, note 59; compare with respect to the duties in relation to a deed given on escrow, *Kingston v. Ambrian Invt. Ltd.*, [1975] 1 All E.R. 120 (C.A.).

64 *Sask. Co-op. Wheat Producers Ltd. v. Luciuk*, [1931] 2 W.W.R. 51 (Sask. C.A.).

65 *Mackay v. Dick* (1881), 6 App. Cas. 251 (H.L.); *Sprague v. Booth*, [1909] A.C. 576 (P.C.); *Kohler v. Thorold Natural Gas Co.* (1916), 52 S.C.R. 514 (S.C.C.) (where the defendant wilfully prevented the plaintiff from delivering gas); *Stuart & Co. v. Clark*, [1917] 2 W.W.R. 1049 (Alta. C.A.) (duty to make a railway "car" available when the contract was to deliver grain "on car").

66 (1978), 85 D.L.R. (3d) 19 at 27 (S.C.C.).

67 Compare *Mackay v. Dick*, above, note 65; see Burrows "Contractual Co-operation and the Implied Term" (1968), 31 M.L.R. 390.

British Columbia case,[68] such an implied term was necessary to give "business efficacy" to the contract.

Thus, in the *Dynamic Transport* case, the Supreme Court of Canada implied a promise by the vendor of land that was sold subject to subdivision approval to apply for such subdivision. In *Multi-Malls Inc. v. Tex-Mall Properties Ltd.; Tex-Mall Properties Ltd. v. Multi-Malls Inc.*,[69] a land sale agreement was subject to a condition that the site be rezoned to permit construction of a shopping centre. The purchaser was impliedly obliged not to perform any act likely to prevent such rezoning. In *Metropolitan Trust Co. of Canada v. Pressure Concrete Services Ltd.*,[70] a sale of land was conditional upon the mortgagee consenting to a new head lease. The vendor was impliedly obliged to obtain the consent of the mortgagee. In *100 Main Street Ltd. v. W.B. Sullivan Construction Ltd.*,[71] similar consent had to be obtained by the vendor from the mortgagee. To obtain such consent, it was necessary for the purchaser to assist the vendor by providing certain financial information. The purchaser refused to co-operate. Hence, the mortgagee's consent was not obtained. The purchaser was in breach of his implied duty to assist the vendor. Therefore, the purchaser could not rely on the vendor's default in fulfilling the condition precedent as a defence to an action for breach of contract.

In the majority of these instances the claim made by the victim of the breach of any implied duty was for damages for breach of contract. However, in *Steiner v. E.H.D. Investments Ltd.*,[72] and *Haupt v. Westcott*,[73] the claim that was successful was for specific performance of the contract that was subject to the unfulfilled condition precedent. Although the condition precedent was a true condition precedent, in the *Turney* sense, and could not be waived unilaterally, in both these cases the court held that the vendor could not frustrate the entire agreement by his failure to apply for the requisite subdivision; hence, he could not resist a claim for specific performance.

5. The present status of the Turney doctrine

Whether the claim is for damages or for specific performance, it looks almost as if the courts are denying or negating the correctness of the *Turney* approach, by giving some kind of recognition to a contract which is subject to a true condition precedent that has not be fulfilled. Yet it has been said consistently that the granting of a remedy for breach of such an implied duty (or an express one where it exists)

---

68 *BEM Enterprises Ltd. v. Campeau Corp.* (1980), 24 B.C.L.R. 244 (B.C.S.C.); varied (1981), 32 B.C.L.R. 116 (B.C.C.A.); compare *Dynamic Tpt. Ltd. v. O.K. Detailing Ltd.*, above, note 66, at 28.

69 (1980), 108 D.L.R. (3d) 399 (Ont. H.C.); affirmed on appeal (1981), 128 D.L.R. (3d) 192 (Ont. C.A.); leave to appeal to S.C.C. refused (1982), 41 N.R. 360n (S.C.C.).

70 (1973), 37 D.L.R. (3d) 649 (Ont. H.C.); affirmed on appeal (1975), 60 D.L.R. (3d) 431 (Ont. C.A.).

71 (1978), 20 O.R. (2d) 401 (Ont. C.A.); leave to appeal to S.C.C. refused (1978), 20 O.R. (2d) 401n (S.C.C.).

72 (1977), 78 D.L.R. (3d) 449 (Alta. C.A.).

73 (1981), 116 D.L.R. (3d) 585 (Alta. Q.B.); reversed (1981), 140 D.L.R. (3d) 573 (Alta. C.A.); leave to appeal to S.C.C. refused (1981), 39 N.R. 540n (S.C.C.).

is not the equivalent of allowing waiver of the condition.[74] Nor does it qualify the strict *Turney* doctrine.[75] Despite such denials, it may be suggested that to admit of a remedy where a condition precedent has not been fulfilled, and especially where the remedy accorded is the enforcement of the conditional contract, is a considerable alleviation or diminution of the *Turney* principle. When these inroads upon that principle are taken into conjunction with the decisions in which *Turney v. Zhilka* has been distinguished by holding that the condition in issue was not a true condition precedent but an internal condition that could be waived unilaterally, it may be seen that Canadian courts have gone a long way towards undermining the doctrine that was first enunciated by the Supreme Court in 1959 and has caused difficulty ever since that date.

What has caused the problems has been not the characterization of some conditions precedent as "true" conditions precedent, external to the contract, making the existence and validity of the contract conditional upon the happening of some event or the conduct of some third party, a stranger to the contract, but the determination that such conditions precedent could not be waived by one party, even where that party alleged that the condition had been inserted for his benefit. To escape from the consequences and ramifications of this doctrine, Canadian courts have been compelled to draw fine distinctions between different instances, to discover express obligations that could exist and bind a party quite separately from the main contract to which the condition precedent was attached, or to imply a term or terms into such contracts so as to achieve the same result. Such developments, it is suggested, have produced inconsistency (as well as dissension between judges in the same case[76]) and have resulted in illogicality, hardship, possibly even absurdity and decisions that smack of unreality.

Change in the law has occurred in one province, British Columbia. In 1978[77] a section was added to the Law and Equity Act by virtue of which waiver of a condition precedent that suspends the performance of a contract (that is, a true condition precedent in the *Turney* sense) may be made unilaterally, provided certain qualifications are satisfied. First of all, the condition precedent must benefit only the party purporting to waive the condition. Second, the contract must be capable of being performed without fulfilment of the condition precedent. Third, where a time is stipulated for fulfilment of the condition precedent waiver occurs before the time stipulated, and where a time is not so stipulated, the waiver is made within a reasonable time.

Adoption of this legislation has probably solved the difficulties inherent in the *Turney* doctrine so far as British Columbia is concerned. It is surprising that

---

74 Compare *Dynamic Transport Ltd. v. O.K. Detailing Ltd.*, above, note 66, at 27.

75 *Haupt v. Westcott*, above, note 73, at 592 *per* Kryska J.

76 See, *e.g., McCauley v. McVey* (1980), 98 D.L.R. (3d) 577 (S.C.C.); *Steiner v. E.H.D. Investments Ltd.*, above, note 72.

77 S.B.C. 1978, c. 11, s. 8; see now the Law and Equity Act, R.S.B.C. 1979, c. 224, s. 49, on which see *McNabb v. Smith* (1981), 124 D.L.R. (3d) 547 (B.C.S.C.); affirmed (1982), 44 B.C.L.R. 295 (B.C.C.A.).

other provinces have not thus far copied the example of British Columbia.[78] Until they do so, if they ever do, courts in the other provinces will be plagued by the problems to which reference has been made. They will be bound to apply the doctrine of "true" conditions precedent, with all its attendant distinctions and qualifications, both real and fictitious.

---

78 Similar provisons to those in the British Columbia statute were recommended for enactment by the Ontario Law Reform Commission's *Report on Amendment of the Law of Contract* (1987), Chapter 13.

12

Terms

1. Express terms

(a) Definition

The parties to a contract, in most instances, will have stated, orally or in writing, the nature, scope and extent of their individual, various obligations thereunder. Insofar as they have made manifest what those obligations are, the parties have *expressly* stipulated the *terms* of the contract. A *term* is a provision of the contract which states or makes explicit an obligation or set of obligations imposed thereunder on one or more of the parties to the contract. An *express term*, therefore, is one which has been specifically mentioned, and agreed upon by the parties, and its form, character and content expressed in the oral or written exchanges between them at the time the contract was made. In consequences, to know and understand the nature and extent of the contents of a contract it is necessary, in the first instance at any rate, to look at the express terms, if any, that have been assented to as between the parties.[1] The express language of the parties is the core of their contractual obligation.

The common law has long differentiated terms of a contract from *representations*. A representation has been defined[2] as "a statement or assertion made by one party to the other before or at the time of the contract of some matter or circumstances relating to it." Such statements may indeed be, or become terms of the contract, in which event they will have effect as such. However, if a representation is not and never becomes a term, its legal character and consequences are different.[3]

Terms are contractual and the failure to fulfil the promise contained in a term gives rise to an action for breach of contract. Representations are non-contractual. If they are not true the appropriate remedy is not an action for breach of contract, but the avoidance or rescission of a contract entered into in consequence of the representation, and, possibly, a tort action for damages. Thus, an untrue representation, or misrepresentation, may: (1) entitle the representee to avoid the contract, if the representation was fraudulently made;[4] (2) entitle the representee to rescind the contract, if the representation was innocently made[5] or; (3) entitle the representee to sue, in tort, for damages if the representation was negligently made.[6] Recent developments have indicated that an action in tort for negligent misrepresentation may be brought, on the basis of the breach of the duty of care owed by one contracting party to another, even though the victim of the misrepresentation may also be suing on the contract entered into as a result of the misrepresentation.[7] Moreover, an action for negligent misrepresentation may be brought alongside an action for breach of a collateral agreement,[8] even though to treat the statement which is the basis of the action as a representation, that is, a non-promissory

---

1 These first five sentences were cited in *Kuhlemeyer v. Sawyer* (1980), 14 R.P.R. 296 at 300-301 (Alta. Q.B.).

2 *Benjamin on Sale*, 8th ed. (1950), p. 554.

3 *Richview Const. Co. v. Raspa* (1975), 66 D.L.R. (3d) 193 at 196 (Ont. C.A.). The discussion in this chapter of the difference between terms and representations was referred to in *Dow & Duggan Prefabrication Ltd. v. Paquet* (1990), 87 Nfld. & P.E.I.R. 144 at 145 (P.E.I.T.D.); affirmed (November 16, 1990), Doc. No. GDC-6502 (P.E.I.C.A.).

4 Above, pp. 294, 300-303.

5 Above, pp. 294, 305.

6 Above, pp. 294-295.

7 *Sodd Corp. Inc. v. Tessis* (1977), 79 D.L.R. (3d) 632 (Ont. C.A.); *Roberts v. Montex Dev. Corp.*, [1979] 4 W.W.R. 306 (B.C.S.C.); *R.E. Lister Ltd. v. Dunlop Can. Ltd.* (1978), 85 D.L.R. (3d) 321 (Ont. H.C.); reversed (1979), 27 O.R. (2d) 168 (Ont. C.A.); reversed on other grounds, [1982] 1 S.C.R. 726 (S.C.C.); *Husky Oil Operations Ltd. v. Oster* (1978), 87 D.L.R. (3d) 86 (Sask. Q.B.); *O'Hara v. Chez Chapeaux Ltd.* (1977), 23 N.S.R. (2d) 610 (N.S.T.D.); Fridman, "The Interaction of Tort and Contract" (1977), 93 L.Q.R. 422.

8 *Esso Petroleum Co. v. Mardon*, [1976] 2 All E.R. 5 (C.A.); *Sodd Corp. Inc. v. Tessis*, above. See also *Sperry Rand Can. Ltd. v. Thomas Equipment Ltd.* (1982), 135 D.L.R. (3d) 197 (N.B.C.A.) (applied in *Morguard Trust Co. v. Lawton Drug Stores Ltd.* (1987), 84 N.B.R. (2d) 14 (N.B.Q.B.), and *Carman Const. Ltd. v. C.P.R.* (1980), 28 O.R. (2d) 232 (Ont. H.C.); affirmed (1981), 33 O.R. (2d) 472 (Ont. C.A.); affirmed [1982] 1 S.C.R. 958 (S.C.C.), where liability was not imposed for different reasons. See further below, pp. 515-516.

statement, and a collateral contractual promise at the same time appears something of a paradox.

Representations, though non-contractual in nature, may sometimes have contractual consequences or effects. First, a representation can be the basis of an independent, collateral contract.[9] Second, a representation may have contractual effects by the operation of the doctrine of estoppel. A statement not originally or subsequently incorporated in the final contract could be so relied upon by the party to whom it was made with the intention that it should be relied and acted upon by him. The representor may not be permitted to retract the statement later or refuse to act upon its accuracy and validity if to do so would be to the detriment of the other party. In this way, the representation, although not a contractual term, *modifies* or *qualifies* the contractual terms.[10] Except when a representation modifies or qualifies an existing contract a representation will not be effective to create a contract by estoppel.[11] To have such effect, the representation must not be as to the future state of affairs, or the future conduct of the representor. If it is of such a kind, then, to be binding and effective it must be a part of the main or original contract, that is, a term, or it must be separately supported by consideration so as to be an independent, collateral contractual obligation.

(b) When is a statement a term?

Not everything that is spoken or written by the parties in the course of the negotiations that lead to the conclusion of a contract will amount to a term of such contract. The intention of the parties is all-important. The basic distinction is between statements which are intended to be terms in the contract and statements which are meant by one party and understood by the other to be mere inducements by their maker to the other to enter into the contract. This is a question of fact,[12] as is made clear by the nineteenth century English case of *Bannerman v. White*[13] in which, during negotiations for the sale of hops, the prospective buyer asked the seller whether sulphur had ever been used in their treatment. If it had, he, the buyer, would not have troubled to ask the price. The seller said sulphur had not been used. A contract of sale ensued. Later the buyer discovered that sulphur had been used with respect to some of the hops. Did the statement bind the seller, so as to justify the buyer in repudiating the contract? Not unless the statement about the sulphur was intended to be a term in the contract. This was found by the jury to be the case. Consequently, the seller was bound and the buyer was entitled to reject the goods. Since the determination whether a particular statement

---

9 Below, pp. 459-462, 507-509, 510-512.

10 Compare above, pp. 121-136. In such instances there is an exception to the doctrine that a representation, to be effective, must be as to existing facts: *Clark's-Gamble of Can. Ltd. v. Grant Park Plaza Ltd.*, [1967] S.C.R. 614 (S.C.C.).

11 Compare above, p. 125.

12 *Irvine v. Parker* (1903), 40 N.S.R. 392 at 395 (N.S.C.A.).

13 (1861), 10 C.B.N.S. 844, 142 E.R. 685. Compare with respect to an express or implied warranty, *Rankin v. Eversfield* (1953), 15 W.W.R. 137 (B.C.S.C.).

was intended to be a term of the contract or must be construed as a representation is a question of fact, it follows that in any given instance a court must analyze the evidence and conclude appropriately.[14] The question then arises whether there are any legal tests applicable by the use of which a court can make the correct determination.

The fact that the agreement between the parties was committed to writing, and such writing omitted an earlier statement might tend to establish that any previous statement was a representation and not intended to be a term. This is what occurred in *Routledge v. McKay*,[15] which was concerned with a statement as to the age of a motorcycle sold by the defendant to the plaintiff. But the opposite is more likely to be true, that is, that a statement included in a later writing was more than a representation. Such was the suggestion made by Denning L.J. in *Oscar Chess Ltd. v. Williams*,[16] another English case concerned with the age of a motor vehicle which was the subject of a contract of sale. Here, however, as in the *Routledge* case, there was no written contract; hence the statement by the learned judge was mere *obiter dictum*. Moreover, in *Richview Construction Co. v. Raspa*[17] it was said that to make a statement into a term it was not enough to prove that oral statements had been included in a written contract. Furthermore, even if the statement is not included in the written contract it could still be interpreted as a term.[18]

A further suggestion made by Denning L.J. in the *Oscar Chess* case,[19] and supported by both English and Canadian authority,[20] was that a statement would more easily be construed as a term, and not a mere representation, where the representor stated a fact which was, or should be within his own knowledge (and of which the other party was ignorant), or where the representor made a statement about something which was, or should be within his control.[21]

---

14 Contrast *Richview Const. Co. v. Raspa* (1975), 66 D.L.R. (3d) 193 (Ont. C.A.); *Beebe v. Robb* (1977), 81 D.L.R. (3d) 349 (B.C.S.C.); *Selig v. Bottcher* (1978), 26 N.S.R. (2d) 247 (N.S.C.A.); *Roberts v. Montex Dev. Corp.*, [1979] 4 W.W.R. 306 (B.C.S.C.) (statements held to be terms), with *Allen v. Allen* (1976), 15 Nfld. & P.E.I.R. 362 (Nfld. Dist. Ct.) (statement neither term nor representation, only statement of opinion and not binding); *Chua v. Van Pelt* (1977), 74 D.L.R. (3d) 244 (B.C.S.C.) (statement a fraudulent misrepresentation). In *Faunatlantic Ltd. v. N.B.* (1977), 20 N.B.R. (2d) 28 (N.B.Q.B.), one disputed statement was a representation, another was a term. See also *Gallen v. Allstate Grain Co.* (1984), 9 D.L.R. (4th) 496 (B.C.C.A.); leave to appeal to S.C.C. refused (1984), 56 N.S.R. 233 (*sub nom. Allstate Grain Co. v. Guichon*) (S.C.C.), where the British Columbia Court of Appeal was divided on this issue.
15 [1954] 1 All E.R. 855 (C.A.).
16 [1957] 1 All E.R. 325 (C.A.).
17 Above, note 14, at 198.
18 See, *e.g, Dick Bentley Productions Ltd. v. Harold Smith (Motors) Ltd.*, [1965] 2 All E.R. 65 (C.A.).
19 Above, note 16, at 329.
20 *Couchman v. Hill*, [1947] K.B. 554 (C.A.); *Harling v. Eddy*, [1951] 2 K.B. 739 (C.A.); *Webster v. Higgin*, [1948] 2 All E.R. 127 (C.A.); *Curtis v. Chemical Cleaning & Dyeing Co.*, [1951] 1 K.B. 805 (C.A.); *Wilson v. Shaver* (1912), 27 O.L.R. 218 (Ont. C.A.); *Scramlin & Smith v. Phalen* (1910), 3 Sask. L.R. 194 (Sask. S.C.).
21 Hence the treatment of the statement in pre-contractual negotiations, as regards future potential sales, as a warranty, not a mere representation, in *Esso Petroleum Co. v. Mardon*, [1976] 2 All E.R. 5 (C.A.).

The validity of these suggested tests is open to question. Indeed the entire area is far from settled. Perhaps the comment can be made that the courts will resort to techniques to create "terms" from representations in order to effect what they consider to be justice, and this more often than not occurs in situations in which there is some kind of exclusionary, exemption, or limitation clause,[22] under which the party to whom the presentation is made will be deprived of a remedy if such statements are ignored or rejected, and the only way to circumvent his difficulties is by giving effect to a representation either as an overriding contract or as a term which has effect independently of the other terms of the contract which may be subject to the exclusionary or other clause in issue.[23]

(c) The interpretation of express terms

The fact that all or many of the different aspects and obligations of the contract have been expressly stipulated evidences the importance placed by the parties upon the language which they have used. The contents of any express term or terms are basic to a true understanding of the nature, scope and extent of the contractual rights and duties of the parties. What has been spoken or written by them as part of the contract is the prime source of knowledge of their intentions. When everything is oral, and there is no written contract at all, proving what has been agreed may be a difficult task, but once it is established what the respective parties said, and what was the nature and content of their undertakings, effect must be given to their express language.[24] In the case of a completely oral contract there is greater flexibility in the nature of the evidence that is admissible to prove the contents of the contract and the meaning of the language used by the parties. In the case of a contract that is in writing the attitude of the law has been stricter. The reason for this is clear. If the parties have seen fit to put their contractual intentions into writing, it must be because they wanted their meaning to be clearly and unequivocally established. There should be no room for argument about what has been agreed. The written word should make plain beyond doubt or question what were the requirements of the contract that was entered into by the parties.[25]

---

22 Below, pp. 571-600.

23 Compare Wedderburn, "Collateral Contracts" [1959] C.L.J. 58 at 69-75.

24 Difficulty of interpretation must not be confused with ambiguity: *C.N.R. v. C.P. Ltd.*, [1979] 1 W.W.R. 358 (B.C.C.A.); affirmed [1979] 6 W.W.R. 96 (S.C.C.); *Edmonton v. I.B.E.W., Loc. 1007* (1978), 14 A.R. 582 (Alta. T.D.); *Northwestern Mechanical Installations Ltd. v. Yukon Const. Co.* (1982), 136 D.L.R. (3d) 685 (Alta. C.A.); *McCain Produce Co. v. C.N.R.: Toner Bros. Ltd. v. C.N.R.* (1979), 25 N.B.R. (2d) 585 (N.B.Q.B.); affirmed (1980), 30 N.B.R. (2d) 476 (N.B.C.A.); affirmed [1981] 2 S.C.R. 219 (S.C.C.). Nor with uncertainty: *Atlantic Shopping Centres Ltd. v. Hutton* (1980), 25 Nfld. & P.E.I.R. 320 (Nfld. T.D.).

25 This paragraph was quoted in *Thuenken v. Schweer* (1987), 83 N.B.R. (2d) 244 at 247 (N.B.C.A.).
    The written word may not make everything plain and clear where there is a patent conflict between two documents or two different parts of the same document making up the contract, even though each separate document or provision is itself plain and clear. In such situations interpretation takes the form of identifying the dominant concept, provision, or document: *Re Tsiribis and Panopoulos; Re Pe Panopoulas and Satellite Restaurant (Kent) Ltd.* (1982) 21 R.P.R. 58 (Ont. H.C.);

There is no doubt that the cases emphasize this fundamental government of the written word, and in particular, the plain, literal and ordinary meaning of the written word in contract.[26] The golden rule is that the literal meaning must be given to the language of the contract, unless this would result in absurdity.[27] Words of ordinary use in a contract must be construed in their ordinary and natural sense. The paramount test of the meaning of words in a contract is the intention of the parties. That is to be determined in the operative sense by reference to the surrounding circumstances at the time of signing the contract.[28]

Side by side with this basic principle there have emerged some general principles of construction, according to which, where there is some question as to the meaning of language used by the parties, such issue may be resolved. At the same time, as if to acknowledge that the written word cannot totally exclude all else, it has been recognized by the common law that there are circumstances in which evidence other than the writing entered into by the parties may be admitted in order to discover the nature and extent of their contractual obligations. In particular, there are situations in which the parties, or others, may be allowed to give oral evidence of what was intended by the parties when they contracted by the language which they used.[29]

The principles, or canons, of construction are rules formulated to aid a court in the interpretation of the intrinsic meaning of the language used by the parties in a written (or even an oral) contract. In a sense they are the rules of the "game" of construing a contract. The function of the court in this respect is not to make

---

Skoko v. Chychrun Const. Co. (1982), 23 R.P.R. 262 (B.C.C.A.); *Freemont Dev. Co. v. Barafield Mortgage Co.* (1983), 46 B.C.L.R. 314 (B.C.S.C.) (the purpose being to discover the real intention of the parties; see *Djukastein v. Warville* (1981), 28 B.C.L.R. 301 (B.C.C.A.)). See also *Ginter v. Sawley Agency Ltd.*, [1967] S.C.R. 451 (S.C.C.).

26 See, *e.g., Re Dickson* (1978), 23 N.B.R. (2d) 392 (N.B.C.A.); reversed (1979), 25 N.B.R. (2d) 634 (S.C.C.). Especially where the language is clear: *Can. Indemnity Co. v. Parsons* (1983), 21 B.L.R. 86 (N.S.C.A.); *Chamberlain v. Parsons* (1978), 91 D.L.R. (3d) 590 (N.S.C.A.). Sometimes the language must be interpreted according to the purpose of the relationship between the parties, *e.g.*, where there is an exemption or exclusion clause: *Delaney v. Cascade River Holidays Ltd.* (1983), 44 B.C.L.R. 24 (B.C.C.A.); below, pp. 578-588.

27 *Suncor Inc. v. Norcen Int. Ltd.* (1988), 89 A.R. 200 (Alta. Q.B.); *North Eastern Railway Co. v. Lord Hastings*, [1900] A.C. 260 (H.L.).

28 *MacMillan Bloedel Ltd. v. B.C. Hydro & Power Authority*, [1993] 2 W.W.R. 127 at 137 (B.C.C.A.) per Cuming J.A. (citing *Matsqui (District) v. Western Power Co. of Can.*, [1934] A.C. 322 (P.C.); *Grand Trunk Pacific Coast S.S. Co. v. Victoria-Vancouver Stevedoring Co.* (1918), 57 S.C.R. 124 (S.C.C.); *Wenzoski v. Klos*, [1940] 2 D.L.R. 195 (Man. C.A.)). Hence the word "strike" was not restricted to the meaning ascribed to it in the British Columbia Industrial Relations Act.

29 The importance of evidence of surrounding circumstances was stressed in *Re Ulster Petroleums Ltd. and Pan-Alta. Gas Ltd.* (1975), 53 D.L.R. (3d) 459 (Alta. C.A.) (contrast *Alta. Energy Co. v. Can. Western Natural Gas Co.*, [1993] 1 W.W.R. 665 (Alta. C.A.), where only the words of the contract could be looked at to interpret the parties' agreement about the price of natural gas that was the subject of the sale). See also *Shore v. Moreshead* (1981), 44 N.S.R. (2d) 47 (N.S.T.D.); *A.E. Hickman Co. v. Roses Aluminum Ltd.* (1982), 36 Nfld. & P.E.I.R. 206 (Nfld. Dist. Ct.); *Hayward v. Mellick* (1982), 23 R.P.R. 265 (Ont. H.C.); reversed (1984), 45 O.R. (2d) 110 (Ont. C.A.); *Trimac Ltd. v. C-I-L Inc.*, [1987] 4 W.W.R. 719 (Alta. Q.B.); reversed in part on other grounds [1987] 6 W.W.R. 66 (Alta. C.A.); *Qualico Devs. Ltd. v. Calgary (City)*, [1987] 5 W.W.R. 361 (Alta. Q.B.); *Hydamacka v. Wiens* (1987), 61 Sask. R. 44 (Sask. C.A.).

a contract where one does not legally speaking exist but to interpret the meaning of a contract into which the parties have clearly entered.[30]

As for the admissibility of extrinsic, parol evidence, the legal rules which have been developed in this respect recognize the impossibility, at least in some circumstances, of confining the parties to the exact words which they have written down in their correspondence or other negotiations. The "parol evidence" rule and its exceptions represent an attempt by the courts to steer a judicious course between the Scylla of strict reliance upon the written words used by the parties, to the exclusion of all else (which might lead to unfair, if not absurd results from time to time) and the Charybdis of such complete flexibility and breadth of interpretation, by the admission of any evidence at any time in any litigation to establish what individual parties "say" that they meant at the time of contracting, that there would never be any certainty about contracts.[31]

Underlying both the principles of construction and the admissibility of parol evidence may be said to be the doctrine of objectivity, that is, that what the parties have agreed should be understood in the way in which their language would appear to the ordinary reasonable man looking at it from the outside.[32] Admittedly, in some situations courts are concerned with how the words employed by party A were understood by party B, since what is involved in all instances are the intentions of the parties. In attempting to discover what party B understood by such language, party B must be treated and regarded as if he were the ordinary reasonable man. Sometimes, exceptionally, party B can assert that he understood the language in question in a special sense, not necessarily that of the "ordinary" man. Such subjectivity depends on whether there were previous dealings between the parties, or whether, for some reason such as the idiosyncrasies of the trade or business in which the parties were engaged, including any relevant and applicable customs or usages, a specialized meaning of words would be justified.

(d) Parol evidence

The fundamental rule is that if the language of the written contract is clear and unambiguous, then no extrinsic parol evidence may be admitted to alter, vary,

---

30 Compare Osborne J. in *Kaymic Devs. (Ont.) Ltd. v. Ont. Housing Corp.* (1986), 31 D.L.R. (4th) 117 at 124 (Ont. H.C.), in which the meaning of "equity" in reference to rent supplements had to be consistent: the expression was given its ordinary meaning, *i.e.*, the difference between the cost of construction and first mortgage financing.

31 But the principle in the *Hawrish* case, below, is not a tool for the unscrupulous to dupe the unwary: *per* Lambert J.A. in *Gallen v. Allstate Grain Co.* (1984), 9 D.L.R. (4th) 496 at 510 (B.C.C.A.); leave to appeal to S.C.C. refused (1984), 56 N.R. 233 (*sub nom. Allstate Grain Co. v. Guichon*) (S.C.C.).

32 *Caisse Populaire de Caraquet Ltée c. Fédération des Caisses Populaires Acadiennes Ltée* (1988), 87 N.B.R. (2d) 33 (N.B.Q.B.). For example the expectations that a "payment bond" would raise among persons in the position of the subcontractor who was successful in its claim in *ICI Paints (Can.) Inc. v. J.M. Breton Plastering (1984) Co.* (1992), 98 D.L.R. (4th) 549 (N.S.C.A.): note, however, the dissent of Hallett J.A.

or interpret in any way the words used in the writing.[33] In *Hawrish v. Bank of Montreal*[34] a written contract was a guarantee for all of a party's present and future debts up to the amount of $6,000. The guarantor attempted to introduce parol evidence to establish that the contract was only meant to be binding in respect of the current overdraft (not future commitments) and only until the bank to which the guarantee was given could obtain the guarantee of certain other persons elected directors of the company whose debts were being guaranteed. It was held that such evidence was inadmissible. The court adverted to the situations in which such evidence may be admitted in order to elucidate a written contract, but held that none of the applicable situations arose in the case to be determined. The language of the guarantee was plain and unequivocal. Hence, it was to be interpreted and applied to the letter. Parol extrinsic evidence may not be admitted where the effect of such evidence would be to contradict the written contract.[35] It is otherwise where the purpose and result of allowing such evidence to be given would be to explain

---

33 *C.N.R. v. C.P. Ltd.*, above, note 24; *Bohna v. Toffoli* (1982), 12 Man. R. (2d) 1 (Man. Q.B.); *Transcanada Pipelines Ltd. v. Nor. & Central Gas Corp.* (1983), 146 D.L.R. (3d) 293 (Ont. C.A.); *Northwestern Mechanical Installations Ltd. v. Yukon Const. Co.* (1982), 136 D.L.R. (3d) 685 (Alta. C.A.). This sentence was quoted by MacCallum J. in *Curlett v. Toronto-Dominion Bank* (1988), 60 Alta. L.R. (2d) 39 at 47 (Alta. Q.B.), and by Tidman J. in *Chernin v. Scotsburn Co-op. Services Ltd.* (1986), 36 B.L.R. 104 at 131 (N.S.T.D.).

  A more recent statutory exception is provided by the Business Practices Act of Ontario and the Trade Practice Act of British Columbia (above, pp. 340-342) under which parol evidence may be admitted to prove that there was the kind of deception or unconscionability which can justify upsetting a contract of the type governed by those Acts: this is a special, legislative instance, justified by the extraordinary nature of the relief provided by these Acts (this last phrase was adopted by Conant Dist. Ct. J. in *Hoffman v. Sportsman Yachts Inc.* (1990), 47 B.L.R. 101 at 105 (Ont. Dist. Ct.); additional reasons (August 17, 1990), Doc. No. York 335051/88 (Ont. Dist. Ct.); affirmed (1992), 89 D.L.R. (4th) 600 (Ont. C.A.).

  The parol evidence rule is a *rule*, not a presumption: *Ahone v. Holloway* (1988), 30 B.C.L.R. (2d) 368 (B.C.C.A.); *Norman Estate v. Norman* (1990), 43 B.C.L.R. (2d) 193 (B.C.S.C.), despite the remarks of Lambert J.A. in *Gallen v. Allstate Grain Co.*, below, note 34.

34 [1969] S.C.R. 515 (S.C.C.); followed in *Bauer v. Bank of Montreal* (1980), 110 D.L.R. (3d) 424 (S.C.C.); *Carman Const. Ltd. v. C.P.R.* (1982), 136 D.L.R. (3d) 193 (S.C.C.); *Exploits Sales & Service Ltd. v. Fox Farm Village Ltd.* (1982), 40 Nfld. & P.E.I.R. 494 (Nfld. Dist. Ct.); *Bank of N.S. v. Zackheim* (1983), 42 O.R. (2d) 592 (Ont. H.C.); reversed on appeal (1983), 44 O.R. (2d) 244 (Ont. C.A.) (but see below, note 39, with respect to misrepresentation); see also *Bank of Montreal v. Wilder* (1983), 149 D.L.R. (3d) 193 (Ont. C.A.). See the discussion of all these cases and the principle in *Hawrish* by Lambert J.A. in *Gallen v. Allstate Grain Co.* (1984), 9 D.L.R. (4th) 496 at 508-512 (B.C.C.A.); leave to appeal to S.C.C. refused (1984), 56 N.R. 233 (*sub nom. Allstate Grain Co. v. Guichon*) (S.C.C.). Even if the purchaser alleges that *his* written copy of the contract differs from that of the seller: *Source Research Bureau v. Fortier*, [1931] 2 D.L.R. 355 (N.S.C.A.). See also *Forman v. Union Trust Co.*, [1927] S.C.R. 448 (S.C.C.); *Aetna Factors Corp. Ltd. v. Breau* (1957), 41 M.P.R. 288 (N.B. Co. Ct.).

35 *Hawrish v. Bank of Montreal*, above, note 34; *Bauer v. Bank of Montreal*, above, note 34; *Carman Const. Ltd. v. C.P.R.*, above, note 34; *C.I.B.C. v. Cooper* (1986), 5 B.C.L.R. (2d) 192 (B.C.C.A.); *Gadbois v. Bonte Foods Ltd.* (1988), 94 N.B.R. (2d) 21 (N.B.Q.B.). This also applies to *affidavit* evidence: *Finning Tractor & Equipment Co. v. British Columbia (Min. of Finance)* (1988), 30 B.C.L.R. (2d) 249 (B.C.C.A.), where such evidence contradicted the express terms of a lease and standby agreement. The evidence would have substituted a new agreement, not explain the true nature of the existing agreement.

or interpret the true intentions of the parties, where such are not clear from the document.[36]

It has been suggested that the parol evidence rule is intended to avoid injustice.[37] Hence the existence of some exceptions to the rule: (a) to explain incomplete documents; (b) to prove that a condition precedent has been unfulfilled; and (c) to assist in ascertaining the intentions of the parties. In all those situations, the implication may be drawn, injustice would be perpetrated if the written document were accepted as the sole source of the contractual obligations of the parties.[38] To judge by the situations in which parol evidence has been freely admitted by courts, despite the fact that the contract was in writing, the contrary argument can be made that the parol evidence rule is the potential cause of injustice, hence the need to qualify its rigidity in appropriate circumstances.

One obvious situation arises where a party alleges that the written contract was obtained by fraud, misrepresentation, mistake, or other vitiating conduct on the part of the other party; he may adduce evidence to establish his allegation, so as to have the written contract nullified at common law,[39] or perhaps, if this would aid him, rectified in accordance with equitable principles.[40] In such circumstances the party in question is not so much seeking interpretation of the written contract by extrinsic evidence as proving its invalidity, or at least its incorrectness as an expression in writing of the intentions of the parties as manifested in their oral negotiations of which the written contract purports to be the result.

The admission of parol evidence in cases in which fraud, misrepresentation, and other reasons for upsetting a transaction may be alleged is not a true exception to the parol evidence rule. Such evidence does not affect the terms of the contract so much as to negate as validity.[41] There are some real exceptions, by virtue of which a party introducing such evidence is at one and the same time upholding the validity of the written contract yet attempting to have its meaning understood in a certain way.[42]

---

36 See, *e.g., Mabey v. Mansonville Plastics Ltd.* (1978), 24 N.B.R. (2d) 689 (N.B.Q.B.).

37 *Hayward v. Mellick* (1982), 23 R.P.R. 265 at 269 (Ont. H.C.) *per* Reid J.; reversed (1984), 45 O.R. (2d) 110 (Ont. C.A.).

38 This and the previous two sentences were quoted by Wells J. in *John Jacobs & Sons Ltd. v. N.D. Dobbin Ltd.* (1988), 70 Nfld. & P.E.I.R. 99 at 102 (Nfld. T.D.).

39 *Petersen v. Parsons* (1959), 21 D.L.R. (2d) 555 (N.S.C.A.); *Kaplan v. Andrews*, [1955] O.W.N. 364 (Ont. C.A.); *C.I.B.C. v. Larsen*, [1983] 5 W.W.R. 179 (B.C.C.A.). Hence, the Ontario Court of Appeal allowed such evidence to be admitted where the defendant was relying on the plea of misrepresentation to defeat an action on a guarantee: the *Bauer* case was distinguished: *Bank of N.S. v. Zackheim* (1983), 44 O.R. (2d) 244 (Ont. C.A.).

40 *Menni v. Ottoman Bank, Haifa; Mansour v. Ottoman Bank, Haifa*, [1940] 1 W.W.R. 415 (P.C.); *Ottoman Bank of Nicosia v. Chakarian*, [1938] A.C. 260 (P.C.); *Chant v. Infinitum Growth Fund Inc.* (1986), 28 D.L.R. (4th) 577 at 580 (Ont. C.A.) (parol evidence not admissible: no mistake to justify rectification); *Norman Estate v. Norman* (1990), 43 B.C.L.R. (2d) 193 (B.C.S.C.) (evidence admitted: rectification). For rectification see below, pp. 821-832.

41 See *Bank of Montreal v. Wilder* (1983), 149 D.L.R. (3d) 193 at 214 (Ont. C.A.) *per* Lambert J.A.

42 But if an exception applies parol evidence is inadmissible: *Block Bros. Realty Ltd. v. 254929 Alta. Ltd.* (1989), 67 Alta. L.R. (2d) 268 (Alta. C.A.).

Where the contract as written is ambiguous,[43] extrinsic evidence can be admitted to resolve such ambiguity.[44] But it must be an ambiguity that exists in the language as it stands, not one that is itself created by the evidence that is sought to be adduced.[45] For example, a contract was signed by the general manager of a company in circumstances which left it uncertain whether he was signing on behalf of the company, as an agent, or in his own name, but with his representative character appended, intending to be personally liable. Evidence of other, surrounding circumstances was therefore admitted in this case, *Automobiles Renault Canada Ltd. v. Maritime Import Autos Ltd.*,[46] to establish that the company, not the manager, was the bailee of the vehicles. So too: where a contract used the expression "orders", which was unclear from the content of the document;[47] or the word "bonus" which was also unclear[48] where the language employed by the parties did not manifest the place where the mortgagee was to be maintained by the mortgagor;[49] whether cancellation had taken place under the terms of the contract;[50] where it was not certain who was the lessee of the premises, a company or its principal shareholder;[51]

---

43 Or absurd: *Gadbois v. Bonte Foods Ltd.* (1988), 94 N.B.R. (2d) 21 (N.B.Q.B.). Economic reality may make a contract absurd or ambiguous: *A.G. Nfld. v. Churchill Falls (Labrador) Corp.* (1983), 49 Nfld. & P.E.I.R. 181 at 219 (Nfld. T.D.) *per* Goodridge J.; affirmed (1985), 56 Nfld. & P.E.I.R. 91 (Nfld. C.A.); which was affirmed (1988), 70 Nfld. & P.E.I.R. 126 (S.C.C.).

44 *Charrington & Co. v. Wooder*, [1914] A.C. 71 at 77 (H.L.) *per* Lord Haldane. Compare Thomson J. in *Bank of Montreal v. Univ. of Sask.* (1953), 9 W.W.R. (N.S.) 193 at 199 (Sask. Q.B.); *Hoefle v. Bongard & Co.*, [1945] 2 D.L.R. 609 at 623-624 (S.C.C.) *per* Kellock J. and 629 *per* Estey J. See also *Warren Gen. Contracting Ltd. v. Robichaud* (1973), 6 N.B.R. (2d) 821 (N.B.C.A.); *Cameron v. Silverglen Farms Ltd.* (1982), 51 N.S.R. (2d) 64 (N.S.T.D.); reversed (1983), 58 N.S.R. (2d) 31 (N.S.C.A.); *East Wind Const. Ltd. v. Chase* (1987), 77 N.S.R. (2d) 274 (N.S.C.A.) (where the expression "the whole building" was ambiguous); *Head v. Inter Tan Can. Ltd.* (1991), 5 O.R. (3d) 192 (Ont. Gen. Div.) (where a limitation clause was ambiguous). Ambiguity in the legal sense is a term that is capable of being understood in more senses than one: *Atl. Shopping Centres Ltd. v. Hutton* (1980), 25 Nfld. & P.E.I.R. 320 at 336 (Nfld. T.D.). See, *e.g.*, *Imperial Oil Ltd. v. N.S. Light & Power Co.* (1977), 77 D.L.R. (3d) 1 (S.C.C.); *Sarafinchan v. Alta. Hail & Crop Ins. Corp.* (1978), 5 Alta. L.R. (2d) 52 (Alta. Dist. Ct.); reversed on other grounds (1979), 8 Alta. L.R. (2d) 323 (Alta. C.A.); *Abernethy Credit Union Ltd. v. Flavel* (1983), 25 Sask. R. 310 (Sask. Q.B.); *Transcanada Pipelines Ltd. v. Nor. & Central Gas Corp.*, (1983), 146 D.L.R. (3d) 293 (Ont. C.A.); *Hydamacka v. Wiens* (1987), 61 Sask. R. 44 (Sask. C.A.).

45 *Alampi v. Swartz*, [1964] 1 O.R. 488 (Ont. C.A.); *Can. Deposit Ins. Corp. v. Can. Commercial Bank*, [1990] 4 W.W.R. 445 (Alta. Q.B.); reversed [1991] 4 W.W.R. 418 (Alta. C.A.); affirmed [1992] 2 S.C.R. 3 (S.C.C.). See *Valois v. Dahl* (1981), 15 Sask. R. 357 (Sask. Q.B.) (disagreement as to nature of the contract). But there are suggestions that extrinsic evidence may be admitted to *establish* and then clarify a latent ambiguity: see *Noranda Metal Industries Ltd. v. I.B.E.W. Loc. 2345* (1983), 1 O.A.C. 187 at 193 (Ont. C.A.) *per* Dubin J.A. Such evidence may explain, but not contradict, the language of the contract: *Paragon Farms Ltd. v. H.D. Linn Dev. Services Inc.*, [1988] 6 W.W.R. 417 (Sask. Q.B.); *Crown Investcorp Ltd. v. Nfld. & Labrador Housing Corp.* (1986), 60 Nfld. & P.E.I.R. 108 (Nfld. T.D.).

46 (1961), 31 D.L.R. (2d) 592 (N.S.S.C.). Compare *Medic v. Taylor*, [1975] 6 W.W.R. 725 (B.C.S.C.).

47 *Can. Atlas Diesel Engines Co. v. McLeod Engine Ltd.*, [1952] S.C.R. 122 (S.C.C.).

48 *Bohna v. Toffoli* (1982), 12 Man. R. (2d) 1 (Man. Q.B.).

49 *Gauvin v. Bouchard*, [1950] 2 D.L.R. 414 (N.B.C.A.).

50 *Adolph Lbr. Co. v. Meadow Creek Lbr. Co.*, [1919] 1 W.W.R. 823 (S.C.C.).

51 *Atlantic Shopping Centres Ltd. v. Hutton* (1980), 25 Nfld. & P.E.I.R. 320 (Nfld. T.D.).

or where the amount of the debt guaranteed in a guarantee was not certain;[52] but not where the word "both" had no significance in the contract.[53]

Second, while it is not possible to admit parol or other extrinsic evidence to alter the contract by adding to or substracting from its terms as written,[54] such evidence may nonetheless be introduced to explain, without contradicting, the language of the contract,[55] for example, by showing the true nature of the transaction or legal relationship of the parties,[56] or by adding a term where to do so is necessary to give effect to the obvious intention of the parties.[57] This may occur when the parties have plainly omitted something which was intended to be, and must be a part of their agreement, that is, to complete the contract,[58] to fill in gaps,[59] such as the consideration which was left unstated or was put in an ambiguous manner in the contract.[60] As Macdonald J. of the Supreme Court of British Columbia said in *Simon Fraser University v. Juliani*,[61] if there has been an inadequate expression of their intention by the parties, then the court can construe the agreement by adding what is necessary and proved by the evidence, "fairly and broadly, without being too astute or subtle in finding defects."[62]

Third, there are situations in which evidence may be given of some *oral* agreement between the parties which does not contradict the written agreement that is being construed, but modifies or qualifies it, or explains its true application.[63] This is what the guarantor attempted to argue in *Hawrish v. Bank of Montreal*,[64] in accordance with the doctrine in the English case of *Pym v. Campbell*,[65] under

---

52 *Abernethy Credit Union Ltd. v. Flavel* (1983), 25 Sask. R. 310 (Sask. Q.B.).

53 *Chernin v. Scotsburn Co-op. Services Ltd.* (1986), 77 N.S.R. (2d) 91 (N.S.T.D.).

54 *Chisholm v. Chisholm* (1915), 49 N.S.R. 174 (N.S.C.A.).

55 *Hoeppner v. Horstman Contracting Ltd.*, [1992] 3 W.W.R. 335 (Man. Q.B.).

56 *Royal Bank v. Hale* (1961), 30 D.L.R. (2d) 138 (B.C.S.C.); *Can. Fur Auction Sales Co. v. Neely*, [1954] 2 D.L.R. 154 (Man. C.A.); *Mabey v. Mansonville Plastics Ltd.* (1978), 245 N.B.R. (2d) 689 (N.B.Q.B.). Even when a *deed* is involved, as long as its meaning is uncertain: see *Saueracker v. Snow* (1974), 47 D.L.R. (3d) 577 (N.S.S.C.), to disclose the real intent of the grantor.

57 *Connors v. McGregor*, [1924] 2 W.W.R. 294 (Alta. C.A.). Contrast *Re Broughton Collieries Ltd.*, [1944] 1 D.L.R. 530 (N.S.C.A.), with *Sutherland v. Cavn & Keay Home Bldrs. Ltd.* (1968), 2 D.L.R. (3d) 54 (B.C.S.C.).

58 *Johnson v. Crocker*, [1954] O.W.N. 352 (Ont. C.A.); *e.g.*, what was to happen on the vendor's death; *Bonnett v. Bonnett* (1980), 112 D.L.R. (3d) 649 (Sask. Q.B.).

59 *Wattie v. Lytton*, [1945] O.W.N. 57 (Ont. C.A.); the *Can. Fur Auction* case, above, note 56; *Slywka v. Gamache*, [1954] 2 D.L.R. 530 (Alta. C.A.). *E.g.*, to prove a condition precedent and whether it has been satisfied or waived: *Samoth Financial Corp. v. Todd* (1979), 14 B.C.L.R. 266 (B.C.S.C.); *Triple Five Corp. v. Crown Zellerbach Stores Ltd.* (1981), 17 Alta. L.R. (2d) 178 (Alta. Q.B.).

60 *Great Eastern Oil & Import Co. v. Chafe* (1956), 40 M.P.R. 21 (Nfld. S.C.). Or to identify a party for the purposes of satisfying the Statute of Frauds; see *Babcock v. Carr* (1981), 127 D.L.R. (3d) 77 (Ont. H.C.).

61 (1969), 5 D.L.R. (3d) 670 at 671 (B.C.S.C.).

62 This entire paragraph was cited in *A.E. Hickman Co. v. Roses Aluminium Ltd.* (1981), 36 Nfld. & P.E.I.R. 206 at 213 (Nfld. Dist. Ct.); and in *Irving Oil Ltd. v. Luby* (1982), 39 Nfld. & P.E.I.R. 295 at 300 (Nfld. Dist. Ct.).

63 This sentence was quoted by MacCallum J. in *Curlett v. Toronto-Dominion Bank* (1988), 60 Alta. L.R. (2d) 39 at 48 (Alta. Q.B.).

64 [1969] S.C.R. 515 (S.C.C.).

65 (1856), 6 E. & B. 370, 119 E.R. 903.

which a qualification could be proved orally, for instance, as in the *Pym* case, that a deed apparently complete was only an escrow. The guarantor in *Hawrish* tried to establish by oral evidence an oral limitation on the scope of the guarantee. This was not permitted. The court in rejecting the guarantor's attempt to use such evidence made it clear that non-contradictory parol evidence was admissible, but only if it established some explanatory or collateral undertaking that affected the written one, and that strict proof of any such collateral undertaking was necessary for it to be admitted so as to affect the written words.[66]

The development of the doctrine of "collateral agreements" has been long and complex.[67] Although the validity and effect of such agreements has been accepted by courts in England[68] and Canada,[69] there are many issues still unresolved. The nature of such agreements, and the way in which, and extent to which they can affect the contractual obligations of parties to the main agreement, to which the collateral agreement is subsidiary, as well as others not parties to such main agreement, will be discussed in more detail elsewhere.[70] One problem that is immediately relevant here is the question of proving such a collateral agreement by means of parol evidence. Such agreements are not usually concluded in writing. In general they take the form of oral statements preceding, or accompanying, the making of a written contract between the maker of the statement and the one to whom the statement is made.[71]

Because of this courts are called upon to allow proof of such agreements by parol evidence even though such an agreement may greatly affect the terms of the main, written contract. In the *Hawrish* case,[72] and two subsequent decisions of the Supreme Court of Canada, *Bauer v. Bank of Montreal*[73] and *Carman Construction Ltd. v. Canadian Pacific Railway Co.*,[74] the attitude adopted was to refuse to allow such evidence where the alleged collateral agreement would have made a significant difference to the obligations created by the main, written contract.

---

66 *Heilbut, Symons & Co. v. Buckleton*, [1913] A.C. 30 (H.L.); *Wenger v. LeMaster* (1962), 36 D.L.R. (2d) 277 (B.C.S.C.).

67 Wedderburn, "Collateral Contracts", [1959] C.L.J. 58. For a definition of "collateral agreement" see *Ahone v. Holloway* (1988), 30 B.C.L.R. (2d) 368 at 373 (B.C.C.A.) per McLachlin J.A.

68 *Lindley v. Lacey* (1864), 17 C.B.N.S. 578; *Erskine v. Adeane* (1873), L.R. 8 Ch. App. 756; *De Lassalle v. Guildford*, [1901] 2 K.B. 215 (C.A.); *Heilbut, Symons & Co. v. Buckleton* above, note 66.

69 *Byers v. McMillan* (1887), 15 S.C.R. 196 (S.C.C.); *Harris v. Robinson* (1892), 21 S.C.R. 390 (S.C.C.); *California Standard Co. v. Chiswell*, [1955] 5 D.L.R. 119 (Alta. S.C.); *Standard Bank v. McCrossan*, [1920] 3 W.W.R. 846 (S.C.C.); *Wells v. Blain*, [1927] 1 W.W.R. 223 (Sask. C.A.); *Blanchette Neon Ltd. v. Charlie Jim* (1956), 17 W.W.R. 404 (Alta. C.A.); *Ferland v. Keith*, [1958] O.W.N. 445 (Ont. C.A.). These are all instances of *contemporaneous* undertakings or agreements: one case, such modification was *subsequent* to the written contract (and operated as an estoppel); *Findlay v. Kowal*, [1945] 2 W.W.R. 423 (Man. Co. Ct.), an illustration of the *High Trees* principle, above, pp. 121-136, but antedating the *High Trees* case; compare *City & Westminister Properties (1934) Ltd. v. Mudd*, [1959] Ch. 129.

70 Below, Chapter 13.

71 Or between the latter and a third party: below, pp. 505-507. But such transactions are not relevant in the present context.

72 [1969] S.C.R. 515 (S.C.C.).

73 (1980), 110 D.L.R. (3d) 424 (S.C.C.).

74 (1982), 136 D.L.R. (3d) 193 (S.C.C.).

To some extent these decisions run counter to earlier cases, in England and Canada, where courts have been prepared to admit parol evidence of what has been called the "inconsistent collateral contract".[75] In some instances the basis for such apparent inconsistency has been an allegation of misrepresentation. In others, however, there appears to be no such reason for admitting evidence which would alter or vary the terms of a written contract between the same parties.

The decision in the *Hawrish* case marks a significant change in the attitude of Canadian courts towards this question.[76] That case, and the subsequent reiteration of the approach in the *Hawrish* case, indicate that Canadian courts may now be less willing than their English counterparts to permit a party to escape the stricter consequences of a written agreement by invoking some oral statement that could modify and soften the harshness of the terms committed to writing (in the absence of fraud or some other vitiating factor). Notwithstanding this approach, which is exemplified in later decisions of lower courts,[77] there are cases in which, after the *Hawrish* decision, parol evidence was admitted to establish such a collateral agreement.[78] In one instance this was because the oral variation of the written agreement was made at the same time as the written agreement and was not inconsistent with it. This was a contract whereby a real estate broker was empowered by a farm owner to sell the latter's property. The broker was given exclusive authority to sell. It was held that this was not inconsistent with an oral statement that the farmer would not sell the property on his own without payment of commission to the broker.[79] In another instance the oral agreement purported to limit the cost of doing some building work to $30,000. It was held that this was valid and could be proved by parol evidence so as to disentitle the builder to recover more than that amount.[80] In a third instance, the representation by the defendant vendor of a farm that the farm was 65 acres in size was held to be a collateral agreement which bound the vendor and made him liable when the farm turned out to be

---

75 McLauchlan, "The Inconsistent Collateral Contract" (1976), 3 Dalhousie L.J. 136. See also, Fridman, "Written Contracts with an Oral Element" (1977), 8 Manitoba L.J. 383. *Gadbois v. Bonte Foods Ltd.* (1988), 94 N.B.R. (2d) 21 (N.B.Q.B.). The doctrine of collateral contracts is irrelevant if the prior oral statement is in fact part of the single written contract between the parties: *Toronto-Dominion Bank v. Griffiths*, [1988] 1 W.W.R. 735 at 744 (B.C.C.A.) *per* Lambert J.A.

76 This and the next sentence were quoted by Roscoe J. in *Sinclair v. Brady* (1991), 111 N.S.R. (2d) 25 at 28 (N.S.T.D.); affirmed (1993), 117 N.S.R. (2d) 178 (N.S.C.A.).

77 *Exploits Sales & Service Ltd. v. Fox Farm Village Ltd.* (1982), 40 Nfld. & P.E.I.R. 494 (Nfld. Dist. Ct.); *Bank of N.S. v. Mabey* (1979), 26 N.B.R. (2d) 536 (N.B.Q.B.); *Cameron v. Silverglen Farms Ltd.* (1982), 51 N.S.R. (2d) 64 (N.S.T.D.); reversed on other grounds (1983), 144 D.L.R. (3d) 544 (N.S.C.A.); *Pan Orient Holdings Ltd. and Nor. Shore Motors Ltd. v. Danyo Enterprises Ltd.* (1979), 11 B.C.L.R. 79 (B.C.S.C.); *Color Your World Inc. v. Robert F. Avery Holdings Ltd.* (1988), 88 A.R. 163 (Alta. Q.B.); *Econo-Malls Ltd. v. Richler* (1989), 77 Nfld. & P.E.I.R. 230 (Nfld. T.D.).

78 *Sodd Corp. v. Tessis* (1977), 79 D.L.R. (3d) 632 (Ont. C.A.); *Smith v. Porter* (1978), 21 N.B.R. (2d) 170 (N.B.S.C.); reversed in part (1979), 27 N.B.R. (2d) 439 (N.B.C.A.); compare *R.E. Lister Ltd. v. Dunlop Can. Ltd.* (1978), 85 D.L.R. (3d) 321 (Ont. H.C.); reversed (1979), 105 D.L.R. (3d) 684 (Ont. C.A.); reversed on other grounds (1982), 135 D.L.R. (3d) 1 (S.C.C.), where the doctrine was accepted, although the facts did not support liability on this basis.

79 *L. & R. Realty Ltd. v. Stevens* (1979), 14 A.R. 37 (Alta. Dist. Ct.).

80 *S. & B. General Contracting Ltd. v. V.I.P. Clothing & Sound Ltd.* (1982), 16 Sask. R. 164 (Sask. Q.B.).

smaller.[81] In *Chrispen v. Topham*[82] parol evidence was admitted to prove an agreement collateral to the written contract between a man and woman undertaking to cohabit whereby the parties agreed to perform certain domestic duties. So, too, in *Ahone v. Holloway*[83] a collateral agreement about interest to be paid did not contradict the written mortgage.

It is not easy to reconcile such decisions with the fundamental propositions set out in *Hawrish v. Bank of Montreal* and later cases in the Supreme Court of Canada. One way might be by saying that such oral statements are not independent contracts modifying or varying another written agreement, but oral terms of the main, written part of the contract. On that basis, such contracts are not to be regarded as wholly in writing but as contracts partly oral and partly in writing. Hence, the problem of the parol evidence rule does not arise. The oral and written parts of the contract must be considered together and interpreted as one inclusive contract. This was the view adopted by Lambert J.A. in *Toronto-Dominion Bank v. Griffiths.*[84] It was the approach adopted previously by two members of the English Court of Appeal in *J. Evans & Son (Portsmouth) Ltd. v. Andrea Merzario Ltd.*,[85] where there was a written contract and an oral statement about the way the goods that were the subject-matter of the contract were to be transported on the ship in respect of which the parties were contracting. Lord Denning, M.R., however, preferred to take the path of "collateral agreement", suggesting that the more restrictive approach to such agreements in the older English case of *Heilbut, Symons & Co. v. Buckleton*[86] was now outmoded.[87] Such might be the situation in England. It cannot be said to be the situation in Canada after the *Hawrish* case and its successors. Hence, perhaps the most rational and acceptable way of admitting collateral agreements and giving them effect is by determining that they are part and parcel of the main, written agreement. To do this, however, gives rise to two problems. The first is the determination whether such collateral statements are truly terms of the contract. The second is whether the collateral agreement and the written contract can be reconciled, where there respective provisions appear to be in conflict. These are important issues.[88]

---

81 *Hayward v. Mellick* (1982), 23 R.P.R. 265 (Ont. H.C.); reversed (1984), 45 O.R. (2d) 110 (Ont. C.A.).

82 (1986), 28 D.L.R. (4th) 754 (Sask. Q.B.); affirmed (1987), 39 D.L.R. (4th) 637 (Sask. C.A.).

83 (1988), 30 B.C.L.R. (2d) 368 (B.C.C.A.): compare *Elm Mercury Sales (1976) Ltd. v. Wiseman* (1988), 71 Nfld. & P.E.I.R. 187 (Nfld. T.D.); *AWS Welding Consulting Ltd. v. Foundation Co. of Can.* (1987), 27 C.L.R. 28 (Alta. Q.B.); *Steeplejack Services (Can.) Ltd. v. Access Scaffold & Ladder Co.* (1989), 98 A.R. 311 (Alta. Master).

84 [1988] 1 W.W.R. 735 (B.C.C.A.).

85 [1976] 2 All E.R. 930 (C.A.); compare *L & R. Realty Ltd. v. Stevens*, above, note 79.

86 Above, note 66.

87 Compare Lord Denning, M.R. in *Howard Marine Ltd. v. Ogden & Sons*, [1978] 2 All E.R. 1134 at 1140 (C.A.).

88 See further below, Chapter 13. For the recommendation that the parol evidence rule be abrogated see Ontario Law Reform Commission, *Report on Amendment of the Law of Contract* (1987), Chapter 8: compare British Columbia Law Reform Commission, *Report on Parol Evidence Rule* (1979); Law Commission, *Report on the Parol Evidence Rule* (1986), Law Comm. No. 154.

(e) The kind of evidence

What type of evidence is admissible, in accordance with what has been stated above, to establish the meaning of the written term or terms which are ambiguous or lacking in completion? How far may the courts go in their search for additional sources of information as to the intentions of the parties, once they have strayed from the precise words used in a written document?[89]

There are three potential sources of such information. One is the conduct, including the statements, of the parties prior to the making of the written agreement. A second is the conduct of the parties contemporaneous with the making of such agreement. Third and lastly, there is the conduct of the parties after the agreement has been put into writing.[90]

What was done, or said, by the parties before the contract was entered into may sometimes be looked at, in cases of ambiguity, or where misrepresentation is alleged or the plea of *non est factum* is raised,[91] to explain the meaning of the written words they have used. Thus, earlier dealings between the parties may explain language in a later contract.[92]

The contents of an oral agreement which preceded the written one may act as an aid in the interpretation of the latter, as long as the latter is not explicit.[93] If it is, and it contradicts the alleged oral agreement, the only reasonable explanation is that the written contract replaces the earlier, oral one insofar as they differ. As Ritchie J. in Nova Scotia said in 1915,

> the negotiation cannot be received to change the terms of a written contract, but interpreting the contract in the light of surrounding circumstances is another matter.[94]

This has been repeated in more modern times.[95]

This may be taken a stage further, in that not only what preceded the contract

---

89 Parties *cannot* by agreement render admissible what by law is inadmissible evidence: *Bahamas Int. Trust Co. v. Threadgold*, [1974] 1 W.L.R. 1516 (H.L.).

90 *C.N.R. v. C.P. Ltd.*, [1979] 1 W.W.R. 358 at 372-373 (B.C.C.A.) *per* Lambert J.A.; appeal dismissed (1979), 105 D.L.R. (3d) 170 (S.C.C.). This paragraph was quoted by MacCallum J. in *Curlett v. Toronto-Dominion Bank* (1988), 60 Alta. L.R. (2d) 39 at 48 (Alta. Q.B.).

91 *Arrale v. Costain Civil Engr. Ltd.*, [1976] 1 Lloyd's Rep. 98 (C.A.).

92 *Cleveland v. Boak* (1906), 39 N.S.R. 39 (N.S.C.A.).

93 *Johnson Invts. Ltd. v. Pagratide*, [1923] 2 W.W.R. 736 (Alta. C.A.).

94 In *Chisholm v. Chisholm* (1915), 49 N.S.R. 174 at 181-182 (N.S. C.A.).

95 *Prenn v. Simmonds*, [1971] 3 All E.R. 237 at 240-241 (H.L.) *per* Lord Wilberforce; *Reardon Smith Line Ltd. v. Hansen-Tangen*, [1971] 3 All E.R. 570 at 574-575 (H.L.) *per* Lord Wilberforce ("what the court must do must be to place itself in thought in the same factual matrix as that in which the parties were"); compare *Amerada Minerals Corp. of Can. v. Mesa Petroleum (N.A.) Co.*, [1985] 4 W.W.R. 607 (Alta. Q.B.); reasons corrected [1985] 6 W.W.R. 767 (Alta. Q.B.).

See further, for applications of this, *Qualico Devs. Ltd. v. Calgary (City)*, [1987] 5 W.W.R. 361 (Alta. Q.B.); *B.C. Hydro & Power Authority v. Cominco Ltd.* (1989), 34 B.C.L.R. (2d) 60 (B.C.C.A.); *Delisle v. Bulman Group Ltd.* (1991), 54 B.C.L.R. (2d) 343 (B.C.S.C.); *Paddon-Hughes Dev. Co. v. Chiles Estate*, [1992] 3 W.W.R. 519 at 524 (Alta. Q.B.). The factual background may be explained by extrinsic evidence, but not the intentions of the parties: *A.G. Nfld. v. Churchill Falls (Labrador) Corp.* (1983), 49 Nfld. & P.E.I.R. 181 (Nfld. T.D.); affirmed (1985), 56 Nfld. & P.E.I.R. 91 (Nfld. C.A.); which was affirmed (1988), 70 Nfld. & P.E.I.R. 126 (S.C.C.).

but also what occurred at the same time that it was put into writing may be used to assist in its interpretation.[96] For example, in *McKean v. Black*,[97] contemporaneous statements were admitted to establish that a conveyance of timber was not intended to be an outright sale, but only by way of giving security until the advance of moneys made on the security of the timber was repaid to the lender. As Newcombe J. of the Supreme Court of Canada said in the later case of *A. R. Williams Machinery Co. v. Moore*,[98] citing and relying on earlier English authority,[99]

> in order to interpret the correspondence we must look to the state of the facts and circumstances as known to and affecting the parties at the time.

The language used in the contract must be interpreted, wherever possible, in the sense which the parties understood it. Hence the relevance of the surrounding circumstances.[100]

The problem, however, is whether the same reliance should be placed upon what the parties said or did *after* the contract was made and put into writing. Here there may be a diversity of opinion between the English and Canadian authorities. As a result of the decision of the House of Lords in *James Miller & Partners Ltd. v. Whitworth Street Estates (Manchester) Ltd.*,[101] there is no doubt that in England regard may not be paid to the subsequent conduct or statements of the parties in the interpretation of a contract.[102]

Canadian courts have adopted the view that subsequent conduct can be a useful guide to the interpretation of a written contract.[103] Cases before the decision of the House of Lords in the *Whitworth* case permitted the admission of such evidence as long as it did not add to, or vary the document to be interpreted but simply helped the court to arrive at a conclusion as to the true intent and meaning

---

96 *Gilks v. Rocca Group Ltd.* (1977), 20 N.B.R. (2d) 1 at 16 (N.B. Q.B.) *per* Stratton J.

97 (1921), 62 S.C.R. 290 (S.C.C.).

98 [1926] S.C.R. 692 at 705 (S.C.C.).

99 *Fowkes v. Manchester & London Life Assur. & Loan Assn.* (1863), 3 B. & S. 917.

100 See *Berthe v. Greggor*, [1983] 2 W.W.R. 515 (Man. Q.B.) on the meaning of a restrictive covenant against competition from the vendor of a hairdressing business. Compare *Delaney v. Cascade River Holidays Ltd.* (1983), 44 B.C.L.R. 24 (B.C.C.A.) on the interpretation of an exemption clause.

These two sentences in the text were quoted by O'Driscoll J. in *CHML/CKDS v. Telemedia Communications Inc.* (1988), 40 B.L.R. 223 at 242 (Ont. H.C.); additional reasons at (1988), 65 O.R. (2d) 753 (Ont. H.C.); leave to appeal to Div. Ct. refused (1988), 65 O.R. (2d) 753 (note) (Ont. H.C.).

101 [1970] A.C. 583 (H.L.). See Lord Denning's attempted distinction in *Wickman Machine Tool Sales Ltd. v. Schuler A.G.*, [1972] 2 All E.R. 1173 at 1181 (C.A.); affirmed [1974] A.C. 235 (H.L.) where the House of Lords refused to accept Lord Denning's reasoning. In consequence Lord Denning deplored the English approach and preferred the Canadian one, in a later case: *Port Sudan Cotton Co. v. Govindasmay Chettiar & Sons*, [1977] 2 Lloyd's Rep. 5 at 11.

102 Except, perhaps in deciding the scope of an ambiguous title to land, in the light of subsequent possession; *Watcham v. A.G. East Africa Protectorate*, [1919] A.C. 533 (P.C.), on which see the *Wickman Machine Tool Sales* case, above, note 101.

103 This sentence was quoted by O'Driscoll J. in *CHML/CKDS v. Telemedia Communications Inc.*, above, note 100.

of the words used in the document.[104] The effect of such conduct was, in a sense, to *fix* the interpretation of the language of the document.[105] In one case, which was concerned with whether a restrictive covenant in a contract was personal to the parties or went with the land,[106] Thomson J. of the Supreme Court of Saskatchewan, said that in cases involving an ambiguity in an agreement, "there is no better way of determining what the parties intended than to look to what they did under it."[107] There is much to be said for this approach, as many Canadian judges have declared. In the words of Lord Denning,[108] when the contract is unclear, the parties "are themselves the very best guides to the way in which it was used." This did not appeal to Lord Reid, who referred to the possibility that a contract might mean one thing the day it was signed, but by reason of subsequent events mean something different a month or a year later.[109] This may be an overreaction, in that the dangers of shifting meaning may have been exaggerated by Lord Reid and others. When the matter came before the Manitoba Court of Appeal and was thoroughly canvassed, the judges in that court found no difficulty in rejecting the more rigid approach of the House of Lords and accepting the admissibility of subsequent conduct in an appropriate case, where there is ambiguity.

In *Manitoba Development Corporation v. Columbia Forest Products Ltd.*[110] the issue was as to the meaning of the phrase "all necessary working capital" in a contract. One party urged that it meant an obligation of a specific, limited kind and duration, and that it had performed such obligation. The other contended that the phrase was intended to mean a continuing obligation, such that the other party had not completed in satisfaction of its contractual duty. To maintain this interpretation, it was sought to introduce evidence of subsequent conduct. This the trial judge allowed, and gave judgment for the original defendant (which was arguing for the liberal admission of evidence). On appeal from the decision, the Court of Appeal upheld this part of the decision (though the appeal was allowed in part on a totally different point). What the Court of Appeal said was that the phrase in question was ambiguous, hence that subsequent conduct was admissible, and this established that the meaning of the phrase indicated that the original

---

104 *Anthony v. F.W. Woolworth Co.* (1965), 35 D.L.R. (2d) 82 at 86 (Ont. H.C.) *per* Grant J. Compare *Hayduk v. Waterton; Flechuk v. Waterton*, [1968] S.C.R. 871 (S.C.C.); *Leitch Gold Mines Ltd. v. Texas Gulf Sulphur Co.* (1969), 3 D.L.R. (3d) 161 at 237 (Ont. H.C.); *Firestone Tire & Rubber Co. v. Commr. of Income Tax*, [1942] S.C.R. 476 (S.C.C.); *Cooke (Barchak Estate) v. Anderson*, [1945] 1 W.W.R. 657 (Alta. C.A.); *Turvey v. Lauder* (1956), 4 D.L.R. (2d) 225 (S.C.C.).

105 *Re C.N.R. and Ottawa*, [1925] S.C.R. 494 (S.C.C.), relied on by Eberle J. in *Corporate Properties Ltd. v. Manufacturers Life Ins. Co.* (1987), 40 D.L.R. (4th) 506 at 521 (Ont. H.C.); reversed (1989), 63 D.L.R. (4th) 703 (Ont. C.A.); leave to appeal to S.C.C. refused (1990), 68 D.L.R. (4th) vii (note) (S.C.C.).

106 *Bank of Montreal v. Univ. of Saskatchewan* (1953), 9 W.W.R. (N.S.) 193 (Sask. Q.B.).

107 *Ibid.*, at 199. Compare *Gatineau Power Co. v. Fraser Co.*, [1941] 2 D.L.R. 487 at 507 (N.B. C.A.) *per* Kellock J.; *Hoefle v. Bongard & Co.*, [1945] S.C.R. 360 at 377 (S.C.C.) *per* Kellock J.; *Krauss v. Jameson* (1951), 4 W.W.R. (N.S.) 139 at 141 (B.C.C.A.) *per* O'Halloran J.A.; *Valois v. Dahl* (1981), 15 Sask. R. 357 (Sask. Q.B.).

108 In *Wickman Machine Tool Sales Ltd. v. Schuler A.G.*, above, note 101.

109 *James Miller & Partners Ltd. v. Whitworth Street Estates (Manchester) Ltd.*, [1970] A.C. 583 (H.L.).

110 [1974] 2 W.W.R. 237 (Man. C.A.).

plaintiff, now the appellant, was in breach of the agreement and could not succeed in its claim of breach of contract. The plaintiff/appellant was itself the party in breach. Later decisions affirmed the same view.[111]

More recently, however, an Alberta judge, without referring to the Manitoba decision, stated that he did not accept the *dicta* of the British Columbia Court of Appeal in *Canadian National Railway v. Canadian Pacific Ltd.*[112] in which evidence of subsequent conduct was held to be admissible. In *Paddon-Hughes Development Co. v. Chiles Estate*,[113] Montgomery J. relied more on language of another Alberta judge, Harradence J.A., in *Northwestern Mechanical Installations Ltd. v. Yukon Construction Co.*[114] to state that the rule as expounded in British Columbia was not the law in Canada or Alberta.[115]

It would appear, therefore, that there is some difference among different Canadian courts in this respect. The reasoning of Lord Reid appealed to Montgomery J. But it has not always commended itself to other judges in Canada. It is suggested that the approach favoured in Manitoba and British Columbia is more realistic and not as dangerous as Lord Reid indicated.

(f) Construction of written documents

Where there is no ambiguity in a written contract it must be given its literal meaning.[116] Thus in *Ritchie v. Webster*,[117] the attempt was made to construe the word "and" in a contract as meaning "so". It was held that this was impossible, since the literal meaning led to no uncertainty, absurdity or injustice and the text was unambiguous and grammatically correct as it stood. Similarly, in *Chamberlain v. Parsons*,[118] a covenant not to "set up business" could not be made to mean "carry on business". Therefore, the vendor of an electrical business could validly

---

111 *C.N.R. v. C.P. Ltd.*, [1979] 1 W.W.R. 358 (B.C.C.A.); appeal dismissed (1980), 105 D.L.R. (3d) 170 (S.C.C.); *Northwestern Mechanical Installations Ltd. v. Yukon Const. Co.* (1982), 135 D.L.R. (3d) 685 (Alta. C.A.); *Valois v. Dahl*, above, note 107; see also *Corporate Properties Ltd. v. Manufacturers Life Ins. Co.*, above, note 105; *Delisle v. Bulman Group Ltd.* (1991), 54 B.C.L.R. (2d) 343 (B.C.S.C.); *B.C. Hydro & Power Authority v. Cominco Ltd.* (1989), 34 B.C.L.R. (2d) 60 (B.C.C.A.).

112 Above, note 111.

113 [1992] 3 W.W.R. 519 (Alta. Q.B.).

114 (1982), 136 D.L.R. (3d) 685 at 691-692 (Alta. C.A.); what was said was *obiter* because there was no ambiguity in the language of the contract. Difficulty in interpretation was not synonymous with ambiguity: *ibid.*, at 692-693.

115 Compare the view of Goodridge J. in *A.G. Nfld. v. Churchill Falls (Labrador) Corp.* (1983), 49 Nfld. & P.E.I.R. 181 at 219-220 (Nfld. T.D.) that subsequent conduct could not be admitted to interpret a contract though it could give rise to an estoppel. This case was affirmed on appeal by the Newfoundland Court of Appeal and the Supreme Court of Canada: (1985), 56 Nfld. & P.E.I.R. 91; (1988), 70 Nfld. & P.E.I.R. 126.

116 *North Eastern Ry. Co. v. Hastings*, [1900] A.C. 260 at 263 (H.L.) *per* Lord Halsbury; *Morel v. Lefrancois* (1906), 38 S.C.R. 75 (S.C.C.); *Reeves v. Huffman* (1951), 3 W.W.R. (N.S.) 176 (Man. K.B.); *Tombill Gold Mines Ltd. v. Hamilton*, [1956] S.C.R. 858 (S.C.C.); compare *Can. Indemnity Co. v. Parsons* (1983), 21 B.L.R. 86 (N.S.C.A.).

117 [1917] 2 W.W.R. 1124 (B.C.C.A.).

118 (1978), 91 D.L.R. (3d) 590 (N.S.C.A.).

undertake electrical work out of his home for customers who required it without breaking the covenant in restraint of trade. So, too, in *Aldo Ippolito & Co. v. Canada Packers Inc.*,[119] the majority of the Ontario Court of Appeal held that the language of a sales-agency agreement respecting its termination was clear and unambiguous: therefore only 30 days' notice had to be given.

In accordance with what is sometimes referred to as the "golden rule",[120] words must be given their plain, ordinary meaning, at least unless to do so would result in absurdity.[121] That is what the parties are presumed to have intended by the words that they used. As Sir Montague Smith said, delivering the opinion of the Privy Council in *McConnel v. Murphy*,[122]

> [i]n mercantile contracts and indeed in all contracts where the meaning of language is to be determined by the court, the governing principle must be to ascertain the intention of the parties through the words they have used. This principle is of universal application. It is seldom in mercantile contracts that any technical or artificial rule of law can be brought to bear upon their construction. The question really is the meaning of the language and must be the same everywhere.

In a case in which the meaning of "may" was involved, that is, whether it referred to a permission or a command,[123] Egbert J. of the Supreme Court of Alberta said

> [t]he cardinal principle of the constructon of contracts is that each word must have assigned to it its plain, ordinary meaning . . .Therefore, when parties choose certain words to express their meaning and to define their relationship there is no excuse for distorting those words out of their ordinary plain meaning.

Hence, in one case,[124] the word "actional" in the phrase "actional drilling operations", since it added nothing to the meaning of the expression, could be left out and given no meaning at all. In another[125] the normal meaning of "rock" was adopted in the construction of an excavation contract. In another case, involving a contract to supply electricity, no technical meaning could be attributed to the expression "similar service". They were "words of ordinary use and must be

---

119 (1986), 57 O.R. (2d) 65 (Ont. C.A.); additional reasons at (1986), 14 C.C.E.L. 76 at 89 (Ont. C.A.) (applied in *Emile State Inc. v. Commodore Business Machines Ltd.* (1988), 19 C.C.E.L. xxix (Ont. C.A.)): compare the "plain meaning" of "salary and related costs" in *Maysfield Property Management Inc. v. Clarkson Gordon Inc.* (1988), 51 D.L.R. (4th) 575 (Ont. H.C.). Compare also the different approach of the New Brunswick Court of Appeal from that of the trial judge in the "hole-in-one" case: *Michaud v. Grand Falls Golf Club Inc.* (1990), 73 D.L.R. (4th) 352 (N.B.C.A.); reversing (1989), 103 N.B.R. (2d) 361 (N.B.Q.B.).

120 *Re Dickson* (1978), 23 N.B.R. (2d) 392 (N.B.C.A.); reversed on other grounds (1979), 25 N.B.R. (2d) 634 (S.C.C.).

121 *Suncor Inc. v. Norcen Int. Ltd.* (1988), 89 A.R. 200 (Alta. Q.B.). Compare *Mercantile Bank of Can v. Sigurdson* (1978), 86 D.L.R. (3d) 680 (B.C.S.C.); *Bowater Nfld. Ltd. v. Nfld. & Labrador Hydro* (1978), 15 Nfld. & P.E.I.R. 301 (Nfld. C.A.).

122 (1873), L.R. 5 P.C. 203 at 218-219. See *Conley Holdings Ltd. v. Can. Metal & Supply Co.* (1986), 47 Sask. R. 299 at 301 (Sask. Q.B.).

123 *Merrill Petroleums v. Seaboard Oil Co.* (1957), 22 W.W.R. 529 at 550 (Alta. S.C.); upheld on appeal (1958), 25 W.W.R. 236 (Alta. C.A.). *Re Baker* (1890), 44 Ch. D. 262 (C.A.).

124 *Risvold and Mallory v. Scott*, [1938] 1 W.W.R. 682 (Alta. S.C.).

125 *Mills v. Continental Bag & Paper Co.* (1918), 4 O.L.R. 71 (Ont. C.A.).

construed in their natural sense in view of the circumstances of the case."[126] Only if to do this would be to create an absurd situation may the court, generally speaking, depart from the basic approach. For it is the duty of the court to avoid any interpretation that would result in a commercial absurdity.[127] In such a situation, there is a patent ambiguity, and the court can go beyond the words and look at the surrounding circumstances and the course of dealing between the parties, if any, to see what the parties intended.[128] Departure from the plain, ordinary meaning of words may also be allowed where adherence to the rule would involve inconsistency or repugnancy between different parts of the contract.[129]

The point here is that, since the parties obviously did not intend to contract in such a manner as to produce an absurd agreement, that interpretation must be placed upon their language as will give it most effect.[130] If there are two possible interpretations, one of which is absurd or unjust, the other of which rational, the latter must be taken as the correct one, on this basis of giving effect to the general contractual intentions of the parties.[131] For example, in *Clergue v. Vivian & Co.*,[132] the Supreme Court of Canada was faced with a contract which referred to "myself *or* assigns". To interpret this literally would have made nonsense of the whole agreement. Hence, in this situation the word "or" was construed as if it had been the word "and", so as to give real effect to the undoubted intentions of the parties. The intention of the parties is the paramount test of the meaning of words in a contract.[133] Although words normally mean what the ordinary man would take them to mean, this is only as long as both parties understand and interpret them in this same way. In that situation such mutual interpretation governs. The court should be guided by the reasonable expectations of the parties, as long as this

---

126 *Western Power Co. v. Matsqui Corp.*, [1934] A.C. 322 at 331 (P.C.) *per* Lord Wright. Compare *Milliken v. Young*, [1929] 3 D.L.R. 64 at 68 (Sask. C.A.) *per* Martin J.A.

127 *Toronto v. W.H. Hotel Ltd.*, [1966] S.C.R. 434 (S.C.C.). Compare *Reddy v. Struple* (1911), 44 S.C.R. 246 at 257 (S.C.C.) *per* Duff J. See *Mercantile Bank of Can. v. Sugurdson*, above, note 121.

128 *Burritt v. Stone*, [1917] 3 W.W.R. 978 (Sask. C.A.).

129 *Bowater Nfld. Ltd. v. Nfld. & Labrador Hydro*, above, note 121. Words of a technical nature may have to be interpreted in a special way (unless the intention of the parties is manifestly to the contrary): compare *Shore v. Wilson* (1842), 9 Cl. & Fin. 355 (H.L.); so might words having a special meaning in consequence of some usage or custom, *e.g.*, the expression "snowed-in", in *Campbell-Bennett Ltd. v. G.L. McNicol Co.*, [1952] 3 D.L.R. 247 (B.C.S.C.).

130 *Morgan v. Hudson Bay Mining & Smelting Co.*, [1930] 2 D.L.R. 587 (Man. K.B.). Compare *Marquest Indust. Ltd. v. Willows Poultry Farms Ltd.* (1968), 66 W.W.R. 477 (B.C.C.A.). For the possibility of *implying* a term if necessary, to achieve this result compare below, pp. 474-481.

131 *Thompson v. North Battlefield*, [1924] 1 W.W.R. 51 (Sask. C.A.). In the light of the purpose of their relationship and the genesis and aim of the transaction: see *Delaney v. Cascade River Holidays Ltd.* (1983), 44 B.C.L.R. 24 at 44 (B.C.C.A.) *per* McFarlane J.A.; *Can. Square Corp. v. Versafood Services* (1981), 130 D.L.R. (3d) 205 at 215-216 (Ont. C.A.). So an interpretation that defies "economic reality" was to be avoided: *A.G. Nfld. v. Churchill Falls (Labrador) Corp.* (1983), 49 Nfld. & P.E.I.R. 181 at 219 (Nfld. T.D.) *per* Goodridge J.; affirmed (1985), 56 Nfld. & P.E.I.R. 91 (Nfld. C.A.); which was affirmed (1988), 70 Nfld. & P.E.I.R. 126 (S.C.C.).

132 (1909), 41 S.C.R. 607 (S.C.C.).

133 *G.T.P. Coast S.S. Co. v. Victoria-Vancouver Stevedoring Co.* (1918), 57 S.C.R. 124 at 126 (S.C.C.) *per* Fitzpatrick C.J.C.; *Cie Française du Phenix v. Travellers Fire Ins. Co.*, [1952] 2 S.C.R. 190 at 217 (S.C.C.) *per* Estey J.

is compatible with the written contract.[134] Only in the absence of such clear indication by the parties will other rules of construction be invoked. "Their own interpretation is accepted as expressing the real will and intention of the parties."[135] That interpretation takes precedence over particular words in the contract.[136] For example, in *Wenzoski v. Klos*,[137] in which the expression "fix the road" was in issue, the test was what was in the contemplation of the parties at the time of signing the contract, that is by, reference to the surrounding circumstances.

Hence, the contract should be construed as a whole,[138] giving effect to everything in it if at all possible.[139] No word should be superfluous[140] (unless of course, as happened in one instance,[141] it is truly meaningless and can be ignored). In *Cooke (Barchak Estate) v. Anderson*,[142] one clause in a contract fixed the price of land at $5,000. A later clause referred to payment not in cash but by the provision of a certain quantity of beets. It was held that these clauses must be read together so as to create harmony, and not dissension among the different terms of the contract. Thus, the later clause to the necessary extent modified or limited the earlier one. In such cases of repugnancy within the contract, therefore, as was stated in *Forbes v. Git*,[143] if the dissonant clauses can be read harmoniously this must be done. If not, then the repugnant part must be rejected in order to give effect to the general intent of the parties, as evidenced by the contract as a whole, rather than any

---

134 *Alex Duff Realty Ltd. v. Eaglecraft Holdings Ltd.* (1983), 44 A.R. 67 (Alta. C.A.) *per* McGillivray C.J.A., citing *Leading Invts. v. New Forest Invts. Ltd.; H.W. Liebig & Co. v. Leading Invts. Ltd.* (1981), 20 R.P.R. 6 at 20 (Ont. C.A.) *per* Brooke J.A. See, *e.g., Fort Francis v. Boise Cascade Can. Ltd.* (1983), 143 D.L.R. (3d) 193 (S.C.C.).

135 *Hendry v. A. Zimmerman*, [1948] 2 D.L.R. 287 at 290 (Man. C.A.) *per* Coyne J.A.

136 *Ford v. Beech* (1848), 11 Q.B. 852; *Coddington v. Paleologo* (1867), L.R. 2 Ex. 193: *Sierichs v. Hughes* (1918), 42 O.L.R. 608 (Ont. C.A.).

137 [1940] 2 D.L.R. 195 (Man. C.A.). Compare *Martin v. Jarvis* (1916), 31 D.L.R. 740 at 743 (Ont. H.C.) *per* Boyd C.; *Can. Law Book Co. v. Boston Book Co.* (1922), 64 S.C.R. 182 at 185-186 (S.C.C.) *per* Duff J.

138 *Can. Deposit Ins. Corp. v. Can. Commercial Bank* (1992), 13 C.B.R. (3d) 183 (S.C.C.); affirming (1991), 79 Alta. L.R. (2d) 294 (Alta. C.A.); which reversed (1990), 73 Alta. L.R. (2d) 230 (Alta. Q.B.); *i.e.,* to interpret an ambiguous expression by reference to the *purpose* of the contract; *National Trust Co. v. Massey Combines Corp.* (1988), 39 B.L.R. 245 (Ont. H.C.), which in that case was to provide security for builders.

139 *North Eastern Ry. v. Hastings*, [1900] A.C. 260 (H.L.); *Milliken v. Young*, [1929] 1 W.W.R. 213 (Sask. C.A.); *Wardle v. Man. Farm Loans Assn.*, [1955] 2 D.L.R. 23 (Man. C.A.); reversed on other grounds, [1956] S.C.R. 3 (S.C.C.); *Jets Hockey Ventures v. Molson Breweries of Can. Ltd.* (1989), 63 D.L.R. (4th) 119 (Man. Q.B.); varied (1990), 63 Man. R. (2d) 239 (Man. C.A.). Compare *Elderslie S.S. Co. v. Borthwick*, [1905] A.C. 93 (H.L.). So a disclaimer clause can limit a travel company's liability for breach of contract: *Bentley v. Touram Inc.* (1990), 87 Nfld. & P.E.I.R. 262 (P.E.I. T.D.).

140 *R. v. Bishop of Oxford* (1879), 4 Q.B.D. 425; affirmed (1880), 5 App. Cas. 214 (C.A.); *Brown Bros. Ltd. v. Popham*, [1939] 4 D.L.R. 662 at 670 (Ont. C.A.) *per* Roberston C.J.O. But it may not have the same meaning throughout the whole document: *Watson v. Hagitt*, [1928] A.C. 127 (P.C.).

141 *Risvold and Mallory v. Scott*, [1938] 2 D.L.R. 238 (Alta. S.C.); compare above, p. 467.

142 [1945] 1 W.W.R. 657 (Alta. C.A.).

143 [1922] 1 A.C. 256 especially at 259 (P.C.) *per* Lord Wrenbury.

particular, and jarring language.[144] If there is conflict between two parts of a document, the dominating purpose must prevail, as indicating the real intentions of the parties.[145]

In cases of doubt, as a last resort, language should always be construed against the grantor or promisor under the contract.[146] *Verba fortius accipiuntur contra proferentem*. In the words of Sir Montague Smith in *McConnel v. Murphy*:[147]

> where a stipulation is capable of two meanings equally consistent with the language employed, that shall be taken which is most against the stipulator and in favour of the other party.

The *contra proferentem* rule is of great importance, especially where the clause being construed creates an exemption, exclusion or limitation of liability.[148] Thus in *Alex Duff Realty Ltd. v. Eaglecraft Holdings Ltd.*,[149] a contract between a real estate broker and a property owner provided for payment of commission to the former on the "sale" of the land. The broker claimed commission when a potential buyer signed an agreement for sale, but was later not ready, willing and able to close the sale. The broker's claim failed. Applying the *contra proferentem* rule, since the contract was ambiguous, the expression "sale" could not be interpreted to include an agreement for sale. Similarly, in *Hillis Oil & Sales Ltd. v. Wynn's*

---

144 *R. v. Peat Fuels Ltd.*, [1930] Ex. C.R. 188 (Ex. Ct.); *Djukastein v. Warville* (1981), 38 B.C.L.R. 301 (B.C.C.A.). But the question whether there is any repugnancy must first be answered: compare *Ottawa Elec. Co. v. St. Jacques* (1901), 31 S.C.R. 636 (S.C.C.) and *Cotter v. Gen. Petroleums Ltd.*, [1951] S.C.R. 154 (S.C.C.).

145 *Ginter v. Sawley Agency Ltd.*, [1967] S.C.R. 451 (S.C.C.); *Skoko v. Chychrun Const. Co.* (1982), 23 R.P.R. 262 (B.C.C.A.); *Freemont Dev. Co. v. Barafield Mortgage Co.* (1983), 46 B.C.L.R. 314 (B.C.S.C.); *Morris v. Hunt Morris & Associates (1982) Ltd.* (1986), 74 A.R. 207 (Alta. Q.B.); additional reasons at (1987), 50 Alta. L.R. (2d) 14 (Alta. Q.B.).

146 *Milliken v. Young*, [1929] W.W.R. 213 (Sask. C.A.); *McCann v. Temiskaming Hotel Co.*, [1943] 2 D.L.R. 741 at 752 (Ont. C.A.) *per* Gillanders J.A.; *Ont. Bus Industries Inc. v. "Federal Calumet" (The)* (1991), 47 F.T.R. 149 (Fed. T.D.); affirmed (1992), 150 N.R. 149 (Fed. C.A.); *Royal LePage Real Estate Services Ltd. v. Harper* (1991), 85 Alta. L.R. (2d) 31 at 38 (Alta. Q.B.). See, *e.g., Saint John Toyota Ltd. v. Levine* (1992), 127 N.B.R. (2d) 1 (N.B.Q.B.); *Meng v. Ford Motor Co. of Can.* (1992), 126 N.B.R. (2d) 324 (N.B.Q.B.); *Winnipeg Waste Disposal Ltd. Partnership v. Portage La Prairie (City)* (1992), 80 Man. R. (2d) 316 (Man. Q.B.); affirmed (1992), 83 Man. R. (2d) 213 (Man. C.A.). *E.g.*, as regards the commission payable under a real estate agency contract: *Block Bros. Realty Ltd. v. Viktora*, [1974] 2 W.W.R. 282 (B.C.C.A.). Contrast *Chin v. Jacobs*, [1972] 2 O.R. 54 (Ont. C.A.) on what was payable to an employee. But not if the grant is *by* the Crown; the rule is reversed: *Viscountess Rhondda's Claim*, [1922] 2 A.C. 339 at 353 (H.L.) *per* Lord Birkenhead.

147 (1873), L.R. 5 P.C. 203 at 218-219. See the citation of this by McIntyre J. in *Conley Holdings Ltd. v. Can. Metal & Supply Co.* (1986), 47 Sask. R. 299 (Sask. Q.B.).

148 *Falcon Lumber Ltd. v. Can. Wood Speciality Co.* (1978), 23 O.R. (2d) 345 (Ont. H.C.); *Consol. Bathurst Export Ltd. v. Mutual Boiler & Mach. Ins. Co.* (1981), 112 D.L.R. (3d) 69 (S.C.C.); *Chabot v. Ford Motor Co. of Can.* (1982), 138 D.L.R. (3d) 417 (Ont. H.C.); *Exchanger Industries Ltd. v. Dominion Bridge Co.* (1986), 69 A.R. 22 (Alta. Q.B.); *Huber v. Conquest Tours (Toronto) Ltd.* (1990), 74 O.R. (2d) 781 (Ont. Div. Ct.). Compare below, pp. 578-579.

149 (1983), 44 A.R. 67 (Alta. C.A.).

Canada Ltd.[150] the rule was applied to resolve ambiguity as between two terms in a contract, with the result that reasonable notice had to be given to terminate a distributorship. The rule is also of great relevance where the contract being construed is a *contrat d'adhesion*, that is, where the signatory does not really have the opportunity to negotiate its terms but is obliged either to agree, and sign, or forgo whatever advantages such a contract might bring him. Hence, in *Davies v. Zurich Life Insurance Co. of Canada*,[151] the question whether a deceased obtained immediate coverage upon signing a "conditional insurance agreement" was answered in favour of the deceased's widow and against the insurance company.

Where the contract is ambiguous, the application of the *contra proferentem* rule ensures that the meaning least favourable to the author of the document prevails.[152] However, the *contra proferentem* rule applies only as between the parties to the contract. It will not assist third parties, who are taken to have knowledge of everything in the contract or document, including ambiguities and errors. Hence, in *Freemont Development Co. v. Barafield Mortgage Co.*,[153] a third party could not invoke the rule in relation to a charge filed under the Land Title Act of British Columbia. In this respect it is to be noted that a contract should be construed so as not to take away property rights or create liability or a disability.[154] It requires very plain words to establish an intention to impose any such consequences, for example, to create an unusual liability in respect of property neither owned nor possessed by the party liable under a contract.[155]

General words may be followed by more specific ones in a document, for example, "all animals, including dogs, tigers, and elephants". Conversely, specific words may be followed by more general ones, for example, "all dogs, tigers, elephants and other animals". It would appear that, in the former case, the general words cannot be construed so as to cover a situation which is not mentioned in

---

150 [1986] 1 S.C.R. 57 (S.C.C.): contrast *Moose Jaw Senior Citizens' Assistance Program Inc. v. Thunder Creek Home Care Dist. No. 6 Inc.* (1986), 52 Sask. R. 295 (Sask. Q.B.), where there was no ambiguity and it was not clear against what party the terms should be construed; *Delisle v. Bulman Group Ltd.* (1991), 54 B.C.L.R. (2d) 343 (B.C.S.C.).

151 (1981), 39 N.R. 457 (S.C.C.).

152 For examples, see *Blue Label Beverages (1971) Ltd. v. Centennial Packers Ltd.* (1986), 44 Alta. L.R. (2d) 68 (Alta. Q.B.); *Wall Bros. Const. Co. v. Canson Enterprises Ltd.* (1986), 70 B.C.L.R. 243 (B.C.C.A.); *Westmore v. Old MacDonald's Farm Ltd.* (1986), 70 B.C.L.R. 332 (B.C.S.C.); *Rody v. Re/Max Moncton Inc.* (1986), 72 N.B.R. (2d) 430 (N.B.Q.B.); *District of Kenora Home for the Aged v. Duck Estate* (1987), 62 O.R. (2d) 696 (Ont. H.C.); *Sign-O Lite Signs Ltd. v. Windsor Plywood (Kelowna) Ltd.* (1988), 61 Alta. L.R. (2d) 21 (Alta. Q.B.); *Vandex Const. Ltd. v. Strata Plan No. VR 738* (1988), 30 C.L.R. 111 (B.C.C.A.); *Charda Holdings Ltd. v. R.* (1988), 24 F.T.R. 121 (Fed. T.D.); *Federal Business Dev. Bank v. A.C. Landry & Son Ltd./A.C. Landry & Fils Ltée* (1988), 95 N.B.R. (2d) 45 (N.B.Q.B.); additional reasons at (December 7, 1988), Doc. No. B/C/351/87, B/C/8/88 (N.B.Q.B.); reversed (1991), 115 N.B.R. (2d) 91 (N.B.C.A.); *Huber v. Conquest Tours (Toronto) Ltd.* (1990), 74 O.R. (2d) 781 (Ont. Div. Ct.).

153 (1983), 46 B.C.L.R. 314 (B.C.S.C.).

154 *Red Lake v. Drawson*, [1964] 1 O.R. 324 (Ont. H.C.); affirmed without written reasons, [1964] 2 O.R. 248 (Ont. C.A.).

155 *Nor. Ont. Power Co. v. La Roche Mines Ltd.*, [1938] 3 D.L.R. 657 at 663 (P.C.) *per* Lord Russell of Killowen. This and the previous sentence were quoted by Foisey J. in *Harris v. Robert Simpson Co.* (1985), 56 A.R. 201 at 209 (Alta. Q.B.).

the subsequent specific language, since the existence of the latter indicates the real, and narrower intention of the parties.[156] So far as the reverse situation is concerned, whether the general words should be construed in their general sense, or given a more limited meaning, by reason of the context in which they are found, depends upon the operation of the *ejusdem generis* rule. "It is a general rule of construction," said Pollock C.B. in 1857,[157] "that, where a particular class is spoken of, and general words follow, the class first mentioned is to be taken as the most comprehensive and the general words treated as referring to matters *ejusdem generis* with such class." The basis of the rule is made clear in the following passage from a more recent judgment by Devlin J., in a case concerning a charter-party:[158]

> The ejusdem generis rule means that there is implied into the language which the parties have used words for restriction which are not there. . . . The so-called rule is, in short, really only a recognition of the fact that parties with their minds concerned with the particular objects which they are contracting are apt to use words, phrases, or clauses which, taken literally, are wider than they intended.

Such a construction can only be employed however, if: (i) the specific words have some common characteristic which constitute them as a *genus*;[159] (ii) the specific words do not exhaust a whole *genus*;[160] or (iii) there is no clear indication that the opposite was intended by the parties.[161]

If a single transaction is carried into effect by several documents, the whole is treated as one document and they must all be read together for the purpose of ascertaining the intention of the parties. Nor does it matter whether or not the documents are actually contemporaneous, as long as they are executed within so short an interval that the court can come to the conclusion that in fact they represented a single transaction.[162] If there is only one document, but it is partly printed and partly written, or there are written words which fill in gaps or replace printed words, then the rule is that the *written* words are more important because their presence indicates that they represent, or are more likely to represent, the real intention of the parties.[163]

---

156 *Shukin v. Demosky*, [1927] 1 D.L.R. 649 (Sask. K.B.).

157 *Lyndon v. Standbridge* (1857), 2 H. & N. 45 at 51.

158 *Chandris v. Isbrandtsen-Mollar Co.*, [1951] 1 K.B. 240 at 245-246 (C.A.).

159 *Anderson v. Anderson*, [1895] 1 Q.B. 749 (C.A.); *Jacobs v. Morris*, [1902] 1 Ch. 816 (C.A.); *Knutsford S.S. Ltd. v. Tillmans & Co.*, [1908] A.C. 406 (H.L.).

160 *Larsen v. Sylvester & Co.*, [1908] A.C. 295 (H.L.); *Ambatielos v. Anton Jurgens Margarine Works*, [1923] A.C. 175 (H.L.).

161 *Harrison v. Blackburn* (1864), 17 C.B.N.S. 678. See *Berthe v. Greggor*, [1983] 2 W.W.R. 515 (Man. Q.B.), involving the construction of a covenant in restraint of trade; compare also, at first instance, *Barton v. Toronto Argonaut Football Club Ltd.* (1978), 86 D.L.R. (3d) 133 (Ont. H.C.); affirmed (1979), 108 D.L.R. (3d) 152 (Ont. C.A.); affirmed (1982), 134 D.L.R. (3d) 1 (*sub nom. Barton v. Agincourt Football Enterprises Ltd.*) (S.C.C.).

162 *Jacobs v. Batavia Trust Ltd.*, [1924] 2 Ch. 329 (C.A.).

163 *Baumwoll Manufactur von Carl Scheibler v. Furness*, [1893] A.C. 8 (H.L.); *Glynn v. Margetson*, [1893] A.C. 351 (H.L.); *Templin v. Alles*, [1944] O.W.N. 96 (Ont. C.A.).

(g) Alteration of documents

The foregoing discussion has been concerned with determining the meaning and effect of a written contract in the form in which it was agreed to by the parties. In some situations a party has altered the contents of such a document after it was agreed to and accepted by both parties, and the issue has arisen whether such alteration has any effect. The general principle is that a material alteration by one party, not assented to by the other and evidenced appropriately, will nullify the original contract.[164]

An alteration will be material if it varies "the legal position of the parties or the legal incidents of the instruments."[165] In *Petro Canada Exploration Incorporated v. Tormac Transport Ltd.*,[166] the defendants gave a personal guarantee for the debts of another owed to the plaintiff. The parties did not intend that this should be under seal. Later an employee of the plaintiff, without authorization, affixed a red wafer seal to the document beside the defendants' signatures. When the plaintiff sued on the guarantee the defendants were held not to be liable. Any material alteration of a document, including sealing, which varied its legal form or effect as originally expressed debars the party responsible from enforcing any covenant contained in it as against a party who might have been prejudiced as a result of the alteration.[167] In this instance, as contrasted with what occurred in *Linton v. Royal Bank of Canada*,[168] the addition of the seal completely altered the nature of the obligation undertaken by the defendants. Similarly, in *Bank of Montreal v. Hache*,[169] the bank increased the interest rate of a guarantee after the bank issued a writ of summons to enforce its right sunder the guarantee. This was held to be a material alteration, rendering the guarantee void. In contrast, in *Bank of Nova Scotia v. Outlook Express (1976) Ltd.*,[170] a change made to the rate of interest on a promissory note due to fluctuations in the prime rate was not a material alteration, so as to release the guarantors of the note from liability. Here the document in question accepted that there might be alterations in the rate, so that the intentions of the parties had not been altered in any significant way, whereas in the *Hache* case the change made by the bank did significantly affect the obligations undertaken by the guarantor. In the same way the change made

---

164 *Pigot's Case* (1614), 11 Co. Rep. 26b; *Master v. Miller* (1791), 4 T.R. 320 (K.B.); *Aldous v. Cornwall* (1868), L.R. 3 Q.B. 573 (Q.B.); *Davidson v. Cooper* (1844), M. & W. 343; *Royal Bank v. Bermuda Holdings Ltd.* (1976), 67 D.L.R. (3d) 316 (B.C.S.C.); *Johnson v. Trobak* (1977), 79 D.L.R. (3d) 684 (B.C.C.A.); *C.I.B.C. v. Skender*, [1985] 1 W.W.R. 405 (B.C.S.C.); affirmed [1986] 1 W.W.R. 284 (B.C.C.A.); *Alta. Treasury Branches v. Acorn* (1987), 83 A.R. 215 (Alta. Master).

165 *Roynat Ltd. v. Sommerville* (1982), 40 N.B.R. (2d) 578 (N.B.C.A.).

166 [1983] 4 W.W.R. 205 (B.C.S.C.).

167 But prejudice may *not* be necessary according to *Roynat Ltd. v. Sommerville*, above, note 165.

168 (1967), 60 D.L.R. (2d) 398 (Ont. H.C.); see also *Bank of N.S. v. Spear* (1973), 37 D.L.R. (3d) 130 (N.B.C.A.).

169 (1982), 38 N.B.R. (2d) 54 (N.B.Q.B.). Compare *Alta. Treasury Branches v. Acorn*, above, note 164, alteration of hypothecation agreement rendered it totally revoked.

170 (1983), 27 Sask. R. 311 (Sask. Q.B.); compare *Royal Bank v. Davidson* (1972), 25 D.L.R. (3d) 202 (N.S.C.A.); *C.I.B.C. v. Skender*, above, note 164, later addition of witness's signature and "B.C." did not affect guarantee.

to the date of a debenture, after the debenture had been executed, did not affect the rights, liabilities, or legal position of the parties, or the legal effect of the debenture, in *Roynat Ltd. v. Sommerville*.[171] It would appear, therefore, that if a party adds something to a document after its execution, by way of filling in a gap or remedying a defect, as long as this does not change the position of the parties under the document, or the document's legal effects, no material alteration will have occurred. Of course if this is done fraudulently, the situation will be different. However, if an alteration is material, it need not have been effected with a fraudulent intent. The change in itself will suffice.[172]

However, there is another qualification to be noted. The alteration must have been made by the party in question or by his authorization, or in consequence of his negligence or fraud.[173] Alteration by a stranger not authorized by a party[174] will not excuse the parties from performance of their obligations or avoid the document. On this principle the decision in the *Petro Canada* case seems contrary to principle, unless it is assumed that the employee who added the seal, though unauthorized expressly, was acting within the course of his employment or scope of his authority as an employee so as to bind his employer notwithstanding lack of express instructions, negligence or fraud.

2. Implied terms

(a) The possibility of implication

The law has long recognized that it is not always possible to confine the terms of a contract, whether written, oral, or partly written and partly oral, to those which have been expressly stipulated between the parties. There are circumstances in whch a court is entitled to conclude that everything agreed by the parties is not contained in the written document or documents, or the oral statements of the parties, that appear to make up the contract. Some additional term or terms must be implied. The acceptance of what Duff J. once called "an unexpressed incident"[175] requires more than that a court might think it reasonable to make such an implication.[176] It is firmly based on the idea that courts are seeking to discover what the parties intended, not what a court thinks reasonable.[177]

---

171 Above, note 165.

172 *Ibid.* But see *Farm Credit Corp. v. Lacombe Nurseries Ltd.* (1992), 2 Alta. L.R. (3d) 20 at 26-27 (Alta. C.A.); leave to appeal to S.C.C. refused (1993), 8 Alta. L.R. (3d) xlv (note) (S.C.C.): below, note 173.

173 *Bank of Montreal v. Hache*, above, note 169; *London Lumber Co. v. Kerrigan*, [1958] O.R. 484 (Ont. C.A.); *Gill v. Doey*, [1933] 4 D.L.R. 753 (Ont. H.C.). There must be a fraudulent or mischievous purpose in making the alteration: *Farm Credit Corp. v. Lacombe Nurseries Ltd.*, above, note 172; *C.I.B.C. v. Skender*, [1986] 1 W.W.R. 284 at 287-288 (B.C.C.A.).

174 Or by a party's solicitor without that party's knowledge: *Sim v. Large* (1981), 22 B.C.L.R. 278 (B.C.S.C.), relying on *Johnson v. Trobak*, above, note 164.

175 *Georgia Const. Co. v. Pac. Great Eastern Ry.*, [1929] S.C.R. 630 at 633 (S.C.C.).

176 *Liverpool City Council v. Irwin*, [1976] 2 All E.R. 39 at 50 (H.L.) *per* Lord Salmon. The original version of this passage, in the first edition, was cited with approval by Jones J.A. in *Royal Bank v. M.F. Schurman* (1984), 64 N.S.R. (2d) 379 at 382 (N.S.C.A.).

177 *J.W. Cowie Enrg. Ltd. v. Allen* (1981), 47 N.S.R. (2d) 705 at 711 (N.S.T.D.) (citing *Lyford v. Cargill*, [1944] 1 D.L.R. 696 (B.C.C.A.)); appeal allowed on other grounds (1982), 26 C.P.C. 241 (N.S.C.A.).

While, as already seen, the courts are not anxious to go beyond the letter of the written word, where the contract is expressed in writing, unless there is some strong justification, such as patent, internal ambiguity in the language employed by the parties, nonetheless, there are circumstances in which it is clear law that, at the invitation of one of the parties in the course of litigation, a court is entitled to conclude that everything that was agreed between the parties is not contained in the written document or documents that make up the contract, and that it is possible, and justifiable to import or imply into the contract some additional term or terms, in order to establish the nature and scope of the contractual obligations binding the respective parties. Naturally, this is not something which the courts will do easily or cavalierly. There has to be strong evidence to support the conclusion that the implication of a term is permissible in the circumstances.[178] It would seem that there are three main instances when this may be done: (i) when it is reasonably necessary, having regard to the surrounding circumstances, and in particular the previous course of dealing between the parties, if any; (ii) when there is an operative trade or business usage or custom that may be said to govern the relationship of the parties; and (iii) when some statute of its own motion implies a term into the kind of contract that is in question.[179]

(b) The doctrine of business efficacy

One illustration of this is where it is necessary to imply the suggested term or terms to make the transaction effecive, to give it what has been called "business efficacy",[180] and thus to prevent such a failure of consideration as cannot have been within the contemplation of either side.

In *Folk Arts Council of N.S. v. O'Donnell*, below, note 180, the court rejected the idea that this was based on *consensus ad idem* and thought its foundation was the reasonable expectations of the parties: *ibid.*, at 577-578.

This paragraph in the text was quoted in *McInerney v. MacDonald* (1990), 103 N.B.R. (2d) 423 at 430 (N.B.C.A.) (affirmed [1992] 2 S.C.R. 138 (S.C.C.)). This paragraph and the succeeding one were quoted by Pace J.A. in *Whitehall Holdings Ltd. v. Hawboldt Metal Fabricators Inc.* (1987), 78 N.S.R. (2d) 346 at 350 (N.S.C.A.); leave to appeal to S.C.C. refused (1988), 89 N.S.R. (2d) 180 (note) (S.C.C.).

178 To be implied a term must be (1) reasonable and equitable; (2) necessary to give business efficacy; (3) so obvious that it goes without saying; (4) capable of clear expression; (5) not contradictory of an express term in the contract: *BP Refinery (Westernport) Pty. Ltd. v. Shire of Hastings* (1977), 16 A.L.R. 363 at 376 (P.C.) *per* Lord Simon of Glaisdale.

179 This paragraph was cited by Long J. in *Odeco Drilling of Can. Ltd. v. Hickey* (1985), 54 Nfld. & P.E.I.R. 116 at 133 (Nfld. T.D.), and part of it by Macdonald J. in *Whitehall Holdings Ltd. v. Hawboldt Metal Fabricators Inc.* (1986), 75 N.S.R. (2d) 34 at 41 (N.S.T.D.); affirmed (1987), 78 N.S.R. (2d)) 346 (N.S.C.A.); leave to appeal to S.C.C. refused (1988), 87 N.R. 399 (note) (S.C.C.). The last sentence was quoted in *Hawes v. Sherwood-Parkdale Metro Junior Hockey Club Inc.* (1991), 88 D.L.R. (4th) 439 at 442 (P.E.I.C.A.).

180 *The "Moorcock"* (1889), 14 P.D. 64 at 68 (C.A.), *per* Bowen L.J. Thus an agreement to buy necessarily imports an agreement to pay the purchase price: *J.J. Bonnie v. Aero Tool Works Ltd.,* [1952] 1 S.C.R. 495 (S.C.C.). Compare *Grieve McClory Ltd. v. Dome Lbr. Ltd.,* [1922] 2 W.W.R. 1282 (Alta. C.A.); affirmed by an equally divided Supreme Court of Canada, [1923] 1 W.W.R. 989 (S.C.C.). Compare *Wallace v. Motton* (1892), 25 N.S.R. 81 (N.S.C.A.). As to agreements to

> The court will imply an unexpressed term in a contract where necessary to implement the parties' presumed intention and give business efficacy to the contract.[181]

The theory behind this doctrine is that had the "officious bystander" drawn the attention of the parties to the matter in issue, they would have agreed that the contract should provide for its resolution in the manner which is subsequently suggested, in later litigation, as the implied term.[182] But another way of expressing the doctrine is in terms of making the contract have real meaning and effect, perhaps regardless of the parties' underlying intentions.[183]

In determining the intention of the parties, attention must be paid to the express terms of the contract in order to see whether the suggested implication is necessary and fits in with what has clearly been agreed upon,[184] and the precise nature of what, if anything, should be implied. For this latter reason, in particular, the House of Lords in two leading cases refused to imply a term into a contract, one being a contract of agency, under which the agent was to receive commission for selling property, the other being a contract of employment as a lorry driver. In neither instance was it possible to formulate a term which could put succinctly what was being suggested as the necessary implication into the contract in question. In the one case, *Luxor (Eastborne) Ltd. v. Cooper*,[185] any implied term would have conflicted with the express rights and liabilities of the parties as set out in the contract. In the other, *Lister v. Romford Ice & Cold Storage Co.*[186] it was not possible to put the implied term in precise enough language, and any of the suggested implied terms, which would have had the effect of making the employer, and not the employee, liable to third parties for the employee's negligence in driving the lorry, was either contrary to public policy or inconsistent with the normal duties of the employee, and hence would have to be spelled out expressly if it was to be effective.

---

share profits and losses, see *Folk Arts Council of N.S. v. O'Donnell* (1977), 37 N.S.R. (2d) 573 (N.S. Co. Ct.); compare *Jenkins v. Cox* (1983), 56 N.S.R. (2d) 301 (N.S.T.D.). But a distribution contract did not necessarily imply that the defendant would provide the plaintiff with supplies of the product: *Solar U.S.A. Inc. v. Sask. Minerals*, [1992] 3 W.W.R. 15 (Sask. Q.B.). However, business efficacy required an implication that a trade that was the subject-matter of the contract was safe, in *Ivo v. Halabura* (1990), 85 Sask. R. 147 (Sask. Q.B.).

181 *Allan v. Bushnell T.V. Co.* (1969), 1 D.L.R. (3d) 534 at 539 (Ont. H.C.) *per* Lieff J.; compare *Twin Cities Co-op. Dairy Ltd. v. Elm Ave. Holdings Ltd.* (1966), 56 D.L.R. (2d) 264 (N.S.S.C.). Compare *McLeod Engines Ltd. v. Can. Atlas Diesel Engines Co.* (1951), 1 W.W.R. (N.S.) 271 (B.C.C.A.); reversed on other grounds [1952] 2 S.C.R. 122 (S.C.C.).

182 *Reigate v. Union Mfg. Co. (Ramsbottom)*, [1918] 1 K.B. 592 at 605 (C.A.) *per* Scrutton L.J.; *Shirlaw v. Southern Foundries (1926) Ltd.*, [1939] 2 K.B. 206 at 227 (C.A.); affirmed [1940] A.C. 701 (H.L.) *per* MacKinnon L.J. Compare *Re Broughton Collieries Ltd.*, [1944] 1 D.L.R. 530 (N.S.C.A.).

183 See *per* Foisey J. in *Knowlton Realty Ltd. v. Mace* (1980), 106 D.L.R. (3d) 667 at 670 (Alta. Q.B.).

184 *Connors v. McGregor*, [1924] 2 W.W.R. 294 (Alta. C.A.). Compare *Lyle v. Baynes Manning Ltd.* (1957), 21 W.W.R. 42 (B.C.C.A.).

185 [1941] A.C. 108 (H.L.). See also *Lyford v. Cargill Co.*, [1944] 1 W.W.R. 273 (B.C.C.A.); *Super S. Drugs Ltd. v. Richfield Properties Ltd.* (1979), 24 A.R. 449 (Alta. T.D.) on the presumption against adding to a contract terms which the parties have not expressed. Contrast the approach in *Knowlton Realty Ltd. v. Mace* (1980), 106 D.L.R. (3d) 667 (Alta. Q.B.).

186 [1957] A.C. 555 (H.L.).

Quite obviously, that is a delicate matter of fact to be determined by reference to all the circumstances of a given case, bearing in mind the general qualification that the alleged implied term must be one that is reasonable, necessary, capable of exact formulation, and clearly justified having regard to the intentions of the parties when they contracted.[187] Once again, as with the admission of parol evidence to supplement the written language of a contract, the distinction must be drawn between a determination by the court, by making the necessary implications, that a contract exists at all, and a finding that, in an undoubted contract, there is to be implied as a matter of fact, some additional term or terms beyond what has been expressed.[188]

Necessary terms have been implied in the following circumstances: into a contract to supply news, so as to import the obligation that the news would be reasonably fit for transmission to the public;[189] into a contract of employment, so as to make the employee the trustee of his employer of information gleaned during the course of employment;[190] into a contract between a stockbroker and his firm, so as to entitle the firm to terminate that relationship when the Toronto Stock Exchange withdrew its approval to its continuance,[191] into a contract to dig a well, so as to involve the conclusion that the party doing the digging must go to a certain depth in order to collect any payment under the contract;[192] into a contract of sale of logs, so as to understand the word "approximately" used therein;[193] into a contract of carriage, so as to involve the obligation to use reasonable care,[194] into an option of pre-emption of land, so as to prevent the land from being given to anyone else before being offered to the optionee;[195] into a contract of repair to involve the obligation to use reasonable care;[196] into a charter-

---

187 This sentence was quoted in *Hawes v. Sherwood-Parkdale Metro Junior Hockey Club Inc.* (1991), 88 D.L.R. (4th) 439 at 443 (P.E.I.C.A.), and in *Law-Woman Management Corp. v. Peel (Regional Municipality)* (1991), 17 R.P.R. (2d) 62 at 81 (Ont. Gen. Div.) *per* Lane J.

188 This paragraph was cited with by Hallet J. in *Midland Doherty Ltd. v. Rohrer* (1984), 62 N.S.R. (2d) 205 at 212 (N.S.T.D.); affirmed (1985), 68 N.S.R. (2d) 103 (N.S.C.A.).

189 *Allan v. Bushnell T.V. Co.*, above, note 181.

190 *W. J. Gage Ltd. v. Sugden*, [1967] 2 O.R. 151 (Ont. H.C.). Compare *Int. Tools Ltd. v. Kollar*, [1968] 1 O.R. 669 (Ont. C.A.); compare as regards other implications into a contract of employment: *Sanko S.S. Co. v. Eacom Timber Sales Co.* (1986), 8 B.C.L.R. (2d) 69 (B.C.S.C.).

191 *Posluns v. Toronto Stock Exchange*, [1964] 2 O.R. 547 (Ont. H.C.); affirmed [1966] 1 O.R. 285 (Ont. C.A.); affirmed [1968] S.C.R. 330 (S.C.C.).

192 *Savidan v. Laplante*, [1924] 2 W.W.R. 1222 (Sask. C.A.). Contrast *Deschênes Drilling Ltd./Forages Deschênes Ltée c. O'Brien* (1989), 97 N.B.R. (2d) 441 (N.B.Q.B.), no implied term that a well to be dug would produce water that was safe to drink; because the party digging the well was not equated with "experts" in respect of whose work a term as to "fitness for purpose" was implied (by law rather than as a matter of fact?).

193 *Burgoyne v. Murphy*, [1951] 2 D.L.R. 556 (N.B.S.C.).

194 *Key v. Key*, [1930] 3 D.L.R. 327 (Ont. C.A.). Nor did it matter that the transport was gratuitous. Contrast *Craven v. Strand Holidays (Can.) Ltd* (1980), 119 D.L.R. (3d) 225 (Ont. H.C.); reversed (1982), 142 D.L.R. (3d) 31 (Ont. C.A.); leave to appeal to S.C.C. refused (1983), 48 N.R. 320 (S.C.C.).

195 *Gardner v. Coutts & Co.*, [1968] 1 W.L.R. 173.

196 *Scott-D'Amboisie Const. Co. v. Reo Motors*, [1958] O.R. 711 (Ont. C.A.). Compare *G.H. Myers & Co. v. Brent Corss Service Co.*, [1934] 1 K.B. 46; *Marktara Ltd. v. Branter* (1981), 6 Sask. R.

party, so as to involve the obligation that the ship would be ready to load timber
having regard to weather conditions;[197] to require repayment of a loan within a
reasonable time;[198] to control termination of a contract;[199] to require the claiming
of goods bailed within a reasonable time;[200] to impose an obligation to pay
reasonable remuneration for work done;[201] to require the return of a chattel in
the same condition as it was leased subject to reasonable wear and tear;[202] to give
a sole agency to a contracting party;[203] to preclude the solicitation of customers
of a company after the sale of the implied promisor's shares in the company;[204]
to involve the performance of work with reasonable care and skill or in a
workmanlike manner;[205] in a contract with a professor as to the proper basis for
the assessment of his performance as a teacher;[206] in a logging contract to the

288 (Sask. Dist. Ct.); *Smith v. Autogo Service Ltd.* (1981), 45 N.S.R. (2d) 520 (N.S.T.D.); *MacLean v. Portland Masonry Ltd.* (1982), 55 N.S.R. (2d) 666 (N.S.T.D.); *Babb Const. Ltd. v. Precision Rebuilding Ltd.* (1989), 80 Nfld. & P.E.I.R. 291 (Nfld. T.D.); additional reasons at (1990), 80 Nfld. & P.E.I.R. 291 at 298 (Nfld. T.D.). Compare also *Young & Marten Ltd. v. McManus Childs Ltd.*, [1969] 1 A.C. 454 (H.L.). See also *S. & M. Carpet Ltd. v. Ledwith* (1990), 80 Nfld. & P.E.I.R. 53 (Nfld. T.D.), implied term that carpet would be installed in a workmanlike manner. As far as the implication of terms into sales or leases of houses are concerned, see, for some discussion, *Barak v. Langtry*, [1954] 4 D.L.R. 135 (B.C.S.C.) and the cases there cited. Compare *Fraser-Reid v. Droumsekas* (1980), 103 D.L.R. (3d) 385 (S.C.C.). As for an implied term in a contract to *visit* premises, see *Finigan v. Calgary* (1967), 62 W.W.R. 115 (Alta. C.A.).

197 *Snow v. Harris*, [1930] 1 D.L.R. 802 (N.S.C.A.).

198 *Surette v. Surette* (1980), 40 N.S.R. (2d) 482 (N.S.T.D.).

199 *Twin City Painting Contractors Ltd. v. Penwood Const. Ltd.* (1980), 44 N.S.R. (2d) 418 (N.S. Co. Ct.); *Philip F. Levine Marketing Ltd. v. 3SM Tours Ltd.*, [1983] 4 W.W.R. 149 (Alta. Q.B.); amending reasons at [1983] 6 W.W.R. 436 (Alta. Q.B.); *Bernard-Norman Specialties Co. v. S.C. Time Inc.* (1989), 31 C.P.R. (3d) 158 (Ont. H.C.); *Helcor Enterprises Ltd. v. Moore & James Food Services Ltd.*, [1990] 5 W.W.R. 596 (Man. Q.B.); *Parsons v. Can. Satellite Communications Inc.* (1990), 47 B.L.R. 112 (Nfld. T.D.); affirmed (1992), 101 Nfld. & P.E.I.R. 356 (Nfld. C.A.).

200 *Davis v. Henry Birks & Sons Ltd.*, [1983] 1 W.W.R. 754 (B.C.C.A.).

201 *McLaughlin v. Stark* (1980), 27 N.B.R. (2d) 340 (N.B.C.A.); contrast *Murdock-Lingley Ltd. v. Crowthers* (1978), 22 N.B.R. (2d) 140 (N.B.C.A.).

202 *Con-force Prods. Ltd. v. Luscar Ltd.* (1982), 27 Sask. R. 299 (Sask. Q.B.).

203 *Smith v. Mosher Limestone Co.* (1981), 121 D.L.R. (2d) 290 (N.S.C.A.); compare *Knowlton Realty Ltd. v. Mace* (1979), 106 D.L.R. (3d) 667 (Alta. Q.B.).

204 *J.L.R. Holdings Ltd. v. Wiseberg* (1977), 17 O.R. (3d) 809 (Ont. H.C.); affirmed (1978), 21 O.R. (2d) 839 (Ont. C.A.); compare *Computer Workshops Ltd. v. Banner Capital Market Brokers Ltd.* (1989), 39 B.L.R. 64 (Ont. H.C.); affirmed (1990), 1 O.R. (3d) 398 (Ont. C.A.), implied term that vendor would not sell computer systems to another party in breach of confidence and fiduciary duty.

205 *Frie v. Sask. Telecommunications*, [1979] 6 W.W.R. 60 (Sask. Q.B.) (with which contrast *Hart v. Bell Telephone Co. of Can.* (1979), 10 C.C.L.T. 335 (Ont. C.A.)); *Matthews v. Godin* (1980), 25 Nfld. & P.E.I.R. 496 (P.E.I.C.A.); compare *Spencer v. Forseth Building Movers Ltd.* (1983), 27 Sask. R. 247 (Sask. Q.B.) (duty to advise of risks in moving building); *Hagerman v. Niagara Falls* (1980), 29 O.R. (2d) 609 (Ont. H.C.) (duty to provide spectator at hockey game with seat in a safe place). And see *G. Ford Homes Ltd. v. Draft Masonry (York) Co.* (1984), 2 O.A.C. 231 (Ont. C.A.) (implication of term that staircase would be installed in conformity with Ontario Building Code). See also *Carrier v. Sterling Trust Co.* (1985), 8 O.A.C. 339 (Ont. Div. Ct.); *Fraser v. U-Need-A-Cab Ltd.* (1983), 43 O.R. (2d) 389 (Ont. H.C.); affirmed (1985), 50 O.R. (2d) 281 (Ont. C.A.).

206 *Cohnstaedt v. University of Regina*, [1989] 1 S.C.R. 1011 (S.C.C.).

effect that the timetable for the required logging was subject to conditions beyond the plaintiff's control, such as the weather;[207] and to require the parties to a franchise agreement, *viz.*, a car dealership, to act towards each other in good faith.[208]

Terms were not implied in the following instances: a sale of shares, when it was alleged that there was an implied obligation on a company to buy back the shares from the original buyer;[209] a contract of employment of a teacher, when it was alleged that every such contract should be in a prescribed form;[210] a contract of agency, in respect of which it was alleged there was an implied term that the principal would continue to pay the agent after the latter terminated the relationship;[211] an option, into whch it was sought to imply a term as to the continuation of the option;[212] a contract of employment between an employee and the Post Office, in which it alleged there was an implied term that the Post Office would continue to recognize the guild of which the employee was a member;[213] a contract between a football player and a football club, in which the schedule had been increased to 16 games;[214] an employment contract, so as to prevent the employer from dismissing the employee;[215] a franchise agreement with respect to advertising, training and assistance to be supplied to the franchisee;[216] a contract of carriage of goods by truck, requiring a party to pay an insurance surcharge;[217] and a distribution agreement to require a party to provide the other with adequate supplies of the product in question.[218]

The situations referred to above involve a multitude of circumstances, making it virtually impossible to draw any general conclusions. What is necessary for any given contract to be effective, despite the failure or neglect of the parties to make this express, must depend upon the particular facts, rather than upon any broad principles of law. However, there is one situation in respect of which, perhaps, some more general principle might be stated. Where a contract requires a party to do or obtain something, in order that the contract can come into existence or

---

207 *Morin v. Nuni (Ye) Forest Products Ltd.* (1990), 49 B.L.R. 179 (N.W.T.S.C.).

208 *McKinlay Motors Ltd.v. Honda Can. Inc.* (1989), 46 B.L.R. 62 (Nfld. T.D.).

209 *Lyle v. Baynes Manning Ltd.*, above, note 184.

210 *MacLeod v. Dominion (Town) School Commrs.* (1958), 16 D.L.R. (2d) 587 (N.S.S.C.).

211 *Grover v. Stirling Bonding Co.*, [1935] 3 D.L.R. 481 (S.C.C.); compare *Woodpulp Inc. (Can.) v. Jannock Indust. Ltd.* (1979), 26 N.B.R. (2d) 358 (N.B.C.A.); varied on other grounds (1979), 33 N.B.R. (2d) 652 (N.B.C.A.).

212 *Clegg v. Pac. Stock Co.*, [1935] 1 W.W.R. 369 (B.C.S.C.).

213 *Gallagher v. Post Office*, [1970] 3 All E.R. 712.

214 *Re Gabriel and Hamilton Tiger-Cat Football Club Ltd.* (1975), 57 D.L.R. (3d) 669 (Ont. H.C.), applying *Trollope & Colls Ltd. v. North West Metro. Hospital Bd.*, [1973] 2 All E.R. 260 (H.L.).

215 *Longman v. Fed. Business Dev. Bank* (1982), 131 D.L.R. (3d) 533 (B.C.S.C.). Compare also *I.S.S. Information System Services Ltd. v. Smyth* (1985), 7 C.C.E.L. 35 (B.C. Co. Ct.) (no implied term in contract of loan with employer that the loan would be forgiven if the employment were terminated without cause).

216 *387071 Ont. Ltd. v. 526770 Ont. Ltd.* (1988), 66 O.R. (2d) 167 (Ont. H.C.).

217 *Atomic Interprovincial Transport (Eastern) Ltd. v. Paul Geiger Trucking Ltd.* (1987), 47 Man. R. (2d) 42 (Man. Q.B.); affirmed (1988), 49 Man. R. (2d) 296 (Man. C.A.).

218 *Solar U.S.A. Inc. v. Sask. Minerals*, [1992] 3 W.W.R. 15 (Sask. Q.B.). Nor could a term be implied so as to create a binding contract with respect to the sharing of season tickets for hockey games in *Eng v. Evans* (1992), 83 Alta. L.R. (2d) 107 (Alta. Q.B.).

be performed, there would seem to be an implied term that such party will do everything reasonably within its power to achieve the fulfilment of this requirement, or will not unreasonable hamper its achievement. In cases involving conditions precedent,[219] there are many statements to the effect that implicit in such transactions is the duty of the party who has some task to perform, for example, to obtain the approval of a third party, or some planning permission, to act reasonably and in good faith with a view to its fulfilment.[220] Such term is implied in order to give business efficacy to the transaction. But it might also be said that whevever a party is obliged by a contract to do something, or refrain from doing something, there is implicit in the contract an obligation of good faith.[221] Parties may not impede the fulfilment of a contract. On the contrary they must do whatever is reasonable to attain the performance of the contract.[222] The standard of performance is objective. What the obligated party must do is not what is reasonable in his eyes, but what would be reasonable in the eyes of the hypothetical reasonable man. In other words, the obligated party can only excuse himself from performance if non-performance was inevitable, pre-determined, beyond doubt.[223]

The classical doctrine of "business efficacy", based upon what was necessary to give a contract meaning and purpose, was the subject of exegesis by Lord Denning M.R. in *Liverpool City Council v. Irwin.*[224] There he suggested that terms could be implied in contracts where it was "reasonable" to do so, as well as where it was "necessary" to do so. He attempted to argue that courts had the power to import terms into a contract not only on the basis that they were simply filling in gaps carelessly or unwittingly left by the parties, but also whenever a court thought that it was reasonable in the interests of one or both of the parties to add something to the written contract. This approach was held incorrect by the House of Lords in that case.[225] Subsequently, Lord Denning acknowledged that his efforts to develop or rephrase the law had been unsuccessful. In a later case,

---

219 See above, pp. 443-446.
220 *BEM Enterprises Ltd. v. Campeau Corp.* (1980), 24 B.C.L.R. 244 (B.C.S.C.); varied (1981), 32 B.C.L.R. 116 (B.C.C.A.); *Hogg v. Wilken* (1974), 5 O.R. (2d) 759 (Ont. H.C.); *Steiner v. E.H.D. Invts. Ltd.* (1977), 78 D.L.R. (3d) 449 (Alta. C.A.); *Dynamic Tpt. Ltd. v. O.K. Detailing Ltd.* (1978), 85 D.L.R. (3d) 19 (S.C.C.); *Multi-Malls Inc. v. Text-Mall Properties Ltd.* (1980), 108 D.L.R. (3d) 339 (Ont. H.C.); affirmed (1981), 128 D.L.R. (3d) 192 (Ont. C.A.); leave to appeal to S.C.C. refused (1982), 41 N.R. 360n (S.C.C.).
221 Compare *McKinlay Motors Ltd. v. Honda Can. Inc.* (1989), 46 B.L.R. 62 (Nfld. T.D.).
222 *MacKay v. Dick* (1881), 7 App. Cas. 251 (H.L.); *100 Main St. Ltd. v. W.B. Sullivan Const. Ltd.* (1978), 20 O.R. (2d) 401 (Ont. C.A.); leave to appeal to S.C.C. refused (1978), 20 O.R. 401n (S.C.C.); compare Burrows, "Contractual Co-Operation and the Implied Term" (1968), 31 M.L.R. 390; compare Stoljar, "Prevention and Co-Operation in the Law of Contract" (1953), 31 Can. Bar Rev. 231. As to the situation in the United States, see Burton, "Breach of Contract and the Common Law Duty to Perform in Good Faith" (1980), 94 H.L.R. 369.
223 *BEM Enterprises Ltd. v. Campeau Corp.*, above, note 220; *Aldercrest Devs. Ltd. v. Hunter* (1970), 11 D.L.R. (3d) 439 (Ont. C.A.); *M.J.B. Enterprises Ltd. v. People's Food Market Ltd.* (1980), 11 B.C.L.R. 130 (B.C.C.A.).
224 [1976] 1 Q.B. 319 (C.A.).
225 [1977] A.C. 239 (H.L.); compare *Cdn. Pacific Ltd. v. Ont. Hydro* (1987), 19 O.A.C. 232 (Ont. Div. Ct.); reversed on other grounds (1987), 24 O.A.C. 143 (Ont. C.A.); leave to appeal to S.C.C. refused (1988), 28 O.A.C. 400 (note) (S.C.C.).

Shell United Kingdom Ltd. v. Lostock Garages Ltd.,[226] he drew a distinction between two types of implied terms, both of which he said emanated from the doctrine of *The "Moorcock"*.[227] The first consisted of those terms which had become implied into contracts over a period of years and were, by now, treated as almost *pro forma* terms in such transactions, for example, those implied into contracts of sale of goods, contracts between master and servant, or landlord and tenant.[228] The second were those which were implied into specific contracts, *ad hoc*, on the basis of necessity, *not* reasonableness alone. His attempt to rid the common law of the "officious bystander" met with failure. The stricter, more traditional approach to the question of the implication of a term, otherwise than by reason of previous dealings or custom, survived Lord Denning's attack. While it may be true that some Canadian judges have been prepared to base the common-law doctrine on the "reasonable expectations of the parties"[229] rather than upon the ascertainment of the parties' intentions,[230] both explanations of the doctrine are grounded on the idea that only what is necessary may be implied, not that which is reasonable in the eyes of the court.

(c) **Previous dealings**[231]

An important instance of the implication of a term under the doctrine just described is where the parties have previously transacted contracts of a similar type to the one the construction of which is in question, and have included certain terms which are not expressly agreed in such later contract. Sometimes it may be possible to infer, as a matter of fact, that the parties must have intended to contract on the same basis as the earlier contracts.[232]

The situation in respect of this possibility has been confused, in recent years, as a result of the decision by the House of Lords in *McCutcheon v. McBrayne Ltd.*

---

226 [1977] 1 All E.R. 481 at 487-488 (C.A.) (where, on the traditional approach, an implied term, that a supplier of petrol would not actively discriminate against a garage proprietor, could not be added to a "solus" agreement between the parties: on which see above, pp. 410-414). See also Denning, *The Discipline of Law* (1979), pp. 31-41.

227 (1889), 14 P.D. 64 (C.A.).

228 Compare *Liverpool City Council v. Irwin*, [1977] A.C. 239 at 257-258 (H.L.) *per* Lord Cross; *National Bank of Greece S.A. v. Pinios Shipping Co. No. 1; The "Maira"*, [1989] 1 All E.R. 213 at 218-219 (C.A.) *per* Lloyd L.J.; compare the distinction referred to by Mason J. in *Codelfa Const. Pty Ltd. v. State Rail Authority of N.S.W.* (1982), 149 C.L.R. 337 at 345, and by Gibson L.J. in *Reid v. Rush & Tompkins Group PLC*, [1989] 2 Lloyd's Rep. 167 at 172, 177-178 (C.A.), and May L.J. in *Bank of N.S. v. Hellenic Mutual War Risks Association (Bermuda) Ltd.*, [1989] 2 Lloyd's Rep. 238 at 268 (C.A.); reversed [1991] 1 Lloyd's Rep. 191 (H.L.).

229 See, *e.g.*, *Folk Arts Council of N.S. v. O'Donnell* (1977), 37 N.S.R. (2d) 573 at 577-578 (N.S. Co. Ct.).

230 *Lyford v. Cargill Co.*, [1944] 1 D.L.R. 696 (B.C.C.A.). *J.W. Cowie Enrg. Ltd. v. Allen* (1981), 47 N.S.R. (2d) 705 at 711 (N.S.T.D.); varied (1982), 26 C.P.C. 241 (N.S.C.A.).

231 There is a general reference to this section in *Abitibi-Price Inc. v. Westinghouse Can. Inc.* (1988), 73 Nfld. & P.E.I.R. 271 at 300 (Nfld. T.D.).

232 *Atomic Interprovincial Transport (Eastern) Ltd. v. Paul Geiger Trucking Ltd.* (1988), 45 D.L.R. (4th) 312 at 316 (Man. C.A.).

and its aftermath. In the *McCutcheon* case,[233] the defendants operated steamers between the Scottish mainland and the islands. The plaintiff had used those steamers on numerous occasions on each of which he had signed a written contract which contained a clause exempting the defendants from liability for negligence. On the occasion in question the plaintiff's agent made an *oral* contract for the shipment of the plaintiff's car by the defendants' steamer. By reason of the latters' negligence the car was lost and the plaintiff sued. The defendants pleaded the exemption clause, to which the plaintiff answered that it was not a term in the particular contract in question. The defendants' response was that, in light of the previous dealings between the parties, such exemption clause had to be implied into the oral contract. The House of Lords held in favour of the plaintiff, and did not permit the implication of the term in question. Lord Devlin, at least, made it clear that merely because of such previous dealings terms were not necessarily to be implied which were omitted in a subsequent contract. "Previous dealings are relevant," his Lordship said,[234] "only if they prove knowledge of the terms, actual and not constructive, and assent to them." In the Canadian case of *A.I.M. Steel Ltd. v. Gulf of Georgia Towing Co.*,[235] a contract for transporting goods from ship to shore was arranged over the telephone. Previous such dealings between the parties had been in writing. In this situation no implication of the usual limitation of liability term was permitted into the oral contract. The written contracts related to a different form of contract, and the parties in the oral contract did not have limitation provisions in mind. Thus, the negligent party was liable for the loss of the goods. In that case, too, no intention to incorporate a limitation clause could be presumed from the conduct of the parties, their contract, and the surrounding circumstances. Nor did business efficacy require any such implication. The contract was perfectly good without it. Indeed, as in the *McCutcheon* case, the injured party was better off without any such implication. Perhaps this is the explanation of these cases. This view is strengthened by the converse situation which arose in *Burnett v. Westminster Bank Ltd.*[236] There the bank, of which the plaintiff was a customer, altered its rules regarding cheques. But the plaintiff did not have notice of this change, and so operated on the previous basis, under which he would have been entitled to act as he did and would have been protected. In the circumstances the court held that the contract between the parties was not affected by the change by the bank. In this case, therefore, the previous dealings governed, because the alteration was against the interests of the plaintiff, in the sense of possibly causing him loss, and notice was consequently imperative.

An English case which, on the facts, seems to comply with the decision in

---

233 [1964] 1 All E.R. 430 (H.L.). For a discussion of this and other *English* cases, see Macdonald, "Incorporation of Contract Terms by a 'Consistent Course of Dealing'" (1988), 8 J. Leg. St. 48.

234 [1964] 1 All E.R. 430 at 437 (H.L.).

235 (1964), 48 D.L.R. (2d) 549 (B.C.S.C.). Contrast the earlier case of *Imp. Grain & Milling Co. v. Slobinsky Bros. & Sons*, [1922] 3 W.W.R. 221 (Man. K.B.) though this may be a case concerned with *custom*, not merely previous dealings; contrast also *A. R. Kitson Trucking Ltd. v. Rivtow Straits Ltd.* (1975), 55 D.L.R. (3d) 462 (B.C.S.C.) below, note 238.

236 [1966] 1 Q.B. 742.

the *McCutceheon* case, is *Hollier v. Rambler Motors (A.M.C.) Ltd.*,[237] in which previous written contracts did not permit the implication of a clause exempting the garage from responsibility for loss from fire into an *oral* contract of repair. However, Salmon L.J.,[238] echoing earlier, similar comments in the Court of Appeal and the House of Lords,[239] suggested that Lord Devlin had gone too far in the *McCutcheon* case when he indicated that actual and not constructive notice of terms was required and assent with such actual knowledge.

Similarly in a Canadian case, *Atomic Interprovincial Transport (Eastern) Ltd. v. Paul Geiger Trucking Ltd.*,[240] a special and onerous term requiring a party to pay an insurance surcharge could not be implied from previous dealings between the parties. Their course of dealings had not been consistent, and the implied term involved a change in the relationship. Here it was pointed out that even one previous dealing may settle the question if it reflects a custom of the trade.[241]

If there is no true course of dealings between the parties then any implication of a term or rule on such basis will be impossible.[242]

(d) Usage and custom[243]

In some circumstances, and under rigorous conditions, a trade, business, or professional usage or custom[244] may be incorporated by implication into a contract, and become one of its terms. Sometimes a relevant usage or custom may be proved to aid in the construction of the language used by the parties.[245]

What is here being discussed goes further than the interpretation of words: it relates to the insertion of some new, or additional obligation into the express terms of the contract.

When does a usage or custom affect a written contract? The answer given by the Supreme Court of Canada in *Georgia Construction Co. v. Pacific Great Eastern*

---

237 [1972] 1 All E.R. 399 (C.A.) with which contrast *Br. Crane Hire Corp. v. Ipswich Plant Hire Ltd.*, [1975] Q.B. 303 (C.A.), where a term was implied, but this latter case involved two commercial undertakings engaged in the same business over a longer period of time.

238 [1972] 1 All E.R. 399 at 403-404 (C.A.); cited with approval in *A. R. Kitson Trucking Ltd. v. Rivtow Straits Ltd.* (1975), 55 D.L.R. (3d) 462 (B.C.S.C.), in which a term as to the issuance of the usual bill of lading could be implied from the previous dealings between the parties.

239 *Hardwick Game Farm v. Suffolk Agricultural & Poultry Producers Assn.*, [1966] 1 All E.R. 309 at 322 (C.A.) *per* Sellers L.J., 344 *per* Diplock L.J.; affirmed [1968] 1 All E.R. 444 (*sub nom. Henry Kendall & Sons v. William Lilico & Sons Ltd.*) at 457 (H.L.) *per* Lord Guest, 481 *per* Lord Pearce, and 496 *per* Lord Wilberforce.

240 Above, note 232.

241 *Ibid.*, at 317, quoting *Br. Crane Hire Corp. v. Ipswich Plant Hire Ltd.*, above, note 237. As to custom see below, pp. 483-485.

242 *Abitibi-Price Inc. v. Westinghouse Can. Inc.* (1988), 73 Nfld. & P.E.I.R. 271 (Nfld. T.D.).

243 This section was referred to as a "useful discussion of the law" by Maurice J. in *Con-Force Products Ltd. v. Luscar Ltd.* (1982), 27 Sask. R. 299 at 301 (Sask. Q.B.).

244 For a detailed analysis of the two expressions and the distinction between them see the judgment of Audette J. in *The "Freiya" v. The "R.S."* (1922), 65 D.L.R. 218 at 222-223 (Ex. Ct.).

245 Above, p. 468, note 129.

Railway,[246] was, when the usage, or custom, was reasonably certain, notorious, and so generally acquiesced in by those in the particular trade, business or profession that was involved in the contract that it may be presumed to form an ingredient of the contract.[247] In that case, the alleged customary meanings of "extra haul" and "overhaul" in a contract to perform work on a railway line were not accepted as being within the criteria just stated; hence, no such special meanings or terms could be implied. This was followed in *David (Steveston Sawmills) v. Arnott-Smith Timber Co.*,[248] with respect to a custom in the timber trade. In that case, the evidence established that the custom was certain, notorious and universally accepted. However, the express terms of the contract ousted the application of the custom. Therefore, the seller was obliged to deliver specific quantities of timber, rather than the customary fair percentage of *different* types of timber. An appeal to custom was also unsuccessful in *Great Northern Petroleum & Mines Ltd. v. Merland Explorations Ltd.*[249] The plaintiff sought to introduce a custom as to a practice in the oil and gas industry that the defendants would notify the plaintiff of the defendants' intention to acquire an interest in lands subject to the agreement or would allow the plaintiff to participate in the acquisition. Shannon J. applied the decision in the *Georgia Construction Co.* case,[250] and held that such a custom was contrary to the express provisions of the formal agreement. The plaintiff could not rely on this custom to prove that the contract impliedly prevented the defendants from acquiring the land in question for themselves.

Thus the alleged custom must not be inconsistent with the specific terms of the contract, else it will not be possible to incorporate the custom on the basis of the presumed intention of the parties.[251] It must also be certain, else there can be no application of such intention, on the ground that the parties will not be presumed to have agreed to something that was not clear. This is why the alleged custom that was supposed to apply to fishing vessels off the coast of British Columbia was rejected by Audette J. of the Exchequer Court in *The "Freiya" v. The "R.S."*[252] And the custom must be generally accepted. To quote from Locke J. of the Supreme Court of Canada in *Schara Tzedeck v. Royal Trust Co.*,

> [i]nsofar as support for the claim is based on custom, it would have been necessary
> . . . to establish that a custom to change the estate of Jewish persons in the manner

---

246 [1929] S.C.R. 630 at 633 (S.C.C.) *per* Duff J. Hence no custom could be relied upon in *Const. Rentals Ltd. v. Nfld.* (1984), 47 Nfld. & P.E.I.R. 299 (Nfld. S.C.).

247 This and the previous sentence were cited by Hallet J. in *Midland Doherty Ltd. v. Rohrer* (1984), 62 N.S.R. (2d) 205 at 212 (N.S.T.D.); affirmed (1985), 68 N.S.R. (2d) 103 (N.S.C.A.).

248 (1952), 7 W.W.R. (N.S.) 306 (B.C.S.C.) but contrast *Cartwright & Crickmore Ltd. v. MacInnes*, [1931] S.C.R. 425 (S.C.C.).

249 (1983), 25 Alta. L.R. (2d) 67 (Alta. Q.B.); affirmed on other grounds (1984), 36 Alta. L.R. (2d) 97 (Alta. C.A.).

250 Above, note 246, and *Palgrave, Brown & Sons v. S.S. Turid*, [1922] 1 A.C. 397 (H.L.).

251 *Imp. Grain & Milling Co. v. Slobinsky Bros. & Sons*, [1922] 3 W.W.R. 221 (Man. K.B.).

252 Above, note 244. See also *Nor. Elevator Co. v. Lake Huron & Man. Milling Co.* (1907), 13 O.L.R. 349 (Ont. C.A.).

described . . . had obtained the force of law in the locality and thus had taken the place of the common law in respect of the matter . . .[253]

That was a case in which the executors of a will were being sued for several thousands of dollars for the burial of a deceased Jewish woman. She had left in her will her desire to be buried according to the Jewish custom and ritual, even though she had virtually disassociated herself from the Jewish religion and Jewish company during her lifetime. The appropriate Jewish authorities conducted her burial and then sought to charge a large sum, more than what the court found was a "reasonable" amount, on the basis of an alleged custom among Jewish people, not only in the particular area but throughout Canada, that payment was based on a number of factors, for example, wealth, contribution to Jewish charities, etc. This custom was not received and given effect to by the courts, and the executors were only liable for the reasonable sum, not the amount settled upon by the burial authority which had made its determination on the basis of the custom.

It would seem that the most likely situation in which a custom can be made effectual is where there is a recognized trade, business or profession, which, over the years, had developed a mode of conducting its business or of understanding its transaction, such as is the case with the buying and selling of shares through stockbrokers.[254]

(e) Under statute[255]

The judicial power to imply a term or terms, so as to effectuate the true contractual intent of the parties has sometimes been pre-empted by legislatures. There are several types of contractual situations in respect of which statutes have enacted that certain terms are necessarily implied into the contract (unless specifically excluded by the parties).[256] Even this exception is not always operative, since, especially in contracts relating to the sale of goods and other consumer transactions, there has been a tendency for legislatures to make it impossible for

---

253 [1953] 1 S.C.R. 31 at 38 (S.C.C.).

254 Compare *Greenshields Inc. v. McDonough*, [1968] 1 O.R. 297 (Ont. H.C.); *Cartwright v. MacInnes*, above, note 248. Compare *Br. Crane Hire Corp. v. Ipswich Plant Hire Ltd.*, [1975] Q.B. 303 (C.A.), when both parties were familiar with the business of hiring out heavy equipment.

255 Note also that apart from, and prior to, statutes which have codified the common law, such as the Sale of Goods Act, the common law implied terms into certain types of contracts not as a matter of effectuating the parties' intentions but from judicial policy: such terms are implied by law, not implied in fact: see the authorities cited above, note 228. Such terms have been implied into conditional sales contracts: *Traders Finance Corp. v. Norray Distributing Ltd.* (1967), 60 W.W.R. 129 (Man. Q.B.); contracts of bailment: *Coleshaw v. Lipsett* (1973), 33 D.L.R. (3d) 382 (Sask. Q.B.); contracts for work and labour: *Associated Siding Applicators Ltd. v. E.S. Jonasson Contr. Ltd.* (1985), 57 A.R. 136 (Alta. Q.B.); *Markland Associates Ltd. v. Lohnes* (1973), 33 D.L.R. (3d) 493 (N.S.T.D.); house building: *Barak v. Langtry*, [1954] 4 D.L.R. 135 (B.C.S.C.). See also *Farnel v. Main Outboard Centre Ltd.* (1987), 50 Man. R. (2d) 13 (Man. C.A.); *Deschênes Drilling Ltd./ Forages Deschênes Ltée c. O'Brien* (1989), 97 N.B.R. (2d) 441 (N.B.Q.B.).

256 Terms implied by the Sale of Goods Act are set out and discussed in Fridman, *Sale of Goods in Canada*, 3rd ed. (1986), pp. 104-117, 174-216: see also *ibid.*, pp. 219-222 for terms implied under other statutes.

parties to exclude by agreement what the particular legislature has deemed sufficiently important to be implied into the contract by statute.[257]

Whenever a statute implies a term into a contract within the scope of the statute, such term is incorporated into the contract as a matter of law and does not require any judicial implication.[258] It becomes an express term.[259]

(f) The theory of implied terms

There are three possible bases for the implication of terms into a contract, other than where this is mandatory under a statute. The first is that the intention of the parties is clear from the contract and its surrounding circumstances; they would have included such a term had they foreseen its necessity or it had been drawn to their attention. The second is that to import such a term is required in order to give effect to what has been called "the reasonable expectations of the parties". The third is that the implication of such a term is needed to give purpose and effect to the rest of the contract.

The first explanation, or theory, which has received the most general acceptance, accords with the notion of *consensus ad idem*, which, it has been suggested,[260] lies at the root of the common-law conception of contract. Courts should be discovering and declaring what the parties have assented to as binding upon them. Implied terms aid in the determination of their agreement by fulfilling their manifest, if unavowed, intentions. Although this explanation seems to involve no construction by courts, and appears to state that courts only extract from the language and nature of the contract something that is really there all the time (if not made obvious), it contains an element of fiction. A court will include what has been expressly excluded by the parties, justifying such inclusion by reference to what might have been in their minds, if not must have been in their minds, at the time of contracting.

The second explanation or theory resembles the first, in that it deals with the deemed intentions of the parties, although expressed in the language of their expectations or desires rather than their intentions.[261] Again, while purporting to be logically derived from the contract and its attendant circumstances, and therefore not requiring any artificial construction by the courts, this explanation also suggests something of a fiction. The court is to attribute to parties what the court regards as being their reasonable expectations. *Ex hypothesi* the parties have not made those expectations perfectly clear. There is an omission in the language of the contract. That omission is filled by the court's later addition of language suggested

---

257 See, *e.g.*, Fridman, *op. cit.*, above, note 256, at pp. 281-282.

258 Compare *Mahoney v. Newcastle Bd. of School Trustees* (1966), 61 D.L.R. (2d) 77 (N.B.C.A.).

259 *Can. Indemnity Co. v. Andrews & George Co.*, [1953] 1 S.C.R. 19 at 24 (S.C.C.) *per* Kerwin and Estey JJ., and at 25 *per* Rand J.

260 Above, pp. 15-16.

261 Compare *Folk Arts Council of N.S. v. O'Donnell* (1977), 37 N.S.R. (2d) 573 at 577-578 (N.S. Co. Ct.). See, generally, Reiter & Swan, "Contract and the Protection of Reasonable Expectations" in Reiter and Swan, *Studies in Contract Law* (1980), Study I.

by one party, presumably over the objection of the other. The courts state that they are acting objectively and by reference to the internal structure of the contract. In effect, they may be acting more subjectively and with reference to extrinsic factors.

The third explanation is more plainly supportive of the idea that a court is entitled to interpret a contract, perhaps regardless of its express language, in a way in which the court thinks is justified and proper, on the basis that a contractual intention, evidenced by the express language of the contract, should be effectuated rather than defeated, even if this involves the addition of terms not included in, or stated by the parties. This seems a more obvious example of legal fiction than the other explanations. It also justifies a more positive, activist role for courts in the interpretation and construction of contracts than the other explanations.

All three explanations have their defects. The problem involved in attempting to rationalize and justify the implication of terms at common law arises because of the essential tension between two opposing views of the function of contract law and the courts. One stresses the importance of the parties' own acts and language, and the limited role of courts in determining what parties have agreed. The other places more emphasis on the extent to which courts can intervene and mould a contract and its terms for parties who have carelessly or inefficiently failed to make their true intentions as clear and explicit as possible. Although courts have often said that they will not make a contract for the parties, it would seem that, to some extent at least, they are prepared to fill in blanks, as long as the parties have manifested a contractual intent, and have provided a bare minimum of expression of that intent.

3. Varieties of terms

(a) The condition-warranty dichotomy[262]

(i) *Introduction*

Not all terms of a contract are of equal weight and importance. They have different characteristics and different effects in law, depending upon their particular nature and the way in which the law had developed with respect to each. Classical legal analysis distinguished between two types of terms: conditions and warranties.[263]

Historically, the concepts of condition and warranty had very broad meanings which, in the process of time, became narrowed to their present-day special

---

262 See the reference to this and subsequent pages by O'Sullivan J.A. in *Kruse v. Oakwood Const. Services Ltd.* (1982), 16 Man. R. (2d) 270 at 274 (Man. C.A.). See, generally, Montrose, "Conditions, Warranties and Other Contractual Terms" (1937), 15 Can. Bar Rev. 309; Stoljar, "Conditions, Warranties and Descriptions of Quality in Sales of Goods" (1952), 15 M.L.R. 425; (1953), 16 M.L.R. 174; Reynolds, "Warranty, Condition and Fundamental Term" (1963), 79 L.Q.R. 534; Stoljar, "The Contractual Concept of Condition" (1953), 69 L.Q.R. 585.

263 Bridge, "Discharge for Breach of the Contract of Sale of Goods" (1983), 28 McGill L.J. 867 at 872-885.

connotations. Originally, "warranty" referred to any sort of promise or "guarantee",[264] while "condition" referred to requirements that had to be satisfied in order to produce a binding contract.[265] Such meaning is still attributable to "condition". However, largely by reason of the development of the law relating to sale of goods, and especially the codification of that law in England in 1893 (which has been copied in all the common-law provinces of Canada), the expressions "warranty" and "condition" acquired somewhat special meanings in the law of contract. Admittedly, those particular meanings, strictly speaking, applied only in relation to the contract of sale of goods, and by reason of the statutory provisions. Not unreasonably or unnaturally those meanings spilled over into other contractual contexts, with the result that the "sale of goods" terminology became of general application.

Under the Sale of Goods Act, the distinction between conditions and warranties was based upon the *effects* of a breach of either. Although this formulation was culled by the draftsman of the statute from the earlier common-law development, it was a strange, and rather upside-down mode of defining such important concepts. The Act said

> [w]hether a stipulation in a contract of sale is a condition, the breach of which may give rise to a right to treat the contract as repudiated, or a warranty, the breach of which may give rise to a claim for damages but not to a right to reject the goods and treat the contract as repudiated, depends in each case on the construction of the contract.[266]

It did not matter what the parties called the term in question; what mattered were its real consequences, because a stipulation "may be a condition, though called a warranty in the contract." Thus, adopting this statutory definition, and applying it more generally than to the contract of sale of goods alone, a "condition" was a term which was so important that failure by the party bound to perform it to do so entitled the other party to treat the contract as at an end and pursue whatever remedies thereupon become available,[267] while a "warranty" was a term the breach of which did not have such a drastic effect, but nevertheless entitled the injured party to sue for damages representing what he lost by such breach, although still bound to perform obligations under the contract.[268]

---

264 "A binding promise": *Oscar Chess Ltd. v. Williams*, [1957] 1 All E.R. 325 at 327 (C.A.) *per* Denning L.J., relied on in *Williams v. Bittner* (1981), 10 Sask. R. 190 (Sask. Dist. Ct.).

265 Namely conditions precedent and subsequent; see above, pp. 435-437.

266 Sale of Goods Act, 1893 (56 & 57 Vict.) c. 71(a), s. 11(1)(*b*); compare *ibid.*, s. 62 (not contained in the Sale of Goods Act, 1979 (U.K.), c. 54). For the correspondence with Canadian statutes, see Fridman, *Sale of Goods in Canada*, 3rd ed. (1986), pp. 4-5.

267 A "vital" term: *Oscar Chess Ltd. v. Williams*, note 262 at 328 *per* Denning L.J. For other possible meanings of "condition" and "warranty", see Stoljar, *loc. cit.*, above, note 262; *Schuler A.G. v. Wickman Machine Tool Sales Ltd.*, [1973] 2 All E.R. 39 at 49 (H.L.) *per* Lord Morris.

268 A "subsidiary term in a contract": *Oscar Chess Ltd. v. Williams*, above, note 264 at 328 *per* Denning L.J. However, in *A.P.T. Industries Ltd. v. Bingo Press & Specialty Ltd.* (1991), 81 Alta. L.R. (2d) 179 (Alta. Q.B.), the complaints about tickets and packaging that were made to one defendant by a third party, on the basis of which the defendant purported to terminate its joint venture contract with the plaintiff, were so petty and easily remedied that they did not amount to breaches

According to this analysis, therefore, all terms are either conditions or warranties. The former are more fundamental or basic than the latter. The character of a term: (a) depends upon the true construction of the contract, that is, the intentions of the parties as manifested and evidenced in the manner already discussed; and (b) determines what is to happen if it is broken. Until recent times it would seem that this dichotomy exhausted the possible categories of terms in a contract. The only confusing or perhaps complicating factor was the use of the expression "condition" to mean, on some occasions, something else, namely a condition upon the necessary fulfilment of which depended the very existence or life of the contract, *i.e.*, a condition precedent. Such conditions, while in one sense terms of a contract, in another were not so much terms of an existing, valid, contract, as what might be called "ante-natal" or "external" terms — a part of, and yet outside, the contract to the life of which they are vital.[269]

(ii) *Conditions*

The classical test of what is a condition goes back to *Boone v. Eyre*[270] in 1779 (at a time when the expression "condition" had the more restricted meaning of "condition precedent"). The question was said to be whether, in the later words of Lord Ellenborough in *Davidson v. Gwynne*[271] in 1810, the term and its non-performance went to the "whole root and consideration" of the contract. This expression "the root of the contract", was generally accepted as the basis of the distinction between conditions and other, lesser terms, in particular warranties.[272] In other words, it was the quality of the term in issue, that is, its potential legal effects, that had to be examined to discover its true legal nature. In *Hong Kong Fir Shipping Co. v. Kawasaki Kisen Kaisha Ltd.*[273] this approach was rejected.[274] In its place the English Court of Appeal purported to put a different test: the *practical consequences* of a breach of the term in question, that is, its potential seriousness

---

of condition (or fundamental breach as MacLeod J. expressed it, *ibid.*, at 191), so as to entitle the defendant to terminate the contract: indeed they did not qualify as breaches of contract.

269 Above, Chapter 11.

270 (1779), 1 Hy. Bl. 273. In this case the statement is made in reference to a *condition precedent*, but the context shows that what is referred to is a condition in the modern general sense, as well as a condition precedent.

271 (1810), 12 East. 381 at 389.

272 The passage from "The classical test" to the end of this sentence was quoted by Stratton J.A. in *First City Trust Co. v. Triple Five Corp.* (1989), 57 D.L.R. (4th) 554 at 563 (Alta. C.A.); additional reasons at (1989), 57 D.L.R. (4th) 554 at 578 (Alta. C.A.); leave to appeal to S.C.C. refused (1989), 70 Alta. L.R. (2d) liii (note) (S.C.C.).

273 [1962] 2 Q.B. 26 (C.A.) especially at 63 *per* Upjohn L.J., and 67-71 *per* Diplock L.J.

274 In *First City Trust Co. v. Triple Five Corp.* (1989), 57 D.L.R. (4th) 554 at 564 (Alta. C.A.), Stratton J.A., after quoting this sentence and the next one, commented that the *Hong Kong Fir* case did not *reject* the earlier concept: "It simply added a new dimension that must be considered under certain circumstances.": compare *ibid.*, at 565, stating that the *Hong Kong Fir* case, as explained in the *Bunge* case (below, p. 493) did not replace earlier, traditional rules but introduced a new test, namely, "one based on a consideration of the gravity of the consequences of a breach, which under certain circumstances should be applied." See also below, pp. 500-503.

to the parties and their contract. The relative importance of terms, therefore, was dependent upon how serious the effect would be, in a practical as contrasted with a legal sense, if the term in question were broken.[275] Subsequently, in *The "Mihalis Angelos"*,[276] a differently constituted Court of Appeal reaffirmed the older attitude, namely, whether the breach relied upon by the innocent party to justify repudiation of a charter-party by the charterers went to the root of the contract. In that case, it was held that the readiness of the ship to load by a certain date was a condition; hence, its breach entitled the charterers to repudiate. In the *Hong Kong Fir* case[277] a term as to seaworthiness could not be construed as a condition of the charter-party; hence, the *owners* committed no breach of condition, with the result that the *charterers* were guilty of a breach of contract when they repudiated the charter-party on the ground of the unreadiness of the ship.

The difference between the classical approach and that propounded in the *Hong Kong Fir* case seems to lie in the extent to which the court will look *outside* the internal language of the contract to determine this issue. What might be considered an attempt to fuse or interrelate these two approaches was made by Salmon L.J. in *Decro-Wall International S.A. v. Practitioners in Marketing Ltd.*[278] If the contract made it clear that a term, expressly or by implication, went to the root of the contract, the situation was plain. If it did not do so, then the court had to look at the practical result of the breach in order to decide whether or not it went to the root of the contract. Clearly what Salmon L.J. was trying to do was to reconcile, without having to decide between, two opposing views or expressions of the law as stated by the Court of Appeal. Subsequently in *Schuler A.G. v. Wickman Machine Tool Sales Ltd.*,[279] two members of the House of Lords, Lords Reid and Wilberforce, made some comments upon this question, though neither they nor the House as a whole were obliged to decide as between the different views.

Lord Reid differentiated conditions precedent from other conditions.[280] The latter were terms of a contract as contrasted with something to be satisfied before the contract comes into operation or something basic to its continuing operation. He also attempted to define what was to be understood by "condition" in the sense of a term which was not a condition precedent. This was on the basis of a breach justifying termination of the contract or an action for damages on the part of the aggrieved party. "Sometimes," his Lordship said,

> a breach of a term gives that option to the aggrieved party because it is of a fundamental

---

275 Compare *Table Stake Const. Ltd. v. Jones* (1977), 82 D.L.R. (3d) 113 (Ont. H.C.); and the language of Goodman J. in *Smale v. Van der Weer* (1977), 17 O.R. (2d) 480 at 492 (Ont. H.C.).

276 [1971] 1 Q.B. 164 especially at 193 (C.A.) *per* Lord Denning M.R. See the discussion of this case in (1973), 89 L.Q.R. 93.

277 Compare *Beaton v. Cooper*, [1938] 1 W.W.R. 604 (Sask. C.A.), as to time for transfer and delivery of shares.

278 [1971] 2 All E.R. 216 at 221-222 (C.A.).

279 [1973] 2 All E.R. 39 (H.L.).

280 *Ibid.*, at 44. Conditions precedent were pre-conditions; other conditions did not have an automatic effect; compare *ibid.*, at 49 *per* Lord Morris.

character going to the root of the contract, sometimes it gives that option because the parties have chosen to stipulate that it shall have that effect.[281]

He then went on to quote from Blackburn J. in the famous case of *Bettini v. Gye*[282] the following sentence:

Parties may think some matter, apparently of very little importance, essential; and if they sufficiently express an intention to make the literal fulfilment of such a thing a condition precedent, it will be one.

As Lord Reid went on to say, what the court is seeking to discover is "intention as disclosed by the contract as a whole."[283] Use of the word "condition" was an indication, even a strong indication, of such an intention but it was by no means conclusive. If a particular construction led to an unreasonable result, this was a relevant consideration. To like effect was Lord Morris, especially when he stated, "words are but the instruments by which meanings or intentions are expressed."[284] Lord Wilberforce was more critical of the views expressed in the *Hong Kong Fir* case. The question in this case was posed by the term in the contract, under which the Wickman company obligated itself to send representatives to visit certain stated firms. Under the contract the Schuler company appointed the Wickman company as its sole agents to sell Schuler products in certain territories. The issue thus raised was

whether it is open to the parties to a contract, not being a contract for the sale of goods, to use the word "condition" to introduce a term, breach of which ipso facto entitles the other party to treat the contract at an end.[285]

His answer was given in this passage:

It is said that this is contrary to modern trends which focus interest rather on the nature of the breach, allowing the innocent party to rescind or repudiate whenever the breach is fundamental, whether the clause breached is called a condition or not: that the affixing of the label "condition" cannot pre-empt the right of the court to estimate for itself the character of the breach. Alternatively it is said that the result contended for can only be achieved if the consequences of a breach of a "condition" . . . are spelt out in the contract. . . .

. . . .The use as a promissory term of "condition" is artificial, as is that of "warranty" in some contexts. But . . . this use is now too deeply embedded in English law to be uprooted by anything less than a complete revision. . . . the *Hong Kong Fir* case, . . . did not reverse the trend. What it did decide . . . was that though a term . . . was not a "condition" in the technical sense, it might still be a term, breach of which if sufficiently serious could go to the root of the contract. Nothing in the judgments . . . cast[s] any doubt upon the meaning or effect of "condition" where that word is technically used.

---

281 *Ibid.*, at 44.
282 (1876), 1 Q.B.D. 183 at 187 (in which a singer obliged to arrive for rehearsals several days prior to the first concert she was to give was not bound by any condition to do so).
283 Above, note 279, at 45.
284 *Ibid.*, at 49.
285 *Ibid.*, at 54.

> The alternative argument . . . is equally precluded by authority. It is not necessary for parties to a contract, when stipulating a condition, to spell out the consequences of breach: these are inherent in the (assumedly deliberate) use of the word.

Against the background the majority of the House of Lords held that the term was not a condition and did not justify repudiation of the contract when the term was unfulfilled by the Wickman company. From this judgment Lord Wilberforce dissented.[286] However, apart from the decision on the facts, their Lordships appear to be in agreement that the older, accepted, even classical use of the expression "condition" was the correct one in modern law, despite the attempts to introduce new concepts.

The matter was taken up again by the English Court of Appeal in *Cehave N.V. v. Bremer Handelgesellschaft m.b.H.*[287] This case concerned a contract of sale of goods, the subject-matter being various shipments of citrus pulp pellets to be used as an ingredient in cattle food. Each shipment was "to be made in good condition," and each shipment was to be considered a separate contract. The buyers paid in advance and received the shipping documents. Nonetheless, when the goods arrived by ship at Rotterdam, some of the cargo which formed the subject-matter of the contract was found to be damaged, and the buyers rejected the whole cargo, on the ground that the goods were not in good condition, as required under the contract. In fact, as subsequently occurred, the cargo was ordered to be sold by a court at Rotterdam. It was bought by a third party, who then sold it to the original buyers at a much lower price than the original contract price. The buyers attempted to recover the original purchase price from the original sellers. In an arbitration the umpire held that the buyers were not entitled to reject, and so were in breach of contract. On appeal to the Board of Appeal of the Grain and Feed Trade Association, it was held that the sellers were in breach of the express condition that the goods were to be shipped in good condition; therefore, the buyers could recover their money. The sellers appealed to a judge, who upheld the Board's award. The sellers then appealed to the Court of Appeal who reversed the decision of the judge and the Board and held that the sellers were entitled to succeed in their claim against the buyer for the latter's breach of contract.

The language of the Sale of Goods Act did not preclude the possibility that, even in contracts of sale of goods, the status and effect of a term may depend upon how it is to be regarded in the light of "the events resulting from the breach, rather than the breach itself."[288] Does a statute, for example, the Sale of Goods Act, or do the intentions of the parties, permit the court to treat the term as one

---

286 Compare the decision in *Zien v. Field* (1963), 43 W.W.R. 577 (B.C.C.A.); reversed on other grounds, [1963] S.C.R. 632 (S.C.C.), in which it was held that a term as to the amount of working capital available on the sale of a business as a going concern went to the root and substance of the contract, and was therefore a condition. See also *Allan v. Bushnell T.V. Co.*, [1969] 1 O.R. 107 (Ont. H.C.), above p. 181 where the condition was *implied*, not express. Compare also *Richview Const. Co. v. Raspa* (1975), 11 O.R. (2d) 377 (Ont. C.A.), where the term was a warranty.

287 *Cehave N.V. v. Bremer Handelgesellschaft m.b.H.*, [1975] 3 All E.R. 739 (C.A.) applied by Zuber J.A. in *Jorian Properties Ltd. v. Zellenrath* (1984), 40 O.R. (2d) 775 at 788 (Ont. C.A.).

288 [1975] 3 All E.R. 739 at 766 (C.A.) *per* Ormrod L.J.

justifying repudiation, rejection of goods, or some other form of the contract as broken and therefore terminated?[289] A term is not necessarily a condition or a warranty; its character must be decided along the lines suggested in the *Hong Kong Fir* case. Roskill L.J. concluded:[290]

> I think the statements of law in the *Hong Kong Fir Shipping* case apply just as much to contracts for the sale of goods as to other contracts. . . . Since I have already held that [the relevant clause] is not a 'condition' in the strict sense of that word, the buyers can rely on the breach of [that clause] if they can show that that breach 'deprived them of the whole of the benefit of the contract' or 'went to the root of the contract' or 'destroyed the consideration which the buyers gave', to use but three of the phrases canvassed in argument before us.

In the circumstances of this case the court held that the term that the goods were to be shipped in good condition was not a condition in the strict sense, nor did its breach go to the root of the contract and justify rejection of the goods by the buyers or permit the buyers to regard the contract as terminated.

The *Hong Kong Fir* approach, though seemingly rejected by Lord Wilberforce in the *Schuler* case, received a more favourable reception by Lord Wilberforce in the later case of *Reardon Smith Line Ltd. v. Hansen-Tangen*.[291] Referring to the *Hong Kong* case, he said:[292]

> The general law of contract has developed, along much more rational lines. . . . . . , in attending to the nature and gravity of a breach or departure rather than in accepting rigid categories which do or do not automatically give a right to rescind . . .

He endorsed the language of Roskill L.J. in the *Cehave* case[293] with reference to the desirability of having the same legal principles apply to the law of contract as a whole, without differentiating contracts for the sale of goods from others, and added " . . . and if the choice were between extending cases under the Sale of Goods Act 1893 into other fields, or allowing more modern doctrines to infect those cases, my preference would be clear."[294] His subsequent discussion of "innominate" or "intermediate" terms,[295] when placed alongside the above statements, indicates that he had accepted the change of emphasis propounded in the *Hong Kong Fir* case, in place of the original, classical definition or description of a condition.

The more recent remarks of Lord Wilberforce and other members of the House of Lords in *Bunge Corporation v. Tradax Export S.A.*[296] would seem to have been

---

289 *Ibid.*, at 766-767.

290 *Ibid.*, at 757.

291 [1976] 3 All E.R. 570 (H.L.).

292 *Ibid.*, at 576-577.

293 Above, note 288, at 756.

294 Above, note 291, at 577.

295 *Bremer Handelsgesellschaft m.b.H. v. Vanden Avenne Izegem P.V.B.A.*, [1978] 2 Lloyd's Rep. 109. On these terms, see below, pp. 500-503.

296 [1981] 2 All E.R. 513 (H.L.). See Appleby & Meisel, "Hong Kong Fir Revisited: The House of Lords and Certainty in Contracts", [1982] Lloyds M. & C.L.Q. 592. See also the discussion of this case by Stratton J.A. in *First City Trust Co. v. Triple Five Corp.* (1989), 57 D.L.R. (4th) 554

designed to minimize the potential effects of the analysis in the *Hong Kong Fir* case, and restrict its scope by interpreting it not as making any significant change in the way the law approached terms in a contract, but as clarifying the earlier, well-established law. Counsel for the appellants in that case, relying on the language of Diplock L.J. in the *Hong Kong Fir* case, suggested that to decide whether a term was a condition or not, one must consider "the breach actually committed and then decided whether that default would deprive the party not in default of substantially the whole benefit of the contract."[297] Such a test, said Lord Wilberforce, "would be commercially most undesirable."[298] It would expose a party after a breach of a short period of time to an argument whether the delay involved would have left time for the seller to provide the goods that were the subject-matter of the contract. It would make it difficult, even impossible, for a supplier to know whether he could do so. It would "fatally remove from a vital provison in the contract," to quote his words in relation to the term dealing with time for performance, "that certainty which is the most indispensable quality of mercantile contracts."[299] This would lead to a large increase in arbitrations. Over and above such practical objections, however, there were legal grounds for rejecting the test suggested above. The judgment of Diplock L.J. in the *Hong Kong Fir* case did not support the proposition of the appellants in the *Bunge* case. That judgment recognized that whether a default entitled the other party to treat the contract as repudiated did not depend upon interpretation or construction of the nature of the default: it was open to the parties to agree that, as regards any particular obligation, any breach should entitle the party not in default to treat the contract as repudiated.[300] Greater flexibility in the law of contracts was commendable, and supported by Roskill L.J. in the *Cehave* case and by Lord Wilberforce in the *Reardon Smith* case. In suitable cases, however, courts should not be reluctant, if the intentions of the parties so indicate, to hold that an obligation has the force of a condition. To such cases the "gravity of the breach" approach of the *Hong Kong Fir* case would be unsuitable.[301]

Lord Wilberforce therefore accepted that it was both incorrect in law and unfortunate in practice to adopt the "gravity of the breach" or "wait and see" approach that seems to have been suggested by Diplock L.J. in the *Hong Kong Fir* case. As Lord Wilberforce and Lord Lowry explained, however, Diplock L.J. was not adopting any such new criterion for deciding by means of hindsight whether or not a term was a condition.[302] In the words of Lord Lowry

---

at 564-565 (Alta. C.A.); additional reasons at (1989), 57 D.L,.R. (4th) 554 at 578 (Alta. C.A.); leave to appeal to S.C.C. refused (1989), 70 Alta. L.R. (2d) liii (note) (S.C.C.). For the facts of the *Bunge* case, see below, p. 502.

297 Above, note 296, at 541.
298 *Ibid.*
299 *Ibid.*
300 *Ibid.*
301 *Ibid.*, at 541-542.
302 Compare *ibid.*, at 549-550 *per* Lord Roskill.

It is by construing a contract (which can be done as soon as the contract is made) that one decides whether a term is, either expressly or by necessary implication, a condition, and not by considering the gravity of the breach of that term (which cannot be done until the breach is imminent or has occurred). The latter process is not an aid to construing the contract, but indicates whether rescission or merely damages is the proper remedy for a breach for which the innocent party might be recompensed in one way or the other according to its gravity. . . .

The "wait and see" method, or . . . the "gravity of the breach" approach, is not the way to identify a condition in a contract. This is done by construing the contract in the light of the surrounding circumstances . . . Diplock L.J. shed a new light on old and accepted principles; he did not purport to establish new ones.[303]

These refutations of anything novel or innovative in the judgment of Diplock L.J. in the *Hong Kong Fir* case are naturally authoritative. They are not convincing. What appears to have occurred in the English courts is that Diplock L.J. attempted to provide a new, more modern analysis of contractual terms, designed to give maximum flexibility and adaptability to the law, so as to accord with commercial requirements and practices.[304] Later courts adopted and extended that analysis. The result was that, ultimately, the logic of that analysis was exposed as leading to great uncertainty as to the law and its application in a given instance. The House of Lords realized this in the *Bunge* case, and, after the tergiversations referred to earlier, finally rejected the idea that whether a term was or not a condition could be decided by a reference to what eventually happened, in the event of a breach of such term. Instead they reiterated that the traditional test was the applicable one, *viz.*, by construction of the language of the contract at the time it was agreed to by the parties in light of the surrounding circumstances.[305]

In Canada, the earlier analysis of Diplock L.J. was largely ignored. The more traditional approach now favoured by English courts in light of the *Bunge* case, was referred to and utilized by the Alberta Court of Appeal in *Bank of British Columbia v. Turbo Resources Ltd.*[306] Under a contract of guarantee, the creditor (a bank) agreed to notify the guarantor of any default on the part of the principal debtor within 15 days, and to make the guarantor a party to any discussions with the principal debtor. The guarantor took great precautions, by means of business arrangements with the principal debtor, to ensure that the debt was duly paid. There was a default by the principal debtor. The bank failed to notify the guarantor of

---

303 *Ibid.*, at 546.

304 See further, below, pp. 500-503, discussing the notion of *innominate* or *intermediate* terms.

305 *Bentsen v. Taylor, Sons & Co. (No. 2)*, [1893] 2 Q.B. 274 at 281 (C.A.) *per* Bowen L.J.; *Reardon Smith Line Ltd. v. Hansen-Tangen*, [1976] 3 All E.R. 570 at 574 *per* Lord Wilberforce; *Bunge Corp. v. Tradax S.A.*, [1981] 2 All E.R. 513 at 538 (H.L.) *per* Megaw L.J., at 542 *per* Lord Wilberforce; *First City Trust Co. v. Triple Five Corp.* (1989), 57 D.L.R. (4th) 554 at 566-567 (Alta. C.A.) *per* Stratton J.A.

306 (1983), 148 D.L.R. (3d) 598 (Alta. C.A.) (referred to and applied in *Trimac Ltd. v. C-I-L Inc.*, [1987] 4 W.W.R. 719 (Alta. Q.B.); reversed in part on other grounds [1987] 6 W.W.R. 66 (Alta. C.A.); *Qualico Devs. Ltd. v. Calgary (City)*, [1987] 5 W.W.R. 361 (Alta. Q.B.); *Alpine Resources Ltd. v. Bowtex Resources Ltd.* (1989), 66 Alta. L.R. (2d) 144 (Alta. Q.B.)). See also *First City Trust Co. v. Triple Five Corp.*, above, note 305, at 566.

the default, and held meetings with the principal debtor without the guarantor. The bank sued the guarantor on the guarantee. At trial the claim succeeded. On appeal, it was held that the requirements of the contract were conditions. Therefore when they were not performed by the bank, the guarantor was discharged from the contract of guarantee. In coming to this conclusion, the court relied on the language of Lord Wilberforce in the *Bunge* case, and looked at the "commercial setting of the contract", the "commercial purpose" of the contract, "the genesis of the transaction, the background, the context", as Lord Wilberforce had referred to them in the *Reardon Smith* case. Applying those tests to the facts of this case, the importance of the terms in the guarantee was obvious, and breach of those terms discharged the guarantor from liability under the agreement.

In contrast the material term in *First City Trust Co. v. Triple Five Corp.*[307] was not the kind of term default in the performance of which by one party would entitle the other party to regard themselves as released from their obligations under the agreement. Breach of this term was treated as entitling the party in question only to a potential damage award. This was because the term provided for the recourse available in the event of breach, and anticipated that the parties intended the agreement should continue notwithstanding a contemplated breach.

(iii) *Warranties*

In the present context the expression "warranty" refers to a term in a contract which does not go to the root of the agreement between the parties but expresses some lesser obligation, the failure to perform which can give rise to an action for damages but never to the right to repudiate the contract. The contrast is with "condition", as previously explained and interpreted. Just as the expression "condition" has many different meanings, according to the context in which it is being used, so the expression "warranty" can vary in its connotation.[308] Sometimes it may be used "to denote one of the meanings that can be given to the word 'condition'."[309] In such event the proper course for a court is to construe the word in accordance with its intended meaning, not that which it might otherwise have.[310] Indeed the Sale of Goods Act enacts this with respect to the use of these expressions in a contract of sale of goods.[311]

The court must determine, by the use of the appropriate techniques of construction, not merely by the mechanical, automatic, unthinking application of the literal technical meaning of the word used by the parties, into which category

---

307 Above, note 305, at 566-567.
308 *Schuler A.G. v. Wickman Machine Tool Sales Ltd.*, [1973] 2 All E.R. 39 at 49 (H.L.) *per* Lord Morris.
309 *Ibid.*
310 For example, in contracts of insurance and in maritime law the expression "warranty" in a contract is often used to mean what is technically a condition: compare Reynolds, "Warranty, Condition & Fundamental Term" (1963), 79 L.Q.R. 534 at 538.
311 Above, p. 488.

a term properly belongs. Once it has been decided which it is, then the different consequences flow.[312]

A Canadian example is provided by *Table Stake Construction Ltd. v. Jones*.[313] In a contract for the sale of land, the vendor "warranted" (the word used in the contract) that on the closing date there would be no outstanding work orders against the property which was the subject of the sale. Prior to the closing date, the purchaser's solicitor discovered that there was a list of deficiencies drawn up against the property by the municipality. No formal work order had been issued. There were indications that such an order might be served on the vendor in the future. The purchaser refused to complete the transaction unless the vendor gave back a cheque for repairs. This the vendor refused. The purchaser sued for specific performance. His success depended upon whether the term as to outstanding work orders was a condition or a warranty.

Osler J., applying the language of Diplock L.J. in the *Hong Kong Fir* case, held that the most flagrant breach of the alleged "warranty" could not give rise to an event that would deprive the purchaser of substantially the whole benefit it was intended he should obtain from the contract. The situation with respect to work orders would not affect the financial advantages the purchaser was to get from the purchase, nor would it mean that the purchaser would not obtain possession of a suitable property. Having decided that the statement about work orders was a term, the learned judge then went on to hold that it amounted to a warranty, not a condition. Non-fulfilment of the term would not affect the substance and foundation of the transaction and the obligation arising from the term did not go so directly to the substance of the contract that its non-performance could be considered non-performance of the contract itself.[314] Thus the purchaser was not entitled to refuse to complete, which meant that the purchaser had wrongfully repudiated the contract, and could not thereafter sue for specific performance.

(b) The breakdown of the dichotomy

(i) *Two developments*

Criticism of what has been called the "warranty-condition set-up"[315] was expressed by many academic writers, as Lord Wilberforce acknowledged in the

---

312 One important difference may be with respect to the operation of the doctrine of *merger into grant, i.e.,* what happens when a contract for the sale of land is perfected as it were, by the subsequent conveyance. Much may depend upon whether the term in question was a condition or a warranty: see *Franz v. Hansen* (1917), 36 D.L.R. 349 especially at 358 (Alta. C.A.) *per* Beck J.; reversed on the facts and the applicaton of law, [1918] 2 W.W.R. 40 (S.C.C.); leave to appeal to the Privy Council refused (1918), 57 S.C.R. vii (S.C.C.); *Richview Const. Co. v. Raspa* (1975), 11 O.R. (2d) 377 (Ont. C.A.), and cases there cited. See also Silverman, "Merger: One Aspect of its Application and Effect in Real Property Contracts" (1962), 5 Can. B.J. 92.

313 (1977), 82 D.L.R. (3d) 113 (Ont. H.C.). See also *Jorian Properties Ltd. v. Zellenrath* (1984), 46 O.R. (2d) 775 (Ont. C.A.).

314 (1977), 82 D.L.R. (3d) 113 at 120, 121 (Ont. H.C.).

315 Llewellyn, "On Warranty of Quality and Society" (1936), 36 Col. L.R. 699 at 731.

Schuler case.[316] As his Lordship indicated, it was not without foundation or justification.[317] The words themselves have undergone much development of meaning, and are possibly by now far removed from what they were originally intended or understood to mean. They do not accurately represent what the law is actually doing. This comment is most particularly true of the expression "condition", since its use has led to the confusion of a party's *promise* with his *performance* of that promise, and to the failure to distinguish between a "true" condition (that is, a condition precedent) with a promise (that is, contractual undertaking). Perhaps more importantly, at least to some critics, the division of terms into conditions and warranties did not adequately solve the problems that can arise in relation to a breach of contract.

The tacit, if not plainly manifested recognition of these drawbacks to the classical dichotomy between conditions and warranties led in recent years to two major developments. Though separate, they may not be entirely unconnected. First in time was the growth of the concept of the "fundamental term", together with its concomitant, the doctrine of "fundamental breach". Second, there was the judgment of Diplock L.J., in *Hong Kong Fir Shipping Co. v. Kawasaki Kisen Kaisha*.[318] The former was perhaps a response to the challenge presented to the law by the emergence and importance of exemption, exclusion, or limitation clauses in a contract.[319] The latter may have been prompted by the confusion and difficulty into which the law had fallen in consequence of the effect of the courts' reactions to such clauses upon the classical dichotomy already outlined, and the resultant need to reformulate the law and clarify the situation.

(ii) *Fundamental terms*

A major factor in the recent history of the law of contract has been the extent to which contracting parties, notably those bargainng from a position of strength, such as transportation companies, insurance companies, sellers of goods, have sought to protect themselves from potential liability for breach of contract by inserting a term therein designed to exclude the operation of "conditions and warranties" (as those terms were traditionally or classically defined). The attitude of the courts, in conformity with the doctrine of strict construction of contracts, and, more especially, the *contra proferentem* rule,[320] was to restrict the operation of such clauses as much as possible. But the decisions reveal that, provided a party drew the relevant clause in satisfactory language, the resultant effect might be to render him completely immune from any type of liability for breach of the contract, no matter how, or in what form, the breach occurred. In other words,

---

316 Above, note 308, at 54.

317 Reynolds, "Warranty, Condition & Fundamental Term" (1963), 79 L.Q.R. 534 at 535-540.

318 [1962] 2 Q.B. 26 at 67-71 (C.A.); compare *ibid.*, at 63 *per* Upjohn L.J.; *Astley Industrial Trust Ltd. v. Grimley*, [1963] 2 All E.R. 33 at 46-47 (C.A.); *Tradex Int. S.A. v. Goldschmidt S.A.*, [1977] 2 Lloyd's Rep. 684 at 712.

319 Below, Chapter 15.

320 Above, pp. 470-471.

whether the breach was total and complete (a breach of "condition"), or subsidiary and relatively collateral (a breach of "warranty"), the guilty party would not be liable. The culmination of this development was the decision in *Suisse Atlantique Société d'Armament Maritime S.A. v. N.V. Rotterdamsche Kolen Centrale*[321] in 1967. In that case, the House of Lords appear to have recognized the possibility of complete or utter exclusion of potential liability by the use of appropriate language. By way of answer to this growth, and even before the *Suisse Atlantique* case, the courts developed a new concept, in order to enable an innocent and injured party to a contract to have some possibility of redress, despite the presence in the contract of a privative clause. This was the notion of the *fundamental term*.

By the expression "fundamental term" was meant a term which was so basic and fundamental to the contract that: (a) its breach involved liability for non-performance of the contract; (b) it could not be excluded by an exclusion or exemption clause (at least until the *Suisse Atlantique* case suggested that it might); and (c) it was neither a condition nor a warranty but a term that was more important than either, a term that went to the "core" of the contract.[322] To cite one statement, which antedated the decision of the House of Lords in the *Suisse Atlantique* case,

> every contract contains a term or terms so fundamental that liability for breach of them cannot be excluded by an exemption clause, however widely drawn, on the grounds that an attempt to contract out of liability for breach of such term would in effect be an attempt to exclude liability for breach of contract altogether.[323]

There were two problems about this, even without the added complications as to exemption fed into the law by the later House of Lords decision. The first was the possibility of confusion or overlap with a condition. The second was the possibility of confusion between the breach of a fundamental term and fundamental breach.

Given the classical definition of a "condition", was there any difference between a condition and a fundamental term? Since the former is in effect an essential term or promise going to the root of the contract, such that its breach would substantially deprive the innocent party of the whole benefit it was intended he should obtain from the contract, what, then, is, or is comprehended by, a "fundamental term"? How much more fundamental is it possible to get? As long as there was no need to construe and apply an exemption or similar clause, the problem remained more theoretical than practical; once a clause of that type was introduced into the situation, courts were faced with subtleties and difficulties that made evident the abundant unreality of the distinction between conditions and fundamental terms.

Prior to the *Suisse Atlantique* case, some commentators preferred to stress the idea of fundamental breach as opposed to the notion of breach of a fundamental term. This was a particularly valid and appropriate an attitude to adopt since the problems emerged not at a time when the parties entered the contract but at a

---

321 [1967] 1 A.C. 361 (H.L.); below, pp. 589-590.
322 To use the expression favoured by Melville, "The Core of a Contract" (1961), 19 M.L.R. 26.
323 Reynolds, above, note 317, at p. 541.

much later stage, if and when one party was guilty of a breach and the question arose as to the nature of his liability (if any, having regard to an exclusion or exemption clause if the contract contained one). As was said at the time,

> the present position seems to be that while lip-service is paid to the notion of breach, the tendency is to approach the contract from the other end and to look for the fundamental term or obligation.[324]

The value, indeed the purpose of such approach, lay in the idea of that some terms were of such a nature that breaches of such terms were not "merely" breaches of condition or warranty but much worse. To such an extent was this so that a party could never protect himself from liability for such a breach and would always be susceptible to appropriate action by the injured or affected party, that is, rejection of goods, repudiation of the contract, or a suit for damages.[325]

Although the House of Lords attempted in the *Suisse Atlantique* case to reconcile the differing views and to put fundamental terms and fundamental breach into a proper perspective and relationship, the *dicta* in that case left much ambiguity in the law. Indeed in *Photo Production Ltd. v. Securicor Transport Ltd.*,[326] Lord Wilberforce admitted the unsatisfactory nature of the speeches in the *Suisse Atlantique* case. At the same time, both he and other members of the House of Lords recognized the past, and possibly continued, utility of the doctrine of fundamental breach.[327] However, in view of the comments of the Supreme Court of Canada in *Hunter Engineering Co. v. Syncrude Canada Ltd.*,[328] the idea of fundamental breach may no longer be of relevance or value. If so, then it may no longer be necessary to formulate a category of fundamental terms distinct from conditions.

(iii) *Innominate terms*

Two reasons may be suggested for the development which began with the judgment of Diplock L.J. in the *Hong Kong Fir* case,[329] in which an attempt was made to clarify the law relating to contractual terms and place it on a more realistic, pragmatic footing. First of all, as long as the law continued to pay lip-service to the classical condition-warranty dichotomy there were problems of a theoretical, as well as practical nature surrounding the analysis of contractual terms and, in particular, the true character and effect of exemption and similar clauses. Second, the classical analysis seemed to be historically inaccurate and logically inept. This was pointed out by Diplock L.J. in the *Hong Kong Fir* case. In the course of his examination of the law, he argued that the extended use of the distinction between

---

324 *Ibid.*, at p. 546.
325 Treitel, "Fundamental Breach" (1966), 29 M.L.R. 546; Silverberg, "The Doctrine of Fundamental Breach Revisited", [1971] J.B.L. 197, 280.
326 [1980] 1 All E.R. 556 at 561 (H.L.).
327 *Ibid.*, at 561, 566-567, 569-570.
328 (1989), 57 D.L.R. (4th) 321 (S.C.C.): below, pp. 597-600.
329 [1962] 2 Q.B. 26 (C.A.); above, pp. 489-490.

conditions and warranties, beyond the law of sale of goods into contracts generally, was incorrect in theory and impracticable so far as concerned the solution of problems arising in contracts other than those of sale of goods. While in most situations the comparatively simply distinction between conditions and warranties sufficed for practical purposes, and could be used to resolve the issue between the parties, by fixing and determining their respective obligations, and the consequences of a breach, there were other situations where that distinction did not provide enough exactitude to permit a court to arrive at a proper and just conclusion. To quote Diplock L.J.[330]

> [t]here are . . . many contractual undertakings of a more complex character which cannot be categorized as being "conditions" or "warranties", if the later nineteenth-century meaning adopted in the Sale of Goods Act, 1893 . . . be given to those terms. Of such undertakings all that can be predicated is that some breaches will and others will not give rise to an event which will deprive the party not in default of substantially the whole benefit which it was intended that he should obtain from the contract; and the legal consequences of a breach of such an undertaking, unless provided for expressly in the contract, depend upon the nature of the event to which the breach gives rise and do not follow automatically from a prior classification of the undertaking as a "condition" or a "warranty".

The subsequent history of the views of Diplock L.J. has been discussed.[331] The English Court of Appeal adopted his more modern analysis, and applied it to contracts of sale of goods, in the *Cehave* case in 1975,[332] despite some earlier doubts expressed by members of that court in *The "Mihalis Angelos"*,[333] and by Lord Wilberforce in the *Schuler* case.[334] In the *Reardon Smith* case,[335] Lord Wilberforce appeared to indicate a change of mind, and a willingness to accede to the ideas of Diplock L.J. Indeed in *Bremer Handelsgesellschaft m.b.H. v. Vandem Avenne Izegem P.V.B.A.*,[336] he went so far as to say

> [a]utomatic and invariable treatment of a clause such as this runs counter to the approach, which modern authorities recognise, of treating such a provision as having the force of a condition (giving rise to rescission or invalidity) or a contractual term (giving rise to damages only) according to the nature and gravity of the breach. The clause is then categorised as an innominate term. . . . In my opinion, the clause may vary appropriately and should be regarded as such an intermediate term: to do so would recognise that while in many, possibly most, instances, breach of it can adequately be sanctioned by damages, cases may exist in which, in fairness to the buyer, it would be proper to treat the cancellation as not having effect. On the other hand, always so to treat it may often be unfair to the seller, and unnecessarily rigid.

This last comment indicates the true nature of the reasons for adopting the category

---

330 Above, note 329, at 70.
331 Above, pp. 490-495.
332 *Cehave N.V. v. Bremer Handelgesellschaft m.b.H.*, [1975] 3 All E.R. 739 (C.A.).
333 [1971] 1 Q.B. 164 at 183 (C.A.) especially at 199 *per* Edmund Davies L.J., 205 *per* Megaw L.J.
334 *Schuler A.G. v. Wickman Machine Tool Sales Ltd.*, [1973] 2 All E.R. 39 at 54 (H.L.).
335 *Reardon Smith Line Ltd. v. Hansen-Tangen*, [1976] 3 All E.R. 570 at 576-577 (H.L.).
336 [1978] 2 Lloyd's Rep. 109 at 113.

of innominate or intermediate terms, namely the avoidance of undue rigidity, which might bring in its train the possibility of injustice to one or the other party. The desirability of such a flexible approach to contractual terms was the basis for the approval afforded to this analysis by some commentators.[337] The disadvantages of flexibility, in a commercial context, leading to uncertainty in such transactions, were the bases for criticism of the newer approach.[338] It would seem that the need for certainty has overcome the distaste felt for rigidity. Such, it would seem, is indicated by the decision of the House of Lords in *Bunge Corporation v. Tradax Export S.A.*[339]

The buyers contracted to purchase a quantity of soya bean meal for shipment from the United States. This was one of a string of contracts, as was the practice in the trade, the shipment contract being an intermediate contract made in the course of the transfer of the goods from the supplier to the eventual receiver. Three shipments were to be made from an American port nominated by the sellers. One shipment was to be in June 1975. The buyers had to provide a vessel at the nominated port and were required to give at least 15 days consecutive notice of the probable readiness of the vessel. This meant that the notice had to be given by the buyers to the sellers by June 13. The buyers did not give the appropriate notice until June 17. This the sellers claimed was a breach of contract amounting to repudiation. They claimed damages from the buyers on the basis that by then the market price for soya bean meal had fallen by over $60 (U.S.) a ton. The dispute was referred to arbitration. The sellers were awarded $317,500 (U.S.) damages. The Commercial Court judge reversed the award on the ground that the term as to when notice was required to be given was not a condition but an intermediate term; therefore, the lateness of the notice did not amount to a breach of contract. The Court of Apeal reversed this, holding that the term was a condition. The buyers' appeal to the House of Lords was dismissed. The House of Lords held, with the Court of Appeal, that stipulations as to time in mercantile contracts were generally to be treated as conditions, and not as innominate or intermediate terms, because the reason for such clause was to enable each party to organize his affairs to meet obligations arising in the future under the contract, not merely to determine, with the benefit of hindsight, the appropriate remedy when a breach occurred. Furthermore, where string contracts were involved, as here, the need for certainty required such a clause to be adhered to strictly.

The case is important not only in relation to its decision with respect to terms

---

337 Grieg, "Condition or Warranty?" (1973), 89 L.Q.R. 93 at 104-106.

338 Cheshire & Fifoot, *Law of Contract*, 8th ed. (1972), p. 123; there is no similar expression to be found in later editions.

339 [1981] 2 All E.R. 513, applied in *Société Italo-Belge Pour le Commerce de l'Industrie S.A. (Antwerp) v. Palm & Vegetable Oils (Malaysia) SDN BHD.*, [1982] 1 All E.R. 19; *Bank of B.C. v. Turbo Resources Ltd.* (1983), 148 D.L.R. (3d) 598 (Alta. C.A.); *First City Trust Co. v. Triple Five Corp.* (1989), 57 D.L.R. (4th) 554 (Alta. C.A.); additional reasons at (1989), 57 D.L.R. (4th) 554 at 578 (Alta. C.A.); leave to appeal to S.C.C. refused (1989), 70 Alta. L.R. (2d) liii (note) (S.C.C.); *Canwest Pacific Television Inc. v. 147250 Can. Ltd.* (1987), 14 B.C.L.R. (2d) 338 (B.C.S.C.); affirmed (1988), 30 B.C.L.R. (2d) 145 (B.C.C.A.). On the *Bunge* case, see Comment (1982), 60 Can. Bar Rev. 335.

as to the time for performance of contractual obligations,[340] but also because of the way the House of Lords dealt with the view propounded by Diplock L.J. in the *Hong Kong Fir* case as to contractual terms and how they were to be defined. The House of Lords did not repudiate the idea that terms may be conditions, warranties or intermediate or innominate terms. They appear to have repudiated, however, the suggestion by Diplock L.J. that the characterization of a term depends upon the effects or consequences of a breach rather than upon traditional methods of construction of contracts. Everything depends first of all upon whether the parties have identified a stipulation as a condition, warranty or innominate term. If the contract does not expressly or by implication make it clear that a term is a condition or a warranty, (the necessary implication arising from the nature, purpose and circumstances of the contract, the "factual matrix", as Lord Wilberforce once called it),[341] the term in question is an innominate term. Only then will the remedy for its breach depend on the nature, consequences and effect of the breach.[342] In other words, the test of the character of a term is the traditional one. A term only becomes an innominate or intermediate term if it has failed to be shown to be a condition or a warranty.[343]

Although the House of Lords has accepted and endorsed the idea that there are more than two classes of terms, at the same time it made perfectly clear that courts should not too facilely conclude that a term was an innominate term, when there were no manifest indications by the parties that a term was a condition. It also made clear that contract breakers should not be permitted too easily to escape from the consequences of their breach by being allowed to plead and prove that the term broken was not a condition, when it was one, but only an innominate term, with the result that the contract breaker could then argue that the consequences were not so serious as to justify treating such term as if it were a condition.[344] The reason for this reluctance to broaden the scope of innominate terms, and be less rigid in the application of the condition-warranty dichotomy, was the desire to ensure that commercial men could rely with a degree of certainty upon the arrangements that they made by contracts.[345] Logically, the endorsement of the rejection of the division of all contractual terms into conditions and warranties is sound. Historically it is correct, for it brings the law back to where it had been left by Lord Mansfield in 1779.[346]

---

340 Below, pp. 524-529.

341 *Reardon Smith Line Ltd. v. Hansen-Tangen*, above, note 335, at 573-575.

342 *Bunge Corp. v. Tradax Export S.A.*, above, note 339, at 543 *per* Lord Scarman; compare *ibid.*, at 549-550 *per* Lord Roskill.

343 The passage from "The House of Lords did not repudiate" to "a condition or a warranty" was quoted by Stratton J.A. in *First City Trust Co. v. Triple Five Corp.* (1989), 57 D.L.R. (4th) 554 at 565 (Alta. C.A.).

344 Above, note 339, at 542 *per* Lord Wilberforce ("courts should not be reluctant, if the intentions of the parties as shown by the contract so indicate, to hold that an obligation has the force of a condition"); *ibid.*, at 550 *per* Lord Roskill.

345 *Ibid.*, at 541 *per* Lord Wilberforce, 544 *per* Lord Scarman, and 546 *per* Lord Lowry.

346 In *Boone v. Eyre* (1779), 1 Hy. Bl. 273; see *Bunge Corp. v. Tradax Export S.A.*, above, note 339, at 543 *per* Lord Scarman.

13

Collateral Contracts

1. Definition and effect[1]

The interpretation of a written contract (and, therefore, the proper ascertainment of the obligations of the parties thereunder) may be complicated by the alleged existence of some additional extrinsic agreement between the parties, affecting the meaning or scope of the written instrument. What is involved is some statement made by one party to the ultimate contract inducing the other party to enter into such contract. The statement in question, if not a term in the contract, could be nothing more than a "mere" representation. It would therefore be legally ineffective, unless the statement were made fraudulently.[2] To give such statements legal consequence, English courts evolved the idea that in appropriate circumstances statements of this kind could have independent contractual status. They were not terms of the contract eventually concluded between the parties. They were more significant than representations inducing such contract. They could amount to a distinct contract "collateral" to the main contract made between the maker of the statement and the one to whom the statement was made.[3]

The process of transforming such statements into contracts began in the

---

1 McLauchlan, "The Inconsistent Collateral Contract" (1977), 3 Dalhousie L.J. 136; Fridman, "Written Contracts with an Oral Element" (1977), 8 Manitoba L.J. 383; Dawson, "Parol Evidence, Misrepresentation and Collateral Contracts" (1982), 27 McGill L.J. 403.

2 Above, pp. 300, 450; but note the possibility of liability for *negligence*: below, pp. 515-516.

3 The passage from "additional extrinsic agreement" to the end of this paragraph was quoted by Egbert J. in *Remillard v. Remillard* (1990), 103 A.R. 110 at 115 (Alta. Q.B.).

In *Ahone v. Holloway* (1988), 30 B.C.L.R. (2d) 368 at 373 (B.C.C.A.), McLachlin J.A. defined a collateral contract as an "oral agreement ancillary to a written agreement".

nineteenth century in England,[4] and was eventually given recognition by the House of Lords in *Heilbut, Symons & Co. v. Buckleton*.[5] There Lord Moulton said:[6]

> [i]t is evident, both on principle and authority, that there may be a contract the consideration for which is the making of some other contract. "If you will make such and such a contract I will give you one hundred pounds," is in every sense of the word a complete legal contract. It is collateral to the main contract, but each has an independent existence, and they do not differ in respect of their possessing to the full the character and status of a contract.

The Supreme Court of Canada accepted the collateral contract doctrine, as stated in the English cases, in *Byers v. McMillan*[7] in 1887. It is thus a part both of English and Canadian contract law.

Since the nineteenth century it has undergone an important extension both in England and Canada. Originally the doctrine was concerned with such "collateral" contracts between the same two parties as were parties to the main contract. Indeed, sometimes such collateral contracts were referred to as "collateral warranties",[8] indicating that they were being treated as ancillary to the main contract, even though they were also accorded an independent status distinct from the main transaction. In more recent years, courts in England and Canada have held that a contract between A and B can be collateral to a contract between B and C.[9] The result of this has been that B might have a remedy against both A and C. His remedy against A is founded on A's breach of the "collateral contract" made with B; his remedy against C might be based on C's breach of the main contract negotiated between C and B. Indeed, if for some reason, such as the presence of an exemption or similar clause in the B-C contract, B had no remedy against C, B might still be able to sue A for breach of their independent, "collateral" contract.

The possibility that a contracting party might have alternative causes of action against the same party, or two different ones, introduced into the law a considerable degree of flexibility. Use of the collateral contract doctrine enabled an aggrieved

---

4 *Lindley v. Lacy* (1864), 17 C.B.N.S. 578; *Morgan v. Griffiths* (1871), L.R. 6 Ex. 70; *Erskine v. Adeane* (1877), L.R. 8 Ch. App. 756; *De Lassalle v. Guildford*, [1901] 2 K.B. 215 (C.A.). See Wedderburn, "Collateral Contracts", [1959] C.L.J. 58.

5 [1913] A.C. 30 (H.L.).

6 *Ibid.*, at 47.

7 (1887), 15 SC.R. 194 (S.C.C.); *Harris v. Robinson* (1892), 21 S.C.R. 390 (S.C.C.); *Brownsberger v. Harvey* (1909), 12 W.W.R. 596 (Sask. S.C.); *Tocher v. Thompson* (1913), 5 W.W.R. 812 (Man. C.A.); *Eisler v. Can. Fairbanks Co.* (1912), 8 D.L.R. 390 (Sask. S.C.).

8 Or even collateral *conditions*: see *Fleischhaker v. Fort Garry Agencies Ltd.* (1957), 23 W.W.R. 390 (Man. C.A.); *Zien v. Field* (1963), 43 W.W.R. 577 (B.C.C.A.); reversed [1963] S.C.R. 632 (S.C.C.). See also *Couchman v. Hill*, [1947] K.B. 554 (C.A.); *Harling v. Eddy*, [1951] 2 K.B. 739 (C.A.). See the criticism of this by Denning L.J. in *Oscar Chess Ltd. v. Williams*, [1957] 1 All E.R. 325 at 328 (C.A.).

9 *Brown v. Sheen & Richmond Car Sales Ltd.*, [1950] 1 All E.R. 1102; *Shanklin Pier Ltd. v. Detel Products Ltd.*, [1951] 2 K.B. 854; *Andrews v. Hopkinson*, [1957] 1 Q.B. 229; *Wells (Merstham) Ltd. v Buckland & Silica Ltd.*, [1965] 2 Q.B. 170; *Traders Finance Corp. v. Haley; Haley v. Ford Motor Co. of Can.* (1966), 57 D.L.R. (2d) 15 (Ont. C.A.); affirmed [1967] S.C.R. 437 (S.C.C.); *Nor. & Central Gas Corp. v. Hillcrest Collieries Ltd.; Byron Creek Collieries Ltd. v. Coleman Collieries Ltd.*, [1976] 1 W.W.R. 481 at 525-527 (Alta. T.D.).

party: (a) to evade the parol evidence rule; (b) to escape the consequences of an exemption or similar clause; and (c) to widen the scope of liability for damage caused to him by a failure to perform contractual duties. Not surprisingly, therefore, courts have sometimes sought to restrict the scope of the doctrine, lest, through too irresponsible and general an application, it undermine settled principles of law. Lord Moulton appreciated the dangers of this in the *Heilbut, Symons* case,[10] when he said that "such collateral contracts must from their very nature be rare." The effect of such a collateral contract, that is, between the same parties as were parties to the main contract, would be to increase the consideration of the main contract, the more natural and usual way of carrying this out being by modifying the main contract, not by executing a concurrent and collateral contract. "Such collateral contracts, the sole effect of which is to vary or add to the terms of the principal contract," he said, "are therefore viewed with suspicion by the law. They must be proved strictly." Although Lord Denning thought that the language of Lord Moulton was entirely out of date, in England in 1976,[11] recent developments in Canadian courts would appear to support the view that the strict approach promulgated by Lord Moulton is still operative and applicable in Canada. Unless it is possible to interpret the oral statement as part of the written contract, making that contract one that is partly written and partly oral, rather than a wholly written contract affected by an oral collateral warranty or contract,[12] the stringent requirements of the doctrine of collateral contracts will have to be met. The consequences of this may be that an attempt to bind the maker of the oral statement, despite his freedom from obligation under the main, written contract, may fail.

2. Requirements of the doctrine

(a) Contractual intention

A party alleging a collateral contract must not only prove the terms of such a contract, he must also show the existence of an *animus contrahendi* on the part of all the parties. Any laxity on these points would enable a party to escape from the full performance of the main contract, proved by the writing assented to by the parties, and would lessen the authority of the written contract by permitting variation simply by suggesting the existence of a verbal collateral agreement relating to the same subject-matter.[13] Thus, to establish a collateral contract requires the same kind of evidence as to certainty of terms and intention to enter into a binding,

---

10 Above, note 5, at 47.

11 *J. Evans & Son (Portsmouth) Ltd. v. Andrea Merzario Ltd.*, [1976] 2 All E.R. 930 at 933 (C.A.). See also *Esso Petroleum Co. v. Mardon*, [1976] 2 All E.R. 5 (C.A.); compare *Howard Marine Ltd. v. Ogden & Sons*, [1978] 2 All E.R. 1134 at 1140 (C.A.).

12 As was the interpretation given by Roskill and Lane L.JJ. to the facts in the *Evans* case, above. This was also the alternative explanation of the situation in *Toronto Dominion Bank v. Griffiths*, [1988] 1 W.W.R. 735 (B.C.C.A.).

13 *Heilbut, Symons & Co. v. Buckleton*, [1913] A.C. 30 at 47 (H.L.) *per* Lord Moulton.

contractual agreement, as is needed where any contract is alleged to exist between the parties.[14]

What this means is that the statement purporting to be the contractual promise in such a collateral contract must amount to more than a broad, general inducement to enter into the main contract, or even a representation in the sense in which that word has been discussed earlier. The statement must constitute a definite, contractual undertaking, a binding promise meant to be taken seriously by the party to whom it is made, and intended to have such effect by the party who made the statement.[15] A good illustration is provided by *Murray v. Sperry Rand Corporation*.[16] The manufacturer and distributor of farm machinery published a sales brochure which included statements about the quality and capacity of a particular type of machine. The descriptions were very detailed. The brochure was strongly promotional. It went far beyond any simple intention to furnish specifications and indicated with some precision the performance of the machine that was being described. It was, as Reid J. found,[17] a sales tool. The statements in the brochure were not representations: they were not designed only to boost the product in question; they were intended to induce purchases of the product. The effect of such statements was that anyone reading the brochure would reasonably conclude that the manufacturer, and distributor, were promising that the described performance would be the actual performance of the product. In the same way, in *Hallmark Pool Corporation v. Storey*,[18] the statement in the brochure put out by the makers of a swimming pool would convey to the average person that a Hallmark pool installed by a Hallmark dealer would have guaranteed durability for 15 years under Canadian climatic conditions. In both these cases, therefore, the manufacturer who published the brochure was liable on the basis of collateral contract, when the product failed to live up to expectations.[19] But in *Gadbois v.*

---

14 Above, pp. 16, 26. Compare *Bauer v. Bank of Montreal* (1980), 110 D.L.R. (3d) 424 at 431 (S.C.C.) *per* McIntyre J.

15 Compare, *e.g., Carman Const. Ltd. v. C.P.R.* (1982), 136 D.L.R. (3d) 193 at 199 (S.C.C.) *per* Martland J.

16 (1979), 23 O.R. (2d) 456 (Ont. H.C.). See also *Sodd Corp. v. Tessis* (1979), 79 D.L.R. (3d) 632 (Ont. C.A.); *Smith v. Porter* (1978), 21 N.B.R. (2d) 170 (N.B.S.C.); reversed in part (1979), 27 N.B.R. (2d) 439 (N.B.C.A.); *Roberts v. Montex Dev. Corp.*, [1979] 4 W.W.R. 306 (B.C.S.C.); *Trueman v. Maritime Auto & Trailer Sales Ltd.* (1977), 19 N.B.R. (2d) 8 (N.B.C.A.). Contrast *R.E. Lister Ltd. v. Dunlop Can. Ltd.* (1978), 85 D.L.R. (3d) 321 (Ont. H.C.); reversed (1979), 105 D.L.R. (3d) 684 (Ont. C.A.); reversed [1982] 1 S.C.R. 726 (S.C.C.), where no collateral warranty was held to arise on the facts.

17 (1979), 23 O.R. (2d) 456 at 465 (Ont. H.C.).

18 (1983), 144 D.L.R. (3d) 56 especially at 65 (N.B.C.A.) *per* La Forest J.A., referring to the first edition of this book at p. 5. See also *Maughan v. Int. Harvester Co. of Can.* (1980), 112 D.L.R. (3d) 243 (N.S.C.A.) on the scope of the manufacturer's liability under his collateral manufacturer's warranty.

19 Compare *Hayward v. Mellick* (1984), 2 O.A.C. 161 (Ont. C.A.), where the Ontario Court of Appeal was divided on the question whether the statement about the size of the farm to be sold was a negligent misrepresentation (majority) or a collateral warranty (*per* Houlden J.A. dissenting).

Bonte Foods Ltd.[20] the plaintiff was unable to prove a collateral agreement by which he claimed to be entitled to certain financial incentives as the employee of the defendant.

(b) Consideration

Since a collateral contract is a contract, the promise contained therein must be supported by consideration.[21] Where a collateral contract is collateral to a main contract between the same two parties, this has not caused any problems. The consideration for the promise contained in the collateral contract is the promise by the party to whom the statement is made that he will enter into a contract with the maker of the statement, or the eventual entering into such a contract. Where the collateral contract is alleged to exist between a stranger to the main contract and one of the parties to the eventual main contract, consideration for the promise said to be contained in such collateral contract is harder to find. How can it be said to be consideration for a promise by A that B enters into a contract with C? Yet courts in England and Canada have consistently held that consideration for such a collateral contract can be found. In the words of Reid J. in *Murray v. Sperry Rand Corporation*,[22] a person may be liable for breach of a warranty notwithstanding that he has no contractual relationship with the person to whom the warranty is given."

The cases in which this has been held concern statements by manufacturers about their products, the purpose and effect of which was to induce a person to whom they were made to enter into a contract with a third party to purchase the product in question.[23] In this way the manufacturer is "benefited" by the act of the party to whom the statement was made. That there has to be some benefit to the promisor, to constitute consideration, is axiomatic. In *Shanklin Pier Ltd. v. Detel Products Ltd.*,[24] a paint manufacturer made representations concerning the qualities of its paint to pier owners. In consequence, as the manufacturer intended, the owners caused the paint to be specified in a contract made with another party for painting the pier. The painting contractor purchased the paint and applied it to the pier. The paint failed to perform as it had been specified it would do. Consequently, the owners of the pier sued the manufacturer. McNair J. held that the manufacturer was liable. As regards the question of consideration, he said[25]

> [i]f, as is elementary, the consideration for the warranty in the usual case is the entering into of the main contract in relation to which the warranty is given, I see no reason why there may not be an enforceable warranty between A and B supported by the

---

20 (1988), 94 N.B.R. (2d) 21 (N.B.Q.B.). Compare *U.M.W. District No. 18 v. Cardinal River Coals Ltd.* (1985), 58 A.R. 371 (Alta. C.A.), extrinsic evidence admitted, but it failed to establish the alleged collateral contract.

21 Above, pp. 81-113.

22 (1979), 23 O.R. (2d) 456 at 466 (Ont. H.C.).

23 See the cases cited above, note 9.

24 [1951] 2 K.B. 854.

25 *Ibid.*, at 856.

consideration that B should cause C to enter into a contract with A or that B should do some other act for the benefit of A.

The same approach is exemplified in other English as well as Canadian decisions.[26] It would seem clearly established by a long list of cases that in a three party situation a collateral contract can be found to have been entered into for consideration as long as the effect of the collateral contract is that one party thereto makes a contract with a third party, to the ultimate financial benefit of the party making the promise in the collateral contract. Manufacturers, for example, will indirectly benefit through the purchase of their products from dealers. In situations of this kind, there is no necessity for the benefit to the promisor to come directly and immediately from the promisee, as long as there is some eventual economic or similar benefit, and it can be traced back to the actions of the promisee, performed in reliance upon, and as a consequence of the promise contained in the collateral contract. If anything, such situations are stronger examples of consideration than those in which a promisee has agreed to perform a duty already owned to a third party under a pre-existing contract, by way of consideration for a promise by a stranger to that pre-existing contractual obligation.[27]

3. Problems

(a) Other difficulties

However, collateral contracts do not only give rise to problems of intention and consideration. Even where a party alleging such a contract can establish these requirements, there may be other difficulties preventing him from relying on such a contract. One has previously been discussed,[28] namely, the problem of inconsistency with a written contract, and the need to overcome the parol evidence rule. The other is the problem that arises where the main contract contains an exemption or similar clause, by virtue of which the promisor can escape from, or limit liability under the main contract. In such circumstances, can the exemption or other clause also affect the liability that might otherwise be alleged under the collateral contract?

(b) Inconsistency

The issue of inconsistency was previously considered in relation to the parol evidence rule.[29] An oral collateral contract which varies or modifies a written contract will not be given effect.[30] Such may not be the view adopted by courts

---

26 Cited above, note 9.

27 Discussed above, pp. 106-108.

28 Above, pp. 460-462.

29 Above, pp. 459-462.

30 *Hawrish v. Bank of Montreal*, [1969] S.C.R. 515 (S.C.C.); *Bauer v. Bank of Montreal* (1980), 110 D.L.R. (3d) 424 (S.C.C.); applied in *Chant v. Infinitum Growth Fund Inc.* (1986), 28 D.L.R. (4th) 577 (Ont. C.A.) to negate a collateral oral agreement, with which contrast *Chrispen v. Topham* (1986), 28 D.L.R. (4th) 754 (Sask. Q.B.); affirmed (1987), 39 D.L.R. (4th) 637 (Sask. C.A.), where

in other parts of the common-law world.[31] The attitude that a collateral contract inconsistent with a written main contract may not be proved by parol evidence has been criticized as being inflexible.[32] It has also been said that inconsistency ought not to operate as a bar to enforcement of an oral agreement as a collateral contract where the making of the oral agreement has been proved to the court's satisfaction, or, as an alternative argument, that where an oral agreement has been satisfactorily proved, the contract should be regarded as partly in writing and partly oral.[33] This, in effect, was the approach adopted by two members of the English Court of Appeal in *J. Evans & Son (Portsmouth) Ltd. v. Andrea Merzario Ltd.*[34] Only Lord Denning adhered to the collateral contract approach, and he was able to do so only by limiting the scope and effect of the language of Lord Moulton in *Heilbut, Symons & Co. v. Buckleton.*[35] The judgments of the Supreme Court of Canada in *Hawrish v. Bank of Montreal,*[36] *Bauer v. Bank of Montreal,*[37] and *Carman Construction Co. v. Canadian Pacific Railway,*[38] which might be thought to preclude such a resolution of the problem have been interpreted in British Columbia differently. In *Toronto Dominion Bank v. Griffiths,*[39] Lambert J.A. indicated that the existence of an oral agreement could be taken to mean that

---

oral evidence established such an agreement to govern the relations between a cohabiting man and woman.

For examples of inconsistency which resulted in the exclusion of an alleged oral collateral contract, see *Jetaway Invts Ltd. v. Salah* (1986), 73 N.S.R. (2d) 12 (N.S.T.D.); *C.I.B.C. v. Cooper* (1986), 5 B.C.L.R. (2d) 192 (B.C.C.A.) (but note the dissenting view of Esson J. which was adopted and followed in *Bank of B.C. v. Sanregret* (1987), 77 A.R. 352 (Alta. M.C.)); *Color Your World Inc. v. Robert F. Avery Holdings Ltd.* (1988), 88 A.R. 163 (Alta. Q.B.); *Steeplejack Services (Can.) Ltd. v. Access Scaffold & Ladder Co.* (1989), 98 A.R. 311 (Alta. Master). Contrast cases where there was no inconsistency: *AWS Welding Consulting Ltd. v. Foundation Co. of Can.* (1987), 27 C.L.R. 28 (Alta. Q.B.); *Elm Mercury Sales (1976) Ltd. v. Wiseman* (1988), 71 Nfld. & P.E.I.R. 187 (Nfld. T.D.); *Toronto Dominion Bank v. Acharya* (1992), 100 Nfld. & P.E.I.R. 1 (Nfld. T.D.). In *Ahone v. Holloway* (1988), 30 B.C.L.R. (2d) 368 (B.C.C.A.), one alleged collateral contract was inconsistent, the other not.

31 See the English cases cited in Fridman, "Written Contracts with an Oral Element" (1977), 8 Manitoba L.J. 383 at 388-393; *Fletcher Bernard-Smith Ltd. v. Shell, B.P. & Todd Oil Services,* a 1979 New Zealand case, cited by Dawson, "Parol Evidence, Misrepresentation and Collateral Contracts" (1982), 27 McGill C.J. 403 at 404. Contrast *Hoyt's Proprietary Ltd. v. Spencer* (1919), 27 C.L.R. 133 (Aus.) relied on by the Supreme Court of Canada in the *Hawrish* case, above, note 30.

32 Dawson, *loc. cit.,* above, note 31 at pp. 412-413. It has been said that it is not *absolute: Gallen v. Allstate Grain Co.* (1984), 9 D.L.R. (4th) 496 at 510 (B.C.C.A.) *per* Lambert J.A.: "The principle in *Hawrish* is not a tool for the unscrupulous to trap the unwary".

33 McLauchlan, "The Inconsistent Collateral Contract" (1976-77), 3 Dalhousie L.J. 136 at 177.

34 [1976] 2 All E.R. 930 (C.A.).

35 [1913] A.C. 30 at 47 (H.L.); see [1976] 2 All E.R. 930 at 933 (C.A.).

36 [1969] S.C.R. 515 (S.C.C.).

37 (1980), 110 D.L.R. (3d) 424 (S.C.C.).

38 (1982), 136 D.L.R. (3d) 193 (S.C.C.). See, however, the judgment of Lambert J.A. in *Gallen v. Allstate Grain Co.* (1984), 9 D.L.R. (4th) 496 at 509-512 (B.C.C.A.); leave to appeal to S.C.C. refused (1984), 56 N.R. 233 (*sub nom. Allstate Grain Co. v. Guichon*) (S.C.C.), seeking to limit the operation of this principle. Contrast the dissenting judgment of Seaton J.A.: *ibid.,* at 501-503.

39 [1988] 1 W.W.R. 735 (B.C.C.A.); see also *Ahone v. Holloway,* above, note 30.

the contract was a single contract, partly oral and partly in writing. This does not appear to have been the attitude of Canadian judges elsewhere.

One way to escape from the logic of these Supreme Court decisions is by treating the promise that is alleged to be a collateral contract not as a contractual statement but as an innocent misrepresentation.[40] If this is done, then: (a) parol evidence may be admitted to establish the statement and prove that it was a misrepresentation which induced the making of the contract; and (b) the main contract may be rescinded on the basis of such misrepresentation, so as to provide a party with a defence to an action brought on the main contract.

This approach to the problem was adopted by the Ontario Court of Appeal in *Bank of Nova Scotia v. Zackheim*.[41] The bank sued on a guarantee given by the defendant. His defence was that the bank manager had orally represented to him that the guarantee would apply only to the future indebtedness of the principal debtor. But the guarantee referred to "all debts and liabilities present and future" of the principal debtor. It also denied any effect to oral representations and promises. Thus, the facts of this case resembled those in earlier Supreme Court of Canada decisions. The bank applied for summary judgment, alleging that there was no defence to its claim under the guarantee against the guarantor. The Master dismissed the application on the ground that the defence of innocent misrepresentation raised a serious issue of law. The bank appealed to the High Court, where Griffiths J. allowed the appeal, on the ground that evidence of the oral statement was excluded by the parol evidence rule, whether the defence was based on innocent misrepresentation or collateral contract. The guarantor appealed to the Court of Appeal. His appeal was successful. The *Bauer* case, on which Griffiths J. relied, was distinguished. Although that case correctly applied the law with respect to collateral contracts, it did leave open the possibility of a valid defence of innocent misrepresentation, to be established by satisfactory oral evidence. Thus, a viable alternative exists where a party alleges an oral collateral contract, namely, that the promise or inducement can be treated as a misrepresentation, proved by parol evidence, It is noteworthy that a similar view has been adopted by the British Columbia Court of Appeal, in *Canadian Imperial Bank of Commerce v. Larsen*.[42] Thus, unless and until the Supreme Court of Canada closes the door to such an interpretation of oral collateral statements, the way is clear for contractual parties to introduce parol evidence that may qualify a written contract.

(c) Exclusion clauses[43]

A major reason for the development of the collateral doctrine was the need felt by some courts to provide a remedy where a party had breached the main

---

40 Below, p. 515.
41 (1983), 42 O.R. (2d) 592 (Ont. H.C.); reversed (1983), 44 O.R. (2d) 244 (Ont. C.A.); see also *C.I.B.C. v. Trapp* (1985), 60 B.C.L.R. 241 (B.C.S.C.); *Gallen v. Allstate Grain Co.*, above, note 32, at 511 *per* Lambert J.A.
42 [1983] 5 W.W.R. 179 (B.C.C.A.).
43 On these generally see below, pp. 571-600.

contract, but was immune from liability (or had contracted for only limited liability) under the terms of that contract. By basing the aggrieved party's claim on the collateral contract, the barrier to liability erected by the main contract was finessed or outflanked. Such an approach could be justified, notwithstanding the strictness of the law of contract, where parties had expressly and clearly contracted for exclusion or limitation of liability, on the ground that, indirectly, through the oral collateral promise, the party who had extracted an agreement for his exemption from, or limitation of liability had reintroduced his (unlimited) liability. That liability could be based either on the contractual promise contained in the collateral agreement or, as will further be examined later, on the idea of negligent misrepresentation, which would give rise to an action for damages (whereas characterization of the collateral statement as an innocent, but not negligent misrepresentation could only operate as a defence to an action brought by the collateral promisor against the collateral promisee).

English and Canadian cases can be cited to support and illustrate this way of dealing with the problem of exclusion clauses.[44] Indeed to such an extent was this done that it gave rise to another problem. In many instances the oral statement was made by a servant or agent of the party protected by the exclusion or limitation clause, and the contract expressly provided that only the provisions of the written contract bound the parties, and they could not be affected by any oral statement or representation made by a servant or agent of the party covered by the clause in question. Yet courts consistently allowed evidence to be introduced of such oral statements and gave effect to them either as collateral contracts or as misrepresentations. Not only did this seem to conflict with the idea of consistency previously discussed, it also raised the issue of the authority of the servant or agent to modify, alter or affect the express terms of the written contract. The courts seem to have avoided any serious consideration of this problem, contenting themselves with concluding that the servant or agent could bind the master or principal, regardless of the express provisions of the written contract, or the vexed question of an agent's authority to endow himself with authority to make such modifications.[45]

In view of recent Canadian decisions this question may have become otiose. In some situations an exclusion or similar clause may now govern the circumstances even if reliance is placed upon some collateral statement or promise as constituting a collateral contract or representation. With respect to liability for negligent misrepresentation this may be said to be clear. As regards collateral contracts, although no decision makes this precisely determined, *dicta* in the Supreme Court of Canada in *Carman Construction Ltd. v. Canadian Pacific Railway*[46] indicate that

---

44 *Mendelssohn v. Normand Ltd.*, [1970] 1 Q.B. 177 (C.A.); *J. Evans & Son (Portsmouth) Ltd. v. Andrea Merzario Ltd.* above, note 34; *Eisler v. Can. Fairbanks Co.* (1912), 8 D.L.R. 390 (Sask. S.C.); *Francis v. Trans-Can. Trailer Sale Ltd.* (1969), 6 D.L.R. (3d) 705 (Sask. C.A.). Contrast *Spelchan v. Long* (1956), 2 D.L.R. (2d) 707 (B.C.C.A.).

45 Fridman, *loc. cit.*, above note 31 at pp. 397-403; Fridman, "The Self-Authorizing Agent" (1983), 13 Man. L.J. 1.

46 Above, note 38, criticized by Hayek (1983), 7 Can. Bus. L.J. 328.

the presence of a suitably worded clause in the main, written contract may exclude the possibility of alternative, extrinsic liability on a collateral contract. The contract in that case was to widen a railway siding, which involved excavation of the site and removal of a quantity of rock. The construction company's tender was based on an estimate of the amount of rock to be removed given by an employee of the railway and based on a survey performed some time earlier by a technician employed by the railway. The construction company's employees had visited the site and had concluded that on the basis of their information they could not submit a price for the work to be done. Only after the estimate as to the rock to be removed had been provided could the construction company submit their bid, which was accepted. The formal contract drawn up in consequence of the tender and its acceptance provided that the agreement had been entered into by the contractor "on his own knowledge respecting the nature and conformtion of the ground upon which the work is to be done, the location, character, quality and quantities of the material to be removed, the character of the equipment and facilities needed, the general and local conditions and all other matters which can in any way affect the work." The contract also stated that the contractor did not rely on any information given or statement made to him in relation to the work by the railway company. The work proved more costly than the contractor had originally calculated, because the rock to be removed was more than had been estimated by the railway. The contractor sued for the price of this extra work, basing his claim both on collateral contract and negligent misrepresentation. At first instance,[47] Griffiths J. held that the claim should be dismissed. Although there was a collateral contract, liability thereunder as well as liability for negligent misrepresentation had been validly excluded by the terms of the contract referred to above. In this regard Griffiths J. followed *dicta* in the earlier decision of Rutherford J. in *R.E. Lister Ltd. v. Dunlop Canada Ltd.*,[48] which had been approved, inferentially, by the Ontario Court of Appeal.[49] The judgment of Griffiths J. was upheld on appeal,[50] by the majority on the ground that the contractor tendered knowing that in the very contract on which it was tendering it had agreed to assume the risk of using any information obtained by it from the railway's employees. Brooke J.A. dissented on the grounds that the railway had authorized its employee to give out the information about the quantity of rock to be removed, and the clause relating to information did not apply on the facts.[51] The construction company appealed to the Supreme Court of Canada and was again unsuccessful.[52] The relevant reason for this failure, in the present context, was the inclusion in the contract of the clause discussed above, by which the railway excluded any possibility of liability

---

47 (1980), 109 D.L.R. (3d) 288 (Ont. H.C.).

48 (1978), 85 D.L.R. (3d) 321 (Ont. H.C.).

49 (1980), 105 D.L.R. (3d) 684 (Ont. C.A.); reversed (1982), 135 D.L.R. (3d) 1 (S.C.C.) on grounds not material here.

50 (1981), 124 D.L.R. (3d) 680 (Ont. C.A.).

51 *Ibid.*, at 684.

52 (1982), 136 D.L.R. (3d) 193 (S.C.C.).

in respect of statements made by its employees outside the scope of the written contract.[53]

However, it may be possible for a collateral contract to be considered as overriding both the main contract and its exclusion clause.[54]

4. Negligent misrepresentation

Discussion of collateral contracts would not be complete without some reference to the possibility that statements made *dehors* the contract may be treated not only as contractual promises giving rise to distinct contractual liability (or a defence to an action under the main contract) but also as representations, giving rise to a defence of innocent misrepresentation or an action for damages for negligent misrepresentation. The possibility of such a statement being an innocent misrepresentation has already been mentioned. In the present context the possibility of liability for negligent misrepresentation must be considered.

A logical difficulty in this respect is the contradiction between contractual terms and representations (whether true or false, fraudulent or innocent). It has been seen elsewhere that the law firmly differentiates contractual terms from representations.[55] Both are types of statements made by contracting parties prior to, or at the same time as the negotiation of a contract. The distinction lies in the intent with which the statement is communicated to the other party. If it is in the form of a promise or undertaking, such a statement may be considered as a part of the eventual contract between the parties. If the maker of such a statement never intended that it should have contractual force and effect, the statement cannot be regarded as more than a representation inducing the contract but not forming a part of it. Given this clear differentiation, it is hard to see how a statement can be a contractual term and a representation at the same time, even if the term in question is a term of a collateral contract, not the main one. As previously noted, such a statement must have been made with contractual intent if it is to be treated as a collateral contractual promise.[56] That being so, it can scarcely be treated also as a representation, not contractual in nature, but having the consequences and legal effects of a representation. Yet English and Canadian courts have been prepared to regard such statements as potentially collateral contracts and misrepresentations, and have been willing to give the recipient of such a statement alternative remedies in contract, for breach of the collateral agreement, or tort, for negligent misrepresentation (or to allow relief from the main contract on the basis of an innocent misrepresentation permitting rescission of the main contract).

The source of this duplicate or concurrent liability is the decision of the English

---

53 The clause was not regarded as a clause exempting from liability but as a non-reliance provision, the effect of which was to prevent liability arising on the part of C.P.R. in respect of statements made or information given by its employees: (1982), 136 D.L.R. (3d) 193 at 204 (S.C.C.).

54 As in *Rose v. Borisko Bros. Ltd.* (1982), 125 D.L.R. (3d) 671 (Ont. H.C.); affirmed (1983), 147 D.L.R. (3d) 191 (Ont. C.A.). Contrast *Hayward v. Mellick* (1984), 2 O.A.C. 161 (Ont. C.A.).

55 Above, pp. 449-451.

56 Above, pp. 507-509.

Court of Appeal in *Esso Petroleum Co. v. Mardon*.[57] Esso sued for possession of premises, rent in arrear and mesne profits under a lease by Esso to Mardon of a service station. Mardon counterclaimed for damages. That claim was founded on two causes of action. One was a collateral warranty alleged to have been given by Esso to Mardon as to the earning capacity of the station prior to the granting of the lease. The other was an allegation that Esso induced Mardon to enter into the lease by falsely, that is, negligently representing the potential sales capacity of the service station. The Court of Appeal found for Mardon on both grounds. There was a breach of warranty and a negligent misrepresentation. Thus, Mardon had a defence to the action by Esso and a claim for damages for lost profits. The Court of Appeal had no difficulty in making these dual holdings notwithstanding the point discussed above as to the conflict or inconsistency between a finding of a contractual warranty and a finding of a negligent misrepresentation based on the same statement made by Esso to Mardon as to the potential sales capacity of the station.

This judgment has been accepted and followed in Canada. For example in *Sodd Corporation v. Tessis*,[58] the Ontario Court of Appeal held that a statement by a chartered accountant who was the trustee in bankruptcy of a company in liquidation as to the retail value of goods in a warehouse owned and operated by the bankrupt company was a collateral warranty on which the purchaser of the goods could sue when he lost money by his purchase of such goods, and a negligent misrepresentation about the goods made in breach of the duty of care owned by the accountant/trustee to the purchaser, under the doctrine enunciated by the House of Lords in *Hedley, Byrne & Co. v. Heller & Partners*.[59] The *Mardon* case was also followed in *R.E. Lister v. Dunlop Canada Ltd.*,[60] although, for reasons already considered, no liability followed on the facts of that case. Similarly in *Carman Construction Ltd. v. Canadian Pacific Railway*,[61] there was potential liability for breach of a collateral warranty and for negligent misrepresentation, although liability was excluded on the facts of that case by virtue of the express provisions of the main contract to which reference has been made.[62]

---

57 [1976] 2 All E.R. 5 (C.A.) (followed in respect of collateral warranty in *Thake v. Maurice*, [1984] 2 All E.R. 513).

58 (1978), 79 D.L.R. (3d) 632 (Ont. C.A.); *Smith v. Porter* (1978), 21 N.B.R. (2d) 170 (N.B.S.C.); reversed in part (1979), 27 N.B.R. (2d) 439 (N.B.C.A.), a case of breach of collateral warranty and *fraudulent* misrepresentation; see also *Rose v. Borisko Bros. Ltd.* (1981), 125 D.L.R. (3d) 671 (Ont. H.C.); affirmed (1983), 147 D.L.R. (3d) 191 (Ont. C.A.).

59 [1964] A.C. 465 (H.L.).

60 (1978), 85 D.L.R. (3d) 321 (Ont. H.C.); reversed (1979), 105 D.L.R. (3d) 685 (Ont. C.A.); reversed (1982), 135 D.L.R. (3d) 1 (S.C.C.).

61 (1982), 136 D.L.R. (3d) 193 (S.C.C.).

62 Contrast *Rose v. Borisko Bros. Ltd.* (1981), 125 D.L.R. (3d) 671 (Ont. H.C.); affirmed (1983), 147 D.L.R. (3d) 191 (Ont. C.A.).

14

Performance

1. The duty to perform

Generally speaking the parties to a contract are obliged to perform in accordance with the express and implied terms of the contract. The duty to perform must be carried out precisely and exactly.[1] Anything less than such performance is a breach of contract and may preclude the party in default from enforcing the provisions of the contract that are for his benefit, for example, the payment of the price agreed upon for goods or services.[2] The strictness of the duty to perform, however, is modified in certain circumstances. Under the doctrine of impossibility or frustration, for example, a party may be excused from performance of the contract

---

1 And, possibly, in good faith: *Gateway Realty Ltd. v. Arton Holdings Ltd.* (1991), 106 N.S.R. (2d) 180, especially at 191-198 (N.S.T.D.); affirmed (1992), 112 N.S.R. (2d) 180 (N.S.C.A.). Compare what is said below, pp. 522-523 with respect to situations where a party has some discretion. Is the issue of good faith in performance of more general relevance?

2 These opening three sentences were quoted by Angers J.A. in *Cameron Auctioneers & Appraisers Ltd. v. G.R. Galbraith Supplies* (1988), 47 D.L.R. (4th) 141 at 145-146 (N.B.C.A.). On the effects of non-performance, *i.e.*, breach, see below, pp. 558 *et seq.* Note, however, the "dependency" of performance, below, pp. 529-534. Note also the possible effects of a partial performance: below, pp. 534-539.

as a whole or that part which has yet to be performed.[3] Performance may be dispensed with completely, or its character altered, by virtue of some subsequent agreement between the parties, or conduct by one party which gives rise to an estoppel, or the waiver of such party's right to demand performance, or a certain previously agreed manner of performance.[4] The duty to perform may also be qualified or otherwise affected by a provision in the contract under which liability for non-performance may be excluded or limited in some way.[5] Failing such modifications of contractual duties, whether intrinsic to the contract or resulting from subsequent unilateral or bilateral conduct,[6] the contract must be performed with strict adherence to its language and meaning.[7]

Thus, if a contract stipulates that no charge is to be made for certain services, it is a breach of contract to purport to claim payment for their provision.[8] So, in *Bank of Nova Scotia v. Guenette*,[9] the bank failed to include the wife in the credit account supposed to be in their joint names in pursuance of their agreement with the bank. Hence, there was a total failure of consideration for the agreement for the loan of money by the bank. In *Clareview Rental Project (Edmonton) Ltd. v. Dockery*,[10] an investor who failed to pay certain cash calls when made by his investment agent was guilty of a failure to perform an obligation that was properly put upon him. On the other hand, where a contract was under seal, and therefore was not required to be supported by consideration, the requirement of nominal consideration contained in the contract under seal did not have to be fulfilled; therefore, the non-payment of such nominal consideration was not a breach of contract by the party on whom payment was imposed, such as to provide the other party with a defence to an action for an alleged breach of contract on his part.[11]

Unless a contract provides for payment otherwise than in cash, the party obliged to pay must perform his duty by giving currency. Payment by cheque may be refused where this has not been agreed upon in advance. The terms of the contract govern.

---

3 Below, Chapter 16.

4 Below, pp. 543-551.

5 Below, pp. 571-600.

6 Including, of course, the possibility of *substituted* performance by *another* party, by virtue of either *novation* or *assignment*: below, pp. 539-542. Contrast substantial performance by the *same* party obliged to perform: below, pp. 536-539.

7 *E.g.*, *Kokotalo v. Ramchuk* (1980), 28 A.R. 127 (Alta. Q.B.) duty to execute a new will. Compare *Paul v. Western Can. Lottery Foundation* (1981), 127 D.L.R. (3d) 502 (Sask. C.A.), duty to pay correct winner of a lottery. *Exchanger Industries Ltd. v. Dominion Bridge Co.* (1986), 69 A.R. 22 (Alta. Q.B.), failure to adhere to instructions from plaintiff in process of annealing certain steel tubes; therefore, breach of contract.

8 *Pierce v. Krahn* (1979), 10 Alta. L.R. (2d) 49 (Alta. T.D.).

9 (1986), 68 A.R. 368 (Alta. Q.B.). And the failure to provide a computer system invented by the plaintiff was a breach of contract in *Orbitron Software Design Corp. v. M.I.C.R. Systems Ltd.* (1990), 48 B.L.R. 147 (B.C.S.C.). But the plaintiff failed to establish other failures in performance that were alleged.

10 (1990), 78 Alta. L.R. (2d) 106 (Alta. Q.B.).

11 *Bay v. Three Hebemick Enterprises Ltd.* (1983), 21 Man. R. (2d) 51 (Man. Q.B.). For the situation where a contract is under seal, see above, pp. 117-119.

Thus, in *Mitchell v. Dares Motors Ltd.*,[12] a credit note was given by a seller on the return of certain goods by the buyer. Later, when the note was presented for encashment, the seller could not argue that he was entitled to repay subject to a discount. The seller was liable for the full face value of the note. Again, in *Blanco v. Nugent*[13] in which the buyer under a crop-sharing agreement desired to pay off the balance of the purchase price in cash, it was held that, since the contract provided for the entitlement of the seller to be paid in wheat and other grain, the buyer was obliged to discharge his obligation in that way, by giving further wheat, etc., although he was allowed credit for repayment in cash already made and accepted by the seller. Substitution was not allowed. So, too, in *California Prune & Apricot Growers Inc. v. Baird & Peters*,[14] a contract of sale of goods provided for the shipment of goods from the Pacific coast to St. John, New Brunswick by way of the C.N.R. It was held that this was an essential term of the contract and had to be performed exactly as stipulated. Hence, the delivery of the goods by C.P.R. was not performance of the contract and the buyer was entitled to reject goods so shipped. Nor was substitution of a boiler with a smaller capacity a proper performance of the contract to supply materials in *Engineering & Plumbing Supplies (Vancouver) Ltd. v. Intervan Acceptance Corporation*.[15] The result was that the supplier was guilty of inducing a breach of contract between the party to whom the boiler was supplied and a third party.

As long as the party obliged to perform has done what he undertook to do in the first place, there can be no complaint by the other party, and no successful attempt by the latter to hold the former liable in any way for breach of contract. Thus, in *Trask Well Co. v. Kinley*,[16] the plaintiffs undertook to drill a well on the defendant's land, for the purpose of providing water for the defendant's hotel. There was no limit to the depth to which the plaintiffs had to go, but the drilling would determine on notification by the defendant that there was a sufficient quantity of water for the defendant's needs. No mention was made of the quality of the water, only that the well should produce ten to twelve gallons a minute. The plaintiffs sank the well and eventually produced the stipulated quantity of water. But the water was salty, in consequence of which the defendant could not use it for *all* purposes of the hotel, though it could be used for some. When the plaintiffs sued for the price of their work it was held at first instance that they were not entitled to succeed since they had not completed their contract. On appeal, it was held that they had done all they had contracted to do, and were therefore entitled to their money. There was no implied term as to the quality of the water to be produced as a result of the drilling. Indeed the plaintiffs had been willing to drill deeper if the defendant had so required, but the latter had stopped the work. In such circumstances, performance of the contract had taken place. In contrast, in *Wood*

12 (1963), 39 D.L.R. (2d) 89 (N.S.S.C.).
13 [1949] 3 D.L.R. 19 (Man. K.B.).
14 [1926] S.C.R. 208 (S.C.C.).
15 (1981), 30 B.C.L.R. 170 (B.C.C.A.).
16 [1948] 3 D.L.R. 721 (N.S.C.A.).

& Wood v. Cuvelier,[17] a contractor undertook to install a furnace in a house, and to ensure that it functioned properly. Because of the configuration of the property a large number of pipes was necessary. Because of improper installation of the pipes, a draft problem emerged when the furnace was lit, and combustion material leaked into the house. The contractor was held liable for failure to install a properly working heating system. The system worked, but it caused damage to the homeowner's property. Therefore, the contract had not been performed in accordance with its terms.[18]

However, a trivial deviation from proper performance of a contract will not amount to a breach. *De minimis non curat lex,* while a potentially dangerous maxim, seemingly excusing non-performance in strict accord with the terms of a contract, has nonetheless been applied in some circumstances. An illustration is *B. & R. Holdings Ltd. v. Western Grocers Ltd.; Westfair Foods Ltd. v. B. & R. Holdings Ltd.*[19] It appeared that, somehow, the tenants were guilty of a shortfall of three cents per annum in the payment of rent over a period of years. This was held not to be a breach of the tenants' contractual duty to pay a stipulated sum by way of rent. A striking contrast is provided by the decision of the House of Lords in *A/S Awilco v. Fulvia S.p.A. di Navigazione, The "Chikuma".*[20] A time charter-party required the charterers to make "punctual and regular payment of the hire" monthly in advance to the owners' bank in Genoa. Failing this the owners were entitled to withdraw the chartered ship from the charterers. When the 81st monthly payment of nearly $US 70,000 was due, the charterers' bank in Norway arranged for an Italian bank to make a credit transfer of the due hire to the owners' bank in Genoa. The transfer was irrevocable, and the owners could have withdrawn the amount transferred. Under Italian law, however, interest in the amount transferred did not run in favour of the owners' bank until a few days' later. If the owners had transferred the amount they would have had to pay their bank interest of between $70 and $100. The owners took the view that the hire had not been paid punctually, in accordance with the contract. They withdrew the ship from the charterers, who then claimed $3,000,000 from the owners. At various levels the decision went for or against the owners. Ultimately the House of Lords held that, although the transfer of the hire payment had been unconditional, in the sense that it was irrevocable and not subject to any condition precedent or

---

17 (1979), 34 N.S.R. (2d) 261 (N.S.T.D.).

18 Note, however, the necessity for establishing that an alleged requirement is a *term* of the contract, *e.g.,* a warranty, and not an innocent misrepresentation: see *Williams v. Bittner* (1981), 10 Sask. R. 190 (Sask. Dist. Ct.); above, pp. 449-453. In *S & M Carpet Ltd. v. Ledwith* (1990), 80 Nfld. & P.E.I.R. 53 (Nfld. T.D.), it seems that it was an implied term of the contract that the customer would complain of defects in the supply and installation of a carpet at the time the work was complete. Hence, his later complaint was not allowed to defeat the supplier's claim for the unpaid price.

19 (1982), 25 R.P.R. 121 (Sask. Q.B.).

20 [1981] 1 All E.R. 652 (H.L.); see also *The "Brimnes",* [1975] Q.B. 929 (C.A.). Note the emphasis upon the context of commercial transactions and the need for certainty in such transactions; compare the attitude of the House of Lords to "innominate terms" in *Bunge Corp. v. Tradax Export S.A.,* [1981] 2 All E.R. 513 (H.L.); above, pp. 502-503.

subsequent, it was not unconditional in the sense of being unfettered or unrestricted. This was only possible if the owners had received the equivalent of cash or something as good as cash. The money could not be used immediately to earn interest: it could only be withdrawn subject to payment of interest. Therefore, it was an overdraft facility rather than cash. The charterers had therefore not performed their contractual obligation to pay the monthly hire, even though there was only a minor failure, and even though the consequence was a harsh result for the charterers. The principle of *de minimis* could not excuse the charterer's behaviour in this instance, although whether it could ever be invoked to excuse such a failure was left undecided.

The strictness of the duty to perform may be qualified by the language of the contract itself. For example, in *Moir v. J.P. Porter Co.*,[21] a company agreed to pay a retiring employee a supplementary pension "in the sole discretion of the Board of Directors." The company suffered financial losses and subsequently terminated the supplementary pension after having paid it for some time. Was this a breach of contract? It was held that as long as the Board of Directors had exercised its discretion in good faith, neither capriciously nor maliciously, the ending of the pension was a legitimate act. The duty to pay was not absolute. It was qualified, inferentially, by the needs of the company. A somewhat similar interpretation of what appeared at first sight to be an absolute duty under the contract was placed upon a contract in a recent British Columbia decision. In *Placer Developments Ltd. v. British Columbia Hydro & Power Authority*,[22] the defendants' power line was downed during a lawful strike that was taking place on the plaintiffs' mine. No electricity was supplied to the mine, causing a loss of productivity. The defendants refused to allow the plaintiffs to repair the line. The defendants failed to do anything to effect repairs because of a fear of violence from the striking employees of the plaintiffs, as well as the fear that the defendants' unionized employees would not cross the picket lines set up by the plaintiffs' employees. Eventually the plaintiffs did do the repairs without asking the defendants' permission. The plaintiffs then sued for the losses incurred by reason of the defendants' delay. The defendants were in breach of their duty to repair, owed under the contract to supply the plaintiffs with electricity. But this was only because they had failed to repair the line within a reasonable time. Gould J. rejected the argument, based on American authorities, that the mere failure to repair was itself a breach of contract.[23] The learned judge

---

21 (1979), 33 N.S.R. (2d) 674 (N.S.C.A.); compare above, pp. 29-31. *Greenberg v. Meffert* (1985), 18 D.L.R. (4th) 548 (Ont. C.A.); leave to appeal to S.C.C. refused (1985), 56 O.R. (2d) 320 (S.C.C.), below, pp. 522-523. Nor was it possible to interpret a dealership contract as depriving a party of the right to terminate the contract without cause or giving reasonable notice. The court could not conceive of a perpetual dealership agreement: *Treen Gloves & Safety Products Ltd. v. Degil Safety Products (1989) Inc.* (1990), 33 C.P.R. (3d) 74 (B.C.S.C.). Note that a court cannot compel a party to exercise a discretion given by contract, nor prevent its exercise. But once the discretion is exercised the court is entitled to examine whether it was exercised properly (as to which, compare below, p. 522): *MicMac Agencies Ltd. v. Prudential Assurance Co.* (1987), 82 N.S.R. (2d) 193 (N.S.T.D.); additional reasons at (1988), 86 N.S.R. (2d) 14 (N.S.T.D.).

22 (1983), 46 B.C.L.R. 329 at (B.C.S.C.).

23 *Ibid.*, at 338.

appears to have taken the view that the duty in this instance was not a completely strict, unqualified one. It was modified by the idea of what was reasonable in the circumstances.

There may be two modes of performance, giving the party obliged to perform a choice as to which mode he will adopt. In such circumstances, the promisee cannot object to the choice ultimately made. Moreover if one mode of performance becomes impossible, the alternative is still open to the promisor and must be taken by him.[24]

Whether performance has occurred may depend upon the ultimate approval of the party on whose behalf or for whose benefit performance has been undertaken. This may be the situation, for example, where the contract states that the purchaser may reject goods not satisfactory to him; that is, the seller must satisfy the purchaser as to the goods he delivers before the seller has performed his duty to deliver the contract goods. Such a provision is a perfectly legitimate one, as Estey J. explained in the Supreme Court of Canada in *Canada Egg Products Ltd. v. Canadian Doughnut Co.*,[25] and the purchaser is within his contractual rights if he honestly rejects the goods. The fact that others might have been satisfied or that he has acted unreasonably, according to Estey J., was not material.[26]

Where a contract is framed in such terms it has been held that only the party entitled to exercise the stipulated judgment must be taken into account, so that even if a jury would regard his refusal to accept goods or services as unreasonable, his decision will be upheld and honoured by the courts.[27] The only limitation or qualification, therefore, would appear to be that he must act honestly and in good faith.[28] Reasonableness would therefore not be a criterion. However, it has also been said that a party who is empowered to act in this way, *e.g.*, by exercising a discretion to accord commission to a sales agent,[29] must act reasonably as well

---

24 *Kirzinger v. Kalthoff* (1965), 45 D.L.R. (2d) 144 at 156 (Sask. Q.B.); compare *Hall v. Conder* (1857), 26 L.J.C.P. 288; *McIlquham v. Taylor*, [1895] 1 Ch. 53 (C.A.).

25 [1955] S.C.R. 398 (S.C.C.).

26 *Ibid.*, at 609. Compare *Fletton Ltd. v. Peat Marwick Ltd.* (1986), 32 B.L.R. 162 (B.C.S.C.); affirmed (1988), 50 D.L.R. (4th) 729 (B.C.C.A.); leave to appeal to S.C.C. refused (1988), 50 D.L.R. (4th) vii (note) (S.C.C.). The issue was the entitlement of a party to reject an insurance proposal made in connection with an intended contract.

27 *Truman v. Ford Motor Co.*, [1926] 1 D.L.R. 960 (Ont. C.A.). But an objective standard of reasonableness was applied in *Jack Wookey Holdings Ltd. v. Tanizul Timber Ltd.* (1988), 27 B.C.L.R. (2d) 221 (B.C.C.A.), citing *Greenberg v. Meffert*, above, note 21.

28 *Fletton Ltd. v. Peat Marwick Ltd.*, above, note 26; *North End Invts. Inc. v. Alsman*, [1989] 4 W.W.R. 545 (Alta. Q.B.), where the plaintiff had to be satisfied by the defendant's financial and leasehold information. To this extent it is valid to speak in terms of an obligation to perform a contract in good faith, as discussed in *Gateway Realty Ltd. v. Arton Holdings Ltd.* (1991), 106 N.S.R. (2d) 180 (N.S.T.D.); affirmed (1992), 112 N.S.R. (2d) 180 (N.S.C.A.); see also *Mesa Operating Ltd. Partnership v. Amoco Can. Resources Ltd.* (1992), 129 A.R. 177 (Alta. Q.B.).

29 *Greenberg v. Meffert*, above, note 21; compare the comment by Judson J., "a vendor . . . must exercise his right reasonably and in good faith not in a capricious or arbitrary manner", in *Mason v. Freedman* (1958), 14 D.L.R. (2d) 529 at 534 (S.C.C.); compare *LeMesurier v. Andrus* (1986), 25 D.L.R. (4th) 424 (Ont. C.A.), on a capricious repudiation of a contract for purchase of land.

as in good faith, *i.e.*, honestly;[30] and the reasonableness or otherwise of his conduct is to be determined objectively, not like matters of taste, personal compatibility or judgment.[31]

Until the right reserved in the other party by the contract has been exercised (or there is clear evidence that it would not be within the requisite period or at all), the performing party cannot claim either that he has performed the contract on his side, or that he is excused performance because the other party would not accept the goods or services in question. Conversely, it would be no defence to an action for breach of contract brought against the party with the power to approve or reject, that such party could have exercised that power so as to render the seller, now suing for breach, unable to perform, and therefore unable to sue the buyer.[32]

There may be some ambiguity about the way the obligation is stated in the contract. Until such ambiguity or uncertainty is resolved, it may not be known whether the contract has been performed (or indeed what performance involves, or when it must take place).[33] Such ambiguity may revolve around the date when something is to occur. Or, it may relate to the way in which a contract is to be performed, perhaps leading to other questions or liabilities, as in *Aga Heat (Canada) Ltd. v. Brockville Hotel Co.*[34] There the liability of a company which contracted to put equipment in a hotel kitchen depended upon whether the additional work done by their employee in that kitchen was an authorized mode of performing the contract, even though it was a variation of or addition to the contract, or was an agreed arrangement as to the mode of performing the contractual obligation. On either basis the company was held liable. Cases like this suggest that sometimes there is scope for straying away from the notion that performance must be within the strict letter of the contract before it will be treated as performance of the contract.

---

30 *Chernin v. Scotsburn Co-op. Services Ltd.* (1986), 36 B.L.R. 104 (N.S.T.D.), relying on *Mason v. Freedman*, above, note 29 (which seems to conflict with *Can. Egg Products Ltd. v. Can Doughnut Co.*, above, note 25, unless they can be distinguished by saying that the two Supreme Court decisions deal with different subject-matter).

31 *Jack Wookey Holdings Ltd. v. Tanizul Timber Ltd.*, above, note 27, a case concerned with whether a party was satisfied with the performance of a logging contract. Compare, on whether concrete supplied under a contract was defective or satisfactory, *Valley Concrete (1979) Ltd. v. Western Caissons Ltd.* (1987), 53 Alta. L.R. (2d) 226 (Alta. Q.B.) and *293360 Alta. Ltd. v. Al Klippert Ltd.* (1988), 90 A.R. 47 (Alta. Q.B.).

32 *Coady Store Fixtures & Equipment Co. v. Tosh*, [1964] 2 O.R. 701 (Ont. H.C.); affirmed (1965), 52 D.L.R. (2d) 506n (Ont. C.A.). Not also that the fact that performance must be approved by a stranger to the contract will not affect the existence or validity of the contract; only whether it has been performed. Hence, in *Fabbi v. Jones; Fleck v. Jones*, [1973] S.C.R. 42 (S.C.C.) the need for approval by the P.U.C. before the contract could be said to have been fulfilled did not prevent the conduct of the defendant from being the inducement of a breach of contract, for which he was liable.

33 See *e.g.*, *Beer v. Lea* (1913), 29 O.L.R. 255 (Ont. C.A.) (when did the option terminate); *Monroe v. Mews; Re Mining Claim K.R.L. 462*, [1937] O.R. 452 (Ont. C.A.) (when did the *day* end); *McMillan Bloedel & Powell River Ltd. v. B.C. Elec. Co.* (1961), 29 D.L.R. (2d) 670 (B.C.C.A.) (the date from which an agreement was operative, namely, the "effective" date, or the date of the contract).

34 [1945] S.C.R. 184 (S.C.C.).

2. Time for performance

The contract may be one which, of its nature, has no particular time within which it is to be performed.[35] In *McBride and Hogaboam v. Johnson*,[36] the Supreme Court of Canada was faced with such a contract, at least according to the way they interpreted it. The plaintiff alleged that the deceased, against whose estate the action was being brought, had promised to marry her; a promise which had been made some years before his death in a road traffic accident. The defendants, on behalf of the deceased's estate, argued that the promise had been repudiated years before and that repudiation had been accepted by the plaintiff. The court held that no such repudiation was effective. The obligation to marry the plaintiff subsisted. Performance of that obligation accrued from day to day, right up to the day on which the deceased met his death. Hence, at the time of that death the deceased had not performed his contract and his estate was liable. However, the death of the deceased was a supervening event which frustrated the contract, thereby relieving the deceased's estate from liability.

That was a special situation, since it would appear that a promise to marry was one that was capable of being fulfilled at *any* time after it was made (unlike a mercantile contract). But other promises or obligations can only be performed within a "reasonable time", and if not performed by then, the party obliged will be in breach.[37] Sometimes such obligation, that is, to perform within a reasonable time, is imposed by statute.[38] More often than not, however, the obligation arises, expressly or by implication, from the contract itself.[39] In such instances it is a question of fact as to what is a reasonable time.[40] An illustration is afforded by the Alberta

---

35 For discussion of specific problems in this connection, see Stoljar, "Untimely Performance in the Law of Contract" (1955), 71 L.Q.R. 527; Carnegie, "Terminability of Contracts of Unspecified Duration" (1969), 85 L.Q.R. 392; Harvard, "Open Terms Relating to Time in Contracts for Sale of Goods" (1973), 19 McGill L.J. 224; Bridge, "Discharge for Breach of Contracts of Sale of Goods" (1983), 28 McGill L.J. 867 at 912-926.

36 [1962] S.C.R. 202 (S.C.C.) (applying various principles in the English cases of: *Mersey Steel & Iron Co. v. Naylor, Benzon & Co.* (1884), 9 App. Cas. 434 (H.L.); *Frost v. Knight* (1872), L.R. 7 Exch. 111; *Avery v. Bowden* (1856), 119 E.R. 1119; *Heyman v. Darwins Ltd.*, [1942] A.C. 356 (H.L.)). See also below, pp. 646, 653, with respect to the application of the doctrine of frustration.

37 If the failure to perform in time is a "fundamental" breach: *Howell v. Ridge View Dev. & Holdings Co.* (1987), 53 Alta. L.R. (2d) 337 (Alta. C.A.); *McCaig v. Nimmo* (1987), 85 N.B.R. (2d) 132 (N.B.Q.B.). Nor if the term as to time of performance does not go to the root of the contract: *Unified Systems Ltd. v. Clearwater Lobsters Ltd.* (1986), 58 Nfld. & P.E.I.R. 138 (Nfld. T.D.). Even if delay is a breach of contract tardy performance may still not deprive a party of the right to be paid: *Western Harvestore Ltd. v. Schwanke Farms Ltd.* (1981), 17 Alta. L.R. (2d) 262 (Alta. Q.B.).

38 E.g., under the Sale of Goods Act, see Fridman, *Sale of Goods in Canada*, 3rd ed. (1986), p. 229, as to time for a seller to deliver goods where no time is fixed by the contract.

39 *Westlake v. Milosevich* (1983), 56 N.S.R. (2d) 631 (N.S.T.D.). For example, in a contract to exercise an option to purchase shares: *Boxer v. Nowan Properties Ltd.* (1986), 33 D.L.R. (4th) 150 (B.C.S.C.); affirmed (1988), 52 D.L.R. (4th) 667 (B.C.C.A.). So, too, in regard to reasonable notice to terminate a contract: *Aldo Ippolito & Co. v. Can. Packers Inc.* (1986), 14 C.C.E.L. 76 (Ont. C.A.); additional reasons at (1986), 14 C.C.E.L. 76 at 89 (Ont. C.A.); *Treen Gloves & Safety Products Ltd. v. Degil Safety Products (1989) Inc.*, above, note 21.

40 This and the previous three sentences were cited by Nathanson J. in *Dockrill v. Walwyn Stodgell Cochran Murray Ltd.* (1983), 61 N.S.R. (2d) 149 at 155 (N.S.T.D.). In calculating a reasonable

case of *Karpa v. O'Shea*.[41] The plaintiff agreed to buy land from the defendant. He had to arrange certain financing in order to raise the purchase price. No time was stipulated for the completion of the contract, and the question was whether the plaintiff could maintain an action for specific performance when he eventually, after much delay, raised the necessary money. It was held that, since this was a contract for the purchase of farming land, a reasonable time for the performance and completion of such a contract *in Western Canada* was within such time as would permit the commencement of preparations for the seeding of next year's crop. Hence, the date when the plaintiff was ready to complete was too late for such purpose and the contract could not be specifically enforced at his suit. Much depends, therefore, on the type of contract, the subject-matter, *e.g.*, land or shares, and the locality of the contract.[42]

The situation is more complex, however, where a contract stipulates that "time is of the essence of the contract." At common law it would seem that, in contracts of sale of goods, time was *prima facie* of the essence where delivery was concerned.[43] In other words, unless the parties expressly determined otherwise, it was essential for the seller to deliver the contract goods on the date specified in the contract (if a date was specified — otherwise a reasonable time was given within which to deliver, as already noted).[44] Whether time was of the essence at common law in other contracts may be questioned, although it has been suggested that it was in all mercantile contracts.[45] It would be if expressly stipulated as such, for example, as a condition of the contract, or a condition precedent to the effectiveness or performance of a contract.[46] In contracts of sale of goods, now, under the statute,

---

time it may be that delays caused by a strike can be excluded: see *Henry Hope & Sons Ltd. v. Can. Foundry Ltd.* (1917), 40 O.L.R. 338 (Ont. C.A.), applying *Hick v. Raymond & Reid*, [1893] A.C. 22 (H.L.), and *Sims & Co. v. Midland Ry. Co.*, [1913] 1 K.B. 103. An illustration of performance within a reasonable time is afforded by *MacDonald v. Matheson* (1986), 57 Nfld. & P.E.I.R. 268 (P.E.I.C.A.).

41 (1969), 3 D.L.R. (3d) 572 (Alta. C.A.) followed in *Dixon v. Wiebe*, [1979] 3 W.W.R. 354 (Sask. Q.B.). Compare also *Webber v. Copeman* (1912), 2 W.W.R. 882 (Sask. S.C.), following *Ford v. Cotesworth* (1870), L.R. 5 Q.B. 544.

42 Compare *Barrick v. Clarke*, [1951] S.C.R. 177 (S.C.C.): above, p. 42; cited by the British Columbia Court of Appeal in *Boxer v. Nowan Properties Ltd.*, above, note 39, at 669, dealing with the time within which a party was able to exercise an option to purchase shares.

43 *Bowes v. Shand* (1877), 2 App. Cas. 455 (H.L.); *Reuter v. Sala* (1879), 4 C.P.D. 239 (C.A.); *Hartley v. Hymans*, [1920] 3 K.B. 475; see Fridman, *op. cit.*, above, note 38, at pp. 226-228.

44 But this might be because a stipulation as to time was a part of the *description* of the goods; as to which see Fridman, *op. cit.*, above, 38, at pp. 176-183.

45 Cheshire, Fifoot & Furmston, *Law of Contract*, 12th ed. (1991), p. 552. See, *e.g.*, *Canwest Pacific Television Inc. v. 147250 Can. Ltd.* (1987), 14 B.C.L.R. (2d) 338 (B.C.S.C.); affirmed (1989), 30 B.C.L.R. (2d) 145 (B.C.C.A.), following and applying *Bunge Corp. v. Tradax Export S.A.*, [1981] 2 All E.R. 513 (H.L.).

46 See, *e.g. Bunge Corp. v. Tradax Export S.A.*, above, note 45, on the time within which a buyer had to notify a seller of a ship's readiness to load; compare above, p. 502. Compare *Howell v. Ridge View Dev. & Holdings Co.*, above, note 37, failure to build a house by the contract date was a fundamental breach that entitled the purchaser to treat the contract as repudiated by the builder (compare below, pp. 561-571); *McCaig v. Nimmo*, above, note 37, failure to perform a "true" condition precedent (above, pp. 437-441).

time is not of the essence with respect to time of payment of the purchase price (unless so stated), and whether time is of the essence with regard to other terms of the contract depends on the contract and its terms.[47] Thus, in such contracts the issue is one of construction. Most probably the same is true of all other contracts.[48] Where time is expressly or by construction of the essence of a contract, this requires both parties to observe their obligations with strictness as to time. Hence, a party who is the cause of the other party's delay and inability to perform within the contract time, cannot complain that such other party has not observed the strict requirements of the contract as to time.[49]

Even where time is of the essence, the requirement that performance be completed within or at the stipulated time may be waived by the party for whose benefit that requirement has been included in the contract. Where such waiver has occurred, the party who would have been in breach for late performance is not liable, unless his conduct amounts to a further breach of contract.[50] The party who has waived the importance of time will be estopped from later arguing that the contract should have been performed by the other party at the originally agreed upon date.[51] Once such waiver has occurred, the time within which the contract must be performed becomes "a reasonable time".[52] However, a vexed question has arisen, in cases in which the original time for performance was waived and a new date fixed. Does the alteration of the due time for performance result in time still being of the essence of the contract (that is, the original terms subsist and bind the parties, subject only to the substitution of a new date for the old one), or does the change of date result in time no longer being of the essence?

Two views may be discovered in the English and Canadian cases. One line of authority,[53] which includes a decision of the Supreme Court of Canada, holds

---

47 Fridman, *op. cit.*, above, note 38, at pp. 226-227, 258-259. See, *e.g.*, *Charles Rickards Ltd. v. Oppenheim*, [1950] 1 K.B. 616 (C.A.); *Lasby v. Walsh*, [1920] 1 W.W.R. 1027 (Sask. C.A.); *Mooney v. Lipka*, [1926] 3 W.W.R. 391 (Sask. C.A.).

48 See, *e.g.*, *Beaton v. Cooper*, [1938] 1 W.W.R. 604 (Sask. C.A.) (sale of shares); *Elec. Power Equip. Ltd. v. R.C.A. Victor Co.* (1964), 49 W.W.R. 193 (B.C.C.A.) (contract for work done and materials supplied); *Canwest Pacific Television Inc. v. 147250 Can. Ltd.*, above, note 45, where time was held not to be of the essence, therefore the defendant could not resist a decree of specific performance. Contrast *Howe Richardson Inc. v. Nfld. Scale Co.* (1990), 41 C.L.R. 175 (Nfld. T.D.), where the time for delivery of an instruction package to go with the goods being supplied was held to be of the essence; therefore, defendant was entitled to cancel the contract and was not in breach (although he was liable on other grounds).

49 *Campbell v. Sovereign Securities & Holdings Co.* (1958), 13 D.L.R. (2d) 195 (Ont. H.C.); affirmed (1958), 16 D.L.R. (2d) 606 (Ont. C.A.); compare *Centurian Ridge Farms Ltd. v. Boyle* (1978), 90 D.L.R. (3d) 649 (Alta. T.D.).

50 *Dufferin Const. Co. v. Thorold*, [1929] 4 D.L.R. 132 (S.C.C.). If there is no waiver then there will be liability: *McCaig v. Nimmo*, above, note 37. The passage from "Even where time is of the essence" to "breach of contract" was quoted by McDermid J. in *Pearson v. Keating* (1992), 56 O.A.C. 398 at 399 (Ont. Div. Ct.).

51 *Lowe v. Englestad* (1977), 16 A.R. 15 (Alta. T.D.). On waiver and estoppel, see below, pp. 545-549.

52 *Lowe v. Englestad, ibid.*; *Dixon v. Wiebe*, [1979] 3 W.W.R. 354 (Sask. Q.B.).

53 *Barclay v. Messenger* (1874), 30 L.T. 351; *Bogue Elec. Ltd. v. Crothers Mfg. Ltd.*, [1961] S.C.R. 108 (S.C.C.).

that despite a change of date for performance time still remains of the essence. Another, which also includes a decision of the Supreme Court of Canada,[54] suggests that once the date for performance is changed time is no longer of the essence. These opposing viewpoints were discussed in *Landbank Minerals Ltd. v. Wesgew Enterprises Ltd.*[55] In a sale of land time was stipulated to be of the essence. The purchaser agreed to the postponement of the original closing date to a specified later date. The vendor failed to satisfy the purchaser's title requirements by the new date. The purchaser gave notice of termination, under the terms of the contract, and requested the return of its deposit. The vendor refused, arguing that time was no longer of the essence once the time for closing had been extended. The purchaser sued to recover the deposit, and was successful. The difference of opinion referred to above was resolved by the argument that there was a possible distinction between mercantile contracts and others, for example, contracts for the purchase of land otherwise than as an investment. Furthermore, the effect of an extension of the period within which a contract was to be performed on the issue of the essentiality of time depended upon the circumstances of the case. Thus, there might be different consequences depending upon the type of contract and its factual context.[56]

Where the original time for performance has been changed, the parties can bilaterally agree that time is to be of the essence with respect to the new time. Moreover, one party can unilaterally make time of the essence again, when a new date is determined, as long as sufficient and clear notice of this is given to the other party.[57] Hence, in *Rados v. Poconla Investments Ltd.*,[58] the purchaser under a contract of sale of land could successfully sue for specific performance, despite the vendor's attempt to withdraw from the contract. Although time had been of the essence of the contract, both parties allowed the date for completion to pass. The vendor's solicitor later telephoned the purchaser's solicitor and stated that unless the contract was closed within one day the vendor would withdraw. The purchaser did not do anything to satisfy this demand for three days, and claimed that the vendor's unilateral attempt to reintroduce the essentiality of time should not be successful. His argument was accepted. The vendor was in default, but the purchaser had waived that default. Hence the purchaser was entitled to sufficient notice that time was to be of the essence in the future, failing which he had a reasonable time within which to complete, meaning a reasonable time after he was asked to complete by the vendor. The notice given by the vendor was not sufficient. It should have been in writing. Moreover it gave the purchaser too short a time within which to comply, and that made the vendor's act unreasonable.

The common-law position must be compared with the approach taken by courts of equity prior to the reorganization of the English courts in 1873. Equity was prepared to be more flexible with regard to time of performance, especially in

---

54 *Hanson v. Cameron*, [1949] S.C.R. 101 (S.C.C.), interpreting *Kilmer v. B.C. Orchard Lands Ltd.*, [1913] A.C. 319 (P.C.), as explained in *Steedman v. Drinkle*, [1916] 1 A.C. 275 (C.A.).

55 [1981] 5 W.W.R. 524 (Alta. Q.B.).

56 *Ibid.*, at 535.

57 *Beacon Indust. Dev. Corp. v. G.C. Farm Supply Ltd.* (1981), 123 D.L.R. (3d) 467 (Alta. Q.B.).

58 (1981), 20 R.P.R. 154 (B.C.S.C.).

relation to contracts for the sale of land, where specific performance was being requested.[59] But time might still be of the essence, even in equity, where it was expressly or by implication made so by the language or conduct of the parties. Hence, the contract and its subject-matter might well involve that time was of the essence of performance even in equity.[60] The result of statutory provisions stemming from the English Judicature Act of 1873, under which the equitable rules as to time became effective in law as well as equity,[61] meant that where equity would disregard a stipulation as to time being of the essence, the same might be done at law, and where equity would not be involved, because the contract could not be specifically enforced in equity, then time might well be essential, at least if it were so stated. The relationship between law and equity, with special reference to the problem of time being of the essence of a contract, was considered at length by the House of Lords in *United Scientific Holdings v. Burnley Borough Council.*[62] Although the actual point in issue in that case, which concerned rent review clauses in leases, might not be relevant in the Canadian context, the comments made on the subject of timely performance of contracts are material, since Canadian legislation has copied the provisions of the English statutes that were under discussion by the House of Lords. The attitude of the House of Lords was that, since the fusion of law and equity under the statutes, it was incorrect to approach the subject of time from different perspectives. The correct way to deal with stipulations as to time in a contract was with reference to the nature of the stipulation, as was the case with all contractual terms.[63] The effect of a stipulation as to time, and its breach, depended on the kind of term involved. In the words of Lord Simon of Glaisdale[64]

> The law may well come to enquire whether a contractual stipulation as to time is (a) so fundamental to the efficacy of the contract that any breach discharges the other party from his contractual obligations ('essence'), or (b) such that a serious breach discharges the other party, a less serious breach giving a right to damages (if any) (or interest), or (c) such that no breach does more than give a right to damges (if any) (or interest) ('non-essential').

This is the result of the more sophisticated approach to contractual terms that has evolved since 1875. On this analysis, it should no longer be necessary to examine the state of the law prior to 1875 at law and in equity, thereafter applying the

---

59 *Stickney v. Keeble*, [1915] A.C. 386 (H.L.).

60 See, *e.g., Lock v. Bell*, [1931] 1 Ch. 35; *Hare v. Nicholl*, [1966] 1 All E.R. 285 (C.A.); compare *Focal Properties Ltd. v. George Wimpey Can. Ltd.* (1974), 6 O.R. (2d) 3 (Ont. H.C.); affirmed (1975), 14 O.R. (2d) 295 (Ont. C.A.); affirmed [1978] 1 S.C.R. 2 (S.C.C.).

61 See, the Judicature Act, R.S.A. 1980, c. J-1, s. 22; R.S.N.B. 1973, c. J-2, s. 32; R.S.N. 1990, c. J-4, s. 104; R.S.N.S. 1989, c. 240, s. 43(8); Queen's Bench Act, R.S.S. 1978, c. Q-1, s. 45 ¶6; Law and Equity Act, R.S.B.C. 1979, c. 224, s. 27; Judicature Act, R.S.N.W.T. 1988, c. J-1, s. 39; R.S.Y.T. 1986, c. 96, s. 24; compare Courts of Justice Act, R.S.O. 1990, c. C.43, s. 96; Supreme Court Act, R.S.P.E.I. 1988, c. S-10, s. 29.

62 [1977] 2 All E.R. 62 (H.L.).

63 Above, pp. 487-503.

64 Above, note 62, at 86.

disparate principles to modern circumstances. The proper approach is to determine the parties' agreement as to time from the standpoint of modern views on the nature and effect of the terms of a contract.

3. Tender

A party need not perform when he has offered to do so and that offer has been rejected by the other party to the contract.[65] This will be so, at any rate, when the tender of performance was within the terms of the contract, and the party who rejected the proffered performance had no legitimate ground for so doing. Thus, wrongful repudiation by the party entitled to performance discharges the party obliged to perform. This will not be the case, however, where the obligation is to pay money. While tender of payment will render the party so tendering not in breach of the duty to pay (which might have led to a claim in damages exceeding the amount of payment being available to the payee), it will not excuse him from the obligation to pay. What amounts to tender of payment? There must be an unqualified proffering of the specific sum required under the contract.[66] But to tender a certified cheque is not to tender the price to be paid under the contract. However, if no objection is taken to the form of the tender, the creditor must be taken to have waived his right to legal tender.[67] There is no need for tender where an offer to pay has been made and rejected or refused by the offeree. In such circumstances, the offeree has repudiated the agreement in pursuance of which the offer to pay has been made, and this will be much the same as where delivery of goods, etc., has been proffered and rejected.[68]

4. Dependency of performance

Performance by one party may be dependent not only upon satisfaction of, or approval by the other party, but upon some performance by that other party.[69] The obligation on A may not arise or accrue until the fulfilment of some obligation that is on B. Sometimes those obligations may be concurrent, as with delivery of

65 *Startup v. Macdonald* (1843), 134 E.R. 1029. But there may be no obligation to tender until the other party has done something, *e.g.*, prepared a conveyance and submitted it to the purchaser for approval: *Blackstock v. Jeamen Farms Ltd.* (1982), 13 Sask. R. 119 (Sask. C.A.). In *Boxer v. Nowan Properties Ltd.* (1986), 33 D.L.R. (4th) 150 (B.C.S.C.); affirmed (1988), 52 D.L.R. (4th) 667 (B.C.C.A.), the defendant unsuccessfully argued that in the circumstances the exercise of an option to purchase shares was not proper without the simultaneous tender of the purchase price.
66 *B.C. Land & Invt. Agency v. Ishitaka* (1911), 45 S.C.R. 302 (S.C.C.); *Mus v. Matlashewski*, [1944] 3 W.W.R. 358 (Man. C.A.). Note the debtor's duty to tender the precise amount; change *need not* be given by the creditor: *Robinson v. Cook* (1815), 6 Taunt. 336.
67 *Murray v. Smith* (1980), 32 Nfld. & P.E.I.R. 191 (P.E.I.S.C.); affirmed (1981), 35 Nfld. & P.E.I.R. 382 (P.E.I.C.A.).
68 *Mackiw v. Rutherford*, [1921] 2 W.W.R. 329 (Man. K.B.).
69 This sentence was quoted by Angers J.A. in *Cameron Auctioneers & Appraisers Ltd. v. G.R. Galbraith Supplies* (1988), 47 D.L.R. (4th) 141 at 145 (N.B.C.A.).

goods and payment of the purchase price under the Sale of Goods Act.[70] Hence, the defendant was justified in not performing his contractual obligation in *McColl-Frontenac Oil Co. v. Angel*,[71] because the plaintiff had not obtained a hoist as required on his part. Similarly, in *White v. Big River Sports & Equipment Ltd.*,[72] the buyer of a business was entitled to refuse to complete the transaction, and to sue for damages, because the seller had failed to provide an accountant's certificate showing that the company being sold had not been materially affected. In *Chaulk v. Fairview Construction Ltd.*,[73] the builder could not complain that the purchaser of the duplexes which the builder was to construct had repudiated the contract, by failing to obtain the agreed financial provision, because the builder was himself at fault in failing or refusing to complete the contract. Nor, in *Mattila Agencies Ltd. v. Bartkewich*,[74] could the real estate broker claim his commission, when he failed to fulfil an obligation that was placed on him by the contract (although the vendor, the broker's principal, by accepting a counter-offer had waived a condition of the contract, and therefore had performed his obligations). In contrast the defendant in *Conwest Exploration Co. v. Letain*[75] had fulfilled his part of the contractual bargain by creating and incorporating the company as intended by the parties; hence, the plaintiffs had no right to the return of a claim held by them under option, nor to the transfer of other claims staked by the defendant. But in *Kagan v. McLachlan*,[76] where a guarantor of a company's debts to a bank promised to pay off the company's debts from the purchase price obtained in the sale of the company, the failure to pay off the debts was so serious that the bank and the purchaser of the company were entitled to terminate their contracts.

What is involved in such instances is the fulfilment of a condition precedent imposed upon one party prior to performance of the other party's obligations.[77] Such conditions precedent are to be distinguished from what have been referred to as "true" conditions precedent, which must be satisfied before a contract can

---

70 Fridman, *Sale of Goods in Canada*, 3rd ed. (1986), pp. 226, 257. So, too, where there is a duty to open or establish a credit on behalf of the other party before delivery of goods: *Nfld. Associated Fish Exporters Ltd. v. A.T. Karelas* (1963), 49 M.P.R. 49 (Nfld. S.C.); *Trans. Trust S.P.R.L. v. Danubian Trading Co.*, [1952] 2 Q.B. 297 (C.A.). Compare also, in another context, *Sherkin v. Winchell* (1982), 37 O.R. (2d) 97 (Ont. C.A.).

71 [1948] 3 D.L.R. 554 (Man. C.A.).

72 (1980), 28 N.B.R. (2d) 308 (N.B.C.A.). Compare *Combitech Medical Inc. v. B.C. Cancer Foundation* (1988), 18 B.C.L.R. (2d) 308 (B.C.C.A.).

73 (1977), 14 Nfld. & P.E.I.R. 13 (Nfld. C.A.).

74 (1983), 19 Sask. R. 257 (Sask. Q.B.). Compare *Maritime Couriers (Int.) Inc. v. Woodstock Int. Export Ltd.* (1986), 33 B.L.R. 309 (B.C.S.C.).

75 [1964] S.C.R. 20 (S.C.C.); and see *Can. Terminal System Ltd. v. Kingston*, [1936] S.C.R. 106 (S.C.C.).

76 (1989), 60 Man. R. (2d) 248 (Man. Q.B.).

77 This sentence was quoted by Angers J.A. in *Cameron Auctioneers & Appraisers Ltd. v. G.R. Galbraith Supplies*, above, note 69, at 145. For an illustration of the non-performance of such a condition precedent, see *Fletton Ltd. v. Peat Marwick Ltd.* (1986), 32 B.L.R. 162 (B.C.S.C.); affirmed (1988), 50 D.L.R. (4th) 729 (B.C.C.A.); leave to appeal to S.C.C. refused (1988), 50 D.L.R. (4th) vii (note) (S.C.C.).

be held to be valid and binding upon the parties.[78] If the condition precedent is of the other kind, that is, an ordinary or internal condition of the contract, one of its terms,[79] or, putting this another way, part of the consideration for the contract,[80] it may be satisfied, or its performance waived by the party entitled to its benefit, unilaterally, without the assent of the other party.[81] When either of these eventualities occurs, the other party's duty to perform arises for satisfaction. Unilateral waiver is not permitted of "true" conditions precedent (although there are other ways to circumvent the strict nature of such provisions[82]).

This straightforward situation with respect to internal conditions precedent, those which relate to performance, and not to the validity or existence of the contract, is affected by two possibilities. The first is where the party obliged by such condition makes it impossible for the condition to be fulfilled or performed.[83] When that occurs such party cannot plead that the other party was in default in not performing his side of the bargain.[84] Nor can he claim that the contract is discharged by reason of the failure of such other party to perform, the inability of that party to perform, or the inutility of that party's performance. The party preventing the fulfilment of the condition precedent is the party in default, and liable accordingly.[85] Second, if fulfilment of the condition precedent is prevented by a "frustrating" act or event,

---

78 Above, pp. 437-441. Such a condition precedent may be implied: *Osesky v. Wolfman; Wolfman v. McCaffery; Osesky v. Starr* (1982), 15 Man. R. (2d) 263 (Man. Q.B.). For examples of situations where the condition precedent was held to be a "true" condition precedent in the *Turney v. Zhilka* sense, see *Sim v. Large* (1981), 22 B.C.L.R. 278 (B.C.S.C.); *King v. Holsmer* (1982), 44 N.B.R. (2d) 290 (N.B.T.D.); *McCaig v. Nimmo* (1987), 85 N.B.R. (2d) 132 (N.B.Q.B.).

79 *White v. Big River Sports & Equipment Ltd.*, above, note 72 at 310 *per* Limerick J.A.

80 *Inkster v. Waite* (1980), 22 B.C.L.R. 213 (B.C.C.A.).

81 In *Pizzo v. Crory* (1986), 71 N.S.R. (2d) 419 (N.S.T.D.), waiver was implied from the conduct of those shareholders who consistently ignored a clause requiring unanimous consent for certain expenditures. See also *Dolan v. Patton* (1986), 75 N.S.R. (2d) 399 (N.S.T.D.), where the plaintiff waived the obligation of the defendant to care for the plaintiff. For an historical discussion, see Beck, "The Doctrine of Substantial Performance: Conditions and Conditions Precedent" (1975), 38 M.L.R. 413 at pp. 416-419.

82 Above, pp. 441-446.

83 See, *e.g.*, *Burchell v. Gowrie & Blockhouse Collieries Ltd.*, [1910] A.C. 614 (P.C.) (principal himself selling property, thereby making it impossible for agent to earn commission); *Alexander Hamilton Institute v. McNally* (1919), 53 N.S.R. 303 (N.S.C.A.) (defendant failing to complete course in which he had enrolled, liable for outstanding fees, as the defendant was responsible for his non-attendance); contrast *Hyland v. Harrison* (1915), 49 N.S.R. 75 (N.S.C.A.). See also *Meeker v. Nicola Valley Lbr. Co.* (1917), 55 S.C.R. 494 (S.C.C.); leave to appeal to Privy Council refused (1918), 55 S.C.R. vii, with which contrast *Kohler v. Thorold Natural Gas Co.* (1916), 52 S.C.R. 514 (S.C.C.); leave to appeal to Privy Council refused (1916), 52 S.C.R. vii.

84 *Nunnelly v. Onsum* (1921), 56 D.L.R. 599 (Alta. C.A.); *Inchbald v. Western Neilgherry Coffee, Tea & Cinchona Plantation Co.* (1866), 17 C.B.N.S. 733. Compare *McDonald v. Bell; Randall v. Bell* (1965), 53 W.W.R. 449 (B.C.S.C.); *Boone v. R.*, [1936] S.C.R. 457 (S.C.C.); *Turnbull v. Eden*, [1929] 4 D.L.R. 261 (B.C.C.A.).

85 Hence the importance of deciding whose fault caused the inability of a party to perform in *Rich v. Nor. America Lbr. Co.* (1913), 17 D.L.R. 25 (B.C.C.A.). For the situation with respect to such contracts where the condition precedent is a "true" condition precedent, see above, pp. 443-446.

beyond the control of the party bound by the condition, the parties are excused from performance.[86]

Leaving these possibilities aside, two issues must be mentioned. The first is the effect of a failure by one party to perform his anterior or concurrent obligation.[87] This has been said to be not a question of interpretation of the contract, but of performance, or the effect of non-performance, of the contract. Hence the party who has performed his obligations may sue the one who has not.[88] But it has been said that a party who seeks to recover from the party who has not performed must show that he, the plaintiff, was always ready, willing and able to perform his concurrent obligation, in a situation in which the mutual obligations are concurrent rather than anterior and posterior.[89] However, there are problems and uncertainties about this where what has occurred is not merely a failure to perform a concurrent or anterior obligation, but amounts to a repudiation by the party entitled to performance before the party obliged to perform, for example, by delivering goods, has actually performed or tendered performance.[90]

Prima facie, repudiation by one party entitles the other to treat the contract as at an end, and unquestionably excuses him from further performance of his obligations thereunder, if he so desires.[91] As was said by McLennan J.A. in *Tanenbaum v. Wright-Winston Ltd.*,[92]

> . . . where one party repudiates a contract by making it clear to the other party that he will not perform his obligation the other party has a choice. He may accept the repudiation, and, if he chooses, sue for damages for breach or he may disregard the repudiation and the contract remains in full force. Repudiation by one party does not terminate the contract. Termination requires repudiation by one party and acceptance of the repudiation by the other.

---

86 Below, Chapter 16. See *Pilson v. J. Rudell Sales & Services Ltd.* (1980), 5 Sask. R. 272 (Sask. Dist. Ct.). Compare *Boligomsetning AS v. Terpstra Management Ltd.* (1989), 42 B.L.R. 252 (Nfld. T.D.), performance of contract frustrated by poor weather.

87 Failure must be distinguished from mere delay in performance: *Dallas v. Dallas Oil Co.*, [1930] 2 D.L.R. 788 (Alta. C.A.); affirmed [1931] S.C.R. 220 (S.C.C.); compare *Unified Systems Ltd. v. Clearwater Lobsters Ltd.* (1986), 58 Nfld. & P.E.I.R. 138 (Nfld. T.D.), where delays did not entitle a party to repudiate the contract. On delay see above, pp. 526-529.

88 *Brunt v. Fairley; Birge v. Fairley*, [1955] O.W.N. 248 (Ont. H.C.); affirmed [1955] 5 D.L.R. 102 (Ont. C.A.). Or he may recover money paid to that other party on the ground of total failure of consideration: *Nyle Int. Corp. v. Depow* (1991), 113 N.B.R. (2d) 91 (N.B.Q.B.); affirmed (1991), 120 N.B.R. (2d) 176 (N.B.C.A.). Or recover property that was given to the defendant in return for a payment that was never made: *Opi Ltd. v. Harway Industrial Enterprises Ltd.* (1986), 44 Alta. L.R. (2d) 122 (Alta. M.C.).

89 *Forrestt & Son Ltd. v. Aramayo* (1900), 83 L.T. 335 (C.A.); *Stuart & Co. v. Clarke*, [1917] 2 W.W.R. 1049 (Alta. C.A.).

90 Compare Fridman, *Sale of Goods in Canada*, 3rd ed. (1986), pp. 276-277, and cases there cited. See also Dawson, "Waiver of Conditions Precedent on Repudiation" (1980), 96 L.Q.R. 239. See also below, pp. 616-617.

91 As to what amounts to repudiation, compare *Can. Egg Products Ltd. v. Can. Doughnut Co.*, [1955] S.C.R. 398 (S.C.C.); *Elec. Power Equip. Ltd. v. R.C.A. Victor Co.* (1964), 49 W.W.R. 193 (B.C.C.A.). On repudiation generally, see below, pp. 600-622.

92 (1965), 49 D.L.R. (2d) 386 at 392 (Ont. C.A.), citing and relying on *Heyman v. Darwins Ltd.*, [1942] A.C. 356 (H.L.); *White & Carter (Councils) Ltd. v. McGregor*, [1962] A.C. 413 (H.L.).

Thus the non-repudiating party *may* elect to be excused from further performance, by treating the contract as at an end. The question that has caused some vexation in the courts, and does not appear to have been resolved, in England or Canada, is whether, in the event of a repudiation that is accepted by the other party, if such party sues for non-performance, the party suing has to establish that he was ready, willing and able to perform *his* obligations with respect to performance, notwithstanding the repudiation in question. In other words, does repudiation by party A amount to a "waiver" by A of the performance by party B of whatever conditions or duties of performance the contract imposes on party B? The whole question, including the precise and true nature of the "conditions" which operate on the party not repudiating, is subject to conflict, ambiguity, and confusion. This is unfortunate, since the resolution of this issue is vital for the clarification of the extent to which a party who has not performed his side of the bargain may nonetheless claim the benefit of the contract and sue the other party for non-performance in the event of that party's wrongful repudiation of the contract.[93]

The second issue raised by the doctrine of dependency of performance, that is, the interrelationship of conditions, is the effect of a partial or incomplete performance by one party of his obligations under the contract. Generally speaking, non-performance in accordance with the terms of the contract, besides being a breach of contract in itself[94] (unless excused on some basis, for example, frustration), precludes the party guilty of such non-performance from enforcing the contract against the other party. Thus, a party who has not performed will be unable to sue the other party for any alleged breach of the contract, for example, non-payment of money due thereunder. If the refusal to pay is by reason of the plaintiff's failure to perform in the manner contemplated by the contract, for example, the defendant will not be liable.[95] This raises the whole question of what has been called

---

93 Below, pp. 615-618.

94 See, *e.g., Winsco Mfg. Co. v. Raymond Distributing Co.* (1957), 10 D.L.R. (2d) 699 (Ont. H.C.); *Yukon Gold Co. v. Can. Klondyke Power Co.* (1919), 47 D.L.R. 146 (B.C.C.A.); *Exchanger Industries Ltd. v. Dominion Bridge Co.* (1986), 69 A.R. 22 (Alta. Q.B.); *Clareview Rental Project (Edmonton) Ltd. v. Dockery* (1990), 78 Alta. L.R. (2d) 106 (Alta. Q.B.). The guilty party may also have to forfeit a deposit given to ensure performance: *Sprague v. Booth,* [1909] A.C. 576 (P.C.); *Howe v. Smith* (1884), 27 Ch. D. 89 (C.A.). But a part-payment may be recovered even by a party in default: *Bradley Bros. (Oshawa) Ltd. v. A to Z Rental Can. Ltd.,* [1973] 1 O.R. 823 (Ont. H.C.); reversed on other grounds (1974), 3 O.R. (2d) 766 (Ont. C.A.); compare *Mitchell v. Agrai-Dairy Mart Ltd.* (1984), 54 A.R. 368 (Alta. Q.B.). As to the unlikelihood of equitable relief from the forfeiture of a deposit, see *Monarch Timber Exporters Ltd. v. Bell* (1963), 41 D.L.R. (2d) 535 (B.C.C.A.); affirmed [1964] S.C.R. 375 (S.C.C.). See also below, pp. 774-775.

95 *Blome v. Regina,* [1920] 1 W.W.R. 311 (Sask. K.B.) (retention of 10 per cent of price of work done, until repairs completed by contractor); *Dryden Const. Co. v. H.E.P.C. of Ont.,* [1958] O.W.N. 349 (Ont. C.A.); affirmed [1960] S.C.R. 694 (S.C.C.) (non-performance of contract to build a road); *Howell v. Ridge View Dev. & Holdings Co.* (1987), 53 Alta. L.R. (2d) 337 (Alta. C.A.) (failure to build home by stipulated date). Contrast *Canwest Pacific Television Inc. v. 147250 Can. Ltd.* (1987), 14 B.C.L.R. (2d) 338 (B.C.S.C.); affirmed (1989), 30 B.C.L.R. (2d) 145 (B.C.C.A.) (defendant liable to decree of specific performance because time was not of the essence, therefore the plaintiff was not guilty of non-performance).

"substantial" performance, and the problem of entire and divisible, or non-entire, contracts.

5. Incomplete performance[96]

(a) Introductory

The common law stated that complete performance of a contractual obligation was necessary before the party under the duty to perform could require payment of the contract price that was promised in return for performance. Nor could the party obliged to perform obtain any payment on a contractual or other basis, for example, by suing upon a *quantum meruit*, in respect of that part of the work or other performance actually completed. The first propostion goes back to the old case of *Pordage v. Cole* in 1669, or perhaps, more accurately, to the note on that case by Serjeant Williams, in his edition of Saunders Reports, which appeared at the end of the eighteenth century,[97] about the same time as the leading case of *Cutter v. Powell.*[98] The second proposition is supported by *Cutter v. Powell* itself, in which the estate of the seaman who did not finish the voyage was unable to claim for the work he did on that part of the voyage before he died. It is also justified, doctrinally, by the argument that where there is an express contract between the parties, it is impossible to imply *another* contract with conflicting terms. Thus, where a contract should have been in writing under the Statute of Frauds,[99] it was not possible for the plaintiff to claim on *quantum meruit* for the work he had done in performance of the contract, throwing aside the express contract and suing on an implied one in its place. This decision, in *Britain v. Rossiter,*[100] may not now be followed in respect of contracts under the Statute of Frauds,[101] but the theoretical reason for denying recovery in such a case would still seem to apply to the problem currently under discussion. This was the reason why in *Sumpter v. Hedges*[102] the plaintiff was refused *quantum meruit* in respect of that part of the work that he had finished prior to his abandonment of the contract (even though the defendant adopted his work, as it were, by completing it). However, it was suggested that a *quantum meruit* claim in such circumstances might be permitted where the defendant was given an option to take or not take the benefit of the work actually done. This involves the substitution of a new agreement, in place of the original

---

96 Waddams, "Restitution for the Part Performer", in Reiter & Swan, *Studies in Contract Law*, p. 151.

97 (1669), 1 Wms. Saund. 319, 85 E.R. 449.

98 (1795), 6 Term Rep. 320. For more modern examples, see *Bank of N.S. v. Guenette; Guenette Holdings Ltd. v. Bank of N.S.* (1986), 68 A.R. 368 (Alta. Q.B.); *Opi Ltd. v. Harway Industrial Enterprises Ltd.* (1986), 44 Alta. L.R. (2d) 122 (Alta. M.C.).

99 Above, pp. 209-218.

100 (1879), 11 Q.B.D. 123 (C.A.).

101 See, *e.g., Delgman v. Guar. Trust Co.,* [1954] S.C.R. 725 (S.C.C.); Waddams, *loc. cit.,* above, note 96 at pp. 169-174. See also Fridman, "Reflections on Restitution" (1976), 8 Ottawa L.R. 156; Fridman, *Restitution,* 2nd ed. (1992), pp. 163-165; 303-305.

102 [1898] 1 Q.B. 673 (C.A.); approved in *Lacroix Bros. & Co. v. Cook,* [1926] 4 D.L.R. 747 (Sask. C.A.).

one. Hence, there are not two conflicting contracts alleged to exist simultaneously, but the replacement of the first one by the new, and inconsistent contract. That is permissible.

The foundation for this attitude by the common law was the idea that the consideration for the promise to pay was complete performance; the promise to pay was dependent upon the performance of the duty to do the work.[103] If an *independent* promise could be established, for example, payment in any event, the situation would be different. Earlier willingness by the courts to construe promises as independent gave way, by the time of Lord Mansfield, to the view that promises were more likely than not dependent, unless something to the contrary could clearly be shown.[104] However, the courts appear to have been willing, in appropriate circumstances, to find that, while the promises were mutually dependent, complete performance of the duty to do the work promised had been "waived" by the subsequent conduct of the party entitled to the benefit of the performance. In such a situation, he was bound to pay, because no longer was he able to insist on performance of the contract in its original form.[105] Thus, there emerged two distinct possibilities for avoiding the harsh, and in some ways unjust consequences of the doctrine of *Pordage v. Cole* and *Cutter v. Powell.* First, a new contract; second waiver of an obligation in the original one.[106] Other ways around the strict rule also developed. Of these perhaps the most important were, and still are: (1) the distinction between entire and divisible contracts; and (2) the doctrine of substantial performance.[107]

(b) Divisible contracts

As early as *Cutter v. Powell* the courts were prepared to accept that some contracts might be treated differently. It if were possible, to "sever" one party's promise from performance of the other party's promise, then performance of the latter was not to be treated as a "condition precedent" of performance of the latter. Of course, the problem is to determine whether in any given instance the intention of the parties was that performance should be entire or the contractual promises can be regarded as separate, divisible, and independent of each other. This happened

---

103 Other reasons were given from time to time, *e.g.*: commercial morality; allocation of risk; the extent of the loss suffered by the innocent. Waddams, *loc. cit.*, above, note 96 at pp. 163-169.

104 *Boone v. Eyre* (1779), 1 Hy. Bl. 273, 126 E.R. 160; *Kingston v. Preston* (1773), 2 Doug. K.B. 689. See also *Duke of St. Albans v. Shore* (1789), 1 Hy. Bl. 270; *Goodisson v. Nunn* (1792), 4 Term. Rep. 761; *Glazebrook v. Woodrow* (1799), 8 Term Rep. 366; *Davidson v. Gwynne* (1810), 12 East. 381.

105 *Ellen v. Topp* (1851), 6 Ex. 424, 155 E.R. 609; *Graves v. Legg* (1854), 9 Ex. 709, 156 E.R. 304; *Carter v. Scargill* (1875), L.R. 10 Q.B. 564.

106 Waddams, *loc. cit.*, above, note 96 at pp. 153-163.

107 Note also the change effected by the Apportionment Act, 1870 (33 & 34 Vict.) c. 35, which permits recovery where payments are intended to be "periodical". This legislation was first introduced in England in 1870. But it may not apply in all provinces: see R.S.N. 1990, c. A-11; R.S.N.S. 1989, c. 16; R.S.P.E.I. 1988, c. A-14; R.S.M. 1987, c. A100; R.S.O. 1990, c. A.23.

in the English case of *Roberts v. Havelock*,[108] in which a contract to repair a ship was held to be divisible, so as to permit the shipwright to recover payment for what he had done before he abandoned the contract, even though the contract required him to put the ship "into through repair". That case was followed in Canada in *Hanson v. Parks*,[109] in which it was said that it was a question of fact whether a party was entitled to payment for work actually done prior to the completion of the whole contract. The court, distinguishing *Cutter v. Powell*, allowed the plaintiff to recover for work done thus far. On the other hand in *Brown v. R.*[110] the doctrine of *Cutter v. Powell* was followed. A contract provided that one half of the fee payable to the plaintiff was to be paid to him on completion of the plans and specifications for the building that was to be construed. Notwithstanding this provision, it was held that the contract was an entire, not a divisible or severable contract. In consequence, the plaintiff could claim for the remainder of the money when the contract was wrongfully terminated by the defendants.[111]

A further category was developed by the courts, that of so-called "lump-sum" contracts, where the contract provided for the payment of a specified sum on completion of the work to be performed, and not before. In one English case, *Hoenig v. Isaacs*,[112] a distinction was drawn between such contracts and entire contracts. More recently, the court in *Bolton v. Mahadeva*[113] purported to coalesce these two categories, so that all lump-sum contracts should be regarded as entire. But it would seem, from the decision of a Canadian court in *McGregor & McIntyre Co. v. Sterling Appraisal Co.*,[114] that even where the contract is a lump-sum contract, if the contractor is negligent in the course of performing the contract, the plaintiff for whom the work is being done may sue for such negligence, and it is no answer that the work has not yet been completed so as to preclude any rights prior to such time.

(c) Substantial performance

Alongside this differentiation between entire and severable, divisible or non-entire contracts, the courts produced the doctrine that even where the contract was entire, if it had been "substantially" performed, the party so performing could obtain payment in respect of what had been completed. This, in its modern form,

---

108 (1832), 3 B. & Ad. 464; compare *Bulton v. Thompson* (1869), L.R. 4 C.P. 330.

109 [1925] 3 D.L.R. 1103 (N.B.C.A.).

110 [1939] Ex. C.R. 252 (Ex. Ct.).

111 Compare *Nugent v. Midland Doherty Ltd.* (1989), 65 D.L.R. (4th) 694 (B.C.C.A.) (no claim for part of promised bonus, since its payment was dependent on an entire year's work: see also *La Plante v. Kinnon* (1915), 21 D.L.R. 293 (Sask. C.A.); *Pimlott v. Marbridge Invts. Ltd.* (1967), 61 D.L.R. (2d) 309 (B.C.C.A.).

112 [1952] 2 All E.R. 176 (C.A.).

113 [1972] 2 All E.R. 1322 (C.A.); compare *Mitchell v. To-Co Const. Ltd.* (1983), 2 C.L.R. 301 (Alta. Q.B.).

114 [1925] 4 D.L.R. 211 (Ont. C.A.); compare *House Repair & Service Co. v. Miller* (1921), 49 O.L.R. 205 (Ont. C.A.); *Fisher v. Cox* (1921), 54 N.S.R. 226 (N.S.C.A.).

stems from the English decision in *Dakin & Co. v. Lee*,[115] which was given approval and perhaps clarification or extension by the Court of Appeal in the subsequent case of *Hoenig v. Isaacs*.[116] From these decisions it would appear that a party is not relieved from payment for what has actually been done, unless: (1) he has obtained no benefit at all; (2) the work done is totally different from the work contracted to be done; or (3) the contractor abandoned the work before completion (unless, of course, there were some subsequent waiver or express agreement to the contrary, or, in modern law, performance or completion of performance were frustrated).[117] The cost of completing the work is relevant, but not decisive; nor is the extent of the defects, in the sense that only trifling lapses will excuse.

These principles have been followed in Canadian cases.[118] Thus in *Yakowchuk v. Crawford*,[119] it was held that there could be no payment for what the contractor had done, where the contract was an entire contract for work and labour not substantially carried out, or the contractor had refused to complete. *Quantum meruit* would not lie. A leading decision of the Supreme Court of Canada is *Fairbanks Soap Co. v. Sheppard*,[120] in which the defendant agreed to construct in the plant of the plaintiff, a soap manufacturer, a machine to make soap chips. When the work was nearly completed, the defendant refused to continue until he had received further payment from the plaintiff. The subsequent litigation involved, *inter alia*, a claim by the defendant for payment in respect of so much of the work as had been done. It was held that what had occurred was a deliberate abandonment by the defendant of the contract before he had substantially completed it, since the machine would not do the work for which it was being constructed. In those circumstances, it was held that the defendant's claim for payment failed.

Abandonment of the contract will therefore deprive the party obliged to perform of any right to payment. But it will also entitle the party for whom performance was to be provided of the right to complete the work himself and charge the cost of doing so to the non-performer.[121] However, the cost of making good such defects or omissions must not be unreasonably high in relation to the value to be gained by the expenditure.[122] In *Kemp v. McWilliams*,[123] however, the Saskatchewan Court of Appeal held that a painter who had agreed to paint a house did not abandon the contract when he stopped after finishing the major part of

---

115 [1916] 1 K.B. 566 (C.A.).

116 Above, note 112; both cases were followed by the Supreme Court of Canada in *Miller v. Advanced Farm Systems Ltd.*, [1969] S.C.R. 845 (S.C.C.).

117 This sentence was quoted in *J.F. Markell Homes Ltd. v. Milne* (1986), 22 C.L.R. 1 at 16 (Ont. Dist. Ct.).

118 See, *e.g., Greg Sheaves Const. Co. v. Channel-Port Aux Basques (Town)* (1989), 77 Nfld. & P.E.I.R. 18 (Nfld. T.D.) (the absence of weight scale slips to be provided by the plaintiff under a contract to supply goods did not mean that the contract was not substantially performed; therefore, the defendant was liable for the price).

119 [1917] 3 W.W.R. 479 (Man. K.B.).

120 [1953] 1 S.C.R. 314 (S.C.C.); compare *Taylor Hardware Co. v. Hunt* (1917), 39 O.L.R. 85 (Ont. C.A.); *Bradley v. Horner* (1957), 10 D.L.R. (2d) 446 (Ont. C.A.).

121 *Westlake v. Milosevich* (1983), 56 N.S.R. (2d) 631 (N.S.T.D.).

122 *Nu-West Homes Ltd. v. Thunderbird Petroleums Ltd.* (1975), 59 D.L.R. (3d) 292 (Alta. C.A.).

123 (1978), 87 D.L.R. (3d) 544 (Sask. C.A.).

the work. He was compelled to stop because the owner of the house refused to make further advances of money, which meant that the painter could not afford to purchase materials to complete the work, although he fully intended to do so at a later stage. The court allowed the painter a percentage of the agreed price, representing the percentage of the work completed, but did not grant the owner a counterclaim in respect of what she had spent to have the job finished. Here the work done was of substantial benefit to the owner, and the painter's reason for leaving the work unfinished was not the intention to abandon, but lack of the necessary expenses.

In other cases, however, it has been held that if there is substantial performance, recovery may be obtained for what had been done, less a sum to cover the cost of making good defects and omissions.[124] The question then arises whether the omissions or defects are of such a nature that what has been done does not amount to substantial performance. Such was the conclusion, on the facts, of the Alberta Appellate Division in *Nu-West Homes Ltd. v. Thunderbird Petroleums Ltd.*[125] In another case[126] the same court held that substantial performance was not to be judged solely by the question of the cost of the work done, where the non-performer's breach of contract caused serious loss. In this instance the plaintiff agreed to cut, bale and stack hay on the defendant's land. Cutting and baling were completed within a reasonable time, but the stacking was delayed for so long that the hay substantially deteriorated. After repeatedly asking the plaintiff to stack the hay, the defendant terminated the contract and sold the damaged hay for its salvage value. The plaintiff sued for the price agreed for his services. At the trial he succeeded. The Appellate Division reversed this decision and refused to allow the plaintiff anything. More recently, it has been held that to determine whether substantial performance has taken place, a court is required to look at such matters as: the percentage of completion; the amount of the contract price earned; the quality of the work still to be performed; the availability of qualified workers and equipment to complete the work; and the ease or facility with which the work may be completed.[127] All these factors, in effect, elaborate the view of the Alberta court with respect to the seriousness to the innocent party of the non-performer's failure to complete.

Summing up the situation, incomplete performance will not necessarily deprive the party guilty of failure to perform in accordance with the contract, where: (i) his non-performance was the fault of the other party; (ii) he has substantially performed, in the sense explained earlier; or (iii) the earlier contract has been replaced by a new agreement allowing payment on a *quantum meruit* basis for

---

124 *Fred Pierce Ltd. v. Troke* (1957), 39 M.P.R. 271 (N.S.C.A.); *Miller v. Advanced Farming Systems Ltd.*, [1969] S.C.R. 845 (S.C.C.); *Markland Associates Ltd. v. Lohnes* (1973), 33 D.L.R. (3d) 493 (N.S.T.D.); *Columbia Bithulithic Ltd. v. D.C. Masonry Const. Ltd.* (1981), 27 B.C.L.R. 220 (B.C. C.A.).

125 Above, note 122.

126 *Veregen v. Red Maple Farms Ltd.* (1976), 59 D.L.R. (3d) 221 (Alta. C.A.).

127 *Mitchell v. To-Co Const. Ltd.* (1983), 2 C.L.R. 301 (Alta. Q.B.).

what has actually been done.[128] The present state of the law has been criticized and it is suggested that the doctrine of restitution requires that a party who has done part, though not all of what he promised or undertook to perform, should be entitled to remuneration on a restitutionary basis.[129] However, there are problems connected with the proper assessment of such payment. Should it be on the basis of the benefit conferred on the party for whom performance was promised? Or should it be on the basis of the value of the proportion of the work that has been completed?[130] Furthermore, should there be a distinction between a party who deliberately abandons the contract and one who fails to complete for some reason other than the other party's default or a frustrating event?[131] On the whole, it is suggested, there is much to be said for the present position under the common law, although suggestions for reform have been made in other jurisdictions.[132]

6. Modification of duty to perform

(a) Change of party

(i) *Novation*

This involves the making of a new contract (usually bringing in a new party in place of one of the original parties[133]) in substitution for a contract already existing between the parties.[134] It is not necessary that the new contract should

---

128 This sentence was quoted in *J.F. Markell Homes Ltd. v. Milne* (1986), 22 C.L.R. 1 at 15 (Ont. Dist. Ct.).

129 Waddams, *loc. cit.*, above, note 96, pp. 169-172. See also Mead, "Restitution Within Contract?" (1991), 11 Legal St. 172, discussing the particular situation with respect to contracts of employment. But see Sales, "Contract and Restitution in the Employment Relationship: No Work, No Pay" (1988), 8 Ox. J. Leg. St. 301.

130 Waddams, loc. cit., pp. 172-175.

131 *Ibid.*, pp. 175-177; and see *ibid.*, pp. 177-179 for other suggested limits on this right to restitution.

132 English Law Commission, Working Paper No. 65, *Law of Contract Pecuniary Restitution on Breach of Contract*, 1975; *Restatement of Law of Contracts*, sect. 357; Palmer, *Law of Restitution* Vol. 1, §5.1; Goff & Jones, *Law of Restitution*, 3rd ed. (1986), pp. 680-683.

133 Note the suggestion that there may be novation where a new contract between the *same* parties is entered into: *King v. Solna Offset of Can. Ltd.* (1984), 3 O.A.C. 178 (Ont. C.A.); *R.J. Ferguson Transit Ltd. v. Air Can.* (1984), 64 N.S.R. (2d) 284 (N.S.T.D.). Compare the decision in *Citech Quartz Corp. v. Grassie Jewellers Ltd. (Receiver of)* (1988), 70 C.B.R. (N.S.) 296 (B.C.S.C.).

134 *Jones v. James Burgess & Sons Ltd.* (1910), 39 N.B.R. 603 (N.B.C.A.); *National Trust Co. v. Mead* (1990), 71 D.L.R. (4th) 488 at 500 (S.C.C.) *per* Wilson J. For examples of novation see *Dom. Oilfields Supply Co. v. T.L. Cleary Drilling Co.* (1958), 25 W.W.R. 1 (Alta. C.A.); *Norton-Palmer Hotel Ltd. v. Windsor Utilities Commn.*, [1942] O.R. 170 (Ont. H.C.); *Farquhar v. Zwicker* (1908), 41 S.C.R. 30 (S.C.C.); *L. Murray Truck & Tractor Ltd. v. Baxter* (1979), 37 N.S.R. (2d) 671 (N.S.T.D.). *Sheehy v. Edmonton World Hockey Enterprises Ltd.* (1979), 22 A.R. 1 (Alta. Q.B.); *Franks v. Vanthuyne* (1982), 16 Sask. R. 316 (Sask. Q.B.); *Kelly v. Greene* (1982), 37 Nfld. & P.E.I.R. 196 (Nfld. T.D.); *Can. Permanent Mtge. Corp. v. Halet Ent. Ltd.* (1983), 30 R.P.R. 240 (B.C.S.C.); *Bank of N.S. v. Vancouver Island Renovating Inc.* (1986), 31 D.L.R. (4th) 560 (B.C.C.A.); *Can. Permanent Trust Co. v. Neumann* (1986), 8 B.C.L.R. (2d) 318 (B.C.C.A.); *Allied-Signal Inc. v. Dome Petroleum Ltd.* (1991), 81 Alta. L.R. (2d) 307 (Alta. Q.B.), an implied novation inferred by O'Leary J. at 321-324 (reversed on other grounds (1992), 3 Alta. L.R. (3d) 155 (Alta. C.A.)). Compare where an original debtor was replaced by the company which the debtor incorporated: *Emco Supply v. Vivian*

be in writing[135] (unless possibly the transaction falls within the Statute of Frauds).[136] But it must be supported by consideration else it will be inoperative, because it is a contract and, as already seen, all contracts, save those under seal, must be made for consideration.[137] Where the contract is one of novation, however, the consideration is normally and substantially the discharge of the old contract. Hence, in *Jones v. James Burgess & Sons Ltd.*[138] no novation took place, because there was no evidence of the discharge of the old contract. Whether a novation has taken place must depend upon the conduct and intentions of the parties.[139] Their conduct may, indeed, establish the requisite intention.[140]

Novation usually involves the substitution of a new party for one of the old,

---

(1984), 46 Nfld. & P.E.I.R. 257 (Nfld. Dist. Ct.) (with which contrast *Irving Oil Ltd. v. Bishop* (1984), 46 Nfld. & P.E.I.R. 283 (Nfld. Dist. Ct.)); *Bancorp Financial Ltd. v. Darwai Invt. Corp.* (1985), 61 B.C.L.R. 130 (B.C.S.C.).

    Contrast *Harris v. Robertson* (1866), 11 N.B.R. 496 (N.B.C.A.); *Dansereau & Richelieu Tpt. Co. v. Lafreniere*, [1926] S.C.R. 138 (S.C.C.); *Pac. Wash-A-Matic Ltd. v. R.O. Booth Holdings Ltd.*, [1978] 5 W.W.R. 525 (B.C.S.C.); reversed [1979] 6 W.W.R. 458 (B.C.C.A.); *Avco Financial Services Can. Ltd. v. T.D. Bank* (1980), 6 Sask. R. 160 (Sask. Dist. Ct.); *Central & Eastern Trust Co. v. Rosebowl Holdings Ltd.* (1981), 34 N.B.R. (2d) 308 (N.B.C.A.); *Can. Permanent Trust Co. v. Carlyle* (1983), 30 R.P.R. 246 (B.C.S.C.); *Eaton Bay Trust Co. v. Pollon* (1983), 30 R.P.R. 256 (B.C.S.C.); *Bank of Montreal v. Miedema* (1983), 30 R.P.R. 264 (B.C.S.C.); *Central Trust Co. v. Bartlett* (1983), 30 R.P.R. 267 (N.S.C.A.); *Harry Freeman & Sons Ltd. v. Neu* (1984), 66 N.S.R. (2d) 255 (N.S. Co. Ct.); *Blue Chip Invts. Inc. v. Kavanagh* (1986), 60 Nfld. & P.E.I.R. 85 (Nfld. T.D.); *Paramount Life Ins. Co. v. Torgerson Dev. Corp.* (1987), 51 Alta. L.R. (2d) 59 (Alta. Q.B.); reversed on other grounds (1988), 58 Alta. L.R. (2d) 13 (Alta. C.A.); *National Trust Co. v. Mead* (1990), 71 D.L.R. (4th) 488 (S.C.C.); reversing the decision on this ground in (1988), 52 D.L.R. (4th) 159 (Sask. C.A.); *Valley Well Drillers Ltd. v. Blueberry Acres Ltd.* (1988), 89 N.S.R. (2d) 236 (N.S.T.D.); *Discovery Trust Co. of Can. v. Schulz* (1990), 83 Sask. R. 284 (Sask. Q.B.).

135 *Strong v. Hesson* (1897), 5 B.C.R. 217 (B.C. Co. Ct.); *Doolaege v. Solid Resources Ltd.* (1990), 108 A.R. 52 (Alta. Master) (when a novation was established); affirmed (1992), 127 A.R. 1 (Alta. C.A.); leave to appeal to S.C.C. refused (1992), 131 A.R. 386 (note) (S.C.C.).

136 Above, p. 226.

137 *Dell v. Saunders* (1914), 6 W.W.R. 657 (B.C.C.A.). The appropriate consideration is the discharge of the original debt in return for a promise to perform some obligation: *National Trust Co. v. Mead*, above, note 134, at 500.

138 Above, note 134.

139 *Polson v. Wulffsohn* (1890), 2 B.C.R. 39 (B.C.S.C.). The statement of the requirement of novation by Begbie C.J., *ibid.*, at 43 was described as a classic statement by Esson J.A. in *Prospect Mortgage Invt. Corp. v. Van-5 Devs. Ltd.*, [1986] 2 W.W.R. 69 at 84; compare *National Trust Co. v. Mead*, above, note 134, at 501 *per* Wilson J. Compare *Walker v. Barclays Bank (Can.) Ltd.; Walker v. Barclays (Can.) Ltd.*, [1941] S.C.R. 491 (S.C.C.); *Avco Financial Services Can. Ltd. v. T.D. Bank* (1980), 6 Sask. R. 160 (Sask. Dist. Ct.); see also *Bank of B.C. v. Firm Holdings Ltd.* (1984), 57 B.C.L.R. 1 (B.C.C.A.).

140 *Rich v. Nor. Amer. Lbr. Co.* (1913), 18 B.C.R. 543 (B.C.C.A.). This and the preceding sentence were cited in *Emco Supply v. Vivian* (1984), 46 Nfld. & P.E.I.R. 257 at 261 (Nfld. Dist. Ct.). This sentence and the following passage were referred to by Grotsky J. in *Discovery Trust Co. of Can. v. Schulz* (1990), 83 Sask. R. 284 at 286 (Sask. Q.B.). For a case where an inference *was* drawn, see *Franks v. Vanthuyne*, above, note 126, with which contrast *Central & Eastern Trust Co. v. Rosebowl Holdings Ltd.*, above, note 134.

original ones.[141] Hence, as Egbert J. explained in *Herold v. British American Oil Co.*[142] the following are required to bring about a novation:

(1) The new debtor must assume complete liability;

(2) the creditor must accept the new debtor as the principal debtor and not as an agent or guarantor;[143]

(3) the creditor must accept the new contract in full satisfaction and substitution for the old contract;[144] and

(4) the new contract must be made with the consent of the old debtor.

In that case there was a novation, because the defendant entered into a contract with a third party despite the prior contract with the plaintiff. This was done with the plaintiff's consent. The transaction between the defendant and the third party was not in breach of the original contract between plaintiff and defendant; it discharged that contract, not broke it.

The addition of a fourth element by Egbert J. to the original three elements in the judgment of Begbie C.J. in *Polson v. Wulffsohn*,[145] was accepted by Lambert J.A. of the British Columbia Court of Appeal,[146] though it was questioned by Esson J.A. in a later case.[147] However, in *National Trust Co. v. Mead*,[148] the Supreme Court of Canada pointed out that Lambert J.A. was in error in suggesting that consent of the old debtor was necessary.[149]

> . . . if the original mortgagor consents to the mortgage being assumed by his assignee on different terms, this would indicate rather that he considers himself to continue to be bound despite the assignment. Consent to changed terms, in other words, does not indicate novation but rather continuing liability. On the other, when changes in the terms have been effected without the knowledge or consent of the original mortgagor, that will be a strong indication in favour of novation.

In this case, reversing the holding of the Saskatchewan Court of Appeal, the Supreme Court of Canada held that no novation had occurred. The execution of an assumption agreement by which the purchaser of a unit for a construction

---

141 *Iriving Oil v. Bishop* (1984), 46 Nfld. & P.E.I.R. 283 (Nfld. Dist. Ct.); *Central Trust Co. v. Adshade* (1983), 60 N.S.R. (2d) 414 (N.S.C.A.); contrast *Emco Supply v. Vivian* (1984), 46 Nfld. & P.E.I.R. 257 (Nfld. Dist. Ct.).

142 (1954), 12 W.W.R. 333 at 340 (Alta. S.C.); see also *A.G. B.C. v. Salter*, [1940] 1 W.W.R. 319 at 327 (B.C.C.A.) *per* Sloan J.A.

143 Compare *McQuay v. Beacon Homes Ltd.* (1980), 13 R.P.R. 147 (Ont. H.C.); *Central & Eastern Trust Co. v. Rosebowl Holdings Ltd.*, above, note 134.

144 It may be on the same terms as the old: *Sheehy v. Edmonton World Hockey Enterprises Ltd.*, above, note 134.

145 Above, note 139.

146 *Bank of B.C. v. Firm Holdings Ltd.* (1984), 57 B.C.L.R. 1 at 3 (B.C.C.A.); *Eaton Bay Trust Co. v. Ling* (1987), 45 D.L.R. (4th) 1 (B.C.C.A.); *Can. Permanent Trust Co. v. Neumann*, above, note 134. And in Nova Scotia: *Valley Well Drillers Ltd. v. Blueberry Acres Ltd.* (1989), 89 N.S.R. (2d) 236 (N.S.T.D.); and by the Saskatchewan Court of Appeal in *National Trust Co. v. Mead*, above, note 134.

147 *Prospect Mortgage Invt. Corp. v. Van-5 Devs. Ltd.*, [1986] 2 W.W.R. 69 at 86-87 (B.C.C.A.).

148 Above, note 134.

149 *Ibid.*, at 504 *per* Wilson J.

company agreed to perform the covenants of a mortgage as though originally made by him and consented to a possible future release of the construction company (the mortgagor) did not amount to a novation. Nor did the action of the mortgagee in discontinuing its action against the construction company establish a novation.[150]

Since what happens in novation is the introduction of a new party, novation appears to resemble other types of transactions which involve new parties, and must therefore be distinguished from them. Thus, it is vital to differentiate a novation which has certain effects and requirements of a formal kind, from, for example: (1) a covenant not to sue a party;[151] (2) a contract of guarantee;[152] (3) waiver or rights, under the original, prior contract;[153] and (4) assignment of rights under the original contract.[154]

There may be novation of part of a debt if the circumstances reveal that this was possible and was the intention of the parties.[155] Whether the contract is novated in part or in whole, the effect of the novation is to release the original debtor completely in respect of what has been novated.[156] Hence, the original debtor is no longer obliged to perform the contract to the extent his duties have been novated.

Novation is not presumed and must clearly be shown.[157] Hence, in *Cabot Trust Co. v. D'Agostino*,[158] the claim that an original mortgage had been novated when land subject to the mortgage was sold by the original mortgagors to a numbered company, which assumed the mortgage, did not succeed. The original mortgagors were liable on the mortgage. The terms of that mortgage, as to what was to happen in the future, included the continuing liability of the original mortgagors.

(ii) *Assignment*

This involves the transfer of the obligation to perform, or more usually, the right to demand performance, from the original debtor or the original creditor, as the case may be, to another party. As with novation, therefore, the duty on the original debtor to perform may be discharged. This is not as clear in the case of assignment, as it is with novation, because not every kind of assignment completely releases the original debtor. Nor will every assignment to a new creditor transfer the right to sue in respect of performance to the assignee.[159]

---

150 *Ibid.*, at 505-509.
151 *Commercial Bank of Tasmania v. Jones*, [1893] A.C. 313 (P.C.).
152 *Morin v. Hammond Lbr. Co.*, [1923] S.C.R. 140 (S.C.C.).
153 *West v. Occidental Fire Ins. Co.*, [1927] 3 D.L.R. 260 (Sask. K.B.).
154 *B.A. Timber Co. v. Jones*, [1944] 2 W.W.R. 577 (B.C.C.A.); *Clareview Rental Project (Edmonton) Ltd. v. Walker* (1993), 8 Alta. L.R. (3d) 18 at 25-26 (Alta. Q.B.); below, Chapter 17.
155 *Weldwood-Westply Ltd. v. Cundy*, [1965] S.C.R. 586 (S.C.C.).
156 *Commercial Bank of Tasmania v. Jones*, above, note 151.
157 *Cabot Trust Co. v. D'Agostino* (1992), 11 O.R. (3d) 144 at 151 (Ont. Gen. Div.) *per* Davidson J.; additional reasons at (January 20, 1993), Doc. Toronto C14534/92 (Ont. Gen. Div.).
158 *Ibid.*, following *National Trust Co. v. Mead* (1990), 71 D.L.R. (4th) 488 (S.C.C.); *Eaton Bay Trust Co. v. Ling* (1987), 45 D.L.R. (4th) 1 (B.C.C.A.).
159 Below, Chapter 17.

(b) Change of duty

Two important methods of changing the original duty to perform created by a contract are by variation of the contract and waiver of rights arising thereunder.[160] These two methods must be carefully distinguished. In cases of variation what happens is that, by mutual agreement, for the benefit or convenience of both parties, there is a later alteration of an original agreement. Hence, a unilateral variation, even if permitted by the original contract, must be accepted by the other party with full knowledge and consent, and must be made for valid consideration, if it is to be valid.[161] Where waiver is alleged to have occurred, however, the change is for the benefit or convenience of one party only, and the other party is said to acquiesce in such change in the original terms of their contract. In both situations there is a later agreement between the parties affecting their earlier transaction. Where variation is the allegation, such agreement, whether written or oral, is express.[162] Where waiver is alleged, the suggested alteration is, at the most, implicit from what has occurred. Furthermore, where the original agreement has been varied by the later one, then, to the extent to which such variation is operative, the first agreement must now be considered to have been completely changed in respect of the variation in question.[163] If waiver is alleged, however, the original rights and duties of the parties remain unchanged, save that, by virtue of the waiver, insofar as it is operative and effective, the party acquiescing in the change cannot enforce his original rights to the extent to which they conflict with the change suggested or initiated by the other party and acquiesced in by the former. Thus, it is important to differentiate variation of a contract from waiver of rights under a contract.

A contract which varies an earlier agreement will be valid to the extent to which it is itself an enforceable agreement. Thus, there must be consideration (unless the variation is contained in a document under seal).[164] If the contract is one which is governed by the Statute of Frauds, the Sale of Goods Act, or any other statute which requires a contract to be in writing or similarly evidenced in writing, the

---

160 Stoljar, "The Modification of Contracts" (1957), 35 Can. Bar. Rev. 485. On the distinction between *waiver* and *repudiation* (below, pp. 600-622); see *Can. Acceptance Corp. v. Fisher*, [1958] S.C.R. 546 at 560-564 (S.C.C.) *per* Rand J. Reference to the original version of this discussion was made in *Weeks v. Rosocha* (1983), 28 R.P.R. 126 at 136 (Ont. C.A.).

161 *Hyslip v. MacLeod Savings & Credit Union Ltd.* (1988), 62 Alta. L.R. (2d) 152 (Alta. Q.B.). But the manufacturer could change the terms and conditions of a contract with which the manufacturer supplied equipment to a dealer, even though this caused hardship to the dealer, by requiring him to pay C.O.D. instead of allowing credit: *Mann v. Belarus Equipment of Can. Ltd.* (1989), 73 Sask. R. 100 (Sask. C.A.); reversing (1988), 69 Sask. R. 19 (Sask. Q.B.).

162 For an example of a later oral variation of an original written agreement, see *Bau-Und Forschungsgesellschaft Thermoform A.G. v. Paszner* (1988), 22 C.P.R. (3d) 193 (B.C.S.C.); additional reasons at (1989), 25 C.P.R. (3d) 536 (B.C.S.C.); reversed (1991), 37 C.P.R. (3d) 349 (B.C.C.A.).

163 See, *e.g., Whitford v. T.D. Bank* (1986), 71 N.S.R. (2d) 408 (N.S.T.D.), new chattel mortgage created in place of original one given to the bank, therefore bank could not repossess vehicle under the terms of the original chattel mortgage.

164 Compare *Guillaume v. Stirton* (1978), 88 D.L.R. (3d) 191 at 203 (Sask. C.A.) *per* Hall J.A.; *Blomidon Mercury Sales Ltd. v. John Piercey's Auto Body Shop Ltd.* (1981), 129 D.L.R. (3d) 630 (Nfld. T.D.); *Hyslip v. MacLeod Savings & Credit Union Ltd.*, above, note 161.

subsequent variation must itself be so effected, else it will be as unenforceable as the original contract would have been had it not been in writing or evidenced in writing. Thus, while a later agreement which rescinds or replaces an earlier one will be effective to achieve such purpose even if it is neither written nor evidenced in writing, such an agreement will be ineffective to vary the earlier contract, if it merely purports to vary. The question in each instance is what was the intention of the parties when they made their *second* agreement. If variation was their ultimate intention, they must follow the same rules as to form as applied to the original contract.[165]

The situation is different, however, where what is alleged is not a variation but a waiver. At common law, a waiver of rights created by and under a contract, not being itself an agreement, did not have to be supported by consideration; nor would it have to be in writing or evidenced by a note or memorandum in writing, if the original contract were within, for example, the Statute of Frauds or the Sale of Goods Act. The common law respected and gave effect to waivers. Thus, if there were a condition precedent to performance by one party,[166] it was possible for the party entitled to require performance of such condition precedent to waive its performance, thereby making it impossible for him to plead that the condition in question had not been performed as a defence to non-performance by him, or to bring an action based upon the alleged non-performance of such condition precedent by the party so obliged. For example, in *Saskatchewan Co-operative Wheat Producers Ltd. v. Luciuk*,[167] the defendant had done business under a contract for several years, and had received benefits from its performance of such contract. In those circumstances, it was not permitted for the defendant to plead non-fulfilment of a condition precedent which, under the contract, was supposed to have been performed before the contract could be effectuated.[168] The defendant had waived the due performance of the condition precedent. However, as previously noted,[169] waiver of a "true" condition precedent by one party is not possible. Hence, in *McCaig v. Nimmo*,[170] no waiver was possible of the condition precedent that the intended purchaser of a property would not be bound to buy unless he sold his Nova Scotia property by a specified date. Nor could a mortgagee waive a

---

165 *Frith v. Alliance Invt. Co.* (1914), 49 S.C.R. 384 (S.C.C.); *Kaulbach v. Eichel*, [1930] 1 D.L.R. 983 (N.S.C.A.); compare *Hawrish v. Bank of Montreal*, [1969] S.C.R. 515 (S.C.C.); compare above, pp. 226-227.

166 Compare above, pp. 437-441.

167 [1931] 2 W.W.R. 51 (Sask. C.A.); compare *Bentsen v. Taylor Sons & Co.*, [1983] 2 Q.B. 193 (C.A.); see also *Pizzo v. Crory* (1986), 71 N.S.R. (2d) 419 (N.S.T.D.), waiver of contractual obligation by the conduct of all the shareholders in the past; therefore the obligation could not be invoked by one shareholder as the basis for an action. See also the division of opinion between Anglin J. and Duff J. in *Davidson v. Norstrant* (1921), 61 S.C.R. 493 (S.C.C.).

168 Compare *Eureka Oil Ltd. v. Colli* (1983), 25 Man. R. (2d) 166 (Man. Q.B.) (late acceptance of a fee for 15 years was waiver, therefore the recipient of the fee could not claim breach of contract by late payment in the 16th year); *Dolan v. Patton* (1986), 75 N.S.R. (2d) 399 (N.S.T.D.) (unilateral waiver by defendant of plaintiff's obligation to feed and care for her).

169 Above, pp. 441-443.

170 (1987), 85 N.B.R. (2d) 132 (N.B.Q.B.).

condition relating to a requirement of a letter of credit before renewal of a mortgage in *Crerar v. Credit Foncier Trust Co.*[171]

Waiver, said Macdonald J.A. in *British American Oil Co. v. Ferguson,*[172] was a voluntary and intentional relinquishment of a known existing legal right, whether arising under contract or by law. To establish waiver, it had to be shown that the person waiving his rights had full knowledge of their existence and their nature. If a party were obliged under the contract to perform in a certain manner, or by a certain time, the beneficiary of performance could be deprived of the right to insist upon proper performance under the contract, or to complain if such performance did not occur, where he informs the party obliged to perform that proper performance was no longer necessary.[173] The common law held the party waiving his rights under the contract to his "indulgence", and did not let him go back on what he had said, at least where it affected the other party's position. Nor could the beneficiary of the waiver repudiate such waiver and later insist upon strict adherence to the original contract.[174]

In view of this, it is not surprising that it was important to differentiate variation and waiver, nor that confusion could arise between them.[175] In both, it would seem, the parties were being held to their later alteration of the original, or former statement of their respective rights and duties. The only difference was with respect to the possible need for: (a) consideration; and (b) writing. Furthermore, whereas variation depended upon the existence of a contract properly so-called, a waiver was effective on some other basis, not "agreement" in a contractual sense.[176] It has been suggested that the true basis for waiver was *estoppel.*[177] In other words, a party who had led the other party to expect a certain state of affairs, could not argue subsequently that the real situation as between the parties was to be governed by their original contract. Unfortunately this conflicts with the fundamental common-law doctrine that, whereas estoppel related to representations as to the past or the present state of affairs, statements as to the situation *in futuro*

---

171 (1987), 37 B.L.R. 1 (Ont. H.C.).

172 [1951] 2 D.L.R. 37 at 44 (Alta. C.A.). An example might be the ratification of a forged signature to a promissory note by the later endorsement of a photocopy by the alleged signatory: *Madawaska Amusements Ltd. v. Ramey* (1990), 96 N.B.R. (2d) 271 (N.B.Q.B.).

173 See *Leather Cloth Co. v. Hieronimus* (1875), L.R. 10 Q.B. 140; *Panoutsos v. Raymond Hadley Corp. of New York,* [1917] 2 K.B. 473 (C.A.); *Hartley v. Hymans,* [1920] 3 K.B. 475.

174 *Hickman v. Haynes* (1875), L.R. 10 C.P. 598; *Levey & Co. v. Goldberg,* [1922] 1 K.B. 688. At least not without giving notice to the other party: *Denmark Productions Ltd. v. Boscobel Productions Ltd.,* [1969] 1 Q.B. 699 at 727 (C.A.) *per* Winn L.J.

175 *Besseler, Waechter, Glover & Co. v. South Derwent Coal Co.,* [1938] 1 K.B. 408. Though to Denning L.J. in *Charles Rickards Ltd. v. Oppenheim,* [1950] 1 K.B. 616 (C.A.), there was no true difference, in modern times, between waiver, forebearance to sue, substituted performance, or variation. All had the same effect. See also Allen J.A. in *Emerald Resources Ltd. v. Sterling Oil Properties Management Ltd.* (1969), 3 D.L.R. (3d) 630 at 643-644 (Alta. C.A.); affirmed (1970), 15 D.L.R. (3d) 256 (S.C.C.).

176 For the suggestion that waiver is based upon "election", see Prowse J.A. in *Mitchell & Jewell Ltd. v. C.P. Express Co.,* [1974] 3 W.W.R. 259 at 270-271 (Alta. C.A.).

177 Compare Sheppard J.A. in *Electric Power Equipment Ltd. v. RCA Victor Co.* (1964), 49 W.W.R. 193 at 218 (B.C.C.A.).

should properly be characterized as promises, and should therefore be in the form of a *contractual* undertaking, involving consideration, etc.[178] There was thus, and may still be said to be, an ambivalence about the common law. On the other hand, there is the insistence that promises as to the future behaviour of a party must be in contractual form and have contractual substance. On the other hand, there is the possibility that conduct by one party might operate to estop him *in the future* from enforcing his strict legal rights. Hence, the problem about differentiating waiver from something similar, such as variation. Hence, also, the view that there is a clear distinction between waiver and estoppel, and the two are not to be confused or equated.[179]

In equity, there was no such difficulty, at least since about the middle of the nineteenth century, following the statements about equitable estoppel made in *Hughes v. Metropolitan Railway Co.*[180] The doctrine there enunciated has developed to permit the modification, in some jurisdictions even the creation, of strict contractual (and other) rights.[181] It has been restated, in perhaps broader terms by Lord Denning M.R. in *Crabb v. Arun District Council*:[182]

> The basis . . . is the interposition of equity. Equity comes in, true to form, to mitigate the rigours of strict law. The early cases did not speak of it as 'estoppel'.[183] They spoke of it as 'raising an equity'. If I may expand that, Lord Cairns said in *Hughes v. Metropolitan Railway Co.*: ' . . . it is the first principle upon which all Courts of equity proceed . . .' that it will prevent a person from insisting on his strict legal rights — whether arising under a contract, or on his title deeds, or by statute — when it would be inequitable for him to do so having regard to the dealings which have taken place between the parties. What then are the dealings which will preclude him from insisting on his strict legal rights? If he makes a binding contract that he will not insist on the strict legal position, a court of equity will hold him to his contract. Short of a binding contract, if he makes a promise that he will not insist on his strict legal rights — *even though that promise may be unenforceable in point of law for want of consideration or want of writing* — and if he makes the promise knowing or intending that the other will act on it, and he does act on it, then again a court of equity will not allow him to go back on that promise: see *Central London Property Trust v. High Trees House, Charles Rickards v. Oppenheim.* Short of an actual promise, if he, by his words or conduct, so behaves as to lead another to believe that he will not insist on his strict legal rights

---

178 *Jorden v. Money* (1854), 5 H.L. Cas. 185 (H.L.).

179 *Anguish v. Maritime Life Assurance Co.* (1987), 51 Alta. L.R. (2d) 376 (Alta. C.A.); additional reasons at (1988), 29 C.C.L.I. 190 (Alta. C.A.); leave to appeal to S.C.C. refused (1988), 91 A.R. 80 (note) (S.C.C.); *Hyslip v. MacLeod Savings & Credit Union Ltd.* (1988), 62 Alta. L.R. (2d) 152 (Alta. Q.B.). But see below, pp. 548-549.

180 (1877), 2 App. Cas. 439 (H.L.) (applied in a case involving *waiver*, not estoppel: *Pizzo v. Crory,* above, note 167, which would suggest that the two modes of varying contractual obligations are the same; compare *Electric Power Equipment Ltd. v. RCA Victor Co.,* above, note 177; contrast *Anguish v. Maritime Life Assurance Co.,* above, note 179).

181 Above, pp. 121-136.

182 [1975] 3 All E.R. 865 at 871 (C.A.) citations are omitted and emphasis added.

183 Lord Denning was referring to what he called "proprietary" estoppel (the case being one of property rights, not contract): but he likened it to "promissory" estoppel generally. The distinction between promissory and proprietary estoppel was not accepted by Scarman L.J. above, note 182, at 875, though the estoppel concept was not repudiated by him; nor its equitable nature.

— knowing or intending that the other will act on that belief — and he does so act, that again will raise an equity in favour of the other, and it is for a court of equity to say in what way the equity may be satisfied. The cases show that this equity does not depend on agreement but on words or conduct.[184]

There would seem now, in modern law, to be a firm foundation for the proposition that even without a technically correct variation of a contract, there may be the alteration (possibly even the extinction) of contractual rights and obligations as a consequence of some words or conduct leading the other party into a certain belief as to the contractual position between the parties, as long as this has led to some reliance by the party to whom the words were spoken or the conduct performed.[185] Once he has changed his position in consequence, the other party cannot return to the original legal situation which obtained between them. He is estopped.[186]

Thus, in *Powell v. Henderson Hail Ltd.*,[187] an insured party gave a release to the insurance company of any claims he had under a crop insurance policy. Subsequently he filed a claim. The insurer promised to investigate, but nothing was done. The plaintiff insured sued in respect of his claim, in answer to which the insurance company pleaded the release. The plaintiff countered by arguing

---

184 Reference is made to *Ramsden v. Dyson* (1866), L.R. 1 H.L. 129; *Birmingham & Dist. Land Co. v. London & North Western Ry.* (1888), 40 Ch. D. 268 (C.A.); *Plimmer v. Mayor of Wellington* (1884), 9 App. Cas. 699 (P.C.); *Inwards v. Baker*, [1965] 2 Q.B. 29 (C.A.); *E.R. Ives Invt. Ltd. v. High*, [1967] 2 Q.B. 379 (C.A.); *Siew Soon Wah v. Yong Tong Hong*, [1973] A.C. 836 (P.C.) (all of which are "property", not "contract" cases).

185 See *Can. Accept. Corp. v. Fisher*, [1958] S.C.R. 546 (S.C.C.). But care must be taken to distinguish true waiver from a mere "indulgence": *Commercial Finance Corp. v. Dunlop Tire & Rubber Goods Co.*, [1942] O.R. 380 (Ont. C.A.); *Glenmore Gdn. Apts. Ltd. v. Todd* (1972), 29 D.L.R. (3d) 242 (Alta. S.C.).

186 This and the preceding two sentences were cited by Montgomery J. in *Bank of N.S. v. Equaton Invts. Ltd.* (1983), 45 A.R. 99 at 110 (Alta. Q.B.); and by Gallant J. in *Jeske v. Maritime Life Assurance Co.* (1990), 105 A.R. 81 at 98 (Alta. Q.B.); affirmed (1991), 117 A.R. 162 (Alta. C.A.).

This form of estoppel must be differentiated from what has become known as estoppel by convention, also referred to as estoppel by contract. Such an estoppel arises where the parties to a transaction have acted on an agreed assumption that a state of facts can be regarded as true for the purposes of that transaction. It resembles estoppel by representation but is different from promissory or equitable estoppel (discussed in the text and above, pp. 121-136). It is a rare type of estoppel and seems to have connections with issues of mistake relating to the contents of a contract, the intention of parties to enter into legal relations, or the existence of a contract or of certain terms in a contract. Estoppel by convention does not specify the legal effects of an assumed promise, it pertains to the question whether a promise has been made. For discussion of this English doctrine (which does not appear to have been invoked in any Canadian case thus far: but see *Litwin Const. (1973) Ltd. v. Pan* (1988), 52 D.L.R. (4th) 459 at 464-468 (B.C.C.A.)) see the following: *Amalgam. Invt. & Property Co. v. Texas Commerce Int. Bank*, [1981] 3 All E.R. 577; *The "Vistafjord"*, [1988] 2 Lloyds. Rep. 343; *The "Amazonia"*, [1990] 1 Lloyds Rep. 236; *Orion Ins. Co. plc. v. Shere Drake Ins. plc.*, [1990] 1 Lloyds Rep. 465 especially at 505-506; *The "Captain Gregos" (No. 2)*, [1990] 2 Lloyd's Rep. 399; *Colchester Borough Council v. Smith*, [1991] 2 All E.R. 29 at 60-63 *per* Ferris J.; Treitel, *Law of Contract*, 8th ed. (1991), at pp. 111-115. Compare, above, p. 129, note 285.

187 [1977] 4 W.W.R. 757 (Sask. Dist. Ct.). Contrast *Gillis v. Bourgard* (1983), 145 D.L.R. (3d) 570 (Ont. C.A.), insurance company negotiating amount of loss estopped from denying liability.

that the promise to investigate gave rise to an estoppel, preventing the insurance company from relying on the release. The plaintiff did not succeed. Even if the promise to investigate the insured's claim constituted an undertaking or promise by the insurance company not to rely on the release, it did not qualify as an instance of promissory estoppel. The undertaking did not induce the plaintiff to change his position in any way. He was neither better nor worse off as a result of the insurance company's promise.[188] All that was present in this case was a bare representation not to enforce a right. So, too, in *Pentagon Construction (1969) Co. v. United States Fidelity & Guarantee Co.*[189] no estoppel could be established. An insured suffered a loss which he alleged came within the scope of his policy. The insurance company relied on an exception clause in the policy, under which the insurance company claimed to have excluded the loss in question. The insured was assured that the insurance company had given an opinion to the effect that the loss incurred by the insured was covered by the policy, despite the clause. This, it was alleged, amounted to an estoppel, precluding the insurance company from relying on the clause. The insured failed. An opinion was not a promise or assurance, one of which was required for estoppel to be proved. Moreover the insured had not relied to his detriment upon the opinion. By way of contrast in *Bank of Nova Scotia v. Equaton Investments Ltd.*[190] a bank customer and his wife guaranteed the debts of a company. Later the bank told the customer that the guarantors were released. This was held to estop the bank from later suing on the guarantee. In *Villa Real Estate & Development Ltd. v. Bloomenthal,*[191] a real estate agent represented to his principal that he waived his commission. This was relied upon by the principal and his solicitor. When the agent attempted to claim commission he was held to be estopped by his earlier conduct.

It has been seen how attempts have been made to utilize this doctrine to "create" contractual obligations.[192] In the present context it is relevant to the modification of an existing contract. In this respect, there may be more scope or legitimacy in the application of this doctrine whether it be called equitable estoppel, quasi-estoppel or promissory estoppel, for the purpose of permitting a party to defend himself from a suit alleging the breach of a contract, when the defendant claims that the original duty under which he was obligated by the contract has been affected by some statement or conduct by the plaintiff which led him, the defendant, in reliance thereon, to alter his position. This now appears to be accepted by English and Canadian courts as a valid way in which contractual rights and duties may be modified or altered even without a formal variation or subsequent agreement in proper contractual form. But it still leaves open, perhaps less so than before,

---

188 But note the possibility that estoppel may be pleaded, in the absence of detrimental reliance, where it would be inequitable to deny an estoppel: *Société Italo-Belge Pour le Commerce et L'Industrie S.A. (Antwerp) v. Palm & Vegetable Oils (Malaysia) SDN BHD: The Post Chaser,* [1982] 1 All E.R. 19; above, p. 134.
189 [1977] 4 W.W.R. 358 (B.C.C.A.).
190 (1983), 45 A.R. 99 (Alta. Q.B.).
191 (1983), 39 A.R. 277 (Alta. Q.B.).
192 Above, pp. 18, 125-127.

the vexed question whether what has occurred is truly some kind of waiver or is properly to be described as a variation of the original contract, for example, by substituting a new or different form or kind of performance. In the latter event there may be no reliance upon the alleged alteration without strict proof of a contract under which it was permitted or justified. In the light of recent statements of the kind cited earlier, perhaps the less strict, equitable view will prevail, and insistence upon truly contractual variation will become less prevalent. Estoppel has probably swallowed up waiver.[193]

(c) Discharge by agreement

(i) Anticipatory release

The contract may provide, in its original terms, for the release of the parties from their obligations in the event of a stipulated occurrence or at some future time. In such circumstances, the parties will have provided by what has been termed an "anticipatory agreement" for the termination of the contract; it then becomes incapable of further performance.[194] The question may arise, however, whether the stipulated event has occurred, and, if so, what its effect is to be upon the contract. This may be a matter for subsequent judicial construction and interpretation.[195] For example, the issue may arise whether a party is entitled to terminate in accordance with the original contract provisions,[196] for example, by giving a notice of default.[197] It may be that notice of determination is required. Failure to give the requisite notice, whether it be for a specific period or for a "reasonable" length of time, will not suffice to discharge the obligations of the party purporting to

---

193 This sentence was quoted by Gallant J. in *Jeske v. Maritime Life Assurance Co.*, above, note 186, at 98.

194 *Garrard v. Lund*, [1921] 1 W.W.R. 329 at 333 (B.C.C.A.) *per* Martin J.A.

195 See, *e.g., Deschenes Elec. Co. v. Royal Trust Co.* (1907), 39 S.C.R. 567 (S.C.C.); *Ottawa Elec. Co. v. St. Jacques* (1901), 31 S.C.R. 636 (S.C.C.); *Nor. Ont. Power Co. v. La Roche Mines Ltd.*, [1938] 3 W.W.R. 252 (P.C.); *Re Desbiens* (1953), 9 W.W.R. (N.S.) 509 (Man. Q.B.). Compare *Schlaut v. Solar*, [1945] 4 D.L.R. 586 (Alta. C.A.), on the effect of a deed given on escrow. On escrow, see *Kingston v. Ambrian Invt. Ltd.*, [1975] 1 All E.R. 120 (C.A.); *Glessing v. Green*, [1975] 2 All E.R. 696 (C.A.).

   Similarly, if parties agree on a settlement that discharges the debtor's original obligation under the contract the question may arise whether the requirements of the settlement have been satisfied, *e.g.*, performed by the debtor under the new agreement. If this has not occurred the creditor can revert to his rights under the original contract: *Northland Bank v. 294427 Alta. Ltd.* (1989), 102 A.R. 152 (Alta. Master), where the time for performance of the settlement had not occurred, therefore the debtor was not in breach.

196 *North v. Victoria Baseball & Athletic Co.*, [1949] 1 W.W.R. 1033 (B.C.S.C.). See *MacNeill Industrial Inc. v. Posnikoff* (1991), 53 B.C.L.R. (2d) 358 (B.C.C.A.), where there was no termination of the contract under its terms. The plaintiff had taken reasonable steps to deal with a lien on the claims in issue; hence, the contract was still operative. Contrast *C. Corp. (Ont.) Inc. v. E. & S. Kramps Holdings Ltd.* (1989), 99 A.R. 178 (Alta. Master), where the franchise agreement was terminated.

197 *Heep v. Thimsen*, [1940] 3 W.W.R. 679 (B.C.C.A.); *Oil City Petroleums (Leduc) Ltd. v. Amer. Leduc Petroleums Ltd.*, [1952] 3 D.L.R. 577 (S.C.C.).

determine the contract in this way.[198] The event which ends the contract may involve an act of one of the parties, such as the giving of notice, or the expression of dissatisfaction with something, such as the lease which is being negotiated between the parties.[199] It may depend upon some extrinsic act. Thus in *Piccinin v. Canada*,[200] a contract for the distribution of Lotto Canada tickets would determine if Lotto Canada Incorporated was liquidated by Parliament or under the Canada Corporations Act. If so, there would be no recourse available to the erstwhile distributors. The shareholders resolved to wind up Lotto Canada Incorporated under the statute dealing with business corporations. This was held enough to determine the distribution contract.

(ii) *Subsequent rescission*

Novation involves a new agreement replacing the old one by new parties. There may be a subsequent agreement *between the same parties*, not involving new ones, under which the original agreement is terminated. The effect of such an agreement depends on the interpretation of the intentions of the parties.[201] As stated by Stratton J. in *Industrial Construction Ltd. v. Lakeview Development Co.*,[202] the parties "will be presumed to have intended to rescind the old contract and to have substituted a new one whenever the new agreement is inconsistent with the original contract to an extent which goes to the very root of it."

There must be a new contract. If it is not possible to establish the appropriate conduct that indicates a new agreement, either in the form of a promise for which there is consideration,[203] or in the form of conduct giving rise to an estoppel,[204]

---

198 *Malley v. Turbo Resources Ltd.* (1980), 19 A.R. 1 (Alta. Dist. Ct.); *A. & K. Lick-A-Chick Franchises Ltd. v. Cordiv Enterprises Ltd.* (1981), 44 N.S.R. (2d) 159 (N.S.T.D.). Note the difference of opinion, on the question of notice, between the trial judge and the Nova Scotia Court of Appeal in *Hillis Oil & Sales Ltd. v. Wynn's Can. Ltd.* (1982), 53 N.S.R. (2d) 421 (N.S.T.D.); reversed (1983), 55 N.S.R. (2d) 351 (N.S.C.A.); reversed by the Supreme Court of Canada restoring the original judgment: [1986] 1 S.C.R. 57; compare *Emile State Inc. v. Commodore Business Machines Ltd.* (1988), 19 C.C.E.L. xxix (Ont. C.A.); reversing (1986), 15 C.C.E.L. 247 (Ont. H.C.).

199 *Highfield Holdings (B.C.) Ltd. v. Canaveral Invts. Ltd.* (1979), 11 B.C.L.R. 245 (B.C.S.C.). Note the importance of distinguishing determination of a binding contract by some act of the parties, and the failure of a contract to become binding under the doctrine of "true" conditions precedent; above, pp. 437-441.

200 (1981), 36 N.R. 247 (S.C.C.).

201 *Mason v. Scott*, [1935] S.C.R. 641 (S.C.C.); *Reeves v. Huffman*, [1951] 4 D.L.R. 324 (Man. K.B.).

202 (1979), 16 N.B.R. (2d) 287 at 298 (N.B.Q.B.). See *e.g.*, *Westcott v. Fitzpatrick* (1978), 21 Nfld. & P.E.I.R. 1 (Nfld. C.A.). The new contract may come about by implication from the conduct of the parties: *Wiboltt v. Westcode Services Ltd.* (1980), 21 B.C.L.R. 258 (B.C.C.A.); compare *King v. Solna Offset of Can. Ltd.* (1984), 3 O.A.C. 178 (Ont. C.A.), where the new, implied contract, resulting from the lack of protest by the employees and from the changed method of remuneration, was called "novation" in the headnote. But it is really an instance of subsequent rescission, not novation; compare above, p. 539, note 133.

203 *Bank of Montreal v. Loomis Armoured Car Services Ltd.* (1980), 21 B.C.L.R. 247 (B.C.S.C.), no promise to abandon claim for loss of banknotes. Compare *Lewitski v. Ogilvie* (1992), 56 O.A.C. 69 (Ont. Div. Ct.).

varying the original agreement, then it cannot be argued that the pristine agreement between the parties does not bind them.

If it is clear that the parties intended that their subsequent agreement should replace the earlier one, for example, by releasing the parties from that original contract, the later contract will be a good defence to an action brought upon the first one, even if the first contract was under seal and the later one was not.[205] The consideration for the new contract is clear; it consists of the mutual releases of the parties from their respective duties under the first contract. Therefore, a seal will not be necessary. However, where the contract is one which is required to be in writing or to be evidenced by a note or memorandum in writing, if the subsequent agreement is not so perpetrated or evidenced, the question has been raised whether the later agreement has the effect of terminating the prior one (as well as the other effects of such later agreement).[206] It was held by the House of Lords in *Morris v. Baron & Co.*[207] that the effect of the later agreement depended upon the intentions of the parties. The question is whether they meant the second agreement to terminate or abrogate the prior contract. If they did, then that contract could not be said to exist any longer, and neither party could sue thereon. This was what occurred in that case, where the later agreement (which failed to satisfy the Sale of Goods Act) did rescind the earlier. If, on the other hand, as in the later case of *United Dominion Corporation (Jamaica) Ltd. v. Shoucair*,[208] no such intention of rescinding the orignal contract could be spelled out of the making of the second contract, the first still stood and could be enforced (as long as it was in the appropriate statutory form). In other words, a contract which was not itself enforceable, by reason of, for example, the Statute of Frauds, or, as in the *Shoucair* case, the Jamaican Moneylenders Act, could have the effect of destroying an earlier agreement (even though the second contract might not itself be enforceable).

(iii) *Accord and satisfaction*[209]

In the two previously discussed situations the parties by a subsequent agreement have disposed of their original contract even before it has been performed by either

---

204 *M.L. Baxter Equip. Ltd. v. GEAC Can. Ltd.* (1982), 133 D.L.R. (2d) 372 (Ont. H.C.); compare above, pp. 129-136.

205 *Berry v. Berry*, [1929] 2 K.B. 316.

206 Above, p. 226.

207 [1918] A.C. 1 (H.L.); see *Shorb v. Public Trustee* (1954), 11 W.W.R. 132 (Alta. C.A.); *Levy Bros. Co. v. Sole*, [1955] O.W.N. 543 (Ont. H.C.). Followed in *Indust. Const. Ltd. v. Lakeview Dev. Co.*, above, note 202.

208 [1969] 1 A.C. 340 (P.C.).

209 Compare above, pp. 104-106, in relation to payment of a lesser sum in settlement of a larger debt and the problem of consideration. Note that even if there is an accord and satisfaction in the technical sense the court can refuse to give effect to it on equitable grounds, *e.g.*, where there is duress or inequality of bargaining power in the negotiation of the agreement: see *D. & C. Builders v. Rees*, [1966] 2 Q.B. 617 (C.A.); *Arrale v. Costain Civil Engr. Ltd.*, [1976] 1 Lloyd's Rep. 98 at 102 (C.A.) *per* Lord Denning M.R.; *Graham v. Voth Bros. Const. (1974) Ltd.*, [1982] 6 W.W.R. 365 (B.C. Co. Ct.).

of them in any respect, or they have rescinded their earlier agreement by a later one. If one party has already performed his obligation under the contract, and it is now sought to discharge the *other* party from performance on his side, this, too, may be achieved by a subsequent agreement between the parties.[210] Such an agreement is called an "accord and satisfaction". It was explained thus by Scrutton L.J., in *British Russian Gazette & Trade Outlook Ltd. v. Associated Newspapers Ltd.*,[211] in words cited with approval by Parlee J. in *Dubord v. Girard*.[212]

> Accord and satisfaction is the purchase of a release from an obligation arising under contract or tort by means of any valuable consideration, not being the actual performance of the obligation itself. The accord is the agreement by which the obligation is discharged. The satisfaction is the consideration which makes the agreement operative. Formerly it was necessary that the consideration should be executed . . . Later it was conceded that the consideration might be executory . . . The consideration on each side might be an executory promise, the two mutual promises making an agreement enforceable in law, a contract.

An accord and satisfaction need not be under seal (even if the original contract which created the obligation now being discharged was under seal).[213] But there must be consideration for the new contract, the discharge of the previously existing obligation.[214] Hence, the whole problem with respect to payment of a lesser sum may have been removed, so far as Canada is concerned, by the legislation referred to earlier, even though that legislation may have given rise to problems of interpretation of its own.[215]

It is a question of fact not of law whether what has occurred amounts to an accord and satisfaction.[216] But there must be both accord *and* satisfaction[217]

---

210 This sentence and the previous one, in their original form, were cited by Steele C.J.D.C. in *Slaney & Slaney v. Edney* (1979), 22 Nfld. & P.E.I.R. 95 at 101-102 (Nfld. Dist. Ct.).

211 [1933] 2 K.B. 616 at 643-644 (C.A.). Hence, in that case, the breach of a promise to discontinue an action, in return for a payment of money, provided a good counterclaim to action when it was continued after the accord and satisfaction.

212 [1945] 1 W.W.R. 641 at 643 (Alta. S.C.).

213 *Cox v. Hourigan*, [1941] S.C.R. 251 at 258 (S.C.C.) *per* Kerwin & Crockett JJ.

214 *Bell v. Quagliotti*, [1918] 2 W.W.R. 915 (B.C.S.C.); *Esquire Heating & Air Conditioning Ltd. v. Hoffman* (1984), 56 A.R. 184 (Alta. M.C.), where it is pointed out that this plea differs from the plea under the statute dealing with part performance of an existing obligation; above, pp. 119-121. *Quaere*: must it be something other than the payment of money when a debt is being settled? *Bell v. Quagliotti, ibid.*, at 918 *per* Gregory J. In *Robichaud v. Caisse populaire de Pokemouche Ltée* (1990), 69 D.L.R. (4th) 589 (N.B.C.A.), the majority of the New Brunswick Court of Appeal, reversing the trial judge ((1989), 101 N.B.R. (2d) 91) held that the immediate receipt of payment and the saving of time, effort and expense were sufficient consideration to make enforceable an agreement to accept $1,000 in satisfaction of a judgment for $3,780.

215 Above, pp. 119-121. But see the *Esquire Heating* case, above, note 214.

216 *Trusts & Guar. Co. v. Dinning*, [1927] 1 W.W.R. 275 (Alta. S.C.). Compare *Weldon v. Vaughan* (1880), 5 S.C.R. 35 at 42 (S.C.C.) *per* Ritchie C.J.; *Armishaw v. Crucil F. & M. Ltd.*, [1947] 2 W.W.R. 945 at 946 (B.C.C.A.) *per* Robertson J.A.; *Household Finance Corp. of Can. v. Carson* (1982), 38 N.B.R. (2d) 315 (N.B.Q.B.). See *Crown Diamond Paints Ltd. v. East Coast Distributors Ltd.* (1972), 5 N.B.R. (2d) 903 (N.B.Q.B.); compare *Johnston v. Precision Homes & Components Ltd.* (1977), 33 N.S.R. (2d) 373 (N.S. Co. Ct.). *Pacholko v. Manastryski* (1983), 26 Sask. R. 154 (Sask. Q.B.). According to McDonald J. in *Rottacker Farms Ltd. v. C. & M. Farms Ltd.*, [1976]

(though the latter may take the form of a "promise" to do something).[218] Hence, the acceptance of a conveyance of land,[219] or the extension of the duration of a promissory note,[220] could be "satisfaction", as long as these things were done as part of an arrangement to discharge an existing debt or other obligation.[221] But not the acceptance of money in discharge of a lien, where the facts revealed that this was not an accord and satisfaction relating to a debt owed by the defendant to the plaintiff on a promissory note for goods supplied.[222]

(d) Discharge by operation of law[223]

(i) Merger

The doctrine of accord and satisfaction is a form of termination or discharge by subsequent agreement between the parties that arises from an act of the parties. The doctrine of merger, however, has been described as "an operation of law not

---

2 W.W.R. 634 (Alta. S.C.); reversed on appeal on the ground of lack of execution (1976), 71 D.L.R. (3d) 263 (Alta. C.A.), this defence must be established by a preponderance of evidence, or of probability.

   If a payment is accepted prior to the giving of notice that this payment is intended to be settlement in full of the debt, this will not necessarily amount to an accord and satisfaction: *Fehr v. Robinson Diesel Injection Ltd.* (1986), 47 Sask. R. 12 (Sask. Q.B.), applied in *Masur v. McKeran* (1990), 115 A.R. 235 (Alta. Master). Compare *Welsh v. Harnish* (1987), 80 N.S.R. (2d) 443 (N.S. Co. Ct.).

217 *Cairns v. Brown*, [1924] 3 W.W.R. 409 (B.C.C.A.). Thus there can be no accord and satisfaction in the absence of an agreement: *Brumby v. Guar. Trust of Can.* (1981), 6 Sask. R. 445 (Sask. Q.B.); *Christie v. Dongen* (1980), 24 B.C.L.R. 61 (B.C.S.C.); nor if what is done is not done as part of such an agreement: *Woodlot Services Ltd. v. Flemming* (1977), 83 D.L.R. (3d) 201 (N.B.C.A.); *Co-op. Fuels v. Doyle* (1981), 30 Nfld. & P.E.I.R. 347 (P.E.I.S.C.) (acceptance of cheque endorsed "account paid in full" was not accord and satisfaction; no agreement to such effect). *Carson v. Luncheonette Ltd.* (1987), 65 Nfld. & P.E.I.R. 318 (Nfld. T.D.); *Welsh v. Harnish*, above, note 216; *Masur v. McKeran*, above, note 216.

218 Which means that as soon as the promise is given the agreement is binding and will discharge the prior obligation (unless that intention is not evident from the circumstances); compare above, note 211. But see *Cox v. Hourigan*, above, note 213. Or else there must be something done, *e.g.*, the delivery of a quit claim (see *Cairns v. Browns*, above, note 217), or the assignment of an interest in mortgaged property (*Slaney & Slaney v. Edney* (1979), 22 Nfld. & P.E.I.R. 95 (Nfld. Dist. Ct.)).

219 *Pither & Leiser v. Manley* (1902), 32 S.C.R. 651 (S.C.C.).

220 *Puicato v. Charles* (1967), 59 W.W.R. 193 (B.C.S.C.).

221 Compare *C.I.B.C. v. Consumer World Marketing Ltd.* (1990), 105 A.R. 364 (Alta. Master), valid accord and satisfaction when debtor agreed to pay bank $200,000 in settlement of a debt of $248,000: a decision which seems to go against the doctrine of *Pinnel's Case*, above, p. 104, which was applied in New Brunswick in *Robichaud v. Caisse populaire de Pokemouche Ltée*, above, note 214.

222 *Beaver Lbr. Co. v. Gellner*, [1945] 3 W.W.R. 657 (Sask. C.A.).

223 In addition to the possibilities mentioned in this section, reference should also be made to: (a) the *suspension* of contractual rights by a statute: see *e.g. Cook v. Ricketson*, [1901] A.C. 588 (P.C.); (b) the *election* of remedies against one of two alternative obligees, *e.g.*, principal and agent: see Fridman, *Law of Agency*, 6th ed. (1990), pp. 204, 218, 237; compare Reynolds, "Election Distributed" (1970), 86 L.Q.R. 318, criticizing the doctrine; (c) the *release* of a joint or several debtor; above, p. 183.

depending upon the intention of the parties."[224] It was outlined in these words, by Lord Russell of Killowen,[225] cited with approval by McDermid J.A. in *Moretta v. Western Computer Investment Corporation.*[226]

> Where parties enter into an executory agreement which is to be carried out by a deed afterwards to be executed, the . . . completed contract is to be found in the deed. The contract is merged in the deed.

The most common instance of this was said to be the contract of sale of land followed by conveyance on completion. All the provisions of the contract which the parties intended should be performed by the conveyance merged in the conveyance and all the rights of the parties in relation to the contract satisfied by the merger. This doctrine involves the submersion of one type of agreement or relationship within another, of wider import, replacing the earlier one;[227] the greater incorporates the lesser.[228] Excluded from the operation of this doctrine were situations in which the later deed was only a collateral agreement, which did not occupy the same total "area" of legal operation as the earlier agreement.[229] But a warranty given on the making of a contract would merge in the later deed of conveyance. So, in the *Moretta* case,[230] a statement as to the date when a first mortgage was due was either an innocent misrepresentation or a warranty. If it were a warranty, the Alberta Court of Appeal held, the doctrine of merger applied. Therefore, once the land had been transferred, the transfer registered, and a certificate of title issued, the purchaser could no longer sue the vendor in respect of the expense of additional financing incurred by reason of the incorrect date given by the vendor to the purchaser.

However in *Fraser-Reid v. Droumsekas,*[231] the Supreme Court of Canada appears to have changed the nature of the doctrine. Dickson J. said[232]

> Although it is the general rule that the acceptance of a deed is prima facie full execution of the agreement to convey, and preliminary agreements and understandings relating to the sale of land become merged in the conveyance, such a rule is not applicable to independent covenants or collateral stipulations in an agreement of sale not intended by the parties to be incorporated in the conveyance.

---

224 *Sharpe v. Gibbs* (1864), 16 C.B.N.S. 527; *Gore Bank v. McWhirter* (1868), 18 U.C.C.P. 293 at 298 *per* Wilson J.

225 *Knight Sugar Co. v. Alta. Ry. & Irrigation Co.*, [1938] 1 D.L.R. 321 at 324 (P.C.).

226 (1983), 50 A.R. 168 at 176 (Alta. C.A.). Compare the view expressed in *Color Your World Inc. v. Robert F. Avery Holdings Ltd.* (1988), 88 A.R. 163 (Alta. Q.B.).

227 *Reese v. R.*, [1957] S.C.R. 794 (S.C.C.). Note also *merger by judgment*, when there has been an action on the contract: *Conquer v. Boot*, [1928] 2 K.B. 336.

228 Hence, the exclusion of oral evidence to establish a collateral agreement: *First National Mtge. Co. v. Grouse Nest Resorts Ltd.* (1977), 2 B.C.L.R. 300 (B.C.C.A.). But the idea of collateral contracts has developed to cope with many different kinds of situation: above, pp. 505-515.

229 *Wenbourne v. J.I. Case Threshing Machine Co.*, [1917] 2 W.W.R. 150 (Alta. S.C.); upheld on appeal by a divided court, [1917] 2 W.W.R. 1262 (Alta. C.A.).

230 Above, note 226.

231 (1980), 103 D.L.R. (3d) 385 (S.C.C.).

232 *Ibid.*, at 394; compare *Hashman v. Anjulin Farms Ltd.*, [1973] S.C.R. 268 (S.C.C.).

The suggestion here is that whether merger operates depends on the parties' intentions, not on the strict application of a rule of law. In the absence of evidence on the point, there is no presumption that the purchaser intended to surrender or abandon the rights acquired by him under the sale agreement. "There is no presumption of merger," said Dickson J.,[233] commenting on the decision of the Ontario Court of Appeal in *Richview Constructon Co. v. Raspa*.[234] The proper inquiry should be to determine whether the facts disclose a common intention to merge the warranty in the deed.[235] Hence, while there was evidence in the *Richview* case to support merger, no such evidence existed in the *Fraser-Reid* case, so that, there being no proof that the parties intended that the conveyance should be taken as performance or satisfaction of the warranty in the sale agreement as to compliance with municipal building by-laws, the doctrine of merger did not apply.

According to the language of Dickson J., therefore, the doctrine of merger would seem to approximate to doctrines dependent upon the express or implicit intentions of the parties. It does not seem to be a doctrine of law. Moreover in the *Moretta* case,[236] Kerans J.A. was very critical of the doctrine, and would have restricted its operation to questions of title to land. The doctrine was distinguishable from rescission by substitution of a new agreement, acceptance or election, and fraud. It was based upon the need for finality and certainty in business affairs.[237] But it resulted in a curious extension of the doctrine of *caveat emptor*. By that principle, the buyer obtained what he bargained for, and nothing more. Under the doctrine of merger, however, the buyer did not even obtain what he had bargained for, since once there was a conveyance, the buyer could no longer complain if his expectations were not realized (in the absence of fraud).

The doctrine is certainly a strange one that is possibly undergoing some more critical examination in recent times. The effect of this may be to restrict its operation to situations where parties have clearly expressed their intention that contractual promises should not outlive their transfer to another agreement, such as a deed, or a conveyance, or to limit its scope so far as concerns the kinds of promises to which the doctrine can apply. For this reason it is difficult to accept that the doctrine of merger explains the cases where the victim of an innocent misrepresentation loses any rights of action he might have had once the property in respect of which the misrepresentation was made has been conveyed to him.[238] This doctrine has never applied to transactions involving personal property, such as goods. Although the doctrine of merger is culled from the law of real property,[239] there seems no good reason why it should be more generously invoked to affect

---

233 Above, note 231, at 397.

234 (1975), 66 D.L.R. (3d) 193 (Ont. C.A.).

235 This was applied by Adams J. in *Roussel v. Saunders* (1990), 85 Nfld. & P.E.I.R. 228 at 241 (Nfld. T.D.), where the learned judge also held that there was fraudulent misrepresentation to which the doctrine of merger did not apply.

236 Above, note 226 at 179-180.

237 Compare *Redican v. Nesbitt*, [1924] S.C.R. 135 at 146 (S.C.C.) *per* Duff J.

238 Above, pp. 306-307. The doctrine will not apply if a misrepresentation is fraudulent: above, note 235.

239 *Fraser-Reid v. Droumsekas*, above, note 231 at 394.

misrepresentations as well as terms of a contract. Indeed, the importance of the discussion of the statement in the *Moretta* case was that only if it amounted to a warranty and was not just a misrepresentation, would it be affected by the doctrine of merger.

(ii) *Impossibility or frustration*

Performance will no longer be required, and, indeed, the contract will be determined, if it becomes impossible to fulfil contractual obligations by reason of some significant factual occurrence, or change of the law. Similarly, performance, will be frustrated, if some act or event renders it no longer feasible or purposeful to fulfil the contract.[240] When this situation arises, there may be rights and liabilties between the parties arising under the common law or modern statutory revisions.[241] Such rights and liabilities, however, stem from the law of quasi-contract, unjust enrichment, or restitution, rather than from the law of contract.[242] It is a debatable question, however, whether the discharge of contractual obligations to perform comes about by reason of some agreement between the parties, express or, more usually, implied, or as a matter of law, under the common-law doctrine of frustration or impossibility. Although in the earlier stages of the development of this doctrine it was considered that the determination of the contract was a matter of tacit agreement (based on the notion of an "implied term"), the modern approach seems to indicate that the effects of impossibility or a frustrating event are imposed as a matter of law.[243] Hence, it may be suggested that one way in which a contract comes to an end, and performance is no longer obligatory, is by reason of this principle of law, namely, that impossibility or frustration operates to discharge parties from such of their contractual obligations as have not yet accrued at the time of the impossibility or frustration intervened.

---

240 Below, Chapter 16.
241 Below, pp. 661-667.
242 Below, pp. 662, 666; and see Fridman, *Restitution*, 2nd ed. (1992), pp. 205-209, 313-315; Maddaugh & McCamus, *Law of Restitution* (1990), Chapter 18.
243 Below, pp. 622-640.

15

Breach

1. Varieties of breach

(a) Distinctions of time and effect

The converse of performance is breach. Non-performance of a contract in any way, or to any degree, and whether deliberate, accidental, through negligence, or unintended, amounts to a breach of contract, unless excused, justified, or otherwise dealt with by the law.[1] In Lord Diplock's words[2] "every failure to perform a primary obligation is a breach of contract." However, different breaches have different effects.

To differentiate varieties of breach would seem to be unnecessary. Yet in a series of cases stretching from at least the middle of the nineteenth century[3] the distinction was drawn between: (1) a failure to perform when performance became due; and (2) a repudiation of the contract in advance of the date for performance which became known as "anticipatory breach" (a phrase that has not gone without criticism as being misleading).[4]

A further, perhaps earlier drawn, distinction was between breaches which would justify the innocent party in treating the contract as at an end and those which only allowed the innocent victim to claim damages for the loss incurred. Whether a breach belonged to the first or second category depended upon the type of contractual term that was breached. Thus was conceived and born the division of contractual terms into "conditions" and "warranties", a dichotomy the development and modern history of which have previously been discussed.[5] As already observed, the modern law of contract also evolved the ideas of (i) "intermediate" or "innominate" terms, and (ii) "fundamental terms".[6] The consequences of a breach of such terms depended upon a number of factors.

First was the question whether the intermediate term was to be treated more like a condition, such that its breach entitled the innocent party to regard the contract as ended as far as his performance was concerned, though not as far as concerned the liability of the contract-breaker, or more like a warranty, so as to entitle the victim only to sue for damages. This, in turn, was dependent upon whether the breach deprived the victim of substantially the whole benefit of the contract that he was supposed to obtain from its performance. Second was the question whether the breach in question was so fundamental, or the term broken was of such a character, that the breach was not simply a failure to fulfil one obligation imposed on the contract-breaker by the contract but constituted a complete non-performance. In effect this, too, involved the issue whether the innocent party had been substantially deprived of the whole benefit of the contract. Third, the relevance of "breach of fundamental term" (or, as it was expressed sometimes, "fundamental breach") was dependent on whether the contract contained an exemption, exclusion,

---

1 *E.g.*, under the doctrine of impossibility or frustration: below, Chapter 16.
2 *Photo Production Ltd. v. Securicor Tpt. Ltd.*, [1980] 1 All E.R. 556 at 566 (H.L.). The onus is always on the innocent party to establish that a breach has occurred: *Hall Motors Ltd. v. F. Rogers & Co.* (1918), 46 D.L.R. 639 (Ont. C.A.) *per* Riddell J.A. See also *North v. Victoria Baseball & Athletic Co.*, [1949] 1 W.W.R. 1033 (B.C.S.C.); *Minto Const. Co. v. Wasson* (1951), 29 M.P.R. 1 (N.B.C.A.) (conduct of defendant was not a breach). Compare *Schrider v. Long Bay Lbr. Co.* (1961), 36 W.W.R. 319 (B.C.C.A.) (conduct was breach).
3 *Hochster v. De La Tour* (1853), 2 E. & B. 678, 118 E.R. 922; below, pp. 600-612.
4 It is not really an anticipatory breach of an act to be done in the future, but the breach of a *presently binding* promise: *Bradley v. H. Newson Sons & Co.*, [1919] A.C. 16 at 53-54 (H.L.) *per* Lord Wrenbury.
5 Above, pp. 487-497.
6 Above, pp. 498-503.

or similar clause.[7] If it did not, then, it would seem, the question of fundamental breach never arose; it was subsumed under the issue of whether the breach was a breach of condition or breach of warranty. If the contract did contain such a clause, then the idea of fundamental breach, or breach of fundamental term, was invoked as one method of circumventing the otherwise applicable clause, thereby permitting the victim of the breach to sue (or to sue for his actual damage, not the amount to which he was limited under the clause).

Thus, the effect of a breach of contract was different according to the nature of the breach. To determine the legal consequences of a breach of contract it may be necessary to consider: (a) the character of the term that has been broken; (b) the practical effects of the breach; (c) the time when the breach occurred; and (d) the nature and effect of an exclusion, exemption or limitation clause upon both the duty to perform imposed by the contract on the party alleged to be in breach and the liability of such party under the contract.

There is a vital difference between, on the one hand, the breach of a condition, a fundamental term, or an intermediate term that is characterized as a condition (whether called so or not in the contract, or construed as such as at the time of contracting), and the breach of a warranty on the other. The latter can never discharge or determine the contract; nor can it relieve the innocent party of his duty to perform under the contract. It entitles the innocent party only to sue for damages.[8] The former kinds of breach entitle the innocent party to treat the contract as ended, to the extent of terminating his obligations, without terminating the liability of the party in breach. Indeed, this difference is relevant whether the breach occurs at the time when performance is due, or prior to the due date for performance, by way of repudiation of the contract.

(b) Discharge by breach

Although it is commonplace to speak of discharge of a contract by breach, meaning the breach of a condition (or its equivalent), the result of such a breach is not the automatic termination of the contract, as has been clarified by recent decisions of the House of Lords.[9] The true effect of a breach which may be said to "discharge" the contract is to relieve the innocent party of his obligations to perform under the contract (and to entitle him to sue for damages in respect of

---

7 See, *e.g., Bagnell's Cleaners & Launderers Ltd. v. Eastern Automobile Co.* (1991), 111 N.S.R. (2d) 51 (N.S.T.D.), in which the court spoke in terms of breach of fundamental term, despite the attitude expressed by the Supreme Court of Canada in *Hunter Engineering Co. v. Syncrude Can. Ltd.* (1989), 57 D.L.R. (4th) 321: below, pp. 597-600.

8 See, *e.g., Carter v. Elm Mercury Sales (1976) Ltd.* (1990), 82 Nfld. & P.E.I.R. 130 (Nfld. T.D.), where the defects in the vehicle, necessitating repairs on several occasions, did not amount to the kind of breach justifying "rescission" of the contract (*i.e.,* the victim's right to treat the contract as terminated: see below, p. 561, on the correct use of "rescission") but did entitle the victim to damages; compare *Magnetic Marketing Ltd. v. Print Three Franchising Corp.* (1991), 38 C.P.R. (3d) 540 (B.C.S.C.).

9 *Johnson v. Agnew*, [1979] 1 All E.R. 883 (H.L.); *Photo Production Ltd. v. Securicor Tpt. Ltd.*, [1980] 1 All E.R. 556 (H.L.); *Afovos Shipping Co. S.A. v. Pagnan*, [1983] 1 All E.R. 449 (H.L.).

his loss, in accordance with principles examined in a later chapter).[10] Other aspects of the contract may remain unaffected. This is of special importance in regard to exemption and similar clauses.[11] For the moment, however, the vital point to stress is that a breach of condition, or of a clause that is treated like a condition, whatever else it may do, does not completely destroy or end the effective operation of the contract except as regards the duties imposed thereunder on the victim of the breach. If the breach occurs prior to the due date for performance, that is, if it is an anticipatory repudiation of the contract, it may not have even that limited effect.[12]

However, a breach of condition will not produce such a discharge of the contract unless the innocent victim elects to make it do so.[13] The innocent party has the option whether to put an end to his obligations under the contract, holding himself no longer bound to perform the duties it placed on him, or to maintain the binding quality of the contract as far as himself and the contract-breaker are concerned.[14] The chief qualification of this is where the breach comes about by reason of impossibility or a frustrating event. In addition, the conduct of the innocent party may also affect his right to elect to determine the contract in the way described. In the first place that party may "waive" the breach, or the proper performance of the contract. If this occurs, he can no longer complain of the breach or the manner of the performance, unless some later conduct of the other party overrides the waiver. Second, the allegedly innocent victim of a breach may be estopped from treating the other party's conduct as a breach justifying discharge or termination along the lines mentioned. Such an estoppel can arise in ways previously discussed, and will operate to debar the alleged victim of a breach from pursuing the usual rights when a breach has occurred, unless and until the estoppel no longer operates to affect the parties' mutual rights and obligations.[15]

Subject to such modifications, the victim of a breach has the right to elect what is to happen as a consequence. At one time the result of his election to determine the contract was said to involve "rescission" of the contract. The use of this expression, much as the improper use of the expressions "termination" and "discharge", caused confusion. It gave the impression that the effect of an election

---

10 Thus, a seller guilty of a fundamental breach (below, pp. 561-571) could not sue for the price of the goods in *Polar Refrigeration Service Ltd. v. Moldenhauer* (1967), 61 D.L.R. (2d) 462 (Sask. Q.B.); compare *Group West Systems Ltd. v. Werner's Refrigeration Co.* (1988), 85 A.R. 82 (Alta. Q.B.); *Montgomery Kone Elevators Co. v. Great-West Life Assurance Co.* (1992), 79 Man. R. (2d) 66 (Man. Q.B.), where the plaintiff guilty of fundamental breach lost its action and was liable on the defendant's counterclaim.

11 Below, pp. 588-600.

12 Below, pp. 612-622.

13 *Denmark Productions Ltd. v. Boscobel Productions Ltd.*, [1969] 1 Q.B. 699 at 724 (C.A.) *per* Salmon L.J.

14 *Photo Production Ltd. v. Securicor Tpt. Ltd.*, above, note 9, at 566-567 *per* Lord Diplock; *Suisse Atlantique Société d'Armament Maritime S.A. v. N.V. Rotterdamsche Kolen Centrale*, [1967] 1 A.C. 361 (H.L.); *Shibamoto & Co. v. Western Fish Producers Inc. (Trustee of)* (1991), 43 F.T.R. 1 at 26 (Fed. T.D.) *per* Rouleau J.; affirmed (1992), 145 N.R. 91 (Fed. C.A.); *Norfolk v. Aikens* (1990), 64 D.L.R. (4th) 1 at 15 (B.C.C.A.).

15 On frustration, see below, Chapter 16; on waiver and estoppel, above, pp. 544-549.

to determine following a breach rendered the contract invalid and not binding, when, in fact, as is now clear, the contract may still have vital consequences, and govern the respective rights and liabilities of the parties. Decisions in England have made explicit that the term "rescission" is inaccurately applied to this situation.[16] A contract may be rescinded (by an act of the party affected or by the court) when it has been entered into as a result of some misconduct which justifies such a course, for example, a fraudulent misrepresentation. When this happens the contract is avoided and is retrospectively treated as being void *ab initio*. It never validly came into existence. Consequently its terms do not bind either party to the purported contract.[17] Where a contract is terminated, or discharged, for breach, the contract is not avoided. The contract may be, in Lord Wilberforce's phrase,[18] "gone". As he said, "what is dead is dead" (in the sense that a party who has chosen to put an end to a contract by accepting the other party's repudiation cannot afterwards seek specific performance). But the contract is very much alive, and is still valid and binding so far as concerns such other matters as the liability of the contract-breaker under its terms, the possible application of an exclusion or similar clause, and the possibility that the dispute between the parties must be submitted to arbitration.[19] Rescission is not the correct way to describe what may occur when a breach of contract has taken place. Rescission refers to the fate of voidable contracts, not to the termination of initially valid, but subsequently broken contracts.

Where the contract contains an exclusion or similar clause, a breach of condition or its equivalent may not give the victim any rights to terminate or discharge the contract or to sue for damages. What happens will depend upon the language of the clause in question, and the way it is interpreted by the courts. Notwithstanding such language and its interpretation, the effect of the clause may be circumvented or circumscribed by the characterization of the breach in question as a fundamental breach. It is important, therefore, to understand the concept of fundamental breach, and to consider exclusion and similar clauses with special reference to the effect of a fundamental breach.

2. Fundamental breach

(a) Fundamental breach and breach of condition

The essence of a "condition", in contrast with a "warranty", was that it went to the root of the contract.[20] Therefore a breach of condition virtually denied the innocent party the benefit of whatever he expected to obtain under the agreement.

---

16 *Buckland v. Farmer & Moody*, [1978] 3 All E.R. 929 (C.A.); *Johnson v. Agnew*, above, note 9. But Canadian courts persist in the usage: see *Carter v. Elm Mercury Sales (1976) Ltd.*, above, note 8; *Magnetic Marketing Ltd. v. Print Three Franchising Corp.*, above, note 8; *Shaganappi Motors (1976) Ltd. v. Hildt* (1992), 128 A.R. 206 (Alta. Q.B.).

17 Compare above, pp. 300-303; below, pp. 807-808.

18 *Johnson v. Agnew*, above, note 9, at 894.

19 *Heyman v. Darwins Ltd.*, [1942] A.C. 356 (H.L.).

20 Above, pp. 489-496.

Until the modern evolution of exemption, exclusion and limitation clauses,[21] the differentiation of breach of condition from breach of warranty sufficed for practical and theoretical purposes. The rise in importance and frequency of exclusion and similar clauses in twentieth century commercial life, coupled with the emergence of so-called standard-form contracts, or *contrats d'adhesion*, made the older, classical analysis inept for the purpose of dealing with the legal problems of parties who were effectively deprived of any true bargaining power. Such standard-form contracts involved the offeree in accepting or rejecting the offer in the terms in which it was made, without any opportunity, or only a limited opportunity, to alter any of its provisions.[22] In particular, the offeror included an exemption or similar clause, for his protection, and would not permit its excision from the contract. Indeed, in many instances the offeree may have been unaware of such clause, or, if aware, was not in any position to object or demand its removal.[23] A further development was the recognition that not all terms could be easily and immediately classified in advance of any litigation as being either conditions or warranties.[24] These factors led to the emergence of the idea of "fundamental terms", the failure to perform which being treated as a "fundamental breach". However, the exposition of such fundamental terms, and the distinction between fundamental breach and other, notionally less fundamental breaches, that is, of conditions or warranties, became confused. Wherein lay the difference between a fundamental term and a condition? What was, or could be, more fundamental to a contract than a condition (as that expression had been understood)? How did a fundamental breach differ from a breach of condition, and in what way was it more fundamental?

The resolution of these problems is to be found in the speeches in the House of Lords in *Photo Production Ltd. v. Securicor Transport Ltd.*,[25] which have been approved, accepted and applied by the Supreme Court of Canada.[26] In the *Photo Production* case[27] Lord Diplock drew an important distinction between fundamental breach and breach of condition. A fundamental breach occurs "where the event resulting from the failure by one party to perform a primary obligation has the effect of depriving the other party of substantially the whole benefit which it was

---

21 Below, pp. 571-600.

22 *A. Schroeder Music Publishing Co. v. Macaulay*, [1974] 3 All E.R. 616 (H.L.).

23 Below, pp. 573-578.

24 Above, pp. 487-497.

25 [1980] 1 All E.R. 556 (H.L.), in which the House of Lords rejected the earlier approach in *Suisse Atlantique Société d'Armament Maritime S.A. v. N.V. Rotterdamsche Kolen Centrale*, [1967] 1 A.C. 361 (H.L.): see [1980] 1 All E.R. 556 at 561 (H.L.) *per* Lord Wilberforce.

26 *Hunter Engineering Co. v. Syncrude Can. Ltd.* (1989), 57 D.L.R. (4th) 321 at 337-340 (S.C.C.) *per* Dickson C.J.C., at 369 *per* Wilson J.; *Beaufort Realties (1964) Inc. v. Chomedey Aluminum Co.* (1980), 116 D.L.R. (3d) 193 (S.C.C.). See also *Cathcart Inspection Services Ltd. v. Purolator Courier Ltd.* (1982), 139 D.L.R. (3d) 371 (Ont. C.A.); *Borg-Warner Accept. Can. Ltd. v. Wynozek* (1981), 122 D.L.R. (3d) 737 (Sask. Q.B.); *Nabel Leasing Division of Citicorp Leasing Can. Ltd. v. Walwyn Stodgell Cochran Murray Ltd.* (1982), 41 N.B.R. (2d) 291 (N.B.Q.B.); *Can. Dom. Leasing Corp. v. George A. Welch & Co.* (1981), 125 D.L.R. (3d) 723 (Ont. C.A.).

27 Above, note 25, at 566-567. For some criticism of the language and analysis of Lord Diplock, see Lord Denning M.R., in *George Mitchell (Chesterhall) Ltd. v. Finney Lock Seeds Ltd..*, [1983] 1 All E.R. 108 at 116 (C.A.); affirmed [1983] 2 All E.R. 737 (H.L.).

the intention of the parties that he should obtain from the contract." A breach of condition occurs

> where the contracting parties have agreed, whether by express words or by implication of law, that any failure by one party to perform a particular primary obligation ("condition" in the nomenclature of the Sale of Goods Act . . .[28]), irrespective of the gravity of the event that has in fact resulted from the breach, shall entitle the other party to put an end to all primary obligations of both parties remaining unperformed.[29]

The distinction between fundamental breach and breach of condition therefore turns upon the factual, as well as legal, consequences of each type of breach. At first sight there would appear to be little or no difference between the two kinds of breach. In practice, as well as in theory, there is a very important distinction. In both situations, the innocent party may elect whether to put an end to the primary obligations of the parties remaining unperformed, in which respect these breaches differ from other breaches of a primary obligation under the contract. A difference appears when the effect of an exclusion or similar clause is being considered.

In England that difference is no longer as important since the passage in 1977 of legislation controlling the extent to which parties may exclude or limit liability under certain contracts.[30] The situation in Canada is not the same, although, as Wilson J. pointed out in *Hunter Engineering Co. v. Syncrude Canada Ltd.*,[31] some provinces have some legislative protection in this area. Where such statutes are inapplicable, as in the *Hunter Engineering* case, the present position in Canada is unclear, in consequence of the speeches in that case.[32] What can be said is that a party can more easily exclude or limit liability for breach of a condition than for a fundamental breach.

(b) Fundamental breach and fundamental term[33]

Prior to the *Photo Production* case it might have been said that fundamental breach and breach of a fundamental term were two different ways of dealing with the same issue: namely, whether the breach in question was of such a character that it was not affected by an exclusion, exemption or limitation clause in the contract.[34] As late as 1977, in one Canadian case,[35] the approach adopted was

---

28 Above, p. 488.

29 For his distinction between primary obligations, in the express words of the contract or incorporated by implication of law from the legal nature of the contract, and secondary obligations substituted on a breach of a primary obligation, see [1980] 1 All E.R. 556 at 566 (H.L.).

30 Unfair Contract Terms Act, 1977 (U.K.), c. 50; Cheshire, Fifoot & Furmston's *Law of Contract*, 12th ed. (1991), pp. 179-198; Treitel, *Law of Contract*, 8th ed. (1991), pp. 226-244.

31 (1989), 57 D.L.R. (4th) 321 at 377-378 (S.C.C.).

32 Below, pp. 597-600.

33 See also above, pp. 498-500.

34 *Cain v. Bird Chevrolet-Oldsmobile Ltd.* (1976), 69 D.L.R. (3d) 484 at 486 (Ont. H.C.); reversed in part (1978), 88 D.L.R. (3d) 607 (Ont. C.A.). But the *Suisse Atlantique* case (itself now discredited) caused some difficulty in this respect: Fridman, "The Effect of Exclusion Clauses" (1969), 7 Alta. L. Rev. 281. Nonetheless the possibility of a breach of a fundamental term was also considered in *Shanganappi Motors (1976) Ltd. v. Hildt* (1992), 128 A.R. 206 (Alta. Q.B.), relying on *Keefe*

to treat the defendant's wrongdoing, selling a new automobile with a worn crankshaft which was defective at the time of purchase, as the breach of a fundamental term of the contract. This changed in later decisions.[36] The language of the Supreme Court of Canada in the *Hunter Engineering* case[37] indicates that the idea of fundamental breach has become endemic. In subsequent cases the issue has been whether what occurred was a fundamental breach (which justified the behaviour of the other party), or was not.[38]

There may have been a valid reason for creating the idea of a fundamental term, and treating its breach as possibly theoretically distinct from a fundamental breach. Before recent developments with respect to exclusion and similar clauses, it might have been said that a clause that purported to exclude liability for breaches of conditions and warranties did not effectively exclude liability for breaches of a fundamental term; whereas a fundamental breach, which might nonetheless have been equated with a breach of condition, albeit not a breach of warranty, fell within the ambit of the exclusion clause, so that the innocent party was deprived of any remedy. Since this issue is now a matter of construction of the contract,[39] there seems little point in marking any distinction between the breach of a fundamental term and a fundamental breach. Indeed, having regard to what has been occurring with respect to the analysis of contractual terms, namely, the breakdown of the condition-warranty dichotomy,[40] the true effect of a breach of contract depends not so much upon the *a priori* classification of a term under the rubric of "condition", "warranty", or "fundamental term", but upon the consequences of a breach on the situation of the innocent party. It is not how the parties viewed the term at the time of making the contract, but how the innocent party is affected by the breach in question. The emphasis has moved from anterior agreement to subsequent non-performance. Thus, as the Supreme Court of Canada clearly recognized in the *Hunter Engineering* case, the concept of fundamental breach is considerably more important and relevant to the determination of the rights of the parties after breach than the categorization of the term that has been breached.[41]

The question now posed for a court when a contract has been broken is the nature of the performance expected of the contract-breaker, and the likely effects

---

v. Fort (1978), 89 D.L.R. (3d) 275 (N.S.C.A.), a case which followed the *Suisse Atlantique* decision and considered whether there had been a fundamental breach; and in *Bagnell's Cleaners & Launderers Ltd. v. Eastern Automobile Ltd.* (1991), 111 N.S.R. (2d) 51 (N.S.T.D.).

35 *Bradley v. Capital Auto Elec.* (1977), 16 Nfld. & P.E.I.R. 491 (P.E.I.S.C.).

36 *E.g., Drake v. Bekins Moving & Storage Co.*, [1982] 6 W.W.R. 640 (B.C. Co. Ct.); *Kerr v. Gingras* (1980), 24 B.C.L.R. 372 (B.C.S.C.).

37 Above, note 31, at 333-343, 368-382.

38 See, *e.g., Dover Corp. (Can.) Ltd. v. Victoria Chinatown Care Society* (1988), 26 B.C.L.R. (2d) 240 (B.C.C.A.) and *Poole v. Tomenson Saunders Whitehead Ltd.* (1987), 43 D.L.R. (4th) 56 (B.C.C.A.); additional reasons at [1988] 4 W.W.R. 300 (B.C.C.A.). See further below, pp. 565-571, 588-600.

39 Below, pp. 592-600.

40 Above, pp. 497-503.

41 Compare Ogilvie, "Fundamental Breach Excluded but not Extinguished: Hunter Engineering v. Syncrude Canada" (1990), 17 Can. Bus. L.J. 75, especially at pp. 86-87.

upon the situation of the innocent party if it is broken.[42] The trend of modern contract law is away from any rigid classification of terms, even if the rigidity is mollified by the invention of new categories of terms, be they "fundamental", "intermediate" or "innominate", and towards the classification of breaches. In order to characterize the kind of breach involved in any given instance, regard must be paid to the promised performance in the light of the expectations thereby raised in the promisee, and the effects of non-performance upon those expectations. Thus, the law has become more interested in fundamental breach than in so-called fundamental terms.

(c) The nature of fundamental breach

The concept of fundamental breach has been variously described. In *Canso Chemicals Ltd. v. Canadian Westinghouse Co. (No. 2)*,[43] MacKeigan C.J.N.S. cited nine different definitions, culled from English and Canadian leading cases. It has been referred to as a breach in consequence of which the performance of the contract becomes something totally different from that which the contract contemplates.[44] It has been called "a breach which goes to the root of the contract."[45] It has been said to involve "such a congeries of defects as to destroy the workable character of the machine" (that is, the machine which was the subject-matter of the contract).[46] A fundamental breach has been defined as one which destroys "the whole

---

42 See, *e.g., Maughan v. Int. Harvester Co. of Can.* (1980), 112 D.L.R. (3d) 243 at 252-253 (N.S.C.A.); doctrine of fundamental breach did not apply to a collateral warranty given by a manufacturer. Nor could the doctrine of fundamental breach apply to a statutory warranty under the Agricultural Implements Act (Saskatchewan), which had been excluded: *Rein v. Machula*, [1977] 2 W.W.R. 244 (Sask. C.A.).

43 (1974), 54 D.L.R. (3d) 517 at 523-524 (N.S.C.A.). See also *Poole v. Tomenson Saunders Whitehead Ltd.* (1987), 43 D.L.R. (4th) 56 at 63-64 (B.C.C.A.).

44 *Suisse Atlantique Société d'Armament Maritime S.A. v. N.V. Rotterdamsche Kolen Centrale*, [1967] 1 A.C. 361 at 393 (H.L.) *per* Viscount Dilhorne; *ibid.*, at 397 *per* Lord Reid; *Leamac Indust. Dev. Ltd. v. Western GMC Truck Centre Ltd.* (1979), 14 A.R. 277 (Alta. Dist. Ct.); *Keefe v. Fort* (1979), 89 D.L.R. (3d) 275 at 279 (N.S.C.A.) *per* Pace J.A.; *Borg-Warner Accept. Can. Ltd. v. Wyonzek* (1981), 122 D.L.R. (3d) 737 (Sask. Q.B.); *Imperial Brass Ltd. v. Jacob Electric Systems Ltd.* (1989), 72 O.R. (2d) 17 at 28 (Ont. H.C.) *per* Lane J.; compare *Bagnell's Cleaners & Launderers Ltd. v. Eastern Automobile Ltd.* (1991), 111 N.S.R. (2d) 51 (N.S.T.D.), with which contrast *Carter v. Elm Mercury Sales (1976) Ltd.* (1990), 82 Nfld. & P.E.I.R. 130 (Nfld. T.D.), especially at 139 *per* Barry J.

45 *Suisse Atlantique* case, above, note 44, at 399 *per* Lord Reid; *Yeoman Credit Ltd. v. Apps*, [1961] 2 All E.R. 281 at 289 (C.A.) *per* Pearce L.J.; *Wells, Monaghan & Co. v. Parsons* (1982), 38 Nfld. & P.E.I.R. 339 (Nfld. T.D.); compare *Unified Systems Ltd. v. Cleanwater Lobsters Ltd.* (1986), 58 Nfld. & P.E.I.R. 138 (Nfld. T.D.); *Citibank Leasing Can. Ltd. v. Action Fasteners Ltd.* (1987), 74 N.B.R. (2d) 241 (N.B.Q.B.); *Mills v. Edmonton (City)* (1987), 46 D.L.R. (4th) 26 (Alta. Q.B.) *per* Berger J.; *Standard Precast Ltd. v. Dywidag Fab Con Products Ltd.* (1989), 56 D.L.R. (4th) 385 at 386 (B.C.C.A.).

46 *Pollock & Co. v. Macrae*, [1922] S.C. 192 at 200 (Scot.); *Schofield v. Gafco Ent. Ltd.* (1983), 43 A.R. 262 (Alta. C.A.).

contractual substratum,"[47] as undermining the whole contract,[48] as involving a totally different performance of the contract from that intended by the parties,[49] as involving an event which deprives the innocent party of substantially the whole benefit which that party was to obtain under the contract.[50] It has been described as a breach which entitles the innocent party to treat the contract as repudiated.[51] Perhaps the idea which most satisfactorily enshrines the idea of fundamental breach is that which appealed to Lord Diplock in the *Photo Production* case,[52] and to Wilson J. in the *Hunter Engineering* case,[53] as differentiating such a breach from breach of condition. This is the notion of some act which substantially deprives the innocent party of the intended benefit such party was to obtain under the contract. However defined, a fundamental breach is one which is more significant in factual terms, and more effective in respect of the rights and liabilities of the parties and the continued existence of the contract and their "primary obligations", in Lord Diplock's phrase, than any other kind of breach.

In every instance, it is a question of fact whether the breach complained of by the innocent party amounts to a fundamental breach. That question, in turn, depends upon: the terms of the contract; the intended benefit to the innocent party; the purpose of the contract; the material consequences of the breach; and, perhaps, though this has never been discussed in the cases, the extent to which the loss incurred by the innocent party can be remedied adequately by an award of damages.[54] One point is clear. Whether a breach is fundamental does not appear to depend upon any express terms of the contract. The determination of a fundamental breach is a teleological question not one that involves construction of the contract in the narrow, literal sense. The concept of fundamental breach

---

47 *Suisse Atlantique* case, above, note 44, at 433 *per* Lord Wilberforce.

48 *Hong Kong Fir Shipping Co. v. Kawasaki Kisen Kaisha Ltd.*, [1962] 1 All E.R. 474 at 479 (C.A.) *per* Sellers L.J.

49 *R.G. McLean Ltd. v. Can. Vickers Ltd.* (1970), 15 D.L.R. (3d) 15 at 20 (Ont. C.A.) *per* Arnup J.A.; compare *Standard Precast Ltd. v. Dywidag Fab Con Products Ltd..*, above, note 45, with which contrast *Sanko S.S. Co. v. Eacom Timber Sales Co.* (1986), 32 D.L.R. (4th) 269 (B.C.S.C.).

50 *Harbutt's Plasticine Ltd. v. Wayne Tank & Pump Co.*, [1970] 1 All E.R. 225 at 239 (C.A.) *per* Widgery L.J.

51 *Suisse Atlantique* case, above, note 44, at 397 *per* Lord Reid, and at 421-422 *per* Lord Upjohn. Compare *Poole v. Tomenson Saunders Whitehead Ltd.*, above, note 43, at 64: "the breach must be tantamount to the frustration of the contract either as a result of the unequivocal refusal of one party to perform his contractual obligation or as a result of conduct which has destroyed the commercial purpose of the contract — thereby entitling the innocent party to be relieved from future performance."; compare *Eagle Dancer Enterprises Ltd. v. Southam Printing Ltd. — Imprimerie Southam Ltée* (1992), 6 B.L.R. (2d) 45 (B.C.S.C.). See also *Montgrand v. Amok Ltd.* (1987), 57 Sask. R. 147 (Sask. Q.B.).

52 [1980] 1 All E.R. 556 at 566-567 (H.L.); and in *Hong Kong Fir Shipping Co. v. Kawasaki Kisen Kaisha Ltd.*, above, note 48, at 485. See *Ontex Resources Ltd. v. Metalore Resources Ltd.* (1993), 13 O.R. (3d) 229 at 249 (Ont. C.A.).

53 *Hunter Engineering Co. v. Syncrude Can. Ltd.* (1989), 57 D.L.R. (4th) 321 at 369 (S.C.C.). Compare *Magnetic Marketing Ltd. v. Print Three Franchising Corp.* (1991), 38 C.P.R. (3d) 540 (B.C.S.C.).

54 Compare the decisions in *Gibbard Hereford Farms v. Smith* (1974), 10 N.S.R. (2d) 272 (N.S.C.A.); *Pic-a-pop Beverages Ltd. v. G. & J. Watt Co.* (1975), 52 D.L.R. (3d) 754 (Sask. C.A.); *Davidson v. N. Amer. Business Equipment Ltd.* (1974), 49 D.L.R. (3d) 533 (Ont. Dist. Ct.).

seems to transcend the normal issues of contractual interpretation. It involves investigation of the underlying nature and purpose of the contract into which the parties have entered, and the respective benefits designed to be obtained or ensured by the agreement.[55]

Providing a truck with a defective steering system was a fundamental breach in *Davis v. Chrysler Canada Ltd.*[56] So, too, was the supply of an unsatisfactory boiler system for a ship in *Peabody Engineering Canada Ltd. v. Johnstone Shipping Ltd.*[57] In *Rosseway v. Canadian Kenworth Ltd.*,[58] a truck sold by the defendants broke down. The seller knew that the buyer needed the truck to earn income. The complete uselessness of the truck in such circumstances was a fundamental breach of the contract of sale, justifying the recovery of the buyer's purchase price, even though he had used the truck for some time prior to its final breakdown. Similarly, in *Bagnell's Cleaners & Launderers Ltd. v. Eastern Automobile Co.*,[59] the defendants were guilty of fundamental breach when they supplied a van to be used in the plaintiff's business and the van had problems with its engine, transmission and radiator that necessitated considerable maintenance and replacement. In *Bartok v. Patrician School of Personal Arts Ltd.*,[60] the plaintiff entered into a fashion merchandising course run by the defendants to obtain a diploma and register with the defendant's placement service. Her purpose was eventually to achieve a position in the fashion world. The plaintiff paid the full fee in advance and then fulfilled all but one month of the course, when the defendants wrongfully discontinued the course. This was held to be a fundamental breach, entitling the plaintiff to the return of the full fee, not just a breach of contract that might have permitted

---

55 This paragraph was quoted by Macdonell J. in *Eagle Dancer Enterprises Ltd. v. Southam Printing Ltd. — Imprimerie Southam Ltée* (1992), 6 B.L.R. (2d) 45 at 53 (B.C.S.C.); the last two sentences were quoted by Taylor J. in *Critchley v. Critchley* (1988), 30 B.C.L.R. (2d) 316 at 318 (B.C.S.C.).

56 (1977), 26 N.S.R. (2d) 410 (N.S.T.D.). See also *Belanger v. Fournier Chrysler Dodge (1975) Ltd.* (1979), 25 N.B.R. (2d) 673 (N.B.C.A.); *Dow Chemical of Can. Ltd. v. R.V. Indust. Ltd.* (1979), 9 Alta. L.R. (2d) 129 (Alta. T.D.); *Borg-Warner Accept. Can. Ltd. v. Wyonzek* (1982), 122 D.L.R. (3d) 737 (Sask. Q.B.); *Reid v. Prowse* (1983), 45 Nfld. & P.E.I.R. 216 (Nfld. Dist. Ct.); *Seich v. Festival Ford Sales Ltd.* (1978), 6 Alta. L.R. (2d) 262 (Alta. Dist. Ct.); *Cain v. Bird Chevrolet-Oldsmobile* (1976), 69 D.L.R. (3d) 484 (Ont. H.C.); appeal allowed on damages only (1978), 20 O.R. (2d) 569 (Ont. C.A.); *Chabot v. Ford Motor Co. of Can.* (1982), 138 D.L.R. (3d) 417 (Ont. H.C.); *Murphy v. Penny Motors Ltd.* (1979), 23 Nfld. & P.E.I.R. 152 (Nfld. T.D.).

57 (1979), 26 N.R. 76 (Fed. C.A.); leave to appeal to S.C.C. refused (1979), 30 N.R. 270n (S.C.C.). As was the total lack of maintenance that led to the dangerous state of a bolt and the collapse of the crane loaned to one of the parties to litigation by another party in *Daigle v. Cape Breton Crane Rentals Ltd.* (1985), 64 N.B.R. (2d) 129 (N.B.Q.B.); additional reasons at (1985), 64 N.B.R. (2d) 403 (N.B.Q.B.); revesed in part on other grounds (1987), 77 N.B.R. (2d) 319 (N.B.C.A.); leave to appeal to S.C.C. refused (1987), 79 N.B.R. (2d) 180 (note) (S.C.C.).

58 (1978), 6 Alta. L.R. (2d) 177 (Alta. Dist. Ct.); compare *Murphy v. Penny Motors Ltd.* (1979), 23 Nfld. & P.E.I.R. 152 (Nfld. T.D.).

59 (1991), 111 N.S.R. (2d) 51 (N.S.T.D.), relying on *Canso Chemicals Ltd. v. Can. Westinghouse Co.* (1974), 54 D.L.R. (3d) 517 (N.S.C.A.).

60 (1977), 2 B.L.R. 275 (Ont. C.A.). So, too, in *Shaganappi Motors (1976) Ltd. v. Hildt* (1992), 128 A.R. 206 (Alta. Q.B.), the defendant failed to drill wells as promised in the contract under which the plaintiff acquired an interest in a petroleum and gas lease in return for providing a special car. The defendant was liable for fundamental breach.

recovery of the unfulfilled portion of the fee. The notion of fundamental breach was explored in *Captain v. Far Eastern Steamship Co.*,[61] where it was held that it involved doing more than performing the contract in a negligent or unreasonable manner. It involved doing something that was right outside the proper performance of the contract. Here the contract was to ship the plaintiff's goods below deck. The defendants knew that the storage containers used by them were not waterproof. They also knew that protecting the plaintiff's goods from water was vital. Hence, leaving the goods on the dock for three weeks after arrival at the port in Canada was a fundamental breach (which had important consequences with respect to the exculpatory clause contained in the contract). The failure to deliver enough material to erect a building, which the buyer was obliged to build, was a fundamental breach in *Nikkel v. Standard Group Ltd.*[62] So was the withdrawal of a senior partner from a firm of lawyers, in *Wells, Monaghan & Co. v. Parsons*,[63] because the earnings of the defendant depended on the amount brought into the partnership by all the participants; therefore, the senior partner's breach went to the root of the contract. In consequence the affected partner could repudiate the contract without having to pay the liquidated damages otherwise due on withdrawal. Furthermore in *Gallant v. Hobbs*,[64] even though the contract for the sale of a racehorse excluded all warranties, the fact that the horse, when delivered, was suffering from rabies (with which it had been infected at the time of the sale) amounted to a fundamental breach. The risk was on the seller of the horse, not on the buyer. A failure to list an orthodontist in the yellow pages was a fundamental breach of contract in *Mills v. Edmonton (City).*[65] So was the failure to perform a contract for cleaning and janitorial services during the contract's probationary period.[66] A purchaser of land who promised, but never intended, to plant alfalfa to be offered for sale to a stipulated party, was guilty of a fundamental breach in *Murray v. Saskatchewan;*[67] so was a promoter of fights who, because of his difficulties with the boxing commission, and other problems, was unable to schedule and promote fights for the boxer whom he represented.[68] Similarly, the failure to provide computer software

---

61 (1978), 97 D.L.R. (3d) 251 (B.C.S.C.); compare *Celgar Ltd. v. Star Bulk Shipping Co.*, [1979] 4 W.W.R. 248 (B.C.C.A.).

62 (1982), 16 Man. R. (2d) 71 (Man. Q.B.).

63 (1982), 38 Nfld. & P.E.I.R. 339 (Nfld. T.D.). And the return of a truck which had been pledged as security for a company's liability: *Brandon Petroleum Sales Ltd. v. Harasewich* (1989), 99 A.R. 81 (Alta. Master).

64 (1982), 37 O.R. (2d) 1 (Ont. Co. Ct.); affirmed (1983), 40 O.R. (2d) 377 (Ont. C.A.).

65 (1987), 46 D.L.R. (4th) 26 (Alta. Q.B.).

66 *Montgrand v. Amok Ltd.* (1987), 57 Sask. R. 147 (Sask. Q.B.); *Dover Corp. (Can.) Ltd. v. Victoria Chinatown Care Society* (1988), 26 B.C.L.R. (2d) 240 (B.C.C.A.); *Montgomery Kone Elevators Co. v. Great-West Life Assurance Co.* (1992), 79 Man. R. (2d) 66 (Man. Q.B.). Contrast *Poole v. Tomenson Saunders Whitehead Ltd.* (1987), 43 D.L.R. (4th) 56 (B.C.C.A.); additional reasons at [1988] 4 W.W.R. 300 (B.C.C.A.); *Signcorp Invts. Ltd. v. Brown Derby Family Restaurants Inc.* (1992), 103 Sask. R. 314 (Sask. Q.B.).

67 [1987] 3 W.W.R. 541 (Sask. C.A.).

68 *Lalonde v. Coleman* (1990), 67 Man. R. (2d) 187 (Man. Q.B.).

as agreed in a contract was a fundamental breach in *Group West Systems Ltd. v. Werner's Refrigeration Co.*[69]

A serious defect in a vehicle or machine sold or leased by the defendant to the plaintiff has not always rendered the defendant guilty of a fundamental breach.[70] Nor has a departure from the terms of the contract always been considered so fundamental as to permit invocation of the doctrine for the purposes of circumventing the application of an exclusionary clause.[71] In one instance,[72] where a finding of fundamental breach was negatived, the court said that in all the cases in which a fundamental breach was found (where a defective chattel was involved) the defects in the chattel were apparent almost immediately after the chattel had been delivered. "I have found no case," said Stevenson J., "where a defect that appeared after the lapse of a considerable time and following intensive use of the chattel has been held to amount to a fundamental breach." In one instance it was said that the buyer of a truck that broke down several times might have alleged fundamental breach the first time a breakdown occurred, but could not do so when later the same thing happened.[73] The defective nature of the thing that was sold or leased must be inherent at the time of the transaction, and must appear within a reasonable time. However, if the buyer or lessee of the chattel fails to object and seek redress, the breach in question might not justify repudiation of the contract on the basis of fundamental breach.[74] Nor can such a breach be alleged where the plaintiff designed the subject-matter of the contract, which subsequently failed to perform properly.[75] There must be some totally different performance from that

---

69 (1988), 85 A.R. 82 (Alta. Q.B.): compare *Woodman's Sea Products Ltd. v. Lush* (1990), 84 Nfld. & P.E.I.R. 79 (Nfld. T.D.); *Imperial Brass Ltd. v. Jacob Electric Systems Ltd.* (1989), 72 O.R. (2d) 17 (Ont. H.C.). Contrast *Unified Systems Ltd. v. Clearwater Lobsters Ltd.* (1986), 58 Nfld. & P.E.I.R. 138 (Nfld. T.D.).

70 *Keefe v. Fort* (1978), 89 D.L.R. (3d) 275 (N.S.C.A.); *Gaklis v. Wells* (1979), 37 N.S.R. (2d) 451 (N.S.C.A.); *Mallaley v. Goiziou* (1980), 27 N.B.R. (2d) 309 (N.B.Q.B.); *Schofield v. Gafco Enterprises Ltd.* (1983), 43 A.R. 262 (Alta. C.A.); *Nabel Leasing Div. of Citicorp Leasing Can. Ltd. v. Walwyn Stodgell Cochran Murray Ltd.* (1982), 41 N.B.R. (2d) 291 (N.B.Q.B.); *R.E. Newell Fisheries Ltd. v. Gow* (1983), 22 B.L.R. 179 (N.S.T.D.); *Citibank Leasing Can. Ltd. v. Action Fasteners Ltd.* (1986), 74 N.B.R. (2d) 241 (N.B.Q.B.); *Savin Can. Inc. v. Wood* (1986), 72 N.B.R. (2d) 206 (N.B.Q.B.) (lessee's own fault); *Michael Ede Leasing Ltd. v. Kleysen Transport Ltd.* (1986), 42 Man. R. (2d) 52 (Man. C.A.); *Carter v. Elm Mercury Sales (1976) Ltd.* (1990), 82 Nfld. & P.E.I.R. 130 (Nfld. T.D.); *Standard Precast Ltd. v. Dywidag Fab Con Products Ltd.* (1989), 56 D.L.R. (4th) 385 (B.C.C.A.).

71 *McCain Produce Co. v. C.N.R.; Pirie Potato Co. v. C.N.R.; Toner Bros. v. C.N.R.* (1979), 25 N.B.R. (2d) 585 (N.B.Q.B.); affirmed (1980), 113 D.L.R. (3d) 584 (N.B.C.A.); affirmed (1981), 123 D.L.R. (3d) 764 (S.C.C.).

72 *Volvo Can. Ltd. v. Fox* (1980), 20 N.B.R. (2d) 1 at 8 (N.B.Q.B.).

73 *Leamac Indust. Dev. Ltd. v. Western GMC Truck Centre Ltd.* (1979), 14 A.R. 277 (Alta. Dist. Ct.).

74 But there may still be repudiation for fundamental breach if the seller or lessor has attempted to repair the defect but has not succeeded in doing so, even if this takes some time and several months have elapsed since the original sale or lease: *Beldessi v. Island Equip. Ltd.* (1973), 41 D.L.R. (3d) 147 (B.C.C.A.); *Burroughs Business Machines Ltd. v. Feed-Rite Mills (1962) Ltd.* (1976), 42 D.L.R. (3d) 303 (Man. C.A.); affirmed (1976), 64 D.L.R. (3d) 767 (S.C.C.); *P.U.C. (Waterloo) v. Burroughs Business Machines Ltd.* (1974), 52 D.L.R. (3d) 481 (Ont. C.A.); *R.G. McLean Ltd. v. Can. Vickers Ltd.* (1970), 15 D.L.R. (3d) 15 (Ont. C.A.).

75 *R.E. Newell Fisheries Ltd. v. Gow,* above, note 70.

contemplated by the parties. Therefore, a plaintiff who provided the plans for the machine built by the defendant ought to have contemplated the possibility that, as designed, the machine would not function as intended. Moreover, a negligent mode of performance must be distinguished from a non-performance. Thus, where cartons of sunglasses were stolen because of the defendant's negligence, this was not a fundamental breach, although it was a breach of the contract.[76] Similarly, in *McCain Produce Co. v. Canadian National Railway Co.; Pirie Potato Co. v. Canadian National Railway Co.; Toner Brothers Ltd. v. Canadian National Railway Co.*,[77] sending potatoes in cars which were not heated (as required by the contract of carriage) so that the potatoes arrived at the ship on which they were to be loaded frozen and damaged, was not a fundamental breach, although it was very nearly a fundamental breach. In *Air Transit Ltd. v. Innotech Aviation of Newfoundland Ltd.*[78] the sale of a business to a third party by one party to the contract that was in issue was held not to be a fundamental breach of that contract. Nor was a driver guilty of such a breach of the contract between himself and a trucking company, where the contract entitled the company to terminate the contract if a driver consumed alchohol or drugs, when the driver, believing that he was not on duty, drank some beer.[79] Nor, in *Carleton Condominium Corp. No. 11 v. Shenkman Corp. Ltd.*,[80] did the poor condition of a parking garage built by one party qualify as a fundamental breach that could overcome the effect of an exculpatory clause. In *Hunter Engineering Co. v. Syncrude Canada Ltd.*[81] it was ultimately held by the Supreme Court of Canada that a fundamental breach had occurred when the gearboxes failed on account of a defect in design in the manner in which the gears were welded. Even a refusal to pay for goods has been held not to be a fundamental breach.[82]

Examination and comparison of the cases is sometimes helpful and can provide some insight into the way the notion of fundamental breach has been understood and applied by the courts. In the final analysis, however, much depends upon the facts of a particular instance. The basic test comes down to the simple, if not obvious one of deciding what is the real purpose of the contract, the true benefit intended to be obtained by the injured party, the extent to which the misperformance by the defendant goes beyond falling short of what was desired by the victim of the breach and involves the complete denial to him of any benefit from the performance that was provided.[83] As the decisions indicate, the line between an ordinary breach of contract and a fundamental breach is very fine, perhaps even nebulous. It does exist, however. In relevant situations courts must make the choice. Those situations, as previously suggested, involve the application of an exclusion,

---

76 *Nat. Drugs Ltd. v. Dom. Storage Ltd.* (1979), 1 Man. R. (2d) 139 (Man. C.A.).

77 Above, note 71.

78 (1989), 78 Nfld. & P.E.I.R. 24 (Nfld. T.D.).

79 *Cable v. Day & Ross Ltd.* (1992), 97 Nfld. & P.E.I.R. 264 (Nfld. T.D.).

80 (1985), 14 D.L.R. (4th) 571 (Ont. H.C.).

81 (1989), 57 D.L.R. (4th) 321 (S.C.C.).

82 *MacDonald v. Island Potato Packers Inc.* (1986), 57 Nfld. & P.E.I.R. 219 (P.E.I.C.A.).

83 This sentence was quoted by Macdonell J. in *Eagle Dancer Enterprises Ltd. v. Southam Printing Ltd. — Imprimerie Southam Ltée* (1992), 6 B.L.R. (2d) 45 at 53 (B.C.S.C.).

exemption, or limitation clause upon the rights and liabilities of the parties where a breach of contract has occurred.

3. Exclusion clauses

(a) Nature and purpose

Sometimes clauses are included in a contract for the purpose of protecting one party from total or partial liablity to the other. A clause of this kind may exempt a party from all, or many forms of liability, for example, negligence;[84] it may exclude potential liability with respect to certain types of activity, for example, while unloading goods from a ship; or it may limit the extent of a party's liability, for example, by setting a financial limit to the amount which may be paid by a party in default.[85] But no clause of this kind (nor indeed any clause) can exempt a party from liability for fraud.[86] What is excludable, or in respect of which liability may be limited, is conduct which is negligent, or produces liability without proof of fault (which occurs when one party is virtually treated as an insurer, for example, in contracts of carriage of goods at common law).

Wherever such a clause is permissible and is included by agreement between the parties, there being no fraud, misrepresentation, or other vitiating element in the agreement, the effect of such a clause is to exclude the liability in question, exempt the otherwise liable party, or limit the extent of his liability.[87] Such a clause excludes or modifies contractual obligations. It affects the nature and scope of a party's performance. This was not always accepted as being the consequence of such a clause. Before the decision in *Photo Production Ltd. v. Securicor Transport Ltd.*[88] it was thought that such clauses related only to the consequences of a breach of contract. This attitude, as the history of these clauses and the doctrine of fundamental breach reveal, produced some now rejected approaches to the question whether a party could validly exclude or limit liability. In the *Photo Production*

---

84 Even liability for negligent misrepresentation in terms of *tort*, not contractual liability: see *Peters v. Parkway Mercury Sales Ltd.* (1975), 58 D.L.R. (3d) 128 (N.B.C.A.).

85 Note also the application of the principles relating exclusionary clauses to indemnity clauses, under which one party agrees to indemnify another against the consequences of the latter's own negligence: *Smith v. South Wales Switchgear Ltd.*, [1978] 1 All E.R. 18 (H.L.); *Fenn v. Peterborough* (1979), 104 D.L.R. (3d) 174 (Ont. C.A.); affirmed (1981), 129 D.L.R. (3d) 507 (*sub nom. Consumers' Gas Co. v. Peterborough*) (S.C.C.); *Browne v. Core Rentals Ltd.* (1983), 23 B.L.R. 291 (Ont. H.C.).

86 *Ballard v. Gaskill*, [1955] 2 D.L.R. 219 (B.C.C.A.). Compare *Peters v. Parkway Mercury Sales Ltd.*, above, note 84, at 137. Nor will it apply to a case of innocent misrepresentation when there has been *error in substantialibus*; see *Alessio v. Jovica*, [1974] 2 W.W.R. 126 (Alta. C.A.); above, p. 305; nor to cases of negligent misrepresentation or other innocent misrepresentation which has misled the other party to enter into the contract with such a clause: *Sodd Corp. v. Tessis* (1977), 79 D.L.R. (3d) 632 (Ont. C.A.); *Davidson v. Three Spruces Realty Ltd.* (1977), 79 D.L.R. (3d) 481 (B.C.S.C.); unless it can be construed as applicable: see *Hayward v. Mellick* (1984), 2 O.A.C. 161 (Ont. C.A.).

87 This sentence and those that followed it in the original, first edition were quoted by Barry J. in *Howell v. Newfoundland (A.G.)* (1987), 65 Nfld. & P.E.I.R. 139 at 151 (Nfld. T.D.).

88 [1980] 1 All E.R. 556 (H.L.). Compare Coote, "The Effect of Discharge by Breach on Exception Clauses" (1970), 28 C.L.J. 221 at 228-231.

case[89] Lord Diplock, having differentiated "primary" from "general secondary" and "anticipatory secondary" obligations, stated that exclusion clauses excluded or modified such obligations. In other words, a clause of this kind affected a party's duty to perform *or* his duty to pay damages in respect of past or future loss incurred by the other party by reason of his failure to perform the primary obligation. Such clauses, therefore, have a dual nature: they relate to performance *and* to liability resulting from failure to perform, that is, breach.

Such clauses are ordinary terms of a contract, which *prima facie* must be given effect to, and applied, in the normal way.[90] However, the courts have adopted a stricter attitude towards such clauses than towards others,[91] although the House of Lords has drawn a distinction between a clause which entirely excludes liability and one which limits liability to a certain sum.[92] Exclusion clauses were to be construed strictly; limitation clauses were to be construed naturally. As Lord Denning pointed out subsequently,[93] there was little to choose between them if one looked at the plain meaning of the words. Both types of clause are designed to protect a party who might be, and subsequently turns out to be, guilty of a breach of contract. Since they have this effect of providing an advantage to one party as against the other, and because they are frequently inserted in contracts where one party has little opportunity to bargain with the party for whose benefit the clause is included (usually the situation arising with standard form contracts), the courts looked very carefully at the validity, meaning and application of such

---

89 Above, note 88, at 567-568.

90 *L'Estrange v. Graucob Ltd.*, [1934] 2 K.B. 394. On this see Samek, "The Objective Theory of Contract and the Rule in *L'Estrange v. Graucob*" (1974), 52 Can. Bar Rev. 351.

But it must be clear that what is involved is an exculpatory clause, not "a series of clauses under which the limits of particular liabilities are drawn *ab initio*"; *per* Laskin C.J.C. in *Agnew-Surpass Shoe Stores Ltd. v. Cummer-Young Ltd.* (1975), 55 D.L.R. (3d) 676 at 684-685 (S.C.C.). Compare *Bank of N.S. v. Buckingham* (1983), 1 O.A.C. 151 (Ont. Div. Ct.); *Carman Const. Ltd. v. C.P.R.* (1982), 136 D.L.R. (3d) 193 (S.C.C.); *C.P. Ltd. v. McCain Produce Co.* (1980), 113 D.L.R. (3d) 584 (N.B.C.A.); affirmed [1981] 2 S.C.R. 219 (S.C.C.). The original version of this sentence and the next one were cited by Hughes C.J.N.B. in *C.I.B.C. v. Haley* (1979), 25 N.B.R. (2d) 304 at 316 (N.B.C.A.).

91 *Photo Production Ltd. v. Securicor Ltd.*, above, note 88, at 567-568 *per* Lord Diplock. Indeed, so have some legislatures, which have enacted statutory provisions prohibiting such clauses in certain types of contract, *e.g.*, sale of goods: see Fridman, *Sale of Goods in Canada*, 3rd ed. (1986), pp. 281-282; *Hunter Engineering Co. v. Syncrude Can. Ltd.* (1989), 57 D.L.R. (4th) 321 at 377-378 (S.C.C.) *per* Wilson J.

92 *Ailsa Craig Fishing Co. v. Malvern Fishing Co.*, [1983] 1 All E.R. 101 (H.L.). Compare *Eagle Dancer Enterprises Ltd. v. Southam Printing Ltd. — Imprimerie Southam Ltée* (1992), 6 B.L.R. (2d) 45 (B.C.S.C.), where it is said that in limitation, as contrasted with exclusion clauses there is no need for such specificity in language for such a clause to be valid and effective. A different view was adopted by the High Court of Australia in *Darlington Futures Ltd. v. Delco Australia Pty. Ltd.* (1986), 161 C.L.R. 500, in which it was said that such a distinction was unwarranted. A limitation clause could be so severe in its operation as to make its effect virtually indistinguishable from that of an exclusion clause.

93 *George Mitchell (Chesterhall) Ltd. v. Finney Lock Seeds Ltd.*, [1983] 1 All E.R. 108 at 116 (C.A.); affirmed [1983] 2 All E.R. 737 (H.L.).

clauses.[94] It is hardly surprising that, in modern times, the traditional notion of freedom of contract has been qualified by the manner in which courts have sought to control the application of exclusion, or limitation, clauses, and have endeavoured to render them powerless to affect the liability of a party guilty of breach of contract.[95] To achieve this, courts have looked at three major aspects of such clauses.

The first is whether the term in question could legitimately be regarded as part of the contract between the parties; this has involved the issue of notice. The second is whether the term could be treated as governing either: (a) the event or act which occurred so as to constitute the breach; or (b) the person or persons actually guilty of the breach. The third is whether the kind of breach that has occurred is within the scope of the exclusion or limitation clause, or is of such a kind that, on a proper construction of the term in question, it cannot be said to be applicable to such a breach. In this respect the doctrine of fundamental breach has become important. However, the judgments of the Supreme Court of Canada in *Hunter Engineering Co. v. Syncrude Canada Ltd.*[96] have indicated possible changes as far as the law in Canada is concerned.

(b) Notice

The applicability of an exclusion or limitation clause can be challenged on the ground that the party seeking its protection did not bring its existence and inclusion in the contract sufficiently to the notice of the other party at the time of, or prior to the making of the contract, with the result that the latter cannot be taken to have assented to the clause.[97] If this is so, then the clause will not be effectuated. Unless a party has taken reasonable steps to draw the other party's attention to the contents, or some particular contents, of the proposed contract, the consent of the offeree to the offer will not be taken to extend as far as the term or terms of which the offeree is ignorant.[98] The test is whether the offeree knew the proposed term or terms or had reasonable means of knowledge of the term or terms as a result of the offeror's actions.[99]

---

94 The courts are loathe to let a party contract out of its own negligence: *Browne v. Core Rentals Ltd.* (1983), 23 B.L.R. 291 at 296 (Ont. H.C.) *per* Montgomery J. But it is different if the parties are equal: *C.P. Ltd. v. McCain Produce Co. Ltd.* (1980), 113 D.L.R. (3d) 584 at 597 (N.B.C.A.); affirmed [1981] 2 S.C.R. 219 (S.C.C.). Compare *Hunter Engineering Co. v. Syncrude Can. Ltd.*, above, note 91, at 343 *per* Dickson C.J.C., at 381-382 per Wilson J.

95 Above, note 93, at 113-114 *per* Lord Denning.

96 (1989), 57 D.L.R. (4th) 321 (S.C.C.): below, pp. 597-600. On this case see Ogilvie, "Fundamental Breach Excluded but not Extinguished: Hunter Engineering v. Syncrude Canada" (1990), 17 Can. Bus. L.J. 75; Flannigan, "*Hunter Engineering*: The Judicial Regulation of Exculpatory Clauses" (1990), 69 Can. Bar Rev. 514.

97 Compare above, pp. 39-41 on the subject of communication of an offer to the offeree. See also Clarke, "Notice of Contractual Terms" (1976), 35 C.L.J. 81.

98 These first three sentences were quoted in *Trigg v. MI Movers Int. Transport Services Ltd.* (1991), 4 O.R. (3d) 562 at 565-566 (Ont. C.A.); leave to appeal to S.C.C. refused (1992), 7 O.R. (3d) xii (note) (S.C.C.).

99 *LeRoy Plow Co. v. J. Clark & Son Ltd.* (1921), 65 D.L.R. 370 (N.B.C.A.); *Provident Savings Life Assur. Society v. Mowat* (1902), 32 S.C.R. 147 (S.C.C.) as long as the offeree can read and is not

In this respect various distinctions have been drawn in the cases. One is between contracts which are well-considered and long thought about before they are assented to, and those where the offeree agrees hastily, lacking the time and the impetus to look carefully at what he is accepting.[100] Where the contract is in the first category, there is less likelihood that the offeree will overlook the existence of an exclusion, exemption or limitation clause, and will probably have an opportunity to bargain with regard to its inclusion (perhaps obtaining some countervailing advantage in return for the protection afforded the offeror by such clause). Where the contract falls into the second category, there will be a correspondingly heavier onus on the party for whose benefit the clause was inserted to establish that proper notice was given of such clause. In *Tilden Rent-a-Car Co. v. Clendenning*,[101] which has become a leading decision, the Ontario Court of Appeal was faced with such a situation. The defendant signed a car rental agreement at an airport. He was in a hurry and did not read through the long complicated rental contract. He was asked if he wanted insurance, which involved a higher fee, to which he agreed, as he thought this gave him protection from liability if the vehicle were damaged while in his possession. On the back of the contract, in small print, was a term to the effect that the insurance cover would not be operative if the hirer had drunk any amount of intoxicating liquor at the time when the damage occurred. It did not state that the driver had to be guilty of any offence, such as driving while intoxicated, nor that the degree of intoxication had to be substantial. It applied to any imbibing of drink, however slight. The car was damaged by an accident which happened while the hirer had been drinking (though it was not clear to what extent). Subsequently, the defendant, the hirer, pleaded guilty to a charge arising out of the accident. This was because the accident occurred in British Columbia, where the car was hired, while the defendant was on a visit, and the defendant was back home in Ontario. He was advised to plead guilty rather than return to British Columbia to defend the charge. The car hire company sued him for the damage to the car. He relied on his insurance cover. The car hire company argued that the clause in the contract precluded his reliance on the insurance. The defendant responded by saying that he was unware of the existence of such clause;

---

misled he is bound; compare Nemetz C.J.B.C., dissenting, in *Delaney v. Cascade River Holidays Ltd.* (1983), 24 C.C.L.T. 6 at 6-21 (B.C.C.A.). This paragraph was quoted by Macdonell J. in *Eagle Dancer Enterprises Ltd. v. Southam Printing Ltd. — Imprimerie Southam Ltée* (1992), 6 B.L.R. (2d) 45 at 58 (B.C.S.C.).

100 *Provident Savings Life Assur. Society v. Mowat*, above, note 99. Contrast *Rogers v. Nfld. Light & Power Co.* (1957), 9 D.L.R. (2d) 56 (Nfld. T.D.) (long negotiations); *City Motors (Nfld.) Ltd. v. Alton* (1987), 64 Nfld. & P.E.I.R. 52 (Nfld. T.D.); affirmed on other grounds (1988), 69 Nfld. & P.E.I.R. 161 (Nfld. C.A.) (hurried signature to car rental agreement because plaintiff had to get back to work after lunch).

101 (1978), 83 D.L.R. (3d) 400 (Ont. C.A.) followed in *Crocker v. Sundance Northwest Resorts Ltd.* (1983), 43 O.R. (2d) 145 (Ont. H.C.); *City Motors (Nfld.) Ltd. v. Alton*, above, note 100; *Davies v. Alta. Motor Assn.* (1991), 32 M.V.R. (2d) 42 (Alta. Prov. Ct.). But it was not relevant in *Hoffman v. Sportsman Yachts Inc.* (1992), 89 D.L.R. (4th) 600 (Ont. C.A.) where the clause that permitted a rise in price was not binding by reason of the misrepresentation of the defendant's salesman. Compare an English case, *Interfoto Picture Library Ltd. v. Stiletto Visual Programmes Ltd.*, [1989] Q.B. 433 (C.A.).

that he was in a hurry at the time he signed the rental contract; that he did not have time to read it; and that there was nothing on the face of the document to indicate that anything in it might have affected his position injuriously. Indeed he was given the impression by the car hire company's agent that the provisions as regards insurance completely covered and immunized him from liability in respect of damage to the car or third parties. The majority of the Court of Appeal held that the defendant's signature on the contract did not amount to a true assent to the exclusion of the insurance cover. The clause in question was an unusual type of clause to find in a contract of this description; it was a stringent and onerous provision, and, therefore, the defendant should have been given a real opportunity to understand and appreciate what he was signing.[102] In this case speed was one of the attractive features of the services provided by the car hire company. Hence, it might be said that they owed a special obligation to inform the defendant of what the hire contract involved.[103] In contrast the contract for a holiday in *Craven v. Strand Holidays (Canada) Ltd.*[104] was not negotiated in a hurried manner. Nor did it involve a standard form contract containing onerous provisions in small type in circumstances where no one could be reasonably expected to read it. Hence, the holidaying plaintiffs were bound by the clause which limited the defendant company's liability to using reasonable care in the selection of the services that constituted the tour.[105]

Whether adequate notice has been given is a question of fact.[106] However, it is also clear that the requisite notice must be given before the other party gives his consent. To notify a contracting party of the presence of an exclusion or similar clause in the contract after the contract has been signed, or otherwise agreed to,

---

102 (1978), 83 D.L.R. (3d) 400 at 408-409 *per* Dubin J.A. Compare *Can. Bank of Commerce v. Foreman,* [1927] 2 D.L.R. 530 at 537 (Alta. C.A.) *per* Beck J.A.; *Colonial Invt. Co. v. Borland* (1912), 5 Alta. L.R. 71 at 86 (Alta. C.A.) *per* Beck J.A.; *Can. Permanent Mtge. Corp. v. Barnard,* [1926] 1 D.L.R. 150 at 158 (Sask. K.B.) *per* Bigelow J.; *Davies v. Alta. Motor Assn.,* above, note 101, where the clause in question limited the defendant's liability to the fee for inspecting the vehicle to be purchased in order to see if it was in reasonable condition. In *Walden v. Haney Garage Ltd.,* [1928] 1 D.L.R. 688 (B.C.C.A.) the term excluding liability for negligence was not outside the contemplation of the parties when the plaintiff left his car at the defendant's garage for repairs. See also *Gray-Campbell Ltd. v. Flynne,* [1923] 1 D.L.R. 51 (Alta. C.A.); *Ball v. Gutschenritter,* [1925] S.C.R. 68 (S.C.C.); *Jadis v. Porte* (1915), 23 D.L.R. 713 (Alta. C.A.). Note also the possibility that such a clause might amount to unconscionability: *Davidson v. Three Spruces Realty Ltd.* (1977), 79 D.L.R. (3d) 481 (B.C.S.C.).

103 So, too, where the lessors of a rental car knew the lessee was in a hurry: *City Motors (Nfld.) Ltd. v. Alton,* above, note 100.

104 (1982), 142 D.L.R. (3d) 31 especially at 40 (Ont. C.A.); leave to appeal to S.C.C. refused (1983), 48 N.R. 320 (S.C.C.).

105 Compare *Roberts v. Montex Dev. Corp.,* [1979] 4 W.W.R. 306 (B.C.S.C.); *Montreal Trust Co. v. C.P. Airlines,* [1977] S.C.R. 793 (S.C.C.) involving construction of the Carriage by Air Act, now R.S.C. 1985, c. C-26, Art. I and the Warsaw Convention of 1929, as amended by the Hague Protocol, 1955, Sched. II; *Nikkel v. Standard Group Ltd.* (1982), 16 Man. R. (2d) 71 (Man. Q.B.).

106 Hence no such adequate notice had been given in *Trigg v. MI Movers Int. Transport Services Ltd.* (1991), 4 O.R. (3d) 562 (Ont. C.A.); leave to appeal to S.C.C. refused (1992), 7 O.R. (3d) xii (note) (S.C.C.), where the plaintiff never read the limitation clause and was not properly advised of its contents.

will not suffice.[107] In *Toronto Blue Jays Baseball Club v. John Doe*[108] the club was seeking to prevent the sale of tickets for baseball games when those tickets had been purchased by "scalpers" who sold them at inflated prices. On the reverse side of the tickets, printed in very fine print, were conditions that stated that the ticket was a personal, revocable licence, that the management could refuse admission to anyone by refunding the purchase price, and that the ticket was not to be sold for trade purposes (including resale as part of a commercial venture) without the express consent of the club. There was no evidence that scalpers had actual notice of these conditions, especially a condition that entitled the club to forfeit a ticket without compensation if such ticket was offered for resale at a premium, a particularly onerous condition. Moreover since such tickets were known to be freely transferred to the public at large, some notice to the general public of such a condition was required: notice to the first buyer, *i.e.*, a scalper, was insufficient. Hence the condition about forfeiture without compensation was not part of the contract. Nor can notice of such a clause be given after the contract is signed but before it is performed.[109]

However, express notice may not have to be given where it can be said that the party to whom otherwise notice would have to be given was aware of the existence of the clause in question, or of the likelihood of such a clause being a part of the contract.[110] Such, for example, was the situation in *Captain v. Far Eastern Steamship Co.*[111] The plaintiff, who owned the goods that were damaged by being left on the docks, had worked in the shipping industry and was familiar with bills of lading. Since the bill of lading that governed the duties of the shippers was in the standard form, it was said that the plaintiff would, or perhaps should have known that the usual terms on which shippers contracted included the kind of exclusion or limitation clause that was at issue. Hence the clause governed, although, for other reasons, it did not apply to the circumstances.[112] A corollary of this is that notice of such a term may be inferred from previous dealings between the parties. In other words, it may be implicit in the contract that the relationship involved is affected by such a term. The extent to which such an inference or implication may be made has previously been discussed.[113] Where to do so is possible, then express notification of an exclusion or limitation clause may not

---

107 *Campbell v. Image*, [1978] 2 W.W.R. 663 (B.C. Co. Ct.); compare *Olley v. Marlborough Court Ltd.*, [1949] 1 K.B. 532 (C.A.); *Mendelssohn v. Normand Ltd.*, [1970] 1 Q.B. 177 (C.A.); *Thornton v. Shoe Lane Parking Ltd.*, [1971] 2 Q.B. 163 (C.A.).

108 (1992), 9 O.R. (3d) 622 (Ont. Gen. Div.).

109 *Trigg v. MI Movers Int. Transport Services Ltd.*, above, note 106.

110 This sentence was quoted by Macdonell J. in *Eagle Dancer Enterprises Ltd. v. Southam Printing Ltd. — Imprimerie Southam Ltée* (1992), 6 B.L.R. (2d) 45 at 58 (B.C.S.C.).

111 (1978), 97 D.L.R. (3d) 250 (B.C.S.C.); compare *Anticosti Shipping Co. v. St.-Amand*, [1959] S.C.R. 372 (S.C.C.); *A.R. Kitson Trucking Ltd. v. Rivtow Straits Ltd.* (1975), 55 D.L.R. (3d) 462 (B.C.S.C.); *Evans Products Ltd. v. Crest Warehousing Ltd.* (1976), 69 D.L.R. (3d) 575 (B.C.S.C.); reversed [1978] 1 W.W.R. 648 (B.C.C.A.); affirmed [1979] 5 W.W.R. 385 (S.C.C.); compare *Patterson v. Branson, Brown & Co.*, [1930] 4 D.L.R. 222 (B.C.S.C.), previous notice of time as to closure of stock transaction where margins were running out.

112 Below, p. 591.

113 Above, pp. 481-483.

have to be given. Where such an inference or implication is not permissible, the party claiming the benefit, protection, or advantage of such a term must have notified the other party that it was in the contract, or taken reasonable steps to draw his attention to that fact.[114]

A further distinction has been drawn between documents that are usually expected to be offers or contracts, in which the offeree would normally expect to find all the relevant terms, and those which, in the ordinary course of things, the reasonable man would expect to serve another purpose, not that of being an offer, but which do contain the offer and the terms or refer to some other document which does contain the terms and is incorporated into the offer by reference. The prime illustration in the cases is where the document is a ticket, for example, to park a car, travel by train or ship, or claim goods deposited for cleaning or in a cloakroom. Is an offeree who accepts the ticket for the purpose for which it is issued, namely, to identify the owner of the goods, permit him to enter the train or ship, *etc.*, bound by terms included expressly on the ticket or in it by reference to another document kept elsewhere, for example, in a railway timetable? Many of the cases involving exclusion or limitation clauses are of this type.

There is no doubt but that the attitude of Canadian courts (relying upon English decisions) is that the onus is on the offeror to take reasonable steps or make reasonable efforts to bring the term in question to the notice of the offeree.[115] Indeed, where such a "ticket" is involved, the onus is heavier than in cases of the kind considered above, that is, where the document is plainly a contractual document, and not a receipt or evidence of some right, licence, or privilege conferred on the offeree by the offeror.[116] As Lord Haldane L.C. said,[117]

> if the contract is one which deprives the passenger of the benefit of a duty of care which he is prima facie entitled to expect that the company has accepted, the latter must discharge the burden of proving that the passenger assented to the special terms imposed.

Whether what has been done is reasonably sufficient for the purpose is a question of fact in each instance.[118] It should be noted, however, that sometimes a sign on the premises to which the offeree's attention is drawn, either expressly or by implication, will suffice, as long as a reasonable person would have been aware of the term in question as a consequence of what the offeror has done in this

---

114 *McCutcheon v. MacBrayne Ltd.*, [1964] 1 All E.R. 430 (H.L.).
115 *Heller v. Niagara Racing Assn.*, [1925] 2 D.L.R. 286 (Ont. C.A.); *Appleton v. Ritchie Taxi*, [1942] 3 D.L.R. 546 (Ont. C.A.); *G.T.P. Coast S.S. Co. v. Simpson* (1922), 63 S.C.R. 361 (S.C.C.) distinguished in *Union S.S. Ltd. v. Barnes*, [1956] S.C.R. 842 (S.C.C.); *Int. Tpt. Assn. v. Capital Storage Co.*, [1928] 4 D.L.R. 480 (Sask. Dist. Ct.); *Reid v. Union Gas Co. of Can.* (1961), 27 D.L.R. (2d) 5 (Ont. H.C.); *Luddit v. Ginger Cote Airways Ltd.*, [1942] S.C.R. 486 (S.C.C.); affirmed on other grounds [1947] A.C. 233 (P.C.).
116 These two sentences were quoted by Lane J. in *Toronto Blue Jays Baseball Club v. John Doe* (1992), 9 O.R. (3d) 622 at 626 (Ont. Gen. Div.).
117 *G.T.R. v. Robinson*, [1915] A.C. 740 at 741 (P.C.).
118 *G.T.P. Coast S.S. Co. v. Simpson* (1922), 63 S.C.R. 361 (S.C.C.), giving the effect of the nineteenth century English cases.

respect, and, it must be stressed, as long as the attention of the offeree was drawn to such sign before the offeree accepted the offer.[119]

(c) Strict construction

(i) *Attitude of the courts*

Once such a clause is included in the contract, by virtue of the operation of the rules referred to above, it now seems clear that the courts will regard it with a critical, even, it might be said, a jaundiced eye.[120] They will approach the interpretation of such a clause strictly,[121] applying the ordinary rules of construction, which have earlier been described.[122]

In this respect, there are certain among the canons of construction which have a greater importance or impact in this context. These are the *contra proferentem* rule,[123] the rules governing the comparative importance of later oral terms and earlier written ones,[124] the doctrine of repugnancy,[125] and the rules concerned with reading the contract as a whole.[126] Of prime relevance is the doctrine that the language of the contract must be read literally, which means that the courts will be sharp to detect any "deviation" from the contract and its proper performance. For a party to claim the protection of an exclusion, exemption or limitation clause,

---

119 *Spooner v. Starkman*, [1937] 2 D.L.R. 582 (Ont. C.A.); compare *Mendelssohn v. Normand Ltd.*, above, note 107, at 182 *per* Lord Denning.

120 *Browne v. Core Rentals Ltd.* (1983), 23 B.L.R. 291 at 296 (Ont. H.C.) *per* Montgomery J.

121 *Davidson v. Three Spruces Realty Ltd.* (1977), 79 D.L.R. (3d) 481 (B.C.S.C.); *C.P. Ltd. v. McCain Produce Co.* (1980), 113 D.L.R. (3d) 584 (N.B.C.A.); affirmed (1981), 123 D.L.R. (3d) 764 (S.C.C.); *Smith v. Horizon Aero Sports Ltd.* (1981), 130 D.L.R. (3d) 91 (B.C.S.C.); *Can. Fracmaster Ltd. v. Grand Prix Natural Gas Ltd.* (1990), 109 A.R. 173 (Alta. Q.B.). Note, however, the alleged distinction between exclusion clauses and limitation clauses: above, p. 572.

122 Above, pp. 454-455.

123 Compare *Indemnity Ins. Co. v. Excel Cleaning Services*, [1954] S.C.R. 169 (S.C.C.) (exemption clause inoperative) with *Stevenson v. Reliance Petroleum Ltd.; Reliance Petroleum Ltd. v. Can. Gen. Ins. Co.*, [1956] S.C.R. 936 (S.C.C.) (exception clause operated); see the discussion in Slayton, "The Supreme Court of Canada and the Common Law of Contract" (1971), 17 McGill L.J. 476 at 505-506.

124 *Couchman v. Hill*, [1947] K.B. 554 (C.A.); *Harling v. Eddy*, [1951] 2 K.B. 739 (C.A.); *Spelchan v. Long* (1956), 2 D.L.R. (2d) 707 (B.C.C.A.); *Fleischhaker v. Fort Garry Agencies Ltd.* (1957), 65 Man. R. 339 (Man. C.A.); *Francis v. Trans-Can. Trailer Sales Ltd.* (1969), 69 W.W.R. 748 (Sask. C.A.); *Sperry Rand Can. Ltd. v. Thomas Equip. Ltd.* (1982), 135 D.L.R. (3d) 197 (N.B.C.A.). Compare also *Peters v. Parkway Mercury Sales Ltd.* (1974), 9 N.B.R. (2d) 288 (N.B.Q.B.); affirmed (1975), 10 N.B.R. (2d) 703 (N.B.C.A.) where the doctrine of neglient misrepresentation could not help a plaintiff buyer who was unable to pursue a contractual remedy because of a disclaimer clause. Contrast with this *Sodd Corp. v. Tessis* (1977), 79 D.L.R. (3d) 632 (Ont. C.A.); *Davidson v. Three Spruces Realty Ltd.*, above, note 121, where negligent misrepresentation overcame the effect of an exclusion clause.

125 *Mendelssohn v. Normand Ltd.*, above, note 107, at 186 *per* Phillimore L.J.; compare *Curtis v. Chemical Cleaning & Dyeing Co.*, [1951] 1 K.B. 805 (C.A.); *J. Evans & Son (Portsmouth) Ltd. v. Andrea Merzario Ltd.*, [1976] 2 All E.R. 930 (C.A.).

126 Above, pp. 466-472.

he must show that he acted "within the four corners" of the contract.[127] If what has occurred does not come within the scope of the contract, or if the party involved, or his conduct, does not fall fairly and squarely within the protection sought to be achieved by the clause, the claim of exemption or limitation will fail.[128]

(ii) *Acts covered*

To come within the protection of such a clause, the alleged protected party must establish that the act or event which gave rise to his potential liability was expressly or by necessary implication comprehended by the language of the clause.[129] Usually what is involved is a claim that the defendant is protected from liability for negligence, especially negligence by his servants or agents, or from liability for any damage whether or not it resulted from his own or his servants' or agents' negligence. In such instances the court will look very carefully at the question whether the act complained of comes within the scope of the acts covered by the protection in the clause, or can be said to stand outside the language of the contract. For example, in *Thornton v. Shoe Lane Parking Ltd.*,[130] since the notice that purported to contain the clause exempting the car-park company from liability used the phrase "at owner's risk" it was held that this could only exempt liability for injury to the car parked, not for *personal* injury suffered by the plaintiff. Similarly, in one Canadian case,[131] the question was whether the conduct causing damage involved the operation of "trucking". In *Smith v. Horizon Aero Sports Ltd.*,[132] the "hold-harmless" clause in a contract under which the defendants undertook to teach the plaintiff parachute jumping was held to apply only to fortuitous occurrences, not to negligence in teaching the plaintiff how to jump safely. In *Punch v. Savoy's Jewellers Ltd.*,[133] the exclusion clause limiting the railway company's liability when a valuable piece of jewellery disappeared while in transit was held not to cover the possibility of theft of the jewellery by an employee of the railway. A more subtle instance is provided by *Canadian Pacific Ltd. v. McCain Produce Co.*[134] A clause in the contract limited the liability of the defendants to the value of the goods carried at the place and time of shipment. It was held that this was designed to fix the valuation of the goods: it was not a clause excluding the carrier's liability for consequential damages. The clause was to be read as relating to the

127 *Gibaud v. Great Eastern Ry. Co.*, [1921] 2 K.B. 426 at 435 (C.A.) *per* Scrutton L.J.
128 These two paragraphs, as they originally appeared in the first edition, were quoted by Barry J. in *Howell v. Newfoundland (A.G.)* (1987), 65 Nfld. & P.E.I.R. 139 at 151-152 (Nfld. T.D.). See also the reference by Lane J. in *Toronto Blue Jays Baseball Club v. John Doe* (1992), 9 O.R. (3d) 622 at 627 (Ont. Gen. Div.).
129 *E.g.*, the negligent misrepresentation by the salesman of the used car in *Peters v. Parkway Mercury Sales Ltd.* (1974), 9 N.B.R. (2d) 288 (N.B.Q.B.); affirmed (1975), 10 N.B.R. (2d) 703 (N.B.C.A.); compare *Hayward v. Mellick* (1984), 5 D.L.R. (4th) 740 (Ont. C.A.).
130 [1971] 2 Q.B. 163 (C.A.).
131 *Burt v. Salmon River Logging Co.*, [1953] 2 S.C.R. 117 (S.C.C.).
132 (1981), 130 D.L.R. (3d) 91 (B.C.S.C.).
133 (1986), 33 B.L.R. 147 (Ont. C.A.).
134 (1980), 113 D.L.R. (3d) 584 (N.B.C.A.); affirmed (1981), 123 D.L.R. (3d) 764 (S.C.C.).

computation of damages, not as limiting liability for loss to a particular head of damages. Here it was not so much the kind of harm suffered by the plaintiff that was outside the scope of the clause but the kind of liability that the defendants argued should be imposed when a breach occurred.

Perhaps the leading authority on the subject of strict construction of the scope of an exclusion or similar clause, as far as the conduct covered by its terms is concerned, is *Canada Steamship Lines Ltd. v. R.*[135] A contract with the Crown with respect to warehousing certain goods contained a clause exempting the Crown from liability in the event of certain stated occurrences. The damage complained of was brought about by the negligent act of a servant of the Crown. It was held by the Privy Council, reversing the Supreme Court of Canada, that, on a strict construction of the language of the clause, the Crown could not rely upon it in the circumstances of the case, but was liable for the damage in question. Lord Morton summarized the applicable law as follows:

> (1) If the clause contains language which expressly exempts the person in whose favour it is made [the proferens] from the consequence of the negligence of his own servants, effect must be given to that provision. . . .
> (2) If there is no express reference to negligence, the court must consider whether the words used are wide enough, in their ordinary meaning, to cover negligence on the part of the servant of the proferens. . . .
> (3) If the words are wide enough for the above purpose, the court must then consider whether "the head of damage may be based on some ground other than of negligence."[136]

An alternative approach is to see whether the conduct which gave rise to the claim was a proper mode of performing the contract, in which event it will be covered by the exclusion clause, or was so removed from such performance that it is outside the ambit of the clause.[137] A good illustration, in that this was the ground relied upon by one of the judges of the Court of Appeal (Edmund Davies L.J.) for his decision against the operation of the exemption clause, is *Mendelssohn v. Normand Ltd.*[138] When the plaintiff parked his car in the defendant's garage the ticket he obtained contained on its back a condition denying liability for loss, and a condition that the contract could not be varied so as to bind the defendant unless the variation was in writing signed by the defendant's manager. On one

---

135 [1952] A.C. 192 (P.C.); followed in *Crocker v. Sundance Northwest Resorts Ltd.* (1983), 43 O.R. (2d) 145 (Ont. H.C.). Compare the *Salmon River* case, above, note 131, where the Supreme Court of Canada was divided on the question whether the exemption clause was limited to acts of negligence.

136 [1952] A.C. 192 at 208 (P.C.); see the reference by de Grandpré J. in *Agnew-Surpass Shoe Stores Ltd. v. Cummer-Young Invts. Ltd.* (1975), 55 D.L.R. (3d) 676 at 694-695 (S.C.C.). Compare *Smith v. South Wales Switchgear Ltd.*, [1978] 1 All E.R. 18 at 25, 30-31 (H.L.); *Browne v. Core Rentals Ltd.* (1983), 23 B.L.R. 291 (Ont. H.C.) (both cases involving *indemnity* clauses).

137 Note the criticism of this proposition by the Court of Appeal in *Gillespie Bros. & Co. v. Roy Bowles Ltd.*, [1973] 1 Q.B. 400 (C.A.), in which it was said that it should not be given its full force. It was a rule of construction, not of law. If the clause covered negligence but could be effective without excluding liability for negligence, it should not be made to apply to negligence.

138 [1970] 1 Q.B. 177 (C.A.).

occasion the plaintiff wanted to lock his car because it contained valuables. The attendant said it was against the rules of the garage to lock the door. When the plaintiff informed the attendant about the valuables, the attendant said that he would lock the car. Later the plaintiff discovered that his valuables had been stolen. Despite the defendant's claim to be protected by the exemption clause, judgment was given in favour of the plaintiff. The reason for the decision in the plaintiff's favour that is most pertinent to the present discussion was that the contract under which the plaintiff parked his car at the defendant's garage could only be performed in one way, in accordance with the rules of the garage, namely, by leaving the car locked. In requiring the plaintiff to refrain from locking his car, and requesting him to leave the keys with him, on the undertaking that he would lock up the car, the attendant was acting wrongfully, in an unauthorized manner. In these circumstances, the exemption clause could not operate in the defendant's favour. Similarly, in *Davidson v. Three Spruces Realty Ltd.; Farr v. Three Spruces Realty Ltd.; Elsdon v. Three Spruces Realty Ltd.*,[139] the defendant, bailee of the plaintiff's valuable property, was supposed to keep it in a safety deposit box. Therefore the exemption clause did not operate in favour of the defendant when the property was kept in bulk storage. In *Drake v. Bekins Moving & Storage Co.*[140] the plaintiff's rug, which had not been covered by an insurance policy, disappeared while in the possession of the defendant bailees. Despite their attempt to limit their liability by a clause in the contract, they were held liable. On a strict construction of the contract, the clause in question did not protect them when there was a disappearance of the rug, as contrasted with damage through negligence or otherwise.

The concept of improper or no performance, or of deviation from proper performance of the contract, is closely connected with the doctrine of fundamental breach. Cases of this kind may, in fact, be treated as examples of such a breach, the effect of which will be considered later.[141] For the moment, however, it may be stated that an exemption clause will only apply: (i) when the contract is being performed in its contemplated manner;[142] and (ii) where the act which is the source of the alleged exemption is one which is expressly or implicitly comprehended by the strictly construed language of the clause.

(iii) *Persons covered*

(A) *Problems* A further qualification may be introduced by reference to the persons whose acts have caused the damage in respect of which the protection of the clause is claimed. There are two problems in this connection. The first is whether the term can be construed so as to extend to cover the acts of the person actually causing the loss or damage complained of, and thereby protect the

---

139 (1978), 79 D.L.R. (3d) 481 (B.C.S.C.).

140 [1982] 6 W.W.R. 640 (B.C. Co. Ct.); compare *Levison v. Patent Steam Carpet Cleaning Co.*, [1978] Q.B. 69 (C.A.).

141 Below, pp. 588-600.

142 Unless, possibly, the deviation or improper performance is the fault of the party claiming, against whom the exemption or other clause is raised as a defence.

defendant. This, as is evident, is another aspect of the question whether the act in issue comes within the scope of the clause. The second problem is whether the clause can be construed as protecting the person who committed the harmful act, even though such person is not the party who made the contract with the plaintiff. This latter problem has been difficult and complex, involving not only the law relating to exclusion and similar clauses but also aspects of the law relating to offer and acceptance, consideration, privity of contract, and agency.

As far as the first issue is concerned, since the language of these clauses is strictly construed, much will depend upon whether the words used by the parties, and in particular the *proferens*, the one in whose favour the clause is included, can be understood to cover acts committed not by the defendant, the *proferens*, personally, but also by the one who actually caused the harm or injury now made the subject of a claim. The passage quoted from the judgment in the *Canada Steamship* case[143] makes this very clear. It is interesting that, whereas the Privy Council were prepared to find that the exemption clause in that case did not protect the Crown from liability for its servants' negligence, the Supreme Court of Canada, on their reading of the language of the contract, were able to come to the opposite conclusion.[144] This is a reflection upon: (a) the difficulties inherent in construing contractual language with a view to discovering the parties' explicit or presumed intentions; and (b) the possibly more conservative approach of the Canadian court, at that time, as contrasted with the attitude of the Privy Council.

The second issue moves the discussion slightly further afield. It involves the question of third party beneficiaries of contracts. In discussing the problem of privity,[145] it was seen that, generally speaking, a contract cannot confer any rights upon a stranger to the contract. Such a stranger: (a) was not a direct party to the contract; and (b) gave no consideration. To this two major exceptions were recognized. The first is where a party to the contract was acting as the agent of the stranger attempting to assert the right in question. The second was where the contract created a trust in favour of such stranger. These exceptions, in particular the first, have been of great relevance in relation to exclusion and similar clauses purporting to confer some "vicarious immunity" on a servant, agent or independent contractor employed by one of the contracting parties. In *London Drugs Ltd. v. Kuehne & Nagel International Ltd.*[146] the majority of the Supreme Court of Canada relaxed the strict duties even further in relation to the issue of the applicability of an exclusion or similar clause. The development of the exceptions to the privity doctrine in this context requires exposition.

(B) *Privity and agency* Initially there was general unwillingness on the part of the courts to construe exemption and similar clauses liberally and a desire to

---

143 Above, p. 580.

144 [1950] S.C.R. 532 (S.C.C.); reversed [1952] A.C. 192 (P.C.). For a case where the language was held to cover someone not actually named in the document, *e.g.*, the plaintiff's broker, see *Moss v. Richardson Greenshields of Can. Ltd.*, [1988] 4 W.W.R. 15 (Man. Q.B.); affirmed [1989] 3 W.W.R. 50 (Man. C.A.).

145 Above, pp. 185-191, 194-200.

146 (1992), 97 D.L.R. (4th) 261 (S.C.C.); below, p. 586.

restrict their operation. Hence the cases indicated that someone not a party to a contract containing an exemption clause would not be protected by such clause, if that person's conduct had been the cause of the plaintiff's loss or injury, even if the person causing the loss in question did so while acting for the benefit of the *proferens*, the party in whose favour the clause was included in the contract, or did so while in pursuance of a duty to the *proferens*. Thus in *Adler v. Dickson*,[147] the master of the ship was liable even though the owners of the ship were protected by an exemption clause in the contract of carriage made with the passenger who was injured through the negligence of the ship's crew. In *Gore v. Van der Lann*,[148] the bus driver could not rely on the exemption clause in favour of the bus company, even where the passenger did not pay for carriage, but was given a free pass on the corporation's buses. Such passenger did not impliedly promise not to sue such employees as a condition of obtaining the pass.[149] In *Midland Silicones Ltd. v. Scruttons Ltd.*,[150] the stevedores could not rely on a clause in the bill of lading limiting the liability of the shipowners as carriers for loss caused to the goods that were being carried. In this latter case the House of Lords suggested that an exemption or similar clause could be invoked by a non-party to the contract if it could be established that one of the direct parties to the contract had contracted as the agent of such non-party. For such an agency to exist, however, it had to be shown that there was some kind of agreement between the party agreeing to the exemption, exclusion or limitation of liability and the non-party seeking to invoke that protection.

The hint contained in the *Midland Silicones* case was sufficient for the Privy Council in *New Zealand Shipping Co. v. A.M. Satterthwaite & Co.*,[151] where a newer approach was adopted. The bill of lading under which cargo was shipped from Liverpool to New Zealand contained a clause under which "no servant or agent of the carrier (including every independent contractor from time to time employed by the carrier) shall in any circumstances whatsoever be under any liability whatsoever to the shipper, consignee or owner of the goods or to any holder of this bill of lading for any loss or damage or delay of whatsoever kind arising or resulting directly or indirectly from any act, neglect or default on his part while acting in the course of or in connection with his employment. . . ." This exemption clause was expressed to apply to and for the protection of every servant, agent or independent contractor of the carrier as well as the carrier himself. It was also

---

147 [1954] 3 All E.R. 397 (C.A.).

148 [1967] 2 Q.B. 31 (C.A.); compare *Genys v. Matthews*, [1965] 3 All E.R. 24.

149 In any event, the case was decided under the provisions of a statute which made such exception clauses void, but the decision has been criticized in this respect, see Odgers (1970), 86 L.Q.R. 69.

150 [1962] A.C. 446 (H.L.); compare *Wilson v. Darling Island Stevedoring & Lighterage Co.*, [1956] 1 Lloyd's Rep. 346 (Aust.). The *Midland Silicones* case was approved and followed by the Supreme Court of Canada in *Can. Gen. Elec. Co. v. Pickford & Black Ltd.*, [1971] S.C.R. 41 (S.C.C.) (discussed and explained by Iacobucci J. in *London Drugs Ltd. v. Kuehne & Nagel Int. Ltd.*, above, note 146, at 352-353). See also *Bill Boivin Plumbing & Heating Ltd. v. Flatt* (1965), 51 D.L.R. (2d) 574 (Ont. C.A.).

151 [1974] 1 All E.R. 1015, [1975] A.C. 154 (P.C.).

stated that such servant, *etc.*, should be deemed to be a party to the contract in the bill of lading. Stevedores were employed by the carrier in New Zealand, as independent contractors. After the plaintiff became the holder of the bill of lading, the stevedores negligently damaged the cargo while unloading. The question arose, therefore, whether the stevedores could claim the protection of this exemption clause. By a majority the Judicial Committee of the Privy Council held that the stevedores could raise this defence. Two reasons were given. One was that, arising from the agency of the carriers acting on behalf of the stevedores, there was a separate contract between the plaintiffs as holders of the bill of lading and the stevedores, based on the performance of services by the latter, which was the consideration provided by them for the promise of exemption or immunity contained in the clause in issue. In this respect the fact that the stevedores were already under a duty to the carrier to perform such services did not affect the independence of the consideration moving from the stevedores to the holder of the bill of lading, the plaintiff.[152] The other reason also involved the notion of agency. The exemption was construed as being intended to cover the whole carriage from loading to discharge, and such performance attracted the exemption in favour of whomever was or became the performer of the services comprehended within the notion of carriage.[153] The bill of lading was an initially unilateral offer of exemption which became a "unilateral" contract binding on the owners, the holders of the bill of lading, when the stevedores performed services by discharging the goods.[154] In other words, the restriction upon the application of the exemption clause found in the *Midland Silicones* case and others was removed by the process of finding, construing, or constructing an entirely separate contract between the holder of the bill of lading, or owner of goods, and the party actually performing the obligations placed upon the original carrier by the bill of lading.

From this conclusion two members of the Judicial Committee of the Privy Council dissented. Lord Simon of Glaisdale[155] thought that it went against the classical common law idea that clauses which limit or exclude liability for negligence are viewed unfavourably. Viscount Dilhorne[156] thought that to invoke the concept of agency in order to produce a secondary or additional contract that can accommodate the clause in question involved "not just . . . straining the language of the contract but rewriting it." Subsequent Canadian decisions applied the *Satterthwaite* case[157] or denied its applicability.[158] For the most part the Canadian

---

152 Compare as to this the discussion of the cases concerned with performance of a pre-existing duty as consideration: above, pp. 106-108.

153 [1974] 1 All E.R. 1015 at 1020 (P.C.) *per* Lord Wilberforce.

154 On unilateral contracts see above, pp. 69-76.

155 [1974] 1 All E.R. 1015 at 1029 (P.C.).

156 *Ibid.*, at 1024. Especially when the concept of "unilateral" contracts is involved and applied to these situations. There seems to be considerable artificiality in holding that the third party performed the requested act in consideration and by way of acceptance of the offer to exclude or limit that party's potential liability for negligence.

157 *ITO-Int. Terminal Operators Ltd. v. Miida Electronics Inc.* (1986), 28 D.L.R. (4th) 641 (S.C.C.) (discussed and explained by Iacobucci J. in *London Drugs Ltd. v. Kuehne & Nagel Int. Ltd.* (1992), 97 D.L.R. (4th) 261 at 355-357 (S.C.C.)); *Ceres Stevedoring Co. v. Eisen & Metall A.G.; Can. Overseas*

decisions turned on the issue of agency, and the problem was to discern whether the elements of the necessary contract between the party granting the exemption and the party seeking its protection were to be found in the facts.[159] In *Dyck v. Manitoba Snowmobile Association*,[160] the Manitoba Court of Appeal was able to find the requisite agency where a plaintiff participated in a snowmobile race. The contract under which he entered the sport provided for the release of the association and its organizers and their respective agents, officials, servants, and representatives, from liability for injury resulting from the race, howsoever caused. The issue was whether the starter could take advantage of this provision when his alleged negligence brought about the accident in which the plaintiff was hurt. The starter's attempt to rely on the release was successful. The form of entry was designed to protect *inter alia* the starter; the language of the form indicated that the association was contracting as agent for the starter. There was evidence that the starter had authorized the association to act as his agent in requiring prospective race participants to complete an entry form including a waiver or release of liability, and consideration moved from the starter to the plaintiff in exchange for the benefits the starter claimed under the release. That consideration was the act of the starter in starting the race, since the contract contemplated that the association would provide officials to conduct the race, including the starter. The act of the starter in starting the race was compared to the offloading of the goods by the stevedores in the *Satterthwaite* case. In *ITO-International Terminal Operators Ltd. v. Miida Electronics Inc.*[161] the Supreme Court of Canada was able to find the necessary agency between the stevedores, seeking protection from liability, and the carriers of goods that were stolen.

In contrast the Supreme Court of Canada could not find any agency in *Greenwood Shopping Plaza Ltd. v. Beattie.*[162] A lease provided that the lessor would not grant subrogation rights for recovery of loss caused by the acts of the lessee to the insurance company with which the lessor insured against loss by fire. Employees of the lessee were responsible by their negligence for a fire which destroyed the leased premises. When the insurance company sought recovery from the employees, they attempted to invoke the protection of this clause in the lease. They were successful before the trial judge[163] and the Nova Scotia Court of

---

Shipping Ltd. v. Eisen & Metall A.G. (1976), 72 D.L.R. (3d) 660 (Que. C.A.); *Circle Sales & Import Ltd. v. Wilhelmsen; Marie-Anne Novelties Inc. v. Wilhelmsen*, [1978] 1 F.C. 269 (Fed. T.D.). See also *Saint John Shipbuilding & Dry Dock Co. v. Kingsland Maritime Corp.* (1981), 126 D.L.R. (3d) 332 (Fed. C.A.); leave to appeal to S.C.C. refused (1981), 126 D.L.R. (3d) 332 (note) (S.C.C.).

158 *Calkins & Burke Ltd. v. Far Eastern S.S. Co.* (1976), 72 D.L.R. (3d) 625 (B.C.S.C.).

159 Compare *Port Jackson Stevedoring Pty. Ltd. v. Salmond & Spraggon (Australia) Pty. Ltd.*, [1980] 3 All E.R. 257 (P.C.).

160 (1982), 136 D.L.R. (3d) 11 (Man. C.A.); affirmed [1985] 4 W.W.R. 319 (S.C.C.); compare *L. & B. Const. Ltd. v. Nor. Can. Power Comm.; Nor. Can. Power Commn. v. L. & B. Const. Ltd.*, [1984] 6 W.W.R. 598 (N.W.T.S.C.).

161 Above, note 157, at 669-671, applying the *Satterthwaite* case.

162 (1980), 111 D.L.R. (3d) 257 (S.C.C.) (discussed and explained by Iacobucci J. in *London Drugs Ltd. v. Kuehne & Nagel Int. Ltd.*, above, note 157, at 353-355).

163 (1978), 31 N.S.R. (2d) 1 (N.S.T.D.), supplementary reasons at 34 N.S.R. (2d) 217 (N.S.T.D.).

Appeal,[164] on the broad ground that the context and purport of the contract were such that it could only be made meaningful if the provisions of the lease were extended to cover the negligence of the lessee's employees. The Supreme Court reversed the lower courts' decisions. They applied the strict doctrine of agency as set out in the *Midland Silicones* case and the *Satterthwaite* case and held that, failing proof that the lessee had contracted as agent for his employees, the latter were not entitled to the same immunity as the lessee. The evidence in this case did not support any finding of such a contractual link between the employer, the lessee, and the employees sufficient to protect the latter from liability for their own separate negligence.

(C) *The London Drugs case* The agency and trust exceptions to the privity doctrine, in general and in relation to the question of third party beneficiaries of an exclusion or similar clause, have not been affected by the case of *London Drugs Ltd. v. Kuehne & Nagel International Ltd.*[165] The judgment of the majority in that case, however, has widened the scope of exceptions to the privity doctrine by adding a new qualification to those previously applicable. In a lengthy judgment on behalf of himself and three other members of the court,[166] Iacobucci J. subjected the privity doctrine to extensive analysis and criticism, and showed how the doctrine had been treated in other jurisdictions, *viz.*, Quebec, New Zealand and the United States.[167] Then he examined previous decisions of the Supreme Court to which reference has been made,[168] after which he considered whether the doctrine should be relaxed, and, since his response was in the affirmative, how such relaxation should be accomplished.[169]

This evolutionary, if not revolutionary attitude of the majority of the court must be examined in the context of the facts in the case. The plaintiff delivered a transformer to the corporate defendant, a warehouseman, for storage pursuant to a warehouse receipt. The contract provided that the corporate defendant's liability would be limited to $40 per pallet unless the holder declared a valuation in excess of $40 and paid an additional charge. The corporate defendant offered the plaintiff all-risk insurance coverage, which the plaintiff declined because the plaintiff decided to include the property on its own insurance policy. The individual defendants were employees of the corporate defendant. When lifting the transformer they damaged it. The plaintiff sued the corporate defendant in bailment, contract and negligence, and sued the individual defendants in negligence. At trial the corporate defendant was liable only for $40 but the individual defendants were held liable for the full value of the transformer.[170] The British Columbia Court of Appeal held the employees' liability was limited to $40.[171] The plaintiff appealed

---

164 (1979), 99 D.L.R. (3d) 298 (N.S.C.A.).

165 (1992), 97 D.L.R. (4th) 261 at 368 (S.C.C.) *per* Iacobucci J.

166 L'Heureux-Dubé, Sopinka and Cory JJ.

167 Above, note 165, at 343-352.

168 *Ibid.*, at 352-358.

169 *Ibid.*, at 358-369.

170 [1986] 4 W.W.R. 183 (B.C.S.C.).

171 (1990), 70 D.L.R. (4th) 51 (B.C.C.A.).

and the employees cross-appealed. In the event the majority of the Supreme Court held that the employees were only liable for $40. La Forest J. decided that they were not liable for any amount, on the ground that the employees were not liable in tort. McLachlin J. held that the exemption clause in the contract did not cover the employees because it referred to "warehouseman" and that meant the employer, the corporate defendant, and did not include the corporate defendant's employees. In reaching this conclusion she clearly adopted a strict construction of the contract. However, she arrived at the same determination of liability as the majority by holding that because of the limitation of liability clause the duty of care in tort owed by the employees to the plaintiff was limited to damage under $40, because the plaintiff had accepted all risk of damage in excess of that amount by this conduct at the time of contracting. In the course of her judgment she disagreed with the tort analysis invoked by La Forest J. which would have introduced major changes into the law of tort.[172] Neither of these judgments is relevant to the issue now under consideration, namely, the relaxation of the privity doctrine to permit third parties to enjoy the benefit of an exemption or similar clause. The majority, however, dealt with the issue of the employees' liability by allowing them to rely on the limitation of liability clause contained in the contract between the plaintiff, the owner of the damaged property, and the corporate defendant, the warehouseman. In doing so they enunciated a new type of situation in which third party beneficiaries could be successful despite the privity doctrine.

Iacobucci J. stressed the special considerations arising from employer-employee and employer-customer relationships: and the identity of interest between an employer and his or her employees with regard to performance of the employer's contractual obligations. In effect, when a customer knows that the employer's obligations will be carried out by the employer's employees, and the contract with the employer contains a term limiting the employer's liability for what both parties contemplate will be performed by the employees, to uphold strict application of the privity doctrine would allow the customer, i.e., the plaintiff in this case, to circumvent or escape the limitation of liability clause to which such customer had expressly consented.[173] It would also be absurd to allow the customer to go around such clause by suing the employees in tort.[174] Moreover there were sound policy reasons for relaxing the privity doctrine: a clause of the kind found in this case, where the owner of the goods did not declare their value and did not pay an additional insurance fee, made perfect commercial sense.[175] Before such employees could obtain the benefit of a clause of this kind, however, the following requirements had to be satisfied:[176]

---

172 Above, note 165, at 320, 324-325.

173 *Ibid.*, at 361.

174 *Ibid.*, at 363.

175 *Ibid.*, at 364. Nor would employees reasonably expect to be subject to unlimited liability for damage occurring in the performance of the contract when the contract specifically limited the warehouseman's liability to a fixed amount: *ibid.*, at 364-365.

176 *Ibid.*, at 366-367.

(1) the limitation of liability clause must, either expressly or impliedly, extend its benefit to the employees (or employee) seeking to rely on it; and

(2) the employees (or employee) seeking the benefit of the limitation of liability clause must have been acting in the course of their employment *and* must have been performing the very services provided for in the contract between their employer and the plaintiff (customer) when the loss occurred.

These principles represented an "incremental" change to the common law. It was incremental and not major because (1) this new exception depended on the intention of the contracting parties; (2) it involved very similar benchmarks to the recognized agency exception; and (3) it was a very specific and limited exception where employees qualified as third party beneficiaries and caused the damage in the course of their employment and while carrying out the very services for which the customer had contracted with the employer. In short Iacobucci J., and those who concurred with him, recognized a limited *jus tertii*.[177]

From the judgment of Iacobucci J. it is now clear that in Canada the qualifications of the strict privity doctrine, insofar as the ability of a third party to rely on an exemption or similar clause is concerned, have been added to in this "incremental" way. Limited though this new qualification may be, it will have an enormous effect upon the liability of a contracting party and those who work for him where a breach of contract has occurred and an exclusion or other exculpatory clause is invoked by way of defence.

(d) The effect of fundamental breach

(i) *Before the Photo Production case*

A further, if external, qualification of the effect of an exclusion or similar clause is to be found in the doctrine of fundamental breach of contract. Prior to 1966, in England, there was "spawned"[178] out of the exercise of determining the reach of an exculpatory provision, a line of cases under which fundamental breach was, as a matter of law, a ground for excluding the application of such a clause. Instead of involving *construction* of a contract, a breach of this kind raised issues of legal principle, of substantive rules. These cases were concerned with deviation from the performance of a contract in different ways, for example, taking the wrong route to deliver goods;[179] abusing a bailment, for example, by applying the goods bailed to a different, and improper use;[180] and delivering not merely unfit goods,

---

177 *Ibid.*, at 367-368.
178 *B.G. Linton Const. Ltd. v. C.N.R.*, [1975] 3 W.W.R. 97 at 107 (S.C.C.) *per* Laskin C.J.C. See also *George Mitchell (Chesterhall) Ltd. v. Finney Lock Seeds Ltd.*, [1983] 1 All E.R. 108 at 113-114 (C.A.) *per* Lord Denning; affirmed [1983] 2 All E.R. 737 (H.L.).
179 *Hain S.S. Co. v. Tate & Lyle Ltd.*, [1936] 2 All E.R. 597 (H.L.); *Sze Hai Tong Bank Ltd. v. Rambler Cycle Co.*, [1959] A.C. 576 (P.C.).
180 *Alexander v. Railway Executive*, [1951] 2 K.B. 882; *Smeaton Hanscomb & Co. v. Sassoon Setty Son & Co.*, [1953] 2 All E.R. 1471; *J. Spurling Ltd. v. Bradshaw*, [1956] 2 All E.R. 121 (C.A.); *Hunt & Winterbotham v. British Road Services*, [1962] 1 Q.B. 617 (C.A.); *Hollins v. Davy Ltd.*, [1963] 1 Q.B. 844.

but goods which were totally different in character from the goods which were the subject of a contract.[181] The doctrine was summarized by Denning L.J., in *Karsales (Harrow) Ltd. v. Wallis*:[182]

> The principle is sometimes said to be that the party cannot rely on an exempting clause when he delivers something 'different in kind' from that contracted for, or has broken a "fundamental term" or a "fundamental contractual obligation." However, I think that these are all comprehended by the general principle that a breach which goes to the root of the contract disentitles the party from relying on the exempting clause.

Or, as the same judge said a little earlier in that case:[183]

> Exempting clauses . . . , no matter how widely they are expressed, only avail the party when he is carrying out his contract in its essential respects. . . . They do not avail him when he is guilty of a breach which goes to the root of the contract.

There are several instances in Canada prior to 1966 of this English principle or doctrine of law being applied.[184]

This development, which was not always accepted by all English judges, some of whom continued to adopt the *construction* approach to this question,[185] culminated in, and was ultimately upset by, the speeches in the House of Lords in *Suisse Atlantique Société d'Armament Maritime S.A. v. N.V. Rotterdamsche Kolen Centrale*.[186] The appellants chartered a vessel from the respondents for two years' consecutive voyages for the carriage of coal from the U.S.A. to Europe. Fewer journeys were made than ought to have been made during the period of the charter-party. In consequence, the appellants argued that they had been deprived of the earnings from freights which could have been carried had the correct number of voyages been undertaken. By way of response, the respondents claimed that their liability was limited under a clause in the charter-party to demurrage, calculated at the rate of $1,000 a day. On this basis, their liability would have been about one quarter of the amount sought by the appellants on the basis of damages calculated at large, in accordance with the normal contractual principles. As it turned out, the real decision in favour of the respondents was founded on the question

---

181   *Chanter v. Hopkins* (1838), 4 M. & W. 399, 150 E.R. 1484; *Nichol v. Godts* (1854), 10 Exch. 191; *Karsales (Harrow) Ltd. v. Wallis*, below, note 182; *Yeoman Credit Ltd. v. Apps*, [1961] 2 All E.R. 281 (C.A.); *Astley Indust. Trust Ltd. v. Grimley*, [1963] 1 All E.R. 33 (C.A.); *Charterhouse Credit Co. v. Tolly*, [1963] 2 Q.B. 683 (C.A.).

182   [1956] 2 All E.R. 866 at 869 (C.A.).

183   *Ibid.*, at 868-869.

184   See *e.g., Knowles v. Anchorage Holdings Co.* (1964), 46 W.W.R. 173 (B.C.S.C.); *Schmidt v. Int. Harvester Co.* (1962), 38 W.W.R. 180 (Man. Q.B.); *Varga v. Stokes Seeds Ltd.* (1962), 32 D.L.R. (2d) 167 (Ont. H.C.); *Western Processing & Cold Storage Ltd. v. Hamilton Const. Co.* (1965), 51 W.W.R. 354 (Man. C.A.); *Can. Dom. Leasing Corp. v. Suburban Superdrug Ltd.* (1966), 55 W.W.R. 396 (Alta. C.A.); *Traders Finance Corp. v. Norray Distributing Ltd.* (1967), 60 W.W.R. 129 (Man. Q.B.); compare *F. & B. Tpt. Ltd. v. White Truck Sales Man. Ltd.* (1965), 51 W.W.R. 124 (Man. C.A.).

185   *E.g.*, Pearson L.J. in *U.G.S. Finance Ltd. v. Nat. Mortgage Bank of Greece, S.A.*, [1964] 1 Lloyd's Rep. 446 at 453 (C.A.).

186   [1967] 1 A.C. 361 (H.L.).

whether the appellants were right in arguing that they had a contractual right to a certain number of voyages. For this reason, it could be said that everything expressed by the House on the issue of fundamental breach was not necessary to the decision. Moreover the speeches in that case were not easy to understand or to reconcile with each other. However, it appears to have been decided by that case that when there was an exemption or similar clause and a fundamental breach, it could not be decided automatically as a matter of law that the exemption clause could not apply. It was a question of construction whether the clause in issue could be read so as to exclude liability in the event of a fundamental breach.[187] There was no rule of law by which liability for fundamental breach could never be precluded under a contract. The parties were always free, by the use of appropriate, clear, unambiguous language to exclude all forms or possibilities of liability.[188]

Despite the seemingly clear statement by the House of Lords that what was to happen in the event of a fundamental breach depended upon the proper construction of the contract, including an exclusion or similar clause, there were doubts and uncertainties in the English cases after 1966. Many went along with the "construction" approach.[189] Some, however, especially where Lord Denning was a member of the court, appear to have endeavoured to reintroduce the strict law approach by various means, including the making of fine, tenuous distinctions between election to determine the contract, waiver of the breach, frustration, deviation as contrasted with misperformance.[190]

The *Suisse Atlantique* case, quite naturally, had a great effect upon Canadian courts. Canadian judges, who had been prepared to hold that the doctrine of fundamental breach operated as a rule of law rendering an exclusion or similar clause potentially ineffectual, preferred to accept and adopt the "construction" approach. As Bull J.A. of the British Columbia Court of Appeal said in *Traders Finance Corporation v. Halverston*,[191]

> whether an exception clause is applicable where there is a fundamental breach of contract is one of construction of the contract and depends on the nature and extent of the exclusions and the presumed intentions of the parties.

Both the definition of "fundamental breach" and the law as to the effects of such a breach upon an exemption or exclusion clause, as set out in the *Suisse Atlantique* case, were adopted and applied by the courts of Ontario in *R.G. McLean Ltd. v.*

---

187 Compare *Inelco Indust. Ltd. v. Venture Well Services* (1975), 59 D.L.R. (3d) 458 at 467 (Alta. C.A.) *per* Sinclair J.A.

188 See, *e.g.*, *Alexander Stephen (Scotland) Ltd. v. J.J. Riley (U.K.) Ltd.*, [1976] S.C. 157 (Scot.) (a Scottish case but the principles were said to be the same).

189 *Kenyon, Son & Craven Ltd. v. Baster Hoare & Co.*, [1971] 2 All E.R. 708; *Wathes (Western) Ltd. v. Austins (Menswear) Ltd.*, [1975] 1 Lloyd's Rep. 14 (C.A.); *Levison v. Patent Steam Carpet Cleaning Co.*, [1978] Q.B. 69 (C.A.); *R.W. Green Ltd. v. Cade Bros. Farms*, [1978] 1 Lloyd's Rep. 602.

190 *Harbutt's Plasticine Ltd. v. Wayne Tank & Pump Co.*, [1970] 1 Q.B. 447 (C.A.); *Farnsworth Finance Facilities Ltd. v. Attryde*, [1970] 2 All E.R. 774 (C.A.); *The "Angelia"; Trade & Transport Inc. v. Iino Kaiun Kaisha Ltd.*, [1973] 2 All E.R. 144; *Photo Production Ltd. v. Securicor Tpt. Ltd.*, [1980] 1 All E.R. 556 (H.L.).

191 (1969), 2 D.L.R. (3d) 666 at 676 (B.C.C.A.).

Canada Vickers Ltd.,[192] a case involving a disclaimer clause in a contract of sale of goods, ousting the operation of conditions and warranties. Notwithstanding this and other decisions,[193] there were indications that in Canada, as in England, after the *Suisse Atlantique* case, the law was uncertain. In several judgments, including one given by the Supreme Court of Canada,[194] language can be found suggesting that the construction approach was not the correct one, or that the construction approach had not completely ousted the strict law doctrine to be found in earlier English and Canadian decisions.[195] Between 1966 and 1980, therefore, the law both in England and Canada was in a dubious state. Judges seeking to find a solution to a problem with which they were faced could pray in aid decisions and dicta in support of either method of dealing with a fundamental breach committed of a contract containing an exclusionary type clause.

(ii) *The Photo Production case*

Any doubts and difficulties were resolved by the decision of the House of Lords in the *Photo Production* case,[196] which was expressly approved and followed by the Supreme Court of Canada in *Beaufort Realties (1964) Inc. v. Chomedey Aluminum Co.*,[197] and subsequently also in *Hunter Engineering Co. v. Syncrude Canada Ltd.*[198]

In the *Photo Production* case the defendants were hired by the plaintiffs to

---

192 [1969] 2 O.R. 249 (Ont. H.C.); varied on appeal, but only as to damages [1971] 1 O.R. 207 (Ont. C.A.); followed by Stewart J. in *Freedhoff v. Pomalift Indust. Ltd.*, [1970] 3 O.R. 571 (Ont. H.C.); reversed on other grounds [1971] 2 O.R. 773 (Ont. C.A.).

193 *Lightburn v. Belmont Sales Ltd.* (1969), 6 D.L.R. (3d) 692 (B.C.S.C.); *Western Tractor Ltd. v. Dyck* (1969), 7 D.L.R. (3d) 535 (Sask. C.A.); *Gibbons v. Trapp Motors Ltd.* (1970), 9 D.L.R. (3d) 742 (B.C.S.C.); *Arrow Transfer Co. v. Royal Bank* (1971), 19 D.L.R. (3d) 420 (B.C.C.A.); affirmed on other grounds [1972] S.C.R. 858 (S.C.C.); *Beldessi v. Island Equip. Ltd.* (1973), 29 D.L.R. (3d) 213 (B.C.S.C.); reversed in part (1973), 41 D.L.R. (3d) 147 (B.C.C.A.); *Henuset Bros. Ltd. v. Highland Stock Farms Ltd.* (1976), 63 D.L.R. (3d) 554 (Alta. T.D.).

194 *B.G. Linton Const. Ltd. v. C.N.R.*, [1975] 2 S.C.R. 678 (S.C.C.).

195 *Heffron v. Imperial Parking Co.* (1974), 46 D.L.R. (3d) 642 (Ont. C.A.); *Tricco v. Hynes* (1971), 2 Nfld. & P.E.I.R. 53 (Nfld. Dist. Ct.); *Philipzyk v. Edmonton Real Estate Bd. Co-op. Listing Bureau Ltd.* (1975), 55 D.L.R. (3d) 424 (Alta. C.A.); *Burlington Leasing Ltd. v. De Moura* (1975), 60 D.L.R. (3d) 71 (Ont. Co. Ct.); *Cain v. Bird Chevrolet-Oldsmobile Ltd.* (1976), 69 D.L.R. 484 (Ont. H.C.); reversed in part (1978), 88 D.L.R. (3d) 607 (Ont. C.A.); *Neilsen v. Maclin Motors Ltd.* (1976), 71 D.L.R. (3d) 744 (Alta. T.D.); *Evans Products Ltd. v. Crest Warehousing Ltd.* (1976), 69 D.L.R. (3d) 575 (B.C.S.C.); reversed on appeal on the ground of lack of fundamental breach (1978), 95 D.L.R. (3d) 631 (B.C.C.A.); affirmed [1979] 5 W.W.R. 385 (S.C.C.); *Findlay v. Couldwell* (1976), 69 D.L.R. (3d) 320 (B.C.S.C.); *Davidson v. Three Spruce Realty Ltd.* (1977), 79 D.L.R. (3d) 481 (B.C.S.C.) (applying the notion of unconscionability or inequality of bargaining power); *Alta. Caterers Ltd. v. R. Vollan (Alta.) Ltd.* (1977), 11 A.R. 181 (Alta. T.D.); *Murray v. Sperry Rand Corp.* (1979), 23 O.R. (2d) 456 (Ont. H.C.); *Captain v. Far Eastern S.S. Co.* (1978), 97 D.L.R. (3d) 250 (B.C.S.C.); *Celgar Ltd. v. Star Bulk Shipping Co.*, [1979] 4 W.W.R. 248 (B.C.C.A.).

196 *Photo Production Ltd. v. Securicor Tpt. Ltd.*, [1980] 1 All E.R. 556 (H.L.); see also the House of Lords decisions in *Ailsa Craig Fishing Co. v. Malvern Fishing Co.*, [1983] 1 All E.R. 101 (H.L.) and *George Mitchell (Chesterhall) Ltd. v. Finney Lock Seeds Ltd.*, [1983] 2 All E.R. 737 (H.L.).

197 (1980), 116 D.L.R. (3d) 193 (S.C.C.).

198 (1989), 57 D.L.R. (4th) 321 (S.C.C.): below, pp. 597-600.

provide security for the plaintiffs' factory. A servant of the defendants, sent to perform the defendants' contractual obligations, deliberately set fire to the factory, destroying it and causing considerable loss to the plaintiffs. When sued by the plaintiffs, the defendants pleaded an exemption clause in the contract, purporting to exclude altogether, or else limit, liability for the acts of their servants. They were successful at the trial. But the Court of Appeal allowed the plaintiffs' action and did not give effect to the exemption clause.[199] Two reasons were given for this. First, on a strict construction of the language of the clause the parties had not agreed to exonerate the defendants in respect of damage caused by malicious, wilful, deliberate misconduct by a servant of the defendants, as opposed to some act of carelessness or neglect. Second, however, a fundamental breach of contract had taken place. The contract was to provide security for the plaintiffs' factory. The defendants had not secured the factory; they had destroyed it. Such a fundamental breach discharged the contract or rendered it void at the moment of breach, so that the contract was effectively destroyed, and the exemption clause could not affect liabilities which arose after, or as a consequence of such fundamental breach, but could only apply to pre-breach liabilities. This approach is more consistent with the views of Lord Denning before the *Suisse Atlantique* case (and in some decisions after the *Suisse Atlantique* case[200]) than with the "constructionist" approach endorsed in the *Suisse Atlantique* and subsequent cases.

Not surprisingly, therefore, the House of Lords reversed the Court of Appeal and held that the exemption clause precluded an action by the plaintiffs. The clause was said to be sufficiently clear, even when interpreted *contra proferentem*,[201] to cover the circumstances of this case. More importantly, in the present context, there was no rule of law by which an exemption or similar clause could be eliminated from consideration when there was a breach of contract, whether fundamental or not. Nor could such a clause be deprived of effect. Parties could agree to exclude or modify their obligations by the use of appropriate words. Therefore, whenever there was a breach of contract, of whatever kind, whether fundamental breach, breach of fundamental term, or breach of some less important term, the effect of an exclusion clause depended on the proper construction of the wording of the whole contract, including the exclusion clause. It is worthy of note that the House of Lords pointed to the strained construction that had been placed upon exclusion clauses in the past, chiefly in consumer contracts or *contrats d'adhesion* (that is, standard form contracts). The inference in this reflection was that courts had adopted such an approach to prevent unfairness, or the imposition of an unreasonable bargain upon an unequal party. In England this has now become an unnecessary judicial exercise by reason of the enactment of the Unfair Contract

---

199 [1978] 3 All E.R. 146 (C.A.).

200 *E.g., Harbutt's Plasticine Ltd. v. Wayne Tank & Pump Co.*, [1970] 1 Q.B. 447 (C.A.), specifically overruled by the House of Lords in the *Photo Production* case: see Ziegel (1980), 30 U.T.L.J. 421.

201 Above, pp. 470-472.

Terms Act, 1977. The situation where parties were contracting at arms' length and on equal terms was different. In the words of Lord Diplock[202]

> [i]n commercial contracts negotiated between businessmen capable of looking after their own interests and of deciding how risks inherent in the performance of various kinds of contract can be most economically borne (generally by insurance), it is…wrong to place a strained construction on words in an exclusion clause which are clear and fairly susceptible of one meaning only. …

Despite this clear statement by the House of Lords, a subsequent attempt was made by the Court of Appeal (especially by Lord Denning in what was his last reported judgment as Master of the Rolls) to reinstate the pre-*Suisse Atlantique* rule of law doctrine, by invoking the idea that an exclusion clause, to be effective, had to be "reasonable".[203] This failed. The House of Lords refused to countenance any such qualification of their decision in the *Photo Production* case.[204] That case, said Lord Bridge,[205] "gave the final quietus to the doctrine that a 'fundamental breach' of contract deprived the party in breach of the benefit of clauses in the contract excluding or limiting his liability."

To this must be added a corollary. In another decision, *Ailsa Craig Fishing Co. v. Malvern Fishing Co.*,[206] which also involved the Securicor company, and concerned the sinking of a ship which the company was contractually bound to look after, the House of Lords held that there was an important distinction between exclusion and limitation clauses. Lord Fraser[207] referred to authorities which laid down very strict principles to be applied when considering the effect of clauses of exclusion or indemnity, but went on to add

> … these principles are not applicable in their full rigour when considering the effect of conditions merely limiting liability. Such conditions will of course be read contra proferentem and must be clearly expressed, but there is no reason why they should be judged by the specially exacting standards which are applied to exclusion or indemnity clauses.

As Lord Wilberforce said,[208]

> clauses of limitation are not regarded by the courts with the same hostility as clauses of exclusion; this is because they must be related to other contractual terms, in particular

---

202 Above, note 196, at 568.
203 *George Mitchell (Chesterhall) Ltd. v. Finney Lock Seeds Ltd.*, [1983] 1 All E.R. 108 (C.A.); but the case could be, and was decided under the Sale of Goods Act 1979 (U.K.), c. 54, Sched. I, para. 11.
204 [1983] 2 All E.R. 737 (H.L.).
205 *Ibid.*, at 741.
206 [1983] 1 All E.R. 101 (H.L.); compare *Eagle Dancer Enterprises Ltd. v. Southam Printing Ltd.* — *Imprimerie Southam Ltée* (1992), 6 B.L.R. (2d) 45 (B.C.S.C.). Contrast the view in the Australian case of *Darlington Futures Ltd. v. Delco Australia Pty. Ltd.* (1986), 161 C.L.R. 500 (Aust. H.C.): above, p. 572, note 92.
207 [1983] 1 All E.R. 101 at 105 (H.L.).
208 *Ibid.*, at 102-103.

to the risks to which the defending party may be exposed, the remuneration which
he receives, and possibly also the opportunity of the other party to insure.

The relevant factors should be noted.

(iii) *Canadian aftermath*

In the *Beaufort Realties* case,[209] the Supreme Court of Canada purported to
determine the issue involved by the approval and application of the decision of
the House of Lords. The Supreme Court's affirmation of the decision of the Ontario
Court of Appeal, however, might appear to have done precisely the opposite. A
builder agreed to waive his rights under a building contract to a mechanics lien.
Subsequently, the building owner refused to make payments as they fell due. This
was held to be a fundamental breach of contract. The Ontario Court of Appeal
held that it was not reasonable to suppose that the parties intended the waiver
of the lien to bind the builder.[210] Wilson J.A., giving the judgment of the court,
pointed out the uncertainty of the English cases at that time (which was before
the decision of the House of Lords in the *Photo Production* case) on the question
of the effect of a fundamental breach on an exclusion clause. She concluded that
the right question to ask in each case was not whether the exclusionary clause
was fair and reasonable in its contractual setting but "whether it is fair and
reasonable that it survive the disintegration of its contractual setting."[211] The
purpose of this question was to discover the intention of the parties. The tenor
of this judgment appears to be in favour of the construction approach.[212]

In the Supreme Court of Canada, where the decision and the language of
the Ontario Court of Appeal were both approved and followed, the application
of the construction approach was supported by the House of Lords' decision in
the *Photo Production* case, in particular the rejection of the rule of law approach
of Lord Denning both before and after the *Suisse Atlantique* decision.[213] However,
in view of the language of the House of Lords in the *Photo Production* case, especially
the ideas contained in the passage from Lord Diplock's speech cited earlier, it
is surprising that both the Ontario Court of Appeal and the Supreme Court of
Canada could conclude that "in the context of the contract as a whole the true
construction to be placed upon" the relevant term in the contract in the *Beaufort
Realties* case, "is that the waiver therein contained ceased to bind the respondent
upon it having communicated to the appellant its election to treat the contract
as at an end."[214] Much of the reasoning of Wilson J.A. that was adopted by the

---

209 *Beaufort Realties (1964) Inc. v. Chomedey Aluminum Co.* (1981), 116 D.L.R. (3d) 193 (S.C.C.).
210 *Chomedey Aluminum Co. v. Belcourt Const. Ltd.* (1979), 97 D.L.R. (3d) 170 (Ont. C.A.).
211 *Ibid.*, at 178.
212 *Note*, however, the idea of what is "fair and reasonable"; compare *Rose v. Borisko Bros. Ltd.* (1981),
       125 D.L.R. (3d) 671 at 679 (Ont. H.C.) *per* O'Brien J.; affirmed (1983), 147 D.L.R. (3d) 191
       (Ont. C.A.).
213 Above, note 209, at 196-197.
214 *Ibid.*, at 198.

Supreme Court seems to have been concerned with the legislation creating and setting out the requirements and effects of mechanics liens.[215] Wilson J.A. seems to have been of the opinion that although the statute permitted waiver of a lien by the signing of an express agreement to such effect, the legislature could not have meant that such a waiver would be effective where the contract so signed was initially enforceable against the party waiving the lien and subsequently ceased to be so. Despite the public interest in waivers being able to be relied on,[216] the Ontario Court of Appeal was able to conclude that a waiver should not be capable of enforcement where the contract was broken by a fundamental breach. But, it may be argued, was not the purpose of the waiver precisely to protect the owner in the event of his non-payment (when, otherwise, the lien would attach)? If non-payment of the builder's charges, as contrasted with some other kind of breach of the contract, was ineffective to bring the waiver into operation, what was the point of inserting the waiver in the contract? In effect, it would seem, the Ontario Court of Appeal, and the Supreme Court of Canada, were adopting the "fair and reasonable" approach introduced by the English Court of Appeal in the *Mitchell* case,[217] and later rejected decisively by the House of Lords,[218] under the guise of applying the construction approach to exclusion clauses and fundamental breach. With the adoption of the construction approach by the Supreme Court of Canada there can be no quarrel. With the actual decision in the *Beaufort Realties* case, there can be no disagreement. It may not be too harsh to suggest that the two superior courts in that case negated by their actual decision the very principle of law which they purported to be approving and applying.

Subsequent decisions in Canada endorsed the construction approach[219] although the party relying on an exclusion clause and the construction approach was not always successful.[220] Courts looked at the risks to which a party was exposing himself, and whether, despite an exclusion clause, such party was accepting a particular risk.[221] They looked at the purpose of the contract, especially the

---

215 Above, note 210, at 178-179, cited in above, note 209, at 197-198.

216 *Shill-Brand v. Belcourt Const. (Ottawa) Ltd.* (1978), 19 O.R. (2d) 606 (Ont. Div. Ct.).

217 Above, note 203.

218 Above, note 204.

219 *I.e.*, that there is no rule of law that a fundamental breach relieves the innocent party of the disclaimer clause: *Hayward v. Mellick* (1984), 2 O.A.C. 161 at 168 (Ont. C.A.) *per* Weatherston J.A. See Wilson J. in *Hunter Engineering Co. v. Syncrude Can. Ltd.* (1989), 57 D.L.R. (4th) 321 at 374 (S.C.C.).

220 Contrast *Can. Dom. Leasing Corp. v. George A. Welch & Co.* (1981), 125 D.L.R. (3d) 723 (Ont. C.A.); *Nabel Leasing Div. of Citicorp Leasing Can. Ltd. v. Walwyn Stodgell Cochran Murray Ltd.* (1982), 41 N.B.R. 291 (N.B.Q.B.); *Delaney v. Cascade River Holidays Ltd.* (1983), 24 C.C.L.T. 6 (B.C.C.A.), with *Woollatt Fuel & Lumber (London) Ltd. v. Matthews Group Ltd.* (1981), 128 D.L.R. (3d) 68 (Ont. C.A.); leave to appeal to S.C.C. refused (1982), 35 O.R. (2d) 140n (S.C.C.); *Gallant v. Hobbs* (1982), 37 O.R. (2d) 1 (Ont. Co. Ct.); affirmed (1983), 40 O.R. (2d) 377 (Ont. C.A.); *Rose v. Borisko Bros. Ltd.* (1983), 147 D.L.R. (3d) 191 (Ont. C.A.). See also Ogilvie, "The Reception of Photo Production Ltd. v. Securicor Transport Ltd. in Canada: *Nec Tamen Consumebatur*" (1982), 27 McGill L.J. 424. The application of the construction approach was uncertain: Wilson J. in *Hunter Engineering Co. v. Syncrude Can. Ltd.*, above, note 219, at 374.

221 *Gallant v. Hobbs*, above, note 220.

relationship between the parties brought about by the contract.[222] They looked at relevant legislation, and at whether the language of the contract sufficed to exclude its operation.[223] Two illustrative, and contrasting cases, merit examination.

In *Peter Cortesis Jeweller Ltd. v. Purolator Courier Ltd.*,[224] a jeweller delivered a package containing pearls to the defendant carrier for delivery. The bill of lading given to the jeweller purported to limit the carrier's liability to $2 per pound. The jeweller did not disclose the contents of the package or its value, which he should have done under the relevant legislation if he wished to enlarge the carrier's liability. When the package was lost while in the possession of the carrier, the jeweller sued for the value of the pearls, and the carrier relied on the limitation clause. He was successful. Despite the fundamental breach by the carrier, the proper construction of the clause limiting the carrier's liability was that it was to apply in such circumstances. The words were clear and unambiguous, and they showed that the parties had contemplated the method for measuring the monetary value of any loss to the jeweller. In *Cathcart Inspection Services Ltd. v. Purolator Courier Ltd.*,[225] the carrier failed to deliver a tender for a construction contract entrusted to the carrier for delivery. As a result the plaintiff lost a contract and a considerable profit. The bill of lading signed by the plaintiff excluded liability for any special, consequential or other damages for any reason whatsoever including delay in delivery. This clause was inserted under a heading entitled "delay and limitation of value". The material legislation limited a carrier's liability to $1.50 per pound unless a higher value was declared. When the plaintiff sued for his lost profits, one defence raised against the claim was the exclusion clause.[226] At the trial of the action it was held[227] that the statutory limitation applied only to loss of or damage to the goods carried, not to consequential losses for non-delivery. It was also said that the clause could not protect the carrier on a proper construction of the contract, taking into consideration the fact that the heading referred to delay and not to non-delivery; that the clause was to be strictly construed against the carrier; that it should be construed so as to give the contract business efficacy; and that it would contradict the main purpose of the contract to construe the clause to enable the carrier to be free of any obligation to deliver. In reaching this conclusion, the Ontario Court of Appeal made use of two notions.[228] The first was the test of what was "fair and reasonable" employed by Wilson J.A. in the *Beaufort Realties* case.[229] "Fair", however, was not meant in a moral sense (as in cases of unconscionability) because parties with equal bargaining power might enter into a contract that was unfair to one or other of them but presumably that

---

222 *Delaney v. Cascade River Holidays Ltd.*, above, note 220.
223 *Chabot v. Ford Motor Co. of Can.* (1982), 138 D.L.R. (3d) 417 (Ont. H.C.).
224 (1981), 35 O.R. (2d) 39 (Ont. Co. Ct.).
225 (1981), 128 D.L.R. (3d) 227 (Ont. H.C.); affirmed (1982), 139 D.L.R. (3d) 371 (Ont. C.A.).
226 Another defence was remoteness of damage: below, p. 723.
227 Following the decision in *Cornwall Gravel Co. v. Purolator Courier Ltd.* (1978), 83 D.L.R. (3d) 267 (Ont. H.C.); affirmed (1980), 115 D.L.R. (3d) 511 (Ont. C.A.); affirmed (1980), 120 D.L.R. (3d) 575 (S.C.C.). This case was before the *Photo Production* and *Beaufort Realties* cases.
228 (1982), 139 D.L.R. (3d) 371 at 374-375 (Ont. C.A.).
229 Compare *Citibank Leasing Can. Ltd. v. Action Fasteners Ltd.* (1986), 74 N.B.R. (2d) 241 (N.B.Q.B.).

was not their intention. It referred, so it would seem, to what was a proper construction of the contract taking into account the *contra proferentem* doctrine, and the need to use clear words to escape from the consequences of one's own, or one's servant's wrongdoing. The other notion was that "when a contract is in issue the court should look for and be guided by the reasonable expectations of the parties as long as it is compatible with their written contract."[230] Both these ideas, it may be suggested, are debatable propositions of law. They seem to involve the division between the strict approach to construction and an approach that brings into play the broader context of the contract, its purposes, intent, and design.

In the light of the ideas and decisions contained in these post-*Photo Production* Canadian cases, it was suggested[231] that, while lip-service was paid to the construction approach to exclusion clauses and fundamental breach, some vestiges of the older "rule of law" doctrine remained to bedevil the issue. Under the guise of "construction", some courts were utilizing something very much akin to the "rule of law" doctrine. What Canadian courts seemed to be doing was applying a concept of "fair and reasonable" construction in relation to the survival of the exclusion clause after a fundamental breach and the application of such a clause where the breach in question involved not just a negligent performance of the contract but the complete failure of the party obliged to fulfil the contract in any way whatsoever.[232]

Far from resolving this and other issues relating to fundamental breach and its effect on exclusion clauses, the decision of the Supreme Court of Canada in *Hunter Engineering Co. v. Syncrude Canada Ltd.*[233] can be said to have left a legacy of more uncertainty. In it two different views were expounded as to the proper method of dealing with such clauses where a fundamental breach occurred, although, in the case in question, no such breach was held to have been involved.

(iv) *The Hunter Engineering case*

The essential facts of this case insofar as the present issue is concerned are these. A contract for the manufacture of gearboxes contained an express warranty relating to the quality of the goods in question. Also it expressly excluded any other warranty "statutory or otherwise". The failure of the gearboxes to perform as required by reason of a defect in the design in the manner in which they were welded was held to entail a breach of the implied warranty (*i.e.*, condition, as it is referred to therein) in s. 15(a) of the Ontario Sale of Goods Act[234] that the goods

---

230 *Leading Invts. Ltd. v. New Forest Invts. Ltd.; H.W. Liebig & Co. v. Leading Invts. Ltd.* (1981), 126 D.L.R. (3) 75 at 85 (Ont. C.A.) *per* Brooke J.A.

231 In the second edition, at pp. 557-558, citing, *e.g., Kehler v. Klumper* (1983), 23 Man. R. (2d) 196 (Man. Co. Ct.).

232 This and the previous sentence, in the form in which they appeared in the second edition, were quoted by Wilson J. in *Hunter Engineering Co. v. Syncrude Can. Ltd.* (1989), 57 D.L.R. (4th) 321 at 374 (S.C.C.).

233 (1989), 57 D.L.R. (4th) 321 (S.C.C.).

234 R.S.O. 1990, c. S.1.

would be reasonably fit for the buyer's purpose.[235] When sued in respect of this failure, the sellers, *i.e.*, manufacturers, relied on the clause which excluded, *inter alia*, statutory warranties. Several members of the court held that the breach in question was not a fundamental breach.[236] However, this does not appear to be material to the ultimate decision in favour of the sellers on this point, because it was also held that the exclusion clause relieved the sellers from liability. In reaching this conclusion, however, the court gave different reasons.

Chief Justice Dickson (with whom La Forest J. concurred) approached this issue on the basis of "unconscionability". Wilson J. (with whom L'Heureux-Dubé J. concurred) adopted the view that an exclusion clause should be enforced and effectuated unless it ought not to be in the circumstances of the breach. An examination of the judgments reveals a division of opinion between the members of the court such that the present state of the law in Canada on this matter seems to be questionable and uncertain.

After examining the leading English and Canadian cases,[237] Dickson C.J.C. expressed the view that the doctrine of fundamental breach should be laid to rest. It created unnecessary complexities and resulting uncertainty. As a tool for averting unfairness it was too unrefined. Chief Justice Dickson preferred to deal explicitly with unconscionability where it was necessary and appropriate. Unconscionability was a much better way to cope with "the protection of the weak from over-reaching by the strong" than "the artificial legal doctrine of 'fundamental breach'".[238]

Wilson J., who also examined the earlier decisions,[239] stated that they left the law in need of clarification.[240] To resolve the uncertainty one of two methods could be adopted. One was to adopt the *Photo Production* case in its entirety, which would mean discarding the concept of fundamental breach. Whatever the nature of the breach the effect of an exclusion clause would be determined by construction. The only relevant question for the court would be: on the true and natural construction of the provisions of the contract, did the parties at the time the contract was made (this is the important factor) succeed in excluding liability?[241] The second method would entail importing some "reasonableness" requirement into the law. Courts could then refuse to enforce an exclusion clause in strict accordance with its terms if to do so would be unfair and unreasonable. The learned judge rejected this approach. Courts were quite unsuited to assess the fairness of reasonableness of contractual provisions as the parties negotiated them.[242] It was a different matter for courts to determine the enforceability of an exclusion clause after a particular breach had occurred.[243] Exclusion clauses did not lose their validity automatically under some hard and fast rule of law. They were to be given a true and natural

---

235 Fridman, *Sale of Goods in Canada*, 3rd ed. (1986), pp. 185-201.
236 Wilson, McIntyre and L'Heureux-Dubé JJ.
237 Above, note 233, at 336-340.
238 *Ibid.*, at 361.
239 *Ibid.*, at 369-374.
240 *Ibid.*, at 374-375.
241 *Ibid.*, at 375.
242 *Ibid.*
243 *Ibid.*, at 376.

construction, to give effect to the meaning the parties agreed to when they negotiated the contract. However, the courts still had to decide, on the basis of the parties' intention when the contract was made, whether the clause should be given effect to in the event of a fundamental breach. Whether fairness was the criterion or the balancing of conflicting values did not matter. The result would be the same because the question was: "in the circumstances that have happened should the court lend its aid to A to hold B to this clause?"[244]

Wilson J., unlike the Chief Justice, wished to retain the concept of fundamental breach. Such a breach would only render an exclusion clause ineffective, however, if it was appropriate to do so. That might entail invoking unconscionability, although there was little to choose between fundamental breach and unconscionability so far as certainty in the law was concerned. Indeed unconscionability was even less certain than fundamental breach. Nonetheless, there had to be some residual power in the court to withhold its assistance on policy grounds in appropriate circumstances.[245]

The difference between these two views seems to lie in this: Dickson C.J.C. took the line that the contract was to be examined as of the time of its making to determine the effect of an exclusion clause, whereas Wilson J. considered that the right moment of time for such examination was after the event which was alleged to have resulted in a breach of contract. Moreover, Dickson C.J.C. rejected fundamental breach, whereas Wilson J. considered that fundamental breach remained vital and relevant. A decision since the *Hunter Engineering* case, *Canadian Fracmaster Ltd. v. Grand Prix Natural Gas Ltd.*,[246] applied strict construction to an exclusion clause, but held that the clause was unambiguous and not unconscionable because the parties possessed equal bargaining power. Therefore the clause was valid and effective. This appears to be an adoption of the view of Dickson C.J.C. In *Kordas v. Stokes Seeds Ltd.*[247] the Ontario Court of Appeal dealt with an exclusion clause which the trial judge had held was inapplicable because of a fundamental breach of contract by the seller of allegedly defective goods. The court considered that a reading of the *Hunter Engineering* case indicated that there was not much life left in the concept of fundamental breach of contract.[248] The *Hunter Engineering* case revealed two different approaches to the issue of the effect of exclusion clauses after a breach of contract: that of Wilson J., which required a determination whether the breach undermined the entire contractual setting or went to the very root of the contract; and that of Dickson C.J.C., dependent on unconscionability. The Court of Appeal did not resolve this debate since the facts of the case before it did not conform to either approach. The cabbages delivered to the plaintiff were not fundamentally different from those for which he bargained. Nor was this a case of unconscionability in the sense of protecting the weak from

---

244 *Ibid.*, at 377.
245 *Ibid.*, at 380-381.
246 (1990), 109 A.R. 173 (Alta. Q.B.).
247 (1992), 11 O.R. (3d) 129 (Ont. C.A.); leave to appeal to S.C.C. refused (1993), 99 D.L.R. (4th) vii (note) (S.C.C.).
248 *Ibid.*, at 135.

over-reaching by the strong.[249] In consequence it seems that the present state of the law is unclear and uncertain.

4. Anticipatory breach[250]

(a) Definition and elements

(i) *Definition*

Anticipatory breach occurs when a party, by express language or conduct, or as a matter of implication from what he has said or done, repudiates his contractual obligations before they fall due. What must be shown before such a breach is said to occur was stated thus by Lord Alverstone in an English case,[251] cited and relied upon by Walsh J. of the Supreme Court of Alberta in *Reed v. McVeigh*:[252]

> The conduct of the party who has broken the contract is such that the other party is entitled to conclude that the party breaching the contract no longer intends to be bound by its provisions.

The authorities reveal that, for this type of breach to occur the following must be established: (1) conduct which amounts to a total rejection of the obligations of the contract; (2) lack of justification for such conduct. If, to these, is added the acceptance by the innocent party of the repudiation, then the effect will be to terminate the contract. This does not mean that the repudiating party is free from all liability. It simply means that the innocent party may be freed from *his* obligations (as in the case of a breach at the due date of performance), and may pursue such remedies as would be available to him if the breach had taken place at the time when performance was due.[253]

(ii) *What amounts to repudiation?*

The problem of what sort of conduct constitutes a repudiation of a contract

---

249 *Ibid.*, at 136-137.

250 See McRae, "Repudiation of Contracts in Canadian Law" (1978), 56 Can. Bar Rev. 232. See also Dawson, "Metaphors and Anticipatory Breach of Contract" (1981), 40 C.L.J. 83; Carter, "The Embiricos Principle and the Law of Anticipatory Breach" (1984), 47 M.L.R. 422; Rose, "The Doctrine of Anticipatory Breach" (1981), 34 Current Legal Problems 235. The original version of this part was referred to with approval by Lang J. in *Odeco Drilling of Can. Ltd. v. Hickey* (1985), 54 Nfld. & P.E.I.R. 116 at 133 (Nfld. T.D.).

251 *Rhymney Ry. Co. v. Brecon & Merthyr Tydfil Junction Ry. Co.* (1900), 69 L.J. Ch. 813 at 818. Compare *Heyman v. Darwins Ltd.*, [1942] A.C. 356 at 378-379 (H.L.) *per* Lord Wright; *Woodar Invt. Dev. Ltd. v. Wimpey Const. (U.K.) Ltd.*, [1980] 1 All E.R. 571 at 575-576 (H.L.) *per* Lord Wilberforce, and at 579-580 *per* Lord Salmon.

252 [1931] 1 W.W.R. 257 at 258 (Alta. S.C.), in which the hypothecation of shares was not a repudiation of a contract, even though the contract stipulated that the party in question was not to encumber or pledge such shares. *Sed quaere?*

253 This and the preceding two sentences in their original form in the first edition were cited by Perry L.J.S.C. in *Saunders v. Multi Bldrs. Ltd.* (1981), 30 B.C.L.R. 236 at 243 (B.C.S.C.).

is one that has exercised the courts for a long time.[254] To some extent it is not unlike (indeed it may even be a variation of) the question of the distinction between terms in a contract which are of a basic, even a fundamental nature, and terms of lesser importance.[255] Breach of the former, as seen earlier, gives rise to rights of repudiation and rescission on the part of the innocent party; breach of the latter entitles the innocent party only to claim damages.[256] The recently declared existence of "innominate" terms, different from the classical "condition" and "warranty",[257] indicates that there may be many varied terms, breach of which at the date of performance produces the right to repudiate on the part of the innocent party. In the same way, an anticipatory breach of such a term might be treated by the innocent party as repudiation by the contract-breaker. In other words the breach of such a term operates in two ways. On the one hand it is a repudiation; on the other it entitles the innocent party to treat the contract as "rescinded". The use of this word in this way has been criticized on the ground that what is happening is not rescission.[258] What is important to point out at this juncture, however, is that the conduct which amounts to repudiation — with whatever consequences flow therefrom — must be of this serious nature, *vis-à-vis* the contents, obligations, and purposes of the contract. Repudiation is not lightly to be inferred from a party's conduct, particularly where prior to the time for performance a party has repeated its intention to carry out the contract.[259] The phrase preferred by Sachs L.J., for

---

254 The nineteenth century English development may be traced in the following cases: *Hochster v. De La Tour* (1853), 2 E. & B. 678, 118 E.R. 922; *Avery v. Bowden* (1856), 6 E. & B. 953, 119 E.R. 1119; *Frost v. Knight* (1872), L.R. 7 Ex. 111; *Freeth v. Burr* (1874), L.R. 9 C.P. 208; *Mersey Steel & Iron Co. v. Naylor, Benzon & Co.* (1882), 9 App. Cas. 434 (H.L.); *Johnstone v. Milling* (1886), 16 Q.B.D. 460 (C.A.). All these cases have been relied upon and used as authority by courts in Canada: McRae, *loc. cit.*, above, note 250, at p. 234.

255 Above, pp. 487-497. Hence, in many cases the issue was whether there was a "fundamental breach" entitling the innocent party to treat the contract as repudiated: see, *e.g.*, *Michael Ede Leasing Ltd. v. Kleysen Transport Ltd.* (1986), 42 Man. R. (2d) 52 (Man. C.A.); *Wells Const. Ltd. v. Thomas Fuller Const. Co. (1958) Ltd.* (1986), 22 C.L.R. 144 (Nfld. T.D.); *Applewood Lane West Ltd. v. Scott*, [1987] 3 W.W.R. 665 (Man. C.A.); *Sanko S.S. Co. v. Eacom Timber Sales Ltd.* (1986), 32 D.L.R. (4th) 269 (B.C.S.C.); *Montgrand v. Amok Ltd.* (1987), 57 Sask. R. 147 (Sask. Q.B.); *Group West Systems Ltd. v. Werner's Refrigeration Co.* (1988), 85 A.R. 82 (Alta. Q.B.); *Dover Corp. (Can.) Ltd. v. Victoria Chinatown Care Society* (1988), 26 B.C.L.R. (2d) 240 (B.C.C.A.); *Capital Placement of Can. (C.P.C.) Ltd. v. Wilson* (1988), 83 N.S.R. (2d) 170 (N.S.C.A.); *Ballantyne v. Grone* (1989), 22 R.F.L. (3d) 217 (B.C.C.A.); *Standard Precast Ltd. v. Dywidag Fab Con Products Ltd.* (1989), 56 D.L.R. (4th) 385 (B.C.C.A.); *Modular Windows of Can. Ltd. v. Niot Invt. Holdings Ltd.* (1988), 31 C.L.R. 43 (Ont. Master); *Brandon Petroleum Sales Ltd. v. Harasewich* (1989), 99 A.R. 81 (Alta. Master); *Imperial Brass Ltd. v. Jacob Electric Systems Ltd.* (1989), 72 O.R. (2d) 17 (Ont. H.C.).

256 Cited by Lang J. in *Odeco Drilling of Can. Ltd. v. Hickey* (1985), 54 Nfld. & P.E.I.R. 116 at 133 (Nfld. T.D.); and by MacIntosh J. in *Tobias v. Nolan* (1985), 71 N.S.R. (2d) 92 at 120 (N.S.T.D.).

257 Above, pp. 500-503.

258 *Buckland v. Farmer*, [1978] 3 All E.R. 929 (C.A.); *Johnson v. Agnew*, [1979] 1 All E.R. 883 (H.L.); compare above, p. 561. But Canadian judges still talk about rescission in such cases, see, *e.g.*, *Imperial Brass Ltd. v. Jacob Electric Systems Ltd.* (1989), 72 O.R. (2d) 17 at 25 (Ont. H.C.) *per* Lane J.

259 *Standard Precast Ltd. v. Dywidag Fab Con Products Ltd.* (1989), 56 D.L.R. (4th) 385 at 386 (B.C.C.A.).

example, in *Decro-Wall International S.A. v. Practitioners in Marketing Ltd.*,[260] a phrase which has a long and respectable ancestry, but has recently become revived in use, is a breach of contract which goes to "the root of that contract". In the same case,[261] Buckley L.J. expressed the test differently:

> . . . not every breach, even if its continuance is threatened throughout the contract or the remainder of its subsistence, will amount to a repudiation. To constitute repudiation, the threatened breach must be such as to deprive the injured party of a substantial part of the benefit to which he is entitled under the contract.

Both versions have been utilized in Canada, where the courts have accepted the doctrine without question.[262] It has been applied in cases of sale of goods,[263] sale of land,[264] performance of services,[265] leases of chattels,[266] promises to marry,[267]

---

260 [1971] 2 All E.R. 216 at 227 (C.A.); compare *Van Wezel v. Risdon*, [1953] 2 D.L.R. 382 (Alta. S.C.). Compare Campbell J. in *MacDonald v. Island Potato Packers Inc.* (1983), 45 Nfld. & P.E.I.R. 224 at 232 (P.E.I.S.C.): "repudiation . . . which goes directly to the substance of the contract" (affirmed on appeal (1986), 57 Nfld. & P.E.I.R. 219 (P.E.I.C.A.)). Compare *Van Dorne v. N. Amer. Van Lines (Can.) Ltd.* (1977), 79 D.L.R. (3d) 42 at 47 (B.C.S.C.) *per* Aikins J.; affirmed (1979), 95 D.L.R. (3d) 358 (B.C.C.A.). See also *Unified Systems Ltd. v. Clearwater Lobsters Ltd.* (1986), 58 Nfld. & P.E.I.R. 138 (Nfld. T.D.).

261 [1971] 2 All E.R. 216 at 232 (C.A.); quoted in *Odeco Drilling of Can. Ltd. v. Hickey* (1985), 54 Nfld. & P.E.I.R. 116 at 133 (Nfld. T.D.); compare Morrow J.A. in *Dresser Industries Inc. v. Raven Muds Ltd.* (1977), 1 A.R. 616 at 636 (Alta. C.A.): "depriving the innocent party of substantially the whole or a major benefit under the agreement." See, *e.g., Nyle Int. Corp. v. Depow* (1991), 113 N.B.R. (2d) 91 (N.B.Q.B.); affirmed (1991), 120 N.B.R. (2d) 176 (N.B.C.A.): failure to issue common stocks and neglect to deposit funds in the account of the joint venture into which the plaintiff had paid money. It was held that the defendant's breach entitled the plaintiff to repudiate the agreement and claim the return of his money. See also *Fed. Commerce & Navigation Ltd. v. Molena Alpha Inc.*, [1979] 1 All E.R. 307 at 316 (H.L.) *per* Lord Wilberforce. *Afovos Shipping Co. S.A. v. Pagnan* [1983] 1 All E.R. 449 at 455 (H.L.) *per* Lord Diplock. Note the connection with fundamental breach: *ibid.*

262 See, *e.g., Cromwell v. Morris*, [1917] 2 W.W.R. 374 (Alta. C.A.); *Amer. Nat. Red Cross v. Geddes Bros.* (1921), 61 S.C.R. 143 at 147 (S.C.C.) *per* Davis C.J.; *Can. Egg Products Ltd. v. Can. Doughnut Co.*, [1955] S.C.R. 398 (S.C.C.). Note the comments by McRae, *loc. cit.*, above, note 250, at pp. 262-263.

263 *Amer. Nat Red Cross v. Geddes Bros.*, above, note 262; *Can. Egg Products Ltd. v. Can. Doughnut Co.*, above, note 262; *Robert Bell Engine & Thresher Co. v. Farquharson*, [1918] 1 W.W.R. 924 (Sask. C.A.); *January Dev. Ltd. v. Millons* (1981), 15 Man. R. (2d) 18 (Man. Q.B.); compare *Dresser Industries Inc. v. Raven Mud Ltd.*, above, note 261; *Peabody Eng. Can. Ltd. v. Johnstone Shipping ltd.* (1979), 26 N.R. 74 (Fed. C.A.); leave to appeal to S.C.C. refused (1979), 30 N.R. 270n (S.C.C.); *Group West Systems Ltd. v. Werner's Refrigeration Co.* (1988), 85 A.R. 82 (Alta. Q.B.). Contrast *MacDonald v. Island Potato Packers Inc.*, above, note 260.

264 *Robinson v. Peters*, [1927] 3 D.L.R. 131 (Sask. C.A.); *Engleblom v. Blakeman*, [1930] 1 W.W.R. 565 (B.C. C.A.); *Kloepfer Wholesale Hardware & Automotive Co. v. Roy*, [1952] 2 S.C.R. 465 (S.C.C.); *Mid Park Const. Ltd. v. Cleland* (1992), 27 R.P.R. (2d) 68 (Ont. Gen. Div.); or a lease of premises: *Applewood Lane West Ltd. v. Scott*, [1987] 3 W.W.R. 665 (Man. C.A.).

265 *Philadelphia Eagles Inc. v. Armstrong* (1951), 3 W.W.R. (N.S.) 637 (Man. K.B.); compare *McCowan v. McKay* (1901), 13 Man. R. 590 (Man. C.A.); *Finelli v. Dee*, [1968] 1 O.R. 676 (Ont. C.A.); *Benoit v. Town of Tracadie* (1978), 21 N.B.R. (2d) 159 (N.B.Q.B.); *Community Invts. Ltd. v. Hardman* (1983), 59 N.S.R. (2d) 273 (N.S.T.D.); *Montgrand v. Amok Ltd.* (1987), 57 Sask. R. 147 (Sask. Q.B.); *Dover Corp. (Can.) Ltd. v. Victoria Chinatown Care Society* (1988), 26 B.C.L.R. (2d) 240 (B.C.C.A.).

and wherever the circumstances show that one party has seriously breached the contract, that is, done something which goes to the root of the contract,[268] or made it impossible for himself to perform the contract,[269] or revealed his intention of no longer being bound.[270] In short, there have been many explanations, in Canada as in England, of the kind of behaviour which amounts to repudiation—whether express or implicit.[271] Two particular varieties of contract have produced problems, however, in England and Canada. One is the contract of employment; the other is the lease.

While there may be repudiation of a contract of employment, by either employer or employee, the courts have been careful not to make any and every misconduct by either party into the sort of conduct which constitutes repudiation (just as, for example, where the contract is one of sale of goods, not every misdelivery will be repudiation, especially if the contract is one to be performed by instalments

---

266 *Car Leasing (Alta.) Ltd. v. Swinhoe* (1978), 15 A.R. 22 (Alta. Dist. Ct.).

267 *McBride and Hogaboam v. Johnson*, [1962] S.C.R. 202 (S.C.C.); compare *Frost v. Knight*, above, note 254.

268 *Van Wezel v. Risdon*, above note 260; *Robert Bell Engine & Thresher Co. v. Farquharson*, above, note 263; *Dresser Industries Inc. v. Raven Muds Ltd.*, above, note 261; *Sanko S.S. Co. v. Eacom Timber Sales Co.* (1986), 32 D.L.R. (4th) 269 (B.C.S.C.) (change of ship); *Kagan v. McLachlan* (1989), 60 Man. R. (2d) 248 (Man. Q.B.) (guarantors' refusal to pay debt guaranteed) (contrast *Northland Bank v. 294427 Alta. Ltd.* (1989), 102 A.R. 152 (Alta. Master).

269 *Brault v. R.* (1921), 20 Ex. C.R. 101 (Ex. Ct.); *R. v. Stewart* (1901), 32 S.C.R. 483 (S.C.C.).

270 *Philadelphia Eagles Inc. v. Armstrong*, above, note 265; *Finelli v. Dee*, above, note 265; *447927 Ont. Inc. v. Pizza Pizza Ltd.* (1987), 62 O.R. (2d) 114 (Ont. H.C.); affirmed (1990), 72 O.R. (2d) 704 (Ont. C.A.) (letter repudiating franchise agreement); *Wells Const. Ltd. v. Thomas Fuller Const. Co. (1958) Ltd.* (1986), 22 C.L.R. 144 (Nfld. T.D.) (refusal to make progress payment on construction job); *Modular Windows of Can. Ltd. v. Niot Invt. Holdings Ltd.* (1988), 31 C.L.R. 43 (Ont. Master) (refusal to correct improper installation of windows); *Murray v. Saskatchewan*, [1987] 3 W.W.R. 541 (Sask. C.A.) (refusal to plant alfalfa). Contrast *Cowie v. McDonald*, [1917] 2 W.W.R. 356 (Sask. C.A.); *Yanik v. Conibear and Nor. Tpt. Co. (No. 2)*, [1945] 1 W.W.R. 33 (Alta. C.A.), when the conduct did not reveal any intention to abandon the contract; see also *MacDonald v. Island Potato Packers Inc.*, above, note 260; *Ballantyne v. Grone* (1989), 22 R.F.L. (3d) 217 (B.C.C.A.). Including a new term, however, is such conduct: *Robinson v. Peters*, above, note 264. Compare also *Samuel v. Black Lake Asbestos & Chrome Co.* (1921), 62 S.C.R. 472 (S.C.C.); *Thompson & Alix Ltd. v. Smith*, [1933] S.C.R. 172 (S.C.C.). However, making a mistake about the meaning and effect of the contract is *not* repudiation: *Anderson v. Anchor Hotel Ltd.*, [1973] 2 W.W.R. 582 (B.C.S.C.); compare *Woodar Invts. Dev. Ltd. v. Wimpey Const. (U.K.) Ltd.*, above, note 251. But attempting to introduce new terms into a contract was held to amount to repudiation in *Wile v. Cook* (1986), 31 D.L.R. (4th) 205 (S.C.C.).

271 But it is a question of fact, ultimately, whether the conduct in question, *e.g.*, sending a letter purporting to repudiate, is repudiation of the contract: *Wellington Oil & Gas Co. v. Alta. Pipe Line Co.*, [1936] 2 D.L.R. 335 (S.C.C.) *per* Kerwin J. See, *e.g.*, *447927 Ont. Inc. v. Pizza Pizza Ltd.*, above, note 270, for an instance of a letter constituting repudiation; and compare *Mid Park Const. Ltd. v. Cleland* (1992), 27 R.P.R. (2d) 68 (Ont. Gen. Div.). As to what amounts to repudiation, see also the judgments of Roberston J.A. and Seaton J.A. in *Ainscough v. McGavin Toastmaster Ltd.* (1974), 45 D.L.R. (3d) 687 at 698-702, 709-713 (B.C.C.A.); affirmed (1975), 54 D.L.R. (3d) 1 (S.C.C.). Note the contrast between a repudiation which is accepted (below, p. 608) and the mutual cancellation of a contract: see *Campbell v. MacMillan Bloedel Ltd.*, [1978] 2 W.W.R. 686 (B.C.S.C.).

of delivery or payment).[272] Not every dismissal of the employee, even if it is wrongful, will be a repudiation; the circumstances may show that the contract is not to be treated as at an end.[273] So, too, not every alleged wrongful act of the employee will be a repudiation by him. In a Canadian case, *Ainscough v. McGavin Toastmaster Ltd.*,[274] there was a strike by employees in response to the employer's plans to reduce operations in a plant. The British Columbia Court of Appeal held that this was not a repudiation by each individual employee of his contract of employment. There was no intention by the employees of bringing their contracts to an end; they only wanted to force the employer to change his plans. This was upheld by the majority of the Supreme Court of Canada.

However, there is another aspect to the problem of repudiation in relation to contracts of employment. A purported repudiation of a contract will not effectively terminate the contract (and so relieve the innocent party of his obligations thereunder) unless it is "accepted".[275] Repudiation, though potentially capable of ending a contract, does not automatically terminate it. The suggestion has been made that the situation is different with respect to contracts of service or employment. That view was expressed in several English decisions prior to 1971.[276] It was based on the thought that the relations between master and servant were of a personal and confidential nature, involving close proximity and trust, such that it was not conceivable that if one party performed a repudiatory act the relationship could continue, at the will of the innocent party, as if nothing wrongful or improper had occurred.[277] In commercial contracts this was not unlikely. In contracts of service or employment, on the contrary, it was thought unreasonable, and therefore inappropriate. In *Campbell v. MacMillan Bloedel Ltd.*,[278] Anderson

---

272 Fridman, *Sale of Goods in Canada*, 3rd ed. (1986), pp. 235-238; compare *Thompson & Alix Ltd. v. Smith*, above, note 270; *Alexander Hamilton Institute v. McNally* (1919), 53 N.S.R. 303 (N.S.C.A.); *Yanik v. Conibear and Nor. Tpt. Co. (No. 2)*, above, note 270. It is a matter of intention.

273 *Hill v. C.A. Parsons & Co.*, [1971] 3 All E.R. 1345 (C.A.). Contrast *Denmark Productions Ltd. v. Boscobel Productions Ltd.*, [1969] 1 Q.B. 699 (C.A.). See the *dicta* of Salmon L.J. in *Decro-Wall Int. S.A. v. Practitioners in Marketing Ltd.*, [1971] 2 All E.R. 216 at 223 (C.A.). See also the discussion, and distinction, of *Hill v. Parsons* by Seaton J.A. in *Philp v. Expo 86 Corp.* (1987), 45 D.L.R. (4th) 449 at 455-456 (B.C.C.A.). There it was held that when such a contract came to an end by repudiation the employee could sue for damages for wrongful dismissal, and not claim outstanding wages or salary under the contract.

274 Above, note 271; with which compare *Morgan v. Fry*, [1968] 1 Q.B. 521; reversed in part [1968] 2 Q.B. 710 (C.A.).

275 Above, p. 600; below, pp. 608-612, 615-618.

276 *Vine v. Nat. Dock Labour Bd.*, [1956] 1 Q.B. 658 (C.A.); varied [1957] A.C. 488 (H.L.); *Francis v. Municipal Councillors of Kuala Lumpur*, [1962] 3 All E.R. 633 (P.C.); *Denmark Productions Ltd. v. Boscobel Productions Ltd.*, [1969] 1 Q.B. 699 (C.A.). See also *Miles v. Wakefield District Council*, [1987] A.C. 539 (H.L.), which is criticized as being inconsistent with the general law of contract as stated in *The "Simma"*, [1988] 3 W.L.R. 200: Mead, "Restitution Within Contract?" (1991), 11 J. Leg. St. 172 at pp. 174-175.

277 Compare *McWhirter v. Univ. of Alta. Governors (No. 2)* (1977), 80 D.L.R. 609 (Alta. Q.B.); reversed on other grounds (1979), 18 A.R. 145 (Alta. C.A.).

278 [1978] 2 W.W.R. 686 (B.C.S.C.). Nor did the demotion of the employee amount to repudiation in *Longman v. Fed. Business Dev. Bank* (1982), 131 D.L.R. (3d) 533 (B.C.S.C.). Compare *Poole v. Tomenson Saunders Whitehead Ltd.* (1987), 43 D.L.R. (4th) 56 (B.C.C.A.); additional reasons

J. of the Supreme Court of British Columbia took the same view. Employment contracts were not like commercial contracts. However, in that case, the learned judge held that there was no repudiation entitling the employee to sue for wrongful dismissal in breach of contract. The original contract had been replaced by a new one, when the demoted employee agreed to take on the junior appointment and worked in it for several months. In England, however, in 1971, the tide of opinion which had originally run in the direction set by Jenkins L.J. in 1956,[279] turned.[280] In various *dicta* English judges began to suggest that there might be circumstances in which wrongful dismissal by an employer, or some equivalent repudiatory conduct by the employee, did not automatically terminate the contract.[281]

These hints finally resulted in a decision by Megarry V.-C., in *Thomas Marshall (Exports) Ltd. v. Guinle*,[282] to the effect that an employee's wrongful act did not terminate the contract where the employer never accepted the repudiation by the employee. In that case the employers were endeavouring to maintain that an employee's covenant not to disclose confidential information received while in their employ survived the employee's purported resignation from the employment, which resignation the employers never accepted. The employee argued that his resignation, without more, sufficed to bring the contract, including the covenant, to an end. The employee was unsuccessful. The employee was still bound by the covenant, and the employers were able to obtain the injunction they sought to restrain the employee from acting in a manner inconsistent with the covenant. In the subsequent case of *Gunton v. London Borough of Richmond Upon Thames*,[283] the Court of Appeal in England, by a majority, endorsed this view. When a repudiatory act occurs, the status or relationship of master and servant determines, but other incidents of that relationship may survive, if the innocent party does not accept the repudiation.[284] Hence, in that case, the wrongful dismissal of the employee by the council did not determine the employee's right under the contract not to be dismissed on disciplinary grounds until prescribed disciplinary procedures had been carried out, nor his right to be compensated beyond the one month's wages in lieu of notice, for breach of the council's duty to observe the proper procedures. Shaw L.J. dissented on the ground that, in accordance with the older view, the dismissal terminated every aspect of the relationship. Since it was not possible

---

at [1988] 4 W.W.R. 300 (B.C.C.A.), failure of employer to pay employee full bonus originally agreed on corporate reorganization to which the employee objected was not constructive dismissal, *i.e.*, fundamental breach or repudiation of the contract of employment on the part of the employer. Contrast *Lafferty v. Ont. Chiropractic Assn.* (1987), 44 D.L.R. (4th) 167 (Ont. H.C.); affirmed (1989), 63 D.L.R. (4th) 448 (Ont. C.A.).

279 *Vine v. Nat. Dock Labour Bd.*, [1956] 1 Q.B. 658 at 674 (C.A.); varied [1957] A.C. 488 (H.L.).

280 *Gunton v. London Borough of Richmond Upon Thames*, [1980] 3 All E.R. 577 at 586 (C.A.) *per* Buckley L.J.

281 *Decro-Wall Int. S.A. v. Practitioners in Marketing Ltd.*, [1971] 2 All E.R. 216 at 223 (C.A.) *per* Salmon L.J., and at 228-229 *per* Sachs L.J.; *Hill v. C.A. Parsons Ltd.*, [1972] Ch. 305 at 319 (C.A.) *per* Sachs L.J.; *Sanders v. Ernest A. Neale Ltd.*, [1974] 3 All E.R. 327 at 333 *per* Donaldson J.

282 [1979] Ch. 227 especially at 239 and 243.

283 [1980] 3 All E.R. 577 (C.A.).

284 *Ibid.*, at 594 *per* Brightman L.J.

to reinstate the employee in his service, because specific performance of a contract of service or employment will not be ordered by the courts,[285] and the only remedy to the employee was damages, it was illogical to say that a contract of service survived repudiation by one side or other. "To preserve the bare contractual relationship," he said,[286] "is an empty formality." Obviously, in view of this dissent, it cannot be said that the problem has been solved definitively, until the House of Lords has had an opportunity to consider the matter. In any event, there is no Canadian decision in which this problem has been settled. Until such time as that occurs, it would appear that the majority view of the English Court of Appeal in the *Gunton* case, apart from being the most authoritative pronouncement to date, is both sound in its reasoning and sensible in its practical effects. Despite the fact that specific performance will not be decreed of contracts of employment (save in exceptional circumstances[287]), there is no logical or practical reason for making any distinction between such contracts and others so far as concerns the doctrine of repudiation. The modern trend, as will be seen in relation to leases in respect of both repudiation and the application of the doctrine of frustration, is to assimilate all types of contracts. Some writers have attempted to argue that different classes of contracts should be treated differently.[288] The present attitude of the common law seems to be opposed to this. Hence, it is more desirable and consistent to apply the normal principles of repudiation to contracts of employment.

Where leases are concerned, it was suggested by Lord Denning[289] prior to recent developments in Canada and England with respect to frustration of leases,[290] that, in the same way as the doctrine of frustration did not apply to a lease, neither did the doctrine of repudiation or anticipatory breach. The converse was held to be the case in *Glenmore Garden Apartments Ltd. v. Todd*,[291] where the lessee purported to rescind the three-year lease, on the ground that the lessor had not completed construction of the building in time for the lessee to take possession on the agreed date. It was held that the lessor's conduct was a sufficient repudiation to entitle the lessee to cancel or rescind the contract. Moreover the language of Laskin J., in the Supreme Court of Canada in *Highway Properties Ltd. v. Kelly, Douglas & Co.*,[292] suggested, long before recent decisions applied the doctrine of

---

285 See *McWhirter v. Univ. of Alta. Governors (No. 2)*, above, note 277 compare below, p. 791.

286 Above, note 283, at 582.

287 Compare the issuance of an injunction in *Hill v. C.A. Parsons Ltd.*, above note 281. For a special case of reinstatement, see *Vine v. National Dock Labour Bd.*, above, note 276; *Francis v. Municipal Councillors of Kuala Lumpur*, above, note 276. See the discussion of the general rule, and the exceptions based on "special circumstances", as well as the English cases referred to, in *Philp v. Expo 86 Corp.* (1987), 45 D.L.R. (4th) 449 especially at 459-461 (B.C.C.A.) *per* Lambert J.A.

288 See Macneil, *The New Social Contract* (1980); Mcneil, "Contracts: Adjustments of Long-Term Economic Relations" (1978), 72 N.W.U.L.R. 856; Macneil, "The Many Futures of Contract" (1974), 67 S. Cal. L.R. 691; Beatty, "Labour is not a Commodity", in Reiter & Swan, *Studies in Contract Law* (1980), p. 313; Swinton, "Contract Law and the Employment Relationship", *ibid.*, p. 357.

289 *Total Oil of G.B. Ltd. v. Thompson Garages (Biggin Hill) Ltd.*, [1972] 1 Q.B. 318 at 324 (C.A.).

290 Below, pp. 658-661.

291 (1972), 29 D.L.R. (3d) 242 (Alta. S.C.).

292 (1971), 17 D.L.R. (3d) 710 at 717 (S.C.C.), applied in *Applewood Lane West Ltd. v. Scott*, [1987] 3 W.W.R. 665 (Man. C.A.).

frustration to leases,[293] that even if a contract is a lease of land, both repudiation and frustration may apply in appropriate circumstances. What the learned judge was saying, in effect, was that archaic notions of estates in land, which in the past prevented the application of normal contractual principles to such contracts, should not now be invoked, in the light of changes in economic, social, and even legal concepts relating to land, to substantiate the earlier attitudes of the courts. A lease should be treated as any other contract, and the ordinary, general principles relating to discharge by frustration or repudiation should be made applicable as and when appropriate. Indeed, in *Applewood Lane West Ltd. v. Scott*,[294] the Manitoba Court of Appeal did so. Tenants made considerable noise when holiday parties were held in the leased premises. This was in violation of the terms of the lease. Their conduct was part of a deliberate scheme to get the landlord to evict them. It was held that this behaviour amounted to a constructive abandonment of the premises, which was a fundamental breach, in other words repudiation of the lease. Hence the landlord was able to sue for lost rent.

(iii) *Must be wrongful*

The kind of repudiation which can give rise to discharge on the basis of anticipatory breach must be unjustified.[295] In other words, if the party repudiating is entitled to do so, by reason of the other party's conduct, the latter cannot rely on the former's repudiatory act so as to invoke the remedies which normally result from a breach of repudiation.[296]

Thus, the employer who summarily dismisses an employee on the ground of the employee's misconduct must justify this by proving that the misconduct of the employee was itself a repudiation of the fundamental obligations of the contract of service. Failure to do so results in the employer being liable for wrongful dismissal,

---

293 Below, pp. 660-661.

294 [1987] 3 W.W.R. 665 (Man. C.A.).

295 For the problem that arises when the repudiating party does not know that the *other* party will break his contract at the date of performance if no repudiation occurs, see Dawson, "Waiver of Conditions Precedent on a Repudiation" (1980), 96 L.Q.R. 239; compare below, p. 617.

296 See *G. Coleman Yacht Sales Ltd. v. C. & C. Yachts Ltd.* (1983), 45 B.C.L.R. 66 (B.C.S.C.); *Brandon Petroleum Sales Ltd. v. Harasewich* (1989), 99 A.R. 81 (Alta. Master); *DSI Management Inc. v. A.T.S. Electro-Lube Ltd.* (1989), 24 C.P.R. (3d) 193 (B.C.S.C.). But the repudiation, *e.g.*, dismissal of an employee, can be justified *ex post facto*, if the repudiating party discovers facts which would have entitled him to repudiate the contract even though he did not know the facts at the time and indeed repudiated for the wrong reason, or no reason at all, *i.e.*, was unjustified at the time of repudiation: *Universal Cargo Carriers Corp. v. Citati*, [1957] 2 Q.B. 401 at 453 *per* Devlin J.; affirmed [1957] 3 All E.R. 234 (C.A.) (discussed by Macdonald J. in *Sanko S.S. Co. v. Eacom Timber Sales Co.* (1986), 32 D.L.R. (4th) 269 at 275-278 (B.C.S.C.)); *Denmark Productions Ltd. v. Boscobel Productions Ltd.*, above, note 276; *Komorowski v. Van Weel* (1993), 12 O.R. (3d) 444 at 457 (Ont. Gen. Div.). Hence, the vendor of land was not guilty of repudiation when he refused to close the deal; the contract was void for uncertainty since the parties disputed the interpretation of an essential term: *259596 Alta. Ltd. v. Richards: Richards v. 259596 Alta. Ltd.* (1983), 45 A.R. 251 (Alta. Q.B.).

The sentence in the text was quoted by Geatros J. in *Paragon Farms Ltd. v. H.D. Linn Dev. Services Inc.*, [1988] 6 W.W.R. 417 at 425 (Sask. Q.B.).

that is, breach of contract, and may entitle the employee, in some situations, to declare the contract of employment terminated by reason of the purported dismissal.[297] In *Estate-Gard Services of Canada Ltd. v. Loewen Management Corp.*,[298] for example, the defendant employer was guilty of wrongful repudiation of the contract in dismissing the plaintiff on the basis of the plaintiff's failure to attend meetings and lack of profitability. So, too, a failure to accept or pay for goods will be a repudiation of the contract of sale, unless the refusal to accept or pay was founded upon, for example, some significant breach by the seller, such as delivery of the wrong goods, or the wrong quantity of goods, or goods which were merchantable or fit for use. Hence in *Unified Systems Ltd. v. Clearwater Lobsters Ltd.*[299] the defendants wrongfully repudiated the contract by destroying or erasing software delivered by the plaintiff under the contract; they were not justified by the plaintiff's breaches of the contract. The misconduct of one party may disqualify him from relying on the other party's failure to perform as a grounds for treating the contract as terminated by repudiation. In such instances the misconduct of the one party was the true cause of the other party's inability to fulfil his obligations, or else, the misconduct of the one party entitled the other to refuse to perform, or to continue to perform those obligations.[300]

If there is a defence, the party repudiating does not have to give a reason for repudiation.[301] His act will not be wrongful.

(iv) *Acceptance of repudiation*[302]

"An unaccepted repudiation," said Asquith L.J. in one English case,[303] "is a

---

297 Compare the situation in *Denmark Productions Ltd. v. Boscobel Productions Ltd.*, above, note 276, at 724 *per* Salmon L.J. See, *e.g.*, *Woods v. Miramichi Hospital* (1965), 67 D.L.R. (2d) 757 (N.B. C.A.).

298 (1989), 38 B.C.L.R. (2d) 362 (B.C.C.A.).

299 (1986), 58 Nfld. & P.E.I.R. 138 (Nfld. T.D.).

300 See *e.g.*, *North v. Victoria Baseball & Athletic Co.*, [1949] 1 W.W.R. 1033 (B.C.S.C.) (misbehaviour at baseball games justified cancellation of plaintiff's season ticket); *Schrider v. Long Bay Lbr. Co.* (1961), 36 W.W.R. 319 (B.C.C.A.) (non-delivery of material); *Meeker v. Nicola Vally Lbr. Co.* (1917), 55 S.C.R. 494 (S.C.C.); leave to appeal to the Privy Council refused (1918), 55 S.C.R. vii (failure of vendor to obtain title was fault of purchaser); *Kohler v. Thorold Natural Gas Co.* (1916), 52 S.C.R. 514 (S.C.C.); leave to appeal to the Privy Council refused (1916), 52 S.C.R. vii (vendor's default was caused by purchaser's wrongful act). Contrast *Alexander Hamilton Institute v. McNally* (1919), 49 D.L.R. 606 (N.S.C.A.).

In *Paragon Farms Ltd. v. H.D. Linn Dev. Services Inc.*, [1988] 6 W.W.R. 417 (Sask. Q.B.), the plaintiff's repudiation was justified when the defendant could not perform its obligations under the contract because the area to which the contract related was designated an "employment centre" by the city. This appears to be more like an instance of frustration than of repudiation. The two modes of termination of a contract must be distinguished. See below, Chapter 16.

301 *259596 Alta. Ltd. v. Richards; Richards v. 259596 Alta. Ltd.* (1983), 45 A.R. 251 at 256 (Alta. Q.B.) *per* Dea J.

302 This section was referred to by Stratton J. in *Benoit v. Town of Tracadie* (1978), 21 N.B.R. (2d) 159 at 167 (N.B.Q.B.). The opening sentences of this paragraph, as far as "does accept the repudiation" were quoted by the court in *B. Mathews Devs. Ltd. v. Humford Devs. Ltd.* (1985), 20 C.L.R. 134 at 140 (B.C. Co. Ct.).

303 *Howard v. Pickford Tool Co.*, [1951] 1 K.B. 417 at 421 (C.A.).

thing writ in water and of no value to anybody; it confers no legal rights of any sort or kind." Although this graphic expression has been said to be limited by the facts of the case in which it occurred,[304] the phrase does have some merit, and does put succinctly an important aspect of the law relating to discharge by repudiation or anticipatory breach. Such repudiation will not effectively terminate the contract unless the innocent party does accept the repudiation, and is prepared to treat the contract as ended. The innocent party, in effect, has an election whether or not to treat the contract as continuing or as ended, once the party has committed an act which, in accordance with what has been said above, can be regarded as repudiating the contract.[305] To quote the language of Beck J. in *Cromwell v. Morris*[306]

> [a] mistaken attempt by one of the parties to an agreement to rescind it, does not, *ipso facto*, operate to rescind it; there is no effective rescission unless the other party recognizes the rescission. . . . The promise may treat a renunication before the time of performance as a breach, but where the promisee has this option, he is bound to exercise it. He cannot treat the renunciation as a breach if he tries to hold the promisor to his contract.

What this means in detail will be considered a little later. For the moment, however, it is important to point out that, from the time that this kind of termination was recogized by the law, it was accepted that there could be no such thing as a *unilateral* repudiation. Just as the making of a contract requires the joint participation of both parties, an offeror and an acceptor, so the discharge of a contract, even where the discharge is by repudiation, renunciation, or refusal to perform, in advance of the time for performance, also requires the conformity and acquiescence of *both* parties.[307]

Because of this, in a number of cases, the issue has arisen whether the innocent party has accepted the other party's anticipatory breach or repudiation, and if so, at what point of time this took place.[308] For example, in *American National Red Cross v. Geddes Brothers*[309] the plaintiff agreed to sell goods to the defendant. Before

---

304 *White & Carter (Councils) Ltd. v. McGregor*, [1962] A.C. 413 at 438 (H.L.) *per* Lord Keith.
305 *G. & R. Const. v. Southern Slope Holdings Ltd.* (1968), 63 W.W.R. 65 at 78 (B.C.S.C.); *Heyman v. Darwins Ltd.* [1942] A.C. 356 (H.L.); *Can. Egg Products Ltd. v. Can. Doughnut Co.*, [1955] S.C.R. 398 at 412-413 (S.C.C.) *per* Locke J. See *Capital Placement of Can. (C.P.C.) Ltd. v. Wilson* (1988), 83 N.S.R. (2d) 170 (N.S.C.A.), where the defendant, a franchisee, continued to operate under the contract after breaches by the franchisor: therefore he elected to affirm the contract, not treat it as repudiated. Compare *Fletton Ltd. v. Peat Marwick Ltd.* (1988), 50 D.L.R. (4th) 729 (B.C.C.A.). Note however the possibility that in the exercise of its general equitable jurisdiction a court may refuse to allow the innocent party to elect to continue the contract: *Clea Shipping Corp. v. Bulk Oil Int. Ltd.*, [1984] 1 All E.R. 129; and see below, p. 620.
306 [1917] 2 W.W.R. 374 at 377 (Alta. C.A.).
307 *Denmark Produtions Ltd. v. Boscobel Productions Ltd.*, [1969] 1 Q.B. 699 (C.A.).
308 *Samuel v. Black Lake Asbestos & Chrome Co.* (1921), 62 S.C.R. 472 (S.C.C.). The Alberta Court of Appeal was divided on this issue in *Dresser Industries Ltd. v. Raven Muds Ltd.* (1977), 1 A.R. 616 (Alta. C.A.).
309 (1921), 61 S.C.R. 143 (S.C.C.). Note the importance of the subsequent conduct of the original buyer, the defendant in the action, according to Anglin J: *ibid.*, at 163-164, citing and relying on *Freeth v. Burr* (1874), L.R. 9 C.P. 208; *Mersey Steel & Iron Co. v. Naylor, Benzon & Co.* (1884), 9 App. Cas. 434 (H.L.); *Gen. Bill Posting Co. v. Atkinson*, [1909] A.C. 118 (H.L.).

the due date for delivery, the plaintiff wrote to say that he would be unable to carry out the contract. The defendant made an entry in his books that the contract was cancelled. When the plaintiff later purported to deliver, and tried to hold the defendant liable for non-acceptance of the goods, the question arose whether the plaintiff's repudiation of the contract, since that was what the letter amounted to when it was received by the defendant, had been accepted by the defendant, even though the latter had not given the plaintiff notice of acceptance of the plaintiff's abandonment of the contract. The subsequent conduct of the plaintiff, in attempting to explain his failure to deliver the goods at the contractually correct time, showed that the plaintiff had treated the original contract as at an end and believed that the defendant had agreed to accept that situation. Hence, the defendant was not liable. The contract was ended, and so had the defendant's obligations with respect to the goods. This may have been repudiation but it was close to abandonment of the contract agreement.[310]

Acceptance of a repudiation of a contract should not be confused with an agreement to terminate a contract.[311] So where a letter was sent to the repudiating party, after repudiation, in which the repudiation was accepted, the contract was rescinded by mutual consent.[312] As it was put by the Supreme Court of Canada in another case,[313] in such a situation the parties may be said to have "walked away from" the contract, and abandoned it. In *Davidson v. Sharpe*[314] the Supreme Court held that the conduct of a party in suing on a contract in British Columbia, and obtaining cancellation of the agreement, was an election of this kind, an acceptance of the repudiation by the other party, with the result that the innocent party could not later bring *another* action on the contract, this time in Saskatchewan. This was carried a little further in *Canada Egg Products Ltd. v. Canadian Doughnut Co.*[315] Here it was held that the issuance of a writ by the buyers of goods from the sellers (who had notified the former in advance of the delivery date that they were not going to deliver) was notice of the buyer's acceptance of the sellers' repudiation of the contract to sell egg yolks and albumen.

On the other hand, in *McBride and Hogaboam v. Johnson*,[316] it was alleged by the estate of the deceased that he had repudiated his promise to marry the

---

310 Compare *Dawson v. Helicopter Exploration Co.*, [1955] 5 D.L.R. 404 (S.C.C.); McRae, 56 Can. Bar Rev. 233.

311 *Gaklis v. Wells* (1979), 37 N.S.R. (2d) 451 at 464 (N.S.C.A.) *per* Jones J.A. Hence possibly, in *Benoit v. Town of Tracadie*, above, note 302, the original contract was abandoned or unilaterally rescinded, rather than ended by repudiation; compare McRae, 56 Can. Bar Rev. 233 at pp. 253-256. The difference between the two arises where the innocent party wishes to sue for damages: McRae, *op. cit.*, at p. 255.

312 *Wellington Oil & Gas Co. v. Alta. Pipe Line Co.*, [1936] 2 D.L.R. 335 (S.C.C.). Contrast *447927 Ont. Inc. v. Pizza Pizza Ltd.* (1987), 62 O.R. (2d) 114 (Ont. H.C.); affirmed (1990), 72 O.R. (2d) 704 (Ont. C.A.), where the letter in reply to the plaintiff's letter was acceptance of the former's repudiation, not rescission by mutual consent.

313 *Chapman v. Ginter*, [1968] S.C.R. 560 (S.C.C.).

314 (1920), 60 S.C.R. 72 (S.C.C.).

315 (1954), 11 W.W.R. 193 especially at 202-206 (Sask. C.A.) *per* Martin C.J.S.; affirmed [1955] S.C.R. 398 (S.C.C.).

316 [1962] S.C.R. 202 (S.C.C.); compare above, p. 524.

plaintiff before he was killed in an automobile accident. It was held that the plaintiff had never accepted such purported repudiation. Consequently the contract remained in existence until the time of his death.[317] Similarly in *Ainscough v. McGavin Toastmaster Ltd.*,[318] it was held by the British Columbia Court of Appeal (for reasons which were not in issue in the Supreme Court) that even if there had been a repudiation the conduct of the employees did not amount to an acceptance by them of the employer's repudiation of their contracts of employment. Hence, the employees were still entitled to severance pay under the original terms of those contracts.

Acceptance of repudiation can take the form of conduct which reveals that the innocent party does not intend to continue with the contract.[319] For example, in *Benoit v. Town of Tracadie*,[320] the plaintiff provided ambulance services to the town. He sent a letter to the effect that if a new price agreement were not reached within 30 days he would terminate the contract. Before the 30 days expired the town made him an offer, which he refused. The town then arranged for a different ambulance service. The letter from the plaintiff was held to be notice of termination, that is, repudiation, which the town had accepted by its conduct. So, too, in *Car Leasing (Alberta) Ltd. v. Swinhoe*,[321] a car lessee's continued failure to pay the monthly rental when it became due was repudiation of the lease agreement, which the lessor accepted by repossessing the rented vehicle. Such conduct, however, is quite clear and unequivocal. Presumably, so was the action of the town in the *Benoit* case in hiring a new ambulance service. In such instances it may be unnecessary to communicate the acceptance to the repudiating party.

However in *Van Dorne v. North American Van Lines (Canada) Ltd.*,[322] it appears to have been suggested that notification of acceptance of repudiation may sometimes be required.[323] A bailor failed to pay the agreed storage for storing goods with the bailee. When the bailee sought to argue that this failure was *per se* a repudiation of the contract (thereby relieving the bailee of his obligations with respect to the safety of the goods), it was held that this was not so unless the bailee notified the bailor whether or not he intended to terminate as a result of the alleged repudiation. His failure to do so meant that the contract was still effective and binding, and the bailee was liable for the destruction of the goods by fire. How is this case to be reconciled with the facts and decisions in *American National Red Cross v. Geddes Brothers?*[324] If communciation of either acceptance of a

---

317 Although it was affected by the doctrine of frustration.

318 [1974] 3 W.W.R. 114 (B.C.C.A.); affirmed [1975] 5 W.W.R. 444 (S.C.C.); above, p. 604.

319 If the conduct leads to no other conclusion than that the repudiation has been accepted: *Van Wezel v. Risdon* (1952), 7 W.W.R. (N.S.) 646 (Alta. S.C.); *Dresser Indust. Inc. v. Raven Muds Ltd.* (1977), 1 A.R. 616 at 639 (Alta. C.A.) *per* Morrow J.A.

320 Above, note 302.

321 (1979), 15 A.R. 22 (Alta. Dist. Ct.).

322 (1978), 79 D.L.R. (3d) 42 (B.C.S.C.); affirmed (1979), 95 D.L.R. (3d) 358 (B.C.C.A.).

323 Compare *Can. Egg Products Ltd. v. Can. Doughnut Co.*, [1955] S.C.R. 398 at 413 (S.C.C.) *per* Locke J.; *Kamlee Const. Ltd. v. Oakville* (1960), 26 D.L.R. (2d) 166 (S.C.C.); *Ginter v. Chapman* (1967), 60 W.W.R. 385 (B.C.C.A.); McRae, *loc. cit.*, above, note 311 at pp. 244-249.

324 Above, note 309.

repudiation or the mutual agreement to terminate the contract is an essential requirement for either: (a) the election by the innocent party to end his obligations under the contract and maintain his right to sue for damages; or (b) an agreement to the ending of the contract so far as both parties' obligations, and the other party's liability to pay damages are concerned, how could the defendant's entry in his books, without some message to the plaintiff, effectively end their contract, when in the *Van Dorne* case the bailee's failure to do anything overt, whatever he may have thought, did not suffice? The distinction might be one that turns on the facts, for example, in the *Geddes Brothers* case all that needed to be done was an entry in the books (which was at least an overt act of some kind), whereas in the *Van Dorne* case the bailee should have done something, namely, sent back the goods, or perhaps put them elsewhere, to indicate his intention to regard the bailment as at an end.

What these an other cases illustrate is that it is sometimes a very difficult task to determine: (a) whether a purported repudiation has been accepted; or (b) whether the parties have agreed to the mutual termination of their respective obligations. It has been argued[325] that terms such as "rescission" and "acceptance" should be abandoned, since they seem to involve some kind of communication, whereas there is no logical necessity for a requirement that an election to terminate must be communicated to the repudiator. Certainly "rescission" is a confusing term to employ in this context (as it is elsewhere except where it is appropriate[326]). But the notion of "acceptance" of a repudiation is neither illogical nor unwarranted. It should be made clear, however, whether, and under what circumstances the innocent party, who elects to treat the repudiation as a breach discharging him from his obligations, is bound to do something, by way of explicit, overt, unequivocal conduct, to inform the repudiator that his choice has been made.

(b) Consequences

(i) *Preliminary points*

An accepted repudiation is of legal effect; a repudiation that is not accepted is not effective in law to determine the contract.[327] The crucial question is whether the innocent party has exercised his option or election in favour of treating the contract as at an end.[328] This choice, which will be binding once it is made,[329] must be made within a reasonable time, that is, after the innocent party has

---

325 McRae, *loc. cit.*, above, note 311, at pp. 255-256; compare below, p. 807, as to "rescission". See also Dawson, "Metaphors and Anticipatory Breach of Contract" (1981), 40 C.L.J. 83 at 103.

326 Compare above, p. 561.

327 But see the discussion of contracts of employment above, pp. 603-607.

328 He may do so even if the repudiation is based upon the repudiator's misunderstanding or misreading of the contract: *Clausen v. Can. Timber & Lands Ltd.*, [1923] 3 W.W.R. 1072 (P.C.). But an act done under an erroneous understanding of the contract may not be repudiation: *Woodar Invts. Dev. Ltd. v. Wimpey Const. (U.K.) Ltd.*, [1980] 1 All E.R. 571 (H.L.).

329 Election to accept repudiation is final; the innocent party cannot afterwards reaffirm the contract: *Osmack v. Stan Reynolds Auto Sales Ltd.*, [1974] 1 W.W.R. 408 (Alta. C.A.); affirmed [1976] 2 W.W.R. 576 (S.C.C.). Compare *Komorowski v. Van Weel* (1993), 12 O.R. (3d) 444 at 460 (Ont. Gen Div.).

discovered the situation giving rise to the choice of action which is open to him. If he delays at sufficient length to prejudice the other party or third parties by his eventual course of action, or so long that his conduct can be regarded as acceptance of the repudiation, the innocent party, in effect, will lose his right of election.[330] As long as he acts with reasonable dispatch, the innocent party has a right of choice. The position was summed up very succinctly by Lord Atkinson in the following passage:

> ...where a contract is to be performed on a future day or is dependent on a contingency and one of the parties to the contract repudiates it and shows by word or act that he does not intend to perform it, the other party is entitled to sue him for breach of the contract without waiting for the arrival of the time fixed for performance, or the happening of the contingency on which the contract is dependent, and is himself absolved from the fruther performance of his part of the contract. If he elects to do this the contract is completely at an end, and the party in default is not entitled to an opportunity to change his mind. But the repudiation of a contract by one of the parties to it does not of itself discharge the contract. It only gives to the other party the option of either treating the contract as at an end, or of waiting until the stipulated time has arrived or the contingency upon which the performance of the contract was dependent has happened.[331]

Thus, the innocent party may elect whether to have the contract "ended", which frees him from further performance, and sue, or to let it continue.[332] If the latter, the contract will continue to exist for *both parties*. In other words, it remains in existence for the benefit of the repudiator as well as the innocent party.[333] This usually means that if, in the meanwhile, between repudiation and time for performance, something happens which would give the repudiator a defence to an action for breach, the repudiator is protected, and the innocent party cannot afterwards say that he could have accepted the repudiation, and *would have done so*, therefore the contract can be treated as broken and the repudiator should be deprived of this subsequent defence.[334] For example, in *Fletton Ltd. v. Peat Marwick*

---

330 *Allen v. Robles*, [1969] 3 All E.R. 154 (C.A.). *Dresser Indust. Inc. v. Raven Muds Ltd.* (1977), 1 A.R. 616 at 637 (Alta. C.A.) *per* Morrow J.A. citing *Cromwell v. Morris*, [1917] 2 W.W.R. 374 (Alta. C.A.).

331 *Martin v. Stout*, [1925] A.C. 359 at 364 (P.C.) citing *Withers v. Reynolds* (1831), 2 B. & Ad. 882; *Hochster v. De La Tour* (1853), 2 E. & B. 678; *Mersey Steel & Iron Co. v. Naylor, Benzon & Co.*, (1882), 9 App. Cas. 434 (H.L.).

332 *Shibamoto & Co. v. Western Fish Producers Inc. (Trustee of)* (1991), 43 F.T.R. 1 at 24 (Fed. T.D.) *per* Rouleau J.; affirmed (1992), 145 N.R. 91 (Fed. C.A.). Compare *Norfolk v. Aikens* (1990), 64 D.L.R. (4th) 1 at 15 (B.C.C.A.). For example, see *Group West Systems Ltd. v. Werner's Refrigeration Co.* (1988), 85 A.R. 82 (Alta. Q.B.) (defendant accepted repudiation, therefore not liable for breach); *Derrickson v. Madsen Marina Ltd.* (1987), 15 B.C.L.R. (2d) 125 (B.C.C.A.) (acceptance of repudiation, therefore party released from future obligations); *Can. Int. Marine Underwriters Ltd. v. Symons General Ins. Co.*, [1986] I.L.R. 1-2042 (Ont. H.C.); varied (March 9, 1988), Doc. No. CA 222/86 (Ont. H.C.), affirmation of contract.

333 *Cromwell v. Morris*, [1917] 2 W.W.R. 374 at 377 (Alta. C.A.) *per* Beck J. citing *Frost v. Knight* (1872), L.R. 7 Ex. 111. Compare also *Johnstone v. Milling* (1886), 16 Q.B.D. 460 (C.A.).

334 *Avery v. Bowden* (1856), 6 E. & B. 953 (subsequent impossiblity, which occurred after repudiation and non-acceptance of such repudiation).

Ltd.,[335] the defendant agreed to sell goods to the plaintiff on condition that the plaintiff secure product liability insurance satisfactory to the defendant or a satisfactory legal opinion that the defendant would not be liable for defects. The defendant repudiated the contract in advance of the date for performance. Although the plaintiff issued a writ for a breach of contract, the plaintiff continued efforts to obtain insurance or a legal opinion, but failed to do so. The British Columbia Court of Appeal, affirming the trial judge, held that the plaintiff's action could not succeed. The plaintiff had elected not to accept the repudiation. Therefore the contract was alive for both parties. Since the plaintiff had not fulfilled the condition precedent to performance by the defendant, the latter was not in breach. But this advantage to the repudiator may not always occur,[336] nor, indeed, will acceptance of repudiation always operate to the detriment of the repudiator.[337] Moreover, where the co-operation of the repudiating party is necessary if the contract is to be continued in operation the innocent party cannot elect: he must accept the repudiation and sue.[338]

Before dealing fully with his problem, other general points must be clarified. First though the conduct of the innocent party who elects to accept repudiation is sometimes referred to as "rescinding" or "rescission of" the contract, this is not accurate.[339] Rescission, a remedy available in instances of fraudulent (and sometimes innocent) misrepresentation, involves treating the contract as if it had never occurred, thus, leaving the parties in the situation they were in prior to the making of the illusory contract.[340] Termination after repudiation does not bring in its train the non-existence of the contract. What happens is that the innocent party is allowed to pursue his normal contractual remedies for breach in advance of the time when they might otherwise have become available — as will be seen.

Second, it is also incorrect to speak of what happens when a repudiation is accepted as "ending" the contract.[341] Repudiation does not "end" a contract: it terminates future further performance by *either* side,[342] but it does not destroy rights of action which thereby accrue as a consequence of the breach (including breaches which may have taken place prior to the breach which amounted to the

---

335 (1988), 50 D.L.R. (4th) 729 (B.C.C.A.).

336 See, *e.g.*, *Roper v. Johnson* (1873), L.R. 8 C.P. 167; *Michael v. Hart & Co.*, [1902] 1 K.B. 482 (C.A.); affirmed (1903), 89 L.T. 422 (H.L.) (involving changes in the price of goods, with subsequent effects on the measure of damages).

337 Below, pp. 616-617.

338 *Shibamoto & Co. v. Western Fish Producers Inc. (Trustee of)* (1991), 43 F.T.R. 1 at 24 (Fed. T.D.) *per* Rouleau J.; affirmed (1992), 145 N.R. 91 (Fed. C.A.).

339 Compare Laskin J. in *Highway Properties Ltd. v. Kelly, Douglas & Co.* (1971), 17 D.L.R. (3d) 710 at 717 (S.C.C.).

340 Above, pp. 300, 561; below, pp. 807-814.

341 *L.E.P. Air Services Ltd. v. Rolloswin Invt.*, [1971] 3 All E.R. 45 at 54 (C.A.) *per* Megaw L.J.; affirmed [1972] 2 W.L.R. 1175 at 1184-1185 *per* Lord Diplock, and 1190 *per* Lord Simon of Glaisdale (H.L.).

342 Thus the innocent party is not obliged to perform his promises under the contract: see, *e.g. Dresser Industries Inc. v. Raven Muds Ltd.* above, note 330 (manufacturer was not obliged to supply goods to the wholesale distributor of the manufacturer's products after repudiation by the distributor by refusing to pay money to the manufacturer).

repudiation).[343] For this reason a guarantor could be liable upon the default of the principal debtor who repudiated the contract and his obligations thereunder.[344] The repudiating debtor, in situations of an accepted repudiation, is in breach of all future obligations, and he is not permitted to perform them, as Lord Atkinson stated. If he changes his mind, and attempts to perform them later, as happened, for example, in *Finelli v. Dee*,[345] the repudiator does not bind the innocent party who has previously accepted the repudiation.

Third, a distinction must be drawn between acceptance of repudiation and "waiver" of an actual or intended breach of contract.[346] When the innocent party "accepts" a repudiation, he is not forgiving the repudiating party. Nor is he bringing the contract, or a particular obligation imposed by the contract, to an end, so that it can never be performed in the future. On the other hand, when it is alleged that the innocent party has "waived" the breach, whether such breach has already occurred or is threatened for the future by the acts or language of the other party, the party "waiving" is relieving the other party of the need to perform the obligation in question, or is condoning and forgiving a breach that has taken place. Furthermore, an obligation that has been "waived" may be revived in certain circumstances, so as to become once again binding on the party in whose favour it was waived.

(ii) *The effects of acceptance of repudiation*

Since the contract is discharged by breach, not agreement, the innocent, injured party has the right to sue.[347] He may sue for damages immediately, without waiting for the time when the contract should have been performed to arrive.[348] Or he may claim on a *quantum meruit*, for the value of services rendered prior to the

---

343 *Mussen v. Van Diemen's Land Co.*, [1938] Ch. 253; *Boston Deep Sea Fishing & Ice Co. v. Ansell* (1883), 39 Ch. D. 339 (C.A.). Compare the situation when a fundamental breach, or breach of condition, occurs at the due date of performance: above, pp. 559-561. Hence, on an anticipatory breach of a contract of sale of land, of which time was of the essence (above, pp. 525-529), no right to cancel the contract arose; the contract survived so far as the defaulting purchaser's liability to pay damages at large, not just forfeit the deposit, was concerned: *E. & B. Mortgages Ltd. v. Skrivanos* (1981), 118 D.L.R. (3d) 139 (B.C.S.C.).

344 *L.E.P. Air Services Ltd. v. Rolloswin Invt.*, above, note 341.

345 [1968] 1 O.R. 676 (Ont. C.A.); compare *Amer. Nat. Red Cross v. Geddes Bros.* (1921), 61 S.C.R. 143 (S.C.C.).

346 For *waiver* see above, pp. 544-545.

347 *Gaklis v. Wells* (1979), 37 N.S.R. (2d) 451 (N.S.C.A.).

348 Can he do this if it is impossible to restore the parties to their original situation, *i.e.*, make *restitutio in integrum*? Rescission will not be allowed unless this can be done. But determination for repudiation is not rescission, as already stated. Hence, it should not matter whether the *status quo ante* can or cannot be restored. To the contrary is an English decision, *Thorpe v. Fasey*, [1949] Ch. 649, which is both criticized and distinguished in Cheshire & Fifoot, *Law of Contract*, 8th ed. (1972), pp. 578-580 (although not referred to in the 12th ed. (1991)). It seems an isolated case which need not and should not be followed.

repudiation.[349] This latter course may be more desirable if that amount exceeds what the innocent party would have recovered if the contract had been performed. The claim in *quantum meruit* in this instance (unlike certain other such claims) is not contractual in nature, since it is not based upon the *contract*; it is quasi-contractual, or based upon the more modern notions of unjust enrichment or restitution.[350]

If the innocent party sues for damages, the normal rules as to measurement of loss and remoteness apply.[351] However, the decision of the English Court of Appeal in *The "Mihalis Angelos"*[352] indicates that there may be some limitation on the claims that can be made by such a party in the event of repudiation or anticipatory breach. The repudiator can justify his repudiation by something discovered after the repudiation, which would have entitled him to repudiate, even though his repudiation, as it stood and for the reasons given, was wrongful;[353] he can take advantage of anything that occurs after repudiation by way of defence, if the repudiation is not accepted and the contract continues in effect.[354] In the same way the repudiator may be able to claim that the damages awarded against him should be *nominal* only, and not substantial, if the facts revealed that the innocent party has really lost nothing, or would have lost nothing as a result of the conduct of the other party, had the contract run its proper course, and not been abruptly terminated in advance. What happened in *The "Mihalis Angelis"* was that a charter-party was repudiated by the charterers on July 17th. The charterers could have cancelled the contract on July 20th if the ship had not been ready to load at a stated port on or before July 20th. The English Court of Appeal held that the charterers were guilty of anticipatory breach, since they could not legitimately cancel before July 20th. But on that date the ship would not have been ready, which would have been a breach of condition on the part of the shipowners. Hence all the charterers had done was anticipate, or prematurely do what they would have been entitled to do a few days later (without cost to themselves or loss to the shipowners). In such circumstances damages were only nominal.

This case also raises another point, about which there has been much

---

349 *Planché v. Colburn* (1831), 5 C. & P. 58, subsequent proceedings 131 E.R. 305; *De Bernardy v. Harding* (1853), 3 Ex. 822, 155 E.R. 1586. But in *Lewis A. Jones Inc. v. Grandma Lee's of Can. Ltd.* (1989), 64 D.L.R. (4th) 538 (Ont. C.A.), the plaintiff lost on appeal because there was no breach of contract: therefore the judge should not have treated it as if based on restitution.

350 *Luxor (Eastborne) Ltd. v. Cooper*, [1941] A.C. 108 (H.L.); Goff & Jones, *Law of Restitution*, 3rd ed. (1986), pp. 465-468; Fridman, *Restitution*, 2nd ed. (1992), pp. 315-318; Maddaugh & McCamus, *Law of Restitution*, pp. 422-438. The choice between damages and *quantum meruit* involves an election between *remedies* not rights: therefore it need not be made until judgment: *Komorowski v. Van Weel* (1993), 12 O.R. (3d) 444 at 461 (Ont. Gen. Div.) (unlike the choice between acceptance and non-acceptance of repudiation, which is an election between inconsistent *rights* and must be made promptly and communicated to the other party: *ibid.*).

351 Below, pp. 711-731.

352 [1971] 1 Q.B. 164 (C.A.).

353 *Universal Cargo Carriers Corp. v. Citati*, [1957] 2 Q.B. 401; affirmed [1957] 1 W.L.R. 979 (C.A.); *Denmark Productions Ltd. v. Boscobel Productions Ltd.*, [1969] 1 Q.B. 699 (C.A.). Compare above, p. 607.

354 Above, p. 613.

controversy. On its resolution the court was divided. The issue is whether a party repudiating can escape from liability if he can show that the *other* party would not have been able to perform the contract, on the due date, if the repudiation had not occurred and the contract allowed to run its full course.[355] To put this another way, can the innocent party succeed in an action for damages against the repudiator, once the repudiation has taken place and has been accepted, without *that* party proving that he was, and *always would have been*, that is, at the contract performance date, ready, willing and able to perform his part of the bargain? There are conflicting decisions and dicta in the English and Canadian courts.[356] In *The "Mihalis Angelos"*,[357] the majority, Edmund Davies and Megaw L.JJ. held that the charterers could not rely on the undoubted breach by the shipowners of *their* breach of condition to have the ship ready to load on the stipulated date, in order to justify the charterers' prior or premature cancellation of the contract, and thereby escape liability (although, as seen, that liability was nominal only). Lord Denning M.R. thought that if the charterers had a right to cancel on July 17th, they could rely on it, even though they gave the wrong reasons for it. Since they were entitled to cancel — even though they were not bound to cancel — before the proper date, that is, July 20th, they could rely on the good reason *ex post facto*.[358] This is in accordance with a dictum of Lord Summer in *British & Benington's Ltd. v. North Western Cachar Tea Co.*[359] It also seems logical in view of what has earlier been said about subsequent justification of an originally wrongful repudiation. But the matter is not without difficulty, in the light of the view taken by the other members of the court that it is a matter of construction of the contract. Possibly, in view of the decision with respect to damages, it may be that the question is one that will not cause serious difficulty in practice. On the other hand, if the innocent party must establish his ability to perform in order to sue when the repudiation is accepted, this might cause some parties in that position to fail. With respect, the approach adopted by Lord Denning M.R. seems more appropriate, logical, and acceptable.[360]

What of the rights, if any, of the repudiating party?[361] As noted already, he may or may not be able to take advantage proleptically of a defence which is not available at the moment of repudiation or acceptance of repudiation, and he

---

355 See Dawson "Waiver of Conditions Precedent on a Repudiation" (1980), 96 L.Q.R. 239; Dawson, "Metaphors and Anticipatory Breach of Contract" (1981), 40 C.L.J. 83 at 104.

356 *Braithwaite v. Foreign Hardwood Co.*, [1905] 2 K.B. 543 (C.A.); *Colley v. Overseas Exporters*, [1921] 3 K.B. 302; *Taylor v. Oakes, Roncoroni & Co.* (1922), 127 L.T. 267 (C.A.); *British & Benington's Ltd. v. North Western Cachar Tea Co.*, [1923] A.C. 48 (H.L.); *Rosenthal (J.) & Sons Ltd. v. Esmail*, [1965] 1 W.L.R. 1117 (H.L.); *Heney v. Bostwick* (1885), 24 N.B.R. 414 (N.B.C.A.); Fridman, *Sale of Goods in Canada*, 3rd ed. (1986), pp. 274-276.

357 Above, note 352, at 200, 207-208.

358 *Ibid.*, at 195-196.

359 Above, note 356, at 71-72.

360 But it does not appeal to Dawson, 96 L.Q.R. 239 at pp. 243-246. He prefers to say that the non-repudiator may have to show ability to perform *at the time of repudiation*, but not at the time for proper performance by him of his obligations under the contract.

361 Goff & Jones, *Law of Restitution*, 3rd ed. (1986), pp. 468-483; Fridman, *Restitution*, 2nd ed. (1992), pp. 215-219, 318-321; Maddaugh & McCamus, *Law of Restitution*, pp. 438-446.

may be able to insist that damages be nominal (even if what later occurs is not a complete defence to liability). But can the repudiating party recover money which has been paid in advance by that party to the other one, for example, as part payment, deposit, or earnest in relation to a contract of sale of land or goods? Sometimes, at least where such money is given as earnest or guarantee of full performance,[362] such money is forfeited if the purchaser wrongfully repudiates.[363] Where it is given as part payment of the price, there is authority for the proposition that such money is recoverable.[364] Equity gave some relief by granting a party time to complete payment, that is, by refusing to regard time as of the essence of a contract.[365] Whether equitable relief is available where the reason for the failure is something other than lack of time, is a vexed question.[366] In cases of unconscionability, there would seem to be little doubt that equity would give relief, as it has done in other situations, for example, mortgages. But if there is no evidence of unconscionable, oppressive, or similar circumstances or conduct, it may be that even equity will not relieve a party from a hard bargain into which he entered freely, but which he now finds he cannot perform through no fault of the other party.[367]

(iii) *Where repudiation is not accepted*

In cases of anticipatory breach the innocent party, instead of treating the contract as broken and suing for damages, may treat the contract as fully discharged, and recover his deposit or part payment. He may also consider the contract as valid and subsisting, and wait until the proper date for performance comes when, if the breach is still continuing, he may sue upon such breach.[368] The innocent party who elects not to accept repudiation may pursue alternative remedies even before the due date for performance.

When damages are eventually claimed by the innocent party, there is a problem

---

362 Which depends on the intentions of the parties: *Mayson v. Clouet*, [1924] A.C. 980 (P.C.).

363 *Howe v. Smith* (1884), 27 Ch. D. 89 (C.A.); *Erickson v. Andrew*, [1943] 2 W.W.R. 70 (Alta. C.A.); *Stevenson v. Colonial Homes Ltd.*, [1961] O.R. 407 (Ont. C.A.); *Frank H. Davis of Georgia v. Rayonier Can. (B.C.) Ltd.* (1968), 65 W.W.R. 251 (B.C.S.C.); *De Palma v. Runnymede Iron & Steel Co.*, [1950] O.R. 1 (Ont. C.A.).

364 *Dies v. British & Int. Mining & Finance Corp.*, [1939] 1 K.B. 724, and the Canadian cases cited in the previous note. The *Dies* case is strongly criticized by Beatson, "Discharge for Breach: The Position of Instalments, Deposits and Other Payments Due Before Completion" (1981), 97 L.Q.R. 389.

365 Above, pp. 527-528; see *Kilmer v. B.C. Orchard Lands Ltd.*, [1913] A.C. 319 (P.C.).

366 Except in the provinces where legislation does give some relief to a depositor: see, *e.g.*, Judicature Act, R.S.A. 1980, c. J-1, s. 17; Courts of Justice Act, R.S.O. 1990, c. C.43, ss. 96, 98. See also *Shiloh Spinners Ltd. v. Harding*, [1973] A.C. 691 especially at 722 (H.L.) *per* Lord Wilberforce.

367 Below, pp. 774-775; and see *Stockloser v. Johnson*, [1954] 1 All E.R. 630 (C.A.); *Bridge v. Campbell Discount Co.*, [1962] A.C. 600 (H.L.); *Galbraith v. Mitchenall Estates*, [1965] 2 Q.B. 473. Such was the decision in respect of the charterer under a time charter-party in *Scandinavian Trading Tanker Co. v. Flota Petrolera Ecuatoriana*, [1983] 2 All E.R. 763 (H.L.).

368 *Macnaughton v. Stone*, [1949] O.R. 853 at 858-859 (Ont. H.C.) *per* McRuer C.J.H.C. Unless, in the meanwhile the contract is terminated by frustration or impossibility: above, p. 613; below, Chapter 16.

as regards the innocent party's common-law duty to mitigate his loss.[369] The decision of the House of Lords in *White & Carter (Councils) Ltd. v. McGregor*[370] has caused some difficulty. There the appellants contracted with the respondents to give the latter advertising space for three years on litter bins which the appellants provided for local authorities. This contract was cancelled by the respondents on the same day that it was made. But the appellants refused to accept the repudiation. Thereafter they proceeded to carry out the contract, by preparing advertisement plates, attaching them to bins, and displaying them for the contract price of three years. Then the appellants sued the respondents for the full contract price. What was unusual about this case was that the appellants could completely fulfil their part of the contract without any co-operation from the respondents.[371] The majority of the House of Lords held that they should be successful. The most that the majority were prepared to say, by way of limiting the power of the innocent party in a case of anticipatory breach to perform after breach and then sue for the contract price or damages, was that this might not follow if, in Lord Reid's words, "it can be shown that a person has no legitimate interest, financial or otherwise, in performing the contract rather than claiming damages."[372] Then perhaps, "he ought not to be allowed to saddle the other party with an additional burden with no benefit to himself." But if there were some benefit, however small, as against claiming damages and reletting the advertising space, which could be shown, as here, then the innocent party was entitled to fulfil the contract and claim what he would have been paid had there been no repudiation by the other party.[373] The dissenting two members of the House of Lords found the proposition startling and in conflict with the general duty to minimize or mitigate loss or damages and capable of producing ridiculous results, whereby the innocent party could insist upon fulfilment of the contract, thereby causing loss to the repudiating party which far exceeded what might be considered the damages ordinarily flowing from the breach and caused to the innocent party.[374] Is this a problem of causation? Or should the law take strictly the liability of a party guilty of anticipatory breach, holding him even more responsible than one who broke his contract when performance was due? The indications in one Canadian case are that the minority rather than the majority opinion will be followed if and when this problem arrives before the Supreme Court of Canada.[375]

---

369 On which see below, pp. 776-783.

370 [1962] A.C. 413 (H.L.); see *Hounslow London B.C. v. Twickenham Garden Dev. Ltd.*, [1971] 1 Ch. 233 at 251-254. Note also the criticism of the majority opinion by Laskin J.A., as he then was, in *Finelli v. Dee*, [1968] 1 O.R. 676 (Ont. C.A.).

371 A point which was very important to Lord Reid; compare *Hounslow London B.C. v. Twickenham Garden Dev. Ltd.*, [1971] Ch. 233. Compare also the remarks of Rouleau J. in *Shibamoto & Co. v. Western Fish Producers Inc. (Trustee of)* (1991), 43 F.T.R. 1 at 24 (Fed. T.D.); affirmed (1992), 145 N.R. 91 (Fed. C.A.), referred to above, p. 614.

372 *White & Carter (Councils) Ltd. v. McGregor*, above, note 370, at 431.

373 *Ibid.*

374 *Ibid.*, at 433, 422, *per* Lord Morton of Henryton, and Lord Keith.

375 Dicta of Laskin J.A. in *Finelli v. Dee*, above, note 370; compare also Tedeschi, "Prevention of Performance by Promisee," (1975), 10 Israel Law Review 153 at 171-173.

What is more, recent authority in England has suggested that there is a possible limitation on the otherwise unfettered right of the innocent party to maintain the contract in existence, perform his part, and sue for damages including what he has spent.[376] As it was put by Lloyd J. in *Clea Shipping Corporation v. Bulk Oil International Ltd.*,[377] "there comes a point at which the court will cease, on general equitable principles, to allow the innocent party to enforce his contract according to its strict legal terms." The point seems to be somewhere between conduct which is unreasonable and conduct which is wholly unreasonable. Although this may upset the idea that in commercial contracts certainty is important, which would seem to exclude the possibility of any equitable jurisdiction to provide relief from contracts or otherwise interfere with the normal consequences of a breach,[378] the idea expressed by Lord Reid, as to absence of any legitimate interest in enforcing the contract, could be utilized to permit a court to force the innocent party to treat the contract as ended and mitigate his damages.

An alternative which appears to be open to the innocent party is that of suing for specific performance.[379] It was held in *Kloepfer Wholesale Hardware & Automotive Co. v. Roy*[380] that after an anticipatory breach, even though the innocent party did not accept the repudiation, he could obtain specific performance of a contract for the sale of land. It did not matter that the innocent party brought his suit before the due date for performance of the contract which had been repudiated, but if he did so, the plaintiff might not get specific performance right away but a declaration that he had the right to such performance on the due date. This was followed and accepted as good law by the Privy Council in *Hasham v. Zenab*,[381] in which, the circumstances being of the kind outlined above, the innocent party was enabled to obtain a decree of specific performance six weeks before the due date for performance of the repudiation contract, though he was not allowed to enforce the decree, and call for conveyance of the land in question, until the date for performance arrived, when, without bringing a new suit, he would be able to enforce his decree.

(iv) *Leases*

There appears to be a conflict between the courts of England and those of Canada with respect to the application of the doctrines enunciated and discussed above to leases of land.[382] In *Total Oil (Great Britain) Ltd. v. Thompson Garages*

---

376 *Attica Sea Carriers Corp. v. Ferrostaal Poseidon Bulk Reederei G.m.b.H.*, [1976] 1 Lloyd's Rep. 250 (C.A.); *Gator Shipping Corp. v. Trans-Asiatic Oil SA*, [1978] 2 Lloyd's Rep. 357.

377 [1984] 1 All E.R. 129 at 136-137.

378 *Scandinavian Trading Tanker Co. AB v. Flota Petrolera Ecuatoriana*, [1983] 2 All E.R. 763 (H.L.).

379 McRuer C.J.H.C. in *Macnaughton v. Stone*, [1949] O.R. 853 at 858-859 (Ont. H.C.). If specific performance is not obtained by the plaintiff he can obtain the alternative remedy of common law damages: *McKenna v. Richey*, [1950] V.L.R. 360; *Johnson v. Agnew*, [1980] A.C. 367 (H.L.); *Fletton Ltd. v. Peat Marwick Ltd.* (1988), 50 D.L.R. (4th) 729 at 733-737 (B.C.C.A.).

380 [1952] 2 S.C.R. 465 (S.C.C.).

381 [1960] A.C. 316 (P.C.).

382 Above, pp. 606-607.

(Biggin Hill) Ltd.[383] a lease was involved with a tying covenant under which the defendants agreed to sell only motor fuel supplied by the plaintiffs. It was suggested that the doctrine of repudiation and acceptance could not apply to bring a lease to an end. The estate survived whatever might have happened in the case of a "pure" contract. The analogy was drawn with the doctrine of frustration, which, it was said, also did not apply to leases.[384]

About the same time, in the Supreme Court of Canada, in *Highway Properties Ltd. v. Kelly, Douglas & Co.*,[385] a different view of frustration and repudiation in relation to leases was taken by Laskin J. He was not prepared to accept views as to the importance and continuance of an "estate" in land, where a lease was concerned, in the light of modern social and legal developments, for example, legislation on the contractual terms operating between landlord and tenant.[386] The actual question in that case concerned the measure of damages attainable by a landlord when the tenant wrongfully repudiated the lease and as a result, the landlord repossessed the premises, could not re-let them as they stood, had to subdivide them, and then leased the various parts piecemeal. In consequence the landlord lost money which he was endeavouring to reclaim from the tenant. In the lower courts, following the doctrine of estates, the repudiation by the tenant constituted a surrender of the lease. Hence, the lease ended with the surrender, and the landlord could only obtain damages for breaches occurring up to the date of surrender, not afterwards. In other words, the ordinary doctrine of repudiation and anticipatory breach could not apply to a lease. This approach the Supreme Court rejected. The court, in the *Roy* case,[387] had accepted that the doctrine of anticipatory breach could apply to a contract for the sale of land, even to the point of allowing an immediate suit for specific performance. It was equally open to the court to consider its application to a contractual lease, even if the lease were partly executed. Its anticipatory feature resulted from the fact that instalments of rent are payable for future periods, and repudiation of the lease raises the question whether the landlord can pursue an immediate remedy for the loss of such rent, etc., for the unexpired part of the lease, even if the estate in the land may have terminted. The law as it had developed up to that case recognized three courses open to the landlord.

> He may do nothing to alter the relationship of landlord and tenant, but simply insist on performance of the terms and sue for rent or damages on the footing that the lease remains in force. Second, he may elect to terminate the lease, retaining, of course, the right to sue for rent accrued due, or for damages to the date of termination for previous breaches of covenant. Third, he may advise the tenant that he proposes to re-let he property on the tenant's account and enter into possession on that basis.[388]

A further, more extensive proposition, suggested by counsel for the landlord, was

---

383 [1972] 1 Q.B. 318 (C.A.).
384 But see below, pp. 658-661.
385 (1971), 17 D.L.R. (3d) 710 (S.C.C.), over-ruling *Goldhar v. Universal Sections & Mouldings Ltd.*, [1963] 1 O.R. 189 (Ont. C.A.).
386 (1971), 17 D.L.R. (3d) 710 at 715-716 (S.C.C.).
387 Above, note 380.
388 Above, note 386, at 716.

eventually accepted by the Supreme Court, since it was a logical extension of the third course stated above, once the "underpinning and implications" of the that third course had been examined. This fourth course was as follows:

> The landlord may elect to terminate the lease but with notice to the defaulting tenant that damages will be claimed on the footing of a present recovery of damages for losing the benefit of the lease over its unexpired term. One element of such damages would be . . .the present value of the unpaid future rent of the premises for that period.[389]

By electing to terminate, the landlord did not limit the damages he may claim. He is not necessarily in the same position as if he had elected to keep the lease alive.[390]

The view expressed by the Supreme Court of Canada seems more reasonable and modern in the light of the way commercial leases really operate today, and, in view of the approach to frustration that has been evidenced by Canadian provincial legislation on tenancies, and recent decisions of the common law.[391] The assimilation of leases to contracts in general is to be welcomed.

---

389 *Ibid.*
390 *Ibid.*, at 721.
391 Below, pp. 658-661.

16

Frustration

1. Development of the doctrine[1]

(a) Impossibility generally no excuse

Where a party undertakes an obligation by an apparently unqualified promise, his *prima facie* duty is to perform. If circumstances intervene between the date of the contract and performance rendering performance impossible, he nevertheless

---

1 Page, "The Development of the Doctrine of Impossibility of Performance" (1920), 18 Mich. L.R. 589; Trakman, "Loser Take Some: Loss Sharing and Commercial Impossibility" (1985), 69 Minn. L.R. 471; Wladis, "Common Law and Uncommon Events: The Development of the Doctrine of Impossibility of Performance in English Contract Law" (1987), 75 Georgetown L.J. 1575.

remains bound unless a term of discharge can be implied into the contract. As Martin C.J. of Saskatchewan said in *McCuaig v. Kilbach*,[2]

> [w]here a person by his own agreement creates a duty or charge upon himself, he is bound to carry it out notwithstanding that he is prevented from so doing by some accident or contingency which he ought to have provided against in his agreement.

Hence, in that case, where a lessee of farm land had agreed to plow the land, it was no excuse or defence to an action for breach of contract that the land was covered in part by water, as a result of flooding, thereby making it impossible for the lessee to plow as arranged. The defendant should have provided against this contingency by agreement.[3] The law was reluctant to admit the kind of conditions subsequent which would permit the termination of a contractual obligation upon the happening of a certain event.[4] As late as 1920, by which time, as will be seen, there had been significant developments in the law, Lord Buckmaster could say in one Privy Council case,[5] that there was

> no phrase more frequently misused than the statement that impossibility of performance excuses breach of contract. Without further qualification such a statement is not accurate; and indeed if it were necessary to express the law in a sentence, it would be more exact to say that precisely the opposite was the real rule.

This general principle first appears in the seventeenth century in the case of *Paradine v. Jane*.[6] There, when the plaintiff claimed arrears of rent, the defendant pleaded that he had had no enjoyment of the lease nor any profit, having been ejected from the land by "Prince Rupert's Horse".[7] This defence failed, on the ground that no exemption had been provided for in the contract and, as explained in a later decision,[8] no term could be implied where it might have been expressed. In the course of the judgment, the court in the *Paradine* case gave vent to the view that contracts were "absolute", in the sense that impossibility would never excuse, unless specifically provided for by the contract itself. It would also seem that underlying the decision in that case was the notion that any doctrine of impossibility

---

2 [1954] 3 D.L.R. 117 at 119 (Sask. C.A.); compare *McKenna v. F.B. McNamee & Co.* (1888), 15 S.C.R. 311 at 317 (S.C.C.) *per* Ritchie C.J., citing *Lindley v. Lacey* (1864), 17 C.B.N.S. 578; *Wallis v. Littell* (1861), 11 C.B.N.S. 369.

3 Hence, as will be seen, if express provisions have been made, they will govern, and nothing else can be implied into the contract: see, *e.g., Cooke v. CKOY Ltd.*, [1963] 2 O.R. 257 (Ont. H.C.). In *Laurwen Invts. Inc. v. 814693 Northwest Territories Ltd.* (1990), 48 B.L.R. 100 (N.W.T.S.C.), the contract dealt with "loss, theft or damage" of videotapes: this did not cover what was to happen if, as occurred, the defendant's house was destroyed by an accidental fire: therefore the law of frustration applied.

4 For the nature and effect of conditions subsequent, see above, pp. 435-437.

5 *Grant, Smith & Co. v. Seattle Const. & Dry Dock Co.*, [1920] A.C. 162 at 169 (P.C.).

6 (1647), Aleyn 26, 82 E.R. 897; compare *Hills v. Sughrue* (1846), 15 M. & W. 253, 153 E.R. 844; *Budgett & Co. v. Binnington & Co.*, [1891] 1 Q.B. 35 (C.A.). On *Paradine v. Jane*, see Wladis, *loc. cit.*, above, note 1, at pp. 1579-1586. On the situation before that case, *ibid.*, at pp. 1576-1578. On later developments, *ibid.*, pp. 1588-1593.

7 *I.e.*, plea of *vis major*.

8 *Atkinson v. Ritchie* (1809), 10 East 530, 103 E.R. 877 *per* Lord Ellenborough C.J.

could not apply where land or proprietary interests were involved. The land could not be destroyed: the interests could survive.[9]

(b) English origins of the modern law

The start of the modern repudiation of the strict common-law doctrine of "absolute" contractual obligations is to be found in two cases of the 1860's,[10] in which the accidental destruction by fire of premises in respect of which there were contracts of hire, or for work to be done, extinguished the rights and liabilities of the parties. In *Taylor v. Caldwell*,[11] when the Surrey music hall was burnt down, this discharged an executory contract of hire of the premises for a series of concerts. In *Appleby v. Myers*,[12] the accidental destruction of the building in which a party was to erect machinery discharged the lump-sum contract under which the machinery was to be installed. It was in these decisions that the courts, and notably Blackburn J., who was instrumental in the enunciation and development of this doctrine,[13] derived the idea of impossibility from the older law relating to conditions precedent.

In *Hong Kong Fir Shipping Co. v. Kawasaki Kien Kaisha Ltd.*,[14] Diplock L.J., giving a historical explanation of the law relating to conditions, gave more credit to Bramwell B. in the formulation of the modern doctrine, when he said that it was not until *Jackson v. Union Marine Insurance Co.*[15]

> that it was recognized that it was the happening of the event and not the fact that the event was the result of a breach by one party of his contractual obligations that relieved the other party from further performance of his obligations.

At that time, to cite the graphic and imaginative language of Diplock L.J.,[16] "the doctrine of frustration was being foaled by 'impossibility of performance' out of 'condition precedent'."

The courts were attempting to extricate themselves from the straitjacket of the absolute theory of contracts, by the employment of other, well-accepted notions. The weapon or instrument to hand was the theory that performance might be dependent upon promises, and such promises might themselves be dependent upon the performance of other conditions. Consequently it could be implied into a

---

9 On the modern law relating to contracts concerning land and interests in land, see below, pp. 658-661.

10 Earlier, isolated instances can be found: *e.g.*, *Williams v. Lloyd* (1628), W.Jo. 179; *Hyde v. Dean & Canons of Windsor* (1597), Cro. Eliz. 552.

11 (1863), 3 B. & S. 826, 122 E.R. 309.

12 (1867), L.R. 2 C.P. 651.

13 See also his decisions in *Bettini v. Gye* (1876), 1 Q.B.D. 183; *Poussard v. Spiers* (1876), 1 Q.B.D. 410, in relation to conditions precedent and impossibility of performance. Compare Wladis, *loc. cit.*, above, note 1, at pp. 1594-1608.

14 [1962] 2 Q.B. 26 at 68-69 (C.A.). Compare McBryde, "Frustration of Contract", [1980] Jur. Rev. 1 at pp. 2-3.

15 (1874), L.R. 10 C.P. 125. See also *Geipel v. Smith* (1872), L.R. 7 Q.B. 404; *Dahl v. Nelson, Donkin & Co.* (1881), 6 App. Cas. 38 (H.L.).

16 [1962] 2 Q.B. 26 at 70 (C.A.).

contract, in some circumstances, even where the parties had not made their promises or their performances expressly dependent upon the happening or occurrence of a certain event, that this was what the parties intended, as reasonable men. Hence, their contract was subject to a condition precedent or a condition subsequent, whichever were the more rationally applicable, that if X happened or did not happen, then their contract would not come into effect, or would determine.[17] If the term to be implied were a condition *precedent*, it was not impossibility or frustration that was involved, but the older law about dependent and independent promises.[18] If the term that was implied was a condition *subsequent*, and could be interpreted as a term excusing further performance of the contract, then the contract was determined by impossibility.

Later, as noted by Diplock L.J. in the *Hong Kong Fir* case, the notion of impossibility broadened through the inclusion within its scope or ambit of the idea of "frustration of the adventure", by such cases as *Jackson v. Union Marine Insurance Co.* An injury to the ship which was being chartered which occurred without fault on the part of either contractual party, caused many months' delay with respect to the availability of the ship for a charter. This occurrence discharged a charter-party under which the ship chartered was to sail with all despatch. The ship could have been sent in due course, but by the time it was ready and available the original purpose of the intended charter-party could not be fulfilled. Therefore, there was "practical" impossibility, or "frustration", even though there was no physical impossibility, as in the earlier *Taylor* and *Appleby* cases. Delays of this kind could render a contract totally nugatory, either because the delay would be so infinite that the contract could never be performed, or else because, while the delay might be limited and comparatively short, the contract should have been performed on or before a certain date and the delay would undoubtedly continue beyond that date. Following the *Jackson* case, English courts treated delays of this kind as "frustrating" the contract (a phrase which eventually came to include within its scope all the various instances of impossibility). In such circumstances, although the contract could be performed ultimately at some time in the future, perhaps even a foreseeable or calculable time, there is, or would be little point in doing so by such time. The commercial purpose of the original contract has been frustrated; to go on when the delaying act or event has concluded its effects would be to bind the parties by a new contract, in new and different circumstances.

A new, or at least different type of impossibility or frustration occurred as a result of the postponement of the coronation procession of Edward VII because of the king's illness. Three cases in England in the years 1903 and 1904 appeared to suggest that, where the "sole purpose" of a contract failed or disappeared, through no fault of either party, the contract could be treated as frustrated in accordance

---

17 For a criticism of this approach to frustration, based upon psychological reasoning, see Fuller & Braucher, *Basic Contract Law* (1964), pp. 554-559, cited in Katz, Goldstein & Dershowitz, *Psychoanalysis, Psychiatry and Law* (1967), pp. 295-297.

18 Above, pp. 529-534.

with the doctrine enunciated in *Taylor v. Caldwell*[19] and subsequent decisions.[20] In *Krell v. Henry*,[21] the contract was for the hire of rooms, at a very high rent, because the rooms overlooked the route of the procession. The defendant hired two rooms for three days, during the period of coronation. Though nothing was said in the contract, it was understood by the parties that the purpose of the hire was to enable the procession to be viewed. The defendant had paid a deposit. When the landlord sued for the remainder of the rent, evidence of the purpose of the contract was admitted, and the plaintiff's claim failed. Nor could the defendant recover his deposit. A subsequent decision, *Chandler v. Webster*[22] held that in a like instance, where rent was expressed payable in advance, the "tenant" was obliged to pay the agreed sum, despite the cancellation of the procession and the frustration. However, in *Herne Bay Steam Boat Co. v. Hutton*,[23] the contract was for the hire of a ship which was to be at the disposal of the defendant for June 28th, to take passengers from Herne Bay to view the fleet and cruise around it. The naval review was cancelled, but it was still possible to cruise around the fleet, which remained at Spithead on the day mentioned in the contract. In these circumstances, the court held that the contract was not frustrated, and the defendant was liable. The only possible basis for distinction between this case and *Krell v. Henry* would seem to be that in the *Herne Bay* case: (1) there was more than one purpose; and (2) at least one of those purposes could still be fulfilled.

The case of *Krell v. Henry* has been criticized,[24] and attempts made to discover its true *ratio decidendi*.[25] On some explanations it adds nothing new either to the concept of frustration or to the theory underlying instances of impossibility or frustration. If the view is taken that the decision was founded on the idea of "frustration of purpose", then the case was innovatory, and marked a departure from earlier decisions.

---

19 Above, note 11.

20 See also *Victoria Seats Agency v. Paget* (1902), 19 T.L.R. 16; *Clark v. Lindsay* (1903), 88 L.T. 198. On all these cases see the discussion in Wladis, *loc. cit.*, above, note 1, at pp. 1608-1622.

21 [1903] 2 K.B. 740 (C.A.). Compare *Minnevitch v. Café de Paris (Londres) Ltd.*, [1936] 1 All E.R. 884 (cancellation of contract with band on death of King George V): cited by Wladis, *loc. cit.*, above, note 1, at pp. 1628-1629.

22 [1904] 1 K.B. 493 (C.A.): see below, p. 662.

23 [1903] 2 K.B. 683 (C.A.).

24 *Larringa & Co. v. Société Franco-Amér. des Phosphates de Médulla*, [1923] All E.R. 1 (H.L) *per* Lord Finley; *Maritime Nat. Fish Ltd. v. Ocean Trawlers Ltd.*, [1935] A.C. 524 at 528 (P.C.) *per* Lord Wright; but contrast his views in *Fibrosa Spolka Akcyjna v. Fairbairn Lawson Combe Barbour Ltd.*, [1943] A.C. 32 (H.L.).

25 See Tedeschi, "Frustration of Purpose" (1975), 10 Israel L.R. 1 pp. 1-7, and the authorities there cited. Wladis, "Common Law and Uncommon Events: The Development of the Doctrine of Impossibility of Performance in English Contract Law" (1987), 75 Georgetown L.J. 1575, at pp. 1608-1622, regards these cases as the product of unique circumstances: and the *Krell* principle has played a relatively insignificant role in the subsequent development of the law of impossibility in England: *ibid.*, at pp. 1620-1622.

(c) Canadian developments

In Canada the doctrine of *Taylor v. Caldwell* was clearly accepted and expressed in two Supreme Court cases which canvassed not only that case and the decision in *Appleby v. Myers*, but also the intervening authorities between 1863 and the 1920's.[26]

In the first of these, *Kerrigan v. Harrison*,[27] a vendor of land gave to the vendee a right of way over a defined road, together with a covenant in the grant by which the vendor promised to maintain the road and keep it in repair. The road was destroyed by the encroachment of lake water, without any fault attributable to the vendor. The vendor was excused from repairing the original road or providing a substituted right of way since the contract did not provide for such alternative arrangement. In arriving at this conclusion the Supreme Court of Canada applied *Taylor v. Caldwell* and *Appleby v. Myers*. To Brodeur J. the destruction of the road was by act of God, therefore the vendor's obligation ceased. The continued existence of the road was at the basis of the contract, and there was an implied condition that impossibility of performance ended the obligation, just as it did in the *Appleby* case.[28]

The second case was *Canadian Government Merchant Marine Ltd. v. Canadian Trading Co.*[29] Here, the opposite conclusion was reached on the facts from that to which the court had come in the earlier decision. There was no frustration or impossibility. In this case under a contract of affreightment goods were to be shipped in certain named vessels. The contract was made conditional upon the service to be provided by a stevedoring company and the sailing of certain steamers between named ports. The defendants were held liable when the plaintiff had to rescind the contract of affreightment because the intended ships were not completed and ready for use in the service of the defendants and for the purposes of the contract in question. Frustration could not succeed as a defence, because the language of the contract negated the implication of a condition that would excuse the defendants. Once again Brodeur J. referred to the basis of the doctrine of impossibility as resting on an implied condition.[30] In a lengthy passage,[31] Duff J. explained both the doctrine and its justification.

The principle of *Taylor v. Caldwell* has unquestionably been extended to cases

---

26 *E.g., Horlock v. Beal*, [1916] 1 A.C. 486 (H.L.); *Tamplin S.S. Co. v. Anglo-Mexican Petroleum Co.*, [1916] 2 A.C. 397 (H.L.); *Metro. Water Bd. v. Dick, Kerr & Co.*, [1918] A.C. 119 (H.L.); *Bank Line v. Arthur Capel & Co.*, [1919] A.C. 435 (H.L.). See Wladis, *loc. cit.*, above, note 25, at pp. 1622-1625. For the approach by Canadian courts to the ideas of delay and frustration of purpose, see below, pp. 655-656.

27 (1921), 62 S.C.R. 374 (S.C.C.). Compare also the earlier case of *McKenna v. F.B. McNamee & Co.* (1888), 15 S.C.R. 311 (S.C.C.) in which the Supreme Court held that a contract was subject to an implied agreement that the contract was subject to a future contractual relationship coming into existence between the defendant and the government of British Columbia.

28 (1921), 62 S.C.R. 374 at 381-383 (S.C.C.).

29 (1922), 64 S.C.R. 106 (S.C.C.).

30 *Ibid.*, at 119.

31 *Ibid.*, at 111-112.

in which parties having entered into a contract in terms unqualified it is found when the time for performance arrives, that a state of things contemplated by both parties as essential to performance according to the true intent of both of them fails to exist. . . .For the purpose of deciding whether a particular case falls within the principle you must consider the nature of the contract . . .whether the parties must have made their bargain on the footing that a particular thing or state of facts should be in existence when the time for performance should occur . . . And if reasonable persons situated as the parties were must have agreed that the promissor's contractual obligations should come to an end if that state of circumstances should not exist then a term to that effect may be implied. . . . But it is most important to remember that no such term should be implied when it is possible to hold that reasonable men could have contemplated the taking the risk of the circumstances being what they in fact proved to be when the time for performance arrived.

The doctrine of English law is that generally a promisor except to the extent to which his promise is qualified warrants his ability to perform it and this notwithstanding he may thereby make himself answerable for the conduct of other persons.

The seeming rigour of this doctrine is mitigated in the case of commercial contracts by the application of the principle above referred to which rests upon the assumption, . . . that in relation to possibilities in the contemplation of the contract but not actually present to the minds of the parties, the parties intended to stipulate for what would be fair and reasonable having regard to their mutual interests and to the main objects of the contract.

The impression that is left by these cases, and the language employed by the judges therein, is that, as seems to have been stated initially in the nineteenth century English cases, the application of the doctrine of impossibility or frustration depends upon the possibility of implying a suitable term to such effect into the contract. For Canadian courts, and for their English counterparts, the basis of the doctrine was originally an "implied term", that is, the possibility of incorporating into the contract some "condition" that would excuse either party or both from further performance of the contract in a certain eventuality.[32]

The idea that the doctrine of impossibility or frustration was founded upon the implication of a term permitting or recognizing the cessation of the contract in certain eventualities, was expressed differently in some Canadian cases. Sometimes it was said that a contract only became impossible of performance, or was frustrated, in the sense of the disappearance of the purpose of the "adventure", when what had occurred went to, or struck at the very root or foundation of the contract. When this happened, the basis of the contract was removed, and what was left was not the contract into which the party now alleging frustration or impossibility originally entered,[33] or would have entered had he known.[34]

---

32 See, *e.g.*, *Smith v. Johnson Bros. Ltd.*, [1954] 1 D.L.R. 392 at 398-400 (Ont. H.C.) *per* Schroeder J.; *McLaughlin v. Colvin*, [1941] 4 D.L.R. 568 at 575-576 (Ont. C.A.) *per* Fisher J.A.; affirmed, [1962] 3 D.L.R. 292 (S.C.C.). Note, however, the failure of consideration approach adopted by Middleton J.A. in *Goulding v. Rabinovitch*, [1927] 3 D.L.R. 820 at 821 (Ont. C.A.).

33 Compare *Tatem Ltd. v. Gamboa*, [1939] 1 K.B. 132 (seizure of ship on outbreak of Spanish Civil War frustrated contract) (cited and relied on in *Laurwen Invts. Inc. v. 814693 Northwest Territories Ltd.* (1990), 48 B.L.R. 100 at 109 (N.W.T.S.C.)); *Sir Lindsay Parkinson & Co. v. Works & Public*

According to Lord Shaw in *Lord Strathcona Steamship Co. v. Dominion Coal Co.*[35]

> [p]ut shortly frustration can only be pleaded when the events and facts on which it is founded have destroyed the subject-matter of the contract, or have, by an interruption of performance thereunder so critical or protracted as to bring to an end in a full and fair sense the contract as a whole, so superseded it that it can be truly affirmed that no resumption is reasonably possible.

It is clear that this related to "the common object of the agreement", not merely a one-sided advantage.[36] Indeed, this explanation of the doctrine was probably more useful to describe what happens in the case of "commercial frustration", as it has sometimes been called, than the original variety of impossibility, namely, destruction of the subject-matter. Mere difficulty in performance is not enough;[37] there must be the annihilation of the foundation of the contract. This is what took place, according to Chisholm C.J. of Nova Scotia in *Lieberman v. Roseland Theatre Ltd.*[38] What was involved was an agreement to sell shares to a certain company. The proposed vendor of the shares was held free to sell them elsewhere when the company sold other shares to X, with the result that the vendor lost control of the company. As the agreement with the company which was to buy the vendor's shares specified that the vendor was not to lose such control, it was held that the act of the company was a supervening event making performance of the original agreement impossible. Therefore, the contract was frustrated, leaving the vendor free to act as he willed. Although it was legally and physically possible for the vendor to sell the shares as arranged, the purpose of such sale was destroyed by what had happened; it was annihilated.

Bldg. Commrs., [1949] 2 K.B. 632 (C.A.); *Davis Contractors Ltd. v. Fareham Urban Dist. Council*, [1956] A.C. 696 (H.L.).

34 *George Eddy Co. v. Noble Corey & Son*, [1951] 4 D.L.R. 90 at 99-100 (N.B.C.A.) *per* Michaud C.J.Q.B.

35 [1926] A.C. 108 at 114 (P.C.).

36 *Hirji Mulji v. Cheong Yue S.S. Co.*, [1926] A.C. 497 at 507 (P.C.) *per* Lord Sumner, quoted by Urquhart J. in *Bayer Co. v. Farbenfabriken*, [1944] 2 D.L.R. 616 at 630 (Ont. H.C.); affirmed [1944] O.R. 488 (Ont. C.A.)—where there was no frustration of a contract when war occurred in 1939; the money could be paid to the Custodian of Enemy Property.

37 Nor mere economic unwisdom: *Samuel v. Black Lake Asbestos & Chrome Co.* (1920), 58 D.L.R. 270 at 276 (Ont. C.A.) *per* Kelly J. (compare *ibid.*, at 285 *per* Hodgins J.A.); varied (1921), 62 S.C.R. 472 (S.C.C.). Compare *Summers Transport Ltd. v. G.M. Smith Ltd.* (1990), 82 Nfld. & P.E.I.R. 1 at 14 (Nfld. T.D.) *per* Adams J., referring to this passage in the text and footnote. Compare Chandler, "Self-Induced Frustration: Foreseeability and Risk" (1990), 41 N. Ireland L.Q. 362 at 366. See also *110843 Can. Ltée v. Canada* (1988), 28 F.T.R. 1 (Fed. T.D.), a case in the Federal Court from Quebec, involving provisions of the Quebec Civil Code, but leading to the same general conclusion on the distinction between impossibility and difficulty of performance.

However, the Ontario Law Reform Commission favours the approach of the *Second Restatement of Contracts*, incorporating provisions of the Uniform Commercial Code, Art. 2 §§2-613—2-616, replacing "impossibility" with "impracticability": *Report on Amendment of the Law of Contract* (1987), pp. 271-279. The *Report* also distinguishes between discharge of a contract and suspension of performance.

38 [1946] 1 D.L.R. 342 (N.S.S.C.).

There are several statements to the effect that, as with the instance just cited, when the fundamental assumption underlying the contract disappears, the contract itself comes to an end by the operation of the doctrine.[39] This approach was utilized in several cases, for example: where drought made enjoyment of leased land virtually impossible;[40] where a mob made employers incapable of operating and maintaining an independent shop not requiring workers to be members of a trade union;[41] where a business which had only one asset was sold, and the asset subsequently disappeared, by reason of the change in the law of Saskatchewan, as a consequence of which there was no longer any need for a list of voters in Regina.[42]

In this last case, Sirois J. suggested that if the foundation of the contract went the contract itself came to end, even if the parties had made provision for what had happened.[43] This seems to go too far. Other statements of this principle put the matter differently. As O'Halloran J.A. said in *Australian Dispatch Line v. Anglo-Canadian Shipping Co.*[44] (in which the outbreak of war between China and Japan did not frustrate or render impossible of performance certain charter-parties),

> [t]he principle of frustration or impossibility of performance . . . when applied to charter-parties, extends beyond the destruction or non-existence of the subject-matter; it includes cases in which some supervening event modifies the circumstances affecting a contract so profoundly as to justify it being said there is an implied condition in the contract that it shall be treated as at an end . . . In other words the principle applies also where there is "cessation or non-existence of an express condition or state of things going to the root of the contract."

And in making a decision as to this, the court must take "what would be intended by a fair and reasonable man."[45] Thus the "root of the contract" notion depended upon what was express or implied, using the test of the reasonable man, in the contract. It was, in effect, only another way of stating the "implied condition" basis of impossibility or frustration. Which suggests that if the parties provided for what is to happen in the event of the alleged "frustrating" occurrence taking place, there was no room for an implied condition or the application of the "root of the contract" or "fundamental assumption" theory.[46]

What the courts did in these cases, however, was to elaborate or amplify the doctrine of the "implied condition", by making it plain that not every alleged "frustrating" circumstance would be effective for the purpose of the operation of

39 See the judgments of Duff J. in *Vancouver Breweries Ltd. v. Dana* (1915), 52 S.C.R. 134 (S.C.C.); *Roche v. Johnson* (1916), 53 S.C.R. 18 (S.C.C.); *Can. Govt. Merchant Marine Ltd. v. Can. Trading Co.* (1922), 64 S.C.R. 106 (S.C.C.).

40 *Cooke v. Moore*, [1935] 1 W.W.R. 374 (Sask. K.B.); affirmed [1935] 3 W.W.R. 256 (Sask. C.A.).

41 *Ziger v. Shiffer & Hillman Co.*, [1933] O.R. 407 (Ont. C.A.).

42 *Indust. Overload Ltd. v. McWatters*, [1972] 2 W.W.R. 760 (Sask. Q.B.); compare *Carr v. Berg*, [1917] 3 W.W.R. 1037 (B.C.C.A.); affirmed [1918] 2 W.W.R. 368 (S.C.C.).

43 (1972), 24 D.L.R. (3d) 231 at 235 (Sask. Q.B.).

44 [1940] 4 D.L.R. 104 at 106-107 (B.C.C.A.), citing *Horlock v. Beal*, [1916] 1 A.C. 486 (H.L.); *The "Penelope"*, [1928] P. 180.

45 [1940] 4 D.L.R. 104 at 107 (B.C.C.A.), citing Lord Watson in *Dahl v. Nelson, Donkin & Co.* (1881), 6 App. Cas. 38 at 59 (H.L.).

46 See below, pp. 640-642.

the law. A party would not be permitted to utilize the doctrine of frustration to escape from a bad bargain.[47] There had to be something which fundamentally, radically, or totally altered the nature of the contractual relationship between the parties, rendering it different character, purpose and effect from what it was, and what it was intended to be at the time when it was first entered into by the parties. Only then would it be legitimate and possible to imply the required term and apply the doctrine.[48]

(d) The doctrine of implied term

The "classical" notion of an implied term or condition meant that as reasonable men, looked at objectively, the parties must have intended discharge by the supervening event, though expressing no such term, either because they did not contemplate such frustration or because they took discharge for granted.[49] Variations on this were suggested, sometimes by judges, at others by textbook writers. Thus, the view discussed immediately above, that is, the "root of the contract" or "fundamental assumption", was, and may still be acceptable if regarded and treated as a method of expressing the implied term theory. If looked upon as a visible alternative explanation of the doctrine of impossibility or frustration, however, it conflicted with long-accepted judicial dicta, and led to the danger of accepting the view that if the "underlying purpose" of the contract goes, that is, if one party loses his economic advantage, that sufficed to permit the operation of the doctrine — a view which is potentially dangerous and misleading.

There were other suggestions, such as that the true basis of frustration was, or was akin to one form of mistake, or that failure of consideration was at the root of the doctrine.[50] Perhaps the most widely formulated theory in opposition to the "classical" notion was that the doctrine of frustration rested on a legal fiction by which the court sought to satisfy the demands of natural justice rather than

---

47 *Galt v. Frank Waterhouse & Co.*, [1944] 2 D.L.R. 158 (B.C.C.A.); *Australian Dispatch Line v. Anglo-Can. Supply Co.*, [1940] 4 D.L.R. 104 (B.C.C.A.). Compare *McDermid v. Food-Vale Stores (1972) Ltd.* (1980), 25 A.R. 301 (Alta. Q.B.); *Luchuck v. Sport B.C.* (1984), 52 B.C.L.R. 145 (B.C.S.C.); supplementary reasons at (1984), 53 B.C.L.R. 143 (B.C.S.C.); compare *Graham v. Wagman* (1976), 73 D.L.R. (3d) 667 (Ont. H.C.); reversed on other grounds (1978), 89 D.L.R. (3d) 282 (Ont. C.A.); *Delta Food Processors Ltd. v. East Pac. Enterprises Ltd.* (1979), 16 B.C.L.R. 13 (B.C.S.C.).

48 Compare *Harry Freeman & Sons Ltd. v. Neu* (1984), 66 N.S.R. (2d) 255 (N.S. Co. Ct.) (no frustration caused by owner of building to be constructed finding fault with workmanship, and giving direct orders to workmen constituting annoyance); *Kesmat Invt. Inc. v. Indust. Machinery Co.* (1985), 66 N.S.R. (2d) 51 (N.S.T.D.) (unsuspected requirement of environmental study not frustration; but difficulty of obtaining study and excessive cost thereof, with municipality's intention to subvert application for subdivision, *was* frustration).

49 Which permitted the merger or impossibility of performance with commercial frustration: see the *Tamplin* case, above, note 26; *Bank Line v. Arthur Capel & Co.*, above, note 26. For a critical examination of the implied term theory, see Trakman, "Frustrated Contracts and Legal Fictions" (1983), 46 M.L.R. 39.

50 *Goulding v. Rabinovitch*, [1927] 3 D.L.R. 820 at 821 (Ont. C.A.) *per* Middleton J.A.; compare Lord Simon of Glaisdale in *Nat. Carriers Ltd. v. Panalpina (Nor.) Ltd.*, [1981] 1 All E.R. 161 at 177 (H.L.).

relying on inferences as to the parties' intent. This was stated strongly by Lord Wright on several occasions,[51] and hints of it appeared in other judgments, even while they paid service to the "implied condition" doctrine.[52] However, it would seem that the House of Lords have denied that this is the true and valid foundation for the invocation of the doctrine of frustration or impossibility. While the House of Lords were prepared to accept the notion of fundamental alteration of the contract, with its consequent effect upon the real or attributed intentions of the parties,[53] they would not go so far as to admit or accept that the court played a more constructive role in such instances. Lord Simon in *British Movietonews v. London & District Cinemas*,[54] for example, said

> The parties to an executory contract are often faced, in the course of carrying it out, with a turn of events which they did not at all anticipate. . . . Yet this does not in itself affect the bargain they have made. If, on the other hand, a consideration of the terms of the contract, in the light of the circumstances existing when it was made, shows that they never agreed to be bound in a fundamentally different situation which has now unexpectedly emerged, the contract ceases to bind at that point — not because the court in its discretion thinks it just and reasonable to qualify the terms of the contract, but because on its true construction it does not apply in that situation. When it is said that in such circumstances the court reaches a conclusion which is "just and reasonable" . . . or one "which justice demands" . . . this result is arrived at by putting a just construction on the contract in accordance with an "implication . . . from the presumed common intention of the parties" . . . If the decisions in "frustration" cases are regarded as illustrations of the power and duty of a court to put the proper construction on the agreement made between the parties, having regard to the terms in which that agreement is expressed and to the surrounding circumstances in which it was made, including any necessary implications, such decisions are seen to be examples of the general judicial function of interpreting a contract when there is disagreement as to its effect.

This suggests that frustration is dealt with by construction of the contract, not by any judicial tinkering with the obligations between the parties.

That "construction theory" appears to be the one now favoured by English courts,[55] The formulation which has received approval is that of Lord Radcliffe in *Davis Contractors Ltd. v. Fareham Urban District Council:*

---

51 *Joseph Constantine S.S. Line Ltd. v. Imperial Smelting Corp.*, [1942] A.C. 154 at 186 (H.L.); *Denny, Mott & Dickson, Ltd. v. Fraser & Co.*, [1944] A.C. 265 at 274-275 (H.L.); *Legal Essays & Addresses, Essay X*, at p. 254.

52 *E.g., Ocean Tramp Tankers Corp. v. V/O Sovfracht*, [1964] 1 All E.R. 161 at 166 (C.A.) *per* Lord Denning M.R.; compare *Morgan v. Manser*, [1948] 1 K.B. 184. See also his statements in *Staffordshire Area Health Authority v. South Staffordshire Waterworks Co.*, [1978] 3 All E.R. 769 (C.A.); *Multiservice Bookbinding Ltd. v. Marden*, [1979] Ch. 84 at 112-113; *Pioneer Shipping Ltd. v. B.T.P. Tioxide Ltd.*, [1980] Q.B. 547 (C.A.); affirmed [1982] A.C. 724 (H.L.).

53 *Tsakiroglou & Co. v. Noblee & Thorl G.m.b.H.*, [1962] A.C. 93 (H.L.); *Davis Contractors Ltd. v. Fareham Urban Dist. Council*, [1956] A.C. 696 (H.L.).

54 [1951] 2 All E.R. 617 at 625 (H.L.).

55 *Nat. Carriers Ltd. v. Panalpina (Nor.) Ltd.*, [1981] 1 All E.R. 161 (H.L.); compare *Amalgam. Invt. & Prop. Co. v. J. Walker & Sons Ltd.*, [1976] 3 All E.R. 509 (C.A.). And those of Australia: see

. . .frustration occurs whenever the law recognises that, without default of either party a contractual obligation has become incapable of being performed because the circumstances in which performance is called for would render it a thing radically different from that which was undertaken by the contract. *Non haec in foedera veni.* It was not this that I promised to do.[56]

Lord Simon of Glaisdale, in *National Carriers Ltd. v. Panalpina (Northern) Ltd.*,[57] suggested that frustration occurred when there was a supervening event (without default of either party and for which the contract made no sufficient provision) which so significantly changed the nature (not merely the expense or onerousness) of the outstanding contractual rights and obligations from what the parties could reasonably have contemplated at the time of its execution that it would be unjust to hold them to the literal sense of its stipulations in the new circumstances. He also thought that certain instances of frustration were best explained by the theory of failure of consideration.[58] However, he did state that the "construction theory", or "theory of a radical change in obligation" was the one most generally accepted, even though the implied term theory still provided a satisfactory explanation of many cases.[59]

Canadian cases suggest that the "construction theory", or "radical change in obligation theory", as expressed by Lord Radcliffe, is the one adopted by Canadian courts in modern times.[60] They may be said to have rejected the classical implied term doctrine.[61] They have also rejected the idea that frustration depends upon the equitable allocation of the risk between the parties.[62] But there are hints in at least one decision[63] that the doctrine of frustration, while apparently dependent

---

Codelfa Const. Pty. Ltd. v. State Rail Authority of New South Wales (1982), 56 A.L.J.R. 800 (Aust.), on which see Swanton (1983), 57 Austr. L.J. 201.

56 [1956] A.C. 696 at 729 (H.L.).
57 Above, note 55, at 175.
58 *Ibid.*, at 177.
59 *Ibid.*, at 186.
60 *Capital Quality Homes Ltd. v. Colwyn Const. Ltd.* (1975), 61 D.L.R. (3d) 385 (Ont. C.A.); *Victoria Wood Dev. Corp. v. Ondrey* (1978), 92 D.L.R. (3d) 229 (Ont. C.A.); leave to appeal to S.C.C. refused (1979), 26 N.R. 267 (S.C.C.); *Re Dom. Coal Co.* (1974), 49 D.L.R. (3d) 390 (N.S.C.A.); *Summers Transport Ltd. v. G.M. Smith Ltd.* (1990), 82 Nfld. & P.E.I.R. 1 (Nfld. T.D.); *Petrogas Processing Ltd. v. Westcoast Transmission Co.* (1988), 59 Alta. L.R. (2d) 118 at 133-135 (Alta. Q.B.); affirmed (1989), 58 D.L.R. (4th) 156 (Alta. C.A.); *111 Niakwa Road Ltd. v. Duraps Corp.* (1985), 37 Man. R. (2d) 250 (Man. Q.B.); additional reasons at (1986), 43 Man. R. (2d) 65 (Man. Q.B.).
   But see the curious judgment of Cummings J. in *Dove v. S. & M. Carpet Ltd.* (1988), 73 Nfld. & P.E.I.R. 354 at 360 (Nfld. T.D.), apparently affirming an implied term approach. The judgment treats what happened to the plaintiff, *i.e.*, a knee injury that incapacitated him from fulfilling the parties' intentions as a fundamental breach of contract that entailed frustration! The judgment was varied on other grounds (1989), 81 Nfld. & P.E.I.R. 105 (Nfld. T.D.).
61 Compare de Weerdt J. in *Laurwen Invts. Inc. v. 814693 Northwest Territories Ltd.* (1990), 48 B.L.R. 100 at 108 (N.W.T.S.C.).
62 *Victoria Wood Dev. Corp. v. Ondrey*, above, note 60, at 241-242, rejecting the ideas of Houlden J.A. in *Focal Properties Ltd. v. George Wimpey Can. Ltd.* (1975), 73 D.L.R. (3d) 387 (Ont. C.A.); affirmed [1978] 1 S.C.R. 2 (S.C.C.).
63 *Capital Quality Homes Ltd. v. Colwyn Const. Ltd.*, above, note 60, at 391; compare *McDermid v. Food-Vale Stores (1972) Ltd.* (1980), 25 A.R. 301 at 309 (Alta. Q.B.) *per* Egbert J.

upon a radical change in the obligation, is founded on "the more realistic view that the court imposes upon the parties the just and reasonable solution that the new situation demands." If this is nothing more than the doctrine expounded by Lord Radcliffe, and given subsequent approval in other English cases, then it accords with the English doctrine, and is acceptable. If it introduces into the equation the notion espoused by Lord Denning, and others,[64] that frustration is a device by which the rules as to absolute contracts can be reconciled with a special exception which justice demands, then it may go too far. It suggests that the doctrine is not a rational attempt to achieve what the parties probably intended to happen in the unforeseen circumstances, but instead permits a court to rewrite, not merely reinterpret, the contract. That goes too far, and may lead to the discharge of contracts for such reasons as additional expense or difficulty involved in their performance and fulfilment in the changed circumstances. Courts in England and Canada have rejected such factors as justifying the invocation of the doctrine. It would be contrary to principle and contradictory of the decided cases to adopt a theory of frustration which could substantiate the opposite.

2. Features of the doctrine

(a) Construction and the implied term

Although the distinction has been drawn between the older "implied term" theory and the more recently approved "construction theory", the difference between them is not as great as might appear at first sight. As Lord Wilberforce explained in the *Panalpina* case,[65] the various theories (namely, a device to reconcile absolute contracts with a special exception demanded by justice, implied term, construction, removal of the foundation of the contract, and total failure of consideration) shade into one another. The choice between them is the choice of what is most appropriate to the particular contract under consideration. The search for a justification of the court's "interference" with a contract may have alighted, for the time being, on the idea that the sole function of the court is to construe the contract in order to find out what the parties *would have* agreed should happen had they conceived of what happened as coming to pass.[66] However, to express the approach of the courts in this way is not too far removed from the use of the idea that the court can imply a term into the contract capable of resolving the issue. After all, before a court can imply a term into a contract, except under the authority of statute, custom, or past practice as between the parties, it must be shown that to do so is necessary and in conformity with the express terms of the contract, as well as its underlying purpose and surrounding circumstances.[67] In effect, therefore, a court implying a term into a contract is construing the contract

---

64 Compare Lord Sumner in *Hirji Mulji v. Cheong Yue S.S. Co.*, [1926] A.C. 497 at 510 (P.C.).
65 [1981] 1 All E.R. 161 at 170 (H.L.).
66 Hence the difference where there is an express term that governs the situation: below, p. 640.
67 Above, pp. 475-483.

in such a way as to give it effect, meaning, and purpose in the light of all the ambient commercial facts.

Recent emphasis on "construction", in contrast with an implied term, simply means that, in place of a more fictional approach, courts are stressing the need to relate the contract and its fate to the ultimate design intended by the parties.[68] Hence the discussion of the idea of a "common venture" by the Ontario Court of Appeal in *Victoria Wood Development Corporation v. Ondrey*,[69] and the rejection by that court of the suggestion that courts should be concentrating upon, and seeking to discern the parties' intentions with respect to the way potential risks under the contract have been allocated, expressly or by implication, by the parties.[70] The reason for the investigation of whether there was some common venture seems to be that only where such a venture can be discerned will a radical, substantial, or material change of circumstances, occurring in an unforeseen way, or to an unforeseen extent, or with an unforeseen consequence, result in the frustration of the contract.[71] In such circumstances it would be contrary to the nature and intent of the original contract to regard the parties as still bound by its terms. Alternative explanations could be given, consistent with other theories underlying the doctrine of frustration. It could be said that to hold the parties bound would be unreasonable, against justice, or not in accord with their implicit agreement. It could also be said that, where a common venture existed, the new development, for example, a change in the law, the destruction of the subject-matter of the contract, the death of a party, went to the "root of the contract", or removed the very "foundation" of the contract, so that there was nothing on which the contract could legitimately be said to rest. Such language is not so much a technical expression of what a court is doing, and the method by which a court achieves its object, as a rationalization of the action being taken by the court. More technical ways of stating or explaining the court's action are by speaking of "a total failure of consideration", such that to hold a party bound by the contract would result in his giving consideration to the other party and receiving nothing in return, or by saying that a term should be implied into the contract that it would terminate if the unforeseen event that actually happened were to occur.

What, then, is the purpose behind replacing the "implied term" theory, or one of its linguistic alternatives, by the "construction theory", with its emphasis on a radical change in the obligation? The answer seems to be the desire by courts to escape from, or avoid the need for fictions, replacing them by a more realistic approach that provides an explanation of what the courts are truly performing rather than an explanation that employs such facile expressions and notions as "implied

---

68 Compare Trakman, "Frustrated Contracts and Legal Fiction" (1983), 46 M.L.R. 39, especially at pp. 39-45.

69 (1978), 92 D.L.R. (3d) 229 (Ont. C.A.); leave to appeal to S.C.C. refused (1979), 26 N.R. 267 (S.C.C.); compare the earlier discussion in *Capital Quality Homes Ltd. v. Colwyn Const. Ltd.* (1975), 61 D.L.R. (3d) 385 at 398 (Ont. C.A.).

70 Which appears to be the Scottish approach: McBryde, "Frustration of Contract", [1980] Jur. Rev. 1 at 4-6.

71 *Victoria Wood Dev. Corp. v. Ondrey*, above, note 69, at 237, 241.

terms". To imply a term in order to resolve the issue is obviously legal sleight-of-hand, concealing what is really being done. To inquire into the true nature of the contractual obligation, for the purpose of discovering whether it is in conformity with that obligation to hold that it can validly outlast and survive the change of circumstances that has occurred is more direct, honest, open, and rational. Such an approach is consistent with what has been happening generally in the law of contract, namely, the realization that contracts cannot be understood and interpreted except by reference to the surrounding circumstances.[72] Courts must have regard to: the situation that existed at the time the contract was made; the intentions of the parties that were to be achieved by the contract; and the general commercial background against which the contract was negotiated. This is not to say that the approach of the courts is subjective. They do not look at the internal desires or intentions of the individual parties. The investigation must be objective. It must take the form of seeking to discover, by the tests of the reasonable onlooker or observer with knowledge of what the parties have said and done, and the other, relevant factors, how the contract is to be understood by reasonable third parties, external to the contract. In this way the doctrine of frustration is consistent with the modern approach to the problem of mistake in relation to contracts, and with the modern law relating to contractual interpretation generally.[73]

(b) A radical change in the obligation

The key to both the understanding and the application of the doctrine of frustration in modern times is the idea of a radical change in the contractual obligation, arising from unforeseen circumstances in respect of which no prior agreement has been reached, those circumstances having come about without default by either party. What would appear essential is that the party claiming that a contract has been frustrated should establish that performance of the contract, as originally agreed, would be impossible.[74] For example, if the subject-matter of the contract has been lost or destroyed, a court will be willing to determine that the contract is ended.[75] The same has been the result where a container that was being rented could not be loaded on a ship for transportation to Newfoundland, when the defendant had promised to supervise the operation;[76] and where revision of a school curriculum occurred so as to render the agreed contract to prepare

---

72 Compare above, pp. 494-496.

73 Compare, above, pp. 247-251, 453-455. The doctrine is not to be lightly invoked and ought not to be extended, since the effect of frustration is to kill the contract and discharge the parties from further liability under it: *J. Lauritzen A/S v. Wijsmuller B.V.; "Super Servant Two" (The)*, [1990] 1 Lloyd's Rep. 1 at 6 (C.A.) *per* Bingham L.J.

74 Or worthless: *Dot Devs. Ltd. v. Fowler* (1980), 118 D.L.R. (3d) 371 at 377 (B.C.S.C.) *per* McKinnon J. Hence, in that case the sales agreement was not frustrated, even though the house to be occupied by the vendor for some months after closing, had been destroyed by fire. The rest of the contract could still be performed.

75 *Marine Const. Ltd. v. Metro Enrg. & Const. Ltd.* (1978), 20 Nfld. & P.E.I.R. 504 (Nfld. T.D.).

76 *Summers Transport Ltd. v. G.M. Smith Ltd.* (1990), 82 Nfld. & P.E.I.R. 1 (Nfld. T.D.).

a textbook impossible to fulfil.[77] So, too, if a contract relating to land was intended to result in certain development of the land, to the knowledge of both parties and as they both intended, a change in planning legislation preventing such development will be held to frustrate the contract.[78] But mere knowledge of the purchaser's intention to develop will not suffice if that development was not a "common venture".[79] Nor will a charter-party be frustrated by reason of the outbreak of war in the area where the ship chartered was to voyage,[80] though in certain circumstances a strike at one of the ports in the charter-party may have this effect,[81] as will the appropriation of the ship that was to be chartered.[82]

Time and again it has been stressed that frustration will not be invoked where the change in circumstances has meant that it would be more expensive or onerous for the contract to be performed.[83] Nor will the fact that the contract has ceased to be advantageous for one party, or has become an uneconomic venture, mean that the contract has been frustrated.[84] In *Staffordshire Area Health Authority v. South Staffordshire Waterworks Co.*,[85] Lord Denning argued that a contract was frustrated for such a reason when the water to be provided thereunder could no longer be provided at a given, small price. No time limit was appointed in the contract. Nor was there any provision for revising the figure. Years later, by reason of fluctuations in the value of the pound sterling and inflationary trends in the economy, the price at which the water was to be provided became derisory, and the party which had undertaken to supply the water argued that the burden under the contract had become onerous and unreasonable. The majority of the Court of Appeal agreed with the argument that the contract should be interpreted to

---

77 *Cassidy v. Can. Publishing Corp.* (1989), 41 B.L.R. 223 (B.C.S.C.): compare *Okanagan College Faculty Assn. v. British Columbia (Labour Relations Bd.)* (1987), 10 B.C.L.R. (2d) 353 (B.C.S.C.); reversed (1988), 33 B.C.L.R. (2d) 149 (B.C.C.A.).

78 *Capital Quality Homes Ltd. v. Colwyn Const. Ltd.*, above, note 69.

79 *Victoria Wood Dev. Corp. v. Ondrey*, above, note 69; compare *Amalgam. Invt. & Property Co. v. J. Walker & Sons Ltd.*, [1976] 3 All E.R. 509 (C.A.).

80 *Finelvet A.G. v. Vinava Shipping Co.*, [1983] 2 All E.R. 658; compare the decision with respect to the closure of the Suez Canal in *Tsakiroglou & Co. v. Noblee & Thorl G.m.b.H.*, [1962] A.C. 93 (H.L.).

81 *Pioneer Shipping Ltd. v. B.T.P. Tioxide Ltd.*, [1981] 2 All E.R. 1030 (H.L.); compare *O'Connell v. Harkema Express Lines Ltd.* (1982), 141 D.L.R. (3d) 291 (Ont. Co. Ct.), strike causing closure of business frustrated contract of employment in the business; on the effect of strikes, see below, p. 655.

82 *Re Dominion Coal Co.* (1974), 49 D.L.R. (3d) 390 (N.S.C.A.), with which compare *Bank Line Ltd. v. Arthur Capel & Co.*, [1919] A.C. 435 (H.L.). Contrast *Tamplin S.S. Co. v. Anglo-Mexican Petroleum Co.*, [1916] 2 A.C. 397 (H.L.); *Port Line v. Ben Line Steamers Ltd.*, [1958] 2 Q.B. 146.

83 *Delta Food Processors Ltd. v. East Pac. Enterprises Ltd.* (1979), 16 B.C.L.R. 13 (B.C.S.C.); *McDermid v. Food-Vale Stores (1972) Ltd.* (1980), 25 A.R. 301 (Alta. Q.B.); *Acadia Forest Products Ltd. v. Neal Forest Products Ltd.* (1983), 48 N.B.R. (2d) 429 (N.B.Q.B.); *Luchuck v. Sport B.C.* (1984), 52 B.C.L.R. 145 (B.C.S.C.); supplementary reasons at (1984), 53 B.C.L.R. 143 (B.C.S.C.); *Smith v. Tamblyn (Alta.) Ltd.* (1979), 9 Alta. L.R. (2d) 274 (Alta. T.D.). Compare *Graham v. Wagman* (1976), 73 D.L.R. (3d) 667 (Ont. H.C.); reversed on other grounds (1978), 89 D.L.R. (3d) 282 (Ont. C.A.).

84 *Acadia Forest Products Ltd. v. Neal Forest Products Ltd.*, above, note 83; *Cairns Homes Ltd. v. Jerol Invts. Ltd.* (1983), 25 Sask. R. 305 (Sask. Q.B.).

85 [1978] 3 All E.R. 769 (C.A.).

end the obligation to supply water; only Lord Denning thought that this result could be achieved by invoking the doctrine of frustration. In somewhat similar circumstances, in *Boise Cascade Canada Ltd. v. R.*[86] the Supreme Court of Canada held that relevant legislation could be interpreted to limit the obligation of the party which had undertaken to supply water at a rate fixed when the value of money was greater. Frustration was raised before the Ontario Court of Appeal as a possible ground for relieving the water supplier of its obligations, but was rejected for the reason that the doctrine had not been developed to the point at which a contract could be determined for such a reason unless its proper construction permitted such a conclusion.[87] In the Supreme Court of Canada it was held that the terms of the agreement governed the situation, precluding the application of the doctrine of frustration.[88] Underlying the decisions in both courts, however, may be seen the view that mere hardship in fulfilment of a contract could not of itself amount to frustration, as long as the contract could still be fulfilled according to its terms. Only if to do this was impossible might it be said that frustration could apply. Hence, in the *Panalpina* case,[89] the House of Lords could hold that the lease was not frustrated, even though developments had interfered with the proper enjoyment of the lease for a period of time during the continuance of the lease's term, since it was still possible for the lessee to enjoy the benefits of the lease when the physical interference that was occurring had ended.

From the decided cases to which reference has been made it is deducible that the basis of frustration is impossibility. By this is meant physical impossibility and impossibility resulting from a legal development that has rendered the contract no longer a lawful one. However frustration goes further, and comprehends situations where the contract may be both physically and legally capable of being performed but would be totally different from what the parties intended were it performed after the change that has occurred. In regard to such situations the greatest difficulty has been met, both as respects the theoretical explanation of the doctrine and its practical application. The distinction is made and drawn between complete fruitlessness and mere inconvenience, hardship, loss of advantage, or the like. It is also necessary to differentiate a disruption that is permanent, *vis-à-vis* the contract (albeit that it may not be permanent in other respects) and one that is temporary or transient. The latter might add to the difficulties of performance. It might make performance less desirable, economically valuable, or more expensive to undertake. But it will not constitute frustration. The courts require an utter and complete transformation of the contractual circumstances. Change, in itself, is insufficient. It must be change that totally alters the nature, meaning, purpose, effect, and consequences of the contract so far as concerns either or both parties.[90]

---

86 (1981), 126 D.L.R. (3d) 649 (Ont. C.A.); varied on other grounds (1983), 143 D.L.R. (2d) 193 (S.C.C.).

87 (1981), 126 D.L.R. (3d) 649 at 655-656 (Ont. C.A.).

88 (1983), 143 D.L.R. (3d) 193 at 209 (S.C.C.).

89 [1981] 1 All E.R. 161 (H.L.). See Robertson, "Frustrated Leases: 'No to Never — But Rarely If Ever'" (1982), 60 Can. Bar Rev. 619. See also below, p. 661.

90 Compare *Lieberman v. Roseland Theatre Ltd.*, [1946] 1 D.L.R. 342 (N.S. S.C.); above, p. 630.

Nor will the courts apply the doctrine of frustration if the act or event that is alleged to have brought about this radical change in the nature of the contract be something foreseeable.[91] If what happened did not go beyond what was contemplated when the contract was made, the doctrine is inoperative. So, in *Cobbold v. Time Canada Ltd.*,[92] a subscription to Time magazine was not frustrated by the fact that the Canadian government changed the tax law governing advertising expenses, the result of which was the termination of the Canadian edition of the magazine to which the subscription had been made. When the parties had contracted the possibility of this occurring had been realized.

(c) The effect of express terms

Under the older implied term theory it was not possible to imply a term permitting a contract to be declared frustrated if the contract expressly covered the situation that was alleged to be dealt with by the implied term, or if any such implied term would be inconsistent with the express terms of the contract. The construction theory of frustration has the same consequences. If the contract is worded in such a way as to make an interpretation of the contract to allow frustration contradictory of what the parties have expressed in the contract, or nonsensical having regard to their language, it is not open to the court to give the contract such a construction and apply the doctrine of frustration.

Thus, the contract may provide specifically for its termination in stated circumstances:[93] no term can therefore be implied, nor any construction entertained which would allow termination in *other* circumstances.[94] It was this issue which divided the British Columbia Court of Appeal in *McDonald Aviation Co. v. Queen Charlotte Airlines Ltd.*[95] The defendant chartered an airplane from the plaintiff for a period of four weeks. He guaranteed payment for a minimum of 200 flying hours,

---

91 See *Leitch Tpt. Ltd.v. Neonex Int. Ltd.* (1979), 8 B.L.R. 257 (Ont. C.A.). Note the difference of opinion on the issue of foreseeability between Houlden J.A. and Lacourcière J.A. in *Focal Properties Ltd. v. George Wimpey Can. Ltd.* (1975), 73 D.L.R. (3d) 387 (Ont. C.A.); affirmed on other grounds, [1978] 1 S.C.R. 2 (S.C.C.).

92 (1980), 28 O.R. (2d) 326 (Ont. H.C.); quoted and relied on in *111 Niakwa Road Ltd. v. Duraps Corp.* (1985), 37 Man. R. (2d) 250 (Man. Q.B.); additional reasons at (1986), 43 Man. R. (2d) 65 (Man. Q.B.).

93 See, *e.g., Petrogas Processing Ltd. v. Westcoast Transmission Co.*, [1988] 4 W.W.R. 699 (Alta. Q.B.); affirmed (1989), 58 D.L.R. (4th) 156 (Alta. C.A.), where the contract provided that the buyer would be exempt from paying for minimum quantities of natural gas if smaller volumes became necessary by "limitations imposed by law." This applied when federal and provincial legislation introduced price regulation which prevented export of gas by the buyer as originally contemplated. The contract was frustrated.

94 *Cooke v. CKOY Ltd.*, [1963] 2 O.R. 257 (Ont. H.C.). See also *Robbins v. Wilson & Cabeldu Ltd.*, [1944] 3 W.W.R. 625 (B.C.C.A.); note: (1) the refusal to apply the *Fibrosa* case, below, p. 662; (2) in an Editor's note to the report it was suggested that the contract was not frustrated but simply *suspended*: compare above, pp. 382-383 on the question of the effect of war upon contractual relations.

95 [1952] 1 D.L.R. 291 (B.C.C.A.). Note that at this time Canadian courts had adopted the implied term theory: above, p. 629.

whether or not the aircraft was in operation for that length of time. The defendant also agreed to pay a *pro rata* share of the insurance of the aircraft. The airplane crashed in flight before the first instalment of the hiring rent was received by the plaintiff. It was held by Coady J. at first instance that the rent could not be recovered by reason of the doctrine of frustration or impossibility, but the defendant's share of the insurance premiums was still payable. On appeal, the majority of the British Columbia Court of Appeal held that the doctrine of frustration or impossibility, applied to the rent and the premiums. O'Halloran J.A. was prepared to agree with the trial judge that the express terms of the contract precluded any implied term as to discharge of the obligation to pay the insurance premiums on the basis of frustration or impossibility.[96] But Robertson J.A. held that this was not so. In order that an express term or terms should exclude the doctrine they

> ... must make provision (that is, full and complete provision, so intended) for a given contingency, otherwise it is not for the Court to import into the contract some other and different provisions for the same contingency, called by a different name ... The contract must provide for the precise state of affairs ... If it does, then it is impossible to imply in the contract any term or condition inconsistent with its express provision ...[97]

In *Smale v. Van der Weer*[98] a condition precedent in a contract for the sale of land provided that municipal approval was to be obtained for subdivision of the land. The purchaser waived the condition precedent. Later the purchaser attempted to argue that the contract was frustrated when the approval was not obtained. He was not successful in thus avoiding liability. The parties had expressly provided for the possibility that such approval would not be granted. They had contemplated what in fact occurred.[99]

Similarly, the contract may make it clear that there are to be no excuses, or none of the kind now sought to be incorporated by implication or construction into the contract. For example, in one instance,[100] involving a charter of a tug, with provisions as to what was to happen in bad weather, which was foreseeable in the area and at the time in question, it was held that the contract could not be read as involving the inference that the work was to be completed within a specific period, with the consequent implication that if it could not, by reason of bad weather, the contract was terminated. If the contract is one which contemplates, either expressly or inferentially, the very situation which has now emerged and in respect of which it is attempting to invoke the doctrine of frustration, the courts

---

96 [1952] 1 D.L.R. 291 at 295-296 (B.C.C.A.).

97 *Ibid.*, at 305.

98 (1977), 80 D.L.R. (3d) 704 (Ont. H.C.); compare *Focal Properties Ltd. v. George Wimpey Can. Ltd.*, above, note 91.

99 Compare *Cobbold v. Time Can. Ltd.*, above, note 92.

100 *B.C. Mills, Tug & Barge Co. v. Kelley*, [1923] 1 D.L.R. 1015 (B.C.C.A.); see especially the judgment of McPhillips J.A. at 1020-1022. Contrast, as regards the effect of unforeseen bad weather, nor provided for in the contract, *Impala Const. Ltd. v. Wade* (1983), 40 Nfld. & P.E.I.R. 437 (Nfld. Dist. Ct.); compare *Marine Const. Ltd. v. Metro. Enrg. & Const. Ltd.* (1978), 20 Nfld. & P.E.I.R. 504 (Nfld. T.D.).

will not do so.[101] Thus, *Lane v. Lane*[102] concerned the effect of a separation agreement when the husband later retired and his income was thereupon reduced. This did not frustrate the contract to pay maintenance, since this was known by the parties to be a possible future occurrence and was considered by the parties when making the agreement.

(d) Self-induced impossibility

Nor will the doctrine be applied where the party seeking to introduce and rely on any such term has himself brought about the event or occurrence which he now claims as the basis for the termination of the contract.

This notion has a long, and respectable ancestry, since it stems from the doctrine that a party cannot rely on the non-performance of a condition precedent which is the result of his own, blameworthy conduct (that is, a party cannot rely on his own wrongdoing to excuse him from liability).[103] It was first clearly expounded in the context of frustration by the Privy Council in *Maritime National Fish Co. v. Ocean Trawlers Ltd.*[104] in 1935. There a party sought to excuse himself from a charter-party on the basis of his failure to obtain licences for the ships chartered from the other contracting party. While this might have resulted in termination of the charter-party on the basis of impossibility, through supervening illegality, since without the appropriate governmental licences it was not lawful to engage in the enterprise, it was found that the charterer had obtained a number of licences, but not enough to cover *all* his vessels, including the chartered ones. When the charterer allocated the licences to other vessels, and then pleaded frustration because of the non-availability of licences for the chartered ships, it was held that he could not rely on the doctrine because the result was his own fault. He could have used the licences for the chartered ships; in which event there would have been no frustration. What had occurred here was what was termed a "self-induced" frustration, and on that the charterer could not found any exemption from liability.

Similarly, in *McDermid v. Food-Vale Stores (1972) Ltd.*,[105] the inability of the supplier of heat, power and water to fulfil the contract stemmed from the defendant's own failure to install new services when a fire destroyed the furnace and power and water lines which the defendant used to supply what was required under the

---

101 *Galt v. Frank Waterhouse & Co.*, [1944] 1 W.W.R. 657 (B.C.C.A.). Compare on the facts, *Smith v. Johnson Bros. Ltd.*, [1954] 1 D.L.R. 392 (Ont. H.C.). Compare *Elec. Power Equip Ltd. v. R.C.A. Victor Co.* (1964), 49 W.W.R. 193 (B.C.C.A.); *Cobbold v. Time Can. Ltd.*, above, note 92.

102 [1935] 3 W.W.R. 592 (Man. K.B.): compare *May v. May*, [1929] 2 K.B. 386 at 393-394 (C.A.) *per* Scrutton L.J. Compare also *Henuset Bros. Ltd. v. Highland Stock Farms Ltd.*, [1976] W.W.D. 5 (Alta. T.D.), where the term that the goods were "at buyer's risk" prevented the application of the doctrine of frustration.

103 *Commr. of Agricultural Loans of Ont. v. Irwin*, [1942] S.C.R. 196 (S.C.C.): compare, above, pp. 443-446.

104 [1935] A.C. 524 (P.C.); compare *Bank Line Ltd. v. Arthur Capel & Co.*, [1919] A.C. 435 at 452 (H.L.) *per* Lord Sumner. See also *J. Lauritzen A/S v. Wijsmuller B.V.; "Super Servant Two" (The)*, [1990] 1 Lloyd's Rep. 1 (C.A.): on which see Chandler, "Self-Induced Frustration: Foreseeability and Risk" (1990), 41 N. Ireland L.Q. 362.

105 (1980), 25 A.R. 301 (Alta. Q.B.).

contract. Hence, the defendant could not rely on the doctrine of frustration by way of defence to the plaintiff's action for breach of the contract of supply. Nor could a footballer rely on the terms of his contract under which he was guaranteed a salary if he were injured or unable to play, when his inability to play for the club which had promised such payment resulted from the player's undertaking to play for another club. This was a deliberate act on his part which put it out of his power to play for the club employing him under the contract.[106] So, too, in *Church of Scientology of British Columbia v. Ahmed*,[107] a tenant induced the local authority to make an order banning occupancy of the demised premises. Therefore, he could not rely on the ban to establish that the lease had been frustrated. Consequently the tenant was liable to the landlord for damages sustained by reason of the tenant's alterations to the premises. In *S.F. Silver Falcon Holding Co. v. Agricultural Development Corp. of Saskatchewan*[108] the defendant, a Crown corporation, claimed that the purchase of shares in a joint venture was conditional on obtaining approval from the Lieutenant Governor in Council, therefore the contract did not bind the defendant since no approval had been obtained. The plea was unsuccessful. The defendant never applied for the approval. Hence the defendant could not rely on the self-inflicted frustration.

By way of contrast, in *Halifax v. Vaughan Construction Co.*[109] it was held by Currie J. of the Nova Scotia Court of Appeal that a company which had received land under an agreement to erect a "first class building" thereon, was not guilty of self-induced frustration when the land was expropriated by the Crown, even though the company had not hastened to perform its contract with the city. It is clearly a question of fact, therefore, whether the conduct of a party can be construed in such a way as to preclude reliance on the doctrine. The onus of proving a self-induced frustration would seem to be on the party raising such allegations.[110]

(e) Frustration and mistake

What links, or may be considered as linking the contractual doctrines of mistake and frustration, which both involve judicial "intervention" or interpretation,

---

106 *Barton v. Toronto Argonaut Football Club* (1978), 86 D.L.R. (3d) 133 (Ont. H.C.); affirmed (1979), 108 D.L.R. (3d) 152 (Ont. C.A.); affirmed (1982), 134 D.L.R. (3d) 1 (*sub nom. Barton v. Agincourt Football Enterprises Ltd.*) (S.C.C.).

107 (1983), 44 B.C.L.R. 297 (B.C.S.C.).

108 (1990), 81 Sask. R. 195 at 212-213 (Sask Q.B.); compare *Graham v. Wagman* (1978), 21 O.R. (2d) 1 (Ont. C.A.); *Steiner v. E.H.D. Invts. Ltd.* (1977), 78 D.L.R. (3d) 449 (Alta. C.A.).

109 (1957), 9 D.L.R. (2d) 431 (N.S.S.C.); reversed on other grounds (1958), 41 M.P.R. 19 (N.S.C.A.). The other members of the court decided the case on other grounds.

110 *Joseph Constantine S.S. Line Ltd. v. Imperial Smelting Corp.*, [1942] A.C. 154 (H.L.) (alleged negligence by owner causing explosion in boiler of ship, could not be established by charterers, therefore charter-party was frustrated). Is the issue of self-induced frustration to be determined by the degree of control the alleged inducing party has over the events? And is it a question of *deliberate* conduct or of *negligence*? See *Paal Wilson & Co. A/S v. Partenreederei Hannah Blumenthal*, [1983] 1 A.C. 854 at 882 (H.L.); *Cheall v. Association of Professional, Executive, Clerical & Computer Staff*, [1983] 2 A.C. 180 at 188-189 (H.L.); Chandler, *loc. cit.*, above, note 104, at pp. 367-368.

is the idea that the courts are looking, in each instance, albeit in different ways and for different purposes, to discover: (1) what the reasonable man would have understood the parties to be agreeing to when they contracted; (2) what they have omitted to say but must have accepted as the basis or fundamental assumption on which they contracted, such as to render it obvious when any question arises as to what they intended; and (3) whether in all the circumstances, having regard to the language of the parties, the type of contract they made, the facts leading up to the making of the contract, and any other relevant matters, it is just and reasonable for the court to interpret the contract in the manner now being suggested by one of the parties. The difference between these various reasons for inquiring as to what underlies the contractual relationship in issue consists in the purpose for which the inquiry is made, and the varying consequences and effects which result.

The court is anxious to identify the real and true nature of the obligations voluntarily assumed by the parties when they contracted. Indeed, that is its function; it is what the court must do in order to decide what, if any, remedy is available to a party. This involves discovering the express and implied terms of the contract, their meaning, and their interrelation. The muted intentions of the parties, if such they may be called, come into play and require to be discovered and understood in three various situations. The first is when the issue arises whether there is a contract at all. Then the question may be whether one party or both contracted under a fundamental, erroneous assumption which was so vital as to render his or their apparent consent nugatory and lead to the conclusion that there is no contract. The second is when the existence of a contract is undeniable, but there is some question as to its contents. Then serious problems arise as to when and with what effect a party is entitled to add to the express terms of the contract by some suggested implication or inference from the facts and the surrounding circumstances. The third is when the question arises whether frustration has brought the contract to an end prior to, or in the middle of its complete performance by both sides. Then the issue falls to be determined by construction of the contract in the light of a radical change in the obligation, possibly by reference to some "fundamental assumption". It is the first and third of these situations which present the most similarities of technique and even character. In respect of both, the question really is: is there a contract?

Where mistake is involved, the issue is whether there ever *was* a contract. Where it is frustration that is the question, the issue is whether there now *is* a contract. In both situations the court is faced with much the same problem, namely, whether to relieve a party from an obligation which he appears to have accepted and undertaken without qualification, but in respect of which he has discovered something which makes the transaction different from what he imagined it was going to be. What makes the transaction different may have occurred before the transaction, or at the same time (mistake), or subsequently to the transaction (impossibility or frustration).[111]

---

111 See, *e.g.*, *Amalgam. Invt. & Property Co. v. John Walker & Sons Ltd.*, [1976] 3 All E.R. 509 (C.A.).

The provisions of the Sale of Goods Act, which juxtaposes sections dealing with the effect of (1) non-existence of the subject-matter of a sale prior to or at the time of the making of a contract and (2) the later destruction, or perishing of the goods, reveal how, at least in the context of one type of contract, indeed what has been called the "master" contract, there is a close relationship between mistake and frustration, at least where these categories of excuse or exemption from liability stem from the physical destruction of the subject-matter of a contract. It is possible that the statutory provisions with respect to contracts of sale of goods are based upon the idea of construction of the contract which, it has been suggested, are inherent, if not explicit, in the leading case of *Couturier v. Hastie*.[112] If mistake can be said to be, sometimes, if not always, a question of contractual construction: if the existence and scope of a contract is also dependent in some instances at least upon the resolution of questions of construction: and if frustration may be determined also by reference to much the same inquiry, then, it may be suggested, all these seemingly different issues are really only aspects of the same one.

An important question is whether, in any of these situations, the test is really the objective test of the reasonable man, as it is often said to be, or is something more subjective.[113] Furthermore, it may be asked whether the function of the courts, in the final analysis, is really to discover the intent of the parties, by reference to admissible evidence, and the making of the kinds of inferences which it is legitimate for courts to make, or whether it is the substitution of the court's view of what is: (1) just; (2) reasonable; and (3) merited by the circumstances, for what would seem to be the bargain struck by the parties by their language or conduct, and the obligations which they have seemingly chosen for themselves. In posing these questions, we are really at the heart of the law of contract. One of the problems that arises from the complexities of the law relating to mistake and frustration (to say nothing of the law dealing with the construction and interpretation of contracts), is that the courts at various times, and in different jurisdictions, have given vent to contradictory opinions, and confusing statements of principle, from which it is not always clear whether they consistently support and promulgate one view of the law's function or the other. While there is much verbal genuflection at the shrine of objectivity and the "reasonable man" or the "reasonable officious bystander", some of the decisions, and some of the *dicta*, appear to give more encouragement to the view that either the courts are attempting to decide a case in the light of what one particular party, or perhaps both parties, actually had in mind at the material time, or are endeavouring to make a contract for the parties

---

In Swan, "The Allocation of Risk in the Analysis of Mistake and Frustration", in Reiter & Swan, *Studies in Contract Law* (1980), p. 182 at pp. 184-185, note 12, the learned author says that he will later analyze this decision, but apparently fails to do so.

112 (1856), 5 H.L. Cas. 673, 10 E.R. 1065 (H.L.); above, p. 279; compare Fridman, *Sale of Goods in Canada*, 3rd ed. (1986), pp. 60-63.

113 See *Hallmark Pool Corp. v. Storey* (1983), 144 D.L.R. (3d) 56 at 65 (N.B.C.A.) *per* La Forest J.A.; compare the remarks of Corbin, *Treatise on the Law of Contract* (1963), Vol. I, paragraph 106.

which the courts think, even if the parties do not, is a reasonable, fair and just one in the circumstances.[114]

3. The doctrine applied and exemplified

(a) Physical incapacity

That the death of a party determined a contract involving personal confidence was recognized in the sixteenth century in *Hyde v. Dean & Canons of Windsor*.[115] This has been accepted in many such instances, such as agency.[116] The death of a party will not always frustrate a contract made by such party during his lifetime.[117] A leading Canadian case is *Chisholm v. Chisholm*.[118] A testator during his lifetime contracted to pay money to the wife of the testator's son, as long as the testator could do so and while the wife was self-dependent (that is, did not re-marry). The wife had to place her daughter, the testator's granddaughter, in a stipulated educational institution until she finished her education. This the wife did. When the testator died, the question arose whether the obligation to pay the contracted sum of money continued, the granddaughter still being in the institution and the other conditions of payment still being operative. It was argued that the contract was determined by the testator's death. But the court found that, since it was not a personal type of contract, it survived the death of the testator, whose estate was liable on the contract. More recently, in *Witwicki v. Midgley*[119] the plaintiff and her husband assigned their interest in land to their son, who agreed to permit them to live on the land and to provide them with maintenance during their lifetimes. The husband died. Then the son died. The plaintiff, the widow, claimed that the contract was frustrated, therefore she could reclaim the land. The contract was held not to have been frustrated by the son's death. It was a contract involving a financial obligation, which could continue despite the son's death. It was not a contract for personal services that could not outlast the death of the party contracted to provide such services.

---

114 Note, also, the analysis of mistake and frustration in terms of "allocation of risk", see Swan, *loc. cit.*, above, note 111 (and the rejection of this approach in the *Victoria Wood* case above, p. 634); or in terms of economics: see, *e.g.*, Kronman, "Mistake, Disclosure, Information and the Law of Contracts" (1978), 7 J. Leg. Stud. 1; Posner & Rosenfield, "Impossibility and Related Doctrines in Contract Law: An Econmic Analysis" (1977), 6 J. Leg. Stud. 83; and Bruce, "An Economic Analysis of the Impossibility Doctrine" (1982), 11 J. Leg. Stud. 311.

115 (1597), Cro. Eliz. 552, 78 E.R. 798; compare *Grant v. Johnson* (1864), 5 N.S.R. 493 (N.S.C.A.).

116 *Stubbs v. Holywell Ry. Co.* (1867), L.R. 2 Exch. 311; *Graves v. Cohen* (1929), 46 T.L.R. 121; *Harvey v. Tivoli, Manchester, Ltd.* (1907), 23 T.L.R. 592. For cases of agency, see *Blades v. Free* (1829), 9 B. & C. 167, 109 E.R. 63; *Pool v. Pool* (1889), 58 L.J.P. 67; *Tasker v. Shepherd* (1861), 6 H. & N. 575, 158 E.R. 237.

117 *Sifton v. Sweezey*, [1939] 2 W.W.R. 580 (P.C.); *Sweezey v. Beaucharnois Power Corp. Ltd.*, [1939] 2 W.W.R. 574 (P.C.).

118 (1912), 46 N.S.R. 27 (N.S.C.A.); compare *Kirk v. Eustace*, [1937] A.C. 491 (H.L.) for the effect of death of a party promising marriage; see *McBride v. Johnson*, [1962] S.C.R. 202 (S.C.C.).

119 [1976] 6 W.W.R. 471 (Man. Q.B.); affirmed [1979] 5 W.W.R. 242 (Man. C.A.).

Whether illness of a party will operate to terminate a contract will depend upon the nature of the contract and the type of illness. If it is of the kind which renders the contract incapable of performance as agreed, for example, to play as a concert on a particular night, it would seem that frustration takes place.[120] If it does not disrupt the ultimate fulfilment of the contract, a different result will occur.[121] No frustration was held to have occurred in *Lafreniere v. Leduc*.[122] The plaintiff sold his business to the defendant and agreed to work for the defendant for some years. A year or so later the plaintiff, afflicted by arthritis, went south for the winter, being unable to work as agreed. This was held to involve a breach of the agreement, in respect of which the defendant could claim damages (to be set off against a claim by the plaintiff). The plaintiff's attempt to argue frustration on account of his illness failed. In *Dove v. S. & M. Carpet Ltd.*,[123] however, the knee injury to the carpet installer that rendered him permanently incapable to install carpets frustrated the agreement between the parties which created a business in which the installation of carpets was an essential ingredient.

(b) Destruction of subject-matter

Where the continued existence or coming into existence of a specific thing is essential to the performance of the contract, proper construction of the contract requires a finding of frustration in the event of its subsequent non-existence.[124] This is what occurred in the leading cases of *Taylor v. Caldwell*[125] and *Appleby*

---

120 *Robinson v. Davidson* (1871), L.R. 6 Exch. 269; compare *Bettini v. Gye* (1876), 1 Q.B.D. 183; *Poussard v. Speirs* (1876), 1 Q.B.D. 410; compare *Condor v. Barron Knights*, [1966] 1 W.L.R. 87; *Hart v. A.R. Marshall & Sons Ltd.*, [1978] 2 All E.R. 413.

121 *Hall v. Wright* (1859), E.B. & E. 765, 120 E.R. 695; *Storey v. Fulham Steel Works Co.* (1907), 24 T.L.R. 89 (C.A.); *Loates v. Maple* (1903), 88 L.T. 288. Compare as to the effect of conscription, *Morgan v. Manser*, [1948] 1 K.B. 184.

122 (1990), 66 D.L.R. (4th) 577 (Ont. H.C.).

123 (1988), 73 Nfld. & P.E.I.R. 354 (Nfld. T.D.); varied on other grounds (1989), 81 Nfld. & P.E.I.R. 105 (Nfld. T.D.); note the way the trial judge characterized what happened as a fundamental breach that frustrated the contract. Such language is internally contradictory.

124 But knowledge of the existence in question, *i.e.*, its importance in the contract, must be mutual: *Re Badische*, [1921] 2 Ch. 331, relied upon by Chisholm C.J. in *Lieberman v. Roseland Theatre Ltd.*, [1946] 1 D.L.R. 342 (N.S.S.C.). Contrast *Blackburn Bobbin Co. v. T.W. Allen & Sons*, [1918] 2 K.B. 467 (C.A.). Note also that this will not operate if the non-existence is the fault of one party, *i.e.*, is caused by his wilful or negligent conduct: *Joseph Constantine S.S. Ltd. v. Imperial Smelting Corp.*, [1942] A.C. 154 (H.L.). *J. Lauritzen A/S v. Wijsmuller B.V.; "Super Servant Two" (The)*, [1990] 1 Lloyd's Rep. 1 (C.A.); Chandler, *loc. cit.*, above, note 104.

125 (1863), 3 B. & S. 826, 122 E.R. 309. Contrast *Dot Devs. Ltd. v. Fowler* (1980), 118 D.L.R. (3d) 371 (B.S.S.C.) where the destruction of the house by fire did not frustrate the contract. But in *Laurwen Invts. Inc. v. 814693 Northwest Territories Ltd.* (1990), 48 B.L.R. 100 (N.W.T.S.C.), the destruction by fire of video tapes that were loaned by the plaintiff to the defendant resulted in the frustration of the rental contract. Therefore the plaintiff was not entitled to further rental payments (but he was entitled, at common law, and under the statute, below, pp. 661-666, to the value of the videotapes on a *quantum meruit* basis). Compare *Can-Truck Transportation Ltd. v. Fenton's Auto Paint Shop Ltd.* (1993), 101 D.L.R. (4th) 562 (Ont. C.A.), where a truck sent to the defendants was destroyed, along with the defendant's premises, in an accidental fire. The

v. Myers, where fire destroyed premises that were the subject-matter of a contract.[126] The same has been held to result: (1) where a ship was stranded for so long as to render her virtually non-existent as a carrier, although still identifiable;[127] (2) where a ship was detained in a German port during hostilities, so as to render the free use of the ship for the ensuing two years, as contemplated in the contract to pay wages, impossible;[128] (3) where a ship was requisitioned after it had been chartered for one season, making it impossible for the charter to be performed, even though the requisition ceased before the expiry of the season and the parties knew of this possibility;[129] (4) where a boom had been placed across a river, so as to make performance of a charter-party impossible;[130] (5) where the boiler of a ship exploded before the ship could commence service under a charter-party;[131] (6) where land which was the subject of a real estate commission contract was expropriated (which is a kind of *legal* destruction, even though physically the land still exists);[132] and (7) where an office was abolished by statute.[133]

In much the same way, where land became inundated, a duty to provide a road ceased to exist;[134] so, too, where a permanent change in the weather made threshing on stipulated land impossible.[135] But the burning of premises adjoining

---

contract of repair was frustrated. Hence the defendant's remedy under the contract, *viz.*, a right of lien, was subject to the common law of frustration and the Frustrated Contracts Act, R.S.O. 1990, c. F.34: below, pp. 663-666.

126 (1867), L.R. 2 C.P. 651. Compare *Marine Const. Ltd. v. Metro. Enrg. & Const. Ltd.* (1978), 20 Nfld. & P.E.I.R. 504 (Nfld. T.D.) (loss of rented barge by reason of severe storm; rental agreement determined by frustration).

127 *Nickoll & Knight v. Ashton, Edridge & Co.*, [1901] 2 K.B. 126 (C.A.). Compare the situation where a strike at one of the nominated ports in a charter-party interfered with the proper fulfilment of the charter-party: *Pioneer Shipping Ltd. v. B.T.P. Tioxide*, [1981] 2 All E.R. 1030 (H.L.).

128 *Horlock v. Beal*, [1916] 1 A.C. 486 (H.L.).

129 *Bank Line v. Arthur Capel & Co.*, [1919] A.C. 435 (H.L.); contrast *Tamplin S.S. Co. v. Anglo-Mexican Petroleum Co.*, [1916] 2 A.C. 397 (H.L.); compare, however, *Tatem, Ltd. v. Gamboa*, [1939] 1 K.B. 132.

130 *Court Line Ltd. v. Dant & Russell Inc.*, [1939] 3 All E.R. 314; contrast *Ashmore & Son v. C.S. Cox & Co.*, [1899] 1 Q.B. 436; *Australian Dispatch Line v. Anglo-Can. Shipping Co.*, [1940] 2 W.W.R. 266 (B.C.C.A.).

131 The *Constantine* case above, note 124.

132 *Oxford Realty Ltd. v. Annette*, [1961] O.W.N. 316 (Ont. H.C.); compare *Baily v. De Crespigny* (1869), L.R. 4 Q.B. 180; contrast *Goulding v. Rabinovitch*, [1927] 3 D.L.R. 820 (Ont. C.A.). Compare also *Some Fine Invts. Ltd. v. Ertolahti* (1991), 107 N.S.R. (2d) 1 (N.S.T.D.); additional reasons at (1991), 107 N.S.R. (2d) 1 at 4 (N.S.T.D.), where a barn that was to be moved from property sold to the defendant was declared to be heritage property, not to be disturbed. The contract was frustrated. On frustration in relation to contracts about interests in land, see below, pp. 658-661.

133 *Reilly v. R.*, [1934] A.C. 176 (P.C.), but contrast the situation where a statute was repealed, in *St. Catharines v. H.E.P.C.*, [1928] 1 D.L.R. 598 (Ont. H.C.); affirmed [1928] 3 D.L.R. 200 (Ont. C.A.); which was affirmed [1930] 1 D.L.R. 409 (P.C.); and where the defendant's licence to distribute lottery tickets was cancelled, the defendant could still employ the plaintiff in some other way: *Luchuck v. Sport B.C.* (1984), 52 B.C.L.R. 145 (B.C.S.C.); supplementary reasons at (1984), 53 B.C.L.R. 143 (B.C.S.C.).

134 *Kerrigan v. Harrison* (1921), 62 S.C.R. 374 (S.C.C.); compare *Cahan v. Fraser*, [1951] 4 D.L.R. 112 (B.C.C.A.).

135 *Klein v. Sanderson*, [1928] 2 W.W.R. 289 (Alta. C.A.).

a stall in a market did not affect the contract of lease of the stall, even though it was contemplated that the defendant, the stall-holder, and other tenants would be making use of the adjoining premises.[136]

(c) Change of law

The state of the law at the time the parties made the contract is considered to have been in the parties' contemplation; hence, any subsequent change rendering performance legally impossible (even though it might be physically possible) may allow a court to hold the contract frustrated.[137] Thus, in a leading case, *Baily v. De Crespigny*,[138] a party covenanted for himself and his assigns only to erect ornamental buildings on a paddock. A railway company compulsorily purchased the paddock under an Act passed 20 years after the contract in question was first made. On the paddock the railway company built a station. It was held that the covenant was discharged by change in the law (and that the word "assigns" in the contract did not cover a purchaser like the railway company which acquired by compulsion). This was applied in the Canadian case of *Oxford Realty Ltd. v. Annette*,[139] where property was expropriated while it was in the hands of a real estate commission agent who was selling it on behalf of the owner-vendor. Since this happened before anything could be done on the owner's behalf by the agent to produce an offer to purchase, it was held that the contract of agency was frustrated, and no commission was payable to the agent. Expropriation did not have a similar effect, however, in the older case of *Goulding v. Rabinovitch*,[140] which concerned land subject to an option to purchase. This was because, according to Middleton J.A., in the meantime the plaintiff had had the benefit of the option, and the defendant, the vendor, had suffered detriment in that he had been unable to deal freely with the land.

A change made by the British Columbia Ministry of Education in the contents of a curriculum frustrated a contract to prepare a textbook based on the old curriculum in *Cassidy v. Canada Publishing Corporation.*[141] Similarly, in *Petrogas Processing Ltd. v. Westcoast Transmission Co.*[142] the introduction of price regulation into the natural gas industry by federal and provincial legislation brought into effect

---

136 *Merkur v. H. Shoom & Co. Ltd.*, [1954] O.W.N. 55 (Ont. C.A.). Compare *Impala Const. Ltd. v. Wade* (1983), 40 Nfld. & P.E.I.R. 437 (Nfld. Dist. Ct.) (effect of extreme wet weather, and act of God, on contract to perform road services including bulldozing).

137 Note that changes in planning law or in zoning arrangements may not always result in frustration: compare *Capital Quality Homes Ltd. v. Colwyn Const. Ltd.* (1975), 61 D.L.R. (3d) 385 (Ont. C.A.) with *Victoria Wood Dev. Corp. v. Ondrey* (1978), 92 D.L.R. (3d) 229 (Ont. C.A.); leave to appeal to S.C.C. refused (1979), 26 N.R. 267 (S.C.C.); *Cairns Homes Ltd. v. Jerol Invts. Ltd.* (1983), 25 Sask. R. 305 (Sask. Q.B.); below, p. 660.

138 (1869), L.R. 4 Q.B. 180; contrast *Walton Harvey Ltd. v. Walker & Homfrays Ltd.*, [1931] 1 Ch. 274 (C.A.).

139 [1961] O.W.N. 316 (Ont. H.C.). Compare the treatment of a barn as heritage property and its effect on the contract in *Some Fine Invts. Ltd. v. Ertolahti*, above, note 132.

140 [1927] 3 D.L.R. 820 (Ont. C.A.); compare *Fong v. Kerwin*, [1929] 3 D.L.R. 612 (Ont. C.A.).

141 (1989), 41 B.L.R. 223 (B.C.S.C.).

142 (1988), 59 Alta. L.R. (2d) 118 (Alta. Q.B.); affirmed (1989), 58 D.L.R. (4th) 156 (Alta. C.A.).

a term in a contract under which the buyer of natural gas was not obliged to take minimum quantities of the gas. This was because the change in price prevented the export of gas by the buyer as originally contemplated by the parties. In contrast a freeze by Canada Mortgage and Housing Corporation on financing, the deterioration of the housing market, and the decline in the availability of M.U.R.B.'s after the making of a contract involving a joint venture agreement to develop M.U.R.B.'s as a tax shelter housing project did not have the effect of frustrating that contract so as to permit unilateral withdrawal by the defendant.[143] So, too, in *110843 Canada Ltée v. Canada*,[144] the inaction of the Quebec Transport Commission, among other reasons, made performance of a contract relating to car rental services at airports more difficult, but not impossible.

If the purpose of the contract is still *legally* possible, as well as physically, no frustration will occur. This is what happened in *Claude Neon General Advertising Ltd. v. Sing*,[145] in which the sign could still be shown as it was not illuminated, and the law only affected illuminations.

In one sense the cases in which "property" of a non-material kind, for example, a public office,[146] has been abolished by legislation subsequent to a contract which dealt with such property, could be regarded as instances of impossibility or frustration by virtue of a change in the law. They are also instances of destruction of the subject-matter of the contract, since, although the destruction was by law, and not by physical acts or events, the practical effect is the same.

(d) Supervening illegality

While this appears to be much the same type of frustration as by change in the law, there are differences. Thus, a change in the law may make it utterly impossible for something to be done, if it involves any kind of legal transaction. Supervening illegality, for example, a statute or proclamation making trading with an enemy in time of war illegal, renders the act or contract illegal, but not impossible to perform. Furthermore, it has been pointed out[147] that this kind of frustration operates as a rule of law, not of construction. It is based not upon the implied will or intentions of the parties (who may indeed wish or desire to continue to trade, despite the fact of war and the illegality of their intended transaction), but upon the doctrine of public policy.[148]

The effect of war upon contracts is subject to some dispute.[149] There may be situations in which the contract is not frustrated, even though the law makes

---

143 *111 Niakwa Road Ltd. v. Duraps Corp.* (1985), 37 Man. R. (2d) 250 (Man. Q.B.); additional reasons at (1986), 43 Man. R. (2d) 65 (Man. Q.B.).

144 (1988), 28 F.T.R. 1 (Fed. T.D.). See also *Mr. Convenience Ltd. v. 040502 N.B. Ltd.* (1992), 129 N.B.R. (2d) 36 (N.B.Q.B.); reversed in part (August 6, 1993), Doc. 231/92/CA (N.B.C.A.), where a change in regulations about video lottery terminals did not frustrate the contract in issue.

145 [1942] 1 D.L.R. 26 (N.S.S.C.).

146 *E.g., Reilly v. R.*, above, note 133.

147 The *Constantine* case above, note 124, at 163 *per* Lord Simon L.C.

148 Above, pp. 370-372.

149 Above, pp. 382-383.

trading with the enemy illegal. As was held in one Canadian case, *Bayer Co. v. Farbenfabriken*,[150] if there is no benefit to, or intercourse with the enemy, there will be no frustration. In that case there was an executory contract to pay an annual sum to a foreign corporation, so as to prevent its competition in a particular market and to oblige it to supply goods. This was not determined by the outbreak of war between Canada and Germany, which was the home of the foreign corporation, as a result of which the corporation became a foreign enemy. Statute required the payment of the money to the Custodian of Enemy Property. This was still possible, and legal. Hence the contract continued in effect. It would seem, also, that some contracts, if not necessarily injurious, may have their operation merely suspended during hostilities.[151] But if the contract might do injury to the public if it were kept in existence, even if suspended, then the outbreak of war and the illegality of the transaction as a consequence may result in the total abrogation of the contract.[152]

(e) Disappearance of sole object of contract

The origins of this kind of frustration in the "coronation" cases has been described.[153] There can be little doubt that these decisions have been cited and applied in Canadian courts. There can be equally little doubt that no attempt has been made by those courts to analyze those cases and seek to discover upon what principles or theories they are based. In no Canadian decision has anything like "frustration of purpose", at any rate as it emerged in the coronation cases, been involved. Perhaps the nearest instances are those in which what occurred was a significant financial change in the surrounding circumstances, for example, the impecuniosity of a party,[154] the rise in costs which made a transaction less economical or profitable,[155] or the inability of a party to obtain a requisite loan.[156]

---

150 [1944] O.R. 305 (Ont. H.C.); affirmed [1944] O.R. 488 (Ont. C.A.); compare also the situation with respect to the payment of money under a separation agreement to an "enemy" wife in *Bevan v. Bevan*, [1955] 2 Q.B. 227.

151 *Schering Ltd. v. Stockholms Enskilda Bank*, [1946] A.C. 219 (H.L.); compare *Arab Bank Ltd. v. Barclay's Bank*, [1954] A.C. 495 (H.L.).

152 *Ertel Bieber & Co. v. Rio Tinto Co.*, [1918] A.C. 260 (H.L.). In the Australian case of *Codelfa Const. Pty Ltd. v. State Rail Authority of New South Wales* (1982), 56 A.L.J.R. 800 (Aust. H.C.) the performance of the contract was impeded (but not made completely impossible) by the fact that certain residents where the contracted work was to be done obtained injunctions on the ground of nuisance, preventing work at certain times and on certain days. This was held to frustrate the original contract, entitling the contractor to claim for extra work on a *quantum meruit* basis: contrast *Peter Kiewit Sons' Co. v. Eakins Const. Co.*, [1960] S.C.R. 361 (S.C.C.).

153 Above, pp. 626-627.

154 *Tingley v. McKeen*, [1954] 4 D.L.R. 392 (N.B.C.A.); *Graham v. Wagman* (1976), 73 D.L.R. (3d) 667 (Ont. H.C.); reversed on other grounds (1978), 89 D.L.R. (3d) 282 (Ont. C.A.).

155 *Swanson Const. Co. v. Govt. of Man.* (1963), 43 W.W.R. 385 (Man. C.A.); affirmed (1964), 47 W.W.R. 640 (S.C.C.); *Peter Kiewit Sons' Co. v. Eakins Const. Co.*, above, note 152; *Elec. Power Equip. Ltd. v. R.C.A. Victor Co.* (1964), 41 D.L.R. (2d) 727 (B.C.S.C.); varied (1964), 46 D.L.R. (2d) 722 (B.C.C.A.); *Acadia Forest Products Ltd. v. Neal Forest Products Ltd.* (1983), 48 N.B.R. (2d) 429 (N.B.Q.B.); *Luchuck v. Sport B.C.* (1984), 52 B.C.L.R. 145 (B.C.S.C.); supplementary reasons at (1984), 53 B.C.L.R. 143 (B.C.S.C.); *Smith v. Tamblyn (Alta.) Ltd.* (1979), 9 Alta. L.R. (2d) 274 (Alta. T.D.).

The argument was put forward that such change either went to the root of the contract, or effectively made the purpose of the transaction disappear. In either event the contract ought to be frustrated. This met with no success. Canadian courts, and in this respect they would seem to be responding in much the same way as English ones,[157] have taken the view that it is not enough to point to the potential loss or unprofitability of a transaction in the light of altered circumstances.[158] The purpose can still be fulfilled. Hence the contract remains unaffected. Motive and object are not the same. Only the frustration of the latter will have legal effect.

However, by the application of the "radical change in the obligation" theory, as set out by Lord Radcliffe in the *Davis Contractors* case,[159] the Ontario Court of Appeal was able to hold the contract frustrated in *Capital Quality Homes Ltd. v. Colwyn Construction Ltd.*,[160] where something akin to "frustration of purpose", or the disappearance of the sole object of the contract occurred. The plaintiff agreed to buy 26 building lots from the defendant. The contract provided 26 separate deeds of conveyance as the purchaser, the plaintiff, was buying the lots with the intention of erecting homes on them, and then selling each home by a separate conveyance. Both parties were aware of this intention. Subsequently, the Ontario Planning Act was amended, in such a way as to prevent the conveyance of the 26 deeds without consent from the relevant committee of adjustment. The plaintiff claimed the return of his deposit. The Court of Appeal, affirming the trial judge, held that this was recoverable because the contract had been frustrated. Once the court determined that the doctrine of frustration was applicable to a contract relating to land,[161] it went on to consider whether the doctrine should be invoked in the circumstances of this case. It was held that in this instance there had been a clear "frustration of the common venture" into which the parties had entered by this contract.[162] Such a result was not possible, however, where the parties had expressly provided for what was to happen in the event that municipal approval for the subdivision of the land was not obtained.[163] Nor was it possible where there was

---

156 *R. v. Guildwood Nursing Home Ltd.*, [1970] Ex. C.R. 298 (Ex. Ct.).

157 See *Davis Contractors Ltd. v. Fareham Urban Dist. Council*, [1956] A.C. 696 (H.L.). But see the different view taken by the High Court of Australia in *Codelfa Const. Pty. Ltd. v. State Rail Authority of New South Wales* (1982), 56 A.L.J.R. 800 (Aust. H.C.), criticized by Swanton (1983), 57 Aust. L.J. 201.

158 Compare what was said by Kelly J., at first instance, in *Samuel v. Black Lake Asbestos & Chrome Co.* (1920), 58 D.L.R. 270 at 276 (Ont. C.A.); varied (1921), 62 S.C.R. 472 (S.C.C.).

159 Above, note 157, at 729; above, p. 634.

160 (1975), 61 D.L.R. (3d) 385 (Ont. C.A.); compare *Focal Properties.Ltd. v. George Wimpey Can. Ltd.* (1975), 73 D.L.R. (3d) 387 (Ont. C.A.); affirmed [1978] 1 S.C.R. 2 (S.C.C.). See also *Summers Transport Ltd. v. G.M. Smith Ltd.* (1990), 82 Nfld. & P.E.I.R. 1 (Nfld. T.D.), which applied the *Capital Quality Homes* case where it became impossible to fit the rented trailer on the ship that was to transport it to Newfoundland. It was particularly relevant that the contractual obligations of the lessor of the trailer extended to supervision of the loading of the trailer in Montreal as well as its discharge from the ship in Newfoundland. In view of the trailer's size, none of this could be done.

161 Below, pp. 658-661.

162 Above, note 160, at 398.

163 *Smale v. Van der Weer* (1977), 80 D.L.R. (3d) 704 (Ont. H.C.).

no such "common venture". That was the situation in *Victoria Wood Development Corporation v. Ondrey.*[164] The mere knowledge of the vendor in that case that land was being bought for development, or even for a particular kind of development, was insufficient to bring into operation the doctrine of frustration when an entirely unexpected governmental enactment made the purchaser's purpose incapable of realization, or so difficult that great hardship was occasioned to the purchaser in carrying out that purpose.[165] What emerges from these cases, once again, is that there is a considerable difference between the motive of one, or both of the parties in entering into the contract alleged to have been frustrated by the unforeseen event, and their mutual or common intention in making the contract. Frustration of, or an impediment to, the former will not have any legal effect. Frustration of the latter may well result in the termination of the parties' obligations.

It is not hard to see why courts are, and should be cautious when accepting or applying a doctrine of "frustration of purpose". It would be all too easy to permit a party to slip out of a bargain or obligation that no longer was as valuable or worthwhile to him. Yet that is the kind of chance that a party presumably accepts when contracting. If it can be said genuinely that the foundation, root, or fundamental assumption underlying the contract has disappeared, so that it would be both fruitless and frustrating to continue to be bound by the contract, then it is reasonable to treat the contract as determined. Even though this involves the courts in discovering (somehow or other) what is the true "object" or "purpose" of the contract, it is suggested that the attitude of the law is not unreasonable.[166]

(f) Delay amounting to commercial frustration

Various events may occur subsequently upon the making of a contract, interfere with its proper performance, and cause delays. There might be: physical manifestations, such as storms, floods, etc.; human activity such as strikes; governmental regulation which prevents continuation with the work in question; or the outbreak of war which makes it impossible to deliver goods from one country to another, or, as resulted from the events of 1956, closes a normal shipping route, such as the Suez Canal, with all the ensuing delays that came about from that historic event. If such an event holds up performance of the contract for a limited period, the contract may not be frustrated, even if the length of the period is unforeseeable or incalculable. An infinite delay, or one which would mean that the performance of the contract would not occur on the contracted date, has frequently been held to result in frustration. Indeed such instances were the paradigm cases of

---

164 (1978), 92 D.L.R. (3d) 229 (Ont. C.A.); leave to appeal to S.C.C. refused (1979), 26 N.R. 267 (S.C.C.). Compare *Amalgamated Invt. & Property Co. v. J. Walker & Sons Ltd.*, [1976] 3 All E.R. 509.

165 Above note 164, at 241.

166 Compare the remarks of Bingham L.J. in *J. Lauritzen A/S v. Wijsmuller B.V.; "Super Servant Two" (The)*, [1990] 1 Lloyd's Rep. 1 at 6 (C.A.): above, note 73.

"frustration", as contrasted with impossibility. They have lent their name to the whole doctrine.[167]

For example, in *Metropolitan Water Board v. Dick, Kerr & Co.*[168] a contract to build a reservoir in six years contained a proviso for extension of time in case of delay. In World War I the Ministry of Munitions stopped all work on the part of the builders of the reservoir and seized their plant. The House of Lords held that this delay was outside the contemplation of the parties in their contract, and that changes in the costs of labour and material in the intervening period would make any resumption of work later, in substance, the performance of a "new" contract. Hence, the contract was discharged on the basis of frustration. But in the *Tamplin* case,[169] in which a ship under charter was requisitioned by the Government for use as a troopship in World War I, a majority of the House of Lords held that this delay did not frustrate anything, that is, did not interfere with the "commercial adventure". There was nothing which was going to be achieved by the contract, save the payment of freight, which could still have been performed. In much the same way, in *Tsakiroglou & Co. v. Noblee & Thorl G.m.b.H.*,[170] which arose out of the closure of the Suez Canal in 1956, the House of Lords held that the new route for delivery, via the Cape of Good Hope, with resultant extra time, expense, etc., instead of through the Canal, was not so radically different a performance. Nor was it going to frustrate the commercial adventure, since no delivery date had been fixed by the contract and no particular route had been determined. In *National Carriers Ltd. v. Panalpina (Northern) Ltd.*,[171] the House of Lords held that the closure of a street giving access to the warehouse which the defendants had leased for ten years from the plaintiffs did not frustrate the contract. Although the effect of the local authority's action in closing the street meant that for two years out of the ten the defendants would lose the use of the warehouse, thereby severely disrupting their business, the closure of access to the warehouse was not sufficiently grave to amount to frustration. The defendants would still have three years' use of the lease and the warehouse after access was re-established. The defendants therefore had no defence to an action by the plaintiffs for unpaid rent. In *Finelvet A.G. v. Vinava Shipping Co.*,[172] charterers under a time charter-party argued that the war between Iraq and Iran frustrated the charter-party. This was because the effect of the war was to make the Shatt al-Arab river, where the ship was to dock at Basrah, dangerous for shipping. Mustill J., dismissing an appeal from an arbitrator, held that the contract was not frustrated. There was a rebuttable presumption that a state of war would continue for an indefinite period. But it depended on the circumstances whether the effects of the war frustrated

---

167 Above, p. 626.
168 [1918] A.C. 119 (H.L.); compare *Denny, Mott & Dickson Ltd. v. Fraser & Co.*, [1944] A.C. 265 (H.L.).
169 *Tamplin S.S. Co. v. Anglo-Mexican Petroleum Co.*, [1916] 2 A.C. 397 (H.L.).
170 [1962] A.C. 93 (H.L.). Compare and contrast *Carapanayoti & Co. v. Green Ltd.*, [1959] 1 Q.B. 131; *Société Franco-Tunisienne D'Armement v. Sidermar S.P.A.*, [1961] 2 Q.B. 278; *Ocean Tramp Tankers Corp. v. V/O Sovfracht*, [1964] 2 Q.B. 226 (C.A.).
171 [1981] 1 All E.R. 161 (H.L.). Compare below, p. 661.
172 [1983] 2 All E.R. 658.

performance of the contract. There was no automatic frustration of a contract when a war broke out in this area.[173] But in *Pioneer Shipping Ltd. v. B.T.P. Tioxide Ltd.*,[174] a strike at a port from which cargo was to be carried from Canada to ports in Europe was held to frustrate a charter-party of the ship carrying the cargo. Seven voyages were contemplated for the season in issue. One had been completed before the strike. In consequence of the strike only two more were possible. Performance of three out of seven contemplated voyages was held by an arbitrator to amount to something radically different from what had been agreed to originally by the owners. This was ultimately upheld by the Court of Appeal, with whom the House of Lords agreed.

It would seem, therefore, that the effect of delay is dependent upon: (1) what were the terms and obligations of the contract; (2) how serious was the delay; and (3) whether its effect is to render the original contract futile, or change its nature so that it is now something utterly different, if performed, from what was contemplated.

Some Canadian cases, in which, through wind or weather, strikes and slow workmanship, performance of a contract has been delayed, have not been too ready to apply the doctrine of frustration.[175] In one instance, *George Eddy Co. v. Noble Corey & Son*,[176] railway strikes and forest fires delayed the performance of a contract to manufacture and deliver lumber by a stipulated date. It was held, however, that these were not the true reasons for the defendant's failure to perform. The defendant had failed to act diligently and was unwilling to perform his contractual obligation. Hence he could not plead "frustration" as the reason for the delay, and was liable for breach of contract. However, the strike which led to the closure of the defendants' business in *O'Connell v. Harkema Express Lines Ltd.*,[177] was considered to have frustrated the contract under which the plaintiff was employed by the defendants as their sales manager. The closure of the business through the strike was not within the contemplation of the parties and radically altered their original agreement. Hence, the defendants were not liable for the alleged wrongful dismissal of the plaintiff (although they were liable for unpaid salary for the months when the strike was on and the business had not been closed).

Three more recent discussions also illustrate that delay sometimes, but not always, affects a contract significantly enough to justify its frustration. In *Bell Island*

---

173 See the discussion of *Geipel v. Smith* (1872), L.R. 7 Q.B. 404; *Horlock v. Beal*, [1916] 1 A.C. 486 (H.L.); *Bank Line Ltd. v. Arthur Capel & Co.*, [1919] A.C. 435 (H.L.); *Denny, Mott & Dickson Ltd. v. Frazer & Co.*, above, note 168; above, note 172, at 664-668.

174 [1981] 2 All E.R. 1030 (H.L.).

175 *B.C. Mills, Tug & Barge Co. v. Kelley*, [1923] 1 W.W.R. 597 (B.C.C.A.); *Can. Govt. Merchant Marine Ltd. v. Can. Trading Co.* (1922), 64 S.C.R. 106 (S.C.C.).

176 [1951] 4 D.L.R. 90 (N.B.C.A.).

177 (1982), 141 D.L.R. (3d) 291 (Ont. Co. Ct.); compare *Ziger v. Shiffer & Hillman Co.*, [1933] 2 D.L.R. 691 (Ont. C.A.), strike which produced a breakdown of law and order frustrated a contract. See also *MacMillan Bloedel Ltd. v. B.C. Hydro & Power Authority* (1992), 72 B.C.L.R. (2d) 273 (B.C.C.A.), on the meaning of "strike" in a *force majeur* clause (it included unofficial strikes and strikes for political purposes): see also *Fishery Products Int. Ltd. v. Midland Transport Ltd.* (1992), 100 Nfld. & P.E.I.R. 222 (Nfld. T.D.).

Fisheries Ltd. v. Ishiwata Trading Co.[178] the contract in issue was one under which the defendant undertook to buy fish from the plaintiff. The fish were to be sold to customers of the defendant. Therefore, prior to buying any fish, they had to be inspected by an inspector on behalf of the customers. One such inspector was assaulted at the plaintiff's plant. This led to a refusal by the defendant to buy the plaintiff's fish for a period of one and one-half days, until a new inspection could take place. The plaintiff alleged that the defendant was in breach of contract. The court held that the defendant was not liable. The circumstances resulted in the suspension of performance of the contract.[179] In *Boligomsetning AS v. Terpstra Management Ltd.*[180] bad weather prevented timely delivery of pulpwood under a supply contract. Although there was a *force majeur* clause in the contract it did not provide for any extension of the time for delivery, which the supplier agreed was the case. Instead the contract was frustrated. However, in *Canwest Pacific Television Inc. v. 147250 Canada Ltd.*,[181] delay by the C.R.T.C. in rendering a decision was not a supervening event that frustrated the contract, entitling the defendant to refuse to perform the agreements.

There are conflicting decisions with respect to the failure of a party to obtain approval for development plans for property that was the subject-matter of a sale. Whether the delay resulting from the inability of a party to obtain such approval can frustrate the contract of sale may depend upon whether time was of the essence of the agreement.[182] In *Allen Heights Development Ltd. v. Ralph Mitchell Ltd.*,[183] time was not stated to be of the essence of a contract of sale of a lot. The developer who sold the lot promised to deliver a warranty deed to the plaintiff-purchaser within 90 days after the transaction was approved by the Planning Board. For five years the developer tried to get such approval. He failed. He then sought to have the contract rescinded for frustration. He was unsuccessful. The contract was not frustrated because the parties could have contemplated that the sale would be determined by failure to obtain the necessary approval, but they had not so provided. On the other hand, time was said to be of the essence of the contract of sale of land in *Focal Properties Ltd. v. George Wimpey (Canada) Ltd.*[184] Approval of the purchaser's plan to subdivide the property was required from the appropriate authority. The purchaser had to obtain registration of the plan. The vendor was to provide the necessary servicing of the land. The closing date of the transaction was five years from the date of the agreement, or some other date that was mutually acceptable. The plaintiff could not get registration of his plan, despite his efforts to do so, by the closing date originally agreed between the parties. He elected to treat the contract as terminated and sued for the return of his deposit. He was

---

178 (1986), 59 Nfld. & P.E.I.R. 345 (Nfld. T.D.).

179 This meant that the contract was not discharged by frustration, a distinction drawn by the Ontario Law Reform Commission, *Report on Amendment of the Law of Contract* (1987), pp. 271, 275, 278.

180 (1989), 75 Nfld. & P.E.I.R. 239 (Nfld. T.D.).

181 (1988), 30 B.C.L.R. (2d) 145 (B.C.C.A.).

182 On which see above, pp. 525-529.

183 (1974), 17 N.S.R. (2d) 667 (N.S.S.C.).

184 (1975), 73 D.L.R. (3d) 387 (Ont. C.A.); affirmed on other grounds, [1978] 1 S.C.R. 2 (S.C.C.).

able to do so, but in the Ontario Court of Appeal different grounds for this decision were given by Jessup and Houlden JJ.A. who made up the majority. Jessup J.A. depended more on the doctrine of conditions precedent for his decision in favour of the purchaser.[185] Houlden J.A. thought that the basis of the purchaser's claim was frustration. The delay was not foreseeable. And the fact that delay made the contract impossible to fulfil within the originally stipulated five years amounted to frustration.

Just as the courts have been chary of declaring a contract frustrated on the basis or ground of disappearance of the "sole object" or purpose of the contract, so they have been careful not to create the impression that any delay that can be attributed to causes beyond the control of a party should justify giving relief from a contractual obligation on the basis of the doctrine of frustration. The interference must be substantial; the event must not be trivial; the consequences must be significant.

(g) Sale of goods

Special mention and consideration must be given to cases involving contracts for the sale of goods. This is because the question of frustration or impossibility is dealt with, to a limited extent, by the provisions of the Sale of Goods Act. Where there is an agreement to sell specific goods, and subsequently the goods, without any fault on the part of the seller or buyer, perish before the risk passes to the buyer, the agreement is thereby avoided.[186] This only provides for the case where the goods themselves disappear, that is, are destroyed wholly or in part. Furthermore, it only applies where the sale is of specific goods. Hence, if what is being sold is something generic, for example, 100 tons of potatoes, as opposed to something specific, for example, my Lincoln Continental, licence plate No. . . ., then it would appear that the statute does not apply: nor does the doctrine of frustration, unless the parties contemplated that the goods were to be of a special kind, or emanate from a special place, which has now become impossible.[187]

This is what caused the dissension in the Ontario Court of Appeal in *Parrish & Heimbecker Ltd. v. Gooding Lumber Ltd.*[188] A contract provided for the sale of corn. The defendant intended to obtain the corn in a certain locality, though this was not specified in the contract. Because of a drought in the area there was not enough corn produced in the area in question to satisfy the requirements of the contract. When the defendant was sued for non-delivery, he attempted to plead frustration. It was held by a majority of the court that since he had not put the particular source of the corn in the contract, he was liable for failing to deliver,

---

185 Above, pp. 437-443.
186 Sale of Goods Act, R.S.O. 1990, c. S.1, s. 8; for other provinces, see Fridman, *Sale of Goods in Canada*, 3rd ed. (1986), pp. 4-5. For discussion of the section, see *ibid.*, pp. 59-65, 299-308. For criticism of the Act, see the Ontario Law Reform Commission, *Report on Sale of Goods*, 1979, Vol. II, pp. 365-368.
187 *Sanschagrin v. Echo Flour Mills Co.*, [1922] 3 W.W.R. 694 (Man. C.A.).
188 (1968), 67 D.L.R. (2d) 495 (Ont. C.A.).

whatever his intention might have been. Laskin J.A., as he then was, dissented. In his opinion there had been a failure of a material assumption underlying the contract.[189] It is suggested however, that this approach was unwarranted, in the light of earlier decisions and general theory, since the defendant never made it known to the plaintiff, nor had it accepted, that his source was to be of a specific kind. In contrast, there are cases when what Laskin J.A. had in mind was the situation, with a very different result.[190]

If the alleged frustrating event is not a failure of the goods which are the subject-matter of the contract, but something else, for example, the failure to obtain a requisite licence or permission from a government,[191] the situation will be regulated by the common law, not the Act. Similarly, where some intervening event makes the performance of the contract illegal. In such cases, the purpose of the contract is frustrated or it is affected by supervening illegality, or, sometimes, there is some other physical reason why the contract cannot be performed.[192] The normal principles and rules will apply to determine whether or not the contract is ended by reason of frustration.

Mention should be made of the argument that, where the Act applies, that is, in the case of physical destruction or perishing of the goods, all that is meant is that the court must decide as a matter of construction whether the contract is avoided. According to this line of reasoning, the contract may still subsist, if it was contemplated by the parties that the goods might not exist, or the seller's or buyer's undertaking was a more absolute one, or could be taken as a representation, even a condition or warranty, that the goods would exist, or that the party in question would be liable even if the goods did not exist at the material time. While this point of view has been strenuously argued, it would appear that there is no fundamental authority supporting it. On the contrary, the language of the Act is intended to be mandatory and of general application in the envisaged circumstances.

(h) Land

Courts in England[193] and Canada[194] originally took the view that, without express provision for relief from liability or obligation, a party would still be bound by a contract relating to land, whether a contract of sale or a lease, when there was an alleged frustrating event, such as that which occurred in *Paradine v. Jane*.[195] In 1945 the House of Lords held that the outbreak of war did not terminate a

---

189 *Ibid.*, at 498.
190 *Howell v. Coupland* (1876), 1 Q.B.D. 258 (C.A.); *Appleby v. Myers* (1867), L.R. 2 C.P. 651; *H.R. & S. Sainsbury Ltd. v. Street*, [1972] 3 All E.R. 1127.
191 *Mayer & Lage Inc. v. Atlantic Sugar Refineries Ltd.*, [1926] 2 D.L.R. 783 (Ont. H.C.).
192 *Holland Amer. Metal Corp. v. Goldblatt*, [1953] O.R. 112 (Ont. C.A.); *Vancouver Milling & Grain Co. v. C.C. Ranch Co.*, [1924] S.C.R. 671 (S.C.C.).
193 *Redmond v. Dainton*, [1920] 2 K.B. 256; *Matthey v. Curling*, [1922] 2 A.C. 180 (H.L.); *Swift v. MacBean*, [1942] 1 K.B. 375; *Eyre v. Johnson*, [1946] K.B. 481.
194 See the cases cited below, notes 198, 199.
195 (1647), Aleyn 26; above, p. 624.

lease for 99 years.[196] They did not decide affirmatively, however, one way or the other whether under any circumstances the doctrine of frustration could apply to proprietary interests.[197] Post-1945 Canadian cases involving leases[198] and such other proprietary interests as options[199] indicated that the contract would survive and would continue to bind the parties whatever happened (unless something different were expressed in the contract). The only suggestion to the contrary, before and after 1945, is to be found in *Cooke v. Moore.*[200] Applying the earlier language of Duff J. in *Vancouver Breweries Ltd. v. Dana,*[201] it was held that a lease could be terminated where the fundamental assumption underlying the contract disappeared, that is, became impossible to fulfil. In the *Cooke* case, drought, dust storms, and similar events rendered the whole purpose of a lease of land on the prairies incapable of fulfilment. It was held that the lease could be dealt with under the modern doctrine of frustration.

To such an extent was the case law antagonistic to the application of the doctrine of frustration to interests in land that some provincial legislatures enacted legislation under which the idea of frustration could be applied to residential tenancies.[202] Commercial premises, however, did not come within the scope of such legislation. Hence, until recently, there was considerable uncertainty as to the state of the law.

Some indication of the ultimate direction in which the law was to go can be found in the judgment of Laskin J. in *Highway Properties Ltd. v. Kelly, Douglas*

---

196 *Cricklewood, Property & Invt. Trust Ltd. v. Leighton's Invts. Trust Ltd.,* [1945] A.C. 221 (H.L.); compare *Cusack-Smith v. London Corp.,* [1956] 1 W.L.R. 1368.

197 Lords Simon and Wright in the *Cricklewood* case thought the doctrine of frustration might apply; Lord Goddard and Lord Russell did not. The arguments of the latter may be supported by (1) the common-law doctrine of non-avoidance of a lease for collateral fraud: *Feret v. Hill* (1854), 15 C.B. 207, 139 E.R. 400, above, p. 426, (2) the equitable refusal to rescind a transfer of property induced by innocent misrepresentation: *Angel v. Jay,* [1911] 1 K.B. 666, above, p. 306. But these doctrines may be questioned today. Hence, so too may the opinion of Lords Goddard and Russell with respect to frustration.

198 *Merkur v. H. Shoom & Co.,* [1954] O.W.N. 55 (Ont. C.A.) (in which no reference was made to the *Cricklewood Invt.* case); *Foster v. Caldwell,* [1948] 4 D.L.R. 70 (N.B.C.A.); *Stanford v. Nicolau,* [1943] R.L. 154 (Que. C.A.); compare *Claude Neon Gen. Advertising Ltd. v. Sing,* [1942] 1 D.L.R. 26 (N.S.S.C.); *Neon Products Ltd. v. Swain,* [1974] 1 W.W.R. 583 (Alta. T.D.).

199 *Goulding v. Rabinovitch,* [1927] 3 D.L.R. 820 (Ont. C.A.); *Fong v. Kerwin,* [1929] 3 D.L.R. 612 (Ont. C.A.). In the *Goulding* case, expropriation did not frustrate the contract, the parties still received interim benefits or were subjected to interim detriment (*per* Middleton J.A. at 821). But note the different result where expropriation affected a real estate commission contract, *i.e.,* a personal contract not involving property interests: *Oxford Realty Ltd. v. Annette,* [1961] O.W.N. 316 (Ont. H.C.).

200 [1935] 1 W.W.R. 374 (Sask. K.B.); affirmed [1935] 3 W.W.R. 256 (Sask. C.A.). See also *Fong v. Kerwin,* above, note 199, with respect to forfeiture of a contract to *create* a lease; and *Re Dennis Commercial Properties Ltd. and Westmount Life Ins. Co.,* [1969] 2 O.R. 850 (Ont. H.C.); affirmed with variation, [1970] 1 O.R. 698n (Ont. C.A.). Further appeal to Supreme Court of Canada discontinued on consent after motion to quash dismissed, [1970] 1 O.R. 698n (S.C.C.).

201 (1915), 52 S.C.R. 134 (S.C.C.); compare the idea expressed in *Ziger v. Shiffer & Hillman Co.,* [1933] O.R. 407 (Ont. C.A.).

202 See, *e.g.,* Residential Tenancies Act, S.N.B. 1975, c. R-10.2, s. 11 [am. S.N.B. 1983, c. 82, s. 7]; R.S.S. 1978, c. R-22, s. 15.

& Co.[203] Although the Supreme Court of Canada was concerned with the extent to which the contractual doctrine of wrongful repudiation could be applied to a lease,[204] the remarks of Laskin J. went beyond that particular point. Rejecting the argument that the landlord was limited to remedies given by the law of property, the learned judge said[205]

> [i]t is no longer sensible to pretend that a commercial law . . .is simply a conveyance and not also a contract. It is equally untenable to persist in denying resort to the full armoury of remedies ordinarily available to redress repudiation of covenants, merely because the covenants may be associated with an estate in land.

The inference to be drawn from this statement is that contracts which create or dispose of estates or interests in land are nonetheless contracts, whatever other effects they may have under the law of property. Therefore, the normal contractual doctrines should apply to them, including the doctrine of frustration.

Such indeed was the approach taken by the Ontario Court of Appeal in 1975 in *Capital Quality Homes Ltd. v. Colwyn Construction Ltd.*,[206] which involved a contract for the sale of land. The doctrine of frustration was held applicable and was applied. So was it in a subsequent case, *Focal Properties Ltd. v. George Wimpey (Canada) Ltd.*,[207] where the members of the Ontario Court of Appeal were divided on the issue of frustration, without denying that the doctrine could be applied to a contract for the sale of land. Following these decisions the same court reinforced the idea that frustration could be invoked where the contract related to the sale of interests in land, even though, on the facts of this case, *Victoria Wood Development Corporation v. Ondrey*,[208] what happened did not amount to frustration. In Canada, therefore, a respectable *corpus* of authority now exists for the proposition that contracts of sale of land may be frustrated if appropriate circumstances occur, such as a change in planning law which affects the "common venture" of the parties. As with other situations it is necessary to prove that the act or event alleged to result in frustration was: (a) unforeseeable; (b) unforeseen; (c) not caused by either party's default; and (d) would make the contract something radically different.

No Canadian case, as yet, has tackled the question of leases.[209] It might be argued, as it was in earlier times, that the obligations of a lease might still be

---

203 (1971), 17 D.L.R. (3d) 710 (S.C.C.).

204 Above, p. 621.

205 Above, note 203, at 721, cited with approval in *National Carriers Ltd. v. Panalpina (Nor.) Ltd.*, [1981] 1 All E.R. 161 at 172 (H.L.) *per* Lord Wilberforce, at 177 *per* Lord Simon of Glaisdale, and at p. 187 *per* Lord Roskill. Compare *Firth v. Halldran* (1926), 38 C.L.R. 261 at 269 (Aust.) *per* Isaacs J.

206 (1975), 61 D.L.R. (3d) 385 (Ont. C.A.): above, p. 652; and see the decision of the English Court of Appeal in *Amalgam. Invt. & Property Co. v. John Walker & Sons Ltd.*, [1976] 3 All E.R. 509 at 516 *per* Buckley L.J., where it was assumed that the doctrine would apply although on the facts it was not applicable.

207 (1975), 73 D.L.R. (3d) 387 (Ont. C.A.); affirmed [1978] 1 S.C.R. 2 (S.C.C.): above, p. 656.

208 (1978), 92 D.L.R. (3d) 229 (Ont. C.A.); leave to appeal to S.C.C. refused (1979), 26 N.R. 267 (S.C.C.); above, p. 653.

209 The topic is exhaustively discussed in Robertson, "Frustrated Leases: 'No to never—But Rarely if Ever'" (1982), 60 Can. Bar Rev. 619.

performed even though no benefit accrued to the party fulfiling those obligations. Since lack of economic advantage is not of itself a basis for holding a contract frustrated,[210] it would be logical to deduce that frustration can never apply to leases of land. That would be illogical in another way, however. There is no doubt that frustration can apply to a lease of a chattel, if, for example, the chattel is destroyed or lost. [211] In modern times there seems to be no justification for marking a distinction between chattels and realty, at least where contracts concerning such property are concerned.[212] The House of Lords has now definitively held that if the circumstances are appropriate a lease can be frustrated. In *National Carriers Ltd. v. Panalpina (Northern) Ltd.*,[213] the circumstances alleged to produce frustration of the commercial lease were not considered to have made serious or grave inroads upon the contract. Nevertheless the House of Lords accepted that frustration was theoretically applicable. The attitude expressed by the House of Lords was that a modern approach to law required the treatment of leases in the same way as other contracts, in particular licences to occupy land or charter-parties.[214] Given the acceptance by courts in Ontario of the relevance of the doctrine of frustration to land sales agreements, it would be surprising if a Canadian court rejected the lead proffered by the House of Lords in the *Panalpina* case with regard to leases. In consequence it would seem reasonable to conclude that the doctrine of frustration can apply to contracts, of whatever sort, concerning land and interests in land. Whether in any given instance the doctrine applies in fact and in law, is a question that will depend upon the circumstances of the individual case and the correct application of the principles which have been examined earlier.[215]

4. The effects of frustration

(a) **At common law**

Prior to statutory alteration of the law, the position was that if a contract were terminated by impossibility or frustration, the situation of the parties was crystallized; all further liability was automatically discharged.[216] Neither party could be liable to the other for breach of contract. The question, however, was as to what happened to money or property which changed hands prior to the frustrating event, as consideration for the performance of something which was now no longer possible, and what was the situation with respect to liabilities which had accrued, such as rent due, the price of goods, etc.

---

210 Above, p. 639.
211 *Laurwen Invts. Inc. v. 814693 Northwest Territories Ltd.* (1990), 48 B.L.R. 100 (N.W.T.S.C.): above, p. 647; compare *Summers Transport Ltd. v. G.M. Smith Ltd.* (1990), 82 Nfld. & P.E.I.R. 1 (Nfld. T.D.): above, p. 637.
212 *Aliter per* Lord Russell of Killowen in the *Panalpina* case, below, note 213, at 181.
213 [1981] 1 All E.R. 161 (H.L); above, p. 654.
214 *Ibid.*, at 177-179 *per* Lord Simon of Glaisdale: compare *ibid.*, at 168 *per* Lord Hailsham L.C.
215 In the case of leases it will appear that this will "hardly ever" happen: above, note 213, at 186-187 *per* Lord Hailsham L.C.
216 *Hirji Mulji v. Cheong Yue S.S. Co.*, [1926] A.C. 497 at 505-506 (P.C.) *per* Lord Sumner.

As a result of the "coronation" cases,[217] notably *Chandler v. Webster*,[218] it was held at common law that when frustration occurred: (1) money already paid over could not be recovered by the payor; and (2) money might still be due if, for example, it were rent payable in advance, and therefore would have been in the hands of the payee if, for some reason or another, the payor had not neglected to fulfil his obligation. Thus, frustration might discharge some, but not all, liabilities. Nor would it mean that an innocent party who had suffered detriment prior to the frustration could recover anything. The loss lay where it fell. It does appear from older cases that payment for work already done prior to the frustration of the contract could be obtained from a party for whom the work had been performed.[219] Moreover if the parties had made provision for what was to happen in the event of frustration, their arrangements would be enforced.[220]

The House of Lords, in the *Fibrosa* case in 1943[221] overruled the coronation cases on the subject of quasi-contractual recovery of money paid prior to the frustration, and held that in such situations there was a total failure of consideration (which it was necessary to establish since a partial failure of consideration would not justify such recovery).[222] On the approach adopted in that case, the deposit for the rent in *Krell v. Henry*[223] might have been recovered, and the rent due in *Chandler v. Webster*[224] would have been discharged, lest there be one action to recover the rent and then a subsequent one by the lessee to recover on the basis of failure of consideration, that is, in quasi-contract, or, in modern terminology, unjust enrichment or restitution.[225]

The House of Lords' decision still left open the possibility of some injustice even after the granting of quasi-contractual restitutionary relief. In that case itself, for example, when enemy occupation of Poland made it impossible for the manufacturers of wool-packing machinery to deliver the goods, although their manufacture was completed, the part-payment of the purchase price was recoverable, and the remainder of that price could not be demanded of the purchasers. But the expenditures incurred by the sellers before the frustration could not be compensated for in any action. In Canada, there are to be found suggestions that, even apart from legislation, the common law could effect rough justice in such

---

217 Above, pp. 626-627.

218 [1904] 1 K.B. 493 (C.A.).

219 See *Klein v. Sanderson*, [1928] 2 W.W.R. 289 (Alta. C.A.); citing *Stubbs v. Holywell Ry. Co.* (1867), L.R. 2 Exch. 311; *Hollingsworth v. Lacharitie* (1910), 13 W.L.R. 492 (Man. C.A.); *Elsom v. Ellis* (1916), 4 Sask. L.R. 294 (Sask. S.C.); *Hill v. Howie*, [1919] 2 W.W.R. 392 (Sask. K.B.).

220 *Robbins v. Wilson & Cabeldu Ltd.*, [1944] 3 W.W.R. 625 (B.C.C.A.).

221 *Fibrosa Spolka Akcyjna v. Fairbairn Lawson Combe Barbour Ltd.*, [1943] A.C. 32 (H.L.).

222 *Whincup v. Hughes* (1871), L.R. 6 C.P. 78.

223 [1903] 2 K.B. 740 (C.A.); above, p. 627.

224 Above, note 218.

225 Goff & Jones, *Law of Restitution*, 3rd ed. (1986), pp. 449-451; Fridman, *Restitution*, 2nd ed. (1992), pp. 205-206; Maddaugh & McCamus, *Law of Restitution*, pp. 405-408. On the comparison of English, Scottish and American law see Dawson, "Judicial Revision of Frustrated Contracts", [1982] Jur. Rev. 86.

situations by granting some recovery on the basis of what was just and reasonable.[226] However, the situation was unsatisfactory and was changed by statute.

(b) Statutory provisions[227]

(i) Where enacted

Improvement of the law was achieved in England by the Law Reform (Frustrated Contracts) Act, 1943. That statute was used as the basis for the Model Act prepared by the Canadian Uniform Law Commissioners, subsequently enacted in every province and territory save British Columbia, Nova Scotia, and Saskatchewan.[228] British Columbia has its own slightly different statute.[229] Hence, it is only in Nova Scotia and Saskatchewan that the common law (that is, the law as it was stated by the House of Lords in the *Fibrosa* case) still applies.

(ii) The Model Act

This does not apply to certain contracts.[230] They are as follows:

(1) contracts for the carriage of goods by sea;

(2) charter-parties, except time charter-parties, and charter-parties by way of demise — in which temporary ownership of the ship passes to the charterer (a most unusual type of charter-party);

(3) contracts of insurance;

(4) contracts for the sale of goods when the goods perish before the contract (which is not truly frustration) or perish afterwards without fault by either party and before risk passes to the buyer;

(5) contracts where the parties have made their own provisions for what is to happen in the event of frustration.

With respect to the above contracts either the agreed arrangements govern

---

226 *Cahan v. Fraser*, [1951] 4 D.L.R. 112 (B.C.C.A.); compare the dissenting judgment of Robertson J.A. in *McDonald Aviation Co. v. Queen Charlotte Airlines Ltd.*, [1952] 1 D.L.R. 291 at 307-309 (B.C.C.A).

227 This section was referred to by the Ontario Court of Appeal in *Can-Truck Transportation Ltd. v. Fenton's Auto Paint Shop Ltd.* (1993), 101 D.L.R. (4th) 562 at 567 (Ont. C.A.).

228 Alberta, R.S.A. 1980, c. F-20; Manitoba, R.S.M. 1987, c. F190; New Brunswick, R.S.N.B. 1973, c. F-24; Newfoundland, R.S.N. 1990, c. F-26; Ontario, R.S.O. 1990, c. F.34; Prince Edward Island, R.S.P.E.I. 1988, c. F-16; Northwest Territories, R.S.N.W.T. 1988, c. F-12; Yukon, R.S.Y. 1986, c. 73. A new uniform statute has been recommended by the Uniformity Commissioners: Maddaugh & McCamus, *Law of Restitution*, at p. 405, note 15, p. 417, note 83. Its provisions, modified in certain respects, are recommended for adoption by the Ontario Law Reform Commission, *Report on Amendment of the Law of Contract*, 1987, pp. 281-285. The Saskatchewan Law Reform Commission recommended proposals for dealing with frustrated contracts in 1987.

229 R.S.B.C. 1979, c. 144.

230 In Ontario it has been held that the Act does not apply to statutory liens under the Mechanics' Lien Act (see now the Construction Lien Act, R.S.O. 1990, c. C.30); a general statute, such as the Frustrated Contracts Act, does not overrule a particular statute such as the Mechanics' Lien Act: *W.J.C. Kaufmann Co. v. Berberi* (1982), 36 O.R. (2d) 774 (Ont. Div. Ct.).

the position of the parties, or the common law (or Sale of Goods Act) will apply. The Act binds the Crown; therefore, contracts made with the Federal Government or with a Province will be subject to the provisions of the Act, as long as the contract is regulated by the law of a Province that has passed the necessary legislation.

The Act only comes into play where a contract[231] to which it can apply, that is, *inter alia*, one governed by the law of the enacting Province, has become impossible of performance or been otherwise frustrated, and the parties have *for that reason* been discharged from the further performance of the contract. Only impossibility or frustration will call the Act into play. What the Act does, broadly speaking, is to change the previous law in two important ways.

In the first place, money paid before discharge is recoverable and debts accrued cease. This confirms the decision in the *Fibrosa* case[232] and the reversal of *Chandler v. Webster*.[233] The provisions of the Act also make clear two things which the House of Lords could not do in the *Fibrosa* case. One is that there does not have to be a total failure of consideration for the payor to be able to recover under the Act what he has paid out prior to discharge. The other is that, where the payee has done something in pursuance of the contract, and has incurred expenses "in connection with the performance", the payee may be allowed to retain, or recover, as appropriate, such expenses from the original payor, up to the extent of the amount paid or payable by the original payor. There was no common-law rule under which an equitable adjustment of the various costs and expenses, losses and gains, could be made as between the parties. Now, under the Act, there may be some recompense for overhead expenses and personal work and services by the payee.[234]

The above provisions regulate the right of a party to recover what he has already paid out, or his immunity from further payments under the contract. The Act makes another important alteration in the previous common law. Where there was only partial performance of an entire contract, and performance remains uncompleted, nothing could be recovered with respect to that part which had actually been performed. So much was derived from *Cutter v. Powell*.[235] Even if the reason for the failure to complete performance was some frustrating event,

---

231 Note, however, that if it is possible to *sever* the frustrated term from the rest of the contract, the provisions with respect to frustration will apply to *that* term; see *Witwicki v. Midgley*, [1976] 6 W.W.R. 471 (Man. Q.B.) (above, p. 646) where at first instance the term which required the son to provide love, affection and personal and individual services to his mother could be severed from the rest of the contract, which meant that the other provisions of the contract were still enforceable; affirmed [1979] 5 W.W.R. 242 (Man. C.A.) on the ground that the son's death did not frustrate the contract.

232 Above, note 221.

233 Above, note 218.

234 For this to occur there must be proper pleadings and evidence on the basis of which the issue can be tried: *Can-Truck Transportation Ltd. v. Fenton's Auto Paint Shop Ltd.* (1993), 101 D.L.R. (4th) 562 (Ont. C.A.).

235 (1795), 6 Term Rep. 320, 101 E.R. 573 (above, p. 534); note (1) the exceptions or qualifications of this: above, pp. 535-539; (2) the decision probably applies when the express terms of the contract are inconsistent with the statute, *i.e.*, when the parties have in fact stated what is to happen in the event of discharge through frustration.

as in *Appleby v. Myers*,[236] nothing could be recovered for what had been done piror to that event, such as the erection of part of the projected machinery on the premises that were burnt down in that case. The Act changes this. Now a court has the power to award a sum respecting the value of whatever "valuable benefit" (other than a payment of money) may have been conferred on one party by the other before the discharge. There are difficulties about the interpretation and application of this provision.[237] Even though it extends to benefits conferred on third parties, as well as the other contracting party, it is not easy to understand what is actually meant by a "valuable benefit". In the light of recent decisions, it would seem that the Act is contemplating some tangible benefit that survives the frustrating act or event.

Until the discussion by Goff J. in England in 1977[238] there was very little judicial consideration of this provision (or, indeed, of the Act as a whole). In an earlier Newfoundland case, *Parsons Brothers Ltd. v. Shea*,[239] the plaintiffs had completed part of the work involved in constructing a heating system for the defendant's building when the building was accidentally destroyed by fire. The plaintiffs claimed in respect of the work done by them prior to that event, relying on the provisions of the Newfoundland Act. What they had done was useless to the defendant; it had been burned in the fire. Nonetheless the plaintiffs argued that they had conferred a "benefit" on the defendant, in that the plaintiffs had performed part of the contract. However there was no evidence that the building owner, the defendant, had really received any benefit from the completed work. Hence nothing was recoverable by the plaintiffs. A more recent decision, from the same jurisdiction, is that in *Impala Construction Ltd. v. Wade*.[240] This involved a contract to perform various services, including bulldozing a road. Only partial performance occurred by reason of extreme wet weather conditions, unusual even for Newfoundland. The plaintiffs sued for the contract price, but were able to recover only for the work actually completed. The court held that the contract had been frustrated by an act of God (namely, the abnormal weather conditions) which brought into effect the provisions of the Newfoundland Frustrated Contracts Act. Since 60 per cent of the work had been completed, 60 per cent of the contract price could be recovered by the plaintiffs under the section of the Act dealing with obtaining a "valuable benefit" prior to the discharge of the contract by frustration.

Neither of these Canadian decisions contains any detailed analysis of the relevant sections of the statute. Such analysis can be found in the judgment of

---

236 (1867), L.R. 2 C.P. 651.

237 Goff & Jones, *Law of Restitution*, 3rd ed. (1986), pp. 489-499; Fridman, *Restitution*, 2nd ed. (1992), pp. 313-315; Maddaugh & McCamus, *Law of Restitution*, pp. 411-414; *B.P. Exploration Co. (Libya) v. Hunt (No. 2)*, [1982] 1 All E.R. 925 at 938-943 *per* Goff J.

238 *B.P. Exploration Co. (Libya) v. Hunt (No. 2)*, above, note 237.

239 (1965), 53 D.L.R. (2d) 86 (Nfld. S.C.).

240 (1983), 40 Nfld. & P.E.I.R. 437 (Nfld. Dist. Ct.).

Goff J. in *B.P. Exploration Co. (Libya) Ltd. v. Hunt (No. 2).*[241] The learned judge makes clear that the task of the court in a situation involving the statute is twofold: identification and valuation of the benefit; and award of a just sum. The defendant's benefit must be identified as the end product of the plaintiff's services, and is to be valued as at the date of the frustration (leaving out of account use of goods, inflation of money, and other irrelevant matters). The underlying rationale of this provision, as indeed of the whole statute, is to prevent the unjust enrichment of one party at the expense of the other. The Act is designed to give effect to principles of restitution or unjust enrichment, not to principles of the law of contract. With this there can be no quarrel, since the principles of contract law relate to what happens when a contract is broken by one party, not to what happens when the contract is discharged, and the parties relieved of their obligations thereunder, in consequence of a frustrating act or event. In this respect the law of restitution, whether originating in the common law or under the statute, fills the gap left by the law of contract.

(iii) *The British Columbia Act*[242]

Criticism and difficulties pointed out by commentators on the Model Act were taken into consideration by the B.C. Law Reform Commission, with the result that the British Columbia legislation on this subject differs slightly from the English and the Model Acts.

Thus, the Act applies to sales of goods within the "perishing" provision of the Sale of Goods Act.[243] The Act speaks of the entitlement to "restitution" of a party for "benefits created by his performance or part performance of the contract."[244] It also permits a claim for damages for consequential loss as a result of failure to fulfil obligations which should have been performed before the frustration but were not.[245] Where restitution is required in respect of benefits, losses may be apportioned between the parties.[246] For these purposes "benefit" means "something done in the fulfilment of contractual obligations, whether or not the person for whose benefit it was done received the benefit."[247] Restitution will not be granted where it was "implied", in one of three ways, that the person conferring the benefit should bear the risk of loss.[248] In this respect the situation

---

241 Above, note 237. His interpretation is criticized by Maddaugh & McCamus, *op. cit.*, at p. 414 who prefer an approach which would consider all requested services as conferring and obtaining a benefit in the required sense: *ibid.*, at p. 411. Compare the recommendation in favour of equal apportionment of reliance expenditures recommended by the Ontario Law Reform Commission, *Report*, above, note 228, at pp. 283, 285.

242 R.S.B.C. 1979, c. 144.

243 *Ibid.*, s. 1(1)(*b*).

244 *Ibid.*, s. 5(1).

245 *Ibid.*, s. 5(2).

246 *Ibid.*, s. 5(3).

247 *Ibid.*, s. 5(4).

248 *Ibid.*, s. 6(1).

with respect to which party generally effects insurance may be telling.[249] More detailed provisions deal with how restitution is to be calculated (that is, with respect to reasonableness of expenditures and the value of property returned by a party)[250] and the irrelevance of loss of profits and insurance money that is payable as a consequence of the frustrating event.[251] The limitation period is the same as if the claim were for breach of contract, the breach being assumed to occur when the frustration takes place.[252]

---

249 *Ibid.*, s. 6(2), (3). For criticism of this section, see the Ontario Law Reform Commission's *Report*, above, note 228, at pp. 283-284; and see Maddaugh & McCamus, *op. cit.*, at pp. 418-419.
250 R.S.B.C. 1979, c. 144, s. 7.
251 *Ibid.*, s. 8.
252 *Ibid.*, s. 9.

17

Assignment

1. The nature of assignment

(a) Characteristics of assignment

Contractual rights are one variety of *choses in action*. This expression describes "all personal rights of property which can only be claimed or enforced by action, and not by taking physical possession."[1] The distinction drawn by the law is between

---

1 *Torkington v. Magee*, [1902] 2 K.B. 427 at 430; reversed on other grounds [1903] 1 K.B. 644 (C.A.) *per* Channell J. This has been held not to include, *e.g.*, (1) a right to repossession under a conditional sales agreement: *Lounsbury Co. v. Duthie*, [1957] S.C.R. 590 (S.C.C.); or (2) a right to foreclose on a mortgage: *B.A. Timber Co. v. Jones (No. 2)*, [1944] 2 W.W.R. 577 (B.C.C.A.).

   Note that a general assignment may be made of all book debts (or accounts receivable): see, for example, *Re M-B Industries Ltd.* (1987), 17 B.C.L.R. (2d) 197 (B.C. Co. Ct.); *Yorkshire Trust Co. v. 304231 Alta. Ltd.* (1986) 46 Alta. L.R. (2d) 47 (Alta. Q.B.); *Alberta v. Can. West Interiors Ltd.* (1986), 43 Alta. L.R. (2d) 155 (Alta. Master). Such an assignment may affect a joint account in the names of the assignor and another person: *Royal Bank v. Fraser Valley Credit Union* (1987), 37 D.L.R. (4th) 169 (B.C.C.A.). On the assignment of book debts, see below, note 36.

choses in action and choses in possession. The latter category embraces all personal property (as distinct from land or realty) which is capable of possession such that title thereto is based upon and enforced by taking possession. Choses in action include, *inter alia*, debts, shares, patents, copyrights, and, what is relevant for present purposes, rights of action arising out of contract.[2] Some choses in action have been made assignable under statute in particular ways and subject to particular safeguards. With these, for example, copyright, the present work is not concerned. This chapter is concerned only with assignment of contractual rights and contractual burdens or liabilities.

Assignment involves the transfer to a stranger, that is a person who is not a party to the original contract, of contractual rights arising under the contract, so as to permit the assignee to sue the debtor under the original contract in his, the assignee's own name, with or without the assent of the debtor.[3] To this must be added the possibility that there may be an assignment, that is a transfer of the obligations upon the original debtor under the contract to a stranger, a third party, with the result that the assignee is the one responsible for performing the contract and therefore liable to be sued if the contract is not performed. The attitude of the common law has varied according to what is purported to be assigned is the benefit or the burden of a contract. Furthermore, while equity and statute have intervened with respect to the assignment of contractual rights, they have had nothing to do with the law relating to the assignment of contractual obligations by the debtor.

Essentially, therefore, assignment of rights or liabilities is the substitution of a creditor or debtor, as the case may be, for the original creditor or debtor, that is, the original promisee or promisor respectively under the contract. To the extent to which a *new* party is introduced to the contract, there is a qualification of the doctrine of privity. Since *substitution*, rather than addition is involved, assignment is only a metaphorical qualification of privity, not a true or real one. On the other hand, since the original contract is still the operative transaction, with a change of one party (or possibly both), what is happening is in effect the creation of an agreement which benefits a third party, a stranger to the original contract, or imposes liabilities on such a stranger, which is, in effect, contrary to the doctrine of privity.[4] Whichever view is adopted, assignment must be distinguished from other legal

---

2 And *tort*; but not all such rights of action: see *Union Gas Co. v. Brown*, [1968] 1 O.R. 524 (Ont. H.C.); reversed on other grounds [1970] 1 O.R. 715 (Ont. C.A.); below. A covenant in restraint of trade (see Chapter 10) has been held to be part of the goodwill of a business and therefore assignable on the sale of the business together with its goodwill: see *Barkett v. Shaw* (1960), 31 W.W.R. 1 (Man. Q.B.).

3 *E.g.*, the bank suing for the payment of losses incurred under an insurance policy taken out by the assignor in *C.I.B.C. v. Ins. Corp. of Ireland*, (1988), 46 D.L.R. (4th) 562 (B.C.S.C.); reversed (1990), 75 D.L.R. (4th) 482 (B.C.C.A.). Compare *Gable v. Osborne Bros. Land & Property Ltd.* (1986), 72 A.R. 108 (Alta. Master), assignee, to whom rights assigned by way of security, entitled to sue to enforce his assigned rights.

4 Above, Chapter 5.

mechanisms which also serve and operate as qualifications of, or exceptions to, the doctrine of privity of contract.

(b) Assignment distinguished from other transactions

Assignment is different from *novation*. In cases of novation the original obligation is discharged by agreement of the parties and a *new* obligation with fresh consideration is undertaken, usually, but not necessarily in the same terms, with a different creditor or debtor.[5]

Assignment must be differentiated from the concept of the trust as it has been used in some instances to get around the strict doctrine of privity. In such instances the third party who is nominated as the beneficiary of a contract made between two others has an *equitable* remedy, which may involve joining one of the parties to the contract as co-plaintiff or co-defendant.[6] What he is enforcing, however, is the original contract, with the original parties; he is not seeking to substitute himself, nor is one of the original parties seeking to substitute him for the other original party.

Assignment must also be distinguished from cases of *agency*, where a party to a contract is really acting on behalf of someone else, his principal, although without authority to do so, and the principal later ratifies the unauthorized agreement, thereby becoming a party to the contract by the operation of the doctrines of agency, in particular the law relating to ratification.[7] This may only be done where the agent was acting for a disclosed principal, that is, where the other contracting party knew of the possible existence of a principal. Where the agent does not reveal such possibility, and acts for an undisclosed principal, ratification by such principal of the unauthorized contract is not permitted so as to entitle the principal to be treated as a party to the contract.[8] Some writers have suggested that the rationale of permitting an undisclosed principal to sue and be sued on a contract made on his behalf by an agent (that is, with authority to do so), is that there is a notional assignment of the agent's rights or liabilities under the contract to the principal.[9] If this suggestion is well-founded, it would make the difference between assignment and agency less clear. However, it is by no means an acceptable explanation of the reason why the law permits an undisclosed principal (as contrasted with one whose existence is always known by the parties to the contract) to be treated as a party to the contract negotiated by his agent. Undisclosed agency must be regarded as an anomaly, allowed by the law for severely practical commercial reasons, though limited in scope by the refusal by the law

---

5 *Liversidge v. Broadbent* (1859), 4 H. & N. 60, 157 E.R. 978; *Re United Rys. of Havana & Regla Warehouses Ltd.*, [1960] Ch. 52; affirmed [1961] A.C. 1007 (H.L.); compare *B.A. Timber Co. v. Jones (No. 2)* above, note 1; *411076 B.C. Ltd. v. McCullagh* (1992), 72 B.C.L.R. (2d) 252 (B.C.S.C.); on novation, see above, p. 539.

6 Above, pp. 196-200.

7 Above, pp. 194-196; see Fridman, *Law of Agency*, 6th ed. (1990), pp. 74-97.

8 *Keighley, Maxsted & Co. v. Durant*, [1901] A.C. 240 (H.L.).

9 Goodhart & Hamson, "Undisclosed Principals in Contract" (1931), 4 Camb. L.J. 320; Stoljar, *Law of Agency*, pp. 231-233.

to apply the doctrine of ratification, and by certain other qualifications upon the broad application of the idea.[10]

Assignment must also be differentiated from *negotiability*. By custom of the law merchant, certain written instruments have the quality of negotiability attached to them by general usage. Chief among these are: bills of exchange, cheques, and promissory notes.[11] But the list may not be closed.[12] Under certain conditions, the transfer of such instruments, which is termed "negotiation", passes title therein, and thereby enables the transferee to sue, or be sued upon the instrument even though it was originally "made" as between two different parties.[13] Negotiation differs from assignment in several respects: for example, consideration does not have to be proved, but is *presumed*, where the transferee is a "holder in due course";[14] such a holder takes free from "equities", that is, obtains a good title not subject to defeasance or qualification by any other party;[15] nothing other than delivery of the instrument payable to the bearer is required to effect a negotiation;[16] no notice to the original debtor is necessary; delivery of the instrument is absolute. It will be seen that there are significant differences in the character and effects of negotiation or negotiability on the one hand and assignment on the other.

From what was decided in *Shamia v. Joory*,[17] there might be a restitutionary claim to funds in the hands of one party to a contract at the suit not of the original other party but someone else to whom the original creditor has "transferred" the whole or part of such fund, without a formal assignment, despite the fact that what is involved is not a negotiable instrument, and even though no agency

---

10 Fridman, above, note 7 at pp. 228-242.
11 See the Bills of Exchange Act, R.S.C. 1985, c. B-4. Mention should also be made of certain other documents, *e.g.*, bills of lading, which can transfer title to goods by "negotiation" in certain circumstances.
12 *Goodwin v. Robarts* (1875), L.R. 10 Exch. 337 at 346 *per* Cockburn C.J.; affirmed (1876), 1 App. Cas. 476 (H.L.); *Edelstein v. Schuler & Co.*, [1902] 2 K.B. 144; Crawford & Falconbridge, *Banking & Bills of Exchange*, 8th ed. (1986), Vol. 2, pp. 1167-1170.
13 See, *e.g.*, Falconbridge, *Law of Negotiable Instruments in Canada*, pp. 52, 117.
14 Bills of Exchange Act, above, note 11, ss. 56-58 (Crawford & Falconbridge, *op cit.*, above, note 12, Vol. 2, pp. 1452-1473): hence the rules about past consideration and consideration moving from the promisee (above, pp. 108, 113) do not apply.
15 *Miller v. Race* (1758), 1 Burr. 452; *London Joint Stock Bank v. Simmons*, [1892] A.C. 201 (H.L.). Contrast where the contract is not negotiable: *Crouch v. Credit Foncier of Eng.* (1873), L.R. 8 Q.B. 374. The holder in due course is presumed to be *bona fide*: *Raphael v. Bank of England* (1855), 17 C.B. 161.

   An assignee, however, does take subject to equities, whether the assignment is statutory or equitable: *London & Western Can. Invts. Co. v. Dolph* (1918), 43 O.L.R. 449 at 450-451 *per* Middleton J.; *First City Capital Ltd. v. Petrosar Ltd.* (1987), 42 D.L.R. (4th) 738 at 746-747 (Ont. H.C.) *per* Callaghan A.C.J. H.C. Compare *Central Trust Co. v. Messenger* (1988), 33 B.C.L.R. (2d) 34 at 37 (B.C.S.C.), to the effect that the assignee steps in the shoes of the assignor, than whom the assignee can have no greater rights or obligations: compare below, p. 678.
16 *Milnes v. Dawson* (1850), 5 Ex. 948. But note the situation if the instrument is payable to *order*, it requires *endorsement* before delivery otherwise what occurs is assignment not negotiation.
17 [1958] 1 Q.B. 448. On which see Fridman, above, note 7 at p. 272; Davies, "Shamia v. Joory: A Forgotten Chapter in Quasi Contract" (1959), 75 L.Q.R. 220; Goff & Jones, *Law of Restitution*, 3rd ed. (1986), pp. 518-521; Fridman, *Restitution*, 2nd ed. (1992), pp. 259-261.

relationship is involved. All that may be necessary is that the debtor "attorn" to the new creditor, that is, acknowledge that he now holds the sum in question to the use of the new creditor. The limits of this quaint, historical survival are by no means clear. Nor is its relevance in modern law. To the extent to which such attornment can be effective, in some circumstances there may be a way around both the doctrine of privity and the law of assignment.

(c) Voluntary and involuntary assignment

In most instances assignment of rights and liabilities under a contract takes place by act of the parties, that is as a consequence of a voluntary disposition or transaction on the part at least of the creditor or debtor. There are some situations in which assignment occurs by operation of law without the need for any assent by the creditor or debtor as the case may be. This will result, for example, in the event of the death of a contracting party or his bankruptcy. Some distinction must therefore be drawn between the operation of the law of assignment in cases of voluntary acts by a party or parties, and the effect of certain legal acts or events upon pre-existing contractual rights or liabilities.

2. Assignment by act of parties

(a) Of the benefit of a contract

(i) *Common law*

Contractual rights were unassignable at common law, as were other choses in action, if by this is meant that the assignee was thereby enabled to sue the debtor for recovery of the debt or other benefit under the contract in his, the assignee's, own name. If a purported assignment occurred the assignor would still have to sue to recover, though what was recovered would enure to the benefit of the assignee. The assignee could sue the assignor under the contract between *them*, for what was promised under the assignment, or, possibly, to force the assignor to bring the appropriate proceedings against the debtor. Or the assignee could be made the agent of the assignor, by a power of attorney, authorizing him to sue on behalf of the assignor, but in such event the situation would be exactly the same as if the assignor had himself sued the debtor. At common law, however, there were two situations in which assignment would have the effect of entitling the assignee to sue in his own name. One was where the assignment was made by or to the Crown, as long as the Crown had assented to the assignment. This was one reason why the assignee of a contract made with the Crown in *R. v. Smith*[18] was not permitted to sue by the Supreme Court of Canada, since there was no evidence of any consent by the Crown of any assignment. The second exception at common

---

18 (1883), 10 S.C.R. 1 (S.C.C.).

law was in the case of a negotiable instrument such as a bill of exchange or a promissory note.[19]

Three reasons appear to have been suggested for this refusal to recognize and allow assignments to have their fullest possible effect. In the first place, to do so would have detracted from the doctrine of privity of contract; it would have interfered with the personal nature of the contractual bond.[20] Second, there was the thought that such assignments savoured of the offence of maintenance, that is, the support of ligitation by someone not originally involved in the suit. This was a purpose which would tend to make a contract illegal at common law.[21] Hence the courts were loathe to permit transactions which, even though not seemingly designed to effect maintenance, might serve such end and thereby promote vexatious litigation. Third, there was the difficulty of creating a method of transferring such intangible choses in action, there being nothing physical to deliver, except in the case of a negotiable instrument, which, as already seen, was capable of being effectively assigned through the medium of negotiations, that is, delivery from hand to hand.

(ii) *Equity*

(A) *A different approach* Whereas the common-law courts took the view that an assignment was to be regarded and treated as a mere assignment of a right to bring an action at law against the debtor (which clearly tended to support the views antagonistic to assignment that have been stated above), courts of equity adopted a different approach. Such courts were prepared to treat a debt as a piece of property, capable of being dealt with like any other property, for example, by assignment, that is, transfer, such that the need to enforce it by an action at law was a mere incident of the transfer, not the essence.[22]

(B) *Earlier developments* From the early seventeenth century, equity assisted assignees. Where the chose in action arose at law, that is, was legal, for example, a debt or other contractual right, equity relieved the assignee in one of three ways. Where the contract was expressly or impliedly for the benefit of "the promisee and his assigns", equity permitted the assignee to sue in his own name.[23] If the assignor was recalcitrant about suing on behalf of the assignee, equity would compel him to allow the use of his name in a common-law court. For this "value" was necessary. Equity will not assist a volunteer; hence, consideration had to be shown for the assignment before courts of equity would use their procedure to make the assignor sue.[24] If there were collusion between assignor and debtor, equity would even compel performance by the debtor to the assignee, joining the assignor as

19 Compare above, p. 192.
20 Compare above, pp. 175, 191.
21 Above, p. 374.
22 *Fitzroy v. Cave*, [1905] 2 K.B. 364 at 372 (C.A.) *per* Cozens-Hardy L.J.
23 *Buckland v. Papillon* (1866), 2 Ch. App. 67.
24 Compare *Richards v. Delbridge* (1874), L.R. 18 Eq. 11; *Holt v. Heatherfield Trust*, [1942] 2 K.B. 1.

a party to prevent any subsequent action by him.[25] In view of the modern assimilation of law and equity, which has occurred in Canada following what happened in England under the Judicature Act of 1873,[26] it is still possible to obtain enforcement of an equitable assignment of a legal chose in action, in much the same way. It is still necessary for the assignor to be joined as a party, either as co-plaintiff, if he is willing, or as co-defendant if he is not.

Where the chose in action was equitable, for example, arising under a trust, no subsequent common-law proceedings against the debtor could arise, as was the case with a legal chose in action (which therefore meant that the original creditor, the assignor, had to be included to prevent duplicity of actions). Hence, the assignee was always allowed by equity to sue in his own name. This was, and still is, a real, complete, fully effective assignment. Equitable assignments still have the same effect in Canada, and in England, as they did prior to 1873. As Macdonald C.J. said in the leading British Columbia case of *Dell v. Saunders*,[27] which discussed both equitable and statutory assignments,

> [i]t is only when the right assigned is an equitable one . . . that the assignee can sue in his own name. The law in this respect has not been changed.

He was referring to changes made by a British Columbia statute (which was, and is in much the same form and to the same effect as the English and other Canadian statutes). Since there is still a difference between statutory and equitable assignments, it is necessary to determine, *inter alia*, whether what is involved in a given instance is an equitable or a statutory assignment. In that particular case it was held, by a majority of the court, that although a good equitable assignment had taken place, it was an assignment of a legal, not an equitable chose in action; hence the statute was inapplicable, and the assignee could not bring the action in his own name. The case concerned a conveyance of land which recited in the deed an agreement between the parties to pay the purchase price by instalments. The conveyance was expressed to be subject to that agreement. The right to payment was assigned by the vendor to a third party, the plaintiff in the action. When the plaintiff sued for the recovery of an overdue instalment which was payable to the original vendor (the assignor), it was held that, because the assignment was not in writing, as required by the statute, it was not a valid statutory assignment, and because it was an equitable assignment of a legal debt, that is, a legal chose in action, the plaintiff could not sue in his own name.

(C) *Requirements of a valid equitable assignment* The nature of the particular transaction is all-important. Two issues arise. First, is it properly to be construed as an assignment at all? Second, if so, is it of an equitable or a legal chose? Sometimes these issues are not clearly differentiated by the courts,[28] but the general

---

25 *Hammond v. Messenger* (1838), 9 Sim. 327.

26 36 & 37 Vict., c. 66.

27 (1914), 17 D.L.R. 279 at 281 (B.C.C.A.).

28 Sometimes the issue is whether there was an assignment: *McAvoy v. Royal Bank*, [1933] 3 W.W.R. 433 (Sask. C.A.); *Can. Credit Men's Trust Assn. v. Heinke* (1957), 23 W.W.R. 305 (B.C.S.C.).

answer is given that the transaction in question was not an equitable assignment. This occurred, for example, in *Handley v. Crows' Nest Pass Lumber Co.*[29] An order signed by employees of the company sent to an officer of the company directing the company to pay some of the wages of the employees to the owner of a hotel at which the employees were lodging was not an equitable assignment. In *Partridge v. Winnipeg Investment Co.*[30] an order directing payment of a sum from the proceeds of a loan to a third party was not an equitable assignment in general; at the most it operated as such an assignment only from the fund specifically described in the order. But as long as the fund is specified,[31] and the amount of the assignment is stated, there may be a good equitable assignment of part of a fund. In *G.F. Stephens & Co. v. Perdue; Werner v. Perdue*[32] the creditor gave a written order to a third party granting him a sum on the general balance owed to the creditor on a mortgage. This was a valid equitable assignment, with the result that the transferee of the mortgage took subject to the assignment in question. So too in *Kidd v. Harden; McConnal v. Harden*[33] a sale was negotiated by an agent. The vendor accepted the agent's cheque on the undertaking that the cheque would be met by a deposit in the agent's account to be made by the agent's principal, the purchaser, on the proceeds of the resale of the goods by the principal. This was held to be an equitable assignment of such proceeds in the principal's hands, when they reached him, in favour of the vendor. Therefore the principal could not withhold the deposit and use the proceeds of the resale to settle accounts between himself and the agent.

Mention of this raises the question of assignments of *future* choses in action, for example, debts which have not yet matured but which will come into existence or be paid in the future. Following the House of Lords decision in the leading case of *Tailby v. Official Receiver,*[34] the Supreme Court of Canada held, in *Fraser v. Imperial Bank of Canada,*[35] that an assignment of future choses in action, to arise in the future out of a contract, bound the conscience of the assignor in equity, and became effective for all purposes when the subject-matter of the assignment came into existence, for example, when the debts were paid by debtors of the assignor.[36]

---

29 (1909), 11 W.L.R. 210 (B.C.C.A.).

30 [1917] 2 W.W.R. 832 (Man. C.A.); reversed [1921] 1 W.W.R. 839 (S.C.C.).

31 *Rodick v. Gandell* (1852), 1 De G.M. & G. 763 at 777-778 *per* Lord Truro: *Palmer v. Carey,* [1926] A.C. 703 (P.C.) (hence there was no assignment in that case because there were no goods or funds on which the order, *i.e.,* the alleged assignment, was to operate).

32 [1931] 3 W.W.R. 90 (Alta. S.C.); compare *Beatty v. Best* (1921), 61 S.C.R. 576 (S.C.C.); *Sterling Collieries v. Jones,* [1924] 3 W.W.R. 955 (Alta. Chambers).

33 [1924] 3 W.W.R. 293 (Alta. C.A.).

34 (1888), 13 App. Cas. 523 (H.L.).

35 (1912), 47 S.C.R. 313 (S.C.C.).

36 If the future choses in action are *book debts, i.e.,* trade debts due to be paid in the future, their assignability and the form of an assignment may be governed in some provinces by statute: *e.g.,* in Ontario the Personal Property Security Act, R.S.O. 1990, c. P.10. This statute also permits and governs the assignment of a "security interest," as defined in that Act. For the possibility of conflict between the provision of the statute and that of the Conveyancing and Law of Property Act, R.S.O.

No special form was, or is required in equity for a valid equitable assignment. As Lamont J.A. said in *Grant v. Morgan*,[37] following and accepting the decision of the House of Lords in *Brandt's Son & Co. v. Dunlop Rubber Co.*,[38] "any form of words is sufficient, so long as they clearly show an intention that the assignee is to have the benefit of the debt assigned." *Lawson Graphics Pacific Ltd. v. Simpson*[39] was a case which Southin J. admitted[40] was close to the line. While it is clear that an oral assignment is possible,[41] the assignor in this case simply said to the assignee, "When we are paid, you will be paid." That was sufficient to constitute an equitable assignment of a debt that, eventually, was paid to the assignor.

But *consideration* is necessary unless there has been a completed transfer, that is, a gift. Thus, there is a distinction between a perfected and an imperfectly constituted transfer, in this respect at least. If the assignor has transferred the equitable title by whatever means are suitable and appropriate, the courts will assist the assignee to enforce his right, whether or not value has been given.[42] If this has not been done,[43] or it cannot be done, since what is being assigned is a future chose in action,[44] consideration must be established, else the courts will not assist the assignee, except, possibly to the extent that the debtor owes the assignor.[45] In the case of future choses, the courts treated the assignment as a contract to assign in the future, hence the need for consideration.[46] But it appears that even if there is no consideration, payment by the debtor of the *assignee* will discharge the debtor.[47]

As between the assignor and the assignee, no notice to the debtor is required.[48]

1990, c. C.34 (below, note 77) see the Ontario Law Reform Commission *Report on Sale of Goods* (1979), vol. 1, pp. 120-121.

37 [1924] 2 D.L.R. 1164 at 1165 (Sask. C.A.); compare *Bank of N.S. v. Nfld. Rebar Co.* (1987), 65 Nfld. & P.E.I.R. 165 (Nfld. T.D.).

38 [1905] A.C. 454 (H.L.).

39 (1987), 12 B.C.L.R. (2d) 126 (B.C.S.C.).

40 *Ibid.*, at 133.

41 *Bank of N.S. v. Nfld. Rebar Co.*, above, note 37.

42 *Kekewich v. Manning* (1851), 42 E.R. 519; compare Beck J.A. in *Dickson v. Chamberland*, [1927] 2 D.L.R. 429 at 438 (Alta. C.A.).

43 *Curtis v. Langrock*, [1922] 1 W.W.R. 316 (Alta. C.A.); *Sanderson v. Halstead*, [1968] 1 O.R. 749 (Ont. H.C.).

44 *Sanderson v. Halstead*, above, note 43.

45 *Grant v. Morgan*, above, note 37.

46 *Tailby v. Official Receiver*, above, note 34.

47 *German v. Yates* (1915), 32 T.L.R. 52; distinguishing *Re Brooks Settlement Trusts*, [1939] Ch. 993.

48 *Holt v. Heatherfield Trust*, [1942] 2 K.B. 1; *Re Trytel*, [1952] 2 T.L.R. 32; contrast the situation with respect to statutory assignments, below, p. 681.

   Note, however, that at first instance in *B.A. Timber Co. v. Jones (No. 2)*, [1943] 2 W.W.R. 654 (B.C.S.C.) it was said that the assignee of a debt could only sue in his own name without providing notice of assignment to the debtor in two instances: (1) where the debtor was a party to or in agreement with the assignment; *or* (2) the assignor was a limited liability company which no longer had any corporate existence. On appeal, however, it was held: (1) that no notice to the debtor was required if the assignment was of a *charge* over property as contrasted with a debt; and (2) that what was involved in this case was *not* assignment: [1944] 2 W.W.R. 577 (B.C.C.A.) following, as regards the first point, *Taylor v. London & County Banking Co.*, [1901] 2 Ch. 231 (C.A.).

However notice to the debtor, though not essential, is desirable for at least two reasons. First of all, to prevent the debtor from paying the assignor, which would discharge him.[49] Second, to give the assignee priority over subsequent encumbrancers, for example, second or later assignees[50] (a doctrine which applies even though the chose in action is a *legal one*).[51] But no formal notice seems to be necessary, where notice is given.[52] As long as the debtor has the knowledge in question, for example, from newspapers, this will suffice for these purposes.[53]

(D) *Effects of valid equitable assignment* Whether the chose in action which is being assigned by the equitable assignment is legal or equitable, the assignee only acquires title to the assigned chose "subject to equities".[54] This means that in any action brought by the assignee to enforce his rights, the debtor or other defendant may raise against the assignee whatever defences would have been available against the original assignor.[55] This would include a claim for unliquidated damages which the debtor might have counterclaimed and if successful set off against the assignor, as long as the damages in question arise out of, and are inseparably connected with the contract which has been the source of the assignment.[56] Two English cases illustrate the operation of this doctrine. In *Roxburghe v. Cox*[57] C assigned the proceeds of the sale of his army commission to A. This money was paid into B's bank, where C was overdrawn. On A's notifying B of the assignment, it was held that A took subject to the bank's set-off against

---

In an English case, in which an option to renew a contract was assigned, *Warner Bros. Records Inc. v. Rollgreen Ltd.*, [1975] 2 All E.R. 105 (C.A.), it was held that, until notice was given to the debtor, *i.e.*, the other party to the option, the assignee of the option obtained no enforceable contractual rights against that party. Note the criticism of this case, as conflicting with earlier authority, in Treitel, *Law of Contract*, 8th ed. (1991), p. 585, note 82.

49 *Stocks v. Dobson* (1853), 4 De G.M. & G. 11, 43 E.R. 411. In the *Warner Bros.* case, above, note 48, it was said by Lord Denning M.R., relying on other cases, that notice of the assignment was necessary to perfect the title of the assignee of a debt or an option.

50 *Dearle v. Hall* (1828), 3 Russ. 1, 38 E.R. 475; *Fraser v. Imperial Bank of Can.*, above, note 35; compare *Colonial Bank v. Butec Int. Chemical Corp.* (1986), 7 B.C.L.R. (2d) 381 (B.C.S.C.) where no proper notice was given to the debtor by the assignee, hence the latter had no claim upon shares allegedly transferred to the assignee, a collateral pledgee, by a blank transfer form.

51 *Marchant v. Morton, Down & Co.*, [1901] 2 K.B. 829.

52 Unless the transaction involves an interest in land, in which event the Statute of Frauds may be involved: above, pp. 212-214. On the need for clarity of the notice see *James Talcott Ltd. v. John Lewis & Co.*, [1940] 3 All E.R. 592 (C.A.).

53 *Lloyd v. Banks* (1868), 3 Ch. App. 488.

54 *First City Capital Ltd. v. Petrosar Ltd.* (1987), 42 D.L.R. (4th) 738 at 746-747 (Ont. H.C.) *per* Callaghan A.C.J.H.C.; compare above, note 15.

55 *E.g.*, that the original creditor, the assignor, precluded payment of the debt by the creditor's own act: *Bryant & May (Holdings) Ltd. v. R.O.C. Tpt. (N.B.) Ltd.* (1978), 23 N.B.R. (2d) 681 (N.B.Q.B.).

56 *Nfld. Govt. v. Nfld. Ry.* (1888), 13 App. Cas. 199 (P.C.). Compare *Central Trust Co. v. Messenger* (1988), 33 B.C.L.R. (2d) 34 (B.C.S.C.). On set-off, see *Springer Dev. Corp. (Receiver of) v. Alta. Mortgage & Housing Corp.* (1987), 79 A.R. 368 (Alta. Q.B.); *New York House Ltd. v. O'Connor-4 Co.* (1988), 1 R.P.R. (2d) 295 (Ont. H.C.); affirmed (September 30, 1991), Doc. CA 524/88, 527/88 (Ont. C.A.). The leading case on set-off is *Telford v. Holt*, [1987] 2 S.C.R. 193 (S.C.C.).

57 (1881), 17 Ch. D. 520 (C.A.).

C, that is, the amount owing by C on his overdraft. On the other hand in *Stoddart v. Union Trust*[58] A fraudulently sold a paper to B. The proceeds of this sale A assigned to C, who, though ignorant of the fraud, only obtained a voidable title to such proceeds. When C sued B for the money, B pleaded the fraud perpetrated by A claiming that he had suffered greater loss than the amount assigned to B. It was held that this defence could not be raised by the debtor against the assignee, because it was personal to the assignor, not connected with the contractual debt assigned by the assignor.

The other important issue which arises where there has been an equitable assignment relates to the right of the assignee to sue in his own name, without involving the assignor as co-plaintiff. This depends upon several factors. One is whether the chose assigned is legal or equitable.[59] Another is whether the assignment is absolute or conditional. A third is whether the assignment is total or partial. An "absolute" assignment is one by which the entire interest of the assignor in the chose in action is for the time being transferred unconditionally to the assignee and placed under his control.[60] Hence if the assignment is to be operative or to cease to be operative on the happening of an uncertain event, it will be conditional, not absolute.[61] But an assignment which is given by way of security only or on a certain trust will be an absolute assignment, not a conditional one.[62] Thus, the fact that there will be a re-assignment at some future time does not destroy the absoluteness of the assignment at the time it is made.[63] On the other hand in *Sardara Singh v. Industrial Mortgage & Finance Corporation*[64] the British Columbia court refused to follow the English case of *Hughes v. Pump House Hotel Co.*,[65] in which the assignor allowed the assignee to settle all accounts for him, and the assignment which included these terms was held to be an absolute assignment. It was held that where the assignor makes an assignment of a debt subject to the possibility of a dispute between the assignor, the creditor, on the one hand and the debtor on the other, the assignment is not absolute. Possibly these cases can be reconciled by saying that in the English decision there was no uncertainty as to the person entitled to be paid, and in the Canadian case it was not clear since the effect of the assignment might have depended on the outcome of a dispute between the assignor and the debtor. An assignment which is by way of charge, that is, entitles the assignee to payment from a particular fund, is not absolute since it does not

---

58 [1912] 1 K.B. 181 (C.A.). This distinction of claims of a strong personal nature was referred to by Barry J. in *Bryant & May (Holdings) Ltd. v. R.O.C. Tpt. (N.B.) Ltd.*, above, note 55, at 686.

59 *Griffiths v. Kenney*, [1917] 1 W.W.R. 800 (B.C.S.C.).

60 *Magrath v. Collins*, [1917] 1 W.W.R. 487 (Alta. S.C.).

61 *Durham Bros v. Robertson*, [1898] 1 Q.B. 765 (C.A.) followed in *Dom. Creosoting Co. v. T.R. Nickson Co.*, [1917] 2 W.W.R. 330 (S.C.C.).

62 *O'Dwyer v. Banks*, [1953] 2 D.L.R. 204 (Alta. C.A.), following *Hughes v. Pump House Hotel*, [1902] 2 K.B. 190 (C.A.); compare *Wilton v. Rochester German Underwriters Agency*, [1917] 2 W.W.R. 782 (Alta. C.A.); *Taylor v. Equitable Fire & Marine Ins. Co.*, [1918] 1 W.W.R. 676 (Alta. C.A.); *Comfort v. Betts*, [1891] 1 Q.B. 737 (C.A.).

63 *Tancred v. Delagoa Bay & East Africa Ry. Co.* (1889), 23 Q.B.D. 239.

64 (1967), 61 W.W.R. 338 (B.C. Co. Ct.).

65 [1902] 2 K.B. 190 (C.A.).

transfer ownership in the fund to the assignee.[66] Nor will a partial assignment be absolute,[67] even though it will be effective as an assignment of the part of the debt assigned.

In all these situations, where the assignment is not absolute, the assignee cannot sue in his own name, any more than he can where the chose assigned is legal as opposed to equitable. This situation must be differentiated from the position where there is more than one equitable assignee,[68] and questions arise as to who should be joined as a party,[69] and where the assignor has retained some interest in the original indebtedness and may therefore have a right of action of his own, quite distinct from that of the assignee.[70]

(iii) *Under statute*

(A) *Statutory intervention* The situation in England was changed by the provisions of the Judicature Act of 1873 (now contained in section 136 of the Law of Property Act, 1925),[71] under which a new form of assignment was introduced in order to alleviate or eradicate some of the problems felt with respect to equitable assignments. In Canada, some provinces adopted the English legislation, *verbatim*. Those which did so are: Alberta,[72] British Columbia,[73] New Brunswick,[74] Newfoundland,[75] Nova Scotia,[76] and Ontario.[77] Two provinces, Manitoba and Saskatchewan, have enacted legislation that is wider in scope. The Northwest Territories and the Yukon have similar legislation to that which exists in Saskatchewan and

---

66 *Jones v. Humphreys*, [1902] 1 K.B. 10. On the distinction between assignment, charge, etc., see the judgment of Anglin J. in *Dom. Creosoting Co. v. T.R. Nickson Co.*, above, note 61.

67 *Re Steel Wing Co.*, [1921] 1 Ch. 349; *Williams v. Atlantic Assur. Co.*, [1933] 1 K.B. 81 (C.A.); *Walter & Sullivan Ltd. v. J. Murphy & Sons Ltd.*, [1955] 2 Q.B. 584 (C.A.).

68 Involving joining the assignor as party: *Beatty v. Best* (1920), 47 O.L.R. 265 (Ont. C.A.); reversed on other grounds (1921), 61 S.C.R. 576 (S.C.C.).

69 *Columbia Grain Milling Co. v. Weins*, [1940] 3 W.W.R. 396 (B.C.S.C.) (when the protection of the debtor is important); compare *Dawson v. Leach*, [1935] 3 W.W.R. 547 (Alta. C.A.); also on parties *McKean v. Jones* (1891), 19 S.C.R. 489 (S.C.C.); *Can. Bank of Commerce v. La Brash*, [1918] 1 W.W.R. 8 (Sask. C.A.); *Mouat Bros. Co. v. Warnier*, [1931] 1 D.L.R. 569 (B.C.C.A.).

70 *Sardara Singh v. Indust. Mtge. & Finance Corp. Ltd.* (1967), 61 W.W.R. 338 (B.C. Co. Ct.); compare *Elliott v. Le Page*, [1929] 3 D.L.R. 912 (Man. K.B.).

71 15 & 16 Geo. 5, c. 20.

72 Judicature Act, R.S.A. 1980, c. J-1, s. 21.

73 Law and Equity Act, R.S.B.C. 1979, c. 224, s. 32.

74 Judicature Act, R.S.N.B. 1973, c. J-2, s. 31.

75 Judicature Act, R.S.N. 1990, c. J-4, s. 103.

76 Judicature Act, R.S.N.S. 1989, c. 240, s. 43(5). The Judicature Act of Prince Edward Island, R.S.P.E.I. 1974, c. J-3 (which dealt with this in s. 15) is not contained in the 1988 Revised Statutes.

77 Conveyancing and Law of Property Act, R.S.O. 1990, c. C.34, s. 53(1). Note the possibility of conflict between this provision and that of the Personal Property Security Act relating to the assignment of a "security interest" or of book debts not intended to be by way of security: above, p. 676, note 36.

Manitoba.[78] Thus, the situation in Canada depends upon which province or territory is the place where the assignment occurred.

The Manitoba and Saskatchewan legislation, and that of the territories, permits any written assignment in any form, whether absolute or not, to have the effect of enabling the assignee to sue in his own name.[79] Thus, in those provinces, the limitations of the earlier equitable assignment have been swept away, and, as long as there is a written assignment signed by the assignor, the assignee has complete freedom to bring an action to enforce the debt without joining the assignor as a party. The position in all the other provinces is different[80] and resembles the present-day position in England. In those provinces, as in England,

> any absolute assignment by writing under the hand of the assignor (not purporting to be by way of charge only) of any debt or other legal thing in action, of which express notice in writing has been given to the debtor, trustee, or other person from whom the assignor would have been entitled to claim such debt or thing in action, is effectual in law (subject to equities having priority over the right of the assignee) to pass and transfer from the date of such notice the legal right to such debt or thing in action, all legal and other remedies for the same, and the power to give a good discharge for the same without the concurrence of the assignor.

The scope and effect of this provision must now be examined.

(B) *Requirements of a valid statutory assignment* One point should be clarified at the outset. Although the statute speaks of "any debt or other legal thing in action", it would seem that the statute applies to *any* chose in action, whether legal or equitable, which could have been assigned in equity prior to the statutory change in the law.[81] There are limitations of the kinds of things which are assignable.[82] As long as the chose is within the ambit of assignability, it may be dealt with in accordance with the statute.

On that basis a valid statutory assignment involves: that the assignment be absolute; that it be written; and that written notice be given to the debtor. What is meant by an "absolute" assignment has been considered earlier.[83] As explained, this excludes from the ambit of the statutory provisions an assignment by way

---

78 The passage from "In Canada, some provinces . . ." to "Saskatchewan and Manitoba" was quoted in *Bank of N.S. v. Nfld. Rebar Co.*, above, note 37 at 172 *per* Steele J.

79 Law of Property Act, R.S.M. 1987, c. L90, s. 31; Choses in Action Act, R.S.S. 1978, c. C-11; Choses in Action Act, R.S.N.W.T. 1988, c. C-7; Choses in Action Act, R.S.Y. 1986, c. 24. See *West v. Shun* (1915), 24 D.L.R. 813 (Sask. S.C.) on the interpretation and application of the Saskatchewan statute. There need be no notice to the debtor but if there is the assignee takes free from equities, defences, etc., that are subsequent to the notice.

80 The passage from "permits any written assignment" to "is different" was quoted in *Manitoba Milk Producers Co-op Inc. v. Manitoba (Milk Producers' Marketing Bd.)* (1987), 52 Man. R. (2d) 225 at 227 (Man. Q.B.) *per* Barkman J.

81 *Re Pain*, [1919] 1 Ch. 38. For example, the assignor's interest in a trust fund: *Nash v. Landry* (1986), 7 B.C.L.R. (2d) 129 (B.C. Co. Ct.); affirmed (January 27, 1988), Doc. Vancouver CA006816 (B.C.C.A.).

82 Below, pp. 683-686.

83 Above, pp. 679-680.

of charge.[84] But a mortgage of a debt may be an absolute assignment.[85] The assignment must be in writing signed by the assignor.[86] It is essential under the statute that the assignee prove that express notice of the assignment, in writing, has been given to the debtor.[87] Hence, in one Ontario case,[88] which involved an assignment of a debt followed by a re-assignment back to the original assignor, it had to be shown that notice of the re-assignment had been given to the debtor.

It would appear that consideration for the assignment need not be shown for it to be effective under the statutory provisions (provided all the other requirements of the statute are satisfied). Whether the chose is legal or equitable, therefore, and whether it is for consideration or by way of gift, whether the gift is perfected or not, the assignment will be enforceable under the statute, because the statutory transaction is a transfer of property, *not* a contract.[89]

(C) *Effect of a valid statutory assignment* Where the statute is satisfied then the assignee may sue in his own name, without joining the assignor as a party.[90] As Macdonald C.J. said in the case of *Dell v. Saunders*,[91]

> [l]egal choses in action could and have been recovered by suit in the name of the assignor. It is here that the law has been changed. The Act gives the assignee of a legal chose in action who complies with its provisions the right to sue in his own name, but when a legal chose in action is assigned otherwise than in conformity to the Act, he must still sue in the name of the assignor.

Except for the apparent differentiation of legal and equitable choses in action, which is not drawn by the statute, the remarks of the learned judge, spoken about the British Columbia statute, express succinctly what has been achieved by the statutory changes. They are procedural rather than substantive; they are designed

---

84 See the cases cited above in notes 60, 61, 68.

85 See the cases cited above in notes 62, 63.

86 Compare the requirements of the Manitoba and Saskatchewan statutes, above, note 79.

87 See, *e.g.*, *Pettit & Johnston v. Foster Wheeler Ltd.*, [1950] O.R. 83 (Ont. H.C.); affirmed subject to variation as to interest [1950] O.W.N. 474 (Ont. C.A.); *Watson v. C.F. Hart Ltd.* (1986), 59 Nfld. & P.E.I.R. 308 (Nfld. Dist. Ct.) (lack of notice in writing defeated assignee's claim). Compare *Dalhousie Lbr. Co. v. Walker* (1916), 44 N.B.R. 455 (N.B.C.A.); *Dell v. Saunders* (1914), 17 D.L.R. 279 (B.C.C.A.); *Griffiths v. Kenney*, [1917] 1 W.W.R. 800 (B.C.S.C.); *Grant v. Cameron* (1891), 18 S.C.R. 716 (S.C.C.). Compare the English case, *Warner Bros. Records Inc. v. Rollgreen Ltd.*, [1975] 2 All E.R. 105 (C.A.). Contrast *Won Wah Low Co. v. Wong*, [1962] O.W.N. 165 (Ont. H.C.). In one English case, *Hockley and Papworth v. Goldstein* (1920), 90 L.J.K.B. 111, it was held that reading the assignment over to a blind man did not fulfil the requirements of the statute (although there was a good equitable assignment).

88 *Allux Ltd. v. McKenna*, [1962] O.W.N. 258 (Ont. Div. Ct.); compare *DiGuilo v. Boland*, [1958] O.R. 384 (Ont. C.A.).

89 *Re Westerton*, [1919] 2 Ch. 104. Contrast the situation where the assignment is equitable: above, p. 677. In *Bank of N.S. v. Nfld. Rebar Co.*, above, note 37, a statutory assignment to the bank had priority over an equitable assignment to the plaintiffs: it was earlier in time. But this might also have been because the statutory assignment transferred property.

90 *Won Wah Low Co. v. Wong*, above, note 87.

91 Above, note 87 at 281. Compare *Trubenizing Process Corp. v. John Forsyth Ltd.*, [1943] S.C.R. 422 at 428-529 (S.C.C.) *per* Davis J.

to simplify and make easier the process for enforcing an assignment,[92] In one respect there is a difference between a statutory assignment and an equitable one, in that notice to the debtor is necessary in the case of the former,[93] and, at most only desirable, for the protection of the assignee,[94] in the case of the latter. But, in both, the assignee takes subject to equities, that is, defences that would be available against the assignor, or the priorities of other assignees.[95]

(D) *Effects of an invalid statutory assignment* As stated by Macdonald C.J., an assignment that does not conform to the requirements of the statute, as long as in other respects it is valid, will be enforceable as an equitable assignment, that is, requiring the assignee to join the assignor as a party.[96] Thus an absolute assignment not in the statutory form, an assignment that is not absolute whether in the statutory form or not, and an assignment that is of a future chose in action, will necessitate the joinder of the assignor to any proceedings to claim under the assignment from the debtor.

(iv) *What is assignable*

Whether an assignment is statutory or equitable, it will not be valid unless the interest, that is, the chose in action, which has been assigned is one that is assignable under the law.[97] The statutes have made no change in this requirement.

The assignment must not destroy a personal tie.[98] Nor may it throw uncontemplated burdens on the debtor, to his prejudice. Thus, it has been held that the assignee of the benefit of a contract under which the defendant agreed to pay money to the assignor could not obtain specific performance of the contract; to have done so would have meant that too harsh a burden was put upon the debtor.[99] In this context, a question which has arisen several times in the courts of England

---

92 Compare *Slattery v. Slattery*, [1946] 1 D.L.R. 304 at 313 (Ont. C.A.) *per* Laidlaw J.A.

93 *W.F. Harrison & Co. v. Burke*, [1956] 1 W.L.R. 419 (C.A.).

94 By virtue of the application of the rule in *Dearle v. Hall*, above, note 50.

95 Compare above, p. 678. The same is true of assignments under the Manitoba and Saskatchewan statutes and the statutes of the territories.
    The passage from "In one respect" to the end of the paragraph was quoted by Steele J. in *Bank of N.S. v. Nfld. Rebar Co.*, above, note 37, at 171. Note, in that case, the question of priorities and how it was solved: above, note 89.

96 *Brandt's Son & Co. v. Dunlop Rubber Co.*, [1905] A.C. 454 (H.L.); approved in *Dom. Creosoting Co. v. T.R. Nickson Co.* (1917), 55 S.C.R. 303 (S.C.C.); *Grant v. Morgan*, [1924] 2 D.L.R. 1164 (Sask. C.A.).

97 Compare Fridman, *Sale of Goods in Canada*, 3rd ed. (1986), pp. 463-467. A debt or other chose in action will not be assignable if the original contract prohibits or forbids any such assignment: *Helstan Securities Ltd. v. Hertfordshire C.C.*, [1978] 3 All E.R. 262.

98 *Cottage Club Estates v. Woodside Estates Co. (Amersham)*, [1928] 2 K.B. 463 (arbitration clause under a building contract); compare *Peters v. General Accident, Fire & Life Assur. Corp.*, [1938] 2 All E.R. 267 (C.A.) (policy covering those driving with the assured's consent). Compare *Nat. Trust Co. v. Miller*, [1977] 1 W.W.R. 481 (Man. Q.B.) (assignment of shares valid, since there was nothing personal about the original contract of purchase of the shares, nor any personal obligations on the original purchaser).

99 *Belgo-Can. Real Estate Co. v. Allan, Killam & McKay Ltd.*, [1924] 3 W.W.R. 833 (Man. C.A.).

and Canada is whether the benefit of a contract, under which A agrees to supply B with certain goods, may be assigned by B. In the leading English case of *Tolhurst v. Associated Portland Cement Co.*,[100] the House of Lords upheld the assignment, made by a small company to a large one, of a contract to supply chalk as required by the assignor's cement works. This was on the basis that the smaller company could have enlarged itself, thereby increasing its requirements of chalk, and an intention to benefit assigns was manifest in the original contract.

On the same basis an assignment was upheld where a contractor covenanted for herself *and her assigns* to supply water from a pump on her land to the purchaser of some of the contractor's land who had bought it to construct a bungalow thereon. When the purchaser sold the land to a third party, with the benefit of this covenant, it was held that the contractor was bound to supply the water, since the possibility of assignment was clearly contemplated by the original contract; it was impersonal in character, and added no greater burden to the obligee, the promisor or debtor.[101] So too, in Canada, a court upheld the assignment of a covenant in restraint of trade,[102] under which the defendant agreed not to compete for a limited period and within a limited area. Although the contract did not specify that it was for the benefit of the covenantee's assigns, when the latter sold the business to the plaintiff, it was held that the defendant was bound to the assignee. The sale of the business included the goodwill of the business; the covenant was part of the goodwill; therefore, it was assignable and upon assignment, that is, sale by the original purchaser to a third party, it operated for the benefit of the assignee, the subsequent buyer of the business. There was no new burden on the debtor, the party under the restraint. In an Australian case, *New Redhead Estate & Coal Co. v. Scottish Australian Mining Co.*,[103] the Privy Council held that a contract, under which the railway agreed to let the coal company transfer coal from its colliery over the railway on payment of an annual fee, was an assignable contract, so that the coal company could assign its benefit to a third party.

However, the same will not be the case, at least unless the debtor assents to the assignment,[104] where the transfer might be too burdensome upon the debtor. For example, in *Kemp v. Baerselman*,[105] the benefit of a contract to supply eggs to the assignor's business was assigned to a limited liability company. It was held to be unenforceable, since it might have involved excessive demands being made upon the egg supplier, over the amount which he had undertaken and could

---

100 [1903] A.C. 414 (H.L.). See the interpretation of this case to cover assignment of benefits, not obligations, unless all the parties agreed, by Puddester J. in *Air Transit Ltd. v. Innotech Aviation of Nfld. Ltd.* (1989), 78 Nfld. & P.E.I.R. 24 at 51 (Nfld. T.D.).

101 *Shayler v. Woolf*, [1946] 2 All E.R. 54.

102 *Barkett v. Shaw* (1960), 31 W.W.R. 1 (Man. Q.B.). Compare *Jacoby v. Whitmore* (1883), 49 L.T. 335 (C.A.); *Berry v. Days* (1903), 5 O.L.R. 629 (Ont. C.A.); *Day v. Trull* (1929), 36 O.W.N. 262 (Ont. H.C.). On restraint of trade see above, pp. 388-415.

103 [1920] 1 W.W.R. 173 (P.C.).

104 *Air Transit Ltd. v. Innotech Aviation of Nfld. Ltd.*, above, note 100. Compare in the case of an assignment by the debtor of his obligations: *Simpson and Ors v. Cousins*, [1923] 1 D.L.R. 106 (P.E.I.C.A.); compare below, pp. 686-687.

105 [1906] 2 K.B. 604 (C.A.).

reasonably contemplate as being necessitated by his original contract. The same result followed where the contract was one involving personal service by the debtor, and the assignor was the party entitled to the benefit of such service.[106] The House of Lords in *Nokes v. Doncaster Amalgamated Collieries Ltd.*,[107] refused to treat such a contract as assignable, even though, in that case, the assignment was the consequence of an amalgamation of companies under the English Companies Act. This was followed in a Manitoba case, *Fisher v. Rosenberg.*[108] There the defendant was the employee of a company which was taken over by the plaintiffs. It was held that the benefit of his contract of service was not assignable without his, the employee's, consent. However, since he had continued to work for the new business, that is, after the takeover, it was held that he was bound by his contract and therefore liable for a breach.

Some contracts are treated, as a matter of public policy (even apart from any specific statutory provisions which may affect them or other contracts) as being unassignable, so far as their benefit is concerned.[109] These include contracts under which pensions and salaries are payable out of national funds to a public officer, and contracts under which alimony is payable to a wife.

A third important category of unassignable contracts is where the purported assignment relates to a bare right of action, whether for breach of contract or tort. This is because such an assignment savours of at the very least the tort of maintenance, that is, assisting a person to bring litigation without the party so assisting having a legitimate interest in the outcome of the proceedings, and may even involve champerty, that is, sharing in the proceeds of litigation.[110] This was stated to be anachronistic even before recent developments in the law of maintenance and champerty in England.[111] But those changes have not come about in Canada, and therefore, the rationale for refusing to recognize such assignments may still be valid and operative in this country. It was held in *Union Gas Co. v. Brown*,[112] that, despite the provisions of the Ontario statute creating statutory assignments, it was not possible for a party entitled to bring an action for trespass against the defendant to assign such right to the assignor company's parent company. It was a bare right of action for unliquidated damages in tort, and, even if not champertous in intent, could not be assigned. Exceptionally, however, some assignments of rights of action are permitted. In the first place, if it is not the right itself that is being assigned, but the proceeds of, that is, the sum to be awarded

---

106 *E.g.*, writing a book: *Stevens v. Benning* (1855), 6 De G.M. & G. 223, 43 E.R. 1218; *Griffith v. Tower Publishing Co.*, [1897] 1 Ch. 21.

107 [1940] A.C. 1114 (H.L.).

108 (1960), 67 Man. R. 336 (Man. Q.B.).

109 *E.g.*, in relation to the assignment of wages, see, for example, the Wages Act, R.S.O. 1990, c. W.1, and the Wage Assignments Act, R.S.A. 1980, c. W-1.

110 *Prosser v. Edmonds* (1835), 160 E.R. 196; for maintenance and champerty, compare above, pp. 374-375.

111 *County Hotel & Wine Co. v. London & North Western Ry. Co.*, [1918] 2 K.B. 251 at 258; affirmed on other grounds [1921] 1 A.C. 85 (H.L.) *per* McCardie J. For the change in the law see above, p. 374.

112 [1968] 1 O.R. 524 (Ont. H.C.); reversed on other grounds [1970] 1 O.R. 715 (Ont. C.A.).

in, the action, it has been held that this amounts to an assignment of future property and will be valid, because nothing passes until the damages in question are awarded, so that there is no question of maintenance.[113] Second, if the right of action accompanies property that is being transferred, for example, where the right to sue on a broken covenant is assigned along with the lease that has been broken, it has been held that more than a right to litigate is being assigned, thereby excluding the possibility of champerty.[114] In such instances the right of action is one of the incidents attached to the property that is being transferred and "an assignment of property is valid, even although that property may be incapable of being recovered without ligitation."[115]

(b) Of the burdens or liabilities under a contract

(i) Non-assignability

In strict speech, as well as in point of law, it is incorrect to talk of the assignment of the liabilities or burdens placed upon a contracting party by a contract.[116] As was clearly stated in *Lounsbury Co. v. Duthie*,[117] a party to a contract may assign rights but not liabilities so as to relieve himself of a contractual obligation. The party obliged under a contract is always under that personal obligation to perform, and will be liable should performance not occur. In the *Lounsbury* case, for example, under a conditional sale contract the vendor was given the right to repossess the goods and resell them in certain circumstances. The purchaser defaulted, whereupon the vendor, as entitled under the contract, seized the goods. But he did not resell them. He transferred his interest in them to a third party, without obtaining the consent of the purchaser to such transfer. It was held that the vendor was liable to the purchaser for breach of his obligation, upon repossessing the goods, to resell them and pay over to the purchaser any surplus obtained from such sale, after deducting what was owed by the purchaser to the vendor. So too, in *Simpson and Ors v. Cousins*,[118] the original debtor was still liable to pay the money due under a contract with the plaintiff, even though the debtor had purported to assign such debt to a new company. There was no evidence either of any assent by the creditor to payment by a new debtor, or of a new contract by the creditor with the new company.

That decision brings home an important point, by way of qualification of what has been stated above, even though it does not really involve either assignment or an evasion of the doctrine of privity. There may be a change of debtors by

---

113 *Glegg v. Bromley*, [1912] 3 K.B. 474 (C.A.) (proceeds of an action for deceit). But why is it not champerty?

114 *Ellis v. Torrington*, [1920] 1 K.B. 399 (C.A.). Compare *Compania Colombiana de Seguros v. Pac. Steam Navigation Co.*, [1965] 1 Q.B. 101. But why is it not maintenance?

115 *Dawson v. Great Nor. & City Ry. Co.*, [1905] 1 K.B. 260 at 271 (C.A.).

116 *Nokes v. Doncaster Amalgam. Collieries*, [1940] 3 All E.R. 549 at 552 (H.L.) *per* Lord Simon L.C.

117 [1957] S.C.R. 590 (S.C.C.).

118 [1923] 1 D.L.R. 106 (P.E.I.C.A.); compare *Natal Land Co. v. Pauline Colliery Syndicate*, [1904] A.C. 120 (P.C.).

the method of novation, that is, as seen earlier, by the making of a new contract between the original parties and a new party, the "assignee" of the debt.[119] Such a new contract will discharge the old debtor from liability to the creditor, and replace him with the "new" debtor. A novation may be express or implied. The latter will occur, for example, where a creditor deals with a partnership after he has knowledge that there has been a change of partners following the retirement of a former partner, who was, prior to his retirement, one of the joint debtors owing the partnership's debts to the creditor in question. This may result in the inference that the creditor has discharged the old partner and looks only to the continuing partners for payment of the debts previously incurred.

(ii) *Substituted or vicarious performance*

While assignment, in the correct and effective sense, is not possible in respect of liabilities under a contract (so as to relieve the original obligee from any liability for non-performance or mal-performance), the law has gone a little way towards permitting the original debtor or obligee to transfer his burdens of obligation to another's shoulders. Occasionally the law has allowed the substitution of another debtor, in the sense of another party to perform the original obligee's task, under agreement between the original debtor and the substitute performer of the contract. This is not agency (although, in some situations a party, even one who is himself an agent, is allowed to delegate performance to another on his behalf).[120] It is not assignment (since the original debtor or obligee is primarily responsible and will be liable in the event of faulty performance). Nor is it permissible in respect of any and every contractual obligation.[121]

In *R. v. Smith*,[122] the Supreme Court of Canada, following earlier English authority, was loathe to admit the possibility of substituted or vicarious performance. In the words of Strong J.[123]

> [t]hat a party who enters into a contract for the performance of work is not entitled by a mere assignment to another person to substitute the assignee for himself, so as to delegate to the assignee his own rights and liabilities under the contract, without the consent of the other party to the agreement, is a proposition of law so well established that it requires scarcely any authority to support it. In such a case there is no privity of contract — no contractual relation of any kind — between the assignee and the party for whom the work is to be performed.

That was a case involving a contract to perform services for the Crown. It was held that, since the Crown had never consented to the assignment of the performance of the contract to a third party, such assignment was invalid, and the assignee could not sue for an alleged breach of the contract by the Crown.

---

119 Above, pp. 539-542.
120 Compare Fridman, *Law of Agency*, 6th ed. (1990), pp. 147-154.
121 Compare Fridman, *Sale of Goods in Canada*, 3rd ed. (1988), pp. 467-470.
122 (1883), 10 S.C.R. 1 (S.C.C.) following *Robson v. Drummond* (1831), 2 B. & Ad. 303, 109 E.R. 1156.
123 (1883), 10 S.C.R. 1 at 55 (S.C.C.).

However, it was recognized by more than one English case in the nineteenth century that there could be vicarious or substituted performance where no personal considerations influenced the choice of the original debtor or obligee.[124] This development was summarized in the following sentence from the *Tolhurst* case[125] cited in a twentieth century Alberta case involving the assignment of the burden to permit the hanging of a neon sign: "there is a clear right to assign a contract where no services depending on individual skill or personal confidence are required."[126] As was said by Hogg J. in the leading Ontario case of *Sullivan v. Gray*,

> The law is well established that where the skill or knowledge or some other personal quality of a party with whom a contract has been made is a material ingredient of the contract, the contract can be performed by the contracting party alone, and not by an assignee.[127]

In the earlier language of King J. of the Supreme Court of Canada in *Maloney v. Campbell*

> Agreements are said to be personal . . . when they are based on confidences, or considerations applicable to special personal characteristics and so cannot be usefully performed by another.[128]

Hence, in that case, an agreement to indemnify against payment of a possible money demand was "no more personal in this sense than is one to indemnify against payment of a definite or matured liability or an agreement to pay a sum of money for another."[129] The obligation was to indemnify the grantor of the mortgage in respect of his personal covenant to pay the sum mortgaged. The purchaser of the mortgaged land gave this indemnity, and it was held that he could assign this obligation so as to entitle the assignee to recover from the original debtor, that is, the grantor of the mortgage, the amount which he had paid under the indemnity.

Similarly, in *Paterson Timber Co. v. Canadian Pacific Lumber Co.*,[130] where there was a contract to sell all a particular company's timber coming for one year from a specified lumber camp, it was held that the obligation under this contract could be assigned to a new company, which replaced the original company. Performance of this contract did not require such personal service as to render it incapable of vicarious or substituted performance. Hence, the original company

---

124 Compare *Robson v. Drummond*, above, note 122 (described by Lord Greene M.R. in *Davies v. Collins*, [1945] 1 All E.R. 247 (C.A.), as "an extreme case") with *British Waggon Co. v. Lea* (1880), 5 Q.B.D. 149.

125 *Tolhurst v. Assoc. Portland Cement Co.*, [1903] A.C. 414 (H.L.).

126 *Blanchette Neon Ltd. v. Charlie Jim* (1956), 17 W.W.R. 404 at 408 (Alta. C.A.) *per* O'Connor C.J.A.

127 [1942] 3 D.L.R. 269 at 271 (Ont. H.C.).

128 (1897), 28 S.C.R. 228 at 233 (S.C.C.).

129 *Ibid.*, at 233. But see the cases cited above, note 118.

130 (1910), 14 W.L.R. 598 (B.C.C.A.); affirmed (1910), 23 W.L.R. 579 (S.C.C.); following *British Waggon Co. v. Lea*, above, note 124; the *Tolhurst* case, above, note 125, and distinguishing *Kemp v. Baerselman*, above, note 105.

could sue the buyers of the timber for wrongful repudiation of the contract. It was no defence to the latter that the former had arranged for *another* company to perform the contract, as a consequence of the "assignment" to the new company. The same situation would have arisen in *Canadian Credit Men's Trust Association Ltd. v. Heinke*,[131] if the contract between the original obligee and the substituted obligee had transferred all the rights of the original obligee to the third party, and so had been a proper "assignment". Since it did not, the purported substitution was ineffective to pass title to the third party. But the contract was "assignable", in the sense which has been used in the present context.

By way of contrast, there was an element of personal skill and confidence in a contract under which a party placed all its insurance business in the hands of another party; hence, when the latter assigned its business to a third party, it was held, in *Royal Financial Insurance Co. v. National Biscuit & Confection Co.*,[132] that the assignee of the business could not sue to enforce the undertaking by the other party to give its insurance business to the "assignor". In *Sullivan v. Gray*[133] the plaintiff, the owner of stores which provided equipment for amusement shows, etc., contracted to supply attractions and similar equipment at certain times to certain fairs. Later he assigned that contract to the defendant. The defendant subsequently cancelled the agreement between himself and the plaintiff. When sued on that contract, the defendant pleaded that the contract was invalid, on the ground of lack of consideration, because, it was argued, the plaintiff had purported to assign to him what was an unassignable contract, in view of the fact that the performance of the obligation to supply the attractions, etc., was personal. This argument was accepted and the defendant could not be made liable. It has been suggested that this decision is incorrect.[134] The argument that there was no consideration for the defendant's promise was said to be bad because: (1) the defendant went into the contract with his eyes open, and should not have been allowed to raise the plea that the obligation on the plaintiff was "unassignable"; and (2) there was no evidence that the defendant was in fact an unacceptable substitute for the plaintiff in the eyes of those to whom the plaintiff had contracted to supply the materials. It is interesting that this case involves a novel dispute, between the parties to an alleged "assignment", not between assignor and creditor, or assignee and creditor. Possibly, whatever the situation between either "assignor" or "assignee" on the one hand, and the creditor on the other, the agreement between the "assignee" and "assignor" should have been upheld, unless there were other grounds for its voidness or invalidity. However, there can be no doubt that Hogg J., in reaching his conclusion, was applying, in a different way, the principles previously established, and discussed above, as to the possibility of "assigning",

---

131 (1957), 23 W.W.R. 305 (B.C.S.C.).

132 [1933] 1 W.W.R. 43 (B.C.S.C.).

133 Above, note 127; following *Robson v. Drummond*, above, note 124; *British Waggon Co. v. Lea*, above, note 124; *Ross v. Fox* (1867), 13 Gr. 683 (U.C. Ch.); *Cohen v. Webber* (1911), 24 O.L.R. 171 (Ont. C.A.); *Wagstaffe v. Cook* (1921), 20 O.W.N. 303 (Ont. H.C.); affirmed (1921), 21 O.W.N. 82 (Ont. C.A.).

134 See the Editorial Note to the report in [1942] 3 D.L.R. 269.

in the limited sense used in this context, a duty arising under a contract. With those principles, it would appear, nobody will quarrel, even though particular applications of the principles may sometimes be criticized.

3. Assignment by operation of law

At common law there was a distinction between the effect of death of a party upon his rights and liabilities in respect of torts committed by or against him and the effect of the death of a party to a contract. Death terminated rights of action in tort, as well as liabilities.[135] However, the death of either party did not interfere with the continuation of the contract or of an action for breach of contract, unless the contract was based on personal considerations, skill or confidence.[136] Any rights of action that accrued to a party or existed against him could be brought by or against his estate. Hence, on death, contractual rights and liabilities passed, and still pass to the executors or administrators of the deceased, that is, his personal representatives, on intestacy or under the will. In consequence, save in respect of "personal" contracts,[137] one may speak of the involuntary and general assignment of all contractual rights and liabilities which results from death, as a matter of law, regardless of any wishes or acts of the deceased contracting party.[138]

Similarly, but in this respect, as a matter of statute,[139] as interpreted by the courts, where a contracting party is made bankrupt, rights of action for breach of contract which are vested in him at the time of bankruptcy may pass to his trustee in bankruptcy.[140] This would seem to depend upon whether such rights relate to his property (which vests in the trustee), or relate to personal feelings, or reputation (when they remain personal rights not capable of being pursued for the benefit of the bankrupt's creditors). In the case of breach of a contract for personal services made with the bankrupt, that is, by wrongful dismissal, much depends upon whether the breach occurred before or after the date when the bankrupt's property vested in the trustee.

Reference should also be made to the possibility that under statute there may be a right to compel the payment of wages or salary due to an employee to some third party, a creditor of the employee, or, in some instances, his spouse. Attachment and garnishment are legal procedures that may be invoked to protect the rights of third parties, to whom the employee is indebted. In a sense, therefore, since by virtue of these procedures the employer is obliged to pay the debt not to the

---

135 This has now been changed by statute. Fridman, *Law of Torts in Canada*, Vol. 1, pp. 608-609.
136 See, generally, *Farrow v. Wilson* (1869), L.R. 4 C.P. 744; *Ahmed Angullia v. Estate & Trust Agencies*, [1938] A.C. 624 (P.C.). Compare p. 646 on the termination of contract by death under the doctrine of frustration.
137 To which assignment probably does not apply anyway: above, pp. 687-690.
138 This paragraph was quoted by Hinds J. in *Rettie Estate v. Tsawwassen Gardens Ltd.* (1989), 42 B.L.R. 78 at 82 (B.C.S.C.).
139 Bankruptcy and Insolvency Act, R.S.C. 1985, c. B-3, s. 67.
140 But bankruptcy may terminate the contract unless the trustee-in-bankruptcy elects within a reasonable time to perform the contract: *Creditel of Can. Ltd. v. Terrace Corp. (Const.) Ltd.* (1983), 50 A.R. 311 (Alta. C.A.); *Re Thompson Knitting Co.* (1924), 56 O.L.R. 625 (Ont. C.A.).

original creditor, his employee, but someone else, for example, the wife of the employee who has rights under a maintenance order, what occurs is a kind of involuntary assignment, but of a specific, not general nature, as compared with what happens on the death or bankruptcy of a contracting party.[141]

---

141 For this purpose it is necessary to refer to the appropriate and relevant statutes, if any, in a given jurisdiction.

18

Damages

1. Recovery of damages for breach of contract

(a) At common law

(i) *Contract and other claims*

When a contract has been broken, whether by non-performance at the time performance is due,[1] repudiation in advance of such time,[2] fraud,[3] or negligent performance,[4] the remedy at common law is generally an action for damages.[5] Liability is strict, in the sense that the aggrieved party does not have to show that the breach was committed deliberately or negligently. As previously seen, the only possible defences or excuses are (1) that the breach was caused by supervening impossibility or frustration;[6] or (2) that the other party failed to perform some condition precedent upon the performance of which depended performance by the party alleged to be in breach;[7] or (3) the existence of an exclusion or other clause that exempts the party alleged to be in breach, or otherwise affects that party's liability.[8] In the absence of any such factor the party who has breached a contract will be liable to pay damages in accordance with principles of remoteness and assessment later considered.[9]

However, there are alternative remedies available to an aggrieved party in the event of certain kinds of breach of contract. The nature of those alternatives depends on how the breach occurred.

(A) *Tort* If the contract is broken by fraud or negligence, there is the possibility of an action in tort instead of an action for breach of contract, if the conduct

---

1 Above, pp. 558-571. But if the contract is for the payment of money the plaintiff's claim is based on the defendant's liability in debt; hence interest may be awarded, in contrast with claims for damages at large: *President of India v. Lips Maritime Corp.; The Lips*, [1987] 3 All E.R. 110; *President of India v. Pintada Compania Navigacion SA*, [1985] A.C. 104 (H.L.).

2 *I.e.*, anticipatory breach, above, pp. 600-622.

3 *Morin Technical Services (1978), Ltd. v. Morin* (1982), 40 A.R. 15 (Alta. Q.B.).

4 For cases before the decision in the *Rafuse* case, see *Kienzle v. Stringer* (1981), 130 D.L.R. (3d) 272 (Ont. C.A.); leave to appeal to S.C.C. refused (1982), 130 D.L.R. (3d) 272n (S.C.C.); *Reid v. Traders Gen. Ins. Co.* (1963), 41 D.L.R. (2d) 148 (N.S. T.D.); *McNeil v. Village Locksmith Ltd.* (1981), 129 D.L.R. (3d) 543 (Ont. H.C.); *Can. Western Natural Gas Co. v. Pathfinder Surveys Ltd.* (1980), 21 A.R. 459 (Alta. C.A.); *John Maryon Int. Ltd. v. N.B. Telephone Co.* (1982), 141 D.L.R. (3d) 193 (N.B. C.A.); leave to appeal to S.C.C. refused (1982), 43 N.B.R. (2d) 468 (S.C.C.). For subsequent cases see *Olson v. New Home Certification Program of Alta.* (1986), 44 Alta. L.R. (2d) 207 (Alta. Q.B.); *Abitibi-Price Inc. v. Westinghouse Can. Inc.* (1988), 73 Nfld. & P.E.I.R. 271 (Nfld. T.D.); *Beninger v. Lasair Const. Services Ltd.* (1989), 102 N.B.R. (2d) 425 (N.B. Q.B.); *Begusic v. Clark, Wilson & Co.* (1991), 57 B.C.L.R. (2d) 273 (B.C.C.A.).

5 See Harris, Ogus & Phillips, "Contract Remedies and the Consumer Surplus" (1979), 95 L.Q.R. 581; Harker, "The Role of Contract and the Object of Remedies for Breach of Contract in Contemporary Western Society" (1984), 101 S.Af. L.J. 121, at pp. 137-141. See generally, Waddams, *The Law of Damages*, 2nd ed. (1991), especially paras. 5.10 - 5.250, 7.10 - 7.320, 8.10 - 8.340, 11.10 - 11.390, 13.70 - 13.410, 14.20 - 14.410, 15.10 - 15.660.

6 Above, pp. 623-667.

7 Above, pp. 529-534.

8 Above, pp. 571-600.

9 Below, pp. 711-744, 753-766.

in question can be held to constitute the tort of deceit or the tort of negligence (frequently, but not exclusively, the tort of negligent misrepresentation). Until recently it was a much-debated question whether a party could sue in tort when the relationship between the parties was governed by a contract.[10]

> Important legal consequences ... turned on the differences in the rules applicable to contractual and tortious liability. The three most important areas in which these differences have been reflected in the decisions on the question of concurrent liability are limitation of actions, measure of damages and apportionment of liability.[11]

In consequence of the decision in *Central Trust Co. v. Rafuse*[12] as interpreted and applied in two subsequent decisions of the Supreme Court of Canada, *Canadian Pacific Hotels Ltd. v. Bank of Montreal*[13] and *BG Checo International Ltd. v. British Columbia Hydro & Power Authority*,[14] it is now clear that, in accordance with what is said therein, there is no objection to the bringing of an action in tort in place of an action for breach of contract in appropriate situations.

In the *Rafuse* case the plaintiff sued a firm of solicitors in respect of loss suffered when a mortgage arranged by the solicitors was subsequently held to be void. Although there was a contractual relationship between the plaintiff and the solicitors, an action in tort for negligence was held by the Supreme Court to be available to the plaintiff. After analyzing and discussing the authorities, Le Dain J., who gave the judgment of the court, summarised the law in the following propositions.[15]

The common law duty of care created by a relationship of sufficient proximity is not confined to relationships that arise apart from contract. A common law duty of care may be created by a relationship of proximity that would not have arisen but for a contract.

What is undertaken by the contract indicates the nature of the relationship that gives rise to the common law duty of care. The scope of that duty, however, does not depend on specific obligations or duties created by the express terms of

---

10 The earlier cases are referred to in the previous edition of this text at pp. 644 and 645, footnotes 22 and 23. The Canadian, English, New Zealand and Australian cases are considered and discussed by Le Dain J. in *Central Trust Co. v. Rafuse* (1987), 31 D.L.R. (4th) 481 at 491-521 (S.C.C.); compare *BG Checo Int. Ltd. v. B.C. Hydro & Power Authority* (1993), 99 D.L.R. (4th) 577 at 606-614 (S.C.C.) *per* Iacobucci J. For English views see *Sayers v. Harlow Urban District Council*, [1958] 2 All E.R. 342; *Midland Bank Trust Co. v. Hett, Stubbs & Kemp*, [1978] 3 All E.R. 571; *Forsikringsaktieselskapet Vesta v. Butcher*, [1988] 2 All E.R. 43 (C.A.).

11 *Central & Eastern Trust Co. v. Rafuse*, above, note 10, at 489 *per* Le Dain J.

12 Above: followed and applied in *Abitibi-Price Inc. v. Westinghouse Can. Inc.* (1988), 73 Nfld. & P.E.I.R. 271 (Nfld. T.D.).

13 (1988), 40 D.L.R. (4th) 385 (S.C.C.).

14 (1993), 99 D.L.R. (4th) 577 (S.C.C.); application for re-hearing refused (1993), 5 C.L.R. (2d) 173n (S.C.C.).

15 *Rafuse*, above, note 10, at 521-522. Le Dain J. also stated that the principles in question applied to solicitors and that the solicitor's liability in negligence derived from the decision in *Hedley Byrne & Co. v. Heller & Partners Ltd.*, [1964] A.C. 465 (H.L.). It applied to all professional services for which the solicitor had been retained: *Midland Bank Trust Co. v. Hett, Stubbs & Kemp*, [1979] Ch. 384; *Tracy v. Atkins* (1979), 105 D.L.R. (3d) 632 (B.C.C.A.).

the contract. In that sense the common law duty of care must be independent of the contract (as Pigeon J. had stated was necessary in the earlier case of *J. Nunes Diamonds Ltd. v. Dominion Electric Protection Co.*[16]). The distinction is between what is to be done and how it is to be done. A claim will not lie in tort if it depends on the manner in which an obligation or duty has been specifically defined in the contract.

No concurrent or alternative liability in tort will be allowed if its effect would be to allow the plaintiff to circumvent or escape a contractual exclusion or limitation of liability that would otherwise apply to the tortious behaviour. (Although if concurrent liability is permitted, the plaintiff can elect whichever cause of action is most advantageous.)

The principles stated above were refined or added to by Le Dain J. in *Canadian Pacific Hotels Ltd. v. Bank of Montreal.*[17] This case concerned the liability of a bank for losses caused by the forgery committed by the plaintiff's accountant. The contract between the plaintiff and the bank contained no "verification agreement", although the daily bank statement contained the requirement that the plaintiff check the statement promptly and report errors, etc., within 30 days of delivery, or else the statement would be considered correct. The trial judge and the Ontario Court of Appeal rejected the plaintiff's action. The Supreme Court allowed the appeal by the plaintiff. The reason for this was that the plaintiff, as a customer of the bank, owed no duty of care with respect to the examination of statements unless expressly created by the contract with the bank or implied into such contract. No such implication of a term to that effect could be made; it was not necessary for "business efficacy", nor was it to be implied from custom, nor could any intention to impose such a duty be presumed.[18] Unlike the Privy Council in the similar case of *Tai Hing Cotton Mill Ltd. v. Liu Chong Hing Bank Ltd.*,[19] which Le Dain J. analyzed in great detail, the Supreme Court of Canada considered the possibility of alternative liability in tort as well as contract in such a situation. Such an action would not lie, however, despite the decision in the *Rafuse* case, because even if a duty of care could be owed by the customer of a bank in the absence of a verification agreement, the principle of concurrent or alternative liability affirmed in the *Rafuse* case "cannot extend to the recognition of a duty of care in tort when that same duty of case has been rejected or excluded by the courts as an implied term of a particular class of contract". In other words, consistent with the principles of the *Rafuse* case, a tort claim would not lie where a contract claim could not.[20]

The Supreme Court returned to the question of concurrent or alternative

---

16 (1972), 26 D.L.R. (3d) 699 at 727-728 (S.C.C.). For a recent example of an independent tort see *Queen v. Cognos Ltd.* (1993), 99 D.L.R. (4th) 626 (S.C.C.), a case of negligent misrepresentation. Compare the earlier case of *Olson v. New Home Certification Program of Alta.* (1986), 44 Alta. L.R. (2d) 356 (Alta. Q.B.).

17 (1987), 40 D.L.R. (4th) 385 at 432 (S.C.C.).

18 Compare above, pp. 474-485, with respect to the implication of terms into a contract.

19 [1986] 1 A.C. 80.

20 La Forest J. gave different reasons for arriving at the same conclusion as the rest of the Court with respect to the decision of the case: (1988), 40 D.L.R. (4th) 385 at 433-434. They are not relevant here.

liability in contract and tort in *BG Checo International Ltd. v. British Columbia Hydro & Power Authority*.[21] Here the alternative grounds of action were breach of contract and misrepresentation, arising out of a statement in tender documents and the ultimate contract awarded to the plaintiff that clearing of a right of way in the area where the plaintff was to erect electric power lines would be done by others and would not form part of the work to be performed by the plaintiff. Further clearing work was never done, and the performance of the contract proved more costly than the plaintiff expected. Fraud was subsequently rejected by the B.C. Court of Appeal, which held that the defendant was liable for negligent misrepresentation, for which damages were awarded, the issue of breach of contract being sent back to the B.C. Supreme Court. The Supreme Court of Canada upheld the finding on fraud. On the question of liability for negligent misrepresentation, however, the Court was divided. The majority agreed that the plaintiff could sue in tort for negligent misrepresentation, or in contract for breach. The contract, when properly construed, required the defendant to clear the right of way. Its terms did not exclude the claim in tort. The principle of the *Rafuse* case was expressed as follows:

> ... where a given wrong *prima facie* supports an action in contract and in tort, the party may sue in either or both, except where the contract indicates that the parties intended to limit or negative the right to sue in tort. This limitation on the general rule of concurrency arises because it is always open to parties to limit or waive the duties which the common law would impose on them for negligence.[22]

Such limitation was vital to preserve individual liberty and commercial flexibility. The only limit on the right to choose one's action is the principle of primacy of private ordering, the right of individuals to arrange their affairs and assume risks in a different way than would be done by the law of tort.

There were three possible situations that could arise when contract and tort applied to the same wrong: (1) contract stipulated a more stringent obligation than the general law of tort, in which event a tort action was unlikely since the plaintiff could not recover in tort for a higher contractual duty (which was the position of the majority of commercial transactions); (2) contract stipulated a lower duty than would be presumed by the law of tort, which occurs when the parties, by their contract, indicate that the usual liability imposed by the law of tort is not to bind them (usually by an exclusion or exemption cause — which, as previously seen, raises problems,[23] not investigated by the Court in this case); in such cases there was little point in suing in tort, unless the clause in question did not entirely negate tort liability; (3) where the duty in contract and the common law duty in tort are co-extensive: here the plaintiff may seek to sue concurrently or alternatively in tort to secure some advantage peculiar to the law of tort, *e.g.*, a more generous limitation period.[24] The contract duty might arise expressly or by implication. A

---

21 Above, note 10.
22 *BG Checo Int. Ltd.*, above, note 10, at 584.
23 Above, pp. 571-600.
24 Below, pp. 698-699.

prime example was provided by the "common calling" cases which have long permitted concurrent actions in contract and tort. Here no private ordering was involved. The source of the action was an objective expectation, defined by the courts, of the obligation and its correlative right. Into this category fell the case before the court.

Unlike Iacobucci J. (with whom Sopinka J. concurred), the majority did not accept that where parties expressly dealt with a particular matter in their contract all right to sue was lost. Nor did they agree with the converse, namely, that implied terms of contracts did not oust liability. Acceptance of the views of Iacobucci J. would entail investigation not only of the express terms of the contract to see whether it dealt with the particular matter in issue, but also of "the elastic distinctions" between commercial and non-commercial contracts, the court's perception of relative bargaining power, and whether the court saw the result as just or unjust. This left such cases too uncertain: and parties ought to be able to predict in advance whether they could sue concurrently in tort or contract or were confined to contract.

The final part of the majority judgment is devoted to the distinction between measurement of damages in tort as contrasted with contract.[25] As will be seen, this is a difficult and vexed question.

The dissent was based on the idea that since the duty of care owed to the plaintiff was defined by and co-extensive with a specific term of the contract, *viz.*, the term dealing with clearing of the right of way, the plaintiff could only sue for breach of contract. Hence, the case should be treated as one of breach of contract, and damages assessed for such breach.[26]

In view of the differing opinions expressed in this case, there would appear to be some uncertainty with respect to the application of the doctrine expounded in the *Rafuse* case. While the notion of concurrency is clearly accepted in Canada,[27] its application in any given instance may depend on how a court views the "independence" of the alleged tort and on the manner in which the terms, express and implied, of a contract are interpreted. The attempt by the majority in the *Checo* case to clarify the results of *Rafuse* may or may not be successful.

Acceptance of the notion of concurrency not only involves resolution of the relationship between exclusion or similar clauses in a contract and a claim in tort,[28] but also of the issues of limitation and damages.

Limitation results in the extinction of a remedy, though not a right, by effluxion

---

25 Below, pp. 699-700.

26 Compare the similar approach in *Beninger v. Lasair Const. Services Ltd.* (1989), 102 N.B.R. (2d) 425 (N.B. Q.B.). In contrast in *Queen v. Cognos Inc.* (1993), 99 D.L.R. (4th) 626 (S.C.C.) Iacobucci J. and Sopinka J. held that the contract in that case did not have the effect of precluding the plaintiff's action in tort. This was not a case of concurrency. All the members of the Court agreed on that.

27 It seems to be accepted in England too: *A.B. Marintrans v. Comet Shipping Co.*, [1985] 3 All E.R. 442, where a claim was allowed in contract, although tort would have been more appropriate, so as to avoid the application of legislation which allowed a defence of contributory negligence to an action in tort.

28 See the language of Le Dain J. in *Central & Eastern Trust Co. v. Rafuse*, above, note 10, at 522, and the language of the majority in the *Checo* case, above, note 10, at 585, and of Iacobucci J., *ibid.*, at 614-616.

of time.[29] Difficulty may result from the possibility that the limitation period for actions in tort and in contract may differ. The English doctrine now seems to be that time begins to run against the plaintiff where the cause of action is tort from the date when the plaintiff discovers or "with reasonable diligence" could have discovered that he has suffered damage (where personal injury is involved) or had both the knowledge required for bringing an action for damage in respect of the relevant damage and a right to bring such action (where damage to property is involved). The "knowledge" referred to means knowledge of material facts about the damage in respect of which the action is brought and other relevant facts.[30] The "discoverability" rule, as it has been termed, was held by the Supreme Court in the *Rafuse* case to apply to actions in tort, whether what occurred was injury to property or financial loss caused by professional negligence. The Supreme Court adopted views expressed in the earlier decision in *City of Kamloops v. Nielsen*,[31] in which the Court followed an English Court of Appeal decision,[32] later rejected by the House of Lords.[33] With respect to contract the English doctrine was, and remains, that time begins to run against the plaintiff from the date of the breach of contract.[34] In Canada, the decisions seem to be conflicting. The Ontario Court of Appeal has held that the "discoverability" rule applies to contract as well as to tort.[35] Prior to the *Rafuse* case the Alberta Court of Appeal held that there was a difference between contract and tort in regard to limitation.[36] The difference was founded on a misunderstanding as to the underlying nature of tort liability, as contrasted with liability in contract, in that the court seems to have assumed that in all tort actions, not only those based on negligence, damage was the gist of the action whereas it was not the gist of an action in contract (an error evident also in the *Rafuse* case).[37] After the *Rafuse* decision the Alberta Court of Appeal adhered to its earlier decision, and in *Fidelity Trust Co. v. 98956 Investments Ltd. (Receiver of)*[38] held that the "discoverability" rule did not apply to a case of contract. Until such time as the Supreme Court of Canada has coped with this particular issue the matter will remain in some doubt.

A further problem with respect to potentially concurrent or alternative claims in tort, or for breach of contract, is the question of damages. There are two issues.

---

29 Below, pp. 704-706.

30 See Limitation Act, 1980 (U.K.), c. 58, as amended by the Latent Damage Act, 1986, c. 37; *Fridman on Torts*, Vol. 2 (1990), pp. 380-381.

31 (1984), 10 D.L.R. (4th) 641 (S.C.C.).

32 *Sparham-Souter v. Town & Country Devs. (Essex) Ltd.*, [1976] Q.B. 858 (C.A.).

33 *Pirelli General Cable Works Ltd. v. Oscar Faber & Partners*, [1983] 1 All E.R. 65 (H.L.). See also *Dove v. Banhams Patent Locks Ltd.*, [1983] 2 All E.R. 833 (Q.B.).

34 See *Schwebel v. Telekes* (1967), 61 D.L.R. (2d) 470 (Ont. C.A.) (on which see *Consumers Glass Co. v. Foundation Co. of Can.* (1985), 20 D.L.R. (4th) 1 26 (Ont. C.A.)); *Power v. Halley* (1981), 124 D.L.R. (3d) 350 at 355 (Nfld. C.A.).

35 *Consumers Glass Co. v. Foundation Co. of Can.* (1985), 20 D.L.R. (4th) 126 (Ont. C.A.), overruling *Schwebel v. Telekes*, above, note 34.

36 *Costigan v. Ruzicka* (1984), 13 D.L.R. (4th) 368 (Alta. C.A.); leave to appeal to S.C.C. refused (1984), 13 D.L.R. (4th) 368n (S.C.C.).

37 Fridman, *Law of Torts in Canada*, Vol. 2 (1990), at p. 381.

38 [1988] 6 W.W.R. 427 (Alta. C.A.).

One is remoteness.[39] It is a matter of debate whether the applicable tests of remoteness are the same for tort and contract.[40] Another is the measurement of loss. There might be greater recovery in one type of suit than in the other. Thus, in *Morin Technical Services (1978) Ltd. v. Morin*,[41] the plaintiff, a purchaser of the assets and business of a corporation, sued the vendor for fraudulent misrepresentation and breach of warranty. It was said that the damages for fraud could exceed the damages that could be awarded in an action for breach of warranty.[42] This seems to have been accepted by the majority in the *Checo* case, although they considered it anomalous to award a different level of damages for what was essentially the same wrong on the sole basis of the form of action chosen (although particular circumstances or policy might dictate such a course).[43] In that case the choice was between contract and, as it emerged, negligent, not fraudulent misrepresentation. The different measure of damages was stated as follows. In contract the plaintiff was to be put back in the position it would have been in had the contract been performed as agreed. In tort the plaintiff was to be put in the position it would have been in had the misrepresentation not been made. In a situation of concurrency the main reason to expect a difference between tort and contract damages was the exclusion of the bargain elements in standard tort compensation.[44] Contract is concerned with "expectation" damges, tort with "reliance" damages. Expectation damages will be denied in a misrepresentation case where but for the misrepresentation the contract would not have been entered into by the plaintiff.[45] But the majority of the court in the *Checo* case noted a tendency towards similar damages in tort and contract, even in situations like that of the *Rainbow* case. Indeed in the *Checo* case the facts suggested that the plaintiff's loss whether calculated in terms of tort liability or contract was much the same; reasonably foreseeable loss. From a practical point of view, if not a logical one, there is much to be said to assimilating the issues of remoteness and assessment when a tort claim is brought concurrently or alternatively with one in contract (even if a distinction can be maintained where the tort action is "independent").

A final issue worthy of mention, though it will be raised again, more appropriately, elsewhere[46] is the question of contributory negligence as a defence. It is clear that it is a defence to an action in tort (with some exceptions that are irrelevant to the present context). But it is by no means clear, at least in Canada

---

39 Below, pp. 711-717.
40 But there may be no practical difference: *Asamera Oil Corp. v. Sea Oil & General Corp.; Baud Corp. N.V. v. Brook* (1978), 89 D.L.R. (3d) 1 at 30 (S.C.C.); *BG Checo Int. Ltd. v. B.C. Hydro & Power Authority* (1993), 99 D.L.R. (4th) 577 at 599 (S.C.C.).
41 (1982), 40 A.R. 15 (Alta. Q.B.).
42 *Ibid.*, at 34 *per* Prowse J., relying on *Doyle v. Olby (Ironmongers) Ltd.*, [1969] 2 Q.B. 158 (C.A.).
43 *BG Checo Int. Ltd.*, above, note 40, at 591.
44 *Ibid.*, at 592.
45 *Rainbow Industrial Caterers Ltd. v. Can. National Railway Co.* (1991), 84 D.L.R. (4th) 291 (S.C.C.).
46 Below, pp. 755-757.

as contrasted with England,[47] whether it will be allowed as a defence in action for breach of contract.

(B) *Other alternatives* In some situations an aggrieved party can properly claim not damages at large for breach of contract but a sum representing the value of services rendered or goods delivered to the other party.[48] Such an action is an action on a *quantum meruit* (where services are rendered) or *quantum valebant* (where goods have been sold and delivered). It may be brought: (a) where no precise sum has been fixed by the parties for the remuneration of the plaintff;[49] or (b) where the original contract has been replaced impliedly by another one, and the action is being brought on the substituted, not the original contract.[50] Such *quantum meruit* claims, which are genuinely contractual in nature, must be distinguished from other such claims which are quasi-contractual in origin, and would now more properly be described as resting upon the ideas of unjust enrichment or restitution.[51] In these latter instances, for example, where the original contract was unenforceable under the Statute of Frauds, or abandoned by the parties, or void or frustrated, the plaintiff's claim is based upon other legal foundations than contract.[52] That being so it follows that: (1) liability does not depend upon *agreement*, but on the principles of unjust enrichment or restitution; and (2) the remoteness of damage rules applicable to contract cases have no application. Nor will the measurement of the amount payable to the plaintiff depend upon the "normal" contractual rules. What the court will award the plaintiff will depend upon what is just, equitable, and reasonable, having regard to all the circumstances.

---

47 See *Forsikringsaktieselskapet Vesta v. Butcher*, [1988] 2 All E.R. 43 (C.A.), allowing contributory negligence as a defence where a defendant's liability in contract is the same as his liability in negligence independently of the existence of any contract. The English Court of Appeal did not follow the contrary judgment of Neill L.J., sitting as a trial judge, in *A.B. Marintrans v. Comet Shipping Co.*, [1985] 3 All E.R. 442.

48 No alternative is possible where the claim for damages is equitable, not common law in nature (below, pp. 706-711) and specific performance is unavailable (below, pp. 708-709). In such circumstances only a *quantum meruit* claim is available: *Garnett v. Armstrong* (1977), 83 D.L.R. (3d) 717 (N.B. C.A.).

49 *E.g.*, under the Sale of Goods Act, R.S.O. 1990, c. S.1, s. 9; see Fridman, *Sale of Goods in Canada*, 3rd ed. (1986), p. 42, where goods are involved. For the situation where services are rendered, see *Syhlonyk v. Syhlonyk* (1983), 20 Sask. R. 354 (Sask. Q.B.). But there must be a contract: see *Hotel Holdings Ltd. v. C.N.R.* (1973), 4 Nfld. & P.E.I.R. 458 (Nfld. S.C.), where the negotiations for the use of the hotel fell through, and there was no obligation to pay for what had been provided thus far.

50 *Steven v. Bromley & Son*, [1919] 2 K.B. 722 at 728 (C.A.) *per* Atkin L.J. See, *e.g.*, *Bancorp Mortgage Ltd. v. Sicon Group Inc.* (1990), 2 B.L.R. (2d) 161 (B.C.S.C.). Hence in *Morrison-Knudsen Co. v. B.C. Hydro & Power Authority (No. 2)* (1978), 85 D.L.R. (3d) 186 (B.C.C.A.) a *quantum meruit* claim could not be brought, because the plaintiffs continued to work under the contract broken by the landowner. They were still bound by the *original* contract. Compare Birks, *An Introduction to the Law of Restitution* (1988), p. 464. This proposition is attacked by Mead, "Restitution Within Contract?" (1991), 11 Legal St. 172, at pp. 182-188; and see *Miles v. Wakefield*, [1987] A.C. 539 (H.L.). But this may be a peculiarity of the contract of employment: compare above, p. 604.

51 Fridman, *Restitution*, 2nd ed. (1992), pp. 285-292.

52 *Ibid.*, pp. 303-311, 313-318. Compare Maddaugh & McCamus, *Law of Restitution* (1990), Chapters 13, 14, 18 19.

In other situations, the injured party will be claiming not damages at large, but the return of money paid to the other party by way of deposit or part payment of the purchase price of goods, land, etc., or as earnest of the plaintiff's good behaviour and proper performance. Such cases raise problems with respect to forfeiture, where the contract may provide that sums of that nature become forfeited to the other party. Much depends upon whether the forfeiture of such sums is to be regarded as a penalty or as the payment of liquidated damages to the other party;[53] and upon whether the reason for the non-completion of the contract was the default of the party giving the deposit or party-payment, that of the other party, or possibly circumstances not attributable to either.[54]

Another possibility is that the plaintiff, having paid all the money due under the contract in advance to the other party, upon the failure of the contract to be performed by the other party as agreed, for example, because of the wilful breach of contract by the other party, or the frustration of the contract, will sue for the return of the money so paid. Such a claim is one founded upon the failure of the consideration for the payment in question. It rests upon a *total* failure of such consideration; a partial failure does not justify or substantiate such a claim.[55] Such a claim is also restitutionary, and not contractual in nature, and now rests upon the ideas of unjust enrichment or restitution.[56] A similar situation occurs where money has been paid under mistake, or as a result of compulsion, or in various other ways which do not necessarily involve a contractual relationship between the party paying the money and the party receiving such money, or the benefit of the money having been paid.[57] Even though in some cases, for example, involving mistake, there may be, or may have been a contract between the parties, the claim by the payor now seeking the return of his money is not a contractual one, based upon agreement, but a restitutionary one, founded upon the payment of the money and the unjust or unjustified enrichment received by the payee as a consequence of such payment.[58]

(ii) *Qualifications of right to sue*

The right to sue for damages for breach of contract does not arise out of the contract itself, that is, it is not a matter of agreement, but is an independent

---

53 Below, pp. 766-774.
54 Fridman, *op. cit.* above, note 51, at p. 212-219.
55 But see the Frustrated Contracts Act, above, pp. 663-666.
56 Fridman, *op. cit.* above, note 51, at pp. 153-158, 205-215; Goff & Jones, *Law of Restitution*, 3d ed. (1986), pp. 449-451, 454-465. Compare Waddams, *Law of Damages*, 2d ed. (1991), paras. 9.200-9.250.
57 Fridman, above, note 56, Chapters 3, 4, 5, 7; Goff & Jones, *op. cit.* above, note 56, Chapters 3, 9, 18-22.
58 These various claims have been characterized as satisfying what has been termed a plaintiff's "restitutionary" interest; which is contrasted with his expectation or expectancy interest or claim and his reliance interest or claim: on which, see below, pp. 720-729. See Fuller & Perdue, "The Reliance Interest in Contract Damages" (1936), 46 Yale L.J. 52.

right given by the law. That right, like others, may be *waived* by the injured party.[59] A contract providing that a seller who does not supply goods satisfactory to the buyer will replace them does not preclude the buyer from suing for damages when the seller does not supply the correct goods.[60] But, if the buyer *does* choose to exercise the remedy given under the contract, for example, replacement of the goods, he may be prevented from suing for damages.[61] In such an instance, he will have elected which remedy to pursue.[62] Election of remedies may be prescribed by a contract,[63] although a party may not be prevented from bringing an action for damages.[64] Similarly, a contract may require a party to submit the claim to settlement in a particular way, for example, to an engineer for his certification as to a party's rights.[65] A party cannot bind himself not to have recourse to the courts, at any rate as long as the contract he makes is one that is to have legal force and effect, since the ouster of the courts' jurisdiction is against public policy and void.[66] The parties may agree that, prior to appeal to the courts, they will submit any dispute to arbitration. Such submission is a condition precedent to an action for damages.[67] The parties may agree that, for instance, no appeal may be made to the courts, unless there is an allegation of some impropriety or mistake in the exercise of the arbitral jurisdiction.[68]

Thus, although the right to sue for breach of contract can never be completely taken away from a contracting party, it may be qualified or modified. The net effect may be to deprive a party of the right to complain about the way he has been treated, or the effects of his contract. If the contractual agreement with respect to the settlement of a dispute is being observed, and there is no contractual wrongdoing or impropriety of law, such as an infringement of the rules of natural justice, a potential right to sue for breach of contract may have been negated. In determining whether or not such wrongdoing or impropriety has occurred, it

---

59 Note also the possibility that the obligations of a party, and therefore his liability to be sued, may be affected by an exemption, exclusion or limitation clause: above, pp. 571-600.

60 *Wellington v. Fraser* (1909), 19 O.L.R. 88 (Ont. C.A.).

61 *Boyd v. Shaw Cassils Co.* (1908), 12 O.W.R. 913 (Ont. H.C.); varied (1919), 13 O.W.R. 991 (Ont. Div. Ct.). See, however, *Celgar Ltd. v. Star Bulk Shipping Co.*, [1979] 4 W.W.R. 248 (B.C.C.A.).

62 *Lennox v. Goold, Shapley & Muir Co.* (1912), 2 W.W.R. 829 (Sask. S.C.); *Edwards v. Pearson*, [1919] 3 W.W.R. 505 (Alta. C.A.); *Bishinsky v. Appleton* (1921), 50 O.L.R. 426 (Ont. C.A.).

63 Compare *Toronto Corp. v. Toronto Ry.*, [1907] A.C. 315 (P.C.).

64 *Beck & Co. v. Szymanowski*, [1924] A.C. 43 at 52 (H.L.); *Elliott v. Brown* (1910), 13 W.L.R. 390 (Sask. S.C.). Note, however, the situation where a contract is expressed to be binding in honour only: above, pp. 27-30.

65 *Wallace v. Temiskaming & Northern Ont. Ry. Commn.* (1906), 12 O.L.R. 126 (Ont. C.A.); affirmed (1906), 37 S.C.R. 696 (S.C.C.).

66 Above, p. 380.

67 *Scott v. Avery* (1856), 5 H.L.C. 811, 10 E.R. 1121 (H.L.); *Caven v. C.P.R.*, [1925] 3 W.W.R. 32 (P.C.); *David v. Swift* (1911), 44 S.C.R. 179 (S.C.C.). As to the need to exhaust all internal remedies prior to going to court, compare *Bertrand v. Can. Nat. Telegraph Co.*, [1948] 1 W.W.R. 49 (Sask. C.A.).

68 *Cipriani v. Burnett*, [1933] A.C. 83 (P.C.).

may be necessary to pay attention to, and apply the law relating to commercial or labour arbitrations,[69] or to the principles of administrative law.[70]

(iii) *Limitation of actions*

A right of action for damages for breach of contract may be compromised as a consequence of a *new* contract under which the claim is settled and withdrawn in consideration of a payment of something by the alleged contract-breaker to the alleged injured party.[71] It may also be destroyed as a result of the injured party's waiver of his right to sue resulting in a detrimental response by the other party, for example, a change of his position in reliance on the "waiver" of the right of action. This can give rise to an "estoppel" against the party who originally had the right to sue.[72] It will also be lost if the party who has the right to sue does not bring his action within the proper, statutory period of limitation.

Under the various statutes which are effective in the common-law provinces of Canada, the period is usually six years.[73] However, there are special provisions with respect to acknowledgement of the obligation after the expiration of the limitation period, part-payment after such expiration, particularly as concerns co-debtors, the effect of fraud, etc., and, in some provinces,[74] the period that is applicable to certain types of contracts.[75] Much depends upon whether the legislation of the province is founded upon the English statute of 1623, the English Act of 1939, or the Uniform Statute produced by the Canadian Uniformity Commissioners.

---

69 In cases involving, respectively, disputes between business men or between employers and employees.

70 In cases involving, respectively, disputes between universities and their faculty members or students: see, *e.g.*, *Re Polten and Governing Council of Univ. of Toronto* (1975), 8 O.R. 749 (Ont. Dist. Ct.); *Vanek v. Univ. of Alta. Govs.*, [1975] 5 W.W.R. 429 (Alta. C.A.); *Kane v. Bd. of Govs. of U.B.C.*, [1980] 1 S.C.R. 1105 (S.C.C.); *Paine v. Univ. of Toronto* (1982), 131 D.L.R. (3d) 325 (Ont. C.A.); leave to appeal to the Supreme Court of Canada refused (1982), 42 N.R. 270 (S.C.C.); *Re Ruiperez and Bd. of Govs. of Lakehead Univ.* (1983), 147 D.L.R. (3d) 154 (Ont. C.A.); *Re Giroux and Ont.* (1983), 2 D.L.R. (4th) 274 (Ont. Div. Ct.); affirmed (1984), 46 O.R. (2d) 276 (Ont. C.A.); *Re McInnes and Simon Fraser Univ.* (1984), 3 D.L.R. (4th) 708 (B.C.C.A.); *Bilson v. Univ. of Saskatchewan* (1984), 16 D.L.R. (4th) 31 (Sask. C.A.); *B. v. W.* (1985), 23 D.L.R. (4th) 248 (Ont. H.C.); *Thomas v. Mount St. Vincent Univ.* (1986), 28 D.L.R. (4th) 230 (N.S.T.D.); *Vinogradov v. Univ. of Calgary* (1987), 37 D.L.R. (4th) 725 (Alta. C.A.). Fridman, "Judicial Intervention into University Affairs" (1973), 21 Chitty's L.J. 181. For the additional complication of the powers of the *Visitor*, affecting rights of action in contract, see *McWhirter v. Univ. of Alta. Govs.* (1975), 63 D.L.R. (3d) 684 (Alta. S.C.).

71 Compare above, pp. 94, 549-553.

72 Compare above, pp. 545-549.

73 R.S.A. 1980, c. L-15; R.S.B.C. 1979, c. 236; R.S.M. 1987, c. L150; R.S.N.B. 1973, c. L-8; R.S.N.S. 1989, c. 258; R.S.N. 1990, c. L-15; R.S.O. 1990, c. L.15; R.S.P.E.I. 1988, c. S-7; R.S.S. 1978, c. L-15; R.S.N.W.T. 1988, c. L-8; R.S.Y.T. 1986, c. 104. See generally, Morton, *Limitation of Civil Actions* (1988); Williams, *Limitation of Actions in Canada*, 2nd ed. (1980). Note that where an equitable remedy is sought, equitable doctrines, not the statutory provisions, affect the time within which the plaintiff can actively pursue his remedy: below, pp. 794-795.

74 *E.g.*, Ontario: see *Schwebel v. Telekes* (1967), 61 D.L.R. (2d) 470 at 472 (Ont. C.A.) *per* Laskin J.A. Compare also Nova Scotia, New Brunswick and British Columbia.

75 *E.g.*, covenants under seal (12 years); compare also actions for an account when the right derives from a fiduciary relationship, as contrasted with that of principal and agent.

These statutes are procedural. They do not affect the substantive rights of the plaintiff. In other words, the expiration of the limitation period deprives the plaintff of the right to pursue his remedy; it operates as a barrier to an action, but it does not affect the *cause* of action. It does not result in the defendant's being innocent of a breach of contract.[76] If the defendant, after the expiration of the limitation period, chooses to pay the plaintiff the damages claimed, the payment will be valid and cannot be recovered on any contractual or restitutionary basis, such as money paid under mistake. Indeed an acknowledgement of the liability, or a part payment of the amount claimed, made or given after the passage of the limitation period, may operate to revive an otherwise statute-barred liability. Such part-payment must not be intended to be payment in full. It must in some way amount to a revival of the original debt.[77] So, too, if there is a valid and operative acknowledgement,[78] it will not create a new cause of action, but will merely resurrect the original right to sue.[79]

When the period begins to run may depend upon the proper construction of the contract.[80] In *Rittinger Construction Ltd. v. Clark Roofing (Saskatchewan) Ltd.*,[81] for example, a contract to construct new roofing provided that the contractor would remedy defects which appeared within one year of the completion of the work. Such defects became manifest within the year, and unsuccessful attempts were made within the next four years to remedy them. When an action was brought against the contractor, it was argued that the cause of action had arisen more than six years previously, so as to bar the suit. It was held that time ran not from the date the contract was completed, but from the time the last attempt was made to remedy the defects, or at least from a year after the contract was completed. In *Schwebel v. Telekes*,[82] Laskin J.A. made several things clear about the operation of the statutes of limitation. First, in contract cases it has been consistently held that the limitation period, when specified as commencing when the cause of action arises, runs from the occurrence of the breach of contract that is alleged.[83] Second, the limitation period runs from the breach of duty, not from the time it was, or

---

76 *Rodriguez v. Parker*, [1967] 1 Q.B. 116. But the question may arise whether by the length of time the plaintiff has shown that he has *abandoned* the contract; compare *Yellowega v. Yellowega* (1968), 66 W.W.R. 241 (Man. Q.B.) with *Thurber v. Tucker* (1951), 2 W.W.R. (N.S.) 575 (B.C.S.C.).

77 *Warner v. Meisner*, [1935] 3 D.L.R. 95 (N.S.C.A.).

78 See *Dungate v. Dungate*, [1965] 1 W.L.R. 1477 (C.A.); *Good v. Parry*, [1963] 2 Q.B. 418 (C.A.); see also *Consol. Agencies Ltd. v. Bertram Ltd.*, [1965] A.C. 470 (P.C.).

79 *Busch v. Stevens*, [1963] 1 Q.B. 1.

80 For the problem of determining the date when the limitation period begins to run where the plaintiff may have an action for breach of contract *or* in tort, see above, pp. 698-699. Note the issue in *Pound v. Nakonechny* (1984), 5 D.L.R. (4th) 427 (Sask. C.A.) as to which section of the Saskatchewan Limitation of Actions Act applied to personal injury suffered through the sale of defective goods.

81 (1967), 65 D.L.R. (2d) 158 (Sask. Q.B.); affirmed (1968), 68 D.L.R. (2d) 670 (Sask. C.A.).

82 (1967), 61 D.L.R. (2d) 470 at 473-475 (Ont. C.A.).

83 *Mott v. Trott*, [1943] S.C.R. 256 (S.C.C.); *McBride v. Vacher*, [1951] O.W.N. 268 (Ont. C.A.); see also *Power v. Halley* (1981), 124 D.L.R. (3d) 350 (Nfld. C.A.); *John Maryon Int. Ltd. v. N.B. Telephone Co.* (1983), 141 D.L.R. (3d) 193 (N.B.C.A.); leave to appeal to S.C.C. refused (1982), 43 N.B.R. (2d) 468 (S.C.C.).

ought to have been discovered.[84] Third, the period is six years from the occurrence of all the facts that must be provided as part of the plaintiff's case.[85] Recently, however, the Ontario Court of Appeal has stated that *Schwebel v. Telekes* is no longer good law in Ontario. Before time will run under the Act, the plaintiff must be aware of his claim.[86]

Under other statutory provisions the period may be extended on the basis of: (1) the plaintiff's disability, for example, through infancy, during the limitation period; or (2) the defendant's fraud, concealing the existence of a cause of action. "Fraud", here does not mean what was understood at common law as fraud, that is, deceitful conduct, but has been construed, at least by the English courts, as comprehending fraud in the equitable sense, that is, any unconscionable conduct which ought in justice to deprive the defendant of the right to plead the statute of limitations.[87]

(b) In equity[88]

The right to seek damages in equity, rather than at common law, derives, in England, from a statute of 1858.[89] Some, but not all Canadian provinces, have enacted the same or equivalent provisions.[90] The power to grant damages in equity did not exist prior to the changes in the mid-nineteenth century which were a precursor, in England, of the merger or fusion of law and equity and the courts which administered both. Damages was the common-law remedy *par excellence*. It is now the case that all courts, whether in England or Canada (even those which

---

84 Referring to *Cartledge v. E. Jopling & Sons Ltd.*, [1963] A.C. 758 (H.L.), a tort case. For changes in the English rule in tort cases, see above, p. 699.

85 *Lewington v. Raycroft*, [1935] O.R. 440 (Ont. H.C.); affirmed, [1935] O.R. 474 (Ont. C.A.).

86 *Consumers Glass Co. v. Foundation Co. of Can.* (1985), 9 O.A.C. 193 (Ont. C.A.), relying on *Kamloops v. Nielsen* (1984), 10 D.L.R. (4th) 641 (S.C.C.). Compare *Callaghan Contracting Ltd. v. Royal Ins. Co. of Can.* (1989), 59 D.L.R. (4th) 753 (N.B.C.A.); leave to appeal to S.C.C. refused (1990), 103 N.B.R. (2d) 90 (note) (S.C.C.): under a contract of indemnity time does not begin to run until the loss is discovered or ought reasonably to have been discovered.

87 *Kitchen v. Royal Air Force Assn.*, [1958] 1 W.L.R. 563 (C.A.); *Eddis v. Chichester Constable*, [1969] 2 Ch. 345 (C.A.); *Applegate v. Moss*, [1971] 1 Q.B. 406 (C.A.); *King v. Victor Parsons & Co.*, [1973] 1 All E.R. 206 (C.A.); *Bartlett v. Barclays Bank Trust Co.*, [1980] 1 All E.R. 139; *UBAF Ltd. v. European Amer. Banking Corp.*, [1984] 2 All E.R. 226 (C.A.).

88 Waddams, *Law of Damages*, 2nd ed. (1991), paras. 1.860-1.990. For other forms of equitable relief see below, Chapter 19.

89 Chancery Amendment Act 1858, (21 & 22 Vict.) c. 27, commonly called Lord Cairns' Act. See Jolowicz, "Damages in Equity — A Study of Lord Cairns' Act", [1975] C.L.J. 224.

90 See Judicature Act, R.S.A. 1980, c. J-1, s. 20; Courts of Justice Act, R.S.O. 1990, c. C.43, s. 99; Queen's Bench Act, R.S.S. 1978, c. Q-1, s. 44(9); Court of Queen's Bench Act, S.M. 1988-89, c. 4, s. 36; Judicature Act, R.S.N.W.T. 1988, c. J-1, s. 42; R.S.Y.T. 1986, c. 96, s. 27. There does not appear to be equivalent legislation in British Columbia, New Brunswick, Nova Scotia, Newfoundland, or Prince Edward Island, but the jurisdiction may arise on general principles since, in England, this power has survived the repeal of the 1858 Act: *Leeds Indust. Co-op. Society Ltd. v. Slack*, [1924] A.C. 851 (H.L.); *Johnson v. Agnew*, [1979] 1 All E.R. 883 at 895 (H.L.). See *Kemp v. Lee* (1983), 44 B.C.L.R. 172 (B.C.S.C.); see *Ansdell v. Crowther* (1984), 11 D.L.R. (4th) 614 at 615 (B.C.C.A.) *per* Lambert J.A.

do not have the statutory power to award damages first granted in Lord Cairns' Act of 1858) can grant a plaintiff common-law damages and/or some form of equitable relief, according to the circumstances of the case, the merits of the plaintiff's case, and the requirements of his particular needs.[91] In some circumstances, however, damages may be awarded in equity in lieu of an otherwise appropriate equitable remedy, namely, an injunction or decree of specific performance.

Under the statutory provisions, whenever a court is empowered to award a decree of specific performance or an injunction, the court may award damages to the plaintiff, in substitution for such equitable remedy, or in addition to it, in order to achieve complete justice in law and in equity.[92] The power to award damages in equity, as contrasted with at common law, only arises where the injured plaintiff has made out a case for an injunction or specific performance *and*, in the circumstances, justice would not be completely done if he were granted such a remedy instead of damages, or if he were not *also* granted damages.

Hence, where there was delay in closing a real estate transaction, damages as well as specific performance were awarded.[93] In contrast, in *Chaulk v. Fairview Construction Ltd.*[94] specific performance was not granted; the plaintiff could be adequately compensated by an award of damages. The purchaser in that case intended to utilize the real estate being bought for investment and resale purposes, not for his own personal use. Hence, it was more reasonable to give him damages for his lost economic opportunity than to enforce the contract of sale. The decision of Megarry J. in *Wroth v. Tyler*,[95] which was not affected on this point by a subsequent

---

91 Sometimes damages at common law are more appropriate than the equitable remedy of rescission: *Field v. Zien*, [1963] S.C.R. 632 (S.C.C.); sometimes damages are inappropriate and an equitable remedy is granted: *Morden v. Armitage*, [1949] 4 D.L.R. 222 (B.C.S.C.). As to an award of damages where the equitable remedy of specific performance cannot be granted because the contract is not in writing as required under the Statute of Frauds, see above, p. 235.

92 If a plaintiff claims damages or specific performance in the alternative, this is not an election of specific performance as a remedy; such election (*i.e.*, of damages in lieu of specific performance) can be made at any time in the course of the litigation; nor can the defendant take away the right of the plaintiff by tendering performance, *i.e.*, by confessing judgment in favour of the plaintiff for specific performance: *Beauchamp v. Coastal Corp.* (1986), 26 D.L.R. (4th) 146 (Fed. C.A.), an action for specific performance of a contract for the sale of a ship with an alternative claim for damages. The plaintiff was awarded damages at trial: this judgment was affirmed by the Federal Court of Appeal.

93 *Holmes v. Alexson* (1976), 69 D.L.R. (3d) 223 (Ont. C.A.); *Re 140 Devs. Ltd. v. Steveston Meat and Frozen Food Lockers (1973) Ltd.* (1975), 59 D.L.R. (3d) 470 (B.C.S.C.).

94 (1977), 14 Nfld. & P.E.I.R. 13 (Nfld. C.A.). Compare *Denovan v. Lee* (1989), 65 D.L.R. (4th) 103 (B.C.C.A.): damages instead of an injunction. For the view that *normally* damages will be an adequate remedy in cases of failure to perform a contract for the sale of land, and that specific performance will only be ordered in very special cases, see Adams J. in *Domowicz v. Orsa Invts. Ltd.* (1993), 15 O.R. (3d) 661 at 680-688 (Ont. Gen. Div.).

95 [1974] Ch. 30; compare *Stewart v. Ambrosina* (1975), 63 D.L.R. (3d) 595 (Ont. H.C.); affirmed (1977), 78 D.L.R. (3d) 125 (Ont. C.A.). See also *Horsler v. Zorro*, [1975] Ch. 302.
     Wroth v. Tyler was followed by Holland J. in *Metro Trust Co. v. Pressure Concrete Services Ltd.* (1973), 37 D.L.R. (3d) 649 at 669-771 (Ont. H.C) without making the basis of the jurisdiction clear (affirmed (1974), 60 D.L.R. (3d) 431 (Ont. C.A.)); see also *Glascar Ltd. v. Polysar Ltd.*

House of Lords case,[96] indicates that where a decree of specific performance is *prima facie* available as a remedy, but would be inappropriate, the court will be more likely to award damages in lieu of such a decree. There the defendant was unwilling to complete a contract for the sale of land. He could not complete because his wife had entered a notice as to her claim in the house under the English Matrimonial Homes Act, 1967, which gave her certain statutory rights in the matrimonial home. To have forced the defendant to complete by a decree of specific performance was inappropriate since it would have meant compelling the defendant, or the plaintiff, the purchaser, to litigate against the wife. Consequently the plaintiff was as well served by an award of damages. Similarly, in *Grant v. Dawkins*,[97] damages rather than specific performance were granted where the defendant's inability to complete a contract for the sale of land was because of the failure to obtain suitable mortgage arrangements.

If specific performance can not be granted, for example, because the contract is for personal services,[98] or there is a want of mutuality,[99] neither can damages be awarded in equity. The plaintiff may be compelled to rely on a common-law action for damages, or an action for a *quantum meruit*.[100] It should be noted, however, that if specific performance is granted, but later becomes impossible, the aggrieved party, whether vendor or purchaser of the land that was the subject-matter of the contract in respect of which the decree was made, may seek to have the decree dissolved or discharged and can claim damages in respect of the breach of contract. This will not be allowed, however, where to do so would be unjust, in the circumstances then existing, to the other party.[101] Prior to the original judgment the plaintiff may have to elect whether to claim damages or specific performance; once that election is made in favour of damages, the right to specific performance will be lost. But if the original election was in favour of specific performance, the right to damages is not lost.[102] This is because the granting of such a decree does not bring the contract to an end. It remains alive, to be performed if possible. Only if such performance is not possible, will the defendant's breach be of such

---

(1975), 61 D.L.R. (3d) 577 (Ont. H.C.); *Kopec v. Pyret* (1987), 36 D.L.R. (4th) 1 at 11-13 (Sask. C.A.), on the time at which damages should be calculated, *viz.*, at the time of the judgment when the order for specific performance would have been made; compare also *306793 Ont. Ltd. v. Rimes* (1979), 100 D.L.R. (3d) 350 (Ont. C.A.); *Hechter v. Thurston* (1978), 80 D.L.R. (3d) 685 (Man. Q.B.); reversed (1979), 98 D.L.R. (3d) 329 (Man. C.A.); but restored by the Supreme Court of Canada (1980), 120 D.L.R. (3d) 576. See further below, p. 709.

96 *Johnson v. Agnew*, [1979] 1 All E.R. 883 (H.L.); below, pp. 709, 754, 808.

97 [1973] 3 All E.R. 897.

98 *Garnett v. Armstrong* (1978), 83 D.L.R. (3d) 717 (N.B.C.A.): below, p. 791.

99 *Price v. Strange*, [1977] 3 All E.R. 371: below, p. 796.

100 Compare *Kaunas v. Smyth* (1976), 75 D.L.R. (3d) 368 (Ont. H.C.).

101 *Johnson v. Agnew*, [1979] 1 All E.R. 883 at 890-895 (H.L.) *per* Lord Wilberforce, overruling *Capital & Suburban Properties Ltd. v. Swycher*, [1976] Ch. 319 (C.A.). See, generally, on this, Hetherington "Keeping the Plaintiff Out of His Contractual Remedies: The Heresies that Survive Johnson v. Agnew" (1980), 96 L.Q.R. 403; Harpum, "Specific Performance with Compensation as a Purchaser's Remedy," [1981] C.L.J. 67.

102 *306793 Ont. Ltd. v. Rimes* (1979), 100 D.L.R. (3d) 350 (Ont. C.A.).

a kind as to terminate the contract and allow the plaintiff to return to court to claim damages.[103]

At one time it was thought that the measure of damages in equity differed from the measurement of damages at common law. Megarry J. in *Wroth v. Tyler*[104] thought that the date for calculating damages in equity was not the same as the date for making such an assessment at common law. He also considered that in equity a more liberal approach to damage assessment was possible, in that a court of equity was not bound by the strict rules of the common law in this respect. Although it appears to have been approved by the English Court of Appeal,[105] the subsequent decision of the House of Lords in *Johnson v. Agnew*[106] held that, following several authorities and on principle, there was no warrant in Lord Cairns' Act for a court to award damages thereunder differently from common-law damages.[107] This decision has been called "an eminently sensible and rational approach," by the Ontario Court of Appeal,[108] which followed the earlier House of Lords case.

In *Johnson v. Agnew*, the House of Lords also held that the question of the date at which damages should be assessed, whether at common law or equity, was left open. Although the general rule was that damages should be calculated as at the date of the breach of contract, the court had the power to fix such other date as might be appropriate in the circumstances.[109] In this way possible injustice might be averted, as was the situation in *Wroth v. Tyler* itself, and in *Johnson v. Agnew*, where the appropriate date was not the date of breach but the date when the remedy of specific performance became aborted without the fault of the vendors. For similar reasons, the Ontario Court of Appeal held that where a vendor defaulted under a contract for the sale of land, the purchaser was entitled to have his damages calculated as of the date of the trial when he claimed damages in lieu of specific performance. That was the date when the defaulting vendor was really guilty of

---

103 Compare *Beauchamp v. Coastal Corp.*, above, note 92.

104 Above, note 95; followed in *Calgary Hardwood & Veneer Ltd. v. C.N.R.* (1977), 74 D.L.R. (3d) 284 (Alta. S.C.); affirmed [1979] 4 W.W.R. 198 (Alta. C.A.); *Hechter v. Thurston* (1978), 80 D.L.R. (3d) 685 (Man. Q.B.); reversed (1979), 98 D.L.R. (3d) 329 (Man. C.A.); reversed (1980), 120 D.L.R. (3d) 576 (S.C.C.); *Metro Trust Co. of Can. v. Pressure Concrete Services Ltd.*, above, note 95; *Kopec v. Tyret*, above, note 95.

105 *Malhotra v. Choudhury*, [1979] 1 All E.R. 186 (C.A.).

106 Above, note 96. Note the discussion of damages in equity compared with damages for tort in *Canson Enterprises Ltd. v. Boughton & Co.* (1991), 85 D.L.R. (4th) 129 where the Supreme Court of Canada expressed differing views.

107 Above, note 96, at 896 *per* Lord Wilberforce.

108 *306793 Ont. Ltd. v. Rimes*, above, note 102, at 354. Hence, where "equitable" damages are claimed, the loss must be reasonably foreseeable and sufficiently certain to merit recovery: *Domowicz v. Orsa Invts. Ltd.*, above, note 94, at 678.

109 Above, note 96, at 896; compare *Horsler v. Zorro*, [1975] Ch. 302, although this case was overruled in respect of other parts of the decision in *Johnson v. Agnew*, above, note 96, at 894; with which contrast the reference to *Horsler v. Zorro* at 896.

a breach that determined the contract.[110] In *Kemp v. Lee*[111] a British Columbia court held that where damages were awarded in equity in lieu of specific performance, there was no inflexible rule that damages were to be assessed as at the date of the trial. It was possible for the court to take the date of the original breach, the date of the trial, or some date in between the two. In this instance the plaintiff had not delayed in bringing an action against the defendant. The plaintiff would have difficulty in selling the property not taken by the defendant; the plaintiff had not missed the market by his actions. Therefore, the measure of his damages was the difference between the contract price and the market value of the property at the date of the trial, not at the date of the defendant purchaser's failure to complete the contract. But in *Kopec v. Pyret*[112] the Saskatchewan Court of Appeal, following Ontario and Manitoba decisions,[113] held that the date of judgment was the appropriate date for calculating damages. The defendant leased land to X for three years, and gave him an option to purchase if the defendant was going to sell the land. The defendant agreed later to sell the land to the plaintiff, without giving notice of this intention to X, as agreed in the lease to X. The latter then filed a caveat claiming an interest in the land under his option to purchase. Then the plaintiff filed a caveat claiming an interest as a purchaser. Then the defendant executed a transfer of the land to X. The plaintiff sued for specific performance or damages. At trial he was awarded damages including damages for loss of bargain and loss of profits, Scheibel J. applying the doctrine that a plaintiff is entitled to recover an amount sufficient to put him in the position he would have been in if the contract had been performed.[114] The Court of Appeal varied the award by deleting loss of profits since that was duplicative of damages for loss of bargain. In addition to the expenses incurred by the plaintiff and an amount in respect of work done by him on the land, the plaintiff was allowed the difference in the value of the land between the purchase price at the time of breach and the date of judgment. The latter was the appropriate date for calculating the loss suffered by the plaintiff. *Wroth v. Tyler* was followed on this point. Thus there appears to be some difference of opinion between different provincial courts on the issue of the date for assessment of damages. At some time the Supreme Court of Canada will have to determine the issue conclusively.

Another aspect of the decision at first instance (it was not dealt with on appeal) is the question of mitigation. Generally, whether the plaintiff sues for damages at common law or in equity, he is under a duty to mitigate his loss.[115] But in *Kopec*

---

110 *306793 Ont. Ltd. v. Rimes*, above, note 102.

111 (1983), 44 B.C.L.R. 172 (B.C.S.C.). However, perhaps the court might have taken a different view if the plaintiff had been at fault in losing opportunities to resell the property so as to reduce his potential damages. But see the discussion of *Kopec v. Pyret*, below.

112 Above, note 95.

113 Referred to above, note 95.

114 *Kopec v. Pyret* (1983), 146 D.L.R. (3d) 242 at 256 (Sask. Q.B.); varied (1987), 36 D.L.R. (4th) 1 (Sask. C.A.); *Asamera Oil Corp. v. Sea Oil & General Corp.; Baud Corp., N.V. v. Brook* (1978), 89 D.L.R. (3d) 1 at 8 (S.C.C.): below, p. 716.

115 Below, pp. 776-782.

v. Pyret[116] Scheibel J. held that where specific performance was claimed but damages are awarded in lieu the plaintiff is under no duty to mitigate when the claim for specific performance has a reasonable chance of success. The reason for this was that otherwise the plaintiff would incur the risk of substantial reduction in his damages if he did not purchase alternative land in order to pursue his remedy of specific performance. Hence his conduct in not pursuing such a purchase was not unreasonable. Some doubt is thrown on these remarks by the subsequent decision of the Court of Appeal that specific performance was not available in the circumstances.[117]

2. Remoteness of damage[118]

(a) Remoteness and measurement of damages distinguished

Whenever a contract is broken, so as to give rise to the common-law remedy of damages, two distinct questions or issues arise.[119] One is whether the damage incurred by the plaintiff is properly remediable by or recoverable in an action for breach of contract. This is the question of remoteness. The second issue is how to measure the loss incurred by the plaintiff, in respect of which the defendant is liable for breach of contract. This is the issue of quantification. Whether the question is one of remoteness or quantification, the rule of the common law, as expounded by Parke B. in *Robinson v. Harman*,[120] is that "where a party sustains a loss by reason of a breach of contract, he is, so far as money can do it, to be placed in the same situation, with respect to damages, as if the contract had been performed." However, for the purposes of the present analysis it is advisable to differentiate the two problems and consider them separately.

(b) Development of rules relating to remoteness

The modern test of remoteness of damage in contract cases stems from the decision in *Hadley v. Baxendale*[121] in 1854. That case was concerned with the liability

---

116 Above, note 114, at 257-258 (Sask. Q.B.).

117 Above, note 114, at 8-9 (Sask. C.A.).

118 Waddams, *Law of Damages*, 2nd ed. (1991), paras. 14.20-14.410. See also Swinton, "Foreseeability: Where Should the Award of Contract Damages Cease?" in Reiter and Swan, *Studies in Contract Law*, p. 61.

119 The *"Argentino"* (1889), 14 App. Cas. 519 (H.L.); *J. D'Almeida Araujo Lda. v. Becker (Sir Frederick) & Co.*, [1953] 2 Q.B. 329.

120 (1848), 1 Ex. 850 at 855. Compare *Wertheim v. Chicoutimi Pulp Co.*, [1911] A.C. 301 at 307 (P.C.); *Sydney Steep Corp. c. Mannesmann Pipe & Steel Corp.* (1986), 75 N.S.R. (2d) 211 at 220 (N.S.T.D.). See also the exhaustive decision of the High Court of Australia in *Commonwealth of Australia v. Amann Aviation Pty. Ltd.* (1991), 66 A.L.J.R. 123. On the utility of money damages as a remedy, compare Yorio, "In Defence of Money Damages for Breach of Contract" (1982), 82 Col. L.R. 1365.

121 (1854), 9 Ex. 341, 156 E.R. 145; Brown, "Developments in the Law of Damages for Breach of Contract" (1975), Special Lectures of Law Society of Upper Canada, 1 at pp. 13-19. For discussion of the economic background, see Barton, "The Economic Basis of Damages for Breach of Contract"

of a common carrier for undue delay in delivering a broken crankshaft to its makers so that they could construct a new one for the plaintiffs, who were mill owners. Without a new crankshaft the mill could not operate, with the consequence that the plaintiffs lost profits. It was held that the plaintiffs' loss of profit during the period of the delay was not an item of damages that could be recovered in the action for breach of the contract of carriage. The only information received by the carrier was that he was to carry a broken crankshaft belonging to the mill and that the plaintiffs were the owners of the mill. In these circumstances, the loss complained of was not reasonably foreseeable as a consequence of the carrier's delay in getting the broken shaft to the makers to use as a pattern for a new one. And, as the court explained, the test of liability was what was reasonably foreseeable. This was stated in language which has now become classical:[122]

> Where two parties have made a contract which one of them has broken, the damages which the other party ought to receive in respect of such breach of contract should be such as may fairly and reasonably be considered either arising naturally, *i.e.*, according to the usual course of things, from such breach of contract itself, or such as may reasonably be supposed to have been in the contemplation of both parties, at the time they made the contract, as the probable result of the breach of it.

The rationale for the exclusion of losses that are not reasonably foreseeable is that it would be unfair to require the defendant to pay full damages where, if he had been aware of them, he might have declined the risk or made other arrangements.[123]

The principles stated in this case have long been accepted by the courts in Canada.[124] As Ritchie J. of the Supreme Court explained in *Brown & Root Ltd. v. Chimo Shipping Ltd.*[125] it has never been seriously questioned since *Hadley v. Baxendale* that damages for breach of contract are limited to the ordinary consequences which would follow in the usual course of things from such breach, or for the consequences of the breach which might reasonably be supposed to have been in the contemplation of the parties at the time they made the contract. These two formulations of the principle reveal clearly its two aspects. The first test is *objective*, that is, what the reasonable man would or ought to have foreseen as being the likely or probable consequences of his breach. This will be, and was intended to be the normal, most usual test. However, exceptionally, it is recognized that, in some instances, the recoverable damages may go beyond what the ordinary, reasonable man would foresee as being likely, and might extend to consequences

---

(1972), 1 J. Leg. Stud. 277; Perloff, "Breach of Contract and the Foreseeability Rule of Hadley v. Baxendale" (1981), 10 J. Leg. Stud. 39.

122 9 Ex. 341 at 354 *per* Alderson B.

123 *Ibid.*, at 355; *Houweling Nurseries Ltd. v. Frisons Western Corp.* (1988), 49 D.L.R. (4th) 205 at 211 (B.C.C.A.).

124 *Walton v. Ferguson* (1914), 7 W.W.R. 611 (Alta. S.C.); *Goodison v. Crow* (1920), 48 O.L.R. 552 (Ont. C.A.); *Prince Rupert Sawmills Ltd. v. M.C. Logging Ltd.* (1967), 65 D.L.R. (2d) 300 (B.C.S.C.); *Parta Indust. Ltd. v. C.P. Ltd.* (1974), 48 D.L.R. (3d) 463 (B.C.S.C.).

125 [1967] S.C.R. 642 at 648 (S.C.C.). Compare *Total Petroleum (North America) Ltd. v. AMF Tuboscope Ltd.* (1987), 54 Alta. L.R. (2d) 13 at 44 (Alta. Q.B.) *per* O'Leary J.

not ordinarily foreseeable, as long as the particular consequences were foreseeable in the light of *their* particular contract and its special circumstances. In such instances the test is *subjective.*[126]

Almost a hundred years later, in a judgment that was, and still is accepted by courts in England[127] and Canada[128] as authoritative (despite some comments that were made later by the House of Lords) Asquith L.J. in *Victoria Laundry (Windsor) Ltd. v. Newman Industries Ltd.*[129] restated, in a more expanded form, having regard to the decisions in the intervening years, the *Hadley v. Baxendale* principle. The *Victoria Laundry* case involved the sale and delivery of a boiler by an engineering firm to a laundry which wanted to extend its business. The boiler was damaged while being removed, with the result that it was delivered several months after the contract date. As a result, the laundry claimed, they lost the extra profit that they would have earned during the period of the delay; also they lost exceptional profits which they would have earned on some highly lucrative dyeing contracts which they would have obtained from a government ministry if they had had the boiler. The defendants, being an engineering firm, in the light of their experience and with the knowledge that they did possess as to the contract and its background, could not argue that they did not foresee some loss of business by the plaintiffs through the later delivery. They could also foresee the possiblity of loss from the inability to perform *normal* dyeing contracts. But they could not be expected to foresee that the plaintiffs would have obtained *exceptional* dyeing contracts, and so incur *exceptional* loss of profits. Thus, damages were recoverable on the basis of the first part of the *Hadley v. Baxendale* rule, the objective test, but not on the basis of the second, the subjective, since the necessary facts were not proved to substantiate such a claim. What Asquith L.J. said in this case was as follows:[130]

> (2) In cases of breach of contract the aggrieved party is only entitled to recover such part of the loss actually resulting as was at the time of the contract reasonably foreseeable as liable to result from the breach.
>
> (3) What was at that time reasonably so foreseeable depends on the knowledge then possessed by the parties, or at all events, by the party who later commits the breach.
>
> (4) For this purpose, knowledge "possessed" is of two kinds; one imputed, the other actual, Everyone, as a reasonable person, is taken to know the 'ordinary course of things' and consequently what loss is liable to result from a breach of contract in that ordinary course. This is the subject matter of the 'first rule' in *Hadley v.*

---

126 The passage from "The first test is objective" to end of the paragraph was quoted by O'Leary J. in *Total Petroleum (North America) Ltd. v. AMF Tuboscope Inc.*, above, note 125, at 43, and by Heald J. in *R. v. Canamerican Auto Lease & Rental Ltd.*, [1987] 3 F.C. 144 at 163 (Fed. C.A.).

127 *East Ham Corp. v. Bernard Sunley & Sons Ltd.*, [1966] A.C. 406 (H.L.); compare *Aruna Mills Ltd. v. Gobindram*, [1968] 1 Q.B. 655.

128 *Prince Rupert Sawmills Ltd. v. M.C. Logging Ltd.*, above, note 124; *Parta Indust. Ltd. v. C.P. Ltd.*, above, note 124; *Houweling Nurseries Ltd. v. Fisons Western Corp.*, above, note 123.

129 [1949] 2 K.B. 528 (C.A.).

130 *Ibid.*, at 539-540; compare *Monarch S.S. Co. v. A.B. Karlshamns Oljefabriker*, [1949] A.C. 196 especially at 234 (H.L.) *per* Lord Du Parcq.

Baxendale. . . . But to this knowledge, which a contract-breaker is assumed to possess whether he actually possesses it or not, there may have to be added a particular case knowledge which he actually possesses, of special circumstances outside the 'ordinary course of things' of such a kind that a breach in those special circumstances would be liable to cause more loss. Such a case attracts the operation of the 'second rule' so as to make additional loss also recoverable.

(5) In order to make the contract-breaker liable under either rule it is necessary that he should actually have asked himself what loss is liable to result from a breach. As has often been pointed out, parties at the time of contracting contemplate not the breach of the contract, but its performance. It suffices that, if he had considered the question, he would as a reasonable man have concluded that the loss in question was liable to result. . . .

(6) Nor, finally, to make a particular loss recoverable, need it be proved that upon a given state of knowledge the defendant could, as a reasonable man, foresee that a breach must necessarily result in that loss. It is enough if he could foresee it was likely so to result. It is indeed enough . . . if the loss (or some factor without which it would not have occurred) is a "serious possibility" or a "real danger". For short, we have used the word "liable" to result. Possibly the colloquialism 'on the cards' indicates the shade of meaning with some approach to accuracy.

This exposition of the law remained uncriticized, and was applied in many subsequent decisions, until the House of Lords became seized of the problem in *The "Heron II"*.[131] In that case shipowners agreed to carry a cargo of sugar belonging to the plaintiffs from Constanza to Basrah. At Basrah, as the shipowners knew, there was a sugar market. The shipowners also knew that the plaintiffs were sugar merchants. But the shipowners did not know that the plaintiffs intended to sell the sugar immediately it arrived, at the then market rate. Nor were they aware of the possibility that the market rate might drop if the sugar were delivered later than the contracted date. Because of the default of the shipowners, the cargo reached Basrah later than agreed, by which time the sugar fetched a lower price on the market than it would have done on the due date for delivery. The plaintiffs sued to recover this loss of profit. The House of Lords held that the shipowners were liable for this loss. Although the special circumstances were not known by the shipowners, it was foreseeable that, if the sugar were delivered late, some financial loss would be suffered or incurred by the plaintiffs. In the course of the speeches in this case, some comments were made by several of their Lordships upon the language of Asquith L.J. in the *Victoria Laundry* case.[132] Exception was taken to the expression "on the cards" as a formulation of the test of what was likely or foreseeable under the principle of *Hadley v. Baxendale*. But in general there appears to have been approval of the approach of Asquith L.J.[133] What their Lordships were anxious to achieve, however, was some distinction between the concept of "reasonable foreseeability" as applicable in tort cases, and the idea that damages, to be recoverable in contract, should be "likely to happen". It was vital to distinguish

---

131 [1969] 1 A.C. 350 (H.L.); compare *S.S. Ardennes v. S.S. Ardennes (Owners)*, [1951] 1 K.B. 55.
132 *Ibid.*, at 388-391 *per* Lord Reid, 399 *per* Lord Morris, 417 *per* Lord Pearce, 423-424 *per* Lord Upjohn.
133 Lord Reid, however, was more critical.

the tort test from the contract one, since different ends and policies were involved. But there was little agreement between their Lordships as to the right phrase to use to describe the contract test. The effect of this decision was expressed in these words from a subsequent English case:[134]

> ... their Lordships expressed varying degrees of enthusiasm for the *Victoria Laundry* case; but, subject to two possible qualifications, it seems ... to remain unimpaired as the classsic authority on the topic. These two qualifications are as follows. First, reference in the judgment in the *Victoria Laundry* case to a loss being "reasonably foreseeable" should perhaps be taken as referring to the loss having been within "actual or assumed contemplation". ... Second, the phrase "liable to result" is not correctly paraphrased by the use of the expression "on the cards", but conveys the relevant shade of likelihood by its own wording ... or when defined (as it was in proposition (6) in the *Victoria Laundry* case) as indicating that a loss is a "serious possibility" or "real danger" ...

The distinction between "reasonable foreseeability" and "reasonable contemplation", and the dispute as to whether the proper test was "probability" or "possibility", which were regarded by Lord Denning as involving purely "semantic" issues, were both subjected to attack by Lord Denning in *Parsons (Livestock) Ltd. v. Uttley, Ingham & Co.*[135] There Lord Denning attempted to develop the law of remoteness of damage in contract further, by stating the rules in such a way as to produce a common point of view or approach, whether the cause of action were in tort or contract. According to Lord Denning,[136] the law should distinguish between loss of profit and physical damage. Where loss of profit, that is, economic damage, was involved, the plaintiff should establish that there was a serious possibility or real danger of such loss. Where physical injury was concerned, it should only be necessary to establish a slight possibility of such injury as a consequence of the breach of contract. This would make cases where physical injury was alleged to be the outcome of a breach of contract the same, for purposes of damages, as actions in tort for physical injury. That would eliminate much of the semantic exercises currently involved in the explanation of the way the courts deal with remoteness problems.[137] Orr and Scarman L.JJ. disagreed with this analysis.[138] All three members of the English Court of Appeal came to the same conclusion on the facts of the particular case in which these comments were made. What occurred in this case was that the manufacturers of a pig-food hopper had negligently, and in breach of contract, omitted to install a proper ventilator in the

---

134 *Aruna Mills Ltd. v. Gobindram*, [1968] 1 Q.B. 655 at 668 *per* Donaldson J. That case concerned loss caused by reason of the devaluation of the pound sterling between the date of delivery under the contract and the date when goods were delivered: the loss was held not to be too remote. Lord Brandon distinguished this case in *President of India v. Lips Maritime Corp.*, [1987] 3 All E.R. 110 at 117 (H.L.) (such loss only to be recognised by an award of interest where a claim for demurrage was concerned, since such a claim was not for a debt but for damages).

135 [1978] 1 All E.R. 525 (C.A.).

136 *Ibid.*, at 532-534.

137 Which were not agreeable to Lord Denning; *ibid.*, at 532.

138 *Ibid.*, at 534, 535.

hopper. In consequence the pig-food stored in the hopper had gone mouldy. A number of the plaintiff's pigs which had eaten the mouldy food had died. For those deaths the manufacturers were held liable.

In contrast with the views of Lord Denning, the other members of the court took a more traditional view of remoteness of damage in breach of contract cases. They accepted the way the law had been stated in *The "Heron II"* and earlier decisions. Scarman L.J., pointed out that the type of consequence, that is, loss of profit or physical injury, would always be an important matter of fact in determining whether, under the circumstances, the loss or injury was of a type which the parties could reasonably be supposed to have contemplated when the contract was made, as being the sort of injury or loss that could occur.[139] Thus, some distinction between loss of profit and physical injury as types of damage did exist, and was relevant in the law, but not in the way suggested by Lord Denning. As Scarman L.J. explained,[140] there were good reasons why it was legitimate and necessary to differentiate tort cases from cases of contract, even where both involved the same kind of injury. The possibility of prior agreement or limitation, for example, could not be eliminated simply by adopting a rule that purported to assimilate the principles applicable in either instance. Hence there was not real point in attempting to do so. However, where the parties had the same actual or imputed knowledge, and the contract contained no term limiting the damages recoverable for breach of contract, the damages recoverable did not depend upon whether, as a matter of legal classification, the plaintiff's cause of action was in breach of contract or tort.[141] In the final analysis, despite the comments of Lord Reid in *The "Heron II"*,[142] the difference between "reasonably foreseeable", the tort test, and "reasonably contemplated", the contract test, was semantic, not substantial.[143]

The Supreme Court of Canada subsequently appears to have agreed with this point of view, in *Asamera Oil Corporation v. Sea Oil & General Corporation; Baud Corporation N.V. v. Brook*.[144] Accepting the language of Scarman L.J. in the *Parsons* case, Estey J., delivering the judgment of the Supreme Court, approved the idea that a differentiation between tort and contract would be made where the agreement or the factual relationship of the parties required such a distinction to be drawn in the interests of justice.[145] More recently, Zuber J.A., in the Ontario Court of Appeal also aligned himself, and Goodman J.A., with those who were unable to see any real difference between the tests of reasonable foreseeability and reasonable contemplation. Neither test was a measure of precision. Indeed, for the purposes

---

139 *Ibid.*, at 535; compare *Monarch S.S. Co. v. A.B. Karlshamns Oljefabriker*, [1949] 1 All E.R. 1 at 14-15 (H.L.) *per* Lord Wright, applied in *C.P. Ltd. v. McCain Produce Co.* (1981), 113 D.L.R. (3d) 584 at 616 (N.B.C.A.); affirmed (1981), 123 D.L.R. (3d) 764 (S.C.C.).
140 [1978] 1 All E.R. 525 at 535 (C.A.). Compare the remarks of Deane J. in *Commonwealth of Australia v. Amann Aviation Pty. Ltd.*, above, note 120, at 144.
141 Above, note 140, at 536.
142 [1969] 1 A.C. 350 at 389, 390 (H.L.).
143 [1978] 1 All E.R. 525 at 531 (C.A.).
144 (1979), 89 D.L.R. (3d) 1 (S.C.C.).
145 *Ibid.*, at 9-10.

of the case in question, *Kienzle v. Stringer*,[146] the learned judge used "reasonable foreseeability" as embracing the test in both tort and contract. That case concerned an action for negligence against a solicitor, but it would seem that the solicitor was also guilty of a breach of his contract with the plaintiff, his client. There would have been serious injustice in holding that the measure of the plaintiff's damages might be different if he sued in contract rather than for negligence. The trial judge, applying an earlier decision,[147] had held that this was indeed so, and awarded what he conceived of as the contract measurement of damages. The Ontario Court of Appeal rejected such approach, without determining whether the liability of a solicitor to his client was for breach of contract or for tort.

There may be a climate of opinion favourable to the view that the difference between the remoteness of damage tests in tort cases and breach of contract cases is merely semantic, and not fundamental in principle. However, the issue has not finally been resolved.[148] What does seem clear is that, in contract cases, the test is the classical one of *Hadley v. Baxendale*, as reaffirmed and reinterpreted by Asquith L.J. and the House of Lords. The appropriate general test is one of "reasonable contemplation" by the parties at the time of the contract, whether or not the results are more serious than would have been reasonably contemplated.[149]

(c) Operation of the rules

(i) *Causation*

Underlying the whole issue, whether the objective or subjective aspect of the rules is bring applied, is the problem of causation. Certainly where the objective doctrine is involved, the issue is also one of directness. This would seem to be

---

146 (1981), 130 D.L.R. (3d) 272 at 275-276 (Ont. C.A.); leave to appeal to S.C.C. refused (1982), 130 D.L.R. (3d) 272n (S.C.C.). Compare *Canlin Ltd. v. Thiokol Fibres Can. Ltd.* (1983), 40 O.R. (2d) 687 at 696-698 (Ont. C.A.) per Cory J.A. (a breach of warranty case); with which compare *Dellelce Const. & Equipment v. Portec Inc.* (1990), 73 O.R. (2d) 396 at 426-428 (Ont. H.C.) per Anderson J.; additional reasons at (1990), 73 O.R. (2d) 396 at 440 (Ont. H.C.).

147 *Messineo v. Beale* (1978), 86 D.L.R. (3d) 713 (Ont. C.A.).

148 But see *Abitibi-Price Inc. v. Westinghouse Can. Inc.* (1988), 73 Nfld. & P.E.I.R. 271 at 304-307 (Nfld. T.D.). Compare the discussion of concurrent liability in contract and tort; above, pp. 694-701.

149 *Vacwell Enrg. Co. v. B.D.H. Chemicals Ltd.*, [1971] 1 Q.B. 111 (C.A.); compare the *talem qualem* rule in tort, *Smith v. Leech Brain & Co.*, [1962] 2 Q.B. 405 (Fridman, *Law of Torts in Canada* (1989), Vol. 1, pp. 325, 328, 330), and note that "financial stringency" may not always disqualify a plaintiff from recovering in tort damages which may have been affected by his financial position: *Dodd Properties (Kent) Ltd. v. Canterbury City Council*, [1980] 1 All E.R. 928 (C.A.), distinguishing *Liesbosch v. S.S. Edison*, [1933] A.C. 449 (H.L.). This last point means that, perhaps, such financial difficulties, exacerbating a plaintiff's losses, may not always make such loss too remote; compare *Freedhoff v. Pomalift Industs. Ltd.* (1971), 19 D.L.R. (3d) 153 (Ont. C.A.).

In *Brown v. Waterloo Regional Bd. of Police Commrs.* (1983), 150 D.L.R. (3d) 729 (Ont. C.A.) and in *Weinstein v. A.E. Le Page (Ont.) Ltd.* (1984), 10 D.L.R. (4th) 717 (Ont. C.A.) Weatherston J.A. adopted the phrase "reasonable expectations" as having the same meaning as, but more in keeping with modern language than the doctrine of foresight or contemplation set out in *Hadley v. Baxendale*.

implicit in the formulation of Alderson B.[150] Thus, before damage is properly treated as recoverable under *Hadley v. Baxendale*, it must have been the direct, physical result or consequence of the breach of contract that is in question.[151] "Direct damage," it has been said,[152] "is that which flows naturally from the breach without other intervening cause, and independently of special circumstances, while indirect damage does not so flow."[153] As Duff J. of the Supreme Court of Canada asked in one case,[154] concerning a fraudulently induced transaction, the question was: what loss did the plaintiff suffer that was directly attributable to the transaction into which the plaintiff was induced to enter? The plaintiff must prove that it was the defendant's breach of contract, and not some intervening factor, that caused the plaintiff's loss. This onus the plaintiff was satisfied in *Eastwalsh Home Ltd. v. Anatal Developments Ltd.*[155] The plaintiff, a builder, agreed to purchase from the defendant, a developer, 147 lots on an unregistered plan of subdivision. The defendant agreed to use its best efforts to satisfy the terms of the contract, especially the obligation forthwith, diligently and in good faith to pursue the registration of the plan prior to the extended closing date of the contract. The plan was not

---

150 Reference to this passage was made by La Forest J.A. in *Doiron v. Caisse Populaire D'Inkerman Ltée* (1985), 17 D.L.R. (4th) 660 (N.B.C.A.).

151 Hence, it would have to be shown that if the defendant had not broken his contract the plaintiff would have acted in a different way so as to avoid the loss which he claims resulted from the defendant's breach: see *Major v. Buchanan* (1975), 9 O.R. (2d) 491 (Ont. H.C.); *Sykes v. Midland Bank Executor & Trustee Co.*, [1971] 1 Q.B. 113 (C.A.).

152 *Saint Line v. Richardsons, Westgarth & Co.*, [1940] 2 K.B. 99 at 103 *per* Atkinson J.; compare *Sayers v. Harlow U.D.C.*, [1958] 2 All E.R. 342 (C.A.).

Note therefore the possibility of there being contributory negligence on the part of the plaintiff cited by La Forest J.A. in *Doiron v. Caisse Populaire D'Inkerman Ltée* (1985), 17 D.L.R. (4th) 660 at 681 (N.B.C.A.). In British Columbia, it has been held that this will bring into play the provisions of the Contributory Negligence Act, *i.e.*, sharing of loss between the parties: *West Coast Finance Ltd. v. Gunderson, Stokes, Walton & Co.*, [1974] 2 W.W.R. 428 (B.C.S.C.); affirmed [1975] 4 W.W.R. 501 (B.C.C.A.); *Palmeri v. Littleton; Renke v. Littleton*, [1979] 4 W.W.R. 577 (B.C.S.C.). See also *Finance Amer. Realty Ltd. v. Speed* (1979), 38 N.S.R. (2d) 374 (N.S.C.A.); *Can. Western Natural Gas Co. v. Pathfinder Surveys Ltd.* (1980), 21 A.R. 459 (Alta. C.A.); *Smith v. McInnis*, [1978] 2 S.C.R. 1357 at 1380-1381 (S.C.C.) *per* Pigeon J. dissenting; *Husky Oil Operations Ltd. v. Oster* (1978), 87 D.L.R. (3d) 86 (Sask. Q.B.); *Tompkins Hardware Ltd. v. North Western Flying Services Ltd.* (1982), 139 D.L.R. (3d) 329 (Ont. H.C.); *Weinstein v. A.E. Le Page (Ont.) Ltd.*, above, note 149. Compare *Caines v. Bank of N.S.* (1978), 90 D.L.R. (3d) 271 (N.B.C.A.). But see, for Ontario, *Dom. Chain Co. v. Eastern Const. Ltd.* (1976), 68 D.L.R. (3d) 385 (Ont. C.A.); affirmed (1978), 84 D.L.R. (3d) 344 (*sub nom. Griffels Associates Ltd. v. Eastern Const. Co.*) (S.C.C.) for a different view; with which compare, *Henuset Bros. Ltd. v. Pan Can. Petroleum Ltd.* (1977), 82 D.L.R. (3d) 345 (Alta. T.D.). Contrast the situation in England where such conduct might result in the plaintiff being totally responsible; compare *Quinn v. Burch Bros. Builders Ltd.*, [1966] 2 Q.B. 370; affirmed [1966] 2 Q.B. 381 (C.A.) with *Hadley v. Droitwich Const. Ltd.* [1967] 3 All E.R. 911 (C.A.). But see *Forsikringsaktieselskapet Vesta v. Butcher*, [1988] 2 All E.R. 43: above, p. 701, note 47. Is the role played by the law of contributory negligence in tort cases played by the law relating to mitigation of damages in contract cases? See below, p. 778.

153 This passage was cited by La Forest J.A. in *Doiron v. Caisse Populaire d'Inkerman Ltée* (1985), 17 D.L.R. (4th) 660 at 681 (N.B.C.A.).

154 *Gosse-Millerd Ltd. v. Devine*, [1928] S.C.R. 101 at 104 (S.C.C.); compare *Allan v. McLennan*, [1917] 1 W.W.R. 513 (B.C.C.A.).

155 (1993), 100 D.L.R. (4th) 469 (Ont. C.A.).

registered in time. The trial judge held that this was a breach of the contract, and that the loss of the building lots was caused by the defendant's failure to satisfy the contract's terms, in particular the term relating to registration of the plan. However, the plaintiff was awarded only nominal damages by the Ontario Court of Appeal, allowing the defendant's appeal from the assessment made by the trial judge, on other grounds relating to the issue of remoteness arising from the fact that what the plaintiff alleged was the loss of a "chance".

Physical causation, as well as the financial consequences of a breach, may be involved.[156] Thus in *Humphries v. Pictou County Power Board*[157] the defendant was in breach of contract in cutting off electricity to the plaintiff's house. While his premises were in the dark, the plaintiff fell and was injured. The question was whether the defendant was liable, in an action for breach of contract, for those injuries. By a majority, the court held that this damage was too remote a consequence of the defendant's breach. The judges who dissented took a somewhat wider view of "cause" than the majority. The physical injury to the plaintiff in this case might not have been "caused", for the purpose of a tort action, by the defendant. However, it could more easily have been regarded as a consequence, both direct and foreseeable, of the defendant's wrongful conduct in a case of contract.[158]

In light of this decision, can it be argued that everything within the parties' "reasonable contemplation" is directly caused by the breach? Or should the issue of "reasonable contemplation" only arise *after*, and not as part of the question of direct physical, financial, or other consequence? The tendency in tort cases, in modern times, is to assimilate the questions of causation, foresight and remoteness. Where the action involves a breach of contract, perhaps the questions should remain distinct.[159]

(ii) *The objective test*

The application of the first branch of the *Hadley v. Baxendale* rule, the objective test, depends upon the nature of the transaction that is involved in any individual case. It is impossible to cover all the various possibilities that might occur. But some elementary differentiation can be made along the lines of the following: loss of profits; expenses; loss of business; loss of earnings; the decrease in the value of goods or property; loss of financial advantage; physical injury to the person

---

156 Compare *C.P. Ltd. v. McCain Produce Co.* (1981), 113 D.L.R. (3d) 584 at 613-615 (N.B.C.A.); affirmed (1981), 123 D.L.R. (3d) 764 (S.C.C.).

157 [1931] 2 D.L.R. 571 (N.S.C.A.); contrast *Kimber v. Willett*, [1947] K.B. 570 (C.A.). Compare also *Varil Bros. v. Hobson* (1933), 149 L.T. 243.

158 This case might be decided differently today: see *Burrard Dry Dock Co. v. Can. Union Lines Ltd.*, [1954] S.C.R. 307 (S.C.C.); applied in *Parallel Productions Ltd. v. Goss Contracting Co.* (1968), 65 W.W.R. 667 (B.C.S.C.).

159 Compare *Eastwalsh Homes Ltd. v. Anatal Devs. Ltd.*, above, note 155, at 484. "In the present case, the trial judge applied the correct approach in separating the question of causation from the question of loss."

or to property.[160] Wherever any of these are within the "reasonable contemplation" of the parties in the ordinary course of events, that is, in the context of the type of transaction that is involved, the loss in question can be recovered.[161]

Damage to the plaintiff personally or to his property usually presents no special difficulty. Problems have arisen, however, where economic loss is alleged to have been the consequence of a breach of contract. Such loss can take several forms.

There may be expenditure by the plaintiff caused by the breach in question. For example, in *Attorney-General for Newfoundland v. Newfoundland Association of Public Employees*,[162] substitute volunteer labour had to be hired when the defendants broke their collective agreement and went on strike. The effect of the strike was to cause a breakdown in a public service. Hence the need to bring in the volunteers. Their cost was a foreseeable consequence of the breach; therefore it was recoverable, less a deduction for the savings in salaries not paid to the striking public employees. Similarly in *R. v. Canamerican Auto Lease & Rental Ltd.*,[163] the plaintiffs recovered the excess amount of rental paid for premises at airports required in consequence of the defendant's acting in breach of contract. Such loss was foreseeable as a likely or probable consequqence of the breach.[164] Another example is provided by the breach of a contract to sell land. If the erstwhile purchaser has to pay more than the contract price for a piece of land, or house, to replace the property that was the subject of the contract, the difference between the contract price and the market price is an expense which is recoverable by way of damages.[165]

---

160 *E.g.*, where defective goods cause physical harm to the person: *McMorran v. Dom. Stores Ltd.* (1977), 74 D.L.R. (3d) 186 (Ont. H.C.); or to property: *Parsons (Livestock) Ltd. v. Uttley, Ingham & Co.*, [1978] 1 All E.R. 525 (C.A.).

161 Even nervous shock, inconvenience, or other "intangible" consequences may be within the scope of recovery: below, pp. 735-744.

162 (1976), 74 D.L.R. (3d) 195 (Nfld. T.D.); compare *Phillips v. Alexander* (1981), 34 N.B.R. (2d) 622 (N.B.Q.B.), cost of installing a well recoverable from defendant who failed to provide adequate water supply as promised.

163 [1987] 3 F.C. 144 (Fed. C.A.): compare *Berta v. Personal Ins. Co. of Can.* (1988), 36 C.C.L.I. 219 (Ont. Dist. Ct.) (rental of substitute car recoverable); *Coleman v. Saskatoon Car Town Ltd.* (1986), 45 Sask. R. 308 (Sask. Q.B.), where the plaintiffs recovered the cost of repairs that had to be made to a used car they purchased. Compare *Woodman's Sea Products Ltd. v. Lush* (1990), 84 Nfld. & P.E.I.R. 79 (Nfld. T.D.), recovery of money paid by way of installments for price of faulty computer accounting system.

164 But not loss of profits resulting from having to locate elsewhere, not at airports: compare *Woodman's Sea Products Ltd. v. Lush*, above, note 163, no recovery of lost business because of faulty computer system delivered by defendants. Note the remarks of Stone J., above, note 163, at 169, that the plaintiff could choose between claiming its *expectation* interest *i.e.*, loss of profits, and its *reliance* interest, *i.e.*, the excessive bid it was forced to make (using the terminology of Fuller & Perdue, "The Reliance Interest in Contract Damages" (1936), 46 Yale L.J. 52).

165 *Wroth v. Tyler*, [1974] Ch. 30 at 56. But see *Clift v. Tonnelier* (1983), 144 D.L.R. (3d) 188 (Sask. Q.B.). It does not matter now whether the claim is for damages at common law or in equity: above, pp. 709-710. Similarly if the vendor is claiming damages for failure by the purchaser to complete; the recoverable loss is the difference between the contract price and the price at which the property could be resold on the market: *100 Main St. Ltd. v. W.B. Sullivan Const. Ltd.* (1978), 88 D.L.R. (3d) 1 (Ont. C.A.); leave to appeal to the S.C.C. refused (1978), 20 O.R. 401n (S.C.C.). Note, however, (a) the problem of the date at which damages are to be assessed and (b) the issue

The same is the situation with respect to the breach of a contract of sale of goods through non-delivery of the goods. Here, as with the obverse situation that arises where the buyer fails to accept the goods in breach of the contract, the appropriate rule is contained in the Sale of Goods Act,[166] which, in effect, restates in statutory form the rule in *Hadley v. Baxendale.* The recalcitrant buyer is obliged to make good any deficiency between the contract price he would have paid and the market price obtained by the seller when he resells the goods, if and where there is an available market and he can resell them. In such circumstances what occurs is what might be called a negative expenditure by the plaintiff. He is out of pocket, not because he has had to pay more, but because he has received less than he would have done under the contract.[167] So, too, if a contract to buy a business is not fulfilled, the measure of damages is the difference between the contract price and what was realised by the vendor on the sale of the vendor's business assets.[168] The situation with respect to contracts of sale of land or goods is paralled by that which arises where the contract is one for the loan of money, or payment of money. If a borrower is put to more expense to obtain alternative funding because of the lender's default, such extra expense may be recoverable.[169] Conversely a borrower who is in default in repaying a loan by the due date may be liable for any loss caused to the lender, who, in turn, is unable to meet some financial commitment. Such might be the case, where the lender is in default in payment

---

of inflation: below, pp. 753-755. Note also the limitation effected by the doctrine of *Bain v. Fothergill,* to the extent to which that doctrine still applies in Canada: below, pp. 731-734.

166 Fridman, *Sale of Goods in Canada,* 3rd ed. (1986), pp. 355-363, 405-410. As to the liability for delivery of faulty goods: see *ibid.,* pp. 395-404; compare *Bacon v. Cooper (Metals) Ltd.,* [1982] 1 All E.R. 397.

167 The passage from "The recalcitrant buyer" to here was quoted by Oliphant J. in *Mount Baker Enterprises Ltd. v. Big Rig Collision Inc.* (1990), 64 Man. R. (2d) 180 at 195-196 (Man. Q.B.); affirmed (1990), 68 Man. R. (2d) 269 (Man. C.A.). As to the situation where there is no available market, see Fridman, *op. cit.,* pp. 363-367: compare *Sydney Steel Corp. v. Mannesmann Pipe & Steel Corp.* (1986), 75 N.S.R. (2d) 211 (N.S.T.D.). Extra work caused by the impecuniosity of the buyer, not reasonably within the contemplation of the parties, will be irrecoverable: *Freedhoff v. Pomalift Indust. Ltd.* (1971), 19 D.L.R. (3d) 153 (Ont. C.A.); *R.G. McLean Ltd. v. Can. Vickers Ltd.* (1971), 15 D.L.R. (3d) 15 (Ont. C.A.) on which see Baer (1973), 51 Can. Bar Rev. 490.

168 *Mount Baker Enterprises Ltd. v. Big Rig Collision Inc.,* above, note 167, in which the plaintiff was also entitled to claim (a) restitution of money received by the defendant for goods sold while the defendant was in possession of the business which the defendant failed to purchase; and (b) expenses incurred by the plaintiff in repairing and replacing the assets of the business.

169 Contrast *Accord Holdings Ltd. v. Excelsior Life Ins. Co.* (1982), 44 A.R. 368 (Alta. Q.B.); reversed in part (1985), 62 A.P.R. 234 (Alta. C.A.) with *Prince Rupert Sawmills Ltd. v. M.C. Logging Ltd.* (1967), 65 D.L.R. (2d) 300 (B.C.C.A.); *Mennie v. Leitch* (1885), 8 O.R. 397 (Ont. C.A.); *Reid v. Garnet B. Hallowell Ltd.* (1978), 10 R.P.R. 308 (Ont. Master) (where it was suggested that the loss of a profitable venture through the deliberate withholding of the loan might also be within the scope of recoverable damages); compare *Wadsworth v. Lydall,* [1981] 2 All E.R. 401 (C.A.); *Bacon v. Cooper (Metals) Ltd.,* above, note 166, where the extra work resulted from the delivery of faulty goods. See also *Martens v. Surrey Credit Union* (1982), 24 R.F.L. (2d) 462 (B.C.S.C.), liability of credit union for wrongfully preventing plaintiff from withdrawing money from an account before a court order to such effect.

of income tax to the Crown by reason of the debtor's failure to fulfil the contract of loan.[170]

The second possibility is that the plaintiff may have lost profits by reason of the defendant's breach of contract. In sale of goods cases, loss of profits through the seller's delivery of faulty goods, or his failure to deliver at all, or only after delay, may be recoverable, where such loss was what would have been expected by the seller, but not otherwise.[171] Loss of earnings caused by an employer's wrongful dismissal of an employee, without the appropriate notice and in circumstances not justifying instant dismissal of the employee, will be recoverable in the normal course of things.[172] Similarly, if the contract is one for the provision of professional services, for example, by a solicitor, the damages recoverable may include what the client has lost in consequence of the breach of contract in issue, for example, by reason

---

170 *Eaton v. R.* (1972), 31 D.L.R. (3d) 723 (Fed. T.D.); affirmed (1972), 42 D.L.R. (3d) 319 (Fed. C.A.).

171 *Whitehead v. R.B. Cameron Ltd.* (1967), 63 D.L.R. (2d) 180 at 184 (N.S.C.A.) *per* Currier C.J.N.S.; *Freedhoff v. Pomalift Industs. Ltd.* (1971), 19 D.L.R. (3d) 153 (Ont. C.A.); *R.G. McLean Ltd. v. Can. Vickers Ltd.* (1971), 15 D.L.R. (2d) 15 (Ont. C.A.); Fridman, *Sale of Goods in Canada*, 3rd ed. (1986), pp. 395-411. See also *Boon v. Bell*, [1932] 2 W.W.R. 304 (Sask. C.A.); *Wingold Const. Co. v. Kramp* (1959), 19 D.L.R. (2d) 358 (Ont. C.A.); affirmed, [1960] S.C.R. 556 (S.C.C.); *Canlin Ltd. v. Thiokol Fibres Can. Ltd.* (1983), 142 D.L.R. (3d) 450 (Ont. C.A.); *MacDonald v. Island Potato Packers Inc.* (1986), 57 Nfld. & P.E.I.R. 219 (P.E.I.C.A.); *Knowlan Corp. v. Ria-Mar Fisheries Ltd.* (1986), 72 N.S.R. (2d) 407 (N.S.T.D.); *Houweling Nurseries Ltd. v. Fisons Western Corp.* (1988), 49 D.L.R. (4th) 205 (B.C.C.A.); leave to appeal to S.C.C. refused (1988), 89 N.R. 398 (note) (S.C.C.) (where damages were reduced by reason of uncertainty); see also *Big Sweeper Building Maintenance Ltd. v. Can. Forest Products Ltd.* (1991), 57 B.C.L.R. (2d) 56 (B.C.C.A.).

In *Sydney Steel Corp. v. Mannesmann Pipe & Steel Corp.*, above, note 167, there was no current market for the goods involved (blast furnace coke), therefore the Sale of Goods Act measure of damages (above) was unfair. Instead the loss of profits suffered by the plaintiff was calculated on the basis of the contract price for the goods less the cost of their production. Compare *MacDonald v. Island Potato Packers Inc.*, above, where again no available market existed: damages were the weighed average selling price of the goods less the contract price and marketing expenses.

172 *Yetton v. Eastwoods Froy Ltd.*, [1966] 3 All E.R. 353; *Woods v. Miramichi Hospital* (1967), 67 D.L.R. (2d) 757 (N.B.C.A.); *Fiddes v. Famous Players*, [1924] 4 D.L.R. 1260 (Man. C.A.). *Guildford v. Anglo-French S.S. Co.* (1883), 9 S.C.R. 303 (S.C.C.); *Fraser-Brace Terminal Contractors v. McKeen*, [1955] 5 D.L.R. 267 (N.B.C.A.); see *Prozak v. Bell Telephone Co. of Can.* (1984), 10 D.L.R. (4th) 382 (Ont. C.A.). But see *Estate-Gard Services of Can. Ltd. v. Loewen Management Corp.* (1989), 38 B.C.L.R. (2d) 362 (B.C.C.A.), where the Court of Appeal reduced damages awarded at trial because they were artificially inflated. The measure of damages is based upon the proper period of notice which the employer did not give, or what would have been reasonable notice. Note the possibility of additional damage for (i) loss of *other* employment: *Hornak v. Paterson* (1967), 62 D.L.R. (2d) 289 (B.C.S.C.) (an action against a trade union, not an employer); (ii) loss of publicity, *Magee v. Channel Seventynine Ltd.* (1976), 75 D.L.R. (3d) 201 (Ont. H.C.); (iii) loss of employment opportunity from loss of reputation: *Abouna v. Foothills Prov. Gen. Hospital Bd.* (1977), 77 D.L.R. (3d) 220 (Alta. T.D.); reversed in part (1978), 83 D.L.R. (3d) 333 (*sub nom. Abouna v. Foothills Prov. Gen. Hosp. Bd. (No. 2)*((Alta. C.A.). Compare *Donna Rae Ltd. v. Seaboard G.M. Diesel Ltd.* (1978), 29 N.S.R. (2d) 413 (N.S.C.A.) where the defendant overloaded a ship's engine causing loss of earnings to the master and crew of the ship. As for damages for mental distress or nervous shock in such cases, see below, pp. 735-744.

of the solicitor's negligence.[173] The damages recoverable are those which would naturally be expected to flow from the solicitor's breach of duty.[174] Hence, the loss resulting from such breach will usually be within the scope of recoverable damages, unless the loss in question was either: (1) the result of the client's own failure to do anything, which would have occurred whatever the conduct of the solicitor; or (2) the result of unknown circumstances, not foreseeable by the solicitor in the ordinary course of events.[175] In sale of land cases, loss of profit is not usually recoverable, unless the transaction is a commercial one, where the parties contemplated that the land in question would be resold, or developed, to the profit of the purchaser.[176] It would seem that loss of profits by reason of a breach of contract is more readily recoverable where the contract was one of sale of goods, or for their manufacture, than where the contract is for the carriage or delivery of goods.[177] In *Scott Maritimes Pulp Ltd. v. B.F. Goodrich Canada Ltd.*,[178] for instance, a carrier contracted to transfer a press roll to a pulp mill. In the course of transfer the press roll was damaged. The liability of the defendants extended only to the cost of repairing the roll. The plaintiffs claimed for loss of profits which ensued from the failure to have the roll in time, which resulted in a delay in production. That loss of profit was not recoverable. It was not within the contemplation of the defendants or someone in the position of the defendants. However in *Cathcart Inspection Services Ltd. v. Purolator Courier Ltd.*,[179] the loss of a construction contract because the defendants failed to deliver a tender for that contract, which had been entrusted to them for delivery, was not only the natural consequence of the

173 There might also be an action in tort for negligence above, pp. 694-695. Note that in a case of breach of a collateral warranty, *Dellelce Const. & Equipment v. Portec Inc.* (1990), 73 O.R. (2d) 396 (Ont. H.C.); additional reasons at (1990), 73 O.R. (2d) 396 at 440 (Ont. H.C.), damages were calculated on the basis of tort, *i.e.*, misrepresentation, not contract.

174 *Kolan v. Solicitor*, [1970] 1 O.R. 41 at 48 (Ont. H.C.) per Lacourcière J.; affirmed (1970), 11 D.L.R. (3d) 672 (Ont. C.A.).

175 See *Major v. Buchanan* (1975), 61 D.L.R. (3d) 46 (Ont. H.C.); *Gouzenko v. Harris* (1976), 72 D.L.R. (3d) 293 (Ont. H.C.); *Messineo v. Beale* (1978), 86 D.L.R. (3d) 713 (Ont. C.A.); *Kienzle v. Stringer* (1981), 130 D.L.R. (3d) 272 (Ont. C.A.); leave to appeal to S.C.C. refused (1982), 42 N.R. 352 (S.C.C.); *Sykes v. Midland Bank Executor & Trustee Co.*, [1971] 1 Q.B. 113 (C.A.); *Otter v. Church, Adams & Tatham & Co.*, [1953] Ch. 280; *Hall v. Meyrick*, [1957] 2 Q.B. 455 (C.A.); *Philips v. Ward*, [1956] 1 All E.R. 874 (C.A.); *Pilkington v. Wood*, [1953] Ch. 770.

   Similarly, in *Prairie Surveys Ltd. v. R.* (1986), 7 F.T.R. 126 (Fed. T.D.), where the defendant's breach of contract caused the plaintiff to suffer a loss of working capital, the resultant closure of an office and consequent loss of business, and therefore profits, were too remote to be recoverable. Such consequences were not reasonably anticipated by the defendant.

176 Compare *Gill v. Kittler* (1983), 44 A.R. 321 (Alta. Q.B.) where the damages also included the cost of obtaining a loan for the purchase price.

177 Compare *Hadley v. Baxendale* (1854), 9 Ex. Ch. 341; *B.C. Saw Mills Co. v. Nettleship* (1868), L.R. 3 C.P. 499; *Horne v. Midland Ry.* (1873), L.R. 8 C.P. 131; *Can. Foundry Co. v. Edmonton Portland Cement Co.*, [1917] 1 W.W.R. 383 (Alta. C.A.); affirmed (1918), 43 D.L.R. 583 (P.C.).

178 (1977), 72 D.L.R. (3d) 680 (N.S.C.A.).

179 (1982), 139 D.L.R. (3d) 371 (Ont. C.A.) (which may have been a case on the subjective test in *Hadley v. Baxendale*; compare *Cornwall Gravel Co. v. Purolator Courier Ltd.* (1978), 83 D.L.R. (3d) 267 (Ont. H.C.); affirmed (1980), 115 D.L.R. (3d) 511 (Ont. C.A.); affirmed [1980] 2 S.C.R. 118 (S.C.C.)).

defendant's breach of contract, it was also within the reasonable contemplation of the parties.[180]

A third way of calculating the economic loss caused to the plaintiff by the defendant's breach of contract is in terms of the diminution in value of the plaintiff's property. Such would be the situation where the seller of goods delivers goods that are faulty, in breach of an express or implied terms of the contract.[181] One way of measuring the damage caused by the breach is by taking the value of the defective goods and subtracting it from the value of the goods that ought to have been delivered.[182] That would be appropriate where the buyer could resell such goods at the lower rate, or where the buyer could restore the original value by an expenditure of the amount by which that value has been reduced. This latter method might be appropriate where there was no market for the defective goods. In the case of other contracts, there appears to be some importance in the distinction between calculating damages in terms of diminished value and calculating them in terms of the cost of replacement, repair, or completed performance after some default or deficiency.[183] In the English case of *Radford v. De Frobeville*,[184] the defendant was in breach of contract in not erecting a brick wall to separate the plaintiff's house from some other property which had been sold to the defendant. Basing the defendant's liability on the "diminution" approach would have resulted in his liability for nominal damages.[185] The plaintiff argued that his loss consisted in the cost of putting up the wall. He was successful. He was entitled to a wall of the kind agreed upon by the parties (even though it cost more to put up at the time of the trial than it would have done had the defendant carried out his

---

180 On the issue of what is sometimes termed "loss of a chance", see the discussion of *Chaplin v. Hicks*, [1911] 2 K.B. 786 (C.A.): below, pp. 751-753.

181 Fridman, *Sale of Goods in Canada*, 3rd ed. (1986), pp. 395-400; on the question whether the goods delivered were worth anything, see *Ford Motor Co. of Can. v. Haley*, [1976] S.C.R. 437 (S.C.C.). Recovery of the cost of repairing faulty goods in a breach of contract case may indicate another difference between remoteness of damage in contract and tort; it is debatable whether such economic loss is recoverable in a tort action: compare *Rivtow Marine Ltd. v. Washington Iron Works*, [1974] S.C.R. 1189 (S.C.C.) and *Kamloops v. Nielsen*, [1984] 5 W.W.R. 1 (S.C.C.).

182 See, e.g., *Flaman v. Regina Motor Products (1970) Ltd.*, [1991] 5 W.W.R. 557 (Sask. C.A.), damages reduced because of lack of evidence of difference in value of a van: no award of damages for high mileage and unanticipated repair, since that would have entitled duplication. But in *Sturge v. Elm Mercury Sales (1976) Ltd.* (1990), 83 Nfld. & P.E.I.R. 37 (Nfld. T.D.) such diminution of value was disallowed: instead the plaintiff was awarded actual financial outlay as special damages, when the car was repossessed by the finance company.

183 See, also *Parallel Productions Ltd. v. Goss Contracting Co.* (1968), 69 D.L.R. (2d) 609 (B.C.S.C.), on the obligation to replace and repair in a *reasonable* way not involving the exact replacement of the object an extra expense. For an example of damages consisting of the cost of repairing defects or completing work contracted to be performed (as well as money paid or due under the contract) less sums which would have been payable under the contract if it had been carried out properly, see *B.J.'s Contracting Ltd. v. Eastern Shredding Ltd.* (1990), 38 C.L.R. 265, 83 Nfld. & P.E.I.R. 121 (Nfld. C.A.).

184 [1978] 1 All E.R. 33; on which see Wallace, "Cost of Repair and Inflation" (1980), 96 L.Q.R. 101; and Harris, Ogus & Phillips, "Contract Remedies and the Consumer Surplus" (1979), 95 L.Q.R. 581.

185 On which see below, pp. 745-746.

obligation in due time). The plaintiff had contracted to do the work, and he had had the benefit of purchasing the plaintiff's land at a lower price than otherwise would have been charged precisely because of his promise to put up a wall that would protect the plaintiff's property and provide the plaintiff with his required privacy. Similarly, in *Dean v. Ainley*[186] the plaintiff was entitled to the cost of sealing the patio of the house he had purchased from the defendant. The latter had covenanted to prevent leakage of water from the patio to the cellar. To perform this task perfectly would have cost more money (which the plaintiff had claimed). Even though the work agreed to be performed would not have been totally satisfactory (which is why the trial judge awarded only nominal damages for breach of covenant), the English Court of Appeal allowed the plaintiff the cost of achieving the less satisfactory solution because this was the least expensive method of dealing with the problem or because this was the cost of what the defendant had contracted to perform. Here, as in *Radford v. De Frobeville*,[187] the plaintiff had suffered a real loss.

However in *Eldon Weiss Home Construction Ltd. v. Clark*,[188] an Ontario County Court judge held that the proper test was not the cost of fulfilment or performance but diminution of value. Here the plaintiff agreed to build a house for the defendants. It was defectively constructed, and $12,000 was needed to make good the deficiencies. The defendants sold the house to a third party for the full market price notwithstanding the deficiencies. When the plaintiffs claimed the remainder of the agreed price for the construction, $4,000, which the defendants had withheld, the judge held that the defendants' measure of damages, in their counterclaim for breach, was not the cost of making up the deficiencies, but the loss in value caused them by those deficiencies. Since they had lost nothing, as evidenced by the sale of the house, they were not entitled to claim anything by way of set-off to the plaintiff's claim. The situation would have been different had the defendants proved that they wanted the work done, in which event they would have been entitled to recover from the plaintiff the cost entailed in doing so.[189] But in *Church of Scientology of British Columbia v. Ahmed*,[190] where a tenant broke his covenant to restore the premises to their original position at the end of a tenancy, it was held that the landlord was entitled to the actual cost of restoration of the premises. His claim was not limited to the diminution in value of the premises by reason of the alterations made by the tenant. The covenant to restore was held to be the equivalent of a covenant to repair.

Thus, one of the difficulties with respect to economic loss is whether the true test of what is recoverable is the actual or required expenditure of the plaintiff

---

186 [1987] 3 All E.R. 748 (C.A.).

187 Above, note 184. Contrast *James v. Hutton*, [1950] 1 K.B. 9, [1949] 2 All E.R. 243 (C.A.); *Wigsell v. School for Indigent Blind* (1882), 8 Q.B.D. 357, in both of which only nominal damages were awarded because the plaintiff never intended to do the work contracted for, but would simply have "pocketed" the damages. In other words, there must be damage or "a real economic loss": *Dean v. Ainley*, above, note 186, at 755 *per* Kerr L.J.

188 (1982), 39 O.R. (2d) (Ont. Co. Ct.).

189 *Ibid.*, at 133; compare *Radford v. De Frobeville*, above, note 184; *Dean v. Ainley*, above, note 186.

190 (1983), 44 B.C.L.R. 297 (B.C.S.C.).

to rectify the defendant's breach or the loss in the value of the property which is the subject-matter of the breach. That is not the only source of difficulty. The cases also reveal some difference of opinion as to whether loss of profit should be awarded or what has been termed "wasted expenditure". This debate rests on the distinction between the plaintiff's so-called *expectation* interest and the plaintiff's so-called *reliance* interest.[191]

The problem with respect to the rival claims of lost profits and wasted expenditure as tests of recovery arises where there is no evidence that, because of the breach of contract, the plaintiff has, or would have lost any profits. In *Anglia Television Ltd. v. Reed*,[192] the English Court of Appeal allowed the plaintiff to claim both pre-contractual[193] and post-contractual expenditures, which had been wasted, when the defendant broke his contract by refusing to perform his obligation to play a leading role in a television play. No question was raised in that case as to the lack of any proof that the film would have recouped that expenditure had it been completed. Nor was the court required to settle the issue of burden of proving whether or not such expenditure would have been recouped. In a subsequent British Columbia case, *Bowlay Logging Ltd. v. Domtar Ltd.*,[194] Berger J. held that expenditure by the plaintiff in preparation for the contract was not recoverable, because the plaintiff would have lost money, not made it, had the contract been completed by the defendant by reason of the plaintiff's inefficiency. That decision was relied on on a later case in the English Court of Appeal, *C. & P. Haulage v. Middleton*.[195] There the plaintiff attempted to claim the cost of work to premises from which he had later been unlawfully evicted. By reason of the eviction the plaintiff was shown to have been better off than if he had been permitted to remain until he could have been required to leave lawfully. The plaintiff was unsuccessful. The reason for this was that to have allowed the plaintiff's claim would have been to compensate him for a bad bargain, not to compensate him for loss caused by, and resulting from the defendant's wrongful conduct. Hence, as was put in a later

---

191 See Fuller & Perdue, "The Reliance Interest in Contract Damages" (1936), 46 Yale L.J. 52, which has been very influential in the United States. Note also the plaintiff's so-called *restitutionary* interest: above, p. 702. In *Commonwealth of Australia v. Amann Aviation Pty. Ltd.* (1991), 66 A.L.J.R. 123, the High Court of Australia allowed the plaintiff reliance damages equivalent to its wasted expenditures as well as damages for loss of profits. There the defendant wrongly repudiated a contract under which the plaintiff was to conduct aerial coastal surveillance for the defendant, to perform which the plaintiff committed large sums and entered into onerous financial arrangements to acquire specially equipped aircraft. On "reliance" damages, see *ibid.*, at 130-131 *per* Mason C.J. and Dawson J.; 139-140 *per* Brennan J.; 148-149 *per* Deane J.; 152-155 *per* Toohey J.; 160-161 *per* Gaudron J.; and 164-166 *per* McHugh J.

192 [1972] 1 Q.B. 60 (C.A.); critized in Waddams, *Law of Damages*, 2nd ed. (1991), paras 2.30, 5.220-5.230. See also *Bell v. Robutka* (1964), 48 D.L.R. (2d) 755 (Alta. Dist. Ct.); affirmed (1966), 55 D.L.R. (2d) 436 (Alta. C.A.). Note also the Australian case of *McRae v. Commonwealth Disposals Commn.* (1951), 84 C.L.R. 377 (Aus.).

193 Compare *Lloyd v. Stanbury*, [1971] 2 All E.R. 267.

194 (1982), 135 D.L.R. (3d) 179 (B.C.C.A.) (distinguished in *Sunshine Vacation Villas Ltd. v. Gov. & Co. of Adventurers of Eng. Trading into Hudson's Bay* (1984), 58 B.C.L.R. 33 at 42-43 (B.C.C.A.)).

195 [1983] 3 All E.R. 94 (C.A.).

English case, *C.C.C. Films (London) Ltd. v. Impact Quadrant Films Ltd.*,[196] "a claim for wasted expenditure cannot succeed in a case where, even had the contract not been broken by the defendant, the returns earned by the plaintiff's exploitation of the chattel or the rights which were the subject-matter of the contract would not have been sufficient to recoup that expenditure." It was also held that the onus was on the defendant to prove that the plaintiff would not have recouped the expenditure if the plaintiff had been able to exploit the contract.[197] Hence, in that case, because the defendant was unable to show that this was the situation, the plaintiff could recover his wasted expenditure. The plaintiff had the choice whether to sue for that amount or claim loss of profits, whether or not he could prove loss of profits or that the loss of profits would have been small. Such "reliance" damages, however, may only be recovered where the loss flows from the breach, not from the plaintiff's own fault in making a bad bargain.[198]

Equally difficult has been the decision whether an aggrieved plaintiff should be awarded the capital loss he has suffered because of the defendant's breach of contract or what he has lost by way of profit. The starting-point for discussion of this question is the decision of the English Court of Appeal in *Cullinane v. British "Rema" Manufacturing Co.*[199] There the court held that, in an action for breach of warranty, the plaintiff had to elect whether to claim damages calculated in accordance with capital loss, that is, the difference in value between the goods contracted for and those supplied by the seller, or his loss of profits, that is, his business losses. The doctrine propounded in the *Cullinane* case was founded on the idea that the plaintiff ought not to have double compensation, which one commentator regarded as "a sound principle."[200] However, commenting on the subsequent Ontario case of *R.G. McLean Ltd. v. Canadian Vickers Ltd.*,[201] which purported to follow the *Cullinane* case, the same writer noted[202] that the English decision forgot that a plaintiff in such instances will usually be able to replace the defective goods (and probably ought to do so, if reasonably possible, in accordance with the doctrine of mitigation of damages[203]). Hence, the plaintiff in that case ought to have recovered the difference in value between a sound and a defective machine and profits lost to the time when the plaintiff, acting reasonably, could have acquired a substitute. Therefore, in the *McLean* case the Ontario Court

---

196 [1984] 3 All E.R. 298 at 306.

197 Compare *Commonwealth of Australia v. Amann Aviation Pty. Ltd.*, above, note 191, distinguishing *Richardson v. Mellish* (1824), 2 Bing. 229, 13 E.R. 294 and *McRae v. Commonwealth Disposals Commissions* (1951), 84 C.L.R. 377.

198 See also *Hayes v. James & Charles Dodd (a firm)*, [1990] 2 All E.R. 815 (C.A.), the capital expenditure thrown away was awarded, not damages for diminution of value, since the property in question was not a readily saleable commodity.

199 [1954] 1 Q.B. 292 (C.A.). This case was considered and explained in the High Court of Australia in *T.C. Industrial Plant Pty. Ltd. v. Robert's Queensland Pty. Ltd.* (1963), 37 A.L.J.R. 289, and in *Commonwealth of Australia v. Amann Aviation Pty. Ltd.*, above, note 191, at 137 *per* Brennan J.; 160-161 *per* Gaudron J.

200 Waddams, *Law of Damages*, 2nd ed. (1991), para. 1.2620.

201 (1970), 15 D.L.R. (2d) 15 (Ont. C.A.).

202 Above, note 200.

203 Below, pp. 776-783.

of Appeal altered the trial judge's award of damages. He had dismissed the seller's counterclaim for the balance of the purchase price of the defective goods (about four-fifths), and gave the plaintiff the profits he would have made had the machine worked. The Court of Appeal reduced the plaintiff's damages by reference to the outstanding amount of the purchase price, and limited the claim for lost profits to the period until the plaintiff could reasonably have acquited a replacement machine. This latter feature distinguishes the Canadian from the English case. It also seems to imply recognition of the possibility of claiming loss of profits, for some period, as well as loss of value. The approach favoured by the *Cullinane* case was rejected by the Alberta Court of Appeal in *Sunnyside Greenhouses Ltd. v. Golden West Seeds Ltd.*[204] There greenhouse panels supplied by the defendants had a shorter life than they should have had. This was a breach of warranty. The damages recoverable by the plaintiffs included the cost of installing the defective panels, some, but not all the costs of removing the panels (since eventually they would have had to be removed and replaced), and the loss of profits based on the amount by which the gross sales for the year in question fell short of the average over a five-year period. In other words, the Alberta court, like that in Ontario, allowed both diminution of value and loss of profits as recoverable damages in an appropriate case. No election was forced on the plaintiff.

This attitude can be found in other Canadian cases.[205] In *Canlin Ltd. v. Thiokol Fibres Canada Ltd.*,[206] the defendant supplied the plaintiff with defective material. From that material the plaintiff was going to manufacture swimming-pool covers. Because of the quality of the material, the plaintiff had to pay the claims of dissatisfied customers and lost anticipated profits. At the trial of the action for breach of contract, the plaintiff was awarded compensation for loss of future business. The Ontario Court of Appeal rejected the defendants' appeal and held that damages could be awarded for loss of future business, when this could be reasonably contemplated or foreseen by the defendant, as was true in this instance. Hence such loss was not too remote.[207] In coming to this conclusion, the court relied on earlier English and Canadian authority,[208] including the *Sunnyside Greenhouses* cases. Although the problem of diminution of value versus loss of profits did not arise directly, it is suggested that the attitude adopted by the Ontario

---

204 (1972), 27 D.L.R. (3d) 434 (Alta. C.A.); affirmed [1973] S.C.R. v (S.C.C.); compare also *Lakelse Dairy Products Ltd. v. Gen. Dairy Mach. & Supply Ltd.* (1970), 10 D.L.R. (3d) 277 (B.C.S.C.); *Beldessi v. Island Equip. Ltd.* (1973), 29 D.L.R. (3d) 213 (B.C.S.C.); reversed in part (1973), 41 D.L.R. (3d) 147 (B.C.C.A.).

205 *Wallace Const. Specialties Ltd. v. Mihalcheon Holdings Ltd.*, [1979] 3 W.W.R. 145 (Sask. Dist. Ct.); *Gill v. Kittler* (1983), 44 A.R. 321 (Alta. Q.B.).

206 (1983), 142 D.L.R. (3d) 450 (Ont. C.A.).

207 Compare the issue of "loss of a chance", below, p. 752: and see *Mills v. Edmonton (City)* (1988), 46 D.L.R. (4th) 26 at 35-36 (Alta. Q.B.). Contrast where all the plaintiff has lost is an opportunity which, on the evidence, could not have been profitable to him anyway: *Findley v. Howard* (1919), 47 D.L.R. 441 (S.C.C.); *Morrison Lamothe Inc. v. Bedok* (1986), 55 O.R. (2d) 129 at 178 (Ont. H.C.) *per* Pennell J.

208 *Simon v. Parsons & Leap Ltd.* (1982), 38 Can. Cas. 151; *Parsons (Livestock) Ltd. v. Uttley, Ingham Co.*, [1978] 1 All E.R. 525 (C.A.); *Richmond Wineries Western Ltd. v. Simpson*, [1940] S.C.R. 1 (S.C.C.).

Court would seem to support the conclusion that, where such loss is appropriate and not remote, such loss can be recovered as well as any other loss attributable to the breach of contract asserted by the plaintiff.[209]

(iii) *The subjective test*

The foundation for the application of the second aspect of the *Hadley v. Baxendale* principle, the "subjective" doctrine, is the defendant's knowledge of some special circumstances which would lead him to realize, as a reasonable man seized of that knowledge, that the plaintiff might suffer some extra, extraordinary, or normally unforeseeable damage, beyond or different from the kind or extent of damage which would otherwise be within the "reasonable contemplation" of the parties.

It is this, for example, which gives rise to the possibility that in an action for breach of a contract of sale of goods, by non-delivery to the buyer, or by delivering goods of the wrong quality, the seller in default may be liable for the loss suffered by the buyer in consequence of what has happened with respect to some sub-sale into which he entered on the strength of the contract with the seller.[210] It is on this basis, also that in *Smith v. Commonwealth Trust Co.*[211] damages could be awarded for loss of reputation on the part of the plaintiff, when the defendant refused to honour cheques drawn on the defendant by the plaintiff. The potential loss of reputation by the plaintiff (a firm) was within the contemplation of the defendant, a bank, at the time of the original deposit of money by the plaintiff in the defendant bank. Similarly, in *General Securities Ltd. v. Don Ingram Ltd.*,[212] the losses suffered by the plaintiff company, in the form of the devaluation of its assets, were recoverable losses, since this was within the contemplation of the defendant company, as a natural and probable result of its failure to provide

---

209 In contrast the British Columbia Court of Appeal suggested that a plaintiff could recover damages for loss of capital *or* damages for loss of profit, but not both, in *Sunshine Vacation Villas Ltd. v. Gov. & Co. of Adventurers of Eng. Trading into Hudson's Bay* (1984), 58 B.C.L.R. 33 (B.C.C.A.). There the loss of profits was more than usually speculative; therefore, damages for loss of cpaital were more appropriate. The comparison was made (*ibid.*, at 46) with *Anglia T.V. v. Reed*, [1972] 1 Q.B. 60 (C.A.); above, p. 726. Compare *Morrison Lamothe Inc. v. Bedok*, above, note 207, relying on *Ronald Elwyn Lister Ltd. v. Dayton Tire Can. Ltd.* (1985), 52 O.R. (2d) 88 (Ont. C.A.). Clearly there is an unresolved dispute here between different courts.

210 *Re Hall & Pim* (1928), 39 L.T. 50 (H.L.); contrast *Williams Bros. v. Agius Ltd.*, [1914] A.C. 510 (H.L.); *The "Heron II"*, [1969] 1 A.C. 350 (H.L.); *Diamond v. Campbell-Jones*, [1961] Ch. 22; see Fridman, *Sale of Goods in Canada*, 3rd ed. (1986), pp. 400-405. Note that actual resale price cannot be used, if known about, to reduce the damages recoverable under the objective rule: *Cory v. Thames Ironworks Co.* (1868), L.R. 3 Q.B. 181; *Rodocanachi v. Milburn* (1886), 18 Q.B.D. 67 (C.A.).

211 (1969), 72 W.W.R. 201 (B.C.S.C.); compare the possibility of *punitive* damages in such a case: *Rolin v. Steward* (1854), 23 L.J. C.P. 148; *Marzetti v. Williams* (1830), 1 B. & Ad. 415, 109 E.R. 842 in which, however, only nominal damages were awarded.

212 [1940] S.C.R. 670 (S.C.C.); compare where a business was sold and the state of the premises was such that purchaser had to undertake repairs and close the business for a period of time, causing loss of profit: *Zauscher v. Earl*, [1943] 2 W.W.R. 697 (B.C.C.A.).

financing for the plaintiffs to buy cars from the defendant, in view of the knowledge of the defendant company of the plaintiff company's financial state and prospects. Hence, under the subjective doctrine of *Hadley v. Baxendale,* the defendant company was responsible for such loss. Similarly, in *Cornwall Gravel Co. v. Purolator Courier Ltd.,*[213] the knowledge by the defendants of the contents of the package sent by their courier service was crucial. The plaintiff sent a tender, that is, an offer to contract, in response to an invitation to submit tenders.[214] The tender was sent by the defendants' courier service, and was to be delivered at a stated time. When it arrived late, the plaintiffs failed to obtain the contract. They sued for the loss of the contract, claiming that this was a foreseeable consequence of the defendants' breach of contract, Since the defendants knew that they were delivering a tender, and could have foreseen the consequences of its late arrival, they were held responsible for the loss of the contract.

On the other hand, however, there are cases in which, because of the failure to establish the requisite knowledge, or that a party with such knowledge could or would reasonably contemplate that what happened would be likely to occur, the defendant was not responsible for all, or some part of the damage alleged to have resulted from the breach in question.[215] For example, in *Brown & Root Ltd. v. Chimo Shipping Ltd.*[216] the defendants tendered cargo for shipment on the plaintiff's ship. The cargo was in bigger pieces than had been agreed. It was alleged that the greater size of the cargo damaged the ship's loading equipment. The Supreme Court of Canada held that this loss was not attributable to the defendant's breach of contract. It was damage which was not within the contemplation of the defendants when they made or broke their contract. In *Parta Industries Ltd. v. Canadian Pacific Ltd.,*[217] goods were shipped by the defendants to the plaintiff from Montreal to British Columbia. There was delay in delivery. By reason of this delay, the plaintiff had to re-order the goods from Belgium. As a result, the plaintiff had to postpone the opening of the plant for which the goods were intended by 105 days. It was held that the defendants, who did not know that the goods were essential to the operation of the plant, were only liable for damage reasonably foreseeable as a result of delay in delivery. They could, or ought to have realized that some delay in the working of the plaintiff's plant would result, since the defendants knew the goods would have to be re-ordered from abroad. Bur they could not be expected to realize the actual length of delay that would occur, that this would entail extra labour costs, interest on money, etc. In consequence, the defendants were not liable for such extra loss suffered by the plaintiff. In *Parallel*

---

213 (1978), 83 D.L.R. (3d) 267 (Ont. H.C.); affirmed (1980), 115 D.L.R. (3d) 511 (Ont. C.A.); affirmed (1980), 120 D.L.R. (3d) 575 (S.C.C.).

214 Above, pp. 31-39.

215 *Walton v. Ferguson* (1914), 7 W.W.R. 611 (Alta. S.C.). Compare two English cases, *Pilkington v. Wood,* [1953] Ch. 770 and *Diamond v. Campbell-Jones,* [1961] Ch. 22.

216 [1967] S.C.R. 642 (S.C.C.).

217 (1974), 48 D.L.R. (3d) 463 (B.C.S.C.).

Productions Ltd. v. Goss Contracting Co.,[218] a bridge collapsed when it was used by the defendants' servant without the permission of the plaintiff, by whom they were employed, and the owner of the bridge. Although they were liable for breach of contract in using the bridge and causing its collapse, the defendants could not be held responsible for replacing the bridge in exactly its original state, which would have involved special materials and greater cost. The defendants had no knowledge of the contract between the plaintiff and the owner of the bridge, under which the plaintiffs were allowed to use the bridge for making a film, on condition that they would put it back in its original condition after filming was concluded. Hence the subjective test of *Hadley v. Baxendale* was not applicable. The defendants were liable under the objective test for the cost of replacing the bridge in a reasonable way, that is, so that it could be used as before.

(iv) *Special problems*

(A) *The doctrine of Bain v. Fothergill*[219] When a vendor fails to complete a contract for the sale of land, the usual way of determining the loss caused by such breach of contract is by reference to the difference between the contract price and the price at which the purchaser can obtain an equivalent piece of property.[220] Under the so-called rule in *Bain v. Fothergill*, damages at large will not be awarded when the reason for such breach is the vendor's inability to make good title, unless the vendor has been guilty of fraud. The only damages recoverable by the purchaser will be the expenses of bringing the action. The reason assigned for this rule in England was that it was difficult for a vendor to prove title. Until recently, this rule was adopted and applied in Canada.[221] It was questioned whether in Canada the rule was necessary in view of the ease with which title can be made, by virtue of various provincial statutes.[222]

In England the rule came under attack.[223] As Megarry J. said in *Wroth v. Tyler*,[224] "the courts have proved ready to find grounds for holding that cases do not fall

---

218 (1968), 69 D.L.R. (2d) 609 (B.C.S.C.) applying *The "Heron II"*, [1969] 1 A.C. 350 (H.L.); *Burrard Dry Dock Co. v. Can. Union Lines Ltd.*, [1954] S.C.R. 307 (S.C.C.); *Biggin & Co. v. Permanite Ltd.*, [1951] 2 K.B. 314 (C.A.).

219 (1874), L.R. 7 H.L. 158 (H.L.); see the earlier case of *Flureau v. Thornhill* (1776), 2 Wm. Bl. 1078.

220 Above, p. 720.

221 *Ont. Asphalt Block Co. v. Montreuil* (1916), 52 S.C.R. 541 (S.C.C.); leave to appeal to Privy Council refused (1916), 52 S.C.R. viii; *Dredge v. Shaw*, [1927] 1 D.L.R. 811 (Sask. K.B.); *Baier v. Bougie* (1963), 44 W.W.R. 608 (B.C.S.C.); *Toth v. Kancz* (1975), 54 D.L.R. (3d) 144 at 149 (Sask. Q.B.); *Kaunas v. Smyth* (1976), 75 D.L.R. (3d) 368 (Ont. H.C.).

222 *E.g.*, Vendors and Purchasers Act, R.S.O. 1990, c. V.2.

223 *Sharneyford Supplies Ltd. v. Edge*, [1987] 1 All E.R. 588 at 594-595 (H.L.) *per* Balcombe L.J., at 599 *per* Kerr L.J., at 600 *per* Parker L.J. (when the rule was held not to apply). Its abolition was recommended by the Law Commission: Working Paper No. 98, 1986; and the later Report, Law Commission, No. 166, 1987: see *Seven Seas Properties Ltd. v. Al-Essa*, [1989] 1 All E.R. 164 (where the rule was applied).

224 [1974] Ch. 30 at 54.

within the rule."[225] That attitude was illustrated by the subsequent English case of *Malhotra v. Choudhury*,[226] in which it was said that the rule was exceptional, applicable only if the vendor, through no fault of his own, was unable to make good title. The vendor had to show that he had used his best endeavours to get good title for the purchaser. Bad faith on his part, even if there were no fraud in the common-law sense, would exclude the operation of the rule in the vendor's favour. A vendor's unwillingness to use his best endeavours to obtain a good title would be the equivalent, or provide evidence of, bad faith. Such was the situation in the *Malhotra* case. Two doctors were in partnership. The contract in question was one by which one partner agreed to buy the other's house. The vendor made all kinds of excuses to prevent the sale of the property to the plaintiff, revealing not his innocent ability to make good title, but his deviousness and general disinclination to sell, as well as his use of technical excuses to hinder the completion and fulfilment of the contract for the sale of the land. Hence, in this instance substantial damages were awarded, not the nominal damages which would be granted under the rule in *Bain v. Fothergill*. So, too, in *Sharneyford Supplies Ltd. v. Edge*,[227] the same court did not apply the rule to a situation in which the vendor of land failed to use his best endeavours to determine a periodic tenancy on the land, so that the purchaser could not obtain vacant possession. The plaintiff, on appeal, was held entitled to damages for loss of profits, and was not restricted to the expenses incurred in the abortive sale. In consequence of judicial and non-judicial criticism the rule has now been abolished in England.[228]

The situation in Canada has also undergone change as a result of the decision of the Supreme Court of Canada in *A.V.G. Management Science Ltd. v. Barwell Developments Ltd.*[229] In British Columbia, where that case originated, the rule has been abrogated by statute.[230] Even where no statutory change has occurred, it may well be that the operation of the rule has been undermined in consequence of the comments of the Supreme Court. The *A.V.G. Management* case involved a sale of land by a vendor to X. The vendor mistakenly believed that the sale to X had fallen through. In consequence he agreed to sell the land to Y. Later X sued the vendor for specific performance of the sales contract with him. He obtained a decree, with which the vendor complied, making it impossible to fulfil the contract with Y, the second purchaser. Y then sued the vendor for damages for breach of the

---

225 See *Day v. Singleton*, [1899] 2 Ch. 320; *Re Daniel*, [1917] 2 Ch. 405; *J.W. Cafés Ltd. v. Brownlow Trust Ltd.*, [1950] 1 All E.R. 894; *Thomas v. Kensington*, [1942] 2 K.B. 181; *Braybrooks v. Whaley*, [1919] 1 K.B. 435. See, more recently, *Ray v. Druce*, [1985] 2 All E.R. 482; *Sharneyford Supplies Ltd. v. Edge*, above, note 223.

226 [1979] 1 All E.R. 186 (C.A.).

227 Above, note 223. Contrast *Seven Seas Properties Ltd. v. Al-Essa*, above, note 223.

228 By the Law of Property (Miscellaneous Provisions) Act, 1989 (U.K.), c. 34, s. 3. A vendor can limit his liability for breach by reason of a defect in title, and this will not be affected by the Unfair Contract Terms Act, 1977 (U.K.), c. 50, but it could be by the Misrepresentation Act, 1967 (U.K.), c. 7: Treitel, *Law of Contract*, 8th ed. (1991), at p. 883.

229 [1979] 2 S.C.R. 43 (S.C.C.).

230 Conveyancing and Law of Property Act, S.B.C. 1978, c. 16, s. 33; see now Property Law Act, R.S.B.C. 1979, c. 340, s. 33.

sales contract made with him. The vendor argued that damages were limited in accordance with the rule in *Bain v. Fothergill* and were not at large, that is, calculable in accordance with the normal doctrine of *Hadley v. Baxendale*. Y argued that the failure to fulfil the contract with him was the fault of the vendor and did not result from an inability outside the vendor's control, therefore ousting the application of the rule. At first instance it was held that the rule applied; the vendor was not fraudulent, therefore the buyer, Y, could only obtain the restricted amount of damages under the rule.[231] This decision was upheld by the British Columbia Court of Appeal.[232] The Supreme Court of Canada reversed the previous decisions and held that the rule did not apply to a situation where a vendor had title when the contract was initially made but voluntarily disabled himself from conveying to a purchaser by entering into concurrent dealings with different purchasers. The vendor here was somewhat greedy, as Laskin C.J. said,[233] and had proceeded in effect to agree to sell the same property twice. On the basis of the origins of the rule, and the limitations on it that developed over the intervening years, Laskin C.J. agreed with Robertson J.A., dissenting in the British Columbia Court of Appeal, that the instant case fell within the exceptions to the rule.

What is even more important about this decision is the analysis of the rationale of the rule, from the point of view of whether it should still be accepted and applied in common-law jurisdictions in Canada. Laskin C.J. considered the reasons given to justify the rule, namely, complexity of real property law, uncertainty of title in England, little variation in the price of property between contract and breach, and concluded that they did not apply in Canada, or were, at the very least, questionable in their application in Canada. The main rationale of the rule had disappeared in provinces which had a Torrens system of registration of title or something similar, namely, British Columbia and the prairie provinces. However, according to Laskin C.J., there was sufficient criticism of the rule in Canadian courts, and sufficient freedom of movement and action on the part of the Supreme Court, to justify rejection of the rule not only in provinces with a Torrens or similar system of registration but also in those provinces which had a system of registration of deeds and documents that governed land transactions. This would cover the Atlantic provinces as well as parts of Ontario and Manitoba. Consequently, in the opinion of Laskin C.J., delivering the judgment of the Supreme Court, the rule in *Bain v. Fothergill* ought not to apply throughout common-law Canada, not just in British Columbia and the "Torrens" provinces. Although all this discussion was *obiter*, since the operation of the rule was excluded by distinguishing the rule not by rejecting it, the statement by Laskin C.J. on behalf of the court was a strong and clear intimation to lower courts across the country that the rule in *Bain v. Fothergill* should not be treated as part of the common law in Canada, even in the absence of legislation achieving that result and regardless of the status of the rule in England.

---

231 (1976), 69 D.L.R. (3d) 741 (B.C.S.C.).

232 (1977), 83 D.L.R. (3d) 702 (B.C.C.A.).

233 (1978), 92 D.L.R. (3d) 289 at 296 (S.C.C.).

However, in *Kopec v. Pyret*[234] in 1987, the Saskatchewan Court of Appeal, quoting and applying what was said in the *A.V.G. Management* case, concluded that the rule in *Bain v. Fothergill* did not apply to the transaction in the case before them. Hence, the court was obliged to consider how to assess the plaintiff's loss of bargain where he was suing for specific performance of a contract of sale of land. From what is said it would appear that, in the absence of any statute abrogating the rule in a particular province, the rule will continue to apply unless the jurisdiction in question has a "Torrens" system of land registry. If the judgment in the *A.V.G. Management* case has not succeeded in abolishing the rule in Canada generally, serious consideration should be given to its abrogation by legislation in provinces other than British Columbia where this has already been achieved.

(B) *Leases* Problems arose in connection with the issue of damages for breach of a lease of land or a lease of a chattel. Until the decision of the Supreme Court of Canada in *Highway Properties Ltd. v. Kelly, Douglas & Co.*,[235] leases of land were not treated as being contractual, but as involving a conveyance. In consequence of this, as previously noted,[236] the doctrines of repudiation and frustration were regarded as being inapplicable to leases of land. The court held that commercial leases were to be treated as contracts. Hence, the proper method of assessing damages for breach of such a contract was to apply general contract principles: and it followed from that conclusion that the doctrines just mentioned were also relevant to such leases. As regards damages, the court held that where a tenant wrongfully repudiated a lease the landlord was entitled to terminate the lease, re-let the property and claim damages that included unpaid future rent, less the actual rental value of the unexpired period, *i.e.*, the prospective loss resulting from the tenant's failure to carry on business, in the shopping centre where the space he had rented was located, for the full term of the lease. Previous decisions had limited the plaintiff's damages, where a lease of chattels was involved, to the rent due at the time of termination of the lease plus any proceeds from resale of the chattel which was repossessed by the plaintiff under the terms of the chattel lease. Damages for loss of future rent were not recoverable. In reaching this conclusion Canadian and English courts had proceeded by analogy to the common law of damages for breach of a lease of land.[237] In relation to leases of land the law in Canada was changed by the decision in the *Highway Properties* case.[238]

---

234 (1987), 36 D.L.R. (4th) 1 (Sask. C.A.).

235 (1971), 17 D.L.R. (3d) 710 (S.C.C.).

236 Above, pp. 606, 621, 660.

237 See *Can. Acceptance Corp. v. Regent Park Butcher Shop Ltd.* (1969), 3 D.L.R. (3d) 304 (Man. C.A.); *Bridge v. Campbell Discount Co.*, [1962] 1 All E.R. 385 (H.L.); *Financings Ltd. v. Baldock*, [1963] 1 All E.R. 443 (C.A.).

238 See *Globe Convestra Ltd. v. Vucetic* (1990), 15 R.P.R. (2d) 220 (Ont. Gen. Div.); contrast *North Sound Ltd. v. Pic Realty Can. Ltd.* (1988), 80 N.B.R. (2d) 415 (N.B.C.A.), where loss of prospective profits on breach of a lease of premises in a mall was too speculative or remote, where the tenant was not yet in possession (the decision would have been different if the tenant had been in possession and the landlord had broken the lease). Compare the remarks of Deyell J. in *Taylor v. Gill*, [1991] 3 W.W.R. 727 at 739 (Alta. Q.B.).

Subsequently, in *Keneric Tractor Sales Ltd. v. Langille*,[239] the Supreme Court of Canada considered the situation where the lease was of a chattel. It was held, whether the lease was determined by express repudiation by the lessee or was determined by the lessor as a result of breach of a term of the contract by the lessee, the same doctrine applied. General contract principles should be applied in both instances. As a result, a lessor of agricultural equipment who was a dealer and had agreed to buy the equipment from a manufacturer, assigning the lease as security for the price, and guaranteeing the payments due under the lease, was entitled to damages representing the losses he would suffer in respect of obligations that would have arisen subsequently. The lessee knew of the arrangements between the dealer and the manufacturer, therefore the loss suffered by the dealer was not too remote.

Thus, leases, whether of land or of chattels, are treated as contracts for all purposes, including the appropriate principles to invoke when damages for breach of a lease are being claimed by the lessor.[240]

(C) *Intangible loss*[241] The prime purpose of an award of damages in cases of breach of contract is to compensate the plaintiff for the economic or physical harm which he has suffered in consequence. Any discussion of the question of remoteness is concerned with the extent of such compensation from the point of view of differentiating damage which can legitimately be said to have been caused and produced by the breach from that which is so far removed, physically and historically, from the original breach as to be unworthy of being the subject of compensation. As in cases of tort, there may be damage resulting from the defendant's wrongful act in respect of which it would be unjust and unfair to make the defendant liable. Hence, in tort cases a limit is drawn. The exact definition of that limit, as previously noted,[242] may be expressed and delineated differently in tort and contract cases, chiefly because the policies in such instances are not the same. Hence, there is not necessarily the same approach in breach of contract cases as in tort situations to certain kinds of harm, and certain kinds of conduct. As will be seen, this may explain the different attitude in contract cases to the issue of punitive or exemplary damages (in respect of which some change is occurring, in Canada if not in England).[243] It may also explain why, in breach

---

239 (1987), 43 D.L.R. (4th) 171 (S.C.C.); affirming (1985), 19 D.L.R. (4th) 652 (*sub nom. Langille v. Keneric Tractor Sales Ltd.*) (N.S.C.A.).

240 Compare *Merger Restaurants v. D.M.E. Foods Ltd.*, [1991] 4 W.W.R. 394 (Man. Q.B.); reversed in part [1992] 1 W.W.R. 667 (Man. C.A.); leave to appeal to S.C.C. refused [1992] 4 W.W.R. lxix (note) (S.C.C.).

241 Bridge, "Contractual Damages for Intangible Loss: A Comparative Study" (1984), 62 C.B.R. 323; Dawson, "General Damages in Contract for Non-Pecuniary Loss" (1983), 10 N.Z.U.L.R 332; Harris, Ogus & Phillips, "Contracts Remedies and the Consumer Surplus" (1979), 95 L.Q.R. 581 at 595-597; Veitch, "Sentimental Damages in Contract" (1977), 16 U.W.O.L.R. 227; Waddams, *Law of Damages*, 2nd ed. (1991), paras. 3.1310-3.1450.

242 Above, pp. 714-717.

243 Below, pp. 747-751.

of contract cases, there was a different approach to non-pecuniary or non-physical harm.[244]

By this reference is meant to the sort of effects of a breach of contract that are not felt in terms of financial loss to the plaintiff, but otherwise cause him detriment. Such detriment is different in that it cannot easily be remedied by providing a substitute for what has been lost or not provided by reason of the breach of contract. Nor can any payment of money enable the plaintiff, easily or at all, to provide for himself what the defendant has caused him to lose.[245] Yet the breach in question has undoubtedly had some ill effects which have affected the plaintiff's situation. Such consequences cannot be fitted in to the scheme that has been suggested to explain the possible consequences of a breach of contract, in terms of the plaintiff's restitution, reliance, and expectation interests.[246] These cover: (1) the value lost to the plaintiff through the unfulfilment of the contract; (2) the loss suffered through the plaintiff's change of position in reliance on the defendant's promise; and (3) the loss of the expectancy which the defendant's promise created. Loss of profits, diminution in the value of goods delivered, expenses incurred but wasted through the defendant's failure to perform, are illustrations of what may occur when these interests are affected. Examples of such situations have previously been considered.[247] Other consequences of a breach of contract do not readily fall within any of these interests nor, indeed, do they easily come within the scope of the doctrine of *Hadley v. Baxendale.* Nevertheless, in modern times such consequences may not be considered outside the scope of liability for breach of contract.

By intangible loss is meant such consequences as loss of reputation, insult, annoyance, aggravation, nervous shock, inconvenience, mental distress, or other emotional or sentimental suffering. In recent years, in England and Canada, there has been a growing realization that such results of a breach of contract should also be the subject of compensation, as long as the doctrine of *Hadley v. Baxendale* is applicable. There has also been a greater acceptance of the idea that such damages can, and should be awarded in appropriate cases.[248]

Not all such damage is recoverable. For example, it has been held that the failure to pay back money due under a contract could not lead to the payment of damages for the effects of such breach on the plaintiff's credit rating. The

---

244 Bridge, *loc. cit.*, above, note 241, at p. 326, prefers the term "intangible loss" which is "more accurately descriptive . . . of a range of injuries affecting feelings, emotional stability, self-esteem, psychic well-being and related phenomena." He equates this with the civilian, *i.e.*, French, idea of "dommage morale" or "préjudice moral".

245 Harris, Ogus & Phillips, *loc. cit.*, above, note 241, at p. 595.

246 Fuller & Perdue, "The Reliance Interest in Contract Damages" (1936), 46 Yale L.J. 52.

247 Above, pp. 720-729.

248 This paragraph was quoted by Wilson J., dissenting, in *Vorvis v. Ins. Corp. of B.C.* (1989), 58 D.L.R. (4th) 193 at 214 (S.C.C.). Note that in *Ribeiro v. C.I.B.C.* (1992), 13 O.R. (3d) 278, the Ontario Court of Appeal thought that any damages for loss of reputation would have been subsumed in the award for mental distress. Hence, it was unnecessary to decide whether damages for loss of reputation could be awarded in an action for wrongful dismissal.

impecuniosity of the plaintiff, even if known to the defendant, was not relevant.[249] Laskin J.A. wondered whether a decline in a party's credit rating could even be compensable in an action for breach of contract.[250] Under the subjective test, it may be suggested, perhaps it might. Under the objective test, it would probably never be a foreseeable consequence of a breach.[251] Such inconvenience to the plaintiff would appear to be irremediable, save under very special circumstances. In *Dunn v. Disc Jockey Unlimited Co.*[252] a disc jockey failed to provide services at a wedding reception as agreed upon with the plaintiff. Damages were based upon the "inconvenience" caused to the plaintiff (not just the annoyance and distress suffered by the plaintiff). This involved the cost of efforts to locate the missing disc jockey, and persuading a guest to take on the job. In *Phillips v. Alexander*,[253] the defendant failed to provide an adequate water supply, in breach of his warranty that his work, when completed, would achieve that result. The plaintiff was awarded not only the cost of digging a well to obtain the necessary supply, he was also awarded a large sum of money to compensate him for the inconvenience he had suffered.

In reliance upon the decision of the House of Lords in *Addis v. The Gramophone Co.*,[254] where it was said that punitive or exemplary damages could not be awarded in cases of breach of contract, it was held by Dupont J. in *McMinn v. Oakville*[255] that in an action for wrongful dismissal, the plaintiff could not recover damages for loss of reputation, nor for the injured feelings he had incurred in consequence of the dismissal. The reason assigned for this was that reputation was not a factor in a contract, except, possibly, where the person claiming for dismissal was an artist (such people being very dependent upon reputation and the opportunity to obtain public performances).[256] In *Cleary v. Cabletronics Inc.*,[257] Montgomery J., on a motion to strike out part of a statement of claim, which included a claim

249 *Andre Knight Ltd. v. Presement* (1967), 63 D.L.R. (2d) 314 (Ont. C.A.); compare as to the effect of the plaintiff's impecuniosity, *Freedhoff v. Pomalift Industs. Ltd.* (1971), 19 D.L.R. (3d) 153 (Ont. C.A.), on which see Baer, 57 Can. Bar Rev. 490 at pp. 500-504. With respect to the relevance of the plaintiff's impecuniosity in tort cases compare *Liesbosch v. S.S. Edison*, [1933] A.C. 449 (H.L.) with *Dodd Properties Ltd. v. Canterbury City Council*, [1980] 1 W.L.R. 433 (C.A.). But damages for customers' loss of confidence in the plaintiff's ability to fulfil its contracts with such customers (loss of reputation?) were awarded in *Knowlan Corp. v. Ria-Mar Fisheries Ltd.* (1986), 72 N.S.R. (2d) 407 (N.S.T.D.).

250 (1967), 63 D.L.R. (2d) 314 at 317 (Ont. C.A.); compare *Trans. Trust S.P.R.L. v. Danubian Trading Co.*, [1952] 1 All E.R. 970 at 977 (C.A.).

251 Compare on a slightly different point, *Gen. Securities Ltd. v. Don Ingram Ltd.*, [1940] S.C.R. 670 (S.C.C.); *Smith v. Commonwealth Trust Co.* (1969), 10 D.L.R. (3d) 181 (B.C.S.C.).

252 (1978), 87 D.L.R. (3d) 408 (Ont. Small Claims Ct.).

253 (1981), 34 N.B.R. (2d) 622 (N.B.Q.B.).

254 [1909] A.C. 488 (H.L.); below, pp. 747-751.

255 (1978), 19 O.R. (2d) 366 (Ont. H.C.). Compare *Wyman & Moscrop Realty Ltd. v. Vancouver Real Estate Bd.* (1959), 27 W.W.R. 476 (B.C.C.A.). Compare also *Knowlan Corp. v. Ria-Mar Fisheries Ltd.*, above, note 249.

256 Compare Grosman & Marcus, "New Developments in Wrongful Dismissal Litigation" (1982), 60 Can. Bar Rev. 656 at 671; see *Withers v. Gen. Theatre Corp.*, [1933] 2 K.B. 536 (C.A.).

257 (1982), 39 O.R. (2d) 456 (Ont. H.C.); and see *Johnston v. Muskoka Lakes Golf & Country Club Ltd.* (1983), 40 O.R. (2d) 762 (Ont. H.C.).

for damages for loss of reputation, dismissed the motion. He held that recent developments in the law relating to damages,[258] had eroded the principle that damages could not be awarded for loss of reputation.[259] Consequently, he allowed the issue to go to trial. However, an attempt by a plaintiff, in a case of wrongful dismissal, to allege that she had suffered an insult because of the dismissal and this insult was compensable, was unsuccessful in *Dobson v. T. Eaton Co.*[260] The law may have developed along the lines of extending the scope of liability for breach of contract beyond the physical or economic consequences to a plaintiff: it has not yet proceeded so far as to permit injured feeling caused by a verbal insult to be brought within the scope of the doctrine of *Hadley v. Baxendale.*

However, there may be situations in which some forms of mental distress can be brought within the doctrine. A series of cases in England and Canada has recognized that, in appropriate circumstances, an allegation of mental upset, annoyance, grief, suffering or disturbance can be counted as damages flowing from a breach of contract, not too remote, and therefore compensable by an award of damages over and above any financial or other normally compensable loss incurred by the plaintiff. Succinctly put, it may be stated that what began as an exceptional allowance of damages for mental illness, or something similar, resulting from a breach of contract has now grown in scope and application, until the emergent doctrine may have undermined the principle in *Addis v. Gramophone Co.* with respect to the types of damages that can and cannot be granted in cases of breach of contract.[261]

The earliest decisions concerned claims against travel agents who had broken contracts with their clients by sending them on holidays that turned out to be different from the promises made at the time the client bought the "package". As a consequence of this difference the client suffered inconvenience, distress, disappointment, aggravation, and the loss of the benefits that would have been expected from a successful holiday.[262] Since those first instances of liability for

---

258 Below, pp. 747-751.
259 See, *e.g.*, *Knowlan Corp. v. Ria-Mar Fisheries Ltd.*, above, note 249. Contrast *Ribeiro v. C.I.B.C.* (1989), 67 O.R. (2d) 385 at 433-439 (Ont. H.C.) *per* Carruthers J.; varied (1992), 13 O.R. (3d) 278 (Ont. C.A.); leave to appeal to S.C.C. refused (1993), 65 O.A.C. 79 (note) (S.C.C.); *Thomas v. Chaleur Auto Sales Ltd.* (1989), 101 N.B.R. (2d) 383 (N.B.C.A.), where it is said that damages for loss of reputation can only be claimed in a defamation action.
260 (1983), 141 D.L.R. (3d) 362 (Alta. Q.B.).
261 This paragraph was quoted by Deyell J. in *Taylor v. Gill*, [1991] 3 W.W.R. 727 at 744-745 (Alta. Q.B.). For a discussion of recent developments in England, Canada, Australia and New Zealand, see Mullany & Handford, *Tort Liability for Psychiatric Damage* (1993), at pp. 51-56.
262 *Jarvis v. Swans Tours Ltd.*, [1973] 1 Q.B. 233 (C.A.); *Jackson v. Horizon Holidays Ltd.*, [1975] 3 All E.R. 92 (C.A.) (which extended the liability to the loss suffered by members of the plaintiff's family, a view which was strongly criticized and held inaccurate by the House of Lords in *Woodar Invt. Ltd. v. Wimpey Const. (U.K.) Ltd.*, [1980] 1 All E.R. 571 (H.L.)); *Elder v. Koppe* (1974), 53 D.L.R. (3d) 705 (N.S.S.C.); *Keks v. Esquire Pleasure Tours Ltd.*, [1974] 3 W.W.R. 406 (Man. Co. Ct.); *Fuller v. Healey Tpt. Ltd.* (1978), 92 D.L.R. (3d) 277 (Ont. Co. Ct.); *Pitzel v. Sask. Motor Club Travel Agency Ltd.* (1983), 149 D.L.R. (3d) 122 (Sask. Q.B.); *Cameron v. Maritime Travel (Halifax) Ltd.* (1983), 58 N.S.R. (2d) 379 (N.S.T.D.). For an earlier case in which the plaintiff

such consequences, the courts have gradually extended the scope of such claims. Thus, it has been held that a solicitor could be liable in breach of contract for the distress caused his client through the solicitor's failure to obtain a remedy which would have protected the client from molestation.[263] In *Tippett v. I.T.U. Local 226*,[264] the plaintiff was wrongfully expelled from his trade union for "ratting". His claim included items for loss of reputation and mental distress. The plaintiff lived in a community largely composed of union members. In consequence of the expulsion, he was treated as an outcast by the people among whom he lived. Because of this, he could successfully claim for both loss of reputation and the mental distress emanating from the expulsion. In *Newell v. Canadian Pacific Airlines Ltd.*,[265] the plaintiff's dogs were transported by air in the cargo compartment of the defendants' airplane. One dog died and the other was seriously injured as a result of the faulty, negligent way the dogs were carried. For this breach of contract the plaintiff claimed, *inter alia*, damages for the upset she suffered because of what had happened, and for the loss of enjoyment of life and the sadness she underwent by reason of the death of the dog. Her claim was successful. Damages for mental distress have also been awarded on the breach of a contract to sell a house,[266] or car;[267] and on breach of a contract to buy a house;[268] where a wedding photographer failed to supply satisfactory photographs.[269]

Not all such claims have proved successful. The plaintiff failed to obtain damages for mental distress in *McNeil v. Forest Lawn Memorial Services Ltd.*[270] There a funeral home cremated the body of the plaintiff's daughter without giving the parents an opportunity to view the deceased prior to the ceremony, in breach of the agreement between the plaintiffs and the funeral home. Damages for distress were not recoverable. In *Turner v. Jatko*,[271] damages for such distress were not awarded, although damages for the physical damage to the plaintiff's property were granted, when the defendant caused damage to the plaintiff's house which had been leased to the defendant while the plaintiff went on sabbatical leave. Nor were such damages allowed for upset caused by an architect who grossly underestimated renovation costs;[272] nor where a university student was not given

recovered damages for nervous shock resulting from breach of contract, when the plaintiff found glass in bread, see *Negro v. Pietro's Bread Co.*, [1933] 1 D.L.R. 490 (Ont. C.A.).

263 *Heywood v. Wellers*, [1976] 1 All E.R. 300 (C.A.), with which contrast *Cook v. Swinfen*, [1967] 1 All E.R. 299 (C.A.); *Kolan v. Solicitor* (1970), 7 D.L.R. (3d) 481 (Ont. H.C.); affirmed (1970), 11 D.L.R. (3d) 672 (Ont. C.A.).
264 (1976), 71 D.L.R. (3d) 146 (B.C.S.C.).
265 (1976), 74 D.L.R. (3d) 574 (Ont. Co. Ct.).
266 *Widdrington v. Dickinson* (1982), 133 D.L.R. (3d) 472 (Ont. H.C.).
267 *Zuker v. Paul* (1982), 135 D.L.R. (3d) 481 (Ont. H.C.).
268 *Taylor v. Gill*, [1991] 3 W.W.R. 727 (Alta. Q.B.); *Smith v. Fearon* (1988), 87 N.S.R. (2d) 119 (N.S.T.D.) (where the failure by the buyer to close was deliberate or reckless, not the result of something beyond his control); compare *Marko v. Perry* (1980), 18 B.C.L.R. 263 (B.C. Co. Ct.) (foreclosure of mortgage).
269 *Wilson v. Sooter Studios Ltd.* (1988), 55 D.L.R. (4th) 303 (B.C.C.A.).
270 (1976), 72 D.L.R. (3d) 556 (B.C.S.C.).
271 (1978), 93 D.L.R. (3d) 314 (B.C. Co. Ct.).
272 *Nfld. Capital Corp. v. Mettam* (1986), 76 N.S.R. (2d) 189 (N.S.T.D.).

a supplementary examination, which was a breach of contract;[273] nor where an insurance company wrongly, but not recklessly refused to pay a life insurance policy;[274] nor where a contract to repair a house was breached, on the ground that there was a commercial contract.[275]

However, the most important type of contract to which the emergent idea of damages for mental distress or its equivalent has been applied, though not on all occasions, is the contract of employment.[276] In actions for wrongful dismissal, plaintiffs have attempted to assert not only economic loss, in the form of lost salary or wages for the period of notice to which they would have been entitled but of which they wree deprived by reason of the summary, and allegedly wrongful, dismissal, but also damages for the anguish, aggravation, emotional shock or disturbance, or other psychic effects of the dismissal. The problem with permitting recovery of such damages in these actions, as with some of the others to which reference has been made, is that normally, in a commercial contract, the only damages which may be awarded by way of compensation are those which relate to the physical or economic loss incurred by the plaintiff.[277] Damages may not be awarded to punish the defendant for his behaviour, however improper or

---

273 *McBeth v. Governors of Dalhousie College & Univ.* (1986), 26 D.L.R. (4th) 321 (N.S.C.A.).
274 *Blouin v. Maritime Life Assur. Co.* (1988), 88 N.S.R. (2d) 23 (N.S.T.D.).
275 *Olson v. New Home Certification Program of Alta.* (1986), 44 Alta. L.R. (2d) 207 (Alta. Q.B.); compare *Can. Trust Mortgage Co. v. 562498 Ont. Ltd.* (1987), 62 O.R. (2d) 741 (Ont. H.C.); affirmed (1990), 72 O.R. (2d) 798 (Ont. C.A.); *Taylor v. Gill*, above, note 268, at 745-747 *per* Deyell J.; compare below, p. 741. See also *Hayes v. James v. Charles Dodd*, [1990] 2 All E.R. 815 (C.A.).
276 Contrast *Pilon v. Peugeot Can. Ltd.* (1980), 114 D.L.R. (3d) 378 (Ont. H.C.); *Luchuck v. Sport B.C.* (1984), 3 C.C.E.L. 117 (B.C.S.C.); supplementary reasons at (1984), 53 B.C.L.R. 143 (B.C.S.C.); *Bohemier v. Storwal Int. Inc.* (1982), 40 O.R. (2d) 264 (Ont. H.C.); reversed on other grounds (1983), 44 O.R. (2d) 361 (Ont. C.A.); leave to appeal to the S.C.C. refused (1984), 3 C.C.E.L. 79 (S.C.C.); *Brown v. Waterloo Regional Bd. of Police Commrs.* (1982), 37 O.R. 277 (Ont. H.C.); reversed on the ground that there was no breach of contract (1983), 150 D.L.R. (3d) 729 (Ont. C.A.); *Pilato v. Hamilton Place Convention Centre Inc.* (1984), 7 D.L.R. (4th) 342 (Ont. H.C.); *Speck v. Greater Niagara General Hospital* (1983), 2 D.L.R. (4th) 84 (Ont. H.C.); *McOnie v. River Pub Ltd.* (1987), 79 N.S.R. (2d) 379 (N.S.T.D.); with *Dobson v. T. Eaton Co.* (1983), 141 D.L.R. (3d) 362 (Alta. Q.B.); *Vorvis v. Ins. Corp. of B.C.* (1982), 134 D.L.R. (3d) 727 (B.C.S.C.); reversed in part (1984), 9 D.L.R. (4th) 40 (B.C. C.A.); affirmed (1989), 58 D.L.R. (4th) 193 (S.C.C.); *Cringle v. Nor. Union Ins. Co.* (1981), 124 D.L.R. (3d) 22 (B.C.S.C.), where shock alone without actual damage was not enough to justify an award. *Lobrutto v. Univ. of St. Jerome's College* (1989), 44 C.P.C. (2d) 104 (Ont. H.C.), claim for mental distress (and punitive damages) struck out. In *Fulton v. Fort Erie* (1982), 40 O.R. (2d) 235 (Ont. H.C.) Krever J. would not allow jury trial of an action for wrongful dismissal where damages for mental distress were claimed, on the ground that the issue was unsettled and therefore was not one appropriate for a jury; compare on the refusal to strike out of pleadings a claim for such damages: *Delmotte v. John Labatt Ltd.* (1978), 92 D.L.R. (3d) 259 (Ont. H.C.); *Cleary v. Cabletronics Inc.* (1982), 39 O.R. (2d) 456 (Ont. H.C.). Reference to this sentence is made by Wilson J., dissenting, in *Vorvis v. Ins. Corp. of B.C.*, *ibid.* (S.C.C.), at 214.
277 This and the next three sentences were quoted by Jones J.A. in *Sunshine Enterprises Ltd. v. Spence* (1988), 87 N.S.R. (2d) 253 at 263 (N.S.C.A.).

outrageous.[278] Nor are damages to be awarded for injured feelings.[279] Nor are damages to compensate the plaintiff for the difficulties he may have experienced by the breach with respect to obtaining some substitute for what he has lost. In particular, where the cause of action is wrongful dismissal, it has been stated more than once that a plaintiff cannot recover anything for loss he may sustain from the fact that his having been dismissed of itself makes it more difficult for him to obtain fresh employment.[280] How, then, have courts been able to escape from the shackles which bound them and would appear to prevent them from giving anything to an aggrieved plaintiff but an amount to compensate him for the economic loss he has sustained?

The answer to this question is to be found in the underlying nature of the doctrine of *Hadley v. Baxendale*.[281] Damages which are foreseeable, or are within the contemplation of a reasonable man in the position of the defendant, will not be too remote but will be recoverable. Hence, if the possibility of mental distress of the kind suffered by a plaintiff, such as vexation, frustration, anguish, aggravation, disturbance, is within the contemplation of the defendant, it will not be out of the ordinary. Nor will it mean that to compensate for such damage would be to punish the defendant rather than to compensate the plaintiff for loss he has incurred. What this entails is that the contract in issue must necessarily involve the possibility of such consequences to the plaintiff should it not be fulfilled in accordance with its terms. In normal commercial contracts, the likelihood of a breach of contract causing mental distress is not to be treated as within the contemplation of the reasonable man. There must be something about the contract which takes it out of the normal run of commercial transactions,[282] such as the particular social background to the trade union membership in the *Tippett* case,[283] or the expectation of enjoyment, relaxation and pleasure that is normally associated with a holiday,

---

278 *Addis v. Gramophone Co.*, [1909] A.C. 488 (H.L.); *Dignan v. Viceroy Const. Co.* (1979), 1 A.C.W.S. (2d) 42 (Ont. H.C.); *Harvey Foods Ltd. v. Reid* (1971), 18 D.L.R. (2d) 90 at 93-96 (N.B.C.A.). But see *Vorvis v. Ins. Corp. of B.C.* (1989), 58 D.L.R. (4th) 193 (S.C.C.): below, p. 748.

279 *Peso Silver Mines Ltd. v. Cropper* (1966), 58 D.L.R. (2d) 1 at 10 (S.C.C.) *per* Cartwright J. Compare, especially as regards reputation, *Abouna v. Foothills Prov. Gen. Hospital Bd. (No. 2)* (1977), 83 D.L.R. (3d) 333 at 344-345 (Alta. C.A.); *McMinn v. Oakville (Town)* (1978), 85 D.L.R. (3d) 131 (Ont. H.C.). Contrast *Perkins v. Brandon Univ.*, [1985] 5 W.W.R. 740 (Man. C.A.).

280 *Peso Silver Mines Ltd., ibid.*, at 10; *Abouna v. Foothills Prov. Gen. Hosp. Bd. (No. 2), ibid.*, at 344 *per* McGillivray C.J. But in an English case, *Cox v. Phillips Indust. Ltd.*, [1976] 1 W.L.R. 638, damages for mental distress were awarded when an employee was denied a promotion in breach of his contract of employment. But this was not a wrongful dimissal case. If it had been no damages for shock would have been recoverable: *ibid.*, at 643; compare *Dobson v. T. Eaton Co.* (1983), 141 D.L.R. (3d) 362 at 363 (Alta. Q.B.) *per* Cavanagh J. See, however, *Knowlan Corp. v. Ria-Mar Fisheries Ltd.* (1986), 72 N.S.R. (2d) 407 (N.S.T.D.).

281 Compare Wilson J., dissenting in *Vorvis v. Ins. Corp. of B.C.*, above, note 276, at 218-220 (S.C.C.).

282 See *Vorvis v. Ins. Corp. of B.C.*, above, note 276; compare *Olson v. New Home Certification Program of Alta.*, above, note 275; *Taylor v. Gill*, above, note 268, at 745-747 *per* Dyell J.

283 (1976), 71 D.L.R. (3d) 146 (B.C.S.C.), distinguishing on this basis both *Addis v. Gramophone Co.*, [1909] A.C. 488 (H.L.) and *Wyman & Moscrop Realty Ltd. v. Vancouver Real Estate Bd.* (1959), 27 W.W.R. 476 (B.C.C.A.).

as was the situation in the "travel-agent" cases.[284] However, it must also be recalled that, under the subjective test in *Hadley v. Baxendale*, an individual defendant may have special facts in his knowledge, bringing in their train the possibility of special consequences should the contract be broken. Where this occurs, there may be liability for damage flowing from such breach even if the damage in question would not ordinarily be contemplated as the kind of damage that might result from breach. Applying this to the mental distress problem, there are indications in the decisions that where a defendant knows of circumstances from which a reasonable man would then be able to contemplate the likelihood of mental distress in the event of a breach of the contract, such a consequence will not be too remote: nor will an award of damages in respect of such consequence be regarded as punitive, rather than compensatory. Thus, in the *Newell* case,[285] the airline knew of the attachment of the plaintiff to her dogs, and her desire for careful, special treatment of them while in transit. Therefore, the possibility that she might be emotionally, and sentimentally affected by any harm to the dogs was within their contemplation when the contract was made. On the other hand, there were no special circumstances known to the defendants in the *McNeil*[286] or *Turner*[287] cases from which such an inference could be drawn.

In wrongful dismissal cases, too, there would have to be some special circumstances taking the particular relationship outside the normal, commercial (or industrial) kind of master and servant contract.[288] This was the case, for example, in *Pilon v. Peugeot Canada Ltd.*,[289] where the employee was told, and believed, that he would have lifetime security, only to be discharged without cause and without notice of the proper kind. So, in *Bohemier v. Storwal International Inc.*,[290] Saunders J., at first instance, in a judgment that was commended by the Ontario Court of Appeal for being correct in its legal analysis,[291] considered that the validity of awarding damages for mental distress on the basis of *Hadley v. Baxendale* was the failure to give adequate notice, not the mere dismissal. It was reasonably foreseeable that if an employer chose to exercise his right to dismiss such action would cause mental distress, anxiety, vexation, frustration, worry and disappointment to the employee. Dismissal with reasonable notice, however, was not a breach

---

284 Above, note 262. Or the kind of situations that existed in the "wedding photograph" case, *Wilson v. Sooter Studios Ltd.*, above, note 269, or those in *Taylor v. Gill*, above, note 268.

285 (1976), 74 D.L.R. (3d) 574 (Ont. H.C.). Does this go a litte too far? But see *Taylor v. Gill*, above, note 268; *Smith v. Fearon*, above, note 268. Contrast *Olson v. New Home Certification Program of Alta.*, above, note 275.

286 (1976), 72 D.L.R. (3d) 556 (B.C.S.C.).

287 (1978), 93 D.L.R. (3d) 314 (B.C. Co. Ct.).

288 Or some special and foreseeable consequences such as the employee's depressive illness: *McOnie v. River Pub Ltd.*, above, note 276; compare *Ribeiro v. C.I.B.C.* (1989), 67 O.R. (2d) 385 (Ont. H.C.); varied (1992), 13 O.R. (3d) 278 (Ont. C.A.), where the plaintiff's damages for mental distress were increased. In this case no decision was made about damages for loss of reputation: above, note 248.

289 (1980), 114 D.L.R. (3d) 378 (Ont. H.C.). Contrast *British Guiana Credit Corp. v. Da Silva*, [1965] 1 W.L.R. 248 (P.C.).

290 (1982), 40 O.R. (2d) 264 at 271-272 (Ont. H.C.).

291 (1983), 44 O.R. (2d) 361 at 362 (Ont. C.A.).

of contract. Dismissal without such notice, in the absence of just cause or excuse, was such a breach. Therefore, it was reasonably foreseeable that dismissal without adequate notice would produce the kinds of consequences set out by the learned judge.[292] In the *Bohemier* case, the employee recognized that he could be dismissed, but did not expect it to happen. Perhaps it may be suggested that Saunders J. was really applying the subjective test in *Hadley v. Baxendale*, in that he founded the employee's claim to damages for mental distress upon the belief by the employee, of which the employer was, or must have been aware, that the employee would not be dismissed. In *Brown v. Waterloo Regional Board of Police Commissioners*,[293] the Ontario Court of Appeal appears to have approved the language of Saunders J. when it was said that, for damages to flow from the wrong of failing to give reasonable notice

> it must have been in the contemplation of both parties, at the time of hiring, that mental distress would be the probable result of a failure to give proper notice, and the mental distress suffered by the discharged employee must flow from the want of reasonable notice and not from the fact of dismissal.

However in the subsequent case of *Pilato v. Hamilton Place Convention Centre Incorporated*,[294] although Fitzpatrick J. relied on, and cited the *Brown* decision, the learned judge appears to have based an award of damages for mental distress not only upon the failure to give proper notice but also on the "severe and unfair manner" in which the employee was dismissed.[295] Is the true test of when such damages may be recovered the lack of proper notice when the employee and employer both contemplated that there would be no dismissal and that dismissal would result in such damage, or the way in which the employee was dismissed? The cases seem to be uncertain as to the proper method of applying the *Hadley v. Baxendale* doctrine in such instances. It can be said, however, that the mere fact that such distress is the result of a wrongful dismissal will not of itself produce liability to compensate for such consequence. There must be something more, some factor which reveals that the likelihood of such damage was within the reasonable contemplation of the parties, either as a consequence of dismissal in the circumstances, or as a consequence of the way in which the dismissal was effectuated. The problem with the latter approach, it may be suggested, is that, if emphasis is placed on the improper or unseemly manner in which the employee is discharged, to award damages for the mental distress that ensues comes very close to making an award of damages to punish the employer rather than to compensate the employee in respect of damage he sustains in consequence of the wrong done to him through the breach of contract. Unless it can also be concluded from the cases that the attitude of the law towards punitive damages in contract cases is changing,[296] there may be raised by these decisions on wrongful dismissal and

---

292 Above, note 290, at 272. Contrast *Cringle v. Nor. Union Ins. Co.* (1981), 124 D.L.R. (3d) 22 (B.C.S.C.).
293 (1983), 150 D.L.R. (3d) 729 at 735 (Ont. C.A.).
294 (1984), 7 D.L.R. (4th) 342 (Ont. H.C.).
295 *Ibid.*, at 354; compare *Speck v. Greater Niagara Gen. Hosp.* (1983), 2 D.L.R. (4th) 84 (Ont. H.C.).
296 Below, pp. 747-751.

mental distress the prospect of punitive or exemplary damages being granted under the guise of compensatory damages. In this respect it should be said that in the *Bohemier* case[297] Saunders J. considered the argument that damages for mental distress could be awarded not as compensatory nor as punitive damages but as aggravated damages. Such was the suggestion of Linden J., at first instance in the *Brown* case.[298] However, Linden J. did not have to award damages for mental distress in that case on that basis, and in the Court of Appeal the plaintiff's claim was dismissed on other grounds, even though the possibility of such damages, on the basis of compensation, not aggravation, was conceded.

As Saunders J. said in the *Bohemier* case,[299] there is "some difficulty in considering mental suffering as a head of damages for breach of contract". To the extent to which English and Canadian courts have allowed such claims, they have done so by the application of the rules laid down in *Hadley v. Baxendale*.[300] Sometimes this has not been achieved without great difficulty. The likelihood of such damage resulting from a breach of contract is much less than in cases where the defendant's act has involved a tort causing, or likely to cause physical harm, whether to the plaintiff or to some other person, in consequence of which the plaintiff has suffered the mental distress in issue. That is because it is now recognized that such damage may flow from certain torts.[301] The prospect that mental distress will flow from a breach of contract is not as obvious, especially where the contract does not give rise to some special personal relationship, perhaps involving trust and confidence on both sides, such as is the case with the contract of employment between master and servant.[302] That claims of this kind have been entertained and allowed by the courts is a significant step in the evolution of the law of contract, as well as the law of damages. The tests of remoteness laid down in *Hadley v. Baxendale* have been pressed into service in an extraordinary and perhaps uniquely modern way.

---

297   Above, note 290, at 272-273.

298   (1982), 37 O.R. (2d) 277 at 288-289 (Ont. H.C.); reversed in part (1983), 150 D.L.R. (3d) 729 (Ont. C.A.). Compare *Thompson v. Zurich Ins. Co.* (1984), 7 D.L.R. (4th) 664 at 678-680 (Ont. H.C.). See also the comments of McIntyre J. in *Vorvis v. Ins. Corp. of B.C* (1989), 58 D.L.R. (4th) 193 at 205; compare *Lobrutto v. Univ. of St. Jerome's College* (1989), 44 C.P.C. (2d) 104 (Ont. H.C.); *Ribeiro v. C.I.B.C.*, above, note 288, at 427-433 *per* Carruthers J.

299   Above, note 290, at 273.

300   Compare *Brown v. Waterloo Regional Bd. of Police Commrs.* (1983), 150 D.L.R. (3d) 729 at 734 (Ont. C.A.), citing *Heywood v. Wellers*, [1976] 1 All E.R. 300 at 310 (C.A.) *per* Bridge L.J. See also Wilson J., dissenting in *Vorvis v. Ins. Corp. of B.C.*, above, note 298, at 215-216.

301   See *McLaughlin v. O'Brian*, [1982] 2 All E.R. 298 (H.L.) for a full discussion of nervous shock or mental distress in tort cases. See also *Attia v. British Gas plc*, [1988] Q.B. 304; *Alcock v. Chief Constable of South Yorkshire Police*, [1992] 1 A.C. 310 (H.L.); *Hicks v. Chief Constable of South Yorkshire Police*, [1992] 2 All E.R. 65 (H.L.); *Mullany & Handford, Tort Liability for Psychiatric Damage* (1993).

302   Reference to this comment is made by Wilson J., dissenting, in *Vorvis v. Ins. Corp. of B.C.*, above, note 298, at 214.

3. Quantification of damages

(a) Purpose of damages

The leading and well-accepted principle is that the plaintiff must be put in as good a position as he would have been had the contract been performed.[303] In the words of Lord Atkinson in *Wertheim v. Chicoutimi Pulp Co.*[304] referred to with approval by Hodgins J.A., for example, in *Cockburn v. Trusts & Guarantee Co.*,[305]

> [a]nd it is the general intention of the law that, in giving damages for breach of contract, the party complaining should, so far as it can be done by money, be placed in the same position as he would have been in if the contract had been performed ... That is a ruling principle. It is a just principle.

The tenor of this language indicates that in some instances the proper award may be not substantial damages but merely nominal ones, recognizing the fact that a breach of contract has occurred, therefore an action will lie, even though no actual loss has been suffered by the plaintiff. Furthermore, in general, damages are intended to be compensatory or restorative, not punitive or exemplary. However, it is also clear that in certain instances the proper assessment of the plaintiff's loss is what he has paid over to the defendant or what he has expended in reliance on the defendant's contractual promise.[306]

(b) Nominal and substantial damages

Thus, if a plaintiff in fact makes a profit out of the defendant's breach by being free to do things which he would otherwise not have been allowed to do, thereby obtaining some financial advantage, that plaintiff will be given only nominal

---

303 This is cited by Nathanson J. in *Mettam Wright Associates Ltd. (Trustee of) v. U.S. Fire Ins. Co.* (1990), 9 R.P.R. (2d) 131 at 141 (N.S.T.D.); affirmed (1991), 102 N.S.R. (2d) 24 (N.S.C.A.); leave to appeal to S.C.C. refused (1991), 106 N.S.R. (2d) 360 (note) (S.C.C.).

    Damages are intended to compensate the plaintiff, not transfer gains made by the defendant out of his breach: *Surrey C.C. v. Bredero Homes Ltd.*, [1993] 3 All E.R. 705 (C.A.); below, pp. 764-765.

304 [1911] A.C. 301 at 307 (P.C.).

305 (1916), 38 O.L.R. 396 at 401 (Ont. C.A.); affirmed (1917), 55 S.C.R. 264 (S.C.C.); see Anglin J. at 268-269. But this does not mean that *interest* on damages could be awarded at common law (unless there was an express or implied agreement between the parties to such effect): see *Eaton v. R.*, [1972] F.C. 185 (Fed. T.D.); affirmed [1972] F.C. 1257 (Fed. C.A.), and the cases therein cited. In a given jurisdiction, however, there may be a statutory provision which gives a court power to award interest at its discretion. *E.g.*, in Ontario this may be done under the Courts of Justice Act, R.S.O. 1990, c. C.43, s. 130; see *Savioli & Morgan Co. v. Vroom Const. Ltd.* (1975), 10 O.R. (2d) 381 (Ont. H.C.); in Saskatchewan under the Queen's Bench Act, R.S.S. 1978, c. Q-1; see *Harrand v. Sask. Govt. Ins. Office* (1978), 88 D.L.R. (3d) 388 (Sask. Q.B.); affirmed [1979] 4 W.W.R. 478 (Sask. C.A.). For the power to award the interest on a debt, see *Prince Albert Pulp. Co. v. Foundation Co. of Can. Ltd.*, [1976] 4 W.W.R. 586 (S.C.C.); *President of India v. Pintada Compania Navigacion SA*, [1985] A.C. 104 (H.L.); *Janred Properties Ltd. v. ENIT*, [1989] 2 All E.R. 444 (C.A.).

306 *I.e.*, recovery of the plaintiff's *restitution* or *reliance* interest: above, pp. 726-729.

damages.[307] So, too, if the plaintiff has lost nothing, or something quite trivial as a result of the defendant's breach, again only nominal damages may be recovered.[308] Indeed, if the plaintiff could have incurred a loss had the contract been completed, he might not be able to recover his expenses, in accordance with the "reliance" doctrine.[309] As suggested in *Prince Rupert Sawmills Ltd. v. M.C. Logging Ltd.*,[310] where there is a breach of a contract to lend or borrow money, the loss to the plaintiff may be nominal, that is, the cost of obtaining an alternative loan, or may be substantial, for example, as where the failure to provide financing caused loss to the assets of the plaintiff's business.[311]

In several cases concerned with options, the Supreme Court of Canada was at pains to point out that, in such instances, the loss to the injured party, whether the grantor or grantee of the option, may be more than nominal. The damages recoverable are not confined to the cost of performance but extend to the value of performance to the injured party.[312] While at first sight, therefore, the injured party may appear to have lost very little by the non-performance of the option contract, there may indeed be a substantial loss to him in consequence. If there is, then it is recoverable in accordance with the normal *Hadley v. Baxendale* principle.[313]

---

307 *Cockburn v. Trusts & Guarantee Co.*, above, note 305; *Valpy v. Oakeley* (1851), 117 E.R. 1142; compare *Messineo v. Beale* (1976), 71 D.L.R. (3d) 31 (Ont. H.C.); affirmed (1978), 86 D.L.R. (3d) 713 (Ont. C.A.).

308 Compare *Corkish v. Dixon* (1957), 21 W.W.R. 618 (B.C.S.C.); *State Vacuum Stores of Can. Ltd. v. Phillips*, [1954] 3 D.L.R. 621 (B.C.C.A.); *Gouzenko v. Harris* (1976), 72 D.L.R. (3d) 293 (Ont. H.C.) (where the plaintiff recovered his expenses, not the loss he alleged, because he could not prove that he had a good cause of action in libel which had been destroyed by the defendant solicitor's negligence); see *Tai Hing Cotton Mill Ltd. v. Kamsing Knitting Factory*, [1978] 1 All E.R. 515 (P.C.), on the plaintiff's obligation to prove what he has lost. So, too, if the plaintiff has helped to bring about his loss by his *own* failure to act: *Caines v. Bank of N.S.* (1978), 90 D.L.R. (3d) 271 (N.B.C.A.). But such damages were refused in *Mid-Western News Agency Ltd. v. Vanpinxteren*, [1976] 1 W.W.R. 299 (Sask. Q.B.), a case of alleged breach of a fiduciary duty by an employee.

309 *Bowlay Logging Ltd. v. Domtar Ltd.* (1982), 135 D.L.R. (3d) 179 (B.C.C.A.); compare *C. & P. Haulage v. Middleton*, [1983] 3 All E.R. 94 (C.A.); *C.C.C. Films (London) Ltd. v. Impact Quandrant Films Ltd.*, [1984] 3 All E.R. 298; above, pp. 726-727.

310 (1967), 65 D.L.R. (2d) 300 (B.C.C.A.). See also *Sommerfeldt v. Petrovich*, [1949] 2 W.W.R. 815 at 821 (Sask. C.A.) *per* Martin C.J.S.

311 *Gen. Securities Ltd. v. Don Ingram Ltd.*, [1940] S.C.R. 670 (S.C.C.); compare *South African Territories Ltd. v. Wallington*, [1898] A.C. 309 (H.L.); *Reid v. Garnet B. Hallowell Ltd.* (1978), 10 R.P.R. 308 (Ont. Master); *Accord Holdings Ltd. v. Excelsior Life Ins. Co.* (1982), 44 A.R. 368 (Alta. Q.B.); reversed in part (1985), 62 A.R. 234 (Alta. C.A.); *Wadsworth v. Lydall*, [1981] 2 All E.R. 401 (C.A.).

312 Compare *Cotter v. Gen. Petroleums Ltd.*, [1951] S.C.R. 154 (S.C.C.); *Cunningham v. Insinger*, [1924] S.C.R. 8 (S.C.C.); *Kinkel v. Hyman*, [1939] S.C.R. 364 (S.C.C.); *Sunshine Explorations v. Dolly Varden Mines Ltd.*, [1970] S.C.R. 2 (S.C.C.). See also *Erie County Natural Gas Co. v. Carroll*, [1911] A.C. 105 (P.C.).

313 See, however, Cartwright J. in *Cotter v. Gen. Petroleums Ltd.*, *ibid.*, at 174-175. For cases in which the breach of an option agreement led to damages representing the market value of the shares to be purchased, at the date they ought to have been delivered in pursuance of the option agreement, but were not, see *William v. Keyes*, [1971] 5 W.W.R. 561 (B.C.S.C.); *McNeil v. Fultz* (1906), 38 S.C.R. 198 (S.C.C.); *W.C. Pitfield & Co. v. Jomac Gold Syndicate Ltd.*, [1938] O.R. 427 (Ont. C.A.).

(c) Exemplary damages[314]

In *Addis v. Gramophone Co.*,[315] the House of Lords laid down that in actions for breach of contract exemplary or punitive damages could not be awarded. The plaintiff was given the six months' notice which his employment required, but he was summarily replaced in breach of the service contract between the parties. In those circumstances, the House of Lords allowed the dismissed employee to recover the salary and commission that he would have earned in the relevant period, but would not award damages for wounded feelings or loss of reputation — which would have been in the nature of a penalty upon the employer in respect of the high-handed way in which the plaintiff was treated. This is consistent with the principle stated in the *Wertheim* case,[316] which was subsequently decided, although it goes back to the dictum of Baron Parke in *Robinson v. Harman*.[317] It is also consistent with the view that damages for breach of contract are given in respect of loss arising from legal obligations created by mutual agreement between the parties, not with expectations, however reasonable, that one contracting party may do something which he is not legally obliged to do, such as give a bonus when to do so was entirely discretionary, not part of the contract between the parties.[318] If the action, although arising out of a contractual situation, is one of tort, for example, where the plaintiff sues in deceit in respect of a fraudulent misrepresentation, the court may award punitive or exemplary damages in tort.[319]

Prior to the decision of the Supreme Court of Canada in *Vorvis v. Insurance Corporation of British Columbia*[320] Canadian courts were divided on the question whether punitive damages could ever be awarded in cases of breach of contract. Some restated the older *Addis* principle on one of two grounds: (a) that damages

---

Note, however, the requirement of *mitigation* in such a case, and its effect upon the value of the shares on which the plaintiff's compensation is based: *Asamera Oil Corp. v. Sea Oil & General Corp.; Baud Corp., N.V. v. Brook* (1979), 89 D.L.R. (3d) 1 (S.C.C.); below, p. 778.

314 Waddams, *Law of Damages*, 2nd ed. (1991), paras. 11.250-11.270; Cormier, "Punitive Damages in Ordinary Contracts" (1981), 42 Manitoba L.R. 93; Note: "Punitive Damages in Contract Actions — Are There Exceptions Swallowing the Rule?" (1980), 20 Washington L.J. 86; Sullivan, "Punitive Damages in the Law of Contracts: The Reality and Illusion of Legal Change" (1977), 61 Minn. L.R. 207. Venour, "Punitive Damages in Contract" (1988), 1 Can. J. of Law & Juris. 87; Feldthusen, "Symposium: Punitive Damages in Contract and Tort: Recent Developments in the Canadian Law of Punitive Damages" (1990), 16 Can. Bus. L.J. 241.

315 [1909] A.C. 488 (H.L.); see *Guildford v. Anglo-French S.S. Co.* (1883), 9 S.C.R. 303 (S.C.C.). On damages for loss of reputation compare the cases cited above, notes 250, 259, 279.

316 Above, note 304. On damages for loss of reputation see *Ribeiro v. C.I.B.C.* (1992), 13 O.R. (3d) 278 (Ont. C.A.), above, p. 736, note 248.

317 (1848), 1 Ex. 850, 154 E.R. 363; above, p. 711.

318 *Lavarack v. Woods of Colchester Ltd.*, [1966] 3 All E.R. 683 (C.A.).

319 *Denison v. Fawcett* (1958), 12 D.L.R. (2d) 537 (Ont. C.A.); *Graham v. Saville*, [1945] 2 D.L.R. 489 (Ont. C.A.). Compare *Cardinal Const. Co. v. R.* (1981), 32 O.R. (2d) 575 (Ont. H.C.); affirmed (1981), 128 D.L.R. (3d) 662 (Ont. C.A.), where the tort argument failed. See also *Harland v. Francsali* (1993), 13 O.R. (3d) 103 (Ont. Gen. Div.), where fraud was found, but not deceit (*sic*) and punitive damages were awarded. On punitive damages in tort cases, see Fridman, "Punitive Damages in the Law of Tort" (1970), 68 Can. Bar Rev. 373.

320 (1989), 58 D.L.R. (4th) 193 (S.C.C.).

are not to be awarded in a breach of contract case, especially one involving wrongful dismissal, for injured feelings, or (b) that vindictive or punitive damages are inappropriate in contract cases.[321] Some cases awarded such damages in circumstances which suggest that the true basis of the claim was not a breach of contract but a tort or the infringement of some statutory right.[322] Still other cases appear to have accepted that punitive or exemplary damages were available to an aggrieved plaintiff in an appropriate case, while denying such damages to the particular plaintiff in the case before the court on the ground that the conduct of the defendant was insufficient to justify such an award.[323] The basis for such awards was described by Linden J. in *Brown v. Waterloo Regional Board of Police Commissioners.*[324] Such damages could be awarded where "a contract has been breached in a high-handed, shocking and arrogant fashion so as to demand condemnation by the Court as a deterrent."[325]

The issue seemingly has been put to rest by the decision in *Vorvis v. Insurance Corporation of British Columbia.*[326] This was a wrongful dismissal case in which the plaintiff claimed damages for mental distress caused by termination of his employment and punitive damages. According to his evidence he was treated in

---

321 *Cardinal Const. Ltd. v. R.* (1981), 32 O.R. (2d) 575 (Ont. H.C.); affirmed (1981), 128 D.L.R. (3d) 662 (Ont. C.A.); *Edwards v. Harris-Intertype (Can.) Ltd.* (1983), 40 O.R. (2d) 558 (Ont. H.C.); affirmed (1984), 46 O.R. (2d) 286 (Ont. C.A.); *Cringle v. Nor. Union Ins. Co.* (1981), 124 D.L.R. (3d) 22 (B.C.S.C.); *Olson v. New Home Certification Program of Alta.* (1986), 44 Alta. L.R. (2d) 207 (Alta. Q.B.); *Wadden v. Guar. Trust Co. of Can.,* [1987] 2 W.W.R. 739 (Alta. Q.B.); *Alpine Resources Ltd. v. Bowtex Resources Ltd.* (1989), 66 Alta. L.R. (2d) 144 (Alta. Q.B.).

322 *Jennett v. Fed. Ins. Co.* (1976), 72 D.L.R. (3d) 20 (Ont. H.C.); *Cornell v. Pfizer C. & G. Inc.* (1981), 23 C.P.C. 286; *Captain Devs. Ltd. v. Nu-West Group Ltd.* (1982), 136 D.L.R. (3d) 502 (Ont. H.C.); supplementary reasons at (1983), 27 R.P.R. 296 (Ont. H.C.); reversed (1984), 6 D.L.R. (4th) 179 (Ont. C.A.); leave to appeal to S.C.C. refused (1984), 55 N.R. 273 (S.C.C.); *Nantel v. Parisien* (1981), 22 R.P.R. 1 (Ont. H.C.); *Centennial Centre of Science & Technology v. VS Services Ltd.* (1982), 40 O.R. (2d) 253 at 254-255 (Ont. H.C.) *per* Dupont J.

323 *Curry v. Advocate General Ins. Co. of Can.* (1986), 9 C.P.C. (2d) 247 (Ont. Master); *Chiusolo v. Royal Ins. Co. of Can.,* [1986] I.L.R. 1-2115 (Ont. H.C.); *Morrison Lamothe Inc. v. Bedok* (1986), 55 O.R. (2d) 129 (Ont. H.C.); *Draft Masonry (York) Co. v. PA Restoration Inc.* (1988), 48 R.P.R. 231 (Ont. Dist. Ct.); *Zarnett v. Adler* (1988), 30 C.L.R. 133 (Ont. H.C.). See also the cases cited by Craig J. in *Fazzari v. Pellizzari* (1988), 28 O.A.C. 38 at 40 (Ont. Div. Ct.).

324 (1982), 37 O.R. (2d) 277 at 293 (Ont. H.C.); reversed on other grounds (1983), 150 D.L.R. (3d) 729 (Ont. C.A.); followed and applied in *Lyons Estate v. Whitworth* (1988), 62 O.R. (2d) 602 (Ont. H.C.). Compare *Fazzari v. Pellizari* above, note 323, where the Ontario Divisional Court, by a majority, held that punitive damages were recoverable in an action for breach of contract.
   Similarly, in *Thompson v. Zurich Ins. Co.* (1983), 45 O.R. (2d) 744 at 752-753 (Ont. H.C.), Pennell J. thought that to differentiate tort and contract cases in respect of such damages was "mechanical", without sound and legitimate basis. However, he seemed to consider that punitive damages were most appropriate where a breach of contract merged with, and assumed the character of, a wilful tort calculated rather than inadvertent and in a wanton and reckless disregard for the contractual rights of others. Compare Linden J. in the *Brown* case, above, at 292-293; Cherniak & Morse, "Aggravated, Punitive and Exemplary Damages in Canada" (1983) *Special Lectures of Law Society of Upper Canada* 151, especially at pp. 176-184.

325 Compare the idea of stronger parties subjugating weaker ones for business reasons in *Nantel v. Parisien,* above, note 322.

326 Above, note 320.

a harsh, humiliating and distressing manner by his employer before the termination. His claims were rejected by the trial judge and the British Columbia Court of Appeal, and by the majority of the Supreme Court of Canada over the dissent of Wilson and L'Heureux-Dubé JJ.

After distinguishing between aggravated and punitive damages,[327] McIntyre J., speaking for the majority, said that the only basis for the imposition of punishment was the finding of the commission of an actionable wrong that caused the injury complained of by the plaintiff.[328] He then illustrated what he meant by reference to *Robitaille v. Vancouver Hockey Club Ltd.*,[329] where the plaintiff was denied proper medical attention by the club by which he was employed. The question was whether the case before the court was of this nature. In this respect, while it was unusual to do so, punitive damages could be awarded in cases of breach of contract.[330] Unlike the situation in tort cases, it will be rare to find a contractual breach appropriate for an award of exemplary or punitive damages. The distinction between tort and contract cases turned on the fact that in contract what was involved was a "private arrangement" between the parties.[331] That distinction did not eliminate an award of punitive damages, but made it rare in contract cases. Then he continued to enunciate the situations when such damages could be awarded.

> ... punitive damages may only be awarded in respect of conduct which is of such nature as to be deserving of punishment because of its harsh, vindictive, reprehensible and malicious nature.... [I]n any case where such an award is made the conduct must be extreme in its nature and such that by any reasonable standard it is deserving of full condemnation and punishment.[332]

The *Vorvis* case did not fall within this category.

The dissenting judgment of Wilson J. relied heavily on the ideas propounded by Linden J. in the *Brown* case[333] and Galligan J. in *Nantel v. Parisien*.[334] Furthermore, the learned judge was not perturbed by the notion that admitting the possibility of awarding such damages in contract cases would narrow the gap between tort and contract.[335] Nor did Wilson J. agree that such damages could only be awarded where the misconduct in itself was an actionable wrong.[336] The correct approach was to assess the conduct in the context of all the circumstances and determine whether it was deserving of punishment because of its shockingly harsh, vindictive, reprehensible and malicious nature.[337] Moreover, Wilson J. did not accept the

---

327 *Ibid.*, at 200-205. Such damages were denied the plaintiff because the treatment of which he complained preceded the wrongful dismissal and the injury it caused did not arise out of the dismissal. Therefore, it did not aggravate the damage caused by the dismissal.
328 *Ibid.*, at 206.
329 (1981), 124 D.L.R. (3d) 228 (B.C.C.A.).
330 *Vorvis*, above, note 320, at 207.
331 *Ibid.*, at 207-208.
332 *Ibid.*, at 208.
333 Above, note 324.
334 Above, note 322.
335 *Vorvis*, above, note 320, at 222.
336 *Ibid.*, at 223-224.
337 *Ibid.*, at 224.

divergence between duties owed a neighbour under the law of tort and duties breached in contract by the type of flagrant and deliberate misconduct meriting an award of punitive damages.[338] In the result, she and L'Heureux-Dubé J. found that the defendant's behaviour in this case justified an award of exemplary damages.

It seems clear that such damages can now be awarded in contract cases. The only question is the determination of an appropriate situation for such an award. The language of McIntyre and Wilson JJ. does not appear to differ too widely in its content or nature. The chief difference seems to be in the requirement by the majority of the commission of a separate actionable wrong that caused the injury complained of by the plaintiff. In *Taylor v. Pilot Insurance Co.*,[339] in which the issue was whether a plaintiff could include in his pleadings in an action for breach of contract brought against insurers a claim for punitive damages, Farley J. suggested that the language of the majority in the *Vorvis* case was ambiguously ambivalent. That view indicated that there could never be an award of punitive damages for breach of an employment contract, or any other contract terminable on notice. This ignored the fact that it was not an actionable wrong to terminate an employment contract on reasonable notice (or by giving severance pay in lieu); but it was an actionable wrong to terminate an employmnt contract without such notice or severance pay in lieu. Furthermore, on the view of the majority, punitive damages seemed to flow from a separate actionable wrong, not the breach of contract *per se*. Taken to its logical conclusion on this basis the punitive damages would be an award for infliction of a tort, such as slapping the plaintiff in the face with a rotting fish when breaking the contract, not purely for the breach of contract. However, the learned judge went on to state, without determining the questions he had raised earlier, that according to the *Vorvis* case it was quite clear that punitive damages may be pleaded in conjunction with a breach of contract case, where the misconduct alleged in the pleadings indicated that a separate actionable wrong had been committed. Since no such wrong was contained in the pleadings in this case, the claim for punitive damages had to be struck out.

Indeed, in the cases since *Vorvis* in which that decision has been applied, most have been cases in which punitive damages were not allowed.[340] In one decision, *Fleck v. Stewart*[341] such damages were awarded because the defendant had behaved

---

338 *Ibid.*

339 (1991), 75 D.L.R. (4th) 370 at 374 (Ont. Gen. Div.).

340 *Lobrutto v. University of St. Jerome's College* (1989), 44 C.P.C. (2d) 104 (Ont. H.C.), where aggravated damages were allowed; *Thomas v. Chaleur Auto Sales Ltd.* (1989), 101 N.B.R. (2d) 383 (N.B.C.A.), where neither punitive nor aggravated damages were allowed, and it was pointed out that in a wrongful dismissal case such damages would not be allowed where the misconduct asserted to justify such damages preceded the dismissal; *Yamaha Can. Music Ltd. v. MacDonald & Oryall Ltd.* (1990), 46 B.C.L.R. (2d) 363 (B.C.C.A.), where there was no actionable wrong causing injury, because there was no harsh, vindictive reprehensible and malicious conduct deserving of condemnation and punishment (the language of McIntyre J.); *Andryechen v. Transit Ins. Co.*, [1992] I.L.R. 1-2830 (Ont. Gen. Div.), where the claim for punitive damages was based on the insurance company's conduct in defending the action for breach of an insurance policy by alleging fraud: in the circumstances this was reasonable, not malicious.

341 (1991), 17 R.P.R. (2d) 132 (Alta. Q.B.).

in a high-handed, aggressive, intimidating manner and his conduct was worthy of condemnation.

Thus, it is reasonable to conclude that although there is now no theoretical objection to an award of exemplary or punitive damages (distinct from aggravated damages which always were recoverable in proper cases) in an action based on breach of contract, the occasions when such damages will be awarded will be severely limited, in accordance with the tenor of the language employed by the majority of the Supreme Court in the *Vorvis* case.

(d) Difficulties of assessment

The fact that it may be difficult, if not virtually impossible, to assess or measure accurately and with definition the value of the loss suffered by the plaintiff — which is attributable to, and not too remote a consequence of the defendant's breach of contract — is not in itself an answer to a claim for damages.[342] The court must and will make an award. As was stated by Duff J. in *Kohler v. Thorold Natural Gas Co.*,[343]

> as against a wrongdoer, and especially when the wrong is of such a character that in itself it is calculated to make and does make the exact ascertainment of damages impossible or extremely difficult and embarrassing, all reasonable presumptions are to be made.

The court must do the best it can and make a reasonable estimate of the plaintiff's loss.[344]

The leading case, which has been followed in Canada, is *Chaplin v. Hicks.*[345]

---

342 *Penvidic Contracting Co. v. Int. Nickel Co.* (1975), 53 D.L.R. (3d) 748 at 756-757 (S.C.C.); *Wood v. Grand Valley Ry. Co.* (1913), 30 O.L.R. 44 (Ont. C.A.); affirmed (1915), 51 S.C.R. 283 (S.C.C.); *Groves-Raffin Const. Ltd. v. Bank of N.S.* (1976), 64 D.L.R. (3d) 78 at 129 (B.C.C.A.) *per* Robertson J.A. The difficulty should not deter the court from doing justice: *Abraham v. Wingate Properties Ltd.* (1986), 36 Man. R. (2d) 264 at 268 (Man. C.A.).

343 (1916), 52 S.C.R. 514 at 530 (S.C.C.); leave to appeal to the Privy Council refused (1916), 52 S.C.R. vii; compare Martin J.A. in *Boon v. Bell*, [1932] 2 W.W.R. 304 at 311 (Sask. C.A.). Compare also *Wilson v. Northampton & Banbury Junction Ry.* (1874), 9 Ch. App. 279; *Mtge. & Agreement Purchasing Co. v. Townsend*, [1920] 3 W.W.R. 968 (Man. C.A.); *Greenwood v. Estevan School Trustees* (1910), 3 Sask. L.R. 433 (Sask. C.A.).

344 *B.J.'s Contracting Ltd. v. Eastern Shredding Ltd.* (1990), 83 Nfld. & P.E.I.R. 121 at 133 (Nfld. C.A.) *per* Marshall J.A. Even if it is a matter of guess work: *Wood v. Grand Valley Ry. Co.* (1915), 51 S.C.R. 283 at 289 *per* Davies J.

345 [1911] 2 K.B. 786 (C.A.). See *Webb & Knapp (Can.) Ltd. v. Edmonton (City)* (1970), 11 D.L.R. (3d) 544 (S.C.C.); *Kinkel v. Hyman*, [1939] S.C.R. 364; *Multi-Malls Inc. v. Tex-Mall Properties Ltd.* (1980), 108 D.L.R. 399 (Ont. H.C.); affirmed (1981), 148 D.L.R. (3d) 192 (Ont. C.A.); leave to appeal to S.C.C. refused [1982] 1 S.C.R. xiii (S.C.C.); *Abraham v. Wingate Properties Ltd.*, above, note 342; *Stan's Power Tong Service v. Argus Machine Co.* (1989), 97 A.R. 314 (Alta. C.A.); affirming on reconsideration (1988), 93 A.R. 18 (Alta. C.A.); varying (1986), 77 A.R. 175 (Alta. Q.B.); *B.J.'s Contracting Ltd. v. Eastern Shredding Ltd.*, above, note 344; *Eastwalsh Homes Ltd. v. Anatal Devs. Ltd.* (1993), 100 D.L.R. (4th) 469 (Ont. C.A.); leave to appeal to S.C.C. refused (1993), 104 D.L.R. (4th) vii (note) (S.C.C.).

There the plaintiff, through the negligence of the defendant, was deprived of the chance to compete in the finals of a beauty competition. The conduct of the defendant was in breach of the contract that existed between him and the plaintiff, in consequence of her entry into the competition. How were damages to be assessed? It was not possible to determine whether or not the plaintiff would have won the competition — for doing which she would have been given a specific sum of money. The defendant argued that, since her winning was a matter of speculation, dependant upon many variable, uncertain factors, the loss of the prize money was also purely speculative. The court thought differently, and awarded the plaintiff what she might have obtained had she won. Since she lost the chance of winning, and the money that would have accompanied victory, *that* was the amount of which she had been deprived by the defendant's breach of contract. In other words, recovery is possible for a "lost chance" where the extent of the loss suffered is contingent on factors outside the control of the plaintiff.[346]

This decision has been applied not only to other cases of a similar kind, involving competitions,[347] but also to situations in which the negligence or other breach of contract by solicitors has resulted in loss of an expected or probable profit or advantage,[348] for example: where architects and planners were deprived of the chance of obtaining a lucrative planning contract by reason of the breach of contract of a city;[349] where the breach of contract by the defendant made the plaintiff unable to fulfil his contract, so as to deprive him of the probable profit he would have made thereunder;[350] where a union and employees were deprived of the opportunity to negotiate a collective agreement because of the employer's unlawful conduct;[351] or where an employee was deprived of the opportunity to earn commission because of his wrongful dismissal;[352] and where an orthodontist was accidentally omitted from a listing of dentists in the yellow pages.[353]

The plaintiff has the onus of proving that a chance had been lost. However, proof of the loss of a mere chance is not enough. The plaintiff must prove that the chance constitutes some reasonable probability of realizing an advantage of

---

346 *Mills v. Edmonton (City)* (1987), 46 D.L.R. (4th) 26 at 36 (Alta. Q.B.) *per* Berger J. Even where the plaintiff claims "equitable" damages, the loss should be reasonably foreseeable and sufficiently certain to merit recovery: *Domowicz v. Orca Invts. Ltd.* (1993), 15 O.R. (3d) 661 at 678 (Ont. Gen. Div.) *per* Adams J.

347 *Hawrysh v. St. John's Sportmens Club* (1964), 49 W.W.R. 243 (Man. Q.B.).

348 Compare *Otter v. Church, Adams Tatham & Co.*, [1953] Ch. 280; *Hall v. Meyrick*, [1957] 2 Q.B. 455 (C.A.); *Sykes v. Midland Bank Executor & Trustee Co.*, [1971] 1 Q.B. 113 (C.A.); *Major v. Buchanan* (1975), 9 O.R. (2d) 491 (Ont. H.C.). Contrast *Gouzenko v. Harris* (1976), 72 D.L.R. (3d) 293 (Ont. H.C.).

349 *Webb & Knapp (Can.) Ltd. v. Edmonton*, [1970] S.C.R. 588 (S.C.C.); compare *Stan's Power Tong Service Ltd. v. Argus Machine Co.*, above, note 345.

350 *Kohler v. Thorold Natural Gas Co.*, above, note 343. *Boon v. Bell*, above, note 343.

351 *Tandy Electronics Ltd. (Radio Shack) v. U.S.W.A.* (1980), 115 D.L.R. (3d) 197 (Ont. Div. Ct.).

352 *Prozak v. Bell Telephone Co. of Can.* (1984), 10 D.L.R. (4th) 382 (Ont. C.A.).

353 *Mills v. Edmonton (City)*, above, note 346.

some real substantial monetary value.[354] In one instance a 50 per cent chance that a tender would have been accepted, to the profit of the plaintiff, was sufficient.[355]

Thus, truly speculative loss is never recoverable, since it is not loss that can be traced to the defendant's breach of contract, nor is necessarily loss which the plaintiff has suffered. Loss that is difficult to assess or calculate is nonetheless definitely loss suffered by the plaintiff attributable to the wrongdoing of the defendant. This is the distinction drawn by the courts. Though hard to make, it is recognizable and capable of being applied. Nevertheless it should be remembered that, in the words of McEachern C.J.B.C. in *Begusic v. Clark, Wilson & Co.*:[356] "The assessment of damages is not a precise science; it is not even a calculation".

(e) Assessment of damages

(i) *Introduction*

The actual quantum of damages to be awarded a successful plaintiff in an action for breach of contract is a question of fact in every case.[357] It is a matter of monetizing the loss suffered by the plaintiff that is attributable to the defendant's wrongdoing in accordance with *Hadley v. Baxendale*.[358] Several specific problems have more recently emerged and should be mentioned.

(ii) *Date of assessment*[359]

The problem is to determine the moment of time when the plaintiff's claim

---

354 *Eastwalsh Homes Ltd. v. Anatal Devs. Ltd.*, above, note 345, at 486. There the plaintiff failed to meet the onus. The evidence showed that it was highly improbable that the plan agreed by the parties, which was not registered in time by the defendant, or any substitute plan, would have been registered by the extended closing date for the contract, even if registration had been diligently pursued by the defendant.

355 *Stan's Power Tong Service v. Argus Machine Co.*, above, note 345.

356 (1991), 57 B.C.L.R. (2d) 273 at 290 (B.C.C.A.); additional reasons at (1992), 66 B.C.L.R. (2d) 253 (B.C.C.A.); leave to appeal to S.C.C. refused (1992), 62 B.C.L.R. (2d) xxii (note) (S.C.C.).

357 *Cockburn v. Trusts & Guar. Co.* (1916), 38 O.L.R. 396 at 399 (Ont. C.A.) *per* Hodgins J.A.; affirmed (1917), 55 S.C.R. 264 (S.C.C.). For some discussion of these difficulties see Brown, (1975), Special Lectures of Law Society of Upper Canada, 1 at 22-34.

358 Compare, *e.g.*, *Lippert v. Ford Hotel of Toronto Ltd.*, [1930] 3 D.L.R. 722 (Ont. C.A.), failure to supply plaintiff with a room in a hotel as agreed between the parties. For examples, see *Miller v. Advanced Farming Systems Ltd.*, [1969] S.C.R. 845 (S.C.C.); *Alkok v. Grymek*, [1968] S.C.R. 452 (S.C.C.) (bad workmanship by defendant); *Wertheim v. Chicoutimi Pulp Co.*, [1911] A.C. 301 (P.C.); *Hathaway v. McIntyre* (1951), 1 W.W.R. (N.S.) 460 (B.C.C.A.); *Williams v. Keyes*, [1971] 5 W.W.R. 561 (B.C.S.C.) (failure to deliver goods, shares or land).

Sometimes damages can take into account not only past and present loss to the plaintiff, but also potential future loss, *e.g.*, where the defendant was to maintain the plaintiff for life, then the damages will include the loss during the prospective life expectancy of the plaintiff: *Zdan v. Hruden* (1912), 4 D.L.R. 255 (Man. C.A.); *Federowicz v. Federowicz (Skvarchuk)* (1951), 3 W.W.R. (N.S.) 230 (Man. K.B.). The justification for this is that damages are a once-for-all assessment when there has been a breach; the plaintiff must establish his total loss at the time of the action.

359 Waddams, *Law of Damages*, 2nd ed. (1991), paras. 1.650-1.1110; Waddams, "The Date of Assessment of Damages" (1981), 97 L.Q.R. 445. See also, Feldman & Libling, "Inflation and the Duty to Mitigate" (1979), 85 L.Q.R. 270; Wallace, "Cost of Repair and Inflation" (1980), 96 L.Q.R. 101.

"crystallizes", that is, falls to be determined in amount.[360] The usual rule was that damages were to be measured or assessed by reference to the position of the plaintiff at the date when the damage or loss was suffered, normally the date of the breach of contract.[361] This may have been the authoritative principle at one time. Recent decisions have shown that inroads have been made on this principle.[362] For example, in *Tai Hing Cotton Mill Ltd. v. Kamsing Knitting Factory*,[363] it was held that in a contract of sale of goods, when no time was fixed for the delivery of the goods, the date at which the value of the goods should be taken for calculating the loss to the buyer was the date the goods ought to have been delivered, after the demand by the buyer that they be delivered. This was not the same date as the date of the seller's letter wrongfully repudiating the contract. This made a considerable difference because of the fluctuations in the price of cotton that was the subject-matter of the contract. Much the same occurred in a case involving delay in effecting repairs, *Costello & Costello v. Cormier Enterprises Ltd.*[364] That delay resulted in an inflationary rise in cost, therefore the date for calculating damages was the date the repairs were done or should have been done once the damage was known to the plaintiff.

Many of the decisions concern contracts for the sale of land. In *Johnson v. Agnew*,[365] Lord Wilberforce pointed out that since the general principle for the assessment of damages was to put the innocent party in the position he would have been in had the contract been performed, this normally means the assessment of damages at the date of breach. However, this was not an absolute rule. If to follow it would give rise to injustice, the court has power to fix such other date as may be appropriate in the circumstances. Hence, it is not surprising to find cases where the contract concerned land in which it was held that the date of the breach was the appropriate date for calculating damages,[366] while others chose

---

360 The expression is that of the Supreme Court of Canada in *Asamera Oil Corp. Ltd. v. Sea Oil & General Corp.; Baud Corp., N.V. v. Brook* (1979), 89 D.L.R. (3d) 1 at 31 (S.C.C.). Compare *Radford v. De Froberville*, [1977] 1 W.L.R. 1262 at 1287 *per* Oliver J.

361 *Philips v. Ward*, [1956] 1 W.L.R. 471 at 474 (C.A.) *per* Denning L.J.

362 Compare *Dodd Properties (Kent) Ltd. v. Canterbury City Council*, [1980] 1 W.L.R. 433 (C.A.). But see *Janred Properties Ltd. v. ENIT*, [1989] 2 All E.R. 444 at 456 (C.A.) *per* Nourse L.J., stressing date of breach, *i.e.*, the contractual date for completion of contract for the purchase of land.

363 [1978] 1 All E.R. 515 (P.C.).

364 (1979), 25 N.B.R. (2d) 8 (N.B.Q.B.); affirmed (1979), 28 N.B.R. (2d) 398 (N.B.C.A.); compare the increased cost in building the wall which the defendant failed to do, in breach of contract: *Radford v. De Froberville*, above, note 360; compare *Nathu v. Imbrook Properties Ltd.* (1990), 75 Alta. L.R. (2d) 126 at 136 *per* Brennan J., difference between earnings of plaintiff during period he was entitled to occupy the leased premises and while his cafe was operating, and what he he should reasonably expect to earn during that period if the cafe was *not* in operation.

365 [1980] A.C. 367 at 400-401 (H.L.). In *Janred Properties Ltd. v. ENIT*, above, note 362, at 457, Nourse L.J. thought that the unusual facts of *Johnson v. Agnew* justified Lord Wilberforce's remarks; but that did not mean they applied generally. Only the House of Lords could say that.

366 *100 Main St. Ltd. v. W.B. Sullivan Const. Ltd.* (1978), 88 D.L.R. (3d) 1 (Ont. C.A.); leave to appeal to S.C.C. refused (1978), 20 O.R. (2d) 401n (S.C.C.); *Richter v. Simpson* (1982), 24 R.P.R. 37 (B.C.S.C.); *Woodford Estates Ltd. v. Pollack* (1978), 93 D.L.R. (3d) 350 (Ont. H.C.); *Kaunas v. Smyth* (1976), 75 D.L.R. (3d) 368 (Ont. H.C.); compare *McCaig v. Reys* (1978), 90 D.L.R. (3d)

a different date, sometimes the date of judgment,[367] sometimes another date altogether.[368] This can be of the utmost importance where, as has occurred with land, rising prices, through inflation or otherwise, have made the value of the land greater than it was either at the date of the contract or at the date of the breach. Is the purchaser/plaintiff to derive the benefit of this? Or is the defendant/vendor?

Two material issues have influenced decisions in this respect. First of all, the plaintiff's claim may be for specific performance, and only in the alternative for damages. Specific performance may be denied, or may be impossible; hence, the plaintiff's only remedy is in damages. Where this is the case, it would seem more reasonable to give the plaintiff the value of the property at the date when he might otherwise have obtained specific performance. What he is getting, by way of damages, is then the true equivalent of what he would have obtained had specific performance been decreed.[369] Second, the date for assessing damages should not be delayed beyond the "normal" date, as it might be termed, namely, the date of breach, if this would permit or encourage a plaintiff to delay bringing his action or otherwise conducting his affairs so as to maximize, rather than minimize his damages.

(iii) *Contributory negligence*

There is no doubt that the conduct of the plaintiff after he has suffered from a breach of contract is material in assessing the ultimate damages payable to him by the defendant. The plaintiff is under a duty to mitigate his damage.[370] However, the relevance of the plaintiff's conduct before, or at the same time as the breach of contract is more questionable. The issue involves a consideration of the extent to which, if at all, any negligence by the plaintifff himself, the effect of which

---

13 (B.C.C.A.), where the majority of the B.C. Court of Appeal allowed an appeal from the trial Judge's grant of an allowance to represent the inflationary rise in the value of land between breach and trial.

367 *Hechter v. Thurston* (1978), 80 D.L.R. (3d) 685 (Man. Q.B.); reversed on appeal (1980), 98 D.L.R. (3d) 329 (Man. C.A.); but restored by the Supreme Court of Canada (1980), 120 D.L.R. (3d) 576 (S.C.C.); *306793 Ont. v. Rimes* (1980), 100 D.L.R. (3d) 350 (Ont. C.A.); *Ribic v. Weinstein* (1983), 140 D.L.R. (2d) 258 (Ont. H.C.); affirmed on other grounds (1984), 10 D.L.R. (4th) 717 (Ont. C.A.); *Metro. Trust Co. of Can. v. Pressure Concrete Services Ltd.* (1973), 37 D.L.R. (3d) 649 (Ont. H.C.); affirmed (1975), 60 D.L.R. (3d) 431 (Ont. C.A.). Compare *Pepper v. Lecoure* (1990), 11 R.P.R. (2d) 235 (Ont. Dist. Ct.), date of trial: damages assessed as at the date of breach would have been unfair to the plaintiff and would have denied him full compensation. In this case the plaintiff abandoned his original claim for specific performance. The date to take was the date when the plaintiff realized or ought to have realized that specific performance was impossible, which, in this instance, was only at the trial of the action. See next note.

368 Date when plaintiff is satisfied specific performance is not obtainable: *Schweickardt v. Thorne*, [1976] 4 W.W.R. 249 (B.C.S.C.); compare *Pepper v. Lecoure*, above, *ibid.* (date of the trial), see previous note; date when purchaser should have complied with decree of specific performance, but did not: *Johnson v. Agnew*, above, note 365; date when the plaintiff, acting reasonably, could have resold the land not taken by the defendant in breach of the contract: *Ansdell v. Crowther* (1984), 11 D.L.R. (4th) 614 (B.C.C.A.).

369 See the cases referred to in the previous note.

370 Below, pp. 776-783.

was to contribute towards causing the damage that he incurred as a consequence of the breach of contract, can be taken into account by a court in quantifying or assessing his damages. Can there be apportionment between the parties in an action for breach of contract in the same way as there may now be such apportionment between plaintiff and defendant in actions in tort, as a result of statutory provisions which have altered the original common law?[371]

Canadian courts have been divided on this issue. In some decisions it has been held that such apportionment can occur, since the language of the provincial statute dealing with the effects of contributory negligence can be made to apply to actions for breach of contract as well as actions in tort.[372] Other decisions suggest that such an approach is untenable.[373] In *Giffels Associates Ltd. v. Eastern Construction Co.*,[374] the Supreme Court of Canada, while stating that a final conclusion on this point was not necessary, went on to say that it was difficult "to see how a contract basis for contribution can be read into one provision of a statute which has interrelated provisions dominated by a reference to tortfeasors." However, in two subsequent decisions two Ontario judges have been able to invoke the idea of contributory negligence by the plaintiff as permitting apportionment of his damage between himself and the defendant in an action for breach of contract by a subtle twist to the concept of mitigation.

In *Tompkins Hardware Ltd. v. North Western Flying Services Ltd.*,[375] the plaintiff's aircraft was damaged when it made a crash landing. This was necessary because skis installed on the aircraft to enable it to be used during the winter dropped out of position. The skis had been installed and maintained by the defendant. There was no doubt that the defendant had been negligent in installing the shock cords which restrained the skis in flight. Hence, the defendant was liable both in tort

---

371 On which see Linden, *Canadian Tort Law*, 5th ed. (1993), pp. 441-447; Fridman, *Law of Torts in Canada* (1989), Vol. 1, pp. 382-385.

372 *Caines v. Bank of N.S.* (1978), 90 D.L.R. (3d) 271 (N.B.C.A.) *per* Bugold J.A. differing from the other members of the Nova Scotia Court of Appeal; *Husky Oil Operation Ltd. v. Oster* (1978), 87 D.L.R. (3d) 86 (Sask. Q.B.); *Palmeri v. Littleton; Renke v. Littleton*, [1979] 4 W.W.R. 577 (B.C.S.C.); *Can. Western Natural Gas Co. v. Pathfinder Surveys Ltd.* (1980), 21 A.R. 459 (Alta. C.A.); *West Coast Finance Ltd. v. Gunderson, Stokes, Walton & Co.* (1974), 44 D.L.R. (3d) 232 (B.C.S.C.); affirmed (1975), 56 D.L.R. (3d) 460 (B.C.C.A.); *Finance Amer. Realty Ltd. v. Speed* (1979), 38 N.S.R. (2d) 374 (N.S.C.A.); *Smith v. McInnis*, [1978] 2 S.C.R. 1357 at 1380 (S.C.C.) *per* Pigeon J.; *Doiron v. Caisse Populaire D'Inkerman Ltée* (1985), 17 D.L.R. (4th) 660 (N.B.C.A.); *Coopers & Lybrand v. H.E. Kane Agencies Ltd.* (1985), 17 D.L.R. (4th) 695 (N.B.C.A.).

In England it has been held by the Court of Appeal that where the defendant's liability in contract is the same as his liability in the tort of negligence independently of contract (on which compare above, pp. 694-701), the court can apportion blame under the relevant legislation and reduce the plaintiff's damages accordingly even though he is suing in contract: *Forsikringsaktieselskapet Vesta v. Butcher*, [1988] 2 All E.R. 43 (C.A.). This suggests that in a "pure" contract case such apportionment for contributory negligence is not possible. The Canadian cases referred to above seem to make no such differentiation: compare *Ribic v. Weinstein*, below, note 377.

373 *Henuset Bros. Ltd. v. Pan Can. Petroleum Ltd.* (1977), 82 D.L.R. (3d) 345 (Alta. T.D.); *Dom. Chain Co. v. Eastern Const. Co.* (1976), 68 D.L.R. (3d) 385 (Ont. C.A.); affirmed on other grounds (1978), 84 D.L.R. (3d) 344 (*sub nom. Giffels Associates Ltd. v. Eastern Const. Co.*) (S.C.C.).

374 (1978), 84 D.L.R. (3d) 344 at 349 (S.C.C.).

375 (1982), 139 D.L.R. (3d) 329 (Ont. H.C.).

and for breach of contract. It was alleged, however, that the plaintiff had also been negligent. One of the skis had previously dropped out of position during an earlier flight. The plaintiff had landed safely and returned the aircraft to the defendant who said that there was no cause for alarm. The defendant argued that the plaintiff should not have flown the aircraft after the first incident, when he could, and should have left the aircraft with the defendant for proper checking. Saunders J. held that the plaintiff was guilty of such contributory negligence, and that this misconduct not only affected the defendant's liability in tort but also its liability in contract. The plaintiff was under an obligation to mitigate its damages and if the pilot had left the aircraft at the defendant's premises after the first incident that action might have been described as "anticipatory mitigation". By negligently taking the aircraft up, the pilot created a situation where the damage occurred because of the inadequate shock cords installed by the defendant. Those circumstances permitted apportionment whether the action was brought in contract or tort.[376]

This idea, namely, "anticipatory mitigation", was adopted and used by Grange J. in *Ribic v. Weinstein*,[377] which concerned the non-fulfilment of a contract to sell land. Out of this situation several actions were brought, including one by the vendor of the land against the estate agent who handled the transaction. In this action the learned judge decided that the vendor was one-third to blame for the ultimate consequences, by retaining a deposit from another, unsuccessful purchaser of the land, and by entering into an unconditional offer to sell the land knowing that there was an outstanding, unresolved, accepted offer affecting the land. Grange J. held that the damages suffered by the vendor were to be apportioned. In this instance, unlike the *Tompkins* case, there was no question of a possible alternate, or concurrent action in tort. This was an action for breach of contract. Yet, through the medium of "anticipatory mitigation", apportionment was allowed.

It would seem that the issue is unresolved by Canadian courts. On principle there should be no barrier to the application of the idea of apportionment in breach of contract cases.[378] Even if the legislation that applies to tort cannot be interpreted to extend to contract situations, the need to establish a casual connection between the plaintiff's loss and the defendant's breach of contract, to which reference has been made,[379] should logically lead to the conclusion that where the plaintiff has been partially responsible for his loss he should bear that proportion by a reduction in his damages. Whether Canadian courts will finally arrive at this conclusion remains to be seen.

---

376 *Ibid.*, at 341. Compare the *Butcher* case, above, note 372.

377 (1982), 140 D.L.R. (3d) 258 (Ont. H.C.); affirmed on other grounds (1984), 10 D.L.R. (4th) 717 (Ont. C.A.).

378 Compare Glanville Williams, *Joint Torts and Contributory Negligence*, at pp. 214-215, cited by Saunders J. in *Tompkins Hardware Ltd. v. North Western Flying Services Ltd.*, above, note 375, at 340.

379 Above, pp. 717-719.

(iv) *Deductions*

In several cases it has been argued that a defendant in breach of contract should not be liable to pay damages in respect of either income tax or unemployment or similar benefits obtained by a plaintiff in consequence of the breach. Wrongful dismissal actions have been the source of these arguments. A plaintiff in such an action obtains damages to compensate him for the salary or wages he would have earned during the period in respect of which he should have received notice of termination.[380] Consequently, the argument runs, those damages represent lost earnings, and since those earnings would have been subject to a payment of income tax by the ex-employee, the defendant, the employer, should not be liable to that extent. The reason for this is that, because of the liability to pay tax, the employee has not really lost such amount. The Supreme Court of Canada has refused to accept this argument in cases of tort,[381] although it has in a case involving compensation for expropriation.[382] In wrongful dismissal actions, some courts have apparently accepted the argument, and deducted the tax that would be payable on the lost earnings.[383] However, in *Jack Cewe Ltd. v. Jorgenson*,[384] the Supreme Court of Canada, while viewing the present situation with respect to income tax on an award of "an identifiable sum for loss of earnings" as "legally insecure",[385] appears to have held that a sum in respect of income tax was not to be deducted from an award of a full year's salary in a successful action for wrongful dismissal. Whatever the position as between the employee and the taxing authority, the employer's liability to pay the employee's earnings should be unaffected.

With respect to benefits accruing to the employee as a result of his being dismissed, it has been held that contributory pension benefits obtained as a consequence of dismissal were not to be deducted from compensation for loss of earnings.[386] Such benefits are derived from the employee's contract with his employer, and the payments under such a pension scheme are akin to payments under an insurance policy. Similarly, where an employee obtains unemployment insurance benefits, these are in consequence, in part, of the payment of contributions by the employer. This is an obligation incurred by reason of the employee's employment. To the extent that payment of these contributions resulted in the provision of unemployment benefits, these are a consequence of the contract of

---

380 Above, p. 722.

381 *R. v. Jennings*, [1966] S.C.R. 532 (S.C.C.): not following *Br. Transport Comm. v. Gourley*, [1956] A.C. 185 (H.L.).

382 *Florence Realty Co. v. R.*, [1968] S.C.R. 42 (S.C.C.).

383 *R. v. Atkins* (1976), 68 D.L.R. (3d) 187 (Fed. C.A.); with which contrast *Quance v. R.*, [1974] C.T.C. 225 (Fed. T.D.).

384 (1980), 111 D.L.R. (3d) 577 (S.C.C.) doubting *R. v. Atkins* (1976), 68 D.L.R. (3d) 187 (Fed. C.A.).

385 *Jack Cewe Ltd., ibid.*, at 579.

386 *Guy v. Trizec Equities Ltd.*, [1979] 2 S.C.R. 756 (S.C.C.), applying *Parry v. Cleaver*, [1970] A.C. 1 (H.L.); *C.P. Ltd. v. Gill*, [1973] S.C.R. 654 (S.C.C.). Compare in the case of tort, *i.e.*, personal injury, the distinction drawn by the majority of the Supreme Court of Canada in *Ratych v. Bloomer* (1990), 69 D.L.R. (4th) 25 between money paid by way of wages under a collective agreement (to be deducted from damages) and money or wages received by way of gifts, or pursuant to an insurance contract paid for by the employee. Can this distinction be applied to dismissal cases?

employment and could not be deducted from damages for wrongful dismissal. Perhaps the consequence might be that the employee would have to return the unemployment insurance benefits. But this was a matter between the employee and the unemployment insurance authorities. It did not concern the former employer.[387]

There were decisions in which such benefits were deductible where the employer had contributed to the unemployment insurance pension or benefits.[388] These must now be regarded as no longer authoritative. The situation with respect to such cases is the same as where the employer has paid nothing by way of unemployment insurance premiums,[389] and where the employee has not claimed unemployment insurance benefits.[390]

(v) *Contracts involving foreign currency*[391]

(A) *The nature of the problem* A contract may require a party to pay money in a foreign, that is, non-Canadian currency. Or the damages payable for breach of a contract may be calculated in terms of such a currency, for example, where the contract is governed by a foreign system of law. Until recent times such situations did not give rise to any problems, because currencies were, on the whole, stable. Recent developments, in particular the emergence of "floating" currencies, which result in fluctuations in the dollar value of foreign currencies, have produced a difficulty. If the dollar value of the foreign debt or the damages due in the foreign currency has altered, either upwards or downwards, by reason of market changes, the consequence may be that the creditor or the debtor, as the case may be, will suffer if the liability of the debtor is considered to be founded on a fixed dollar amount. Since the purpose of awards of damages for breach of contract is to compensate the victim of a breach for the loss he has incurred by reason of the

---

387 *Jack Cewe Ltd. v. Jorgenson*, above, note 384, at 581.

388 *Gardner v. Rockwell Int. of Can. Ltd.* (1975), 59 D.L.R. (3d) 513 (Ont. H.C.); *Burton v. MacMillan Bloedel Ltd.*, [1976] 4 W.W.R. 267 (B.C.S.C.); *Allison v. Amoco Production Co.* (1975), 58 D.L.R. (3d) 233 (Alta. S.C.); *Sublett v. Facit-Addo Can. Ltd.* (1977), 79 D.L.R. (3d) 286 (Ont. H.C.).

389 *Gordie's Auto Sales Ltd. v. Pitre* (1976), 73 D.L.R. (3d) 559 (N.B.C.A.); *Olson v. Motor Coach Industs. Ltd.* (1978), 81 D.L.R. (3d) 132 (Man. C.A.); *Dewitt v. A. & B. Sound Ltd.* (1978), 85 D.L.R. (3d) 604 (B.C.S.C.); *Rooney v. Reed Ltd.* (1978), 88 D.L.R. (3d) 414 (Ont. H.C.).

390 *Douglas v. Sandwell & Co.* (1978), 81 D.L.R. (3d) 508 (B.C.S.C.). For a discussion of the position in the U.S.A. see Fleming, "The Collateral Source Rule and Contract Damages" (1983), 71 Calif. L.R. 56.

391 Waddams, *Law of Damages*, 2nd ed. (1991), paras. 7.80-7.320. Law Reform Commission of British Columbia, *Working Paper No. 33: Foreign Money Liabilities*, 1982; Libling, "Questions and Answers(?); *Miliangos v. Frank (Textiles) Ltd.*" (1977), 93 L.Q.R. 212; Riordon, "The Currency of Suit in Actions for Foreign Debts" (1978), 24 McGill L.J. 422; Lapres, "Comment" (1977), 55 Can. Bar Rev. 132; Note: "The Inflation Factor in Damages for Breach of Contract" (1980), 12 Ottawa L.R. 489. For discussion of a New Zealand case, *Isaac Nayland & Sons Ltd. v. N.Z. Co-op. Wool Marketing Assn. Ltd.*, [1981] 1 N.Z.L.R. 361, see Reckett, "Contract damages for exchanges losses — A New Zealand development," [1982] Lloyds M. & C.L.Q. 566.

breach,[392] to adopt a "nominalist" approach to this issue[393] may be to fail to provide adequate compensation. The plaintiff may receive a sum of money which, superficially, equals what he has lost, but, when converted into Canadian dollars, is short of being a true equivalent. Alternatively, the plaintiff may reap an unexpected windfall if the currency in question has risen in value. Is there some method whereby the parties can be protected against unforeseen, and unforeseeable, fluctuations in currency values? If the contract produces a fixed, determinate debt that is owed by one party to the other, for example, if it is a contract for the sale of goods at a settled price, the parties can agree in advance that the sum payable shall be whatever amount of the foreign currency is required, at the date when payment is due, to produce an agreed number of Canadian dollars. The debtor will then have to provide more or less of the foreign currency depending on what, if anything, has happened to that currency in the period before payment is due under the contract. If, as is often the case, no such prior agreement has been made, what is the situation?

There are really two issues in this respect. The first is whether a court can order payment of a debt or damages for breach of contract in a foreign currency, so as to enable a suitable amount of such currency to be paid by a defendant. The second, and perhaps more important issue, is the determination of the appropriate date at which the value of the amount owed, by conversion of the foreign currency into Canadian dollars, is to be made.

(B) *The currency of a judgment* At common law the principle was that courts had no authority to enter money judgments in terms of a foreign currency. They were obliged to do so in the currency of the forum. This was the doctrine embraced by the English courts, until recently,[394] and it was also adopted by courts in Canada.[395] However, after some indications that the principle should be abandoned or changed,[396] the House of Lords ultimately held that, where a claim was for a debt, that is, a fixed, pre-determined amount of money, an English court did have the power to order payment of the sum in a foreign currency, if that was

---

392 Above, p. 711.

393 *I.e.*, that the debt in a particular currency involves the obligation to pay the nominal amount of that debt in whatever is the legal tender for that currency at the date of payment regardless of any fluctuation in the exchange value of the currency with other currencies.

394 *Manners v. Pearson & Son*, [1898] 1 Ch. 581 (C.A.); *Di Ferdinando v. Simon, Smits & Co.*, [1920] 3 K.B. 409 (C.A.); *S.S. Celia v. S.S. Volturno*, [1921] 2 A.C. 544 (H.L.); *Re United Rys. of Havana & Regla Warehouses Ltd.*, [1961] A.C. 1007 (H.L.).

395 *Custodian v. Blucher*, [1927] S.C.R. 420 (S.C.C.); *Gatineau Power Co. v. Crown Life Ins. Co.*, [1945] S.C.R. 655 (S.C.C.). Contrast, however, *Smith v. C.P.R.* (1963), 41 D.L.R. (2d) 249 (Sask. Q.B.).

396 *Teh Hu v. Nippon Salvage Co.*, [1970] P. 106 (C.A.); *Jugoslavenska Oceanska Plovidba v. Castle Invt. Co.*, [1974] Q.B. 292 (C.A.); *Schorsch Meier G.m.b.H. v. Hennin*, [1975] Q.B. 416 (C.A.); *The "Halcyon the Great"*, [1975] 1 All E.R. 882. But if the parties contemplated the possibility of a currency change, the situation might be different on the application of the subjective test in *Hadley v. Baxendale*: see *Aruna Mills Ltd. v. Gobindram*, [1968] 1 Q.B. 655. See also *President of India v. Lips Maritime Corp.; The Lips*, [1987] 3 All E.R. 110 at 117-118 (H.L.) *per* Lord Brandon, where the express provisions of the contract, a charterparty, made all the difference.

provided for in the contract, rather than in sterling.[397] In a subsequent decision the House of Lords also decided that the same order could be made where the claim was in tort or for damages at large for breach of contract.[398] The situation in Canada, however, is complicated by the provisions of the Currency Act,[399] section 13 of which states that

> [a]ll public accounts throughout Canada shall be kept in the currency of Canada; and any statement as to money or money value in any indictment or legal proceeding shall be stated in the currency of Canada.

Canadian courts appear to have held that this statutory provision makes it impossible in Canada to adopt the change in the common law entertained by the House of Lords.[400] However, it has been suggested that the views of Canadian courts on this matter are all by way of *obiter dicta*: that there is no binding authority, certainly not at the level of the Supreme Court of Canada, that makes it impossible to adopt the English approach, and that the provisions of section 13 of the Currency Act may be *ultra vires* the Canadian Parliament.[401] It has also been indicated that section 13, if valid, might be avoided by the invention of a form of judgment that orders the defendant to pay the sum due in the foreign currency or the equivalent, at the time of payment, in Canadian currency.[402]

(C) *The date of conversion* Given that a judgment for a debt or for damages for breach of contract must be rendered in Canadian dollars, whatever the contract may say as to the currency of account, it becomes vital to determine the date at which conversion from the currency of account into Canadian dollars is to occur. There are several possibilities. The appropriate date could be the date when the debt became due for payment, or the breach of contract occurred; it could be the date of the issuance of the proceedings that gave rise to a judgment; it could be the date of the judgment; or it could be the date of levying execution should that prove necessary. The chief contenders seem to be the date of the accrual of the debt or the occurrence of the breach, and the date of judgment.

The English rule was that the court should have regard to the exchange rate

---

397 *Miliangos v. George Frank (Textiles) Ltd.*, [1976] A.C. 443 (H.L.).

398 *The "Despina"*, [1979] A.C. 685 (H.L.); compare *President of India v. Lips Maritime Corp.*, above, note 396. See also *Fed. Commerce & Navigation Co. v. Tradax Export S.A.*, [1977] Q.B. 324 (C.A.); reversed [1978] A.C. 1 (H.L.); *Kraut v. Albany Fabrics Ltd.*, [1977] Q.B. 182; *Barclays Bank v. Levin Bros. (Bradford) Ltd.*, [1977] Q.B. 270.

399 R.S.C. 1985, c. C-52.

400 *Batavia Times Publishing Co. v. Davis* (1977), 82 D.L.R. (3d) 247 (Ont. H.C.); affirmed (1979), 102 D.L.R. (3d) 192n (Ont. C.A.); *Baumgartner v. Carsley Silk Co.* (1971), 23 D.L.R. (2d) 255 (Que. C.A.); *Gross v. Marvel Office Furniture Mfg. Ltd.* (1979), 93 D.L.R. (3d) 342 (Ont. H.C.); *Am-Pac Forest Products Inc. v. Phoenix Doors Ltd.* (1979), 14 B.C.L.R. 63 (B.C.S.C.); *Williams & Glyn's Bank Ltd. v. Belkin Packaging Ltd.* (1979), 108 D.L.R. (3d) 585 (B.C.S.C.); reversed on other grounds (1981), 123 D.L.R. (3d) 612 (B.C.C.A.); affirmed (1983), 147 D.L.R. (3d) 577 (S.C.C.).

401 Law Reform Commission of British Columbia, *Working Paper No. 33; Foreign Money Liabilities*, 1982, pp. 86-92.

402 *Ibid.*, pp. 92-93.

prevailing on the date of breach, or the date when the obligation to pay arose.[403] This "breach-date" rule was applied by Canadian courts.[404] However, as indicated by the Law Reform Commission of British Columbia,[405] although the Bills of Exchange Act[406] provides for conversion into Canadian currency according to the rate of exchange for sight drafts at the place of payment on the day a bill is payable, other statutes make the appropriate date the date of a judgment or order. Where a statute governs the situation, there is clearly no room for argument.[407] In other situations, however, the question arises whether the "breach date" rule is still applicable, and whether it should be applicable.

In *Miliangos v. George Frank (Textiles) Ltd.*,[408] the House of Lords also reversed the previous English law and held not only that payment could be made in a foreign currency, but that conversion into sterling could be ordered at the rate prevailing on the date of payment, that is, under the judgment of the court, rather than that which obtained at the date when payment was originally due. Since this change in the law is at odds with the prior law in Canada, it remains to be seen whether Canadian courts will adopt the newer approach or adhere to the older doctrine. The recent Canadian cases, to quote the British Columbia Law Reform Commission,[409] "seem to demonstrate considerable dissatisfaction among the judiciary with the date of breach rule and, in some cases, they have been willing to depart from it." However, the cases are confusing and contradictory. The attitude of the courts in Canada has ranged from a reluctant adherence to the date of breach rule, through the endorsement of a date of writ rule, to taking the date of judgment as appropriate for currency conversion.[410]

The older rule was subjected to much criticism,[411] and the result of the *Miliangos* case has been to accelerate and add fuel to the critical comment that the older rule has attracted. Although most commentators agree that the breach-date rule is outmoded and causes unnecessary hardship, they are not in accord as to the proper approach. To allow a plaintiff a choice of date might wreak undue hardship

---

403 See the cases cited above, in note 394.

404 See the cases cited above, in note 395. Contrast *Quartier v. Farah* (1921), 64 D.L.R. 37 (Ont. C.A.), which allowed the plaintiff's claim for an unpaid fee to be collected in Canadian dollars according to the value of French currency at the date of judgment, not at the date of breach.

405 *Loc. cit.*, above, note 401, at pp. 10-12.

406 R.S.C. 1985, c. B-4, s. 162.

407 *E.g.*, Court Order Enforcement Act, R.S.B.C. 1979, c. 75, s. 33; Carriage by Air Act, R.S.C. 1985, c. C-26, s. 2(6).

408 [1976] A.C. 443 (H.L.).

409 *Loc. cit.*, above, note 401, at p. 35.

410 Compare *Batavia Times Publishing Co. v. Davis*, above, note 400; *Am-Pac Forest Products Inc. v. Phoenix Doors Ltd.*, above, note 400; *Williams & Glyn's Bank Ltd. v. Belkin Packaging Ltd.*, above, note 400; *Airtemp Corp. v. Chrysler Airtemp Can. Ltd.* (1981), 121 D.L.R. (3d) 236 (Ont. Div. Ct.); *Min. of State Principality of Monaco v. Project Planning Assoc. (Int.) Ltd.* (1980), 32 O.R. (2d) 438 (Ont. Master); affirmed (1980), 32 O.R. (2d) at 440 (Ont. Div. Ct.); affirmed (1981), 32 O.R. (2d) 438n (Ont. C.A.); leave to appeal to S.C.C. refused (1981), 32 O.R. (2d) 438n (S.C.C.); *Clinton v. Ford* (1982), 137 D.L.R. (3d) 281 (Ont. C.A.); *Nat. Westminster Bank v. Burston* (1980), 28 O.R. (2d) 701 (Ont. Master).

411 Law Reform Commission of B.C., *loc. cit.*, above, note 401, at pp. 39-44.

on the defendant; to give the courts full and free discretion is to abandon principle; to adhere to the breach date approach as a basic rule but permit damages for delay in making the due payment, or give interest on the due sum by way of compensation for loss resulting from changes in currency values, have also been suggested as possible alternative solutions that might be consistent with general policy and principles.[412] The British Columbia Law Reform Commission pointed out that the breach-date rule was based on an inappropriate analogy with commodity contracts, led to unfair results, and was inconsistently applied (apart from the statutory exceptions).[413] That Commission, like the English Law Commission,[414] was in favour of the rejection of the older, stricter rule. Despite the forceful dissent by Lord Simon of Glaisdale in the *Miliangos* case,[415] where the attempt was made to prevent the reversal of the *Havana Railways* case,[416] the British Columbia Law Reform Commission sees merit in the ultimate result, which was to permit the court to depart from the breach-date rule where to achieve justice between the parties required such a departure.[417]

It would appear that other commentators have taken the same view,[418] although at least one suggests that Canadian courts should be cautious before departing from the breach-date rule of conversion, and still more cautious before adopting a rule of practice of actually ordering payment in a foreign currency.[419] This caution seems to be based on the idea that the plaintiff, the creditor, might reasonably have been able to protect himself from loss if he had taken steps to guard against changes in currency values. Moreover, to permit conversion at the later date is somewhat similar to ordering specific performance, which is hardly appropriate where what is involved is non-payment of a sum of money.

In truth, it is suggested, there is no completely satisfactory answer to the problem. The underlying philosophy of damages is compensation for what the plaintiff has lost. Giving the plaintiff the nominal value of his debt or damages

---

412 *Ibid.*, at pp. 62-79.

413 *Ibid.*, at pp. 36-39, 45-48.

414 *Private International Law: Foreign Money Liabilities* (1981), Working Paper No. 80: see Law Reform Commission of British Columbia, *loc. cit.*, above, note 401, at pp. 54-56.

415 [1976] A.C. 443 at 482-483, 487 *et seq.* (H.L.); on which see Libling, "Questions and Answers (?): Miliangos v. Frank (Textiles) Ltd." (1977), 93 L.Q.R. 212.

416 [1961] A.C. 1007 (H.L.).

417 *Loc. cit.*, above, note 401, at pp. 57-61, 79-80, 99-101.

418 Riordan, "Currency of Suit in Actions for Foreign Debts" (1978), 24 McGill L.J. 442; Waddams, *Law of Contracts*, 2nd ed. (1984), at p. 541 (note the change of the author in the 3rd ed. (1993), at p. 489); Castel, *Canadian Conflict of Laws*, Vol. 1 at p. 531, vol. 2 at 573; Note: "The Inflation Factor in Damages for Breach of Contract" (1980), 12 Ottawa L.R. 489 at 497.

This would seem to be consistent with the approach to the general question of the appropriate date at which assessment of damages should be made: above, pp. 753-755. It has considerable connection also with the problem of *inflation* as affecting the calculation or assessment of damages. This seems to be as yet an unresolved issue: see *Johnson v. Agnew*, [1980] A.C. 367 (H.L.) and compare *306793 Ont. Ltd. v. Rimes* (1979), 100 D.L.R. (3d) 360 (Ont. C.A.); *Tanu v. Ray* (1981), 20 R.P.R. 22 (B.C.S.C.).

419 Waddams, *Law of Damages*, 2nd ed. (1991), para. 7.300: compare Waddams, *Law of Contract*, 3rd ed. (1993), at p. 489.

is, in one sense, compensating him. Allowing the debtor to pay off the creditor in devalued currency results in no realistic compensation of the plaintiff. Conversely, the creditor may reap an unexpected windfall by an appreciation of the currency. Can the law ever ensure perfect justice in this respect? Can it guard against every conceivable possibility of this kind? The law certainly recognizes that physical events cannot always be taken into account in assessing liability, or the extent of liability. Why should the law have to concern itself with fiscal or economic events that might even be thought of as within the foresight of the parties and, therefore, something with respect to which *they* should plan?

(vi) *Non-compensatory damages*

In assessing the damages incurred by a plaintiff emphasis has been placed upon the need to compensate the plaintiff for economic, or physical, loss actually suffered.[420] The aim of the law is to replace the economic value of what has been lost by reason of the defendant's conduct. Hence, the importance of determining the date at which damages should be assessed, the possible relevance of the plaintiff's conduct, the materiality of extraneous payments to the plaintiff, and the problem associated with alterations in foreign currencies. However, two issues have recently been raised, by commentators rather than by the courts, as potentially affecting the way that damages for breach of contract are to be assessed.

The first is whether a contract-breaker should be entitled to keep the profits made by his breach of contract, where the victim of the breach can be shown to have incurred no, or no significant loss by reason of the breach. The second is whether the victim of a breach should be able to recover more than the economic value of what he has lost where he can show that, over and above such loss, he has incurred a loss stemming from the utility of the contract and its performance to him. If these two suggestions were to be given credence by the courts, and were accepted, the result would be that damages would be calculated in some instances in a very different way from the way in which, under the classical doctrines considered earlier, they are currently assessed.

The idea that a contract-breaker should be made to disgorge the profits or benefits he may have gained by his breach, is connected with the notion of "efficient breach", which has been propounded by writers who favour an economic analysis of law.[421] That notion asserts that there may be economic advantage in permitting,

---

420 Above, pp. 719, 735-736.
421 Sharpe, *Injunctions and Specific Performance*, 2nd ed. (1992), paras. 7.120-7.170; Posner, *Economic Analysis of Law*, 2nd ed. (1977), 89-90; Macneil, "Efficient Breach of Contract: Circles in the Sky" (1982), 68 Va. L.R. 947; compare Goetz & Scott, "Liquidated Damages: Some Notes on an Enforcement Model and a Theory of Efficient Breach" (1977), 77 Col. L.R. 554. See also Farnsworth, "Your Loss or My Gain? The Dilemma of the Disgorgement Principle in Breach of Contract" (1985), 94 Yale L.J. 1339; Friedmann, "Restitution of Benefits Obtained Through the Appropriation of Property or the Commission of a Wrong" (1980), 80 Col. L.R. 506; Friedman, "Restitution of Profits Gained by Party in Breach of Contract" (1988), 104 L.Q.R. 383; Birks, "Restitutionary Damages for Breach of Contract", [1987-1988] Lloyd's Maritime & Commer-

indeed encouraging parties to break their contracts, deliberately, if to do so would be to promote "wealth maximization". Indeed, the adoption of such an approach would lead to the recognition of a distinction that has never existed at common law, namely, the distinction between deliberate breaches of contract on the one hand and negligent, or completely innocent breaches on the other.[422] Protagonists of the "efficient breach" doctrine would, therefore, not be in favour of allowing the victim of the breach to obtain any share in the profits made by the deliberate contract breaker. Indeed they applaud the current state of the law, which is to deny any such right of recovery to the victim of a breach.[423] However, bearing in mind the gradual evolution of the modern doctrine of restitution, which has gained greater acceptance in Canada, and the United States, than in England,[424] it might be argued that the time is ripe for a further evolution of the common law in favour of extending the scope of damage claims in cases of breach of contract. If Canadian courts are prepared to invoke the idea of punitive damages in certain instances,[425] they might ultimately come to recognize the need to allow restitutionary remedies where a wilful breach of contract has occurred so as to enable the defendant to make a profit out of the injury inflicted on the plaintiff.[426] At the present time, however, the prevailing case law does not support either the "efficient breach" doctrine, or the notion of restitutionary recovery (unless there is some other relationship between the parties over and above that arising from contract, for example, where a fiduciary or quasi-fiduciary relationship exists).[427]

The second problem is also one on which there is no judicial authority. It raises the economists' notion of "consumer surplus", namely, "the excess utility or subjective value obtained from a good over and above the utility associated with its market price.[428] To some extent the law recognizes this notion when it grants a decree of specific performance. However, since such decrees are not always obtainable,[429] there are situations where all the victim of a breach of contract can

---

cial L.Q. 421; Maddaugh & McCamus, *Law of Restitution* (1990), pp. 432-438; Friedmann, "The Efficient Breach Fallacy" (1989), 18 J. Leg. St. 1.

422 Compare Fleming, "The Collateral Source Rule and Contract Damages" (1983), 70 Calif. L.R. 56 at 64-72; compare *Asamera Oil Corp. v. Sea Oil & General Corp.; Baud Corp., N.V. v. Brook* (1979), 89 D.L.R. (3d) 1 at 30 (S.C.C.) *per* Estey J.: ". . . the motives or unjust enrichment of the defendant on breach are generally of no concern in the assessment of contractual damages."

423 Jones, "The Recovery of Benefits Gained from a Breach of Contract" (1983), 99 L.Q.R. 443 at pp. 452-654.

424 Goff & Jones, *Law of Restitution*, 3rd ed. (1986), Chapters 1, 2; Fridman, *Restitution*, 2nd ed. (1992), Chapter 1. But the situation in England may be changing. For the use of restitution in contract cases, see Waddams, *Law of Damages*, 2nd ed. (1991), paras. 9.200-9.250.

425 Above, pp. 747-751.

426 This is the argument of Jones, *loc. cit.*, above, note 423.

427 Goff & Jones, *op. cit.*, above, note 424, Chapter 34; Fridman, *op. cit.*, above, note 424, pp. 367-384. See the judgment of the English Court of Appeal in *Surrey C.C. v. Bredero Homes Ltd.*, [1993] 3 All E.R. 705 (C.A.), indicating that damages compensate the plaintiff, and are not intended to transfer the defendant's gains to the plaintiff.

428 Harris, Ogus & Phillips, "Contract Remedies and the Consumer Surplus" (1979), 95 L.Q.R. 581 at p. 582.

429 Below, pp. 790-795.

obtain is a sum of money that may not truly represent the value to him of his loss.[430] The problem arose in a way in *Radford v. De Froberville*,[431] where the plaintiff recovered the cost of replacing the wall, although that was now greater than the original price, and not simply the diminution in value of his land by reason of the defendant's failure to erect the wall. The latter was minimal: the former was considerable. Although Oliver J. recognized the need to award the higher sum, it does not appear that his reasoning was founded upon any economic principles. Instead he purported to derive the solution from accepted principles of common-law damages, such as they were. The question is not without its complexity, since, to recognize this idea might in some situations permit a plaintiff artifically to inflate his damages or loss. The problem is to draw a reasonable line between properly compensating the plaintiff and unreasonably damnifying the defendant. In this respect it is noteworthy that it has been suggested[432] that "the judges already have an intuitive perception of the problem raised by the consumer surplus and . . . have attempted to find a solution to it (though not always with consistency) within the accepted principles of contract law." It may well be that, without any radical modification of the existing law as to contractual remedies, room may be found for the compensation of a plaintiff in this way.

Both these questions involve a more intimate connection between principles of law and economic ideas. They have come to the fore in recent times largely because of the emergence of the economic analysis of law. That form of legal analysis has not gone unchallenged. Although economic analysis may assist in the understanding of the way the law functions, and the purposes it is designed to achieve, there are many serious objections to an approach to law entirely founded on the notion of economic analysis with its emphasis on economic efficiency.

(f) Pre-assessment

(i) *Introduction*

Sometimes the parties will agree in advance, in the contract itself, what is to happen, by way of compensation of the injured party, in the event of breach, for example, by non-performance of the contract. Such attempts to dictate or regulate the remedy to an injured party give rise to several problems. As a matter of general principle it must be stated that, by and large, the parties are not entirely free to regulate their contractual situation in this manner. The courts have shown in various ways that they will still decide what remedies are available, and in what circumstances.

An agreement to fix the remedy available to an injured party may take one of three forms. In the first place, it could limit damages payable by the wrongdoer

---

430 Hence, perhaps, the decision in *Pepper v. Lecoure* (1990), 11 R.P.R. (2d) 235 (Ont. Dist. Ct.) that the date of the trial was the most suitable moment of time for calculating the plaintiff's loss when specific performance was no longer to be obtained.

431 [1978] 1 E.R. 33; above, p. 724, and see *Tito v. Waddell (No. 2)*, [1977] Ch. 106; *Dean v. Ainley*, [1987] 3 All E.R. 748 (C.A.).

432 Harris, Ogus & Phillips, *loc. cit.*, above note 428, at p. 609.

to a sum which cannot be regarded as being a true measure of the actual or foreseeable loss (and may even be a derisory figure). In such circumstances, what the parties are purporting to do is to limit the contract-breaker's liability. Second, the contract may purport to exclude altogether any possibility of an action for damages in the event of a breach. What is happening in such cases is that the contract-breaker is trying to stipulate for some alternative remedy, such as the replacement of faulty goods, or the making of repairs. Third, the contract may provide for the payment of a sum of money (or the forfeiture of something which has already been paid over, or given by way of a bond to secure performance) and the sum in question is expressed to be a pre-assessment of the injured party's loss. Indeed the contract may state that the amount in question is to be regarded as "liquidated damages", that is, a calculation in advance of the loss that is, would, or should be recoverable by the injured party on the application of the principles in *Hadley v. Baxendale*. Each of the possible situations or provisions in a contract presents its own peculiar difficulties.

Clauses which purport to limit the extent of a wrongdoer's liability raise problems already discussed.[433] In such situations, the normal right to sue for damages at large, under the principles of *Hadley v. Baxendale*, may be ousted. But this will not always be the case. Indeed, in some circumstances, the court may be able to defeat the operation of such a limitation clause, and proceed to grant the general remedy. Similarly where a party purports to deny an injured party the right to sue for damages, by including in the contract a term which provides for an alternative remedy, purporting to make that the *sole* recourse available to the innocent, injured party, sometimes this will not be effective.[434] Much depends upon the nature of the term in question and the way in which it is construed by the courts.[435]

Equally complex is the question whether an attempt to lay down in advance what is to be payable to, or to be retained by the innocent party, in the form of "liquidated damages", is to be successful.[436] At common law, a distinction was drawn, and has been developed, between truly valid, and enforceable agreements as to liquidated damages, and invalid provisions which merely seek to impose a *penalty* upon the guilty party.[437] In addition, equity has been prepared, in some

---

433 Above, pp. 571-600.

434 Above, pp. 702-704.

435 Compare *Edwards v. Pearson*, [1919] 3 W.W.R. 505 (Alta. C.A.); *Arnott v. Can. Fairbanks Morse Co.*, [1921] 1 W.W.R. 261 (Sask. K.B.).

436 A claim for liquidated damages is distinct from a claim to a sum owed as a debt. It is an action for damages. Therefore (a) it can be challenged as involving a penalty (below, p. 771); (b) the defendant can require that the plaintiff mitigate his loss (below, pp. 776-783): see *Bayliss Sign Ltd. v. Advantage Holdings Ltd.* (1986), 8 B.C.L.R. (2d) 230 at 235-240 (B.C. Co. Ct.).

437 For criticism of this distinction from the point of view of economic analysis, see Posner, "Some Uses and Abuses of Economics in Law" (1979), 46 U. Chi. L.R. 201 at 290. See also MacNeil, "Power of Contract and Agreed Remedies" (1962), 47 Cornell L.Q. 495; Note: "A Critique of the Penalty Limitation on Liquidated Damages" (1977), 50 S. Cal. L.R. 1055; Rea, "Efficiency Implications of Penalties and Liquidated Damages" (1984), 13 J. Leg. Stud. 147; Clarkson, Miller & Muris, "Liquidated Damages v. Penalties: Sense or Nonsense?," [1978] Wis. L.R. 351; Goetz

circumstances, to afford even a party guilty of a breach of contract some relief from an otherwise valid forfeiture or penalty. Statutory provisions can also provide a measure of relief from otherwise enforceable terms.

(ii) *Liquidated damages*

As long ago as 1829, Tindal C.J. said that the courts saw "nothing illegal or unreasonable in the parties, by their mutual agreement, settling the amount of damages, uncertain in their nature, at any sum upon which they may agree."[438] Such an agreement must be differentiated from one which settles upon an amount of money (which might even cover the damages suffered by the injured party but is not based thereon) and is intended to ensure the performance of the contract.[439] In other words, it is not meant to be a genuine pre-estimate of loss suffered, but is a threat, something held over the other party *in terrorem*.[440] It is a question of construction whether the clause in question creates a penalty or fixes liquidated damages.[441] It is the language of the contract as a whole, as Estey J. explained in one case,[442] that must determine the intent and purpose of the parties, and while the particular words used are important, the mere use of the words "liquidated damages" or "penalty" is not conclusive.[443] It is a question of law, in every case, whether the conventional sum is a penalty or liquidated damages, and it is decided on a consideration of the whole agreement.[444]

& Scott, "Some Notes on an Enforcement Model and a Theory of Efficient Breach" (1977), 77 Co. L.R. 554.

438 *Kemble v. Farren* (1829), 6 Bing. 141 at 148; compare the earlier case of *Astley v. Weldon* (1801), 2 Bos. & P. 346, 126 E.R. 1318.

439 So as to be forfeited upon the *slightest* breach of *any* promise of the contract: *Waugh v. Pioneer Logging Co.*, [1949] S.C.R. 299 at 300 (S.C.C.) *per* Kerwin J.; compare *Public Works Comm. v. Hills*, [1906] A.C. 368 (P.C.).

440 *Calgary v. Janese-Mitchell Const. Co.* (1919), 59 S.C.R. 101 at 105 (S.C.C.) *per* Duff J.

441 *Wallis v. Smith* (1882), 21 Ch. D. 243 at 249 (C.A.) *per* Fry L.J. For the difficulties created by this, see *Meunier v. Cloutier* (1984), 9 D.L.R. (4th) 486 (Ont. H.C.), a case of breach of a covenant not to compete given by the vendor of a hotel business. The sum agreed to be paid in advance as "liquidated damages" was held to be a penalty. No actual loss was proved. Therefore, the action was dismissed.

442 *Waugh v. Pioneer Logging Co.*, [1949] S.C.R. 299 at 311 (S.C.C.); compare Riddell J. in *St. Catharines Improvement Co. v. Rutherford* (1914), 19 D.L.R. 662 at 667 (Ont. C.A.).

443 Compare *Townsend v. Rumbold* (1909), 19 O.L.R. 433 (Ont. C.A.); *McManus v. Rothschild* (1911), 25 O.L.R. 138 (Ont. C.A.). Indeed, it has been held that even calling a sum liquidated damages in a contract will not necessarily suffice (even if it is construed as a penalty). It must still be a genuine pre-estimate of loss, or else the court will determine for itself which damages are recoverable: *Lozcal Holdings Ltd. v. Brassos Devs. Ltd.* (1980), 111 D.L.R. (3d) 598 (Alta. C.A.); *John Labatt Ltd. v. Financial Trustco Capital Ltd.* (1989), 96 A.R. 56 (Alta. Q.B.). Compare below, note 451 and text, for a different view. Compare also *Fern Invts. Ltd. v. Golden Nugget Restaurant (1987) Ltd.*, below, note 449.

444 *Reimer v. Rosen*, [1919] 1 W.W.R. 429 (Man. C.A.). But there may be a strong presumption that a fixed sum is a penalty, since the modern law of contract favours and emphasizes compensation: *Meunier v. Cloutier*, above, note 441, at 491 *per* Smith J., relying on *H.F. Clarke Ltd. v. Thermidaire Corp. Ltd.* (1976), 54 D.L.R. (3d) 385 (S.C.C.); varied (1976), 54 D.L.R. (3d) 399n (S.C.C.); below, p. 771.

In the famous case of *Dunlop Pneumatic Tyre Co. v. New Garage & Motor Co.*,[445] Lord Dunedin laid down some general rules for the guidance of the courts. These were culled from earlier decisions, and have been accepted by courts in Canada, which, indeed operated on those principles before 1915[446] and still do so.

(1) The sum in question will be a penalty if it is extravagant and unconscionable in amount in comparison with the greatest loss that could possibly follow from the breach.[447]

(2) If the obligation of the promisor is to pay a certain sum of money and it is agreed that if he fails to do so he will pay a larger sum, this larger sum is a penalty.

(3) If there is only one event on which the sum agreed is to be paid, the sum is liquidated damages.[448]

(4) If a single lump sum is made payable upon the occurrence of one or more or all of several events, some of which may occasion serious and others only trifling damage, there is a presumption, but no more, that the sum is a penalty.[449] But not necessarily if it is difficult to prove actual loss.[450]

It has sometimes been held that if the conventional sum is liquidated damages, the injured party can only sue for *that* amount, and not for damages at large.[451]

---

445 [1915] A.C. 79 at 86 *et seq.* (H.L.). The statement by Lord Dunedin is subjected to considerable criticism by Waddams, *Law of Damages*, 2nd ed. (1991), paras. 8.80-8.130.

446 See *St. Catharines Improvement Co. v. Rutherford*, above, note 442; *Can. Gen. Elec. Co. v. Can. Rubber Co. of Montreal* (1915), 52 S.C.R. 349 (S.C.C.).

447 *Clydebank Enrg. & Shipbuilding Co. v. Yzquierdo y Castenada (Don Jose Ramos)*, [1905] A.C. 6 (H.L.), Anglin J. in *Can. Gen. Elec. Co. v. Can. Rubber Co. of Montreal*, above, note 446, at 371. Compare *Sask. Co-op. Wheat Producers Ltd. v. Zurowski*, [1926] 2 W.W.R. 604 (Sask. C.A.). Hence, a mortgage commitment fee was not a penalty in *B.L.T. Holdings Ltd. v. Excelsior Life Ins. Co.*, [1986] 6 W.W.R. 534 (Alta. C.A.): it was not extravagant and unconscionable in comparison with the greatest loss that could have been suffered. But the fact that a court might not award a comparable amount by way of damages might make the sum a penalty: see Waddams, *Law of Damages*, above, note 445, at para. 8.300 and cases there cited. Even if an amount is a penalty it may still be a fair estimate of the damage suffered by the plaintiff: *Calgary (City) v. Nor. Const. Co.*, [1986] 2 W.W.R. 426 (Alta. C.A.); affirmed [1987] 2 S.C.R. 757 (S.C.C.).

448 *Law v. Redditch Local Bd.*, [1892] 1 Q.B. 127 (C.A.); *Reimer v. Rosen*, above, note 444, at 6 *per* Perdue C.J.M., and at 14 *per* Cannon J.A.; compare *Ellis v. Fruhtman* (1912), 3 W.W.R. 558 (Alta. C.A.).

449 *Lord Elphinstone v. Monkland Iron & Coal Co.* (1886), 11 App. Cas. 332 (H.L.); *St. Catharines Improvement Co. v. Rutherford*, above, note 442, at 667 *per* Riddell J.; *Reimer v. Rosen*, above, note 444. See the application of this in *Fern Invts. Ltd. v. Golden Nugget Restaurant (1987) Ltd.* (1992), 6 Alta. L.R. (3d) 86 (Alta. Q.B.), sum of $100,000 payable on *any*, even a trivial, default was a penalty, although described as liquidated damages.

450 *Sask. Co-op. Wheat Producers Ltd. v. Zurowski*, above, note 447. But even then *it might* be a penalty: see Laskin C.J.C. in *Clarke Ltd. v. Thermidaire Corp.* (1976), 54 D.L.R. (3d) 385 at 398 (S.C.C.); varied (1976), 54 D.L.R. (3d) 399n (S.C.C.).

451 See, *e.g.*, *Elsley v. J.G. Collins Ins. Agencies Ltd.* (1978), 83 D.L.R. (3d) 1 (S.C.C.); *Gisvold v. Hill* (1963), 37 D.L.R. (2d) 606 (B.C.S.C.); *Seeley v. Condroy* (1977), 19 N.B.R. (2d) 1 (N.B.C.A.). Hence the *Hadley v. Baxendale* principles do *not* apply: *Stewart (Robert) & Sons Ltd. v. Carapanyoti Ltd.*, [1962] 1 All E.R. 418; *Dorge v. Dumesnil* (1973), 39 D.L.R. (3d) 750 (Man. Q.B.). Nor can a party claim forfeiture of a stipulated sum *and* damages at large: *Sanitary Refuse Collectors Inc. v. Ottawa*, [1972] 1 O.R. 296 (Ont. H.C.); nor the stipulated sum *and* an injunction (except in

Nor can he argue that the sum is really a penalty, so as to be able to evade that limitation of the other party's liability, and sue for damages in accordance with the general principles. Thus in one case, where the liquidated damages were fixed at a dollar, the plaintiff attempted to argue that this was a penalty, so as to obtain a greater sum. He was unsuccessful.[452] Nor can it be argued that a sum is liquidated damages in respect of some breaches of a contract, but a penalty in respect of others. It is one or the other; the decision must be made.[453]

On the principles which have been stated above, it has been held that the following were liquidated damages, and not a penalty, so as to limit the plaintiff to the amount stipulated in the contract, and therefore fix the damages in advance.[454] 25 dollars to be deducted from a contract price for every day's delay in delivering machinery to be manufactured by the defendant for the plaintiff;[455] a specified sum for delay in removing certain articles from the plaintiff's land;[456] the rent for part of premises, not within a lease, which would be waived if the lease were complied with, but would be exigible if the lease were not;[457] a deposit of $5,000

---

respect of an injunction to restrain *future* breaches of the contract); compare *Gen. Accident Assur. Corp. v. Noel*, [1902] 1 K.B. 377 with *Clarke Ltd. v. Thermidaire Corp.*, above, note 450, at 396 *per* Laskin C.J.C.

    This view is criticized by Waddams, *Law of Damages*, above, note 445, at paras. 8.220-8.250; see *Lozcal Holdings Ltd. v. Brassos Devs. Ltd.*, above, note 443; *E. & B. Mortgages Ltd. v. Skrivanos* (1980), 118 D.L.R. (3d) 139 (B.C.S.C.). Compare above, note 443.

452 *Gisvold v. Hill* (1963), 41 W.W.R. 549 (B.C.S.C.).

453 *R. v. London Guar. & Accident Co.*, [1920] 2 W.W.R. 83 (Ex. Ct.).

454 See also *Reimer v. Rosen*, above, note 444, which was not followed by Galt J. in *St. Denis v. Western Prods. Ltd.*, [1923] 3 W.W.R. 858 (Man. K.B.); affirmed [1924] 1 W.W.R. 174 (Man. C.A.). For other examples, see *Nor. Trust Co. v. Rasmussen*, [1924] 2 W.W.R. 1015 (Alta. S.C.); *Pitman v. Pletzke*, [1949] 1 W.W.R. 808 (Sask. C.A.); *Giese Bros. v. Bell* (1915), 9 W.W.R. 826 (Alta. C.A.); *Pine Wyn Invts. Ltd. v. Banhap Invts. Ltd.* (1974), 3 O.R. (2d) 566 (Ont. H.C.); affirmed (1975), 8 O.R. (2d) 647n (Ont. C.A.); *Direct Leasing Ltd. v. Chu* (1976), 71 D.L.R. (3d) 303 (B.C.S.C.) (entire rental under an equipment lease payable in acceleration in the event of default by the lessee; liquidated damages, not a penalty, because in such a situation the equipment was of no value to the lessor; his only recourse was to obtain full payment of the agreed rental); compare *Francis Fuels Ltd. v. Taggart* (1976), 72 D.L.R. (3d) 22 (Ont. Small Claims Ct.); *Emerald Christmas Tree Co. v. Revcon Holdings Ltd.* (1978), 89 D.L.R. (3d) 485 (B.C. Chambers); reversed (1979), 8 R.P.R. 143 (*sub nom. Emerald Christmas Tree Co. v. Boel & Sons Enterprises Ltd*) (B.C.C.A.); *O'Leary v. G.M. Gaudet Enterprises Ltd.* (1977), 27 N.S.R. (2d) 95 (N.S.T.D.). *Michael Ede Leasing Ltd. v. Kleysen Transport Ltd.* (1986), 42 Man. R. (2d) 52 (Man. C.A.); *Sign-O-Lite Signs Ltd. v. Windsor Plywood (Kelowna) Ltd.* (1988), 61 Alta. L.R. (2d) 21 (Alta. Q.B.); *Alwest Neon Signs Ltd. v. Henze* (1989), 105 A.R. 343 (Alta. C.A.) (in all three of which cases the outstanding rent for the whole period of a chattel lease was recoverable in acceleration on default by the lessee). Contrast a case where this was held a penalty: *Caravan Trailer Rental Co. v. Westward Park Ltd.* (1990), 65 Man. R. (2d) 281 (Man. Q.B.).

    A similar difference in different situations is found in Australia: see *O'Dea v. Allstates Leasing System (W.A.) Pty Ltd.* (1983), 152 C.L.R. 359; *Esanda Finance Corp. v. Plessnig* (1989), 166 C.L.R. 131 (liquidated damages); *AMEV-UDC Finance Ltd. v. Austin* (1986), 68 A.L.R. 185 (penalty).

455 *Can. Gen. Elec. Co. v. Can. Rubber Co. of Montreal*, above, note 446.

456 *St. Catharine's Improvement Co. v. Rutherford*, above, note 446.

457 *Fried v. Georges*, [1930] 3 D.L.R. 664 (N.S.C.A.).

on a purchase of property for $59,500;[458] and $50 a day for delay in performing a building contract.[459]

In *H.F. Clarke Ltd. v. Thermidaire Corporation* there was a difference of opinion between the Ontario Court of Appeal and the Supreme Court of Canada on the application of these principles to the facts of the case. A contract in restraint of trade provided for the payment of a sum of money, calculated by reference to the gross trading profit obtained by the defendants through the sale of a certain product which they were prevented from selling under the contract, by way of competition with the plaintiffs. The question was whether this sum was liquidated damages or penalty. In the Court of Appeal,[460] Brooke J.A. considered that the amount of money in issue, though large, that is, in excess of $200,000, was nonetheless liquidated damages. In the circumstances of this case it was difficult to assess the actual loss suffered by the plaintiffs, and the amount arrived at was not unreasonable or extravagant bearing in mind the situation and the kind of harm that could be inflicted on the plaintiffs by the breach of contract. But in the Supreme Court of Canada a different view was taken; it was held that to stipulate for the forfeiture of the gross trading profit made by the defendant, albeit in breach of the contract with the plaintiffs, was in the nature of a penalty.[461]

(iii) *Penalties*[462]

It has already been suggested that a penalty is a sum that is fixed in advance as being subject to forfeiture or payment in the event of non-performance of a contract, or some kind of misperformance.[463] A distinction has been drawn between

---

458 *Hughes v. Lukuvka* (1970), 14 D.L.R. (3d) 110 (B.C.C.A.); compare *John Labatt Ltd. v. Financial Trustco Capital Ltd.*, above, note 443; contrast *Re Provinces & Central Properties Ltd. and Halifax* (1969), 5 D.L.R. (3d) 28 (N.S.C.A.). Contrast also *Frank H. Davis of Georgia Inc. v. Rayonier Can. (B.C.) Ltd.* (1968), 65 W.W.R. 251 (B.C.S.C.).

459 *Westholme Lbr. Co. v. St. James Ltd.* (1915), 8 W.W.R. 122 (B.C.C.A.); compare *Clydebank Enrg. & Shipbuilding Co. v. Yzquierdo y Castenada (Don Jose Ramos)*, [1905] A.C. 6 (H.L.). See also *Upper Lakes Shipping Ltd. v. St. John Shipbuilding & Dry Dock Co.* (1988), 86 N.R. 40 (Fed. C.A.) ($1,000 a day for up to 15 days to a maximum of $200,000 for delay in completing the building of a ship).

460 (1973), 9 C.P.R. (2d) 203 at 214-215 (Ont. C.A.); compare on slightly different facts, Plaxton J. in *R. v. Freeman*, [1942] 4 D.L.R. 182 at 192 (Ont. H.C.).

461 (1976), 54 D.L.R. (3d) 385 (S.C.C.); varied, [1976] 1 S.C.R. 340n (S.C.C.).

462 The Ontario Law Reform Commission, *Report on Amendment of the Law of Contract* (1987), pp. 139-147, recommended that such provisions in a contract should only be struck down as penal if unconscionable, in accordance with the Commission's recommendations relating to unconscionability: on which see *ibid.*, Chapter 6, above, pp. 325-336.

For the history of the development of the law relating to penalties see *AMEV-UDC Finance Ltd. v. Austin*, above note 454, at 196-199 *per* Mason and Wilson JJ., and at 207-208 *per* Deane J.

463 Some contractual provisions achieve the same result as penalty clauses and are treated the same way, though phrased differently: see *Deber Invts. Ltd. v. Roblea Estates Ltd.* (1976), 21 N.S.R. (2d) 158 (N.S.T.D.), forfeiture of sum pre-paid by purchaser of land, treated as a penalty, therefore recoverable; *Unilease Inc. v. York Steel Const. Ltd.* (1978), 83 D.L.R. (3d) 275 (Ont. C.A.), acceleration clause in equipment lease held to involve penalty; compare *Int. Harvester Credit Corp. v. Dolphin* (1978), 88 D.L.R. (3d) 326 (Alta. T.D.); *Caravan Trailer Rental Co. v. Westward Park*

payment of a sum in the event of non-performance of a contractual obligation (when the sum may amount to a penalty) and payment of a sum of money on the happening of an event. In the latter situation no question of a penalty arises, and the courts will not grant relief.[464] The penalty area has been limited to a "narrow field".[465] The doctrine is not designed to relieve a party from the consequences of what might in the event prove to be an onerous or even commercially imprudent bargain.[466] However, it is clear that the doctrine of penalties applies whether a payment is enforced or a payment is withheld by reason of the other party's non-performance.[467]

In *Waugh v. Pioneer Logging Co.*[468] an agreement provided that a special fund would be set up by the purchaser out of the sale price of the timber which was the subject-matter of the contract being augmented as the logging progressed. This was not to exceed $14,000. Its purpose was "to guarantee the due and proper logging by the plaintiff." That sum was to be forfeited in the event of a default by the plaintiff in carrying out the work contracted for between the parties. It was held that this was penalty, not liquidated damages. Again in *Frank H. Davis of Georgia Incorporated v. Rayonier Canada (British Columbia) Ltd.*,[469] a clause which provided for the forfeiture of $10,000 which was deposited towards the purchase of some machinery at a cost of $50,000, was held to be a clause creating a penalty, not one laying down the liquidated damages that could be claimed in the event of default. In *Zielinski v. Saskatchewan Beef Stabilization Board*,[470] an employment contract provided that if the employee were dismissed he would be entitled to 2.5 times his final average salary for a year. When the employee sued for wrongful dismissal this was held to be a penalty, not liquidated damages. Hence, the sum claimed by the employee under this provision was not recoverable. In *Canadian Acceptance Corporation v. Regent Park Butcher Shop Ltd.*,[471] the contract in question was a lease of chattels. In the event of a failure to pay the rent, the lessee was

---

Ltd., above, note 454 (where the contract defined what was called the "termination value" of the leased chattel, *Reit-Syd Equipment Ltd. v. Trush* (1989), 60 Man. R. (2d) 153 (Man. Q.B.)). See also *Graham v. Wagman* (1978), 89 D.L.R. (3d) 282 (Ont. C.A.) reduction in rent for parking space treated as involving a penalty. For a novel mode of achieving the same result, to which the same approach was applied, see *The "Mihalios Xilas"*, [1979] 1 All E.R. 657 (C.A.); reversed on other grounds, [1979] 2 All E.R. 1044 (H.L.). A claim which required a forced resale of shares at a price which left the purchaser damnified in the event of default on payment of any instalment of the purchase price was also a penalty clause in *Jobson v. Jobson*, [1989] 1 All E.R. 621 (C.A.).

464 *Export Credits Guar. Dept. v. Universal Oil Products Co.*, [1983] 2 All E.R. 205 at 215 (H.L.); *Re Apex Supply Co.*, [1942] Ch. 108; *Alder v. Moore*, [1961] 2 Q.B. 57 (C.A.).

465 *Export Credits Guar. Dept. v. Universal Oil Products Co.*, [1983] 2 All E.R. 205 at 219 (H.L.).

466 *Ibid.*, at 224.

467 *Gilbert-Ash (Northern) Ltd. v. Modern Enrg. (Bristol) Ltd.*, [1974] A.C. 689 (H.L.).

468 [1949] S.C.R. 299 (S.C.C.).

469 Above, note 458.

470 [1992] 5 W.W.R. 324 (Sask. Q.B.).

471 (1969), 67 W.W.R. 297 (Man. C.A.); and see *Neonoex Int. Ltd. v. Wassill*, [1974] 1 W.W.R. 587 (Sask. Dist. Ct.). Compare *Bridge v. Campbell Discount Co.*, [1962] A.C. 600 (H.L.). Contrast *Robophone Facilities v. Blank*, [1966] 1 W.L.R. 1428 (C.A.). See the discussion of these cases in *Bayliss Sign Ltd. v. Advantage Holdings Ltd.* (1986), 8 B.C.L.R. (2d) 230 (B.C. Co. Ct.).

liable for the instalments of rent in arrears, and for the accelerated payment of *future* rent. This latter part of the agreement was the creation of a penalty, not an attempt to fix the liquidated damages in advance. In coming to this conclusion the Manitoba Court of Appeal followed earlier English authority. But Dickson J.A. took pains to state that not all "acceleration clauses" necessarily involved the creation of a penalty.[472] In some mortgage or sales situations, such a clause would be valid.[473] The test would seem to be whether the sum to be paid bears a reasonable relation to the injured party's loss or is out of proportion to such loss.[474] Moreover, if the plaintiff's real loss can be established a pre-estimated sum might be a penalty.[475]

The onus is on the party seeking to invalidate a clause, to show that it inflicts a penalty, rather than determines the damages payable by the guilty party.[476] But even where a clause does inflict a penalty, it will not always be unenforceable, as the Supreme Court of Canada made clear in *Dimensional Investments Ltd. v. R.*,[477] for example, where it is not unconscionable or where it is protected by statute.

Where a penalty clause is bad, the innocent party is relegated to his right to claim that lesser amount of damages to which he would have been entitled at common law for the breach actually committed if there had been no penalty clause in the contract.[478] But the question remains unanswered whether such clauses are always totally bad, that is, void, in the same way as covenants in unreasonable restraint of trade. The judgment of Diplock L.J. in *Robophone Facilities Ltd. v. Blank*[479] leaves this matter unsolved, and suggests that courts should not be "astute

---

472 (1969), 3 D.L.R. (3d) 304 at 310 (Man. C.A.).

473 Compare *Wallingford v. Mutual Society* (1880), 5 App. Cas. 685 (H.L.). Compare *Direct Leasing Ltd. v. Chu*, above, note 454, with *Unilease Inc. v. York Steel Const. Ltd.*, above, note 463. See also other cases referred to in this connection in notes 454 and 463.

474 Compare *Prince Albert Credit Union Ltd. v. Johnson* (1982), 131 D.L.R. (3d) 710 (Sask. Q.B.). In *B.L.T. Holdings Ltd. v. Excelsior Life Ins. Co.* (1984), 52 A.R. 1 (Alta. Q.B.), a "standby" fee was held to be a penalty, not liquidated damages; reversed in part (1986), 72 A.R. 217 (Alta. C.A.).

475 *Car Leasing (Alta.) Ltd. v. Swinhoe* (1978), 15 A.R. 22 (Alta. Dist. Ct.). But that does not mean that a pre-estimate of damages will be a penalty if it exceeds what a court would award: *H.F. Clarke Ltd. v. Thermidaire Ltd.* (1976), 54 D.L.R. (3d) 385 (S.C.C.); varied (1976), 54 D.L.R. (3d) 399n (S.C.C.); Waddams, *Law of Damages*, 2nd ed. (1991), paras. 8.280-8.290.

476 *Robophone Facilities Ltd. v. Blank*, above, note 471, at 142 *per* Diplock L.J.

477 [1968] S.C.R. 93 (S.C.C.). But see *Jobson v. Jobson*, above, note 463, at 627 *per* Dillon L.J., at 632 *per* Nicholls L.J., and at 638 *per* Kerr L.J. Whether such clauses are void or only unenforceable was left open by Deane J. in *AMEV-UDC Finance Ltd. v. Austin*, above, note 454, at 208-209.

478 *Charterhouse Leasing Corp. v. Sanmac Holdings Ltd.* (1966), 57 W.W.R. 615 (Alta. S.C.); *Caravan Trailer Rental Co. v. Westward Park Ltd.*, above, note 454; *Reit-Syd Equipment Ltd. v. Trush*, above, note 463. But if the penalty is valid and enforceable it has been suggested that the plaintiff can recover a larger sum if his damage is greater than the penalty: *Lozcal Holdings Ltd. v. Brassos Devs. Ltd.*, above, note 443; *E. & B. Mtges. Ltd. v. Skrivanos*, above, note 451. Waddams, *op. cit.*, above, note 475, paras. 8.220-8.250.

479 Above, note 476, at 142-143; compare *Cellulose Acetate Silk Co. v. Widnes Foundry (1925) Ltd.*, [1933] A.C. 20 (H.L.). See also *Elsley v. J.G. Collins Ins. Agencies Ltd.* (1978), 83 D.L.R. (3d) 1 at 15 (S.C.C.) on the need to relieve against oppression as the only justification for interference with freedom of contract. See also the comments of Deane J. in *AMEV-UDC Finance Ltd. v. Austin*, above, note 454.

to descry 'a penalty clause' in every provision of a contract which stipulates a sum to be payable by one party to the other in the event of a breach by the former." This should not be done since it might deter parties from the very reasonable activity of determining damages in advance, which is useful because: (1) there are cases when damages are difficult to assess; (2) it saves expensive litigation; and (3) it enables parties to know what their liabilities are going to be in advance. What is more, as the judgment makes clear, a sum which looks extravagant under the first part of the *Hadley v. Baxendale* principle, the objective test, may turn out to be quite acceptable if the case is one to which the second part, the subjective test, properly applies.[480] Such enhanced loss may indicate that the stipulated sum, though seemingly large, is a genuine pre-estimate of the damages. In such circumstances, there should be greater scope for such clauses. As the Supreme Court of Canada made clear in *Elsley v. J.G. Collins Insurance Agencies Ltd.*,[481] a penalty clause should only be struck down if it is oppressive, not simply because it might be termed a penalty.

(iv) *Relief against forfeiture*[482]

In some jurisdictions, there may exist some statutory provisions under which a court can grant relief against forfeiture of deposits or other penalties, either generally or in relation to specific kinds of contracts, for example, mortgages.[483] Apart from such specialized, statutory relief, there are indications in the decisions that, under some, very special circumstances, where a forfeiture is not otherwise open to attack as being a penalty, in accordance with the general principles already discussed, a court of equity may grant relief to the party whose money is subjected to the forfeiture.[484]

It has already been noted that, under equitable principles, a court may grant relief from a provision in a contract purporting to make time of the essence. In other words a party may obtain relief against forfeiture, even though the due date for performance of the contract has passed.[485] What if the core of the defendant's

---

480 Above, pp. 729-731. See *Taylor v. Gill*, [1991] 3 W.W.R. 727 at 740-741 (Alta. Q.B.).

481 (1978), 83 D.L.R. (3d) 1 at 15-16 (S.C.C.). Hence the argument that the real issue in such instances is that of "unconscionability": Waddams, *Law of Damages*, 2nd ed. (1991), paras. 8.130-8.160, 8.200. Compare the recommendation of the Ontario Law Reform Commission, above, note 462.

482 The Ontario Law Reform Commission, *loc. cit.*, above, note 462, at pp. 147-153 recommends (a) there should be no distinction between penalty clauses and relief from forfeiture clauses; (b) relief from forfeiture should be based on the same test of unconscionability that is suggested for penalty clauses: above, note 462. On the common origin of the principles applying to both types of clause, see *Jobson v. Jobson*, above, note 463, at 631 *per* Nicholls L.J. For differences that have developed, see *ibid.*, at 633-634.

483 See, *e.g.*, Law and Equity Act, R.S.B.C. 1979, c. 224, s. 4 (on which see *Emerald Christmas Tree Inc. v. Revcon Holdings Ltd.* (1978), 89 D.L.R. (3d) 485 (B.C. Chambers); reversed (1979), 8 R.P.R. 143 (*sub nom. Emerald Christmas Tree Co. v. Boel & Sons Enterprises Ltd.*) (B.C.C.A.)); Courts of Justice Act, R.S.O. 1990, c. C.43, s. 98; Judicature Act, R.S.A. 1980, c. J-1, s. 17.

484 *Jobson v. Jobson*, [1989] 1 All E.R. 621 at 633-634 (C.A.) *per* Nicholls L.J.

485 Above, pp. 527-529. Compare *Legione v. Hateley* (1983), 152 C.L.R. 406 (Aus.); Nicholson, "Breach of an Essential Time Stipulation, and Relief Against Forfeiture" (1983), 57 Aust. L.J. 632.

argument is not the question of time but of amount, that is, that the sum in question is large and should not therefore be forfeited? If he fails to establish, at common law, that the magnitude of the amount renders the forfeiture invalid, as involving a penalty, he may still have recourse to another, equitable doctrine. In *Stockloser v. Johnson*[486] while Romer L.J. thought this jurisdiction could only be invoked when there was fraud, sharp practice or other unconscionable conduct, such as to justify the intervention of equity (which courts in Canada has been willing to act upon in other contexts, for example, where the contract is unconscionable and merits rescission), Somervell and Denning L.JJ. considered that the jurisdiction was broader-based, and could be invoked wherever it was unreasonable to impose such a liability upon the defendant, for example, where the sum forfeited was wholly disproportionate to the damage suffered.[487] This appears to resemble the common-law doctrine on penalties, until it is recalled that not always will such imbalance render the stipulated amount a penalty at common law.

It is clear that courts will not lightly or easily rewrite a contract or remake a bargain between the parties.[488] On the other hand, there are indications, certainly in Canada, that sometimes relief will be granted from an unconscionable forfeiture.[489]

---

486 [1954] 1 Q.B. 476 (C.A.).

487 Compare *Shiloh Spinners Ltd. v. Harding*, [1973] A.C. 691 (H.L.). But such relief from forfeiture may not be applicable in cases not involving the transfer of proprietary or possessory rights: see *Scandinavian Trading Tanker Co. v. Flota Petrolera Ecuatoriana*, [1983] 2 A.C. 694 (H.L.); *Sport Int. Bussum BV v. Inter-Footwear Ltd.*, [1984] 2 All E.R. 321 (H.L.). See also *BICC plc v. Burndy Corp.*, [1985] 1 All E.R. 417 (C.A.).

In *Jobson v. Jobson*, above, note 484, the circumstances were such that the Court of Appeal offered the plaintiff seeking to enforce what was a penalty clause against the defendant, two alternative forms of relief which had the effect of not subjecting the defendant to an unconscionable result. Kerr L.J., *ibid.*, at 640, would have created a further alternative since the others did not offer sufficient justice to the plaintiff.

488 Compare *Bridge v. Campbell Discount Co.*, above, note 471; *Galbraith v. Mitchenall*, [1965] 2 Q.B. 473. Compare what is said by Ritchie J. in *Dimensional Invts. Ltd. v. R.*, above, note 477, at 100-101.

489 *Popyk v. Western Savings & Loan Assn.* (1969), 3 D.L.R. (3d) 511 (Alta. C.A.); *Thorsten & Tate v. Gill* (1980), 19 B.C.L.R. 389 (B.C.S.C.); *World Land Ltd. v. Daon Dev. Corp.* (1982), 20 Alta. L.R. (2d) 33 (Alta. Q.B.); *MacDonald v. Paterson Park Ltd.* (1983), 42 A.R. 272 (Alta. Q.B.); *Coronado Devs. Ltd. v. W.E.D. Devs. Ltd.* (1982), 42 A.R. 283 (Alta. Q.B.). Relief will not be granted where the party seeking relief was the cause of the events leading to forfeiture: *Deber Invts. Ltd. v. Roblea Estates Ltd.* (1976), 21 N.S.R. (2d) 158 (N.S.T.D.); *O'Leary v. G.M. Gaudet Enterprises Ltd.* (1977), 27 N.S.R. (2d) 95 (N.S.T.D.). Such would be the case where the party seeking relief from forfeiture of a deposit had wrongfully repudiated the contract: *Greschuk v. Bizon; Bizon v. Greschuk*, [1977] 2 W.W.R. 262 (Alta. C.A.); *Can. Union College v. Camsteel Indust. Ltd.* (1979), 9 Alta. L.R. (2d) 167 (Alta. Dist. Ct.); *Mitchell v. Agrai-Dairy Mart Ltd.* (1984), 54 A.R. 368 (Alta. Q.B.). Compare above, pp. 612-618, on the effects of repudiation.

4. Mitigation of damages[490]

(a) The duty to mitigate[491]

The innocent injured plaintiff, who claims damages for breach of the contract, is not entitled to sit back, after the breach, and place all the blame on the defendant for what happens thereafter, even if it comes within the *Hadley v. Baxendale* principles. The plaintiff is under an obligation which has both positive and negative aspects. The fundamental principle of compensation for pecuniary loss flowing from the breach of contract "is qualified by a second, which imposes on the plaintiff the duty of taking all reasonable steps to mitigate the loss consequent on the breach, and debars him from claiming in respect of any part of the damage which is due to his neglect to take such steps."[492] In *Yetton v. Eastwoods Froy Ltd.*,[493] it was said

> [t]he basic principle of damages is restitutio in integrum: the plaintiff should have what he has lost through the defendant's fault; but of course, if a plaintiff in fact, in the case of a contract of service, earns something elsewhere through being at liberty to do so, then he has lost that much less as the consequence of the default. Moreover if he can minimize his loss by a reasonable course of conduct, he should do so, though the onus is on the defaulting defendant to show that it could be, or could have been, done and is not being, and has not been done.

Laskin C.J.C., in *Red Deer College v. Michaels*[494] posed the issue thus: "has the plaintiff taken reasonable steps to avoid their [that is, his losses'] unconscionable accumulation."

Thus the plaintiff may not be able to claim from the defendant all the loss which he alleges flows, naturally and probably, from the latter's breach of contract. The onus

---

490 Waddams, *Law of Damages*, above, note 481, Chapter 15; Bridge, "Mitigation of Damages in Contract and the Meaning of Avoidable Loss" (1989), 105 L.Q.R. 398. This section of the Chapter, as it appeared in the first edition, was referred to in *Ermineskin Place Ltd. v. Collins* (1989), 99 A.R. 161 at 164 (Alta. Master).

491 It has been suggested that the term "duty" is inappropriate, because the plaintiff's failure to mitigate does not give the defendant an affirmative right of action; it may reduce the damages for which the defendant is liable; *Darbishire v. Warran*, [1963] 1 W.L.R. 1067 at 1075 *per* Pearson L.J.; *Janiak v. Ippolito* (1985), 16 D.L.R. (4th) 1 at 17 (S.C.C.); Goetz & Scott, "The Mitigation Principle: Toward a General Theory of Contractual Obligation" (1983), 69 Va. L.R. 967. Note that the duty to mitigate does not apply where the plaintiff's claim is for a debt owed by the defendant: *Ermineskin Place Ltd. v. Collins*, above, note 490, at 165.

492 *Br. Westinghouse Electric & Manufacturing Co. v. Underground Elec. Rys., Co.*, [1912] A.C. 673 at 689 (H.L.) *per* Viscount Haldane L.C. The matter is discussed in *Cockburn v. Trusts & Guar. Co.* (1916), 38 O.L.R. 396 (Ont. C.A.); affirmed (1917), 52 S.C.R. 264 (S.C.C.). See also *Karas v. Rowlett*, [1944] S.C.R. 1 at 8 (S.C.C.) *per* Rand J. Compare *Cemco Electrical Mfg. Co. v. Van Snellenberg*, [1947] S.C.R. 121 (S.C.C.); *Can. Ice Machine Co. v. Sinclair*, [1955] S.C.R. 777 (S.C.C.).
    This paragraph, down to "take such steps", was quoted by Ryan J.A. in *Bank of Montreal v. MacInnis* (1988), 47 R.P.R. 188 at 193 (N.B.C.A.); leave to appeal to S.C.C. refused (1988), 47 R.P.R. 188n (S.C.C.).

493 [1966] 3 All E.R. 353 at 362 *per* Blain J.

494 (1975), 57 D.L.R. (3d) 386 at 390 (S.C.C.).

of proving failure to mitigate is on the defendant.[495] While the onus on the defendant of establishing a failure to mitigate, in accordance with the duty, is a heavy one, if it is discharged, then the defendant is relieved of liability for such damages as can be traced to the plaintiff's own inactivity, or his conduct which exacerbates, rather than mitigates his loss.[496] Moreover it has been held that the plaintiff is not relieved of this duty to mitigate by any impecuniosity from which he suffers,[497] unless, possibly it was reasonably foreseeable by the defendant that the plaintiff would have insufficient funds to mitigate his loss following the breach of contract[498] (which seems to raise the issue of causation[499]). However, the plaintiff will be relieved of the duty to mitigate if it is unreasonable to expect him to do anything, or if what the defendant alleges he ought to have done was totally unreasonable.

The duty to mitigate applies to all kinds of contracts.[500] Thus in *Philipzyk*

---

495 *Shulist v. Hunt* (1987), 51 Alta. L.R. (2d) 69 (Alta. Q.B.); *Metal Fabrication (Vic.) Pty. Ltd. v. Kelcey*, [1986] V.R. 507 (Aust.); compare the situation in tort actions, as indicated by *Janiak v. Ippolito*, above, note 491, disapproving *Selvanayagam v. Univ. of West Indies*, [1983] 1 All E.R. 824. For an instance of failure by the defendant to prove that the plaintiff had not mitigated his loss, see *Yamaha Can. Music. Ltd./Yamaha Can. Musique Ltée v. MacDonald & Oryall Ltd.* (1990), 46 B.C.L.R. (2d) 363 (B.C.C.A.).

496 And if the plaintiff had made a profit through the breach, such profit *may* reduce the defendant's liability: *Erie County Natural Gas & Fuel Co. v. Carrol*, [1911] A.C. 105 (P.C.); *Cockburn v. Trusts & Guarantee Co.* (1917), 55 S.C.R. 264 (S.C.C.); contrast *Apeco of Can. Ltd. v. Windmill Place* (1978), 82 D.L.R. (3d) 1 (S.C.C.); *Royal Bank v. Clark* (1978), 88 D.L.R. (3d) 76 (N.B.C.A.); affirmed (1980), 105 D.L.R. (3d) 85 (S.C.C.); *Oshawa Group Ltd. v. Great Amer. Ins. Co.* (1982), 132 D.L.R. (3d) 453 (Ont. C.A.).

  If the profit is through resale of property, it must be shown that the resale is part of a continuous transaction commencing with the original purchase of the property by the plaintiff brought about by, and involving the defendant's wrongful act, *e.g.*, a negligent misrepresentation: *Hussey v. Eels*, [1990] 1 All E.R. 449 (C.A.).

497 *Western Processing & Cold Storage Ltd. v. Hamilton Const. Co.* (1964), 47 W.W.R. 150 (Man. Q.B.); affirmed on the question of damages (1965), 51 W.W.R. 354 (Man. C.A.); *R.G. McLean Ltd. v. Can. Vickers Ltd.* (1970), 15 D.L.R. (3d) 15 (Ont. C.A.); *Freedhoff v. Pomalift Industs. Ltd.* (1971), 19 D.L.R. (3d) 153 (Ont. C.A.). But see *Trans. Trust S.P.R.L. v. Danubian Trading Co. Ltd.*, [1952] 2 Q.B. 297 (C.A.); *General Securities Ltd. v. Don Ingram Ltd.*, [1940] S.C.R. 670 (S.C.C.); *Kienzle v. Stringer* (1981), 130 D.L.R. (3d) 272 (Ont. C.A.); leave to appeal to S.C.C. refused (1982), 130 D.L.R. 272n (S.C.C.); compare *Dodd Properties (Kent) Ltd. v. Canterbury City Council*, [1980] 1 W.L.R. 433 (C.A.).

498 *Marigold Holdings Ltd. v. Norem Const. Ltd.* (1988), 60 Alta. L.R. (2d) 289 at 343 (Alta. Q.B.) *per* Conrad J.; *Pelletier v. Pe Ben Industries Co.*, [1976] 6 W.W.R. 640 (B.C.S.C.).

499 Compare *Alta. Caterers Ltd. v. R. Vollan (Alta.) Ltd.* (1977), 81 D.L.R. (3d) 672 at 683-684 (Alta. T.D.); varied (1977), 11 A.R. 181 (Alta. T.D.). Compare the comments of the Supreme Court of Canada in *Janiak v. Ippolito*, above, note 491, at 17 on the alignment between mitigation and *novus actus interveniens* and the connection with general principles of foreseeability and remoteness; compare the discussion in *Haida Inn Partnership v. Touche Ross & Co.* (1989), 64 D.L.R. (4th) 305 at 313-316 (B.C.S.C.).

500 And whether damages are claimed at common law or in equity: *Kemp v. Lee* (1983), 44 B.C.L.R. 172 (B.C.S.C.). (see, however, *Kopec v. Pyret* (1983), 146 D.L.R. (3d) 242 (Sask. Q.B.); varied (1987), 36 D.L.R. (4th) 1 (Sask. C.A.): above, p. 710). But it may not go so far as to require the plaintiff to prevent an increase in damages resulting from inflation: Feldman & Leibling, "Inflation and the Duty to Mitigate" (1979), 95 L.Q.R. 220. Nor will it apply to a claim for a debt: above, note 491.

v. Edmonton Real Estate Board Co-operative Listing Bureau Ltd.,[501] someone wrongfully expelled from membership of the Board, which affected his ability to earn a living as a realtor, was obliged to mitigate his loss, even though the situation was not the equivalent of that which occurred in cases of wrongful dismissal of an employee. However, the scope of the duty, and its fulfilment, may depend on the nature of the transaction that is in issue. In *Asamera Oil Corporation v. Sea Oil & General Corporation; Baud Corp. N.V. v. Brook*,[502] the Supreme Court of Canada held that in an action for breach of the duty to return shares under a contract of bailment, the principles of mitigation applicable to cases of sale of goods did not apply without reservation to the duty to mitigate where the contract related to shares.[503] The reason for this was because the price of the shares had fluctuated considerably during the period of the litigation. The plaintiff was held obliged to mitigate his loss by purchasing like shares on the open market when he learned of the breach or within a reasonable time thereafter. He could not wait until the action or its result. He was still obliged to mitigate when an injunction could be granted to restrain the defendant from disposing of the shares. He was not obliged to mitigate, however, if and when a decree of specific performance of the contract could be decreed,[504] in other words, when the plaintiff had such a substantial and legitimate interest in the specific return of the shares that no other remedy, that is, damages, would adequately cope with his potential loss.

It has also been suggested that alleged contributory negligence by a plaintiff might be regarded as an anticipatory failure to mitigate his loss.[505] Hence such misconduct by the plaintiff could be treated in the same was as a post-breach failure by him to mitigate his loss. In both instances, if the conduct of the plaintiff was unreasonable, the award of damages could be reduced in proportion to the extent to which the loss had been caused by the plaintiff's misconduct.[506]

(b) Forms of mitigation

In a commercial context, the duty to mitigate might require the plaintiff to replace defective machinery supplied by the defendant, with other machinery which turned out to be superior in quality (so that the plaintiff gained a profit, rather

---

501 (1977), 9 A.R. 568 (Alta. T.D.).

502 (1978), 89 D.L.R. (3d) 1 (S.C.C.).

503 *Ibid.*, at 20 *per* Estey J.

504 Compare the discussion of *Kopec v. Pyret*, above, pp. 710-711.

505 *Tompkins Hardware Ltd. v. North Western Flying Services Ltd.* (1982), 139 D.L.R. (3d) 329 (Ont. H.C.); *Ribic v. Weinstein* (1983), 140 D.L.R. (3d) 258 (Ont. H.C.); affirmed on other grounds (1984), 10 D.L.R. (4th) 717 (Ont. C.A.); above, pp. 756-757.

506 *Janiak v. Ippolito*, above, note 491, at 17 (S.C.C.), on the connection between mitigation and contradictory negligence: see above, note 499. For an example of failure to mitigate being treated as contributory negligence, see *Bank of Montreal v. Maddox & MacInnis* (1987), 83 N.B.R. (2d) 342, where the New Brunswick Court of Appeal reversed the trial judge and held that the failure to sue corporate debtors was *not* contributory negligence (or failure to mitigate) because the outcome of such litigation was speculative.

than suffered a loss in consequence of the defendant's breach).[507] It might even involve the plaintiff in dealing with the defaulting defendant. In *Payzu Ltd. v. Saunders*,[508] the defendants, sellers of goods, wrongfully repudiated when they refused to deliver goods, after failure by the plaintiffs, the buyers, to pay an instalment of the purchase price punctually. The sellers offered to deliver as against cash. Their offer was rejected. When the price of the goods rose, the buyers sued for non-delivery, that is, breach of contract. It was held that, though the sellers were in breach, the buyers had failed to mitigate since they should have accepted the sellers' offer to supply the goods on a cash basis. Hence, the damages payable to the buyers could only be measured in accordance with what would have been lost if the sellers' offer had been accepted. In cases of sale of goods, the innocent plaintiff may have to buy goods elsewhere (if he is claiming that the seller failed to deliver, or delivered the wrong goods), or, may have to sell them as best he can, if he can, where he is a seller claiming a failure by the buyer to accept. Where these courses are open to an injured buyer or seller, and are not taken, then this will have an effect upon the damages otherwise recoverable.[509] Other kinds of mitigation which are illustrated in the cases include the following: repairing of machinery;[510] reselling property after a contracted purchase has failed;[511] obtaining alternative financing for the purchase of property;[512] suing another party;[513] selling bonds to reduce loss;[514] reletting property after the original lessee wrongfully repudiated the lease.[515]

The problem also arises very frequently in cases of wrongful dismissal of an employee. When an employee has been dismissed, in circumstances which support an action by him against his employer for breach of the contract of employment, the authorities make it perfectly plain that the ex-employee is obliged to mitigate

---

507 The *British Westinghouse* case, above, note 492; but contrast *Jewelowski v. Propp*, [1944] 1 K.B. 510; and *Hussey v. Eels*, above, note 496.

508 [1919] 2 K.B. 581 (C.A.); compare *Hounsditch Warehouse Co. v. Waltex*, [1944] 1 K.B. 579. But see *Can. Sander Mfg. Co. v. Can. Gen. Elec. Co.* (1921), 64 D.L.R. 214 (Ont. C.A.).

509 Compare the conduct of the buyers, which was very curious indeed, since they bought at cut price goods which they had previously *rejected*, in *Cehave N.V. v. Bremer Handelgellschaft m.b.H.*, [1976] Q.B. 44 (C.A.).

510 *Exchanger Industries Ltd. v. Dom. Bridge Co.* (1986), 69 A.R. 22 (Alta. Q.B.); compare *Total Petroleum (North America) Ltd. v. AMF Tuboscope Inc.* (1987), 54 Alta. L.R. (2d) 13 (Alta. Q.B.). Or repairing waterproofing: *Marigold Holdings Ltd. v. Norem Const. Ltd.*, above, note 498.

511 *Russell v. Wispinksi* (1987), 13 B.C.L.R. (2d) 196 (B.C.S.C.).

512 *Shulist v. Hunt*, above, note 495.

513 *Caisse Populaire de Richibouctou Ltée v. Savoie* (1986), 75 N.B.R. (2d) 38 (N.B.C.A.); contrast *Bank of Montreal v. Maddox & MacInnis* (1987), 83 N.B.R. (2d) 342 (N.B.C.A.); leave to appeal to S.C.C. refused (1988), 47 R.P.R. 188n (S.C.C.).

514 *Higgins v. Edington* (1987), 11 B.C.L.R. (2d) 171 (B.C.S.C.); affirmed (1988), 31 B.C.L.R. (2d) 203 (B.C.C.A.), with which contrast *Hong Kong Bank of Can. v. Richardson Greenshields of Can. Ltd.* (1990), 72 D.L.R. (4th) 161 (B.C.C.A.).

515 *Grouse Mechanical Co. v. Griffin* (1990), 14 R.P.R. (2d) 233 (B.C.S.C.).

his loss by taking reasonable steps to find alternative employment.[516] Hence in *Brace v. Calder*,[517] when the plaintiff's employment with a partnership was wrongfully terminated by the dissolution of the partnership, giving rise to an action by him against the partnership, in respect of the salary for the remainder of the original term of his contract of service, it was held that the employee's refusal to accept employment from the two partners to whom the business had been transferred, when such employment was on the same terms as his original contract, was an unreasonable failure or refusal to mitigate his loss. The important point here is that the alternative employment was of the same kind, with the same status and salary, as the employment from which the plaintiff was wrongfully dismissed. In the *Yetton* case,[518] however, the plaintiff was dismissed from his position as managing director of a company, in circumstances which justified his action for wrongful dismissal. It was held that he had not failed to perform his duty to mitigate, by seeking alternative employment, when he refused to accept an alternative position with the same salary, but involving a lower status, and when he sought employment which was at a level at least comparable to his previous salary. Hence, his claim for damages for wrongful dismissal based on his loss of salary for the uncompleted period of his contract to service was successful.[519] The same principles, with the same result, were applied by the Supreme Court of Canada in *Red Deer College v. Michaels*,[520] which was concerned with the wrongful termination of the contract of service of a college instructor.

(c) What is reasonable?

The plaintiff is not obliged to act unreasonably, in order to reduce the damages otherwise payable by the defendant. Nor will what he does, even if it results in some mitigation of his loss, assist the defendant if it is not done as a consequence of the breach and is to be regarded as a reasonable and prudent course arising quite naturally out of the circumstances in which the plaintiff was placed by the breach. In other words, the reasonable conduct of the plaintiff must be attributable to the breach. It must not be something which might, or would have happened

---

516 *Beckham v. Drake* (1849), 2 H.L.Cas. 579 at 606 (H.L.) *per* Erle J. Hence, if he obtained other employment he might recover no damages: *Reid v. Explosives Co.* (1887), 19 Q.B.D. 264 (C.A.). But there must be a breach before the duty arises: *Longman v. Fed. Business Dev. Bank* (1982), 131 D.L.R. (3d) 533 (B.C.S.C.).

517 [1895] 2 Q.B. 253 (C.A.).

518 Above, note 493; compare *Shindler v. Nor. Raincourt Co.*, [1960] 1 W.L.R. 1038. See also the Canadian cases of *Thiessen v. Leduc*, [1975] 4 W.W.R. 387 (Alta. S.C.), and *O'Grady v. Ins. Corp. of B.C.* (1975), 63 D.L.R. (3d) 370 (B.C.S.C.).

519 Accepting a demotion from the same employer *is* mitigation, not the abandonment of a claim for wrongful dismissal: *Campbell v. MacMillan Bloedel*, [1978] 2 W.W.R. 686 (B.C.S.C.). But non-acceptance of such demotion is not a failure to mitigate: *Herrschaft v. Vancouver Community College* (1978), 91 D.L.R. (3d) 328 (B.C.S.C.).

520 Above, note 494.

in any event, and so is to be treated as *res inter alios acta*.[521] Hence, in *Petrosar Ltd. v. Ontario Hydro*,[522] the mitigation alleged to have been undertaken by the plaintiff was for a purpose unconnected with the default of the defendant on which the plaintiff's claim was founded; therefore it would not be taken into account.

Mitigation principles, it has been said, are closely related to remoteness, and, it might be added, to causation. In relation to all three ideas, the essential ingredient seems to be foresight.[523] Conduct that ought to be undertaken by the plaintiff must be foreseeable, and therefore reasonably to be expected from the plaintiff, if it is to constitute mitigation. In *Windmill Place v. Apeco of Canada Ltd.*,[524] for example, a lessee was in breach of a contract to lease. The lessee was liable for unpaid rent over the period of the lease, less what might have been obtained by the lessor by way of mitigation. The question, therefore, was whether the lessor was obliged to relet the premises in order to mitigate. In the circumstances of this case it was foreseeable by the lessee that it might be difficult for the lessor to relet the premises by reason of current market conditions. Hence the lessor's failure to relet was not an unreasonable failure on his part, and he was not guilty of failing to mitigate his loss. Similarly, in *Seafood Exporters Corporation of Newfoundland & Labrador v. Donnelly Farms Ltd.*,[525] the delay in reselling fish that had been rejected by the original purchaser because of the effects of the defendant carrier's negligence, was not a failure to mitigate because there was no evidence that the plaintiff would have obtained a better price on such resale if it had taken place earlier. Nor was failure to sue a corporate debtor an instance of failure to mitigate because such litigation would not necessarily have given the plaintiff any remedy; its outcome was speculative.[526]

In contrast, in *Caines v. Bank of Nova Scotia*,[527] the plaintiff's failure to mitigate when he ought to have done so, and could have been expected to do so, limited his claim to nominal damages. The plaintiff discovered that his insurance policy had lapsed. That had occurred before his property was destroyed by fire. The lapse occurred because the bank failed to make the necessary payment, although contractually bound to do so. The plaintiff had relied on the bank's assurance that the premium had been paid. He did not make independent inquiries, nor did he ensure that the premium had been paid to the insurance company. This was treated as failure to mitigate. He could have been expected to take appropriate steps. One

---

521 The *British Westinghouse* case, above, note 492, at 691 *per* Viscount Haldane L.C. For an illustration of reasonable conduct, in this instance laying tile over a floor that was not coloured by the defendant as it should have been, see *Wallace Const. Specialties Ltd. v. Mihalcheon Holdings Ltd.*, [1979] 3 W.W.R. 145 (Sask. Dist. Ct.).

522 (1986), 33 B.L.R. 24 (Ont. H.C.).

523 Waddams, *Law of Damages*, 2nd ed. (1991), para. 15.110; compare above, notes 499, 506.

524 (1978), 82 D.L.R. (3d) 1 (S.C.C.). Compare *Grouse Mechanical Co. v. Griffin*, above, note 515, where the landlord had to re-let the promises with four months free rent: this was reasonable mitigation.

525 (1989), 81 Nfld. & P.E.I.R. 173 (Nfld. T.D.).

526 *Bank of Montreal v. Maddox & MacInnis*, above, note 513. Contrast the *Caisse Populaire* case, above, note 513.

527 (1978), 90 D.L.R. (3d) 271 (N.B.C.A.).

member of the Nova Scotia Court of Appeal preferred to regard the plaintiff's conduct as contributory negligence (which, as previously noted, has sometimes been treated as a form of anticipatory failure to mitigate[528]). So, too, in *Russell v. Wispinski*,[529] the plaintiffs failed to act reasonably in mitigation of the loss resulting from the collapse of a projected sale of their property, when they advertised the property for resale themselves and did not employ the defendant. In *Hong Kong Bank of Canada v. Richardson Greenshields of Canada Ltd.*,[530] a customer did not mitigate his loss by selling bonds earlier than he eventually did, at the moment when the broker made clear he accepted no liability for his failure to sell the bonds.

Even foreseeable conduct will not be treated as conduct that ought to be undertaken by a plaintiff in order to mitigate if it involves the plaintiff in incurring expense that is excessive in the circumstances.[531] A plaintiff is not expected to become involved in litigation to clear the title to some property in order to relieve the defendant, the plaintiff's solicitor, from any liability for the consequences of the defendant's negligence while acting on behalf of the plaintiff.[532] But in *Canso Chemicals Ltd. v. Canadian Westinghouse Co. (No. 2)*,[533] it was held that a plaintiff who could have relied on a *force majeure* clause in contracts with sub-purchasers, but did not do so, thereby remaining liable to such sub-purchasers, could not claim the damages thus payable from the defendants, who were his original suppliers, and whose breach of contract with him resulted in the plaintiff's liability over to his sub-purchasers. Clearly, this is a question of fact, and one that can be difficult to resolve.[534]

(d) Mitigation and anticipatory breach[535]

One situation in respect of which there may not be a duty to mitigate, despite what has been said above, is where the defendant has repudiated the contract in advance of the due date for performance. The decision of the House of Lords in

---

528 Above, p. 757.

529 Above, note 511. See also *Brownstone Press Ltd. v. Rosenfeld, Malcolmson, Lampkin & Levine* (1988), 27 C.I.P.R. 149 (Ont. H.C.); affirmed (1992), 40 C.P.R. (3d) 575 (Ont. C.A.) (failure to mitigate solicitor's failure to register a trade mark); *Shulist v. Hunt* (1987), 51 Alta. L.R. (2d) 69 (failure to obtain alternative financing to enable plaintiff to buy house).

530 Above, note 514. Contrast *Higgins v. Edington*, above, note 514.

531 *Jewelowski v. Propp*, [1944] 1 Q.B. 510.

532 *Pilkington v. Wood*, [1953] Ch. 770, referred to in *Bank of Montreal v. Maddox & MacInnis*, above, note 513.

533 (1974), 10 N.S.R. (2d) 306 (N.S.C.A.).

534 Compare *Farish v. Nat. Trust Co.*, [1975] 3 W.W.R. 499 (B.C.S.C.); *Compania Naviera Maropan S.A. v. Bowaters Lloyd Pulp & Paper Mills Ltd.*, [1955] 2 Q.B. 68 (C.A.); *Rooney v. Reed Ltd.* (1978), 88 D.L.R. (3d) 414 (Ont. H.C.); *McMorran's Cordova Bay Ltd. v. Harman & Co.* (1979), 106 D.L.R. (3d) 495 (B.C.C.A.). As to the valuation of the chance to mitigate loss by the plaintiff's failure to act, see *Ippolito v. Janiak* (1981), 126 D.L.R. (3d) 623 (Ont. C.A.); affirmed (1985), 16 D.L.R. (4th) 1 (sub nom. *Janiak v. Ippolito*) (S.C.C.); *Emeny v. Butters* (1982), 36 O.R. (2d) 328 (Ont. Co. Ct.).

535 Waddams, *Law of Damages*, above, note 523, at paras. 15.400-15.650.

White & Carter (Councils) Ltd. v. McGregor[536] has been discussed in an earlier chapter.[537] It was seen that, according to the House of Lords, the plaintiff was not obliged to forego or abandon the contract, and avoid incurring any expense in its furtherance, but, on the contrary, could continue with an appropriate course of action, as if the contract were still accepted by the defendant, and then claim the loss resulting from his actions. Here, in fact, the plaintiff had exacerbated, indeed had caused, his loss, which could have been avoided altogether at the stage at which the defendant repudiated, however wrongful that repudiation may have been. Nonetheless, the defendant was held liable.

This case has been critically examined in England, and its scope limited by reference to the criteria laid down by Lord Reid as having to be met before mitigation is unnecessary.[538] However it has also been rejected by the Ontario Court of Appeal.[539] In the *Asamera* case,[540] the Supreme Court of Canada seems to have been prepared to accept the approach in *White & Carter (Councils) Ltd. v. McGregor* "where there is a substantial and legitimate interest in looking to performance of a contractual obligation." Such would be the case where a plaintiff who has agreed to purchase a particular piece of real estate, or a block of shares which represent control of a company, has entered into performance of his own obligations, and to discontinue performance might aggravate his losses. In such situations the plaintiff might require a decree of specific performance, and it would be unreasonable to make him mitigate by seeking alternative property or shares. If damages would be a reasonable way of compensating the plaintiff, however, the position might be very different.

---

536 [1962] A.C. 413 (H.L.).
537 Above, pp. 618-620.
538 Above, p. 619.
539 *Finelli v. Dee*, [1968] 1 O.R. 676 (Ont. C.A.).
540 Above, note 502, at 26.

19

Equitable Remedies

1. Specific performance[1]

(a) Nature and purpose

A decree of specific performance is an order issued by a court by which a party is enjoined to do what he has promised or contracted to do. Failure to obey is a contempt of court and may be punished as such. The power to order performance

---

1 Sharpe, *Injunctions and Specific Performance*, 2nd ed. (1992), Chapters 7, 10, 11.

of contracts, though exercised minimally at common law in certain ways,[2] became of great importance as a result of the intervention of the Court of Chancery acting in accordance with its concept of *in personam* jurisdiction.[3] In more modern times some suggestion has been made that the basis for the use of the remedy of specific performance is the notion of property, and it has been argued, though not without dispute, that the remedy of specific performance ought to be more widely employed by courts, on the grounds of economic efficiency.[4] In Anglo-Canadian law, however, there would seem to be doctrinal reasons why a broader use of the remedy is not possible.

Although there are many situations in which a plaintiff will be severely hindered or hampered in his expectations if the contract is not performed, with the consequence that an award of damages will not adequately compensate the plaintiff, not every instance of breach of contract will give rise to the possibility of a decree of specific performance. A court will always entertain a claim for specific performance, or other equitable relief, as well as a claim for damages as an alternative.[5] The result may be that damages are awarded instead of specific performance, either under the common law or the statutory jurisdiction of the court;[6] sometimes damages only, and sometimes specific performance plus compensation rather than damages.[7] The House of Lords has now made it clear that if a decree of specific performance is granted, but not obeyed, the party who originally obtained the decree is not thereby prejudiced in respect of a later claim for damages instead of the decree.[8] Thus the relationship between the common law and equitable

---

2 Sharpe, *op. cit.*, para. 7.10, note 2, referring to the prerogative writ of *mandamus*, delivery of a chattel in detinue and the old writ of covenant.

3 For the idea that the nature of the remedy might be changing, see *Coulls v. Bagot's Executor & Trustee Co.* (1967), 119 C.L.R. 460 at 563 (Aust. H.C.) *per* Windeyer J., quoted by Lord Pearce in *Beswick v. Beswick*, [1968] A.C. 58 at 91 (H.L.).

   Since provincial courts, *i.e.*, courts of lesser jurisdiction have no jurisdiction to grant equitable relief, in Ontario under the Courts of Justice Act, R.S.O. 1990, c. C.43, s. 96(3), equitable remedies such as specific performance, or the making of an apology and a retraction of a libel, cannot be ordered by such a court: *Moore v. Can. Newspapers Co.* (1989), 60 D.L.R. (4th) 113 (Ont. Div. Ct.).

4 Kronman, "Specific Performance" (1978), 45 U. Chi. L.R. 357; Schultz, "The Case for Specific Performance" (1979), 89 Yale L.J. 271; Linzer, "On the Amorality of Contract Remedies — Efficiency, Equity and the Second Restatement" (1981), 81 Col. L.R. 111, Yorio, "In Defence of Money Damages for Breach of Contract" (1982), 82 Col. L.R. 1365. See, however, *Domowicz v. Orsa Invts. Ltd.* (1993), 15 O.R. (3d) 661 especially at 680-688 (Ont. Gen. Div.).

5 *Dobson v. Winton & Robbins Ltd.*, [1959] S.C.R. 775 (S.C.C.). Indeed specific performance *and* damages may both be granted: *Matheson v. Poirier* (1990), 95 N.S.R. (2d) 261 (N.S.T.D.).

6 Above, pp. 706-711.

7 Sharpe, *op. cit.*, above, note 1, paras. 11.20-11.190; Harpum, "Specific Performance with Compensation as a Purchaser's Remedy — A Study in Contract and Equity," [1981] C.L.J. 47. Or damages, above, note 5.

8 *Johnson v. Agnew*, [1979] 1 All E.R. 883 (H.L.) (disapproving *Capital & Suburban Properties v. Swycher*, [1976] Ch. 319 (C.A.) and *Biggin v. Minton*, [1977] 2 All E.R. 647). *Gaspari v. Creighton Holdings Ltd.* (1984), 13 D.L.R. (4th) 570 (B.C.S.C.). If the plaintiff accepts an award of damages in lieu of specific performance, this is an election by the plaintiff, such that if the defendant alters his position by raising and paying over the damages into a bank account in the name of the plaintiff's

remedies, once thought to be alternatives, has been harmonized. Specific performance, however, remains a discretionary remedy.[9]

(b) When obtainable

It would seem to be immaterial whether the defendant has broken his contract at the time when performance is due, or has done so in advance, by way of an "anticipatory breach".[10] Just as the court may issue an injunction to restrain a threatened breach of contract,[11] so it may grant a decree of specific performance *before* the date when performance is due, although its enforcement will be suspended until such date.[12] The kind of contract that is involved will be most material.

It has never been disputed that specific performance of a contract for the sale of land may be obtained, unless the circumstances are such that the decree should not be granted.[13] This may even be possible where the contract is subject

---

solicitors to be held by them as stakeholders, pending the outcome of the defendant's appeal, the plaintiff cannot change his mind on the appeal, and seek specific performance, even if specific performance could have been claimed at the trial, as it was erroneously held that it could not be: *Meng Leong Dev. Pte. Ltd. v. Jip Hong Trading Co. Pte.*, [1985] 1 All E.R. 120 (P.C.).

9 Hence, *e.g.*, the refusal to aid a "volunteer", *i.e.*, one who has not given consideration: *Cannon v. Hartley*, [1949] Ch. 213 at 217 *per* Romer J.; even if a contract is under seal: Sharpe, *op. cit.*, above, note 1, para. 10.400. But the creation of an equitable interest may suffice: *Mountford v. Scott*, [1974] 1 All E.R. 248; affirmed on other grounds, [1975] 1 All E.R. 198 (C.A.). As at common law, inadequacy of consideration is irrelevant: Sharpe, *op. cit.*, para. 10.390.

However, specific performance will not be granted where the defendant cannot transfer title since the defendant lacked such title: *Klippert v. Western Service Agreements Ltd.* (1988), 70 Sask. R. 136 (Sask. Q.B.). On the other hand specific performance is particularly appropriate where the defendant is insolvent and cannot return the money paid by the plaintiff on account of the purchase price: *Kristian Equipment Ltd. v. Urano Rentals Ltd.* (1988), 68 Sask. R. 134 (Sask. Q.B.).

10 As to which see above, pp. 600-622. See, *e.g.*, *Matheson v. Poirier*, above, note 5.

11 Below, pp. 798-799.

12 *Kloepfer Wholesale Hardware & Automotive Co. v. Roy*, [1952] 2 S.C.R. 465 at 477 (S.C.C.) *per* Locke J.; accepted and followed in *Hasham v. Zenab*, [1960] A.C. 316 (P.C.).

13 *E.g.*, *Wroth v. Tyler*, [1974] Ch. 30; *Horsler v. Zorro*, [1975] Ch. 302; *Glascar Ltd. v. Polysar Ltd.* (1975), 9 O.R. (2d) 705 (Ont. H.C.). Specific performance can even be ordered of a contractual licence of short duration, *e.g.*, for a day: *Verrall v. Great Yarmouth B.C.*, [1980] 1 All E.R. 839 (C.A.). See Sharpe, *op. cit.*, above, note 1, paras. 8.10-8.20. And, it would seem, even if damages would provide the plaintiff with a complete remedy: if the necessary conditions are satisfied, a party is entitled to specific performance of a land sale agreement: *Citation Realty Inc. v. 463879 Ont. Ltd.* (1989), 67 D.L.R. (4th) 450 (Ont. H.C.); affirmed (1990), 77 D.L.R. (4th) 384 (Ont. C.A.). Contrast, however, the very different view expressed in *Domowicz v. Orsa Invts. Ltd.*, above, note 4, which did not refer to the *Citation Realty* case.

For examples of different contracts involving land that have been ordered specifically performed, see *Cross v. Currie* (1989), 5 R.P.R. (2d) 121 (N.S.T.D.); *Matheson v. Poirier*, above, note 5; *Leung v. Leung* (1990), 75 O.R. (2d) 786 (Ont. Gen. Div.); *Rosenberg v. Waterloo Terrace Ltd.* (1990), 9 R.P.R. (2d) 23 (Ont. H.C.) (option to purchase); *Schedlosky v. Schedlosky* (1988), 69 Sask. R. 121 (Sask. C.A.). One method of combining specific performance with damages is to order specific performance and abatement of the purchase price: see *Zylberstein v. Can-York Devs. Ltd.* (1988), 48 R.P.R. 314 (Ont. H.C.). Compare *Gelakis v. Giouroukos* (1991), 18 R.P.R. (2d) 161 (Ont. Gen. Div.): compare *407478 Alta. Ltd. v. Pennant Properties Can. Ltd.* (1990), 113 A.R. 188 (Alta. Q.B.); affirmed (March 4, 1992), Edmonton Appeal 9003-0902-AC, 9103-0104-AC (Alta. C.A.).

to a "true" condition precedent.[14] Specific performance has been decreed where a vendor failed to use his best efforts to secure fulfilment of the condition.[15] But specific performance has also been refused where a contract for the sale of land was subject to such a condition precedent,[16] in one instance, at least,[17] on the ground that the non-fulfilment of the condition made the so-called "agreement" merely an offer, so that there was no contract specific performance of which could be ordered. That would seem to be the test, namely the difference between the possibility and the inappropriateness of specific performance.

Where time is not of the essence of a contract,[18] specific performance may be obtained.[19] If the contract is not in writing or evidenced by the requisite note or memorandum under the Statute of Frauds, or equivalent legislation,[20] then no specific performance can be obtained,[21] any more than the plaintiff could be awarded damages at common law.[22] However, where the equitable doctrine of part performance is applicable,[23] the court can admit parol evidence to establish the contract, and thereafter decree specific performance.

Contracts of sale of goods are now dealt with by the Sale of Goods Act,[24] under which specific performance of such a contract may be granted where the sale is of specific or ascertained goods.[25] It would appear that, notwithstanding the statutory provision which merely enacts the older equitable doctrine, such a remedy will not be granted unless the goods are "exceptional" in some way, for

---

14 Above, pp. 437-441.

15 *Haupt v. Westcott* (1980), 116 D.L.R. (3d) 585 (Alta. Q.B.); reversed (1981), 140 D.L.R. (3d) 573 (Alta. C.A.); leave to appeal to S.C.C. refused (1981), 39 N.R. 540 (S.C.C.).

16 *Schickedanz v. Smith* (1987), 50 Alta. L.R. (2d) 395 (Alta. Q.B.): compare *471011 Ont. Inc. v. Bukville Holdings Ltd.* (1988), 50 R.P.R. 192 (Ont. H.C.).

17 *Kitsilano Enterprises Ltd. v. G. & A. Devs. Ltd.,* [1990] 6 W.W.R. 38 at 52-53 (B.C.S.C.) *per* Macdonell J.

18 Above, pp. 525-529.

19 *Beacon Indust. Dev. Corp. v. G.C. Farm Supply Ltd.* (1981), 123 D.L.R. (3d) 467 (Alta. Q.B.). For examples of specific performance after delay in closing a real estate transaction, see *Re 140 Devs. Ltd. v. Steveston Meat & Frozen Food Lockers (1973) Ltd.* (1975), 59 D.L.R. (3d) 470 (B.C.S.C.); *Holmes v. Alexson* (1976), 69 D.L.R. (3d) 223 (Ont. C.A.); *Law-Woman Management Corp. v. Peel (Regional Municipality)* (1991), 17 R.P.R. (2d) 62 (Ont. Gen. Div.).

20 Above, pp. 209, 240, 244.

21 *Babcock v. Carr* (1981), 127 D.L.R. (3d) 77 (Ont. H.C.). Nor can the contract be *rectified* and then specifically enforced: *Sweitzer v. Granger* (1923), 54 O.L.R. 70 (Ont. C.A.); *Rudd v. Manahan (No. 2)* (1913), 11 D.L.R. 37 at 39 (Alta. C.A.) *per* Simmons J.

22 *Carter v. Irving Oil Co.,* [1952] 4 D.L.R. 128 (N.S.S.C.). Nor could damages in equity (see *Horsler v. Zorro,* above, note 13) though the point was left open by Macdonald J. ([1952] 4 D.L.R. at 133), who said that Lord Cairns' Act, and the former Ontario Judicature Act, above, p. 706, did not affect the common law's inability to award damages in such a case.

23 Above, pp. 227-236.

24 Fridman, *Sale of Goods in Canada,* 3rd ed. (1986), pp. 415-417; and see Sharpe, *op. cit.,* above, note 1, paras. 8.240-8.510.

25 For the meaning of "specific" and "ascertained", see Fridman, *op. cit.,* pp. 56-57. Note the suggestion that the remedy is not so limited in *Sky Petroleum v. V.I.P. Petroleum,* [1974] 1 All E.R. 954.

example, by being unique,[26] or by not being capable of being replaced on an "available market"[27] or unless damages would not be an adequate remedy.[28] If appropriate, however, the remedy will be granted,[29] notwithstanding that property in the goods has not passed to the plaintiff, the buyer, under the terms of the contract or the provisions of the Sale of Goods Act.[30]

Shares are not goods.[31] However, specific performance of a contract to purchase the plaintiff's shares in a private corporation was allowed; otherwise the intentions of the shareholders under the buy-sell provisions of an agreement would have been thwarted.[32] Specific performance was also granted of a contract which involved the compulsory buy-out by one partner of a dental practice.[33]

It was considered that equity would not usually decree specific performance of a contract to give or pay money to the plaintiff, damages being an appropriate way of ensuring that the plaintiff was not harmed by the failure to pay. To this there were undoubtedly exceptions, for example, in cases concerning sureties, who were entitled to reimbursement by the principal debtor whose liability the surety had discharged.[34] However, the decision of the House of Lords in *Beswick v. Beswick*,[35] which has been followed in this respect in Canada,[36] now makes it clear that, whenever it would not be suitable to leave the plaintiff to his common-law remedy in damages, for example, because such damages would only be nominal, equity can order the defendant to pay the sums promised under the contract. *Beswick*

---

26 See, *e.g., Pusey v. Pusey* (1684), 23 E.R. 465; *Lowther v. Lowther* (1806), 33 E.R. 230; *Behnke v. Bede Shipping Co.*, [1927] 1 K.B. 649. A similar situation can arise in the case of a contract of sale of *land*, if the land in question has no unique value for the purchaser, *e.g.*, where he did not want it for personal use but only as an investment or business proposition: *Chaulk v. Fairview Const. Ltd.* (1977), 14 Nfld. & P.E.I.R. 13 (Nfld. C.A.); *McNabb v. Smith* (1981), 124 D.L.R. (3d) 547 (B.C.S.C.); affirmed (1982), 132 D.L.R. (3d) 523 (B.C.C.A.); compare *Domowicz v. Orsa Invts. Ltd.*, above, note 4.

27 *Simmons & McBride Ltd. v. Kirkpatrick*, [1945] 3 W.W.R. 557 (B.C.S.C.).

28 Hence the award of an injunction to restrain the defendant from withholding supplies from the plaintiff (a form of negative or inverse specific performance) in *Sky Petroleum v. V.I.P. Petroleum*, [1974] 1 All E.R. 954; contrast *Cohen v. Roche*, [1927] 1 K.B. 169; *Dom. Coal Co. v. Dom. Iron & Steel Co.*, [1909] A.C. 293 (P.C.).

29 See, *e.g., Fraser v. Sam Kee* (1916), 9 W.W.R. 1281 (B.C. Co. Ct.); *Can. Credit Men's Trust Assn. v. Edmonton Lbr. Co.*, [1930] 2 W.W.R. 97 (Alta. S.C.). For instance, if the defendant is insolvent and cannot refund payments already made by the plaintiff for the goods in issue: *Kristian Equipment Ltd. v. Urano Rentals Ltd.* (1988), 68 Sask. R. 134 (Sask. Q.B.) (where the third party to whom the goods had been sold had not complied with the Saskatchewan Personal Property Security Act).

30 *Re Western Can. Pulpwood Co. and Man. Paper Co.*, [1929] 3 W.W.R. 81 (Man. K.B.); affirmed [1929] 3 W.W.R. 544 (Man. C.A.). For when property passes, see Fridman, *op. cit.*, above, note 24, pp. 70-95.

31 Fridman, *op. cit.*, above, note 24, p. 17.

32 *Fleisher v. Rosenbloom* (1988), 53 Man. R. (2d) 247 (Man. Q.B.). See also Sharpe, *Injunctions and Specific Performance*, 2nd ed. (1992), paras. 8.520-8.560.

33 *Hornby v. Nugent* (1989), 64 D.L.R. (4th) 765 (B.C.C.A.), where the British Columbia Court of Appeal held that, in appropriate cases, the court could depart from the literal terms of a contract.

34 *Gray v. Cameron*, [1950] S.C.R. 401 at 407-411 (S.C.C.) *per* Locke J.

35 [1968] A.C. 58 (H.L.).

36 *Waugh v. Slavik*, [1976] 1 W.W.R. 273 (B.C.S.C.); see above, pp. 180-181.

v. Beswick[37] involved a promise to pay a third person, the wife of the deceased, not a party to the original contract. The plaintiff, the widow, sued as the personal representative of the deceased, and as such was able to bring the action (which would not have been maintainable in her own name). But damages for breach of the contract would not have been substantial, since the only truly damaged party was the plaintiff in her personal, not representative capacity. Hence the House of Lords agreed that the technicalities of the doctrine of privity of contract could be avoided in this instance, by ordering the defendant to fulfil the contract and pay the agreed sum to the widow.

(c) When unobtainable

A contract may not be capable of being specifically performed for one of two reasons: either it belongs to a category of contracts which are not capable of being enforced in that way, or else the particular contract, in the particular circumstances, is not susceptible to such remedy.

It has been stated frequently that a contract to lend or to borrow money cannot be specifically enforced by such a decree.[38] As noted above, there was a bias against enforcing contracts involving the payment of money, and it would seem that this underlay the unwillingess of courts of equity to grant specific performance of such borrowing contracts.[39] However, following the rationale of the *Beswick* case, presumably, if it could be established by the plaintiff that, where the defendant failed or refused to perform his promise to lend or to repay money already lent, an award of damages might be inadequate; for example, where such an award, on *Hadley v. Baxendale* principles, could only be nominal,[40] possibly the court could, and would decree specific performance. This remains to be seen; though, it is suggested, there is no good reason, now, in principle why this should not be done.

A more important category of contracts to which the doctrine of specific performance appears to be inapplicable, as a class and not simply in individual

---

37 Above, note 35; compare *Gasparini v. Gasparini* (1978), 87 D.L.R. (3d) 282 (Ont. C.A.).

38 *Prince Rupert Sawmills Ltd. v. M.C. Logging Ltd.* (1967), 65 D.L.R. (2d) 300 at 308 (B.C.C.A.) per Bull J.A., citing *South African Territories Ltd. v. Wallington*, [1898] A.C. 309 (H.L.); *Western Wagon & Property Co. v. West*, [1892] 1 Ch. 271; *Rogers v. Challis* (1859), 54 E.R. 68; *Sichel v. Mosenthal* (1862), 54 E.R. 932. See also *Anderson v. Luoma* (1984), 14 D.L.R. (4th) 749 (B.C.S.C.) involving an agreement between two female homosexuals relating to the pooling of incomes and the support of children produced by artificial insemination.

    Nor will the courts specifically enforce contracts of a *continuing* kind, requiring a series of acts to be performed, since to do so would involve continual supervision: *Seven Seas Restaurant v. Central & Eastern Tour Co.* (1978), 24 N.B.R. (2d) 491 (N.B.Q.B.) although this attitude may be changing; Sharpe, *op. cit.*, above, note 32, paras. 7.340-7.530. See also *Beswick v. Beswick*, above, note 35; *Tito v. Waddell (No. 2)*, [1977] Ch. 106 at 321-322; *Price v. Strange*, [1978] Ch. 337 at 359-360 (citing *C.H. Giles & Co. v. Morris*, [1972] 1 All E.R. 960 at 970).

39 Another reason may be the requirement of "mutuality": *Loan Inventure Corp. of Australasia v. Bonner*, [1970] N.Z.L.R. 744 (P.C.); Sharpe, *op. cit.*, above, note 32, para. 10.450.

40 Above, p. 745; compare Sharpe, *op. cit.*, above, note 32, paras. 7.180-7.200.

cases, is that of contracts of, or for personal services.[41] As Allen J.A. explained in *Emerald Resources Ltd. v. Sterling Oil Properties Management Ltd.*,[42]

> An example of a contract of which the Court will not compel specific performance is a contract of personal service, or one which requires the use of personal skill such as the one we have under consideration. . . . this seems to be based on the grounds of public policy; that it would be improper to make one man serve another against his will.

That case involved a contract to pay certain royalties produced by the oil, etc., coming from a certain property. For various reasons the court refused to order the defendants to fulfil the contractual obligations by paying the royalties in question. One reason was concerned with the doctrine of specific performance of contracts to deliver chattels; another was the inappropriateness of that remedy in cases of personal service, since the plaintiff had agreed to work for the defendants in return for such royalties, as well as other remuneration.

The proposition that contracts of personal service will only give rise to an action for damages if they are broken is one that, in general, has been upheld and applied strictly. For example, in *Francis v. Municipal Councillors of Kuala Lumpur*,[43] the Privy Council held that this meant that the plaintiff could not obtain a declaration that he was still employed by the defendants, notwithstanding their purported dismissal of him. However, it was pointed out in that case[44] that, exceptionally, such a declaration could be granted, which might have the same effect as a decree of specific performance, though the circumstances in which this could be done might be very special, for example, where the plaintiff was employed under a statutory scheme.[45] Possibly under special labour legislation such remedies of declaration and specific performance or reinstatement may be obtained, but

---

41 Sharpe, *op. cit.*, above, note 32, paras. 7.540-7.630. Contrast the attempt by Megarry V.-C. to assimilate contracts of employment with other contracts in *C.H. Giles & Co. v. Morris*, above, note 38; *Thomas Marshall Exports Ltd. v. Guinle*, [1978] 3 All E.R. 193 (on which see above, pp. 605-606).

Such contracts must be contrasted with contracts under which a party agrees to construct a building for the plaintiff, which is part of the agreement to buy land; *Webster v. Garnet Lane Devs. Ltd.* (1989), 70 O.R. (2d) 65 (Ont. H.C.); reversed in part (1992), 10 O.R. (3d) 576 (Ont. C.A.); leave to appeal to S.C.C. refused (1993), 154 N.R. 240 (note) (S.C.C.); *Lawrie v. Gentry Devs. Inc.* (1989), 72 O.R. (2d) 512 (Ont. H.C.).

42 (1969), 3 D.L.R. (3d) 630 at 647 (Alta. C.A.); affirmed (1970), 15 D.L.R. (3d) 256 (S.C.C.); compare *Garnett v. Armstrong* (1978), 83 D.L.R. (3d) 717 (N.B.C.A.); *McWhirter v. Univ. of Alta. Govs. (No. 2)* (1977), 80 D.L.R. (3d) 609 (Alta. Q.B.); reversed on other grounds (1979), 18 A.R. 145 (Alta. C.A.). To grant specific performance of such a contract would show lack of respect for human dignity and freedom of choice: *Philp v. Expo 86 Corp.* (1987), 45 D.L.R. (4th) 449 at 459 (B.C.C.A.) *per* Lambert J.A.

43 [1962] 3 All E.R. 633 (P.C.).

44 *Ibid.*, at 637-638 *per* Lord Morris.

45 *Vine v. Nat. Dock Labour Bd.*, [1957] A.C. 488 (H.L.). See *Philp v. Expo 86 Corp.* (1987), 45 D.L.R. (4th) 449 at 454-456 (B.C.C.A.) *per* Seaton J.A., and the cases there cited: *ibid.*, at 459-461 *per* Lambert J.A.

not in equity.[46] However, there is at least one modern English case[47] in which the court, by the use of the injunction, does appear to have given countenance to the notion that a contract of service can be enforced by judicial process, apart from the grant of damages for its breach. Such instances are, and probably will continue to be rare.

Apart from such special categories, however, the courts will refuse to decree specific performance, even of a contract that is normally one that will be enforced in that way, where such a contract is vague, ambiguous or uncertain, such that it is not clear what the court is specifically enforcing.[48] Nor will specific performance be granted where the contract has been induced by misrepresentation, even if innocent,[49] or where the contract has been entered into by mistake,[50] unless the mistake is not so fundamental as to alter the essential nature of the transaction

---

46 Compare Sharpe, *op. cit.*, above, note 32, para. 7.600.

47 *Hill v. C.A. Parsons & Co.*, [1971] 3 All E.R. 1345 (C.A.): Sharpe, *op. cit.*, above, note 32, paras. 7.620-7.630. Contrast certain cases under human rights legislation, in respect of mandatory age retirement: *Stevenson v. Air Can.* (1981), 126 D.L.R. (3d) 242 (Ont. H.C.); reversed (1982), 132 D.L.R. (3d) 406 (Ont. Div. Ct.); *Lamont v. Air Can.* (1981), 126 D.L.R. (3d) 266 (Ont. H.C.); *Chambers v. C.P. Air Ltd.* (1981), 128 D.L.R. (3d) 673 (B.C.S.C.); *University of Alberta v. Alberta (Human Rights Commission)* (1988), 53 D.L.R. (4th) 46 (Alta. Q.B.). See now *McKinney v. University of Guelph* (1990), 76 D.L.R. (4th) 545 (S.C.C.); *Stoffman v. Vancouver General Hospital* (1990), 76 D.L.R. (4th) 700 (S.C.C.).

48 *Campbell v. Barc.* [1917] 1 W.W.R. 283 (Man. C.A.); *Sweitzer v. Granger* (1923), 54 O.L.R. 70 (Ont. C.A.); *McSorley v. Murphy*, [1928] 3 W.W.R. 589 (B.C.C.A.); affirmed [1929] S.C.R. 542 (S.C.C.); *304498 B.C. Ltd. v. Garibaldi Whistler Dev. Co.* (1989), 39 B.C.L.R. (2d) 328 (B.C.C.A.); *Maxwell Taylor's Restaurants Inc. v. Carcasole* (1990), 72 Alta. L.R. (2d) 376 (Alta. Q.B.); affirmed (1990), 75 Alta. L.R. (2d) 97 (Alta. C.A.). Nor where there is no enforceable contract: *Bay Tower Homes v. St. Andrew's Land Corp.* (1990), 10 R.P.R. (2d) 193 (Ont. H.C.); *Decorby v. Decorby Estate* (1989), 57 Man. R. (2d) 241 (Man. C.A.); *Leonard H. Cook's Const. Ltd. v. Scott* (1989), 9 R.P.R. (2d) 69 (N.B.C.A.). Nor where no breach has occurred and the contract came to an end: *Young Estate v. 503708 Ont. Ltd.* (1988), 67 O.R. (2d) 40 (Ont. H.C.). Nor, perhaps, where the contract is subject to a condition precedent still unfulfilled: *471011 Ont. Inc. v. Bukville Holdings Ltd.* (1988), 50 R.P.R. 192 (Ont. H.C.) — not a "true" condition precedent case: compare above, p. 788, note 16.

49 *Johnston v. Dowsett* (1913), 4 W.W.R. 971 (Man. K.B.); *Whitney v. MacLean*, [1932] 1 W.W.R. 417 (Alta. C.A.); application for extension of time for appealing to S.C.C. refused, [1932] 2 W.W.R. 73 (Alta. C.A.). Nor where the plaintiff's conduct has been unconscionable: see, *e.g.*, *Knupp v. Bell* (1968), 67 D.L.R. (2d) 256 (Sask. C.A.); *Huttges v. Verner* (1975), 12 N.B.R. (2d) 473 (N.B.C.A.); see also *Orangeville Raceway (Ont.) Inc. v. Frieberg, Leonard H. Cook's Const. Ltd. v. Scott*, below, note 53; contrast *Cross v. Currie* (1989), 5 R.P.R. (2d) 121 (N.S.T.D.), where the daughter had not been guilty of undue influence in getting her mother to agree to convey a lot for a small sum. But not where a party resisting specific performance complains that he made a bad bargain: *O'Neil v. Arnew* (1976), 78 D.L.R. (3d) 671 (Ont. H.C.).

50 *Hobbs v. Esquimalt & Nanaimo Ry. Co.* (1899), 29 S.C.R. 450 at 467-468 (S.C.C.) *per* King J; *Smith v. Hall* (1945), 62 B.C.R. 81 (B.C.C.A.); but note the possibility of *rectification* first and then specific performance: *U.S.A. v. Motor Trucks Ltd.*, [1924] A.C. 196 (P.C.). See below, pp. 821-824. If there is a mistake on the part of the defendant it will not be effective to preclude specific performance if (a) it was not induced by the plaintiff, and (b) there was no reasonable excuse for the mistake: *Foderaro v. Future Homes Const. Ltd.* (1991), 17 R.P.R. (2d) 258 (Ont. Gen. Div.); additional reasons at (1991), 17 R.P.R. (2d) 271 (Ont. Gen. Div.).

into which the defendant entered.[51] Nor will there be specific performance where the plaintiff is himself in default,[52] for example, where a buyer of goods has not paid the balance of the purchase price by a certain time, and time was of the essence of the contract.[53] Nor when to grant specific performance might cause difficulties, for example, giving rise to litigation between spouses, or causing a breach between the wife of a party and her daughter, as in *Wroth v. Tyler*.[54] Nor will specific performance be ordered where it has become impossible for the defendant to perform the contract,[55] which will be the situation where the defendant has no title[56] or has created third party rights in the property.[57]

Hardship to third parties is a very strong discretionary reason for refusing to grant a decree of specific performance.[58] But hardship to the defendant can also have the same result. As recently pointed out by Goulding J. in the English case of *Patel v. Ali*,[59] it may no longer be accurate to say that the hardship in question must have existed at the time the contract was made.[60] In that case the hardship arose by reason of a change of the defendant's circumstances after the contract under which the defendant agreed to sell her house to the plaintiff, by reason of her husband's bankruptcy and the birth of two children following her development of cancer which necessitated amputation of her leg. In those circumstances specific performance was denied the plaintiff, who was allowed damages by way of compensation.

A further possibility is that to grant specific performance would be contrary to public policy or otherwise against the public interest. For this reason specific

---

51 Compare *Freeman v. Kaltio* (1963), 39 D.L.R. (2d) 496 (B.C.S.C.); *Solle v. Butcher*, [1950] 1 K.B. 671 (C.A.). See also *Grist v. Bailey*, [1967] Ch. 532; *Magee v. Pennine Ins. Co.*, [1969] 2 Q.B. 507. But not where the contract is clear and there is no good reason for refusing to enforce it: *Tamplin v. James* (1880), 15 Ch. D. 215 (C.A.).

52 *E.g.*, he could not complete on the date for closing: *Calmar Housing Ltd. v. Tarmansen* (1990), 10 R.P.R. (2d) 100 (B.C.S.C.). Or he has not fulfilled a condition precedent to performance by the defendant, *e.g.*, by not paying a required deposit: *471011 Ont. Inc. v. Bukville Holdings Ltd.*, above, note 48.

53 *Mosdell v. Jardine*, [1929] 3 W.W.R. 95 (B.C.S.C.); contrast *Beacon Indust. Dev. Corp. v. G.C. Farm Supply Ltd.* (1981), 123 D.L.R. (3d) 467 (Alta. Q.B.). Or the plaintiff is guilty of some inequitable behaviour, *e.g.*, breach of his duty to the other party, whose agent he was: see *Palinko v. Bower*, [1976] 4 W.W.R. 118 (Alta. C.A.); compare *Orangeville Raceway (Ont.) Inc. v. Frieberg* (1988), 34 C.P.C. (2d) 75 (Ont. H.C.); affirmed (1990), 40 O.A.C. 73 (Ont. Div. Ct.); *Leonard H. Cook's Const. Ltd. v. Scott* (1988), 1 R.P.R. (2d) 76 (N.B.Q.B.); affirmed (1989), 9 R.P.R. (2d) 69 (N.B.C.A.) (on other grounds: see above, note 48). He must come with "clean hands".

54 [1974] Ch. 30. Compare *Thibault v. Parker* (1987), 86 N.B.R. (2d) 159 (N.B.Q.B.), attempt to dispose of marital property contrary to the New Brunswick Marital Property Act, S.N.B. 1980, c. M-1.1, s. 19.

55 *Kopec v. Pyret*, [1987] 3 W.W.R. 449 at 458 (Sask. C.A.) *per* Vancise J.A.

56 *Klippert v. Western Service Agreements Ltd.* (1988), 70 Sask. R. 136 (Sask. Q.B.).

57 *Island Properties Ltd. v. Entertainment Enterprises Ltd.* (1986), 26 D.L.R. (4th) 347 (Nfld. C.A.); *John Labatt Ltd. v. Financial Trustco Capital Ltd.* (1989), 96 A.R. 56 (Alta. Q.B.).

58 Sharpe, *op. cit.*, above, note 32, paras. 10.230-10.380.

59 [1984] 1 All E.R. 978 at 981-982; compare *Mitz v. Wiseman* (1971), 22 D.L.R. (3d) 513 (Ont. H.C.).

60 Contrast *Stewart v. Ambrosina* (1975), 63 D.L.R. (3d) 595 (Ont. H.C.); affirmed (1977), 78 D.L.R. (3d) 125 (Ont. C.A.).

performance was refused in *Finney v. Township of McKellar.*[61] There to have ordered the contract performed would have resulted in the fettering of the municipality's freedom to be influenced by a public hearing relating to the diversion of a road (which was involved in the contract with the plaintiff under which property was purchased from him and other property was exchanged). The Ontario Court of Appeal held that specific performance could not be granted. In contrast the English Court of Appeal in *Verrall v. Great Yarmouth Borough Council*[62] would not refuse specific performance of a contract to allow a political party to use a hall belonging to a municipal council for its convention, although the party was unpopular and the letting of the hall could have caused political problems for the council. The argument put forward by the council was that to allow the hall to be used by the political party in question would have resulted in public disorder and breaches of the peace. On this aspect of the case the Court of Appeal upheld the values of freedom of speech and association, and thought that it would be improper to intervene in such a way as to deny the party in question the right to hold its meeting. The public interest, in this instance, was served by enforcing the contract through specific performance rather than by denying such a remedy and permitting only an award of damages.

Specific performance will not be granted where damages would be an adequate remedy in all the circumstances. It is a discretionary remedy, supplementary to the common-law remedy of damages, as Allen J.A. said,[63] and therefore not normally granted where damages provide adequate relief. Hence, if there is something unique about the subject-matter of the contract it is most likely that specific performance, rather than damages, will be ordered.[64]

Finally, there is the question of delay as affecting the granting of a decree of specific performance.[65] The statutes relating to limitation of actions[66] originally only applied to the common-law remedy of damages. Under modern limitation

---

61 (1982), 133 D.L.R. (3d) 351 (Ont. C.A.).

62 [1980] 1 All E.R. 839 (C.A.).

63 *Emerald Resources Ltd. v. Sterling Oil Properties Ltd.*, above, note 42 at 646; *Ryan v. Mutual Tontine Westminister Chambers Assn.*, [1893] 1 Ch. 116 (C.A.). See Sharpe, *op. cit.*, above, note 32, paras. 7.50-7.330. But see the comments made in *Citation Realty Inc. v. 463879 Ont. Ltd.* (1989), 67 D.L.R. (4th) 450 (Ont. H.C.); affirmed (1990), 77 D.L.R. (4th) 384 (Ont. C.A.): above, note 13.

64 See, *e.g., Webster v. Garret Lane Devs. Ltd.* (1989), 70 O.R. (2d) 65 (Ont. H.C.); reversed in part (1992), 10 O.R. (3d) 576 (Ont. C.A.); leave to appeal to S.C.C. refused (1993), 154 N.R. 240 (note) (S.C.C.); *Lawrie v. Gentry Devs. Inc.* (1989), 72 O.R. (2d) 512 (Ont. H.C.) (although the action turned into a claim for damages because the home that was to have been built for the plaintiff was sold to a third party); *Meadowland Dev. Co. v. Haverstock Estate* (1990), 10 R.P.R. (2d) 160 (N.S.T.D.).

Note also the possibility of *election* by the plaintiff between specific performance and damages: *Beauchamp v. Coastal Corp.* (1986), 26 D.L.R. (4th) 146 (Fed. C.A.); *407478 Alta. Ltd. v. Pennant Properties Can. Ltd.* (1990), 113 A.R. 188 (Alta. Q.B.); affirmed (March 4, 1992), Doc. Edmonton Appeal 9003-0902-AC, 9103-0104-AC (Alta. C.A.), where it is pointed out that specific performance avoids the difficulties inherent in assessing damages (and the court obliged the purchaser to choose between specific performance with abatement of the price and damages).

65 Or an injunction: below, p. 797-802.

66 Above, pp. 704-706.

statutes the same is still true. Equitable remedies are not normally subject to the statutory periods of limitation. However, equity developed its own, very comparable doctrine, that of *laches*, under which undue delay in pursuing an equitable remedy, or equitable relief, might disentitle a plaintifff.[67] What that doctrine is has been well described in *Lindsay Petroleum Co. v. Hurd*[68] which has frequently been cited and followed in Canada:

> ...the doctrine of laches in Courts of Equity is not an arbitrary or a technical doctrine. Where it would be practically unjust to give a remedy, either because the party has, by his conduct, done that which might fairly be regarded as equivalent to a waiver of it, or where by his conduct and neglect he has, though perhaps not waiving that remedy, yet put the other party in a situation in which it would not be reasonable to place him if the remedy were afterwards to be asserted, in either of these cases, lapse of time and delay are most material. But in every case, if an argument against relief, which otherwise would be just, is founded upon mere delay, that delay of course not amounting to a bar by any statute of limitations, the validity of that defence must be tried upon principles substantially equitable. Two circumstances, always important in such cases, are, the length of the delay and the nature of the acts done during the interval . . .

Fundamentally what the court is looking at, in such circumstances, is whether the effect of granting equitable relief after the length of time in question, would operate unreasonably to the prejudice of the other party, even though that party was originally guilty of wrongdoing in the form of a breach of contract.[69] Thus, except where the equitable claim is analogous to a claim which is expressly provided for by the limitation statute, for example, a claim for account, in which event the court will apply the statutory period of limitation by analogy, the court will proceed on discretionary lines, permitting the relief where it is appropriate, denying it where to allow it would perpetrate a greater inequity or injustice than to refuse it.[70]

(d) Obligations of plaintiff

As Lord Radcliffe pointed out in *Australian Hardwoods Party v. Railways Commissioner*,[71] there are various reasons why a claim for specific performance is liable to be defeated on grounds of equity. Thus, the plaintiff who "asks the court to enforce by mandatory order in his favour some stipulation of an agreement which itself consists of interdependent undertakings between the plaintiff and the defendant cannot succeed in obtaining such relief if he is at the time in breach of his own obligations."[72] Thus, a buyer who is in default of payment will not

---

67 Megarry J. in *Wroth v. Tyler*, [1974] Ch. 30. See, *e.g., 370866 Ont. Ltd. v. Chizy* (1987), 57 O.R. (2d) 587 (Ont. H.C.).

68 (1874), L.R. 5 P.C. 221 at 239-240 (P.C.) *per* Lord Selborne.

69 *Croft v. Tress* (1967), 61 W.W.R. 201 (B.C.S.C.).

70 Sharpe, *Injunctions and Specific Performance*, 2nd ed. (1992), paras. 1.820-1.1020.

71 [1961] 1 All E.R. 737 at 742 (P.C.); compare *Chappell v. Times Newspapers Ltd.*, [1975] 2 All E.R. 233 (C.A.).

72 [1961] 1 All E.R. 737 at 742 (P.C.): Sharpe, *op. cit.*, above, note 70, paras. 10.580-10.620.

get specific delivery of chattels under a contract of sale.[73] A party who endeavours to establish a contract under the Statute of Frauds by the doctrine of part performance, and then to have that contract specifically enforced, will fail if he is in default with respect to the making of certain payments under the very contract which he is trying to establish and have enforced.[74]

Second, as Lord Radcliffe went on to explain,[75]

> where the agreement is one which involves continuing or future acts to be performed by the plaintiff, he must fail unless he can show that he is ready and willing on his part to carry out those obligations, which are in fact part of the consideration for the undertaking of the defendant that the plaintiff seeks to have enforced.

That was the reason why specific performance was refused in that particular case. It concerned a contract to purchase a sawmill business under an option which was given with a contract by which the plaintiff company took over and operated the defendant company's sawmill for a term of years. The plaintiff company did not prove that it was ready and willing to perform its own obligations under the contract in question. In this respect Lord Radcliffe explained that, despite earlier judicial statements,[76] there was no distinction for this purpose between an executed and an executory contract. The remedy of specific performance was not confined to executory contracts, nor did its application to contracts that were not wholly or in part still executory invite the court to ignore considerations that were properly applicable in instances of executory contracts, for example, the plaintiff's conduct and position.[77] However, where the plaintiff is ready, willing and able to close or complete the transaction, specific performance can and will be granted.[78]

A third requirement is that of "mutuality", a doctrine that has given rise to considerable uncertainty and controversy.[79] In the *Emerald Resources* case,[80] Allen

---

73 Above, note 53; compare *Measures Bros. Ltd. v. Measures*, [1910] 2 Ch. 248; *471011 Ont. Inc. v. Bukville Holdings Ltd.* (1988), 50 R.P.R. 192 (Ont. H.C.), failure by purchaser to pay required second deposit on purchase of land: specific performance denied since a condition precedent to performance by vendor of obligation to convey had not been fulfilled.

74 *Toombs v. Mueller*, [1974] 6 W.W.R. 577 (Alta. S.C.); reversed on appeal without written reasons, [1975] 3 W.W.R. 96 (Alta. C.A.).

75 Above, note 71; compare *Harris v. Robinson* (1892), 21 S.C.R. 390 at 400 (S.C.C.) *per* Strong J; *Stephens v. Gulf Oil Can. Ltd.* (1974), 45 D.L.R. (3d) 161 at 206 (Ont. H.C.) *per* Henry J.; reversed (1976), 11 O.R. (2d) 129 (Ont. C.A.); leave to appeal to S.C.C. refused (1976), 65 D.L.R. (3d) 193n (S.C.C.); Sharpe, *op. cit.*, above, note 70, paras. 10.630-10.640. Compare *471011 Ont. Inc. v. Bukville Holdings Ltd.* (1988), 50 R.P.R. 192 (Ont. H.C.) (citing *Mills v. Haywood* (1877), 6 Ch. D. 196 (C.A.); *Labelle v. O'Connor* (1908), 15 O.L.R. 519 (Ont. C.A.); *Wandoan Holdings Ltd. v. Pieter Vos. Ltd.* (1974), 47 D.L.R. (3d) 202 (Ont. H.C.)).

76 *Wolverhampton & Walsall Ry. Co. v. London & North Western Ry. Co.* (1873), L.R. 16 Eq. 433 at 439 *per* Lord Selborne L.C.; *J.C. Williamson Ltd. v. Lukey* (1931), 45 C.L.R. 282 (Aust. H.C.).

77 Above, note 71, at 743.

78 *Rosenberg v. Waterloo Terrace Ltd.* (1990), 9 R.P.R. (2d) 23 (Ont. H.C.); *Matheson v. Poirier* (1990), 95 N.S.R. (2d) 261 (N.S.T.D.). Contrast *Calmar Housing Ltd. v. Tarmansen* (1990), 10 R.P.R. (2d) 100 (B.C.S.C.).

79 Sharpe, *op. cit.*, above, note 70, paras. 7.820-7.880.

80 *Emerald Resources Ltd. v. Sterling Oil Properties Management Ltd.* (1969), 3 D.L.R. (3d) 630 at 647 (Alta. C.A.); affirmed (1970), 15 D.L.R. (3d) 256 (S.C.C.).

J.A. referred to this doctrine or principle, and cited textbook authority for the proposition that it could mean either: (1) that the court will not grant specific performance to one party when it could not do so at the suit of the other; or (2) that a party who has completed his side of the contract, whether or not he could have been specifically compelled to do so, is entitlted to the remedy. The better view, which was accepted in the United States, was stated to be the latter, that is, that mutuality need not exist at the time of the agreement provided it exists at the time of the hearing. Under the first view, specific performance could not be granted against an infant, since he could never be compelled to perform,[81] nor of a contract which involved the performance of personal services on the part of the plaintiff,[82] even though the defendant had to do something else, for example, as in the *Emerald Resources* case, pay money and royalties. On the second view, if the infant has in fact performed his part of the contract, or the personal services have been rendered, then the plaintiff ought to be able to obtain specific performance of the defendant's side of the bargain. The point was not determined in the *Emerald Resources* case because of other grounds for refusing specific performance, for example, the doctrine that it was not, in general, applicable to contracts involving goods, and the uncertainty whether the interest to be transferred to the plaintiff by the defendant was an interest in land or a chattel.[83] The principle of mutuality, therefore, is still open to discussion.[84] However, it must be noted that there is at least one important exception to its operation. If a contract is required to be in writing or evidenced by a note or memorandum, for example, under the Statute of Frauds, the party who has not signed, may still obtain specific performance against the party who has, even though the latter could not obtain a decree, or any remedy, against the former.[85]

2. Injunctions[86]

(a) Nature and scope

An injuction is an order by a court requiring the defendant to do, or refrain from doing something. If the former, it is a mandatory injunction; if the latter, it is a prohibitory injunction.[87] Such a remedy is closely allied to and indeed may be the converse of a decree of specific performance. To order someone to do

---

81 *Flight v. Bolland* (1828), 4 Russ. 298, 38 E.R. 817; *Lumley v. Ravenscroft*, [1895] 1 Q.B. 683 (C.A.).

82 *Stocker v. Wedderburn* (1857), 3 K. & J. 393.

83 Above, note 80, at 647-648.

84 In *Price v. Strange*, [1977] 3 All E.R. 371, the English Court of Appeal held that the proper date for determining mutuality was the date of *trial*, not the date of the contract, therefore as long as the plaintiff's obligations had been performed, although normally specific performance of such obligations could not have been granted, the plaintiff could be awarded a decree against the defendant.

85 *Morgan v. Holford* (1852), 1 Sm. & G. 101, 65 E.R. 45; and see other exceptions noted in Sharpe, *op. cit.*, above, note 70, para. 7.870, footnote 175.

86 Sharpe, *op. cit.*, above, note 70, chapters 1, 2.

87 Compare *Saskatchewan (Min. of Environment) v. Redberry Dev. Corp.* (1987), 58 Sask. R. 134 (Sask. Q.B.); affirmed (1992), 100 Sask. R. 36 (Sask. C.A.), with *R.E. Newman Exploration Consultants Ltd. v. Veritas Geophysical Ltd.* (1989), 66 Alta. L.R. (2d) 317 (Alta. C.A.).

something may involve specific performance of a contract. To restrain him from doing something, for example, breaking his contract, may be indirectly to compel him to perform the contract. The nature of this remedy, therefore, leads to some difficult problems, especially in relation to contracts to perform some kind of personal service for another party. Everything as will be seen, depends upon whether the obligation can be regarded, and understood, as involving a positive act or a negative bargain.

The problems stem from the unwillingess of courts of equity to compel the performance of certain contracts, notably those which involve a party in performing personal services.[88] To do this smacks a little of slavery or repression; it is against public policy to make one person serve another when he is unwilling to do so. Also it is unwise to force a person to take another into his employment against his will, especially when the employment may involve some fiduciary, or confidential relationship. Furthermore, it is impossible for the court to supervise the performnce in any satisfactory manner. Can the courts do indirectly what they will not do directly? This raises the issue of the injunction.

(b) Availability

Clearly, in general, a court can issue an injunction to make a party perform his contract, or refrain from breaking it, at least where the above-mentioned difficulties do not arise. Thus, for example, injunctions have been issued to force a party to remove the surface of a road which had been raised too high in breach of the contract between parties,[89] to restrain a defendant from using material relating to the life of William Lyon Mackenzie in a way contrary to the spirit of the agreement under which the defendant was given access to the documents in question,[90] to prevent the breach of an agreement under which the plaintiff obtained from the defendant exclusive rights to the manufacture and distribution in two provinces of certain patent and proprietary remedies,[91] to prevent the improper termination of an automobile franchise agreement,[92] to prevent a party from selling property

---

88 *Rigby v. Connol* (1880), 14 Ch. D. 482 at 487 *per* Jessel M.R.; compare above, p. 791. The notion of "personal services" extends to all situations in which there is some personal relationship between the parties, *e.g.*, agency, partnership, apprenticeship, charitable activities, as well as services. For the use of the injunction in the context of labour disputes, however, see the judgment of Cartwright J. in *I.B.E.W., Loc. 2085 v. Winnipeg Bldrs.' Exchange*, [1967] S.C.R. 628 at 638-640 (S.C.C.); compare Sharpe, *op. cit.*, above, note 70, para. 7.580, and the authorities there cited.

89 *Charrington v. Simons & Co.*, [1971] 2 All E.R. 588 (C.A.).

90 *Lindsey v. Le Sueur* (1913), 29 O.L.R. 648 (Ont. C.A.) in which Meredith C.J.O. relied on *Morison v. Moat* (1851), 9 Hare 241, 68 E.R. 492; affirmed (1852), 21 L.J. Ch. 248; *Lamb v. Evans*, [1893] 1 Ch. 218 (C.A.); *Amber Size & Chemical Co. v. Menzel*, [1913] 2 Ch. 239.

91 *Pasen v. Dom. Herb Distributors Inc.*, [1968] 1 O.R. 688 (Ont. H.C.); affirmed [1968] 2 O.R. 516 (Ont. C.A.).

92 *Baxter Motors Ltd. v. Amer. Motors (Can.) Ltd.*, [1973] 6 W.W.R. 501 (B.C.S.C.); compare *Sky Petroleum Ltd. v. V.I.P. Petroleum Ltd.*, [1974] 1 All E.R. 954.

which would have involved that party in a breach of contract *vis-à-vis* the plaintiff.[93] In all these instances, it would appear, no suggestion was raised that by compelling the performance, or preventing the breach, in question the court was transgressing the principle that personal services cannot be enforced, even though the effect of the injunction was to interfere with the freedom of a party to act as he wished. Once that freedom had been circumscribed by contract, then the courts will be prepared, in an appropriate, suitable case, to enjoin the party in question from loosening himself from the fetters which have been self-imposed.[94]

In cases where a party has undertaken to perform personal services, as contrasted with other obligations such as those which have been referred to in the previous paragraph, an injunction in the face of an actual or threatened breach of such contract has been denied if it would require the employer to keep employing the employee, or the employee to remain in the service of the employer.[95] Thus, for example, in *Kapp v. British Columbia Lions Football Club*,[96] the court refused to grant the plaintiff, a football player, an injunction against the club, to restrain the club from suspending the plaintiff and reporting him to the Canadian Football League, as they claimed to be able to do under his contract with the club. To have granted such an injunction would have compelled the club to employ him. Similarly, in *Page One Records Ltd. v. Britton*[97] an English court refused to grant an injunction to the manager of a song group to restrain the latter from engaging as its manager anyone but the plaintiff, during the time that the plaintiff was bringing an action against the group for breach of his contract of employment with them. The contract between them was in fact a contract for personal services, since the plaintiff was engaged to manage the group's affairs. The reason why the injunction was refused was because the plaintiff had to perform duties of a personal and fiduciary nature, the group had lost confidence in the plaintiff, and the plaintiff might fail in his duty to the group. It would obviously be injudicious to compel

---

93 *P.E.I. Packers Ltd. v. P.E.I. Dev. Agency* (1986), 59 Nfld. & P.E.I.R. 339 (P.E.I.S.C.); *Canmar Grain Inc. v. Radloff* (1986), 52 Sask. R. 161 (Sask. Q.B.); *Saskatoon Funeral Home Co. v. Westwood Holdings Ltd.* (1988), 69 Sask. R. 113 (Sask. C.A.) (contrast *Canwest Pacific Television Inc. v. 147250 Can. Ltd.* (1987), 14 B.C.L.R. (2d) 104 (B.C.C.A.)). But there must be a a breach (or apprehended breach) of the contract: *Patsalas v. National Ballet of Can.* (1986), 13 C.P.R. (3d) 522 (Ont. H.C.).

94 Hence injunctions may be issued to prevent the breach of a contract in restraint of trade, as long as the contract is one that is valid and not void as against public policy: see, *e.g.*, *Wallace Welding Supplies Ltd. v. Wallace* (1986), 8 C.P.C. (2d) 157 (Ont. H.C.); *Tsambalieros v. McKean* (1986), 11 C.P.C. (2d) 1 (Ont. H.C.); *Miller v. Toews*, [1991] 2 W.W.R. 604 (Man. C.A.). On restraint of trade see above, pp. 388-415. Similarly in *Premier Propane Inc. v. Inter-Valley Propane Ltd.* (1990), 49 B.L.R. 167 (B.C.S.C) a contract to make the plaintiff the exclusive supplier of propane to the defendant was not regarded as a negative covenant, but an injunction was refused on other grounds, *viz.*, no proof of irreparable harm to the plaintiff for losing the defendant as a customer: compare below, pp. 800, 804.

95 Sharpe, *op. cit.*, above, note 70, paras. 7.540-7.630.

96 (1967), 61 W.W.R. 31 especially at 41-42 (B.C. Chambers) *per* Dyer J. Compare the converse situation in *Detroit Football Co. v. Dublinski; Detroit Football Co. v. Mains*, [1955] O.W.N. 805 (Ont. H.C.) (which became an action for damages by the time it was on appeal: *Detroit Football Club v. Dublinski*, [1956] O.R. 744 (Ont. H.C.); reversed [1957] O.R. 58 (Ont. C.A.)).

97 [1967] 3 All E.R. 822.

these parties to work and act together, just as it would have been foolhardy to force the football club to use the plaintiff on the team when there were, or might have been grounds for suspecting his ability or loyalty.

(c) Negative obligations[98]

Nonetheless, there are cases where an injunction can be issued, even though the contract in question is one involving personal services. The origin of the jurisdiction to do this is the decision in the famous case of *Lumley v. Wagner*,[99] in which Lord St. Leonards issued an injunction to prevent the opera singer, Joanna Wagner, from performing anywhere but the place in which she had contracted to sing, that is, the plaintiff's opera house. The court could not force her to sing *for* the plaintiff, but it could prevent her from singing for anyone *except* the plaintiff. Thus this jurisdiction arises where there is not only a positive stipulation, for example, to sing for P, but also a negative one, that is, not to sing for anyone other than P. As Lord Cairns explained in the later case of *Doherty v. Allman*,[100]

> [i]f parties, for valuable consideration, with their eyes open, contract that a particular thing shall not be done, all that a Court of Equity has to do is to say, by way of injunction, that which the parties have already said by way of covenant, that the thing shall not be done; and in such case the injunction does nothing more than give the sanction of the process of the Court to that which already is the contract between the parties. It is not then a question of the balance of convenience or inconvenience, or of the amount of damage or of injury—it is the specific performance, by the Court, of that negative bargain which the parties have made, with their eyes open, between themselves.

On this basis there have been a number of instances in which such negative stipulations have been enforced by injunction.[101]

Though there is such a stipulation in a contract, that will not necessarily suffice to permit the court to enforce in this indirect way what it cannot specifically order performed. As Stamp J. made clear in the *Page One Records* case,[102] there is a distinction between a covenant that only involves payment of money and one which is designed to tie the parties together in a relationship of mutual confidence, mutual

---

98   Sharpe, *op. cit.*, above, note 70, paras. 9.10-9.120. Note that some negative covenants or obligations may be *implied*, *e.g.*, a covenant of quiet enjoyment. In such instances it is not necessary for the plaintiff to prove that he would suffer irreparable harm if he were obliged only to claim damages: *Chevron Can. Resources Ltd. v. Heaman* (1990), 66 Man. R. (2d) 66 (Man. Q.B.); reversed in part (1991), 75 Man. R. (2d) 41 (Man. C.A.); *Montreal Trust Co. v. Montreal Trust Co. of Can.* (1988), 24 B.C.L.R. (2d) 238 (B.C.C.A.); compare *Petro-Can. Inc. v. Shaganappi Village Shopping Centre Ltd.* (1990), 108 A.R. 289 (Alta. Q.B.); reversed [1991] 1 W.W.R. 169 (Alta. C.A.).

99   (1852), 1 De G.M. & G. 604, 42 E.R. 687. See Sharpe, *op. cit.*, above, note 70, paras. 9.210-9.300.

100 (1878), 3 App. Cas. 709 at 720 (H.L.), applied in *Dobell v. Cowichan Copper Co.* (1967), 61 W.W.R. 594 (B.C.S.C.).

101 See, *e.g.*, *William Robinson & Co. v. Heuer*, [1898] 2 Ch. 451 (C.A.); *Warner Bros. Pictures Inc. v. Nelson*, [1936] 3 All E.R. 160; the *Dobell* case, above, note 100: *Decro-Wall Int. S.A. v. Practitioners in Marketing Ltd.*, [1971] 2 All E.R. 216 (C.A.).

102 Above, note 97, at 826.

endeavour, and reciprocal obligations, although the fact that some degree of mutual co-operation or confidence is needed will not necessarily preclude the court from granting negative injunctions designed to encourage the party in breach to perform his part.[103] Moreover, if the effect of the injunction, where there is a negative stipulation, would be to compel the defendant to perform the contract for personal services or else be unfree to do anything at all, the court will deny the injunction.[104] In the words of Stamp J.[105]

> where a contract of personal services contains negative covenants, the enforcement of which will amount either to a decree of specific performance of the positive covenants of the contract or to the giving of a decree under which the defendant must either remain idle or perform those positive covenants, the court will not enforce those negative covenants.

The courts will not necessarily import or imply negative covenants into a contract that contains positive stipulations, for the purpose of finding a negative covenant to enforce by injunction. The parties must have made an independent negative stipulation which falls within the narrow confines of such stipulations that are enforceable.[106] The courts are not anxious to extend the scope of the *Lumley v. Wagner* principle, even though they recognize and accept its existence.[107]

(d) Adequacy of damages[108]

The courts will not grant an injunction where an award of damages (or some other remedy) would be an adequate compensation or protection of the interests of the plaintiff.[109] In *Hill v. C.A. Parsons & Co.*[110] the English Court of Appeal

---

103 *Evans Marshall & Co. v. Bertola S.A.*, [1973] 1 All E.R. 992 at 1004-1005 (C.A.) *per* Sachs L.J.
104 *Whitwood Chemical Co. v. Hardman*, [1891] 2 Ch. 415 (C.A.); *Geometrics v. Smith* (1975), 65 D.L.R. (3d) 62 (Ont. H.C.).
105 Above, note 97, at 827.
106 *Mortimer v. Beckett*, [1920] 1 Ch. 571; *Whitwood Chemical Co. v. Hardman*, above, note 104. But an injunction will not be issued for breach of a negative covenant where the parties are in dispute about the facts: *Atlantic Speedy Propane Ltd. v. St. John Raquet Club Ltd.* (1986), 75 N.B.R. (2d) 238 (N.B.Q.B.).
107 See however the vigorous remarks of Lord Denning M.R. in *Hill v. C.A. Parsons & Co.*, [1971] 3 All E.R. 1345 at 1350 (C.A.), with which contrast *Chappell v. Times Newspapers Ltd.* [1975] 2 All E.R. 233 (C.A.).
108 Sharpe, *Injunctions and Specific Performance*, 2nd ed. (1992), paras. 1.60-1.250. Note the statement in *Miller v. Toews*, [1991] 2 W.W.R. 604 (Man. C.A.), in relation to interim or interlocutory injunctions, below, pp. 803-806, that the test was not whether damages would be an adequate remedy, but whether it was "just" to confine the plaintiff to a remedy in damages: this was a restraint of trade case, in which, perhaps, the applicable principles might differ.
109 Nor will the courts issue an injunction to restrain the breach of a contract which could be rescinded on the grounds of unconscionability: *Clifford Davis Mgmt. Ltd. v. W.E.A. Records Ltd.*, [1975] 1 All E.R. 237 (C.A.). Note also the problem of awarding an injunction which might involve supervision by the court: Sharpe, *op. cit.*, above, note 108, paras. 1.260-1.480; and the effect of delay, Sharpe, paras. 1.820-1.1020.
110 [1971] 3 All E.R. 1345 (C.A.). Contrast with this the refusal to grant an injunction in *Chappell v. Times Newspapers Ltd.*, [1975] 2 All E.R. 233 (C.A.).

was prepared to grant an injunction to restrain the employers from treating the plaintiff's contract of employment with them as at an end. Because of the shortness of the notice, the effect of certain statutory provisions about to come into effect, and the continuance of the personal relationship between the parties, damages were not adequate and an injunction was a reasonable remedy, even though the case involved a contract of employment. As Sachs L.J. explained in the later case of *Evans Marshall & Co. v. Bertola S.A.*,[111]

> The courts have repeatedly recognized that there can be claims under contracts in which, as here, it is unjust to confine a plaintiff to his damages for their breach. Great difficulty in estimating these damages is one factor that can be and has been taken into account. Another factor is the creation of certain areas of damage which cannot be taken into monetary account in a common law action for breach of contract: loss of goodwill and trade reputation are examples . . .Generally, indeed, the grant of injunctions in contract cases stems from such factors.

So in *Denison v. Carrousel Farms Ltd.*,[112] Cromarty J. and the Ontario Court of Appeal granted a permanent injunction in a case where the lessee of commercial premises used them for purposes other than those for which he was entitled to use them under the lease. Since the covenant in question was not in restraint of trade, it could be enforced by injunction, as long as the injury to the plaintiff could not be adequately compensated by a small money payment and injunction would not be oppressive to the defendant. Such was the situation in that instance. However, where damages would be an adequate form of remedy, *e.g.*, where the subject-matter of a contract was not so unique and irreplaceable that it would be necessary to prevent the defendant from disposing of it,[113] an injunction will be refused.[114]

(e) Duration

(i) *Two kinds of injunction*

Aside from the division of injunctions into prohibitory and mandatory, there is another important distinction that must be drawn. This depends on the length of time for which the injunction is to endure. The law distinguishes between permanent or perpetual injunctions and interlocutory or interim injunctions.

---

111 [1973] 1 All E.R. 992 at 1005 (C.A.). For the later history of this litigation see [1975] 2 Lloyds' Rep. 373; [1976] 2 Lloyd's Rep. 17. See also *Sky Petroleum Ltd. v. V.I.P. Petroleum Ltd.*, [1974] 1 All E.R. 954, where specific performance could be ordered, therefore an injunction could be granted to restrain the defendants from withholding supplies from the plaintiff; damages would not have compensated the plaintiff.

112 (1981), 129 D.L.R. (3d) 334 (Ont. H.C.); affirmed (1982), 138 D.L.R. (3d) 381 (Ont. C.A.).

113 *Taylor v. Eisner* (1989), 80 Sask. R. 84 (Sask. C.A.).

114 *Relais Nordik Inc. v. Secunda Marine Services Ltd.* (1988), 24 F.T.R. 256 (Fed. T.D.); *Atlantic Speedy Propane Ltd. v. St. John Raquet Club Ltd.* (1988), 75 N.B.R. (2d) 238 (N.B.Q.B.); *Donovan v. Lee* (1989), 65 D.L.R. (4th) 103 (B.C.C.A.); *Sam Vézina Inc. v. Laurentian Pilotage Authority* (1988), 21 F.T.R. 290 (Fed. T.D.); *Imperial Chemical Industries PLC v. Apotex Inc.* (1989), 26 C.I.P.R. 1 (Fed. C.A.).

(ii) *Permanent injunctions*

A permanent, or perpetual, injunction is directed towards the final settlement and enforcement of the rights of the parties which are in dispute. It is none the less perpetual because those rights are restricted in point of time.[115] Hence, an injunction may be classified as permanent or perpetual even though it is to last for a limited period of time, as long as its purpose is to resolve the issue finally between the parties. In *Nili Holdings Ltd. v. Rose,*[116] an interim injunction was granted the plaintiff to restrain the defendant from performing at another restaurant in Victoria contrary to the defendant's covenant with the plaintiff not to do so. On the application to make the injunction permanent, it was held that the interim injunction had been properly granted, since the covenant was not in restraint of trade. Hence the injunction could be continued. However, in the circumstances of this case to continue the injunction would have worked too harsh a burden economically and socially on the defendant. Hence the restrictive covenant was held to expire, as of the date of the judgment, although the contract had not yet terminated, and the injunction was not to continue because there was no contractual basis for its being granted.[117]

(iii) *Interlocutory and interim injunctions*

An interlocutory injunction is directed to ensure that particular defined acts do not take place pending the final determination by the court of the rights of the parties, so that, in the absence of a subsequent order to the contrary, it continues up to, but not beyond, the final hearing of the proceedings.[118] An interim injunction is a particular variety of interlocutory injunction which may be granted for a very short period until an application for an interlocutory injunction can be made. This can occur only in exceptional circumstances.[119] Such injunctions may be granted ex parte, that is, on the application of one party alone, without necessarily hearing the other side. Such injunctions restrain the defendant not until the final hearing or further order, but until a named date or further order, from performing the acts which are in question.[120]

In recent years there has been much debate in Canadian courts on the question whether the test for granting such interlocutory or interim injunctions should be the older test or the newer more flexible, less rigorous one enunciated by the House of Lords in *American Cyanamid Co. v. Ethicon.*[121] Under the older test, the basis

---

115 Spry, *Equitable Remedies*, 2nd ed. (1980), p. 355.
116 (1981), 123 D.L.R. (3d) 454 (B.C.S.C.). See above, p. 394.
117 (1981), 123 D.L.R. (3d) 454 at 466 (B.C.S.C.).
118 Spry, *op. cit.*, above, note 115, p. 417.
119 *Ibid.*, at p. 466.
120 *Ibid.*, at p. 469; see also Sharpe, *op. cit.*, above, note 108, paras. 2.20-2.50.
121 [1975] A.C. 396 (H.L.); see Sharpe, *op. cit.*, above, note 108, paras. 2.60-2.630. See also *N.W.L. Ltd. v. Woods*, [1979] 1 W.L.R. 1294 (H.L.) (see *Popsicle Industries Ltd. v. Ault Foods Ltd.* (1987), 17 C.I.P.R. 86 (Fed. T.D.)); *Hadmor Productions Ltd. v. Hamilton*, [1983] A.C. 191 (H.L.), modifying the *Ethicon* formula.

for the granting of such an injunction was whether the plaintiff had made out a *prima facie* case which might have stood a good chance of success at the trial, such that it would be both unfair and inconvenient to make the plaintiff wait for the eventual outcome of the trial, by which time, even if ultimately successful, he might have suffered such loss that he could not then be adequately compensated or relieved by an award of damages. In the *Ethicon* case, the test was whether a court would be satisfied that the plaintiff's case was not frivolous and that there was a substantial issue or question to be tried.[122] If such were the case, then the court had to take into account whether the harm threatened to the plaintiff and his interests was irreparable, whether this harm would be compensable by an award of damages,[123] and whether it would be convenient to compel the defendant to act or refrain from acting as he was doing, or as he intened to do.[124] The function of the court was to determine the "balance of convenience" between the parties.[125]

It has been suggested[126] that the formula set out in the *Ethicon* case "will not be applied automatically or mechanically by the courts." A comparison of the Canadian cases in which this issue has arisen reveals that there are different approaches. Sometimes the courts, applying the *Ethicon* approach, have rejected the need to show a *prima facie* case as a threshold test, a development welcomed by one writer.[127] On other occasions, however, courts have employed the *prima*

---

122 Sharpe, *op. cit.*, above, note 108, paras. 2.130-2.380. But see *Chevron Can. Resources Ltd. v. Heaman* (1990), 66 Man. R. (2d) 66 (Man. Q.B.); reversed in part (1991), 75 Man. R. (2d) 41 (Man. C.A.), on when proof of irreparable harm is *not* required: above, note 98. See also *Miller v. Toews*, [1991] 2 W.W.R. 604 (Man. C.A.).

123 Sharpe, *op. cit.*, above, note 108, paras. 2.390-2.520.

124 *Ibid.*, paras. 2.530-2.540. Compare the remarks of McLachlin J.A., as to a "two-pronged" test, in *British Columbia (A.G.) v. Wale*, [1987] 2 W.W.R. 331 at 343 (B.C.C.A.). The learned judge considered that the issue of "irreparable harm" was integral to the issue of "balance of convenience".

125 And not to alter the *status quo*: see *Stevenson v. Air Can.* (1981), 126 D.L.R. (3d) 242 (Ont. H.C.); reversed (1982), 132 D.L.R. (3d) 406 (Ont. Div. Ct.); but to maintain the *status quo*, though not so as to allow a party to pursue a remedy before a statutory body over which the court had no control: *Lamont v. Air Can.* (1981), 126 D.L.R. (3d) 266 (Ont. H.C.); *Aetna Financial Services Ltd. v. Feigelman* (1985), 15 D.L.R. (4th) 161 (S.C.C.).

126 Sharpe, *op. cit.*, above, note 108, para. 2.600.

127 *Ibid.*, para. 2.620. See *Abouna v. Foothills Prov. Gen. Hosp. Bd.* (1975), 65 D.L.R. (3d) 337 (Alta. T.D.) (*prima facie* case *or* serious question to be tried, then applying "balance of covenience" test); *Labelle v. Ottawa Real Estate Bd.* (1977), 78 D.L.R. (3d) 558 (Ont. H.C.); *Yule Inc. v. Atlantic Pizza Delight Franchise (1968) Ltd.* (1977), 80 D.L.R. (3d) 725 (Ont. Div. Ct.); *A.G. Ont. v. Harry; A.G. Ont. v. Yeotes* (1979), 93 D.L.R. (3d) 332 (Ont. H.C.); *Morgan Earl Sounds Inc. v. Eleven Yorkville Ltd.* (1979), 9 R.P.R. 197 (Ont. H.C.); *Hoskin v. Price Waterhouse Ltd.* (1982), 35 O.R. (2d) 350 (Ont. H.C.); *Sony of Can. Ltd. v. Hi-Fi Express Inc.* (1982), 38 O.R. (2d) 505 (Ont. H.C.); *Waxoyl A.G. v. Waxoyl Can. Ltd.* (1982), 38 O.R. (2d) 672 (Ont. H.C.); *Chantler v. Metro. Toronto Hockey League* (1983), 44 O.R. (2d) 85 (Ont. H.C.); *Law Soc. of Alta. v. Black* (1983), 8 D.L.R. (4th) 346 (Alta. C.A.); *Heathview Devs. Ltd. v. Credit Foncier* (1982), 37 O.R. (2d) 262 (Ont. H.C.); Sharpe, *op. cit.*, above, note 108, para. 2.280, footnote 42. See also, *Pacific Western Airlines Ltd. v. B.C.F.L.* (1986), 26 D.L.R. (4th) 87 (B.C.C.A.); *P.E.I. Packers Ltd. v. P.E.I. Dev. Agency* (1986), 59 Nfld. & P.E.I.R. 339 (P.E.I.S.C.); *Corona Minerals Corp. v. CSA Management Ltd.* (1989), 68 O.R. (2d) 425 (Ont. H.C.); *Petro-Can. Inc. v. Shaganappi Village Shopping Centre Ltd.* (1990), 108 A.R. 289 (Alta. Q.B.); reversed [1991] 1 W.W.R. 169 (Alta. C.A.); *Atlantic Speedy Propane Ltd. v. St. John Raquet Club Ltd.* (1986), 75 N.B.R. (2d) 238 (N.B.Q.B.); *Int. Paints (Can.) Ltd.*

facie case test, either as well as the formula from the *Ethicon* case, or as a basis for making determination.[128] It has been suggested that the *Ethicon* formula may not apply in all instances, for example, in patent cases, where the older *prima facie* case test might be more appropriate,[129] and that the nature of the discretion to be exercised by the court cannot be defined precisely, therefore making the older test and the *Ethicon* test both relevant.[130] The *Ethicon* test or formula may be a guide to the exercise of the court's discretion, but it should not necessarily be used as an inflexible guide that must be followed in each consecutive step if the court is to act properly and in accordance with principle:

> The checklist of factors which the courts have developed — relative strength of the case, irreparable harm, and balance of convenience — should not be employed as a series of independent hurdles [although often they are]. They should be seen in the

---

v. Consolidated Coatings Corp. (1986), 4 F.T.R. 203 (Fed. T.D.); *Cougar Helicopters Inc. v. Clearwater Holdings Ltd.* (1986), 74 N.S.R. (2d) 203 (N.S.T.D.); *Ikea Ltd. v. Idea Design Ltd.* (1987), 8 F.T.R. 215 (Fed. T.D.); *Malloway v. Tzeachten Indian Band* (1987), 17 F.T.R. 196 (Fed. T.D.); *Chieftain Products Inc. v. Coleco Industries Inc.* (1988), 21 C.P.R. (3d) 386 (Ont. H.C.); *Sam Vézina Inc. v. Laurentian Pilotage Authority* (1988), 21 F.T.R. 290 (Fed. T.D.); *Turbo Resources Ltd. v. Petro-Can. Inc.* (1989), 24 C.P.R. (3d) 1 (Fed. C.A.); *Imperial Chemical Industries PLC v. Apotex Inc.* (1989), 26 C.I.P.R. 1 (Fed. C.A.); *Ledrew v. Lundrigans-Comstock Ltd.* (1990), 85 Nfld. & P.E.I.R. 19 (Nfld. T.D.).

128 *Reiser & Co. v. Nadore Food Processing Equip. Ltd.* (1977), 81 D.L.R. (3d) 278 (Ont. H.C.); *Toronto Marlboro Major Junior "A" Hockey Club v. Tonelli* (1975), 67 D.L.R. (3d) 214 (Ont. H.C.); *Lambair Ltd. v. Aero Trades (Western) Ltd.* (1978), 87 D.L.R. (3d) 500 (S.C.C.); *Lido Indust. Products Ltd. v. Melnor Mfg. Ltd.*, [1968] S.C.R. 769 (S.C.C.); and see *London v. Talbot Square Ltd.* (1978), 93 D.L.R. (3d) 364 (Ont. Div. Ct.); *Cantol Ltd. v. Brodi Chemicals Ltd.* (1978), 94 D.L.R. (3d) 265 (Ont. H.C.); *ATV Music Publishing of Can. Ltd. v. Rogers Radio Broadcasting Ltd.* (1982), 35 O.R. (2d) 417 (Ont. H.C.); Sharpe, *op. cit.*, above, note 108, para. 2.280, footnote 44. *Petro-Can. Inc. v. Landcorp Ont. Ltd.* (1988), 50 R.P.R. 126 (Ont. H.C.); affirmed (1988), 50 R.P.R. xxxi (Ont. Div. Ct.); *Saskatoon Funeral Home Co. v. Westwood Holdings Ltd.* (1988), 69 Sask. R. 113 (Sask. C.A.); *Tsambalieros v. McKean* (1986), 11 C.P.C. (2d) 1 (Ont. H.C.); *Popsicle Industries Ltd. v. Ault Foods Ltd.* (1987), 17 C.P.R. (3d) 1 (Fed. T.D.); *Ainley & Associates Ltd. v. Tatham* (1989), 46 B.L.R. 104 (Ont. H.C.); *Alnor Services Ltd. v. Sawyer* (1990), 31 C.C.E.L. 34 (B.C.S.C.); *Mercury Marine Ltd. v. Dillon* (1986), 30 D.L.R. (4th) 627 (Ont. H.C.).
    Note the criticism of the *Ethicon* principle in subsequent English cases, *e.g.*, *Fellowes & Sons v. Fisher*, [1976] Q.B. 122 (C.A.). See also, generally Baker, "Interlocutory Injunctions — A Discussion of the 'New Rules'" (1977), 42 Sask. L.R. 53; Hammond, "Interlocutory Injunctions: Time for a New Model" (1980), 30 U. of T. L.J. 240; Rogers and Habetz, "Getting the Pre-Trial Injunction" (1982), 60 Can. Bar Rev. 1.

129 *Yule Inc. v. Atlantic Pizza Delight Franchise (1968) Ltd.* (1977), 17 O.R. (2d) 505 at 513 (Ont. Div. Ct.), citing *Teledyne Industries Inc. v. Lido Industrial Products Ltd.* (1977), 79 D.L.R. (3d) 446 (Ont. H.C.); affirmed (1977), 86 D.L.R. (3d) 446 (Ont. C.A.). Contrast *Imperial Chemical Industries PLC v. Apotex Inc.* (1989), 26 C.I.P.R. 1 (Fed. C.A.).

130 *Carlton Realty Co. v. Maple Leaf Mills Ltd.* (1978), 93 D.L.R. (3d) 106 (Ont. H.C.); compare *Esquimalt Anglers' Assoc. v. R.* (1989), 21 F.T.R. 304; see also *Sacred Heart Academy Corp. v. Regina Roman Catholic Separate School Division No. 81*, [1989] 5 W.W.R. 652 at 661 (Sask. Q.B.) (affirmed [1989] 6 W.W.R. 193 (Sask. C.A.)), suggesting that in breach of contract cases the test should be whether a *prima facie* case can be made out by the plaintiff, whereas the *Ethicon* test might be appropriate in other cases. For example, the lesser test might be applicable in a case of breach of fiduciary duty: *Ainley & Associates Ltd. v. Tatham* (1989), 46 B.L.R. 104 (Ont. H.C.); compare *Metropolitan Stores (MTS) Ltd. v. Man. Food & Commercial Workers, Local 832* below, note 132.

nature of evidence relevant to the central issue of assessing the relative risks of harm to the parties from granting or withholding interlocutory relief.[131]

In a case concerning whether proceedings should be stayed, an issue that resembles the question whether an interlocutory injunction should be granted, *Metropolitan Stores (MTS) Ltd. v. Manitoba Food & Commercial Workers, Local 832*,[132] the Supreme Court of Canada refused to choose between the older, traditional test of a *prima facie* case and the lesser test of the *Ethicon* case, although it appears to have been suggested that in contract cases the appropriate test was that of a "serious question", *i.e.*, the test proposed in the *Ethicon* case. In a later case, however, the *Metro Stores* case was distinguished, and the test held appropriate was whether it was just and reasonable to grant a stay of proceedings.[133] In relation to such relief the situation seems to be as confused as it is in regard to the issuance of interim or interlocutory injunctions. The idea that the true test is whether it is just and reasonable to grant such relief has also been propounded in several cases.[134]

Some of this uncertainty may be derived from the decision of the Supreme Court of Canada in *Aetna Financial Services Ltd. v. Feigelman*.[135] In this case, which was concerned with the issuance of a "Mareva" injunction, the court made quite clear that injunctions of this, or apparently any other type, should not be issued if their effect would be to determine the outcome of the issue between parties before any trial of the matter. Hence in some cases, in which this decision was applied,[136] the *Ethicon* doctrine was not invoked because to have done so would have settled the issue between the parties without a proper trial.

Such conflicting decisions make it difficult to state with any certainty what the law relating to the issuance of interim or interlocutory injunctions is in cases of breach of contract. Certainty waits on the resolution of these conflicts by the Supreme Court of Canada as and when occasion arises.

---

131 Sharpe, *op. cit.*, above, note 108, para. 2.630. Note also the development of interim injunctions to restrain a defendant from dealing with his property before judgment ("Mareva" injunctions): Sharpe, *op. cit.*, above, note 108, paras. 2.750-2.1090; *Can. Pacific Airlines Ltd. v. Hind* (1981), 122 D.L.R. (3d) 498 (Ont. H.C.) (on which see the limitations placed by the Supreme Court of Canada in *Aetna Financial Services Ltd. v. Feigelman* (1985), 15 D.L.R. (4th) 161 (S.C.C.); and orders to permit a plaintiff access to a defendant's premises to inspect documents and remove items belonging to the plaintiff ("Anton Piller" injunctions): Sharpe, *op. cit.*, above, note 108, paras. 2.1100-2.1300; *Nintendo of America Inc. v. Coinex Video Games Inc.* (1982), 46 N.R. 311 (Fed. C.A.).

132 [1987] 1 S.C.R. 110 (S.C.C.). See also *Toth v. Canada (Min. of Employment & Immigration)* (1988), 86 N.R. 302 (Fed. C.A.).

133 *Vanbrabant v. Alberta (Min. of Education)* (1989), 37 C.P.C. (2d) 113 (Alta. C.A.).

134 *J.W. Bird & Co. v. Levesque* (1988), 82 N.S.R. (2d) 435 (N.S.T.D.); *Miller v. Toews*, [1991] 2 W.W.R. 604 (Man. C.A.); *Arton Holdings Ltd. v. Gateway Realty Ltd.* (1990), 96 N.S.R. (2d) 82 (N.S.C.A.).

135 Above, note 131.

136 *Canwest Pacific Television Inc. v. 147250 Can. Ltd.* (1987), 14 B.C.L.R. (2d) 104 (B.C.C.A.); *Relais Nordik Inc. v. Secunda Marine Services Ltd.* (1988), 24 F.T.R. 256 (Fed. T.D.).

3. Rescission

(a) Common-law rescission

A party may be able to rescind a contract, that is, treat it as a nullity, without having to pray in aid the action of a court. Such rescission is possible wherever a party has entered into a contract which is voidable at his option, and only requires some conduct by that party with respect to the other, for example, informing him of his decision to rescind,[137] that amounts to a clear election that he intends to avoid the contract. The distinction between this kind of rescission and rescission under equitable doctrines is quite clear from the language of Lord Summer in *Hirji Mulji v. Cheong Yue Steamship Co.*:[138]

> Rescission (except by mutual consent or by a competent court) is the right of one party, arising upon conduct by the other, by which he intimates his intention to abide by the contract no longer. It is a right to treat the contract as at an end, if he chooses, and to claim damages for its total breach, but it is a right in his option and does not depend in theory on any implied term providing for its exercise, but is given by the law in vindication of a breach.

Such rescission operates by virtue of the common law, not equity. It may occur where an infant has entered into a contract which is not binding upon him, and is not void *ab initio*,[139] where a contract has been induced by fraud, even though no damage may have been suffered by the party rescinding,[140] where a contract has been procured by duress.[141]

There is another sense, or use, of the term rescission at common law. The expression was sometimes used to refer to what happened when one party accepted the repudiation of the contract by the other party, in consequence of the latter's breach of an essential term of the contract. In *Buckland v. Farmer*,[142] where the English Court of Appeal considered these two meanings of "rescission" at common law, it was left open whether, after repudiation by breach of an essential term, the innocent party could unilaterally rescind the contract so as to annul it and treat it as if it had never been made. If he could have done this, the innocent party could have sough *restitutio in integrum*, rather than damages which would

---

137 Compare *Car & Universal Finance Co. v. Caldwell*, [1964] 1 All E.R. 290 (C.A.), a case concerning avoidance of a voidable sale of goods by informing the Automobile Association and the police; Fridman, *Sale of Goods in Canada*, 3rd ed. (1986), pp. 134-135.

138 [1926] A.C. 497 at 509-510 (P.C.).

139 Above, pp. 147, 151.

140 *Pomehichuk v. Gale*, [1950] 2 W.W.R. 66 (Man. K.B.); *Muise v. Whalen* (1990), 96 N.S.R. (2d) 298 (N.S.T.D.); *TWT Enterprises Ltd. v. Westgreen Devs. (North) Ltd.*, [1991] 3 W.W.R. 80 (Alta. Q.B.); affirmed [1992] 5 W.W.R. 341 (Alta. C.A.).

141 Above, pp. 313-320. See, *e.g.*, *Byle v. Byle* (1990), 65 D.L.R. (4th) 641 (B.C.C.A.). Contrast *N.A.B.E.T., Loc. 913 v. Cramm* (1986), 63 Nfld. & P.E.I.R. 347 (Nfld. T.D.); *Gordon v. Roebuck* (1989), 64 D.L.R. (4th) 568 (Ont. H.C.); reversed in part (1992), 92 D.L.R. (4th) 670 (Ont. C.A.); *Victorov v. Davison* (1988), 20 C.P.R. (3d) 481 (Ont. H.C.) (no economic duress); *Stott v. Merit Invt. Corp.* (1988), 48 D.L.R. (4th) 288 (Ont. C.A.); leave to appeal to S.C.C. refused (1988), 49 D.L.R. (4th) viii (note) (S.C.C.) (economic duress but subsequent affirmation by plaintiff).

142 [1978] 3 All E.R. 929 (C.A.).

have been claimed after his election to affirm the contract following the breach. Goff L.J., at least,[143] thought that this idea was incorrect; the innocent party was not put to any election; he could only sue for damages if he affirmed the contract or treated it as discharged by breach. Subsequently, in *Johnson v. Agnew*,[144] the House of Lords made it clear that to use the term "rescission" in this context and in this way was to produce confusion. Under the general law of contract, said Lord Wilberforce,[145] " . . . acceptance of a repudiatory breach does not bring about 'rescission ab initio'." It follows, therefore, that if an innocent party, the victim of a breach of contract that is sufficiently important, chooses to treat the contract as discharged, for example, where goods sold to a buyer are defective and the buyer rejects them,[146] his conduct is not to be looked upon as involving rescission of the contract.

(b) Equitable rescission

(i) *In general*

In contrast with the common-law idea of rescission, it is sometimes possible for a party to seek the equitable remedy of rescission, by applying to a court for relief from a transaction in respect of which it would be inequitable to hold the applicant bound.[147]

The jurisdiction of the courts to grant rescission of a contract on equitable grounds, which involves a restoration of the parties to their original rights and property,[148] extends beyond the situations and circumstances in which, at common law, a party, acting unilaterally, can treat the contract as a legal nullity, and then pursue such common-law remedies as may be available. Although there is a degree of overlap between the common-law right to rescind for fraud, and the equitable jurisdiction of the court to grant rescission of a contract which has been entered into as a consequence of a false representation or some other fraud,[149] the equitable power to order rescission is wider in scope. Indeed, the limits of this jurisdiction have not been fixed. Wherever a court considers, on general equitable grounds, that a contract should not be allowed to stand, and that the request by one party

---

143 *Ibid.*, at 942-943.

144 [1979] 1 All E.R. 883 (H.L.).

145 *Ibid.*, at 889.

146 *Nyuli v. Hill*, [1942] 1 W.W.R. 85 (Sask. C.A.); compare *Sumner v. Squires*, [1923] 2 W.W.R. 243 (Sask. C.A.); *Dobson v. Barr*, [1923] 2 W.W.R. 260 (Sask. C.A.); *Royal Bank v. Frank*, [1924] 2 W.W.R. 949 (Sask. C.A.). Breach of a fundamental term would seem to be necessary: *Valmada Ltée v. Boulay* (1981), 34 N.B.R. (2d) 74 (N.B.Q.B.). For a case where the plaintiff's (seller's) conduct was *not* rescission but an attempt to mitigate his damages see *Conary v. Harvey Hooper Lobsters Ltd.* (1982), 38 N.B.R. (2d) 670 (N.B.Q.B.).

147 See, *e.g.*, *Lamers v. Lamers* (1978), 6 R.F.L. (2d) 283 (Ont. H.C.); *Iwaskow v. Kondruk* (1982), 36 A.R. 168 (Alta. Q.B.); *E. & R. Distributors v. Atlas Drywall* (1980), 118 D.L.R. (3d) 339 (B.C.C.A.).

148 *Fleming v. Mair* (1921), 58 D.L.R. 318 at 321 (Sask. C.A.) *per* Lamont J.A.

149 Compare *Albert v. Legere* (1978), 88 D.L.R. (3d) 62 at 67 (N.B.C.A.) *per* Hughes C.J., referring to rescission for fraud, mutual mistake of a fundamental nature, or unilateral mistake induced by fraud.

that it be annulled and avoided should be granted, the court has the power to do so.[150] For example, although it has been noted that damages are not recoverable for failure to sell land when the failure is due to the vendor's lack of title, unless the vendor was guilty of fraud,[151] the court can grant rescission of the contract at the suit of the purchaser, and the recovery of any purchase money which may have been paid over to the vendor.[152] Even if there has been no warranty given by the vendor and no innocent misrepresentation has occured, the court is not powerless to relieve the purchaser from a contract which might be to his disadvantage, albeit that he might be bound at common law. In *Morang & Co. v. LeSueur*,[153] the court could rescind a contract under which a publishing company was to publish a particular work, when the company refused to publish the completed manuscript, and could then order the return of the manuscript to the author, despite the passage of title from one party to the other. The conduct of the company being inequitable, the court could provide the author with a suitable remedy.

These are exceptional, and unusual cases. More frequently the jurisdiction of the court to rescind a contract on equitable grounds is invoked in three main instances. The first is where the contract resulted from some fraud, which induced a mistake on the part of the defrauded party.[154] The second is where the mistake in question was the result of an innocent, non-fraudulent misrepresentation.[155] The third, which comprehends a somewhat mixed variety of instances, though sharing a general underlying character, is where the contract was procured, without fraud in the common-law sense, but as a consequence of what in equity is regarded as fraud, that is, by the use of undue influence, or some unconscionable conduct which renders the bargain questionable on equitable grounds, even though it may be perfectly valid at common law.[156]

Rescission may be granted even where the contract is not susceptible of attack at common law.[157] When it is, the purpose of the court is to produce *restitutio in integrum*.[158] This has two major consequences. In the first place, there cannot be rescission of part of a contract: all of it must be rescinded, or else none.[159] Second, there may have to be, and the court has the power to order adjustments,

---

150 This sentence was quoted by Creaghan J. in *Poirier v. Goguen* (1989), 99 N.B.R. (2d) 91 at 105 (N.B.Q.B.).

151 *Bain v. Fothergill* (1874), L.R. 7 H.L. 158 (H.L.); see above, pp. 731-734.

152 *Reeve v. Mullen* (1913), 5 W.W.R. 128 (Alta. C.A.).

153 (1911), 45 S.C.R. 95 (S.C.C.); compare *Lindsey v. Le Sueur* (1913), 29 O.L.R. 648 (Ont. C.A.); above, p. 798.

154 Above, pp. 295-303.

155 Above, pp. 303-308. But perhaps only if there has been a total failure of consideration: see *Komarniski v. Marien*, [1979] 4 W.W.R. 267 (Sask. Q.B.).

156 Above, pp. 320-336. This paragraph, from "More frequently" to the end, was quoted by Bayda J.A. in *Carlson v. Big Bud Tractors of Can. Ltd.* (1981), 7 Sask. R. 337 at 356 (Sask. C.A.).

157 *Ivanochko v. Sych* (1967), 58 W.W.R. 633 (Sask. C.A.).

158 *Stephenson v. Bromley*, [1928] 4 D.L.R. 737 at 742 (Man. C.A.) *per* Fullarton J.A., citing *Clough v. London & North Western Ry.* (1871), L.R. 7 Ex. 26.

159 *Fleming v. Mair*, [1921] 2 W.W.R. 421 (Sask. C.A.); *Kingu v. Walmar Ventures Ltd.* (1986), 10 B.C.L.R. (2d) 15 (B.C.C.A.).

810   EQUITABLE REMEDIES

perhaps involving monetary payments by way of compensation for use of property, or reimbursement of expenses, so as to ensure that, so far as is within the capability of the court, the parties are restored to their original situations, before the contract was ever concluded between them.[160]

Rescission is only possible where to grant such remedy would not operate to the prejudice of a third and innocent party, who was not implicated in the original contract and so ought not to be affected adversely by the subsequent, later avoidance of that transaction.[161] If granting rescission would have such an effect, a court of equity will refuse that remedy, leaving the plaintiff to his common-law remedy, that is, damages, if it is available in the circumstances.[162] Nor will rescission be granted if the plaintiff's contract is inequitable or he has been guilty of delay, or *laches*.[163]

(ii) *Fraud*[164]

Wherever a party can successfully allege that he was induced to enter into a contract by reason of the fraudulent conduct of the other party (or the other party's agent),[165] the contract in question may be rescinded by the court.[166] This

---

160 See *e.g., Stephenson v. Bromley,* above, note 158; *Lambert v. Slack,* [1926] 2 D.L.R. 166 at 172 (Sask. C.A.) *per* Lamont J.A.; *Int. Casualty Co. v. Thomson* (1913), 48 S.C.R. 167 (S.C.C.); *Stearns v. Neys,* [1929] 3 W.W.R. 177 (Alta. S.C.); *Fleischhaker v. Fort Garry Agencies Ltd.* (1957), 11 D.L.R. (2d) 599 (Man. C.A.); *Bell v. Robutka* (1966), 55 D.L.R. (2d) 436 (Alta. C.A.); *Jarvis v. Maguire* (1961), 35 W.W.R. 289 (B.C.C.A.); *Walters v. Capron* (1964), 50 W.W.R. 444 (B.C.S.C.); *Kupchak v. Dayson Holding Ltd.; Dayson Holding Ltd. v. Palms Motel Ltd.* (1965), 53 D.L.R. (2d) 482 at 487-488 (B.C.C.A.) *per* Davey J.A.

161 *Consol. Invts. Ltd. v. Acres,* [1917] 1 W.W.R. 1426 (Alta. C.A.); *Barry v. Stoney Point Canning Co.* (1917), 55 S.C.R. 51 at 66 (S.C.C.) *per* Idington J. See, however, *Stewart v. Complex 329 Ltd.,* below, note 166, where the fact that a third party had acquired an interest in the business that was the subject-matter of the contract to be rescinded did not prevent rescission.

162 Compare the language of Lamont J.A. in *Fleming v. Mair,* [1921] 2 W.W.R. 421 (Sask. C.A.) and that of MacFarlane J. in *Guest v. Beecroft* (1957), 22 W.W.R. 481 at 486 (B.C.S.C.).

163 Compare what is said in respect of specific performance and injunctions, above, p. 794. See also below, pp. 817-819.

164 Compare above, pp. 295-303.

165 *Hitchcock v. Sykes* (1914), 49 S.C.R. 403 (S.C.C.); compare as to fiduciaries, *Gunning v. Lusby,* [1925] 1 D.L.R. 101 (P.C.). Lack of diligence on the part of the plaintiff will not be a defence: *Stewart v. Complex 329 Ltd.,* below, note 166.

166 *Kupchak v. Dayson Holding Ltd.; Dayson Holding Ltd. v. Palms Motel Ltd.,* above, note 139; *Krahnbiel v. Dondaneau* (1955), 17 W.W.R. 436 (B.C.S.C.); *Pigott & Pigott Const. Co. v. Nesbitt, Thomson & Co.,* [1941] S.C.R. 520 (S.C.C.); *Keatley v. Churchman* (1921), 62 D.L.R. 139 (Alta. S.C.); affirmed [1922] 2 W.W.R. 993 (Alta. C.A.); *Muise v. Whalen* (1990), 96 N.S.R. (2d) 298 (N.S.T.D.); *Stewart v. Complex 329 Ltd.* (1990), 109 N.B.R. (2d) 115 (N.B.Q.B.); *TWT Enterprises Ltd. v. Westgreen Devs. (North) Ltd.,* [1991] 3 W.W.R. 80 (Alta. Q.B.); affirmed [1992] 5 W.W.R. 341 (Alta. C.A.). Or the defrauded party can plead *non est factum: Brown v. Prairie Leaseholds Ltd.* (1953), 9 W.W.R. (N.S.) 577 (Man. Q.B.); affirmed (1954), 12 W.W.R. 464 (Man. C.A.); on *non est factum* see above, pp. 282-292.

The plaintiff will also be able to recover common-law damages for deceit: *Bank of Montreal v. Weisdepp* (1917), 34 D.L.R. 26 at 31 (B.C.C.A.) *per* McPhillips J.A.; *Goulet v. Clarkson,* [1949] 1 D.L.R. 847 (B.C.S.C.) (where the remedy of rescission was barred by the plaintiff's own conduct

will be the case even if the contract is executed,[167] even if the contract is one transferring an interest in land.[168]

The plaintiff must establish the fraud,[169] and its effect upon him.[170] Since an allegation of fraud is a serious one it must be proved by strong and clear evidence.[171] But this does not mean that the plaintiff must discharge the criminal law burden of proof beyond a reasonable doubt. It simply means that before a court will conclude that the defendant is guilty of fraud there must be satisfactory proof of the validity of the allegation.[172] The fraud in question must relate to matters of fact. A fraudulent misrepresentation is one that misstates some existing or past fact, on which the plaintiff relies to contract.[173] It does not consist of a misstatement of law.[174] Nor will an incorrect opinion be a fraudulent misrepresentation.[175]

An exemption clause in a contract cannot exclude any liability on the part of the beneficiary of the clause for his fraud, including the possibility of rescission of the contract. Fraud vitiates a contract, including any exemption or exclusion clause therein. It is not likely that the clause will say, in precise words, that there is to be no liability for fraud. What is more usual is a statement in the contract to the effect that each party will rely on his own judgment and will not expect to hold the other party responsible for statements, etc., which are the foundation of the contract. Such a provision can never constitute an agreement in advance not to hold the other party liable for his fraud. It may operate with the respect to the exclusion of conditions, warranties, etc. It may even exclude the possibility

---

after discovery of the fraud); compare also *Peek v. Derry* (1889), 37 Ch. D. 541 (C.A.); reversed (1889), 14 App. Cas. 337 (H.L.); *Barron v. Kelly* (1918), 56 S.C.R. 455 (S.C.C.); *TWT Enterprises Ltd. v. Westgreen Devs. (North) Ltd.*, above. An alternative claim might be for breach of collateral warranty: *Muise v. Whalen*, above; or for negligent misrepresentation: *Terri-Grant Enterprises Inc. v. 82506 Can. Ltd.* (1986), 47 Sask. R. 63 (Sask. Q.B.).

167 *Burns v. Ambler* (1963), 42 W.W.R. 254 (B.C.S.C.).

168 *Redican v. Nesbitt*, [1924] S.C.R. 135 at 146-147 (S.C.C.) *per* Duff J.; *Kingu v. Walmar Ventures Ltd.* (1986), 10 B.C.L.R. (2d) 15 at 21 (B.C.C.A.) *per* McLachlin J.A.; compare above, pp. 306-307.

169 *Popowich v. Dromarsky*, [1946] 1 W.W.R. 570 (Alta. C.A.).

170 *Alexander v. Enderton* (1914), 15 D.L.R. 588 at 591 (Man. K.B.); affirmed (1914), 25 Man. R. 82 (Man. C.A.) *per* Martin C.J.; compare *Smith v. Chadwick* (1884), 9 App. Cas. 187 (H.L.); *Pioneer Tractor Co. v. Peebles* (1913), 15 D.L.R. 275 (Sask. S.C.); affirmed (1914), 18 D.L.R. 477 (Sask. C.A.); affirmed (1915), 8 W.W.R. 632 (S.C.C.); compare *Aaron's Reefs v. Twiss*, [1896] A.C. 273 (H.L.).

171 *Lasby v. Johnson*, [1928] 3 W.W.R. 447 (Sask. C.A.).

172 *Scott v. Cresswell*, [1975] 3 W.W.R. 193 (Alta. C.A.); *Nor. & Central Gas Corp. v. Hillcrest Collieries Ltd.; Byron Creek Collieries Ltd. v. Coleman Collieries Ltd.*, [1976] 1 W.W.R. 481 at 528-529 (Alta. T.D.).

173 *Enfield v. London Guar. & Accident Co.*, [1926] 4 D.L.R. 37 at 42 (Sask. C.A.) *per* Martin J.A.; *Ry. Passengers' Assur. Co. v. Standard Assur. Co.* (1921), 65 D.L.R. 470 at 477-478 (S.C.C.) *per* Duff J.; *Arnprior v. U.S. Fidelity & Guar. Co.* (1915), 21 D.L.R. 343 at 349-350 (S.C.C.) *per* Duff J.

174 *Rule v. Pals*, [1928] 2 W.W.R. 123 (Sask. C.A.); contrast *Graham v. Legault*, [1951] 3 D.L.R. 423 (B.C.S.C.); compare above, p. 298.

175 Unless the party giving the opinion is an expert or particularly knowledgeable in respect of the matters in question: above, p. 296.

of liability for an *innocent* misrepresentation.[176] It can never free the guilty party from an action for damages, or a suit for rescission, in respect of any fraudulent representation.[177]

(iii) *Innocent misrepresentation*[178]

If fraud is not established, it may still be possible to obtain rescission of the contract on the ground that the plaintiff was induced to enter into it as a result of a misrepresentation that was innocently, that is, non-fraudulently, made.[179] In such a case, however, the court cannot order the payment of damages to the plaintiff, in addition to granting rescission. However, with a view to restoring the plaintiff to the position in which he was before the making of the contract, the court can award some kind of indemnity to compensate the plaintiff for the losses which he has incurred as a consequence of the misrepresentation.[180] This would also involve the possibility of making the plaintiff pay the defendant for any benefits the former may have received in the interim, for example, by the use of the chattel that was the subject-matter of the contract.[181] The purpose of an indemnity is to ensure that the party claiming rescission is no worse off than if he had never entered into the contract. It is not to compensate that party in respect of consequential loss emerging from the failure of the contract. Hence the distinction is drawn between restitution to the *status quo ante* and the recovery of foreseeable loss. It may sometimes be difficult to draw the appropriate line between a loss which stems from the rescinded contract, and justifies indemnification, and one that is a consequential economic loss that might support an action for damages, if the contract were treated as broken instead of rescinded. However, it is important to maintain the distinction between loss of anticipated benefits and recoupment of legitimate expenses or similar losses. These stem from the discharge of obligations created by the contract, not from obligations entered into under the contract.[182]

Rescission for innocent misrepresentation may be obtained when the representation in question induced the plaintiff to enter into the contract. Such was the

---

176 Compare *Carman Const. Ltd. v. C.P.R.* (1982), 136 D.L.R. (3d) 193 (S.C.C.); above, pp. 513-514.
177 *Ballard v. Gaskill*, [1955] 2 D.L.R. 219 (B.C.C.A.); compare *Pearson & Son Ltd. v. Dublin Corp.*, [1907] A.C. 351 (H.L.); *Campbell v. Hamill*, [1925] 3 W.W.R. 628 (Sask. C.A.).
178 Above, pp. 303-308.
179 *Corbeil v. Appell*, [1950] 1 D.L.R. 159 (B.C.S.C.); *Wiley v. Fortin*, [1946] 2 W.W.R. 93 (B.C.S.C.). There must, of course, be a representation: *Thuenken v. Schweer* (1987), 83 N.B.R. (2d) 244 especially at 249-250 (N.B.C.A.) *per* Rice J.A.: it must be a *misrepresentation: 447927 Ont. Inc. v. Pizza Pizza Ltd.* (1987), 144 D.L.R. (3d) 366 (Ont. H.C.); affirmed (1990), 69 D.L.R. (4th) 160 (Ont. C.A.).
180 *Fleischhaker v. Fort Garry Agencies Ltd.* (1957), 65 Man. R. 339 (Man. C.A.). The passage from "If fraud is not established" to here was quoted by Huband J.A. in *Ennis v. Klassen* (1990), 70 D.L.R. (4th) 321 at 326 (Man. C.A.).
181 *Walters v. Capron* (1964), 50 W.W.R. 444 (B.C.S.C.); compare *Stephenson v. Bromley*, [1928] 3 W.W.R. 370 (Man. C.A.).
182 See the English decisions in *Whittington v. Seale-Hayne* (1900), 82 L.T. 49 and *Newbigging v. Adam* (1886), 34 Ch. D. 582 (C.A.) (the point did not arise in the House of Lords: *Adam v. Newbigging* (1888), 13 App. Cas. 308 (H.L.)).

case when the misrepresentation related to the amount of oil a well would produce and the price at which the oil could be sold, in consequence of which the plaintiff purchased the well,[183] and where it related to the rate of interest on a mortgage.[184] But in *Leggett v. Taylor*[185] the misrepresentation as to the type of engine in the machine the plaintiff was buying did not justify rescission of the contract. On the other hand a serious discrepancy in the amount of timber on some land was a ground for rescission of a contract for the purchase and sale of a timber licence, in *Fukukawa and Queen Charlotte Timber Holding Co. v. American Timber Holding Co.; American Timber Holding Co. v. Fukukawa.*[186] In *Ennis v. Klassen*[187] the misdescription of the car that was being sold as a BMW 733i, when in fact it was a different model substantially inferior to the car the plaintiff believed he was buying, was sufficient to justify rescission. In other words equity will not relieve a party from the consequences of a mistaken bargain, unless the party requesting such relief has been seriously inconvenienced or prejudiced by the mistake in question, and that mistake was the product of an innocent misrepresentation by the other party.[188]

There appears to be a limitation on the extent to which rescission may be obtained where there has been no fraud. If the contract involves land and it has been executed, for example, by conveyance of the property, it will be too late for the plaintiff who contracted under a mistake to obtain rescission. This has been established by a number of Canadian cases, commencing with the decision of the Supreme Court of Canada in 1899 in *Cole v. Pope.*[189] The fact that the contract has been executed may not be a barrier to rescission if the contract concerned chattels.[190] But a contract of sale of land is treated differently; so much so that, even if an express warranty of quality was given by the vendor, there can be no

---

183 *Eisenschiml v. Western Drilling Co.*, [1943] 1 W.W.R. 605 (Alta. C.A.); compare *Shortt v. MacLennan*, [1959] S.C.R. 3 (S.C.C.).

184 *Comeller v. Billinkoff* (1953), 11 W.W.R. 279 (Man. Q.B.).

185 (1965), 50 D.L.R. (2d) 516 (B.C.S.C.). See also *Rasch v. Horne*, [1930] 3 D.L.R. 647 (Man. C.A.); *Freeman v. Kultio* (1963), 39 D.L.R. (2d) 496 (B.C.S.C.); *Cancarp Const. Ltd. v. P.D.I. Structures (1982) Inc.* (1987), 62 O.R. (2d) 161 (Ont. H.C.). But contrast the idea that a misrepresentation must be material, rather than go to "the root of the contract": *George v. Dominick Corp. of Can.*, [1973] S.C.R. 97 (S.C.C.).

186 [1928] 2 W.W.R. 37 (B.C.S.C.).

187 (1990), 70 D.L.R. (4th) 321 (Man. C.A.).

188 Compare *Field v. Zien*, [1963] S.C.R. 632 (S.C.C.).

189 (1898), 29 S.C.R. 291 (S.C.C.). See also *Redican v. Nesbitt*, [1924] S.C.R. 135 (S.C.C.); *Shortt v. MacLennan*, [1959] S.C.R. 3 (S.C.C.); *Schonekess v. Bach* (1968), 62 W.W.R. 673 (B.C.S.C.); *Kingu v. Walmar Ventures Ltd.* (1986), 10 B.C.L.R. (2d) 15 at 21 (B.C.C.A.). See also above, pp. 306-308.

190 See, *e.g.*, *Geggie v. Kerr Motors Ltd.*, [1922] 2 W.W.R. 1256 (Alta. C.A.); *McKinnon v. Brockinton*, [1921] 2 W.W.R. 437 (Man. C.A.); *Fleischhaker v. Fort Garry Agencies Ltd.* above, note 180; *Bevan v. Anderson* (1957), 23 W.W.R. 508 (Alta. S.C.); *Ennis v. Klassen*, above, note 187. Contrast *Diamond v. B.C. Thoroughbred Breeders' Society* (1965), 52 W.W.R. 385 (B.C.S.C.). Compare a recent Australian case: *Leason Pty. v. Prince Farm Pty. Ltd.*, [1983] 2 N.S.W.L.R. 381 (Aust.). See also the dissenting judgement of Twaddle J.A. in *Ennis v. Klassen*, above, note 187.

rescission on its breach.[191] However, apart from fraud, there is one situation in which an executed contract for the sale of land may be rescinded. This is where there has been a failure of consideration, and the purchaser has, in fact, obtained something very different from that for which he bargained,[192] for example, a smaller quantity of land,[193] or a different kind of tenancy.[194] Sometimes this is referred to as *error in substantialibus*.[195] In essence, however, what is involved is a significant variation from the contract as it was believed to be, and the contract as, in fact, it is.[196]

(iv) *Unconscionable bargains*

The equitable remedy of rescission may also be invoked where the contract is open to attack on the ground of being brought about by undue influence or unconscionable conduct.[197] The original power of courts of equity was in respect of contracts produced by the exercise of undue influence by one party against the other.[198] In modern times a broader equitable doctrine enables the court to intervene and rescind a contract which is made between parties of unequal bargaining power, where the conduct of one party is viewed as being unconscionable with respect to the other, even though the situation is not one strictly within the equitable doctrine of undue influence.[199]

---

191 *Franz v. Hansen*, [1917] 3 W.W.R. 77 (Alta. C.A.); reversed on other grounds, [1918] 2 W.W.R. 40 (S.C.C.); leave to appeal to the Privy Council refused (1918), 57 S.C.R. vii (S.C.C.).

192 *Cole v. Pope*, above, note 189; *F. & B. Tpt. Ltd. v. White Truck Sales Man. Ltd.* (1965), 51 W.W.R. 124 (Man. C.A.).

193 *Fukukawa and Queen Charlotte Timber Hldg. Co. v. Amer. Timber Holding Co.; Amer. Timber Hldg. Co. v. Fukukawa*, [1928] 2 W.W.R. 37 (B.C.S.C.); compare *Thurston v. Streilen*, [1951] 4 D.L.R. 724 (Man. K.B.), where rescission was refused on other grounds. Contrast *Aberg v. Rafuse* (1979), 8 R.P.R. 216 (N.S.T.D.); *Komarniski v. Marien* [1979] 4 W.W.R. 267 (Sask. Q.B.); *John Bosworth Ltd. v. Pro. Syndicated Devs. Ltd.* (1979), 24 O.R. (2d) 97 (Ont. H.C.).

194 *Ruscheinsky v. A. Spencer Co.*, [1948] 2 W.W.R. 392 (B.C.S.C.).

195 *Redican v. Nesbitt*, above, note 189, at 146-147 *per* Duff J.; compare *Alessio v. Jovica* (1974), 42 D.L.R. (3d) 243 at 256-257 (Alta. C.A.) *per* Sinclair J.A.; *Nor. & Central Gas Const. Co. v. Hillcrest Collieries; Byron Creek Collieries Ltd. v. Coleman Colieries Ltd.*, [1976] 1 W.W.R. 481 at 553-554 (Alta. T.D.) *per* Lieberman J.; Fridman, "Error in Substantialibus: A Canadian Comedy of Errors" (1978), 56 Can. Bar Rev. 603; above, pp. 307-308.

196 Note also the denial of rescission in cases of undue delay or where restitution of benefits obtained by the plaintiff is impossible: *Terri-Grant Enterprises Inc. v. 82506 Can. Ltd.* (1986), 47 Sask. R. 63 (Sask. Q.B.); and where the contract is affirmed by the plaintiff (unless such affirmation is not effective, *e.g.*, by reason of estoppel: *Revell v. O'Brian Financial Corp.* (1988), 30 B.C.L.R. (2d) 330 (B.C.S.C.); affirmed (1991), 62 B.C.L.R. (2d) 314 (B.C.C.A.)): below, pp. 817-821.

197 Compare the refusal to grant decrees of specific performance, or an injunction, on the same ground: *Hnatuk v. Chretian* (1960), 31 W.W.R. 130 (B.C.S.C.); *Clifford Davis Mgmt. Ltd. v. W.E.A. Records*, [1975] 1 All E.R. 237 (C.A.). Compare as to *rectification*, *Longley v. Barbrick* (1962), 36 D.L.R. (2d) 672 (N.S.S.C.).

198 *Burris v. Rhind* (1899), 29 S.C.R. 498 (S.C.C.); *McKay v. Clow*, [1941] S.C.R. 643 (S.C.C.); compare above, pp. 320-321.

199 *Morrison v. Coast Finance Ltd.* (1965), 54 W.W.R. 257 (B.C.C.A.); *Knupp v. Bell* (1968), 67 D.L.R. (2d) 256 (Sask. C.A.); *Mundinger v. Mundinger* (1969), 3 D.L.R. (3d) 338 (Ont. C.A.); affirmed (1970), 14 D.L.R. (3d) 256n (S.C.C.); *Marshall v. Can. Permanent Trust Co.* (1968), 69 D.L.R.

It must be stressed, however, that, wide though the equitable jurisdiction may be, and broad though its application can sometimes appear, even a court applying equitable powers is not able, nor is it willing to interfere with a concluded contract which is otherwise not exceptionable, merely on the ground that a party now finds the original bargain he made is not to his taste, or will not be as profitable or as valuable as he had hoped and intended. The equitable power is to give relief in cases involving unconscionable transactions, not all those which may, originally or subsequently, prove to be foolhardy, burdensome, or otherwise undesirable and improvident.[200]

The notion of undue influence has been discussed earlier.[201] It was seen that it is important to differentiate from other examples of undue influence those situations which involve parties whose relationship is such that it gives rise to a presumption, which is rebuttable by suitable evidence, that undue influence was asserted by the one over the other.[202] Where the presumption does operate, the party seeking to uphold the agreement must discharge the burden of establishing that no undue influence was used or manifested, for example, by proving that independent advice was made available to the other party (though it is not necessary

---

(2d) 260 (Alta. S.C.); *Paris v. Machnick* (1972), 32 D.L.R. (3d) 723 (N.S.T.D.); *Adams v. Fahrngruber* (1975), 10 O.R. (2d) 96 at 102 (Ont. H.C.) *per* Grant J.; *Buchanan v. C.I.B.C.* (1980), 125 D.L.R. (3d) 394 (B.C.C.A.); *Bertolo v. Bank of Montreal* (1986), 33 D.L.R. (4th) 610 (Ont. C.A.); *Dominion Home Improvements Ltd. v. Knuude* (1986), 20 C.L.R. 192 (Ont. Dist. Ct.); *Doan v. Ins. Corp. of B.C.* (1987), 18 B.C.L.R. (2d) 286 (B.C.S.C.); *Turner Estate v. Bonli Estate* (1989), 77 Sask. R. 49 (Sask. Q.B.); affirmed (1990), 86 Sask. R. 235 (Sask. C.A.); compare above, pp. 325-336. For English developments in this respect, see *Lloyd's Bank Ltd. v. Bundy*, [1974] 3 All E.R. 757 (C.A.); *Schroeder Music Publishing Co. v. Macaulay*, [1974] 3 All E.R. 616 (H.L.); *Clifford Davis Mgmt. Ltd. v. W.E.A. Records*, above, note 197; but note *Nat. Westminister Bank v. Morgan*, [1985] 1 All E.R. 821 (H.L.).

200 This passage, from "It must be stressed . . .", in its original form, was cited by Stratton J.A. in *Beaulieu v. Nat. Bank of Can.* (1984), 55 N.B.R. (2d) 154 at 171-172 (N.B.C.A.). For cases where rescission was denied after allegations of unconscionability, see *Johnson v. Johnson Estate* (1986), 69 N.B.R. (2d) 408 (N.B.Q.B.); *DeWolfe v. Mansour* (1986), 73 N.S.R. (2d) 110 (N.S.T.D.); *Eagle Const. Ltd. v. Chaytor* (1986), 58 Nfld. & P.E.I.R. 23 (Nfld. T.D.); *370866 Ont. Ltd. v. Chizy* (1987), 57 O.R. (2d) 587 (Ont. H.C.); *Principal Invts. Ltd. v. Thiele Estate* (1987), 12 B.C.L.R. (2d) 258 (B.C.C.A.); *Boisonault v. Block Bros. Realty Ltd.* (1987), 47 Man. R. (2d) 148 (Man. Q.B.); *Cameron v. Dorcic* (1987), 80 N.S.R. (2d) 152 (N.S.T.D.); affirmed (1988), 83 N.S.R. (2d) 85 (N.S.C.A.); *Sebastian v. Bonitatibus* (1988), 31 C.C.L.I. 80 (Ont. Dist. Ct.); *Halifax West Aquinas Credit Union Ltd. v. Owens* (1989), 91 N.S.R. (2d) 256 (N.S.T.D.); *Ahone v. Holloway* (1988), 30 B.C.L.R. (2d) 368 (B.C.C.A.); *Kielly Estate v. Knox* (1989), 76 Nfld. & P.E.I.R. 96 (P.E.I.T.D.).

201 Above, pp. 320-325.

202 *E.g.*, parent and child: *Vanzant v. Coates* (1917), 40 O.L.R. 556 (Ont. C.A.); *Schwartz v. Guerin*, [1922] 2 W.W.R. 145 (Alta. C.A.); brothers and sister: *Geffen v. Goodman Estate* (1991), 81 D.L.R. (4th) 211 (S.C.C.); reversing (1989), 61 D.L.R. (4th) 431 (sub nom. *Goodman Estate v. Geffen*) (Alta. C.A.) [additional reasons at (1990), 67 D.L.R. (4th) 765 (Alta. C.A.)]; which reversed (1987), 52 Alta. L.R. (2d) 210 (*sub nom. Goodman v. Geffen*) (Alta. Q.B.); above, p. 323. But not husband and wife: *Bank of Montreal v. Stuart*, [1911] A.C. 120 (P.C.). But see the cases referred to above, p. 322. Note also the decision in *Cox v. Adams* (1904), 35 S.C.R. 393 (S.C.C.), which may still be good law: *Krys v. Krys*, [1929] S.C.R. 153 (S.C.C.).

to prove it was taken).[203] The best way of discharging the burden, however, is by showing that the transaction was entered into after its nature and effect had been fully explained to the contracting party by some independent and qualified person so completely as to satisfy the court that the party in question was acting independently of any influence from the other party and with the full appreciation of what he was doing.[204] This principle can be seen at work in *Iwanchuk v. Iwanchuk*,[205] where the father, who contracted with his son, could not read or write English. The son had to prove that his father knew what he was doing when he contracted to transfer property to his son.

Where the presumption does not apply, it becomes necessary for the party seeking rescission on this ground to prove the pressure or influence alleged to have brought about the contract. This is a question of fact, depending upon the comparative positions of the parties, economically and otherwise, the kind of influence that could be exerted by the defendant on the plaintiff, the knowledge and understanding possessed by the plaintiff, and the means employed by the defendant to obtain the contract.[206]

As was pointed out in *Morrison v. Coast Finance Ltd.*,[207] rescission of a contract on the ground that it is the product of undue influence differs from rescission based upon the contract's being an unconscionable bargain. The former relates to the validity of the consent which one party has manifested. The fact that such consent was obtained by such means vitiates, or can vitiate the apparent agreement between the parties. Where a bargain is claimed, and held to be unconscionable, it is not the consent of the party making that claim that is being impugned by him or by the court. Rather it is the reasonableness of the bargain, the conscientiousness of the defendant, the equitable character of the whole transaction. Hence, the language of Lord Denning M.R., in *Lloyd's Bank Ltd. v. Bundy*,[208] in which he purported to expound a wider conception of undue influence and term it "inequality of

---

203 See, *e.g.*, *Brooks v. Alker* (1975), 9 O.R. (2d) 409 (Ont. H.C.). Compare also *Murray v. Smith* (1980), 32 Nfld. & P.E.I.R. 191 (P.E.I.S.C.); affirmed (1981), 35 Nfld. & P.E.I.R. 382 (P.E.I. C.A.); *Malicki v. Yankovich* (1981), 33 O.R. (2d) 537 (Ont. H.C.); additional reasons at (1982), 42 O.R. (2d) 522 (Ont. H.C.); affirmed (1983), 41 O.R. (2d) 160 (Ont. C.A.). See also *Johnson v. Johnson Estate* (1986), 69 N.B.R. (2d) 408 (N.B.Q.B.); *Gammon v. Steeves* (1986), 72 N.B.R. (2d) 239 (N.B.Q.B.); reversed in part (1987), 83 N.B.R. (2d) 397 (N.B.C.A.); *Goguen v. Goguen* (1988), 92 N.B.R. (2d) 158 (N.B.Q.B.) (no rebuttal of the presumption).

204 *Inche Noriah v. Shaik Allie Bin Omar*, [1929] A.C. 127 (P.C.).

205 [1919] 3 W.W.R. 363 (Alta. C.A.). Contrast *Murray v. Smith*, above, note 203; *Laderoute v. Laderoute* (1978), 81 D.L.R. (3d) 433 (Ont. H.C.).

206 Contrast *Needles v. Slovarp*, [1922] 2 W.W.R. 649 (Sask. C.A.); *Sutherland v. Sutherland*, [1946] 4 D.L.R. 605 (B.C.S.C.); *Brock & Petty v. Gronbach*, [1953] 1 S.C.R. 207 (S.C.C.); with *Hnatuk v. Chretian* (1960), 31 W.W.R. 130 (B.C.S.C.); and *Mulholland v. Bartsch*, [1939] 2 W.W.R. 108 (Alta. S.C.). See also *McCormack Estate v. Feehan Estate* (1986), 59 Nfld. & P.E.I.R. 215 (P.E.I.S.C.); *MacDonald v. Creelman* (1988), 83 N.S.R. (2d) 415 (N.S.T.D.); affirmed (1989), 88 N.S.R. (2d) 403 (N.S.C.A.); *Land v. McPherson* (1989), 42 B.L.R. 23 (B.C.S.C.); affirmed (May 10, 1990), Doc. No. V00960 (B.C.C.A.); *Thom v. Saltner*, [1989] 1 W.W.R. 456 (Man. Q.B.); *Kielly Estate v. Knox* (1989), 76 Nfld. & P.E.I.R. 96 (P.E.I.T.D.).

207 (1965) 54 W.W.R. 257 at 259 (B.C.C.A.) *per* Davey J.A.

208 [1974] 3 All E.R. 757 at 765 (C.A.); cited above, p. 329.

bargaining power", is open to question. The other members of the Court of Appeal were able to hold that the transaction could be upset and rescinded on the ground that the bank had failed in its duty to provide its customer with independent advice or the opportunity for independent advice, and so could not take advantage of the charge made by the plaintiff on his house in favour of the bank for the purpose of securing a loan made to the plaintiff's son. Lord Denning, however, enunciated a broader principle. The nature of this principle, and its subsequent history in England and Canada, have been examined earlier.[209] As previously noted, there is considerable uncertainty as to the application and limits of this principle, and with respect to its present and future status in the law. However, it must be conceded that Canadian courts feel free to rescind contracts, of whatever sort, on the broad "equitable" idea of unconscionability.[210]

(c) Barriers to rescission

Since the remedy of rescission is equitable, it is discretionary in nature. Hence, if there are equitable grounds for refusing a plaintiff this remedy, it will be denied, even though a *prima facie* case for rescission has been established. They were summarized by McLachlin J.A., in *Kingu v. Walmar Ventures Ltd.*,[211] as (i) lack of prompt action by the plaintiff; (ii) the acquisition of rights by innocent third parties; and (iii) the impossibility of restoring the parties to their pre-contractual position.[212]

Laches is unreasonable delay in pursuing the remedy of rescission.[213] The plaintiff must elect to rescind within a reasonable time.[214] What is a reasonable time, and whether the length of delay and the plaintiff's conduct amount to laches are questions of fact which depend upon the circumstances of the case.[215]

---

209 Above, pp. 329-334.

210 Which, according to McLachlin J.A. in *Principal Invts. Ltd. v. Thiele Estate* (1987), 12 B.C.L.R. (2d) 258 at 263 (B.C.C.A.), involves (i) proof of inequity in position of the parties, arising from ignorance, need or distress of the weaker party, and (ii) substantial unfairness in the bargain obtained by the stronger party.

211 (1986), 10 B.C.L.R. (2d) 15 at 21 (B.C.C.A.).

212 McLachlin J.A. also mentioned that in the absence of fraud an executed contract for the sale of land could not be rescinded: but note the doctrine of *error in substantialibus*: above, pp. 307-308. If the contract is for the sale of goods, *e.g.*, a car, rescission for innocent misrepresentation is possible even if the contract is executed: *Ennis v. Klassen* (1990), 70 D.L.R. (4th) 321 (Man. C.A.): note, however, the dissent of Twaddle J.A., *ibid.*, at 334-336, 338-339.

213 Above, pp. 794-795.

214 *Ruscheinsky v. A. Spencer Co.*, [1948] 2 W.W.R. 392 at 399 (B.C.S.C.) *per* Coady J.; *Hudson Bay Invt. Co. v. Thompson*, [1924] 1 W.W.R. 933 (Man. K.B.).

215 *Consol. Invts. Ltd. v. Acres*, [1917] 1 W.W.R. 1426 (Alta. C.A.); *Monticello State Bank v. Guest*, [1920] 3 W.W.R. 14 (Alta. Q.B.); *Wallbridge v. W.H. Moore & Co.; W.H. Moore & Co. v. Baldry* (1964), 48 W.W.R. 321 (B.C.S.C.) (in all of which delay did not bar rescission); compare *Richmond v. Lafontaine* (1899), 30 S.C.R. 155 (S.C.C.); *Timmins v. Kuzyk* (1962), 32 D.L.R. (2d) 207 (B.C.S.C.) (where delay was a good ground for refusing rescission); *United Shoe Machinery Co. v. Brunet*, [1909] A.C. 330 (P.C.); *N.S. Const. Co. v. Que. Streams Comm.*, [1933] S.C.R. 220 (S.C.C.); *Terri-Grant Enterprises Inc. v. 82506 Can. Ltd.* (1986), 47 Sask. R. 63 (Sask. Q.B.); *Alex v. Tiede*, [1986] 5 W.W.R. 599 (Man. Q.B.).

Closely connected with this, and sometimes overlapping, is the question whether the plaintiff has disentitled himself from obtaining rescission by his own conduct since he discovered the circumstances and knew of the facts and the behaviour of the defendant that supported and justified a claim for rescission. Has he affirmed the contract? Or adopted it? Has he acquiesced in the misconduct of the defendant, in such a way as to show that he has elected to be bound by the contract[216] (leaving open only a claim for damages, if such a claim can be brought at common law, for example, in cases of fraudulent, but not cases of innocent misrepresentation)?[217] Sometimes the length of time which has passed since knowledge and appreciation of the situation was possessed by the plaintiff may reveal his intention to elect to affirm the contract, or may be treated by the court as sufficient to be considered as acquiescence.[218] In this respect, therefore, delay has a twofold effect or importance. It is a potential bar in itself, and it is the foundation for the distinct barrier of election, affirmation or acquiescence.

Delay is not the only basis for a claim of affirmation, etc. The plaintiff's positive conduct may reveal that he has chosen to affirm,[219] or may indicate that it would be inequitable to grant the remedy of rescission.[220] This again is a question of fact.[221] Dealing with property, after discovery of the fraud, may not amount to affirmation or election.[222] Even using a chattel for a period of time with knowledge of the conduct which could entitle a party to rescind may not amount to affirmation or election.[223] But attempting to get a mare in foal after discovery of an innocent misrepresentation, on the basis of which the plaintiff had bought the mare, was a ground for refusing rescission in *Monticello State Bank v. Guest*[224] In deciding whether the conduct of the plaintiff bars him from obtaining rescission, the court must look at the realities of the situation as opposed to the mere technicalities relating to the application of the priniciples of equity.[225] Moreover conduct that might otherwise amount to affirmation will not have such effect if the plaintiff's behaviour was the result of the defendant's behaviour, such as his failure to disclose

---

216 As in *Panzer v. Zeifman* (1978), 88 D.L.R. (3d) 131 (Ont. C.A.).

217 *Barron v. Kelly*, [1918] 2 W.W.R. 131 (S.C.C.); *Goulet v. Clarkson*, [1949] 1 D.L.R. 847 (B.C.S.C.); compare *Guest v. Beecroft* (1957), 22 W.W.R. 481 (B.C.S.C.).

218 See *Consol. Invt. Ltd. v. Acres*, above, note 215.

219 *Brauchle v. Lloyd* (1915), 7 W.W.R. 1343 (Alta. C.A.); *Panzer v. Zeifman*, above, note 216; contrast *Perry v. Prudential Trust Co.; Thomas v. Crown Trust Co.* (1958), 25 W.W.R. 193 (Man. C.A.).

220 *Pepper v. Prudential Trust Co.*, [1965] S.C.R. 417 (S.C.C.).

221 *Mankovsky v. Jacob*, [1922] 2 W.W.R. 684 (Man. K.B.). See the dissent in *Wiebe v. Butcharts Motors Ltd.*, [1949] 2 W.W.R. 688 (B.C.C.A.).

222 *Kupchak v. Dayson Hldgs. Ltd.; Dayson Hldgs. Ltd. v. Palms Motel Ltd.* (1965), 53 W.W.R. 65 (B.C.C.A.); *Boulter v. Stocks* (1913), 47 S.C.R. 440 (S.C.C.) (Note the doctrine of *reviver* of the right to rescind for *subsequent* discovery of *other* misconduct by the defendant).

223 *Paproski v. Neuman* (1957), 20 W.W.R. 294 (Sask. C.A.); *Freeman v. Consol. Motors Ltd.* (1968), 65 W.W.R. 234 (Man. Q.B.). Nor did painting a kitchen: *Guest v. Beecroft*, above, note 217.

224 [1920] 3 W.W.R. 14 (Alta. Q.B.).

225 *Guest v. Beecroft*, above, note 217, at 486 *per* MacFarlane J.

material facts (when the defendant will be estopped from relying on affirmation as an answer to rescission).[226]

One thing is clear. It is immaterial that the plaintiff has been guilty of carelessness in contracting, or in asserting his rights after discovery of the truth.[227] A negligent or neglectful plaintiff does not lose his equitable remedies, unless his neglect amounts to laches or affirmation. Or unless his conduct, whether neglectful or not, has produced a situation in which, to allow him to rescind, at this stage, would result in the prejudicing of some innocent third party. The court will not upset a contract when to do so would have unfortunate consequences for strangers to the contract who have subsequently transacted with one of the original parties on the faith of the validity of the original contract.[228] In this respect, also, delay by the plaintiff may be material.[229]

(d) The importance of *restitutio*

There is another relevant matter which must be taken into account by the court when deciding whether or not to exercise its discretion and grant the equitable remedy of rescission. This is the possibility of being able to effect a true *restitutio in integrum* between the parties. Since the purpose or aim of the equitable remedy of rescission is to return the plaintiff to the position in which he was before the contract was made, and since one of the essential features of an equitable remedy is *mutuality*, that is, the potential availability of the remedy to both parties equally, it follows that unless *both* parties can be restored to their respective original situations, it should not be open to a court to rescind the contract.[230] However, the issue has often arisen whether complete restitution in every respect is necessary, and what in effect amounts to restitution.

It has been held that there is no need for a complete *restitutio* where the rescission is brought about by mutual agreement between the parties.[231] It has also been said, despite other judicial statements to the contrary,[232] that restitution is not always a condition precedent to rescission, though it will be so in most instances. The court will do what is just.[233] In this respect rescission was not granted where the plaintiff had received the full benefit of the defendant's work performed under

226 *Revell v. O'Brian Financial Corp.* (1988), 30 B.C.L.R. (2d) 330 (B.C.S.C.) [affirmed (1991), 62 B.C.L.R. (2d) 314 (B.C.C.A.)], relying on *Amalgamated Invt. & Property Co. v. Texas Commerce Int. Bank Ltd.*, [1981] 1 All E.R. 923 (Q.B.), on which see above, p. 129.
227 *Van Hyfte v. Dejonkheere* (1953), 8 W.W.R. (N.S.) 581 (Man. Q.B.); *Holund Holding Ltd. v. Lewicky* (1970), 12 D.L.R. (3d) 398 (B.C.S.C.). Compare *Stewart v. Complex 329 Ltd.* (1990), 109 N.B.R. (2d) 115 (N.B.Q.B.).
228 *Domenco v. Domenco* (1963), 44 W.W.R. 549 (Man. Q.B.). Contrast *Stewart v. Complex 329 Ltd.*, above, note 227, where the fact that third parties had acquired interests did not prelude rescission.
229 *Consol. Invts. Ltd. v. Acres*, above, note 215.
230 *Kingu v. Walmar Ventures Ltd.* (1986), 10 B.C.L.R. (2d) 15 at 21 (B.C.C.A.) *per* McLachlin J.A.
231 *Pyramid Const. (Calgary) Ltd. v. Feil* (1957), 22 W.W.R. 497 (Alta. S.C.).
232 *Guest v. Beecroft*, above, note 215.
233 *Hudson Bay Invt. Co. v. Thompson*, [1924] 1 W.W.R. 933 at 938 (Man. K.B.) *per* Macdonald J.

the contract sought to be rescinded, and the plaintiff was neither able nor willing to make restitution to the defendant.[234] But there will be no need for restitution where the subject-matter of the contract has been destroyed, and therefore cannot be restored to the defendant, and that destruction has been the fault of the defendant. Such was the result when the defendant sold goods which were the subject-matter of the original contract of which rescission was being sought.[235]

Rescission has been denied where the plaintiff exercised acts of ownership and use in relation to a large proportion of the subject-matter of the contract, namely, equipment installed by the defendant,[236] and where the contract was for the sale of a car, the defendant, the seller, providing the plaintiff, buyer, with a loan to enable the latter to buy the car.[237] Rescission was also denied where land acquired by the plaintiff was no longer available in the condition in which it was at the time of the original transfer to the plaintiff because he had adopted a different farm system.[238] In *Thurston v. Streilen*[239] the plaintiff bought land from the defendant. On the land there were some buildings and some chattels, which were part of the subject-matter of the sale to the plaintiff. Subsequently the plaintiff sold some of the chattels, and consumed others. Later he found out that the defendant did not have title to a part of the land which had been sold to the plaintiff. The plaintiff sought rescission of the contract. This would have been possible, on the grounds of innocent misrepresentation. But the court refused the remedy because restitution was not possible. The land could have been restored to the defendant, but not all the chattels. Consequently, because the sale of the land and the sale of the chattels constituted one transaction, it was not possible to rescind where restitution of the land was possible but not restitution of the chattels. The judgment of Montague J. considers in depth the question of restitution. In the words of the learned judge, to entitle a plaintiff to rescind, one of the law's requirements is that it must be possible for both parties to the contract to be restored to their original positions.[240] Some relaxation of this requirement appears to have been suggested by Dysart J. in *Hines v. McCallum*,[241] following the language of earlier English cases,[242] and taken up in later Canadian ones.[243] But, as Montague J. said,

---

234 *Ruiter Engineering & Const. Ltd. v. 430216 Ont. Ltd.* (1989), 32 C.L.R. 23 (Ont. C.A.); varying (1986), 23 C.L.R. 287 (Ont. H.C.). Compare *Terri-Grant Enterprises Inc. v. 82506 Can. Ltd.* (1986), 47 Sask. R. 63 (Sask. Q.B.), where no restitution was possible of benefits received by the plaintiff as a result of his purchase of a franchise which he made as a result of innocent misrepresentations by the defendant (although damages were awarded for breach of collateral warranty and negligent misrepresentation).

235 *Sager v. Man. Windmill Co.* (1914), 6 W.W.R. 265 (Sask. C.A.); affirmed (1914), 7 W.W.R. 1213 (S.C.C.) a strong case, since it concerned *fraud* by the defendant.

236 *Frigidaire Corp. v. Steedman*, [1932] 3 W.W.R. 544 (P.C.); compare *Weibelzahl v. Symbaluk* (1963), 44 W.W.R. 666 (B.C.C.A.).

237 *Lee v. Chapin* (1915), 9 W.W.R. 228 (Alta. C.A.).

238 *Alex v. Tiede*, [1986] 5 W.W.R. 599 (Man. Q.B.).

239 [1951] 4 D.L.R. 724 (Man. K.B.).

240 *Ibid.*, at 728.

241 [1925] 2 D.L.R. 403 at 410 (Man. K.B.).

242 *Erlanger v. New Sombrero Phosphate Co.* (1878), 3 App. Cas. 1218 (C.A.); *Adam v. Newbigging* (1888), 13 App. Cas. 308 (H.L.); *Hulton v. Hulton*, [1917] 3 K.B. 813 (C.A.).

the tendency to relax the rule in rescission cases which requires restoration to the status quo has . . . been exhibited only in cases where the overriding fiduciary principle has applied, or when the impossibility to restore has been due to the act of the party against whom rescission was claimed; or, again, where there has been deterioration for which compensation may be made by money.[244]

There are cases from which it may be concluded that the court has the power to make monetary adjustments, thereby giving effect in principle to the notion of restitution, even though exact restitution *in specie* cannot be made. These would indicate, it is suggested, despite the apparent strictness of the language of Montague J., that the courts are willing and prepared to be more flexible and lenient than in former times.[245] While restitution is a guiding principle for the courts, it will not be the master of their actions. If it is absolutely impossible to obtain restitution, formally or in effect, rescission may be denied. If some kind of satisfactory adjustment of the rights of the parties can be made, perhaps by the transfer of money between them, rescission will not be ruled out as a possible remedy in appropriate cases. Similarly, if restitution is not possible because the defendant's own conduct caused the plaintiff to be unable to return what was purchased, rescission will not be denied.[246]

4. Rectification[247]

(a) Nature and problems

Rectification is a very powerful weapon in the armoury of equity, capable of dealing with cases of mistake, even where the common law could, and would do nothing to relieve a party from the consequences of the transaction into which he had entered. When this remedy is successfully invoked the courts can vary the terms of a written document, which was not possible at common law.[248] Rectification is concerned with contracts and documents, not intentions.[249] The essence

---

243 *Can. Farm Implement Co. v. Alta. Foundry & Machine Co.*, [1927] 1 W.W.R. 1025 (Alta. S.C.); *Carter v. Golland*, [1937] O.R. 881 (Ont. C.A.).

244 Above, note 239, at 735.

245 See, *e.g., Wandinger v. Lake* (1977), 78 D.L.R. (3d) 305 (Ont. H.C.), a case of fraud which involved the purchase of a motel. Rescission was ordered although the purchaser had removed certain chattels and had occupied the premises for several months. The value of the chattels and the rent received by the purchaser were deducted from the price he had paid, to which he was entitled on rescission. In this way the benefit received by the purchaser was restored to the vendor.

246 *Stewart v. Complex 329 Ltd.* (1990), 109 N.B.R. (2d) 115 (N.B.Q.B.).

247 Reference to this section was made by Malone J. in *Klippert v. Western Service Agreements Ltd.* (1988), 70 Sask. R. 136 at 138 (Sask. Q.B.).

248 And may order specific performance of the contract as rectified: *Freeman v. Kaltio* (1963), 39 D.L.R. (2d) 496 (B.C.S.C.); or damages as well: *Carroll v. Erie County Natural Gas & Fuel Co.* (1899), 29 S.C.R. 591 (S.C.C.); *Connor v. Ferguson*, [1920] 3 W.W.R. 403 (Man. K.B.). A promissory note may be rectified, even after it has been sued upon and tendered in evidence: *Polish Combatants' Assn. Credit Union Ltd. v. Moge*, [1984] 5 W.W.R. 97 (Man. C.A.).

249 *Frederick E. Rose (London) Ltd. v. William H. Pim Junior & Co.*, [1953] 2 Q.B. 450 at 461 (C.A.) per Denning L.J.; *Distillery Int. Union of Amer. Loc. No. 153 v. Can. Park & Tilford Distilleries Ltd.* (1973), 36 D.L.R. (3d) 632 (B.C.S.C.).

of rectification is to bring the document which was expressed or intended to be in pursuance of a prior agreement into harmony with that prior agreement.[250] It deals with the situation where, contracting parties having reduced into writing the agreement reached by their negotiations, some mistake was made in the wording of the final, written contract, altering the effect, in whole or in part, of the contract. What the court does is to alter the document, in accordance with the evidence, and then enforce the document as changed.[251] Rectification is not used to vary the intentions of the parties, but to correct the situation where the parties have settled upon certain terms but have written them down incorrectly.[252] But the court will not give a remedy for a party who is displeased with what the contract has brought him.[253]

This jurisdiction is of great antiquity,[254] but it is still very much an active jurisdiction of the court. However, as pointed out by Duff J. more than once,[255] it is a jurisdiction that must be exercised with great caution, and only after a heavy onus of proof has been discharged, and the court is convinced by evidence which is "strong and irrefragable",[256] involving "a high degree of conviction",[257] leaving no "fair and reasonable doubt"[258] that the document before the court does not

---

250 *Lovell & Christmas Ltd. v. Wall* (1911), 104 L.T. 85 (C.A.), discussed in *Joscelyne v. Nissen*, [1970] 2 Q.B. 86 (C.A.). This may include harmonizing the written terms of an agreement with the knowledge of the parties as to the background of the contract and their previous conduct: *Sky Ranches Ltd. v. Nelson* (1977), 4 B.C.L.R. 97 (B.C.S.C.); affirmed (1980), 30 B.C.L.R. 162 (B.C.C.A.). In such circumstances, even if there was a fraudulent misrepresentation, rectification, not rescission, may be an appropriate remedy: *Metropolitan Stores of Can. Ltd. v. Nova Const. Co.* (1988), 50 D.L.R. (4th) 508 (N.S.C.A.).

251 This and the two previous sentences were cited by Hallett J. in *Fed. Business Dev. Bank. v. Elcon Petroleum Maintenance Ltd.* (1983), 58 N.S.R. (2d) 246 at 258 (N.S.T.D.); and in *Kootenay Savings Credit Union v. Toudy* (1987), 17 B.C.L.R. (2d) 203 at 218 (B.C.S.C.) (varied on reconsideration on other grounds (1987), 22 B.C.L.R. (2d) 201 (B.C.S.C.)). But while rectification was granted in *Glascar Ltd. v. Polysar Ltd.* (1975), 9 O.R. (2d) 705 (Ont. H.C.), the court would not order specific performance, and awarded damages for breach, since the effect of the rectification was to introduce a condition that made the contract conditional (even though it was probable that the condition would have been fulfilled).

252 *Saskatoon Drug & Stationery Co. v. Saskatoon Bldg. & Dev. Co.* (1981), 8 Sask. R. 421 at 427 (Sask. Q.B.) per Noble J. The passage beginning "Rectification is concerned with contracts" to here was quoted by Hunter J. in *Building Design 2 Ltd. v. Wascana Rehabilitation Centre*, [1992] 6 W.W.R. 343 at 358 (Sask. Q.B.).

253 Hence, rectification is not available where the contract could never execute the intention of the parties, and there was no mistake as to its contents: *Distillery Int. Union of Amer., Loc. No. 153 v. Can. Park & Tilford Distilleries Ltd.*, above, note 249. But rectification could be ordered where the contract as written infringed the rule against perpetuities: the contract was rectified so as to make it valid: *Caroline (Village) v. Roper* (1987), 37 D.L.R. (4th) 761 (Alta. Q.B.).

254 *Shelburne v. Earl of Inchiquin* (1784), 1 Bro. C.C. 338, 59 E.R. 1167; *Townshend v. Stangroom* (1801), 6 Ves. 328, 31 E.R. 1076.

255 *Hart v. Boutilier* (1916), 56 D.L.R. 620 at 630 (S.C.C.); *The "M.F. Whalen" v. Point Anne Quarries Ltd.* (1922), 63 S.C.R. 109 at 126-127 (S.C.C.); compare *Sky Ranches Ltd. v. Nelson*, note 250, at 105 per Bouck J. But see *Augdome Corp. v. Gray*, [1975] 2 S.C.R. 354 (S.C.C.).

256 Lord Thurlow in *Shelburne v. Inchiquin*, above, note 254.

257 *Crane v. Hegeman-Harris Co.*, [1939] 4 All E.R. 68 at 71 (C.A.) per Lord Greene M.R.

258 Duff J. in *Hart v. Boutilier*, above, note 255. See below, p. 830.

truly represent the concluded agreement between the parties. Hence, rectification is not a remedy which is available *after* there has been a breach of contract, but only at the stage when there is some disagreement as to what the contract really was.[259] Nor is it available where there is sufficient evidence to satisfy the requirements of the Statute of Frauds[260] (though it would seem that, if the contract is within the Statute, rectification of the written contract may be allowed, so as to show what was the true agreement between the parties, despite the common law's refusal to admit parol evidence to establish such a contract).[261] Nor will rectification be the appropriate remedy where the contract does not have to be, and is not wholly in writing, but is partly written and partly oral, which permits parol, extrinsic evidence to be admitted to explain and interpret the contract between the parties.[262]

There are two problems with the remedy of rectification. One is the question of upsetting an apparent agreement between parties, that is, replacing it with something else, or, as it were, permitting a party to say that the bargain as it was reached between them was not the bargain he intended. This savours somewhat of allowing a party to have second thoughts, of letting him change his mind. To do this seems to conflict with the basic idea, shared by the common law and equity, that bargains once reached cannot be upset, merely because they turn out to be not as desirable as they were thought to have been.[263] They may only be rescinded on grounds of fraud, mistake, or unconscionability.[264] The second problem relates to the admission of parol evidence to explain a contract. At common law such evidence cannot be admitted to contradict a written contract.[265] This, it would seem, is just what is happening when the court grants the remedy of rectification. The distinction seems to lie in the difference between *construction* of a contract (the correctness of which is not in dispute), and *rectification* of a document, the accuracy of which, in terms of the agreement between the parties, is open to doubt.[266] Unfortunately, as Lord Denning M.R. pointed out in another context,[267] once parol evidence is admitted for the purpose of determining the validity of a claim for

---

259 *Murray & Murray v. Brown* (1975), 16 W.W.R. 397 (B.C.S.C.). The passage from "This jurisdiction" to here was quoted by Hunter J. in *Building Design 2 Ltd. v. Wascana Rehabilitation Centre*, above, note 252, at 360.

260 *Shaffer v. O'Neal*, [1943] 3 W.W.R. 676 (Sask. C.A.).

261 *U.S.A. v. Motor Trucks Ltd.*, [1924] A.C. 196 (P.C.); *Allen v. Frith*, [1940] 3 W.W.R. 463 (Man. C.A.). Contrast the earlier case of *Lesiuk v. Schneider* (1917), 36 D.L.R. 598 (Alta. S.C.); compare the remarks as to the admissibility of parol evidence in a rectification action made by McGillivray C.J.A. in *Re Whissel Enterprises Ltd. and Eastcal Dev. Ltd.* (1980), 116 D.L.R. (3d) 174 at 176 (Alta. C.A.). See also *Davidson v. Eaton/Bay Trust Co.* (1986), 71 A.R. 184 (Alta. Q.B.), where parol evidence was admitted.

262 *Wood v. Grand Valley Ry. Co.* (1913), 30 O.L.R. 44 (Ont. C.A.); affirmed (1915), 51 S.C.R. 283 (S.C.C.).

263 *Wells v. Blain*, [1927] 1 D.L.R. 687 at 695 (Sask. C.A.) *per* Turgeon J.A.

264 Above, pp. 808-817.

265 Above, pp. 455-462.

266 *Bercovici v. Palmer* (1966), 59 D.L.R. (2d) 513 at 517-518 (Sask. C.A.) *per* Culliton C.J.S.

267 *Arrale v. Costain Civil Enrg. Ltd.*, [1976] 1 Lloyd's Rep. 98 (C.A.).

rectification, such evidence may have an effect upon the mind of the court in deciding issues of construction. However, the distinction must be made and upheld.

These two problems were well stated by Brooke J.A., delivering the judgment of the Ontario Court of Appeal, which was subsequently reversed by the Supreme Court of Canada on other grounds, in *H.F. Clarke Ltd. v. Thermidaire Corporation*:[268]

> When may the Court exercise its jurisdiction to grant rectification? In order for a party to succeed on a plea of rectification, he must satisfy the Court that the parties, all of them, were in complete agreement as to the terms of their contract but wrote them down incorrectly. It is not a question of the Court being asked to speculate about the parties' intention, but rather to make an inquiry to determine whether the written agreement properly records the intention of the parties as revealed in their prior agreement. The Court will not write a contract for businessmen or others but rather through the exercise of its jurisdiction to grant rectification in appropriate circumstances, it will reproduce their contract in harmony with the intention clearly manifested by them, and so defeat claims or defences which would otherwise unfairly succeed to the end that business may be fairly and ethically done.

This is in accord with the general equitable doctrine, which may be contrasted with the approach of the common law, that parol evidence is admitted to show the circumstances whenever the defences of fraud, accident or mistake are raised to an action on a contract.[269] Thus, equity will not allow either the strict common-law doctrine of apparent agreement, nor that of exclusion of contradictory parol evidence, to stand in the way of achieving a just and equitable result where an action is brought, or is going to be brought, upon a contract, even a written one.[270]

(b) Requirements of rectification

(i) *Essential elements*

What must be shown by a party claiming rectification, either in a suit for such remedy, or by way of a defence to an action on a contract, is a mistake in putting down the parties' intentions, and some earlier agreement which shows that there was such a mistake. These important qualifications for, or ingredients of, a successful claim for rectification must be established, as noted earlier, by strong,

---

268 (1973), 33 D.L.R. (3d) 13 at 20-21 (Ont. C.A.); reversed [1976] 1 S.C.R. 319 (S.C.C.); varied [1976] 1 S.C.R. 340n (S.C.C.); see above, p. 771.

269 *Jadis v. Porte* (1915), 8 W.W.R. 768 (Alta. C.A.); compare *Colonial Invt. Co. v. Borland* (1912), 5 Alta. L.R. 71 (Alta. C.A.); *Edmonton Securities Co. v. LePage* (1913), 5 W.W.R. 188 (Alta. C.A.); *Bathurst Lbr. Co. v. Harris* (1919), 46 N.B.R. 411 (N.B.C.A.).

270 Compare *Riverlate Properties Ltd. v. Paul*, [1974] 2 All E.R. 656 at 660 (C.A.) *per* Russell L.J.

Indeed in *Augdome Corp. v. Gray*, [1975] 2 S.C.R. 354 (S.C.C.) it seems to have been suggested that rectification would be granted to permit a contract to express the parties' true intentions even when no action for rectification was being brought, nor any oral evidence submitted to establish the basis for such rectification (unless rectification could affect the rights of third parties: compare *Syrett v. Transcona-Springfield S.D. No. 12* (1976), 67 D.L.R. (3d) 568 (Man. Q.B.)). This must go too far; it does not seem to accord with the stringent views on rectification that have been expressed in the Supreme Court on other occasions.

clear, and convincing proof, which leads to a consideration of the kind of evidence that may be introduced by that party to make his case.[271]

(ii) *Mistake*

Rectification can be granted, said Fitzpatrick C.J. dissenting in the Supreme Court of Canada,[272] only if the mistake is mutual and the evidence of this mistake is clear and unambiguous. Nor will it be granted if the mistake is the fault of the plaintiff, for example, through his negligence. This statement suggests that both parties must be mistaken as to what they had agreed and that, in consequence, a unilateral mistake will be inoperative or ineffectual as a basis for rectification.[273] The essential idea is that the written document must not defeat the spirit and terms of the accord reached between the parties.[274]

Thus, courts have allowed rectification: where a document did not state that the contract was for the sale and purchase of all the premises occupied by the vendor,[275] where it failed to specify that the transfer of land would be on the same conditions as it was held by the transferor, that is, with reservations only as to coal, but instead also included reservations as to mines and minerals other than coal,[276] where the land was misdescribed in the conveyance or contract;[277] where the contract omitted the year,[278] where the contract, incorrectly, included the words "reserving all mines and minerals" in a contract for the transfer of land;[279] where a policy of insurance stated that the amount to be paid was $2,000 instead of

---

271 This passage was said to state the law correctly by Bayda J.A. in *Carlson v. Big Bud Tractors of Can. Ltd.* (1981), 7 Sask. R. 337 at 346 (Sask. C.A.) and in *Red's Camps (71) Ltd. v. Red's Camp Ltd.* (1983), 27 Sask. R. 293 at 295 (Sask. Q.B.). It was also quoted by Creaghan J. in *Poirier v. Goguen* (1989), 99 N.B.R. (2d) 91 at 106 (N.B.Q.B.). The conditions for rectification are put slightly differently by Egbert J. in *Davidson v. Eaton/Bay Trust Co.* (1986), 71 A.R. 184 at 191 (Alta. Q.B.): note, in particular, his statement that proof must be beyond a reasonable doubt which conflicts with other judicial statements: below, p. 830.

272 *Hart v. Boutilier* (1916), 56 D.L.R. 620 at 622 (S.C.C.); compare Stuart J.A. in *Royal Trust Co. v. Fairbrother* (1922), 63 D.L.R. 637 at 638 (Alta. C.A.).

273 See, however, below, p. 827.

274 This sentence was cited by Hallett J. in *Fed. Business Dev. Bank v. Elcon Petroleum Maintenance Ltd.* (1983), 58 N.S.R. (2d) 246 at 258 (N.S.T.D.); see also *B.C. Forest Products Ltd. v. Nordal* (1954), 11 W.W.R. 403 at 406 (B.C.S.C.) *per* Wilson J.; compare *Shukin v. Demosky*, [1927] 1 D.L.R. 649 at 651 (Sask. K.B.) *per* Mackenzie J. As to when the mistake is one of *law*, not fact, see *Stone v. Godfrey* (1854), 5 De G.M. & G. 76, 43 E.R. 798; *Burroughes v. Abbott*, [1922] 1 Ch. 86.

275 *Hart v. Boutilier*, above, note 272; compare *Johnson v. Trobak* (1977), 79 D.L.R. (3d) 684 (B.C.C.A.) mistake about the extent of an option to purchase; rectification granted of *altered* contract, since the vendor acquiesced in this by his conduct.

276 *Halwa v. Olson*, [1948] 1 W.W.R. 1049 (Alta. C.A.).

277 *Masters v. Azaroff*, [1944] 3 W.W.R. 465 (Sask. C.A.); *Conkin v. Konschuh* (1984), 54 A.R. 326 (Alta. Q.B.) where the option of rectification was granted.

278 *Clark v. Moore*, [1923] 3 D.L.R. 818 (Sask. K.B.).

279 *Henderson v. Montreal Trust Co.*, [1955] 2 D.L.R. 528 (Alta. C.A.): note the strong dissent by Clinton Ford J.A.

the $1,000 that had actually been agreed,[280] where there was a mistake as to the method of calculating the price of gas, the contract referring to "Canadian" gallons instead of U.S. gallons,[281] where the title deed to a house was made in favour of the husband only instead of husband and wife,[282] where there was a mistake in the executed contract with respect to the amount of work to be done under the contract;[283] where a "farmout" agreement erred as to the calculation of the assignor's percentage of profits to be paid under the assignment;[284] where a mortgage referred to the wrong land as being the subject of the mortgage;[285] where a guarantee bond was rectified to make the defendant liable as guarantor of a loan;[286] where a deed related to the plaintiff's property;[287] where the parties mistakenly drafted a contract so as to infringe the rule against perpetuities;[288] and where the mistake was the result of a fraudulent misrepresentation.[289]

Rectification was refused, however: where the mistake was a mere mistake in the advice of the conveyancer, or in his knowledge as to what needs or does not need to go in the contract or document;[290] where a contract of towage referred only to "barges", but one party attempted to have it altered so as to include "scows",[291] where the plaintiff could not prove a mutual mistake as to the exclusion of a part of some land from the sale;[292] and where there was no mistake in a trust deed under which property was conveyed by the husband and wife to the

---

280 *Aetna Life Ins. Co. v. Brodie* (1880), 5 S.C.R. 1 (S.C.C.); compare *MacKey v. Goebel* (1983), 25 Sask. R. 316 (Sask. Q.B.), mistake about the balance owed by the purchaser of land. And where a beneficiary was omitted: *Cockell v. Cockell*, [1944] 3 W.W.R. 328 (Sask. C.A.); *Cornwall v. Halifax Banking Co.; Re Cornwall* (1902), 32 S.C.R. 442 (S.C.C.). And to identify the character in which parties signed a contract, see *O'Brien v. Kunson*, [1919] 3 W.W.R. 480 (B.C.C.A.).

281 *Pac. Petroleums Ltd. v. Concordia Propane Gas Marketers Ltd.* (1977), 5 A.R. 421 (Alta. T.D.).

282 *Armstrong v. Armstrong* (1978), 22 O.R. (2d) 223 (Ont. H.C.). Contrast *Fancy v. Whynot* (1990), 98 N.S.R. (2d) 20 (N.S.T.D.).

283 *Standard Const. Co. v. Founation Co. of Can.* (1980), 28 N.B.R. (2d) 483 (N.B.Q.B.); affirmed (1980), 33 N.B.R. (2d) 124 and (1981), 37 N.B.R. (2d) 61 (N.B.C.A.).

284 *Oriole Oil & Gas Ltd. v. American Eagle Petroleum Ltd.* (1981), 27 A.R. 411 (Alta. C.A.); leave to appeal to S.C.C. refused (1981), 36 N.R. 449 (S.C.C.).

285 *Fed. Business Dev. Bank v. Elcon Petroleum Maintenance Ltd.* (1983), 58 N.S.R. (2d) 246 (N.S. T.D.).

286 *Kootenay Savings Credit Union v. Toudy* (1987), 17 B.C.L.R. (2d) 203 (B.C.S.C.); varied on reconsideration on other grounds (1987), 22 B.C.L.R. (2d) 201 (B.C.S.C.).

287 *Wilbur v. Steeves* (1990), 10 R.P.R. (2d) 68 (N.B.Q.B.).

288 *Caroline (Village) v. Roper* (1987), 37 D.L.R. (4th) 761 (Alta. Q.B.).

289 *Metropolitan Stores of Can. Ltd. v. Nova Const. Co.* (1988), 50 D.L.R. (4th) 508 (N.S.C.A.). Unconscionability, as well as mistake, was stressed in *Consolidated Parts Distributors of Can. Ltd. v. Monro* (1992), 80 Man. R. (2d) 65 (Man. Q.B.).

290 *Royal Trust Co. v. Fairbrother*, above, note 272. Nor where the contract was to give a security and the security had been given and realized: *Georgeson v. Dom. Bank*, [1924] 2 W.W.R. 931 (Alta. C.A.).

291 *The "M.F. Whalen" v. Pointe Anne Quarries Ltd.* (1921), 63 S.C.R. 109 (S.C.C.).

292 *Brown v. Hillar*, [1951] O.R. 634 (Ont. H.C.). Compare *Amos & Amos v. Helmke* (1981), 45 N.S.R. (2d) 69 (N.S.C.A.) (reversing (1980), 39 N.S.R. (2d) 675 (N.S.T.D.), on the grounds that the land that had been delivered to the purchaser was in possession); leave to appeal S.C.C. refused (1981), 47 N.S.R. 360 (S.C.C.).

husband in trust for their daughter.[293] Nor would the court permit rectification where a party argued that the contract was not certain enough, and contained ambiguity. As Davey C.J.B.C. pointed out in *Silver Standard Mines Ltd. v. Granbu Mining Co.*,[294] rectification is not designed to make more certain an agreement that carries out the intention of the parties as originally written. It operates as a remedy in instances of mistake, not of ambiguity.

Perhaps this explains why courts have been reluctant to grant this remedy where the mistake is one-sided, that is, *unilateral*.[295] As McKeown C.J. said in *Lee v. Arthurs*,[296]

> [t]he whole principle of rectifying or reforming a conveyance rests upon the idea that the document as written is not evidential of the contract as made, and if both parties agree on the point, the Court will proceed to reform the deed or writing in accordance with the common intent, but a deed cannot be reformed or rectified against the protest of one party thereto who says it is right already.

However, it would appear that, while this is generally true, there may be instances of rectification for unilateral mistake. Such situations may be exceptional, but they can arise.[297] One example is where the document is a deed poll, that is, a document that is made by one party only.[298] Another such situation is where to allow the other party, denying the mistake, to take advantage of the document would be tantamount to fraud.[299] Thus, proof by one party that it was intended the contract

---

293 *Lavallee v. Lavallee* (1982), 45 N.B.R. (2d) 19 (N.B.Q.B.). For other instances where rectification was refused on the ground that the necessary mistake was not proved, see *Chant v. Infinitum Growth Fund Inc.* (1986), 28 D.L.R. (4th) 577 (Ont. C.A.); *BCE Dev. Corp. v. Cascade Invts. Ltd.* (1987), 55 Alta. L.R. (2d) 22 (Alta. Q.B.); affirmed (1987), 56 Alta. L.R. (2d) 349 (Alta. C.A.); leave to appeal to S.C.C. refused (1988), 58 Alta. L.R. (2d) xlix (note) (S.C.C.); *Klippert v. Western Service Agreements Ltd.* (1988), 70 Sask. R. 136 (Sask. Q.B.); *Calmont Truck Centre Ltd. v. Dziwenka* (1991), 112 A.R. 206 (Alta. Q.B.); *Building Design 2 Ltd. v. Wascana Rehabilitation Centre*, [1992] 6 W.W.R. 343 (Sask. Q.B.).

294 (1970), 72 W.W.R. 241 (B.C.S.C.); reversed (1971), 19 D.L.R. (3d) 598 (B.C.C.A.).

295 *Brittain v. Gartner* (1963), 46 W.W.R. 112 (Alta. S.C.); *Shorb v. Public Trustee* (1953), 8 W.W.R. (N.S.) 657 (Alta. S.C.); affirmed (1954), 11 W.W.R. 132 (Alta. C.A.); *Nfld. Liquor Corp. v. N.A.P.E.* (1980), 22 Nfld. & P.E.I.R. 62 (Nfld. T.D.); *United Grain Growers Ltd. v. Agri-Bldrs. (Regina) Ltd.* (1982), 18 Sask. R. 316 (Sask. Q.B.); affirmed (1984), 33 Sask. R. 241 (Sask. C.A.); *Saanich Police Assn. v. Saanich Police Bd.* (1983), 43 B.C.L.R. 132 (B.C.C.A.).

296 (1919), 48 D.L.R. 78 at 85 (N.B.C.A.).

297 *McNeil v. Iona Gypsum Products Ltd.*, [1925] 2 D.L.R. 659 (N.S.C.A.).

298 *C.P.R. v. Gilbert Plains* (1960), 67 Man. R. 241 (Man. Q.B.); compare *Cockell v. Cockell*, above, note 280. Compare *Re Northland Properties Ltd.*, below, note 303, and the English cases relied on therein.

299 *Bourgeois v. Smith* (1921), 48 N.B.R. 212 (N.B.S.C.); *Amer. Merchant Marine Ins. Co. v. Buckley-Tremaine Lbr. etc. Co.*, [1920] 3 W.W.R. 878 (B.C.S.C.); *McMillen v. Chapman*, [1953] O.R. 399 (Ont. C.A.); *Nfld. Liquor Corp. v. N.A.P.E.*, above, note 295; *United Grain Growers Ltd. v. Agri-Bldrs. (Regina) Ltd.* (1982), 18 Sask. R. 316 (Sask. Q.B.); affirmed (1984), 33 Sask. R. 241 (Sask. C.A.); *Building Design 2 Ltd. v. Wascana Rehabilitation Centre*, [1992] 6 W.W.R. 343 at 361-362 (Sask. Q.B.). The basis of this seems to be unconscionability: *Murphy's Ltd. v. Fabricville Co.* (1981), 117 D.L.R. (3d) 668 (N.S.T.D.); *Avco Financial Services Realty Ltd. v. Tracey* (1979), 59 N.S.R. (2d) 333 (N.S.T.D.). Compare the English decisions in *Garrard v. Frankel* (1862), 30 Beav. 445, 54 E.R. 961; *Harris v. Pepperell* (1867), L.R. 5 Eq. 1; *Paget v. Marshall* (1884), 28 Ch. D. 255;

should contain a term beneficial to himself, but that the other party omitted the term, knowing that the plaintiff was ignorant of such omission, was held to be a ground for rectification in the English case of *A. Roberts & Co. v. Leicestershire County Council.*[300] There would appear to be a basis for allowing rectification in such circumstances in that the party not mistaken was guilty of sharp practice.[301] But a more recent English case[302] suggests that sharp practice may not have to be proved.[303] However, the mere ignorance by one party that a condition was included on the reverse of a contractual document was not enough of itself to justify granting that party rectification of the contract in the absence of proof of fraud or some kind of concealment or unconscionable behaviour by the other party.[304]

(iii) *Common intention*

Until the decision of the English Court of Appeal in *Joscelyne v. Nissen,*[305] there was a dispute about the need to show a concluded agreement between the parties prior to the written document of which rectification was being sought. One view was that, even if no formal contract had been created, there had to be proof of such a contract or agreement.[306] Other decisions indicated that even if no prior contract had been concluded, as long as there was convincing sufficient evidence that the parties had achieved and manifested a common intention, which was not in fact carried out by the written document, there could be rectification based upon

May v. Platt, [1900] 1 Ch. D. 616; *Riverlate Properties Ltd. v. Paul,* [1975] Ch. 133 (C.A.); note the criticism there of the Canadian decision in *Devald v. Zigeuner,* [1958] O.W.N. 381 (Ont. H.C.).

300 [1961] Ch. 555 (followed and relied upon in *Nfld. Liquor Corp. v. N.A.P.E.,* above, note 295 where the union knew that the collective agreement contained a grant of benefits to which the employer had never agreed; rectification was granted).

301 *ITT Industries of Can. Ltd. v. Toronto Dominion Bank* (1988), 63 Alta. L.R. (2d) 87 (Alta. Q.B.); *Metropolitan Stores of Can. Ltd. v. Nova Const. Co.* (1988), 50 D.L.R. (4th) 508 (N.S.C.A.).

302 *T. Bates & Son Ltd. v. Wyndham's (Lingerie) Ltd.,* [1981] 1 All E.R. 1077; compare *Saanich Police Assn. v. Saanich Police Bd.* (1983), 43 B.C.L.R. 132 (B.C.C.A.), no sharp practice in collective bargaining where employer thought a clause conferred no benefit and the union knew that the benefit was conferred and that the employer did not realize that the benefit was conferred.

303 Compare *Re Northland Properties Ltd.* (1989), 74 C.B.R. (N.S.) 231 (B.C.S.C.), in which the court was asked to give directions about an agreement made by petitioners on a liquidation which led to a settlement of the corporation's liabilities; the court ordered rectification of a document by which the petitioners elected a variable rate of interest on a mortgage. This was a unilateral mistake of a voluntary nature. The court followed the English cases involving trusts or deeds (rather than contracts): *Re Butlin's Settlement Trusts,* [1976] 2 All E.R. 483; *Re Slocock's Will Trusts,* [1979] 1 All E.R. 358 (Ch.).

304 *United Grain Growers Ltd. v. Agri-Bldrs. (Regina) Ltd.,* above, note 299.

305 [1970] 2 Q.B. 86 (C.A.).

306 *Baynton v. Amery,* [1945] 2 W.W.R. 523 (Alta. S.C.); reversed on other grounds, [1945] 4 D.L.R. 659 (Alta. C.A.); *Ferguson v. Saunders* (1958), 12 D.L.R. (2d) 688 (Alta. C.A.) in which there was no evidence of a prior *consensus*; and see *Poirier v. Goguen* (1989), 99 N.B.R. (2d) 91 (N.B.Q.B.). Compare also, *Walsh v. Trevannion* (1848), 16 Sim. 178, 60 E.R. 841; *MacKenzie v. Coulson* (1869), L.R. 8 Eq. 368; *Faraday v. Tamworth Union* (1916), 86 L.J. Ch. 436; *Lovell & Christmas Ltd. v. Wall* (1911), 104 L.T. 85 (C.A.); *Craddock Bros. v. Hunt,* [1923] 2 Ch. 136 (C.A.); *Fredrick E. Rose (London) Ltd. v. W.H. Pim Junior & Co.,* [1953] 2 Q.B. 450 at 461-462 (C.A.) *per* Denning L.J.

the mistake in carrying out that intention that was indicated by the evidence.[307] In the *Joscelyne* case, the court came down in favour of the latter view, which would seem to be in accordance with both common sense and the principle underlying the whole concept of rectification. In that case there was a contract between a father and his daughter under which the father sold or transferred his business to the daughter in return for the latter's promise to pay certain costs and expenses. The daughter paid some household expenses for a time and then refused to continue to do so, saying that those expenses were not included in the written agreement. The father sought rectification on the ground that the inclusion of those expenses was understood between the parties, even though nothing may have been formally concluded. The court granted the remedy sought.

More recent cases in Canada reveal that this approach has been accepted and adopted by Canadian courts.[308] As Woods J.A. said in *Mitchell v. MacMillan*,[309] referring to the earlier Saskatchewan case of *Bercovici v. Palmer*,[310]

> there must be evidence which leaves no fair and reasonable doubt that there was an intention in the minds of the parties which continued down to the time of the creation of the instrument, which by error did not appear in the writing.

In that case, for example, a lessee successfully contended that an option to purchase the land, the inclusion of which had been intended by the parties, was inadvertently omitted from the lease. Rectification, and then specific performance, were ordered. Similarly, in *Duck Lake Feed Processors Ltd. v. Folliet*,[311] a lease contained a clause granting the lessee an option to purchase. It should also have contained a clause giving a right of first refusal to the lessee, as the parties had intended. Rectification was granted. In *Eaton v. Eaton*[312] a separation agreement dealt with certain land. It was subsequently argued that the intention of the parties was that this land should belong to the ex-husband, but that this had not been included in the agreement. Hence, the court ordered rectification of the agreement, thereby denying the ex-wife a beneficial interest in one half the land in issue. So, too, in *Qualico Developments Ltd. v. Calgary (City)*,[313] the parties had agreed on the terms of a

---

307 *Fordham v. Hall* (1914), 6 W.W.R. 769 (B.C.C.A.); *U.S.A. v. Motor Trucks Ltd.*, [1924] A.C. 196 (P.C.); *Yanik v. Conibear and Nor. Tpt. Co. (No. 2)*, [1944] 2 W.W.R. 273 (Alta. S.C.); reversed [1945] 1 W.W.R. 33 (Alta. C.A.); *Bercovici v. Palmer* (1967), 58 W.W.R. 111 (Sask. C.A.); compare *Shipley U.D.C. v. Bradford Corp.*, [1936] Ch. 375 (C.A.); *Crane v. Hegeman-Harris Co.*, [1939] 4 All E.R. 68 (C.A.). Part of this sentence in the text is quoted by Wakeling J.A. in *Montreal Trust Co. v. Maley* (1992), 105 Sask. R. 195 at 200 (Sask. C.A.); leave to appeal to S.C.C. refused [1992] 6 W.W.R. lvi (note) (S.C.C.).

308 *Ludlow v. Beattie* (1978), 87 D.L.R. (3d) 561 (Ont. H.C.); *Armstrong v. Armstrong* (1978), 22 O.R. (2d) 223 (Ont. H.C.); *Peter Pan Drive-In Ltd. v. Flambro Realty Ltd.* (1978), 22 O.R. (2d) 291 (Ont. H.C.); affirmed (1980), 26 O.R. (2d) 746 (Ont. C.A.); leave to appeal to S.C.C. refused (1980), 32 N.R. 538 (S.C.C.). But in *Poirier v. Goguen*, above, note 306, there was never an agreement about a precondition in a contract: hence there was no contract to rectify.

309 (1980), 5 Sask. R. 160 at 162 (Sask. C.A.).

310 (1966), 58 W.W.R. 111 (Sask. C.A.).

311 (1982), 16 Sask. R. 355 (Sask. Q.B.).

312 (1981), 21 R.F.L. (2d) 322 (Ont. H.C.).

313 (1987), 53 Alta. L.R. (2d) 129 (Alta. Q.B.).

contract concerning the acquisition of land on which a freeway was to be constructed, but had written down those terms incorrectly: rectification was ordered. In *Caroline (Village) v. Roper*[314] the parties had mistakenly written down their agreement in terms that infringed the rule against perpetuities. Rectification was ordered to give effect to the underlying intention that the land in question should always be used for a community hall.

In contrast rectification was refused in *Trecartin v. Flame Bar-B-Q Ltd.*[315] The plaintiff sued on a demand promissory note. The defendant pleaded that the debt covered by the note was owed under a long-term loan agreement instead of under the note. There was no proof of this. The defendant claimed rectification of the promissory note so as to make it conform to the alleged loan agreement. Rectification was inappropriate in this instance, because there was no evidence of a common intention that the note and the agreement should be part of one document. The terms of the agreement and the note were incompatible.[316]

(iv) *The evidence*

The proof must be clear and convincing, by incontrovertible testimony, as regards the agreement actually made by the parties and their mutual mistake.[317] All the circumstances must be looked at to see whether the plaintiff has discharged the onus, which is on him, and is a heavy one,[318] of establishing the ingredients

---

314 (1987), 37 D.L.R. (4th) 761 (Alta. Q.B.). See also *Unilux Manufacturing Co. v. Prime Boilers Inc.* (1990), 74 O.R. (2d) 270 (Ont. H.C.), effect given to implied term by rectifying the written contract.

315 (1978), 23 N.B.R. (2d) 567 (N.B.C.A.).

316 For other cases where rectification was refused for the same reason see *Alex v. Tiede*, [1986] 5 W.W.R. 599 (Man. Q.B.) (where both parties sought the remedy which was granted to the defendant, not the plaintiff); *Bank of Montreal v. Vancouver Professional Soccer Ltd.* (1987), 15 B.C.L.R. (2d) 34 (B.C.C.A.); *Cominco Ltd. v. Can. Pacific Ltd.* (1988), 24 B.C.L.R. (2d) 124 (B.C.S.C.); *209991 Ont. Ltd. v. C.I.B.C.* (1988), 39 B.L.R. 44 (Ont. H.C.); *Can. Deposit Ins. Corp. v. Can. Commercial Bank* (1990), 105 A.R. 368 (Alta. Q.B.); reversed (1991), 113 A.R. 371 (Alta. C.A.): which was affirmed [1992] 2 S.C.R. 3 (S.C.C.); *Ont. Cruisemarine Ltd. v. R.* (1990), 35 F.T.R. 241 (Fed. T.D.); *Can. Mortgage & Housing Corp. v. Edinburgh House Apartments Ltd.* (1991), 112 A.R. 104 (Alta. Q.B.); affirmed (1993), 135 A.R. 244 (Alta. C.A.).

317 *Prov. Fox Co. v. Tennant* (1915), 48 N.S.R. 555 (N.S.C.A.); *Cyr v. Dionne* (1936), 11 M.P.R. 107 (N.B.S.C.); *Gauvin v. Bouchard*, [1950] 2 D.L.R. 414 (N.B.C.A.). *Peter Pan Drive-In Ltd. v. Flambro Realty Ltd.*, above, note 308; *Carlson v. Big Bud Tractors of Can. Ltd.* (1981), 7 Sask. R. 337 (Sask. C.A.); *Smith v. Horizon Aero Sports Ltd.* (1981), 7 Sask. R. 337 (Sask. C.A.); *Smith v. Horizon Aero Sports Ltd.* (1981), 130 D.L.R. (3d) 91 at 106-107 (B.C.S.C.) *per* Spencer J. citing *U.S.A. v. Motor Trucks Ltd.*, [1924] A.C. 196 (P.C.).

318 *Smith v. Hemeon*, [1953] 4 D.L.R. 157 (N.S.S.C.); *Tatarchuk v. Sidor & Imperial Oil Ltd.*, [1950] 2 W.W.R. 953 (Alta. S.C.); affirmed (1951), 1 W.W.R. (N.S.) 435 (Alta. C.A.); *Re Whissel Enterprises Ltd. and Eastcal Dev. Ltd.* (1980), 116 D.L.R. (3d) 174 at 176 (Alta. C.A.); contrast *Fuhr and Fuhr v. Davidson*, [1948] 1 W.W.R. 1057 (Alta. S.C.); varied on appeal [1949] 1 W.W.R. 221 (Alta. C.A.); *Tobias v. Nolan* (1985), 71 N.S.R. (2d) 92 (N.S.T.D.); varied on other grounds (1987), 78 N.S.R. (2d) 271 (N.S.C.A.): followed in *Fancy v. Whynot* (1990), 98 N.S.R. (2d) 20 (N.S.T.D.).
In *Coderre (Wright) v. Coderre*, [1975] 2 W.W.R. 193 (Alta. S.C.), McDonald J. of the Alberta Supreme Court suggested that there was a conflict in this respect between the decision in *Joscelyne v. Nissen*, above, note 305, and the language of Duff J. in the *Whalen* case, above, note 291, which

of a case of rectification.[319] Although it has been said that the standard of proof for establishing a case for rectification is "stringent",[320] and has been described in various terms,[321] it remains an open question[322] whether the test is the almost criminal test of "no fair or reasonable doubt"[323] or the less demanding, but still demanding one of "convincing proof".[324] But there is no special rule of evidence. The court must come to a conclusion using good sense and in the light of such documentary and strong oral evidence as is adduced.[325]

While parol or oral evidence is plainly admissible to establish this case,[326] everything depends upon the weight of such evidence.[327] The plaintiff's oral evidence will suffice, if it proves clearly what was the intention of the parties. In this respect even evidence of the subsequent conduct of the parties may be introduced.[328] Cases of this kind must be differentiated from situations in which

---

was supported by the decision of the Supreme Court of Canada, on another point, in *Hanes v. Wawanesa Mut. Ins. Co.*, [1963] S.C.R. 154 (S.C.C.). The English case repeats the older view as to strict proof. Some Canadian cases appear to suggest that the *civil* burden, *i.e.*, preponderance of probability, is the test (compare McDonald J. in *Rottacker Farms Ltd. v. C. & M. Farms Ltd.*, [1976] 2 W.W.R. 634 (Alta. S.C.); reversed [1976] 6 W.W.R. 601 (Alta. C.A.) and Lieberman J. in *Nor. & Central Gas Corp. v. Hillcrest Collieries; Byron Creek Collieries Ltd. v. Coleman Collieries Ltd.*, [1976] 1 W.W.R. 481 (Alta. T.D.)). Is this only a semantic quarrel? Surely all that is involved is care in establishing the relevant facts and ingredients. See Fridman, "A Dispute That Never Was" (1977), 25 Chitty's Law Journal 51. See also the cases referred to below, notes 320-324.

319 *Shorb v. Public Trustee* (1953), 8 W.W.R. (N.S.) 657 (Alta. S.C.); affirmed (1954), 11 W.W.R. 132 (Alta. C.A.). Proof "beyond doubt" was required, but not provided in *Saskatoon Drug & Stationery Co. v. Saskatoon Building & Dev. Co.* (1981), 8 Sask. R. 421 (Sask. Q.B.); compare *Overwater v. Better Homes Ltd.* (1984), 31 Man. R. (2d) 146 (Man. Q.B.).

320 *Bank of Montreal v. Vancouver Professional Soccer Ltd.* (1987), 15 B.C.L.R. (2d) 34 at 36 (B.C.C.A.) per McLachlin J.A.

321 Above, notes 256-258.

322 *Farm Credit Corp. v. Lacombe Nurseries Ltd.* (1992), 2 Alta. L.R. (3d) 20 (Alta. C.A.); leave to appeal to S.C.C. refused (1993), 8 Alta. L.R. (3d) xlv (note) (S.C.C.), relying on *Augdome Corp. v. Gray*, [1975] 2 S.C.R. 354 (S.C.C.).

323 Applied in *Farm Credit Corp. v. Lacombe Nurseries Ltd.*, above, note 322.

324 *B.P. Resources Can. Ltd. v. General American Oils Ltd.* (1989), 66 Alta. L.R. (2d) 82 (Alta. Q.B.) (although it was hinted that rather more was required); *Building Design 2 Ltd. v. Wascana Rehabilitation Centre*, [1992] 6 W.W.R. 343 at 361 (Sask. Q.B.) per Hunter J., suggesting that the cases referred to by him, *viz.*, *Bercovici v. Palmer* (1966), 58 W.W.R. 111 (Sask. C.A.), *Mitchell v. MacMillan* (1980), 5 Sask. R. 160 (Sask. C.A.), *Proto Manufacturing Ltd. v. Deutsch* (1982), 37 O.R. (2d) 528 (Ont. H.C.), and *Coderre (Wright) v. Coderre*, [1975] 2 W.W.R. 193 (Alta. T.D.), do not reflect the criminal standard of proof.

325 This paragraph as it appeared in the second edition was cited by Hallett J. in *Fed. Business Dev. Bank v. Elcon Petroleum Maintenance Ltd.* (1983), 58 N.S.R. (2d) 246 at 258 (N.S.T.D.). *Johnson Invt. Co. v. Fisher*, [1921] 3 W.W.R. 680 (Alta. C.A.).

326 As in *Davidson v. Eaton/Bay Trust Co.* (1986), 71 A.R. 184 (Alta. Q.B.).

327 *Shukin v. Demosky*, [1927] 1 D.L.R. 649 (Sask. K.B.); *Johnson Invt. Co. v. Fisher*, above, note 325; *Smith v. Hemeon*, above, note 318; *Lings v. Zbryski*, [1930] 3 W.W.R. 415 (Alta. C.A.).

328 *Smith v. Hemeon*, above, note 318; compare *Silver Standard Mines Ltd. v. Granby Mining Co.* (1970), 72 W.W.R. 241 (B.C.S.C.); reversed (1971), 19 D.L.R. (3d) 578 (B.C.C.A.).

what is being sought is construction or clarification of a written contract,[329] and no mistake is alleged.[330]

(c) Bars to rectification

Since this remedy is equitable, the usual equitable defences, or bars, can be raised to a claim for rectification. Thus, delay may operate to destroy whatever possible right the plaintiff might have had to allege the incorrectness of the document.[331] So may his affirmation of the written contract as it stands, by his conduct in not objecting to it, but carrying it out.[332] This may amount to neglect of his right.[333] If he has been negligent in not asserting his rights or challenging the inaccuracy of the contract, he ought not to be allowed to attack its propriety at too late a stage.[334] Nor will the courts permit rectification if it will affect third parties, who were not originally involved in the transaction;[335] nor where the parties cannot be restored to their original positions.[336]

---

329 *Jackson v. Drake* (1906), 37 S.C.R. 315 (S.C.C.).

330 *Whitney v. MacLean*, [1932] 1 W.W.R. 417 (C.A.); application for extension of time for appealing to S.C.C. refused, [1932] 2 W.W.R. 73 (Alta. C.A.).

331 *Hart v. Boutilier* (1916), 56 D.L.R. 620 (S.C.C.); which might result in its being too late to give an effective remedy; *Georgeson v. Dom. Bank*, [1924] 2 W.W.R. 931 (Alta. C.A.).

332 *E.g.*, by the owner's acceptance of the house built by the contractor under the building contract of which, later, rectification was sought: *A.L. Gullison & Sons Ltd. v. Corey* (1979), 24 N.B.R. (2d) 638 (N.B.Q.B.); affirmed (1980), 29 N.B.R. (2d) 86 (N.B.C.A.); compare *Amos & Amos v. Helmke* (1984), 45 N.S.R. (2d) 69 (N.S.C.A.); leave to appeal to S.C.C. refused (1981), 47 N.S.R. (2d) 360 (S.C.C.).

333 *Shorb v. Public Trustee* (1953), 8 W.W.R. (N.S.) 657 at 672-673 (Alta. S.C.); affirmed (1954), 11 W.W.R. 132 (Alta. C.A.).

334 Re *Christensen; Tom v. Everett*, [1928] 4 D.L.R. 668 at 671 (B.C.C.A.) *per* Macdonald C.J.A.

335 *Dom. Bank v. Marshall* (1922), 63 S.C.R. 352 (S.C.C.); *Shorb v. Public Trustee*, above, note 333; *Carlson v. Big Bud Tractors of Can. Ltd.* (1981), 7 Sask. R. 337 at 349 (Sask. C.A.) *per* Bayda J.A.; *Consortium Capital Projects Ltd. v. Blind River Veneer Ltd.* (1988), 63 O.R. (2d) 761 (Ont. H.C.); affirmed (1990), 72 O.R. (2d) 703 (Ont. C.A.).

336 *Jackson v. Irwin* (1913), 4 W.W.R. 1301 (B.C.C.A.). Compare *Georgeson v. Dom. Bank*, above, note 331.

Index